Whitaker's
ALMANACK

INTERNATIONAL
SPORTS
RECORDS
—AND—
RESULTS
1998/9

PETER MATTHEWS

LONDON: THE STATIONERY OFFICE

First published 1998
The Stationery Office Ltd
51 Nine Elms Lane, London SW8 5DR

ISBN 0 11 702248 9

A CIP catalogue record for this book is available
from the British Library. A Library of Congress
CIP catalogue record has been applied for.

Published by The Stationery Office and
available from:

The Publications Centre
(mail, telephone and fax orders only)
PO Box 276, London SW8 5DT
General enquiries 0171 873 0011
Telephone orders 0171 873 9090
Fax orders 0171 873 8200

The Stationery Office Bookshops
123 Kingsway, London WC2B 6PQ
0171 242 6393   Fax 0171 242 6394
68–69 Bull Street, Birmingham B4 6AD
0121 236 9696   Fax 0121 236 9699
33 Wine Street, Bristol BS1 2BQ
0117 9264306   Fax 0117 9294515
9–21 Princess Street, Manchester M60 8AS
0161 834 7201 Fax 0161 833 0634
16 Arthur Street, Belfast BT1 4GD
01232 238451 Fax 01232 235401
The Stationery Office Oriel Bookshop
The Friary, Cardiff CF1 4AA
01222 395548 Fax 01222 384347
71 Lothian Road, Edinburgh EH3 9AZ
0131 228 4181 Fax 0131 622 7017

The Stationery Office's Accredited Agents
(see Yellow Pages)

and through good booksellers

Titles published by Whitaker's Almanack
Whitaker's Almanack 1999
Whitaker's Almanack 1900: Facsimile Edition
*Whitaker's Almanack International Sports Records
and Results 1998/9*

Pocket-books
Whitaker's Almanack Pocket Reference
Whitaker's Almanack Pocket World 1999

Forthcoming
*Whitaker's London Almanack 1999: What's What
in London*

Edited by Anne Mathew and Jane Franklin

Text designed and typeset by James Crew

Jacket designed by Bob Eames

Printed and bound in Great Britain by
Albert Gait Ltd, Grimsby

Acknowledgements
Information for this book has come from a huge range
of sources. In particular I would like to thank Paulo
Abbiati, Ove Karlsson, Ian Morrison, Jean-Jacques
Tissier, Günter Weinert and Mark Young, as well as
the many experts, and officials of governing bodies that
I have consulted over the years.

Contents

Contents   v

Preface

I have been putting the finishing touches to this book after a wonderful week of top-class sport. I have seen, either in person or on television, drama of the highest order, accompanied by the supreme skill and fitness of some of the world's greatest sportsmen and women. In Rome's Olympic Stadium I saw and commentated on a superb new world record for 1500 metres by the majestic Moroccan, Hicham El Guerrouj. His time of 3:26.00 took 1.37 seconds off the old record time, a huge margin these days, when records are more likely to be broken by tiny fragments, and was 4.77 seconds inside the then-world record set by my co-commentator Steve Ovett in 1983.

I have come to appreciate golf as the greatest individual game and, on my return, I sat entranced by the closing stages of the British Open. The drama unfolded over days of riveting action, accompanied by sportsmanship of the highest order. Relative unknown Brian Watts played steadily and resolutely throughout, and came up with a bunker shot of the highest skill on the very last hole, to force a play-off. That followed the comeback for a brilliant finish by the prodigiously talented Tiger Woods. Ultimately, the coveted title went to grey-haired veteran, Mark O'Meara, who had won his first Major earlier in the year at the US Masters. Above all, there was the joy of watching 17-year-old Justin Rose, who did not just thrust his way into contention on the second day, but stayed there. He played throughout the last two days with the coolness of a seasoned professional, and achieved the best result by an amateur in the Open since 1953. His finish – holing out a pitch at the final hole – was a sporting moment to treasure for ever.

My weekend was made complete by the highlights of a cricket match staged at Lord's to commemorate the 150th birthday of W G Grace, who in his day dominated the world of sport more than any other man. Sachin Tendulkar produced a breathtaking innings, good enough to rival any played on that greatest of grounds. Cricket, the finest of all team games, was my first sporting love, and from the initial excitements of that game in the 1950s, I have been avidly following all sport and collecting its statistics over the past 45 years. Packed into this book are the fruits of that enthusiasm over the years.

I have aimed to provide a comprehensive record of the statistics of international sport. There are concise introductions to each individual sport, and to the leading events within those sports, with detailed lists of records and winners. Comprehensive coverage is given to the Olympic Games, and to world championships and major international events within each sport, as well as to the major national events in the UK, USA, Europe, Australia and elsewhere.

Such has been the magnitude of this task that, in order to contain the extent of the book to a reasonable size, I have had to face difficult decisions about what to include and what to leave out. Many sports are practised all over the world, and I have tried to include as many as possible, and, in particular, all those that are widespread.

The question of what is and what is not a sport is always a matter for debate. The primary consideration is that of competition, but I have determined that human physical activity should also be a factor. Therefore, greyhound racing has been omitted, being a purely animal activity (although the trainers are men and women), as have the games of bridge and chess, where intellectual rather than physical skills are prevalent.

Space has not always permitted the inclusion of complete lists for long-established events; where such lists have had to be restricted to more recent winners, I have given summaries to include the champions who have won most titles, thus ensuring that the 'greats' of the past are recognized. Complete lists of Olympic champions are included, but under each sport, rather than in the separate Olympic section.

In lists of team champions I have summarized the wins by each team. In these and other lists, I have shown consecutive wins as, for example, 1983-7, for wins in each year from 1983 to 1987. Seasons that encompass two calendar years have been shown as, for example, 1994/5.

We have tried to make the book as topical as possible, including events as late as we dare in a tight publishing schedule, and have included a special section on FRANCE 98, football's World Cup.

I have been collecting sports records since the age of eight. One of my first sporting memories is England's regaining of the Ashes at The Oval in 1953, and that was also the year when I first pored over my father's collection of Wisden's Cricketers' Almanacks. The following year, Roger Bannister's first sub four-minute mile, and Chris Chataway's epic victory over Vladimir Kuts over 5000 metres at the White City Stadium in London, triggered in me a lifetime's devotion to athletics.

I am particularly pleased that Whitaker's Almanack is publishing my work. I first discovered that marvellous reference work in Jarrold's bookshop in Norwich, at the age of nine or ten, and have used it extensively. In the years since then, I have filled many notebooks with data from a wide range of sources to provide a basis for this work. My research has led me to a huge range of books, newspapers, magazines and web sites, and to many experts around the world. I am most grateful to them all for the help they have given me over the years.

Peter Matthews
20 July 1998

Abbreviations

cc	cubic capacity
d	days
ft	feet
hr	hours
in	inches
kg	kilograms
km	kilometres
km/h	kilometres per hour
m	metres
min	minutes
mph	miles per hour
m/s	metres per second
sec	seconds
w	wind-assisted (athletics; after times)
y	yards
yr	years

Cricket

av.	average
c	caught
dec	declared
St	stumped
*	not out

Dates are given in the style 12 Jul 1998, with the month abbreviated to its first three characters.

Countries

Alb	Albania
Alg	Algeria
Ant	Antigua
Arg	Argentina
Arm	Armenia
Aus	Australia
Aut	Austria
Bah	Bahamas
Ban	Bangladesh
Bar	Barbados
Bel	Belgium
Ber	Bermuda
Bhn	Bahrain* (BRN)
Blr	Belarus
Bra	Brazil
Bul	Bulgaria
Bur	Burma (now Myanmar)* (MYA)
Cam	Cameroon* (CMR)
Can	Canada
Chl	Chile* (CHI)
Chn	China (People's Republic)
Col	Colombia
Con	Congo* (CGO)
CR	Costa Rica (CRC)
Cro	Croatia
Cs	Czechoslovakia* (TCH)
Cub	Cuba
Cyp	Cyprus
Cze	Czech Republic
Den	Denmark
Dji	Djibouti
Dom	Dominican Republic
Ecu	Ecuador
Egy	Egypt
Eng	England
Est	Estonia
Eth	Ethiopia
Fij	Fiji
Fin	Finland
Fra	France
FRG	Federal Republic of Germany
Gab	Gabon
Gam	The Gambia
GDR	German Democratic Republic
Geo	Georgia
Ger	Germany
Gha	Ghana
Gre	Greece
Gua	Guatemala
Guy	Guyana
Haw	Hawaii
HK	Hong Kong* (HKG)
Hol	Holland/Netherlands (NED)
Hun	Hungary
Ice	Iceland* (ISL)
Ina	Indonesia
Ind	India
IOM	Isle of Man
Ire	Ireland* (IRL)
Irn	Iran
Irq	Iraq
Isr	Israel
Ita	Italy
IvC	Ivory Coast/Côte d'Ivoire* (CIV)
Jam	Jamaica
Jap	Japan* (JPN)
Ken	Kenya
Kgz	Kyrgyzstan
Kuw	Kuwait
Kzk	Kazakhstan
Lat	Latvia
Leb	Lebanon
Lie	Liechtenstein
Lit	Lithuania
Lux	Luxembourg
Mal	Malaysia
Maw	Malawi
Mex	Mexico
Mgl	Mongolia
Mlt	Malta
Mol	Moldova
Mon	Monaco
Mor	Morocco* (MAR)
NI	Northern Ireland
Nic	Nicaragua* (NCA)
Nig	Nigeria* (NGR)
NKo	North Korea (Korean DPR)* (PRK)
Nor	Norway
NZ	New Zealand* (NZL)
Pak	Pakistan
Pan	Panama
Par	Paraguay
Per	Peru
Phi	Philippines
PNG	Papua New Guinea
Pol	Poland
Por	Portugal
PR	Puerto Rico* (PUR)
Qat	Qatar
Rho	Rhodesia
Rom	Romania
Rus	Russia
SAf	South Africa (RSA)
Sco	Scotland
Sen	Sénégal
Sin	Singapore
SKo	Korea (South)* (KOR)
Slo	Slovenia
Som	Somalia
Spa	Spain* (ESP)
SRho	Southern Rhodesia (now Zimbabwe)
Sri	Sri Lanka
Sud	Sudan
SVI	St Vincent
Svk	Slovakia
Sur	Surinam
Swe	Sweden
Swi	Switzerland* (SUI)
Syr	Syria
Tai	Taiwan (Chinese Taipeh)* (TPE)
Tan	Tanzania
Tha	Thailand
Tjk	Tadjikstan
Tkm	Turkmenistan
Tri	Trinidad and Tobago
Tun	Tunisia
Tur	Turkey
Uga	Uganda
UK	United Kingdom of Great Britain and Northern Ireland* (GBR)
Ukr	Ukraine
Uru	Uruguay
USA	United States
USSR	Soviet Union* (URS) (1917-91)
UVI	US Virgin Islands
Uzb	Uzbekistan
Ven	Venezuela
Wal	Wales
WI	West Indies
Yug	Yugoslavia
Zai	Zaire
Zam	Zambia
Zim	Zimbabwe (formerly Rhodesia)

* These abbreviations differ in some cases from those used by the IOC (which are shown in brackets). The latter are always three characters, and are often based on the French-language version of the country's name (for example, MAR for Maroc – Morocco); I have preferred English, or the local language of the country concerned.

Governing Bodies and Sports Organizations

Specified here in English. See respective sports for other abbreviations, original-language titles, and dates of founding.

AAA	Amateur Athletic Association (UK)
AAU	Amateur Athletic Union (USA)
AIBA	International Amateur Boxing Federation
ATP	Association of Tennis Professionals
CMSB	World Confederation of Boules Sports
FAI	International Aeronautics Federation
FEI	International Equestrian Federation
FIA	International Automobile Federation
FIAC	International Amateur Cycling Federation
FIBA	International Basketball Federation
FIBT	International Bobsleigh and Tobogganing Federation
FIC	International Canoe Federation
FIE	International Fencing Federation
FIFA	International Association Football Federation
FIG	International Gymnastic Federation
FIH	International Hockey Federation
FIL	International Luge Federation
FILA	International Amateur Wrestling Federation
FIM	International Motorcycling Federation
FINA	International Amateur Swimming Federation
FIP	Federation of International Polo
FIPJP	International Federation of Pétanque and Jeu Provençal
FIPV	International Pelota Vasca Federation
FIQ	International Bowling Federation
FIRA	International Amateur Rugby Federation
FIRS	International Roller Skating Federation
FIS	International Ski Federation
FISA	International Rowing Federation
FISB	Interntional Skibob Federation
FISU	International University Sport Federation
FIT	International Trampolining Federation
FITA	International Archery Federation
FIVB	International Volleyball Federation
FMK	International Karate Federation
GAA	Gaelic Athletic Association
IAAF	International Amateur Athletic Federation
IBA	International Baseball Association
IBF	International Badminton Federation
	International Bandy Federation
	International Boxing Federation
IBSF	International Billiards and Snooker Federation
ICC	International Cricket Council
IFNA	International Federation of Netball Associations
IFSS	International Federation of Sleddog Sports
IHF	International Handball Federation
IIHF	International Ice Hockey Federation
IJF	International Judo Federation
IKF	International Korfball Federation
IOC	International Olympic Committee
IOF	International Orienteering Federation
IPF	International Powerlifting Federation
IRF	International Racquetball Federation
IRFB	International Rugby Football Board
ISA	International Surfing Association
ISAF	International Sailing Federation
ISBF	International Billiards and Snooker Federation
ISF	International Softball Federation
ISRF	International Squash Rackets Federation
ISU	International Skating Union
ITF	International Tennis Federation
ITTF	International Table Tennis Federation
ITU	International Triathlon Union
IWF	International Weightlifting Federation
IWSF	International Water Ski Federation
IYRU	International Yacht Racing Union
LPGA	Ladies' Professional Golf Association
MCC	Marylebone Cricket Club
NASCAR	National Association for Stock Car Auto Racing (USA)
NBA	National Basketball Federation (USA)
NBL	National Basketball League (USA)
NCAA	National Collegiate Athletic Association (USA)
NFL	National Football League (USA)
NHL	National Hockey League (USA)
PGA	Professional Golfers Association
PRCA	Professional Rodeo Cowboys Association
TCCB	Test and County Cricket Board
TWIF	Tug-of-War International Federation
UCI	International Cycling Union
UIM	International Powerboating Union
UIPMB	International Union of Modern Pentathlon and Biathlon
UIT	International Shooting Union
WBA	World Boxing Association
WBC	World Boxing Council
WBO	World Boxing Organization
WCBS	World Confederation of Billiards Sports
WCF	World Curling Federation
WPA	World Pool Federation
WSF	World Snooker Federation
	World Squash Federation
WTF	World Taekwondo Federation
WWSU	World Water Skiing Union

American Football

American football evolved from the British games of soccer and rugby in the latter part of the nineteenth century. There were conflicting versions of football, but an important development was the first match under Harvard Rules between Harvard University and McGill University, Montreal, in May 1874. In 1876 the Intercollegiate Football Association was formed, and in that year Harvard agreed to reduce the number of players per side from 15 to 11. The first professional game was between Latrobe and Jeanette in Pennsylvania on 31 Aug 1895, and by the end of the century this version of football had become the national game of the USA. It was exceptionally rough at the time and, after many fatalities in the early part of the twentieth century, considerable modifications were made to the rules, including the introduction of the forward pass, in 1906. The first Rose Bowl game between the leading college teams was held in 1902.

The American Professional Football Association was formed in 1920. Twelve teams contested the first league season, with Akron Pros designated the first champions. The association became the National Football League (NFL) in 1922.

Governing bodies: National Football League, 280 Park Avenue, New York, NY 10017, USA. Tel: (1) 212 450 2000. Commissioner: Paul Tagliabue, President: Neil Austrian.

World League of American Football, 26A Albemarle Street, London W1X 3FA. Tel: 0171 355 1995, Fax: 0171 499 8098.

Abbreviations for positions

CB Cornerback; DE Defensive end; DT Defensive tackle; KR Kick returner; LB Linebacker; Q Quarterback; RB Running back; S Safety; WR Wide receiver

League Football (NFL and AFL)

There was just one league to 1932, the National Football League (or NFL).

National Football League (NFL)

NFL to 1932

Champions:

Year	Champion	Year	Champion
1921	Chicago Staleys	1927	New York Giants
1922	Canton Bulldogs (Ohio)	1928	Providence Steam Roller
1923	Canton Bulldogs (Ohio)	1929	Green Bay Packers
1924	Cleveland Bulldogs	1930	Green Bay Packers
1925	Chicago Cardinals	1931	Green Bay Packers
1926	Frankford Yellow Jackets	1932	Chicago Bears

NFL 1933-59

From 1933, the NFL was divided into two divisions, Eastern and Western, with the respective winners playing off for the NFL Championship. In 1950-2 the divisions were named the American Conference (Eastern) and National Conference (Western). In 1953-9 they were known as the Eastern and Western Conferences.

Divisional winners and championship game results:

Year	Eastern/American Conf.	Western/National Conf.	Championship game
1933	New York Giants	Chicago Bears	Chicago 23 New York 21
1934	New York Giants	Chicago Bears	New York 30 Chicago 13
1935	New York Giants	Detroit Lions	Detroit 26 New York 7
1936	Boston Redskins	Green Bay Packers	Green Bay 21 Boston 6
1937	Washington Redskins	Chicago Bears	Washington 28 Chicago 21
1938	New York Giants	Green Bay Packers	New York 23 Green Bay 17
1939	New York Giants	Green Bay Packers	Green Bay 27 New York 0
1940	Washington Redskins	Chicago Bears	Chicago 73 Washington 0
1941	New York Giants	Chicago Bears	Chicago 37 New York 9
1942	Washington Redskins	Chicago Bears	Washington 14 Chicago 6
1943	Washington Redskins	Chicago Bears	Chicago 41 Washington 21
1944	New York Giants	Green Bay Packers	Green Bay 14 New York 7
1945	Washington Redskins	Cleveland Rams	Cleveland 15 Washington 14
1946	New York Giants	Chicago Bears	Chicago Bears 24 New York 14

1947	Philadelphia Eagles	Chicago Cardinals	Chicago Cardinals 28 Philadelphia 21
1948	Philadelphia Eagles	Chicago Cardinals	Philadelphia 7 Chicago Cardinals 0
1949	Philadelphia Eagles	Los Angeles Rams	Philadelphia 14 Los Angeles 0
1950	Cleveland Browns	Los Angeles Rams	Cleveland 30 Los Angeles 28
1951	Cleveland Browns	Los Angeles Rams	Los Angeles 24 Cleveland 17
1952	Cleveland Browns	Detroit Lions	Detroit 17 Cleveland 7
1953	Cleveland Browns	Detroit Lions	Detroit 17 Cleveland 16
1954	Cleveland Browns	Detroit Lions	Cleveland 56 Detroit 10
1955	Cleveland Browns	Los Angeles Rams	Cleveland 38 Los Angeles 14
1956	New York Giants	Chicago Bears	New York 47 Chicago 7
1957	Cleveland Browns	Detroit Lions	Detroit 59 Cleveland 14
1958	New York Giants	Baltimore Colts	Baltimore 23 New York 17
1959	New York Giants	Baltimore Colts	Baltimore 31 New York 16

NFL 1960-9

Divisional winners and championship game results: (a) Capitol Division (b) Century Division (c) Coastal Division (d) Central Division

Year	Eastern	Western	Play-off
1960	Philadelphia Eagles	Green Bay Packers	Philadelphia 17 Green Bay 13
1961	New York Giants	Green Bay Packers	Green Bay 37 New York 0
1962	New York Giants	Green Bay Packers	Green Bay 16 New York 7
1963	New York Giants	Chicago Bears	Chicago 14 New York 10
1964	Cleveland Browns	Baltimore Colts	Cleveland 27 Baltimore 0
1965	Cleveland Browns	Green Bay Packers	Green Bay 23 Cleveland 12
1966	Dallas Cowboys	Green Bay Packers	Green Bay 34 Dallas 27
1967	(a) Dallas Cowboys	(c) Los Angeles Rams	
	(b) Cleveland Browns	(d) Green Bay Packers	Green Bay 21 Dallas 17
1968	(a) Dallas Cowboys	(c) Baltimore Colts	
	(b) Cleveland Browns	(d) Minnesota Vikings	Baltimore 34 Cleveland 0
1969	(a) Dallas Cowboys	(c) Los Angeles Rams	
	(b) Cleveland Browns	(d) Minnesota Vikings	Minnesota 27 Cleveland 7

American Football League (AFL)

The American Football League (AFL) was formed in 1960 as a rival to the NFL. It had Eastern and Western Divisions, while the NFL still had its Eastern and Western Conferences. Both the AFL and NFL had end-of-season championships and, at the end of the 1966 season, the AFL and NFL champions met for the first Super Bowl (played January 1967).

Divisional winners and championship game results 1960-9:

Year	Eastern winners	Western winners	Play-off
1960	Houston Oilers	Los Angeles Chargers	Houston 24 Los Angeles 16
1961	Houston Oilers	San Diego Chargers	Houston 10 San Diego 3
1962	Houston Oilers	Dallas Texans	Dallas 20 Houston 17
1963	Boston Patriots	San Diego Chargers	San Diego 51 Boston 10
1964	Buffalo Bills	San Diego Chargers	Buffalo 20 San Diego 7
1965	Buffalo Bills	San Diego Chargers	Buffalo 23 San Diego 0
1966	Buffalo Bills	Kansas City Chiefs	Kansas City 31 Buffalo 7
1967	Houston Oilers	Oakland Raiders	Oakland 40 Houston 7
1968	New York Jets	Oakland Raiders	New York Jets 27 Oakland 23
1969	New York Jets	Oakland Raiders	Kansas City Chiefs 17 Oakland 7

In 1969 the top two in each division qualified for AFL play-offs.

AFC and NFC

In 1970 the NFL and AFL merged under the National Football League banner and divided into two conferences – American (AFC) and National (NFC) – each with three divisions – Eastern, Central and Western. End-of-season play-offs culminate in the American and National Conference Championship games, with the two winners meeting in the Super Bowl (*see* page 6).

AFC divisional winners from 1970

Year	Eastern	Central	Western
1970	Baltimore Colts	Cincinnati Bengals	Oakland Raiders
1971	Miami Dolphins	Cleveland Browns	Kansas City Chiefs
1972	Miami Dolphins	Pittsburgh Steelers	Oakland Raiders
1973	Miami Dolphins	Cincinnati Bengals	Oakland Raiders
1974	Miami Dolphins	Pittsburgh Steelers	Oakland Raiders
1975	Baltimore Colts	Pittsburgh Steelers	Oakland Raiders
1976	Baltimore Colts	Pittsburgh Steelers	Oakland Raiders
1977	Baltimore Colts	Pittsburgh Steelers	Denver Broncos
1978	New England Patriots	Pittsburgh Steelers	Denver Broncos
1979	Miami Dolphins	Pittsburgh Steelers	San Diego Chargers
1980	Buffalo Bills	Cleveland Browns	San Diego Chargers
1981	Miami Dolphins	Cincinnati Bengals	San Diego Chargers
1983	Miami Dolphins	Pittsburgh Steelers	Los Angeles Raiders
1984	Miami Dolphins	Pittsburgh Steelers	Denver Broncos
1985	Miami Dolphins	Cleveland Browns	Los Angeles Raiders
1986	New England Patriots	Cleveland Browns	Denver Broncos
1987	Indianapolis Colts	Cleveland Browns	Denver Broncos
1988	Buffalo Bills	Cincinnati Bengals	Seattle Seahawks
1989	Buffalo Bills	Cleveland Browns	Denver Broncos
1990	Buffalo Bills	Cincinnati Bengals	Los Angeles Raiders
1991	Buffalo Bills	Houston Oilers	Denver Broncos
1992	Miami Dolphins	Pittsburgh Steelers	San Diego Chargers
1993	Buffalo Bills	Houston Oilers	Kansas City Chiefs
1994	Miami Dolphins	Pittsburgh Steelers	San Diego Chargers
1995	Buffalo Bills	Pittsburgh Steelers	Kansas City Chiefs
1996	New England Patriots	Pittsburgh Steelers	Denver Broncos
1997	New England Patriots	Pittsburgh Steelers	Kansas City Chiefs

AFC championship games

1970	Baltimore 27 Oakland 17	1984	Miami 45 Pittsburgh 28
1971	Miami 21 Baltimore 0	1985	New England 31 Miami 14
1972	Miami 21 Pittsburgh 17	1986	Denver 23 Cleveland 20
1973	Miami 27 Oakland 10	1987	Denver 38 Cleveland 33
1974	Pittsburgh 24 Oakland 13	1988	Cincinnati 21 Buffalo 10
1975	Pittsburgh 16 Oakland 10	1989	Denver 37 Cleveland 21
1976	Oakland 24 Pittsburgh 7	1990	Buffalo 51 Los Angeles 3
1977	Denver 20 Oakland 17	1991	Buffalo 10 Denver 7
1978	Pittsburgh 34 Houston 5	1992	Buffalo 29 Miami 10
1979	Pittsburgh 27 Houston 13	1993	Buffalo 30 Kansas City 13
1980	Oakland 34 San Diego 27	1994	San Diego 17 Pittsburgh 13
1981	Cincinnati 27 San Diego 7	1995	Pittsburgh 20 Indianapolis 16
1982	Miami 14 New York Jets 0	1996	New England 20 Jacksonville 6
1983	Los Angeles 30 Seattle 14	1997	Denver 24 Pittsburgh 21

NFC divisional winners from 1970

Year	Eastern	Central	Western
1970	Dallas Cowboys	Minnesota Vikings	San Francisco 49ers
1971	Dallas Cowboys	Minnesota Vikings	San Francisco 49ers
1972	Washington Redskins	Green Bay Packers	San Francisco 49ers
1973	Dallas Cowboys	Minnesota Vikings	Los Angeles Rams
1974	St Louis Cardinals	Minnesota Vikings	Los Angeles Rams
1975	St Louis Cardinals	Minnesota Vikings	Los Angeles Rams
1976	Dallas Cowboys	Minnesota Vikings	Los Angeles Rams
1977	Dallas Cowboys	Minnesota Vikings	Los Angeles Rams
1978	Dallas Cowboys	Minnesota Vikings	Los Angeles Rams
1979	Dallas Cowboys	Tampa Bay Buccaneers	Los Angeles Rams

Year	Eastern	Central	Western
1980	Philadelphia Eagles	Minnesota Vikings	Atlanta Falcons
1981	Dallas Cowboys	Tampa Bay Buccaneers	San Francisco 49ers
1983	Washington Redskins	Detroit Lions	San Francisco 49ers
1984	Washington Redskins	Chicago Bears	San Francisco 49ers
1985	Dallas Cowboys	Chicago Bears	Los Angeles Rams
1986	New York Giants	Chicago Bears	San Francisco 49ers
1987	Washington Redskins	Chicago Bears	San Francisco 49ers
1988	Philadelphia Eagles	Chicago Bears	San Francisco 49ers
1989	New York Giants	Minnesota Vikings	San Francisco 49ers
1990	New York Giants	Chicago Bears	San Francisco 49ers
1991	Washington Redskins	Detroit Lions	New Orleans Saints
1992	Dallas Cowboys	Minnesota Vikings	San Francisco 49ers
1993	Dallas Cowboys	Detroit Lions	San Francisco 49ers
1994	Dallas Cowboys	Minnesota Vikings	San Francisco 49ers
1995	Dallas Cowboys	Green Bay Packers	San Francisco 49ers
1996	Dallas Cowboys	Green Bay Packers	Carolina Panthers
1997	New York Giants	Green Bay Packers	San Francisco 49ers

NFC championship games

1970	Dallas 17 San Francisco 10		1984	San Francisco 23 Chicago 0
1971	Dallas 14 San Francisco 3		1985	Chicago 24 Los Angeles Rams 0
1972	Washington 26 Dallas 3		1986	New York 17 Washington 0
1973	Minnesota 27 Dallas 10		1987	Washington 17 Minnesota 10
1974	Minnesota 14 Los Angeles 10		1988	San Francisco 28 Chicago 3
1975	Dallas 37 Los Angeles 7		1989	San Francisco 30 Los Angeles Rams 3
1976	Minnesota 24 Los Angeles 13		1990	New York 15 San Francisco 13
1977	Dallas 23 Minnesota 6		1991	Washington 41 Detroit 10
1978	Dallas 28 Los Angeles 0		1992	Dallas 30 San Francisco 20
1979	Los Angeles 9 Tampa Bay 0		1993	Dallas 38 San Francisco 21
1980	Philadelphia 20 Dallas 7		1994	San Francisco 38 Dallas 28
1981	San Francisco 28 Dallas 27		1995	Dallas 38 Green Bay 27
1982★	Washington 31 Dallas 17		1996	Green Bay 30 Carolina 13
1983	Washington 24 San Francisco 21		1997	Green Bay 23 San Francisco 10

★ A players' strike shortened the season, and the top eight teams played off to decide the championship.

Major NFL Records

General

Most games: 340 George Blanda (Chicago Bears, Baltimore, Houston, Oakland 1949-75)

Most seasons as head coach: 40 (with record 325 wins) George Halas (Chicago Bears 1920-9, 1933-42, 1946-55, 1958-67)

Scoring

Most points (career): 2002 George Blanda (Chicago Bears, Baltimore, Houston, Oakland 1949-75)

Most points (season): 176 Paul Hornung (Green Bay 1960)

Most points (game): 40 Ernie Nevers (Chicago Cardinals v Chicago Bears 28 Nov 1929)

Most touchdowns (career): 165 Jerry Rice (San Francisco 49ers 1985-96)

Most touchdowns (season): 25 Emmitt Smith (Dallas 1995)

Most touchdowns (game): 6 Ernie Nevers (Chicago Cardinals v Chicago Bears 28 Nov 1929), William Jones (Cleveland v Chicago Bears 25 Nov 1951), Gale Sayers (Chicago v San Francisco 12 Dec 1965)

Most field goals (career): 383 Nick Lowery (New England Patriots, Kansas City Chiefs, New York Jets 1978, 1980-96)

Most field goals (season): 37 John Kasay (Carolina Panthers 1996)

Most field goals (game): 7 Jim Bakken (St Louis v Pittsburgh 24 Sep 1967), Rich Karlis (Minnesota v Los Angeles Rams 5 Nov 1989), Chris Boniol (Dallas v Green Bay 18 Nov 1996)

Rushing

Most yards gained (career): 16,726 Walter Payton (Chicago 1975-87)
Most yards gained (season): 2105 Eric Dickerson (Los Angeles Rams 1984)
Most yards gained (game): 275 Walter Payton (Chicago v Minnesota 20 Nov 1977)

Passing

Most passes completed (career): 4453 Dan Marino (Miami 1983-97)
Most passes completed (season): 404 (from record 655 attempts) Warren Moon (Houston Oilers 1991)
Most passes completed (game): 45 Drew Bledsoe (New England v Minnesota 13 Nov 1994)
Most yards gained (career): 55,146 Dan Marino (Miami 1983-97)
Most yards gained (season): 5084 Dan Marino (Miami 1984)
Most yards gained (game): 554 Norm Van Brocklin (Los Angeles Rams v New York Yanks 28 Sep 1951)

All-Time Leading NFL Players

(As at end of 1997 season)

Most points

George Blanda	2002
Nick Lowery	1711
Jan Stenerud	1699
Gary Anderson	1681
Morten Anderson	1641
Norm Johnson	1558
Eddie Murray	1532
Pat Leahy	1470
Jim Turner	1439
Matt Bahr	1422

Most touchdowns

Jerry Rice	166
Marcus Allen	145
Jim Brown	126
Walter Payton	125
Emmitt Smith	119
John Riggins	116
Lenny Moore	113
Don Hutson	105
Barry Sanders	105
Steve Largent	101
Franco Harris	100

Most passes completed

Dan Marino	4453
John Elway	3913
Warren Moon	3827
Fran Tarkenton	3686
Joe Montana	3409
Dan Fouts	3297
Dave Krieg	3092
Boomer Esiason	2969
Jim Kelly	2874
Steve DeBerg	2844

Most yards gained passing

Dan Marino	55,416
John Elway	48,369
Warren Moon	47,465
Fran Tarkenton	47,003
Dan Fouts	43,040
Joe Montana	40,551
Johnny Unitas	40,239
Dave Krieg	37,948
Boomer Esiason	37,920
Jim Kelly	35,467

Most yards gained rushing

Walter Payton	16,726
Barry Sanders	13,778
Eric Dickerson	13,259
Tony Dorsett	12,739
Jim Brown	12,312
Marcus Allen	12,243
Franco Harris	12,120
Thurman Thomas	11,405
John Riggins	11,352
O J Simpson	11,236
Emmitt Smith	11,234

Fewest games to reach 10,000 yards rushing

Eric Dickerson	91
Barry Sanders	103
O J Simpson	110
Walter Payton	113

Barry Sanders has the NFL record with over 1500 yards in four successive seasons 1994-7.

Franchise Changes

Since the formation of the AFL, in 1960, the following teams have changed their franchise:

	From	To
1960	Chicago Cardinals	St Louis Cardinals
1961	Los Angeles Chargers	San Diego Chargers
	New York Titans	New York Jets
1963	Dallas Texans	Kansas City Chiefs
1971	Boston Patriots	New England Patriots
1982	Oakland Raiders	Los Angeles Raiders
1984	Baltimore Colts	Indianapolis Colts
1988	St Louis Cardinals	Phoenix Cardinals
1994	Phoenix Cardinals	Arizona Cardinals
1995	Los Angeles Rams	St Louis Rams
	Los Angeles Raiders	Oakland Raiders
1996	Cleveland Browns	Baltimore Ravens
1997	Houston Oilers	Tennessee Oilers

New franchises since NFL and AFL merger, in 1970:
1995   Carolina Panthers (Charlotte) and Jacksonville Jaguars

Super Bowl

Inaugurated in 1966, the Super Bowl, the contest between the AFC and NFC champions, has become the greatest sporting event in the USA. Tickets for the game are highly prized and the game often attracts record television audiences. It is held in January each year, at the end of the regular season. The contests are traditionally referred to using Roman numerals; the January 1998 game was Super Bowl XXXII.

Results:

Year	Venue	Winners	Runners-up	Attendance
1967	Los Angeles	Green Bay Packers 35	Kansas City Chiefs 10	61,946
1968	Miami	Green Bay Packers 33	Oakland Raiders 14	75,546
1969	Miami	New York Jets 16	Baltimore Colts 7	75,389
1970	New Orleans	Kansas City Chiefs 23	Minnesota Vikings 7	80,562
1971	Miami	Baltimore Colts 16	Dallas Cowboys 13	79,204
1972	New Orleans	Dallas Cowboys 24	Miami Dolphins 3	81,023
1973	Los Angeles	Miami Dolphins 14	Washington Redskins 7	90,182
1974	Houston	Miami Dolphins 24	Minnesota Vikings 7	71,882
1975	New Orleans	Pittsburgh Steelers 16	Minnesota Vikings 6	80,997
1976	Miami	Pittsburgh Steelers 21	Dallas Cowboys 17	80,187
1977	Pasadena	Oakland Raiders 32	Minnesota Vikings 14	103,438
1978	New Orleans	Dallas Cowboys 27	Denver Broncos 10	75,583
1979	Miami	Pittsburgh Steelers 35	Dallas Cowboys 31	79,484
1980	Pasadena	Pittsburgh Steelers 31	Los Angeles Rams 19	103,985
1981	New Orleans	Oakland Raiders 27	Philadelphia Eagles 10	76,135
1982	Pontiac	San Francisco 49ers 26	Cincinnati Bengals 21	81,270
1983	Pasadena	Washington Redskins 27	Miami Dolphins 17	103,667
1984	Tampa	Los Angeles Raiders 38	Washington Redskins 9	72,920
1985	Stanford	San Francisco 49ers 38	Miami Dolphins 16	84,059
1986	New Orleans	Chicago Bears 46	New England Patriots 10	73,818
1987	Pasadena	New York Giants 39	Denver Broncos 20	101,063
1988	San Diego	Washington Redskins 42	Denver Broncos 10	73,302
1989	Miami	San Francisco 49ers 20	Cincinnati Bengals 16	75,179
1990	New Orleans	San Francisco 49ers 55	Denver Broncos 10	72,191
1991	Tampa	New York Giants 20	Buffalo Bills 19	73,818
1992	Minneapolis	Washington Redskins 37	Buffalo Bills 24	63,130
1993	Pasadena	Dallas Cowboys 52	Buffalo Bills 19	98,374
1994	Atlanta	Dallas Cowboys 30	Buffalo Bills 13	72,817
1995	Miami	San Francisco 49ers 49	San Diego Chargers 26	74,107
1996	Phoenix	Dallas Cowboys 27	Pittsburgh Steelers 17	76,347
1997	New Orleans	Green Bay Packers 35	New England Patriots 21	72,301
1998	San Diego	Denver Broncos 31	Green Bay Packers 24	69,912

Most wins: 5 San Francisco 49ers; Dallas Cowboys; 4 Pittsburgh Steelers

Career records

Most games (player): 5 – all wins Charles Haley (San Francisco 1989-90, Dallas 1993-4, 1996) (the only player to have achieved this); also 5 Marv Fleming (Green Bay 1967-8, Miami 1972-4), Larry Cole (Dallas 1971-2, 1976, 1978-9), Cliff Harris (Dallas 1971-2, 1976, 1978-9), D D Lewis (Dallas 1971-2, 1976, 1978-9), Mike Lodosh (Denver), Preston Pearson (Baltimore 1969, Pittsburgh 1975, Dallas 1976, 1978-9), Charlie Waters (Dallas 1971-2, 1976, 1978-9), Rayfield Wright (Dallas 1971-2, 1976, 1978-9)

Most games (coach): 6 Don Shula (Baltimore 1969, Miami 1972-4, 1983, 1985)

Most points: 42 Jerry Rice (San Francisco 1989-95)

Most touchdowns: 7 Jerry Rice (San Francisco 1989-95)

Most touchdown passes: 11 Joe Montana (San Francisco 1982-90)

Most yards gained passing: 1142 Joe Montana (San Francisco 1982-90)

Most passes completed: 83 Joe Montana (San Francisco 1982-90)

Most pass receptions: 28 Jerry Rice (San Francisco 1989-95)

Most yards gained receiving: 512 Jerry Rice (San Francisco 1989-95)

Most yards gained rushing: 354 Franco Harris (Pittsburgh 1975-80)

Most field goals: 5 Ray Wersching (San Francisco 1982-5)

Single game records
Most points: 18 Roger Craig (San Francisco 1985), Jerry Rice (San Francisco 1990 & 1995)
Most touchdowns: 3 Roger Craig (San Francisco 1985), Terrell Davis (Denver 1998), Jerry Rice (San Francisco 1990 & 1995), Ricky Walters (San Francisco 1995)
Touchdown passes: 6 Steve Young (San Francisco 1995)
Yards gained passing: 357 Joe Montana (San Francisco 1989)
Passes completed: 31 Jim Kelly (Buffalo 1994)
Pass receptions: 11 Jerry Rice (San Francisco 1989), Dan Ross (Cincinnati 1982)
Yards gained receiving: 215 Jerry Rice (San Francisco 1989)
Yards gained rushing: 204 Timmy Smith (Washington 1988)
Most field goals: 4 Don Chandler (Green Bay v Oakland, 1968), Ray Wersching (San Francisco v Cincinnati, 1982)

MVPs (Most Valuable Players)

1967	Bart Starr (QB), Green Bay
1968	Bart Starr (QB), Green Bay
1969	Joe Namath (QB), New York
1970	Len Dawson (QB), Kansas City
1971	Chuck Howley (LB), Dallas
1972	Roger Staubach (QB), Dallas
1973	Jake Scott (S), Miami Dolphins
1974	Larry Csonka (RB), Miami
1975	Franco Harris (RB), Pittsburgh
1976	Lynn Swann (WR), Pittsburgh
1977	Fred Biletnikoff (WR), Oakland
1978	Randy White (DT) & Harvey Martin (DE), Dallas
1979	Terry Bradshaw (QB), Pittsburgh
1980	Terry Bradshaw (QB), Pittsburgh
1981	Jim Plunkett (QB), Oakland
1982	Joe Montana (QB), San Francisco
1983	Joe Riggins (RB), Washington
1984	Marcus Allen (RB), Los Angeles
1985	Joe Montana (QB), San Francisco
1986	Richard Dent (DE), Chicago
1987	Phil Simms (QB), New York
1988	Doug Williams (QB), Washington
1989	Jerry Rice (WR), San Francisco
1990	Joe Montana (QB), San Francisco
1991	Ottis Anderson (RB), New York
1992	Mark Rypien (QB), Washington
1993	Troy Aikman (QB), Dallas
1994	Emmitt Smith (RB), Dallas
1995	Steve Young (QB), San Francisco
1996	Larry Brown (CB), Dallas
1997	Desmond Howard (KR) Green Bay
1998	Terrell Davis (WR), Denver

US College Football

More than 650 colleges, affiliated to the National Collegiate Athletic Association (NCAA), compete throughout the USA each year. The NCAA is now divided into four divisions: 1-A, 1-AA, II, III.

National College Football Champions

At the end of December each year, journalists throughout the USA engage in a national poll to vote for the outstanding college team of the year. The Associated Press poll has been conducted since 1936; United Press, now UPI, had a coaches' poll 1950–90, and *USA Today*/CNN introduced a poll from 1991.
Winners:
(Where winners of the two polls differ, both teams are shown, AP winner first, UPI or USA Today/CNN winner second.)

1936	Minnesota	1955–6	Oklahoma	1972	South Carolina
1937	Pittsburgh	1957	Auburn & Ohio State	1973	Notre Dame
1938	Texas Christian	1958	Louisiana State	1974	Oklahoma & Southern California
1939	Texas A & M	1959	Syracuse		
1940–1	Minnesota	1960	Minnesota	1975	Oklahoma
1942	Ohio State	1961	Alabama	1976	Pittsburgh
1943	Notre Dame	1962	South Carolina	1977	Notre Dame
1944–5	Army	1963	Texas	1978	Alabama & Southern California
1946–7	Notre Dame	1964	Alabama		
1948	Michigan	1965	Alabama & Michigan State	1979	Alabama
1949	Notre Dame	1966	Notre Dame	1980	Georgia
1950	Oklahoma	1967	South Carolina	1981	Clemson
1951	Tennessee	1968	Ohio State	1982	Penn State
1952	Michigan State	1969	Texas	1983	Miami (Florida)
1953	Maryland	1970	Texas & Nebraska	1984	Brigham Young
1954	Ohio State & UCLA	1971	Nebraska	1985	Oklahoma

1986	Penn State	1990	Colorado & Georgia Tech	1994–5	Nebraska
1987	Miami (Florida)	1991	Miami & Washington	1996	Florida
1988	Notre Dame	1992	Alabama	1997	Michigan & Nebraska
1989	Miami (Florida)	1993	Florida State	**Most wins:**	8 Notre Dame

Bowl Games

The ultimate aim of all teams in the NCAA is to reach one of the end-of-season Bowl finals, which represent the highlight of the College season. The 'Big Four' are the Rose Bowl (first played 1902), Orange Bowl (1935), Sugar Bowl (1935), and Cotton Bowl (1937). Most wins in each are listed below.

Rose Bowl

20 Southern California (USC); 8 Michigan; 6 Washington, Ohio State; 5 Stanford, UCLA; 4 Alabama; 3 Illinois, Michigan State

Orange Bowl

11 Oklahoma; 8 Nebraska; 5 Miami; 4 Alabama; 3 Florida State, Georgia Tech, Penn State; 2 Georgia, Louisiana State, Texas, Clemson, Notre Dame, Colorado

Sugar Bowl

8 Alabama; 5 Mississippi; 4 Georgia Tech, Oklahoma, Tennessee; 3 Louisiana State, Nebraska, Florida State; 2 Texas Christian, Santa Clara, Georgia, Pittsburgh, Notre Dame, Florida

Cotton Bowl

9 Texas; 5 Notre Dame; 4 Texas A & M; 3 Rice, Southern Methodist; 2 Texas Christian, Louisiana State, Alabama, Arkansas, Georgia, Penn State, Houston, Tennessee

Bowl records

Most 'Big Four' appearances: 31 Alabama; 29 USC; 25 Nebraska; 23 Texas; 21 Oklahoma; 18 Louisiana State
Most 'Big Four' wins: 21 USC; 18 Alabama; 15 Oklahoma; 12 Texas, Nebraska; 11 Notre Dame, Alabama,
   Georgia, Georgia Tech and Notre Dame have won all four major Bowls.

NCAA Division I-A Career Records

Most points scored: 423 Roman Anderson (Houston 1988–91)
Most touchdowns: 65 Anthony Thompson (Indiana 1986–9)
Most field goals: 80 Jeff Jaeger (Washington 1983–6)
Most yards gained rushing: 6082 Tony Dorsett (Pittsburgh 1973–6)
Most yards gained passing: 15,031 Ty Detmer (Brigham Young 1988–91)
Most passes completed: 958 Ty Detmer (Brigham Young 1988–91)

Heisman Trophy

Awarded annually since 1935 by the Downtown Athletic Club of New York to the top college footballer, as determined by a poll of journalists. It was originally called the DAC Trophy, but it was renamed in 1936 as the John W Heisman Memorial Trophy, after the first athletic director of the Downtown Club.
Winners:

1935	Jay Berwanger (Chicago)	1947	John Lujack (Notre Dame)	1957	John Crow (Texas A & M)
1936	Larry Kelley (Yale)			1958	Pete Dawkins (Army)
1937	Clint Frank (Yale)	1948	Doak Walker (Southern	1959	Billy Cannon (Louisiana
1938	Davey O'Brien		Methodist)		State)
	(Texas Christian)	1949	Leon Hart (Notre Dame)	1960	Joe Bellino (Navy)
1939	Nile Kinnick (Iowa)	1950	Vic Janowicz (Ohio State)	1961	Ernie Davis (Syracuse)
1940	Tom Harmon (Michigan)	1951	Dick Kazmaier (Princeton)	1962	Terry Baker (Oregon
1941	Bruce Smith (Minnesota)	1952	Billy Vessels (Oklahoma)		State)
1942	Frank Sinkwich (Georgia)	1953	John Lattner (Notre	1963	Roger Staubach (Navy)
1943	Angelo Bertelli (Notre		Dame)	1964	John Huarte (Notre
	Dame)	1954	Alan Ameche (Wisconsin)		Dame)
1944	Les Horvath (Ohio State)	1955	Howard Cassady (Ohio	1965	Mike Garrett (USC)
1945	Doc Blanchard (Army)		State)	1966	Steve Spurrier (Florida)
1946	Glenn Davis (Army)	1956	Paul Hornung (Notre	1967	Gary Beban (UCLA)
			Dame)		

1968	O J Simpson (USC)	1980	George Rogers (South	1990	Ty Detmer (Brigham
1969	Steve Owens (Oklahoma)		Carolina)		Young)
1970	Jim Plunkett (Stanford)	1981	Marcus Allen (USC)	1991	Desmond Howard
1971	Pat Sullivan (Auburn)	1982	Herschel Walker (Georgia)		(Michigan)
1972	Johnny Rogers (Nebraska)	1983	Mike Rozier (Nebraska)	1992	Gino Torretta (Miami)
1973	John Cappelletti (Penn	1984	Doug Flutie (Boston	1993	Charlie Ward (Florida
	State)		College)		State)
1974-5	Archie Griffin (Ohio	1985	Bo Jackson (Auburn)	1994	Rashaan Salaam
	State)	1986	Vinny Testaverde (Miami)		(Colorado)
1976	Tony Dorsett (Pittsburgh)	1987	Tim Brown (Notre Dame)	1995	Eddie George (Ohio State)
1977	Earl Campbell (Texas)	1988	Barry Sanders (Oklahoma)	1996	Danny Wuerffel (Florida)
1978	Billy Sims (Oklahoma)	1989	Andre Ware (Houston)	1997	Charles Woodson
1979	Charles White (USC)				(Michigan)

World League

In 1991 the NFL inaugurated the World League of American Football as an international spring league. Franchises were granted to teams in the USA, Canada, Mexico, the UK, Germany, Italy and Spain, and the event was contested for two years.

The NFL agreed at the end of 1993 to end the World League, and to create an all-European league from 1995, with the return of the World Bowl as its final.

World Bowl

Results:

1991	London Monarchs 21 Barcelona Dragons 0	1996	Scottish Claymores 32 Frankfurt Galaxy 27
1992	Sacramento Surge 21 Orlando Thunder 17	1997	Barcelona Dragons 38 Rhein Fire 24
1995	Frankfurt Galaxy 26 Amsterdam Admirals 22	1998	Rhein Fire 34 Frankfurt Galaxy 10

European Championships

Winners:

Italy	1983, 1987
Finland	1985, 1993, 1995, 1997
Great Britain	1989, 1991

Eurobowl Winners

Winners:

1986	Taft Vantaa (Fin)	1991-2	Amsterdam Crusaders (Hol)
1988	Helsinki Roosters (Fin)	1993-4	London Olympians (UK)
1989	Legnano Frogs (Ita)	1995	Düsseldorf Panthers (Ger)
1990	Manchester Spartans (UK)	1996-8	Hamburg Blue Devils (Ger)

Canadian Football

Canadian football differs in several respects from American football, including having teams of 12 rather than 11 players. The earliest recorded game of football in Canada was between students at the University of Toronto in 1861. The Canadian Football League (CFL) was founded as a professional organization in 1958.

Governing body: Canadian Football League, CFL Building, 110 Eglinton Avenue West, 5th Floor, Toronto, Ontario M4R 1A3. Tel: (1) 416 322 9650. Chairman: John Tory.

Grey Cup

In 1909 Earl Grey, the Governor-General of Canada, donated a trophy to be awarded annually to the Canadian rugby football champion. From 1954 however, the Earl Grey Cup was awarded to the champion of the CFL.
Winners:

14	Toronto Argonauts 1914, 1921, 1933, 1937-8, 1945-7, 1950, 1952, 1983, 1991, 1996-7
12	Hamilton Tigers (Tiger-Cats from 1953) 1913, 1915, 1928-9, 1932, 1953, 1957, 1963, 1965, 1967, 1972, 1986
11	Edmonton Eskimos 1954-6, 1975, 1978-82, 1987, 1993 (most CFL wins)

9	Winnipeg Blue Bombers 1939, 1941, 1958-9, 1961-2, 1984, 1988, 1990
7	Ottawa Senators 1925-6, 1960, 1968-9, 1973, 1976
4	Montreal Alouettes 1949, 1970, 1974, 1977
4	University of Toronto 1909-11, 1920
3	Queen's University 1922-4
3	Calgary Stampeders 1948, 1971, 1992
3	British Columbia Lions 1964, 1985, 1994
2	Ottawa Rough Riders 1940, 1951
2	Sarnia Imperials 1934, 1936
2	Sasketchewan Roughriders 1966, 1989
2	Toronto Balmy Beach 1927, 1930
1	Hamilton Alerts 1912, Montreal AAA Winged Wheelers 1931, Winnipeg 1935, Toronto Hurricanes 1942, Hamilton Flying Wildcats 1943, St Hyacinthe-Donnacona Navy 1944, Baltimore Stallions (USA) 1995

CFL Most Outstanding Player
Most wins: 5 Doug Flutie (Calgary, Toronto, QB 1991-4, 1996); 3 Jackie Parker (Edmonton, QB 1957-8, 1960)

Angling

Angling is the art of catching fish with rod, line and hook. The activity dates back to civilized man's earliest days. The oldest club still in existence is the Ellem fishing club in Scotland, formed in 1829. English national championships were first held in 1906.
International governing body: Confédération Internationale de la Pêche Sportive (CIPS), formed in Rome in 1952.

World Championships

The first World Fresh Water Championship was held in 1957, three years after the staging of the first European championship. A separate women's championship was first held in 1994.
Winners:

	Men's individual	Men's team		Men's individual	Men's team
1957	Mandeli (Ita)	Italy	1983	Wolf-Rüdiger Kremkus (FRG)	Belgium
1958	Garroit (Bel)	Belgium	1984	Bobby Smithers (Ire)	Luxembourg
1959	Robert Tesse (Fra)	France	1985	Dave Roper (Eng)	England
1960	Robert Tesse (Fra)	Belgium	1986	Lud Wever (Hol)	Italy
1961	Ramon Legogue (Fra)	GDR	1987	Clive Branson (Wal)	England
1962	Raimondo Tedasco (Ita)	Italy	1988	Jean-Pierre Fouquet (Fra)	England
1963	William Lane (Eng)	France	1989	Tom Pickering (Eng)	Wales
1964	Joseph Fontanet (Fra)	France	1990	Bob Nudd (Eng)	France
1965	Robert Tesse (Fra)	Romania	1991	Bob Nudd (Eng)	England
1966	Henri Guiheneuf (Fra)	France	1992	David Wesson (Aus)	Italy
1967	Jacques Isenbaert (Bel)	Belgium	1993	Mario Barros (Por)	Italy
1968	Günter Grebenstein (FRG)	France	1994	Bob Nudd (Eng)	England
1969	Robin Harris (Eng)	Holland	1995	Paul Jean (Fra)	France
1970	Marcel Van den Eynde (Bel)	Belgium	1996-7	Alan Scotthorne (Eng)	Italy
1971	Dino Bassi (Ita)	Italy	**Most individual wins:** 3 Tesse, Nudd		
1972	Hubert Levels (Hol)	France	**Most team wins:** 13 France		
1973	Pierre Michiels (Bel)	Belgium			
1974	Aribert Richter (FRG)	France		Women's individual	Women's team
1975	Ian Heaps (Eng)	France	1994	Astrid Block (Ger)	Italy
1976	Dino Bassi (Ita)	Italy	1997	Wendy Locker (Eng)	England
1977	Jean Mainil (Bel)	Luxembourg			
1978	Jean-Pierre Fouquet (Fra)	France			
1979	Gérard Heulard (Fra)	France			
1980	Wolf-Rüdiger Kremkus (FRG)	F R Germany			
1981	Dave Thomas (Eng)	France			
1982	Kevin Ashurst (Eng)	Holland			

World Fly-Fishing Championships

The world fly-fishing championships, organized by the CIPS, were first held in 1981.
Winners:

Year	Venue	Individual	Team
1981	Lake Echternach (Lux)	C Wittkamp (Hol)	Netherlands
1982	Narcea River (Spa)	Viktor Diez (Spa)	Italy
1983	Sesia River (Ita)	Segismondo Fernandez (Spa)	Italy
1984	Tormes River (Spa)	Tony Pawson (Eng)	Italy
1985	San River (Pol)	Leslaw Frasik (Pol)	Poland
1986	Ourthe River (Bel)	Slivoj Svoboda (Cs)	Italy
1987	Various locations (Eng)	Brian Leadbetter (Eng)	England
1988	Tasmania (Aus)	John Pawson (Eng)	England
1989	Kuusinski and Kitka Rivers (Fin)	Wladyslaw Trzebuinia (Pol)	Poland
1990	River Dee and Llyn Brenig (Wal)	Franciszek Szajnik (Pol)	Czechoslovakia
1991	Rotorua (NZ)	Brian Leadbetter (Eng)	New Zealand
1992	Three rivers in Italy	Pierluigi Coccito (Ita)	Italy
1993	Lakes in Kamloops area (Can)	Russell Owen (Wal)	England
1994	Ringebu & Lillehammer (Nor)	Pascal Cognard (Fra)	Czech Republic
1995	Loughs Conemara and Corrib (Ire)	Jeremy Hermann (Eng)	England
1996	Rivers Vlatova and Olava (Czc)	Picrluigi Coccito (Ita)	Czech Republic
1997	River Snake, Wyoming (USA)	Pascal Cognard (Fra)	France

Archery

From the use of bow and arrow in hunting and in warfare, archery developed as one of man's earliest-known organized sports. Practitioners can remain at the top for a long time. A notable example is Alice Blanche Legh, who won a record 23 British ladies' titles between 1881 and 1922, when she was 67.

International governing body: Fédération Internationale de Tir à l'Arc (FITA), Avenue de Cour 135, 1007 Lausanne, Switzerland. Tel: (41) 21 614 3050, Fax: (41) 21 614 3055. President: James L Easton, Executive Director: Tom Dielen. Founded 1931. 116 member nations (and 16 associate) in 1998.

Olympic Games

Archery was included in the Olympic Games from 1900 to 1908, then again in 1920 (at the Belgian style of shooting), and was reintroduced in 1972. Scores for 1972 to 1984 were for double FITA rounds (36 arrows at 90m, 70m, 50m and 30m for men; 70m, 60m, 50m and 30m for women), while in 1988 there was an open FITA round, then a series of elimination rounds with nine arrows shot at each distance. In 1992 the top 32, and in 1996 the top 64, competed in a knock-out competition after the initial ranking round. Team events for men and women were contested from 1988.
Winners:

Individual

Year	Men	Women
1972	John Williams (USA) 2528	Doreen Wilber (USA) 2424
1976	Darrell Pace (USA) 2571	Luann Ryon (USA) 2499
1980	Tomi Poikolainen (Fin) 2455	Keto Lossaberidze (USSR) 2491
1984	Darrell Pace (USA) 2616	Seo Hyang-soon (SKo) 2568
1988	Jay Barrs (USA) 338	Kim Soo-nyung (SKo) 344
1992	Sébastien Flute (Fra)	Cho Youn-jeong (SKo)
1996	Justin Huish (USA)	Kim Kyung-wook (SKo)

Team

Year	Men	Women
1988	South Korea 986	South Korea 982
1992*	Spain	South Korea
1996	USA	South Korea

* Conducted on a knock-out basis.

Olympic records for double FITA rounds

Men: Darrell Pace (USA) 2616 in 1984
Women: Kim Soo-nyung (SKo) 2683 in 1988

Most medals

Hubert Van Innis (Bel) won a record six gold and three silver medals: two gold, one silver 1900, the rest in 1920.

World Championships

World target archery championships were first staged in 1931 and are now held biennially. From 1957 to 1985 the contests were over double FITA rounds and scores are given for these. From 1987-91 the championships were conducted on a knock-out basis, with scores not being accumulated over the rounds; the scores given are for the final round of 36 arrows. Now there is a knock-out head-to-head competition for the top 64 from the ranking round of 72 arrows.

Winners:

Men's individual

1931	Michal Sawicki (Pol)	1958	Stig Thysell (Swe) 2101	1979	Darrell Pace (USA) 2474
1932	Laurent Reith (Bel)	1959	James Caspers (USA) 2247	1981	Kyösti Laasonen (Fin)
1933	Donald Mackenzie (USA)	1961	Joseph Thornton (USA)		2541
1934	Henry Kjellson (Swe)		2310	1983	Richard McKinney (USA)
1935	Adriaan van Kohlen (Bel)	1963	Charles Sandlin (USA)		2617
1936	Emil Heilborn (Swe)		2332	1985	Richard McKinney (USA)
1937	George De Rons (Bel)	1965	Matti Haikonen (Fin)		2601
1938	Frantisek Hadas (Cs)		2313	1987	Vladimir Yesheyev
1939	Roger Beday (Fra)	1967	Ray Rogers (USA) 2298		(USSR) 329
1946	Einar Tang Holbek (Den)	1969	Hardy Ward (USA) 2423	1989	Stanislav Zabrodskiy
1947-50	Hans Deutgen (Swe)	1971	John Williams (USA) 2445		(USSR) 332
1952	Stellan Andersson (Swe)	1973	Viktor Sidoruk (USSR)	1991	Simon Fairweather (Aus)
1953	Bror Lundgren (Swe)		2185		334
1955	Nils Andersson (Swe)	1975	Darrell Pace (USA) 2548	1993	Park Kyung-mo (SKo)
1957	Ozziek Smathers (USA)	1977	Richard McKinney (USA)	1995	Lee Kyung-chul (Kor)
	2231		2501	1997	Kim Kyung-ho (SKo)

Most wins: 4 Deutgen; 3 McKinney

Men's team

14	USA	1957, each title from 1959-83
5	Sweden	1934, 1948, 1952-3, 1955
4	Czechoslovakia	1936, 1938, 1947, 1949
4	South Korea	1985, 1991, 1995, 1997
3	France	1931, 1939, 1993
2	Poland	1932, 1937
2	Belgium	1933, 1935
2	Denmark	1946, 1950
1	Finland 1958, F R Germany 1987, USSR 1989	

Women's individual

1931-4	Janina Kurkowska (Pol)		1952	Jean Lee (USA)
1935	Ina Catani (Swe)		1953	Jean Richards (USA)
1936	Janina Kurkowska (Pol)		1955	Katarzyna Wisniowska (Pol)
1937	Ingo Simon (UK)		1957	Carole Meinhart (USA) 2120
1938	Nora Weston Martyr (UK)		1958	Sigrid Johansson (Swe) 2053
1939	Janina Kurkowska (Pol)		1959	Ann Corby (née Weber) (USA) 2023
1946	Nilla de Wharton Burr (UK)		1961	Nancy Vanderheide (USA) 2173
1947	Janina Kurkowska (Pol)		1963	Victoria Cook (USA) 2253
1948	Nilla de Wharton Burr (UK)		1965	Maire Lindholm (Fin) 2214
1949	Barbara Waterhouse (UK)		1967	Maria Maczynska (Pol) 2240
1950	Jean Lee (USA)		1969	Dorothy Lidstone (Can) 2361

1971	Emma Gapchenko (USSR) 2380		1985	Irina Soldatova (USSR) 2595
1973	Linda Myers (USA) 2204		1987	Ma Xangjun (Chn) 330
1975	Zebiniso Rustamova (USSR) 2465		1989	Kim Soo-nyung (SKo) 338
1977	Luann Ryon (USA) 2515		1991	Kim Soo-nyung (SKo) 333
1979	Kim Jin-ho (SKo) 2507		1993	Kim Hyo-jung (Sko)
1981	Natalya Butuzova (USSR) 2514		1995	Natalya Valeyeva (Mol)
1983	Kim Jin-ho (SKo) 2616		1997	Kim Du-ri (SKo)

Most wins: 7 Kurkowska (née Spychajowa)

Women's team

8	USA	1952, 1957-9, 1961, 1963, 1965, 1977
7	Poland	1933-4, 1936, 1938-9, 1967, 1971
7	South Korea	1979, 1983, 1989, 1991, 1993, 1995, 1997
6	USSR	1969, 1973, 1975, 1981, 1985, 1987
5	United Kingdom	1935, 1937, 1946, 1949, 1955
2	Finland	1950, 1953
1	Denmark 1947, Czechoslovakia 1948	

Compound bow – men

1995	Gary Broadhead (USA)
1997	Dee Wilde (USA)

Compound bow – women

1995	Angela Moscarelli (USA)
1997	Fabiola Palazzini (Ita)

Compound bow – men's team

1995	France
1997	Hungary

Compound bow – women's team

1995	USA
1997	Italy

World Records

For single FITA rounds (maximum 360 points for each set).

Men

Olympic FITA	1368	Oh Kyo-moon (SKo) 1995
Olympic 90m	330	Vladimir Yesheyev (USSR) 1990
Olympic 70m	345	Fear Jackson (Aus) 1997
Olympic 50m	351	Kim Kyung-ho (SKo) 1997
Olympic 30m	360	Han Seung-hoon (SKo) 1994
Olympic Team	4053	South Korea (Oh Kyo-moon, Lee Eun-kyung, Kim Jae-rak) 1995
Compound FITA	1379	Brian Politis (Aus) 1998
Compound 90m	329	Brian Politis (Aus) 1998
Compound 70m	347	Adam Richards (Aus) 1998
Compound 50m	346	Brian Politis (Aus) 1998
Compound 30m	358	Brian Politis (Aus) 1998
Compound Team	3977	USA (Gary Broadhead, Tom Crowe, John Vozzy) 1995

Women

Olympic FITA	1377	Kim Jung-rye (SKo) 1995
Olympic 70m	341	Chung Chang-sook (SKo) 1997
Olympic 60m	349	Ying He (Chn) 1995
Olympic 50m	345	Kim Moon-sun (SKo) 1996
Olympic 30m	357	Joanne Edens (UK) 1990
Olympic Team	4094	South Korea (Cho Youn-jeong, Kim Soo-nyung, Lee Eun-kyung) 1992
Compound FITA	1363	Nicole Bartlett (Aus) 1998
Compound 70m	334	Marie Hulbert (Aus) 1998
Compound 60m	347	Nicole Bartlett (Aus) 1998
Compound 50m	336	Petra Ericsson (Swe) 1997
Compound 30m	358	Madeline Ferris (Aus) 1998
Compound Team	3954	France (Michèle Deloraine, Valérie Fabre, Catherine Pellen)

World Indoor Championships

First held in 1991.
Winners:

Year	Individual	Team	Year	Individual	Team
Men freestyle (Olympic)			**Women freestyle (Olympic)**		
1991	Sébastien Flûte (Fra)		1991	Natalya Valeyeva (USSR)	
1993	Gennadiy Metrofanov (Rus)		1993	Jennifer O'Donnell (USA)	
1995	Magnus Pattersson (Swe)	USA	1995	Natalya Valeyeva (Mol)	Ukraine
1997	Chung Jae-hun (SKo)	S Korea	1997	Tetyana Muntyan (Ukr)	USA
Men compound bow			**Women compound bow**		
1991	Joe Asay (USA)		1991	Lucia Panico (Ita)	
1993	Kirk Ethridge (USA)		1993	Inga Low (USA)	
1995	Mike Hendrikse (USA)	USA	1995	Glenda Penaz (USA	USA
1997	Dee Wilde (USA)	Sweden	1997	Valérie Fabre (Fra)	USA

World Indoor Records

For FITA rounds, maximum score 600.

Men

Olympic 18m	596	Magnus Pattersson (Swe) 1995
Olympic 25m	593	Magnus Pattersson (Swe) 1993
Compound 18m	596	Dee Wilds (USA) 1994
Compound 25m	592	Tom Henriksen (Den) 1998

Women

Olympic 18m	590	Natalya Valeyeva (Mol) 1995
Olympic 25m	592	Petra Ericsson (Swe) 1991
Compound 18m	589	Petra Ericsson (Swe) 1997
Compound 25m	570	Susanne Kessler (Den) 1995

World Field Archery Championships

Held (now biennially) in three bow divisions: bare bow (from 1959), recurve (1969) and compound (1990).
Most wins: 4 Anders Rosenberg (Swe), men's bare bow 1978, 1980, 1982 and 1992

Athletics

Competition in running, jumping or throwing dates back to pre-history. The earliest evidence of organized running is from about 3800BC in Egypt, and athletic achievements were particularly prized at the ancient Olympic Games in Greece. Those Games were more than just sporting contests; they were also great artistic and cultural festivals, maintaining the Greek ideal of perfection of mind and body. They provided the inspiration for the modern Olympic Games, which have provided the focus for world athletics since their reintroduction in 1896. Separate World Championships for all events were instituted in 1983, and nowadays there is a plethora of top-class competition.

The first National Championships were those of England in 1866, organized by the Amateur Athletic Club. These preceded the formation of the Amateur Athletic Association, in 1880. The International Amateur Athletic Federation was formed in 1912, and ratified the first list of world records in 1914.

International governing body: The International Amateur Athletic Federation (IAAF), 17 rue Princesse Florestine, B.P.359, Monte Carlo 98007, Monaco. Tel: (377) 93 307070, Fax: (377) 93 159515. President: Dr Primo Nebiolo, General Secretary: István Gyulai. Formed in 1912, initially with 17 members. 209 affiliated nations by 1998.

(Times are given in minutes: seconds; distances in metres; w denotes wind-assisted result.)

Olympic Games

At the first Olympic Games of the modern era, in Athens, Greece, 6-15 April 1896, just 59 athletes from ten nations contested the athletics events. The 1900 and 1904 Games were also small-scale affairs, with just over 100 athletes at each; from 1908 the Games grew rapidly in importance, to become true world championships. Women's events were first included in 1928, and the number of contestants in athletics exceeded 1000 for the first time at the 1960 Games. Automatic timing was first used at the Olympic Games in 1932.

(Automatic times are given, where known, for proper comparisons. OR denotes Olympic record.)

Men

100 metres

1896	Thomas Burke (USA) 12.0
1900	Francis Jarvis (USA) 11.0
1904	Archie Hahn (USA) 11.0
1906	Archie Hahn (USA) 11.2
1908	Reginald Walker (SAf) 10.8
1912	Ralph Craig (USA) 10.8
1920	Charles Paddock (USA) 10.8
1924	Harold Abrahams (UK) 10.6
1928	Percy Williams (Can) 10.8
1932	Eddie Tolan (USA) 10.38
1936	Jesse Owens (USA) 10.3
1948	Harrison Dillard (USA) 10.3
1952	Lindy Remigino (USA) 10.79
1956	Bobby Morrow (USA) 10.62
1960	Armin Hary (FRG) 10.32
1964	Robert Hayes (USA) 10.06
1968	James Hines (USA) 9.95
1972	Valeriy Borzov (USSR) 10.14
1976	Hasely Crawford (Tri) 10.06
1980	Allan Wells (UK) 10.25
1984	Carl Lewis (USA) 9.99
1988	Carl Lewis (USA) 9.92
1992	Linford Christie (UK) 9.96
1996	Donovan Bailey (Can) 9.84 OR

200 metres

1900	Walter Tewksbury (USA) 22.2
1904	Archie Hahn (USA) 21.6
1908	Robert Kerr (Can) 22.6
1912	Ralph Craig (USA) 21.7
1920	Allen Woodring (USA) 22.0
1924	Jackson Scholz (USA) 21.6
1928	Percy Williams (Can) 21.8
1932	Eddie Tolan (USA) 21.12
1936	Jesse Owens (USA) 20.7
1948	Melvin Patton (USA) 21.1
1952	Andrew Stanfield (USA) 20.81
1956	Bobby Morrow (USA) 20.75
1960	Livio Berruti (Ita) 20.62
1964	Henry Carr (USA) 20.36
1968	Tommie Smith (USA) 19.83
1972	Valeriy Borzov (USSR) 20.00
1976	Donald Quarrie (Jam) 20.22
1980	Pietro Mennea (Ita) 20.19
1984	Carl Lewis (USA) 19.80
1988	Joe DeLoach (USA) 19.75

1992	Michael Marsh (USA) 20.01
1996	Michael Johnson (USA) 19.32 OR

400 metres

1896	Thomas Burke (USA) 54.2
1900	Maxie Long (USA) 49.4
1904	Harry Hillman (USA) 49.2
1906	Paul Pilgrim (USA) 53.2
1908	Wyndham Halswelle (UK) 50.0
1912	Charles Reidpath (USA) 48.2
1920	Bevil Rudd (SAf) 49.6
1924	Eric Liddell (UK) 47.6
1928	Ray Barbuti (USA) 47.8
1932	Bill Carr (USA) 46.28
1936	Archie Williams (USA) 46.66
1948	Arthur Wint (Jam) 46.2
1952	George Rhoden (Jam) 46.09
1956	Charles Jenkins (USA) 46.86
1960	Otis Davis (USA) 45.07
1964	Michael Larrabee (USA) 45.15
1968	Lee Evans (USA) 43.86
1972	Vincent Matthews (USA) 44.66
1976	Alberto Juantorena (Cub) 44.26
1980	Viktor Markin (USSR) 44.60
1984	Alonzo Babers (USA) 44.27
1988	Steve Lewis (USA) 43.87
1992	Quincy Watts (USA) 43.50
1996	Michael Johnson (USA) 43.49 OR

800 metres

1896	Edwin Flack (Aus) 2:11.0
1900	Alfred Tysoe (UK) 2:01.2
1904	James Lightbody (USA) 1:56.0
1906	Paul Pilgrim (USA) 2:01.5
1908	Mel Sheppard (USA) 1:52.8
1912	James Meredith (USA) 1:51.9
1920	Albert Hill (UK) 1:53.4
1924	Douglas Lowe (UK) 1:52.4
1928	Douglas Lowe (UK) 1:51.8
1932	Tom Hampson (UK) 1:49.70
1936	John Woodruff (USA) 1:52.9
1948	Malvin Whitfield (USA) 1:49.2
1952	Malvin Whitfield (USA) 1:49.34
1956	Thomas Courtney (USA) 1:47.75
1960	Peter Snell (NZ) 1:46.48
1964	Peter Snell (NZ) 1:45.1
1968	Ralph Doubell (Aus) 1:44.40
1972	David Wottle (USA) 1:45.86

1976	Alberto Juantorena (Cub) 1:43.50
1980	Steve Ovett (UK) 1:45.40
1984	Joaquim Cruz (Bra) 1:43.00
1988	Paul Ereng (Ken) 1:43.45
1992	William Tanui (Ken) 1:43.66
1996	Vebjørn Rodal (Nor) 1:42.58 OR

1500 metres

1896	Edwin Flack (Aus) 4:33.2
1900	Charles Bennett (UK) 4:06.2
1904	James Lightbody (USA) 4:05.4
1906	James Lightbody (USA) 4:12.0
1908	Mel Sheppard (USA) 4:03.4
1912	Arnold Jackson (UK) 3:56.8
1920	Albert Hill (UK) 4:01.8
1924	Paavo Nurmi (Fin) 3:53.6
1928	Harri Larva (Fin) 3:53.2
1932	Luigi Beccali (Ita) 3:51.20
1936	Jack Lovelock (NZ) 3:47.8
1948	Henry Eriksson (Swe) 3:49.8
1952	Josef Barthel (Lux) 3:45.28
1956	Ron Delany (Ire) 3:41.49
1960	Herbert Elliott (Aus) 3:35.6
1964	Peter Snell (NZ) 3:38.1
1968	Kipchoge Keino (Ken) 3:34.91
1972	Pekka Vasala (Fin) 3:36.33
1976	John Walker (NZ) 3:39.17
1980	Sebastian Coe (UK) 3:38.40
1984	Sebastian Coe (UK) 3:32.53 OR
1988	Peter Rono (Ken) 3:35.96
1992	Fermin Cacho (Spa) 3:40.12
1996	Noureddine Morceli (Alg) 3:35.78

5000 metres

1912	Hannes Kolehmainen (Fin) 14:36.6
1920	Joseph Guillemot (Fra) 14:55.6
1924	Paavo Nurmi (Fin) 14:31.2
1928	Ville Ritola (Fin) 14:38.0
1932	Lauri Lehtinen (Fin) 14:29.91
1936	Gunnar Höckert (Fin) 14:22.2
1948	Gaston Reiff (Bel) 14:17.6
1952	Emil Zátopek (Cs) 14:06.72
1956	Vladimir Kuts (USSR) 13:39.86
1960	Murray Halberg (NZ) 13:43.4
1964	Robert Schul (USA) 13:48.8

1968	Mohamed Gammoudi (Tun) 14:05.0
1972	Lasse Viren (Fin) 13:26.42
1976	Lasse Viren (Fin) 13:24.76
1980	Miruts Yifter (Eth) 13.20.91
1984	Saïd Aouita (Mor) 13:05.59 OR
1988	John Ngugi (Ken) 13:11.70
1992	Dieter Baumann (Ger) 13:12.52
1996	Vénuste Niyongabo (Bur) 13:07.96

10,000 metres

1912	Hannes Kolehmainen (Fin) 31:20.8
1920	Paavo Nurmi (Fin) 31:45.8
1924	Ville Ritola (Fin) 30:23.2
1928	Paavo Nurmi (Fin) 30:18.8
1932	Janusz Kusocinski (Pol) 30:11.4
1936	Ilmari Salminen (Fin) 30:15.4
1948	Emil Zátopek (Cs) 29:59.6
1952	Emil Zátopek (Cs) 29:17.0
1956	Vladimir Kuts (USSR) 28:45.60
1960	Pyotr Bolotnikov (USSR) 28:32.18
1964	William Mills (USA) 28:24.4
1968	Naftali Temu (Ken) 29:27.4
1972	Lasse Viren (Fin) 27:38.35
1976	Lasse Viren (Fin) 27:40.38
1980	Miruts Yifter (Eth) 27:42.69
1984	Alberto Cova (Ita) 27:47.54
1988	Brahim Boutayeb (Mor) 27:21.46
1992	Khalid Skah (Mor) 27:46.70
1996	Haile Gebrselassie (Eth) 27:07.34 OR

Marathon (42.195km)

1896	Spyridon Louis (Gre) 2:58:50 (40km)
1900	Michel Théato (Lux) 2:59:45 (40.26km)
1904	Thomas Hicks (USA) 3:28:53 (40km)
1906	William Sherring (Can) 2:51:23.6 (41.86km)
1908	John Hayes (USA) 2:55:18.4
1912	Kenneth McArthur (SAf) 2:36:54.8 (40.2km)
1920	Hannes Kolehmainen (Fin) 2:32:35.8 (42.75km)
1924	Albin Stenroos (Fin) 2:41:22.6
1928	Mohamed Boughéra El Ouafi (Fra) 2:32:57.0

1932	Juan Carlos Zabala (Arg) 2:31:36.0
1936	Kitei Son (Jap)★ 2:29:19.2
1948	Delfo Cabrera (Arg) 2:34:51.6
1952	Emil Zátopek (Cs) 2:23:03.2
1956	Alain Mimoun (Fra) 2:25:00.0
1960	Abebe Bikila (Eth) 2:15:16.2
1964	Abebe Bikila (Eth) 2:12:11.2
1968	Mamo Wolde (Eth) 2:20:26.4
1972	Frank Shorter (USA) 2:12:19.8
1976	Waldemar Cierpinski (GDR) 2:09:55
1980	Waldemar Cierpinski (GDR) 2:11:03
1984	Carlos Lopes (Por) 2:09:21 OR
1988	Gelindo Bordin (Ita) 2:10:32
1992	Hwang Young-cho (SKo) 2:13:23
1996	Josiah Thugwane (SAf) 2:12:36

★ Actually the Korean Sohn Kee-chung.

110 metres hurdles

1896	Thomas Curtis (USA) 17.6
1900	Alvin Kraenzlein (USA) 15.4
1904	Fred Schule (USA) 16.0
1906	Robert Leavitt (USA) 16.2
1908	Forrest Smithson (USA) 15.0
1912	Fred Kelly (USA) 15.1
1920	Earl Thomson (Can) 14.8
1924	Daniel Kinsey (USA) 15.0
1928	Sydney Atkinson (SAf) 14.8
1932	George Saling (USA) 14.57
1936	Forrest Towns (USA) 14.2
1948	William Porter (USA) 13.9
1952	Harrison Dillard (USA) 13.91
1956	Lee Calhoun (USA) 13.70
1960	Lee Calhoun (USA) 13.98
1964	Hayes Jones (USA) 13.67
1968	Willie Davenport (USA) 13.33
1972	Rodney Milburn (USA) 13.24
1976	Guy Drut (Fra) 13.30
1980	Thomas Munkelt (GDR) 13.39
1984	Roger Kingdom (USA) 13.20
1988	Roger Kingdom (USA) 12.98
1992	Mark McKoy (Can) 13.12
1996	Allen Johnson (USA) 12.95 OR

400 metres hurdles

1900	Walter Tewksbury (USA) 57.6
1904	Harry Hillman (USA) 53.0
1908	Charles Bacon (USA) 55.0
1920	Frank Loomis (USA) 54.0
1924	Morgan Taylor (USA) 52.6
1928	Lord Burghley (UK) 53.4
1932	Robert Tisdall (Ire) 51.67
1936	Glenn Hardin (USA) 52.4
1948	Roy Cochran (USA) 51.1
1952	Charles Moore (USA) 51.06
1956	Glenn Davis (USA) 50.29
1960	Glenn Davis (USA) 49.51
1964	Rex Cawley (USA) 49.69
1968	David Hemery (UK) 48.12
1972	John Akii-Bua (Uga) 47.82
1976	Edwin Moses (USA) 47.63
1980	Volker Beck (GDR) 48.70
1984	Edwin Moses (USA) 47.75
1988	Andre Phillips (USA) 47.19
1992	Kevin Young (USA) 46.78 OR
1996	Derrick Adkins (USA) 47.54

Steeplechase

1900	George Orton (Can) 7:34.4 (2500m)
1900	John Rimmer (UK) 12:58.4 (4000m)
1904	James Lightbody (USA) 7:39.6 (2590m)
1908	Arthur Russell (UK) 10:47.8 (3200m)

3000 metres steeplechase

1920	Percy Hodge (UK) 10:00.4
1924	Ville Ritola (Fin) 9:33.6
1928	Toivo Loukola (Fin) 9:21.8
1932	Volmari Iso-Hollo (Fin) 10:33.4★
1936	Volmari Iso-Hollo (Fin) 9:03.8
1948	Tore Sjöstrand (Swe) 9:04.6
1952	Horace Ashenfelter (USA) 8:45.68
1956	Christopher Brasher (UK) 8:41.35
1960	Zdzislaw Kryszkowiak (Pol) 8:34.31
1964	Gaston Roelants (Bel) 8:30.8
1968	Amos Biwott (Ken) 8:51.0
1972	Kipchoge Keino (Ken) 8:23.64
1976	Anders Gärderud (Swe) 8:08.02
1980	Bronislaw Malinowski (Pol) 8:09.70

1984 Julius Korir (Ken) 8:11.80
1988 Julius Kariuki (Ken) 8:05.51
      OR
1992 Matthew Birir (Ken) 8:08.94
1996 Joseph Keter (Ken) 8:07.12
* Due to lap-counting error, distance
was 3460 metres.

High jump
1896 Ellery Clark (USA) 1.81
1900 Irving Baxter (USA) 1.90
1904 Samuel Jones (USA) 1.80
1906 Con Leahy (UK/Ire) 1.77
1908 Harry Porter (USA) 1.90
1912 Alma Richards (USA) 1.93
1920 Richmond Landon (USA)
      1.94
1924 Harold Osborn (USA) 1.98
1928 Robert King (USA) 1.94
1932 Duncan McNaughton (Can)
      1.97
1936 Cornelius Johnson (USA)
      2.03
1948 John Winter (Aus) 1.98
1952 Walter Davis (USA) 2.04
1956 Charles Dumas (USA) 2.12
1960 Robert Shavlakadze (USSR)
      2.16
1964 Valeriy Brumel (USSR) 2.18
1968 Dick Fosbury (USA) 2.24
1972 Jüri Tarmak (USSR) 2.23
1976 Jacek Wszola (Pol) 2.25
1980 Gerd Wessig (GDR) 2.36
1984 Dietmar Mögenburg (FRG)
      2.35
1988 Gennadiy Avdeyenko
      (USSR) 2.38
1992 Javier Sotomayor (Cub) 2.34
1996 Charles Austin (USA) 2.39
      OR

Pole vault
1896 William Hoyt (USA) 3.30
1900 Irving Baxter (USA) 3.30
1904 Charles Dvorak (USA) 3.50
1906 Fernand Gonder (Fra) 3.40
1908 Edward Cooke & Alfred
      Gilbert (USA) 3.71
1912 Harry Babcock (USA) 3.95
1920 Frank Foss (USA) 4.09
1924 Lee Barnes (USA) 3.95
1928 Sabin Carr (USA) 4.20
1932 Bill Miller (USA) 4.31
1936 Earle Meadows (USA) 4.35
1948 Guinn Smith (USA) 4.30
1952 Robert Richards (USA) 4.55
1956 Robert Richards (USA) 4.56
1960 Donald Bragg (USA) 4.70

1964 Frederick Hansen (USA) 5.10
1968 Bob Seagren (USA) 5.40
1972 Wolfgang Nordwig (GDR)
      5.50
1976 Tadeusz Slusarski (Pol) 5.50
1980 Wladyslaw Kozakiewicz (Pol)
      5.78
1984 Pierre Quinon (Fra) 5.75
1988 Sergey Bubka (USSR) 5.90
1992 Maksim Tarasov (CIS/Rus)
      5.80
1996 Jean Galfione (Fra) 5.92 OR
      (also 5.92 OR: Igor
      Trandenkov (Rus), Andrei
      Tivontchik (Ger))

Long jump
1896 Ellery Clark (USA) 6.35
1900 Alvin Kraenzlein (USA) 7.18
1904 Myer Prinstein (USA) 7.34
1906 Myer Prinstein (USA) 7.20
1908 Francis Irons (USA) 7.48
1912 Albert Gutterson (USA) 7.60
1920 William Pettersson (Swe)
      7.15
1924 William De Hart Hubbard
      (USA) 7.44
1928 Edward Hamm (USA) 7.73
1932 Edward Gordon (USA) 7.64
1936 Jesse Owens (USA) 8.06
1948 William Steele (USA) 7.82
1952 Jerome Biffle (USA) 7.57
1956 Gregory Bell (USA) 7.83
1960 Ralph Boston (USA) 8.12
1964 Lynn Davies (UK) 8.07
1968 Bob Beamon (USA) 8.90
      OR
1972 Randy Williams (USA) 8.24
1976 Arnie Robinson (USA) 8.35
1980 Lutz Dombrowski (GDR)
      8.54
1984 Carl Lewis (USA) 8.54
1988 Carl Lewis (USA) 8.72
1992 Carl Lewis (USA) 8.67
1996 Carl Lewis (USA) 8.50

Triple jump
1896 James Connolly (USA) 13.71
1900 Myer Prinstein (USA) 14.47
1904 Myer Prinstein (USA) 14.325
1906 Peter O'Connor (UK/Ire)
      14.07
1908 Tim Ahearne (UK/Ire) 14.91
1912 Gustaf Lindblom (Swe) 14.76
1920 Vilho Tuulos (Fin) 14.50
1924 Anthony Winter (Aus) 15.52
1928 Mikio Oda (Jap) 15.21
1932 Chuhei Nambu (Jap) 15.72

1936 Naoto Tajima (Jap) 16.00
1948 Arne Åhman (Swe) 15.40
1952 Adhemar Ferreira da Silva
      (Bra) 16.22
1956 Adhemar Ferreira da Silva
      (Bra) 16.35
1960 Jozef Schmidt (Pol) 16.81
1964 Jozef Schmidt (Pol) 16.85
1968 Viktor Saneyev (USSR)
      17.39
1972 Viktor Saneyev (USSR)
      17.35
1976 Viktor Saneyev (USSR)
      17.29
1980 Jaak Uudmäe (USSR) 17.35
1984 Al Joyner (USA) 17.26
1988 Khristo Markov (Bul) 17.61
1992 Mike Conley (USA) 18.17w
1996 Kenny Harrison (USA) 18.09
      OR

Shot
1896 Robert Garrett (USA) 11.22
1900 Richard Sheldon (USA)
      14.10
1904 Ralph Rose (USA) 14.80
1906 Martin Sheridan (USA) 12.32
1908 Ralph Rose (USA) 14.21
1912 Patrick McDonald (USA)
      15.34
1920 Ville Pörhölä (Fin) 14.81
1924 Clarence Houser (USA)
      14.99
1928 John Kuck (USA) 15.87
1932 Leo Sexton (USA) 16.00
1936 Hans Woellke (Ger) 16.20
1948 Wilbur Thompson (USA)
      17.12
1952 Parry O'Brien (USA) 17.41
1956 Parry O'Brien (USA) 18.57
1960 William Nieder (USA) 19.68
1964 Dallas Long (USA) 20.33
1968 Randy Matson (USA) 20.54
1972 Wladyslaw Komar (Pol)
      21.18
1976 Udo Beyer (GDR) 21.05
1980 Vladimir Kiselyov (USSR)
      21.35
1984 Alessandro Andrei (Ita) 21.26
1988 Ulf Timmermann (GDR)
      22.47 OR
1992 Mike Stulce (USA) 21.70
1996 Randy Barnes (USA) 21.62

Discus
1896 Robert Garrett (USA) 29.15
1900 Rudolf Bauer (Hun) 36.04
1904 Martin Sheridan (USA) 39.28

1906	Martin Sheridan (USA) 41.46
1908	Martin Sheridan (USA) 40.89
1912	Armas Taipale (Fin) 45.21
1920	Elmer Niklander (Fin) 44.685
1924	Clarence Houser (USA) 46.155
1928	Clarence Houser (USA) 47.32
1932	John Anderson (USA) 49.49
1936	Ken Carpenter (USA) 50.48
1948	Adolfo Consolini (Ita) 52.78
1952	Sim Iness (USA) 55.03
1956	Al Oerter (USA) 56.36
1960	Al Oerter (USA) 59.18
1964	Al Oerter (USA) 61.00
1968	Al Oerter (USA) 64.78
1972	Ludvik Danek (Cs) 64.40
1976	Mac Wilkins (USA) 67.50
1980	Viktor Rashchupkin (USSR) 66.64
1984	Rolf Danneberg (FRG) 66.60
1988	Jürgen Schult (GDR) 68.82
1992	Romas Ubartas (Lit) 65.12
1996	Lars Riedel (Ger) 69.40 OR

Hammer

1900	John Flanagan (USA) 49.73
1904	John Flanagan (USA) 51.23
1908	John Flanagan (USA) 51.92
1912	Matt McGrath (USA) 54.74
1920	Patrick Ryan (USA) 52.87
1924	Fred Tootell (USA) 53.29
1928	Patrick O'Callaghan (Ire) 51.39
1932	Patrick O'Callaghan (Ire) 53.92
1936	Karl Hein (Ger) 56.49
1948	Imre Németh (Hun) 56.07
1952	József Csermak (Hun) 60.34
1956	Harold Connolly (USA) 63.19
1960	Vasiliy Rudenkov (USSR) 67.10
1964	Romuald Klim (USSR) 69.74
1968	Gyula Zsivótzky (Hun) 73.36
1972	Anatoliy Bondarchuk (USSR) 75.50
1976	Yuriy Sedykh (USSR) 77.52
1980	Yuriy Sedykh (USSR) 81.80
1984	Juha Tiainen (Fin) 78.08
1988	Sergey Litvinov (USSR) 84.80 OR
1992	Andrey Abduvaliyev (CIS/Tjk) 82.54
1996	Balázs Kiss (Hun) 81.24

Javelin

1906	Erik Lemming (Swe) 53.90
1908	Erik Lemming (Swe) 54.82
1912	Erik Lemming (Swe) 60.64
1920	Jonni Myyrä (Fin) 65.78
1924	Jonni Myyrä (Fin) 62.96
1928	Erik Lundkvist (Swe) 66.60
1932	Matti Järvinen (Fin) 72.71
1936	Gerhard Stöck (Ger) 71.84
1948	Tapio Rautavaara (Fin) 69.77
1952	Cyrus Young (USA) 73.78
1956	Egil Danielsen (Nor) 85.71
1960	Viktor Tsibulenko (USSR) 84.64
1964	Pauli Nevala (Fin) 82.66
1968	Janis Lusis (USSR) 90.10
1972	Klaus Wolfermann (FRG) 90.48
1976	Miklós Németh (Hun) 94.58 OR
1980	Dainis Kula (USSR) 91.20

New-specification javelin

1984	Arto Harkönen (Fin) 86.76
1988	Tapio Korjus (Fin) 84.28
1992	Jan Zelezny (Cs) 89.66 OR
1996	Jan Zelezny (Cze) 88.16

Decathlon

(There have been several different scoring tables, for comparision all points re-scored on 1984 tables.)

1912	Jim Thorpe (USA) 6564#
1920	Helge Lövland (Nor) 5804
1924	Harold Osborn (USA) 6476
1928	Paavo Yrjölä (Fin) 6587★
1932	James Bausch (USA) 6735★
1936	Glenn Morris (USA) 7254
1948	Robert Mathias (USA) 6628
1952	Robert Mathias (USA) 7592
1956	Milton Campbell (USA) 7614
1960	Rafer Johnson (USA) 7926
1964	Willi Holdorf (FRG) 7794 (estimated)
1968	Bill Toomey (USA) 8144
1972	Nikolay Avilov (USSR) 8466
1976	Bruce Jenner (USA) 8634
1980	Daley Thompson (UK) 8522
1984	Daley Thompson (UK) 8847 OR
1988	Christian Schenk (GDR) 8488
1992	Robert Zmelík (Cs) 8611
1996	Dan O'Brien (USA) 8824

Disqualified for professionalism, and gold given to Hugo Weislander (Swe) 5965; Thorpe was posthu-mously reinstated in 1982.

★ On the 1984 tables, the second-placed Akilles Järvinen scored 6645 in 1928 and 6879 in 1932.

20 kilometres walk

1956	Leonid Spirin (USSR) 1:31:27.4
1960	Vladimir Golubnichiy (USSR) 1:34:07.2
1964	Kenneth Matthews (UK) 1:29:34.0
1968	Vladimir Golubnichiy (USSR) 1:33:58.4
1972	Peter Frenkel (GDR) 1:26:42.4
1976	Daniel Bautista (Mex) 1:24:40.6
1980	Maurizio Damilano (Ita) 1:23:35.5
1984	Ernesto Canto (Mex) 1:23:13
1988	Jozef Pribilinec (Cs) 1:19:57 OR
1992	Daniel Plaza (Spa) 1:21:45
1996	Jefferson Pérez (Ecu) 1:20:07

50 kilometres walk

1932	Thomas Green (UK) 4:50:10.0
1936	Harold Whitlock (UK) 4:30:41.4
1948	John Ljunggren (Swe) 4:41:52.0
1952	Giuseppe Dordoni (Ita) 4:28:07.8
1956	Norman Read (NZ) 4:30:42.8
1960	Don Thompson (UK) 4:25:30.0
1964	Abdon Pamich (Ita) 4:11:12.4
1968	Christoph Höhne (GDR) 4:20:13.6
1972	Bernd Kannenberg (FRG) 3:56:11.6
1980	Hartwig Gauder (GDR) 3:49:24
1984	Raúl Gonzales (Mex) 3:47:26
1988	Vyacheslav Ivanenko (USSR) 3:38:29 OR
1992	Andrey Perlov (CIS/Rus) 3:50:13
1996	Robert Korzeniowski (Pol) 3:43:30

4 x 100 metres relay

1912	UK 42.4
1920	USA 42.2
1924	USA 41.0

1928	USA 41.0
1932	USA 40.1
1936	USA 39.8
1948	USA 40.6
1952	USA 40.26
1956	USA 39.59
1960	F R Germany 39.66
1964	USA 39.06
1968	USA 38.23
1972	USA 38.19
1976	USA 38.33
1980	USSR 38.26
1984	USA 37.83
1988	USSR 38.19
1992	USA 37.40 OR
1996	Canada 37.69

Medley relay

(200m, 200m, 400m, 800m)

1908	USA 3:29.4

4 x 400 metres relay

1912	USA 3:16.6
1920	UK 3:22.2
1924	USA 3:16.0
1928	USA 3:14.2
1932	USA 3:08.14
1936	UK 3:09.0
1948	USA 3:10.4
1952	Jamaica 3:04.04
1956	USA 3:04.80
1960	USA 3:02.37
1964	USA 3:00.71
1968	USA 2:56.16
1972	Kenya 2:59.83
1976	USA 2:58.66
1980	USSR 3:01.08
1984	USA 2:57.91
1988	USA 2:56.16
1992	USA 2:55.74 OR
1996	USA 2:55.99

Women

100 metres

1928	Elizabeth Robinson (USA) 12.2
1932	Stanislawa Walasiewicz (Pol) 11.9
1936	Helen Stephens (USA) 11.5
1948	Fanny Blankers-Koen (Hol) 11.9
1952	Marjorie Jackson (Aus) 11.65
1956	Betty Cuthbert (Aus) 11.82
1960	Wilma Rudolph (USA) 11.18w
1964	Wyomia Tyus (USA) 11.49
1968	Wyomia Tyus (USA) 11.08
1972	Renate Stecher (GDR) 11.07

1976	Annegret Richter (FRG) 11.08
1980	Lyudmila Kondratyeva (USSR) 11.06
1984	Evelyn Ashford (USA) 10.97
1988	Florence Griffith-Joyner (USA) 10.54w (10.62 OR in quarter-final)
1992	Gail Devers (USA) 10.82
1996	Gail Devers (USA) 10.94

200 metres

1948	Fanny Blankers-Koen (Hol) 24.4
1952	Marjorie Jackson (Aus) 23.89
1956	Betty Cuthbert (Aus) 23.55
1960	Wilma Rudolph (USA) 24.03
1964	Edith Maguire (USA) 23.05
1968	Irena Szewinska (Pol) 22.58
1972	Renate Stecher (GDR) 22.40
1976	Bärbel Eckert (GDR) 22.37
1980	Bärbel Wöckel (née Eckert) (GDR) 22.03
1984	Valerie Brisco-Hooks (USA) 21.81
1988	Florence Griffith-Joyner (USA) 21.34 OR
1992	Gwen Torrence (USA) 21.81
1996	Marie-José Pérec (Fra) 22.12

400 metres

1964	Betty Cuthbert (Aus) 52.01
1968	Colette Besson (Fra) 52.03
1972	Monika Zehrt (GDR) 51.08
1976	Irena Szewinska (Pol) 49.29
1980	Marita Koch (GDR) 48.88
1984	Valerie Brisco-Hooks (USA) 48.83
1988	Olga Bryzgina (USSR) 48.65 OR
1992	Marie-José Pérec (Fra) 48.83 OR
1996	Marie-José Pérec (Fra) 48.25 OR

800 metres

1928	Lina Radke (Ger) 2:16.8
1960	Lyudmila Shevtsova (USSR) 2:04.50
1964	Ann Packer (UK) 2:01.1
1968	Madeline Manning (USA) 2:00.92
1972	Hildegard Falck (FRG) 1:58.55
1976	Tatyana Kazankina (USSR) 1:54.94
1980	Nadezhda Olizarenko (USSR) 1:53.43 OR
1984	Doina Melinte (Rom) 1:57.60

1988	Sigrun Wodars (GDR) 1:56.10
1992	Ellen van Langen (Hol) 1:55.54
1996	Svetlana Masterkova (Rus) 1:57.73

1500 metres

1972	Lyudmila Bragina (USSR) 4:01.38
1976	Tatyana Kazankina (USSR) 4:05.48
1980	Tatyana Kazankina (USSR) 3:56.56
1984	Gabriella Doria (Ita) 4:03.25
1988	Paula Ivan (Rom) 3:53.96 OR
1992	Hassiba Boulmerka (Alg) 3:55.30
1996	Svetlana Masterkova (Rus) 4:00.83

3000 metres

1984	Maricica Puica (Rom) 8:35.96
1988	Tatyana Samolenko (USSR) 8:26.53 OR
1992	Yelena Romanova (CIS/Rus) 8:46.04

5000 metres

1996	Wang Junxia (Chn) 14:59.88

10,000 metres

1988	Olga Bondarenko (USSR) 31:05.21
1992	Derartu Tulu (Eth) 31:06.02
1996	Fernanda Ribeiro (Por) 31:01.63 OR

Marathon (42.195km)

1984	Joan Benoit (USA) 2:24:52 OR
1988	Rosa Mota (Por) 2:25:40
1992	Valentina Yegorova (CIS/Rus) 2:32:41
1996	Fatuma Roba (Eth) 2:26:05

80 metres hurdles

1932	Mildred Didrikson (USA) 11.7
1936	Trebisonda Valla (Ita) 11.75
1948	Fanny Blankers-Koen (Hol) 11.2
1952	Shirley Strickland (Aus) 11.03
1956	Shirley Strickland (Aus) 10.96
1960	Irina Press (USSR) 10.94
1964	Karin Balzer (GDR) 10.54
1968	Maureen Caird (Aus) 10.39

100 metres hurdles

1972   Annelie Ehrhardt (GDR) 12.59
1976   Johanna Schaller (GDR) 12.77
1980   Vera Komisova (USSR) 12.56
1984   Benita Fitzgerald-Brown (USA) 12.84
1988   Yordanka Donkova (Bul) 12.38 OR
1992   Paraskevi Patoulidou (Gre) 12.64
1996   Ludmila Engquist (Swe) 12.58

400 metres hurdles

1984   Nawal El Moutawakil (Mor) 54.61
1988   Debbie Flintoff-King (Aus) 53.17
1992   Sally Gunnell (UK) 53.23
1996   Deon Hemmings (Jam) 52.82 OR

High jump

1928   Ethel Catherwood (Can) 1.59
1932   Jean Shiley (USA) 1.65
1936   Ibolya Csák (Hun) 1.60
1948   Alice Coachman (USA) 1.68
1952   Esther Brand (SAf) 1.67
1956   Mildred McDaniel (USA) 1.76
1960   Iolanda Balas (Rom) 1.85
1964   Iolanda Balas (Rom) 1.90
1968   Miloslava Rezková (Cs) 1.82
1972   Ulrike Meyfarth (FRG) 1.92
1976   Rosemarie Ackermann (GDR) 1.93
1980   Sara Simeoni (Ita) 1.97
1984   Ulrike Meyfarth (FRG) 2.02
1988   Louise Ritter (USA) 2.03
1992   Heike Henkel (Ger) 2.02
1996   Stefka Kostadinova (Bul) 2.05 OR

Long jump

1948   Olga Gyarmati (Hun) 5.69
1952   Yvette Williams (NZ) 6.24
1956   Elzbieta Krzesinska (Pol) 6.35
1960   Vyera Krepkina (USSR) 6.37
1964   Mary Rand (UK) 6.76
1968   Viorica Viscopoleanu (Rom) 6.82
1972   Heide Rosendahl (FRG) 6.78
1976   Angela Voigt (GDR) 6.72

1980   Tatyana Kolpakova (USSR) 7.06
1984   Anisoara Stanciu (Rom) 6.96
1988   Jackie Joyner-Kersee (USA) 7.40 OR
1992   Heike Drechsler (Ger) 7.14
1996   Chioma Ajunwa (Nig) 7.12

Triple jump

1996   Inessa Kravets (Ukr) 15.33 OR

Shot

1948   Micheline Ostermeyer (Fra) 13.75
1952   Galina Zybina (USSR) 15.28
1956   Tamara Tishkyevich (USSR) 16.59
1960   Tamara Press (USSR) 17.32
1964   Tamara Press (USSR) 18.14
1968   Margitta Gummel (GDR) 19.61
1972   Nadezhda Chizhova (USSR) 21.03
1976   Ivanka Khristova (Bul) 21.16
1980   Ilona Slupianek (GDR) 22.41 OR
1984   Claudia Losch (FRG) 20.48
1988   Natalya Lisovskaya (USSR) 22.24
1992   Svetlana Krivelyova (CIS/Rus) 21.06
1996   Astrid Kumbernuss (Ger) 20.56

Discus

1928   Halina Konopacka (Pol) 39.62
1932   Lillian Copeland (USA) 40.58
1936   Gisela Mauermayer (Ger) 47.63
1948   Micheline Ostermeyer (Fra) 41.92
1952   Nina Ponomaryeva (USSR) 51.42
1956   Olga Fikotová (Cs) 53.69
1960   Nina Romashkova (USSR) 55.10
1964   Tamara Press (USSR) 57.27
1968   Lia Manoliu (Rom) 58.28
1972   Faina Melnik (USSR) 66.62
1976   Evelin Schlaak (GDR) 69.00
1980   Evelin Jahl (née Schlaak) (GDR) 69.96
1984   Ria Stalman (Hol) 65.36
1988   Martina Hellmann (GDR) 72.30 OR

1992   Maritza Martén (Cub) 70.06
1996   Ilke Wyludda (Ger) 69.66

Javelin

1932   Mildred Didrikson (USA) 43.68
1936   Tilly Fleischer (Ger) 45.18
1948   Herma Bauma (Aut) 45.57
1952   Dana Zátopková (Cs) 50.47
1956   Inese Jaunzeme (USSR) 53.86
1960   Elvira Ozolina (USSR) 55.98
1964   Mihaela Penes (Rom) 60.54
1968   Angéla Németh (Hun) 60.36
1972   Ruth Fuchs (GDR) 63.88
1976   Ruth Fuchs (GDR) 65.94
1980   Maria Caridad Colón (Cub) 68.40
1984   Tessa Sanderson (UK) 69.56
1988   Petra Felke (GDR) 74.68 OR
1992   Silke Renk (Ger) 68.34
1996   Heli Rantanen (Fin) 67.94

Pentathlon

80m hurdles, high jump, shot, long jump, 200m 1964-8. 100m hurdles replaced 80m hurdles from 1972 and 800m replaced 200m from 1976. *(All scored on 1971 tables.)*

1964   Irina Press (USSR) 4702
1968   Ingrid Becker (FRG) 4559
1972   Mary Peters (UK) 4801
1976   Sigrun Siegl (GDR) 4745
1980   Nadezhda Tkachenko (USSR) 5083

Heptathlon

1984   Glynis Nunn (Aus) 6387
1988   Jackie Joyner-Kersee (USA) 7291 OR
1992   Jackie Joyner-Kersee (USA) 7044
1996   Ghada Shouaa (Syr) 6780

10 kilometres walk

1992   Chen Yueling (Chn) 44:32
1996   Yelena Nikolayeva (Rus) 41:49 OR

4 x 100 metres relay

1928   Canada 48.4
1932   USA 46.86
1936   USA 46.9
1948   Netherlands 47.5
1952   USA 46.14
1956   Australia 44.65
1960   USA 44.72
1964   Poland 43.69

1968   USA 42.87
1972   F R Germany 42.81
1976   GDR 42.55
1980   GDR 41.60 OR
1984   USA 41.65
1988   USA 41.98
1992   USA 42.11
1996   USA 41.95

4 x 400 metres relay
1972   GDR 3:22.95
1976   GDR 3:19.23
1980   USSR 3:20.12
1984   USA 3:18.29
1988   USSR 3:15.18 OR
1992   CIS United team 3:20.20
1996   USA 3:20.91

Discontinued events (men)

60 metres
1900   Alvin Kraenzlein (USA) 7.0
1904   Archie Hahn (USA) 7.0

5 miles
1906   Henry Hawtrey (UK)
          26:11.8
1908   Emil Voigt (UK) 25:11.2

Team race
1900   Great Britain (5000m)
1904   USA (4 miles)
1908   Great Britain (3 miles)
1912   USA (3000m)
1920   USA (3000m)
1924   Finland (3000m)

Cross-country individual
1912   Hannes Kolehmainen (Fin)
          45:11.6 (12km)
1920   Paavo Nurmi (Fin) 27:15.0
          (8km)
1924   Paavo Nurmi (Fin) 32:54.8
          (10km)

Cross-country team
1912   Sweden
1920   Finland
1924   Finland

200 metres hurdles
1900   Alvin Kraenzlein (USA) 25.4
1904   Harry Hillman (USA) 24.6

Pentathlon
1906: standing long jump, Greek-
style discus, javelin, 192m race and
Greco-Roman wrestling. 1912-24:
long jump, javelin, 200m, discus and
1500m.

1906   Hjalmar Mellander (Swe)
1912   Jim Thorpe (USA)★
          Ferdinand Bie (Nor)
1920   Eero Lehtonen (Fin)
1924   Eero Lehtonen (Fin)
★ Posthumously reinstated as winner.

Standing high jump
1900   Ray Ewry (USA) 1.655
1904   Ray Ewry (USA) 1.50
1906   Ray Ewry (USA) 1.565
1908   Ray Ewry (USA) 1.575
1912   Platt Adams (USA) 1.63

Standing long jump
1900   Ray Ewry (USA) 3.21
1904   Ray Ewry (USA) 3.476
1906   Ray Ewry (USA) 3.30
1908   Ray Ewry (USA) 3.335
1912   Konstantin Tsiklitiras (Gre)
          3.37

Standing triple jump
1900   Ray Ewry (USA) 10.58
1904   Ray Ewry (USA) 10.55

56lb weight
1904   Etienne Desmarteau (Can)
          10.465
1920   Patrick McDonald (USA)
          11.265

Stone (6.4kg) put
1906   Nicolaos Georgantas (Gre)
          19.925

Shot – both hands
*(Aggregate of throws with right and left
hands.)*
1912   Ralph Rose (USA) 27.70

Discus – Greek style
1906   Werner Järvinen (Fin) 35.17
1908   Martin Sheridan (USA) 38.00

Discus – both hands
1912   Armas Taipale (Fin) 82.86

Javelin – freestyle
1908   Erik Lemming (Swe) 54.445

Javelin – both hands
1912   Julius Saaristo (Fin) 109.42

1500 metres walk
1906   George Bonhag (USA)
          7:12.6

3000 metres walk
1906   György Sztantics (Hun)
          15:13.2
1920   Ugo Frigerio (Ita) 13:14.2

3500 metres walk
1908   George Larner (UK) 14:55.0

10,000 metres walk
1912   George Goulding (Can)
          46:28.4
1920   Ugo Frigerio (Ita) 48:06.2
1924   Ugo Frigerio (Ita) 47:49.0
1948   John Mikaelsson (Swe)
          45:13.2
1952   John Mikaelsson (Swe)
          45:02.8

10 miles walk
1908   George Larner (UK)
          1:15:57.4

Most medals
(G – Gold, S – Silver, B – Bronze)

Men		G	S	B	Years
12	Paavo Nurmi (Fin)	9	3	–	1920-8
10	Raymond Ewry (USA)	10	–	–	1900-8
10	Carl Lewis (USA)	9	1	–	1984-96
9	Martin Sheridan (USA)	5	3	1	1906-8
8	Ville Ritola (Fin)	5	3	–	1924-8
7	Erik Lemming (Swe)	4	–	3★	1906-12

★ Including one for tug-of-war.

Four gold medals: Alvin Kraenzlein (USA) 1900; Archie Hahn (USA)
       1904-6; James Lightbody (USA) 1904-6; Myer Prinstein (USA)
       1900-6; Mel Sheppard (USA) 1908-12; Hannes Kolehmainen (Fin)
       1912-20; Jesse Owens (USA) 1936; Emil Zátopek (Cs) 1948-52;
       Harrison Dillard (USA) 1948-52; Al Oerter (USA) 1956-68; Lasse Viren
       (Fin) 1972-76

Women	G	S	B	Years
7 Shirley de la Hunty (Aus)	3	1	3	1948-56
7 Irena Szewinska (Pol)	3	2	2	1964-76
7 Merlene Ottey (Jam)	0	2	5	1980-96

Four gold medals: Fanny Blankers-Koen (Hol) 1948; Betty Cuthbert (Aus) 1956-64; Bärbel Wöckel (GDR) 1976-80; Evelyn Ashford (USA) 1984-92; Gail Devers (USA) 1992-6

Most gold medals at one Games

Men: 5 Paavo Nurmi (Fin) 1924; 4 Alvin Kraenzlein (USA) 1900, Ville Ritola (Fin) 1924, Jesse Owens (USA) 1936, Carl Lewis (USA) 1984
Women: 4 Fanny Blankers-Koen (Hol) 1948

Most medals at one Games

6 Ville Ritola (Fin) 4 gold, 2 silver 1924

Oldest gold medallists

Men: 42yr 23d Pat McDonald (USA) 56lb weight 1920
Women: 36yr 176d Lia Manoliu (Rom) discus 1968

Oldest medallists

Men: 48yr 115d Tebbs Lloyd Johnson (UK) 3rd 50km walk 1948
Women: 37yr 348d Dana Zátopková (Cs) 2nd javelin 1960

Youngest gold medallists

Men: 17yr 263d Bob Mathias (USA) decathlon 1948
Women: 15yr 123d Barbara Pearl Jones (USA) 4x100m relay 1952

Most Games contested

6 Lia Manoliu (Rom) 1952-72, women's discus, successively 6th, 9th, 3rd, 3rd, 1st, 9th; Tessa Sanderson (UK) 1976-96, women's javelin

Medal table of leading nations 1896-1996

(Totals include 1906 Games.)

	Men			Women			Total
Nation	*Gold*	*Silver*	*Bronze*	*Gold*	*Silver*	*Bronze*	**Medals**
USA	259	187	161	39	25	17	688
USSR/CIS	37	37	42	34	29	35	214
United Kingdom	42	58	42	5	20	14	181
GDR	14	19	14	25	28	24	124
Germany★	13	26	38	16	13	16	122
Finland	47	33	30	1	2	–	113
Sweden	17	25	41	1	–	3	87
Australia	6	9	12	11	10	12	60
France	8	19	17	6	1	3	54
Italy	13	7	20	3	6	3	52
Canada	12	10	16	2	5	7	52
Poland	9	7	5	6	8	7	42
Hungary	6	13	16	3	1	2	41
Kenya	13	15	11	–	1	–	40
Jamaica	4	11	5	1	5	5	31
Czechoslovakia	8	7	3	3	2	2	25
Romania	–	–	1	9	9	6	25
Greece	3	8	12	1	1	–	25
Cuba	3	6	4	2	2	4	21

★ Germany 1896-1952 and 1992, Federal Republic of Germany 1956-88. Medals won by the combined German teams of 1956, 1960 and 1964 have been allocated to FRG or GDR according to the athlete's origin.

In all, 68 nations have won medals at track and field sports, with Algeria, Bahamas, Colombia, Korea, Lithuania, Namibia and Qatar added to the list in 1992, and Russia (10), Ukraine, Belarus, Czech Republic (3) and Burundi in 1996.

World Championships

Athletics events at the Olympic Games have had World Championship status, but the first championships for athletics alone were staged in the Olympic Stadium, Helsinki, Finland in 1983. Originally held every four years, the championships are now biennial.

Venues

1983	Helsinki, Finland
1987	Rome, Italy
1991	Tokyo, Japan
1993	Stuttgart, Germany
1995	Göteborg, Sweden
1997	Athens, Greece

The 1999 championships will be held in Seville, Spain.

Men

100 metres

1983	Carl Lewis (USA) 10.07
1987	Carl Lewis (USA) 9.93*
1991	Carl Lewis (USA) 9.86
1993	Linford Christie (UK) 9.87
1995	Donovan Bailey (Can) 9.97
1997	Maurice Greene (USA) 9.86

* Ben Johnson (Can) won in 9.83, but following his admission of drug-taking had his world record and title stripped from him by the IAAF.

200 metres

1983	Calvin Smith (USA) 20.14
1987	Calvin Smith (USA) 20.16
1991	Michael Johnson (USA) 20.01
1993	Frank Fredericks (Nam) 19.85
1995	Michael Johnson (USA) 19.79
1997	Ato Boldon (Tri) 20.04w

400 metres

1983	Bert Cameron (Jam) 45.05
1987	Thomas Schönlebe (GDR) 44.33
1991	Antonio Pettigrew (USA) 44.57
1993	Michael Johnson (USA) 43.65
1995	Michael Johnson (USA) 43.39
1997	Michael Johnson (USA) 44.12

800 metres

1983	Willi Wülbeck (FRG) 1:43.65
1987	Billy Konchellah (Ken) 1:43.06
1991	Billy Konchellah (Ken) 1:43.99
1993	Paul Ruto (Ken) 1:44.71
1995	Wilson Kipketer (Den) 1:45.08
1997	Wilson Kipketer (Den) 1:43.38

1500 metres

1983	Steve Cram (UK) 3:41.59
1987	Abdi Bile (Som) 3:36.80
1991	Noureddine Morceli (Alg) 3:32.84
1993	Noureddine Morceli (Alg) 3:34.24
1995	Noureddine Morceli (Alg) 3:33.73
1997	Hicham El Guerrouj (Mor) 3:35.83

5000 metres

1983	Eamonn Coghlan (Ire) 13:28.53
1987	Saïd Aouita (Mor) 13:26.44
1991	Yobes Ondieki (Ken) 13:14.45
1993	Ismael Kirui (Ken) 13:02.75
1995	Ismael Kirui (Ken) 13:16.77
1997	Daniel Komen (Ken) 13:07.38

10,000 metres

1983	Alberto Cova (Ita) 28:01.04
1987	Paul Kipkoech (Ken) 27:38.63
1991	Moses Tanui (Ken) 27:38.74
1993	Haile Gebrselassie (Eth) 27:46.02
1995	Haile Gebrselassie (Eth) 27:12.95
1997	Haile Gebrselassie (Eth) 27:24.58

Marathon

1983	Rob de Castella (Aus) 2:10:03
1987	Douglas Wakiihuri (Ken) 2:11:48
1991	Hiromi Taniguchi (Jap) 2:14:57
1993	Mark Plaatjes (USA) 2:13:57
1995	Martin Fíz (Spa) 2:11:41
1997	Abel Antón (Spa) 2:13:16

3000 metres steeplechase

1983	Patriz Ilg (FRG) 8:15.06
1987	Francesco Panetta (Ita) 8:08.57
1991	Moses Kiptanui (Ken) 8:12.59
1993	Moses Kiptanui (Ken) 8:06.36
1995	Moses Kiptanui (Ken) 8:04.16*
1997	Wilson Boit (Ken) 8:05.84

110 metres hurdles

1983	Greg Foster (USA) 13.42
1987	Greg Foster (USA) 13.21
1991	Greg Foster (USA) 13.06
1993	Colin Jackson (UK) 12.91
1995	Allen Johnson (USA) 13.00
1997	Allen Johnson (USA) 12.93

400 metres hurdles

1983	Edwin Moses (USA) 47.50
1987	Edwin Moses (USA) 47.46
1991	Samuel Matete (Zam) 47.64
1993	Kevin Young (USA) 47.18
1995	Derrick Adkins (USA) 47.98
1997	Stéphane Diagana (Fra) 47.70

High jump

1983	Gennadiy Avdeyenko (USSR) 2.32
1987	Patrik Sjöberg (Swe) 2.38
1991	Charles Austin (USA) 2.38
1993	Javier Sotomayor (Cub) 2.40
1995	Troy Kemp (Bah) 2.37
1997	Javier Sotomayor (Cub) 2.37

Pole vault

1983	Sergey Bubka (USSR) 5.70
1987	Sergey Bubka (USSR) 5.85
1991	Sergey Bubka (USSR) 5.95
1993	Sergey Bubka (Ukr) 6.00
1995	Sergey Bubka (Ukr) 5.92
1997	Sergey Bubka (Ukr) 6.01

Long jump

1983	Carl Lewis (USA) 8.55
1987	Carl Lewis (USA) 8.67
1991	Mike Powell (USA) 8.95
1993	Mike Powell (USA) 8.59
1995	Iván Pedroso (Cub) 8.70
1997	Iván Pedroso (Cub) 8.42

Triple jump

1983	Zdzislaw Hoffmann (Pol) 17.42
1987	Khristo Markov (Bul) 17.92
1991	Kenny Harrison (USA) 17.78
1993	Mike Conley (USA) 17.86
1995	Jonathan Edwards (UK) 18.29
1997	Yoelbi Quesada (Cub) 17.85

Shot

1983	Edward Sarul (Pol) 21.39
1987	Werner Günthör (Swi) 22.23
1991	Werner Günthör (Swi) 21.67
1993	Werner Günthör (Swi) 21.97
1995	John Godina (USA) 21.47
1997	John Godina (USA) 21.44

Discus

1983	Imrich Bugár (Cs) 67.72
1987	Jürgen Schult (GDR) 68.74
1991	Lars Riedel (Ger) 66.20
1993	Lars Riedel (Ger) 67.72
1995	Lars Riedel (Ger) 68.76
1997	Lars Riedel (Ger) 68.54

Hammer

1983	Sergey Litvinov (USSR) 82.68
1987	Sergey Litvinov (USSR) 83.06
1991	Yuriy Sedykh (USSR) 81.70
1993	Andrey Abduvaliyev (Tjk) 81.64
1995	Andrey Abduvaliyev (Tjk) 81.56
1997	Heinz Weis (Ger) 81.78

Javelin

1983	Detlef Michel (GDR) 89.48 (old specification)
1987	Seppo Räty (Fin) 83.54
1991	Kimmo Kinnunen (Fin) 90.82
1993	Jan Zelezny (Cze) 85.98
1995	Jan Zelezny (Cze) 89.58 (90.12q)
1997	Marius Corbett (SAf) 88.40

Decathlon

1983	Daley Thompson (UK) 8714
1987	Torsten Voss (GDR) 8680
1991	Dan O'Brien (USA) 8812
1993	Dan O'Brien (USA) 8817
1995	Dan O'Brien (USA) 8695
1997	Tomás Dvořák (Cze) 8837

4 x 100 metres relay

1983	USA 37.86
1987	USA 37.90
1991	USA 37.50
1993	USA 37.48 (37.40sf CBP)
1995	Canada 38.31
1997	Canada 37.86

4 x 400 metres relay

1983	USSR 3:00.79
1987	USA 2:57.29
1991	Great Britain 2:57.53
1993	USA 2:54.29
1995	USA 2:57.32
1997	USA 2:56.47

20 kilometres walk

1983	Ernesto Canto (Mex) 1:20:49
1987	Maurizio Damilano (Ita) 1:20:45
1991	Maurizio Damilano (Ita) 1:19:37
1993	Valentin Massana (Spa) 1:22:31
1995	Michele Didoni (Ita) 1:19:59
1997	Daniel García (Mex) 1:21:43

50 kilometres walk

1976	Venyamin Soldatenko (USSR) 3:54:40
1983	Ronald Weigel (GDR) 3:43:08
1987	Hartwig Gauder (GDR) 3:40:53
1991	Aleksandr Potashov (USSR) 3:53:09
1993	Jesús Angel García (Spa) 3:41:41
1995	Valentin Kononen (Fin) 3:43:42
1997	Robert Korzeniowski (Pol) 3:44:46

Women

100 metres

1983	Marlies Göhr (GDR) 10.97
1987	Silke Gladisch (GDR) 10.90
1991	Katrin Krabbe (Ger) 10.99
1993	Gail Devers (USA) 10.82
1995	Gwen Torrence (USA) 10.85
1997	Marion Jones (USA) 10.83

200 metres

1983	Marita Koch (GDR) 22.13
1987	Silke Gladisch (GDR) 21.74
1991	Katrin Krabbe (Ger) 22.09
1993	Merlene Ottey (Jam) 21.98
1995	Merlene Ottey (Jam) 22.12

| 1997 | Zhanna Pintusevich (Ukr) 22.32 |

400 metres

1983	Jarmila Kratochvílová (Cs) 47.99
1987	Olga Bryzgina (USSR) 49.38
1991	Marie-José Pérec (Fra) 49.13
1993	Jearl Miles (USA) 49.82
1995	Marie-José Pérec (Fra) 49.28
1997	Cathy Freeman (Aus) 49.77

800 metres

1983	Jarmila Kratochvílová (Cs) 1:54.68
1987	Sigrun Wodars (GDR) 1:55.26
1991	Lilia Nurutdinova (USSR) 1:57.50
1993	Maria Mutola (Moz) 1:55.43
1995	Ana Quirot (Cub) 1:56.11
1997	Ana Quirot (Cub) 1:57.14

1500 metres

1983	Mary Decker (USA) 4:00.90
1987	Tatyana Samolenko (USSR) 3:58.56
1991	Hassiba Boulmerka (Alg) 4:02.21
1993	Liu Dong (Chn) 4:00.50
1995	Hassiba Boulmerka (Alg) 4:02.42
1997	Carla Sacramento (Por) 4:04.24

3000 metres

1980	Birgit Friedmann (FRG) 8:48.05
1983	Mary Decker (USA) 8:34.62
1987	Tatyana Samolenko (USSR) 8:38.73
1991	Tatyana Dorovskikh (née Samolenko) (USSR) 8:35.82
1993	Qu Yunxia (Chn) 8:28.71

5000 metres (first held 1995)

| 1995 | Sonia O'Sullivan (Ire) 14:46.47 |
| 1997 | Gabriela Szabo (Rom) 14:57.68 |

10,000 metres (first held 1987)

1987	Ingrid Kristiansen (Nor) 31:05.85
1991	Liz McColgan (UK) 31:14.31
1993	Wang Junxia (Chn) 30:49.30
1995	Fernanda Ribeiro (Por) 31:04.99
1997	Sally Barsosio (Ken) 31:32.92

Marathon

1983	Grete Waitz (Nor) 2:28:09
1987	Rosa Mota (Por) 2:25:17
1991	Wanda Panfil (Pol) 2:29:53
1993	Junko Asari (Jap) 2:30:03
1995	Manuela Machado (Por) 2:25:39 (*400m short*)
1997	Hiromi Suzuki (Jap) 2:29:48

100 metres hurdles

1983	Bettine Jahn (GDR) 12.35
1987	Ginka Zagorcheva (Bul) 12.34
1991	Lyudmila Narozhilenko (later Engquist) (USSR) 12.59
1993	Gail Devers (USA) 12.46
1995	Gail Devers (USA) 12.68
1997	Ludmila Engquist (Swe) 12.50

400 metres hurdles

1980	Bärbel Broschat GDR 54.55
1983	Yekaterina Fesenko (USSR) 54.14
1987	Sabine Busch (GDR) 53.62
1991	Tatyana Ledovskaya (USSR) 53.11
1993	Sally Gunnell (UK) 52.74
1995	Kim Batten (USA) 52.61
1997	Nezha Bidouane (Mor) 52.97

High jump

1983	Tamara Bykova (USSR) 2.01
1987	Stefka Kostadinova (Bul) 2.09
1991	Heike Henkel (Ger) 2.05
1993	Ioamnet Quintero (Cub) 1.99
1995	Stefka Kostadinova (Bul) 2.01
1997	Hanne Haugland (Nor) 1.99

Long jump

1983	Heike Daute (GDR) 7.27w
1987	Jackie Joyner-Kersee (USA) 7.36
1991	Jackie Joyner-Kersee (USA) 7.32
1993	Heike Drechsler (née Daute) (Ger) 7.11
1995	Fiona May (Ita) 6.98w
1997	Lyudmila Galkina (Rus) 7.05

Triple jump (first held 1993)

1993	Ana Biryukova (Rus) 15.09
1995	Inessa Kravets (Ukr) 15.50
1997	Sárka Kaspárková (Cze) 15.20

Shot

1983	Helena Fibingerová (Cs) 21.05
1987	Natalya Lisovskaya (USSR) 21.24
1991	Huang Zhihong (Chn) 20.83
1993	Huang Zhihong (Chn) 20.57
1995	Astrid Kumbernuss (Ger) 21.22
1997	Astrid Kumbernuss (Ger) 20.71

Discus

1983	Martina Opitz (GDR) 68.94
1987	Martina Hellmann (née Opitz) (GDR) 71.62
1991	Tsvetanka Khristova (Bul) 71.02
1993	Olga Burova (Rus) 67.40
1995	Ellina Zvereva (Blr) 68.64
1997	Beatrice Faumuina (NZ) 66.82

Javelin

1983	Tiina Lillak (Fin) 70.82
1987	Fatima Whitbread (UK) 76.64
1991	Xu Demei (Chn) 68.78
1993	Trine Hattestad (Nor) 69.18
1995	Natalya Shikolenko (Blr) 67.56
1997	Trine Hattestad (Nor) 68.78

Heptathlon

1983	Ramona Neubert (GDR) 6770
1987	Jackie Joyner-Kersee (USA) 7128
1991	Sabine Braun (Ger) 6672
1993	Jackie Joyner-Kersee (USA) 6837
1995	Ghada Shouaa (Syr) 6651
1997	Sabine Braun (Ger) 6739

10 kilometres walk (first held 1987)

1987	Irina Strakhova (USSR) 44:12
1991	Alina Ivanova (USSR) 42:57
1993	Sari Essayah (Fin) 42:59
1995	Irina Stankina (Rus) 42.13
1997	Annarita Sidoti (Ita) 42:55.49 (*track*)

4 x 100 metres relay

1983	GDR 41.76
1987	USA 41.58
1991	Jamaica 41.94
1993	Russia 41.49
1995	USA 42.11
1997	USA 41.47

4 x 400 metres relay

1983	GDR 3:19.73
1987	GDR 3:18.63
1991	USSR 3:18.43
1993	USA 3:16.79
1995	USA 3:22.39
1997	Germany 3:20.82

Most medals

Men

10 Carl Lewis (USA) gold 100m, long jump, 100m & 4x100m 1983; long jump & 4x100m 1987, long jump & 4x100m 1991; silver 100m 1987, long jump 1991; bronze 200m 1993

7 Michael Johnson USA gold 200m 1991 & 1995, 400m 1993, 1995 & 1997, 4x400m 1993 & 1995

Women

14 Merlene Ottey (Jam) gold 4x100m 1991, 200m 1993 & 1995; silver 200m 1983, 100m 1993 & 1995, 4x100m 1995; bronze 4x100m 1983, 100m & 200m 1983, 1987 & 1997, 4x100m 1993

8 Gwen Torrence (USA) gold 4x400m 1993, 100m & 4x100m 1995; silver 100m 1991, 200m 1991 & 1993, 4x100m 1993; bronze 100m 1993

7 Jearl Miles (later Miles-Clark) USA gold 400m 1993, 4x400m 1993 & 1995; silver 4x400m 1991, 1997; bronze 400m 1995 & 1997

World Indoor Championships

First held as the World Indoor Games at Bercy, Paris, France 19–20 January 1985. Official Championships are now staged biennially.

Winners:

Men

60 metres

1985   Ben Johnson (Can) 6.62
1987   Lee McRae (USA) 6.50*
1989   Andrés Simon (Cub) 6.52
1991   Andre Cason (USA) 6.54
1993   Bruny Surin (Can) 6.50
1995   Bruny Surin (Can) 6.46
1997   Haralambros Papadias (Gre) 6.50

* Original winner, Ben Johnson (Can) 6.41, was later disqualified after admitting long-term drug use.

200 metres

1985   Aleksandr Yakovlyev (USSR) 20.95
1987   Kirk Baptiste (USA) 20.73
1989   John Regis (UK) 20.54
1991   Nikolai Antonov (Bul) 20.67
1993   James Trapp (USA) 20.63
1995   Geir Moen (Nor) 20.58
1997   Kevin Little (USA) 20.40

400 metres

1985   Thomas Schönlebe (GDR) 45.60
1987   Antonio McKay (USA) 45.98
1989   Antonio McKay (USA) 45.59
1991   Devon Morris (Jam) 46.17
1993   Butch Reynolds (USA) 45.26
1995   Darnell Hall (USA) 46.17
1997   Sunday Bada (Nig) 45.51

800 metres

1985   Colomán Trabado (Spa) 1:47.42
1987   José Luiz Barbosa (Bra) 1:47.49
1989   Paul Ereng (Ken) 1:44.84
1991   Paul Ereng (Ken) 1:47.08
1993   Tom McKean (UK) 1:47.29
1995   Clive Terrelonge (Jam) 1:47.30
1997   Wilson Kipketer (Den) 1:42.67

1500 metres

1985   Mike Hillardt (Aus) 3:40.27
1987   Marcus O'Sullivan (Ire) 3:39.04
1989   Marcus O'Sullivan (Ire) 3:36.64
1991   Noureddine Morceli (Alg) 3:41.57
1993   Marcus O'Sullivan (Ire) 3:45.00
1995   Hicham El Guerrouj (Mor) 3:44.54
1997   Hicham El Guerrouj (Mor) 3:35.31

3000 metres

1985   João Campos (Por) 7:57.63
1987   Frank O'Mara (Ire) 8:03.32
1989   Saïd Aouita (Mor) 7:47.94
1991   Frank O'Mara (Ire) 7:41.14
1993   Gennaro Di Napoli (Ita) 7:50.26
1995   Gennaro Di Napoli (Ita) 7:50.89
1997   Haile Gebrselassie (Eth) 7:34.71

60 metres hurdles

1985   Stéphane Caristan (Fra) 7.67
1987   Tonie Campbell (USA) 7.51
1989   Roger Kingdom (USA) 7.43
1991   Greg Foster (USA) 7.45
1993   Mark McKoy (Can) 7.41
1995   Allen Johnson (USA) 7.39
1997   Anier García (Cub) 7.48

High jump

1985   Patrik Sjöberg (Swe) 2.32
1987   Igor Paklin (USSR) 2.38
1989   Javier Sotomayor (Cub) 2.43
1991   Hollis Conway (USA) 2.40
1993   Javier Sotomayor (Cub) 2.41
1995   Javier Sotomayor (Cub) 2.38
1997   Charles Austin (USA) 2.35

Pole vault

1985   Sergey Bubka (USSR) 5.75
1987   Sergey Bubka (USSR) 5.85
1989   Radion Gataullin (USSR) 5.85
1991   Sergey Bubka (USSR) 6.00
1993   Rodion Gataullin (Rus) 5.90
1995   Sergey Bubka (Ukr) 5.90
1997   Igor Potapovich (Kaz) 5.90

Long jump

1985   Jan Leitner (Cs) 7.96
1987   Larry Myricks (USA) 8.23
1989   Larry Myricks (USA) 8.37
1991   Dietmar Haaf (Ger) 8.15
1993   Iván Pedroso (Cub) 8.23
1995   Iván Pedroso (Cub) 8.51
1997   Iván Pedroso (Cub) 8.51

Triple jump

1985   Khristo Markov (Bul) 17.22
1987   Mike Conley (USA) 17.54
1989   Mike Conley (USA) 17.65
1991   Igor Lapshin (USSR) 17.31
1993   Pierre Camara (Fra) 17.59
1995   Brian Wellman (Ber) 17.72
1997   Yoel García (Cub) 17.30

Shot

1985   Remigius Machura (Cs) 21.22
1987   Ulf Timmermann (GDR) 22.24
1989   Ulf Timmermann (GDR) 21.75
1991   Werner Günthör (Swi) 21.17
1993   Mike Stulce (USA) 21.27
1995   Mika Halvari (Fin) 20.74
1997   Yuriy Belonog (Ukr) 21.02

5000 metres walk

(Discontinued)

1985   Gérard Lélièvre (Fra) 19:06.22
1987   Mikhail Shchennikov (USSR) 18:27.79
1989   Mikhail Shchennikov (USSR)18:27.10
1991   Mikhail Shchennikov (USSR) 18:23.55
1993   Mikhail Shchennikov (Rus) 18:32.10

4 x 400 metres relay

1991   Germany 3:03.05
1993   USA 3:04.20
1995   USA 3:07.37
1997   USA 3:04.93

Heptathlon (official from 1995)

1993   Dan O'Brien (USA) 6476
1995   Christian Plaziat (Fra) 6246
1997   Robert Zmelík (Cze) 6228

Women

60 metres

1985   Silke Gladisch (GDR) 7.20
1987   Nellie Fiere-Cooman (Hol) 7.08
1989   Nellie Cooman (Hol) 7.05
1991   Irina Privalova (USSR) 7.02
1993   Gail Devers (USA) 6.95
1995   Merlene Ottey (Jam) 6.97
1997   Gail Devers (USA) 7.06

200 metres

1985	Marita Koch (GDR) 23.09
1987	Heike Drechsler (GDR) 22.27
1989	Merlene Ottey (Jam) 22.34
1991	Merlene Ottey (Jam) 22.24
1993	Irina Privalova (Rus) 22.15
1995	Melinda Gainsford (Aus) 22.64
1997	Ekaterini Koffa (Gre) 22.76

400 metres

1985	Diane Dixon (USA) 53.35
1987	Sabine Busch (GDR) 51.66
1989	Helga Arendt (FRG) 51.52
1991	Diane Dixon (USA) 50.64
1993	Sandie Richards (Jam) 50.93
1995	Irina Privalova (Rus) 50.23
1997	Jearl Miles-Clark (USA) 50.96

800 metres

1985	Cristeana Cojocaru (Rom) 2:04.22
1987	Christine Wachtel (GDR) 2:01.32
1989	Christine Wachtel 1:59.24
1991	Christine Wachtel (Ger) 2:01.51
1993	Maria Mutola (Moz) 1:57.55
1995	Maria Mutola (Moz) 1:57.62
1997	Maria Mutola (Moz) 1:58.96

1500 metres

1985	Elly van Hulst (Hol) 4:11.41
1987	Doina Melinte (Rom) 4:05.68
1989	Doina Melinte (Rom) 4:04.79
1991	Lyudmila Rogachova (USSR) 4:05.09
1993	Yekaterina Podkopayeva (Rus) 4:09.29
1995	Regina Jacobs (USA) 4:12.61
1997	Yekaterina Podkopayeva (Rus) 4:05.19

3000 metres

1985	Debbie Scott (Can) 9:04.99
1987	Tatyana Samolenko (USSR) 8:46.52
1989	Elly van Hulst (Hol) 8:33.82
1991	Marie-Pierre Duros (Fra) 8:50.69
1993	Yvonne Murray (UK) 8:50.55
1995	Gabriela Szabo (Rom) 8:54.50
1997	Gabriela Szabo (Rom) 8:45.75

60 metres hurdles

1985	Xénia Siska (Hun) 8.03
1987	Cornelia Oschkenat (GDR) 7.82
1989	Yelisaveta Chernyshova (USSR) 7.82
1991	Lyudmila Narozhilenko (USSR) 7.88
1993	Julie Baumann (Swi) 7.96
1995	Aliuska López (Cub) 7.92
1997	Michelle Freeman (Jam) 7.82

High jump

1985	Stefka Kostadinova (Bul) 1.97
1987	Stefka Kostadinova (Bul) 2.05
1989	Stefka Kostadinova (Bul) 2.02
1991	Heike Henkel (Ger) 2.00
1993	Stefka Kostadinova (Bul) 2.02
1995	Alina Astafei (Ger) 2.01
1997	Stefka Kostadinova (Bul) 2.02

Pole vault

1997	Stacy Dragila (USA) 4.40

Long jump

1985	Helga Radtke (GDR) 6.86
1987	Heike Drechsler (GDR) 7.10
1989	Galina Chistyakova (USSR) 6.98
1991	Larisa Berezhnaya (USSR) 6.84
1993	Marieta Ilcu (Rom) 6.84
1995	Lyudmila Galkina (Rus) 6.95
1997	Fiona May (Ita) 6.86

Triple jump

1991	Inessa Kravets (USSR) 14.44 *(demonstration event)*
1993	Inessa Kravets (USSR) 14.47
1995	Iolanda Chen (Rus) 15.03
1997	Inna Lasovskaya (Rus) 15.01

Shot

1985	Natalya Lisovskaya (USSR) 20.07
1987	Natalya Lisovskaya (USSR) 20.52
1989	Claudia Losch (FRG) 20.45
1991	Sui Xinmei (Chn) 20.54
1993	Svetlana Krivelyova (Rus) 19.57
1995	Larisa Peleshenko (Rus) 19.93
1997	Victoriya Pavlysh (Ukr) 20.00

Pentathlon (official from 1995)

1993	Liliana Nastase (Rom) 4686★
1995	Svetlana Moskalets (Rus) 4834
1997	Sabine Braun (Ger) 4780

★ Original winner Irina Belova (Rus) 4787 was disqualified following a positive drugs test.

3000 metres walk

(Discontinued)

1985	Giuliana Salce (Ita) 12:53.42
1987	Olga Krishtop (USSR) 12:05.49
1989	Kerry Saxby (Aus) 12:01.65
1991	Beate Anders (Ger) 11:50.90
1993	Yelena Nikolayeva (Rus) 11:49.73

4 x 400 metres relay

1991	Germany 3:27.22
1993	Jamaica 3:32.32
1995	Russia 3:29.29★
1997	Russia 3:26.84

★ Original winners, Russia 3:28.90, disqualified following a positive drugs test.

IAAF World Cup

First held in 1977. The competing teams represent each of the five continents, with national teams from the USA and the top two men's and women's teams from the European Cup. Host nations Italy and Spain competed as ninth teams in 1981 and 1989. Each team enters one competitor per event. From 1994 the event has been staged every four years.

Winners:

Year	Venue	Men	Women
1977	Düsseldorf	GDR	Europe
1979	Montreal	USA	GDR
1981	Rome	Europe	GDR
1985	Canberra	USA	GDR
1989	Barcelona	USA	GDR
1992	Havana	Africa	CIS
1994	London	Africa	Europe

Men's individual events

100 metres
1977   Steve Williams (USA) 10.13
1979   James Sanford (USA) 10.17
1981   Allan Wells (Eur/UK) 10.20
1985   Ben Johnson (Ame/Can) 10.00
1989   Linford Christie (UK) 10.10
1992   Linford Christie (UK) 10.21
1994   Linford Christie (UK) 10.21

200 metres
1977   Clancy Edwards (USA) 20.17
1979   Silvio Leonard (Ame/Cub) 20.34
1981   Mel Lattany (USA) 20.21
1985   Robson da Silva (Ame/Bra) 20.44
1989   Robson da Silva (Ame/Bra) 20.00
1992   Robson da Silva (Ame/Bra) 20.56
1994   John Regis (UK) 20.45

400 metres
1977   Alberto Juantorena (Ame/Cub) 45.36
1979   Hassan El Kashief (Afr/Sud) 45.39
1981   Cliff Wiley (USA) 44.88
1985   Mike Franks (USA) 44.47
1989   Roberto Hernández (Ame/Cub) 44.58
1992   Sunday Bada (Afr/Nig) 44.99
1994   Antonio Pettigrew (USA) 45.26

800 metres
1977   Alberto Juantorena (Ame/Cub) 1:44.04
1979   James Maina (Afr/Ken) 1:47.69
1981   Sebastian Coe (Eur/UK) 1:46.16
1985   Sammy Koskei (Afr/Ken) 1:45.14
1989   Tom McKean (UK) 1:44.95
1992   David Sharpe (UK) 1:46.06
1994   Mark Everett (USA) 1:46.02

1500 metres
1977   Steve Ovett (Eur/UK) 3:34.45
1979   Thomas Wessinghage (Eur/FRG) 3:46.00
1981   Steve Ovett (Eur/UK) 3:34.95

1985   Omer Khalifa (Afr/Sud) 3:41.16
1989   Abdi Bile (Afr/Som) 3:35.56
1992   Mohammed Suleiman (Asi/Qat) 3:39.37
1994   Noureddine Morceli (Afr/Alg) 3:34.70

5000 metres
1977   Miruts Yifter (Afr/Eth) 13:13.82
1979   Miruts Yifter (Afr/Eth) 13:35.9
1981   Eamonn Coghlan (Eur/Ire) 14:08.39
1985   Doug Padilla (USA) 14:04.11
1989   Saïd Aouita (Afr/Mor) 13:23.14
1992   Fita Bayissa (Afr/Eth) 13:41.23
1994   Brahim Lahlafi (Afr/Mor) 13:27.96

10,000 metres
1977   Miruts Yifter (Afr/Eth) 28:32.3
1979   Miruts Yifter (Afr/Eth) 27:53.07
1981   Werner Schildhauer (GDR) 27:38.43
1985   Woldajo Bulti (Afr/Eth) 29:22.96
1989   Salvatore Antibo (Eur/Ita) 28:05.26
1992   Addis Abebe (Afr/Eth) 28:44.38
1994   Khalid Skah (Afr/Mor) 27:38.74

3000 metres steeplechase
1977   Michael Karst (FRG) 8:21.6
1979   Kiprotich Rono (Afr/Ken) 8:25.97
1981   Boguslaw Maminski (Eur/Pol) 8:19.89
1985   Julius Kariuki (Afr/Ken) 8:39.51
1989   Julius Kariuki (Afr/Ken) 8:20.84
1992   Phillip Barkutwo (Afr/Ken) 8:26.81
1994   Moses Kiptanui (Afr/Ken) 8:28.28

110 metres hurdles
1977   Thomas Munkelt (GDR) 13.41

1979   Renaldo Nehemiah (USA) 13.39
1981   Greg Foster (USA) 13.32
1985   Tonie Campbell (USA) 13.35w
1989   Roger Kingdom (USA) 12.87w
1992   Colin Jackson (UK) 13.07
1994   Tony Jarrett (UK) 13.23

400 metres hurdles
1977   Ed Moses (USA) 47.58
1979   Ed Moses (USA) 47.53
1981   Ed Moses (USA) 47.37
1985   Andre Phillips (USA) 48.42
1989   David Patrick (USA) 48.74
1992   Samuel Matete (Afr/Zam) 48.88
1994   Samuel Matete (Afr/Zam) 48.77

High jump
1977   Rolf Beilschmidt (GDR) 2.30
1979   Franklin Jacobs (USA) 2.27
1981   Tyke Peacock (USA) 2.28
1985   Patrik Sjöberg (Eur/Swe) 2.31
1989   Patrik Sjöberg (Eur/Swe) 2.34
1992   Yuriy Sergiyenko (CIS/Ukr) 2.29
1994   Javier Sotomayor (Ame/Cub) 2.40

Pole vault
1977   Mike Tully (USA) 5.60
1979   Mike Tully (USA) 5.45
1981   Konstantin Volkov (USSR) 5.70
1985   Sergey Bubka (USSR) 5.85
1989   Philippe Collet (Eur/Fra) 5.75
1992   Igor Potapovich (CIS/Kzk) 5.60
1994   Okkert Brits (Afr/SAf) 5.90

Long jump
1977   Arnie Robinson (USA) 8.19
1979   Larry Myricks (USA) 8.52
1981   Carl Lewis (USA) 8.15
1985   Mike Conley (USA) 8.20
1989   Larry Myricks (USA) 8.29
1992   Iván Pedroso (Ame/Cub) 7.97
1994   Fred Salle (UK) 8.10

Triple jump

1977 João de Oliveira (Ame/Bra) 16.68

1979 João de Oliveira (Ame/Bra) 17.02

1981 João de Oliveira (Ame/Bra) 17.37

1985 Willie Banks (USA) 17.58

1989 Mike Conley (USA) 17.49

1992 Jonathan Edwards (UK) 17.34

1994 Yoelbi Quesada (Ame/Cub) 17.61

Shot

1977 Udo Beyer (GDR) 21.74

1979 Udo Beyer (GDR) 20.45

1981 Udo Beyer (GDR) 21.40

1985 Ulf Timmermann (GDR) 22.00

1989 Ulf Timmermann (GDR) 21.68

1992 Mike Stulce (USA) 21.34

1994 C J Hunter (USA) 19.92

Discus

1977 Wolfgang Schmidt (GDR) 67.14

1979 Wolfgang Schmidt (GDR) 66.02

1981 Armin Lemme (GDR) 66.38

1985 Gennadiy Kolnootchenko (USSR) 69.08

1989 Jürgen Schult (GDR) 67.12

1992 Tony Washington (USA) 64.86

1994 Vladimir Dubrovshchik (Eur/Blr) 64.54

Hammer

1977 Karl-Hans Riehm (FRG) 75.64

1979 Sergey Litvinov (USSR) 78.70

1981 Yuriy Sedykh (USSR) 77.42

1985 Jüri Tamm (USSR) 82.12

1989 Heinz Weis (Eur/FRG) 77.68

1992 Tibor Gécsek (Eur/Hun) 80.44

1994 Andrey Abduvaliyev (Asi/Tjk) 81.72

Javelin

1977 Michael Wessing (FRG) 87.46

1979 Wolfgang Hanisch (GDR) 86.48

1981 Dainis Kula (USSR) 89.74

1985 Uwe Hohn (GDR) 96.96

1989 Steve Backley (UK) 85.90

1992 Jan Zelezny (Eur/Cs) 88.26

1994 Steve Backley (UK) 85.02

4 x 100 metres relay

1977 USA 38.03

1979 Americas 38.70

1981 Europe 38.73

1985 USA 38.10

1989 USA 38.29

1992 USA 38.48

1994 UK 38.46

4 x 400 metres relay

1977 F R Germany 3:01.34

1979 USA 3:00.70

1981 USA 2:59.12

1985 USA 3:00.71

1989 Americas 3:00.65

1992 Africa 3:02.14

1994 UK 3:01.34

Women's individual events

100 metres

1977 Marlies Oelsner (GDR) 11.16

1979 Evelyn Ashford (USA) 11.06

1981 Evelyn Ashford (USA) 11.02

1985 Marlies Göhr (née Oelsner) (GDR) 11.10

1989 Sheila Echols (USA) 11.18

1992 Natalya Voronova (CIS/Rus) 11.33

1994 Irina Privalova (Eur/Rus) 11.32

200 metres

1977 Irena Szewinska (Eur/Pol) 22.72

1979 Evelyn Ashford (USA) 21.83

1981 Evelyn Ashford (USA) 22.18

1985 Marita Koch (GDR) 21.90

1989 Silke Möller (GDR) 22.46

1992 Marie-José Pérec (Eur/Fra) 23.07

1994 Merlene Ottey (Ame/Jam) 22.23

400 metres

1977 Irena Szewinska (Eur/Pol) 49.52

1979 Marita Koch (GDR) 48.97

1981 Jarmila Kratochvílová (Eur/Cs) 48.61

1985 Marita Koch (GDR) 47.60

1989 Ana Quirot (Ame/Cub) 50.60

1992 Jearl Miles (USA) 50.64

1994 Irina Privalova (Eur/Rus) 50.62

800 metres

1977 Totka Petrova (Eur/Bul) 1:59.20

1979 Nikolina Shtereva (Eur/Bul) 2:00.52

1981 Lyudmila Veselkova (USSR) 1:57.48

1985 Christine Wachtel (GDR) 2:01.57

1989 Ana Quirot (Ame/Cub) 1:54.44

1992 Maria Mutola (Afr/Moz) 2:00.47

1994 Maria Mutola (Afr/Moz) 1:58.27

1500 metres

1977 Tatyana Kazankina (USSR) 4:12.7

1979 Totka Petrova (Eur/Bul) 4:06.46★

1981 Tamara Sorokina (USSR) 4:03.33

1985 Hildegard Körner (GDR) 4:10.86

1989 Paula Ivan (Eur/Rom) 4:18.60

1992 Yekaterina Podkopayeva (CIS/Rus) 4:17.60

1994 Hassiba Boulmerka (Afr/Alg) 4:01.05

3000 metres

1977 Grete Waitz (Eur/Nor) 8:43.5

1979 Svyetlana Ulmasova (USSR) 8:36.32

1981 Angelika Zauber (GDR) 8:54.89

1985 Ulrike Bruns (GDR) 9:14.65

1989 Yvonne Murray (Eur/UK) 8:44.32

1992 Derartu Tulu (Afr/Eth) 9:05.89

1994 Yvonne Murray (UK) 8:56.81

10,000 metres

1985 Aurora Cunha (Por) 32:07.50

1989 Kathrin Ullrich (GDR) 31:33.92

1992 Derartu Tulu (Afr/Eth) 33:38.97

1994 Elana Meyer (Afr/SAf) 30:52.51

100 metres hurdles

1977	Grazyna Rabsztyn (Eur/Pol) 12.70
1979	Grazyna Rabsztyn (Eur/Pol) 12.67
1981	Tatyana Anisimova (USSR) 12.85
1985	Cornelia Oschkenat (GDR) 12.71
1989	Cornelia Oschkenat (GDR) 12.60
1992	Aliuska López (Ame/Cub) 13.06
1994	Aliuska López (Ame/Cub) 12.91

400 metres hurdles

1979	Barbara Klepp (GDR) 55.83
1981	Ellen Neumann (GDR) 54.82
1985	Sabine Busch (GDR) 54.45
1989	Sandra Farmer-Patrick (USA) 53.84
1992	Sandra Farmer-Patrick (USA) 55.38
1994	Sally Gunnell (UK) 54.80

High jump

1977	Rosemarie Ackermann (GDR) 1.98
1979	Debbie Brill (Ame/Can) 1.96
1981	Ulrike Meyfarth (Eur/FRG) 1.96
1985	Stefka Kostadinova (Eur/Bul) 2.00
1989	Silvia Costa (Ame/Cub) 2.04
1992	Ioamnet Quintero (Ame/Cub) 1.94
1994	Britta Bilac (Eur/Slo) 1.91

Long jump

1977	Lynette Jacenko (Oce/Aus) 6.54
1979	Anita Stukane (USSR) 6.64
1981	Sigrid Ulbricht (GDR) 6.80
1985	Heike Drechsler (GDR) 7.27
1989	Galina Chistyakova (USSR) 7.10
1992	Heike Drechsler (Ger) 7.16
1994	Inessa Kravets (Eur/Ukr) 7.00

Triple jump

1992	Li Huirong (Asi/Chn) 13.88
1994	Anna Biryukova (Eur/Rus) 14.46

Shot

1977	Ilona Slupianek (GDR) 20.93*

1979	Ilona Slupianek (GDR) 20.98
1981	Ilona Slupianek (GDR) 20.60
1985	Natalya Lisovskaya (USSR) 20.69
1989	Huang Zhihong (Asi/Chn) 20.73
1992	Belsy Laza (Ame/Cub) 19.19
1994	Huang Zhihong (Asi/Chn) 19.45

Discus

1977	Faina Melnik (USSR) 68.10
1979	Evelin Jahl (GDR) 65.18
1981	Evelin Jahl (GDR) 66.70
1985	Martina Opitz (GDR) 69.78
1989	Ilke Wyludda (GDR) 71.54
1992	Maritza Martén (Ame/Cub) 69.30
1994	Ilke Wyludda (Ger) 65.30

Javelin

1977	Ruth Fuchs (GDR) 62.36
1979	Ruth Fuchs (GDR) 66.10
1981	Antoaneta Todorova (Eur/Bul) 70.08
1985	Olga Gavrilova (USSR) 66.80
1989	Petra Felke (GDR) 70.32
1992	Tessa Sanderson (Eur/GBR) 61.86
1994	Trine Hattestad (Eur/Nor) 66.48

4 x 100 metres relay

1977	Europe 42.51
1979	Europe 42.19
1981	GDR 42.22
1985	GDR 41.37
1989	GDR 42.21
1992	Asia (Chn) 43.63
1994	Africa (Nig) 42.92

4 x 400 metres relay

1977	GDR 3:24.04
1979	GDR 3:20.38
1981	GDR 3:20.62
1985	GDR 3:19.49
1989	Americas 3:23.05
1992	Americas 3:29.73
1994	UK 8:27.36

Most individual event wins

Men: 4 Miruts Yifter (Afr/Eth); 3 Ed Moses (USA), João de Oliveira (Ame/Bra), Udo Beyer (GDR), Robson da Silva (Ame/Bra), Linford Christie (UK)

Women: 4 Evelyn Ashford (USA); 3 Ilona Slupianek* (GDR), Marita Koch (GDR)

* Subsequently disqualified for infringing the doping regulations, Slupianek having tested positive at the preceding European Cup and therefore retrospectively ineligible.

IAAF World Race Walking Cup

This competition is held biennially for the Lugano Trophy (men) and the Eschborn Cup (women). It has been officially recognized by the IAAF with the above name since 1977.

Lugano Trophy

Contested by men's national teams walking over 20km and 50km.
Wins:

5	GDR	1965, 1967, 1970, 1973, 1985
4	USSR	1975, 1983, 1987, 1989
4	Mexico	1977, 1979, 1993, 1995
2	United Kingdom	1961, 1963
2	Italy	1981, 1991
1	Russia	1997

Individual winners – 20 kilometres

1961	Ken Matthews (UK) 1:30:54
1963	Ken Matthews (UK) 1:30:10
1965	Dieter Lindner (GDR) 1:29:10
1967	Nikolay Smaga (USSR) 1:28:39
1970	Hans-Georg Reimann (GDR) 1:26:55
1973	Hans-Georg Reimann (GDR) 1:29:31
1975	Karl-Heinz Stadtmüller (GDR) 1:26:12
1977	Daniel Bautista (Mex) 1:24:03

1979	Daniel Bautista (Mex) 1:18:49
1981	Ernesto Canto (Mex) 1:23:52
1983	Jozef Pribilinec (Cs) 1:19:30
1985	José Marin (Spa) 1:21:42
1987	Carlos Mercenario (Mex) 1:19:24
1989	Frants Kostyukevich (USSR) 1:20:21
1991	Mikhail Shchennikov (USSR) 1:20:43
1993	Daniel García (Mex) 1:24:26
1995	Li Zewen (Chn) 1:19:44
1997	Jefferson Pérez (Ecu) 1:18:24

**Individual winners –
50 kilometres**

1961	Abdon Pamich (Ita) 4:25:38
1963	István Havasi (Hun) 4:17·16
1965	Christoph Höhne (GDR) 4:03:14
1967	Christoph Höhne (GDR) 4:09:09
1970	Christoph Höhne (GDR) 4:04:36
1973	Bernard Kannenberg (FRG) 3:56:51
1975	Yevgeniy Lyungin (USSR) 4:03:42
1977	Raúl González (Mex) 4:04:17
1979	Martín Bermudez (Mex) 3:43:36
1981	Raúl González (Mex) 3:48:30
1983	Raúl González (Mex) 3:45:37
1985	Hartwig Gauder (GDR) 3:47:31
1987	Ronald Weigel (GDR) 3:42:52
1989	Simon Baker (Aus) 3:43:13
1991	Carlos Mercenario (Mex) 3:42:03
1993	Carlos Mercenario (Mex) 3:50:28
1995	Zhao Yongsheng (Chn) 3:41:20
1997	Jesús Angel García (Spa) 3:39:54

Eschborn Cup

Contested by women's national teams walking over 10km (5km 1979-81).
Wins:

4	USSR 1981, 1987, 1989, 1991
3	China 1983, 1985, 1995
1	UK 1979, Italy 1993, Russia 1997

Individual winners

5 kilometres

1979	Marion Fawkes (UK) 22:51
1981	Siw Gustavsson (Swe) 22:57

10 kilometres

1983	Xu Yongjiu (Chn) 45:14

IAAF World Cup Marathon

Staged biennially after the first event, at Hiroshima, Japan in 1985. From 1997 the event has been incorporated with the marathon race in the World Championships (qv).
Winners:

Year	Team	Individual
Men		
1985	Djibouti	Ahmed Salah (Dji) 2:08:09
1987	Italy	Ahmed Salah (Dji) 2:10:55
1989	Ethiopia	Metaferia Zeleke (Eth) 2:10:28
1991	UK	Yakov Tolstikov (USSR) 2:09:17
1993	Ethiopia	Richard Nerurkar (UK) 2:10:03
1995	Italy	Douglas Wakiihuri (Ken) 2:12:01
1997	Spain	*As World Championships*
Women		
1985	Italy	Katrin Dörre (GDR) 2:33:30
1987	USSR	Zoya Ivanova (USSR) 2:30:39
1989	USSR	Sue Marchiano (USA) 2:30:48
1991	USSR	Rosa Mota (Por) 2:26:14
1993	China	Wang Junxia (Chn) 2:28:16
1995	Romania	Anuta Catuna (Rom) 2:31:10
1997	Japan	*As World Championships*

IAAF Women's World Road Race Championship

Held at 10km 1983-4 and 15km 1985-91, then replaced by half-marathon championship.
Winners:

Year	Team	Individual
1983	USA	Wendy Sly (UK) 32:23
1984	UK	Aurora Cunha (Por) 33:04
1985	UK	Aurora Cunha (Por) 49:17
1986	USSR	Aurora Cunha (Por) 48:31
1987	Portugal	Ingrid Kristiansen (Nor) 47:17
1988	USSR	Ingrid Kristiansen (Nor) 48:24
1989	China	Wang Xiuting (Chn) 49:34
1990	Portugal	Iulia Negura (Rom) 50:12
1991	Germany	Iulia Negura (Rom) 48:42

IAAF World Half Marathon Championship

Held annually from 1992.
Winners:

Year	Team	Individual
Men		
1992	Kenya	Benson Masya (Ken) 60:24
1993	Kenya	Vincent Rousseau (Bel) 61:06

(Individual winners)

1985	Yan Hong (Chn) 46:22
1987	Olga Krishtop (USSR) 43:22
1989	Beate Anders (GDR) 43:08
1991	Irina Strakhova (USSR) 43:55
1993	Wang Yan (Chn) 45:10
1995	Gao Hongmiao (Chn) 42:19
1997	Irina Stankina (Rus) 41:52

1994	Kenya	Khalid Skah (Mor) 60:27
1995	Kenya	Moses Tanui (Ken) 61:45
1996	Italy	Stefano Baldini (Ita) 61:17
1997	Kenya	Shem Kororia (Ken) 59:56

Women

1992	Japan	Liz McColgan (UK) 68:53
1993	Romania	M Conceição Ferreira (Por) 70:07
1994	Romania	Elana Meyer (SAf) 68:36
1995	Romania	Valentina Yegorova (Rus) 69:58
1996	Romania	Ren Xiujuan (Chn) 70:39
1997	Romania	Tegla Loroupe (Ken) 68:14

IAAF World Road Relay Championship

Held biennially from 1992, with relay teams of five men (six in 1992) and six women combining for the marathon distance of 42.195km.

Winners:

Year	Men	Women
1992	Kenya 2:00:02	Portugal 2:20:14
1994	Morocco 1:57:56	Russia 2:17:19
1996	Kenya 2:00:40	Ethiopia 2:16:04
1998	Kenya 2:01:13	Ethiopia 2:21:15

Commonwealth Games

See Commonwealth Games section for all winners.

Most gold medals

Men: 6 Don Quarrie (Jam) 1970-8

Women: 7 Marjorie Nelson (née) Jackson (Aus) 1950-4, Raelene Boyle (Aus) 1970-82; 6 Pam Kilborn/Ryan (Aus) 1962-70

Most wins at one event

Men: 3 Howard Payne (Eng) hammer 1962, 1966, 1970, Don Quarrie (Jam) 100m 1970, 1974, 1978, Daley Thompson (Eng) decathlon 1978, 1982, 1986

Women: 3 Valerie Young (NZ) shot 1962, 1966, 1970, Pam Ryan (Aus) 80mh 1962, 1966, 100mh 1970, Jennifer Lamy (Aus) 4x100m 1966, 1970, 1974, Kathy Cook (Eng) 4x100m 1978, 1982, 1986, Tessa Sanderson (Eng) javelin 1978, 1986, 1990

Most medals

(G – Gold, S – Silver, B – Bronze)

		G	S	B	Years
Men					
6	Don Quarrie (Jam)	6	-	-	1970-78
6	Harry Hart (SAf)	4	1	1	1930-34
6	Allan Wells (Sco)	4	1	1	1978-82
Women					
9	Raelene Boyle (Aus)	7	2	-	1970-82
8	Denise Boyd (Aus)	2	3	3	1974-82
7	Marjorie Jackson (Aus)	7	-	-	1950-4
7	Valerie Young (NZ)	5	1	1	1958-74
7	Kathy Cook (Eng)	3	3	1	1978-86

| 7 | Debbie Flintoff (Aus) | 3 | 3 | 1 | 1982-90 |
| 7 | Angella Issajenko (Can) | 3 | 2 | 2 | 1982-6 |

(Boyd née Robertson, Young née Sloper, Cook née Smallwood, Issajenko née Taylor, Ryan née Kilborn)

Most medals at one Games

| 5 | Decima Norman (Aus) | 5 | - | - | 1938 |
| 5 | Shirley Strickland (Aus) | 3 | 2 | - | 1950 |

European Cup

Contested by European nations, with each team entering one athlete per event and one team in each relay. Originally held biennially, but annually from 1994. The Cup is dedicated to the memory of Dr Bruno Zauli, the former President of the European Committee of the IAAF, who died suddenly in 1963 soon after the decision had been made to start this event.

From 1965 until 1981 the competition was staged with a qualifying round, semifinals and final, but from 1983 the nations have been arranged into groups according to strength, with eight men's and eight women's teams in A and B groups, and additional nations in C1 and C2 groups. There is two up and two down promotion and relegation between the groups (one up and down between A and B prior to 1989). The groups for 1991 were rearranged with the merging of the FRG and GDR teams into a combined Germany, and in 1993, to take account of the ex-Soviet and Yugoslav republics. In 1993 the top group was renamed as the Super League, with a First League and three groups in the Second League, and the competition became an annual one.

Men's wins

6	GDR	1970, 1975, 1977, 1979, 1981, 1983
6	USSR	1965, 1967, 1973, 1985, 1987, 1991
3	Germany	1994-6
3	UK	1989, 1997-8
1	Russia	1993

Women's wins

9	GDR	1970, 1973, 1975, 1977, 1979, 1981, 1983, 1987, 1989
4	Russia	1993, 1995, 1997-8
3	USSR	1965, 1967, 1985
3	Germany	1991, 1994, 1996

Most individual event wins in finals

Men: 13 Linford Christie (GBR) 100m 1987, 1989, 1991, 1993-7; 200m 1987, 1994-7; 5 Harald Schmid (FRG) 400m 1979, 400mh 1979, 1983, 1985, 1987

Women: 6 Marlies Göhr (GDR) 100m 1977, 1979, 1981, 1983, 1985, 1987, Heike Drechsler (GDR/Ger) long jump 1983, 1987, 1991, 1993-5; 5 Renate Stecher (GDR) 100m 1973, 1975, 200m 1970, 1973, 1975

1986 Romas Ubartas (USSR)
67.08
1990 Jürgen Schult (GDR) 64.58
1994 Vladimir Dubrovshchik (Blr)
64.78
Most wins: 3 Adolfo Consolini (Ita)
1946, 1950, 1954

Hammer
1978 Yuriy Sedykh (USSR) 77.28
1982 Yuriy Sedykh (USSR) 81.66
1986 Yuriy Sedykh (USSR) 86.74
CBP
1990 Igor Astapkovich (USSR)
84.14
1994 Vasiliy Sidorenko (Rus)
81.10
Most wins: 3 Sedykh

Javelin
(New specification from 1986.)
1978 Michael Wessing (FRG)
89.12
1982 Uwe Hohn (GDR) 91.34
1986 Klaus Tafelmeier (FRG)
84.76
1990 Steve Backley (UK) 87.30
CBP
1994 Steve Backley (UK) 85.20
Most wins: 4 Janis Lusis (USSR)
1962, 1966, 1969 (CBP old
javelin 91.52), 1971; 2 Matti
Järvinen (Fin) 1934, 1938, Janusz
Sidlo (Pol) 1954, 1958, Backley

Decathlon
1978 Aleksandr Grebenyuk
(USSR) 8340
1982 Daley Thompson (UK) 8744
1986 Daley Thompson (UK) 8811
CBP
1990 Christian Plaziat (Fra) 8574
1994 Alain Blondel (Fra) 8453
Most wins: 3 Vasiliy Kuznetsov
(USSR) 1954, 1958, 1962;
2 Joachim Kirst (GDR) 1969,
1971, Thompson

4 x 100 metres relay
1978 Poland 38.53
1982 USSR 38.60
1986 USSR 38.29
1990 France 37.79 CBP
1994 France 38.57

4 x 400 metres relay
1978 F R Germany 3:02.03
1982 F R Germany 3:00.51
1986 United Kingdom 2:59.84

1990 United Kingdom 2:58.22 CBP
1994 United Kingdom 2:59.13

20 kilometres walk
1978 Roland Wieser (GDR)
1:23:12
1982 José Marin (Spa) 1:23:43
1986 Jozef Pribilinec (Cs) 1:21:15
CBP
1990 Pavol Blazek (Cs) 1:22:05
1994 Mikhail Shchennikov (Rus)
1:18:45

50 kilometres walk
1978 Jordi Llopart (Spa) 3:53:30
1982 Reima Salonen (Fin) 3:55:29
1986 Hartwig Gauder (GDR)
3:40:55 CBP
1990 Andrey Perlov (USSR)
3:54:36
1994 Valeriy Spitsyn (Rus) 3:41:07
Most wins: 2 Abdon Pamich (Ita)
1962, 1966, Christoph Höhne
(GDR) 1969, 1974

Women

100 metres
1978 Marlies Göhr (GDR) 11.13
1982 Marlies Göhr (GDR) 11.01
1986 Marlies Göhr (GDR) 10.91
1990 Katrin Krabbe (GDR) 10.89
CBP
1994 Irina Privalova (Rus) 11.02
Most wins: 3 Göhr

200 metres
1978 Lyudmila Kondratyeva
(USSR) 22.52
1982 Bärbel Wöckel (GDR) 22.04
1986 Heike Drechsler (GDR)
21.71 CBP
1990 Katrin Krabbe (GDR) 21.95
1994 Irina Privalova (Rus) 22.32
Most wins: 2 Irena Szewinska (Pol)
1966, 1974

400 metres
1978 Marita Koch (GDR) 48.94
1982 Marita Koch (GDR) 48.15
CBP
1986 Marita Koch (GDR) 48.22
1990 Grit Breuer (GDR) 49.50
1994 Marie-José Pérec (Fra) 50.33
Most wins: 3 Koch; 2 Mariya Itkina
(USSR) 1958, 1962

800 metres
1978 Tatyana Providokhina
(USSR) 1:55.80

1982 Olga Mineyeva (USSR)
1:55.41 CBP
1986 Nadezhda Olizarenko
(USSR) 1:57.15
1990 Sigrun Wodars (GDR)
1:55.87
1994 Lyubov Gurina (Rus) 1:58.55
Most wins: 2 Vera Nikolic (Yug)
1966, 1971

1500 metres
1978 Giana Romanova (USSR)
3:59.01
1982 Olga Dvirna (USSR) 3:57.80
CBP
1986 Ravilya Agletdinova (USSR)
4:01.19
1990 Snezana Pajkic (Yug) 4:08.12
1994 Lyudmila Rogachova (Rus)
4:18.93

3000 metres
1978 Svetlana Ulmasova (USSR)
8:33.16
1982 Svetlana Ulmasova (USSR)
8:30.28 CBP
1986 Olga Bondarenko (USSR)
8:33.99
1990 Yvonne Murray (UK)
8:43.06
1994 Sonia O'Sullivan (Ire)
8:31.84
Most wins: 2 Ulmasova

10,000 metres
1986 Ingrid Kristiansen (Nor)
30:23.25 CBP
1990 Yelena Romanova (USSR)
31:46.83
1994 Fernanda Ribeiro (Por)
31:08.75

Marathon
1982 Rosa Mota (Por) 2:36:04
1986 Rosa Mota (Por) 2:28:38
CBP
1990 Rosa Mota (Por) 2:31:27
1994 Manuela Machado (Por)
2:29:54
Most wins: 3 Mota

100 metres hurdles
1978 Johanna Klier (GDR) 12.62
1982 Lucyna Kalek (Pol) 12.45
1986 Yordanka Donkova (Bul)
12.38 CBP
1990 Monique Ewanje-Épée (Fra)
12.79
1994 Svetla Dimitrova (Bul) 12.72

Most wins: 3 Karin Balzer (GDR)
1966 (80mh), 1969, 1971;
2 Fanny Blankers-Koen (Hol)
1946, 1950 (both at 80mh)

400 metres hurdles

1978	Tatyana Zelentsova (USSR) 54.89	
1982	Ann-Louise Skoglund (Swe) 54.58	
1986	Marina Styepanova (USSR) 53.32 CBP	
1990	Tatyana Ledovskaya (USSR) 53.62	
1994	Sally Gunnell (UK) 53.33	

High jump

1978   Sara Simeoni (Ita) 2.01
1982   Ulrike Meyfarth (FRG) 2.02 CBP
1986   Stefka Kostadinova (Bul) 2.00
1990   Heike Henkel (FRG) 1.99
1994   Britta Bilac (Slo) 2.00
Most wins: 2 Iolanda Balas (Rom) 1958, 1962

Long jump

1978   Vilma Bardauskiené (USSR) 6.88
1982   Vali Ionescu (Rom) 6.79
1986   Heike Drechsler (GDR) 7.27
1990   Heike Drechsler (GDR) 7.30 CBP
1994   Heike Drechsler (GDR) 7.14
Most wins: 3 Drechsler

Triple jump

1994   Ana Biryukova (Rus) 14.89

Shot

1978   Ilona Slupianek (GDR) 21.41
1982   Ilona Slupianek (GDR) 21.59 CBP
1986   Heidi Krieger (GDR) 21.10
1990   Astrid Kumbernuss (GDR) 20.38
1994   Viktoriya Pavlysh (Ukr) 19.61
Most wins: 4 Nadezhda Chizhova (USSR) 1966, 1969, 1971, 1974; 2 Slupianek

Discus

1978   Evelin Jahl (GDR) 66.98
1982   Tsvetanka Khristova (Bul) 68.34
1986   Diane Sachse (GDR) 71.36 CBP
1990   Ilke Wyludda (GDR) 68.46

1994   Ilke Wyludda (Ger) 68.72
Most wins: 2 Nina Dumbadze (USSR) 1946, 1950, Tamara Press (USSR) 1958, 1962, Faina Melnik (USSR) 1971, 1974, Wyludda

Javelin

1978   Ruth Fuchs (GDR) 69.16
1982   Anna Verouli (Gre) 70.02
1986   Fatima Whitbread (UK) 76.32 (77.44 CBP qual)
1990   Päivi Alafranti (Fin) 67.68
1994   Trine Hattestad (Nor) 68.00
Most wins: 2 Dana Zátopková (Cs) 1954, 1958, Fuchs 1974, 1978

Heptathlon

1978   Margit Papp (Hun) 4655 (Pentathlon)
1982   Ramona Neubert (GDR) 6664
1986   Anke Behmer (GDR) 6717 CBP
1990   Sabine Braun (FRG) 6688
1994   Sabine Braun (Ger) 6419
Most wins: 2 Galina Bystrova (USSR) (pentathlon) 1958, 1962, Braun

4 x 100 metres relay

1978   USSR 42.54
1982   GDR 42.19
1986   GDR 41.84

Most medals
(G - Gold, S - Silver, B – Bronze)

1990   GDR 41.68 CBP
1994   Germany 42.90

4 x 400 metres relay

1978   GDR 3:21.20
1982   GDR 3:19.05
1986   GDR 3:16.87 CBP
1990   GDR 3:21.02
1994   France 3:22.34

10 kilometres walk

1986   Maria Cruz Diaz (Spa) 46:09
1990   Annarita Sidoti (Ita) 44:00
1994   Sari Essayah (Fin) 42:37 CBP

Most gold medals at all events

Men
5   Harald Schmid (FRG) 1978-86
5   Roger Black (UK) 1986-94
4   Janis Lusis (USSR) 1962-71
4   Valeriy Borzov (USSR) 1969-74

Women
6   Marita Koch (GDR) 1978-86
5   Fanny Blankers-Koen (Hol) 1946-50
5   Irena Szewinska (Pol) 1966-74
5   Marlies Göhr (GDR) 1978-86
4   Maria Itkina (USSR) 1954-62
4   Nadezhda Chizhova (USSR) 1966-74
4   Renate Stecher (GDR) 1969-74
4   Heike Drechsler (GDR/GER) 1986-90

		G	S	B	Years
Men					
6	Harald Schmid (FRG)	5	1	-	1978-86
6	Pietro Mennea (Ita)	3	2	1	1971-74
6	Roger Black (UK)	5	1	-	1986-94
Women					
10	Irena Szewinska (Pol)	5	1	4	1966-78
8	Fanny Blankers-Koen (Hol)	5	1	2	1938-50
8	Renate Stecher (GDR)	4	4	-	1969-74
7	Marlies Göhr (GDR)	5	1	1	1978-86
6	Yevgeniya Sechenova (USSR)	2	2	2	1946-50
6	Marita Koch (GDR)	6	-	-	1978-86

Most medals at one event

5	Igor Ter-Ovanesyan (USSR) (long jump)	3	2	-	1966-71

Most medals at one Championships

		G	S	B	Years
Men					
4	John Regis (UK)	2	1	1	1990
Women					
4	Fanny Blankers-Koen (Hol)	3	1	-	1950
4	Irena Kirszenstein/Szewinska (Pol)	3	1	-	1966
4	Stanislawa Walasiewicz (Pol)	2	2	-	1938

European Indoor Championships

European Indoor Games were held for the first time on 27 March 1966 at the Westfallenhalle in Dortmund. From 1970 they received IAAF sanction as the official European Indoor Championships, and were held annually until 1990; since then they have been biennial.

Most wins

Men

7	Valeriy Borzov (USSR) 60m 1970-1, 1974-7; 50m 1972
6	Viktor Saneyev (USSR) triple jump 1970-2, 1975-7
5	Marian Woronin (Pol) 60m 1979-82, 1987
5	José Luis González (Spa) 1500m 1982, 1985-6; 3000m 1987-8
5	Dietmar Mögenburg (FRG) high jump 1980, 1982, 1984, 1986, 1989

Women

8	Helena Fibingerová (Cs) shot 1973-4, 1977-8, 1980, 1983-5
6	Nellie Cooman/Fiere (Hol) 60m 1985-9, 1994
5	Karin Balzer (GDR) 50m hurdles 1967-9, 60m hurdles 1970-1
5	Nadezhda Chizhova (USSR) shot 1967-8, 1970-2
5	Marlies Göhr (GDR) 60m 1977-9, 1982-3

World Records – Men

World records for athletics were first officially recognized by the IAAF in 1913. Initially, records were accepted for 96 men's events; this list has been reduced at various times, including the elimination of Imperial distances (except the 1 mile), in 1977. From 1977, all records at sprint distances up to 400 metres have been accepted only if timed fully automatically. Prior to that date the best hand-timed results have been listed.

Records are shown, at 15-year intervals from 1900 to 1990 and all those from 1990, for each of the currently recognized events. Pre-1900 performances were not ratified by the IAAF; neither were those indicated by 'u', for various reasons, but they are considered to be the best acceptable. Also listed are those athletes to have set most records at each event.

(a = set at high altitude (over 1000m); u = not ratified by the IAAF; y = 120 yards rather 110m; 220 yards rather than 200m; 440 yards rather than 400m; 880 yards rather than 800m; est = estimated; w = wind-assisted. Timing is indicated as hand or automatic.)

100 metres

1900	10.8	Luther Cary (USA) 4 Jul 1891
	10.8	eight other men
1915	10.5u	Emil Ketterer (Ger) 9 Jul 1911
	10.5u	Richard Rau (Ger) 13 Aug 1911
1930	10.2u	Charles Paddock (USA) 18 Jun 1921
1945	10.2u	Charles Paddock (USA) 18 Jun 1921
	10.2	Jesse Owens (USA) 20 Jun 1936
	10.2	Hal Davis (USA) 6 Jun 1941
	10.2u	Lloyd La Beach (Pan) 8 Aug 1943
1960	10.0	Armin Hary (FRG) 21 Jun 1960 (10.25 auto)
	10.0	Harry Jerome (Can) 15 Jul 1960
1975	9.9 (hand)	seven men
	9.95a	Jim Hines (USA) 14 Oct 1968
1990	9.92	Carl Lewis (USA) 24 Sep 1988
	9.83	Ben Johnson (Can) 30 Aug 1987★
	9.90	Leroy Burrell (USA) 14 Jun 1991
	9.86	Carl Lewis (USA) 25 Aug 1991
	9.85	Leroy Burrell (USA) 6 Jul 1994
	9.84	Donovan Bailey (Can) 27 Jul 1996

★ Johnson's time was officially ratified but later dropped after his admission that he had taken steroids for many years. He ran 9.79 in the Olympic Games at Seoul on 24 Sep 1988, but was disqualified after a positive drugs test. **Most wins:** 4 Steve Williams (USA), all at 9.9 1974-6

200 metres

1900	21.2y★	Bernie Wefers (USA) 30 May 1896
1915	21.2y	William Applegarth (UK) 4 Jul 1914
	20.8y★	Albert Robinson (USA) 2 May 1913
1930	21.0u	Helmut Körnig (Ger) 26 Aug 1928
	20.6★	Roland Locke (USA) 1 May 1926
1945	20.6yu	James Carlton (Aus) 18 Jun 1932
	20.3y★	Jesse Owens (USA) 25 May 1935
1960	20.5y	Peter Radford (UK) 28 May 1960
	20.5	Stonewall Johnson (USA) 2 Jul 1960
	20.5	Ray Norton (USA) 2 Jul 1960
	20.5	Livio Berruti (Ita) 3 Sep 1960 (20.62a)
	20.0★	Dave Sime (USA) 9 Jun 1956
1975	19.83a	Tommie Smith (USA) 16 Oct 1968
	19.5★	Tommie Smith (USA) 7 May 1966
1990	19.72a	Pietro Mennea (Italy) 12 Sep 1979
	19.66	Michael Johnson (USA) 23 Jun 1996
	19.32	Michael Johnson (USA) 1 Aug 1996

★ Straight track (c.0.3–0.4 sec faster) – prior to 1951, records could be set on any type of course; from 1951 to 1975, separate records were maintained for straight and turn; thereafter, all records must be made around a full turn. **Most wins:** 5 Ray Norton (USA) 20.6–20.5 (1959-60)

400 metres

1900	47.8y	Maxie Long (USA) 29 Sep 1900
1915	47.8y	As above
1930	47.0	Emerson Spenser (USA) 12 May 1928
1945	46.0	Rudolf Harbig (Ger) 12 Aug 1939
	46.0	Grover Klemmer (USA) 29 Jun 1941
1960	44.9	Otis Davis (USA) 6 Sep 1960
	44.9	Carl Kaufmann (FRG) 6 Sep 1960 (auto: 45.07 Davis, 45.08 Kaufmann)
1975	43.86a	Lee Evans (USA) 18 Oct 1968
1990	43.29	Butch Reynolds (USA) 17 Aug 1988

Most wins: 4 Herb McKenley (Jam) 46.2y–45.9 (1946-8)

800 metres

1900	1:53.4y	Charles Kilpatrick (USA) 21 Sep 1895
1915	1:51.9	Ted Meredith (USA) 8 Jul 1912
1930	1:50.6	Séraphin Martin (Fra) 14 Jul 1928
1945	1:46.6	Rudolf Harbig (Ger) 15 Jul 1939
1960	1:45.7	Roger Moens (Bel) 3 Aug 1955
1975	1:43.7	Marcello Fiasconaro (Ita) 27 Jun 1973
	1:44.1y	Rick Wohlhuter (USA) 8 Jun 1974
1990	1:41.73	Sebastian Coe (UK) 10 Jun 1981
	1:41.73	Wilson Kipketer (Den) 7 Jul 1997
	1:41.24	Wilson Kipketer (Den) 13 Aug 1997
	1:41.11	Wilson Kipketer (Den) 24 Aug 1997

Most wins: 5 Lawrence 'Lon' Myers (USA) 1:56.2y–1:55.4y (1880-5)

1000 metres

1900	2:36.8	Henri Deloge (Fra) 10 Jun 1900
1915	2:31.0u	Emilio Lunghi (Ita) 31 May 1908
1930	2:23.6	Jules Ladoumègue (Fra) 19 Oct 1930
1945	2:21.5	Rudolf Harbig (Ger) 24 May 1941
1960	2:16.7	Siegfried Valentin (GDR) 29 Jul 1960
1975	2:13.9	Rick Wohlhuter (USA) 30 Jul 1974
1990	2:12.18	Sebastian Coe (UK) 11 Jul 1981

Most wins: 3 Auden Boysen (Nor) 2:20.4–2:19.0 (1953-5)

1500 metres

1900	4:06.2	Charles Bennett (UK) 15 Jul 1900
1915	3:55est	Norman Taber (USA) 16 Jul 1915
1930	3:49.2	Jules Ladoumègue (Fra) 5 Oct 1930
1945	3:43.0	Gunder Hägg (Swe) 7 Jul 1944
1960	3:35.6	Herb Elliott (Aus) 6 Sep 1960
1975	3:32.16	Filbert Bayi (Tan) 2 Feb 1974
1990	3:29.46	Saïd Aouita (Mor) 23 Aug 1985
	3:28.86	Noureddine Morceli (Alg) 6 Sep 1992
	3:27.37	Noureddine Morceli (Alg) 12 Jul 1995
	3:26.00	Hicham El Guerrouj (Mor) 14 Jul 1998

Most wins: 3 Abel Kiviat (USA) 3:59.2–3:55.8 (1912), Gunder Hägg (Swe) 3:47.6–3:43.0 (1941-4), Steve Ovett (UK) 3:32.09–3:30.77 (1980-3)

1 mile

1900	4:12fl	Walter George (UK) 23 Aug 1886 (pro)
	4:15.6	Thomas Conneff (USA) 30 Aug 1895
1915	4:12.6	Norman Taber (USA) 16 Jul 1915
1930	4:10.4	Paavo Nurmi (Fin) 23 Aug 1923
1945	4:01.3	Gunder Hägg (Swe) 17 Jul 1945
1960	3:54.5	Herb Elliott (Aus) 6 Aug 1958
1975	3:49.4	John Walker (NZ) 12 Aug 1975
1990	3:46.32	Steve Cram (UK) 27 Jul 1985
	3:44.39	Noureddine Morceli (Alg) 5 Sep 1993

Most wins: 3 Gunder Hägg (Swe) 4:06.1–4.01.3 (1942-5), Arne Andersson (Swe) 4:06.2–4:01.6 (1942-4), Sebastian Coe (UK) 3:48.95–3:47.33 (1979-81)

2000 metres

1900	5:38.8★	Thomas Conneff (USA) 2 Sep 1895
1915	5:37.0★	Alfred Shrubb (UK) 11 Jun 1904
1930	5:23.4	Eino Borg (Purje) (Fin) 9 Aug 1927
1945	5:11.8	Gunder Hägg (Swe) 23 Aug 1942
1960	5:02.2	István Rozsavölgyi (Hun) 2 Oct 1955
1975	4:56.2	Michel Jazy (Fra) 12 Oct 1966
1990	4:50.81	Saïd Aouita (Mor) 16 Jul 1987
	4:47.88	Noureddine Morceli (Alg) 3 Jul 1995

★ Time at 1¼ mile (2011.68m).

3000 metres

1900	9:18.2	Henri Deloge (Fra) Paris 22 Oct 1895
1915	8:36.9	Hannes Kolehmainen (Fin) 12 Jul 1912
1930	8:20.4	Paavo Nurmi (Fin) 13 Jul 1926
1945	8:01.2	Gunder Hägg (Swe) 28 Aug 1942
1960	7:52.8	Gordon Pirie (UK) 4 Sep 1956
1975	7:35.2	Brendan Foster (UK) 3 Aug 1974
1990	7:29.45	Saïd Aouita (Mor) 20 Aug 1989
	7:28.96	Moses Kiptanui (Ken) 16 Aug 1992
	7:25.11	Noureddine Morceli (Alg) 2 Aug 1994
	7:20.67	Daniel Komen (Ken) 1 Sep 1996

Most wins: 4 Paavo Nurmi (Fin) 8:28.6–8:20.4 (1922-6)

5000 metres

1900	15:20.0	Charles Bennett (UK) 22 Jul 1900
1915	14:36.6	Hannes Kolehmainen (Fin) 10 Jul 1912
1930	14:28.2	Paavo Nurmi (Fin) 19 Jun 1924
1945	13:58.1	Gunder Hägg (Swe) 20 Sep 1942
1960	13:35.0	Vladimir Kuts (USSR) 13 Oct 1957
1975	13:13.0	Emiel Puttemans (Bel) 20 Sep 1972
1990	12:58.39	Saïd Aouita (Mor) 22 Jul 1987
	12:56.96	Haile Gebrselassie (Eth) 4 Jun 1994
	12:55.30	Moses Kiptanui (Ken) 8 Jun 1995
	12:44.39	Haile Gebrselassie (Eth) 16 Aug 1995
	12:41.86	Haile Gebrselassie (Eth) 13 Aug 1997
	12:39.74	Daniel Komen (Ken) 22 Aug 1997
	12:39.36	Haile Gebrselassie (Eth) 13 Jun 1998

Most wins: 4 Vladimir Kuts (USSR) 13:56.6-13:35.0 (1954-7), Ron Clarke (Aus) 13:34.4–13:16.6 (1965-6), 4 Haile Gebrselassie (Eth) as above

10,000 metres

1900	31:40.0	Walter George (UK) 28 Jul 1884
1915	30:58.8	Jean Bouin (Fra) 16 Nov 1911
1930	30:06.1	Paavo Nurmi (Fin) 31 Aug 1924
1945	29:35.4	Viljo Heino (Fin) 25 Aug 1944
1960	28:18.8	Pyotr Bolotnikov (USSR) 5 Oct 1960
1975	27:30.80	David Bedford (UK) 13 Jul 1973
1990	27:08.23	Arturo Barrios (Mex) 18 Aug 1989
	27:07.91	Richard Chelimo (Ken) 5 Jul 1993
	26:58.38	Yobes Ondieki (Ken) 10 Jul 1993
	26:52.23	William Sigei (Ken) 22 Jul 1994
	26:43.53	Haile Gebrselassie (Eth) 5 Jun 1995

26:38.08   Salah Hissou (Mor) 23 Aug 1996
26:31.32   Haile Gebrselassie (Eth) 4 Jul 1997
26:27.85   Paul Tergat (Ken) 22 Aug 1997
Most wins: 5 Emil Zátopek (Cs) 29:28.2–28:54.2
(1949-54)

Marathon

Note that records are not officially recognized for the marathon, as times are affected by the nature of the road courses. The distance of 26 miles 385 yards (42.195km) was that used for the race at the 1908 Olympic Games, run from Windsor to the White City Stadium. This distance became standard from 1924.

Best times:

1915   2:36:06.6   Alexis Ahlgren (Swe) 31 May 1913
1930   2:29:01.8   Al Michelsen (USA) 12 Oct 1925
1945   2:26:42   Sohn Kee-chung (Kor) 3 Nov 1935
1960   2:15:16.2   Abebe Bikila (Eth) 10 Sep 1960
1975   2:08:33.6   Derek Clayton (Aus) 30 May 1969
1990   2:06:50   Belayneh Dinsamo (Eth) 17 Apr 1988
Most wins: 4 Jim Peters (UK) 2:20:42.2–2:17:39.4
(1952-4)

3000 metres steeplechase

1930   9:21.8u   Toivo Loukola (Fin) 4 Aug 1928
1945   8:59.6u   Erik Elmsäter (Swe) 4 Aug 1944
1960   8:31.4   Zdzislaw Krzyszkowiak (Pol) 26 Jun
                  1960
1975   8:09.70   Anders Gärderud (Swe) 1 Jul 1975
1990   8:05.35   Peter Koech (Ken) 4 Jul 1989
       8:02.08   Moses Kiptanui (Ken) 19 Aug 1992
       7:59.18   Moses Kiptanui (Ken) 16 Aug 1995
       7:59.08   Wilson Boit Kipketer (Ken) 13 Aug
                  1997
       7:55.72   Bernard Barmasai (Ken) 24 Aug 1997
Most wins: 4 Anders Gärderud (Swe) 8:20.7–8:08.02
(1972-6)

110 metres hurdles

1900   15.4y   Stephen Chase (USA) 28 Sep 1895
1915   15.0   Forrest Smithson (USA) 25 Jul 1908
1930   14.4y   Earl Thomson (USA) 29 May 1920
       14.4   Eric Wennström (Swe) 25 Aug 1929
       14.4y   Stephen Anderson (USA) 23 Aug
               1930
1945   13.7   Forrest Towns (USA) 27 Aug 1936
       13.7   Fred Wolcott (USA) 29 Jun 1941
1960   13.2   Martin Lauer (FRG) 7 Jul 1959
               (13.56 auto)
       13.2   Lee Calhoun (USA) 21 Aug 1960
1975   13.0y   Rod Milburn (USA) 25 Jun 1971
               Rod Milburn (USA) 20 Jun 1973
       13.0   Guy Drut (Fra) 22 Aug 1975
       13.24   Rod Milburn (USA) 7 Sep 1972
1990   12.92   Roger Kingdom (USA) 16 Aug 1989
       12.91   Colin Jackson (UK) 20 Aug 1993
Most wins: 6 Forrest Towns (USA) 14.1–13.7 (1936),
Rod Milburn (USA) 13.2–13.0y/13.24 (1971-5)

400 metres hurdles

1900   57.2   Godfrey Shaw (UK) 12 Aug 1891
1915   54.6yu William Meanix (USA) 16 Jul 1915
1930   52.0   F Morgan Taylor (USA) 5 Jul 1928
1945   50.6   Glenn Hardin (USA) 26 Jul 1934
1960   49.2   Glenn Davis (USA) 6 Aug 1958
       49.3y   Gert Potgieter (SAf) 16 Apr 1960
1975   47.82   John Akii-Bua (Uga) 2 Sep 1972
1990   47.02   Edwin Moses (USA) 31 Aug 1983
       46.78   Kevin Young (USA) 6 Aug 1992
Most wins: 4 Edwin Moses (USA) 47.63–47.02
(1976-83)

High jump

1900   1.97m   Michael Sweeney (USA) 21 Sep 1895
1915   2.01m   Edward Beeson (USA) 2 May 1914
1930   2.03m   Harold Osborn (USA) 27 May 1924
1945   2.11m   Lester Steers (USA) 17 Jun 1941
1960   2.22m   John Thomas (USA) 1 Jul 1960
1975   2.30m   Dwight Stones (USA) 11 Jul 1973
1990   2.44m   Javier Sotomayor (Cub) 29 Jul 1989
       2.45m   Javier Sotomayor (Cub) 27 Jul 1993
Most wins: 6 Valeriy Brumel (USSR) 2.23–2.28
(1961-3); 4 John Thomas (USA) 2.17–2.22 (1960)

Pole vault

1900   3.62m   Raymond Clapp (USA) 16 Jun 1898
1915   4.02m   Marcus Wright (USA) 8 Jun 1912
1930   4.30m   Lee Barnes (USA) 28 Apr 1930
1945   4.77m   Cornelius Warmerdam (USA) 23 May
                1942 (and 4.78m indoors 20 Mar 1943)
1960   4.82mu   Bob Gutowski (USA) 15 Jun 1957
       4.80m   Don Bragg (USA) 2 Jul 1960
1975   5.65m   Dave Roberts (USA) 28 Mar 1975
1990   6.06m   Sergey Bubka (USSR) 10 Jul 1988
       6.07m   Sergey Bubka (USSR) 6 May 1991
       6.08m   Sergey Bubka (USSR) 9 Jun 1991
       6.10m   Sergey Bubka (USSR) 5 Aug 1991
       6.11m   Sergey Bubka (Ukr) 13 Jun 1992
       6.12m   Sergey Bubka (Ukr) 30 Aug 1992
       6.13m   Sergey Bubka (Ukr) 19 Sep 1992
       6.14m   Sergey Bubka (Ukr) 31 Jul 1994
Most wins: 17 Sergey Bubka (USSR) 5.85–6.14
(1984-94); 9 John Pennel (USA) 4.95–5.44 (1963-9)
(5u); 7 Cornelius Warmerdam (USA) 4.57–4.77
(1940-2); 6 Bob Seagren (USA) 5.32–5.63 (1966-72);
5 Thierry Vigneron (Fra) 5.75–5.91 (1980-4)

Long jump

1900   7.51m   Peter O'Connor (Ire) 29 Aug 1900
1915   7.61m   Peter O'Connor (Ire) 5 Aug 1901
1930   7.93m   Silvio Cator (Haiti) 9 Sep 1928
1945   8.13m   Jesse Owens (USA) 25 May 1935
1960   8.21m   Ralph Boston (USA) 12 Aug 1960
1975   8.90ma   Bob Beamon (USA) 18 Oct 1968
1990   As above
       8.95m   Mike Powell (USA) 30 Aug 1991
Most wins: 6 Ralph Boston (USA) 8.21–8.35 (1960-5);
5 Peter O'Connor (Ire) 7.51–7.61 (1900-1)

Triple jump

1900	14.78m	Edwin Bloss (USA) 16 Sep 1893
1915	15.52m	Daniel Ahearne (USA) 30 May 1911
1930	15.52m	Daniel Ahearne (USA) 30 May 1911
	15.52m	Anthony Winter (Aus) 12 Jul 1924
1945	16.00m	Naoto Tajima (Jap) 6 Aug 1936
1960	17.03m	Jozef Schmidt (Pol) 5 Aug 1960
1975	17.89ma	João Carlos de Oliveira (Bra) 15 Oct 1975
1990	17.97m	Willie Banks (USA) 16 Jun 1985
	17.98m	Jonathan Edwards (UK) 18 Jul 1995
	18.16m	Jonathan Edwards (UK) 7 Aug 1995
	18.29m	Jonathan Edwards (UK) 7 Aug 1995

Most wins: 5 Adhemar Ferreira da Silva (Bra) 16.00–16.56 (1951-5)

Shot

1900	14.75m	George Gray (Can) 1 Aug 1898
1915	15.54m	Ralph Rose (USA) 21 Aug 1909
1930	16.04m	Emil Hirschfeld (Ger) 26 Aug 1928
1945	17.40m	Jack Torrance (USA) 5 Aug 1934
1960	20.06m	Bill Nieder (USA) 12 Aug 1960
1975	22.86m	Brian Oldfield (USA) 10 May 1975 (pro)
	22.02m	George Woods (USA) 8 Feb 1974 *(indoors)*
	21.82m	Al Feuerbach (USA) 5 May 1973
1990	23.12m	Randy Barnes (USA) 19 May 1990

Most wins: 15 Parry O'Brien (USA) 18.00–19.30 (1953-9); 10 Dallas Long (USA) 19.25–20.68 (1959-64); 7 George Gray (USA) 13.76–14.75 (1889-98), Ralph Rose (USA) 14.81–15.54 (1904-9); 5 Jack Torrance (USA) 16.30–17.40 (1934)

Discus

1915	47.85mu	Armas Taipale (Fin) 20 Jul 1913
1930	51.73m	Paul Jessup (USA) 23 Aug 1930
1945	53.34m	Adolfo Consolini (Ita) 26 Oct 1941
1960	59.91m	Edmund Piatkowski (Pol) 14 Jun 1959
	59.91m	Rink Babka (USA) 12 Aug 1960
1975	69.08m	John Powell (USA) 4 May 1975
	70.38mu	Jay Silvester (USA) 16 May 1971
1990	74.08m	Jürgen Schult (GDR) 6 Jun 1986

Most wins: 6 Jay Silvester (USA) 60.56–70.38 (1961-71); 5 Martin Sheridan (USA) from 2.5m circle 36.77–43.69 (1901-5); 4 Fortune Gordien (USA) 56.46–59.28 (1949-53), Al Oerter (USA) 61.10–62.94 (1962-4), Mac Wilkins (USA) 69.18–70.86 (1976)

Hammer

1900	51.61m	John Flanagan (USA) 29 Sep 1900
1915	57.77m	Pat Ryan (USA) 17 Aug 1913
1930		*As above*
1945	59.00m	Erwin Blask (Ger) 27 Aug 1938
	59.55mu	Pat O'Callaghan (Ire) 22 Aug 1937
1960	70.33m	Hal Connolly (USA) 12 Aug 1960
1975	79.30m	Walter Schmidt (FRG) 14 Aug 1975
1990	86.74m	Yuriy Sedykh (USSR) 30 Aug 1986

Most wins: 19 John Flanagan (USA) 44.46–56.19 (1895-1909); 7 Hal Connolly (USA) 66.71–71.26 (1956-65), Mikhail Krivonosov (USSR) 63.34–67.32 (1954-6), James Mitchell (USA) 36.40–44.21 (1886-92); 6 Yuriy Sedykh (USSR) 80.38–86.74 (1980-6)

Javelin

(Old specification)

1900	49.32m	Eric Lemming (Swe) 18 Jun 1899
1915	64.81mu	Jonni Myyrä (Fin) 18 Jul 1915
1930	72.93m	Matti Järvinen (Fin) 14 Sep 1930
1945	78.70m	Yrjö Nikkanen (Fin) 11 Oct 1938
1960	86.04m	Albert Cantello (USA) 5 Jun 1959
1975	94.08m	Klaus Wolfermann (FRG) 5 May 1973
Last	104.80m	Uwe Hohn (GDR) 20 Jul 1984

Most wins: 10 Matti Järvinen (Fin) 71.57–77.23 (1930-6); 9 Eric Lemming (Swe) 49.32–62.32 (1899-1912); 5 Jonni Myrrä (Fin) 63.29–68.56 (1914-25)

Javelin

(New specification, introduced 1987)

1990	89.58m	Steve Backley (UK) 2 Jul 1990
	89.66mR	Jan Zelezny (Cs) 14 Jul 1990
	90.98mR	Steve Backley (UK) 20 Jul 1990
	91.98mR	Seppo Räty (Fin) 6 May 1991
	96.96mR	Seppo Räty (Fin) 2 Jun 1991
	91.46m	Steve Backley (UK) 25 Jan 1992
	94.74m*	Jan Zelezny (Cs) 4 Jul 1992
	95.54m	Jan Zelezny (Cze) 6 Apr 1993
	95.66m	Jan Zelezny (Cze) 26 Aug 1993
	98.48m	Jan Zelezny (Cze) 25 May 1996

'R' denotes performances made with a javelin with a roughened surface, banned in 1991; Backley's 89.58 was reinstated as the world record.

* Not recognized due to javelin specification.

Decathlon

(All records re-scored on the 1984 tables.)

1915	6564u	Jim Thorpe (USA) 13/15 Jul 1912
1930	6865	Akilles Järvinen (Fin) 19/20 Jul 1930
1945	7254	Glenn Morris (USA) 7/8 Aug 1936
1960	7982	Rafer Johnson (USA) 8/9 Jul 1960
1975	8420	Bruce Jenner (USA) 9/10 Aug 1975
1990	8847	Daley Thompson (UK) 8/9 Aug 1984
	8891	Dan O'Brien (USA) 4/5 Sep 1992 (100m 10.43w, long jump 8.08m, shot 16.69m, high jump 2.07m, 400m 48.51, 110m hurdles 13.98, discus 48.56m, pole vault 5.00m, javelin 62.58m, 1500m 4:42.10)

Most wins: 4 Paavo Yrjöla (Fin) 6460–6700 (1926-30), Daley Thompson (UK) 8648–8847 (1980-4)

4 x 100 metres relay

1915	42.3	Germany 8 Jul 1912
1930	40.8	Germany 2 Sep 1928
	40.8	four other times

1945	39.8	USA 9 Aug 1936
1960	39.59	USA 1 Dec 1956
1975	38.19	USA 10 Sep 1972
1990	37.79	France 1 Sep 1990
	37.79	Santa Monica TC (USA) 3 Aug 1991
	37.67	USA 7 Aug 1991
	37.50	USA 1 Sep 1991
	37.40	USA 8 Aug 1992 (Michael Marsh, Leroy Burrell, Dennis Mitchell, Carl Lewis)
	37.40	USA 21 Aug 1993 (Jon Drummond, Andre Cason, Dennis Mitchell, Leroy Burrell)

4 x 400 metres relay

1915	3:16.6	USA 15 Jul 1912
1930	3:14.2	USA 5 Aug 1928
1945	3.08.2	USA / Aug 1932
1960	3:02.37	USA 8 Sep 1960
1975	2:56.16A	USA 20 Oct 1968
1990	2:56.16	USA 1 Oct 1988
	2:55.74	USA 8 Aug 1992
	2:54.29	USA 22 Aug 1993
	2:54.20	USA 22 Jul 1998 (Jerome Young, Andrew Pettigrew, Tyree Washington, Michael Johnson)

Other current relay world records

4 x 200m   1:18.68

Santa Monica Track Club, USA 17 Apr 1994 (Michael Marsh, Leroy Burrell, Floyd Heard, Carl Lewis)

4 x 800m   7:03.89

UK 30 Aug 1982 (Peter Elliott, Garry Cook, Steve Cram, Sebastian Coe)

4 x 1500m   14:38.8

F R Germany 17 Aug 1977 (Thomas Wessinghage, Harald Hudak, Michael Lederer, Karl Fleschen)

World Records – Women

Women's athletics effectively started in the 1920s, but 1915 'records' are shown for some events, recognizing the efforts of dedicated early pioneers. Women's records were first accepted by the Fédération Sportive Féminine Internationale (FSFI) from its formation in 1921. The FSFI merged with the IAAF in 1936.

Women's records at distances from 1500m upwards have been added to the official lists only from 1967. The years in which the IAAF first officially recognized records for such events are shown as IAAF 19? (e.g. 1984 for 1000m).

100 metres

1915	13.1	Nina Popova (Russia) 22 Aug 1913
1930	12.0	Elizabeth Robinson (USA) 2 Jun 1928
	12.0	Myrtle Cook (Can) 2 Jul 1928
	12.0	Tollien Schuurman (Hol) 31 Aug 1930
1945	11.5u	Helen Stephens (USA) 15 May 1936
	11.5	Helen Stephens (USA) 10 Aug 1936
1960	11.3	Shirley Strickland (Aus) 4 Aug 1955
	11.3	Vera Krepkina (USSR) 13 Sep 1958
1975	10.8	Renate Stecher (GDR) 20 Jul 1973
	11.07	Renate Stecher (GDR) 2 Sep 1972
1990	10.49	Florence Griffith-Joyner (USA) 16 Jul 1988

Most wins: 10 Stanislawa Walasiewicz★ (Pol) 11.9–11.6 (1932-7); 9 Renate Stecher (née Meissner) (GDR) 11.0–10.8 (1970-3)

★ Walasiewicz's femininity has subsequently been in question.

200 metres

1930	25.2y	Nellie Halstead (UK) 16 Aug 1930
	24.7#	Kitomi Hitomi (Jap) 19 May 1929
1945	24.1	Helen Stephens (USA) 19 Aug 1936
	23.6	Stanislawa Walasiewicz★ (Pol) 4 Aug 1935
1960	22.9	Wilma Rudolph (USA) 9 Jul 1960
1975	22.21	Irena Szewinska (Pol) 13 Jun 1974 (22.0 *hand*)
1990	21.34	Florence Griffith-Joyner (USA) 29 Sep 1988

Most wins: 4 Irena Szewinska (née Kirszenstein) (Pol) 22.7–22.21 1965-74, Marita Koch (GDR) 22.06–21.71 (1978-84), Eileen Edwards (UK) 26.2y = 25.3 (1924-7)

Straight tracks.

★ See note above.

400 metres (IAAF 1957)

1930	59.0#	Kinue Hitomi (Jap) 5 May 1928
	59.2y	Marion King (USA) 13 Jul 1929
1945	56.8y	Nellie Halstead (UK) 9 Jul 1932
1960	53.0u	Shin Keum Dan (NKo) 22 Oct 1960
	53.4	Mariya Itkina (USSR) 12 Sep 1959
1975	49.9	Irena Szewinska (Pol) 22 Jun 1974
	50.14	Riitta Salin (Fin) 4 Sep 1974
1990	47.60	Marita Koch (GDR) 6 Oct 1985

Most wins: 7 Marita Koch (GDR) 49.19–47.60 (1978-85); 5 Shin Keum Dan (NKo) 53.0–51.2 (1962-4)

Nearly straight track.

800 metres

1930	2:18.2y	Gladys Lunn (UK) 16 Aug 1930
1945	2:12.0u	Yekdokiya Vasilyeva (USSR) 5 Aug 1943
1960	2:04.3	Lyudmila Lysenko/Shevtsova (USSR) 3 Jul 1960
		Lyudmila Lysenko/Shevtsova 7 Sep 1960
1975	1:57.48	Svetla Zlateva (Bul) 24 Aug 1973
1990	1:53.28	Jarmila Kratochvílová (Cs) 26 Jul 1983

Most wins: 7 Nina Otkalenko (née Pletnyova) 2:12.0–2:05.0 (1951-5)

1000 metres (IAAF 1984)

1990	2:30.6	Tatyana Providokhina (USSR) 20 Aug 1978
	2:30.67	Christine Wachtel (GDR) 17 Aug 1990
	2:29.34	Maria Mutola (Moz) 25 Aug 1995
	2:28.98	Svetlana Masterkova (Rus) 23 Aug 1996

1500 metres (IAAF 1967)

1930	5:18.2	Anna Mushkina (USSR) 19 Aug 1927
1945	4:38.0	Yevdokiya Vasilyeva (USSR) 17 Aug 1944
1960	4:25.0u	Diane Leather (UK) 21 Sep 1955
1975	4:01.38	Lyudmila Bragina (USSR) 9 Sep 1972
1990	3:52.47	Tatyana Kazankina (USSR) 13 Aug 1980
	3:50.46	Qu Yunxia (Chn) 11 Sep 1993

Most wins: 4 Lyudmila Bragina (USSR) 4:06.9–4:01.38 (1972)

1 mile (IAAF 1967)

1945	5:15.3	Evelyne Forster (UK) 22 Jul 1939
1960	4:45.0	Diane Leather (UK) 21 Sep 1955
1975	4:28.5	Francie Larrieu (USA) 3 Mar 1975
	indoor	
	4:28.8u	Adrienne Beames (Aus) 7 Jan 1972
	4:29.5	Paola Pigni (Ita) 8 Aug 1973
1990	4:15.61	Paula Ivan (Rom) 10 Jul 1989
	4:12.56	Svetlana Masterkova (Rus) 14 Aug 1996

Most wins: 5 Diane Leather (UK) 5:07.6–4:45.0 (1953-5)

2000 metres (IAAF 1984)

1990	5:28.69	Maricica Puica (Rom) 11 Jul 1986
	5:25.36	Sonia O'Sullivan (Ire) 8 Jul 1994

3000 metres (IAAF 1974)

1975	8:46.6	Grete Waitz (Nor) 24 Jun 1975
1990	8:22.62	Tatyana Kazankina (USSR) 26 Aug 1984
	8:22.06	Zhang Linli (Chn) 12 Jun 1993
	8:12.19	Wang Junxia (Chn) 12 Sep 1993
	8:06.11	Wang Junxia (Chn) 13 Sep 1993

Most wins: 4 Paola Cacchi (née Pigni) (Ita) 9:42.8-9:09.4 (1969-72); 3 Lyudmila Bragina (USSR) 8:53.0–8:27.12 (1972-6)

5000 metres (IAAF 1981)

1975	15:48.5u	Adrienne Beames (Aus) 5 Jan 1972
1990	14:37.33	Ingrid Kristiansen (Nor) 5 Aug 1986
	14:36.45	Fernanda Ribeiro (Por) 15 Jul 1995
	14:31.27	Dong Yanmei (Chn) 21 Oct 1997
	14:28.09	Jiang Bo (Chn) 23 Oct 1997

Most wins: 3 Ingrid Kristiansen (Nor) 15:28.43-14:37.33 (1981-6)

10,000 metres (IAAF 1981)

1975	34:01.4	Christa Vahlensieck (FRG) 20 Aug 1975
1990	30:13.74	Ingrid Kristiansen (Nor) 5 Jul 1986
	29:31.78	Wang Junxia (Chn) 8 Sep 1993

Marathon

Records are not officially recognized for the marathon, as times are affected by the nature of the road courses.
Best times:

1960	3:40:22	Violet Piercy (UK) 3 Oct 1926
1975	2:38:19	Jackie Hansen (USA) 1 Dec 1974
1990	2:21:06	Ingrid Kristiansen (Nor) 21 Apr 1985
	2:20:47	Tegla Loroupe (Ken) 19 Apr 1998

Most wins: 4 Grete Waitz (Nor) 2:32:30–2:25:29 (1978-83)

80 metres hurdles

From 1927 the standard women's hurdles distance was 80 metres, over seven flights of 2ft 6in (76cm) hurdles. In 1969, this was replaced by a distance of 100m over eight flights of 2ft 9in (84cm) hurdles.

1930	12.1	Maj Jacobsson (Swe) 2 Sep 1930
1945	11.3	Claudia Testoni (Ita) 23 Jul 1939
	11.3	Claudia Testoni (Ita) 13 Aug 1939
	11.3	Fanny Blankers-Koen (Hol) 20 Sep 1942
1960	10.5	Gisela Birkemeyer (GDR) 24 Jul 1960
1969	10.2	Vera Korsakova (USSR) 16 Jun 1968
	10.39	Maureen Caird (Aus) 18 Oct 1968
	(auto)	

Most wins: 6 Irina Press (USSR) 10.6–10.3 (1960-5); 5 Claudia Testoni (Ita) 11.6–11.3 (1938-9)

100 metres hurdles

Replaced the 80 metres hurdles in 1969.

1975	12.3/12.68	Annelie Ehrhardt (GDR) 22 Jul 1973
	12.59	Annelie Ehrhardt (GDR) 8 Sep 1972
1990	12.21	Yordanka Donkova (Bul) 20 Aug 1988

Most wins: 6 Karin Balzer (GDR) 13.3–12.6 (1969-71); 5 Yordanka Donkova (Bul) 12.36–12.21 (1986-8)

400 metres hurdles (IAAF 1974)

1975	56.51	Krystyna Kacperczyk (Pol) 13 Jul 1974
1990	52.94	Marina Styepanova (USSR) 17 Sep 1986
	52.74	Sally Gunnell (UK) 19 Aug 1993
	52.61	Kim Batten (USA) 11 Aug 1995

Most wins: 3 Marina Styepanova (née Makeyeva) (USSR) 54.78–52.94 1979-86

High jump

1915	1.47m★	Margaret Belasco (UK) 6 Jun 1914
1930	1.625m★	Joan Belasco (UK) 27 May 1920
	1.60m	Carolina Gisolf (Hol) 18 Aug 1929
1945	1.71m	Fanny Blankers-Koen (Hol) 30 May 1943

1960	1.86m	Iolanda Balas (Rom) 10 Jul 1960
1975	1.95m	Rosemarie Witschas (GDR) 8 Sep 1974
1990	2.09m	Stefka Kostadinova (Bul) 30 Aug 1987

Most wins: 14 Iolanda Balas (Rom) 1.75–1.91 (1956-61); 7 Rosemarie Ackermann (née Witschas) (GDR) 1.94–2.00 (1974-7)

* In schools meetings, not subject to official measurements.

Pole vault (IAAF 1995)

From 4.20m upwards:

1995	4.20m	Dániela Bartová (Cze) 18 Aug 1995
	4.21m	Dániela Bartová (Cze) 21 Aug 1995
	4.22m	Dániela Bartová (Cze) 9 Sep 1995
	4.23m	Sun Caiyun (Chn) 5 Nov 1995
	4.25m	Emma George (Aus) 30 Nov 1995
	4.28m	Emma George (Aus) 17 Dec 1995
	4.32m	Emma George (Aus) 28 Jan 1996
	4.41m	Emma George (Aus) 28 Jan 1996
	4.42m	Emma George (Aus) 29 Jun 1996
	4.45m	Emma George (Aus) 14 Jul 1996
	4.50m	Emma George (Aus) 8 Feb 1997
	4.55m	Emma George (Aus) 20 Feb 1997
	4.57m	Emma George (Aus) 21 Feb 1998
	4.58m	Emma George (Aus) 15 Mar 1998
	4.59m	Emma George (Aus) 21 Mar 1998

Long jump

1915	5.00m	Ellen Hayes (USA) 7 Apr 1913
1930	5.98m	Kinue Hitomi (Jap) 20 May 1928
1945	6.25m	Fanny Blankers-Koen (Hol) 19 Sep 1943
1960	6.40m	Hildrun Claus (FRG) 7 Aug 1960
1975	6.84m	Heide Rosendahl (FRG) 3 Sep 1970
1990	7.52m	Galina Chistyakova (USSR) 11 Jun 1988

Most wins: 4 Tatyana Shchelkanova (USSR) 6.48–6.70 (1962-4), Anisoara Cusmir (Rom) 7.15–7.43 (1982-3)

Triple jump (IAAF 1990)

1990	14.54m	Li Huirong (Chn) 25 Aug 1990
	14.95m	Inessa Kravets (Ukr) 10 Jun 1991
	14.97m	Yolanda Chen (Rus) 18 Jun 1993
	15.09m	Anna Biryukova (Rus) 21 Aug 1993
	15.50m	Inessa Kravets (Ukr) 10 Aug 1995

Shot

1930	12.85m	Grete Heublein (Ger) 21 Jul 1929
1945	14.89m	Tatyana Sevryukova (USSR) 14 Oct 1945
1960	17.78m	Tamara Press (USSR) 13 Aug 1960
1975	21.60m	Marianne Adam (GDR) 6 Aug 1975
1990	22.63m	Natalya Lisovskaya (USSR) 7 Jun 1987

Most wins: 14 Galina Zybina (USSR) 15.19–16.76 (1952-6); 10 Nadezhda Chizhova (USSR) 18.67–21.45 (1968-73); 9 Grete Heublein (Ger)

10.86–13.70 (1927-31); 6 Tamara Press (USSR) 17.25–18.59 (1959-65); 5 Ruth Lange (Ger) 10.84–11.52 (1927-8)

Discus

1930	39.62m	Halina Konopacka (Pol) 31 Jul 1928
1945	49.88m	Nina Dumbadze (USSR) 14 Aug 1944
1960	57.15m	Tamara Press (USSR) 12 Sep 1960
1975	70.20m	Faina Melnik (USSR) 20 Aug 1975
1990	76.80m	Gabriele Reinsch (GDR) 9 Jul 1988

Most wins: 11 Faina Melnik (USSR) 64.22–70.50 (1971-6); 10 Gisela Mauermayer (Ger) 44.34–48.31 (1935-6); 9 Jadwiga Wajsowna (Pol) 40.34–44.19 (1932-4); 7 Nina Dumbadze (USSR) 49.11–57.04 (1939-52); 6 Halina Konopacka (Pol) 31.24–39.62 (1925-8), Tamara Press (USSR) 57.15–59.70 (1960-5)

Hammer (IAAF 1995)

1995	61.96m	Larisa Baranova (Rus) 11 Feb 1990
	64.44m	Alla Fyodorova (Rus) 24 Feb 1991
	65.40m	Olga Kuzenkova (Rus) 4 Jun 1992
	66.84m	Olga Kuzenkova (Rus) 23 Feb 1994
	67.34mu	Svetlana Sudak (Blr) 5 Jun 1994
	66.86m	Mihaela Melinte (Rom) 4 Mar 1995
	67.08m	Olga Kuzenkova (Rus) 24 May 1995
	68.16m	Olga Kuzenkova (Rus) 5 Jun 1995
	68.16m	Olga Kuzenkova (Rus) 17 Jun 1995
	69.44mu	Olga Kuzenkova (Rus) 17 Feb 1996
	69.42m	Mihaela Melinte (Rom) 11 May 1996
	69.58m	Mihaela Melinte (Rom) 8 Mar 1997
	70.78mu	Olga Kuzenkova (Rus) 11 Jun 1997
	71.22m	Olga Kuzenkova (Rus) 22 Jun 1997
	73.10m	Olga Kuzenkova (Rus) 22 Jun 1997
	73.80mu	Olga Kuzenkova (Rus) 15 May 1998

Javelin

1930	42.32m	Elisabeth Schumann (Ger) 8 Aug 1930
1945	48.39mu	Lyudmila Anokina (USSR) 15 Sep 1945
1960	59.55m	Elvira Ozolina (USSR) 4 Jun 1960
1975	67.22m	Ruth Fuchs (GDR) 3 Sep 1974
1990	80.00m	Petra Felke (GDR) 9 Sep 1988

Most wins: 6 Ruth Fuchs (GDR) 65.06–69.96 (1972-80); 4 Elvira Ozolina (USSR) 57.92–61.38 (1960-4)

Heptathlon (scored on the 1984 tables)

The heptathlon has been the standard women's multi-event competition since 1981.

| 1990 | 7291 | Jackie Joyner (USA) 23/24 Sep 1988 (100m hurdles 12.69, high jump 1.86m, shot 15.80m, 200m: 22.56, long jump 7.27m, javelin 45.66m, 800m 2:08.51) |

Most wins: 4 Ramona Neubert (GDR) 6670–6935 (1981-3), Jackie Joyner-Kersee (USA) 7148–7291 (1986-8)

Pentathlon

Until 1980 the pentathlon was the standard multi-events competition for women. The events changed several times. (Totals re-scored on the 1984 tables.)

Most: 8 Irina Press (USSR) 4121–4602 (1959–64); 5 Aleksandra Chudina (USSR) 3564–4024 (1947-55)

4 x 100 metres relay

1930	48.4	Canada 5 Aug 1928
1945	46.4	Germany 8 Aug 1936
1960	44.51	USA 7 Sep 1960
1975	42.51	GDR 8 Sep 1974
1990	41.37	GDR 6 Oct 1985 (Silke Gladisch, Sabine Rieger, Ingrid Auerswald, Marlies Göhr)

4 x 400 metres relay (IAAF 1969)

1975	3:22.95	GDR 10 Sep 1972
1990	3:15.17	USSR 1 Oct 1988 (Tatyana Ledovskaya, Olga Nazarova, Mariya Pinigina, Olga Bryzgina)

Other current relay world records

4 x 200m	1:28.15	GDR 9 Aug 1980 (Marlies Göhr, Romy Müller, Bärbel Wöckel, Marita Koch)
4 x 800m	7:50.17	USSR 5 Aug 1984 (Nadezhda Olizarenko, Lyubov Gurina, Lyudmila Borisova, Irina Podyalovskaya)

World Indoor Records

World indoor records have been recognized by the IAAF since 1 Jan 1987. Track performances around a turn must be made on a track no larger than 200 metres.

Men

Event	Mark	Athlete (Nation)	Venue	Date
50 metres	5.56a	Donovan Bailey (Can)	Reno	9 Feb 1996
	5.61	Manfred Kokot (GDR)	Berlin	4 Feb 1973
	5.61	James Sanford (USA)	San Diego	20 Feb 1981
	5.55¶	Ben Johnson (Can)	Ottawa	31 Jan 1987
60 metres	6.39	Maurice Greene (USA)	Madrid	3 Feb 1998
200 metres	19.92	Frank Fredericks (Nam)	Liévin	18 Feb 1996
400 metres	44.63	Michael Johnson (USA)	Atlanta	4 Mar 1995
800 metres	1:42.67	Wilson Kipketer (Den)	Paris (Bercy)	9 Mar 1997
1000 metres	2:15.26	Noureddine Morceli (Alg)	Birmingham	22 Feb 1992
1500 metres	3:31.18	Hicham El Guerrouj (Mor)	Stuttgart	2 Feb 1997
1 mile	3:48.45	Hicham El Guerrouj (Mor)	Ghent	12 Feb 1997
2000 metres*	4:52.86	Haile Gebrselassie (Eth)	Birmingham	16 Feb 1998
3000 metres	7:24.90	Daniel Komen (Ken)	Budapest	6 Feb 1998
5000 metres	12:51.48	Daniel Komen (Ken)	Stockholm	19 Feb 1998
50 metres hurdles	6.25	Mark McKoy (Can)	Kobe	5 Mar 1986
60 metres hurdles	7.30	Colin Jackson (UK)	Sindelfingen	6 Mar 1994
High jump	2.43	Javier Sotomayor (Cub)	Budapest	4 Mar 1989
Pole vault	6.15	Sergey Bubka (USSR)	Donetsk	21 Feb 1993
Long jump	8.79	Carl Lewis (USA)	New York	27 Jan 1984
Triple jump	17.83	Aliecer Urrutia (Cub)	Sindelfingen	1 Mar 1997
Shot	22.66	Randy Barnes (USA)	Los Angeles	20 Jan 1989
35lb weight	25.86	Lance Deal (USA)	Atlanta	4 Mar 1995
5000 metres walk	18:07.08	Mikhail Shchennikov (Rus)	Moscow	14 Feb 1995
4 x 200 metres relay	1:22.11	United Kingdom	Glasgow	3 Mar 1991
		(Linford Christie, Darren Braithwaite, Ade Mafe, John Regis)		
4 x 400 metres relay	3:03.05	Germany	Seville	10 Mar 1991
		(Rico Lieder, Jens Carlowitz, Karsten Just, Thomas Schönlebe)		
Heptathlon	6476	Dan O'Brien (USA)	Toronto	13/14 Mar 1993
		(6.67 60m, 7.84 LJ, 16.02 SP, 2.13 HJ, 7.85 60mh, 5.20 PV, 2:57.96 1000m)		

Women

Event	Mark	Athlete (Nation)	Venue	Date
50 metres	5.96	Irina Privalova (Rus)	Madrid	9 Feb 1995
60 metres	6.92	Irina Privalova (Rus)	Madrid	11 Feb 1993
	6.92	Irina Privalova (Rus)	Madrid	9 Feb 1995
200 metres	21.87	Merlene Ottey (Jam)	Liévin	13 Feb 1993
400 metres	49.59	Jarmila Kratochvílová (Cs)	Milan	7 Mar 1982
800 metres	1:56.40	Christine Wachtel (GDR)	Vienna	22 Feb 1988

Event	Mark	Athlete (Nation)	Venue	Date
1000 metres	2:31.23	Maria Mutola (Moz)	Stockholm	25 Feb 1996
1500 metres	4:00.27	Doina Melinte (Rom)	East Rutherford	9 Feb 1990
1 mile	4:17.14	Doina Melinte (Rom)	East Rutherford	9 Feb 1990
2000 metres*	5:30.53	Gabriela Szabo (Rom)	Sindelfingen	8 Mar 1998
3000 metres	8:33.82	Elly van Hulst (Hol)	Budapest	4 Mar 1989
5000 metres	15:03.17	Liz McColgan (UK)	Birmingham	22 Feb 1992
50 metres hurdles	6.58	Cornelia Oschkenat (GDR)	East Berlin	20 Feb 1988
60 metres hurdles	7.69	Lyudmila Narozhilenko (USSR)	Chelyabinsk	4 Feb 1990
	7.63¶	Lyudmila Narozhilenko (Rus)	Seville	4 Mar 1993
High jump	2.07	Heike Henkel (Ger)	Karlsruhe	9 Feb 1992
Pole vault	4.55	Emma George (Aus)	Adelaide	26 Mar 1998
Long jump	7.37	Heike Drechsler (GDR)	Vienna	13 Feb 1988
Triple jump	15.16	Ashia Hansen (UK)	Valencia	28 Feb 1998
Shot	22.50	Helena Fibingerová (Cs)	Jablonec	19 Feb 1977
20lb weight*	22.92	Dawn Ellerbe (USA)	Laramie	16 Jan 1998
3000 metres walk	11:44.00	Alina Ivanova (Ukr)	Moscow	7 Feb 1992
4 x 200 metres relay	1:32.55	SC Eintracht Hamm (FRG)	Dortmund	20 Feb 1988
		(Helga Arendt, Silke-Beate Knoll, Mechthild Kluth, Gisela Kinzel)		
4 x 400 metres relay	3:26.84	Russia	Paris (Bercy)	9 Mar 1997
		(Tatyana Chebykina, Svetlana Goncharenko, Olga Kotlyarova, Tatyana Alekseyeva)		
Pentathlon	4991	Irina Belova (Rus)	Berlin	14/15 Feb 1992
		(8.22 60mh, 1.93 HJ, 13.25 SP, 6.67 LJ, 2:10.26 800m)		

* Unofficial record.

¶ Disqualified for a positive drugs test. The IAAF stripped Johnson of his records in January 1990, after he had admitted long-term steroid use.

World Records and Bests – Long-Distance Track Events

Men

Event	hr:min:sec	Name	Venue	Date
15km	42:34.0	Arturo Barrios (Mex)	La Flèche	30 Mar 1991
10 miles	45:57.6	Jos Hermens (Hol)	Papendal	14 Sep 1975
20km	56:55.6	Arturo Barrios (Mex)	La Flèche	30 Mar 1991
15 miles	1:11:43.1	Bill Rodgers (USA)	Saratoga, Cal.	21 Feb 1979
25km	1:13:55.8	Toshihiko Seko (Jap)	Christchurch, NZ	22 Mar 1981
30km	1:29:18.8	Toshihiko Seko (Jap)	Christchurch, NZ	22 Mar 1981
20 miles	1:39:14.4	Jack Foster (NZ)	Hamilton, NZ	15 Aug 1971
30 miles	2:42:00	Jeff Norman (UK)	Timperley, Cheshire	7 Jun 1980
50km	2:48:06	Jeff Norman (UK)	Timperley, Cheshire	7 Jun 1980
40 miles	3:48:35	Don Ritchie (UK)	Hendon, London	16 Oct 1982
50 miles	4:51:49	Don Ritchie (UK)	Hendon, London	12 Mar 1983
100km	6:10:20	Don Ritchie (UK)	Crystal Palace	28 Oct 1978
150km	10:36:42	Don Ritchie (UK)	Crystal Palace	15 Oct 1977
100 miles	11:30:51	Don Ritchie (UK)	Crystal Palace	15 Oct 1977
200km	15:10:27	Yiannis Kouros (Gre)	Adelaide	4-5 Oct 1997
200 miles	27:48:35	Yiannis Kouros (Gre)	Montauban, Fra	15-16 Mar 1985
500km	60:23.00	Yiannis Kouros (Gre)	Colac, Aus	26-29 Nov 1984
500 miles	105:42:09	Yiannis Kouros (Gre)	Colac, Aus	26-30 Nov 1984
1000km	136:17:00	Yiannis Kouros (Gre)	Colac, Aus	26-31 Nov 1984
1500km	10d 17:28:26	Petrus Silkinas (Lit)	Nanango, Qld	11-21 Mar 1998
1000 mile	11d 13:54:58	Petrus Silkinas (Lit)	Nanango, Qld	11-22 Mar 1998
	kilometres			
1 hour	21.101	Arturo Barrios (Mex)	La Flèche	30 Mar 1991
2 hrs	37.994	Jim Alder (UK)	Walton-on-Thames	17 Oct 1964
24 hrs	303.506	Yiannis Kouros (Gre)	Adelaide	4-5 Oct 1997
48 hrs	473.797	Yiannis Kouros (Gre)	Surgères, Fra	3-5 May 1996
6 days - indoors	1030.000	Jean-Gilles Bousiquet (Fra)	La Rochelle, Fra	16-23 Nov 1992
6 days - outdoors	1023.200	Yiannis Kouros (Gre)	Colac, Aus	26 Nov-1 Dec 1984
15km	49:44.0	Silvana Cruciata (Ita)	Rome	4 May 1981

Women

Event	hr:min:sec	Name	Venue	Date
10 miles	54:21.8	Lorraine Moller (NZ)	Auckland	9 Jan 1993
20km	1:06:48.8	Isumi Maki (Jap)	Amagasaki	19 Sep 1993
25km	1:29:29.2	Karolina Szabó (Hun)	Budapest	23 Apr 1988
30km	1:47:05.6	Karolina Szabó (Hun)	Budapest	23 Apr 1988
20 miles	1:59:09*	Chantal Langlacé (Fra)	Amiens	3 Sep 1983
30 miles	3:12:25	Carolyn Hunter-Rowe (UK)	Barry, Wales	3 Mar 1996
50km	3:18:52	Carolyn Hunter-Rowe (UK)	Barry, Wales	3 Mar 1996
40 miles	4:26:43	Carolyn Hunter-Rowe (UK)	Barry, Wales	7 Mar 1993
50 miles	5:55:41	Valentina Lyakhova (Rus)	Nantes	28 Sep 1996
100km	7:23:28	Valentina Lyakhova (Rus)	Nantes	28 Sep 1996
100 miles	14:29:44	Ann Trason (USA)	Santa Rosa, Cal.	18-19 Mar 1989
200km	19:28:48	Eleanor Adams (UK)	Melbourne	19-20 Aug 1989
200 miles	39:09:03	Hilary Walker (UK)	Blackpool	5-7 Nov 1988
500km	77:53:46	Eleanor Adams (UK)	Colac, Aus.	13-15 Nov 1989
500 miles	130:59:58	Sandra Barwick (NZ)	Campbelltown, Aus	18-23 Nov 1990
1000km	8d 00:27:06	Eleanor Robinson (UK)	Nanango, Qld	11-18 Mar 1998
1500km	12d 06:52:12	Eleanor Robinson (UK)	Nanango, Qld	11-22 Mar 1998
1000km	13d 01:54:02	Eleanor Robinson (UK)	Nanango, Qld	11-23 Mar 1998
	kilometres			
1 hour	18.084	Silvana Cruciata (Ita)	Rome	4 May 1981
2 hrs	32.652	Chantal Langlacé (Fra)	Amiens	3 Sep 1983
24 hrs	242.624	Irina Reutovich (Rus)	Moscow	9-10 May 1998
48 hrs	377.892	Sue Ellen Trapp (USA)	Surgères	2-4 May 1997
6 days	883.631	Sandra Barwick (NZ)	Campbelltown, NSW	18-24 Nov 1990

* Timed on one running watch only.

Indoors (where superior to track best)

200km	19:00:31	Eleanor Adams (UK)	Milton Keynes	3/4 Feb 1990
24 hours	248.901km	Yelena Siderenkova (Rus)	Podolsk	10-11 Feb 1996

Long-Distance Road Bests

Where superior to track bests, and run on properly measured road courses. Road times should be assessed with care, as course conditions can vary considerably.

Men

Event	hr:min:sec	Name	Venue	Date
15km	42:22	Todd Williams (USA)	Washington, DC	11 Mar 1995
10 miles	44:45	Paul Koech (Ken)	Zaandam	21 Sep 1997
Half mar	59:17	Paul Tergat (Ken)	Milan	4 Apr 1998
	58:51*	Paul Tergat (Ken)	Milan	30 Mar 1996
30km	1:28:40	Steve Jones (UK)	Chicago	10 Oct 1985
20 miles	1:35:22	Steve Jones (UK)	Chicago	10 Oct 1985
30 miles	2:37:31	Thompson Magawana (RSA)	Claremont-Kirstenbosch	12 Apr 1988
50km	2:43:38	Thompson Magawana (RSA)	Claremont-Kirstenbosch	12 Apr 1988
40 miles	3:45:39	Andy Jones (Can)	Houston	23 Feb 1991
50 miles	4:50:21	Bruce Fordyce (RSA)	London-Brighton	25 Sep 1983
1000 miles	10d 10:30:35	Yiannis Kouros (Gre)	New York	21-30 May 1988
6 days	1028.370km	Yiannis Kouros (Gre)	New York	21-26 May 1988

* 49 metres short.

Women

10km	30:38	Liz McColgan (UK)	Orlando	12 Feb 1989
15km	46:57	Elana Meyer (SAf)	Cape Town	2 Nov 1991
10 miles	51:16	Colleen de Reuck (SAf)	Washington, DC	5 Apr 1998
	50:31u	Ingrid Kristiansen (Nor)	Amsterdam	11 Oct 1989

Event	hr:min:sec	Name	Venue	Date
Half mar	1:06:43	Masako Chiba (Jap)	Tokyo (33m drop)	19 Jan 1997
	1:06:40u	Ingrid Kristiansen (Nor)	Sandnes	5 Apr 1987
25km	1:21:21	Ingrid Kristiansen (Nor)	London	10 May 1987
30km	1:38:27	Ingrid Kristiansen (Nor)	London	10 May 1987
20 miles	1:46:04	Ingrid Kristiansen (Nor)	London	10 May 1987
30 miles	3:01:16	Frith van der Merwe (SAf)	Claremont – Kirstenbosch	25 Mar 1989
50km	3:08:39	Frith van der Merwe (SAf)	Claremont – Kirstenbosch	25 Mar 1989
40 miles	4:26:13	Ann Trason (USA)	Houston	23 Feb 1991
50 miles	5:40:18	Ann Trason (USA)	Houston	23 Feb 1991
100km	7:00:48	Ann Trason (USA)	Winschoten	16 Sep 1995
100 miles	13:47.41	Ann Trason (USA)	New York	4 May 1991
200km	19:08:21*	Sigrid Lomsky (Ger)	Basel	1-2 May 1993
500km	82:10#	Annie van der Meer (Hol)	Paris-Colmar	8-11 Jun 1983
1000km	7d 01:11:00	Sandra Barwick (NZ)	New York	16-23 Sep 1991
1000 miles	12d 14:38:40	Sandra Barwick (NZ)	New York	16-29 Sep 1991
	kilometres			
24 hours	243.657	Sigrid Lomsky (Ger)	Basel	1-2 May 1993

* Timed at 201km on one running watch.
# 518 kilometres.

Walking

The IAAF currently ratifies records at four track walking events – 20, 30 and 50 kilometres and 2 hours. At one time the list covered a large number of distances, but the shorter distance records were dropped, due, in particular, to difficulties in judging whether walkers were adhering to the strict disciplines of the event. The standard road-walking events for men have become established at 20 and 50 kilometres.

World records and bests – track walks

Men

Event	hr:min:sec	Name	Venue	Date
1500 metres	5:12.0	Antanas Grigaliunas (Lit)	Vilnius	12 May 1990
1 mile	5:33.53i	Tim Lewis (USA)	New York	5 Feb 1988
	5:36.9	Antanas Grigaliunas (Lit)	Vilnius	12 May 1990
3000 metres	10:47.11	Giovanni De Benedictis (Ita)	San Giovanni Valdermo	19 May 1990
5000 metres	18:05.49	Hatem Ghoula (Tun)	Tunis	1 May 1997
10km	38:02.60	Jozef Pribilinec (Cs)	Banská Bystrica	30 Aug 1985
15km	58:22.4	Jozef Pribilinec (Cs)	Hildesheim	6 Sep 1986
20km	1:17:25.6	Bernardo Segura (Mex)	Fana	7 May 1994
25km	1:44:54.0	Maurizio Damilano (Ita)	San Donato Milanese	5 May 1985
30km	2:01:44.1	Maurizio Damilano (Ita)	Cuneo, Italy	4 Oct 1992
40km	2:55:54.0	Raúl Gonzales (Mex)	Fana	2 May 1980
50km	3:40:57.9	Thierry Toutain (Fra)	Héricourt, France	29 Sep 1996
100km	9:16:32.3	Fréderic Marie (Fra)	Etrechy	19 Apr 1987
	kilometres			
1 hour	15.577	Bernardo Segura (Mex)	Fana	7 May 1994
2 hrs	29.572	Maurizio Damilano (Ita)	Cuneo, Italy	4 Oct 1992

Women

The IAAF has ratified records for women's track walking at 5000m and 10 000m since 1981.

Event		Name	Venue	Date
1500 metres	5:50.51	Kerry Saxby (Aus)	Sydney	20 Jan 1991
1 mile	6:16.72i	Sada Eidikite (Lit)	Kaunas	24 Feb 1990
	6:19.39	Ileana Salvador (Ita)	Siderno	15 Jun 1991
3000 metres	11:48.24	Ileana Salvador (Ita)	Padova	29 Aug 1993
5000 metres	20:03.0u	Kerry Saxby-Junna (Aus)	Sydney	11 Feb 1996
	20:13.26	Kerry Saxby-Junna (Aus)	Hobart	25 Feb 1996
10,000 metres	41:56.23	Nadezhda Ryashkina (USSR)	Seattle	24 Jul 1990

Event	hr:min:sec	Name	Venue	Date
15,000 metres	1:15:37.9	Ann Jansson (Swe)	Stockholm	25 Oct 1987
20,000 metres	1:35:29.5	Madeleine Svensson (Swe)	Borås	10 Jul 1991
100km	11:17:42	Sandra Brown (UK)	Etrechy, Fra	27-28 Oct 1990
	kilometres			
1 hour	13.194	Victoria Herazo (USA)	Santa Monica	12 May 1992
2 hours	22.239	Jana Zarubová (Cs)	Prague	12 Oct 1985
24 hours	193.306	Sandra Brown (UK)	Etrechy, Fra	27-28 Oct 1990

i = indoors, * unratified.

World bests – road walks

Where superior to track bests, and walked on properly measured road courses.

Men

Event	hr:min:sec	Name	Venue	Date
25km	1:42:14	Andrey Perlov (USSR)	Sochi	19 Feb 1989
35km	2:28:30	Robert Korzeniowski (Pol)	Eschborn	12 Jun 1993
40km	2:53:59	Andrey Perlov (USSR)	Leningrad	5 Aug 1989
50km	3:37:41	Andrey Perlov (USSR)	Leningrad	5 Aug 1989
100km	8:58:12	Gérard Lelièvre (Fra)	Laval	7 Oct 1984
200km	19:55:07	Zbigniew Klapa (Pol)	Chapelle	22-23 Oct 1983
	kilometres			
24 hours	228.930	Jesse Casteneda (USA)	Albuquerque	18-19 Sep 1976

Women

10km	41:04	Yelena Nikolayeva (Rus)	Sochi	20 Apr 1996
15km	1:09:33	Kerry Saxby (Aus)	Canberra	13 Jul 1985
20km	1:27:30	Liu Hongyu (Chn)	Beijing	1 May 1995
25km	2:12:38	Sue Cook (Aus)	Canberra	20 Jun 1981
30km	2:42:46	Lynda Brusbaker (USA)	Atlanta	31 Oct 1993
40km	3:39:43	Ann Jansson (Swe)	New York	27 Oct 1985
50km	4:41:57	Kora Boufflert (Fra)	Ay-Champagne	17 Sep 1995
50 miles	7:54:54	Sandra Brown (UK)	Manchester-Blackpool	27 Jul 1991
100km	10:57:50	Annie van den Meer (Hol)	Rouen	10 May 1986
200km	24:04:20	Sandra Brown (UK)	Vallorbe, Switzerland	20/21 Sep 1991
	kilometres			
24 hours	211.250	Annie van den Meer (Hol)	Rouen	10-11 May 1986

Major Marathon Races

The marathon distance of 26 miles 385 yards (42.195km), run at the 1908 Olympic Games, from Windsor to the White City Stadium, London, has been standard from 1924.

Boston

The Boston marathon is the world's oldest annual race. It was first run by 15 men on 19 April 1897 over a distance of 24 miles 1232 yards (39.75km). Since then, it has been run every year on or about 19 April, Patriot's Day, which honours the famed ride of Paul Revere through Boston. The full marathon distance was first run in 1927. Although the race director tried to prevent her, Kathy Switzer (USA) ran in 1967; her pioneering efforts helped bring about the acceptance of women runners, who were admitted officially for the first time in 1972.

There were 38,706 finishers – a world record for a marathon – in the centennial race, on 15 April 1996. *Winners from 1970*:

Men

1970	Ron Hill (UK) 2:10:30	1976	Jack Fultz (USA) 2:20:19
1971	Alvaro Mejia (Col) 2:18:45	1977	Jerome Drayton (Can) 2:14:46
1972	Olavi Suomalainen (Fin) 2:15:39	1978	Bill Rodgers (USA) 2:10:13
1973	Jon Anderson (USA) 2:16:03	1979	Bill Rodgers (USA) 2:09:27
1974	Neil Cusack (Ire) 2:13:39	1980	Bill Rodgers (USA) 2:12:11
1975	Bill Rodgers (USA) 2:09:55	1981	Toshihiko Seko (Jap) 2:09:26
		1982	Alberto Salazar (USA) 2:08:51

1983	Greg Meyer (USA) 2:09:01	
1984	Geoff Smith (UK) 2:10:34	
1985	Geoff Smith (UK) 2:14:05	
1986	Rob de Castella (Aus) 2:07:51	
1987	Toshihiko Seko (Jap) 2:11:50	
1988	Ibrahim Hussein (Ken) 2:08:43	
1989	Abebe Mekonnen (Eth) 2:09:06	
1990	Gelindo Bordin (Ita) 2:08:19	
1991	Ibrahim Hussain (Ken) 2:11:06	
1992	Ibrahim Hussain (Ken) 2:08:14	
1993	Cosmas Ndeti (Ken) 2:09:33	
1994	Cosmas Ndeti (Ken) 2:07:15	
1995	Cosmas Ndeti (Ken) 2:09:22	
1996	Moses Tanui (Ken) 2:09:16	
1997	Lameck Aguta (Ken) 2:10:34	
1998	Moses Tanui (Ken) 2:07:34	

Most wins: 7 Clarence De Mar (USA) 1911, 1922-4, 1927-8, 1930; 4 Gérard Coté (Can) 1940, 1943-4, 1948, Rodgers

Women

1972	Nina Kuscsik (USA) 3:08:58
1973	Jackie Hansen (USA) 3:05:59
1974	Miki Gorman (USA) 2:47:11
1975	Liane Winter (FRG) 2:42:24
1976	Kim Merritt (USA) 2:47:10
1977	Miki Gorman (USA) 2:48:33
1978	Gayle Barron (USA) 2:44:52
1979	Joan Benoit (USA) 2:35:15
1980	Jacqueline Gareau (Can) 2:34:28
1981	Allison Roe (NZ) 2:26:46
1982	Charlotte Teske (FRG) 2:29:33
1983	Joan Benoit (USA) 2:22:43
1984	Lorraine Moller (NZ) 2:29:28
1985	Lisa Weidenbach (USA) 2:34:06
1986	Ingrid Kristiansen (Nor) 2:24:55
1987	Rosa Mota (Por) 2:25:21
1988	Rosa Mota (Por) 2:24:30
1989	Ingrid Kristiansen (Nor) 2:24:35
1990	Rosa Mota (Por) 2:25:24
1991	Wanda Panfil (Pol) 2:24:18
1992	Olga Markova (Rus) 2:23:43
1993	Olga Markova (Rus) 2:25:27
1994	Uta Pippig (Ger) 2:21:45
1995	Uta Pippig (Ger) 2:25:11
1996	Uta Pippig (Ger) 2:27:06
1997	Fatuma Roba (Eth) 2:26:24
1998	Fatuma Roba (Eth) 2:23:21

Most wins: 3 Mota, Pippig

Chicago

First held in 1977 as the Mayor Daley Marathon, world-class fields were attracted from 1983. Not held in 1987.
Winners from 1983:

Men

1983	Joseph Nzau (Ken) 2:09:45
1984	Steve Jones (UK) 2:08:05

1985	Steve Jones (UK) 2:07:13
1986	Toshihiko Seko (Jap) 2:08:27
1988	Alejandro Cruz (Mex) 2:08:57
1989	Paul Davies-Hale (UK) 2:11:25
1990	Martin Pitayo (Mex) 2:09:41
1991	Joseildo Silva (Bra) 2:14:33
1992	José Cesar Souza (Bra) 2:16:14
1993	Luiz dos Santos (Bra) 2:13:14
1994	Luiz dos Santos (Bra) 2:11:16
1995	Eamonn Martin (UK) 2:11:18
1996	Paul Evans (UK) 2:08:51
1997	Khalid Khannouchi (Mor) 2:07:10

Women

1983	Rosa Mota (Por) 2:31:12
1984	Rosa Mota (Por) 2:26:01
1985	Joan Benoit (USA) 2:21:21
1986	Ingrid Kristiansen (Nor) 2:27:08
1988	Lisa Weidenbach (USA) 2:29:17
1989	Lisa Weidenbach (USA) 2:28:15
1990	Aurora Cunha (Por) 2:30:11
1991	Midde Hamrin (Swe) 2:36:21
1992	Linda Somers (USA) 2:37:14
1993	Ritva Lemettinen (Fin) 2:33:18
1994	Kristy Johnston (USA) 2:31:34
1995	Ritva Lemettinen (Fin) 2:28:39
1996	Marian Sutton (UK) 2:30:41
1997	Marian Sutton (UK) 2:29:03

Fukuoka

The Asahi marathon was first run in 1947 at Kumamoto. It was first held at Fukuoka in 1951, and has been held there every year in early December since 1964. In 1967, Derek Clayton set a world record to win. The race is open to men only.
Winners from 1967:

1967	Derek Clayton (Aus) 2:09:37
1968	Bill Adcocks (UK) 2:10:48
1969	Jerome Drayton (Can) 2:11:13
1970	Akio Usami (Jap) 2:10:38
1971	Frank Shorter (USA) 2:12:51
1972	Frank Shorter (USA) 2:10:30
1973	Frank Shorter (USA) 2:11:45
1974	Frank Shorter (USA) 2:11:32
1975	Jerome Drayton (Can) 2:10:09
1976	Jerome Drayton (Can) 2:12:25
1977	Bill Rodgers (USA) 2:10:56
1978	Toshihiko Seko (Jap) 2:10:21
1979	Toshihiko Seko (Jap) 2:10:35
1980	Toshihiko Seko (Jap) 2:09:45
1981	Rob de Castella (Aus) 2:08:18
1982	Paul Ballinger (NZ) 2:10:15
1983	Toshihiko Seko (Jap) 2:08:52
1984	Takeyuki Nakayama (Jap) 2:10:00
1985	Masanari Shintaku (Jap) 2:09:51
1986	Juma Ikangaa (Tan) 2:10:06
1987	Takeyuki Nakayama (Jap) 2:08:18

1988	Toshihiru Shibutani (Jap) 2:11:04	
1989	Manuel Matias (Por) 2:12:54	
1990	Belayneh Dinsamo (Eth) 2:11:35	
1991	Shuichi Morita (Jap) 2:10:58	
1992	Tena Negere (Eth) 2:09:04	
1993	Dionicio Cerón (Mex) 2:08:51	
1994	Boay Akonay (Tan) 2:09:45	
1995	Luiz dos Santos (Bra) 2:09:30	
1996	Lee Bong-ju (Kor) 2:10:48	
1997	Josiah Thugwane (SAf) 2:07:28	

Most wins: 4 Shorter, Seko

London

The first London marathon was run on 29 March 1981. Organized and inspired by the 1956 Olympic steeplechase gold medallist, Chris Brasher, it caught the public's imagination and was a great success; 7055 runners started and 6418 finished. There were 15,011 finishers in 1982, new records each year to 24,953 finishers in 1990, and then 25,194 in 1994, 29,135 in 1997 and 29,924 in 1998.

Men

1981	Dick Beardsley (USA) & Inge Simonsen (Nor) 2:11:48
1982	Hugh Jones (UK) 2:09:24
1983	Mike Gratton (UK) 2:09:43
1984	Charlie Spedding (UK) 2:09:57
1985	Steve Jones (UK) 2:08:16
1986	Toshihiko Seko (Jap) 2:10:02
1987	Hiromi Taniguchi (Jap) 2:09:50
1988	Henrik Jørgensen (Den) 2:10:20
1989	Douglas Wakiihuri (Ken) 2:09:03
1990	Allister Hutton (UK) 2:10:10
1991	Yakov Tolstikov (USSR) 2:09:17
1992	António Pinto (Por) 2:10:02
1993	Eamonn Martin (UK) 2:10:50
1994	Dionicio Cerón (Mex) 2:08:53
1995	Dionicio Cerón (Mex) 2:08:30
1996	Dionicio Cerón (Mex) 2:10:00
1997	António Pinto (Por) 2:07:55
1998	Abel Antón (Spa) 2:07:57

Women

1981	Joyce Smith (UK) 2:29:57
1982	Joyce Smith (UK) 2:29:43
1983	Grete Waitz (Nor) 2:25:29
1984	Ingrid Kristiansen (Nor) 2:24:26
1985	Ingrid Kristiansen (Nor) 2:21:06
1986	Grete Waitz (Nor) 2:24:54
1987	Ingrid Kristiansen (Nor) 2:22:48
1988	Ingrid Kristiansen (Nor) 2:25:41
1989	Véronique Marot (UK) 2:25:56
1990	Wanda Panfil (Pol) 2:26:31
1991	Rosa Mota (Por) 2:26:14
1992	Katrin Dörre (Ger) 2:29:39
1993	Katrin Dörre (Ger) 2:27:09
1994	Katrin Dörre (Ger) 2:32:34
1995	Malgorzata Sobanska (Pol) 2:27:43

1996	Liz McColgan (UK) 2:27:54
1997	Joyce Chepchumba (Ken) 2:26:51
1998	Catherina McKiernan (Ire) 2:26:26

New York

The New York Marathon was run annually in Central Park from 1970 to 1976; in 1976, to celebrate the US Bicentennial, the course was changed to follow a route through all five boroughs of the city. From that year, when there were 2090 runners, the race has become one of the world's great sporting occasions; in 1997 there were a record 30,427 finishers.

Winners since 1976:

Men

1976	Bill Rodgers (USA) 2:10:10
1977	Bill Rodgers (USA) 2:11:29
1978	Bill Rodgers (USA) 2:12:12
1979	Bill Rodgers (USA) 2:11:42
1980	Alberto Salazar (USA) 2:09:41
1981*	Alberto Salazar (USA) 2:08:13
1982	Alberto Salazar (USA) 2:09:29
1983	Rod Dixon (NZ) 2:08:59
1984	Orlando Pizzolato (Ita) 2:14:53
1985	Orlando Pizzolato (Ita) 2:11:34.
1986	Gianni Poli (Ita) 2:11:06
1987	Ibrahim Hussein (Ken) 2:11:01
1988	Steve Jones (UK) 2:08:20
1989	Juma Ikangaa (Tan) 2:08:01
1990	Douglas Wakiihuri (Ken) 2:12:39
1991	Salvador García (Mex) 2:09:24
1992	Willie Mtolo (SAf) 2:09:29
1993	Andrés Espinosa (Mex) 2:10:04
1994	Germán Silva (Mex) 2:11:21
1995	Germán Silva (Mex) 2:11:00
1996	Giacomo Leone (Ita) 2:09:54
1997	John Kagwe (Ken) 2:08:12

Women

1976	Miki Gorman (USA) 2:39:11
1977	Miki Gorman (USA) 2:43:10
1978	Grete Waitz (Nor) 2:32:30
1979	Grete Waitz (Nor) 2:27:33
1980	Grete Waitz (Nor) 2:25:41
1981*	Allison Roe (NZ) 2:25:29
1982	Grete Waitz (Nor) 2:27:14
1983	Grete Waitz (Nor) 2:27:00
1984	Grete Waitz (Nor) 2:29:30
1985	Grete Waitz (Nor) 2:28:34
1986	Grete Waitz (Nor) 2:28:06
1987	Priscilla Welch (UK) 2:30:17
1988	Grete Waitz (Nor) 2:28:07
1989	Ingrid Kristiansen (Nor) 2:25:30
1990	Wanda Panfil (Pol) 2:30:45
1991	Liz McColgan (UK) 2:27:32
1992	Lisa Ondieki (Aus) 2:24:40
1993	Uta Pippig (Ger) 2:26:24
1994	Tegla Loroupe (Ken) 2:27:37

1995	Tegla Loroupe (Ken)	2:28:08
1996	Anuta Catuna (Rom)	2:28:18
1997	Franziska Rochat-Moser (Swi)	2:28:43

* The course used 1981-3 was found to be 170 yards (155m) short (around 30 seconds at top men's pace), so the world-best times set by Salazar and Roe in 1981 were invalidated.

Rotterdam

First run in 1981.

Winners:

Men

1981	John Graham (UK)	2:09:28
1982	Rodolfo Gomez (Mex)	2:11:57
1983	Rob de Castella (Aus)	2:08:37
1984	Gidamis Shahanga (Tan)	2:11:12
1985	Carlos Lopes (Por)	2:07:12
1986	Abebe Mekonnen (Eth)	2:09:08
1987	Belayneh Dinsamo (Eth)	2:12:58
1988	Belayneh Dinsamo (Eth)	2:06:50
1989	Belayneh Dinsamo (Eth)	2:08:39
1990	Hiromi Taniguchi (Jap)	2:10:56
1991	Rob de Castella (Aus)	2:09:42
1992	Salvador García (Mex)	2:09:16
1993	Dionicio Cerón (Mex)	2:11:06
1994	Vincent Rousseau (Bel)	2:07:51
1995	Martin Fíz (Spa)	2:08:57
1996	Belayneh Dinsamo (Eth)	2:10:30
1997	Domingos Castro (Por)	2:07:51
1998	Fabián Roncero (Spa)	2:07:26

Women

1983	Rosa Mota (Por)	2:32:27
1984	Carla Beurskens (Hol)	2:34:56
1985	Wilma Rusman (Hol)	2:35:32
1986	Ellinor Ljungros (Swe)	2:41:06
1987	Nelly Aerts (Bel)	2:41:24
1988	Xiao Hong-yan (Chn)	2:37:46
1989	Elena Murgoci (Rom)	2:32:03
1990	Carla Beurskens (Hol)	2:29:47
1991	Joke Kleyweg (Hol)	2:34:18
1992	Aurora Cunha (Por)	2:29:15
1993	Anne van Schuppen (Hol)	2:34:15
1994	Miyoko Asahina (Jap)	2:25:52
1995	Monica Pont (Spa)	2:30:34
1996	Lieve Slegers (Bel)	2:28:06
1997	Tegla Loroupe (Ken)	2:22:07
1998	Tegla Loroupe (Ken)	2:20:47

World Cross-Country Championships

The International Cross-Country Championships were first held at Hamilton Park Racecourse, Glasgow in 1903 over 8 miles (12.87km), contested by the four countries from the British Isles. The race was held annually, with France first entering in 1907, Belgium in 1923, and thereafter the event steadily gained in international prestige. A junior race was first added in 1961, although there had been an international race for juniors between England, France and Belgium in 1940, and the first women's race was held in 1967. There were two women's races in 1970; included here is the one in the USA, the other, in France, was won by Paula Pigni (Ita), with the Netherlands team winners. The event has had official world championship status from 1973, when the IAAF took control of the event from the International Cross-Country Union. A junior women's race was run for the first time in 1989 and short-distance races for seniors in 1998.

The distances raced from 1998 are: men 12km and 4km, women 8km and 4km, junior men 8km, junior women 6km. Teams are of six runners, with four to score, although the senior men had six scorers from a team of nine up to 1997.

Most wins

Senior team – men

45	England	1903-14, 1920-1, 1924-5, 1930-8, 1951, 1953-5, 1958-60, 1962, 1964-72, 1976, 1979-80
14	France	1922-3, 1926-9, 1939, 1946-7, 1949-50, 1952, 1956, 1978
13	Kenya	1986-98
7	Belgium	1948, 1957, 1961, 1963, 1973-4, 1977
5	Ethiopia	1981-5
1	New Zealand	1975

Senior team – women

8	USA	1968-9, 1975, 1979, 1983-5, 1987
8	USSR	1976-7, 1980-2, 1988-90
7	England	1967, 1970-74, 1986
6	Kenya	1991-3, 1995-6, 1998
1	Romania 1978, Portugal 1994, Ethiopia 1997

4 kilometres senior team – men

| 1 | Kenya | 1998 |

4 kilometres senior team – women

| 1 | Morocco | 1998 |

International winners – men

1903-4	Alfred Shrubb (Eng)
1905	Albert Aldridge (Eng)
1906	Charles Straw (Eng)
1907	Adam Underwood (Eng)
1908	Archie Robertson (Eng)
1909-10	Edward Wood (Eng)
1911-3	Jean Bouin (Fra)
1914	Arthur Nicholls (Eng)
1920	James Wilson (Sco)
1921	Walter Freeman (Eng)
1922	Joseph Guillemot (Fra)
1923	Charles Blewitt (Eng)
1924	William 'Joe' Cotterell (Eng)
1925	Jack Webster (Eng)

1926	Ernest Harper (Eng)
1927	Lewis Payne (Eng)
1928	Harry Eckersley (Eng)
1929	William 'Joe' Cotterell (Eng)
1930	Thomas Evenson (Eng)
1931	Tim Smythe (Ire)
1932	Thomas Evenson (Eng)
1933-5	Jack Holden (Eng)
1936	William Eaton (Eng)
1937	James Flockhart (Sco)
1938	John Emery (Eng)
1939	Jack Holden (Eng)
1946-7	Raphael Pujazon (Fra)
1948	John Doms (Bel)
1949	Alain Mimoun (Fra)
1950	Lucien Theys (Bel)
1951	Geoffrey Saunders (Eng)
1952	Alain Mimoun (Fra)
1953	Franjo Mihalic (Yug)
1954	Alain Mimoun (Fra)
1955	Frank Sando (Eng)
1956	Alain Mimoun (Fra)
1957	Frank Sando (Eng)
1958	Stan Eldon (Eng)
1959	Fred Norris (Eng)
1960	Rhadi ben Abdesselem (Mor)
1961	Basil Heatley (Eng)
1962	Gaston Roelants (Bel)
1963	Roy Fowler (Eng)
1964	Francesco Arizmendi (Spa)
1965	Jean Fayolle (Fra)
1966	Ben Assou El Ghazi (Mor)
1967	Gaston Roelants (Bel)
1968	Mohammed Gammoudi (Tun)
1969	Gaston Roelants (Bel)
1970	Michael Tagg (Eng)
1971	David Bedford (Eng)
1972	Gaston Roelants (Bel)

International winners – women

1967-71	Doris Brown (USA)
1972	Joyce Smith (Eng)

IAAF World Champions – men

1973	Pekka Paivarinta (Fin)
1974	Eric De Beck (Bel)
1975	Ian Stewart (Sco)
1976	Carlos Lopes (Por)
1977	Leon Schots (Bel)
1978	John Treacy (Ire)
1979	John Treacy (Ire)

1980	Craig Virgin (USA)
1981	Craig Virgin (USA)
1982	Mohamed Kedir (Eth)
1983	Bekele Debele (Eth)
1984	Carlos Lopes (Por)
1985	Carlos Lopes (Por)
1986	John Ngugi (Ken)
1987	John Ngugi (Ken)
1988	John Ngugi (Ken)
1989	John Ngugi (Ken)
1990-1	Khalid Skah (Mor)
1992	John Ngugi (Ken)
1993-4	William Sigei (Ken)
1995-8	Paul Tergat (Ken)

Most wins: 5 Ngugi; 4 Holden, Mimoun, Roelants, Tergat

Most placings in first three: 7 Roelants four wins, three second 1960-72

Most placings in first ten: 10 Jack Holden 1930-46

Most appearances: 20 Marcel Van de Wattyne 1946-65

IAAF World Champions – women

1973	Paola Cacchi (Ita)
1974	Paola Cacchi (Ita)
1975	Julie Brown (USA)
1976	Carmen Valero (Spa)
1977	Carmen Valero (Spa)
1978	Grete Waitz (Nor)
1979	Grete Waitz (Nor)
1980	Grete Waitz (Nor)
1981	Grete Waitz (Nor)
1982	Maricica Puica (Rom)
1983	Grete Waitz (Nor)
1984	Maricica Puica (Rom)
1985	Zola Budd (Eng)
1986	Zola Budd (Eng
1987	Annette Sergent (Fra)
1988	Ingrid Kristiansen (Nor)
1989	Annette Sergent (Fra)
1990-2	Lynn Jennings (USA)
1993	Albertina Dias (Por)
1994	Helen Chepngeno (Ken)
1995	Derartu Tulu (Eth)
1996	Gete Wami (Eth)
1997	Derartu Tulu (Eth)
1998	Sonia O'Sullivan (Ire)

Most wins: 5 Brown, Waitz

Most placings in first three: 7 Waitz, five wins, two thirds 1978-84

Most placings in first ten: 7 Waitz 1978-84

Most appearances: 16 Jean Lochhead (Wal) 1967-84

Greatest winning margins

Men: 56 sec Jack Holden (Eng) 1934

Women: 40 sec Grete Waitz (Nor) 1980

Men's 4 kilometres

1998	John Kibowen (Ken)

Women's 4 kilometres

1998	Sonia O'Sullivan (Ire)

European Cross-Country Championship

First held in 1994.
Winners:

Men's individual

1994-5	Paulo Guerra (Por)
1996	Jon Brown (UK)
1997	Carsten Jorgensen (Den)

Women's individual

1994	Catherina McKiernan (Ire)
1995	Annemari Sandell (Fin)
1996	Sara Wedlund (Swe)★
1997	Josiane Llado (Fra)

★ Iulia Negura (Rom) disqualified for drugs use.

Men's team

1994	Portugal
1995	Spain
1996	Portugal
1997	Portugal

Women's team

1994	Romania
1995	Russia
1996-7	France

Australian Rules Football

'Aussie Rules' is predominantly a kicking game, played by teams of 18-a-side. Its principal initiators were Henry Colden Harrison and Thomas Wills, who helped to form the Melbourne Football Club in 1858. In 1877 the Victorian Football Association was founded, from which eight clubs broke away to form the Victorian Football League (VFL). Four more teams had been admitted by 1925, and in 1987 teams from Queensland and Western Australia joined the league, which was renamed the Australian Football League in 1990.

Governing body: Australian Football League, GPO Box 1449. Melbourne, Victoria 3001, Australia. Tel: (61) 3 9653 1946, Fax: (61) 3 9650 1303. Chairman: John Kennedy, Chief Executive Officer: Wayne Jackson.

Australian Football League

Australia's premier game is the Grand Final, played annually since 1897 at the Melbourne Cricket Ground, except in 1945, when it was staged at North Carlton.

Most premierships (winning Grand Final)

16	Carlton	1906-8, 1914-5, 1938, 1945, 1947, 1968, 1970, 1972, 1979, 1981-2, 1987, 1995
15	Essendon	1897, 1901, 1911-2, 1923-4, 1942, 1946, 1949-50, 1962, 1965, 1984-5, 1993
14	Collingwood	1902-3, 1910, 1917, 1919, 1927-30, 1935-6, 1953, 1958, 1990
12	Melbourne	1900, 1926, 1939-41, 1948, 1955-7, 1959-60, 1964
10	Richmond	1920-1, 1932, 1934, 1943, 1967, 1969, 1973-4, 1980
9	Hawthorn	1961, 1971, 1976, 1978, 1983, 1986, 1988-9, 1991
8	Fitzroy	1898-9, 1904-5, 1913, 1916, 1922, 1944 (now Brisbane Lions)
6	Geelong	1925, 1931, 1937, 1951-2, 1963
3	South Melbourne	1909, 1918, 1933
3	North Melbourne	1975, 1977, 1996
2	West Coast	1992*, 1994
1	Footscray 1954, St Kilda 1966, Adelaide Crows 1997	

* West Coast Eagles of Perth became the first non-Victorian winners.

Most premierships

South Australia: 32 Port Adelaide 1884-1994
Western Australia: 29 East Fremantle 1900-94

AFL records

Highest aggregate score: 345 St Kilda beat Melbourne 204-141, 6 May 1978
Team score: 239 (37 goals, 17 behinds) Geelong v Brisbane 3 May 1992
Record margin in Grand Final: 96 Hawthorn beat Melbourne 152 to 56, 24 Sep 1988
Goals in career: 2191 Peter Hudson 1963-81
Goals in season: 150 Bob Pratt (South Melbourne) 1934, Peter Hudson (Hawthorn) 1971
Goals in Grand Final: 9 Gordon Coventry for Collingwood v Richmond 1928, Gary Ablett for Geelong v Hawthorn 1989
Most matches: 426 Michael Tuck (Hawthorn) 1972-91
Greatest attendance: 121,696 for the Grand Final, 26 Sep 1970

Australian National Football League Championship

The first inter-state game was between Victoria and South Australia in 1879 and the first inter-state carnival in 1908. *Winners:*

17	Victoria	1908, 1914, 1924, 1927, 1930, 1933, 1937, 1947, 1950, 1953, 1956, 1958, 1966, 1969, 1972, 1980, 1989
6	Western Australia	1921, 1961, 1979, 1983, 1984, 1986
4	South Australia	1911, 1985, 1987-8

National Football League

Contested by the leading teams from all over Australia. Held from 1976 to 1986, but Victoria withdrew in 1977-8, when it ran its own Premiership series (winners: 1977 Hawthorn, 1978 Fitzroy).

Winners:

1976	Hawthorn (Vic)		1981	Essendon (Vic)
1977	Norwood (SA)		1982	Sydney Swans (NSW)
1978	South Adelaide (SA)		1983	Carlton (Vic)
1979	Collingwood (Vic)		1984	Essendon (Vic)
1980	North Melbourne (Vic)		1985-6	Hawthorn (Vic)

Badminton

The name of the game comes from its playing in the 19th century at Badminton House in Gloucestershire, England, by the family and guests of the Duke of Beaufort. Its origins, however, are most directly from the children's game of battledore and shuttlecock, and a similar game was played in China over 2000 years ago. Badminton was popular with Army officers in the 1870s in India, where the first modern rules were codified. The Badminton Association was founded in England in 1893.

International governing body: International Badminton Federation (IBF), Manor Park Place, Rutherford Way, Cheltenham, Gloucestershire GL51 9TU, England. Tel: 01242 234904, Fax: 01242 221030. President: Lu Shengrong, Executive Director: Neil Cameron. Formed in 1934. 133 member nations in 1998.

World Team Championships (Thomas Cup)

For men's teams of six players, who play five singles and four doubles in each contest, held every three years until 1982 when it became a biennial event. The cup was donated in 1940 by Sir George Thomas, winner of 21 All-England titles, but the competition could not start until after the war.

Wins:

11	Indonesia	1958, 1961, 1964, 1970, 1973, 1976, 1979, 1984, 1994, 1996, 1998
5	Malaysia	Malaya 1949, 1952, 1955
		Malaysia 1967, 1992
4	China	1982, 1986, 1988, 1990

Women's World Team Championships (Uber Cup)

The women's equivalent of the Thomas Cup, was also contested triennially until 1984 and biennially thereafter. The cup was presented by Betty Uber who represented England a then-record 37 times, between 1926 and 1951. Each tie consists of three singles and four doubles.

Wins:

6	China	1984, 1986, 1988, 1990, 1992, 1998
5	Japan	1966, 1969, 1972, 1978, 1981
3	United States	1957, 1960, 1963
3	Indonesia	1975, 1994, 1996

World Championships

Individual championships were instituted in 1977; initially they were held every three years, but are now held biennially.

Winners:

Men's singles		**Women's singles**
1977	Flemming Delfs (Den)	Lene Köppen (Den)
1980	Rudy Hartono (Ina)	Wiharjo Verawaty (Ina)
1983	Icuk Sugiarto (Ina)	Li Lingwei (Chn)
1985	Han Jian (Chn)	Han Aiping (Chn)
1987	Yang Yang (Chn)	Han Aiping (Chn)
1989	Yang Yang (Chn)	Li Lingwei (Chn)
1991	Zhao Jianhua (Chn)	Tang Jiuhong (Chn)
1993	Joko Suprianto (Ina)	Susi Susanti (Ina)
1995	Heryanto Arbi (Ina)	Ye Zhaoying (Chn)
1997	Peter Rasmussen (Den)	Ye Zhaoying (Chn)

Men's doubles

1977	Johan Wahjudi & Tjun Tjun (Ina)
1980	Ade Chandra & Hadinata Christian (Ina)
1983	Steen Fladberg & Jesper Helledie (Den)
1985	Park Joo-bong & Kim Moon-soo (SKo)
1987	Li Yongbo & Tian Bingyi (Chn)
1989	Li Yongbo & Tian Bingyi (Chn)
1991	Kim Moon-soo & Park Joo-bong (SKo)
1993	Ricky Subagya & Rudy Gunawan (Ina)
1995	Rexy Mainaky & Ricky Subagya (Ina)
1997	Budiarto Sigit & Candra Wajaga (Ina)

Women's doubles

1977	Etsuko Tuganoo & Emiko Vero (Jap)
1980	Nora Perry & Jane Webster (UK)
1983	Lin Ying & Wu Dixi (Chn)
1985	Han Aiping & Li Lingwei (Chn)
1987	Lin Ying & Guan Weizhen (Chn)
1989	Lin Ying & Guan Weizhen (Chn)
1991	Guan Weizhen & Nong Qunhua (Chn)
1993	Nong Qunhua & Zhou Lei (Chn)
1995	Gil Young-ah & Jang Hye-ock (SKo)
1997	Gu Jun & Ge Fei (Chn)

Mixed doubles

1977	Steen Stovgaard & Lene Køppen (Den)
1980	Hadinata Christian & Imelda Wigoeno (Ina)
1983	Thomas Kihlström (Swe) & Nora Perry (UK)
1985	Park Joo-bong & Yoo Sang-hee (SKo)
1987	Wang Pengrin & Shi Fagjing (Chn)
1989	Park Joo-bong & Chung Myung-hee (SKo)
1991	Park Joo-bong & Chung Myung-hee (SKo)
1993	Thomas Lund (Den) & Catrine Bengtsson (Swe)
1995	Thomas Lund & Marlene Thomsen (Den)
1997	Liu Yong & Ge Fei (Chn)

Team (mixed) – for the Sudirman Trophy

1989	Indonesia
1991	South Korea
1993	South Korea
1995	China
1997	China

Olympic Games

Badminton was played as a demonstration sport in 1972 and 1988, and it became a medal sport in 1992. *Winners since 1992:*

Men's singles

1992	Alan Budi Kusuma (Ina)
1996	Poul-Erik Høyer-Larsen (Den)

Women's singles

	Susi Susanti (Ina)
	Bang Soo-hyun (SKo)

Men's doubles

1992	Kim Moon-soo & Park Joo-bong (SKo)
1996	Rexy Mainaky & Ricky Subagja (Ina)

Women's doubles

1992	Hwang Hye-young & Chung So-young (SKo)
1996	Ge Fei & Gu Jun (Chn)

Mixed doubles

1996	Kim Dong-moon & Gil Young-ah (SKo)

All-England Championships

First played in 1899, until the advent of the World Championships, this was the premier tournament in the world.

Men's singles

1900	Sydney Smith (Eng)	1934	Ralph Nichols (Eng)	1966	Tan Aik Huang (Mal)
1901	H Davies (Eng)	1935	Raymond White (Eng)	1967	Erland Kops (Den)
1902-3	Ralph Watling (Eng)	1936-8	Ralph Nichols (Eng)	1968-74	Rudy Hartono (Ina)
1904-5	Henry Marrett (Eng)	1939	Tage Madsen (Den)	1975	Svend Pri (Den)
1906-7	Norman Wood (Eng)	1947	Conny Jepsen (Swe)	1976	Rudy Hartono (Ina)
1908	Henry Marrett (Eng)	1948	Jørn Skaarup (Den)	1977	Flemming Delfs (Den)
1909-10	Frank Chesterton (Eng)	1949	Dave Freeman (USA)	1978-9	Liem Swie King (Ina)
1911-2	George Sautter (Eng)	1950-2	Wong Peng Soon (Mal)	1980	Prakash Padukone (Ina)
1920	George Thomas (Eng)	1953-4	Eddie Choong (Mal)	1981	Liem Swie King (Ina)
1924	'Curly' Mack (Ire)	1955	Wong Peng Soon (Mal)	1982	Morten Frost (Den)
1925-9	Frank Devlin (Ire)	1956-7	Eddie Choong (Mal)	1983	Luan Jin (Chn)
1930	Donald Hume (Eng)	1958	Erland Kops (Den)	1984	Morten Frost (Den)
1931	Frank Devlin (Ire)	1959	Tan Joe Hok (Ina)	1985	Zhao Jianhua (Chn)
1932	Ralph Nichols (Eng)	1960-3	Erland Kops (Den)	1986-7	Morten Frost (Den)
1933	Raymond White (Eng)	1964	Knud Nielsen (Den)	1988	Ib Frederiksen (Den)
		1965	Erland Kops (Den)	1989	Yang Yang (Chn)

1990	Zhao Jianhua (Chn)
1991	Ardy Wiranata (Ina)
1992	Liu Jun (Chn)
1993-4	Heryanto Arbi (Ina)
1995-6	Poul-Erik Høyer-Larsen (Den)
1997	Dong Jiong (Chn)
1998	Sun Jun (Chn)

Most wins: 8 Rudy Hartono (Ina)

Women's singles

1900-1	Ethel Thomson (Eng)
1902	Meriel Lucas (Eng)
1903-4	Ethel Thomson (Eng)
1905	Meriel Lucas (Eng)
1906	Ethel Thomson (Eng)
1907-10	Meriel Lucas (Eng)
1911	Margaret Larminie (Eng)
1912	Margaret Tragett (née Larminie) (Eng)
1913-4	Lavinia Radeglia (Eng)
1920-2	Kitty McKane (Eng)
1923	Lavinia Radeglia (Eng)
1924	Kitty McKane (Eng)
1925	Margaret Stocks (Eng)
1926-7	Marjorie Barrett (Eng)
1928	Margaret Tragett (Eng)
1929-31	Marjorie Barrett (Eng)
1932	Leonie Kingsbury (Eng)
1933	Alice Woodroffe (Eng)
1934	Leonie Kingsbury (Eng)
1935	Betty Uber (Eng)
1936-7	Thelma Kingsbury (Eng)
1938	Daphne Young (Eng)
1939	Dorothy Walton (Can)
1947	Marie Ussing (Den)
1948	Kirsten Thorndahl (Den)
1949	Aase Jacobsen (Den)
1950	Tonny Olsen-Ahm (Den)
1951	Aase Jacobsen (Den)
1952	Tonny Olsen-Ahm (Den)
1953	Marie Ussing (Den)
1954	Judy Devlin (USA)
1955-6	Margaret Varner (USA)
1957-8	Judy Devlin (USA)
1959	Heather Ward (Eng)
1960	Judy Devlin (USA)
1961-4	Judy Hashman (née Devlin) (USA)
1965	Ursula Smith (Eng)
1966-7	Judy Hashman (USA)
1968	Eva Twedberg (Swe)
1969	Hiroe Yuki (Jap)
1970	Etsuko Takenaka (Jap)
1971	Eva Twedberg (Swe)
1972	Noriko Nakayama (Jap)
1973	Margaret Beck (Eng)
1974-5	Hiroe Yuki (Jap)
1976	Gillian Gilks (Eng)
1977	Hiroe Yuki (Jap)

1978	Gillian Gilks (Eng)
1979-80	Lene Køppen (Den)
1981	Sun Ai-hwang (SKo)
1982-3	Zang Ailing (Chn)
1984	Li Lingwei (Chn)
1985	Han Aiping (Chn)
1986	Kim Yun-ja (SKo)
1987	Kirsten Larsen (Den)
1988	Gu Jiaming (Chn)
1989	Li Lingwei (Chn)
1990-1	Susi Susanti (Ina)
1992	Tang Jiuhong (Chn)
1993-4	Susi Susanti (Ina)
1995	Lim Xiaoqing (Swe)
1996	Bang Soo-hyun (Kor)
1997-8	Ye Zhaoying (Chn)

Most wins: 10 Judy Hashman (née Devlin) (USA)

Men's doubles

1899	D Oakes & Stewart Massey (Eng)
1900-2	H Mellersh & F Collier (Eng)
1903	Stewart Massey & E Huson (Eng)
1904	Albert Prebble & Henry Marrett (Eng)
1905	Stewart Massey & C Barnes (Eng)
1906	George Thomas & Henry Marrett (Eng)
1907	Albert Prebble & Norman Wood (Eng)
1908	George Thomas & Henry Marrett (Eng)
1909	Albert Prebble & Frank Chesterton (Eng)
1910	George Thomas & Henry Marrett (Eng)
1911	P Fitton & Edward Hawthorn (Eng)
1912	George Thomas & Henry Marrett (Eng)
1913-4	George Thomas & Frank Chesterton (Eng)
1920	Alfred Engelbach & Robert du Roveray (Eng)
1921	George Thomas & Francis Hodge (Eng)
1922	Frank Devlin (Ire) & George Sautter (Eng)
1923	Frank Devlin & 'Curly' Mack (Ire)
1924	George Thomas & Francis Hodge (Eng)
1925	Herbert Huber & A Jones (Eng)
1926-7	Frank Devlin & 'Curly' Mack (Ire)
1928	George Thomas & Francis Hodge (Eng)
1929-31	Frank Devlin & 'Curly' Mack (Ire)
1932-5	Donald Hume & Raymond White (Eng)
1936-8	Ralph Nichols & Leslie Nichols (Eng)
1939	Tom Boyle & James Rankin (Ire)
1947	Tage Madsen & Poul Holm (Den)
1948	Preben Dabelsteen & Borge Fredricksen (Den)
1949	Ooi Teik Hock & Teoh Seng Khoon (Mal)
1950	Preben Dabelsteen & Jørn Skaarup (Den)
1951-3	Eddie Choong & David Choong (Mal)
1954	Ooi Teik Hock & Ong Poh Lim (Mal)
1955-6	Finn Kobbero & Jørgen Hammergaard Hansen (Den)
1957	Joseph Alston (USA) & Hock Aun Heah (Mal)
1958	Erland Kops & Per Nielsen (Den)
1959	Lim Say Hup & Teh Kew San (Mal)
1960	Finn Kobbero & Per Neilsen (Den)

1961–4	Finn Kobbero & Jørgen Hammergaard Hansen (Den)
1965–6	Ng Boon Bee & Tan Yee Khan (Mal)
1967–9	Erland Kops & Henning Borch (Den)
1970	Tom Backer & Paul Petersen (Den)
1971	Ng Boon Bee & Punch Gunalan (Mal)
1972–3	Hadinata Christian & Ade Chandra (Ina)
1974–5	Tjun Tjun & Johan Wahjudi (Ina)
1976	Bengt Froman & Thomas Kihlström (Swe)
1977–80	Tjun Tjun & Johan Wahjudi (Ina)
1981	Hariamanto Kartono & Rudy Heryanto (Ina)
1982	Razif Sidek & Jalaini Sidek (Mal)
1983	Stefan Karlsson & Thomas Kihlström (Swe)
1984	Hariamanto Kartono & Rudy Heryanto Ina)
1985–6	Kim Moon-soo & Park Joo-bong (SKo)
1987–8	Li Yongbo & Tian Bingyi (Chn)
1989	Lee Sang-bok & Park Joo-bong (SKo)
1990	Kim Moon-soo & Park Joo-bong (SKo)
1991	Li Yongbo & Tian Bingyi (Chn)
1992	Rudy Gunawan & Eddy Hartono (Ina)
1993	Jon Holst-Christensen & Thomas Lund (Den)
1994	Rudy Gunawan & Bambang Suprianto (Ina)
1995–6	Rexy Mainaky & Ricky Subagya (Ina)
1997	Ha Tae-kwon & Kang Kyung-jin (SKo)
1998	Lee Dong-soo & Yoo Yong-somg (SKo)

Women's doubles

1899–1900	Meriel Lucas & Miss Graeme (Eng)
1901	Miss St John & E Moseley (Eng)
1902	Meriel Lucas & Ethel Thomson (Eng)
1903	M Hardy & Dorothea Douglass (Eng)
1904–6	Meriel Lucas & Ethel Thomson (Eng)
1907–9	Meriel Lucas & G Murray (Eng)
1910	Mary Bateman & Meriel Lucas (Eng)
1911–2	Alice Gowenlock & Dorothy Cundall (Eng)
1913	Hazel Hogarth & Mary Bateman (Eng)
1914	Margaret Tragett (née Larminie) & Eveline Peterson (Eng)
1920	Lavinia Radeglia & Violet Elton (Eng)
1921	Kitty McKane & Margaret McKane (Eng)
1922–3	Margaret Tragett & Hazel Hogarth (Eng)
1924	Margaret Stocks (née McKane) & Kitty McKane (Eng)
1925	Margaret Tragett & Hazel Hogarth (Eng)
1926	A Head & Violet Elton (Eng)
1927	Margaret Tragett & Hazel Hogarth (Eng)
1928–30	Marjorie Barrett & Violet Elton (Eng)
1931	Betty Uber & Marianne Horsley (Eng)
1932	Marjorie Barrett & Leonie Kingbury (Eng)
1933–6	Thelma Kingsbury & Marjorie Bell-Henderson (Eng)
1937–8	Betty Uber & Diana Doveton (Eng)
1939	Ruth Dalsgard & Tonny Olsen (Den)
1947–8	Tonny Olsen-Ahm & Kirsten Thorndahl (Den)
1949	Betty Uber & Queenie Allen (Eng)
1950–1	Tonny Olsen-Ahm & Kirsten Thorndahl (Den)

1952	Tonny Olsen-Ahm & Aase Jacobsen (Den)
1953	Iris Cooley & June White (Eng)
1954	Judy Devlin & Susan Devlin (USA)
1955	Iris Cooley & June White (Eng)
1956	Judy Devlin & Susan Devlin (USA)
1957	Kirsten Granlund (née Thorndahl) & Ami Hammergaard Hansen (Den)
1958	Margaret Varner (USA) & Heather Ward (Eng)
1959	Iris Cooley-Rogers & June White-Timperley (Eng)
1960	Judy Devlin & Susan Devlin (USA)
1961	Judy Hashman (née Devlin) (USA) & Susan Peard (née Devlin) (Ire)
1962	Judy Hashman (USA) & Tonny Holst-Christensen (Den)
1963	Judy Hashman (USA) & Susan Peard (Ire)
1964–5	Karen Jørgensen & Ulla Rasmussen (Den)
1966	Judy Hashman (USA) & Susan Peard (Ire)
1967	Irme Rietveld (Hol) & Ulla Strand (née Rasmussen) (Den)
1968	Retno Koestijah & Miss Minarni (Ina)
1969–70	Margaret Boxall & Sue Whetnall (Eng)
1971	Noriko Takagi & Hiroe Yuki (Jap)
1972–3	Machiko Aizawa & Etsuko Takenaka (Jap)
1974	Margaret Beck & Gillian Gilks (Eng)
1975	Machiko Aizawa & Etsuko Takenaka (Jap)
1976	Gillian Gilks & Sue Whetnall (Eng)
1977	Etsuko Tuganoo (née Takenaka) & Emiko Ueno (Jap)
1978	Atsuko Tokuda & Mikiko Takada (Jap)
1979	Wiharjo Verawaty & Imelda Wigoeno (Ina)
1980	Gillian Gilks & Nora Perry (Eng)
1981	Nora Perry & Jane Webster (Eng)
1982	Lin Ying & Wu Dixi (Chn)
1983	Xu Rong & Wu Jianqiu (Chn)
1984	Liu Ying & Wu Dixi (Chn)
1985	Li Lingwei & Han Aiping (Chn)
1986–7	Chung Myung-hee & Hwang Hye-young (SKo)
1988	Chung So-young & Kim Jun-ja (SKo)
1989	Chung Myung-hee & Chung So-young (SKo)
1990	Chung Myung-hee & Hwang Hye-young (SKo)
1991	Chung So-young & Hwang Hye-young (SKo)
1992	Lin Yanfen & Yao Fen (Chn)
1993–4	Chung So-young & Gil Young-ah (SKo)
1995	Gil Young-ah & Jang Hye-ock (SKo)
1996–8	Ge Fei & Gu Jun (Chn)

Mixed doubles

1899–1900	D Oakes & Miss St John (Eng)
1901	F Collier & Miss E Stawell-Brown (Eng)
1902	L Ransford & Miss E Moseley (Eng)

1903	George Thomas & Ethel Thomson (Eng)
1904	Henry Marrett & Dorothea Douglass (Eng)
1905	Henry Marrett & Hazel Hogarth (Eng)
1906	George Thomas & Ethel Thomson (Eng)
1907	George Thomas & Miss G Murray (Eng)
1908	Norman Wood & Meriel Lucas (Eng)
1909	Albert Prebble & Dora Boothby (Eng)
1910	George Sautter & Dorothy Cundall (Eng)
1911	George Thomas & Margaret Larminie (Eng)
1912	Edward Hawthorn & Hazel Hogarth (Eng)
1913	George Sautter & Miss M Mayston (Eng)
1914	George Thomas & Hazel Hogarth (Eng)
1920-2	George Thomas & Hazel Hogarth (Eng)
1923	'Curly' Mack (Ire) & Margaret Tragett (née Larminie) (Eng)
1924-5	Frank Devlin (Ire) & Kitty McKane (Eng)
1926-7	Frank Devlin (Ire) & Eveline Peterson (Eng)
1928	A Harbot & Margaret Tragett (Eng)
1929	Frank Devlin (Ire) & Marianne Horseley (Eng)
1930-2	Herbert Uber & Betty Uber (Eng)
1933-6	Donald Hume & Betty Uber (Eng)
1937	Ian Maconachie (Ire) & Thelma Kingsbury (Eng)
1938	Raymond White & Betty Uber (Eng)
1939	Ralph Nichols & Bessie Staples (Eng)
1947	Poul Holm & Tonny Olsen-Ahm (Den)
1948	Jørn Skaarup & Kirsten Thorndahl (Den)
1949	Cliton Stephens & Patsey Stephens (USA)
1950-2	Poul Holm & Tonny Olsen-Ahm (Den)
1953	Eddie Choong (Mal) & June White (Eng)
1954	John Best & Iris Cooley (Eng)
1955	Finn Kobbero & Kirsten Thorndahl (Den)
1956	Tony Jordan & June Timperley (née White) (Eng)
1957	Finn Kobbero & Kirsten Granlund (née Thorndahl) (Den)
1958	Tony Jordan & June Timperley (Eng)
1959	Per Nielsen & Inge Birgit Hansen (Den)
1960-1	Finn Kobbero & Kirsten Granlund (Den)
1962-3	Finn Kobbero & Ulla Rasmussen (Den)
1964	Tony Jordan & Jennifer Pritchard (Eng)
1965-6	Finn Kobbero & Ulla Strand (née Rasmussen) (Den)
1967	Svend Andersen & Ulla Strand (Den)

1968	Tony Jordan & Sue Pound (Eng)
1969	Roger Mills & Gillian Perrin (Eng)
1970	Per Walsøe & Pernille Mølgaard Hansen (Den)
1971-2	Svend Pri & Ulla Strand (Den)
1973	Derek Talbot & Gillian Gilks (Eng)
1974	David Eddy & Sue Whetnall (Eng)
1975	Elliott Stuart & Nora Gardner (Eng)
1976-7	Derek Talbot & Gillian Gilks (Eng)
1978	Mike Tredgett & Nora Perry (née Gardner) (Eng)
1979	Hadinata Christian & Imelda Wigoeno (Ina)
1980-1	Mike Tredgett & Nora Perry (Eng)
1982	Martin Dew & Gillian Gilks (Eng)
1983	Thomas Kihlstrom (Swe) & Nora Perry (Eng)
1984	Martin Dew & Gillian Gilks (Eng)
1985	Billy Gillibrand & Nora Perry (Eng)
1986	Park Joo-bong & Chung Myung-hee (SKo)
1987	Lee Deuk-choon & Chung Myung-hee (SKo)
1988	Wang Pengren & Shi Fangjing (Chn)
1989-91	Park Joo-bong & Chung Myung-hee (SKo)
1992	Thomas Lund & Pernille Dupont (Den)
1993	Jon Holst-Christensen & Grethe Morgensen (Den)
1994	Nick Ponting & Joanne Wright (UK)
1995	Thomas Lund & Marlene Thomsen (Den)
1996	Park Joo-bong & Ra Kyung-min (Kor)
1997	Liu Yong & Ge Fei (Chn)
1998	Kim Dong-moon & Ma Kyung-min (SKo)

Most titles

Men: 21 George Thomas 4 singles, 9 men's doubles, 8 mixed doubles 1903-28; 18 Frank Devlin 6 singles, 7 men's doubles, 5 mixed doubles 1922-31

Women: 17 Meriel Lucas 6 singles, 10 women's doubles, 1 mixed doubles 1899-1910, Judy Hashman (née Devlin) 10 singles, 7 women's doubles 1954-67

Badminton champions who also won Wimbledon titles at lawn tennis

Men: Sydney Smith 1900-6

Women: Ethel Larcombe (née Thomson) 1900-14; Dorothea Lambert Chambers (née Douglass) 1903-14; Dora Boothby 1909-13; Kitty Godfree (née McKane) 1920-6

World Cup/Grand Prix Final

Men's singles

1991	Ardy B Wiranata (Ina)
1992	Joko Suprianto (Ina)
1993	Alan Budi Kusuma (Ina)
1994	Heryanto Arbi (Ina)
1995	Joko Suprianto (Ina)
1996	Dong Jiong (Chn)
1997	Jun Sung (Chn)

Women's singles

| Huang Hwa (Chn) |
| Tang Jiuhong (Chn) |
| Susi Susanti (Ina) |
| Susi Susanti (Ina) |
| Ye Zhaoying (Chn) |
| Susi Susanti (Ina) |
| Susi Susanti (Ina) |

European Championships

The European Badminton Union was formed in 1967, and has staged biennial championships from 1968.

	Men's singles	Women's singles
1968	Sture Johnsson (Swe)	Irmgard Latz (FRG)
1970	Sture Johnsson (Swe)	Eva Twedberg (Swe)
1972	Wolfgang Bochow (FRG)	Margaret Beck (Eng)
1974	Sture Johnsson (Swe)	Gillian Gilks (Eng)
1976	Flemming Delfs (Den)	Gillian Gilks (Eng)
1978	Flemming Delfs (Den)	Lene Køppen (Den)
1980	Flemming Delfs (Den)	Liselotte Blumer (Swi)
1982	Jens Peter Nierhoff (Den)	Lene Køppen (Den)
1984	Morten Frost (Den)	Helen Troke (Eng)
1986	Morten Frost (Den)	Helen Troke (Eng)
1988	Darren Hall (Eng)	Kirsten Larsen (Den)
1990	Steve Baddeley (Eng)	Pernille Nedergaard (Den)
1992	Poul-Erik Höyer-Larsen (Den)	Pernille Nedergaard (Den)
1994	Poul-Erik Höyer-Larsen (Den)	Lim Xiaoqing (Swe)
1996	Poul-Erik Höyer-Larsen (Den)	Camilla Martin (Den)
1998	Peter Gade Christensen (Den)	Camilla Martin (Den)

European team champions

7	Denmark	1976, 1980, 1986, 1988, 1990, 1996, 1998
4	England	1974, 1978, 1982, 1984
2	Sweden	1992, 1994

Most doubles titles

10	Gillian Gilks (Eng) women's 1972, 1974, 1976, 1982, mixed 1972, 1974, 1976, 1982, 1984, 1986
6	Mike Tredgett (Eng) men's 1976, 1978, 1984, mixed 1978, 1980
5	Sue Whetnall (Eng) women's 1968, 1970, 1976, mixed 1968, 1970

Bandy

Bandy is an 11-a-side game similar to hockey, but played on an ice rink between 90 and 110m long and 45-65m wide. Unlike ice hockey, however, bandy is played with a ball rather than a puck. It may have originated in England c.1790, and Bury Fen Bandy Club in the north-east of England is the original home of the modern game. Some well-known soccer clubs, such as Sheffield United and Nottingham Forest, originally had bandy in their titles as well as football. The game is now played principally in the Baltic regions, with more than half a million players in Russia, Finland, Norway and Sweden.

The National Bandy Association was formed in England in 1891, but soon the game was forced into the background by ice hockey. The game was introduced into Sweden in 1894 by C G Tebbutt of Bury Fen, who had also organized the first international match, between Bury Fen and Haarlem (Hol) in 1891. The first Swedish club was established in Stockholm in 1895. Bandy was first played in Russia in 1898. It was included as a demonstration sport at the 1952 Winter Olympics in Oslo, when Sweden were the winners.

International governing body: International Bandy Federation (IBF), c/o The Swedish Bandy Federation, Box 78, 641 21, Katrineholm, Sweden. Tel: (46) 150 72200, Fax: (46) 150 72201. President: Albert Pomortsev, Secretary General: Seppo Vaihela. Formed in 1955.

World Championships

These are held for men's teams, first in 1957, then every two years from 1961.

Champions:

14	USSR	1957, 1961, 1963, 1965, 1967, 1969, 1971, 1973, 1975, 1977, 1979, 1985, 1989, 1991
6	Sweden	1981, 1983, 1987, 1993, 1995, 1997

Record score in a World Championship match: USSR beat USA 21-1 at Skövde, Sweden on 1 Feb 1987

Most gold medals by an individual: 8 Valeriy Maslov (USSR) 1961, 1963, 1965, 1967, 1971, 1973, 1975, 1977

Baseball

A special commission sponsored by Albert G Spalding was set up in the United States in 1907 to establish the true 'birth' of baseball; a year later, they concluded that Abner Doubleday, a West Point cadet, had invented the game at Cooperstown, New York in 1839. This legend has become deeply embedded in American folklore, but is entirely mythical. The game almost certainly evolved from such English games as cricket, paddleball, trap ball and rounders. Printed references to 'base ball' in England date back to 1700 and in the USA to the mid-18th century.

The first rules of the modern game were drawn up by Alexander Cartwright Jr in 1845. The first match under these rules was played on 19 June 1846, when the New York Nine defeated a team from the sport's first organized club, the New York Knickerbockers, 23-1 in four innings. In 1871 the National Association of Professional Base Ball Players was formed, the first professional league.

International governing body: International Baseball Association (IBA), Avenue de Mon Repos 24, Case Postale 131 0-1000, Lausanne 5, Switzerland. Tel: (41) 21 318 8240, Fax: (41) 21 318 8241. President: Aldo Notari, Executive Director: Miquel Ortín. Founded 1938. 106 member nations in 1998.

US governing body: Major League Baseball, 350 Park Avenue, New York, NY 10022, USA. Tel: (1) 212 339 7800. President: Paul Beeston.

World Series

There are two major leagues in America – the National League (NL), which was formed in 1876, and the American League (AL), formed in 1900 and officially founded in 1901. A total of 26 teams made up the two leagues until two expansion franchises were granted at the end of the 1992 season, to bring the total to 28. After a regular season of 162 matches against other teams in their own league, a series of play-offs decides the teams to represent each league in the best-of-seven game World Series, played each October.

In 1994 the AL and NL were realigned so that each had three divisions: Eastern and Central, each with five teams, and a Western division of four teams. The three divisional winners plus the runner-up with the best record play off for the right to contest the World Series.

Year	Winners	Runners-up	Score
1903	Boston Red Sox (AL)	Pittsburgh Pirates (NL)	5-3
1904	*Not held*		
1905	New York Giants (NL)	Philadelphia Athletics (AL)	4-1
1906	Chicago White Sox (AL)	Chicago Cubs (NL)	4-2
1907	Chicago Cubs (NL)	Detroit Tigers (AL)	4-0★
1908	Chicago Cubs (NL)	Detroit Tigers (AL)	4-1
1909	Pittsburgh Pirates (NL)	Detroit Tigers (AL)	4-3
1910	Philadelphia Athletics (AL)	Chicago Cubs (NL)	4-1
1911	Philadelphia Athletics (AL)	New York Giants (NL)	4-2
1912	Boston Red Sox (AL)	New York Giants (NL)	4-3★
1913	Philadelphia Athletics (AL)	New York Giants (NL)	4-1
1914	Boston Braves (NL)	Philadelphia Athletics (AL)	4-0
1915	Boston Red Sox (AL)	Philadelphia Phillies (NL)	4-1
1916	Boston Red Sox (AL)	Brooklyn Dodgers (NL)	4-1
1917	Chicago White Sox (AL)	New York Giants (NL)	4-2
1918	Boston Red Sox (AL)	Chicago Cubs (NL)	4-2
1919	Cincinnati Reds (NL)	Chicago White Sox (AL)	5-3
1920	Cleveland Indians (AL)	Brooklyn Dodgers (NL)	5-2
1921	New York Giants (NL)	New York Yankees (AL)	4-3
1922	New York Giants (NL)	New York Yankees (AL)	4-0★
1923	New York Yankees (AL)	New York Giants (NL)	4-2
1924	Washington Senators (AL)	New York Giants (NL)	4-3
1925	Pittsburgh Pirates (NL)	Washington Senators (AL)	4-3
1926	St Louis Cardinals (NL)	New York Yankees (AL)	4-3
1927	New York Yankees (AL)	Pittsburgh Pirates (NL)	4-0
1928	New York Yankees (AL)	St Louis Cardinals (NL)	4-0
1929	Philadelphia Athletics (AL)	Chicago Cubs (NL)	4-1
1930	Philadelphia Athletics (AL)	St Louis Cardinals (NL)	4-2
1931	St Louis Cardinals (NL)	Philadelphia Athletics (AL)	4-3

1932	New York Yankees (AL)	Chicago Cubs (NL)	4-0
1933	New York Giants (NL)	Washington Senators (AL)	4-1
1934	St Louis Cardinals (NL)	Detroit Tigers (AL)	4-3
1935	Detroit Tigers (AL)	Chicago Cubs (NL)	4-2
1936	New York Yankees (AL)	New York Giants (NL)	4-2
1937	New York Yankees (AL)	New York Giants (NL)	4-1
1938	New York Yankees (AL)	Chicago Cubs (NL)	4-0
1939	New York Yankees (AL)	Cincinnati Reds (NL)	4-0
1940	Cincinnati Reds (NL)	Detroit Tigers (AL)	4-3
1941	New York Yankees (AL)	Brooklyn Dodgers (NL)	4-1
1942	St Louis Cardinals (NL)	New York Yankees (AL)	4-1
1943	New York Yankees (AL)	St Louis Cardinals (NL)	4-1
1944	St Louis Cardinals (NL)	St Louis Browns (AL)	4-2
1945	Detroit Tigers (AL)	Chicago Cubs (NL)	4-3
1946	St Louis Cardinals (NL)	Boston Red Sox (AL)	4-3
1947	New York Yankees (AL)	Brooklyn Dodgers (NL)	4-3
1948	Cleveland Indians (AL)	Boston Braves (NL)	4-2
1949	New York Yankees (AL)	Brooklyn Dodgers (NL)	4-1
1950	New York Yankees (AL)	Philadelphia Phillies (NL)	4-0
1951	New York Yankees (AL)	New York Giants (NL)	4-2
1952	New York Yankees (AL)	Brooklyn Dodgers (NL)	4-3
1953	New York Yankees (AL)	Brooklyn Dodgers (NL)	4-2
1954	New York Giants (NL)	Cleveland Indians (AL)	4-0
1955	Brooklyn Dodgers (NL)	New York Yankees (AL)	4-3
1956	New York Yankees (AL)	Brooklyn Dodgers (NL)	4-3
1957	Milwaukee Braves (NL	New York Yankees (AL)	4-3
1958	New York Yankees (AL)	Milwaukee Braves (NL)	4-3
1959	Los Angeles Dodgers (NL)	Chicago White Sox (AL)	4-2
1960	Pittsburgh Pirates (NL)	New York Yankees (AL)	4-3
1961	New York Yankees (AL)	Cincinnati Reds (NL)	4-1
1962	New York Yankees (AL)	San Francisco Giants (NL)	4-3
1963	Los Angeles Dodgers (NL)	New York Yankees (AL)	4-0
1964	St Louis Cardinals (NL)	New York Yankees (AL)	4-3
1965	Los Angeles Dodgers (NL)	Minnesota Twins (AL)	4-3
1966	Baltimore Orioles (AL)	Los Angeles Dodgers (NL)	4-0
1967	St Louis Cardinals (NL)	Boston Red Sox (AL)	4-3
1968	Detroit Tigers (AL)	St Louis Cardinals (NL)	4-3
1969	New York Mets (NL)	Baltimore Orioles (AL)	4-1
1970	Baltimore Orioles (AL)	Cincinnati Reds (NL)	4-1
1971	Pittsburgh Pirates (NL)	Baltimore Orioles (AL)	4-3
1972	Oakland Athletics (AL)	Cincinnati Reds (NL)	4-3
1973	Oakland Athletics (AL)	New York Mets (NL)	4-3
1974	Oakland Athletics (AL)	Los Angeles Dodgers (NL)	4-1
1975	Cincinnati Reds (NL)	Boston Red Sox (AL)	4-3
1976	Cincinnati Reds (NL)	New York Yankees (AL)	4-0
1977	New York Yankees (AL)	Los Angeles Dodgers (NL)	4-3
1978	New York Yankees (AL)	Los Angeles Dodgers (NL)	4-2
1979	Pittsburgh Pirates (NL)	Baltimore Orioles (AL)	4-3
1980	Philadelphia Phillies (NL)	Kansas City Royals (AL)	4-2
1981	Los Angeles Dodgers (NL)	New York Yankees (AL)	4-2
1982	St Louis Cardinals (NL)	Milwaukee Brewers (AL)	4-3
1983	Baltimore Orioles (AL)	Philadelphia Phillies (NL)	4-1
1984	Detroit Tigers (AL)	San Diego Padres (NL)	4-1
1985	Kansas City Royals (AL)	St Louis Cardinals (NL)	4-3
1986	New York Mets (NL)	Boston Red Sox (AL)	4-3
1987	Minnesota Twins (AL)	St Louis Cardinals (NL)	4-3
1988	Los Angeles Dodgers (NL)	Oakland Athletics (AL)	4-1

1989	Oakland Athletics (AL)	San Francisco Giants (NL)	4-0
1990	Cincinnati Reds (NL)	Oakland Athletics (AL)	4-0
1991	Minnesota Twins (AL)	Atlanta Braves (NL)	4-3
1992	Toronto Blue Jays (AL)	Atlanta Braves (NL)	4-2
1993	Toronto Blue Jays (AL)	Philadelphia Phillies (NL)	4-2
1994	*Cancelled due to players' strike*		
1995	Atlanta Braves (NL)	Cleveland Indians (AL)	4-2
1996	New York Yankees (AL)	Atlanta Braves (NL)	4-2
1997	Florida Marlins (NL)	Cleveland Indians (AL)	4-3

* Includes one drawn game.

Most individual appearances: 14 (75 games) Lawrence 'Yogi' Berra (New York Yankees) 1947, 1949-53, 1955-8, 1960-3 (he was on the winning team 10 times, and also has the records for 259 at bats and 71 base hits); 12 (65 games) Mickey Mantle (New York Yankees)

World Series records

Most games: 75 Yogi Berra (in record 14 series) (New York Yankees) 1947-63

Most home runs in one game: 3 'Babe' Ruth (New York Yankees v St Louis Cardinals, 4th game) 6 Oct 1926, Reggie Jackson (New York Yankees v Los Angeles Dodgers, 6th game) 18 Oct 1977 (Jackson hit three consecutive pitches out of the park for his homers.)

Most runs in a career: 42 (from 65 games) Mickey Mantle (New York Yankees) 1951-64 (and record 18 home runs and 40 runs batted in)

Most runs and home runs in a series: 10 (5 home runs) Reggie Jackson (New York Yankees) 1977

Most strikeouts in a career: 94 (in 22 games) Whitey Ford (New York Yankees) 1950-64

Most strikeouts in a series: 35 (in 22 games) Bob Gibson (St Louis Cardinals) 1968

Perfect pitch (9 innings): Don Larsen (New York Yankees v Brooklyn Dodgers, 5th game) 8 Oct 1956

Record attendance (series): 420,784 Los Angeles Dodgers v Chicago White Sox 1-8 Oct 1959

Record attendance (single game): 92,706 Los Angeles Dodgers v Chicago White Sox (5th game) at Memorial Coliseum, Los Angeles, 6 Oct 1959

Most Valuable Player award

The only men to have won the coveted award twice are: Sandy Koufax (Los Angeles, NL 1963, 1965), Bob Gibson (St Louis, NL 1964, 1967), Reggie Jackson (Oakland, AL 1973, New York, AL 1977)

World Series team records

Most wins: 23 New York Yankees; 9 St Louis Cardinals, Philadelphia/Kansas City/Oakland Athletics/A's; 6 Brooklyn/Los Angeles Dodgers; 5 Boston Red Sox, Pittsburgh Pirates, New York/San Francisco Giants, Cincinnati Reds

Most appearances: 34 New York Yankees; 18 Brooklyn/Los Angeles Dodgers; 16 New York/San Francisco Giants; 15 St Louis Cardinals; 14 Philadelphia/Kansas City/Oakland Athletics/A's; 10 Chicago White Sox; 9 Boston Red Sox, Cincinnati Reds, Detroit Tigers

Most National League titles (from 1876)

21 Brooklyn/Los Angeles Dodgers; 19 New York/San Francisco Giants; 16 Chicago Cubs; 16 Boston/Milwaukee/Atlanta Braves; 15 St Louis Cardinals; 9 Pittsburgh Pirates

Most American League titles (from 1901)

34 New York Yankees; 15 Philadelphia/Oakland Athletics; 10 Boston Red Sox; 9 Detroit Tigers

Note: slashes indicate franchise name changes for same team.

Major League Records

Career batting

Best batting average: .367 Ty Cobb (Detroit AL, Philadelphia AL) 1905-28

Most runs: 2245 Ty Cobb (Detroit AL, Philadelphia AL) 1905-28

Most home runs: 755 Hank Aaron (Milwaukee NL, Atlanta NL, Milwaukee AL) 1954-76

Most runs batted in: 2297 Hank Aaron (Milwaukee NL, Atlanta NL, Milwaukee AL) 1954-76

Most base hits: 4256 Pete Rose (Cincinnati NL, Philadelphia NL) 1963-86

Total bases: 6856 Hank Aaron (Milwaukee NL, Atlanta NL, Milwaukee AL) 1954-76

Season's batting

Best batting average: .438 Hugh Duffy (Boston NL) 1894

Most runs: 192 William Hamilton (Philadelphia NL) 1894

Most home runs: 61 Roger Maris (New York AL) 1961

Most runs batted in: 190 Hack Wilson (Chicago NL) 1930

Most base hits: 257 George Sisler (St Louis AL) 1920

Total bases: 457 Babe Ruth (New York AL) 1921

General

Consecutive hits: 12 Pinky Higgins (Boston AL) 19-21 Jun 1938; Moose Dropo (Detroit AL) 14-15 Jul 1952

Consecutive games batted safely: 56 Joe DiMaggio (New York AL) 15 May-16 Jul 1941
Consecutive games played: 2543 Cal Ripken (Baltimore Orioles, AL) 1982-97

Career pitching

Games won: 511 Cy Young (Cleveland NL, St Louis AL, Boston NL, Boston AL, Cleveland AL) 1890-1911
Shutouts: 113 Walter Johnson (Washington AL) 1907-27
Strikeouts: 5714 Nolan Ryan (New York NL, California AL, Houston NL, Texas AL) 1968-93
No-hit games: 7 Nolan Ryan (4 for California AL 1973-5, 1 Houston NL 1981, 2 Texas AL 1990-1)
Complete games: 751 Cy Young (Cleveland NL, St Louis AL, Boston NL, Boston AL, Cleveland AL) 1890-1911
Consecutive games won: 24 Carl Owen Hubbell (New York NL) 1936-7

Season's pitching

Games won: 60 Charles Radbourne (Providence NL) 1884
Shutouts: 16 George Bradley (St Louis NL) 1876; Grover Alexander (Philadelphia NL) 1916
Strikeouts: 383 Nolan Ryan (California AL) 1973

Base running – stolen bases

Career: 1231 Rickey Henderson (Oakland AL, New York AL, Toronto AL) 1979-97
Season: 130 Rickey Henderson (Oakland AL) 1982

All-Time Top Tens

Batting – most runs

Ty Cobb	2245
Babe Ruth	2174
Hank Aaron	2174
Pete Rose	2165
Willie Mays	2062
Stan Musial	1949
Rickey Henderson	1913
Lou Gehrig	1888
Tristram Speaker	1882
Melvin Ott	1859
Frank Robinson	1829

Batting – most hits

Pete Rose	4256
Ty Cobb	4191
Hank Aaron	3771
Stan Musial	3630
Tristram Speaker	3514
Carl Yastrzemski	3419
John P 'Honus' Wagner	3418
Eddie Collins	3313
Willie Mays	3283
Eddie Murray	3255

Batting – most home runs

Hank Aaron	755
Babe Ruth	714
Willie Mays	660
Frank Robinson	586
Harmon Killibrew	573
Reggie Jackson	563
Michael Schmidt	548
Mickey Mantle	536
James Foxx	534
Ted Williams	521
Willie McCovey	521

Pitching – most wins

Cy Young	511
Walter Johnson	416
Chris Matthewson	373
Grover Alexander	373
Warren Spahn	363
Charles 'Kid' Nichols	361
James 'Pud' Galvin	361
Timothy Keefe	342
Steve Carlton	329
Eddie Plank	327

Pitching – most strikeouts

Nolan Ryan	5714
Steve Carlton	4136
Bart Blyleven	3701
Tom Seaver	3640
Don Sutton	3574
Gaylord Perry	3534
Walter Johnson	3508
Phil Niekro	3342
Ferguson Jenkins	3192
Robert Gibson	3117

League Leaders

Post-war leaders – taking the best of the AL or NL each year:

Best batting average

1946	Stan Musial (St Louis) NL	.365
1947	Harry Walker (St Louis/Philadelphia) NL	.363
1948	Stan Musial (St Louis) NL	.376
1949	George Kell (Detroit) AL	.343
1950	Billy Goodman (Boston) AL	.354
1951	Stan Musial (St Louis) NL	.355
1952	Stan Musial (St Louis) NL	.336
1953	Carl Furillo (Brooklyn) NL	.344
1954	Willie Mays (New York Giants) NL	.345
1955	Al Kaline (Detroit) AL	.340
1956	Mickey Mantle (New York Yankees) AL	.353
1957	Ted Williams (Boston) AL	.388
1958	Richie Ashburn (Philadelphia) NL	.350
1959	Hank Aaron (Milwaukee) NL	.355
1960	Dick Groat (Pittsburgh) NL	.325
1961	Norm Cash (Detroit) AL	.361
1962	Tommy Davis (Los Angeles) NL	.346

1963	Tommy Davis (Los Angeles) NL	.326
1964	Roberto Clemente (Pittsburgh) NL	.339
1965	Roberto Clemente (Pittsburgh) NL	.329
1966	Maria Alou (Pittsburgh) NL	.342
1967	Roberto Clemente (Pittsburgh) NL	.357
1968	Pete Rose (Cincinnati) NL	.335
1969	Pete Rose (Cincinnati) NL	.348
1970	Rico Carty (Atlanta) NL	.366
1971	Joe Torre (St Louis) NL	.363
1972	Billy Williams (Chicago) NL	.333
1973	Rod Carew (Minnesota) AL	.350
1974	Rod Carew (Minnesota) AL	.364
1975	Rod Carew (Minnesota) AL	.359
1976	Bill Madlock (Chicago) NL	.339
1977	Rod Carew (Minnesota) AL	.388
1978	Dave Parker (Pittsburgh) NL	.334
1979	Keith Hernandez (St Louis) NL	.344
1980	George Brett (Kansas City) AL	.390
1981	Bill Madlock (Pittsburgh) NL	.341
1982	Willie Watson (Kansas City) AL	.332
1983	Wade Boggs (Boston) AL	.361
1984	Tony Gwynn (San Diego) NL	.341
1985	Wade Boggs (Boston) AL	.368
1986	Wade Boggs (Boston AL	.357
1987	Tony Gwynne (San Diego) NL	.370
1988	Wade Boggs (Boston) AL	.366
1989	Kirby Puckett (Minnesota) AL	.339
1990	Willie McGee (St Louis) NL	.335
1991	Julio Franco (Texas) AL	.341
1992	Edgar Martinez (Seattle) AL	.343
1993	Andres Galarraga (Colorado) NL	.370
1994	Tony Gwynn (San Diego) NL	.394
1995	Tony Gwynn (San Diego) NL	.368
1996	Alex Rodriguez (Seattle) AL	.358
1997	Tony Gwynn (San Diego) NL	.372

Highest-ever average

American League: .421 Napolean Lajoie (Philadelphia) 1901

National League: .438 Hugh Duffy (Boston NL) 1894

Most seasons with best average

American League: 12 Ty Cobb (Detroit) 1907-15, 1917-19; 7 Rod Carew (Minnesota) 1969, 1972-5, 1977-8; 6 Ted Williams (Boston) 1941-2, 1947-8, 1957-8

National League: 8 John P Wagner (Pittsburgh) 1900, 1903-4, 1906-9, 1911; 7 Rogers Hornsby (St Louis) 1920-5, 1928, Stan Musial (St Louis) 1943, 1946, 1948, 1950-2, 1957, Tony Gwynn (San Diego) 1987-9, 1994-7

Most home runs

1946	Hank Greenberg (Detroit) AL	44
1947	Ralph Kiner (Pittsburgh) NL &	
	Johnny Mize (New York Giants) NL	51
1948	Ralph Kiner (Pittsburgh) NL &	
	Johnny Mize (New York Giants) NL	40

1949	Ralph Kiner (Pittsburgh) NL	54
1950	Ralph Kiner (Pittsburgh) NL	47
1951	Ralph Kiner (Pittsburgh) NL	42
1952	Ralph Kiner (Pittsburgh) NL &	
	Hank Sauer (Chicago) NL	37
1953	Eddie Mathews (Milwaukee) NL	47
1954	Ted Kluszewski (Cincinnati) NL	49
1955	Willie Mays (New York Giants) NL	51
1956	Mickey Mantle (New York Yankees) NL	52
1957	Hank Aaron (Milwaukee) NL	44
1958	Ernie Banks (Chicago) NL	47
1959	Eddie Mathews (Milwaukee) NL	46
1960	Ernie Banks (Chicago) NL	41
1961	Orlando Cepeda (San Francisco) NL	46
1962	Willie Mays (San Francisco) NL	49
1963	Harmon Killebrew (Minnesota) AL	45
1964	Harmon Killebrew (Minnesota) AL	49
1965	Willie Mays (San Francisco) NL	52
1966	Frank Robinson (Baltimore) AL	49
1967	Carl Yastrzemski (Boston) AL &	
	Harmon Killebrew (Minnesota) AL	44
1968	Frank Howard (Washington) AL	44
1969	Harmon Killebrew (Minnesota) AL	49
1970	Johnny Bench (Cincinnati) NL	45
1971	Willie Stargel (Pittsburgh) NL	48
1972	Johnny Bench (Cincinnati) NL	40
1973	Willie Stargel (Pittsburgh) NL	44
1974	Mike Schmidt (Philadelphia) NL	36
1975	Mike Schmidt (Philadelphia) NL	38
1976	Mike Schmidt (Philadelphia) NL	38
1977	George Foster (Cincinnati) NL	52
1978	Jim Rice (Boston) AL	46
1979	Dave Kingman (Chicago) NL	48
1980	Mike Schmidt (Philadelphia) NL	48
1981	Mike Schmidt (Philadelphia) NL	31
1982	Gorman Thomas (Milwaukee) AL &	
	Reggie Jackson (California) AL	39
1983	Mike Schmidt (Philadelphia) NL	40
1984	Tony Armas (Boston) AL	43
1985	Darrell Evans (Detroit) AL	60
1986	Jesse Barfield (Toronto) AL	40
1987	Mark McGwire (Oakland) AL &	
	Andre Dawson (Chicago) NL	49
1988	Jose Canseco (Oakland) AL	42
1989	Kevin Mitchell (San Francisco) NL	47
1990	Cecil Fielder (Detroit) AL	51
1991	Cecil Fielder (Detroit) AL &	
	Jose Canseco (Oakland) AL	44
1992	Juan Gonzalez (Texas) AL	43
1993	Juan Gonzalez (Texas) AL &	
	Barry Bonds (San Francisco) NL	46
1994	Matt Williams (San Francisco) NL	43
1995	Albert Belle (Cleveland) AL	50
1996	Mark McGwire (Oakland) AL	52
1997	Ken Griffey Jr (Seattle) AL	56

Most seasons leading

American League: 12 Babe Ruth (New York) 1918-21, 1923-4, 1926-31; 6 Harmon Killebrew 1959, 1962-4, 1967, 1969

National League: 8 Mike Schmidt 1974-6, 1980-1, 1983-4, 1986; 7 Ralph Kiner (Pittsburgh) 1946-52; 6 Gavvy Crovath (Philadelphia) 1913-15, 1917-19, Melvin Ott (New York) 1932, 1934, 1936-8, 1942

Earned run average

1946	Hal Newhouser (Detroit) AL	1.94
1947	Warren Spahn (Boston) NL	2.33
1948	Harry Brecheen (St Louis) NL	2.24
1949	Dave Koslo (New York) NL	2.50
1950	Jim Hearn (St Louis/New York) NL	2.49
1951	Saul Rogovin (Detroit/Chicago) AL	2.78
1952	Allie Reynolds (New York) AL	2.07
1953	Warren Spahn (Milwaukee) NL	2.10
1954	John Antonelli (New York) NL	2.29
1955	Billy Pierce (Chicago) AL	1.57
1956	Whitey Ford (New York) AL	2.47
1957	Bobby Schantz (New York) AL	2.45
1958	Whitey Ford (New York) AL	2.01
1959	Hoyt Wilhelm (Baltimore) AL	2.19
1960	Frank Baumann (Chicago) AL	2.68
1961	Richard Donovan (Washington) AL	2.40
1962	Hank Aguirre (Detroit) AL	2.21
1963	Sandy Koufax (Los Angeles) NL	1.88
1964	Dean Chance (Los Angeles) AL	1.64
1965	Sandy Koufax (Los Angeles) NL	2.04
1966	Sandy Koufax (Los Angeles) NL	2.04
1967	Phil Niekro (Atlanta) NL	1.87
1968	Bob Gibson (St Louis) NL	1.12
1969	Juan Marichal (San Francisco) NL	2.10
1970	Diego Segui (Oakland) AL	2.56
1971	Tom Seaver (New York) NL	1.76
1972	Luis Tiant (Boston) AL	1.91
1973	Tom Seaver (New York) NL	2.07
1974	Buzz Capra (Atlanta) NL	2.28

1975	Jim Palmer (Baltimore) AL	2.09
1976	Mark Fidrych (Detroit) AL	2.34
1977	John Candelaria (Pittsburgh) NL	2.34
1978	Ron Guidry (New York) AL	1.74
1979	J R Richard (Houston) NL	2.71
1980	Don Sutton (Los Angeles) NL	2.21
1981	Nolan Ryan (Houston) NL	1.69
1982	Steve Rogers (Montreal) NL	2.40
1983	Atlee Hammaker (San Francisco) NL	2.25
1984	Alejandro Pena (Los Angeles) NL	2.56
1985	Dwight Gooden (New York) NL	1.53
1986	Mike Scott (Houston) AL	2.22
1987	James E Key (Toronto) AL &	2.76
	Nolan Ryan (Houston) NL	2.76
1988	Allan Anderson (Minnesota) AL &	
	Teodoro Higuera (Milwaukee) AL	2.45
1989	Scott Garrelts (San Francisco) NL	2.28
1990	Roger Clemens (Boston) AL	1.93
1991	Dennis Martinez (Montreal) NL	2.39
1992	Bill Swift (San Francisco) NL	2.08
1993	Greg Maddux (Atlanta) NL	2.36
1994	Greg Maddux (Atlanta) NL	1.56
1995	Greg Maddux (Atlanta) NL	1.63
1996	Kevin Brown (Florida) NL	1.89
1997	Pedro Martinez (Montreal) NL	1.90

Most times leader

American League: 9 Lefty Grove (Philadelphia, Boston) 1926, 1929-32, 1935-6, 1938-9; 5 Walter Johnson (Washington) 1912-13, 1918-9, 1924, Roger Clemens (Boston) 1986, 1990-2, 1997

National League: 5 Christy Mathewson (New York) 1905, 1908-09, 1911, 1913, Pete Alexander (Philadelphia, Chicago) 1915-7, 1919-20, Sandy Koufax (Los Angeles) 1962-6; 3 Dazzy Vance (Brooklyn) 1924, 1928, 1930, Carl Hubbell (New York) 1933-4, 1936, Warren Spahn (Boston, Milwaukee) 1947, 1953, 1961, Tom Seaver (New York) 1970-1, 1973, Greg Maddux (Atlanta) 1993-5

Most Valuable Player awards

Annually since 1931 the Baseball Writers' Association votes for the Most Valuable Player of the Year in both the American and National leagues.

Post-war winners:

	American League	National League
1946	Ted Williams (Boston)	Stan Musial (St Louis)
1947	Joe DiMaggio (New York)	Bob Elliott (Boston)
1948	Louis Boudreau (Cleveland)	Stan Musial (St Louis)
1949	Ted Williams (Boston)	Jack Robinson (Brooklyn)
1950	Philip Rizzuto (New York)	Jim Konstanty (Philadelphia)
1951	'Yogi' Berra (New York)	Roy Campanella (Brooklyn)
1952	Robert Shantz (Philadelphia)	Hank Sauer (Chicago)
1953	Albert Rosen (Cleveland)	Roy Campanella (Brooklyn)
1954	'Yogi' Berra (New York)	Willie Mays (New York)
1955	'Yogi' Berra (New York)	Roy Campanella (Brooklyn)
1956	Mickey Mantle (New York)	Don Newcombe (Brooklyn)
1957	Mickey Mantle (New York)	Hank Aaron (Milwaukee)
1958	Jack Jensen (Boston)	Ernest Banks (Chicago)

	American League	National League
1959	Nelson Fox (Chicago)	Ernest Banks (Chicago)
1960	Roger Maris (New York)	Dick Groat (Pittsburgh)
1961	Roger Maris (New York)	Frank Robinson (Cincinnati)
1962	Mickey Mantle (New York)	Maurice Wills (Los Angeles)
1963	Elston Howard (New York)	Sandy Koufax (Los Angeles)
1964	Brooks Robinson (Baltimore)	Kenton Boyer (St Louis)
1965	Zoilo Versalles (Minnesota)	Willie Mays (San Francisco)
1966	Frank Robinson (Baltimore)	Roberto Clemente (Pittsburgh)
1967	Carl Yastrzemski (Boston)	Orlando Cepeda (St Louis)
1968	Dennis McLain (Detroit)	Robert Gibson (St Louis)
1969	Harmon Killebrew (Minnesota)	Willie McCovey (San Francisco)
1970	John Powell (Baltimore)	Johnny Bench (Cincinnati)
1971	Vida Blue (Oakland)	Joe Torre (St Louis)
1972	Dick Allen (Chicago)	Johnny Bench (Cincinnati)
1973	Reggie Jackson (Oakland)	Pete Rose (Cincinnati)
1974	Jeffrey Burroughs (Texas)	Steve Garvey (Los Angeles)
1975	Fredric Lynn (Boston)	Joe Morgan (Cincinnati)
1976	Thurman Munson (New York)	Joe Morgan (Cincinnati)
1977	Rod Carew (Minnesota)	George Foster (Cincinnati)
1978	Jim Rice (Boston)	Dave Parker (Pittsburgh)
1979	Donald Baylor (California)	Keith Hernandez (St Louis) & Willie Stargell (Pittsburgh)
1980	George Brett (Kansas City)	Mike Schmidt (Philadelphia)
1981	Rollie Fingers (Milwaukee)	Mike Schmidt (Philadelphia)
1982	Robin Yount (Milwaukee)	Dale Murphy (Atlanta)
1983	Cal Ripken Jr (Baltimore)	Dale Murphy (Atlanta)
1984	Willie Hernandez (Detroit)	Ryne Sandberg (Chicago)
1985	Don Mattingly (New York)	Willie McGee (St Louis)
1986	Roger Clemens (Boston)	Mike Schmidt (Philadelphia)
1987	George Bell (Toronto)	Andre Dawson (Chicago)
1988	Jose Canseco (Oakland)	Kirk Gibson (Los Angeles)
1989	Robin Yount (Milwaukee)	Kevin Mitchell (San Francisco)
1990	Rickey Henderson (Oakland)	Barry Bonds (Pittsburgh)
1991	Cal Ripken Jr (Baltimore)	Terry Pendleton (Atlanta Braves)
1992	Dennis Eckersley (Oakland)	Barry Bonds (Pittsburgh)
1993	Frank Thomas (Chicago)	Barry Bonds (Pittsburgh)
1994	Frank Thomas (Chicago)	Jeff Bagwell (Houston)
1995	Mo Vaughan (Boston)	Barry Larkin (Cincinnati)
1996	Juan Gonzalez (Texas)	Ken Caminiti (San Diego)
1997	Ken Griffey Jr (Seattle)	Larry Walker (Colorado)

Most selections

American League: 3 James E Foxx (Philadelphia) 1932-3, 1938, Joe Di Maggio 1939, 1941, 1947, Berra, Mantle, Bonds

National League: 3 Stan Musial 1943, 1946, 1948, Campanella, Schmidt

Cy Young Award

Awarded from 1956 to the outstanding pitcher on the major leagues. From 1967, awards have been made for both American and National leagues.

Recent winners:

	American League	National League
1980	Steve Stone (Baltimore)	Steve Carlton (Philadelphia)
1981	Rollie Fingers (Milwaukee)	Fernando Valenzuela (Los Angeles)
1982	Pete Vukovich (Milwaukee)	Steve Carlton (Philadelphia)
1983	LaMarr Hoyt (Chicago)	John Denny (Philadelphia)
1984	Willie Hernandez (Detroit)	Rick Sutcliffe (Chicago)
1985	Bret Saberhagen (Kansas City)	Dwight Gooden (New York)
1986	Roger Clemens (Boston)	Mike Scott (Houston)
1987	Roger Clemens (Boston)	Steve Bedrosian (Philadelphia)

	American League	National League
1988	Frank Viola (Minnesota)	Orel Hershiser (Los Angeles)
1989	Bret Saberhagen (Kansas City)	Mark Davis (San Diego)
1990	Bob Welch (Oakland)	Doug Drabek (Pittsburgh)
1991	Roger Clemens (Boston)	Tom Glavine (Atlanta)
1992	Dennis Eckersley (Oakland)	Greg Maddux (Oakland)
1993	Jack McDowell (Chicago)	Greg Maddux (Atlanta)
1994	Dave Cone (Kansas City)	Greg Maddux (Atlanta)
1995	Randy Johnson (Seattle)	Greg Maddux (Atlanta)
1996	Pat Hentgen (Toronto)	John Smoltz (Atlanta)
1997	Roger Clemens (Toronto)	Pedro Martinez (Montreal)

Most wins

4 Steve Carlton (Philadelphia NL) 1972, 1977, 1980, 1982, Clemens (AL), Maddux (NL); 3 Sandy Koufax (Los Angeles AL) 1963, 1965-6, James Palmer (Baltimore AL) 1973, 1975-6, Thomas Seaver (New York NL) 1969, 1973, 1975

NCAA Championship

The College World Series for Division 1 colleges has been held annually from 1947. Since 1950 every championship final has been played at Rosenblatt Stadium, Omaha, Nebraska.
Wins:

11	Southern California	1948, 1958, 1961, 1963, 1968, 1970-4, 1978
5	Arizona State	1965*, 1967, 1969, 1977, 1981
4	Texas	1949-50, 1975, 1983
4	Louisiana State	1991, 1993, 1996-7
3	Minnesota	1956, 1960, 1964
3	Arizona	1976, 1980, 1986
3	Cal State Fullerton	1979, 1984, 1995
2	California 1947, 1957, Oklahoma 1951, 1994, Michigan 1953, 1962, Miami (Florida) 1982, 1985, Stanford 1987-8	
1	Holy Cross 1952, Missouri 1954, Wake Forest 1955, Oklahoma State 1959, Ohio State 1966, Wichita State 1989, Georgia 1990, Pepperdine 1992	

* Arizona State's match v Ohio State was not resolved until the 15th innings; Arizona won 2-1.

World Amateur Championship

Instituted 1938, and held biennially since 1974.
Winners:

21	Cuba	1939-40, 1942-3, 1950, 1952-3, 1961, 1969-73*, 1976, 1978, 1980, 1984, 1986, 1988, 1990, 1994
3	Venezuela	1941, 1944-5
2	Colombia	1947, 1965, USA 1973*-4
1	United Kingdom 1938, Dominican Republic 1948, Puerto Rico 1951, South Korea 1982	

* In 1973, Cuba and USA shared the title.

Olympic Games

American baseball has appeared at six Olympic Games as a demonstration sport. A variation of the game, Finnish baseball, was included in 1952 in Helsinki. Baseball became a medal sport for the first time in 1992.
Winners:

1912	USA	1984	Japan
1936	'World Amateurs'	1988	USA
1956	American Services team	1992	Cuba
1964	USA	1996	Cuba

Basketball

The modern game of basketball was invented by Dr James Naismith at the Training School of the International YMCA College at Springfield, Massachussets, USA in December 1891. Games bearing a resemblance to basketball have been played for thousands of years, however, the earliest being perhaps 'Pok-ta-Pok', played by the Olmecs in Mexico in the 10th century BC.

The early games of basketball had large numbers of players, but five-a-side was agreed as standard in 1895. The AAU organized the first national tournament in the USA in 1897. The first professional league was the National Basketball League (NBL), founded in 1898, but this league only lasted two seasons. The American Basketball League was formed in 1925, but declined and the NBL was refounded in 1937. This organization merged with the Basketball Association of America in 1949 to form the National Basketball Association (NBA). The sport was added to the Olympic programme in 1936.

International governing body: Fédération Internationale de Basketball Amateur (FIBA), PO Box 700607, D-81306, München, Germany. Tel: (49) 89 748 1580, Fax: (49) 89 748 1583. President: George E Killian, General Secretary: Borislav Stankovic. Founded in 1932. 202 member nations in 1998.

US governing body: National Basketball Association (NBA), Olympic Tower, 645 Fifth Avenue, New York, NY 10022, USA. Tel: (1) 212 407 8000. Commissioner: David Stern.

Olympic Games

First played by men in 1936 and by women in 1976.
Wins:

Men

11	USA	1936, 1948, 1952, 1956, 1960, 1964, 1968, 1976, 1984, 1992, 1996
2	USSR	1972, 1988
1	Yugoslavia	1980

Women

3	USSR	1976, 1980, 1992 (CIS)
3	USA	1984, 1988, 1996

World Championships

First held for men in Buenos Aires in 1950, and for women in 1953. They are each now held quadrennially.
Wins:

Men

3	USA	1954, 1986, 1994
3	USSR	1967, 1974, 1982
3	Yugoslavia	1970, 1978, 1990
2	Brazil	1959, 1963
1	Argentina	1950

Women

6	USSR	1959, 1964, 1967, 1971, 1975, 1983
6	USA	1953, 1957, 1979, 1986, 1990, 1998
1	Brazil	1994

European Championships

Contested by European nations. Held biennially.
Wins:

Men

14	USSR	1947, 1951, 1953, 1957, 1959, 1961, 1963, 1965, 1967, 1969, 1971, 1979, 1981, 1985
7	Yugoslavia	1973, 1975, 1977, 1989, 1991, 1995, 1997
2	Lithuania	1937, 1939
1	Latvia 1935, Czechoslovakia 1946, Egypt 1949, Hungary 1955, Italy 1983, Greece 1987, Germany 1993	

Women

21	USSR	1950, 1952, 1954, 1956, 1960, 1962, 1964, 1966, 1968, 1970, 1972, 1974, 1976, 1978, 1980, 1981, 1983, 1985, 1987, 1989, 1991
1	Italy 1938, Bulgaria 1958, Spain 1993, Ukraine 1995, Lithuania 1997	

European Championships for Clubs

First held as the European Champions' Cup in 1958 for men and in 1959 for women.

Wins:

Men

8	Real Madrid (Spa)	1964-5, 1967-8, 1974, 1978, 1980, 1995
5	Varese (Ita)	1970, 1972-3, 1975-6
4	CSKA Moskva (USSR)	1961, 1963, 1969, 1971
3	ASK Riga (USSR)	1958-60
3	Milan (Ita)	1966, 1987-8
3	Split (Yug)	1989-90 Jugoplastika 1991 Pop 84
2	Cantu (Ita)	1982-3
2	Maccabi Tel Aviv (Isr)	1977, 1981
2	Cibona Zagreb (Yug)	1985-6
1	Dynamo Tbilisi (USSR) 1962, Bosna Sarajevo (Yug) 1979, Banco di Roma (Ita) 1984, Partizan Belgrade (Yug) 1992, CSP Limoges (Fra) 1993, Joventut Badalona (Spa) 1994, Panathanaikos (Gre) 1996, Olympiakos Piraeus (Gre) 1997, Kinder Bologna (Ita) 1998	

Women

18	Daugava Riga (USSR)	1960-2, 1964-75, 1977, 1981-2
5	AS Vicenza (Ita)	1983, 1985-8
2	Slavia Sofia (Bul)	1959, 1963, 1984
2	Dorna Valencia (Spa)	1992-3
2	SFT Como (Ita)	1994-5
2	CJM Bourges (Fra)	1997-8
1	CKD Praha (Cs) 1976, Sesto San Giovanni (Ita) 1978, Red Star Belgrade (Yug) 1979, Turin (Ita) 1980, Levski Spartak Sofia (Bul) 1984, Jedinstvo Aida Tuzia (Yug) 1989, Enimont Priolo (Ita) 1990, Cesena (Ita) 1991, Wuppertal (Ger) 1996	

NBA

The 29 American professional teams are divided into two conferences, the Eastern, sub-divided into the Atlantic and Central Divisions, and the Western, sub-divided into the Midwest and Pacific Divisions. The best teams contest play-offs annually to determine the champions. The American Basketball Association, which had begun in 1967, merged with the NBA in 1976.

National League Champions

1938	Goodyears
1939-40	Firestones
1941-2	Oshkosh
1943-5	Fort Wayne Pistons
1946	Rochester Royals
1947	Chicago Stags
1948	Minneapolis Lakers
1949	Anderson Packers

NBA Champions

16	Boston Celtics 1957, 1959-66, 1968-9, 1974, 1976, 1981, 1984, 1986
11	Minneapolis (1947-60)/Los Angeles Lakers 1949-50, 1952-4, 1972, 1980, 1982, 1985, 1987-8

6   Chicago Bulls 1991-3, 1996-8
3   Philadelphia (1946-62)/Golden State Warriors
    1947, 1956, 1975
3   Syracuse Nationals (1949-63)/Philadelphia 76ers
    1955, 1967, 1983
2   New York Knicks 1970, 1973
2   Detroit Pistons 1989-90
2   Houston Rockets 1994-5
1   Baltimore Bullets 1948, Rochester Royals 1951,
    St Louis Hawks 1958, Milwaukee Bucks 1971,
    Portland Trail Blazers 1977, Washington Bullets
    1978, Seattle Supersonics 1979

NBA records

Highest match aggregate: 370 Detroit Pistons beat
Denver Nuggets 186-184, Denver, 13 Dec 1983
(extra time was played following a 145-145 tie in
regulation time)

Most points in game: 100 Wilt Chamberlain,
Philadelphia v New York, 2 Mar 1962
Most points in play-offs game: 63 Michael Jordan,
Chicago v Boston, 20 Apr 1986
Season's record points: 4029 Wilt Chamberlain for
Philadelphia 1962 (at a record average 50.4 points
per game)
Career record points: 38,387 Kareem Abdul-Jabbar
for Milwaukee Bucks & Los Angeles Lakers 1969-89
(in 1560 games, average 24.61 points per game, with
a record 15,837 field goals. He also scored 5762
points, including 2396 field goals, in play-off games.
Career record assists: 12,713 John Stockton for Utah
Jazz 1984-98 (av. 11.3 per game, including a record
nine seasons, 1988-96, leading NBA); 10,141 Magic
Johnson
Career record rebounds: 23,924 Wilt Chamberlain
1960-73; 21,620 Bill Russell; 17,834 Moses Malone

Leading career scorers (NBA and ABA)

Points	Name	Games	Av.	Years
38,387	Kareem Abdul-Jabbar	1560	24.6	1970-89
31,419	Wilt Chamberlain	1045	30.1	1960-73
30,026	Julius Erving	1243	24.2	1972-87
29,580	Moses Malone	1455	20.3	1975-95
29,067	Michael Jordan	930	31.3	1984-98
27,782	Karl Malone	1061	26.2	1985-98
27,482	Dan Issel	1218	22.6	1971-85
27,313	Elvin Hayes	1303	21.0	1969-84
26,710	Oscar Robertson	1040	25.7	1961-74
26,595	George Gervin	1061	25.1	1973-86
26,534	Dominique Wilkins	1047	25.3	1982-97
26,395	John Havlicek	1270	20.8	1963-78
25,466	Alex English	1184	21.5	1977-90
25,279	Rick Barry	1020	24.8	1966-80
25,192	Jerry West	932	27.0	1961-74
24,941	Artis Gilmore	1329	18.8	1972-88
24,422	Hakeem Olajuwon	1025	23.8	1984-98
23,334	Robert Parish	1611	14.5	1976-97
23,177	Adrian Dantley	955	24.3	1977-91
23,149	Elgin Baylor	846	27.4	1959-72

Other averages over 25.0 for more than 10,000 points

22,586	Larry Bird	897	25.1	1980-92
20,880	Bob Pettit	792	26.4	1955-65
15,940	David Robinson	630	25.3	1989-98

Leading career scorers in NBA play-offs to 1997

Points	Name	Games	Av.
5987	Michael Jordan	179	33.4
5762	Kareem Abdul-Jabbar	237	24.3
4457	Jerry West	153	29.1
3897	Larry Bird	164	23.8
3776	John Havlicek	172	22.0
3701	Magic Johnson	190	19.5
3691	Karl Malone	137	26.9
3674	Hakeem Olajuwan	136	27.0
3623	Elgin Baylor	134	27.0

3607	Wilt Chamberlain	160	22.5
3217	Scottie Pippen	178	18.1
3182	Kevin McHale	169	18.8
3116	Dennis Johnson	180	17.3
3088	Julius Irving	141	21.9
3022	James Worthy	143	21.1

Other averages over 25.0 for over 1500 points

2240	Bob Pettit	88	25.5
1592	George Gervin	59	27.0
1549	Shaquille O'Neal	58	26.7

NBA leading scorers each season

Based on points to 1970 and subsequently on points per game average.

Year	Name (club)	Games	Points	Av.
1950	George Mikan (Minneapolis)	68	1865	
1951	George Mikan (Minneapolis)	68	1932	
1952	Paul Arizin (Philadelphia)	66	1674	
1953	Neil Johnston (Philadelphia)	70	1564	
1954	Neil Johnston (Philadelphia)	72	1759	
1955	Neil Johnston (Philadelphia)	72	1631	
1956	Bob Pettit (St Louis)	72	1849	
1957	Paul Arizin (Philadelphia)	71	1817	
1958	George Yardley (Detroit)	72	2001	
1959	Bob Pettit (St Louis)	72	2105	
1960	Wilt Chamberlain (Philadelphia)	72	2707	
1961	Wilt Chamberlain (Philadelphia)	79	3033	
1962	Wilt Chamberlain (Philadelphia)	80	4029	
1963	Wilt Chamberlain (San Francisco)	80	3586	
1964	Wilt Chamberlain (San Francisco)	80	2948	
1965	Wilt Chamberlain (SF/Philadelphia)	80	2534	
1966	Wilt Chamberlain (Philadelphia)	79	2649	
1967	Rick Barry (San Francisco)	78	2775	
1968	Dave Bing (Detroit)	79	2142	
1969	Elvin Hayes (San Diego)	82	2327	
1970	Jerry West (Los Angeles)	74	2309	31.2
1971	Lew Alcindor★ (Milwaukee)	82	2596	31.7
1972	Kareem Abdul-Jabbar (Milw'kee)	81	2822	34.8
1973	Nate Archibald (Kansas City/Omaha)	80	2719	34.0
1974	Bob McAdoo (Buffalo)	74	2261	30.6
1975	Bob McAdoo (Buffalo)	82	2831	34.5
1976	Bob McAdoo (Buffalo)	78	2427	31.1
1977	Pete Maravich (New Orleans)	73	2273	31.1
1978	George Gervin (San Antonio)	82	2232	27.2
1979	George Gervin (San Antonio)	80	2365	29.6
1980	George Gervin (San Antonio)	78	2585	33.1
1981	Adrian Dantley (Utah)	80	2452	30.7
1982	George Gervin (San Antonio)	79	2551	32.3
1983	Alex English (Denver)	82	2326	28.4
1984	Adrian Dantley (Utah)	79	2418	30.6
1985	Bernard King (New York)	55	1809	32.9
1986	Dominique Wilkins (Atlanta)	78	2366	30.3
1987	Michael Jordan (Chicago)	82	3041	37.1
1988	Michael Jordan (Chicago)	82	2868	35.0
1989	Michael Jordan (Chicago)	81	2633	32.5
1990	Michael Jordan (Chicago)	82	2753	33.6
1991	Michael Jordan (Chicago)	82	2580	31.5
1992	Michael Jordan (Chicago)	80	2404	30.1
1993	Michael Jordan (Chicago)	78	2541	32.6

1994	David Robinson (San Antonio)	80	2383	29.8
1995	Shaquille O'Neal (Orlando)	79	2315	29.3
1996	Michael Jordan (Chicago)	82	2491	30.4
1997	Michael Jordan (Chicago)	82	2431	29.6
1998	Michael Jordan (Chicago)	82	2357	28.7

★ Took name of Kareem Abdul-Jabbar from 1971/2 season.

Highest-scoring runners-up:

1963	Elgin Baylor (Los Angeles)	80	2719
1990	Karl Malone (Utah Jazz)	82	2540
1961	Elgin Baylor (Los Angeles)	73	2538
1982	Moses Malone (Houston)	81	2520

Most seasons leading

10 Michael Jordan; 7 Wilt Chamberlain; 3 Neil Johnston, Bob McAdoo

Most seasons over 2000 points

Years shown are those of second half of the season.

11	Michael Jordan	1985, 1987-93, 1996-8
11	Karl Malone	1988-98
9	Kareem Abdul-Jabbar	1970-4, 1976-7, 1980-1
8	Alex English	1982-9
8	Dominique Wilkins	1985-91, 1993
7	Wilt Chamberlain	1960-6
7	Oscar Robertson	1961-7
6	George Gervin	1978-83

NBA Most Valuable Player

Voted annually by NBA players from 1956 for the Maurice Podoloff Trophy, named after the first commissioner of the NBA, 1946-63.

1956	Bob Pettit (St Louis)
1957	Bob Cousy (Boston)
1958	Bill Russell (Boston)
1959	Bob Pettit (St Louis)
1960	Wilt Chamberlain (Philadelphia)
1961-3	Bill Russell (Boston)
1964	Oscar Robertson (Cincinnati)
1965	Bill Russell (Boston)
1966-8	Wilt Chamberlain (Philadelphia)
1969	Wes Unseld (Baltimore)
1970	Willis Reed (New York)
1971-2	Kareem Abdul-Jabbar★ (Milwaukee)
1973	Dave Cowens (Boston)
1974	Kareem Abdul-Jabbar (Milwaukee)
1975	Bob McAdoo (Buffalo)
1976-7	Kareem Abdul-Jabbar (Los Angeles)
1978	Bill Walton (Portland)
1979	Moses Malone (Houston)
1980	Kareem Abdul-Jabbar (Los Angeles)
1981	Julius Erving (Philadelphia)
1982	Moses Malone (Houston)
1983	Moses Malone (Philadelphia)
1984-6	Larry Bird (Boston)
1987	Earvin 'Magic' Johnson (Los Angeles)
1988	Michael Jordan (Chicago)
1989-90	Earvin 'Magic' Johnson (Los Angeles)
1991-2	Michael Jordan (Chicago)
1993	Charles Barkley (Phoenix)
1994	Hakeem Olajuwon (Houston Rockets)
1995	David Robinson (San Antonio)
1996	Michael Jordan (Chicago)
1997	Karl Malone (Utah)
1998	Michael Jordan (Chicago)

Most wins: 6 Kareem Abdul-Jabbar★; 5 Bill Russell, Michael Jordan; 4 Wilt Chamberlain; 3 Moses Malone, Larry Bird, 'Magic' Johnson

★ Still known as Lew Alcindor in 1971.

NCAA

NCAA Championships

First contested in 1939; run under the auspices of the National Collegiate Athletic Association.

Division I wins:

11	UCLA	1964-5, 1967-73, 1975, 1995
7	Kentucky	1948-9, 1951, 1958, 1978, 1996, 1998
5	Indiana	1940, 1953, 1976, 1981, 1987
3	North Carolina	1957, 1982, 1993
2	Oklahoma A&M	1945-6
2	Kansas	1952, 1988
2	San Francisco	1955-6
2	Cincinnati	1961-2
2	North Carolina State	1974, 1983
2	Louisville	1980, 1986
2	Duke	1991-2
1	Oregon 1939, Wisconsin 1941, Stanford 1942, Wyoming 1943, Utah 1944, Holy Cross 1947, City College of New York 1950, LaSalle 1954, California 1959, Ohio State 1960, Loyola (Ill) 1963, Texas Western 1966, Marquette 1977, Michigan State 1979, Georgetown 1984, Villanova 1985, Michigan 1989, Nevada – Las Vegas 1990, Arkansas 1994, Arizona 1997	

Most Valuable Player in the NCAA final three times: Lew Alcindor of UCLA 1967-9. He subsequently changed his name to Kareem Abdul-Jabbar.

Highest match aggregate: 399 Troy State (258) beat De Vry Institute, Atlanta (141) at Troy 12 Jan 1992

Most points in game: 113 Clarence 'Bevo' Francis for Rio Grande v Hillsdale on 2 Feb 1954 (Div II)

NCAA Division I career scoring average leaders

Points	Name (College)	Games	Av.	Years
3667	Pete Maravich★ (LSU)	83	44.2	1968-70
2560	Austin Carr (Notre Dame)	74	34.6	1969-71
2973	Oscar Robertson (Cincinnati)	88	33.8	1958-60
2548	Calvin Murphy (Niagara)	77	33.1	1968-70
Scoring over 3200 points in four years:				
3249	Freeman Williams (Portland St)	106	30.7	1975-8
3217	Lionel Simmons (La Salle)	131	24.6	1987-90

★ Maravich averaged over 40 points per game in each season of his college career: 1968 – 1138 pts av.43.8, 1969 – 1148 pts av.44.2, 1970 – 1381 pts av.44.5.

In Division II, Travis Grant scored a record 4045 points (av. 33.4) in 121 games for Kentucky State 1969-72.

NCAA Women's Championship

First contested 1982.

Division I winners:

6	Tennessee	1987, 1989, 1991, 1996-8
2	Louisiana Tech	1982, 1988
2	Southern California	1983-4
2	Stanford	1990, 1992
1	Old Dominion 1985, Texas 1986, Texas Tech 1993, North Carolina 1994, Connecticut 1995	

Highest match aggregate: 261 St Joseph's (Indiana) beat Northern Kentucky 131-130 on 27 Feb 1988

Biathlon

Combined cross-country skiing and rifle shooting. Competitors ski (freestyle) over prepared courses carrying a 22-calibre rifle weighing 4.54kg. Men compete individually over 10km or 20km distances. During the former they have two shooting competitions and in the latter four, prone and standing, at a target 50 metres away. The relay event is 4 x 7.5km, each member shooting once prone and once standing. Penalties are imposed for missing the target. The women's equivalent distances are now 7.5km, 15km, and their relay is 4 x 7.5km.

International governing body: International Biathlon Union, Airportcenter, Postfach 1, A-5071 Wals-Himmelreich, Austria. President: Anders Besseberg, Secretary General: Peter Bayer. 57 member nations in 1998.

Umbrella organization: L'Union Internationale de Pentathlon Moderne et Biathlon (UIPMB), Stade Louis II Entrée E, 13 avenue des Casrelans, MC 98000, Monaco. The UIPMB took on the administration of biathlon in 1957, and staged the first world championships the following year.

Olympic Games

Men's biathlon has been on the Olympic programme since 1960. Women's events were added in 1992.

Winners:

Men

10 kilometres

1980	Frank Ullrich (GDR)
1984	Eirik Kvalfoss (Nor)
1988	Frank-Peter Rötsch (GDR)
1992	Mark Kirchner (Ger)
1994	Sergey Chepikov (Rus)
1998	Ole Einar Björndalen (Nor)

20 kilometres

1960	Klas Lestander (Swe)
1964	Vladimir Melanin (USSR)
1968	Magnar Solberg (Nor)
1972	Magnar Solberg (Nor)
1976	Nikolay Kruglov (USSR)
1980	Anatoliy Alyabyev (USSR)
1984	Peter Angerer (FRG)
1988	Frank-Peter Rötsch (GDR)
1992	Yevgeniy Redkin (CIS)
1994	Sergey Tarasov (Rus)
1998	Halvard Hanevold (Nor)

4 x 7.5 kilometres relay

USSR	1968, 1972, 1976, 1980, 1984, 1988
Germany	1992, 1994, 1998

Most gold medals: 4 Aleksandr Tikhonov (USSR) relay 1968, 1972, 1976, 1980

Most medals: 5 Aleksandr Tikhonov 4 relay gold, 20km silver 1968, Peter Angerer (FRG) gold 20km 1980; silver 10km 1984, relay 1988; bronze relay 1980, 1984

Women

7.5 kilometres

1992	Anfisa Restzova (CIS)
1994	Myriam Bédard (Can)
1998	Galina Kukleva (Rus)

15 kilometres

1992	Antje Misersky (Ger)
1994	Myriam Bédard (Can)
1998	Yekaterina Dafovska (Bul)

3 x 7.5 kilometres relay

1992	France

4 x 7.5 kilometres relay

1994	Russia
1998	Germany

Most individual gold medals: 2 Myriam Bédard (Can) 7.5km & 15km 1994

Most medals: 3 Myriam Bédard (Can) two gold 1994, bronze 15km 1992, Antje Misersky

(Ger) gold 15km 1992, silver
7.5km & relay 1992, Anfisa
Restzova (Rus) gold 7.5km
1992, relay 1994; bronze relay
1992

World Championships

Held annually from 1958 for men
and 1984 for women, except in
Olympic years.
Winners:

Men

20 kilometres

1958	Adolf Wiklund (Swe)
1959	Vladimir Melanin (USSR)
1961	Kalevi Huuskonen (Fin)
1962	Vladimir Melanin (USSR)
1963	Vladimir Melanin (USSR)
1965	Olav Jordet (Nor)
1966	Jon Istad (Nor)
1967	Viktor Mamatov (USSR)
1969	Aleksandr Tikhonov (USSR)
1970	Aleksandr Tikhonov (USSR)
1971	Dieter Speer (GDR)
1973	Aleksandr Tikhonov (USSR)
1974	Juhani Suutarinen (Fin)
1975	Heikki Ikola (Fin)
1977	Heikki Ikola (Fin)
1978	Odd Lirhus (Nor)
1979	Klaus Siebert (GDR)
1981	Heikki Ikola (Fin)
1982	Frank Ullrich (GDR)
1983	Frank Ullrich (GDR)
1985	Yuriy Kashkarov (USSR)
1986	Valeriy Medvetsev (USSR)
1987	Frank-Peter Rötsch (GDR)
1989	Eirik Kvalfoss (Nor)
1990	Valeriy Medvetsev (USSR)
1991	Mark Kirchner (Ger)
1993	Andreas Zingerle (Ita)
1995	Tomas Sykora (Pol)
1996	Sergey Tarasov (Rus)
1997	Ricco Gross (Ger)

10 kilometres

1974	Juhani Suutarinen (Fin)
1975	Nikolay Kruglov (USSR)
1976-7	Aleksandr Tikhonov (USSR)
1978	Frank Ullrich (GDR)
1979	Frank Ullrich (GDR)

1981	Frank Ullrich (GDR)
1982	Eirik Kvalfoss (Nor)
1983	Eirik Kvalfoss (Nor)
1985	Frank-Peter Rötsch (GDR)
1986	Valeriy Medvetsev (USSR)
1987	Frank-Peter Rötsch (GDR)
1989	Frank Luck (GDR)
1990	Mark Kirchner (GDR)
1991	Mark Kirchner (Ger)
1993	Mark Kirchner (Ger)
1995	Patrice Bailly-Salins (Fra)
1996	Vladimir Drachev (Rus)
1997	Wilfried Pallhuber (Ita)

12.5 kilometres pursuit

1997	Viktor Maygurov (Rus)

4 x 7.5 kilometres relay

9	USSR	1969-71, 1973-4, 1977, 1983, 1985-6
6	GDR	1978-9, 1981-2, 1987, 1989
3	Norway	1965-7
3	Germany	1991, 1995, 1997
2	Italy	1990, 1993
1	Finland 1975, Russia 1996	

Team
(20km to 1994, 10km from 1995)

6	USSR/CIS 1959, 1962-3, 1989, 1992-3	
2	Norway	1965, 1995
2	Italy	1991, 1994
2	Belarus	1996-7
1	Sweden 1958, Finland 1961, GDR 1990, Germany 1993	

Women

5 kilometres

1984	Venera Chernyshova (USSR)
1985	Sanna Grönlid (Nor)
1986	Kaya Parve (USSR)
1987	Yelena Golovina (USSR)
1988	Petra Schaaf (FRG)

7.5 kilometres

1989	Anne-Elinor Elvebakk (Nor)
1990	Anne-Elinor Elvebakk (Nor)
1991	Grete Ingeborg Nykkelmo (Nor)
1993	Myriam Bédard (Can)
1995	Anne Briand (Fra)
1996-7	Olga Romasko (Rus)

10 kilometres

1984	Venera Chernyshova (USSR)
1985	Kaya Parve (USSR)
1986	Eva Korpela (Swe)
1987	Sanna Grönlid (Nor)
1988	Anne-Elinor Elvebakk (Nor)

15 kilometres

1989	Petra Schaaf (FRG)
1990	Svetlana Davydova (USSR)
1991	Petra Schaaf (Ger)
1993	Petra Schaaf (Ger)
1995	Corinne Niogret (Fra)
1996	Emmanuelle Claret (Fra)
1997	Magdalena Forsberg-Wallin (Swe)

10 kilometres pursuit

1997	Magdalena Forsberg-Wallin (Swe)

Relay
(3 x 5km 1984-9, 3 x 7.5km 1990-1, 4 x 7.5km 1993-7)

7	USSR	1984-91
3	Germany	1995-7
1	Czech Republic 1993	

Team
(15km to 1993, 7.5km from 1995)

3	USSR	1989-91
3	Germany	1992, 1995-6
2	Norway	1995, 1997
1	France 1993, Belarus 1994	

Most World and Olympic titles

Men (individual/relay): 15
Aleksandr Tikhonov (USSR)
(5/10) 1968-80; 10 Frank Ullrich
(GDR) (6/4) 1978-83;
7 Vladimir Melanin (USSR)
(4/3) 1959-64
Women: 6 Kaya Parve (USSR)
(2/4) 1984-8

World Cup

Contested at 10km and 20km over
a series of five events during each
winter.
Winners:

Men

1978	Frank Ullrich (GDR)
1979	Klaus Siebert (GDR)
1980-2	Frank Ullrich (GDR)
1983	Peter Angerer (FRG)
1984-5	Frank-Peter Rötsch (GDR)

1986	André Sehmisch (GDR)			
1987	Frank-Peter Rötsch (GDR)			
1988	Fritz Fischer (GDR)			
1989	Eirik Kvalfoss (Nor)			
1990-1	Sergey Chepikov (USSR)			
1992	Jon–Åge Tyldum (Nor)			
1993	Mikael Löfgren (Swe)			
1994	Patrice Bailly-Salins (Fra)			
1995	Jon–Åge Tyldum (Nor)			
1996	Vladimir Drachev (Rus)			
1997	Sven Fischer (Ger)			
1998	Ole Einar Björndalen (Nor)			

Women (7.5 kilometres and 15 kilometres)

1988	Anne-Elinor Elvebakk (Nor)
1989	Yelena Golovina (USSR)
1990	Jirina Adamicková (Cs)
1991	Svetlana Davydova (USSR)
1992-3	Anfisa Restzova (Rus)
1994	Svetlana Paramygina (Blr)
1995	Anne Briand (Fra)
1996	Emmanuelle Claret (Fra)
1997-8	Magdalena Forsberg-Wallin (Swe)

Nations Cup

Men

Official from 1987.

5	Germany	FRG 1988, Ger 1993-4, 1997-8
2	GDR	1987, 1989
2	Italy	1991, 1992
1	USSR 1990, Norway 1992, Russia 1996	

Women

Official from 1989.

4	Germany	1991, 1994, 1997-8
3	France	1993, 1995-6
2	Norway	1989, 1992
1	USSR 1990, Russia 1997	

Billiards

The earliest-known reference to billiards, which is related to the outdoor game of *paille-malle* (or pall mall), played on grass, was in 1429 in France. Louis XI, King of France (1461-83), is believed to have had a billiard table. The game became popular in Britain in the 19th century and the Billiards Association was formed and drew up a code of rules in 1885. The BA amalgamated with the Billiards Control Club (formed in 1908) in 1919, to form the Billiards Association and Control Council (BACC), later the Billiards and Snooker Control Council.

International governing body (for all cue sports): The World Confederation of Billiard Sports (WCBS), PO Box 1089, Jalan Semangat 46870, Petaling Jaya, Malaysia. Tel: (60) 776 1175, Fax: (60) 777 1618. President: Jörgen Sandman, Secretary General: W Y Chin. Founded 1992. The WCBS has three divisions:

1. World Pool Association (WPA). Tel: 010 43 641 2763520, Fax: 010 43 641 2763615. President: Jorgen Sandeman;
2. World Snooker Federation (WSF), 27 Oakfield Road, Bristol, BS8 2AT, UK. Tel: 0117 974 4491, Fax: 0117 974 4931. The WSF comprises, for the professional game, the World Professional Billiards and Snooker Association (WPBSA), address as above. Chairman: Rex Williams. Founded 1982. For the amateur game: the International Billiards and Snooker Federation (IBSF), 82 Meyer Road, Singapore 437909. Tel: (65) 3441197. Chairman: Manmohanjit Singh, Secretary: Gloria Ruane, House of Sport, Long Mile Road, Dublin 12, Ireland. Tel: (353) 1 4509850, Fax: (353) 1 4502805. For the women's game: the World Ladies' Billiards and Snooker Association (WLBSA), 66 The Crescent, Horley, Surrey RH6 7NU, UK. Tel: 01293 507273, Fax: 01293 545349. Secretary: Jane O'Neill.
3. (for Carom games) Union Mondiale de Billiard (UMB), Av. de Rhodanie 2, Lausanne, Switzerland.

World Professional Championships

First held in 1870, the championship was organized on a challenge basis until 1909. From 1909 it was run on a knock-out basis under Billiard Control Club rules, until becoming dormant in 1934. It was revived on a challenge basis in 1951. In 1980 it was restored to a tournament event and, since 1982, has been held annually.

Winners:

1870	William Cook (Eng)
1870	John Roberts, Jnr (Eng)
1870	Joseph Bennett (Eng)
1871	John Roberts, Jnr (Eng)
1871	William Cook (Eng)
1875	John Roberts, Jnr (Eng)
1880	Joseph Bennett (Eng)
1885	John Roberts, Jnr (Eng)
1889	Charles Dawson (Eng)
1901	H W Stevenson (Eng)
1901	Charles Dawson (Eng)
1901	H W Stevenson (Eng)
1903	Charles Dawson (Eng)
1908	Melbourne Inman (Eng)
1909-11	H W Stevenson (Eng)
1912-4	Melbourne Inman (Eng)
1919	Melbourne Inman (Eng)
1920	Willie Smith (Eng)
1921-2	Tom Newman (Eng)
1923	Willie Smith (Eng)
1924-7	Tom Newman (Eng)
1928-30	Joe Davis (Eng)
1931	Not held
1932	Joe Davis (Eng)
1933-4	Walter Lindrum (Aus)
1951	Clark McConachy (NZ)
1968	Rex Williams (Eng)
1971	Leslie Driffield (Eng)
1971	Rex Williams (Eng)
1980	Fred Davis (Eng)
1982	Rex Williams (Eng)
1983	Rex Williams (Eng)
1984	Mark Wildman (Eng)
1985	Ray Edmonds (Eng)
1986	Robbie Foldvari (Aus)
1987-8	Norman Dagley (Eng)
1989	Mike Russell (Eng)

1990	Not held	1935	Horace Coles (Wal)	1979	Rex Williams
1991	Mike Russell (Eng)	1936	Robert Marshall (Aus)	1980	Jack Karnehm
1992-3	Geet Sethi (Ind)	1938	Robert Marshall (Aus)	1981	Rex Williams
1994	Peter Gilchrist (Eng)	1951	Robert Marshall (Aus)	1983	Mark Wildman
1995	Geet Sethi (Ind)	1952	Leslie Driffield (Eng)	1987	Norman Dagley
1996	Mike Russell (Eng)	1954	Tom Cleary (Aus)	1988	Ian Williamson

Most wins: pre-1909, John Roberts, Jr made 8 successful defences of his title 1870-85; post-1909, 7 Rex Williams 1968-76 (including 5 successful challenges); Tom Newman won a record 6 titles under knock-out conditions, 1921-7

1958	Wilson Jones (Ind)
1960	Herbert Beetham (Eng)
1962	Robert Marshall (Aus)
1964	Wilson Jones (Ind)
1967	Leslie Driffield (Eng)
1969	Jack Karnehm (Eng)
1971	Norman Dagley (Eng)
1973	Mohammed Lafir (Sri)
1975	Norman Dagley (Eng)
1977	Michael Ferreira (Ind)
1979	Paul Mifsud (Malta)
1981	Michael Ferreira (Ind)
1983	Michael Ferreira (Ind)
1985	Geet Sethi (Ind)
1987	Geet Sethi (Ind)
1990	Manoj Kothari (Ind)
1997	Joe Grech (Mlt)

1979	Rex Williams
1980	Jack Karnehm
1981	Rex Williams
1983	Mark Wildman
1987	Norman Dagley
1988	Ian Williamson
1989-91	Mike Russell
1992-3	Robbie Foldvari (Aus)
1994	Mike Russell
1995	Subhash Agarwal (Ind)
1996-7	Mike Russell
1997	Geet Sethi (Ind)
(Nov)	

Most wins: 7 Joe Davis

World Matchplay Championship

Winners:

1990	Mike Russell (Eng)
1996	Mike Russell (Eng)
1997	Robbie Feldvari (Aus)
1998	Mike Russell (Eng)

World Amateur Championships

Inaugurated in 1926, generally held on a biennial basis to 1938 and, from 1951 to 1990, organized by the International Billiards and Snooker Federation (IBSF). Held again in 1997, when it was played under amateur rules and also open to professionals ranked ninth and below on the WPBSA list.

Winners:

1926	Joe Earlham (Eng)
1927	Allan Prior (SAf)
1929	Les Hayes (Aus)
1931	Laurie Steeples (Eng)
1933	Sydney Lee (Eng)

Most wins: 4 Marshall

United Kingdom Professional Championships

Instituted in 1934, but discontinued in 1951. It was revived from 1979 to 1983, when it was taken off the professional calender. It was revived again in 1987.

Winners:

1934-9	Joe Davis
1946	John Barrie
1947	Joe Davis
1948	Sidney Smith
1950	John Barrie
1951	Fred Davis

Record Breaks

Highest break including the now outlawed cradle cannon: 499,135 Tom Reece 3 Jun-6 Jul 1907

Highest certified break using the anchor cannon: 42,746 William Cook 29 May-7 Jun 1907

Official world record break (since introduction of the 25-hazard rule in 1926): 4137 Walter Lindrum 1932

Highest break under the baulk-line rule: 1784 Joe Davis 29 May 1936

Highest official break in amateur competition: 1149 Michael Ferreira 15 Dec 1978

Highest break under current 'two pot' rule: 962 (unfinished) Michael Ferreira 29 Apr 1986

Highest break under 100 point baulk-line rule: (strictest ever): 713 Mike Russell 1 Mar 1996

Three-Cushion Billiards

Played on a table without pockets, this variation of billiards, popular in the USA and Europe, dates back to 1878. The governing body, the Union Mondiale de Billard (UMB), was formed in 1928. The lack of pockets makes this a 'cannons-only' game, but there are several variations that demand a high level of skill. In Europe is it known as Carom.

The greatest American exponent, Willie Hoppe, won a total of 51 three-cushion championships throughout the USA.

UMB World Three-Cushion Billiards Championships

First held in 1928, annually to 1938, then in 1948, 1952-3, 1958 and annually from 1960. From 1988 the World Cup winner over a series of events has been declared the champion. Raymond Ceulemans (Bel) won a record 20 world titles: 1963-73, 1975-80, 1983, 1985, 1990.

World champions since 1963:

1974	Nobuaki Kobayashi (Jap)
1975-80	Raymond Ceulemans (Bel)
1981	Ludo Dielis (Bel)
1982	Rini van Bracht (Hol)
1983	Raymond Ceulemans (Bel)

1984	Nobuaki Kobayashi (Jap)
1985	Raymond Ceulemans (Bel)
1986	Avelino Rico (Spa)
1987-8	Torbjörn Blomdahl (Swe)
1989	Ludo Dielis (Bel)
1990	Raymond Ceulemans (Bel)
1991-2	Torbjörn Blomdahl (Swe)
1992/3	Sang Chun Lee (USA)
1993/4	Torbjörn Blomdahl (Swe)
1994	Rini van Bracht (Hol)
1995	Jozef Philipoom (Bel)
1996	Christian Rudolph (Ger)
1997	Torbjörn Blomdahl (Swe)

Nine-Ball Pool

World Pool-Billiard Association (WPA) World
Championships were inaugurated in 1990.

Winners:

Men

1990-1	Earl Strickland (USA)
1992	Johnny Archer (USA)
1993	Chao Fong-Pang (Tai)
1994	Takeshi Okumura (Jap)
1995	Oliver Ortmann (Ger)
1996	Ralf Souquet (Ger)
1997	Johnny Archer (USA)

Women

1990-1	Robin Bell (USA)
1992	Franziska Stark (Ger)
1993	Lori Jon Jones (USA)
1994	Ewa Mataya-Laurence (USA)
1995	Gerda Hofstatter (Aut)
1996-7	Allison Fisher (Eng)

Bobsleigh and Toboganning

The first-known bobsleigh races were run by British enthusiasts in Switzerland in the 1880s, when improvements were made to sleighs to make them go faster. Luge races had been held a few years earlier, and two special luge runs were constructed at Davos, Switzerland in 1879. The earliest-known sledge is dated *c.*6500BC, and was found at Heinola, Finland.

The first purpose-built bobsleigh run was constructed at St Moritz in Switzerland in 1902. There are now Olympic bobsleigh events for two- and four-man teams, who sit in the bob. Skeleton one-man toboggans, in which the riders lie face down, are used on the Cresta Run at St Moritz, which dates from 1884. There was an Olympic event for them in 1924 and 1948, but this form of tobogganing has been superseded in the Olympics by Luge Tobogganing, in which the rider sits up or lies back.

Bobsleigh runs are between 1100m and 1600m in length. The two-man bob has a maximum length of 2.7m and a maximum weight (bob and crew) of 390kg; for a four-man bob the maxima are 3.8m and 630kg; luges are 1.28–1.35m in length, and the maximum weight of the luge is 23kg for a single-seater, or 27kg for a two-seater. Luge runs are over a minimum of 1000m.

Women are not permitted in international bobsleigh events, but they do contest single-seater Luge races; this has been an Olympic event since 1964.

International governing bodies: Fédération Internationale de Bobsleigh et de Tobogganing (FIBT), Via Piranese 44/b, I-20137 Milano, Italy. Tel: (39) 2 757 3319, Fax: (39) 2 738 0624. President: Robert H Storey, General Secretary: Ermano Gardella. Founded 1923.

Luge Tobogganing originally came under the auspices of the FIBT, but from 1957 has had its own governing body: Fédération Internationale de Luge de Course (FIL), Rathausplatz 9, D-83471 Berchtesgaden, Germany. Tel: (49) 8652 66960, Fax: (49) 8652 66969. President: Josef Fendt, Executive Director: Hartmut Kardaetz.

Bobsleigh

Olympic Games

A bob competition for four-man sleds was first held in 1924. The two-man event was introduced in 1932, and both events have been staged at each subsequent Games except for those of 1960, when no run was built at Squaw Valley. *Winners:*

Two-man bob

1932	Hubert Stevens & Curtis Stevens (USA)
1936	Ivan Brown & Alan Washbond (USA)
1948	Felix Endrich & Friedrich Waller (Swi)
1952	Andreas Ostler & Lorenz Nieberl (FRG)
1956	Lamberto Dalla Costa & Giacomo Conti (Ita)
1964	Tony Nash & Robin Dixon (UK)
1968	Eugenio Monti & Luciano de Paolis (Ita)
1972	Wolfgang Zimmerer & Peter Utzschneider (FRG)
1976	Meinhard Nehmer & Bernhard Germeshausen (GDR)
1980	Erich Schärer & Josef Benz (Swi)
1984	Wolfgang Hoppe & Dietmar Schauerhammer (GDR)
1988	Janis Kipurs & Vladimir Kozlov (USSR)

1992	Gustav Weder & Donad Acklin (Swi)
1994	Gustav Weder & Donad Acklin (Swi)
1998	Günther Huber & Antomie Tartaglia (Ita) & Pierre Lueders & David MacEachern (Can)

Four-man bob

1924	Switzerland
1928	USA
1932	USA
1936	Switzerland
1948	USA
1952	Germany (FRG)
1956	Switzerland
1964	Canada
1968	Italy
1972	Switzerland
1976	GDR
1980	GDR
1984	GDR
1988	Switzerland
1992	Austria
1994	Germany
1998	Germany

Skeleton bob

| 1928 | Jennison Heaton (USA) |
| 1948 | Nino Bibbia (Ita) |

Most gold medals

3 Meinhard Nehmer & Bernhard Germeshausen (GDR) two-man 1976, four-man 1976 and 1980

Most medals

7 Bogdan Musiol (GDR) gold four-man 1980, 5 silver two-man 1984, 1988; four-man 1984, 1988, 1992; bronze two-man 1980; 6 Eugenio Monti (Ita) 2 gold 1968, 2 silver 1956, 2 bronze 1964

World Championships

Held annually from 1930 for the four-man bob and 1931 for the two-man bob. The Olympic events (qv) are the World Championships in those years.
Winners:

Two-man bob

1931	Hanns Killian & Sebastian Huber (Ger)
1933	Alexandru Papana & Dumitru Hubert (Rom)
1934	Alexandru Frim & Vasile Dumitrescu (Rom)
1935	Reto Capadrutt & Emil Diener (Swi)
1937	Freddie McEvoy & B H Black (UK)
1938	Bibo Fischer & Rolf Thielacke (Ger)
1939	René Lundnen & J Kuffer (Bel)
1947	Fritz Feierabend & Stephan Waser (Swi)
1949	Felix Endrich & Friedrich Waller (Swi)
1950	Fritz Feierabend & Stephan Waser (Swi)
1951	Andreas Osterl & Lorenz Nieberl (FRG)
1953	Felix Endrich & Fritz Stoeckli (Swi)
1954	Guglielmo Scheibmeier & Andrea Zambelli (Ita)

1955	Fritz Feierabend & Harry Warburton (Swi)
1957-60	Eugenio Monti & Renzo Alverà (Ita)
1961	Eugenio Monti & Sergio Siorpaes (Ita)
1962	Rinaldo Ruatti & Enrico De Lorenzo (Ita)
1963	Eugenio Monti & Sergio Siorpaes (Ita)
1965	Tony Nash & Robin Dixon (UK)
1966	Eugenio Monti & Sergio Siorpaes (Ita)
1967	Erwin Thaler & Reinhold Durnthaler (Aut)
1969	Nevio de Zordo & Adriano Frassinelli (Ita)
1970	Horst Floth & Pepi Bader (FRG)
1971	Gianfranco Gaspari & Mario Armano (Ita)
1973-4	Wolfgang Zimmerer & Peter Utzschneider (FRG)
1975	Giorgio Alverà & Franco Perruquet (Ita)
1977	Hans Hiltebrand & Heinz Meier (Swi)
1978-9	Erich Schärer & Josef Benz (Swi)
1981	Bernhard Germeshausen & Hans-Jürgen Gerhardt (GDR)
1982	Erich Schärer & Josef Benz (Swi)
1983	Ralf Pichler & Urs Leuthold (Swi)
1985-6	Wolfgang Hoppe & Dietmar Schauerhammer (GDR)
1987	Ralf Pichler & Celest Poltera (Swi)
1989	Wolfgang Hoppe & Bogdan Musiol (GDR)
1990	Gustav Weder & Bruno Gerber (Swi)
1991	Rudi Lochner & Markus Zimmermann (Ger)
1993	Christoph Langen & Peer Jöchel (Ger)
1995	Christoph Langen & Olaf Hempel (Ger)
1996	Christoph Langen & Markus Zimmermann (Ger)
1997	Reto Götschi & Guido Acklin (Swi)

Four-man bob

Not decided in 1966, due to a fatal accident, nor in 1967, because of a thaw.

Most wins:

15	Switzerland	1939, 1947, 1954-5, 1957, 1971, 1973, 1975, 1982-3, 1986-7, 1989-90, 1993
6	F R Germany	1951, 1958, 1962, 1969, 1974, 1979
6	Germany	1931, 1934-5, 1991, 1995-7
5	Italy	1930, 1960, 1961, 1963, 1970
4	USA	1949-50, 1953, 1959
4	GDR	1977-8, 1981, 1985
2	United Kingdom	1937-8
1	Canada	1965

Most World and Olympic titles

(two-man/four-man)

11	Eugenio Monti (Ita) 8/3
8	Wolfgang Hoppe (GDR/Ger) 4/4
7	Erich Schärer (Swi) 4/3
6	Fritz Feierabend (Swi) 3/3
6	Bernhard Germeshausen (GDR) 2/4

World Cup

First held over a series of events in 1984/5 at two-man and four-man, with an overall title as well.
Winners:

Two-man		Four-man		Combined	
1985	Anton Fischer (FRG)	1985	Jeffrey Jost (USA)	1985	Anton Fischer (FRG)
1986	Maris Poikans (USSR)	1986	Ekkehard Fasser (Swi)	1986	Ekkehard Fasser (Swi)
1987	Anton Fischer (FRG)	1987	Matt Roy (USA)	1987	Matt Roy (USA)
1988	Janis Kipurs (USSR)	1988-9	Ingo Appelt (Aut)	1988	Ingo Appelt (Aut)
1989	Gustav Weder (Swi)	1990	Chris Lori (Can)	1989	Gustav Weder (Swi)
1990	Christian Schebitz (FRG)	1991	Gustav Weder (Swi)	1990	Maris Poikans (USSR)
1991	Wolfgang Hoppe (Ger)	1992	Wolfgang Hoppe (Ger)	1991	Gustav Weder (Swi)
1992-3	Günther Huber (Ita)	1993	Brian Shimer (USA)	1992	Wolfgang Hoppe (Ger)
1994-5	Pierre Lueders (Can)	1994	Hubert Schösser (Swi)	1993	Brian Shimer (USA)
1996	Christoph Langen (Ger)	1994-5	Pierre Lueders (Can)	1994-5	Pierre Lueders (Can)
1997-8	Pierre Lueders (Can)	1996	Wolfgang Hoppe (Ger)	1996	Christoph Langen (Ger)
		1997	Marcel Rohner (Swi)	1997	Günther Huber (Ita)
		1998	Harald Czudaj (Ger)	1998	Pierre Lueders (Can)

Luge Toboganning

Olympic Games

Single-seater

	Men	Women
1964	Thomas Köhler (GDR)	Ortrun Enderlein (GDR)
1968	Manfred Schmid (Aut)	Erica Lechner (Ita)
1972	Wolfgang Scheidel (GDR)	Anna-Maria Müller (GDR)
1976	Detlef Günther (GDR)	Margit Schumann (GDR)
1980	Bernhard Glass (GDR)	Vera Sosulya (USSR)
1984	Paul Hildgartner (Ita)	Steffi Martin (GDR)
1988	Jens Müller (GDR)	Steffi Walter (née Martin) (GDR)
1992	Georg Hackl (Ger)	Doris Neuner (Aut)
1994	Georg Hackl (Ger)	Gerda Weissensteiner (Ita)
1998	Georg Hackl (Ger)	Silke Kraushaar (Ger)

Men's two-seater

1964	Josef Feistmantl & Manfred Stengl (Aut)
1968	Thomas Köhler & Klaus Bonsack (GDR)
1972	Paul Hildgartner & Walter Plaikner (Ita) and Horst Hörnlein & Reinhard Bredow (GDR)
1976	Hans Rinn & Norbert Hahn (GDR)
1980	Hans Rinn & Norbert Hahn (GDR)
1984	Hans Stanggasinger & Franz Wembacher (FRG)
1988	Jörg Hoffmann & Jochen Pietzsch (GDR)
1992	Stefan Krausse & Jan Behrendt (Ger)
1994	Kurt Brugger & Wilfried Huber (Ita)
1998	Stefan Krausse & Jan Behrendt (Ger)

World Championships

Held in 1955, annually from 1957 – with the exception of years in which luge events were included in the Olympics, with which they are now merged – to 1981, and now biennially on artificial runs. Separate world championships on natural runs were held in 1979 and biennially from 1980.
Winners:

Men's single-seater

1955	Anton Salvesen (Nor)
1957	Hans Schaller (FRG)
1958	Jerzy Wojnar (Pol)
1959	Herbert Thaler (Aut)
1960	Helmuth Berndt (FRG)
1961	Jerzy Wojnar (Pol)
1962	Thomas Köhler (GDR)
1963	Fritz Nachmann (FRG)
1965	Hans Plenk (FRG)
1967	Thomas Köhler (GDR)
1969	Josef Feistmantl (Aut)
1970	Josef Fendt (FRG)
1971	Karl Brunner (Ita)
1973	Hans Rinn (GDR)
1974	Josef Fendt (FRG)
1975	Wolfram Fiedler (GDR)
1977	Hans Rinn (GDR)
1978	Paul Hildgartner (Ita)
1979	Detlef Günther (GDR)
1981	Sergey Danilin (USSR)
1983	Miroslav Zajonc (Can)
1985	Michael Walter (GDR)

1987	Markus Prock (Aut)
1989-90	Georg Hackl (FRG)
1991	Arnold Huber (Ita)
1993	Wendel Suckow (USA)
1995	Armin Zoggler (Ita)
1996	Markus Prock (Aut)
1997	Georg Hackl (Ger)

Men's two-seater

1955	Hans Krausner & Herbert Thaler (Aut)
1957-8	Josef Strillinger & Fritz Nachmann (FRG)
1960	Reinhold Frosch & Ewald Walch (Aut)
1961	Roman Pichler & Raimondo Prinoth (Ita)
1962	Giovanni Graber & Gianpoulo Ambrosi (Ita)
1963	Ryszard Pedrak & Lucjan Kudzia (Pol)
1965	Wolfgang Scheidel & Michael Köhler (GDR)
1967	Klaus Bonsack & Thomas Köhler (GDR)
1969-70	Manfred Schmid & Ewald Walch (Aut)
1971	Paul Hildgartner & Walter Plaikner (Ita)
1973	Horst Hörnlein & Reinhard Bredow (GDR)
1974-5	Bernd Hann & Ulrich Hann (GDR)
1977	Hans Rinn & Norbert Hahn (GDR)
1978	Dainis Bremse & Aigars Krikis (USSR)
1979	Hans Brandner & Balthasar Schwarm (FRG)
1981	Bernd Hann & Ulrich Hann (GDR)
1983	Jörg Hoffmann & Jochen Pietzsch (GDR)
1985	Jörg Hoffmann & Jochen Pietzsch (GDR)
1987	Jörg Hoffmann & Jochen Pietzsch (GDR)
1989	Stefan Krausse & Jan Behrendt (GDR)
1990	Hansjörg Raffl & Norbert Huber (Ita)
1991	Stefan Krausse & Jan Behrendt (Ger)
1993	Stefan Krausse & Jan Behrendt (Ger)
1995	Stefan Krausse & Jan Behrendt (Ger)
1996-7	Tobias Schiegl & Markus Schiegl (Aut)

Women's single-seater

1955	Karla Kienzl (Aut)
1956	Maria Isser (Aut)
1957	Maria Semczyszak (Pol)
1959	Elly Lieber (Aut)
1960	Maria Isser (Aut)
1961	Elisabeth Nagele (Swi)
1962-3	Ilse Geisler (GDR)
1965	Ortrun Enderlein (GDR)
1967	Ortrun Enderlein (GDR)
1969	Petra Tierlich (GDR)
1970	Barbara Piecha (Pol)
1971	Elisabeth Demleitner (FRG)
1973-5	Margrit Schumann (GDR)
1977	Margrit Schumann (GDR)
1978	Vera Sosulya (USSR)
1979	Melitta Sollmann (GDR)
1981	Melitta Sollmann (GDR)
1983	Steffi Martin (GDR)
1985	Steffi Martin (GDR)
1987	Cerstin Schmidt (GDR)
1989	Susi Erdmann (GDR)
1990	Gabriele Kohlisch (GDR)

1991	Susi Erdmann (Ger)
1993	Gerda Weissensteiner (Ita)
1995	Gabriele Kohlisch (Ger)
1996	Jana Bode (Ger)
1997	Susi Erdmann (Ger)

Team

1989	Italy
1990	GDR
1991	Germany
1993	Germany
1995	Germany
1996-7	Austria

Most Luge World and Olympic titles

Men: 6 Georg Hackl; 5 Thomas Köhler, Hans Rinn
Women: 5 Margrit Schumann

World Cup

Held over a series of events annually from the 1977/8 season.

Winners:

Men's single-seater

1978	Anton Winkler (FRG)
1979	Paul Hildgartner (Ita)
1980	Ernst Haspinger (Ita)
1981	Ernst Haspinger (Ita) & Paul Hildgartner (Ita)
1982	Ernst Haspinger (Ita)
1983	Paul Hildgartner (Ita)
1984	Michael Walter (GDR)
1985-7	Norbert Huber (Ita)
1988	Markus Prock (Aut)
1989-90	Georg Hackl (FRG)
1991-7	Markus Prock (Aut)
1998	Armin Zöggeler (Ita)

Men's two-seater

1978-9	Peter Gschnitzer & Karl Brunner (Ita)
1980-2	Günther Lemmerer & Reinhold Sulzbacher (Aut)
1983	Hansjörg Raffl & Norbert Huber (Ita)
1984	Jörg Hoffmann & Jochen Pietzsch (GDR)
1985-6	Hansjörg Raffl & Norbert Huber (Ita)
1987	Thomas Schwab & Wolfgang Staudinger (FRG)
1988	Yevgeniy Belousov & Aleksandr Belyukov (USSR)
1989-93	Hansjörg Raffl & Norbert Huber (Ita)
1994-6	Stefan Krausse & Jan Behrendt (Ger)
1997	Chris Thorpe & Gordy Sheer (USA)
1998	Mark Grimette & Brian Martin (USA)

Women's single-seater

1978	Regina König (FRG)
1979-81	Angelika Schafferer (Aut)
1982	Vera Sosulya (USSR)
1983	Ute Weiss (GDR)

1984	Steffi Martin (GDR) & Bettina Schmidt (GDR)	1991-2	Susi Erdmann (Ger)
		1993	Gerda Weissensteiner (Ita)
1985	Cerstin Schmidt (GDR)	1994	Gabriele Kohlisch (Ger)
1986	Maria Rainer (Ita)	1995	Sylke Otto (Ger)
1987	Cerstin Schmidt (GDR)	1996	Jana Bode (Ger)
1988	Yuliya Antipova (USSR)	1997	Andrea Tagwerker (Aut)
1989	Ute Oberhoffner (GDR)	1998	Gerda Weissensteiner (Ita)
1990	Yuliya Antipova (USSR)		

Bowling (Tenpin)

Bowling at 'pins' can be traced back as a pastime to c.5200BC, taking shape in its present form in the early 19th century. Dutch or German migrants took the game of ninepins to the United States, where it became immensely popular – so popular, in fact, that it attracted too much gambling and was banned as a consequence! To get round the law, a tenth pin was added, and the pins were laid out in a diamond shape. The new game also became very popular. The American Bowling Congress, formed in 1895, standardized the rules.

International governing body: Fédération Internationale des Quilleurs (FIQ), 1631 Mesa Ave, Suite A, Colorado Springs, CO 80906, USA. President: Gerald L Koenig, Secretary General: Dr Abdulla Kareem Al-Reyes. 91 member nations in 1998. The FIQ succeeded the pre-war body, the International Bowling Association (IBA).

US governing bodies: American Bowling Congress (ABC), 5301 South 76th St, Greendale, WI 53129. Tel: (1) 414 421 6400.

Professional Bowlers' Association (PBA), 1720 Merriman Road, PO Box 5118, Akron, OH 44334, USA. Tel: (1) 330 836-5568. Commissioner: Mark Gerberich. Founded 1958.

Women's International Bowling Congress (WIBC), 5301 South 76th St, Greendale, WI 53129. Tel: (1) 414 421 9000. President: Joyce Deitch. Formed in 1916.

World Championships

The IBA organized four world championships between 1923 and 1936. Since 1954 the championships have been organized by the FIQ, and since 1963 have been held every four years. Women took part for the first time in 1963. *Winners:*

Men

Individual

Year	Winner	Score	Games	Av.
1923	Thure Sandström (Swe)	414	2	207.00
1926	Hugo Lillier (Swe)	829	4	207.25
1929	Mike Schirgio (USA)	836	4	209.00
1936	Karl Goldtammer (Ger)	921	4	230.25
1954	Gösta Algeskog (Swe)	4932	25	197.28
1955	Nils Böckström (Swe)	4838	25	193.52
1958	Kaarlo Asukas (Fin)	5034	25	201.36
1960	Tito Reynolds (Mex)	4963	25	198.52
1963	Les Zikes (USA)	5519	28	197.11
1967	David Pond (UK)	5708	28	203.86
1971	Ed Luther (USA)	5963	28	212.96
1975	Bud Staudt (USA)	5816	28	207.71
1979	Ollie Ongtawco (Phi)	1278	6	213.00
1983	Armando Marino (Col)	1357	6	226.17
1987	Rolland Patrick (Fra)	1332	6	222.00
1991	Ma Ying-chei (Tai)	1327	6	221.17
1995	Marc Doi (Can)	1364	6	227.33

Doubles

5	Sweden	1923, 1955, 1958, 1987, 1995
3	Great Britain	1967, 1975, 1983 (=)
3	United States	1936, 1963, 1991
2	Finland	1926, 1954

2   Australia   1979, 1983 (=)
1   Mexico 1960, Puerto Rico 1971
Best average score: 225.16 Sweden (1995) 2702 pts from 6 games

Trios

2   United States   1987, 1991
1   Malaysia 1979, Sweden 1983, Netherlands 1995
Best average score: 219.66 Netherlands (1995) 3954 pts from 6 games

Teams of five players

4   Finland   1958, 1967, 1975, 1983
4   Sweden   1923, 1926, 1954, 1987
3   United States   1936, 1963, 1971
1   F R Germany 1955, Venezuela 1960, Australia 1979, Taiwan 1991, Netherlands 1995
Best average score: 211.83 Finland (1983) 6355 pts from 6 games

All-events

(Scores based on all four events: singles, doubles, trios and team)

1983	Mats Karlsson (Swe)	5242	24	218.42
1987	Rick Steelsmith (USA)	5261	24	219.21
1991	Ma Ying-chei (Tai)	5048	24	210.33
1995	Michael Sassen (Hol)	5496	24	229.00

Teams of eight players

(Discontinued 1975)

3   United States   1963, 1967, 1971
2   Sweden   1954, 1958
1   Finland 1955, Mexico 1960, F R Germany 1975
Best average score: 198.30 United States (1971) 12,691 pts from 8 games

Masters

1979	Gerry Bugden (UK)
1983	Tony Cariello (USA)
1987	Roger Pieters (Bel)
1991	Mika Koivuniemi (Fin)
1995	Yang Chen-min (Tai)

Women

Individual

Year	Winner	Score	Games	Av.
1963	Helen Shablis (USA)	4535	24	188.96
1967	Helen Weston (USA)	4585	24	191.04
1971	Ashie Gonzales (PR)	4535	24	188.96
1975	Annedore Haefker (FRG)	4615	24	192.29
1979	Lita de la Rosa (Phi)	1220	6	203.33
1983	Lena Sulkanen (Swe)	1293	6	215.50
1987	Edda Piccini (Ita)	1259	6	209.83
1991	Martina Beckel (Ger)	1272	6	212.00
1995	Debby Ship (Can)	1318	6	219.66

Doubles

2   United States   1963, 1987
2   Japan   1971, 1991
1   Mexico 1960, Sweden 1975, Philippines 1979, Denmark 1983, Thailand 1995
Best average score: 213.83 United States (1987) 2566 pts from 6 games

Trios

2   USA   1979, 1987
1   F R Germany 1983, Canada 1991, Australia 1995
Best average score: 201.44 Australia (1995) 3626 pts from 6 games

Teams of five players

3	USA	1971, 1979, 1987
2	Finland	1967, 1995
1	Japan 1975, Sweden 1983, S Korea 1991	

Best average score: 200.37 United States (1987) 6011 pts from 6 games

All-events

(Scores based on all four events)

1983	Bong Coo (Phi)	4806	24	200.25
1987	Sandra Jo Shiery (USA)	4894	24	203.92
1991	Helle Andersen (Den)	4821	24	200.87
1995	Jaana Puhakka (Fin)	4916	24	204.83

Teams of four players

(Discontinued 1975)

2	United States 1963★, 1971 ★ Two titles in 1963.
1	Mexico 1963★, Finland 1967, Japan 1975

★ Two titles in 1963.

Best average score: 194.00 United States (1971) 4656 pts from 6 games

Masters

1979	Lita de la Rosa (Phi)
1983	Lena Sulkanen (Swe)
1987	Annette Hagre (Swe)
1991	Catherine Willis (Can)
1995	Celia Flores (Mex)

The only perfect game (300) in the world championships was rolled by Rick Steelsmith (USA) during the Trios event at the 1987 championships.

Professional Bowlers' Association

The PBA's annual Tournament of Champions is held at its home in Akron, Ohio, and is sponsored by Firestone.

Year	Tournament of Champions	PBA leading money-winners	$US
1962	Joe Joseph	Don Carter	22,525
1963	*Not held*	Dick Weber	26,280
1964	*Not held*	Don Carter	49,972
1965	Billy Hardwick	Dick Weber	46,333
1966	Wayne Zahn	Bob Strampe	33,592
1967	Jim Stefanich	Dick Weber	47,674
1968	Dave Davis	Jim Stefanich	54,720
1969	Jim Godman	Billy Hardwick	64,160
1970	Don Johnson	Mike McGrath	52,049
1971	Johnny Petraglia	Johnny Petraglia	85,065
1972	Mike Durbin	Don Johnson	56,648
1973	Jim Godman	Don McCune	69,000
1974	Earl Anthony	Earl Anthony	99,585
1975	Dave Davis	Earl Anthony	107,585
1976	Marshall Holman	Earl Anthony	110,833
1977	Mike Berlin	Mark Roth	105,583
1978	Earl Anthony	Mark Roth	134,500
1979	George Pappas	Mark Roth	124,517
1980	Wayne Webb	Wayne Webb	116,700
1981	Steve Cook	Earl Anthony	164,735
1982	Mike Durbin	Earl Anthony	134,760
1983	Joe Berardi	Earl Anthony	135,605
1984	Mike Durbin	Mark Roth	158,712
1985	Mark Williams	Mike Aulby	201,200
1986	Marshall Holman	Walter Williams	145,550
1987	Pete Weber	Pete Weber	179,516

1988	Mark Williams	Brian Voss	225,485
1989	Del Ballard, Jr	Mike Aulby	298,237
1990	Dave Ferraro	Amleto Monacelli	204,775
1991	David Ozio	David Ozio	225,585
1992	Mike McDowell	Mike McDowell	174,215
1993	George Branham	Walter Williams	296,370
1994	Norm Duke	Norm Duke	273,753
1995	Mike Aulby	Mike Aulby	219,792
1996	Dave D'Entremont	Walter Williams	241,330
1997	John Gant	Walter Williams	240,544

Career money leader: Walter Ray Williams, Jr $2,242,917, Pete Weber $2,178,198

Most titles: 41 Earl Anthony; 34 Mark Roth; 26 Pete Weber, Don Johnson; Dick Weber; 25 Mike Aulby

American Bowling Congress

The ABC organizes an annual Masters Bowling Tournament.
Winners (from 1980):

1980	Neil Burton
1981	Randy Lightfoot
1982	Joe Berardi
1983	Mike Lastowski
1984	Earl Anthony
1985	Steve Wunderlich
1986	Mark Fahy
1987	Rick Steelsmith
1988	Del Ballard Jr.
1989	Mike Aulby
1990	Chris Warren
1991	Doug Kent
1992	Ken Johnson
1993	Norm Duke
1994	Steve Fehr
1995	Mike Aulby
1996	Ernie Schlegel
1997	Jason Queen
1998	Mike Aulby

Most wins: 3 Aulby

Women's International Bowling Congress

The Women's National Bowling Association was founded in 1916, and was renamed the Women's International Bowling Congress in 1971. Championships have been held annually from 1916, except for 1943-5. The WIBC tournament attracted a record 75,480 entrants in 1983, when the event was held over a three-month period.

WIBC Queens Tournament

WIBC's most prestigious event, first held in 1961.
Winners (from 1980):

1979-80	Donna Adamek
1981-2	Katsuko Sugimoto (Jap)
1983	Aleta Sill
1984	Kazue Inahashi (Jap)
1985	Aleta Sill
1986	Cora Fiebig
1987	Cathy Almeida
1988	Wendy Macpherson
1989	Carol Gianotti (Aus)
1990	Patty Ann
1991	Dede Davidson
1992	Cindy Coburn-Carroll
1993	Jan Schmidt
1994	Anne Marie Duggan
1995	Sandra Postma
1996	Lisa Wagner
1997	Sandra Jo Shiery-Odom
1998	Lynda Norry

WIBC career money leader: Aleta Sill $821,462 (to end 1996), with season's record $126,325 in 1994

Most titles: 30 Lisa Wagner 1980-96

Bowls

The ancient Egyptians are believed to have played a game similar to bowls around 5200BC, but the earliest recorded green was at Southampton in 1299, although one was claimed in Chesterfield in 1294. The modern rules for bowls were drawn up in Scotland in 1848-9 by Glasgow solicitor William Mitchell. The English Bowling Association was founded in 1903 with Test cricketer W G Grace as its first president. This was preceded by the founding of the International (later Imperial) Bowling Association in 1899, but this lasted only until 1905, when the present world governing body, originally called the International Bowling Board, was formed. The Women's International Bowling Board was formed in 1969.

International governing body: World Bowls Board, c/o David W Johnson, EBA, Lyndhurst Road, Worthing, West Sussex BN11 2AZ. Tel: 01903 820222, Fax: 01903 820444.

World Outdoor Championships

Instituted in 1966 for men and in 1969 for women, the championships are now held every four years. The Leonard Trophy for men is presented to the winning team based on performances in all categories at the world championship.

Winners:

Men's singles		Men's pairs
1966	David Bryant (Eng)	Geoff Kelly & Bert Palm (Aus)
1972	Malwyn Evans (Wal)	Clementi Delgado & Eric Liddell (HK)
1976	Doug Watson (SAf)	Doug Watson & William Moseley (SAf)
1980	David Bryant (Eng)	Alf Sandercock & Peter Rheuben (Aus)
1984	Peter Belliss (NZ)	George Adrain★ & Skippy Arculli (USA)
1988	David Bryant (Eng)	Rowan Brassey & Peter Belliss (NZ)
1992	Tony Allcock (Eng)	Richard Corsie & Alex Marshall (Sco)
1996	Tony Allcock (Eng)	Sam Allen & Jeremy Henry (Ire)

★ Scotsman who substituted for Jim Candelet.

Men's triples		Men's fours	Leonard Trophy
1966	Australia	New Zealand	Australia
1972	United States	England	Scotland
1976	South Africa	South Africa	South Africa
1980	England	Hong Kong	England
1984	Ireland	England	Scotland
1988	New Zealand	Ireland	England
1992	Israel	Scotland	Scotland
1996	Scotland	England	Scotland

Most wins overall: 6 David Bryant (singles 1966, 1980, 1988, triples 1980, team 1980, 1988)

Women's singles		Women's pairs
1969	Gladys Doyle (PNG)	Elsie McDonald & May Cridlan (SAf)
1973	Elsie Wilke (NZ)	Lorna Lucas & Dot Jenkinson (Aus)
1977	Elsie Wilke (NZ)	Helen Wong & Elvie Chok (HK)
1981	Norma Shaw (Eng)	Eileen Bell & Nan Allely (Ire)
1985	Merle Richardson (Aus)	Merle Richardson & Fay Craig (Aus)
1988	Janet Ackland (Wal)	Margaret Johnston & Phyllis Nolan (Ire)
1992	Margaret Johnston (Ire)	Margaret Johnston & Phyllis Nolan (Ire)
1996	Carmen Anderson (Norfolk I)	Margaret Johnston & Phyllis Nolan (Ire)

Women's triples		Women's fours	Team
1969	South Africa	South Africa	South Africa
1973	New Zealand	New Zealand	New Zealand
1977	Wales	Australia	Australia
1981	Hong Kong	England	England
1985	Australia	Scotland	Australia
1988	Australia	Australia	England
1992	Scotland	Scotland	Scotland
1996	South Africa	Australia	South Africa

Most wins overall: 4 Johnston; 3 Richardson (including fours 1977), Nolan

World Indoor Championships

Instituted 1979 for singles and 1986 for pairs.

Winners:

Singles

1979	David Bryant (Eng)
1980	David Bryant (Eng)
1981	David Bryant (Eng)
1982	John Watson (Sco)
1983	Bob Sutherland (Sco)
1984	Jim Baker (Ire)
1985	Terry Sullivan (Wal)
1986-7	Tony Allcock (Eng)
1988	Hugh Duff (Sco)
1989	Richard Corsie (Sco)
1990	John Price (Wal)
1991	Richard Corsie (Sco)
1992	Ian Schuback (Aus)
1993	Richard Corsie (Sco)
1994-5	Andy Thomson (Eng)
1996	David Gourlay Jr (Sco)
1997	Hugh Duff (Sco)
1998	Paul Foster (Sco)

Most wins: 3 Bryant, Corsie

Pairs

1986-7	David Bryant & Tony Allcock (Eng)
1988	Ian Schuback & Jim Yates (Aus)
1989-92	David Bryant & Tony Allcock (Eng)
1993	Gary Smith & Andy Thomson (Eng)
1994	Cameron Curtis & Ian Schuback (Aus)
1995	Alex Marshall & Richard Corsie (Sco)
1996	Kelvin Kerkow & Ian Schuback (Aus)
1997	Mervyn King & Tony Allcock (Eng)
1998	Graham Robertson & Richard Corsie (Sco)

Women's World Indoor Championships

First held in 1988.

Winners:

1988-9	Margaret Johnston (Ire)	1992	Sarah Gourlay (Sco)	1997	Norma Shaw (Eng)
1990	Fleur Bougourd (UK)	1993	Kate Adams (Sco)	1998	Caroline McAllister (Sco)
1991	Mary Price (UK)	1994	Jan Woodley (Sco)		

Boxing

From the beginning of time, man has fought his fellow man, and pugilism was included in the ancient Olympic Games. The first record of a formally staged boxing match was in 1681, when the Duke of Albemarle organized a match between one of his footmen and a butcher. In 1719 James Figg of Oxfordshire, regarded as the first boxing champion, set up his school of arms in London. The earliest prize ring code of rules was formulated in England in 1743 by the champion pugilist Jack Braughton, and in 1865 the 8th Marquess of Queensberry drew up his famous rules for the sport of boxing, directed to fighting with gloves rather than with bare knuckles, as earlier.

The British Boxing Board of Control (BBBC) was formed in 1929, earlier title fights having been largely under the control of the National Sporting Club.

International governing bodies: International Boxing Federation (IBF), 134 Evergreen Place, 9th Floor, East Orange, NJ 07018, USA. Tel: (1) 201 414-0300. President: Bob Lee. Founded 1983.

World Boxing Association (WBA), PO Box 377, Maracay 2110-A, Venezuela. Tel: (58) 44 631584, Fax: (58) 44 633177. President: Gilberto Mendoza, Executive Director: Gilberto Jesus Mendoza. Founded as the National Boxing Association (NBA) in the USA in 1920, taking WBA name in 1962.

World Boxing Council (WBC), Genova 33-503, Col. Juárez, 06600 D F México, México. Tel: (52) 5533-3787. Founded 1963. President: José Sulaiman.

World Boxing Organization (WBO), 1st Federal Bldg, 1056 Ave Munoz Revera, Suite 714, Puerto Rico 00927. Tel: (1 787) 756-6740. President: Francisco Valcarcel. Founded 1988.

Association Internationale de Boxe Amateur (AIBA), PO Box 700141, D-10321 Berlin, Germany. Tel: (49) 30 423 6766, Fax: (49) 30 423 5943. President: Prof. Anwar Chowdhry, General Secretary: Karl-Heinz Wehr. Formed in 1946. 188 member nations.

World Champions

The first world championship fight with gloves and conducted under the Queensberry Rules was on 30 July 1884, when Irish-born Jack Dempsey beat George Fulljames of the USA, in New York for the middleweight title. There has been a proliferation of world champions, with an increase in recent years in the number of weight divisions. Now, the sport is in the curious and unsatisfactory situation of having a number of governing bodies recognizing 'world champions'.

All titleholders recognized by the WBA, WBC, IBF and WBO are shown in the following lists of champions, but other bodies have also been formed in recent years. For each weight the current weight limits (generally in force from 1970) are indicated. The names for the new intermediate weight categories vary, but the WBC versions have been shown in bold print, with the WBA, IBF and WBO terms beneath. The following weight limits were established following discussions in 1910 between boxing authorities in the UK and the USA:

Heavyweight	over 175lb	**Heavyweight**	1930	Max Schmeling (Ger)
Light-heavy	175lb	*Over 190lb (86.2kg)*	1932	Jack Sharkey (USA)
Middleweight	154lb		1933	Primo Carnera (Ita)
Welterweight	142lb	**Undisputed**	1934	Max Baer (USA)
Lightweight	133lb	1882 John L Sullivan (USA)	1935	James J Braddock (USA)
Featherweight	122lb	1892 James J Corbett (USA)	1937	Joe Louis (USA)
Bantamweight	116lb	1897 Bob Fitzsimmons (UK)	1949	Ezzard Charles (USA)
Flyweight	112lb	1899 James J Jefferies (USA)	1951	Jersey Joe Walcott (USA)
Paperweight	105lb	1905 Marvin Hart (USA)	1952	Rocky Marciano (USA)
Weight limits for the current		1906 Tommy Burns (Can)	1956	Floyd Patterson (USA)
categories are shown in the lists		1908 Jack Johnson (USA)	1959	Ingemar Johansson (Swe)
that follow.		1915 Jess Willard (USA)	1960	Floyd Patterson (USA)
		1919 Jack Dempsey (USA)	1962	Sonny Liston (USA)
		1926 Gene Tunney (USA)	1964	Cassius Clay (USA)

1970	Joe Frazier (USA)
1973	George Foreman (USA)
1974	Muhammad Ali (USA)
1978	Leon Spinks (USA)
1987-90	Mike Tyson (USA)

WBA

1965	Ernie Terrell (USA)
1968	Jimmy Ellis (USA)
1978	Muhammad Ali (USA)
1979	John Tate (USA)
1980	Mike Weaver (USA)
1982	Mike Dokes (USA)
1983	Gerrie Coetzee (SAf)
1984	Greg Page (USA)
1985	Tony Tubbs (USA)
1986	Tim Witherspoon (USA)
1986	James Smith (USA)
1987	Mike Tyson (USA)
1990	James 'Buster' Douglas (USA)
1990	Evander Holyfield (USA)
1992	Riddick Bowe (USA)
1993	Evander Holyfield (USA)
1994	Michael Moorer (USA)
1994	George Foreman (USA)
1995	Bruce Seldon (USA)
1996	Mike Tyson (USA)
1996	Evander Holyfield (USA)

WBC

1978	Ken Norton (USA)
1978	Larry Holmes (USA)
1984	Tim Witherspoon (USA)
1984	Pinklon Thomas (USA)
1986	Trevor Berbick (Jam)
1989	Mike Tyson (USA)
1990	James 'Buster' Douglas (USA)
1990	Evander Holyfield (USA)
1992	Riddick Bowe (USA)
1992	Lennox Lewis (UK)
1994	Oliver McCall (USA)
1995	Frank Bruno (UK)
1996	Mike Tyson (USA)
1997	Lennox Lewis (UK)

IBF

1984	Larry Holmes (USA)
1985	Michael Spinks (USA)
1987	Tony Tucker (USA)
1989	James 'Buster' Douglas (USA)
1990-4	*Same as WBA*
1994	George Foreman (USA)
1995	Francois Botha (SAf)*
1996	Michael Moorer (USA)
1997	Evander Holyfield (USA)

* Lost title due to positive drugs test.

WBO

1989	Francesco Damiani (Ita)
1991	Ray Mercer (USA)
1992	Michael Mourer (USA)
1993	Tommy Morrison (USA)
1993	Michael Bentt (USA)
1994	Herbie Hide (UK)
1995	Riddick Bowe (USA)
1996	Henry Akinwande (UK)
1997	Herbie Hide (UK)

Cruiserweight

(Junior heavyweight WBO)
Limit 190lb (86.2kg)

Undisputed

1988	Evander Holyfield (USA)

WBA

1982	Ossie Ocasio (PR)
1984	Piet Crous (SAf)
1985	Dwight Muhammad Qawi (USA)
1986	Evander Holyfield (USA)
1989	Taoufik Belbouli (Fra)
1989	Robert Daniels (USA)
1991	Bobby Czyz (USA)
1993	Orlin Norris (USA)
1995	Nate Miller (USA)
1997	Fabrice Tiozzo (Ita)

WBC

1979	Marvin Camel (USA)
1980	Carlos de Leon (PR)
1982	S T Gordon (USA)
1983	Carlos de León (PR)
1985	Alfonso Ratliff (USA)
1985	Bernard Benton (USA)
1986	Carlos de León (PR)
1988	Evander Holyfield (USA)
1989	Carlos de Léon (PR)
1990	Massimiliano Duran (Ita)
1991	Anaclet Wamba (Fra)
1995	Marcelo Dominguez (Arg)
1998	Juan Carlos Gómez (Cub)

IBF

1983	Marvin Camel (USA)
1984	Lee Roy Murphy (USA)
1986	Rickey Parkey (USA)
1987	Evander Holyfield (USA)
1989	Glenn McCrory (UK)
1990	Jeff Lampkin (USA)
1991	James Warring (USA)
1992	Alfred Cole (USA)
1996	Adolfo Washington (USA)
1997	Uriah Grant (Jam)
1997	Imamu Mayfield (USA)

WBO

1989	Richard Pultz (USA)
1990	Magne Havnå (Nor)
1992	Tyrone Booze (USA)
1993	Markus Bott (Ger)
1993	Nestor Giovannini (Arg)
1994	Dariusz Michalczewski (Ger)
1995	Ralf Rocchigiani (Ger)
1997	Carl Thompson (UK)

Light-heavyweight

Limit 175lb (79.4kg)

Undisputed

1903	Jack Root (Aut)
1903	George Gardner (Ire)
1903	Bob Fitzsimmons (Eng)
1905	Jack O'Brien (USA)
1912	Jack Dillon (USA)
1916	Battling Levinsky (USA)
1920	Georges Carpentier (Fra)
1922	Battling Siki (Sen)
1923	Mike McTigue (Ire)
1925	Paul Berlenbach (USA)
1926	Jack Delaney (Can)
1927	Jim Slattery (USA)
1927	Tommy Loughran (USA)
1930	Jim Slattery (USA)
1930	Maxie Rosenbloom (USA)
1934	Bob Olin (USA)
1935	John Henry Lewis (USA)
1939	Melio Bettina (USA)
1939	Billy Conn (USA)
1941	Anton Christoforidis (Gre)
1941	Gus Lesnevich (USA)
1948	Freddie Mills (UK)
1950	Joey Maxim (USA)
1952	Archie Moore (USA)
1962	Harold Johnson (USA)
1963	Willie Pastrano (USA)
1965	José Torres (PR)
1966	Dick Tiger (Nig)
1968	Bob Foster (USA)
1983	Michael Spinks (USA)

WBA

1971	Vicente Rondon (Ven)
1974	Victor Galindez (Arg)
1978	Mike Rossman (USA)
1979	Victor Galindez (Arg)
1979	Marvin Johnson (USA)
1980	Eddie Mustafa Muhammad (USA)
1981	Michael Spinks (USA)
1986	Marvin Johnson (USA)
1987	Leslie Stewart (Jam)
1987	Virgil Hill (USA)

1991	Thomas Hearns (USA)			
1992	Iran Barkley (USA)			
1992	Virgil Hill (USA)			
1997	Dariusz Michalczewski (Ger)			
1997	Louis del Valle (USA)			
1998	Roy Jones, Jr (USA)			

WBC

1974	John Conteh (UK)
1977	Miguel Cuello (Arg)
1978	Mate Parlov (Yug)
1978	Marvin Johnson (USA)
1979	Matthew Saad Muhammad (USA)
1981	Dwight Muhammah Qawi (USA)
1985	J B Williamson (USA)
1986	Dennis Andries (UK)
1987	Thomas Hearns (USA)
1988	Donny Lalonde (Can)
1988	Sugar Ray Leonard (USA)
1989	Dennis Andries (UK)
1989	Jeff Harding (Aus)
1990	Dennis Andries (UK)
1991	Jeff Harding (Aus)
1994	Mike McCallum (Jam)
1995	Fabrice Tiozzo (Fra)
1996	Roy Jones (USA)
1997	Montell Griffin (USA)
1997	Roy Jones, Jr (USA)
1998	Graziano Rocchigiani (Ger)

IBF

1985	Slobodan Kacar (Yug)
1986	Bobby Czyz (USA)
1987	Prince Charles Williams (USA)
1993	Henry Maske (Ger)
1996	Virgil Hill (USA)
1997	Dariusz Michalczewski (Ger)
1997	William Guthrie (USA)

WBO

1988	Michael Moorer (USA)
1991	Leeonzer Barber (USA)
1994	Dariusz Michalczewski (Ger)

Super-middleweight
Limit 168lb (76.2kg)

WBA

1984	Park Chong-pal (SKo)
1988	Fulgencio Obelmejias (Ven)
1989	Baek In-chul (SKo)
1990	Christophe Tiozzo (Fra)

1991	Victor Cordoba (Pan)
1992	Michael Nunn (USA)
1994	Steve Little (USA)
1994	Frank Liles (USA)

WBC

1988	Sugar Ray Leonard (USA)
1990	Mauro Galvano (Ita)
1992	Nigel Benn (UK)
1996	Thulane Malinga (SAf)
1996	Vincenzo Nardiello (Ita)
1996	Robin Reid (UK)
1997	Thulane Malinga (SAf)
1998	Richie Woodhall (UK)

IBF

1984	Murray Sutherland (Can)
1988	Graziano Rocchigiani (FRG)
1990	Lindell Holmes (USA)
1991	Darrin van Horn (USA)
1992	Iran Barkley (USA)
1993	James Toney (USA)
1994	Roy Jones, Jr (USA)
1997	Charles Brewer (USA)

WBO

1988	Thomas Hearns (USA)
1991	Chris Eubank (UK)
1995	Steve Collins (UK)
1997	Joe Calzaghe (UK)

Middleweight
Limit 160lb (72.6kg)

Undisputed

1891	Nonpareil Jack Dempsey (Ire)
1891	Bob Fitzsimmons (UK)
1897	Kid McCoy (USA)
1898	Tommy Ryan (USA)
1908	Stanley Ketchel (USA)
1908	Billy Papke (USA)
1908	Stanley Ketchel (USA)
1910	Billy Papke (USA)
1911	Cyclone Thompson (USA)
1911	Billy Papke (USA)
1912	Frank Mantell (USA)
1912	Billy Papke (USA)
1913	Frank Klaus (USA)
1913	George Chip (USA)
1914	Al McCoy (USA)
1917	Mike O'Dowd (USA)
1920	Johnny Wilson (USA)
1923	Harry Greb (USA)
1926	Tiger Flowers (USA)
1926	Mickey Walker (USA)
1931	Gorilla Jones (USA)
1932	Marcel Thil (Fra)
1937	Fred Apostoli (USA)

1939	Ceferino Garcia (Phi)
1940	Ken Overlin (USA)
1941	Billy Soose (USA)
1941	Tony Zale (USA)
1947	Rocky Graziano (USA)
1948	Tony Zale (USA)
1948	Marcel Cerdan (Alg)
1949	Jake la Motta (USA)
1951	Sugar Ray Robinson (USA)
1951	Randolph Turpin (UK)
1951	Sugar Ray Robinson (USA)
1953	Carl Bobo Olsen (Haw)
1955	Sugar Ray Robinson (USA)
1957	Gene Fullmer (USA)
1957	Sugar Ray Robinson (USA)
1957	Carmen Basilio (USA)
1958	Sugar Ray Robinson (USA)
1960	Paul Pender (USA)
1961	Terry Downes (UK)
1962	Paul Pender (USA)
1962	Dick Tiger (Nig)
1963	Joey Giardello (USA)
1965	Dick Tiger (Nig)
1966	Emile Griffith (USA)
1968	Nino Benvenuti (Ita)
1970	Carlos Monzon (Arg)
1976	Carlos Monzon (Arg)
	Reunited (see WBA)
1977	Rodrigo Valdez (Col)
1978	Hugo Corro (Arg)
1979	Vito Antuofermo (Ita)
1980	Alan Minter (UK)
1980	Marvin Hagler (USA)

WBA

1987	Sambu Kalambay (Zai)
1989	Mike McCallum (Jam)
1992	Reggie Johnson (USA)
1993	John David Jackson (USA)
1994	Jorge Castro (Arg)
1995	Shinji Takahara (Jap)
1996	William Joppy, Jr (USA)
1997	Julio César Green (Dom)
1998	William Joppy, Jr (USA)

WBC

1974	Rodrigo Valdez (Col)
1987	Sugar Ray Leonard (USA)
1987	Thomas Hearns (USA)
1988	Iran Barkley (USA)
1989	Roberto Duran (Pan)
1990	Julian Jackson (UVI)
1993	Gerald McClellan (USA)

1995	Julian Jackson (UVI)
1995	Quincy Taylor (USA)
1996	Keith Holmes (USA)
1998	Hacine Cherifi (Fra)

IBF

1987	Frank Tate (USA)
1988	Michael Nunn (USA)
1991	James Toney (USA)
1993	Roy Jones, Jr (USA)
1995	Bernard Hopkins (USA)

WBO

1989	Doug De Witt (USA)
1990	Nigel Benn (UK)
1990	Chris Eubank (UK)
1991	Gerald McClellan (USA)
1993	Chris Pyatt (UK)
1994	Steve Collins (UK)
1995	Lonnie Bradley (USA)
1997	Otis Grant (Can)

Super-welterweight

(Junior middleweight WBA, IBF, WBO)

Limit 154lb (69.9kg)

Undisputed

1962	Denny Moyer (USA)
1963	Ralph Dupas (USA)
1963	Sandro Mazzinghi (Ita)
1965	Nino Benvenuti (Ita)
1966	Kim Ki-soo (SKo)
1968	Sandro Mazzinghi (Ita)
1969	Freddie Little (USA)
1970	Carmelo Bossi (Ita)
1971	Koichi Wajima (Jap)
1974	Oscar Albarado (USA)
1975	Koichi Wajima (Jap)

WBA

1975	Yuh Jae-do (SKo)
1976	Koichi Wajima (Jap)
1976	José Duran (Spa)
1976	Angel Castellini (Arg)
1977	Eddie Gazo (Nic)
1978	Masashi Kudo (Jap)
1979	Ayube Kalule (Uga)
1981	Sugar Ray Leonard (USA)
1981	Tadashi Mihara (Jap)
1982	Davey Moore (USA)
1983	Roberto Duran (Pan)
1984	Mike McCallum (Jam)
1988	Julian Jackson (UVI)
1991	Gilbert Délé (Fra)
1991	Vinny Pazienza (USA)
1992	Julio César Vásquez (Arg)
1995	Pernell Whitaker (USA)
1995	Carl Daniels (USA)

1995	Julio César Vásquez (Arg)
1996	Laurent Boudouani (Fra)

WBC

1975	Miguel de Oliviera (Bra)
1975	Elisha Obed (Bah)
1976	Eckhard Dagge (FRG)
1977	Rocky Mattioli (Ita)
1979	Maurice Hope (UK)
1981	Wilfred Benitez (USA)
1982	Thomas Hearns (USA)
1986	Duane Thomas (USA)
1987	Lupe Aquino (Mex)
1988	Gianfranco Rosi (Ita)
1988	Don Curry (USA)
1989	René Jacquot (Fra)
1989	John Mugabi (Uga)
1990	Terry Norris (USA)
1993	Simon Brown (USA)
1994	Terry Norris (USA)
1994	Luis Santana (Dom)
1995	Terry Norris (USA)
1997	Keith Mullings (USA)

IBF

1984	Mark Medal (USA)
1984	Carlos Santos (PR)
1986	Buster Drayton (USA)
1987	Matthew Hilton (Can)
1988	Robert Hines (USA)
1989	Darrin Van Horn (USA)
1989	Gianfranco Rosi (Ita)
1994	Vincent Pettway (USA)
1995	Paul Vaden (USA)
1996	Terry Norris (USA)
1997	Raul Marquez (Mex)
1997	Yory Boy Campas (Mex)

WBO

1988	John David Jackson (USA)
1993	Vernon Phillips (USA)
1995	Gainfranco Rosi (Ita)
1995	Paul Jones (UK)
1996	Ronald Wright (USA)
1996	Bronco McKart (USA)
1996	Ronald Wright (USA)

Welterweight

Limit 147lb (66.7kg)

Undisputed

1892	Billy Smith (USA)
1894	Tommy Ryan (USA)
1898	Billy Smith (USA)
1900	Rube Ferns (USA)
1900	Matty Matthews (USA)
1901	Rube Ferns (USA)
1901	Joe Walcott (Bar)
1904	Dixie Kid (USA)

1905	Joe Walcott (Bar)
1906	Honey Mellody (USA)
1907	Mike Sullivan (USA)
1908	Harry Lewis (USA)
1914	Waldemar Holberg (Den)
1914	Tom McCormick (Ire)
1914	Matt Wells (UK)
1915	Mike Glover (USA)
1915	Jack Britton (USA)
1915	Ted Kid Lewis (UK)
1916	Jack Britton (USA)
1917	Ted Kid Lewis (UK)
1919	Jack Britton (USA)
1922	Mickey Walker (USA)
1926	Pete Latzo (USA)
1927	Joe Dundee (Ita)
1928	Jack Thompson (USA)
1929	Jackie Fields (USA)
1930	Jack Thompson (USA)
1930	Tommy Freeman (USA)
1931	Jack Thompson (USA)
1931	Lou Brouillard (Can)
1932	Jackie Fields (USA)
1933	Young Corbett III (Ita)
1933	Jimmy McLarnin (Ire)
1934	Barney Ross (USA)
1934	Jimmy McLarnin (Ire)
1935	Barney Ross (USA)
1938	Henry Armstrong (USA)
1940	Fritzie Zivic (USA)
1941	Red Cochrane (USA)
1946	Marty Servo (USA)
1946	Sugar Ray Robinson (USA)
1951	Johnny Bratton (USA)
1951	Kid Gavilan (Cub)
1954	Johnny Saxton (USA)
1955	Tony de Marco (USA)
1955	Carmen Basilio (USA)
1956	Johnny Saxton (USA)
1956	Carmen Basilio (USA)
1958	Virgil Atkins (USA)
1958	Don Jordon (Dom)
1960	Benny Kid Paret (Cub)
1961	Emile Griffith (USA)
1961	Benny Kid Paret (Cub)
1962	Emile Griffith (USA)
1963	Louis Rodriguez (Cub)
1963	Emile Griffith (USA)
1966	Curtis Cokes (USA)
1969	José Napoles (Cub)
1970	Billy Backus (USA)
1971	José Napoles (Cub)
1981	Sugar Ray Leonard (USA)
1985	Don Curry (USA)
1986	Lloyd Honeyghan (UK)

WBA

1975	Angel Espada (PR)
1976	Pipino Cuevas (Mex)
1980	Thomas Hearns (USA)
1983	Don Curry (USA)
1987	Mark Breland (USA)
1987	Marlon Starling (USA)
1988	Tomas Molinares (Col)
1989	Mark Breland (USA)
1990	Aaron Davis (USA)
1991	Meldrick Taylor (USA)
1992	Crisanto España (Ven)
1994	Ike Quartey (Gha)

WBC

1975	John H Stracey (UK)
1976	Carlos Palomino (Mex)
1979	Wilfred Benitez (USA)
1979	Sugar Ray Leonard (USA)
1980	Roberto Duran (Pan)
1980	Sugar Ray Leonard (USA)
1983	Milton McCrory (USA)
1987	Lloyd Honeyghan (UK)
1987	Jorge Vaca (Mex)
1988	Lloyd Honeyghan (UK)
1989	Marlon Starling (USA)
1990	Maurice Blocker (USA)
1991	Simon Brown (Jam)
1991	James 'Buddy' McGirt (USA)
1993	Pernell Whitaker (USA)
1997	Oscar De La Hoya (USA)

IBF

1984	Don Curry (USA)
1987	Lloyd Honeyghan (UK)
1988	Simon Brown (Jam)
1991	Maurice Blocker (USA)
1993	Félix Trinidad (PR)

WBO

1989	Genaro Leon (Mex)
1989	Manning Galloway (USA)
1993	Gert Bo Jacobsen (Den)
1993	Eamonn Loughran (Ire)
1996	José Luis López (Mex)
1997	Michael Löwe (Rom/Ger)

Super-lightweight

(Junior welterweight WBA, IBF, WBO)

Limit 140lb (63.5kg)

Undisputed

1922	Pinky Mitchell (USA)
1926	Mushy Callahan (USA)
1930	Jackie Kid Berg (UK)
1931	Tony Canzoneri (USA)
1932	Johnny Jaddick (USA)
1933	Battling Shaw (Mex)
1933	Tony Canzoneri (USA)

1933	Barney Ross (USA)
1946	Tippy Larkin (USA)
1959	Carlos Ortiz (PR)
1960	Duilio Loi (Ita)
1962	Eddie Perkins (USA)
1962	Duilio Loi (Ita)
1963	Roberto Cruz (Phi)
1963	Eddie Perkins (USA)
1965	Carlos Hernández (Ven)
1966	Sandro Lopopolo (Ita)
1967	Paul Fujii (Haw)

WBA

1968	Nicolino Loche (Arg)
1972	Alfonso Frazer (Pan)
1972	Antonio Cervantes (Col)
1976	Wilfred Benitez (USA)
1977	Antonio Cervantes (Col)
1980	Aaron Pryor (USA)
1984	Johnny Bumphus (USA)
1984	Gene Hatcher (USA)
1985	Ubaldo Sacco (Arg)
1986	Patrizio Oliva (Ita)
1987	Juan Martin Coggi (Arg)
1990	Loreto Garza (USA)
1991	Edwin Rosario (PR)
1992	Akinobu Hiranaka (Jap)
1992	Morris East (Phi)
1993	Juan Martin Coggi (Arg)
1994	Frankie Randall (USA)
1995	Juan Martin Coggi (Arg)
1996	Frankie Randall (USA)
1997	Khalid Rahilou (Fra)

WBC

1968	Pedro Adigue (Phi)
1970	Bruno Acari (Ita)
1974	Perico Fernández (Spa)
1975	Saensak Muangsurin (Tha)
1976	Miguel Velasquez (Spa)
1976	Saensak Muangsurin (Tha)
1978	Kim Sang-hyun (SKo)
1980	Saoul Mamby (USA)
1982	Leroy Haley (USA)
1983	Bruce Curry (USA)
1984	Billy Costello (USA)
1985	Lonnie Smith (USA)
1986	Tsuyoshi Hamada (Jap)
1987	René Arredondo (Mex)
1988	Roger Mayweather (USA)
1989	Julio César Chávez (Mex)
1994	Frankie Randall (USA)
1994	Julio César Chávez (Mex)
1996	Oscar De La Hoya (USA)

IBF

1983	Aaron Pryor (USA)
1986	Gary Hinton (USA)
1986	Joe Louis Manley (USA)

1987	Terry Marsh (UK)
1988	James Buddy McGirt (USA)
1988	Meldrick Taylor (USA)
1990	Julio César Chávez (Mex)
1991	Rafael Pineda (Col)
1992	Pernell Whitaker (USA)
1993	Charles Murray (USA)
1994	Jake Rodriguez (USA)
1995	Konstantin Tszyu (Rus)
1997	Vince Phillips (USA)

WBO

1989	Hector Camacho (PR)
1991	Greg Haugen (USA)★
1991	Hector Camacho (PR)
1992	Carlos González (Mex)
1993	Zack Padilla (USA)
1995	Sammy Fuentes (PR)
1996	Giovanni Parisi (Ita)

★ Lost title after testing positive for marijuana.

Lightweight

Limit 135lb (61.2kg)

Undisputed

1886	Jack McAuliffe (Ire)
1896	George Lavigne (USA)
1899	Frank Erne (Swi)
1902	Joe Gans (USA)
1908	Battling Nelson (Den)
1910	Ad Wolgast (USA)
1912	Willie Ritchie (USA)
1914	Freddie Welsh (UK)
1917	Benny Leonard (USA)
1925	Jimmy Goodrich (USA)
1925	Rocky Kansas (USA)
1926	Sammy Mandell (USA)
1930	Al Singer (USA)
1930	Tony Canzeroni (USA)
1933	Barney Ross (USA)
1935	Tony Canzeroni (USA)
1936	Lou Ambers (USA)
1938	Henry Armstrong (USA)
1939	Lou Ambers (USA)
1940	Lew Jenkins (USA)
1941	Sammy Angott (USA)
1942	Beau Jack (USA)
1943	Bob Montgomery (USA)
1943	Sammy Angott (USA)
1944	Juan Zurita (Mex)
1945	Ike Williams (USA)
1951	Jimmy Carter (USA)
1952	Lauro Salas (Mex)
1952	Jimmy Carter (USA)
1954	Paddy de Marco (USA)
1954	Jimmy Carter (USA)
1955	Wallace Bud Smith (USA)

1956	Joe Brown (USA)
1962	Carlos Ortiz (PR)
1965	Ismael Laguna (Pan)
1965	Carlos Ortiz (PR)
1968	Carlos Teo Cruz (Dom)
1969	Mando Ramos (USA)
1970	Ismael Laguna (Pan)
1978	Roberto Duran (Pan)

WBA

1970	Ken Buchanan (UK)
1972	Roberto Duran (Pan)
1979	Ernesto Espana (Ven)
1980	Hilmer Kenty (USA)
1981	Sean O'Grady (USA)
1981	Claude Noel (Tri)
1981	Arturo Frias (USA)
1982	Ray Mancini (USA)
1984	Livingstone Bramble (USA)
1986	Edwin Rosario (PR)
1987	Julio César Chávez (Mex)
1989	Edwin Rosario (USA)
1990	Juan Nazario (PR)
1990	Pernell Whitaker (USA)
1992	Joey Gamache (USA)
1992	Tony Lopez (USA)
1993	Dingaan Thobela (SAf)
1993	Orzubek Nazarov (Kgz)
1998	Jean-Baptiste Mendy (Fra)

WBC

1971	Pedro Carrasco (Spa)
1972	Mando Ramos (USA)
1972	Chango Carmona (Mex)
1972	Rodolfo Gonzalez (Mex)
1974	Guts Ishimatsu (Jap)
1976	Esteban de Jesús (PR)
1979	Jim Watt (UK)
1981	Alexis Arguello (Nic)
1983	Edwin Rosario (PR)
1984	José Luis Ramirez (Mex)
1985	Hector Camacho (PR)
1987	José Luis Ramirez (Mex)
1988	Julio César Chávez (Mex)
1989	Pernell Whitaker (USA)
1992	Miguel Angel González (Mex)
1996	Jean-Baptiste Mendy (Fra)
1997	Steve Johnston (USA)
1998	César Bazan (Mex)

IBF

1984	Charlie Brown (USA)
1984	Harry Arroyo (USA)
1985	Jimmy Paul (USA)
1986	Greg Haugen (USA)
1987	Vinny Pazienza (USA)
1988	Greg Haugen (USA)

1989	Pernell Whitaker (USA)
1992	Freddie Pendleton (USA)
1994	Rafael Ruelas (USA)
1995	Oscar De La Hoya (USA)
1995	Phillip Holiday (SAf)
1997	Shane Mosley (USA)

WBO

1989	Amancio Castro (Col)
1989	Mauricio Aceves (Mex)
1990	Dingaan Thobela (SAf)
1992	Giovanni Parisi (Ita)
1994	Oscar De La Hoya (USA)
1996	Artur Grigoryan (Uzb)

Super-featherweight

(Junior lightweight WBA, IBF, WBO)

Limit 130lb (59kg)

Undisputed

1921	Johnny Dundee (Ita)
1923	Jack Bernstein (USA)
1923	Johnny Dundee (Ita)
1924	Kid Sullivan (USA)
1925	Mike Ballerino (USA)
1925	Tod Morgan (USA)
1929	Benny Bass (USA)
1931	Kid Chocolate (Cub)
1933	Frankie Klick (USA)
1959	Harold Gomes (USA)
1960	Flash Elorde (Phi)
1967	Yoshiaki Numata (Jap)
1967	Hiroshi Kobayashi (Jap)

WBA

1971	Alfredo Marcano (Ven)
1972	Ben Villaflor (Phi)
1973	Kuniaki Shibata (Jap)
1973	Ben Villaflor (Phi)
1976	Sam Serrano (PR)
1980	Yasutsune Uehara (Jap)
1981	Sam Serrano (PR)
1983	Roger Mayweather (USA)
1984	Rocky Lockridge (USA)
1985	Wilfredo Gomez (PR)
1986	Alfredo Layne (Pan)
1986	Brian Mitchell (SAf)
1991	Joey Gamache (USA)
1991	Genaro Hernández (USA)
1995	Choi Yong-soo (SKo)

WBC

1969	René Barrientos (Phi)
1970	Yoshiaki Numata (Jap)
1971	Ricardo Arredondo (Mex)
1974	Kuniaki Shibata (Jap)
1975	Alfredo Escalera (PR)
1978	Alexis Arguello (Nic)
1980	Rafael Limon (Mex)

1981	Cornelius Boza Edwards (Uga)
1981	Rolando Navarette (Phi)
1982	Rafael Limon (Mex)
1982	Bobby Chacon (USA)
1983	Hector Camacho (PR)
1984	Julio César Chávez (Mex)
1988	Azumah Nelson (Gha)
1994	Jesse James Leija (USA)
1995	Gabe Ruelas (USA)
1995	Azumah Nelson (Gha)
1997	Genaro Hernández (Mex)

IBF

1984	Yuh Hwan-kil (SKo)
1985	Lester Ellis (Aus)
1985	Barry Michael (Aus)
1987	Rocky Lockridge (USA)
1988	Tony Lopez (USA)
1989	Juan Molina (PR)
1990	Tony Lopez (USA)
1991	Brian Mitchell (SAf)
1992	John John Molina (PR)
1995	Eddie Hopson (USA)
1995	Tracey Patterson (USA)
1995	Arturo Gatti (USA)
1998	Roberto Garcia (USA)

WBO

1989	Juan Molina (PR)
1989	Kamel Bou Ali (Tun)
1992	Daniel Londas (Fra)
1992	Jimmy Bredhal (Den)
1994	Oscar De La Hoya (USA)
1994	Regilio Tuur (Hol)
1997	Barry Jones (UK)
1998	Anatoliy Aleksandrov (Kzk)

Featherweight

Limit 126lb (57.2kg)

Undisputed

1891	Young Griffo (Aus)
1892	George Dixon (Can)
1897	Solly Smith (USA)
1898	Dave Sullivan (Ire)
1898	George Dixon (Can)
1900	Terry McGovern (USA)
1901	Young Corbett II (USA)
1904	Jimmy Britt (USA)
1904	Tommy Sullivan (USA)
1906	Abe Attell (USA)
1912	Johnny Kilbane (USA)
1923	Eugene Criqui (Fra)
1923	Johnny Dundee (Ita)
1925	Kid Kaplan (USA)
1927	Benny Bass (USA)
1928	Tony Canzoneri (USA)
1928	Andre Routis (Fra)

1929	Battling Battalino (USA)	
1932	Kid Chocolate (Cub)	
1933	Freddie Miller (USA)	
1936	Petey Sarron (USA)	
1937	Henry Armstrong (USA)	
1938	Joey Archibald (USA)	
1940	Harry Jeffra (USA)	
1941	Joey Archibald (USA)	
1941	Chalky Wright (Mex)	
1942	Willie Pep (USA)	
1948	Sandy Saddler (USA)	
1949	Willie Pep (USA)	
1950	Sandy Sadler (USA)	
1957	Hogan Kid Bassey (Nig)	
1959	Davey Moore (USA)	
1963	Sugar Ramos (Cub)	
1964	Vicente Saldivar (Mex)	

WBA

1968	Raul Rojas (USA)
1968	Shozo Saijyo (Jap)
1971	Antonio Gómez (Ven)
1972	Ernesto Marcel (Pan)
1974	Ruben Olivares (Mex)
1974	Alexis Arguello (Nic)
1977	Rafael Ortega (Pan)
1977	Cecilio Lastra (Spa)
1978	Eusebio Pedroza (Pan)
1985	Barry McGuigan (Ire)
1986	Steve Cruz (USA)
1987	Antonio Esparragoza (Ven)
1991	Park Young-kyun (SKo)
1993	Eloy Rojas (Ven)
1996	Wilfredo Vázquez (PR)
1998	Freddie Norwood (USA)

WBC

1968	Howard Winstone (UK)
1968	José Legra (Cub)
1969	Johnny Famechon (Fra)
1970	Vicente Saldivar (Mex)
1970	Kuniaki Shibata (Jap)
1972	Clemente Sánchez (Mex)
1972	José Legra (Cub)
1973	Eder Jofre (Bra)
1974	Bobby Chacon (USA)
1975	Ruben Olivares (Mex)
1975	David Kotey (Gha)
1976	Danny Lopez (USA)
1980	Salvador Sánchez (Mex)
1982	Juan Laporte (PR)
1984	Wilfredo Gomez (PR)
1984	Azumah Nelson (Gha)
1988	Jeff Fenech (Aus)
1990	Marcos Villasana (Mex)
1991	Paul Hodkinson (UK)
1993	Gregorio Vargas (Mex)
1993	Kevin Kelley (USA)

1995	Alejandro González (Mex)
1995	Manuel Medina (Mex)
1995	Luisito Espinosa (Phi)

IBF

1984	Oh Min-keum (SKo)
1985	Chung Ki-young (SKo)
1986	Antonio Rivera (PR)
1988	Calvin Grove (USA)
1988	Jorge Paez (Mex)
1991	Troy Dorsey (USA)
1991	Manuel Medina (Mex)
1993	Tom Johnson (USA)
1997	Naseem Hamed (UK)
1997	Hector Lizarraga (Mex)

WBO

1989	Maurizio Stecca (Ita)
1989	Louie Espinoza (USA)
1990	Jorge Paez (Mex)
1991	Maurizio Stecca (Ita)
1992	Colin McMillan (UK)
1992	Ruben Palacios (Col)
1993	Steve Robinson (UK)
1995	Naseem Hamed (UK)

Super-bantamweight

(Junior featherweight WBA, IBF, WBO)

Limit 122lb (55.3kg)

Undisputed

1922	Jack Kid Wolfe (USA)
1923	Carl Duane (USA)

WBA

1977	Hong Soo-hwan (SKo)
1978	Ricardo Cardona (Col)
1980	Leo Randolph (USA)
1980	Sergio Palma (Arg)
1982	Leo Cruz (Dom)
1984	Loris Stecca (Ita)
1984	Victor Callejas (PR)
1987	Louis Espinoza (USA)
1987	Julio Gervacio (Dom)
1988	Bernardo Pinango (Ven)
1988	Juan José Estrada (Mex)
1989	Jesús Salud (USA)
1990	Luis Mendoza (Col)
1991	Raúl Pérez (Mex)
1992	Wilfredo Vázquez (PR)
1995	Antonio Cermeno (Ven)

WBC

1976	Rigoberto Riasco (Pan)
1976	Royal Kobayashi (Jap)
1976	Yum Dong-kyun (SKo)
1977	Wilfredo Gomez (PR)
1983	Jaime Garza (USA)
1984	Juan Meza (Mex)

1985	Lupe Pintor (Mex)
1986	Samart Payakarun (Tha)
1987	Jeff Fenech (Aus)
1988	Daniel Zaragoza (Mex)
1990	Paul Banke (USA)
1990	Pedro Decima (Arg)
1991	Kiyoshi Hatanaka (Jap)
1991	Daniel Zaragoza (Mex)
1992	Thierry Jacob (Fra)
1993	Tracy Harris Patterson (USA)
1994	Héctor Acero-Sánchez (Dom)
1995	Daniel Zaragoza (Mex)
1997	Erik Morales (Mex)

IBF

1983	Bobby Berna (Phi)
1984	Suh Seung-il (SKo)
1985	Kim Ji-won (SKo)
1987	Lee Seung-hoon (SKo)
1988	José Sanabria (Ven)
1989	Fabrice Benichou (Fra)
1990	Welcome Ncita (SAf)
1992	Kennedy McKinney (USA)
1994	Vuyani Bungu (SAf)

WBO

1989	Kenny Mitchell (USA)
1989	Valerio Nati (Ita)
1990	Orlando Fernandez (PR)
1991	Jesse Benevides (USA)
1992	Duke McKenzie (UK)
1993	Daniel Jiménez (PR)
1995	Marco Antonio Berrera (Mex)
1996	Junior Jones (USA)
1997	Kennedy McKinney (USA)

Bantamweight

Limit 118lb (53.5kg)

Undisputed

1891	George Dixon (Can)
1892	Billy Plimmer (UK)
1895	Pedlar Palmer (UK)
1899	Terry McGovern (USA)
1901	Harry Forbes (USA)
1903	Frankie Neil (USA)
1904	Joe Bowker (UK)
1905	Jimmy Walsh (USA)
1907	Owen Moran (UK)
1908	Johnny Coulon (Can)
1914	Kid Williams (Den)
1917	Pete Herman (USA)
1920	Joe Lynch (USA)
1921	Pete Herman (USA)

1921	Johnny Buff (USA)
1922	Joe Lynch (USA)
1924	Abe Goldstein (USA)
1924	Eddie Martin (USA)
1925	Charlie Rosenberg (USA)
1927	Bud Taylor (USA)
1928	Bushy Graham (Ita)
1929	Al Brown (Pan)
1935	Baltazar Sangchilli (Spa)
1936	Tony Marino (USA)
1936	Sixto Escobar (Spa)
1937	Harry Jeffra (USA)
1938	Sixto Escobar (Spa)
1940	Lou Salica (USA)
1942	Manuel Ortiz (USA)
1947	Harold Dade (USA)
1947	Mauel Ortiz (USA)
1950	Vic Toweel (SAf)
1952	Jimmy Carruthers (Aus)
1954	Robert Cohen (Alg)
1956	Mario D'Agata (Ita)
1957	Alphonse Halimi (Alg)
1959	Joe Becerra (Mex)
1960	Eder Jofre (Bra)
1965	Fighting Harada (Jap)
1968	Lionel Rose (Aus)
1969	Ruben Olivares (Mex)
1970	Chucho Castillo (Mex)
1971	Ruben Olivares (Mex)
1972	Rafael Herrera (Mex)
1972	Enrique Pinder (Pan)

WBA

1973	Romeo Anaya (Mex)
1973	Arnold Taylor (SAf)
1974	Hong Soo-hwan (SKo)
1975	Alfonso Zamora (Mex)
1977	Jorge Lujan (Pan)
1980	Julian Solis (PR)
1980	Jeff Chandler (USA)
1984	Richard Sandoval (USA)
1986	Gaby Canizales (USA)
1986	Bernardo Pinango (Ven)
1987	Takuya Muguruma (Jap)
1987	Park Chang-young (SKo)
1987	Wilfredo Vasquez (PR)
1988	Khaokor Galaxy (Tha)
1988	Moon Sung-kil (SKo)
1989	Khaokor Galaxy (Tha)
1989	Luisito Espinosa (Phi)
1991	Israel Contreras (Ven)
1992	Eddie Cook (USA)
1992	Jorge Eliecer Julio (Col)
1993	Junior Jones (USA)
1994	John Michael Johnson (USA)
1994	Daorung Chuvatana (Tha)

1995	Veeraphol Sahaprom (Tha)
1996	Nana Yaw Konadu (Gha)
1996	Daorung Chor Siriwat (Tha)
1997	Nana Yaw Konadu (Gha)

WBC

1973	Rafael Herrera (Mex)
1974	Rodolfo Martinez (Mex)
1976	Carlos Zarate (Mex)
1979	Lupe Pintor (Mex)
1983	Alberto Davila (USA)
1985	Daniel Zaragoza (Mex)
1985	Miguel Lora (Col)
1988	Raul Perez (Mex)
1991	Greg Richardson (USA)
1991	Joichiro Tatsuyoshi (Jap)
1992	Victor Rabanales (Mex)
1993	Byun Jong-il (SKo)
1993	Yasuei Yakushiji (Jap)
1995	Wayne McCullough (Ire)
1996	Sirimongkol Singmanasak (Tha)
1997	Joichiro Tatsuyoshi (Jap)

IBF

1984	Satoshi Shingaki (Jap)
1985	Jeff Fenech (Aus)
1987	Kelvin Seabrooks (USA)
1988	Orlando Canizales (USA)
1995	Harold Mestre (Col)
1995	Mbulelo Botile (SAf)
1997	Tim Austin (USA)

WBO

1989	Israel Contreras (Ven)
1991	Gaby Canizales (USA)
1991	Duke McKenzie (UK)
1992	Rafael Del Valle (PR)
1994	Alfred Kotey (Gha)
1995	Daniel Jiménez (PR)
1996	Robbie Regan (UK)
1997	Jorge Eliecer Julio (Col)

Super-flyweight

(Junior bantamweight WBA, IBF, WBO)
Limit 115lb (52.2kg)

WBA

1981	Gustavo Ballas (Arg)
1981	Rafael Pedroza (Pan)
1982	Jiro Watanabe (Jap)
1984	Khaosai Galaxy (Tha)
1992	Katsuya Onizuka (Jap)
1994	Lee Hyung-chul (SKo)
1995	Alima Goitia (Ven)
1996	Yokthai Sith-Oar (Tha)
1998	Satoshi Iida (Jap)

WBC

1980	Rafael Orono (Ven)
1981	Kim Chul-ho (SKo)
1982	Rafael Orono (Ven)
1983	Payao Poontarat (Tha)
1984	Jiro Watanabe (Jap)
1986	Gilberto Román (Mex)
1987	Santos Laciar (Arg)
1987	Jesús Rojas (Col)
1988	Gilberto Román (Mex)
1989	Nana Yaw Konadu (Gha)
1990	Moon Sung-kil (SKo)
1993	José Luis Bueno (Mex)
1994	Hiroshi Kawashima (Jap)
1997	Gerry Penalosa (Phi)

IBF

1983	Chun Joo-do (SKo)
1985	Ellyas Pical (Ina)
1986	Cesar Polanco (Dom)
1986	Chang Tae-il (SKo)
1987	Ellyas Pical (Ina)
1989	Juan Polo Pérez (Col)
1990	Robert Quiroga (USA)
1993	Julio César Borboa (Mex)
1994	Harold Grey (Col)
1995	Carlos Salazar (Arg)
1996	Harold Grey (Col)
1996	Danny Romero (Mex)
1997	Johnny Tapia (USA)

WBO

1989	José Ruiz (PR)
1992	José Quirino (Mex)
1992	Johnny Bredahl (Den)
1994	Johnny Tapia (USA)

Flyweight

Limit 112lb (50.8kg)

Undisputed

1913	Sid Smith (UK)
1913	Bill Ladbury (UK)
1914	Percy Jones (UK)
1915	Joe Symonds (UK)
1916	Jimmy Wilde (UK)
1923	Pancho Villa (Phi)
1925	Fidel La Barba (USA)
1928	Frankie Genaro (USA)
1929	Emile Pladner (Fra)
1929	Frankie Genaro (USA)
1931	Young Perez (Tun)
1932	Jackie Brown (UK)
1935	Benny Lynch (UK)
1938	Peter Kane (UK)
1943	Jackie Paterson (UK)
1948	Rinty Monaghan (UK)
1950	Terry Allen (UK)
1950	Dado Marino (Haw)

1952	Yoshio Shirai (Jap)
1954	Pascual Pérez (Arg)
1960	Pone Kingpetch (Tha)
1962	Fighting Harada (Jap)
1963	Pone Kingpetch (Tha)
1963	Hiroyuki Ebihara (Jap)
1964	Pone Kingpetch (Tha)
1965	Salvatore Burruni (Ita)

WBA

1966	Horacio Accavallo (Arg)
1969	Hiroyuki Ebihara (Jap)
1969	Bernabe Villacampo (Phi)
1970	Berkrerk Chartvanchai (Tha)
1970	Masao Ohba (Jap)
1973	Chartchai Chionoi (Tha)
1974	Susumu Hanagata (Jap)
1975	Erbito Salavarria (Phi)
1976	Alfonso López (Pan)
1976	Guty Espadas (Mex)
1978	Betulio Gonzalez (Ven)
1979	Luis Ibarra (Pan)
1980	Kim Tae-shik (SKo)
1980	Shoji Oguma (Jap)
1980	Peter Mathebula (SAf)
1981	Santos Laciar (Arg)
1981	Luis Ibarra (Pan)
1981	Juan Herrera (Mex)
1982	Santos Laciar (Arg)
1985	Hilario Zapata (Pan)
1987	Fidel Bassa (Col)
1989	Jesús Rojas (Ven)
1990	Lee Yul-woo (SKo)
1990	Yukihito Tamakama (Jap)
1991	Elvis Alvárez (Col)
1991	Kim Yong-kang (SKo)
1992	Aquiles Guzman (Ven)
1992	David Griman (Ven)
1994	Saen Sor Ploenchit (Tha)
1996	José Bonilla (Ven)
1998	Hugo Soto (Arg)

WBC

1966	Walter McGowan (UK)
1966	Chartchai Chionoi (Tha)
1969	Efren Torres (Mex)
1970	Chartchai Chionoi (Tha)
1970	Erbito Salavarria (Phi)
1972	Venice Borkorsor (Tha)
1973	Betulio González (Ven)
1974	Shoji Oguma (Jap)
1975	Miguel Canto (Mex)
1979	Park Chan-hee (SKo)
1981	Antonio Avelar (Mex)
1982	Prudencio Cardona (Col)
1982	Freddie Castillo (Mex)
1982	Eleoncio Mercedes (Dom)

1983	Charlie Magri (UK)
1983	Frank Cedeno (Phi)
1984	Koji Kobayashi (Jap)
1984	Gabriel Bernal (Mex)
1984	Sot Chitalada (Tha)
1988	Kim Yong-kang (SKo)
1989	Sot Chitalda (Tha)
1991	Muangchai Kittikasem (Tha)
1993	Yuriy Arbachakov (Rus)
1997	Chatchai Sasakul (Tha)
1998	Alex Baba (Gha)

IBF

1983	Kwon Soon-chun (SKo)
1985	Chung Chong-kwan (SKo)
1986	Chung Bi-won (SKo)
1986	Shin Hi-sup (SKo)
1987	Dodie Penalosa (Phi)
1987	Choi Chang-ho (SKo)
1988	Rolando Bohol (Phi)
1988	Duke McKenzie (UK)
1989	Dave McAuley (UK)
1992	Rodolfo Blanco (Col)
1992	Pichit Sitbangprachan (Tha)
1995	Francisco Tejedor (Col)
1995	Danny Romero (USA)
1996	Mark Johnson (USA)

WBO

1989	Elvis Alvarez (Col)
1990	Isidro Pérez (Mex)
1992	Pat Clinton (USA)
1993	Baby Jake Matlala (SAf)
1995	Alberto Jiménez (Mex)
1996	Carlos Salazar (Arg)

Light-flyweight

(Junior flyweight WBA, IBF, WBO)
Limit 108lb (49kg)

WBA

1975	Jaime Rios (Pan)
1976	Juan José Guzman (Dom)
1976	Yoko Gushiken (Jap)
1981	Pedro Flores (Mex)
1981	Kim Hwan-jin (SKo)
1981	Katsuo Takashiki (Jap)
1983	Lupe Madera (Mex)
1984	Francisco Quiroz (Dom)
1985	Joey Olivo (USA)
1985	Yuh Myung-woo (SKo)
1992	Hiroki Ioka (Jap)
1992	Yuh Myung-woo (SKo)
1993	Leo Gamez (Ven)
1995	Choi Hi-yong (SKo)
1996	Carlos Murillo (Pan)
1996	Keiji Yamaguchi (Jap)

1996	Phichitnoi Chor Siriwat (Tha)

WBC

1975	Franco Udella (Ita)
1975	Luis Estaba (Ven)
1978	Freddie Castillo (Mex)
1978	Netrnoi Vorasingh (Tha)
1978	Kim Sung-jun (SKo)
1980	Shigeo Nakajima (Jap)
1980	Hilario Zapata (Pan)
1982	Amado Ursua (Mex)
1982	Tadashi Tomori (Jap)
1982	Hilario Zapata (Pan)
1983	Chang Jung-koo (Kor)
1988	German Torres (Mex)
1989	Lee Yul-woo (SKo)
1989	Humberto González (Mex)
1990	Rolando Pascua (Phi)
1991	Melchor Cob Castro (Mex)
1991	Humberto González (Mex)
1993	Michael Carbajal (USA)
1994	Humberto González (Mex)
1995	Saman Sor Jaturong (Tha)

IBF

1983	Dodie Penalosa (Phi)
1986	Choi Chong-hwan (SKo)
1988	Tacy Macalos (Phi)
1989	Muancgchai Kittikasem (Tha)
1990	Michael Carbajal (USA)
1994	Humberto González (Mex)
1995	Saman Sor Jaturong (Tha)
1996	Michael Carbajal (USA)
1997	Mauricio Pastrana (Col)

WBO

1989	José de Jesús (PR)
1992	José Camacho (PR)
1994	Michael Carbajal (USA)
1994	Paul Weir (UK)
1995	Jake Matlala (SAf)
1997	Jesús Chong (Mex)
1997	Melchior Cob Castro (Mex)
1998	Juan Cordobá (Arg)

Strawweight

(Mini-flyweight WBA, IBF, WBO)
Limit 105lb (47.6kg)

WBA

1988	Leo Gamez (Dom)
1989	Kim Bong-jun (SKo)
1991	Choi Hi-yong (SKo)
1992	Hideyuki Ohashi (Jap)
1993	Chana Por Pao-in (Tha)
1995	Rosendo Álvarez (Nic)

WBC		IBF		WBO	
1987	Lee Kyung-yung (SKo)	1988	Samuth Sithnaruepol (Tha)	1989	Rafael Torres (Dom)
1988	Hiroki Ioka (Jap)	1989	Nico Thomas (Ina)	1993	Paul Weir (UK)
1988	Napa Kiatwanchai (Tha)	1989	Eric Chavez (Phi)	1993	Alex Sánchez (PR)
1989	Choi Jeum-hwan (SKo)	1990	Phahlan Lookmingkwan	1997	Ricardo López (Mex)
1990	Hideyuki Ohashi (Jap)		(Tha)	1998	Kermin Guardia (Col)
1990	Ricardo López (Mex)	1992	Manuel Melchor (Phi)		
		1992	Ratanapol (Sor Voraphin)		
			Dutchboygym (Tha)		
		1997	Zolani Lapetelo (SAf)		

World titles at most weights

6   Thomas Hearns WBA Welterweight 1980, WBC Junior middleweight 1982, WBC Light-heavyweight 1987, WBC Middleweight 1987, WBO Super-middleweight 1988, WBA Light-heavyweight 1991

5   Sugar Ray Leonard WBC Welterweight 1979, WBA Junior middleweight 1981, WBC Middleweight 1987, WBC Super-middleweight 1988, WBC Light-heavyweight 1988

4   Roberto Duran WBA Lightweight 1972, Welterweight 1980, WBA Junior middleweight 1983, WBC Middleweight 1989

4   Pernell Whitaker IBF/WBC Lightweight 1989 (WBA 1990), IBF Junior welterweight 1992, WBC Welterweight 1993, WBA Junior middleweight 1995

4   Oscar De La Hoya (USA) WBO Junior lightweight 1994, WBO Lightweight 1994 (IBF 1995), WBC Super-lightweight 1996, WBC Welterweight 1997

3   Bob Fitzsimmons Middleweight 1891, Heavyweight 1897, Light-heavyweight 1903

3   Tony Canzoneri Featherweight 1928, Lightweight 1930, Junior welterweight 1931

3   Barney Ross Lightweight 1933, Junior welterweight 1933, Welterweight 1934

3   Henry Armstrong Featherweight 1937, Welterweight 1938, Lightweight 1938

3   Wilfredo Benitez Junior welter–Super-welterweight 1976-81

3   Alexis Arguello Feather–Lightweight 1974-81

3   Wilfredo Gomez Junior feather–Junior lightweight 1977-85

3   Jeff Fenech Bantam–Featherweight 1985-8

3   Julio César Chávez Junior light–Junior welterweight 1984-9

3   Hector Camacho Junior light–Junior welterweight 1983-9

3   Duke McKenzie Feather–Super-bantamweight 1989-92

3   Mike McCallum Junior middle–Light-heavyweight 1984-94

3   Wilfredo Vasquez Bantam–Featherweight 1987-96

Emile Griffith won the welterweight title in 1961 and the middleweight title in 1966. He also claimed to be the first Junior middleweight champion in 1962, but his title was recognized in Austria only.

Most world title fights: 34 Julio César Chávez; 27 Joe Louis

Most world title fight wins: 31 Julio César Chávez; 26 Joe Louis. Louis made a record 25 defences of his heavyweight title, the most in any weight division.

Longest reigning champion: Joe Louis (USA), heavyweight, 11yr 252d

Oldest world champion: 48yr 59d Archie Moore (USA), light-heavyweight. Moore may have been only 45, because of a doubt over his date of birth. In that case, George Foreman at 46 (b.22 Jan 1949) would be the oldest.

Youngest world champion: 17yr 176d Wilfred Benitez (USA), light-welterweight

Heaviest world champion: 270lb (122kg) Primo Carnera (Ita)

Tallest world champion: 6ft 6in (1.98m) Ernie Terrell (USA), heavyweight. Jess Willard is often incorrectly quoted as being 6ft 6½in tall.

Amateur Boxing

Administered by the International Amateur Boxing Association (AIBA), formed in 1946, whose membership had reached 188 nations by 1998. The first national association was the Amateur Boxing Association (ABA) of England, founded in 1880, which staged its first championships in 1881 at four weights: feather, light, middle and heavy.

Olympic Games

Boxing was included on the Olympic programme in 1904 and 1908 and has been at each Games since 1920. Weight limits shown are those currently in use, with previous limits on the following line.

Champions:

Super-heavyweight – over 91kg

1984	Tyrell Biggs (USA)
1988	Lennox Lewis (Can)
1992	Roberto Balado (Cub)
1996	Vladimir Klichko (Ukr)

Heavyweight – 91kg

Over 156lb (71.7kg) 1904-08, over 175lb (79.4kg) 1920-36, over 80kg 1948, over 81kg 1952-80

1904	Samuel Berger (USA)
1908	Albert Leonard Oldham (UK)
1912	*Not held*
1920	Ronald Rawson (UK)
1924	Otto von Porat (Nor)
1928	Arturo Rodriguez Jurado (Arg)
1932	Santiago Lovell (Arg)
1936	Herbert Runge (Ger)
1948	Rafael Iglesias (Arg)
1952	Edward Sanders (USA)
1956	Peter Rademacher (USA)
1960	Francesco De Piccoli (Ita)
1964	Joe Frazier (USA)
1968	George Foreman (USA)
1972	Teofilo Stevenson (Cub)
1976	Teofilo Stevenson (Cub)
1980	Teofilo Stevenson (Cub)
1984	Henry Tillman (USA)
1988	Ray Mercer (USA)
1992	Félix Savon (Cub)
1996	Félix Savon (Cub)

Light-heavyweight – 81kg

Limit 175lb (79.4kg) 1920-36, 80kg 1948

1920	Eddie Eagan (USA)
1924	Harry Mitchell (UK)
1928	Victor Avendano (Arg)
1932	David Carstens (SAf)
1936	Roger Michelot (Fra)
1948	George Hunter (SAf)
1952	Norvel Lee (USA)
1956	James Boyd (USA)
1960	Cassius Clay (USA)
1964	Cosimo Pinto (Ita)
1968	Dan Poznyak (USSR)
1972	Mate Parlov (Yug)
1976	Leon Spinks (USA)
1980	Slobodan Kacar (Yug)
1984	Anton Jospovic (Yug)
1988	Andrew Maynard (USA)
1992	Torsten May (Ger)
1996	Vasiliy Zhirov (Ukr)

Middleweight – 75kg

Limit 158lb (71.7kg) 1904-08, 160lb (72.6kg) 1920-36, 73kg 1948

1904	Charles Mayer (USA)
1908	John Douglas (UK)
1920	Harry Mallin (UK)
1924	Harry Mallin (UK)
1928	Piero Toscani (Ita)
1932	Carmen Barth (USA)
1936	Jean Despeaux (Fra)
1948	László Papp (Hun)
1952	Floyd Patterson (USA)
1956	Gennadiy Schatkov (USSR)
1960	Edward Crook (USA)
1964	Valeriy Popenchenko (USSR)
1968	Chris Finnegan (UK)
1972	Vyacheslav Lemechev (USSR)
1976	Michael Spinks (USA)
1980	José Gomez (Cub)
1984	Shin Joon-sup (Sko)
1988	Henry Maske (GDR)
1992	Ariel Hernández (Cub)
1996	Ariel Hernández (Cub)

Light-middleweight – 71kg

1952	László Papp (Hun)
1956	László Papp (Hun)
1960	Wilbert McClure (USA)
1964	Boris Lagutin (USSR)
1968	Boris Lagutin (USSR)
1972	Dieter Kottysch (FRG)
1976	Jerzy Rybicki (Pol)
1980	Armando Martinez (Cub)
1984	Frank Tate (USA)
1988	Park Si-hun (Kor)
1992	Juan Carlos Lemus (Cub)
1996	David Reid (USA)

Welterweight – 67kg

Limit 143.75lb (65.3kg) 1904, 147lb (66.7kg) 1920-36

1904	Albert Young (USA)
1908	*Not held*
1920	Albert Schneider (Can)
1924	Jean Delarge (Bel)
1928	Edward Morgan (NZ)
1932	Edward Flynn (USA)
1936	Sten Suvio (Fin)
1948	Július Torma (Cs)
1952	Zygmunt Chychla (Pol)
1956	Nicolae Linca (Rom)
1960	Giovanni Benvenuti (Ita)
1964	Marian Kasprzyk (Pol)
1968	Manfred Wolke (GDR)
1972	Emilio Correa (Cub)

1976	Jochen Bachfeld (GDR)
1980	Andrés Aldama (Cub)
1984	Mark Breland (USA)
1988	Robert Wangila (Ken)
1992	Michael Carruth (Ire)
1996	Oleg Saitov (Rus)

Light-welterweight – 63.5kg

1952	Charles Adkins (USA)
1956	Vladimir Yengibaryan (USSR)
1960	Bohumil Nemecek (Cs)
1964	Jerzy Kulej (Pol)
1968	Jerzy Kulej (Pol)
1972	Ray Seales (USA)
1976	Ray Leonard (USA)
1980	Patrizio Oliva (Ita)
1984	Jerry Page (USA)
1988	Vyacheslav Janovskiy (USSR)
1992	Héctor Vinent (Cub)
1996	Héctor Vinent (Cub)

Lightweight – 60kg

Limit 135lb (61.2kg) 1904, 1920-36, 140lb (63.5kg) 1908, 62kg 1948

1904	Harry Spanger (USA)
1908	Frederick Grace (UK)
1920	Samuel Mosberg (USA)
1924	Hans Nielsen (Den)
1928	Carlo Orlando (Ita)
1932	Lawrence Stevens (SAf)
1936	Imre Harangi (Hun)
1948	Gerald Dreyer (SAf)
1952	Aureliano Bolognesi (Ita)
1956	Dick McTaggart (UK)
1960	Kazimierz Pazdzior (Pol)
1964	Józef Grudzien (Pol)
1968	Ron Harris (USA)
1972	Jan Szczepanski (Pol)
1976	Howard Davis (USA)
1980	Angel Herrera (Cub)
1984	Pernell Whitaker (USA)
1988	Andreas Zuelow (GDR)
1992	Oscar De La Hoya (USA)
1996	Hocine Soltani (Alg)

Featherweight – 57kg

Limit 125lb (56.7kg) 1904, 126lb (57.1kg) 1908-36, 58kg 1948

1904	Oliver Kirk (USA)
1908	Richard Gunn (UK)
1920	Paul Fritsch (Fra)
1924	John Fields (USA)
1928	Lambertus van Klaveren (Hol)
1932	Carmelo Robledo (Arg)
1936	Oscar Casanovas (Arg)

1948	Ernesto Formenti (Ita)	1936	Ulderico Sergo (Ita)	1948	Pascual Perez (Arg)
1952	Ján Zachara (Cs)	1948	Tibor Csik (Hun)	1952	Nathan Brooks (USA)
1956	Vladimir Safronov (USSR)	1952	Pentti Hämäläinen (Fin)	1956	Terry Spinks (UK)
1960	Francesco Musso (Ita)	1956	Wolfgang Behrendt (GDR)	1960	Gyula Török (Hun)
1964	Stanislav Stepashkin (USSR)	1960	Oleg Grigoryev (USSR)	1964	Fernando Atzori (Ita)
		1964	Takao Sakurai (Jap)	1968	Ricardo Delgado (Mex)
1968	Antonio Roldan (Mex)	1968	Valeriy Sokolov (USSR)	1972	Georgi Kostadinov (Bul)
1972	Boris Kuznetsov (USSR)	1972	Orlando Martinez (Cub)	1976	Leo Randolph (USA)
1976	Angel Herrera (Cub)	1976	Gu Yung-jo (NKo)	1980	Petar Lessov (Bul)
1980	Rudi Fink (GDR)	1980	Juan Hernández (Cub)	1984	Steve McCrory (USA)
1984	Meldrick Taylor (USA)	1984	Maurizio Stecca (Ita)	1988	Kim Kwang-sun (SKo)
1988	Giovanni Parisi (Ita)	1988	Kennedy McKinney (USA)	1992	Choi Chol-su (NKo)
1992	Andreas Tews (Ger)	1992	Joel Casamayor (Cub)	1996	Malkro Romero (Cub)
1996	Samluck Kamsing (Tha)	1996	István Kovács (Hun)		

Bantamweight – 54kg

Flyweight – 51kg

Light-flyweight – 48kg

				1968	Francisco Rodriguez (Ven)
				1972	György Gedo (Hun)
				1976	Jorge Hernández (Cub)
				1980	Shamil Sabirov (USSR)
1904	Oliver Kirk (USA)	1908	Not held	1984	Paul Gonzales (USA)
1908	Henry Thomas (UK)	1920	Frankie Genaro (USA)	1988	Ivailo Khristov (Bul)
1920	Clarence Walker (SAf)	1924	Fidel La Barba (USA)	1992	Rogelio Marcelo (Cub)
1924	William Smith (SAf)	1928	Antal Kocsis (Hun)	1996	Daniel Petrov (Bul)
1928	Vittorio Tamagnini (Ita)	1932	István Énekes (Hun)		
1932	Horace Gwynne (Can)	1936	Willi Kaiser (Ger)		

Limit 114lb (52.2kg) 1904, 116lb (52.6kg) 1908, 118lb (53.5kg) 1920-36

Limit 105lb (47.6kg) 1904, 112lb (50.8kg) 1920-36

1904 George Finnegan (USA)

Leading medal-winning nations

(G – Gold, S – Silver, B – Bronze)

	G	S	B	Total
United States	48	20	33	101
USSR/CIS	14	20	18	52
United Kingdom	12	10	21	43
Poland	8	9	26	43
Cuba	23	13	5	41
Italy	14	12	13	39
Germany (inc FRG)	6	12	13	31
Argentina	7	7	10	24

Most individual gold medals

3 László Papp (Hun) middleweight 1948, light-middleweight 1952, 1956, Teofilo Stevenson (Cub) heavyweight 1972, 1976, 1980

Oldest champion: 37yr 254d Richard Gunn (UK), featherweight 1908

Youngest champion: 16yr 162d Jackie Fields (USA), featherweight 1924

Olympic Champions to Win Professional World Titles

	Olympic title		First pro title	
Fidel LaBarba (USA)	1924	fly	1925	fly
Willie Smith (SAf)	1924	bantam	1927	bantam*
Frankie Genaro (USA)	1920	fly	1928	fly
Jackie Fields (USA)	1924	feather	1929	welter
Pascual Pérez (Arg)	1948	fly	1954	fly
Floyd Patterson (USA)	1952	middle	1956	heavy
Cassius Clay (USA)	1960	light-heavy	1964	heavy
Nino Benvenuti (Ita)	1960	welter	1965	junior middle
Joe Frazier (USA)	1964	heavy	1968	heavy
George Foreman (USA)	1968	heavy	1973	heavy
Mate Parlov (Yug)	1972	light-heavy	1978	light-heavy
Leon Spinks (USA)	1976	light-heavy	1978	heavy
Sugar Ray Leonard USA	1976	light-welter	1979	junior middle

Leo Randolph (USA)	1976	fly	1980	junior fly
Michael Spinks (USA)	1976	middle	1981	light-heavy
Slobodan Kacar (Yug)	1980	light-heavy	1985	middle
Patrizio Oliva (Ita)	1980	light-welter	1986	junior welter
Mark Breland (USA)	1984	welter	1987	welter
Frank Tate (USA)	1984	light-middle	1987	middle
Meldrick Taylor (USA)	1984	feather	1988	junior welter
Maurizio Stecca (Ita)	1984	bantam	1989	feather
Pernell Whittaker (USA)	1984	light	1989	light
Ray Mercer (USA)	1988	heavy	1991	heavy
Lennox Lewis (UK)	1988	super-heavy	1992	heavy
Giovanni Parisi (Ita)	1988	feather	1992	light
Kennedy McKinney US	1988	bantam	1992	junior feather
Henry Maske (Ger)	1988	middle	1993	light-heavy
Oscar De La Hoya USA	1992	light	1994	junior light

* Smith won the British version of the world title only.

World Amateur Championships

First held in Havana in 1974, these championships are now held biennially. A challenge series, involving seven of the 1982 champions, was organized in Reno in March 1983, and a second series of challenge bouts for the remaining champions took place in Tokyo two months later. These winners have been included in the tables that follow.

Super-heavyweight – over 91kg

1982	Tyrell Biggs (USA)
1983	Tyrell Biggs (USA)
1986	Teofilo Stevenson (Cub)
1989	Roberto Balado (Cub)
1991	Roberto Balado (Cub)
1993	Roberto Balado (Cub)
1995	Aleksey Lezin (Rus)
1997	George Kandelaki (Geo)

Heavyweight – 91kg

1974	Teofilo Stevenson (Cub)
1978	Teofilo Stevenson (Cub)
1982	Aleksandr Lagubkin (USSR)
1983	Willie DeWitt (Can)
1986	Félix Savón (Cub)
1989	Félix Savón (Cub)
1991	Félix Savón (Cub)
1993	Félix Savón (Cub)
1995	Félix Savón (Cub)
1997	Félix Savon (Cub)*

* Original winner Ruslan Chagayev (Uzb) was disqualified.

Light-heavyweight – 81kg

1974	Mate Parlov (Yug)
1978	Sixto Soria (Cub)
1982	Pablo Romero (Cub)
1983	Pablo Romero (Cub)
1986	Pablo Romero (Cub)
1989	Henry Maske (GDR)
1991	Torsten May (Ger)
1993	Ramon Garbey (Cub)
1995	Antonio Tarver (USA)
1997	Aleksandr Lebziak (Rus)

Middleweight – 75kg

1974	Rufat Riskiyev (USSR)
1978	José Gomez (Cub)
1982	Bernardo Comas (Cub)
1983	Bernardo Comas (Cub)
1986	Darin Allen (USA)
1989	Andrey Kurnyavka (USSR)
1991	Tommaso Russo (Ita)
1993	Ariel Hernández (Cub)
1995	Ariel Hernández (Cub)
1997	Zsolt Erdei (Hun)

Light-middleweight – 71kg

1974	Rolando Garbey (Cub)
1978	Viktor Savchenko (USSR)
1982	Aleksandr Koshkin (USSR)
1983	Shawn O'Sullivan (Can)
1986	Angel Espinosa (Cub)
1989	Israel Akopkokhyan (USSR)
1991	Juan Lemus (Cub)
1993	Francisc Vastag (Rom)
1995	Francisc Vastag (Rom)
1997	Alfredo Duvergel (Cub)

Welterweight – 67kg

1974	Emilio Correa (Cub)
1978	Valeriy Rachkov (USSR)
1982	Mark Breland (USA)
1983	Mark Breland (USA)
1986	Kenneth Gould (USA)
1989	Francisc Vastag (Rom)
1991	Juan Hernández (Cub)
1993	Juan Hernández (Cub)
1995	Juan Hernández (Cub)
1997	Oleg Saitov (Rus)

Light-welterweight – 63.5kg

1974	Ayub Kalule (Uga)
1978	Valeriy Lvov (USSR)
1982	Carlos Garcia (Cub)
1983	Carlos Garcia (Cub)
1986	Vasiliy Shishov (USSR)
1989	Igor Ruzhnikov (USSR)
1991	Konstantin Tszyu (USSR)
1993	Héctor Vinent (Cub)
1995	Héctor Vinent (Cub)
1997	Dorel Simion (Rom)

Lightweight – 60kg

1974	Vasiliy Solomin (USSR)
1978	Andeh Davison (Nig)
1982	Angel Herrera (Cub)
1983	Pernell Whitaker (USA)
1986	Adolfo Horta (Cub)
1989	Julio González (Cub)
1991	Marco Rudolph (Ger)
1993	Damian Austin (Cub)
1995	Leonard Doroftei (Rom)
1997	Aleksandr Maletin (Rus)

Featherweight – 57kg

1974	Howard Davis (USA)
1978	Angel Herrera (Cub)
1982	Adolfo Horta (Cub)
1983	Adolfo Horta (Cub)
1986	Kelcie Banks (USA)
1989	Airat Khamatov (USSR)
1991	Kirkor Kirkorov (Bul)
1993	Serafim Todorov (Bul)
1995	Serafim Todorov (Bul)
1997	István Kovács (Hun)

Bantamweight – 54kg		Flyweight – 51kg		Light-flyweight – 48kg	
1974	Wilfredo Gomez (PR)	1974	Douglas Rodriguez (Cub)	1974	Jorge Hernández (Cub)
1978	Adolfo Horta (Cub)	1978	Henryk Srednicki (Pol)	1978	Stephen Muchoki (Ken)
1982	Floyd Favors (USA)	1982	Yuriy Aleksandrov (USSR)	1982	Ismail Mustafov (Bul)
1983	Floyd Favors (USA)	1983	Steve McCrory (USA)	1983	Rafael Saiz (Cub)
1986	Moon Sung-kil (SKo)	1986	Pedro Reyes (Cub)	1986	Juan Torres (Cub)
1989	Enrique Carrion (Cub)	1989	Yuriy Arbachakov (USSR)	1989	Eric Griffin (USA)
1991	Serafim Todorov (Bul)	1991	István Kovács (Hun)	1991	Eric Griffin (USA)
1993	Alexander Khristov (Bul)	1993	Waldemar Font (Cub)	1993	Nshan Muntjian (Arm)
1995	Raimkul Malachbekov (Rus)	1995	Zoltan Lunke (Ger)	1995	Daniel Petrov (Bul)
		1997	Manuel Mantilla (Cub)	1997	Maikro Romero (Cub)
1997	Raimkul Malachbekov (Rus)				

Most titles: 6 Félix Savón;
3 Teofilo Stevenson, Adolfo
Horta (and 1983 world challenge),
Roberto Balado, Juan Hernández.
Pablo Romero won two and a
world challenge in 1983.

Canoeing

International canoe racing is practised in kayaks or Canadian canoes over flat water or, for canoe slalom, on wild water. Kayak is the Inuit word for a canoe made of sealskin, originally stretched over a whalebone frame. Kayak canoeists use a paddle with a blade at each end, and Canadian canoes are propelled by a paddle with a single blade, from a half-kneeling position. Races are designated with K for kayak and C for Canadian canoes followed by the number of canoeists, eg K1, K2, K4, C1, C2.

The most important pioneer of canoeing as a sport was John MacGregor, who founded the Canoe Club in Surrey, England in 1866. European Championships were first held in 1933, with racing at six categories: K1, C1 and C2 over 1000m; K1, and C1 and C2 for folding crafts, over 10,000m. Wild-water and slalom canoeing were introduced in the 1930s.

Speed races on still water are contested at 500m and 1000m in a straight line; formerly, they were also contested over 10,000m on a circuit. Slalom competitions are contested over a rapid river course of maximum extent 600m, through a series of 25 gates, with scoring both for time and as penalty points for faults in negotiating the course. Wild-water competitions are contested on a course of at least 3km in length.

International governing body: International Canoe Federation (FIC), Dozsa György ut 1-3, 1143 Budapest, Hungary. Tel: (36) 1 3634832, Fax: (36) 1 2214130. President: Sergio Orsi, Secretary-General: Otto Bonn. Founded 1924, until 1946 the 'Champst für Kanusport'. 93 member nations in 1996.

Olympic Games

The sport has been part of each Olympic Games from 1936, with slalom events also in 1972 and 1992.
Winners:

Men

Canoe racing – K1 500 metres

1976	Vasile Diba (Rom) 1:46.41
1980	Vladimir Parfenovich (USSR) 1:43.43
1984	Ian Ferguson (NZ) 1:47.84
1988	Zsolt Gyulay (Hun) 1:44.82
1992	Mikko Kolehmainen (Fin) 1:40.34
1996	Antonio Rossi (Ita) 1:37.42

Canoe racing – K1 1000 metres

1936	Gregor Hradetzky (Aut) 4:22.9
1948	Gert Fredriksson (Swe) 4:33.2
1952	Gert Fredriksson (Swe) 4:07.9
1956	Gert Fredriksson (Swe) 4:12.8
1960	Erik Hansen (Den) 3:53.00
1964	Rolf Peterson (Swe) 3:57.13
1968	Mihály Hesz (Hun) 4:02.63
1972	Aleksandr Shaparenko (USSR) 3:48.06
1976	Rüdiger Helm (GDR) 3:48.20
1980	Rüdiger Helm (GDR) 3:48.77
1984	Alan Thompson (NZ) 3:45.73
1988	Greg Barton (USA) 3:55.27
1992	Clint Robinson (Aus) 3:37.26
1996	Knut Holmann (Nor) 3:25.78

Canoe racing – K1 10,000 metres

1936	Ernst Krebs (Ger) 46:01.6
1948	Gert Fredriksson (Swe) 50:47.7
1952	Thorvald Strömberg (Fin) 47:22.8
1956	Gert Fredriksson (Swe) 47:43.4

Canoe racing – K1 4 x 500 metres relay

1960	Germany 7:39.43

Canoe racing – K2 500 metres

1976	Joachim Mattern & Bernd Olbricht (GDR) 1:35.87
1980	Vladimir Parfenovich & Sergey Chukrai (USSR) 1:32.38
1984	Ian Ferguson & Paul McDonald (NZ) 1:34.21
1988	Ian Ferguson & Paul McDonald (NZ) 1:33.98
1992	Kay Bluhm & Torsten Gütsche (Ger) 1:28.27
1996	Kay Bluhm & Torsten Gütsche (Ger) 1:28.69

Canoe racing – K2 1000 metres

1936	Adolf Kainz & Alfons Dorfner (Aut) 4:03.8
1948	Hans Berglund & Lennart Klingström (Swe) 4:07.3
1952	Kurt Wires & Yrjö Hietanen (Fin) 3:51.1
1956	Michel Scheuer & Meinrad Miltenberger (FRG) 3:49.6
1960	Gert Fredriksson & Sven-Olov Sjödelius (Swe) 3:34.7
1964	Sven-Olov Sjödelius & Nils Utterberg (Swe) 3:38.54
1968	Aleksandr Shaparenko & Vladimir Morozov (USSR) 3:37.54
1972	Nikolay Gorbachev & Viktor Kratassyuk (USSR) 3:31.23
1976	Sergey Nagorny & Vladimir Romanovsky (USSR) 3:29.01
1980	Vladimir Parfenovich & Sergey Chukrai (USSR) 3:26.72
1984	Hugh Fisher & Alwyn Morris (Can) 3:24.22
1988	Greg Barton & Norman Bellingham (USA) 3:32.42
1992	Kay Bluhm & Torsten Gütsche (Ger) 3:16.10
1996	Antonio Rossi & Daniele Scarpa (Ita) 3:09.19

Canoe racing – K2 10,000 metres

1936	Paul Weavers & Ludwig Landen (Ger) 41:45.0
1948	Gunnar Åkerlund & Hans Wetterström (Swe) 46:09.4
1952	Kurt Wires & Yrjö Hietanen (Fin) 44:21.3
1956	János Urányi & László Fábián (Hun) 43:37.0

Canoe racing – K4 1000 metres

1964	USSR 3:14.67
1968	Norway 3:14.38
1972	USSR 3:14.02
1976	USSR 3:08.69
1980	GDR 3:13.76
1984	New Zealand 3:02.28
1988	Hungary 3:00.20
1992	Germany 2:54.18
1996	Germany 2:51.52

Canoe racing – C1 500 metres

1976	Aleksandr Rogov (USSR) 1:59.23
1980	Sergey Postrekhin (USSR) 1:53.37
1984	Larry Cain (Can) 1:57.01
1988	Olaf Heukrodt (GDR) 1:56.42

1992	Nikolai Boukhalov (Bul) 1:51.15
1996	Martin Doktor (Cze) 1:49.93

Canoe racing – C1 1000 metres

1936	Francis Amyot (Can) 5:32.1
1948	Josef Holecek (Cs) 5:42.0
1952	Josef Holecek (Cs) 4:56.3
1956	Leon Rotman (Rom) 5:05.3
1960	János Parti (Hun) 4:33.93
1964	Jürgen Eschert (GDR) 4:35.14
1968	Tibor Tatai (Hun) 4:36.14
1972	Ivan Patzaichin (Rom) 4:08.94
1976	Matija Ljubek (Yug) 4:09.51
1980	Lubomir Lubenov (Bul) 4:12.38
1984	Ulrich Eicke (FRG) 4:06.32
1988	Ivan Klementjevs (USSR) 4:12.78
1992	Nikolai Boukhalov (Bul) 4:05.92
1996	Martin Doktor (Cze) 3:54.41

Canoe racing – C1 10,000 metres

1948	Frantisek Capek (Cs) 62:05.2
1952	Frank Havens (USA) 57:41.1
1956	Leon Rotman (Rom) 56:41.0

Canoe racing – C2 500 metres

1976	Sergey Petrenko & Aleksandr Vinogradov (USSR) 1:45.81
1980	László Foltan & István Vaskuti (Hun) 1:43.39
1984	Matija Ljubek & Mirko Nisovic (Yug) 1:43.67
1988	Viktor Reneyskiy & Nikolay Zhuravskiy (USSR) 1:41.77
1992	Aleksandr Maseikov & Dmitriy Dovgalenok (CIS/Blr) 1:41.54
1996	Csaba Horváth & György Kolonics (Hun) 1:40.42

Canoe racing – C2 1000 metres

1936	Vladimir Syrovátka & Jan-Felix Brzák (Cs) 4:50.1
1948	Jan-Felix Brzák & Bohumil Kudrna (Cs) 5:07.1
1952	Bent Peder Rasch & Finn Haunstoft (Den) 4:38.3
1956	Alexe Dumitru & Simion Ismailciuc (Rom) 4:47.4
1960	Leonid Geyshtor & Sergey Makarenko (USSR) 4:17.94
1964	Andrey Khimich & Stepan Oschepkov (USSR) 4:04.64
1968	Ivan Patzaichin & Serghei Covaliov (Rom) 4:07.18
1972	Vladas Chessyunas & Yuriy Lobanov (USSR) 3:52.60
1976	Sergey Petrenko & Aleksandr Vinogradov (USSR) 3:52.76
1980	Ivan Patzaichin & Toma Simionov (Rom) 3:47.65
1984	Ivan Patzaichin & Toma Simionov (Rom) 3:40.60

1988	Viktor Reneyskiy & Nikolay Zhuravskiy (USSR) 3:48.36
1992	Ulrich Papke & Ingo Spelly (Ger) 3:37.42
1996	Andreas Dittmer & Gunar Kirchbach (Ger) 3:31.87

Canoe racing – C2 10,000 metres

1936	Václav Mottl & Zdenek Skrdlant (Cs) 50:33.5
1948	Stephen Lysack & Stephen Macknowski (USA) 55:55.4
1952	Georges Turlier & Jean Laudet (Fra) 54:08.3
1956	Pavel Kharin & Gratsian Botev (USSR) 54:02.4

Folding kayak

| 1936 | K1: Gregor Hradetzky (Aut) 50:01.2 |
| 1936 | K2: Sven Johansson & Eric Bladström (Swe) 45:48.9 |

K1 slalom

1972	Siegbert Horn (GDR)
1992	Pierpaolo Ferrazzi (Ita)
1996	Oliver Fiz (Ger)

C1 slalom

1972	Reinhard Eiben (GDR)
1992	Lukas Pollert (Cs)
1996	Michal Martikan (Svk)

C2 slalom

1972	Walter Hofmann & Rolf-Dieter Amend (GDR)
1992	Scott Strausbaugh & Joe Jacobi (USA)
1996	Frank Adisson & Wilfrid Forgues (Fra)

Most gold medals: 6 Gert Fredriksson (Swe) 1948-60; 4 Ivan Patzaichin (Rom) 1968-84, Ian Ferguson (NZ) 1984-8

Most gold medals at one Games: 3 Vladimir Parfenovich (USSR) 1980, Ian Ferguson (NZ) 1984

Most medals: 8 Gert Fredriksson 6 gold as above, silver K1 10,000m 1952, bronze K1 1000m 1960; 7 Ivan Patzaichin 4 gold as above, 3 silver C2 500m 1980-84, C2 1000m 1972

Women

Canoe racing – K1 500 metres

1948	Karen Hoff (Den) 2:31.9
1952	Sylvi Saimo (Fin) 2:18.4
1956	Yelisaveta Dementyeva (USSR) 2:18.9
1960	Antonina Seredina (USSR) 2:08.08
1964	Lyudmila Khvedosyuk (USSR) 2:12.87
1968	Lyudmila Pinayeva (USSR) 2:11.09
1972	Yulia Ryabchinskaya (USSR) 2:03.17
1976	Carola Zirzow (GDR) 2:01.05
1980	Birgit Fischer (GDR) 1:57.96
1984	Agneta Andersson (Swe) 1:58.72
1988	Vania Gecheva (Bul) 1:55.19
1992	Birgit Schmidt (Ger) 1:51.60
1996	Rita Kóbán (Hun) 1:47.65

Canoe racing – K2 500 metres

1960	Maria Zhubina & Antonina Seredina (USSR) 1:54.76
1964	Anne-Marie Zimmermann & Roswitha Esser (FRG) 1:56.95
1968	Anne-Marie Zimmermann & Roswitha Esser (FRG) 1:56.44
1972	Lyudmila Pinayeva & Yekaterina Kuryshko (USSR) 1:53.50
1976	Nina Gopova & Galina Kreft (USSR) 1:51.15
1980	Carsta Genäuss & Martina Bischof (GDR) 1:43.88
1984	Agneta Andersson & Anna Olsson (Swe) 1:45.25
1988	Birgit Schmidt & Anke Nothnagel (GDR) 1:43.46
1992	Ramona Portwich & Anke Von Seck (Ger) 1:40.29
1996	Agneta Andersson & Susanne Gunnarsson (Swe) 1:39.32

Canoe racing – K4 500 metres

1984	Romania 1:38.54
1988	GDR 1:40.78
1992	Hungary 1:38.32
1996	Germany 1:31.07

K1 slalom

1972	Angelika Bahmann (GDR)
1992	Elisabeth Micheler (Ger)
1996	Stepana Hilgertová (Cze)

Most gold medals: 5 Birgit Schmidt (née Fischer) 1980-96; 3 Lyudmila Pinayeva (née Khevedosyuk) 1964-8, Anke von Seck (née Nothnagel) 1988-92

Most medals: 8 Birgit Schmidt, 5 gold, and 3 silver K1 500m 1988, K2 500m 1996; 4 Lyudmila Pinayeva, 3 gold as above, bronze K2 500m 1968, Vanya Gecheva gold K1 500m 1988, silver K1 500m 1980 & K2 500m 1988, bronze K4 500m 1988

Canoe Racing World Championships

First held in 1938, then in 1948, 1950, 1954, 1958, 1963, 1966 and annually from 1970 with the exception of Olympic years. Races at 200 metres were introduced in 1994 when the men's 10,000 metres and women's 5000 metres events were abandoned.

Recent winners:

Men

K1 200 metres

1994	Sergey Kalesnik (Blr) 36.737
1995	Piotr Marliewicz (Pol) 37.292
1997	Vince Fehervari (Hun) 37.100

K1 500 metres

1989	Martin Hunter (Aus) 1:41.65
1990	Sergey Kalesnik (SU) 1:43.58
1991	Renn Crichlow (Can) 1:42.14

1993 Mikko Kolehmainen (Fin)
1:41.96
1994 Zsombor Borhi (Hun)
1:42.236
1995 Piotr Marliewicz (Pol)
1:40.135
1997 Bolond Storcz (Hun)
1:45.979

K1 1000 metres

1989 Zsolt Gyulay (Hun)
3:38.87
1990 Knut Holmann (Nor)
3:33.18
1991 Knut Holmann (Nor)
3:35.19
1993 Knut Holmann (Nor)
3:42.49
1994 Clint Robinson (Aus)
3:38.714
1995 Knut Holmann (Nor)
3:37.27
1997 Bolond Storcz (Hun)
3:31.625

K1 10,000 metres

1989 Attila Szabó (Hun)
42:48.94
1990 Philippe Boccara (Fra)
42:24.03
1991 Greg Barton (USA)
41:54.73
1993 Thor Nielsen (Den)
42:12.07

K2 200 metres

1994 Maciej Freimut & Adam
Wysocki (Pol) 36.156
1995 Stein Jorgensen & John
Mooney (USA) 34.279
1997 Vince Fehervari & Robert
Hegedus (Hun) 34.152

K2 500 metres

1989 Kay Bluhm & Torsten
Gütsche (GDR) 1:31.58
1990 Sergey Kalesnik &
Anatoliy Tishchenko
(USSR) 1:33.82
1991 Juan José Román & Juan
Manuel Sánchez (Spa)
1:31.70
1993 Kay Bluhm & Torsten
Gütsche (Ger) 1:32.77
1994 Kay Bluhm & Torsten
Gütsche (Ger) 1:33.108
1995 Beniamino Bonomi &
Daniele Scarpa (Ita)
1:30.561

K2 1000 metres

1989 Kay Bluhm & Torsten
Gütsche (GDR) 3:11.62
1990 Kay Bluhm & Torsten
Gütsche (GDR) 3:15.77
1991 Kay Bluhm & Torsten
Gütsche (GDR) 3:15.16
1993 Kay Bluhm & Torsten
Gütsche (Ger) 3.21.80
1994 Jesper Staal & Thor
Nielsen (Den) 3:21.268
1995 Antonio Rossi & Daniele
Scarpa (Ita) 3:18.11
1997 Antonio Rossi & Luca
Negri (Ita) 3:12.514

K2 10,000 metres

1989 Attila Abrahám & Sándor
Hódosi (Hun) 39:24.99
1990 Ivan Lawler & Grayson
Bourne (UK) 39:48.21
1991 Philippe Boccara & Pascal
Boucherit (Fra) 38:58.69
1993 Zsombor Borhi & Attila
Abrahám (Hun) 38:43.34

K4 200 metres

1994 Russia 32.180
1995 Hungary 31.227
1997 Russia 32.128

K4 500 metres

1989 USSR 1:22.50
1990 USSR 1:25.20
1991 Germany 1:23.25
1993 Russia 1:24.80
1994 Russia 1:21.488
1995 Russia 1:23.187
1997 Hungary 1:26.689

K4 1000 metres

1989 Hungary 2:55.30
1990 Hungary 2:57.89
1991 Hungary 2:58.15
1993 Germany 3:04.80
1994 Russia 3:01.488
1995 Germany 2:59.99
1997 Germany 2:52.568

K4 10,000 metres

1989 USSR 35:58.54
1990 USSR 35:21.86
1991 Germany 35:37.98
1993 Germany 35:23.38

C1 200 metres

1994 Nikolai Boukhalov (Bul)
41.869

C1 200 metres (right column)

1995 Nikolai Boukhalov (Bul)
42.757
1997 Bela Belicza (Hun) 43.097

C1 500 metres

1989 Mikhail Slivinsky (USSR)
1:53.17
1990 Mikhail Slivinsky (USSR)
1:55.95
1991 Mikhail Slivinsky (USSR)
1:52.28
1993 Nikolai Boukhalov (Bul)
1:54.02
1994 Nikolai Boukhalov (Bul)
1:55.264
1995 Nikolai Boukhalov (Bul)
1:51.848
1997 Martin Doktor (Cze)
2:01.569

C1 1000 metres

1989 Ivan Klementjevs (USSR)
4:00.04
1990 Ivan Klementjevs (USSR)
4:01.06
1991 Ivan Klementjevs (USSR)
4:02.61
1993 Ivan Klementjevs (Lat)
4:11.20
1994 Ivan Klementjevs (Lat)
4:08.144
1995 Imre Pulai (Hun) 4:03.58
1997 Andreas Dittmer (Ger)
3:59.082

C1 10,000 metres

1989 Ivan Klementjevs (USSR)
46:49.96
1990 Zsolt Bohács (Hun)
48:48.24
1991 Zsolt Bohács (Hun)
46:57.58
1993 Zsolt Bohács (Hun)
47:11.29

C2 200 metres

1994 Aleksandr Maseykov &
Dmitriy Dovgalenok (Blr)
39.792
1995 Csaba Horváth & György
Kolonics (Hun) 38.825
1997 Thomas Zereske &
Christian Gille (Ger)
39.153

C2 500 metres

1989 Nikolay Zhuravsky &
Viktor Reneysky (USSR)
1:40.90

1990	Nikolay Zhuravsky & Viktor Reneysky (USSR) 1:46.01
1991	Attila Paliza & Attila Szabó (Hun) 1:42.00
1993	Csaba Horváth & György Kolonics (Hun) 1:46.40
1994	Gheorghe Andriev & Grigore Obreja (Rom) 1:47.780
1995	Csaba Horváth & György Kolonics (Hun) 1:42.741
1997	Csaba Horváth & György Kolonics (Hun) 1:49.400

C2 1000 metres

1989	Christian Fredriksen & Arne Nielsson (Den) 3:37.08
1990	Ulrich Papke & Ingo Spelly (GDR) 3:38.45
1991	Ulrich Papke & Ingo Spelly (Ger) 3:43.42
1993	Christian Fredriksen & Arne Nielsson (Den) 3:49.52
1994	Andreas Dittmer & Gunar Kirchbach (Ger) 3:50.100
1995	Csaba Horváth & György Kolonics (Hun) 3:45.56
1997	Gunar Kirchbcah & Matthias Röder (Ger) 3:38.550

C2 10,000 metres

1989	Christian Fredriksen & Arne Nielsson (Den) 42:42.59
1990	Christian Fredriksen & Arne Nielsson (Den) 43:04.38
1991	István Gyulai & Pap Petervari (Hun) 42:58.20
1993	Christian Fredriksen & Arne Nielsson (Den) 42:18.58

C4 200 metres

1994	Russia 35.412
1995	Hungary 35.1.53
1997	Belarus 35.649

C4 500 metres

1989	USSR 1:31.10
1990	USSR 1:37.00
1991	USSR 1:32.42

1993	Hungary 1:33.95
1994	Hungary 1:30.464
1995	Hungary 1:34.197
1997	Hungary 1:38.137

C4 1000 metres

1989	USSR 3:19.94
1990	USSR 3:24.74
1991	USSR 3:19.50
1993	Hungary 3:30.67
1994	Hungary 3:26.708
1995	Romania 3:22.96
1997	Romania 3:17.903

Women

K1 200 metres

1994	Rita Köbán (Hun) 42.904
1995	Rita Köbán (Hun) 42.970
1997	Caroline Brunet (Can) 42.927

K1 500 metres

1989	Katrin Borchert (GDR) 1:53.38
1990	Josefa Idem (Ita) 1:57.58
1991	Katrin Borchert (Ger) 1:53.59
1993	Birgit Schmidt (Ger) 1:53.00
1994	Birgit Schmidt (Ger) 1:53.552
1995	Rita Köbán (Hun) 1:50.976
1997	Caroline Brunet (Can) 1:58.566

K1 5000 metres

1989	Katrin Borchert (GDR) 22:15.80
1990	Katrin Borchert (GDR) 22:34.17
1991	Josefa Idem (Ita) 22:30.70
1993	Susanne Gunnarsson (Swe) 22:39.76

K1 1000 metres

1997	Caroline Brunet (Can) 3:53.674

K2 200 metres

1994	Rita Köbán & Eva Laky (Hun) 40.252
1995	Corinna Kennedy & Marie Josée Gibeau (Can) 39.811
1997	Birgit Fischer & Anett Schuck (Ger) 40.300

K2 500 metres

1989	Anke Nothnagel & Heike Singer (GDR) 1:43.17
1990	Ramona Portwich & Anke Von Seck (GDR) 1:46.92
1991	Ramona Portwich & Anke Von Seck (Ger) 1:43.21
1993	Anna Olsson & Agneta Andersson (Swe) 1:48.56
1994	Elzbieta Urbanczyk & Barbara Hajcel (Pol) 1:49.684
1995	Ramona Portwich & Anett Schuck (Ger) 1:42.611
1997	Birgit Fischer & Anett Schuck (Ger) 1:47.178

K2 1000 metres

1997	Birgit Fischer & Manuela Bednar (Ger) 3:36.924

K2 5000 metres

1989	Monike Bünke & Ramona Portwich (GDR) 20:27.05
1990	Ramona Portwich & Anke Von Seck (GDR) 20:46.63
1991	Ramona Portwich & Anke Von Seck (Ger) 20:43.92
1993	Ramona Portwich & Anett Schuck (Ger) 21:33.51

K4 200 metres

1994	Hungary 37.120
1995	Canada 36.602
1997	Germany 36.850

K4 500 metres

1989	GDR 1:32.90
1990	GDR 1:35.58
1991	Germany 1:36.58
1993	Germany 1:37.99
1994	Germany 1:35.58
1995	Germany 1:36.00
1997	Germany 1:37.40

Most wins at World Championships and Olympic Games

Men:

13 Gert Fredriksson (Swe) K1 500m 1948, 1954; K1 1000m 1948, 1950, 1952, 1954, 1956; K1 10,000m 1948, 1956; K1 4x500m relay 1948, 1950, 1954; K2 1000m 1960

13 Rüdiger Helm (GDR) K1 1000m 1976, 1978-83; K2 500m 1978; K4 500m 1983; K4 10,000m 1978-81

13 Ivan Patzaichin (Rom) C1 1000m 1972-3, 1977; C1 10,000m 1978; C2 500m 1979; C2 1000m 1968, 1970, 1972, 1980-1, 1983-4; C2 10,000m 1982

12 Vladimir Parfenovich (USSR) K1 500m 1979-83; K2 500m 1979-82; K2 1000m 1980-2

11 Yuriy Lobanov (USSR) C2 500m 1974-5, C2 1000m 1972, 1974, 1977, 1979; C2 10,000m 1973-5, 1977, 1979

Women:

31 Birgit Fischer (GDR/Ger) K1 500m 1980-3, 1985, 1987, 1992-4; K2 200m 1997; 500m 1981-3, 1985, 1987-8, 1997; K2 1500m 1997; K4 200m 1997; 500m 1979, 1981-3, 1985, 1987-8, 1993-7

16 Ramona Portwich (GDR/Ger) K2 500m 1990-92, 1995; 5000m 1989-91, 1993; K4 500m 1987-8, 1990-1, 1993-6

Most wins at one individual event

Men: 7 Tamas Wichmann (Hun) C1 10,000m 1970-1, 1974, 1977, 1979, 1981-2; 6 Rüdiger Helm (GDR) K1 1000m 1976, 1978-83; 5 Vladimir Parfenovich (USSR) K1 500m 1979-83

Women: 9 Birgit Fischer (GDR) K1 500m as above; 5 Lyudmila Pinayeva (USSR) K1 500m 1964, 1966, 1968, 1970-1

Canoe Slalom World Championships

Held biennially since 1949.

Men C1 slalom

1949	Pierre d'Alencon (Fra)
1951	Charles Dussuet (Swi)
1953	Charles Dussuet (Swi)
1955	Vladimir Jirasek (Cs)
1957	Manfred Schubert (GDR)
1959	Vladimir Jirasek (Cs)
1961	Manfred Schubert (GDR)
1963	Manfred Schubert (GDR)
1965	Gert Kleinert (GDR)
1967	Wolfgang Peters (FRG)
1969	Wolfgang Peters (FRG)
1971	Reinhard Kauder (FRG)
1973	Reinhard Eiben (GDR)
1975	Peter Sodomka (Cs)
1977	Peter Sodomka (Cs)
1979	Jon Lugbill (USA)
1981	Jon Lugbill (USA)
1983	Jon Lugbill (USA)
1985	David Hearn (USA)
1987	Jon Lugbill (USA)
1989	Jon Lugbill (USA)
1991	Martin Lang (Ger)
1993	Martin Lang (Ger)
1995	David Hearn (USA)
1997	Michal Martikan (Svk)

Men K1 slalom

	Othmar Eiterer (Aut)
	Hans Frühwirth (Aut)
	Walter Kirschnaum (FRG)
	Sigi Holzbauer (FRG)
	Manfred Vogt (GDR)
	Paul Farrant (UK)
	Eberhard Gläser (GDR)
	Jürgen Bremer (GDR)
	Kurt Presslmayr (Aut)
	Jürgen Bremer (GDR)
	Claude Peschier (Fra)
	Siegbert Horn (GDR)
	Norbert Sattler (Aut)
	Siegbert Horn (GDR)
	Albert Venn (UK)
	Peter Fauster (Aut)
	Richard Fox (UK)
	Richard Fox (UK)
	Richard Fox (UK)
	Anton Prijon (FRG)
	Richard Fox (UK)
	Shaun Pearce (UK)
	Richard Fox (UK)
	Oliver Fix (Ger)
	Thomas Becker (Ger)

Women K1 slalom

	Hedi Pillwein (Aut)
	Gerti Pertlweiser (Aut)
	Fritzi Schwingl (Aut)
	Rosanne Biesinger (FRG)
	Brigitte Magnus (GDR)
	Hilde Urbaniak (FRG)
	Ludmilla Veberová (Cs)
	Ludmilla Veberová (Cs)
	Ursula Gläser (GDR)
	Ludmilla Polesová (Cs)
	Ludmilla Polesová (Cs)
	Angelika Bahmann (GDR)
	Sybille Spindler (GDR)
	Marija Cwierniewicz (Pol)
	Angelika Bahmann (GDR)
	Cathy Hearn (USA)
	Ulrike Deppe (FRG))
	Elizabeth Sharman (UK)
	Margit Messelhäuser (FRG)
	Elizabeth Sharman (UK)
	Myriam Jérusalmi (Fra)
	Elisabeth Micheler (Ger)
	Myriam Jérusalmi (Fra)
	Lynn Simpson (UK)
	Brigitte Guibal (Fra)

Men C2 slalom

1989	Frank Hemmer & Thomas Loose (FRG)
1991	Franck Adisson & Wilfried Forgues (Fra)
1993	Miroslav Simek & Jiří Rohan (Cze)
1995	Krzysztof Kolomanski & Michel Staniszewski (Pol)
1997	Franck Adisson & Wilfried Forgues (Fra)

Men C1 team		Men C2 team	Men K1 team	Women K1 team
1989	USA	France	Yugoslavia	France
1991	USA	France	France	France
1993	Slovenia	Czech Republic	UK	France
1995	Germany	Czech Republic	Germany	France
1997	Slovakia	France	UK	Germany

Most individual wins

5 Jon Lugbill (USA) men's C1 (also 7 at C1 team 1979-91)
5 Richard Fox (UK) men's K1 (also 5 at K1 team 1981-7, 1993)

Wild-Water World Championships

Held biennially since 1959.

Most individual wins

Men: 4 Jean-Pierre Burny (Bel) K1 1969, 1973, 1975, 1979, Gilles Zok (Fra) C1 1981, 1983, 1985, 1987 (also 5 at C1 team 1977-85)
Women: 3 Gisela Grothaus (FRG) K1 1973, 1975, 1977 (also 4 K1 team 1973-83)

Individual winners from 1989

Men K1

1989	Marco Previde-Massara (Ita)
1991	Markus Gickler (Ger)
1993	Markus Gickler (Ger)
1995	Markus Gickler (Ger)
1998	Thomas Koelmann (Ger)

Men C1

1989	Andrej Jelenc (Yug)
1991	Tomislav Crnkovic (Yug)
1993	Vladi Panato (Ita)
1995	Vladi Panato (Ita)
1998	Vladi Panato (Ita)

Men C2

1989	Andrej Grobisa & Srecko Maslé (Yug)
1991	Eric Archambaut & Thierry Carlin (Fra)
1993	Damien Faysse & Pierre Roos (Fra)
1995	Vladimir Vala & Jaroslav Slicik (Svk)
1998	Gregor Simon & Peter Müller (Ger)

Men team K1

1989	France
1991	Italy
1993	France
1995	New Zealand
1998	France

Men team C1

1989	France
1991	Yugoslavia
1993	France
1995	Germany
1998	France

Men team C2

1989	F R Germany
1991	Germany
1993	Germany
1995	France
1998	Slovakia

Women K1

1989	Sabine Kleinhentz (Fra)
1991	Karin Wahl (Ger)
1993	Uschi Profanter (Aut)
1995	Uschi Profanter (Aut)
1998	Claudia Brokof (Ger)

Women team K1

1989	France
1991	France
1993	France
1995	France
1998	France

Canoe Marathon World Championships

First held at Holme Pierrepont, Nottingham, England in 1988.

Men K1

1988	John Jacoby (Aus)
1990	Kalman Petrovics (Hun)
1992	Ivan Lawler (UK)
1994	Lars Koch (Den)
1996	Chad Meek (Aus)

Men K2

1988	Thor Nielsen & Lars Koch (Den)
1990	Thor Nielsen & Lars Koch (Den)
1992	Ramon Andersson & Steve Wood (Aus)
1994	Ivan Lawler & Steven Harris (UK)
1996	Ivan Lawler & Steven Harris (UK)

Men C1

1988	Pál Pétervári (Hun)
1990	Stig Jepsen (Den)
1992	Gábor Kolozsvári (Hun)
1994	Arne Nielsson (Den)
1996	Arne Nielsson (Den)

Men C2

1988	Stephen Train & Andrew Train (UK)
1990	Arne Nielsen & Christian Frederiksen (Den)
1992	Arne Nielsen & Christian Frederiksen (Den)
1994	Zsolt Bohacs & István Gyulai (Hun)
1996	Stephen Train & Andrew Train (UK)

Women K1

1988	Jane Hall (Aus)
1990	Ingeborg Rasmussen (Nor)
1992	Susanne Gunnarsson (Swe)
1994	Susanne Gunnarsson (Swe)
1996	Susanne Gunnarsson (Swe)

Women K2

1988	Gayle Mayes & Denise Cooper (Aus)
1990	Agnés Erdody & Andrea Baranyai (Hun)
1992	Anett Schuck & Antje Manfroni (Ger)
1994	Denise Cooper & Shelly Jesney (Aus)
1996	Susanne Rosenqvist & Maria Haglund (Swe)

Canoe Sailing World Championships

First held in 1938, and then every three or four years from 1961.

Recent winners:

1984	Steve Clark (USA)
1987	Robin Wood (UK)
1990	Lars Guck (USA)
1993	Robin Wood (UK)
1996	Robin Wood (UK)

Most wins: 3 Alain Emus (UK) 1961, 1965, 1969, Wood

Canoe Polo World Championships

First held in 1994.

Winners:

Men		**Women**
1994	Australia	Australia
1996	Australia	Great Britain

Cricket

Cricket originated in England in the Middle Ages. Its exact origins are obscure, but bat and ball games were played from the 13th century and games similar to the modern one from around 1550. The earliest major match for which the full score survives was England against Kent in London in 1744. In that year the first known laws of the game were issued. The Marylebone Cricket Club (MCC) was founded in 1787, and until the formation of the Cricket Council in 1968 was accepted as the ruling body of the game. Its headquarters was (and still is) at Lord's Cricket Ground, London. The MCC remains responsible for the Laws of Cricket.

The Imperial (International from 1965) Cricket Conference was formed by representatives of England, Australia and South Africa in 1909. India, New Zealand and West Indies were elected members in 1926, Pakistan in 1953 and Sri Lanka in 1981. South Africa ceased to be a member in 1961, but was readmitted to Test cricket in 1992, and later that year Zimbabwe became the ninth Test cricketing nation. The ICC was renamed the International Cricket Council in 1989.

International governing body: International Cricket Council (ICC), The Clock Tower, Lord's Cricket Ground, London NW8 8QN. Tel: 0171 266 1818, Fax: 0171 266 1777. President: J Dalmiya, Chief Executive: D L Richards. 9 full members, 23 associate members and 13 affiliate members.

Test Cricket

The first Test match was played in Melbourne, Australia, on 15-19 March 1877 between Australia and England, represented by James Lillywhite's touring side. Neither side was truly representative of its country; indeed, this was the case for many matches, now accepted as Test matches, played over the next fifty years or so. The first match in England was against Australia at the Oval on 6-8 September 1880. First Tests played by other nations were as follows: South Africa 1889, West Indies 1928, New Zealand 1930, India 1932, Pakistan 1952, Sri Lanka 1982, Zimbabwe 1992.

Summary of Test Match Results

First figure is number of wins by team on left over team in that column; second figure is number of draws. Thus in England v Australia Tests, England have won 90, Australia 111, with 84 Tests drawn (to series completed by 16 June 1998).

	A	E	I	NZ	P	SA	SL	WI	Z	Wins	Tests
Australia	–	114/85	25/17★	15/13	14/15	34/17	7/3	35/21★	–	244	581
England	92/85	–	32/38	36/38	14/32	47/43	3/1	28/42	0/2	252	746
India	11/17★	14/38	–	13/16	4/33	2/4	7/11	7/35	1/1	59	318

	A	E	I	NZ	P	SA	SL	WI	Z	Wins	Tests
New Zealand	7/13	4/38	6/16	–	5/16	3/6	6/7	4/14	2/5	39	262
Pakistan	11/15	9/32	7/33	18/16	–	1/3	9/7	10/12	6/3	71	248
South Africa	14/17	20/43	4/3	12/6	3/3	–	3/2	0/0	1/0	57	220
Sri Lanka	0/3	1/1	1/11	4/7	3/7	0/2	–	0/2	4/3	13	83
West Indies	29/21★	51/42	28/35	10/14	12/12	1/0	1/2	–	–	132	343
Zimbabwe	–	0/2	0/1	0/5	1/3	0/0	0/3	–	–	1	30

★ Plus one tie.

There have been two tied Tests: 9-14 Dec 1960 at Brisbane, Australia v West Indies; 18-22 Sep 1986 at Madras, Australia v India.

Team Records

Highest innings totals

952-6 dec	Sri Lanka v I	Colombo	3-6 Aug 1997
903-7 dec	England v A	The Oval	20-23 Aug 1938
849	England v WI	Kingston	3-5 Apr 1930
790-3 dec	West Indies v P	Kingston	27 Feb-1 Mar 1958
758-8 dec	Australia v WI	Kingston	13-15 Jun 1955
729-6 dec	Australia v E	Lord's	28-30 Jun 1930
708	Pakistan v E	The Oval	6-8 Aug 1987
701	Australia v E	The Oval	18-20 Aug 1934

Highest match aggregates

1981 runs   South Africa (530 & 481) v England (316 & 654-5) at Durban 3-14 Mar 1939 – the 'Timeless Test'. The total playing time was 43 hours 16 minutes, over ten days, and the match was left drawn because England had to catch the boat home at the end of their tour.

1815 runs   West Indies (286 & 408-5) v England (849 & 272-9 dec) at Kingston 3-12 Apr 1930

1764 runs   Australia (533 & 339-9) v West Indies (276 & 616) at Adelaide 24-29 Jan 1969 – the record for a five-day Test

The above three Tests were left drawn.

Highest winning margin

Innings and 579 runs England (903-7 dec) beat Australia (201 & 123) at the Oval 20-24 Aug 1938

Lowest completed innings totals

26	New Zealand v E	Auckland	28 Mar 1955
30	South Africa v E	Port Elizabeth	14 Feb 1896
30	South Africa v E	Birmingham	16 Jun 1924

Lowest match aggregate

234 runs Australia (153) beat South Africa (36 & 45) 12-15 Feb 1932

Individual Test Records

Most Tests

156	Allan Border (Aus) 1978-94★
131	Kapil Dev (Ind) 1978-94
125	Sunil Gavaskar (Ind) 1971-87
124	Javed Miandad (Pak) 1976-94
121	Vivian Richards (WI) 1974-91
118	Graham Gooch (Eng) 1975-95
117	David Gower (Eng) 1978-92
116	Desmond Haynes (WI) 1978-94
116	Dilip Vengsarkar (Ind) 1976-92

114	Colin Cowdrey (Eng) 1954-75
110	Clive Lloyd (WI) 1966-85
108	Geoffrey Boycott (Eng) 1964-82
108	Gordon Greenidge (WI) 1974-91
107	David Boon (Aus) 1984-96
103	Steve Waugh (Aus) 1985-98
103	Ian Healy (Aus) 1988-98
102	Ian Botham (Eng) 1977-92
102	Courtney Walsh (WI) 1984-97

★ Including a record 153 consecutive Tests 1979-94.

Most Test appearances as captain

(No. matches won in brackets)

93	(32)	Allan Border (Aus)	1984-94
74	(36)	Clive Lloyd (WI)	1974-85
52	(13)	Michael Atherton (Eng)	1993-98
50	(27)	Vivian Richards (WI)	1980-91
48	(21)	Greg Chappell (Aus)	1975-83
48	(14)	Imran Khan (Pak)	1982-92
47	(9)	Sunil Gavaskar (Ind)	1976-85
41	(20)	Peter May (Eng)	1955-61
40	(9)	Nawab of Pataudi, Jr (Ind)	1962-75

Other captains to have won 15 or more Tests:

31	(18)	Mike Brearley (Eng)	1977-81
30	(15)	Ian Chappell (Aus)	1971-75
24	(15)	Don Bradman (Aus)	1936-48

Youngest player: 15yr 124d Mushtaq Muhammad (Pak) v WI, Lahore 26 Mar 1959. Hassan Raza (Pak) was alleged to be 14yr 227d v Zimbabwe, Faisalabad 24 Oct 1996, but was then thought to be over 15
Oldest player: 52yr 165d Wilfred Rhodes (Eng) v WI, Kingston 12 Apr 1930
Longest Test career: 30yr 314d Wilfred Rhodes (Eng) 1 Jun 1899 to 12 Apr 1930

Test Match Batting

Highest individual innings scores (over 300)

375	Brian Lara (WI) v E	St John's, Antigua	16-18 Apr 1994
365*	Garfield Sobers (WI) v P	Kingston	27 Feb-1 Mar 1958
364	Leonard Hutton (Eng) v A	The Oval	20-23 Aug 1938
340	Sanath Jayasuriya (Sri) v I	Colombo	4-6 Aug 1997
337	Hanif Muhammad (Pak)# v WI	Bridgetown	20-23 Jan 1958
336*	Walter Hammond (Eng) v NZ	Auckland	31 Mar-1 Apr 1933
334	Don Bradman (Aus) v E	Leeds	11-12 Jul 1930
333	Graham Gooch (Eng) v I	Lord's	26-27 Jul 1990
325	Andrew Sandham (Eng) v WI	Kingston	3-4 Apr 1930
311	Bobby Simpson (Aus) v E	Manchester	23-25 Jul 1964
310*	John Edrich (Eng) v NZ	Leeds	8-9 Jul 1965
307	Bob Cowper (Aus) v E	Melbourne	12-16 Feb 1966
304	Don Bradman (Aus) v E	Leeds	21-23 Jul 1934
302	Lawrence Rowe (WI) v E	Bridgetown	7-10 Mar 1974

* Not out.
# Longest-ever innings at 16 hr 39 min.
The highest match aggregate in a Test is 456 by Graham Gooch, with 333 and 123 for England v India at Lord's on 26-31 Jul 1990.

Fastest scoring

100: 70 min (67 balls) Jack Gregory, Aus v SA, Johannesburg, 12 Nov 1921 56 balls (81 min) Vivian Richards, WI v E, St John's, 15 Apr 1986
200: 214 min (259 balls) Don Bradman, Aus v E, Leeds, 11 Jul 1930 220 balls (268 min) Ian Botham, Eng v I, The Oval, 8-9 Jul 1982
300: 288 min Walter Hammond, Eng v NZ, Auckland, 31 Mar-1 Apr 1933
During his innings of 336 not out in 318 min, Hammond hit ten sixes, then a record for a Test innings. His third 100 took just 47 min, the fastest in Test cricket.

Most runs in a Test career

Runs	Name	Av.	Tests	100s	200s	Years
11,174	Allan Border (Aus)	50.56	156	27	2	1978-94
10,122	Sunil Gavaskar (Ind)	51.12	125	34	4	1971-87
8900	Graham Gooch (Eng)	42.58	118	20	2	1975-95
8832	Javed Miandad (Pak)	52.57	124	23	6	1976-94
8540	Vivian Richards (WI)	50.23	121	24	3	1974-91

Runs	Name	Av.	Tests	100s	200s	Years
8231	David Gower (Eng)	44.25	117	18	2	1978-92
8114	Geoffrey Boycott (Eng)	47.72	108	22	1	1964-82
8032	Garfield Sobers (WI)	57.78	93	26	2	1954-74
7624	Colin Cowdrey (Eng)	44.06	114	22	0	1954-75
7558	Gordon Greenidge (WI)	44.72	108	19	4	1974-91
7515	Clive Lloyd (WI)	46.67	110	19	1	1966-85
7487	Desmond Haynes (WI)	42.29	116	18	0	1978-94
7422	David Boon (Aus)	43.65	107	21	1	1984-96
7249	Walter Hammond (Eng)	58.45	85	22	7	1927-47
7110	Greg Chappell (Aus)	53.86	87	24	4	1970-84
6996	Don Bradman* (Aus)	99.94	52	29	12	1928-48
6971	Leonard Hutton (Eng)	56.67	79	19	4	1937-55
6868	Dilip Vengsarkar (Ind)	42.13	116	17	0	1976-92
6806	Ken Barrington (Eng)	58.67	82	20	1	1955-68
6784	Mark Taylor (Aus)	42.57	96	15	1	1989-98
6480	Steve Waugh (Aus)	48.72	103	14	1	1985-98
6227	Rohan Kanhai (WI)	47.53	79	15	2	1957-74
6149	Neil Harvey (Aus)	48.41	79	21	2	1948-63
6080	Gundappa Viswanath (Ind)	41.93	91	14	1	1969-83
5949	Richie Richardson (WI)	44.39	86	16	0	1983-95
5807	Denis Compton (Eng)	50.06	78	17	2	1937-57
5697	Mohammad Azharuddin (Ind)	45.94	91	20	0	1984-98
5528	Saleem Malik (Pak)	45.68	96	15	1	1982-97
5444	Martin Crowe (NZ)	45.36	77	17	1	1982-95
5442	Mike Atherton (Eng)	38.87	79	11	0	1989-98
5410	Jack Hobbs (Eng)	56.94	61	15	1	1908-30
5357	Doug Walters (Aus)	48.26	74	15	2	1965-81
5345	Ian Chappell (Aus)	42.42	75	14	0	1964-80
5334	John Wright (NZ)	37.83	82	12	0	1978-93
5248	Kapil Dev (Ind)	31.05	127	8	0	1978-94
5234	Bill Lawry (Aus)	47.15	67	13	2	1961-71
5219	Mark Waugh (Aus)	43.13	78	14	0	1991-8
5200	Ian Botham (Eng)	33.54	102	14	1	1977-92
5153	Alec Stewart (Eng)	41.22	75	10	0	1990-8
5138	John Edrich (Eng)	43.54	77	12	1	1963-76
5062	Zaheer Abbas (Pak)	44.79	78	12	4	1969-85

In addition, the following have averages of over 50 for 4500 runs or over 55 for more than 10 Tests:

4555	Herbert Sutcliffe (Eng)	60.73	54	16	0	1924-35
4552	Sachin Tendulkar (Ind)	54.84	61	16	0	1989-98
4550	Brian Lara (WI)	51.70	54	10	2	1990-98
4455	Everton Weekes (WI)	58.61	48	15	2	1948-58
3798	Clyde Walcott (WI)	56.68	44	15	1	1948-60
2256	Graeme Pollock (SAf)	60.97	23	7	2	1963-70
2190	George Headley (WI)	60.83	22	10	2	1930-54
1540	Edward Paynter (Eng)	59.23	20	4	2	1931-39
1072	Sidney Barnes (Aus)	63.05	13	3	1	1938-48
995	K S Duleepsinhji (Eng)	58.52	12	3	0	1929-31
990	Ernest Tyldesley (Eng)	55.00	14	3	0	1921-29
910	Charles Russell (Eng)	56.87	10	5	0	1920-23
723	Stewart Dempster (NZ)	65.72	10	2	0	1930-33

* Bradman at 99.94 has the highest average in Test cricket.

Fewest innings to reach

1000 runs: 12 Herbert Sutcliffe, Everton Weekes
2000/3000/4000/5000/6000 runs: 22/33/48/56/68 Don Bradman
7000 runs: 131 Walter Hammond
8000 runs: 157 Garfield Sobers
9000 runs: 192 Sunil Gavaskar
10,000 runs: 212 Sunil Gavaskar

Most runs in a Test series

Runs	Av.		Tests	Season
974	139.14	Don Bradman (Aus)	5 v E	1930
905	113.12	Walter Hammond (Eng)	5 v A	1928/9
839	83.90	Mark Taylor (Aus)	6 v E	1989
834	92.66	Neil Harvey (Aus)	5 v SA	1952/3
829	118.42	Vivian Richards (WI)	4 v E	1976
827	82.70	Clyde Walcott (WI)	5 v A	1955
824	137.33	Garfield Sobers (WI)	5 v P	1958
810	90.00	Don Bradman (Aus)	5 v E	1936/7
806	201.50	Don Bradman (Aus)	5 v SA	1931/2

Most runs in a series of three Tests or less

752	125.33	Graham Gooch (Eng)	3 v I	1990*
583	194.33	Zaheer Abbas (Pak)	3 v I	1978
571	190.33	Sanath Jayasuriya (Sri)	2 v I	1997
563	563.00	Walter Hammond (Eng)	2 v NZ	1933
558	111.60	Seymour Nurse (WI)	3 v NZ	1969

* Gooch also scored 306 in 3 Tests v NZ in 1990 for a record English summer Test aggregate of 1058 runs av. 96.18.

Most series scoring 500 runs

7 Don Bradman; 6 Sunil Gavaskar, Garfield Sobers

Most centuries in a Test series

5 Clyde Walcott (WI) v A 1955

Most sixes in a Test innings

12 Wasim Akram in 257*, Pakistan v Zimbabwe at Sheikhupura, 19-20 Oct 1996
* Not out.

Test Match Bowling

Best-ever bowling in a Test

10-53	Jim Laker (Eng) v A	Manchester	30-31 Jul 1956

Nine wickets in an innings

9-28	George Lohmann (Eng) v SA	Johannesburg	3 Mar 1896
9-37	Jim Laker (Eng) v A	Manchester	27-30 Jul 1956
9-52	Richard Hadlee (NZ) v A	Brisbane	8-9 Nov 1985
9-56	Abdul Qadir (Pak) v E	Lahore	25 Nov 1987
9-57	Devon Malcolm (Eng) v SA	The Oval	20 Aug 1994
9-69	Jasubhai Patel (Ind) v A	Kanpur	20 Dec 1959
9-83	Kapil Dev (Ind) v WI	Ahmedabad	14-16 Nov 1983
9-86	Sarfraz Nawaz (Pak) v A	Melbourne	14-15 Mar 1979
9-95	John Noreiga (WI) v I	Port-of-Spain	7-9 Mar 1971
9-102	Subhash Gupte (Ind) v WI	Kanpur	12 Dec 1958
9-103	Sydney Barnes (Eng) v SA	Johannesburg	29-30 Dec 1913
9-113	Hugh Tayfield (SAf) v E	Johannesburg	19-20 Feb 1957
9-121	Arthur Mailey (Aus) v E	Melbourne	14-16 Feb 1921

Most wickets in a match

19-90	Jim Laker (Eng) v A	Manchester	26-31 Jul 1956
17-159	Sydney Barnes (Eng) v SA	Johannesburg	26-30 Dec 1913
16-136	Narendra Hirwani* (Ind) v WI	Madras	11-15 Jan 1988
16-137	Bob Massie* (Aus) v E	Lord's	22-26 Jun 1972

* Hirwani (8-81 & 8-75) and Massie (8-84 and 8-53) were both on their Test début.

Most wickets in a Test career

Fifth column shows times five wickets taken in an innings, and the sixth ten wickets in a Test.

Wkts	Name	Av.	Tests	5wi	10wm	Years
434	Kapil Dev (Ind)	29.64	131	23	2	1978-90
383	Ian Botham (Eng)	28.40	102	27	4	1977-92
376	Malcolm Marshall (WI)	20.94	81	22	4	1978-91
375	Courtney Walsh (WI)	25.78	102	13	2	1984-97
362	Imran Khan (Pak)	22.81	88	23	6	1971-92
355	Dennis Lillee (Aus)	23.92	70	23	7	1971-84
341	Wasim Akram (Pak)	22.68	79	21	4	1985-96
337	Curtley Ambrose (WI)	21.16	80	20	3	1988-97
325	Bob Willis (Eng)	25.20	90	16	0	1971-84
314	Shane Warne (Aus)	24.70	67	15	3	1992-98
309	Lance Gibbs (WI)	29.09	79	18	2	1958-76
307	Fred Trueman (Eng)	21.57	67	17	3	1952-65
297	Derek Underwood (Eng)	25.83	86	17	6	1966-82
291	Craig McDermott (Aus)	28.63	71	14	2	1985-96
267	Waqar Younis (Pak)	21.53	53	21	5	1989-98
266	Bishen Bedi (Ind)	28.71	67	14	1	1966-79
259	Joel Garner (WI)	20.97	58	7	0	1977-87
252	Brian Statham (Eng)	24.84	70	9	1	1951-65
249	Michael Holding (WI)	23.68	60	13	2	1975-87
248	Richie Benaud (Aus)	27.03	63	16	1	1952-64
246	Graham McKenzie (Aus)	29.78	60	16	3	1961-71
242	Bhagwant Chandrasekhar (Ind)	29.74	58	16	2	1964-79
236	Alec Bedser (Eng)	24.89	51	15	5	1946-55
236	Abdul Qadir (Pak)	32.80	67	15	5	1977-90
235	Garfield Sobers (WI)	34.03	93	6	0	1954-74
228	Ray Lindwall (Aus)	23.03	61	12	0	1946-60
216	Clarrie Grimmett (Aus)	24.21	37	21	7	1925-36
212	Merv Hughes (Aus)	28.38	53	7	1	1985-93
204	Allan Donald (SA)	22.45	42	10	2	1992-8
202	Andy Roberts (WI)	25.61	47	11	2	1974-83
202	John Snow (Eng)	26.66	49	8	1	1965-76
200	Jeff Thomson (Aus)	28.00	51	8	0	1972-85
197	Anil Kumble (Ind)	28.44	46	11	1	1990-8
193	Jim Laker (Eng)	21.24	46	9	3	1948-59
192	Wes Hall (WI)	26.38	48	9	1	1958-69
189	Sydney Barnes (Eng)	16.43	27	24	7	1901-14
189	Erapalli Prasanna (Ind)	30.38	49	10	2	1962-78
186	Alan Davidson (Aus)	20.53	44	14	2	1953-63
180	Geoff Lawson (Aus)	30.56	46	11	2	1980-89
177	Sarfraz Nawaz (Pak)	32.75	55	4	1	1969-84
174	Tony Lock (Eng)	25.58	49	9	3	1952-68
171	Iqbal Qasim (Pak)	28.11	50	8	2	1976-89
170	Keith Miller (Aus)	22.97	55	7	1	1946-56
170	Hugh Tayfield (SAf)	25.91	37	14	2	1949-60
170	Terry Alderman (Aus)	27.15	41	14	1	1981-91

Fewest Tests to reach

100 wickets: 16 George Lohmann (Eng)
200 wickets: 35 Clarrie Grimmett (Aus)
300 wickets: 56 Dennis Lillee (Aus)

In his Test career Lohmann took 112 wickets 1886-96 at 10.75, the lowest average for any bowler taking 25 or more wickets in a Test career. At 34.11 balls per wicket, he also has the best striking rate. The next best for both these categories are: John Ferris (Eng/Aus) 61 wickets av. 12.70, 36.9 balls/wkt; Michael Proctor (SAf) 41 wickets av. 15.02, 37.7 balls/wkt.

Most wickets in a Test series

Wkts	Av.		Tests	Season
49	10.93	Sydney Barnes (Eng)	4 v SA	1913/4
46	9.60	Jim Laker (Eng)	5 v A	1956
44	14.59	Clarrie Grimmett (Aus)	5 v SA	1935/6
42	21.26	Terry Alderman (Aus)	6 v E	1981
41	12.85	Rodney Hogg (Aus)	6 v E	1978/9
41	17.36	Terry Alderman (Aus)	6 v E	1989
40	13.95	Imran Khan (Pak)	6 v I	1982/3

Most wickets in a three-Test series

35	5.80	George Lohmann (Eng)	3 v SA	1896
34	8.29	Sydney Barnes (Eng)	3 v SA	1912
33	12.15	Richard Hadlee (NZ)	3 v A	1985

Most series taking 20 wickets

9 Fred Trueman, Dennis Lillee, Malcolm Marshall; 8 Curtley Ambrose; 7 Lance Gibbs; 6 Clarrie Grimmett, Alan Davidson, Jeff Thomson, Imran Khan, Kapil Dev

---

Test Match Wicket-Keeping

(C – caught, St – stumped, Dis - dismissals)

Most dismissals in an innings

7 (all c) Wasim Bari (Pak) v NZ, Auckland 23 Feb 1979, Bob Taylor (Eng) v I, Bombay 15 Feb 1980, Ian Smith (NZ) v Sri, Hamilton 23-24 Feb 1991

Most dismissals in a Test match

11 (all c) Jack Russell (Eng) v SA, Johannesburg 1-4 Dec 1995

Most dismissals in a Test career

Dis		C	St	Tests	Years
355	Rodney Marsh (Aus)	343	12	96	1970-84
353	Ian Healy (Aus)	328	25	103	1988-98
272	Jeffrey Dujon (WI)	267	5	81	1981-91
269	Alan Knott (Eng)	250	19	95	1967-81
228	Wasim Bari (Pak)	201	27	81	1967-84
219	Godfrey Evans (Eng)	173	46	91	1946-59
198	Syed Kirmani (Ind)	160	38	88	1976-86
189	Deryck Murray (WI)	181	8	62	1963-80
187	Wally Grout (Aus)	163	24	51	1957-66
176	Ian Smith (NZ)	168	8	63	1980-92
174	Bob Taylor (Eng)	167	7	57	1971-84
165	Jack Russell (Eng)	153	12	54	1988-98
152	Dave Richardson (SAf)	150	2	42	1992-8
141	John Waite (SAf)	124	17	50	1951-65
130	Kieran More (Ind)	110	20	49	1986-93
130	Bert Oldfield (Aus)	78	52	54	1920-37

Most dismissals in a Test series

Dis		C	St	Tests	Season
28	Rodney Marsh (Aus)	28	-	5 v E	1982/3
27	Jack Russell (Eng)	25	2	5 v SA	1995/6
26	John Waite (SAf)	23	3	5 v NZ	1961/2
26	Rodney Marsh (Aus)	26	-	6 v WI	1975/6
26	Ian Healy (Aus)	21	5	6 v E	1993
25	Ian Healy (Aus)	23	2	5 v E	1994/5
24	Deryck Murray (WI)	22	2	5 v E	1963
24	Denis Lindsay (SAf)	24	-	5 v A	1966/7
24	Alan Knott (Eng)	21	3	6 v A	1970/1

Most dismissals in a three-Test series

22	Amal Silva (Sri)	21	1	3 v I	1985

Test Match Catches

(By fielders, not wicket-keepers)

Most catches in an innings

5	Victor Richardson (Aus) v SA	Durban	3 Mar 1936
5	Yajurvindra Singh (Ind) v E	Bangalore	29-30 Jan 1977
5	Mohammad Azharuddin (Ind) v Pak	Karachi	15-16 Nov 1989
5	Krishnamachari Srikkanth (Ind) v A	Perth	1-2 Feb 1992

Most catches in a Test career

		Tests	Years
156	Allan Border (Aus)	156	1978-94
144	Mark Taylor (Aus)	96	1989-98
122	Greg Chappell (Aus)	87	1970-84
122	Vivian Richards (WI)	121	1974-91
120	Ian Botham (Eng)	102	1977-92
120	Colin Cowdrey (Eng)	114	1954-75
110	Bobby Simpson (Aus)	62	1957-78
110	Walter Hammond (Eng)	85	1927-47
109	Garfield Sobers (WI)	93	1954-74
108	Sunil Gavaskar (Ind)	125	1971-87
105	Ian Chappell (Aus)	75	1964-80
103	Graham Gooch (Eng)	118	1975-95
101	Mohammad Azharuddin (Ind)	91	1984-98
99	David Boon (Aus)	107	1984-95
96	Gordon Greenidge (WI)	108	1974-91
93*	Javed Miandad (Pak)	124	1976-94
90	Richie Richardson (WI)	86	1983-95
90	Clive Lloyd (WI)	110	1966-85
89	Mark Waugh (Aus)	78	1991-8
87	Tony Greig (Eng)	58	1972-77

* And 1 stumping.

Most catches in a Test series

		Tests	Season
15	Jack Gregory (Aus)	5 v E	1920-1
14	Greg Chappell (Aus)	6 v E	1974-5
13	Bob Simpson (Aus)	5 v SA	1957-8
13	Bob Simpson (Aus)	5 v WI	1960-1

Most catches in a three-Test series

11	Tony Greig (Eng)	3 v P	1974

All-Rounders

Over 2000 runs and 150 wickets in Tests

(The final column is the ratio of batting average to bowling average, a good test of ability.)

	Tests	Runs	Wkts	Catches	Ratio
Garfield Sobers (WI)	93	8032	235	109	1.70
Imran Khan (Pak)	88	3807	362	28	1.65
Keith Miller (Aus)	55	2958	170	38	1.61
Richard Hadlee (NZ)	83	3124	431	39	1.22
Ian Botham (Eng)	102	5200	383	120	1.18
Kapil Dev (Ind)	131	5248	434	64	1.05
Vinoo Mankad (Ind)	44	2109	162	33	0.97
Wasim Akram (Pak)	79	2021	341	30	0.96
Richie Benaud (Aus)	63	2201	248	65	0.90
Ravi Shastri (Ind)	80	3830	151	36	0.87

	Tests	Runs	Wkts	Catches	Ratio
Others with ratios of 1.5 or more, and 1000 runs/50 wickets:					
Walter Hammond (Eng)	85	7249	83	110	1.55
Aubrey Faulkner (SAf)	25	1754	82	20	1.53

Fewest Tests to reach

1000 runs 100 wickets: 21 Ian Botham; 23 Vinoo Mankad; 25 Kapil Dev
2000 runs 200 wickets: 42 Ian Botham; 50 Kapil Dev, Imran Khan
3000 runs 300 wickets: 71 Ian Botham; 75 Imran Khan; 83 Kapil Dev, Richard Hadlee

300 runs and 20 wickets in a Test series

Runs	Wkts	Name	Tests	Season
475	34	George Giffen (Aus)	5 v E	1894-5
399	34	Ian Botham (Eng)	6 v A	1981
329	30	Richie Benaud (Aus)	5 v SA	1957-8
545	29	Aubrey Faulkner (SAf)	5 v E	1909-10
430	24	Tony Greig (Eng)	5 v WI	1974
442	23	Jack Gregory (Aus)	5 v E	1920-1
424	23	Garfield Sobers (WI)	5 v I	1962
318	22	Kapil Dev (Ind)	6 v E	1981-2
301	21	Richard Hadlee (NZ)	4 v E	1983
722	20	Garfield Sobers (WI)	5 v E	1966
439	20	Keith Miller (Aus)	5 v WI	1955
362	20	Keith Miller (Aus)	5 v WI	1951-2
322	20	Garfield Sobers (WI)	5 v E	1963

Limited-Overs Internationals

The first-ever 'one-day international' match was played at Melbourne on 5 Jan 1971, when Australia beat England by 5 wickets. Such matches have proliferated in recent years.

Overall record for each team to 7 Jul 1998:

Team	Played	Won	Lost	Tied	No result
West Indies	350	219	121	4	6
Australia	402	217	171	3	11
Pakistan	402	204	183	5	10
India	367	164	184	3	16
England	276	141	125	2	8
New Zealand	309	126	167	4	12
Sri Lanka	274	103	157	1	13
South Africa	145	88	54	0	3
Zimbabwe	100	21	73	4	2
Kenya	20	5	14	0	1
Bangladesh	25	1	24	0	0
United Arab Emirates	7	1	6	0	0

Losing all their games: Netherlands 5; Canada, East Africa 3

Records

Innings records

Total: *see* World Cup.
Best v Test nations: 363-7 off 55 overs England v Pakistan at Nottingham 20 Aug 1992
Lowest: 43 Pakistan v West Indies at Cape Town 25 Feb 1993
Individual: 194 Saeed Anwar, Pakistan v India at Chennai 21 May 1997
Best bowling: 7-37 Aaqib Javed, Pakistan v India at Sharjah 25 Oct 1991

Career records (to 7 Jul 1998)

Most runs		Av.	100s	Games
8648	Desmond Haynes (WI)	41.37	17	238
8285	Mohammad Azharuddin (I)	38.17	6	291
7605	Aravinda de Silva (Sri)	36.73	11	238
7381	Javed Miandad (Pak)	41.70	8	233
7089	Sachin Tendulkar (Ind)	41.09	17	196
6882	Saleem Malik (Pak)	33.57	5	268
6778	Arjuna Ranatunga (Sri)	37.24	4	241
6721	Vivian Richards (WI)	47.00	11	187
6524	Allan Border (Aus)	30.62	3	273
6248	Richie Richardson (WI)	33.41	5	224
6068	Dean Jones (Aus)	44.61	7	164
5964	David Boon (Aus)	37.04	5	181
5841	Rameez Raja (Pak)	32.09	9	198
5639	Steve Waugh (Aus)	31.67	1	245
5551	Saeed Anwar (Pak)	40.51	15	153
5449	Brian Lara (WI)	46.97	12	130
5385	Mark Waugh (Aus)	38.19	11	158
5173	Ijaz Ahmed (Pak)	31.93	7	204
5134	Gordon Greenidge (WI)	45.03	11	128
5084	Inzaman-ul-Haq (Pak)	38.51	5	163
4841	Roshan Mahanama (Sri)	30.63	4	195
4704	Martin Crowe (NZ)	38.55	4	143
4357	Geoff Marsh (Aus)	39.97	9	117
4312	Sanath Jayasuriya (Sri)	29.33	7	161
4290	Graham Gooch (Eng)	36.98	8	125

Most wickets		Av.	Games
356	Wasim Akram (Pak)	22.79	247
281	Waqar Younis (Pak)	23.11	171
253	Kapil Dev (Ind)	27.45	224
204	Curtley Ambrose (WI)	23.13	151
204	Courtney Walsh (WI)	30.94	185
203	Craig McDermott (Aus)	24.71	138
199	Anil Kumble (Ind)	27.00	146
184	Steve Waugh (Aus)	34.15	245
182	Imran Khan (Pak)	26.62	175
179	Javagal Srinath (Ind)	27.89	135
178	Allan Donald (SAf)	21.25	105
177	Aaqib Javed (Pak)	31.24	157
158	Richard Hadlee (NZ)	21.56	115
157	Malcolm Marshall (WI)	26.96	136
157	Manoj Prabhakar (Ind)	28.87	129
155	Saqlain Mushtaq (Pak)	19.12	79
150	Shane Warne (Aus)	24.68	96
148	Carl Hooper (WI)	33.33	167
146	Joel Garner (WI)	18.84	98
145	Ian Botham (Eng)	28.54	116
144	Mushtaq Ahmed (Pak)	33.62	130
142	Michael Holding (WI)	21.36	102
140	Ewen Chatfield (NZ)	25.86	114
140	Sanath Jayasuriya (Sri)	33.47	161

Most dismissals

		C	St	Games
234	Ian Healy (Aus)	195	39	168
204	Jeffrey Dujon (WI)	183	21	169
165	David Richardson (SAf)	148	17	122
128	Moin Khan (Pak)	92	36	106
124	Rodney Marsh (Aus)	120	4	92
122	Rashid Latif (Pak)	94	28	101
117	Nayan Mongla (Ind)	81	36	103
103	Saleem Yousuf (Pak)	81	22	86

Most catches by fielder

		Games
140	Mohammed Azharuddin (Ind)	291
127	Allan Border (Aus)	273
101	Vivian Richards (WI)	187
100	Roshan Mahanama (Sri)	195
84	Steve Waugh (Aus)	245
81	Carl Hooper (WI)	167

All-round – over 2000 runs and 100 wickets

Ratio is batting average to bowling average.

	Games	Runs	Wkts	Catches	Ratio
Vivian Richards (WI)	187	6721	118	101	1.31
Imran Khan (Pak)	167	3709	182	37	1.26
Carl Hooper (WI)	167	4174	148	81	1.08
Steve Waugh (Aus)	245	5639	184	84	0.93
Sanath Jayasuriya (Sri)	161	4312	140	56	0.88
Kapil Dev (Ind)	224	3783	253	71	0.87
Ian Botham (Eng)	116	2113	145	36	0.81
Ravi Shastri (Ind)	150	3108	129	40	0.81
Mudassar Nazar (Pak)	122	2653	111	21	0.81
Wasim Akram (Pak)	247	2384	356	59	0.66

Most consecutive matches

182 Sachin Tendulkar for India from 25 Apr 1990 to 24 Apr 1998

131 Richie Richardson for West Indies, 17 Jan 1987–1 Nov 1993

World Cup

The first World Cup was held in England in 1975, contested by the six Test-playing nations plus Sri Lanka and East Africa at 60-over matches. This tournament, and the next World Cup competitions, held in England in 1979 and 1983, were sponsored by the Prudential Assurance Company. From 1979 the non-Test playing members of the International Cricket Conference (ICC) have played off for the ICC Trophy and the right to enter the following World Cup tournament. The 1987 World Cup was held in India and Pakistan, where the matches were contested at 50 overs per innings, as they were in 1992 in Australia and New Zealand.

World Cup finals

Year	Venue	Result
1975	Lord's	West Indies (291-8) beat Australia (274) by 17 runs
1979	Lord's	West Indies (286-9) beat England (194) by 92 runs
1983	Lord's	India (183) beat West Indies (140) by 43 runs
1987	Calcutta	Australia (253-5) beat England (246-8) by 7 runs
1992	Melbourne	Pakistan (249-6) beat England (227) by 22 runs
1996	Lahore	Sri Lanka (245-3) beat Australia 241-7) by 7 wickets

World Cup innings records

Total: 398-5 Sri Lanka v Kenya at Kandy 6 Mar 1996

Lowest: 45 Canada v England at Manchester 14 Jun 1979

Individual: 181 Vivian Richards, West Indies v Sri Lanka at Karachi 13 Oct 1987

Best bowling: 7-51 Winston Davis, West Indies v Australia at Leeds 11-12 Jun 1983

Dismissals: 5 Syed Kirmani (5 *C*), India v Zimbabwe at Leicester 11 Jun 1983, Jimmy Adams (4 *C*, 1 *St*), West Indies v Kenya at Pune 29 Feb 1996, Rashid Latif (4 *C*, 1 *St*), Pakistan v New Zealand at Lahore 6 Mar 1996
Economical bowling: 1-6 in 12 overs Bishen Bedi, India v East Africa at Leicester 11 Jun 1975
Hat-trick: Chetan Sharma, India v New Zealand at Nagpur 31 Oct 1987

World Cup career records

Most runs	Runs	100s	Av.
Javed Miandad (Pak)	1083	1	43.32
Vivian Richards (WI)	1013	3	63.31
Graham Gooch (Eng)	897	1	44.85
Martin Crowe (Nz)	880	1	55.00
Desmond Haynes (WI)	854	1	37.13
Arjuna Rantunga (Sri)	835	–	52.18
David Boon (Aus)	815	2	54.33
Sachin Tendulkar (Ind)	806	2	67.16
Aravinda de Silva (Sri)	724	2	45.25
Rameez Raja (Pak)	700	3	53.84
Kapil Dev (Ind)	669	1	37.16
Imran Khan (Pak)	666	1	35.05
Mohammad Azharuddin (Ind)	665	–	44.33
Allan Lamb (Eng)	656	1	50.46
Richie Richardson (WI)	639	1	37.58
Mark Waugh (Aus)	629	3	62.90
Glenn Turner (NZ)	612	2	61.20
Brian Lara (WI)	602	1	50.16

Most wickets	Wickets	Av.
Imran Khan (Pak)	34	19.26
Ian Botham (Eng)	30	25.40
Phil DeFreitas (Eng)	29	25.58
Wasim Akram (Pak)	28	27.43
Kapil Dev (Ind)	28	31.85
Andy Roberts (WI)	26	21.23
Craig McDermott (Aus)	26	22.57
Abdul Qadir (Pak)	24	21.08
Manoj Prabakhar (Ind)	24	26.66
Steve Waugh (Aus)	24	30.08
Richard Hadlee (NZ)	22	19.13
Madan Lal (Ind)	22	19.36
Allan Donald (SAf)	21	21.66
Chris Harris (NZ)	21	22.71
Michael Holding (WI)	20	17.05

Most dismissals
22 Wasim Bari (Pak) (18 *C*, 4 *St*)

ICC Trophy winners
1979	Sri Lanka
1982	Zimbabwe
1986	Zimbabwe
1990	Zimbabwe
1994	United Arab Emirates
1997	Bangladesh

Highest innings total: 455-9 off 60 overs Papua New Guinea v Gibraltar at Rugeley 18 Jun 1986

First-Class Cricket

First-class matches are contested over three or more days. They are now specified by the members of the ICC, but prior to 1947, when the term was first defined, there are doubts about the first-class status of many matches. The Association of Cricket Statisticians (ACS) has done much work in studying the problem and deciding the status of matches. As a consequence of their deliberations, consistency can be achieved in statistical compilations. However there is still disagreement about the status of various matches, and figures compiled as a result are sometimes at variance with traditional figures. I have respected tradition although incorporating corrections agreed by leading statisticians. First-class cricket is taken as having originated in 1815.

Team Records

Highest innings totals

1107	Victoria v New South Wales at Melbourne 27-28 Dec 1926
1059	Victoria v Tasmania at Melbourne 2-5 Feb 1923
952-6 dec	Sri Lanka v India at Colombo 3-6 Aug 1997
951-7 dec	Sind v Baluchistan at Karachi 18-20 Feb 1974
944-6 dec	Hyderabad v Andhra at Secunderabad 9-11 Jan 1994
918	New South Wales v South Australia at Sydney 5-8 Jan 1901
912-8 dec	Holkar v Mysore at Indore 2-4 Mar 1946
910-6 dec	Railways v Dera Ismail Khan at Lahore 2-4 Dec 1964
903-7 dec	England v Australia at The Oval 20-23 Aug 1938

Highest match aggregate

2376 runs Bombay (651 & 714-8 dec) beat Maharashtra (407 & 604) at Pune over 7 days on 5-11 Mar 1949

Largest margin of victory

Innings & 851 runs Railways (910-6 dec) beat Dera Ismail Khan (32 & 27) at Lahore on 2-4 Dec 1964

Lowest completed innings totals

12 Oxford University (batted one short) v MCC and Ground at Oxford 24 May 1877
12 Northamptonshire v Gloucestershire at Gloucester 11 Jun 1907
13 Auckland v Canterbury at Auckland 31 Dec 1877
13 Nottinghamshire v Yorkshire at Nottingham 20-21 Jun 1901

Lowest aggregate in a completed first-class match

105 Australians (41 & 12-1) beat MCC (33 & 19) at Lord's 27 May 1878

Individual Records – Batting

Highest innings (scores of over 400)

501*	Brian Lara	Warwickshire v Durham	Edgbaston	3, 6 Jun 1994
499	Hanif Muhammad	Karachi v Bahawalpur	Karachi	8-11 Jan 1959
452*	Don Bradman	New South Wales v Queensland	Sydney	4-6 Jan 1930
443*	Bhausahib Nimbalkar	Maharashtra v Kathiawar	Pune	16-18 Dec 1948
437	Bill Ponsford	Victoria v Queensland	Melbourne	16-17 Dec 1927
429	Bill Ponsford	Victoria v Tasmania	Melbourne	3-5 Feb 1923
428	Aftab Baloch	Sind v Baluchistan	Karachi	18-20 Feb 1974
424	Archie McLaren	Lancashire v Somerset	Taunton	15-16 Jul 1895
405*	Graeme Hick	Worcestershire v Somerset	Taunton	5-6 May 1988

* Not out.

Fastest scoring

Minutes or balls received for the following scores (!! denotes runs given away to expedite a declaration):

Score	Mins	Balls				
50	!!8	13	Clive Inman	Leicestershire v Notts	Nottingham	20 Aug 1965
100	!!21	27	Glen Chapple	Lancashire v Glamorgan	Manchester	19 Jul 1993
	!!26	36	Tom Moody	Warwickshire v Glamorgan	Swansea	27 Jul 1990
	35	40-46	Percy Fender	Surrey v Northants	Northampton	26 Aug 1920
	43	34	David Hookes	South Australia v Victoria	Adelaide	25 Oct 1982
200	113	123	Ravi Shastri	Bombay v Baroda	Bombay	10 Jan 1985

120	121	Clive Lloyd	West Indians v Glamorgan	Swansea	9 Aug 1976
120		Gilbert Jessop	Gloucestershire v Sussex	Hove	1 Jun 1903
300	181	Denis Compton	MCC v NE Transvaal	Benoni	3-4 Dec 1948

Edwin Alletson scored 189 runs in 90 mins for Nottinghamshire v Sussex at Hove 20 May 1911, his final 142 runs being hit off 51 balls in 40 minutes.

Gilbert Jessop scored 191 in 90 minutes (passing 150 in 63 mins) for the Gentlemen of the South v Players at Hastings 3 Sep 1907.

Six sixes from a six-ball over

Garfield Sobers (Notts) off Malcolm Nash (Glam) at Swansea 31 Aug 1968
Ravi Shastri (Bombay) off Tilak Raj (Baroda) at Bombay 10 Jan 1985

Playing in a Shell Trophy match for Wellington v Canterbury at Christchurch on 20 Feb 1990, in a deliberate attempt to give away runs Bert Vance, bowled an over containing 22 balls, 17 of which were deliberate no-balls (the umpire lost count and declared over one ball early!). Lee German of Canterbury hit 70 runs, including 8 sixes and 5 fours, and Richard Petrie scored 5 runs including 1 four; with 2 runs from no-balls off which no runs were hit, a total of 77 runs was conceded for the over.

Most sixes in an innings

16 Andrew Symonds 254* for Gloucestershire v Glamorgan at Abergavenny 24-25 Aug 1995. He added a further 4 sixes in his second innings score of 76, and therefore also holds the record (20) in a match.
* Not out.

Most runs in a first-class career and most 100s, 200s, 300s

(To the end of the 1997 season. All England unless stated. Penultimate column shows innings per century.)

Runs	Name	Av.	100s	200s	300s	Inns/100	Years
61,237*	Jack Hobbs	50.65	197	16	1	6.7	1905-34
58,959	Frank Woolley	40.77	145	9	1	10.6	1906-38
57,611	Patsy Hendren	50.80	170	22	1	7.6	1907-38
55,061	Philip Mead	47.67	153	13	–	8.8	1905-36
54,896*	W G Grace	39.55	126	13	3	11.8	1865-1908
50,551	Walter Hammond	56.10	167	36	4	6.0	1920-51
50,138*	Herbert Sutcliffe	51.95	149	17	1	7.3	1919-45
48,426	Geoffrey Boycott	56.83	151	10	1	6.7	1962-86
47,793	Tom Graveney	44.91	122	7	–	10.0	1948-72
44,841	Graham Gooch	49.11	128	13	1	7.7	1973-97
43,551	Tom Hayward	41.79	104	8	1	10.3	1893-1914
43,423	Dennis Amiss	42.86	102	3	–	11.2	1960-87
42,719	Colin Cowdrey	42.89	107	3	2	10.6	1950-76
41,284	Andrew Sandham	44.82	107	11	1	9.3	1911-38
40,140	Len Hutton	55.51	129	11	1	6.3	1934-60
39,832	Mike Smith	41.84	66	3	–	16.5	1951-75
39,802*	Wilfred Rhodes	30.83	58	3	–	26.3	1896-1930
39,790	John Edrich	45.47	103	4	1	9.5	1956-78
39,405	Bob Wyatt	40.04	85	2	–	13.4	1923-57
38,942	Denis Compton	51.85	123	9	1	6.8	1936-64
38,874	Ernest Tyldesley	45.46	102	7	–	9.4	1909-36
37,897	Johnny Tyldesley	40.66	86	13	–	11.6	1895-1923
37,665	Keith Fletcher	37.77	63	2	–	18.5	1962-88
37,354	Gordon Greenidge (WI)	45.88	92	12	–	9.7	1971-92
37,252	Jack (J W) Hearne	40.98	96	11	–	10.7	1909-36
37,248	Leslie Ames	43.51	102	9	–	9.0	1926-51
37,002	Don Kenyon	33.63	74	7	–	15.7	1946-67
36,965	Bill Edrich	42.39	86	9	–	11.2	1934-58
36,673	Jim Parks	34.76	51	1	–	24.1	1949-76
36,479*	David Denton	33.37	69	3	–	16.8	1894-1920
36,323	George Hirst	34.13	60	4	1	20.2	1891-1929
36,212	Vivian Richards (WI)	49.33	114	10	1	7.0	1971-93
36,049	Alan Jones	32.89	56	1	–	20.9	1957-83

Runs	Name	Av.	100s	200s	300s	Inns/100	Years
36,012	Billy Quaife	35.38	72	4	-	16.7	1894-1928
35,725	Roy Marshall	35.95	68	3	-	15.5	1945-72
35,410	Mike Gatting	49.73	92	9	-	9.0	1975-97
35,208	George Gunn	35.96	62	1	-	17.1	1902-32

Others with career averages over 50 and 20,000 runs, or 80 100s or 10 200s:

Runs	Name	Av.	100s	200s	300s	Inns/100	Years
34,843	Zaheer Abbas (Pak)	51.54	108	10	-	7.1	1965-87
34,346	Glenn Turner (NZ)	49.70	103	10	1	7.7	1964-83
33,660	Maurice Leyland	40.50	80	5	-	11.6	1920-48
32,650	Alvin Kallicharan (WI)	43.64	87	6	-	9.6	1966-90
32,502	Allan Lamb	48.94	86	3	-	8.7	1972-95
31,847	Joe Hardstaff Jnr	44.35	83	10	-	9.8	1930-55
30,886	Charles Fry	50.22	94	16	-	7.0	1892-1921
30,574	Percy Holmes	42.11	67	12	2	12.1	1913-35
30,546	Reg Simpson	38.32	64	10	-	13.3	1944-63
28,774	Rohan Kanhai (WI)	49.01	83	7	-	8.1	1955-82
28,647	Javed Miandad (Pak)	53.44	80	11	1	7.9	1973-94
28,473	Graeme Hick	56.27	96	10	2	6.2	1983-97
28,358	Barry Richards (SAf)	54.74	80	6	1	7.2	1964-83
28,315	Garfield Sobers (WI)	54.87	86	6	1	7.1	1953-74
28,067	Don Bradman (Aus)	95.14	117	37	6	2.9	1927-49
27,592	Peter May	51.00	85	5	-	7.3	1948-63
27,131	Allan Border (Aus)	51.38	70	3	-	8.9	1976-96
26,439	Arthur Shrewsbury	36.66	59	10	-	13.7	1875-1902
25,834	Sunil Gavaskar (Ind)	51.46	81	10	1	7.0	1966-87
24,692	K S Ranjitsinhji (Ind)	56.37	72	14	-	6.9	1893-1920
24,535	Greg Chappell (Aus)	52.20	74	4	-	7.3	1966-84
23,493	Kepler Wessels (SAf)	50.41	62	4	-	8.3	1973-97
21,699	Neil Harvey (Aus)	50.93	67	7	-	6.9	1946-63
21,143	Jimmy Cook (SAf)	50.58	64	5	1	7.4	1972-95
21,029	Bobby Simpson (Aus)	56.22	60	12	2	7.3	1952-78
20,940	Graeme Pollock (SAf)	54.67	64	5	-	6.8	1960-87
20,925	Mark Waugh (Aus)	54.06	67	5	-	6.6	1985-98

Others with career averages over 55 and 10,000 runs, or a century more often than every six innings:

Runs	Name	Av.	100s	200s	300s	Inns/100	Years
19,608	Martin Crowe (NZ)	56.02	71	4	-	5.9	1979-96
18,635	Vijay Hazare (Ind)	57.87	60	10	2	6.1	1934-67
16,890	Lindsay Hassett (Aus)	58.24	59	8	-	5.5	1932-54
13,819	Bill Ponsford (Aus)	65.18	47	13	4	5.0	1920-35
13,392	Bill Woodfull (Aus)	65.00	49	7	-	5.0	1921-35
13,248	Vijay Merchant (Ind)	71.22	44	11	1	5.2	1929-51
12,762	Alan Kippax (Aus)	57.22	43	7	1	6.0	1918-36
12,614	Arthur Morris (Aus)	53.67	46	4	-	5.4	1940-64
12,010	Everton Weekes (WI)	55.34	36	9	1	6.7	1944-64
11,820	Clyde Walcott (WI)	56.55	40	4	1	5.9	1941-64
9,921	George Headley (WI)	69.80	33	9	1	5.0	1928-54

★ Denotes ACS figures, which are at considerable variance:
Hobbs 61,760 runs (av. 50.66), 199 100s; W G Grace 54,211 runs (av. 39.45, 124) centuries (11.9 inns per 100);
Sutcliffe 50,670 runs (av. 52.02), 150 100s; Rhodes 39,969 runs (av. 30.81); Denton 36,440 runs (av. 33.40).

Fewest innings to reach 100 centuries
295 Don Bradman, 552 Denis Compton, 619 Len Hutton, 645 Geoffrey Boycott, 658 Zaheer Abbas, 658 Vivian Richards, 680 Walter Hammond, 700 Herbert Sutcliffe

Most times scoring two centuries in a match
8 Zaheer Abbas (including 200 and 100 four times); 7 Walter Hammond; 6 Jack Hobbs, Glenn Turner; 5 Charles Fry, Graham Gooch.
   Uniquely, Arthur Fagg scored two double centuries in a match – 244 and 202★ for Kent v Essex at Colchester 13-15 Jul 1938.

Most centuries in successive innings

6 Charles Fry for Sussex (5) and Rest of England 1901, Don Bradman for his XI and for South Australia (5) 1938-9, Mike Proctor for Rhodesia 1970-1

Most runs in an English season

Runs	Name	100s	Av.	Year
3816	Denis Compton	18	90.85	1947
3539	Bill Edrich	12	80.43	1947
3518	Tom Hayward	13	66.37	1906
3429	Len Hutton	12	68.58	1949
3352	Frank Woolley	12	60.94	1928
3336	Herbert Sutcliffe	14	74.13	1932
3323	Walter Hammond	13	67.81	1933
3311	Patsy Hendren	13	70.44	1928
3309	Bobby Abel	7	55.15	1901
Also 14 or more centuries:				
3024	Jack Hobbs	16	70.32	1925
3011	Walter Hammond	15	75.27	1938
Highest average:				
2429	Don Bradman	13	115.66	1938
1538	Geoffrey Boycott	6	102.53	1979
2746	Graham Gooch	12	101.70	1990
2503	Geoffrey Boycott	13	100.12	1971

Most seasons scoring 3000 runs

3 Herbert Sutcliffe 1928, 1931, 1932, Patsy Hendren 1923, 1928, 1933, Walter Hammond 1933, 1937, 1938

Most seasons scoring 2000 runs

17 Jack Hobbs; 15 Patsy Hendren, Herbert Sutcliffe; 13 Frank Woolley; 12 Walter Hammond; 11 James Langridge, Philip Mead; 10 Tom Hayward; 9 Bill Edrich, Len Hutton, Jack Robertson

Most seasons (English or overseas) scoring 1000 runs

28 W G Grace, Frank Woolley; 27 Colin Cowdrey, Philip Mead; 26 Geoffrey Boycott, Jack Hobbs; 25 Patsy Hendren; 24 Billy Quaife, Herbert Sutcliffe, Dennis Amiss; 23 Alan Jones

Most sixes in a season

80 Ian Botham 1985 (in 1530 runs, av. 69.54)

Individual Records – Bowling

Best bowling

The taking of all ten wickets in an innings by a single bowler has been recorded more than 70 times in first-class cricket. Bowlers to have achieved this feat more than once are: 3 times Alfred 'Tich' Freeman, Kent 1929, 1930, 1931; twice Vyell Walker, England 1859 and Middlesex 1865, W G Grace, MCC 1873, 1886, Hedley Verity, Yorkshire 1931, 1932, Jim Laker, Surrey and England 1956

The least expensive ten wickets analyses

10-10	Hedley Verity	Yorkshire v Nottinghamshire	Leeds	12 Jul 1932
10-18	George Geary	Leicestershire v Glamorgan	Pontypridd	15 Aug 1929
10-20	Premansu Chatterjee	Bengal v Assam	Jorhat	28 Jan 1957
10-26	Bert Vogler	Eastern Province v Griqualand West	Johannesburg	28 Dec 1906
10-28	A E Moss★	Canterbury v Wellington	Christchurch	27-28 Dec 1889
10-28	William Howell	Australians v Surrey	The Oval	15 May 1899
10-28	Naeem Akhtar	Rawalpindi B v Peshaware	Peshawar	2-3 Dec 1995
10-30	Colin Blythe	Kent v Northants	Northampton	1 Jun 1907

★ On his first-class début.

Most wickets in a match

19 (9-37, 10-53) Jim Laker for England v Australia, The Oval 26-31 Jul 1956
17 wickets in a match has been achieved on 18 occasions: least expensive, for 48 runs, Colin Blythe (10-30 and 7-18) Kent v Northants 1 Jun 1907

Most successive wickets

4 wickets with consecutive balls has been achieved on 31 occasions. The only man to do this twice was Bob Crisp for Western Province in Currie Cup matches in 1931-2 and 1934. The most notable spell was by Pat Pocock for Surrey v Sussex at Eastbourne 15 Aug 1972; his records included five wickets in one over, six wickets in nine balls and seven in eleven.

Most hat-tricks (three wickets with consecutive balls)

7 Douglas Wright (Eng) 1937-49; 6 Charlie Parker (Eng) 1922-30, Tom Goddard (Eng) 1924-47

Most wickets in a first-class career

All England unless stated. Fourth and fifth columns show the number of occasions on which bowler has taken 5 wickets in an innings and 10 wickets in a match.

Wkts	Name	Av.	5wi	10wm	Years
4187★	Wilfred Rhodes	16.71	287	67	1898-1930
3776	Alfred 'Tich' Freeman	18.42	386	140	1914-36
3278	Charlie Parker	19.46	277	91	1903-35
3061	Jack (J T) Hearne	17.75	255	64	1888-1923
2979	Tom Goddard	19.84	251	86	1922-52
2876★	W G Grace	17.92	240	64	1865-1908
2874	Alex Kennedy	21.43	225	45	1907-36
2857	Derek Shackleton	18.65	194	38	1948-69
2844	Tony Lock	19.23	196	50	1946-71
2830	Fred Titmus	22.37	168	26	1949-82
2784	Maurice Tate	18.16	195	44	1912-37
2739★	George Hirst	18.72	184	40	1891-1929
2506	Colin Blythe	16.81	218	71	1899-1914
2465	Derek Underwood	20.28	153	47	1963-87
2431	Ewart Astill	23.76	140	22	1906-39
2356	Jack White	18.57	193	58	1909-37
2323	Eric Hollies	20.94	182	40	1932-57
2304	Fred Trueman	18.29	126	25	1949-69
2260	Brian Statham	18.36	123	11	1950-68
2233	Reg Perks	24.07	143	24	1930-55
2221	Johnny Briggs	15.93	200	52	1879-1900
2218	Don Shepherd	21.32	123	28	1950-72
2151	George Dennett	19.82	211	57	1903-26
2105	Tom Richardson	18.42	200	72	1892-1904

★ ACS figures: Rhodes 4204 wickets (av.16.72), W G Grace 2808 (av.18.15), Hirst 2742 (av.18.73).

Others with career average below 15 and 1500 wickets, or more than 50 times taking 10 wickets in a match

2028	Alfred Shaw	12.12	177	44	1864-97
1956	Hedley Verity	14.90	164	54	1930-39
1841	George Lohmann	13.74	176	57	1884-98
1681	James Southerton	14.46	192	59	1854-79
1673	Arthur Mold	15.54	152	56	1889-1901
1571	Tom Emmett	13.56	121	29	1866-88

Best non-English players

1674	Albert Trott (Aus)	21.09	131	41	1893-1911
1651	Malcolm Marshall (WI)	19.10	85	13	1977-96
1571	Intikhab Alam (Pak)	27.67	85	13	1957-82
1560	Bishen Bedi (Ind)	21.69	106	20	1961-82
1465	Courtney Walsh (WI)	22.24	86	16	1982-97
1424	Clarrie Grimmett (Aus)	22.28	127	33	1911-41
1417	Mike Proctor (SAf)	19.53	70	15	1965-89

Fewest matches to reach 1000 wickets

134 Tom Richardson 1892-6; 147 George Dennett 1903-9; 149 Arthur Mold 1899-1905; 156 Jack (J T) Hearne 1888-96; 159 George Lohmann 1884-8

Fewest matches to reach 2000 wickets

327 Tom Richardson 1892-1903; 347 Jack (J T) Hearne 1888-1902; 349 George Dennett 1903-24; 350 Colin Blythe 1899-1912; 350 'Tich' Freeman 1914-29

Most wickets in an English season

Wickets		Av.	Year
304	Alfred 'Tich' Freeman	18.05	1928
298	Alfred 'Tich' Freeman	15.26	1933
290	Tom Richardson	14.37	1895
283	Charlie Turner	11.68	1888
276	Alfred 'Tich' Freeman	15.60	1931
275	Alfred 'Tich' Freeman	16.84	1930
273	Tom Richardson	14.45	1897

Best average while taking at least 100 wickets in a season

186	Alfred Shaw	8.54	1880

200 wickets in a season most often

8 'Tich' Freeman; 5 Charlie Parker; 4 Tom Goddard; 3 Jack (J T) Hearne, George Lohmann, Wilfred Rhodes, Tom Richardson, Maurice Tate, Hedley Verity

100 wickets in a season most often

23 Wilfred Rhodes; 20 Derek Shackleton; 17 'Tich' Freeman; 16 Tom Goddard, Charlie Parker, Reg Perks, Fred Titmus; 15 Jack (J T) Hearne, George Hirst, Alex Kennedy

Individual Records – All-Rounders

Best career figures

Determined by the best ratios of batting average divided by bowling average (the figure in the first column), for those with at least 10,000 runs and 1000 wickets, plus one with over 25,000 runs and 2000 wickets.

	Ratio	Runs	Av.	Wkts	Av.	Years
W G Grace (Eng)	2.21	54,896	39.55	2876	17.92	1865-1908
Frank Tarrant (Aus)	2.06	17,857	36.36	1489	17.66	1898-1936
Frank Woolley (Eng)	2.05	58,959	40.77	2068	19.85	1906-38
Garfield Sobers (WI)	1.98	28,315	54.87	1043	27.74	1953-74
Wilfred Rhodes (Eng)	1.85	39,802	30.83	4187	16.71	1895-1930
Mike Proctor (SAf)	1.84	21,936	36.01	1417	19.53	1965-89
George Hirst (Eng)	1.82	36,272	34.12	2742	18.73	1891-1929
Jack (J W) Hearne (Eng)	1.68	37,252	40.98	1839	24.43	1909-36
Imran Khan (Pak)	1.65	17,771	36.79	1287	22.32	1969-92
Trevor Bailey (Eng)	1.44	28,642	33.42	2082	23.13	1945-67

Best season's figures in England

2000 runs and 150 wickets in a season:

George Hirst	2.78	2385	45.86	208	16.50	1906
Frank Woolley	2.66	2101	42.87	167	16.14	1921
Frank Woolley	2.50	2022	45.95	163	18.37	1922

3000 runs and 100 wickets in a season:

James Parks	1.97	3003	50.89	101	25.83	1937

Ratios of over 3.00 for 1000 runs and 100 wickets:

W G Grace	4.09	1664	52.00	140	12.71	1875
Richard Hadlee (NZ)	3.65	1179	51.26	117	14.05	1981
W G Grace	3.30	2622	62.42	130	18.90	1876
Wilfred Rhodes	3.26	1511	39.76	119	12.19	1922
George Hirst	3.16	1844	47.28	128	14.94	1903

| W G Grace | 3.11 | 1474 | 39.83 | 179 | 12.81 | 1877 |
| Jack (J W) Hearne | 3.09 | 2148 | 55.07 | 142 | 17.83 | 1920 |

Best match

George Giffen (Aus) scored 271 and took 9-96 and 7-70, South Australia v Victoria 7-11 Nov 1891

Individual Records – Wicket-Keeping

(C – caught, St – stumped, Dis – dismissals)

Most dismissals in an innings

9	(8 C, 1 St)	Tahir Rashid (Pak)	Habib Bank v Pakistan Automobile C	Gujranwala	29 Nov 1992
9	(7 C, 2 St)	Wayne James (Zim)	Matabeleland v Masonaland C D	Bulawayo	19-20 Apr 1996
8	(all C)	Wally Grout (Aus)	Queensland v Western Australia	Brisbane	15 Feb 1960
8	(all C)	David East	Essex v Somerset	Taunton	27 Jul 1985
8	(all C)	Steve Marsh	Kent v Middlesex	Lord's	31 May–1 Jun 1991
8	(6 C, 2 St)	Tim Zoehrer	Australians v Surrey	The Oval	27 May 1994
8	(7 C, 1 St)	Darren Berry	Victoria v South Australia	Melbourne	16 Nov 1996

Most stumpings in an innings

6 Hugo Yarnold Worcestershire v Scotland, Broughty Ferry 2 Jul 1951

Most dismissals in a match

13	(11 C, 2 St)	Wayne James (Zim)	Matabeleland v Masonaland C D	Bulawayo	19-21 Apr 1996
12	(8 C, 4 St)	Edward Pooley	Surrey v Sussex	The Oval	6-7 Jul 1868
12	(9 C, 3 St)	Don Tallon (Aus)	Queensland v New South Wales	Sydney	2-4 Jan 1939
12	(9 C, 3 St)	Brian Taber (Aus)	New South Wales v South Australia	Adelaide	13-17 Dec 1968

Most dismissals in a first-class career

English players:

Dis	Name	C	St	Per match	Career
1649	Bob Taylor	1473	176	2.6	1960-88
1527	John Murray	1270	257	2.4	1952-75
1497	Herbert Strudwick	1242	255	2.2	1902-27
1344	Alan Knott	1211	133	2.6	1965-85
1310	Frederick Huish	933	377	2.6	1895-1914
1294	Brian Taylor	1081	213	2.3	1949-73
1253	David Hunter	906	347	2.3	1889-1909
1228	Harry Butt	953	275	2.3	1890-1912
1207	Jack Board	852	355	2.3	1891-1915
1206	Harry Elliott	904	302	2.3	1920-47
1181	Jim Parks	1088	93	1.6	1949-76
1126	Roy Booth	949	177	2.4	1951-70
1121	Les Ames	703	418	1.9	1926-51
1099	David Bairstow	961	138	2.4	1970-90
1095	George Duckworth	754	341	2.2	1923-47
1082	Harold Stephenson	748	334	2.3	1948-64
1071	Jimmy Binks	895	176	2.1	1955-69
1066	Godfrey Evans	816	250	2.3	1939-69

Best non-English players:

869	Rodney Marsh (Aus)	804	65	3.4	1968-84
849	Deryck Murray (WI)	741	108	2.3	1961-80
824	Farokh Engineer (Ind)	703	121	2.5	1958-76
812	Wasim Bari (Pak)	667	145	2.9	1964-83

Over 380 dismissals and over 3 per match:

667	Ian Healy (Aus)	612	55	3.3	1986-98
621	Ray Jennings (SAf)	567	54	3.9	1973-93
587	Wally Grout (Aus)	473	114	3.2	1946-66
585	David Richardson (SA)	549	36	3.1	1977-97
461	Tim Zoehrer (Aus)	423	38	3.1	1980-94

422	Richard Ryall (SAf)	384	38	3.4	1980-95
395	Brian Taber (Aus)	345	50	3.1	1964-74
385	John Maclean (Aus)	354	31	3.6	1968-79

Most dismissals in an English season

Dis	Name	C	St	Year
127	Leslie Ames	79	48	1929
122	Leslie Ames	70	52	1928
110	Hugo Yarnold	62	48	1949
107	George Duckworth	77	30	1928
107	Jimmy Binks	96	11	1960
104	Leslie Ames	40	64	1932
104	John Murray	82	22	1957
102	Frederick Huish	70	32	1913
102	John Murray	95	7	1960

Individual Records – Fielders

Most catches in an innings

7 Tony Brown for Gloucestershire v Notts, Nottingham 26 Jul 1966, Micky Stewart for Surrey v Northants, Northampton 7 Jun 1957

Most catches in a match

10 (4 & 6) Walter Hammond for Gloucestershire v Surrey, Cheltenham 16-17 Aug 1928

Most catches in a first-class career

(All English unless stated.)

Catches		Per match	Career
1018	Frank Woolley	1.04	1906-38
887	W G Grace (874 *ACS figure*)	1.00	1865-1908
830	Tony Lock	1.27	1946-71
819	Walter Hammond	1.29	1920-51
813	Brian Close	1.04	1949-86
784	John Langridge	1.37	1928-55
764	Wilfred Rhodes	0.61	1896-1930
758	Arthur Milton	1.22	1948-74
754	Patsy Hendren	0.91	1907-38
697	Peter Walker	1.49	1956-72
695	John Tunnicliffe	1.40	1891-1907
675	James Seymour	1.22	1900-26
671	Philip Mead	0.82	1905-36
644	Keith Fletcher	0.88	1962-88
638	Colin Cowdrey	0.92	1950-76
634	Micky Stewart	1.19	1954-72

Highest averages per match of those taking 300 or more:

602	Graham Roope	1.50	1964-86
383	Bobby Simpson (Aus)	1.49	1952-78
328	Hugh Trumble (Aus)	1.54	1887-1904

Most catches in an English season

78	Walter Hammond	1928
77	Micky Stewart	1957
73	Peter Walker	1961
71	Philip Sharpe	1962
70	John Tunnicliffe	1901

County Championship

The first recorded inter-county match was contested in 1709 between Kent and Surrey, and the first county to be acclaimed as champions was Sussex in 1827. Such references became more frequent from 1864, the year in which overarm bowling was legalized, but it was not until the 1890 season that the County Championship was officially recognized and a points system introduced.

From 1827 to 1862 the southern counties of Kent, Surrey and Sussex generally proved the best, with an occasional challenge from Nottinghamshire. From 1864, when eight counties took part in inter-county matches, to 1889, the following champion counties were proclaimed, principally on the basis of fewest matches lost.

Surrey	1864, 1887-8, 1889*
Gloucestershire	1873*, 1874, 1876-7
Nottinghamshire	1865, 1868, 1869*, 1871-2, 1873*, 1875, 1879*, 1880, 1882*, 1883-6, 1889*
Middlesex	1866
Yorkshire	1867, 1869*, 1870
Lancashire	1879*, 1881, 1882*, 1889*

Undecided in 1878
* Shared.

County Champions from 1890

The Championship was sponsored by Schweppes in 1977-83 and by Britannic Assurance from 1984 to 1998.

Wins:

30*	Yorkshire	1893, 1896, 1898, 1900-2, 1905, 1908, 1912, 1919, 1922-5, 1931-3, 1935, 1937-9, 1946, 1949*, 1959-60, 1962-3, 1966-8
16*	Surrey	1890-2, 1894-5, 1899, 1914, 1950*, 1952-8, 1971
12#	Middlesex	1903, 1920-1, 1947, 1949*, 1976, 1977*, 1980, 1982, 1985, 1990, 1993
8*	Lancashire	1897, 1904, 1926-8, 1930, 1934, 1950*
7*	Kent	1906, 1909-10, 1913, 1970, 1977*, 1978
6	Essex	1979, 1983-4, 1986, 1991-2
5	Worcestershire	1964-5, 1974, 1988-9
5	Warwickshire	1911, 1951, 1972, 1994-5
4	Nottinghamshire	1907, 1929, 1981, 1987
3	Glamorgan	1948, 1969, 1997
2	Hampshire	1961, 1973
2	Leicestershire	1975, 1996
1	Derbyshire	1936

* Including one tie.
# Including two ties.

Most appearances: 763 Wilfred Rhodes (Yorkshire) 1898-1930; 707 Frank Woolley (Kent) 1906-38

Gillette Cup/NatWest Bank Trophy

Introduced as the Gillette Cup in 1963 as a one-day knock-out event contested by the first-class counties over one innings of 65 overs per side (60 overs from 1964). From 1981 it has been contested for the NatWest Bank Trophy, and Ireland, Scotland and the leading Minor Counties have also taken part, with, most recently, the British Universities and Holland.

Wins:

6	Lancashire	1970-2, 1975, 1990, 1996
5	Warwickshire	1966, 1968, 1989, 1993, 1995
4	Sussex	1963-4, 1978, 1986
4	Middlesex	1977, 1980, 1984, 1988
2	Yorkshire	1965, 1969
2	Kent	1967, 1974
2	Somerset	1979, 1983
2	Northamptonshire	1976, 1992
2	Essex	1985, 1997
1	Gloucestershire 1973, Derbyshire 1981, Surrey 1982, Nottinghamshire 1987, Hampshire 1991, Worcestershire 1994	

Team records (all 60-over innings)

Highest innings: 413-4 Somerset v Devon at Torquay 27 Jun 1990
Highest in final: 322-5 Warwickshire v Sussex at Lord's 4 Sep 1993
Lowest completed innings: 39 Ireland v Sussex at Hove 3 Jul 1985
Largest runs margin: 346 Somerset beat Devon (67) at Torquay 27 Jun 1990

Individual innings records

Highest innings: 206 Alvin Kallicharran for Warwickshire v Oxfordshire, Birmingham 4 Jul 1984
Best bowling: 8-21 Michael Holding for Derbyshire v Sussex, Hove 22 June 1988
Most economical bowling: 1-3 in 12 overs Jack Simmons for Lancashire v Suffolk, Bury St Edmunds 3 Jul 1985
Most dismissals: 7 (all C) Alec Stewart for Surrey v Glamorgan, Swansea 27 Jul 1994

Individual career records 1963-97

Most runs

	Names	Per match	Career
2547	Graham Gooch (Essex)	48.98	1973-96
2113	Mike Gatting (Middlesex)	43.12	1975-97
1950	Dennis Amiss (Warwicks)	39.00	1963-87
1920	Clive Lloyd (Lancashire)	54.85	1969-86

Most wickets

81	Geoff Arnold (Surrey, Sussex)	14.85	1963-80
79	Jack Simmons (Lancashire)	22.72	1970-89
78	Peter Lever (Lancashire)	17.12	1963-76
77	Derek Underwood (Kent)	22.22	1963-87

Most dismissals (C/St)

66	Bob Taylor (Derbyshire)	58/8	1963-84
65	Alan Knott (Kent)	59/6	1965-85
61	Paul Downton (Kent, Middlesex)	54/7	1978-90

Most catches by fielder

26	Graham Gooch (Essex)	1973-97
26	Jack Simmons (Lancashire)	1970-89
25	Geoff Cook (Northants, Durham)	1972-92

Most match awards

9   Graham Gooch; 8 Clive Lloyd, Chris Smith, Robin Smith

Benson & Hedges Cup

A one-day competition played at 55 overs per innings 1972-95, and at 50 overs 1996-8. Contested by 22 teams – the 18 first-class counties and teams representing the Minor Counties, Ireland, Scotland and the Combined Universities. Played on a zonal basis of four groups of five and then by knock-out, except for 1993-4 when it was all by knock-out.

Wins:

4	Lancashire	1984, 1990, 1995-6
3	Kent	1973, 1976, 1978
3	Leicestershire	1972, 1975, 1985
2	Somerset	1981-2
2	Middlesex	1983, 1986
2	Hampshire	1988, 1992
2	Surrey	1974, 1997
2	Essex	1979, 1998
1	Gloucestershire 1977, Northamptonshire 1980, Yorkshire 1987, Nottinghamshire 1989, Worcestershire 1991, Derbyshire 1993, Warwickshire 1994

Team records

Highest innings: 388-7 Essex v Scotland at Chelmsford 30 Apr 1992
Lowest completed innings: 50 Hampshire v Yorkshire at Leeds 4 May 1991

Individual innings records

Highest innings: 198* Graham Gooch for Essex v Sussex, Hove 25 May 1982
Best bowling: 7-12 Wayne Daniel for Middlesex v Minor Counties (East), Ipswich 22 Apr 1978
Most economical bowling: 1-3 in 11 overs Chris Old for Yorkshire v Middlesex, Lord's 6 Jun 1979
Most dismissals: 8 (all C) Derek Taylor for Somerset v Combined Universities, Taunton 8 May 1982
★ Not out.

Individual career records 1972-97

Most runs

	Names	Per match	Career
5176	Graham Gooch (Essex)	52.28	1973-97
2921	Mike Gatting (Middlesex)	40.56	1976-97
2761	Chris Tavare (Univs, Kent, Som)	32.49	1975-93
2663	Derek Randall (Notts)	32.87	1972-93
2636	Allan Lamb (Northants)	47.07	1978-95

Most wickets

149	John Lever (Essex)	18.71	1972-89
132	Ian Botham (Somerset, Worcs, Durham)	21.35	1974-93
107	Stuart Turner (Essex, Minor Counties)	20.96	1972-88
107	Derek Underwood (Kent)	22.75	1972-87

Most dismissals (C/St)

122	David Bairstow (Yorkshire)	117/5	1972-90
94	Stephen Rhodes (Worcs)	85/9	1985-97
88	Alan Knott (Kent)	78/10	1972-85
83	Geoff Humpage (Warwicks)	80/3	1976-90

Most catches by fielder

68	Graham Gooch (Essex)		1973-97
55	Chris Tavare (Univs, Kent, Somerset)		1975-93
53	Ian Botham (Somerset, Worcs, Durham)		1974-93

Most match awards

22 Graham Gooch; 11 Kim Barnett, Mike Gatting, Graeme Hick, Trevor Jesty, Barry Wood

Sunday League

Introduced in 1969 and played on Sundays by the first-class counties in matches of 40 overs per innings (50 in 1993). John Player League 1969-86, Refuge Assurance League 1987-91, no sponsor 1992, Axa Life from 1993.

Wins:

4	Kent	1972-3, 1976, 1995
3	Essex	1981, 1984-5
3	Hampshire	1975, 1978, 1986
3	Worcestershire	1971, 1987-8
3	Lancashire	1969-70, 1989
3	Warwickshire	1980, 1994, 1997
2	Leicestershire	1974, 1977
1	Somerset 1979, Sussex 1982, Yorkshire 1983, Derbyshire 1990, Nottinghamshire 1991, Middlesex 1992, Glamorgan 1993, Surrey 1996	

Refuge Assurance Cup

In 1988-91 the first four teams in the Refuge Assurance League met in semi-finals, and then a final.
Winners: 1988 Lancashire, 1989 Essex, 1990 Middlesex, 1991 Worcestershire

Sunday League team records

Highest innings: 375-4 Surrey v Yorkshire at Scarborough 11 Sep 1994
Lowest completed innings: 23 Middlesex v Yorkshire at Leeds 23 Jun 1974
Largest runs margin: 220 runs Somerset (360-3) beat Glamorgan (140) at Neath 22 Jul 1990

Individual innings records

Highest innings: 203 Alistair Brown for Surrey v Hampshire, Guildford 20 Jul 1997
Best bowling: 8-26 Keith Boyce for Essex v Lancashire, Manchester 30 May 1971; 4 wickets in 4 balls Alan Ward for Derbyshire v Sussex, Derby 7 Jun 1970
Most economical bowling: 0-0 in 8 overs Brian Langford for Somerset v Essex, Yeovil 27 Jul 1969
Most dismissals: 7 (6 C, 1 St) Bob Taylor for Derbyshire v Lancashire, Manchester 4 May 1975

Season's records

Most runs: 917 (av. 70.53) Tom Moody (Worcestershire) 1991
Most wickets: 39 (av. 12.15) Adam Hollioake (Surrey) 1996
Most dismissals: 29 (26 C, 3 St) Steven Rhodes (Worcs) 1987

Individual career records 1969-97

Most runs

	Names	Per match	Career
8573	Graham Gooch (Essex)	34.99	1973-97
7499	Wayne Larkins (Northants, Durham)	28.84	1972-95
7504	Bill Athey (Yorkshire, Gloucs, Sussex)	31.93	1976-97
7389	Kim Barnett (Derbyshire)	34.85	1979-97
7062	Derek Randall (Notts)	33.46	1971-93
7040	Dennis Amiss (Warwicks)	32.14	1969-87
6671	Mike Gatting (Middlesex)	31.61	1975-97
6650	Clive Radley (Middlesex)	29.55	1969-87
6639	David Turner (Hampshire)	29.50	1969-89

Most wickets

386	John Lever (Essex)	19.73	1969-89
368	John Emburey (Middlesex, Northants)	23.47	1975-97
346	Derek Underwood (Kent)	16.89	1969-87
307	Jack Simmons (Lancs)	26.39	1969-89
303	Stuart Turner (Essex)	23.86	1969-86
284	Norman Gifford (Worcs/Warwicks)	26.55	1969-88
281	Eddie Hemmings (Warks, Notts, Sussex)	29.44	1969-94
267	John Shepherd (Kent, Gloucester)	21.46	1969-87

Most dismissals (C/St)

264	Stephen Rhodes (Worcs)	206/58	1985-97
257	David Bairstow (Yorkshire)	234/23	1970-90
236	Bob Taylor (Derby)	187/49	1969-84
223	Eifion Jones (Glamorgan)	184/39	1969-83
218	Alan Knott (Kent)	183/45	1969-85

Most catches by fielder

103	Paul Terry (Hants)	1978-95
101	John Steele (Leics, Glamorgan)	1970-86
100	Graham Gooch (Essex)	1973-97

First-Class Counties

Placings in the first three in the County Championship 1890-1997 and Sunday League (SL) 1969-97, and wins (W), runners-up (RU) or losing semi-finalists (SF) in the Gillette Cup/NatWest Bank Trophy (GC/NW) 1963-97 and Benson & Hedges Cup (B&H) 1972-97. Final column shows year in which counties first took part in the Championship, or in preceding inter-county matches from 1864.

County	County Champs 1st	2nd	3rd	GC/NW W	RU	SF	B&H W	RU	SF	SL 1st	2nd	3rd	First Year
Derbyshire	1	2	4	1	1	1	1	2	1	1	-	1	1871
Durham	-	-	-	-	-	-	-	-	-	-	-	-	1992
Essex	6	3	2	2	1	3	1	4	3	3	5'	3	1895
Glamorgan	3	2	3	-	1	3	-	-	1	1	-	-	1921
Gloucestershire	-	6	7	1	-	3	1	-	1	-	1	1	1870
Hampshire	2	3	5	1	-	8	2	-	3	3	1	3	1864
Kent	7'	10	9"	2	3	2	3	4	5	4	4	4	1864
Lancashire	8'	13'	10'	6	3	5	4	2	4	3	2	3	1865
Leicestershire	2	2	3'	-	1	2	3	1	3	2	1	2	1895
Middlesex	12"	12	13	4	2	7	2	1	2	1	1	3	1864

County	County Champs			GC/NW			B&H			SL			First
	1st	2nd	3rd	W	RU	SF	W	RU	SF	1st	2nd	3rd	Year
Northamptonshire	-	4	5	2	5	3	1	2	3	-	-	1	1905
Nottinghamshire	4	5	5	1	1	1	1	2	3	1	3	1	1864
Somerset	-	-	5	2	2	5	2	-	6	1	6'	-	1882
Surrey	16'	7	12	1	3	7	2	2	4	1	-	1	1864
Sussex	-	7	2'	4	4	4	-	-	1	1	1	1	1864
Warwickshire	5	3	1	5	5	6	1	1	5	3	1	1	1895
Worcestershire	5	5'	2	1	3	6	1	4	3	3	3	2	1899
Yorkshire	30'	13"	11'	2	-	4	1	1	4	1	1	1	1864

' Including one tie for place, " including two ties for place.

Australia

Most runs in a season

Runs	Av.	Player	Season
1690	93.88	Don Bradman (NSW)	1928/9
1659	63.80	Neil Harvey (Vic)	1952/3
1586	113.28	Don Bradman (NSW)	1929/30
1553	91.35	Walter Hammond (Eng)	1928/9
1552	86.22	Don Bradman (SA)	1936/7

Don Bradman exceeded 1000 runs in a record 12 Australian seasons.

Most wickets in a season

Wkts	Av.	Player	Season
106	13.59	Charlie Turner (NSA)	1887/8
93	22.54	George Giffen (SA) ★	1894/5
82	23.69	Clarrie Grimmett (SA)	1929/30
82	19.25	Richie Benaud (NSW)	1958/9
81	22.53	Arthur Mailey (NSW)	1920/1

★ George Giffen also scored 902 runs (av. 50.11) in 1894/5 for the best-ever all-round figures.

Most dismissals in a season

67 (63 C, 4 St) Rodney Marsh (WA) 1975/6

Sheffield Shield

The annual first-class inter-state competition has been contested for the shield, purchased with money donated by the 3rd Earl of Sheffield, from 1891/2. The original three states were joined by Queensland in 1926/7, Western Australia 1947/8 and Tasmania 1977/8. From 1983 the Shield winner has been determined by a final between the top two teams.

Winners (year shown is that of second half of the season):

42 New South Wales
    1896-7, 1900, 1902-7, 1909, 1911-2, 1914, 1920-1, 1923, 1926, 1929, 1932-3, 1938, 1940, 1949-50, 1952, 1954-62, 1965-6, 1983, 1985-6, 1990, 1993-4

25 Victoria
    1893, 1895, 1898-9, 1901, 1908, 1915, 1922, 1924-5, 1928, 1930-1, 1934-5, 1937, 1947, 1951, 1963, 1967, 1970, 1974, 1979-80, 1991

13 South Australia
    1894, 1910, 1913, 1927, 1936, 1939, 1953, 1964, 1969, 1971, 1976, 1982, 1996

11 Western Australia
    1948, 1968, 1972-3, 1975, 1977-8, 1981, 1984, 1987-9, 1992, 1998

2 Queensland
    1995, 1997

Limited-overs competitions

The Australian states currently contest a knock-out competition for the Mercantile Mutual Cup, with matches of 50 overs per innings. Sponsors have been V&G 1969-71, Coca-Cola 1971-3, Gillette 1973-9, McDonald's 1978-88, Federated Automobile Insurance 1988-92, and Mercantile Mutual from 1992/3. New Zealand also took part in the first six years.

Winners (year shown is for second half of the season):

9 Western Australia
   1971, 1974, 1977-8, 1983, 1986, 1990-1, 1997

5 New South Wales
   1985, 1988, 1992-4

5 Queensland
   1976, 1981-2, 1989, 1996, 1998

3 New Zealand
   1970, 1973, 1975

2 Victoria
   1972, 1980, 1995

2 South Australia
   1984, 1987

1 Tasmania
   1979

Innings records

Highest team score: 325-6 S Australia v Tasmania in final at Hobart 15 Mar 1987

Highest individual innings: 164 Rick McCosker for NSW v S Australia, Sydney 3 Dec 1981

Best bowling: 7-34 Carl Rackemann, Queensland v S Australia, 19 Feb 1989

Most economical bowling: 1-8 in 10 overs Graham Porter for W Australia v Victoria, Perth 10 Oct 1986

Most dismissals: 6 (all C) Ken Wadsworth for New Zealand v NSW, Sydney 30 Dec 1969

India

Most runs in a season: 1604 (av. 64.16) Chandu
Borde 1964/5. Vijay Hazare scored 1423 runs in
1943/4 at an average of 177.87, the highest ever
recorded for 1000 runs in a season

Most wickets in a season: 88 Bishen Bedi 1974/5
(av. 15.02) and 1976/7 (av. 19.30)

Most dismissals in a season: 55 (47 C, 8 St) Samir
Dighe 1994/5

In the Indian sub-continent (India, Pakistan, Sri Lanka and Burma)

Most runs in a season: 2121 (av. 88.37), including a
record 10 centuries, Sunil Gavaskar (Ind) 1978/9

Most wickets in a season: 116 (av. 13.78) Maurice
Tate (Eng) 1926/7

Ranji Trophy

The annual Indian first-class inter-state competition was
instituted in 1934 in memory of K S Ranjitsinhji. It is
contested on a zonal basis, culminating in a knock-out
competition.

Winners (year given is that of the second half of the season):

33   Bombay/Mumbai
     1935-6, 1942, 1945, 1949, 1952, 1954, 1956-7,
     1959-73, 1975-7, 1981, 1984-5, 1994-5, 1997
 6   Delhi
     1979-80, 1982, 1986, 1989, 1992
 5   Karnataka
     1974, 1978, 1983, 1996, 1998
 4   Baroda
     1943, 1947, 1950, 1958
 4   Holkar
     1946, 1948, 1951, 1953
 2   Maharashtra
     1940-1
 2   Hyderabad
     1938, 1987
 2   Bengal
     1939, 1990
 2   Madras/Tamil Nadu
     1955 (M), 1988 (TN)
 1   Nawanagar 1937, Western India 1944,
     Haryana 1991, Punjab 1993

New Zealand

Most runs in a season: 1676 (av. 93.11) Martin
Crowe 1986/7

Most wickets in a season: 66 (av. 16.48) Stephen
Boock 1977/8

Most dismissals in a season: 41 Ervin McSweeney
1984/5 (31 C, 10 St) and 1989/90 (35 C, 6 St)

Plunket Shield

First-class competition run on a challenge basis 1906-21,
and on a league basis 1921/2 to 1974/5. The Shield was
presented by Lord Plunket, Governor-General of New
Zealand.

Challenge holders: 1906-7 Canterbury, 1907-11
Auckland, 1911-2 Canterbury, 1912-3 Auckland,
1913-8 Canterbury, 1918-9 Wellington, 1919-20
Canterbury, 1920-1 Auckland, 1921 Wellington

League wins:

(Year given is that of second half of the season.)

14   Wellington
     1924, 1926, 1928, 1930, 1932, 1936, 1950, 1955,
     1957, 1961-2, 1966, 1973-4
12   Auckland
     1922, 1927, 1929, 1934, 1937-40, 1947, 1959,
     1964, 1969
 9   Canterbury
     1923, 1931, 1935, 1946, 1949, 1952, 1956, 1960,
     1965,
 9   Otago
     1925, 1933, 1948, 1951, 1953, 1958, 1970, 1972,
     1975
 4   Central Districts
     1954, 1967-8, 1971
 1   Northern Districts
     1963

Shell Series

From 1975-6 the first-class provincial competition has
been sponsored by Shell. In the first four years the Shell
Cup was awarded to the League winners and the Shell
Trophy to winners of a knock-out competition. From
1979/80 the Shell Trophy has been won by the League
winners, and the Shell Cup by the winners of the
limited-overs competition. The latter was previously
sponsored by the NZ Motor Corporation, 1971-7 and
Gillette 1977-9.

Shell Cup

Winners:

1976	Canterbury
1977	Northern Districts
1978	Canterbury
1979	Otago

Shell Trophy

Wins:

 6   Auckland
     1978, 1981, 1989, 1991, 1995-6
 5   Canterbury
     1976, 1984, 1994, 1997-8
 4   Otago
     1977, 1979, 1986, 1988
 4   Wellington
     1982, 1983, 1985, 1990
 3   Northern Districts
     1980, 1992★, 1993
 2   Central Districts
     1987, 1992★

★ Shared.

Limited-overs competition

Wins:

10   Canterbury
     1972, 1976-8, 1986, 1992-4, 1996-7
7   Auckland
     1973, 1979, 1981, 1983-4, 1987, 1990
5   Wellington
     1974-5, 1982, 1989, 1991
3   Northern Districts
     1980, 1995, 1998
1   Central Districts 1985, Otago 1988

Pakistan

Most runs in a season: 1649 (av. 63.42) Saadat Ali
    1983/4

Most wickets in a season: 107 (av. 16.06) Ijaz Faqih
    1985/6

Most dismissals in a season: 70 (62 C, 8 St) Ashraf
    Ali 1986/7

Quaid-e-Azam Trophy

Pakistan's major national first-class championship is
named after Mohammad Ali Jinnah, who was known
as Quaid-e-Azam, or 'Great Leader'.

Winners (year given is that of second half of the season):

10   Karachi
     1955, 1959-60, 1963 (Karachi A), 1967, 1986,
     Karachi Whites 1991-3
7   Karachi Blues
     1962, 1964, 1965, 1971, 1995-6, 1998
5   National Bank
     1976, 1979, 1982, 1984, 1987
4   United Bank
     1977, 1981, 1983, 1985
3   PIA
     1970, 1980, 1990
3   Lahore (City)
     Lahore 1969, Lahore City 1994, 1997
2   Bahawalpur
     1954, 1958
2   Punjab
     1957, 1975 (Punjab A)
2   Railways
     1973-4
2   Habib Bank
     1978, 1988
1   ADBP
     1989

South Africa

Most runs in a season: 1915 (av. 68.39) John Reid
    (NZ) 1961/2

Most wickets in a season: 106 (av. 19.39) Richie
    Benaud (Aus) 1957/8

Most dismissals in a season: 65 (57 C, 8 St) Ray
    Jennings 1982/3

Currie Cup/Castle Cup/Super Sport Series

The annual first-class competition for the South African
provinces. The Currie Cup was presented by Sir
Donald Currie and first contested in the 1889/90
season. Until 1966 it was not normally contested in
the seasons when a touring team visited South Africa.
The competition was for the Castle Cup 1990-6 and
for the Super Sport Series from 1996/7.

Winners (year given is that of second half of the season):

28 (4*)   Transvaal
          1890, 1895, 1903-5, 1907, 1922*, 1924,
          1926-7, 1930, 1935, 1938*, 1951, 1959,
          1966*, 1969, 1970*, 1971-3, 1979-80,
          1983-5, 1987-8
23 (3*)   Natal
          1911, 1913, 1922*, 1934, 1937, 1938*,
          1947-8, 1952, 1955, 1960-1, 1963-4, 1966*,
          1967-8, 1974, 1976-7, 1981, 1995, 1997
18 (3*)   Western Province
          1893-4, 1897-8, 1909, 1921, 1922*, 1932,
          1953, 1956, 1970*, 1975, 1978, 1982, 1986,
          1990*, 1991, 1996
3 (1*)   Eastern Province
          1989, 1990*, 1992
3   (Orange) Free State
          1993-4, 1998
1   Kimberley (now Griqualand West)
          1891

* Shared wins.

Limited-overs competition

The South African limited-overs competition was
contested for the Gillette Cup from 1969-77, Datsun
Shield 1977-83, Nissan Shield 1983-92, Total Power
Shield 1992/3. Not held since then.

Winners:

9   Transvaal
     1974, 1979-81, 1983-6, 1991
5   Western Province
     1970-1, 1973, 1982, 1989
4   Eastern Province
     1972, 1976, 1988, 1990
3   Natal
     1975, 1977, 1987
2   (Orange) Free State
     1992-3
1   Rhodesia
     1978

Night Trophy

A limited-overs competition, played at night under
floodlights, was introduced in 1981/2. It was sponsored
by Benson & Hedges 1981-96, and became the
Standard Bank Cup from 1996/7.

Winners:

5   Transvaal/Gauteng   1982-3, 1985, 1991, 1993;
                           Gauteng 1998

4	(Orange) Free State	1989, 1994-6
3	Western Province	1986-8
2	Eastern Province	1990, 1992
1	Natal	1984, 1997

West Indies

Most runs in a season: 1765 (av. 135.76) Patsy Hendren (Eng) 1929/30

Most wickets in a season: 80 (av. 12.46) Edward Dowson (Eng) 1901/02

Most dismissals in a season: 42 (40 C, 2 St) Courtney Browne 1996/7

Shell Shield 1966-87, Red Stripe Cup 1988-97, President's Cup 1998

This annual first-class competition for the West Indian teams has been contested annually from 1966, except in 1968.

Winners:

15	Barbados
	1966-7, 1972, 1974, 1976*, 1977-80, 1982, 1984, 1986, 1991, 1995, 1997
6	Guyana
	1973, 1975, 1983, 1987, 1993, 1998 (=)
4	Trinidad & Tobago
	1970-1, 1976*, 1985
4	Jamaica
	1969, 1988-9, 1992
4	Leeward Islands
	1990, 1994, 1996, 1998 (=)
1	Combined Islands
	1981

* Shared.

There was a triangular inter-colonial tournament first held in 1893, up to 1939, but not resumed after the war.

Wins: 11 Trinidad, 10 Barbados, 5 Demerara/ British Guiana

Other post-war tournaments prior to the Shell Shield were won by British Guiana in 1957, 1962 and 1964.

Women's Cricket

The first women's cricket match recorded was at Gosden Common in Surrey, England in 1745. The first women's club was the White Heather Club, founded at Nun Appleton, Yorkshire in 1887 and the first women's Test match was played between England and Australia at Brisbane on 28-31 December 1934.

The Women's Cricket Association (WCA) was formed in England in 1926 and the International Women's Cricket Council (IWCC) in 1958. The WCA amalgamated with the England and Wales Cricket Board in 1998.

World Cup

First held in 1973.
Winners:

1973	England
1978	Australia
1982	Australia
1988	Australia
1993	England
1997	Australia

Highest team score

412-3	Australia v Denmark at Bombay 16 Dec 1997
376-2	England v Pakistan at Vijayavada 12 Dec 1997
324-3	England v Ireland at Pune 16 Dec 1997

Highest individual scores

229*	Belinda Clark, for Australia v Denmark, Bombay 16 Dec 1997
173*	Charlotte Edwards for England v Ireland, Pune 16 Dec 1997
143*	Lindsay Reeler for Australia v Netherlands 29 Nov 1988

* Not out.

Best bowling

6-10	Jackie Lord for New Zealand v India 14 Jan 1982
6-20	Glenys Page for New Zealand v Trinidad & Tobago 23 Jun 1973

Test Records

Team records

Highest innings: 525 Australia v India, Ahmedabad 4-5 Feb 1984; 517-8 New Zealand v England, Scarborough 26-27 Jun 1996; 503-5 dec. England v New Zealand, Christchurch 16-18 Feb 1935

Lowest innings: 35 England v Australia, St Kilda, Melbourne 22 Feb 1958

Individual records

Highest innings

204	Kirsty Flavel for New Zealand v England, Scarborough 26-27 Jun 1996 (555 min)
193	Denise Annetts for Australia v England, Collingham, 23-24 Aug 1987 (381 min)
190	Sandiya Aggarwal for India v England, Worcester, 14 July 1986 (563 min)
189	Betty Snowball for England v New Zealand, Christchurch, 16 Feb 1935 (222 min)

Best bowling

8-53	Neetu David for India v England, Jamshedpur 26-27 Nov 1995
7-6	Mary Duggan for England v Australia, St Kilda, Melbourne, 22 Feb 1958

7-7   Betty Wilson for Australia v England, St Kilda, Melbourne, 22 Feb 1958 (including the only hat-trick in women's Test cricket)

Best match analysis

11-16 Betty Wilson, 7-7 and 4-9, as above 22 Feb 1958
11-63 Julia Greenwood, 6-46 and 5-17, for England v West Indies, Canterbury, 16-18 June 1979

Most dismissals

8 in an innings Lisa Nye (6 C, 2 St) for England v New Zealand, New Plymouth, 12-15 Feb 1992

Career records

Most Tests: 25 Rachael Heyhoe-Flint, England 1960-79
Most runs: 1594 av. 45.54 Rachael Heyhoe-Flint (Eng) in 22 Tests, (inc 3 unofficial: 1814 av. 49.02) 1960-79
Highest average: 81.90 Denise Annetts (Aus) 819 runs in 10 Tests 1987-92
Most centuries: 4 Enid Bakewell (Eng), Sandhya Agarwal (Ind), Deborah Hockley (NZ)
Most wickets: 77 Mary Duggan (Eng) in 17 Tests, av 13.49 1949-63
Most dismissals: 58 (46 C, 12 St) Christina Matthews (Aus) in 20 Tests
England have played Australia in 33 Tests from 1934 to 1987; England have won 6, Australia 7, and 20 have been drawn.

European Cup

First held in 1989, and won by England then and in 1990, 1991 and 1995

National Club League Competition

Run annually by the WCA from 1988, with English clubs playing in area competitions leading to national semi-finals and final. The 1988 Finals were abandoned due to bad weather; Somerset Wanderers, Wakefield, Redoubtables and Vagabonds were semi-finalists.
Subsequent winners:

1989-90	Wakefield
1991	Wolverhampton
1992-3	Wakefield
1994	Redoutables
1995	Wakefield and Redoutables
1997	Kent Invicta

National Club Knock-Out Competition

Organized annually by the WCA, but not held in 1976, 1986, or 1992.
Winners:

1974	Edgbaston
1975	Wallington
1977	Wallington
1978	Riverside
1979-82	Gunnersbury
1983	Vagabonds
1984	Invicta
1985	Somerset Wanderers
1987	Vagabonds
1988	Wolverhampton
1989-90	Wakefield
1991	North Riding
1993	Wakefield
1994-5	Sherwood and Newark
1996-7	Wakefield

Area championships

Organized annually since 1980 (except for 1983-4, and 1987) by the WCA.
Wins:

Middlesex	1980-1, 1985, 1986 (tied with Kent)
East Midlands	1988-91
West Midlands	1982
Yorkshire	1992-7

Croquet

Croquet is played with ball and mallet, and six hoops and a peg laid out on a grass lawn 35 yd (31.9m) long by 28 yd (25.6m) wide. While its exact origins are obscure, it was probably derived from the French game *Jeu de Mail*, played from the 12th century. A game resembling croquet, probably of foreign origin, was played in Ireland in the 1830s. Jean Jaques, the sports-goods manufacturers, made the first croquet sets in England in the 1850s and published a book on the game in 1857. Ten years later the first championships were held at Evesham, Worcestershire.

The All-England Croquet Club was founded at Wimbledon, south London in 1869 and the current governing body, the Croquet Association, was formed in 1896. The game was played at the 1900 Olympic Games in Paris, when all the contestants were French.

International governing body: World Croquet Federation (WCF). Formed in 1986, with 12 member nations. Membership at 20 by 1997.

The Croquet Association, The Hurlingham Club, Ranelagh Gardens, London SW6 3PR. Tel: 0171 736 3148, Fax: 0171 736 3148. Chairman: W H Arliss, Secretary: Paul Campion. Founded 1897.

World Championships

First held at Hurlingham in 1989.
Cancelled in 1993.

1989	Joe Hogan (NZ)
1990	Robert Fulford (UK)
1991	John Walters (UK)
1992	Robert Fulford (UK)
1994	Robert Fulford (UK)
1995	Chris Clarke (UK)
1997	Robert Fulford (UK)

MacRobertson International Shield

Contested by Australia, Great Britain and New Zealand, for the first time in 1925.
Wins:

9   Great Britain
     1925, 1937, 1956, 1963, 1969, 1974, 1982, 1990, 1993, 1996
3   Australia
     1928, 1930, 1935
3   New Zealand
     1950, 1979, 1986

Croquet Championship

First held in 1867.
Recent champions and most wins:

Open Championship

1977	Michael Heap
1978	Nigel Aspinall
1979	David Openshaw
1980	William de R Prichard
1981	David Openshaw
1982-4	Nigel Aspinall
1985	David Openshaw
1986	Joe Hogan (NZ)
1987	Mark Avery
1988	Stephen Mulliner
1989	Joe Hogan (NZ)
1990	Stephen Mulliner
1991-2	Robert Fulford
1993-5	Reg Bamford (SAf)
1996	Robert Fulford
1997	Chris Clarke

Most wins

10   John W Solomon 1953, 1956, 1959, 1961, 1963-8
8   Nigel Aspinall 1969, 1974-6, 1978, 1982-4
7   Humphrey Hicks 1932, 1939, 1947-50, 1952
5   Cyril Corbally 1902-3, 1906, 1908, 1913

Most wins by a woman

4   Dorothy Steel 1925, 1933, 1935-6

Open doubles

First played in 1924.

1977-8	Nigel Aspinall & William Ormerod
1979	Bernard Neal & S R Hemsted
1980	William de B Prichard & Stephen Mulliner
1981	Stephen Mulliner & Mark Ormerod
1982	Martin Murray & Andrew Hope
1983	John McCullough & Phil Cordingley
1984	Nigel Aspinall & Stephen Mulliner
1985	David Openshaw & Mark Avery
1986	Nigel Aspinall & Stephen Mulliner
1987	David Openshaw & Mark Avery
1988	Nigel Aspinall & Stephen Mulliner
1989	Joe Hogan & Bob Jackson (NZ)
1990-3	Chris Clarke & Robert Fulford
1994	Reg Bamford (SAf) & Stephen Mulliner
1995	Steve Cornish & David Maugham
1996	Chris Clarke & Robert Fulford
1997	Reg Bamford (SAf) & Stephen Mulliner

Most wins

10   John W Solomon & Pat Cotter 1954-5, 1958-9, 1961-5, 1969
10   Nigel Aspinall, with William Ormerod 1971-2, 1975-6, 1977-8, with J W Simon 1966, 1968, 1970, with Stephen Mulliner 1984, 1986, 1988

Most titles at all events

31   John W Solomon 10 open, 10 men's, 10 doubles, 1 mixed doubles
31   Dorothy Steel 4 open, 15 women's, 5 doubles, 7 mixed doubles
27   Humphrey Hicks 7 open, 9 men's, 7 doubles, 4 mixed doubles

President's Cup – British Masters

An annual invitation event for the best eight players, first held in 1934, renamed the British Masters from 1992.

Most wins

11   Nigel Aspinall 1969-70, 1973-6, 1978, 1980, 1982, 1984-5
9   John W Solomon 1955, 1957-9, 1962-4, 1968, 1971
6   Pat Cotter 1949-50, 1952-3, 1956, 1960
5   Humphrey Hicks 1947-8, 1951, 1954, 1961
5   Stephen Mulliner 1981, 1983, 1986-7, 1992

Other recent winners

1988	Chris Clarke
1989	Robert Fulford
1990	David Maugham
1991	Chris Clarke
1993-4	David Maugham
1995-6	Chris Clarke
1997	Steve Cornish

Lowest-ever handicap: minus 5.5 Humphrey Hicks. The limit is now fixed at minus 5.

Curling

Curling, a bit like bowls on ice, is known as the 'roaring game', due to the noise made by the curling stone (c.40lb/18kg) as it runs over the ice rink. The curlers use brooms to sweep the rink ahead of their stone to remove impediments and smooth the ice. The game became popular in Scotland, but it may have originated in the Netherlands more than 400 years ago. The Grand Caledonian Curling Club was formed in Edinburgh in 1838. Five years later it added Royal to its title and eventually became the international governing body of the sport.

Scots introduced curling to Canada, where the first club was the Royal Montreal Curling Club, founded in 1807. The first club in the USA was the Orchard Lake Club, formed in Michigan in 1832.

The first international match was between Canada and the USA in 1884, the start of the Gordon International Medal series, now contested annually by clubs representing the Canadian branch of the Royal Caledonian Curling Club and the Grand National Curling Club of America. The Strathcona Cup series between Canada and Scotland started in 1903.

International governing body: World Curling Federation, 81 Great King Street, Edinburgh EH3 6RN. Tel: 0131 556 4884, Fax: 0131 556 9400. President: Günther Hummelt, Secretary General: Mike Thomson. Founded in 1966. 33 member nations affiliated in 1998.

World Championships

Men

Played annually for the Scotch Whisky Cup 1959-67 and for the Air Canada Silver Broom 1968-86.

Winners:

Year	Nation	Skip
1959-60	Canada	Ernie Richardson
1961	Canada	Hec Gervais
1962-3	Canada	Ernie Richardson
1964	Canada	Lyall Dagg
1965	USA	Bud Somerville
1966	Canada	Ron Northcott
1967	Scotland	Chuck Hay
1968-9	Canada	Ron Northcott
1970-1	Canada	Don Duguid
1972	Canada	Orest Meleschuk
1973	Sweden	Kjell Oscarius
1974	USA	Bud Somerville
1975	Switzerland	Otto Danielli
1976	USA	Bruce Roberts
1977	Sweden	Ragnar Kamp
1978	USA	Bob Nichols
1979	Norway	Kristian Sørum
1980	Canada	Rick Falk
1981	Switzerland	Jürg Tanner
1982	Canada	Al Hackner
1983	Canada	Ed Werenich
1984	Norway	Eigel Ramsfjell
1985	Canada	Al Hackner
1986	Canada	Ed Lukovich
1987	Canada	Russ Howard
1988	Norway	Eigel Ramsfjell
1989	Canada	Pat Ryan
1990	Canada	Ed Werenich
1991	Scotland	David Smith
1992	Switzerland	Markus Eggler
1993	Canada	Russ Howard
1994	Canada	Rick Folk
1995	Canada	Kerry Burtnyk
1996	Canada	Jeff Stroughton
1997	Sweden	Peter Lindholm
1998	Canada	Wayne Middaugh

Most wins: 24 Canada; 4 USA
Most times as winning skip: 4 Ernie Richardson;
   3 Ron Northcott

Women

Played annually from 1979.

Winners:

1979	Switzerland	Gaby Casanova
1980	Canada	Mary Mitchell
1981	Sweden	Elisabeth Högström
1982	Denmark	Marianne Jørgensen
1983	Switzerland	Erika Müller
1984	Canada	Connie Laliberte
1985	Canada	Linda Moore
1986	Canada	Marilyn Darte
1987	Canada	Pat Saunders
1988	F R Germany	Andrea Schöpp
1989	Canada	Heather Euston
1990-1	Norway	Djordy Nordby
1992	Sweden	Elisabet Johansson
1993-4	Canada	Sandra Peterson
1995	Sweden	Elisabet Gustafson
1996	Canada	Marilyn Badogh
1997	Canada	Sandra Schmirler
1998	Sweden	Elisabet Gustafson

Most wins: 10 Canada
Most times as winning skip: 3 Elisabet Gustafson

Olympic Games

Curling was included as a demonstration sport at the Games of 1924, 1932 and 1964, and again in 1988 and 1992. It became a medal sport in 1998. A specialized German version of the game was demonstrated in 1936.

Recent winners:

Men

1988	Norway	Eigil Ramsfjell
1992	Switzerland	Urs Dick
1998	Switzerland	Patrick Hürlimann

Women

1988	Canada	Linda Moore
1992	Germany	Andrea Schöpp
1998	Canada	Sandra Schmirler

Cycling

The forerunner of the bicycle, the *célerifère*, was demonstrated in the garden of the Palais Royal, Paris in 1791. The first treadle-propelled bicycle was designed by Scottish blacksmith Kirkpatrick Macmillan in 1839, but the first practical bicycle was the *vélocipède* built in March 1861 by Pierre Michaux and his son Ernest of Paris. The first cycling club, the Liverpool Velocipede Club, was formed in 1867 and the first race took place the following year, over 1200 metres at the Parc St Cloud, Paris; it was won by Englishman James Moore. The first international organization was the International Cyclist Association (ICA), founded in 1892, which promoted the first world championships the following year.

International governing body: Union Cycliste International, 37 route de Chavannes, Case Postale, CH-1000 Lausanne 23, Switzerland. Tel: (41) 21 626 0080, Fax: (41) 21 626 0088. President: Hein Verbruggen, General Secretary: Jean-Pierre Dick. Founded 1900. 162 member nations by 1994. In 1965 two federations were formed within the UCI – the Fédération de Cyclisme Amateur (FICA) and the Fédération Internationale de Cyclisme Professional (FICP).

Olympic Games

Cycling was included in the first Olympics of 1896 and at every Games since, except 1904 when there were no official events. A women's road race was introduced in 1984, and the sprint added in 1988.

Winners:

Men

Sprint

In 1896 and 1900 over 2000 metres, since then at 1000 metres. Now raced over the best of three races.

1896	Paul Masson (Fra) 4:56.0
1900	Georges Taillandier (Fra) 2:52.0
1906	Francesco Verri (Ita) 1:42.2
1908	*Declared void as riders exceeded time limit*
1920	Maurice Peeters (Hol) 1:38.3
1924	Lucien Michard (Fra)
1928	Roger Beaufrand (Fra)
1932	Jacobus van Egmond (Hol)
1936	Toni Merkens (Ger)
1948	Mario Ghella (Ita)
1952	Enzo Sacchi (Ita)
1956	Michel Rousseau (Fra)
1960	Sante Gaiardoni (Ita)
1964	Giovanni Pettenella (Ita)
1968	Daniel Morelon (Fra)
1972	Daniel Morelon (Fra)
1976	Anton Tkáč (Cs)
1980	Lutz Hesslich (GDR)
1984	Mark Gorski (USA)
1988	Lutz Hesslich (GDR)
1992	Jens Fiedler (Ger)
1996	Jens Fiedler (Ger)

1000 metres time trial

In 1896 and 1906 raced over 333.33m.

1896	Paul Masson (Fra) 24.0
1906	Francesco Verri (Ita) 22.8
1928	Willy Falck-Hansen (Den) 1:14.4
1932	Edgar Gray (Aus) 1:13.0
1936	Arie van Vliet (Hol) 1:12.0
1948	Jacques Dupont (Fra) 1:13.5
1952	Russell Mockridge (Aus) 1:11.1
1956	Leandro Faggin (Ita) 1:09.8
1960	Sante Gaiardoni (Ita) 1:07.27
1964	Patrick Sercu (Bel) 1:09.59
1968	Pierre Trentin (Fra) 1:03.91
1972	Niels-Christian Fredborg (Den) 1:06.44
1976	Klaus-Jürgen Grünke (GDR) 1:05.927
1980	Lothar Thoms (GDR) 1:02.955
1984	Freddy Schmidtke (FRG) 1:06.10
1988	Aleksandr Kirichenko (USSR) 1:04.499
1992	José Manuel Moreno (Spa) 1:03.342
1996	Florian Rousseau (Fra) 1:02.712

4000 metres individual pursuit

1964	Jiri Daler (Cs) 5:04.75
1968	Daniel Rebillard (Fra) 4:41.71
1972	Knut Knudsen (Nor) 4:45.74
1976	Gregor Braun (FRG) 4:47.61
1980	Robert Dill-Bundi (Swi) 4:35.66
1984	Steve Hegg (USA) 4:39.55
1988	Gintautas Umaras (USSR) 4:32.00
1992	Chris Boardman★ (UK)
1996	Andrea Collinelli (Ita) 4:20.893

★ Boardman caught his opponent Jens Lehmann a lap from the finish and thus the full distance was not completed; he achieved a record time of 4:24.496 in a preliminary round.

50 kilometres points race

Introduced in 1984.

1984	Roger Ilegems (Bel) 37 pts
1988	Dan Frost (Den) 38 pts
1992	Giovanni Lombardi (Ita) 44 pts
1996	Silvio Martinello (Ita) 37 pts

4000 metres team pursuit

1908	Great Britain 2:18.6 (1810.5m)
1920	Italy 5:20.0
1924	Italy 5:15.0
1928	Italy 5:01.8
1932	Italy 4:53.0
1936	France 4:45.0

1948	France 4:57.8
1952	Italy 4:46.1
1956	Italy 4:37.4
1960	Italy 4:30.90
1964	F R Germany 4:35.67
1968	Denmark 4:22.44
1972	F R Germany 4:22.14
1976	F R Germany 4:21.06
1980	USSR 4:15.70
1984	Australia 4:25.99
1988	USSR 4:13.31
1992	Germany 4:08.791
1996	France 4:05.930

Team road race

1912-20 combined times of best 4 riders in the individual race. 1924-52 best 3. 1956 based on placings.

1912	Sweden 44:35:33.6
1920	France 19:16:43.2
1924	France 19:30:14.0
1928	Denmark 15:09:14.0
1932	Italy 7:27:15.2
1936	France 7:39:16.2
1948	Belgium 15:58:17.4
1952	Belgium 15:20:46.6
1956	France 22 points

100 kilometres team time trial

1960	Italy 2:14:33.53
1964	Netherlands 2:26:31.19 (110km)
1968	Netherlands 2:07:49.06 (104km)
1972	USSR 2:11:17.8
1976	USSR 2:08:53.0
1980	USSR 2:01:21.74 (101km)
1984	Italy 1:58:28.0
1988	GDR 1:57:47.7
1992	Germany 2:01:39

Individual road race

Distance in kilometres shown for each year.

1896	87km	Aristidis Konstantinidis (Gre) 3:22:31.0
1906	84	Fernand Vast (Fra) 2:41:28.0
1912	320	Rudolph Lewis (SAf) 10:42:39.0
1920	175	Harry Stenqvist (Swe) 4:40:01.8
1924	188	Armand Blanchonnet (Fra) 6:20:48.0
1928	168	Henry Hansen (Den) 4:47:18.0
1932	100	Attilio Pavesi (Ita) 2:28:05.6
1936	100	Robert Charpentier (Fra) 2:33:05.0
1948	194.63	José Beyaert (Fra) 5:18:12.6
1952	190.4	André Noyelle (Bel) 5:06:03.4
1956	187.73	Ercole Baldini (Ita) 5:21:17.0
1960	175.38	Viktor Kapitonov (USSR) 4:20:37.0
1964	194.83	Mario Zanin (Ita) 4:39:51.63
1968	196.2	Pierfranco Vianelli (Ita) 4:41:25.24
1972	182.4	Hennie Kuiper (Hol) 4:14:37.0

1976	175	Bernt Johansson (Swe) 4:46:52.0
1980	189	Sergey Sukhoruchenkov (USSR) 4:48:28.9
1984	190.2	Alexi Grewal (USA) 4:59:57.0
1988	196.8	Olaf Ludwig (GDR) 4:32:22.0
1992	195	Fabio Casartelli (Ita) 4:35:21.00
1996	221.9	Pascal Richard (Fra) 4:53:56

Individual road time trial

| 1996 | Miguel Induráin (Spa) 1:04:05 (52.2km) |

Women

Road race

1984	79km	Connie Carpenter-Phinney (USA) 2:11:14
1988	82	Monique Knol (Hol) 2:00:52
1992	81	Kathryn Watt (Aus) 2:04:42
1996	104.4	Jeanne Longo-Ciprelli (Fra) 2:36:13

Individual road time trial

| 1996 | Zulfiya Zabirova (Rus) 36:40 (261km) |

Sprint (1000 metres)

1988	Erika Salumäe (USSR)
1992	Erika Salumäe (Est)
1996	Félicia Ballanger (Fra)

3000 metres individual pursuit

| 1992 | Petra Rossner (Ger) 3:41.753 |
| 1996 | Antonella Bellutti (Ita) 3:33.595 |

Points

| 1996 | Nathalie Lancien (Fra) 24 pts |

Superseded men's track events

660yd	1908	Victor Johnson (UK) 51.2
5km	1906	Francesco Verri (Ita) 8:35.0
	1908	Benjamin Jones (UK) 8:36.2
10km	1896	Paul Masson (Fra) 17:54.2
20km	1906	William Pett (UK) 29:00.0
	1908	Charles Kingsbury (UK) 34:13.6
50km	1920	Henry George (Bel) 1:16:43.2
	1924	Jacobus Willems (Hol) 1:18:24.0
100km	1896	Léon Flameng (Fra) 3:08:19.2
	1908	Charles Bartlett (UK) 2:41:48.6
12hrs	1896	Adolf Schmal (Aut) 314.997km

In 1904 track races were won by Marcus Hurley (USA) at quarter-mile, third-mile, half-mile and 1 mile; Burton Downing (USA) 2 and 25 miles; Charles Schlee (USA) 5 miles.

Men's 2000 metres tandem

From 1924-72, times recorded only over last 200m.

1906	John Matthews & Arthur Rushen (UK) 2:57.0
1908	Maurice Schilles & André Auffray (Fra) 3:07.8
1920	Harry Ryan & Thomas Lance (UK) 2:49.4
1924	Lucien Choury & Jean Cugnot (Fra) 12.6
1928	Bernhard Leene & Daan van Dijk (Hol) 11.8
1932	Maurice Perrin & Louis Chaillot (Fra) 12.0

1936	Ernst Ihbe & Carl Lorenz (Ger) 11.8
1948	Renato Perona & Ferdinando Terruzzi (Ita) 11.3
1952	Lionel Cox & Russell Mockridge (Aus) 11.0
1956	Ian Browne & Anthony Marchant (Aus) 10.8
1960	Giuseppe Beghetto & Sergio Bianchetto (Ita) 10.7
1964	Sergio Bianchetto & Angelo Damiano (Ita) 10.75
1968	Daniel Morelon & Pierre Trentin (Fra) 9.83
1972	Vladimir Semenets & Igor Tselovalnikov (USSR) 10.52

Most Olympic gold medals: 3 Paul Masson (Fra) 1896, Francisco Verri (Ita) 1906, Robert Charpentier (Fra) 1936, Daniel Morelon (Fra) 1968-72

Most Olympic medals: 5 Morelon, as above, and also a silver in 1976 and bronze in 1964, both in the sprint

World Championships

World Championships were first held in 1893 in Chicago, with two events: the sprint and the motor-paced race over 100km. A road race was first held in 1921 and women's events were introduced in 1959. Separate world championships are not contested in Olympic years for events on the Olympic programme (qv). The distinction between amateurs and professionals for track races was abolished in 1993. Events currently contested, with those to have won most often, and winners from 1970 are listed below.

Men

Sprint (amateur)

First held 1893.

1969-71	Daniel Morelon (Fra)
1973	Daniel Morelon (Fra)
1974	Anton Tkáč (Cs)
1975	Daniel Morelon (Fra)
1977	Hans-Jürgen Geschke (GDR)
1978	Anton Tkáč (Cs)
1979	Lutz Hesslich (GDR)
1981-2	Sergey Kopylov (USSR)
1983	Lutz Hesslich (GDR)
1985	Lutz Hesslich (GDR)
1986	Michael Hübner (GDR)
1987	Lutz Hesslich (GDR)
1989-90	Bill Huck (GDR)
1991	Jens Fiedler (Ger)

Most wins: 7 Morelon 1966-7, 1969-71, 1973, 1975; 4 William Bailey (UK) 1909-11, 1913; Hesslich

Sprint

Professional to 1992, then Open.

1970	Gordon Johnson (Aus)
1971	Leijin Loevesijn (Hol)
1972-3	Robert van Lancker (Bel)
1974	Peder Pedersen (Den)
1975-6	John Nicholson (Aus)

1977-86	Koichi Nakano (Jap)
1987	Noboyuki Tawara (Jap)
1988	Stephen Pate (Aus)
1989	Claudio Golinelli (Ita)
1990	Michael Hübner (GDR)
1991	*Vacant*★
1992	Michael Hübner (Ger)
1993	Gary Niewand (Aus)
1994	Martin Nothstein (USA)
1995	Darryn Hill (Aus)
1996-7	Florian Rousseau (Fra)

★ Left vacant after winner Carey Hall (Aus) failed drugs test.

Most wins: 10 Nakano; 7 Jeff Scherens (Bel) 1932-7, 1947, Antonio Maspes (Ita) 1955-6, 1959-62, 1964; 6 Thorvald Ellegaard (Den) 1901-3, 1906, 1908, 1911; 5 Piet Moeskops (Hol) 1921-4, 1926; 4 Lucien Michard (Fra) 1927-30, Reg Harris (UK) 1949-51, 1954

Olympic sprint

Teams of three over three laps.

1995	Germany
1996	Australia
1997	France

1 kilometre time trial

Amateur 1966-91, now Open.

1970	Niels Fredborg (Den)
1971	Eduard Rapp (USSR)
1973	Janusz Kierzkowski (Pol)
1974	Eduard Rapp (USSR)
1975	Klaus Grünke (GDR)
1977-9	Lothar Thoms (GDR)
1981	Lothar Thoms (GDR)
1982	Fredy Schmidtke (FRG)
1983	Sergey Kopylov (USSR)
1985	Jens Glücklich (GDR)
1986	Maik Malchow (GDR)
1987	Martin Vinnicombe (Aus)
1989	Jens Glücklich (GDR)
1990	Aleksandr Kirichenko (USSR)
1991	José Manuel Moreno (Spa)
1993-4	Florian Rousseau (Fra)
1995-7	Shane Kelly (Aus)

Most wins: 4 Thoms; 3 Niels Fredborg (Den) 1967-8, 1970

4 kilometres pursuit

First held 1946. Amateur to 1991, now Open.

1970	Xavier Kurmann (Swi)
1971	Martin-Emilio Rodriguez (Col)
1973	Knut Knudsen (Nor)
1974	Hans Lutz (FRG)
1975	Thomas Huschke (GDR)
1977	Norbert Durpisch (GDR)
1978	Detlef Macha (GDR)
1979	Nikolay Makarov (USSR)

1981-2	Detlef Macha (GDR)	7	USSR		

1981-2   Detlef Macha (GDR)
1983   Viktor Kupovets (USSR)
1985-6   Vyacheslav Yekimov
         (USSR)
1987   Gintautas Umaras
         (USSR)
1989   Vyacheslav Yekimov
         (USSR)
1990   Yevgeniy Berzin (USSR)
1991   Jens Lehmann (Ger)
1993   Graeme Obree (UK)
1994   Chris Boardman (UK)
1995   Graeme Obree (UK)
1996   Chris Boardman (UK)
1997   Philippe Ermenault (Fra)
Most wins: 3 Tiemen Groen (Hol)
   1964-6, Macha, Yekimov

Professional 5 kilometres pursuit

First held in 1939, when it was left
unfinished, and then in 1946.

1970   Hugh Porter (UK)
1971   Dirk Baert (Bel)
1972-3   Hugh Porter (UK)
1974-5   Roy Schuiten (Hol)
1976   Francesco Moser (Ita)
1977-8   Gregor Braun (FRG)
1979   Bert Osterbosch (Hol)
1980   Tony Doyle (UK)
1981-2   Alain Bondue (Fra)
1983   Steele Bishop (Aus)
1984-5   Hans-Henrik Oersted
         (Den)
1986   Tony Doyle (UK)
1987   Hans-Henrik Oersted
         (Den)
1988   Lech Piasecki (Pol)
1989   Colin Sturgess (UK)
1990   Vyacheslav Yekimov
         (USSR)
1991   Francis Moreau (Fra)
1992   Mike McCarthy (USA)
Most wins: 4 Hugh Porter (UK)
   1968, 1970, 1972-3; 3 Guido
   Messina (Ita) 1954-6, Roger
   Rivière (Fra) 1957-9, Leandro
   Faggin (Ita) 1963, 1965-6, Oersted

Team pursuit

First held 1962. Amateur to 1991,
now Open.

Wins:
8   Germany FRG
    1962, 1964, 1970, 1973-5,
    1983
    Ger 1991, 1994

7   USSR
    1963, 1965, 1967, 1969, 1982,
    1987, 1990
6   Italy
    1966, 1968, 1971, 1985, 1996-7
5   GDR
    1977-9, 1981, 1989
2   Australia
    1993, 1995
1   Czechoslovakia
    1986

Keirin

First held 1980. Professional to 1992,
now Open.
1980-1   Danny Clark (Aus)
1982   Gordon Singleton (Can)
1983   Urs Freuler (Swi)
1984   Robert Dill-Bundi (Swi)
1985   Urs Freuler (Swi)
1986   Michel Vaarten (Bel)
1987   Harumi Honda (Jap)
1988   Claudio Golinelli (Ita)*
1989   Claudio Golinelli (Ita)
1990-2   Michael Hübner
         (GDR/Ger)
1993   Gary Niewand (Aus)
1994   Marty Nothstein (USA)
1995   Frédéric Magne (Fra)
1996   Marty Nothstein (USA)
1997   Frédéric Magne (Fra)
* Vacant, after winner failed drugs
test in sprint.
Most wins: 3 Hübner

50 kilometres points race (amateur)

First held 1976.
1976   Walter Baumgartner (Swi)
1977   Constant Tourne (Bel)
1978   Noel de Jonckheere (Bel)
1979   Jiří Slama (Cs)
1980   Gary Sutton (Aus)
1981   Lutz Haueisen (GDR)
1982   Hans-Joachim Pohl
         (GDR)
1983   Michael Marcussen (Den)
1985   Martin Penc (Cs)
1986   Dan Frost (Den)
1987   Marat Ganeyev (USSR)
1989   Marat Satybyldiev
         (USSR)
1990   Stephen McGlede (Aus)
1991   Bruno Risi (Swz)

Points

First held 1980. Professional to 1992,
now Open.
1980   Stan Tourne (Bel)
1981-7   Urs Freuler (Swi)
1988   Daniel Wyder (Swi)
1989   Urs Freuler (Swi)
1990   Laurent Biondi (Fra)
1991   Vyacheslav Yekimov
         (USSR)
1992   Bruno Risi (Swz)
1993   Etienne De Wilde (Bel)
1994   Bruno Risi (Swz)
1995   Silvio Martinello (Ita)
1996   Rosselló Llaneras (Spa)
1997   Silvio Martinello (Ita)
Most wins: 8 Freuler

Motor-paced (amateur)

Held at 100km 1893-1914, for
1 hour 1958-71, and at 50km
from 1972.
1970   Cees Stam (Hol)
1971-3   Horst Gnas (FRG)
1974   Jean Breuer (FRG)
1975-7   Gaby Minneboo (Hol)
1978   Rainer Podlesch (GDR)
1979   Matthe Pronk (Hol)
1980   Gaby Minneboo (Hol)
1981   Matthe Pronk (Hol)
1982   Gaby Minneboo (Hol)
1983   Rainer Podlesch (GDR)
1984   Jan de Nijs (Hol)
1985   Roberto Dotti (Ita)
1986-7   Mario Gentili (Ita)
1988   Vacant after winner
         Vincenzo Colamartino
         (Ita) failed drugs test
1989-91 Roland Königshofer
         (Aut)
1992   Carsten Podlesch (Ger)
Most wins: 7 Leon Meredith (UK)
   1904-5, 1907-9, 1911, 1913;
   5 Minneboo; 3 Gnas, Königshofer

Motor-paced

First held 1895. Held at 100km
1895-1971, over 1 hour from 1972.
Professional to 1992, now Open.
1970   Ehrenfried Rudolph
         (FRG)
1971-2   Theo Verschueren (Bel)
1973-4   Cees Stam (Hol)
1975   Dieter Kemper (FRG)
1976   Wilfried Peffgen (FRG)
1977   Cees Stam (Hol)
1978   Wilfried Peffgen (FRG)
1979   Martin Venix (Hol)

1980	Wilfried Peffgen (FRG)
1981	René Kos (Hol)
1982	Martin Venix (Hol)
1983	Bruno Vicini (Ita)
1984	Horst Schütz (FRG)
1985-6	Bruno Vicini (Ita)
1987	Max Hürtzler (Swi)
1988	Danny Clark (Aus)
1989	Giovanni Renosto (Ita)
1990	Walter Brugna (Ita)
1991	Danny Clark (Aus)
1992	Peter Steiger (Swi)
1993	Jens Veggerby (Den)
1994	Carsten Podlesch (Ger)

Most wins: 6 Guillermo Timoner
(Spa) 1955, 1959-60, 1962,
1964-5; 4 Victor Linart (Bel)
1921, 1924, 1926-7

Amateur road race

1970	Jørgen Schmidt (Den)
1971	Regis Ovion (Fra)
1973	Ryszard Szurkowski (Pol)
1974	Janusz Kowalski (Pol)
1975	André Gevers (Hol)
1977	Claudio Corti (Ita)
1978	Gilbert Glaus (Swi)
1979	Gianni Giacomini (Ita)
1981	Andrey Vedernikov (USSR)
1982	Bernd Drogan (GDR)
1983	Uwe Raab (GDR)
1985	Lech Piasecki (Pol)
1986	Uwe Ampler (GDR)
1987	Richard Vivien (Fra)
1989	Joachim Halupczok (Pol)
1990	Mirko Gualdi (Ita)
1991	Viktor Ryaksinskiy (USSR)
1993	Jan Ullrich (Ger)
1994	Alex Pedersen (Den)
1995	Danny Nelissen (Hol)

Most wins: 2 Giuseppe Martano
(Ita) 1930, 1932, Gustav Adolf
Schur (GDR) 1958-9

Team time trial (amateur)

First held 1962. Contested on the
roads over c.100km.
Wins:

7 Italy
  1962, 1964-5, 1987, 1991,
  1993, 1994
5 USSR
  1970, 1977, 1983, 1985, 1990
3 Sweden
  1967-9, 1974

3 Netherlands
  1978, 1982, 1986
3 GDR
  1979, 1981, 1989
2 Poland
  1973, 1975
1 France 1963, Denmark 1966,
  Belgium 1971

Tandem sprint

First held 1966. Amateur to 1991,
now Open.

1970	Jürgen Barth & Rainer Müller (FRG)
1971	Jürgen Geschke & Werner Otto (GDR)
1973-4	Vladimir Vackár & Miroslav Vymazal (Cs)
1976	Benedykt Kocot & Janusz Kotlinski (Pol)
1977-8	Vladimir Vackár & Miroslav Vymazal (Cs)
1979	Yave Cahard & Frank Depine (Fra)
1980-2	Ivan Kucirek & Pavel Martinek (Cs)
1983	Philippe Vernet & Frank Depine (Fra)
1984	Jürgen Greil & Frank Weber (FRG)
1985-6	Vitezlav Voboril & Roman Rehousek (Cs)
1987-9	Fabrice Colas & Frédéric Magné (Fra)
1990	Gianluca Capitano & Federico Paris (Ita)
1991	Eyk Pokorny & Emanuel Raasch (Ger)
1992	Gianluca Capitano & Federico Paris (Ita)
1993	Federico Paris & Roberto Chiappa (Ita)
1994	Fabrice Colas & Frédéric Magné (Fra)

Most wins: 4 Vackár & Vymazal,
Colas & Magné

Madison 50 kilometres

First held 1995.

1995-6	Silvio Martinello & Mario Villa (Ita)
1997	Miguel Alzamora & Juan Llaneras (Spa)

Professional road race

First held 1927. Open from 1996.

1927	Alfredo Binda (Ita)
1928-9	Georges Ronsse (Bel)
1930	Alfredo Binda (Ita)
1931	Learco Guerra (Ita)
1932	Alfredo Binda (Ita)
1933	Georges Speicher (Fra)
1934	Karel Kaers (Bel)
1935	Jean Aerts (Bel)
1936	Antonin Magne (Fra)
1937	Eloi Meulenberg (Bel)
1938	Marcel Kint (Bel)
1946	Hans Knecht (Swi)
1947	Theo Middelkamp (Hol)
1948	Alberic Schotte (Bel)
1949	Rik van Steenbergen (Bel)
1950	Alberic Schotte (Bel)
1951	Ferdinand Kübler (Swi)
1952	Heinz Müller (Ger)
1953	Fausto Coppi (Ita)
1954	Louison Bobet(Fra)
1955	Stan Ockers (Bel)
1956-7	Rik van Steenbergen (Bel)
1958	Ercole Baldini (Ita)
1959	André Darrigade (Fra)
1960-1	Rik van Looy (Bel)
1962	Jean Stablinski (Fra)
1963	Benoni Beheyt (Bel)
1964	Jan Janssen (Hol)
1965	Tom Simpson (UK)
1966	Rudi Altig (Ger)
1967	Eddy Merckx (Bel)
1968	Vittorio Adorni (Ita)
1969	Harm Ottenbros (Hol)
1970	Jean-Pierre Monseré (Bel)
1971	Eddy Merckx (Bel)
1972	Marino Basso (Ita)
1973	Felice Gimondi (Ita)
1974	Eddy Merckx (Bel)
1975	Hennie Kuiper (Hol)
1976	Freddy Maertens (Bel)
1977	Francesco Moser (Ita)
1978	Gerrie Knetemann (Hol)
1979	Jan Raas (Hol)
1980	Bernard Hinault (Fra)
1981	Freddy Maertens (Bel)
1982	Giuseppe Saronni (Ita)
1983	Greg LeMond (USA)
1984	Claude Criquielion (Bel)
1985	Joop Zoetemelk (Hol)
1986	Moreno Argentin (Ita)
1987	Stephen Roche (Ire)
1988	Maurizio Fondriest (Ita)
1989	Greg LeMond (USA)
1990	Rudy Dhaenens (Bel)
1991-2	Gianni Bugno (Ita)
1993	Lance Armstrong (USA)
1994	Luc Leblanc (Fra)

1995	Abraham Olano (Spa)
1996	Johan Museeuw (Bel)
1997	Laurent Brochard (Fra)

Most wins: 3 Binda, van Steenbergen, Merckx

Individual road time trial
First held in 1994 over 42km.

1994	Chris Boardman (UK)
1995	Miguel Induráin (Spa)
1996	Alex Zülle (Swi)
1997	Laurent Jalabert (Fra)

Women

Sprint
First held 1958.

1969-71	Galina Tsareva (USSR)
1972	Galina Yermolayeva (USSR)
1973	Sheila Young (USA)
1974	Tamara Piltsikova (USSR)
1975	Sue Novarra (USA)
1976	Sheila Young (USA)
1977-9	Galina Tsareva (USSR)
1980	Sue Reber (Novarra) (USA)
1981	Sheila Ochowitz (née Young) (USA)
1982-4	Connee Paraskevin (USA)
1985	Iasabelle Nicoloso (Fra)
1986	Christa Rothenburger (GDR)
1987	Erika Salumäe (USSR)
1989	Erika Salumäe (USSR)
1990	Connie Young-Paraskevin (USA)
1991	Ingrid Haringa (Hol)
1993	Tatyana Dubnicoff (Can)
1994	Galina Yenyukhina (Rus)
1995-7	Félicia Ballanger (Fra)

Most wins: 6 Galina Yermolayeva (USSR) 1958-61, 1963, 1972, Tsareva

500 metres time trial
1995-7	Félicia Ballanger (Fra)

3 kilometres pursuit
1970-4	Tamara Garkushina (USSR)
1975-6	Keetie van Oosten-Hage (Hol)
1977	Vera Kuznetsova (USSR)
1978-9	Keetie van Oosten-Hage (Hol)
1980-1	Nadezhda Kibardina (USSR)
1982	Rebecca Twigg (USA)

1983	Connie Carpenter (USA)
1984-5	Rebecca Twigg (USA)
1986	Jeannie Longo (Fra)
1987	Rebecca Twigg (USA)
1988-9	Jeannie Longo (Fra)
1990	Leontien van Moorsel (Hol)
1991	Petra Rossner (Ger)
1993	Rebecca Twigg (USA)
1994	Marion Clignet (Fra)
1995	Rebecca Twigg (USA)
1996	Marion Clignet (Fra)
1997	Judith Arndt (Ger)

Most wins: 6 Tamara Garkushina (USSR) 1967, 1970-4, Twigg; 5 Beryl Burton (UK) 1959-60, 1962-3, 1966; 4 van Oosten-Hage

30 kilometres points
1988	Sally Hodge (UK)★
1989	Jeannie Longo (Fra)
1990	Karen Holliday (NZ)
1991-4	Ingrid Haringa (Hol)
1995-6	Svetlana Samokhvalova (Rus)
1997	Natalya Karimova (Rus)

★ Demonstration event

Most wins: 4 Haringa

Women's road race
First held 1958.

1970-1	Anna Konkina (USSR)
1972	Geneviève Gambillon (Fra)
1973	Nicole Vandenbroeck (Bel)
1974	Geneviève Gambillon (Fra)
1975	Trijntje Fopma (Hol)
1976	Keetie van Oosten-Hage (Hol)
1977	Josiane Bost (Fra)
1978	Beate Habetz (FRG)
1979	Petra de Bruin (Hol)
1980	Beth Heiden (USA)
1981	Ute Enzenauer (FRG)
1982	Mandy Jones (UK)
1983	Marianne Berglund (Swe)
1985-7	Jeannie Longo (Fra)
1989	Jeannie Longo (Fra)
1990	Catherine Marsal (Fra)
1991	Leontien van Moorseel (Hol)
1993	Leontien van Moorseel (Hol)
1994	Monica Valvik (Nor)
1995	Jeannie Longo (Fra)

1996	Barbara Heeb (Swi)
1997	Alessandra Cappellotto (Ita)

Most wins: 4 Yvonne Reynders (Bel) 1959, 1961, 1963, 1966, Longo

50 kilometres team trial
First held 1987.

1987	USSR
1988	Italy
1989	USSR
1990	Netherlands
1991	France
1992	USA
1993-4	Russia

Individual road time trial
First held 1994.

1994	Karen Kurreck (USA)
1995-7	Jeannie Longo (Fra)

Beth Heiden, Sheila Young and Christa Rothenburger have all won world titles at cycling and speed skating.

Tour de France

First held in 1903, the Tour de France is the greatest cycle race in the world. It regularly attracts the largest attendance at any sporting event, with more than 10 million people watching the annual race at different venues. The riders cover a course which varies each year, but always includes several mountain stages as well as time trials, over a three-week period. The distance in recent years has been around 4000km (3635km in 1995), but from 1911 to 1929 it was always over 5000km.

Winners:

1903	Maurice Garin (Fra)
1904	Henri Cornet (Fra)
1905	Louis Trousselier (Fra)
1906	René Pottier (Fra)
1907-8	Lucien Petit-Breton (Fra)
1909	François Faber (Lux)
1910	Octave Lapize (Fra)
1911	Gustave Garrigou (Fra)
1912	Odile Defraye (Bel)
1913-4	Philippe Thys (Bel)
1919	Firmin Lambot (Bel)
1920	Philippe Thys (Bel)
1921	Léon Scieur (Bel)
1922	Firmin Lambot (Bel)
1923	Henri Pélissier (Fra)

1924-5	Ottavio Bottecchia (Ita)
1926	Lucien Buysse (Bel)
1927-8	Nicholas Frantz (Lux)
1929	Maurice De Waele (Bel)
1930	André Leducq (Fra)
1931	Antonin Magne (Fra)
1932	André Leducq (Fra)
1933	Georges Speicher (Fra)
1934	Antonin Magne (Fra)
1935	Romain Maës (Bel)
1936	Sylvère Maës (Bel)
1937	Roger Lapébie (Fra)
1938	Gino Bartali (Ita)
1939	Sylvère Maës (Bel)
1947	Jean Robic (Fra)
1948	Gino Bartali (Ita)
1949	Fausto Coppi (Ita)
1950	Ferdinand Kübler (Swi)
1951	Hugo Koblet (Swi)
1952	Fausto Coppi (Ita)
1953-5	Louison Bobet (Fra)
1956	Roger Walkowiak (Fra)
1957	Jacques Anquetil (Fra)
1958	Charly Gaul (Lux)
1959	Federico Bahamontès (Spa)
1960	Gastone Nencini (Ita)
1961-4	Jacques Anquetil (Fra)
1965	Felice Gimondi (Ita)
1966	Lucien Aimar (Fra)
1967	Roger Pingeon (Fra)
1968	Jan Janssen (Hol)
1969-72	Eddy Merckx (Bel)
1973	Luis Ocaña (Spa)
1974	Eddy Merckx (Bel)
1975	Bernard Thévenet (Fra)
1976	Lucien van Impe (Bel)
1977	Bernard Thévenet (Fra)
1978-9	Bernard Hinault (Fra)
1980	Joop Zoetemelk (Hol)
1981-2	Bernard Hinault (Fra)
1983-4	Laurent Fignon (Fra)
1985	Bernard Hinault (Fra)
1986	Greg LeMond (USA)
1987	Stephen Roche (Ire)
1988	Pedro Delgado (Spa)
1989-90	Greg LeMond (USA)
1991-5	Miguel Induráin (Spa)
1996	Bjarne Riis (Den)
1997	Jan Ullrich (Ger)
1998	Marco Pantani (Ita)

Fastest average speed:
39.504km/h Miguel Induráin over 3983km in 1992

Longest race: 5745km (3569 miles) 1926

Most starters: 210 in 1986

Most finishers: 158 in 1991
Most races: 16 Joop Zoetemelk 1970-86
Greatest victory margin: 2 hr 49 mins Maurice Garin 1903
Narrowest victory margin: 8 secs Greg LeMond over Laurent Fignon in 1989

Most stage wins: 35 Eddy Merckx, 28 Bernard Hinault, 25 André Leducq, 22 André Darrigade, 20 Nicolas Frantz
Most stage wins in one year: 8 Charles Pelissier 1930, Eddy Merckx 1970 & 1974, Freddy Maertens 1976

Most successful Tour de France riders

6 points for a win, 4-3-2-1 for 2nd to 5th places.

Rider	Years	1st	2nd	3rd	4th	5th	Pts
Bernard Hinault	1978-86	5	2	-	-	-	38
Joop Zoetemelk	1970-82	1	6	-	3	1	37
Eddy Merckx	1969-75	5	1	-	-	-	34
Jacques Anquetil	1957-64	5	-	1	-	-	33
Lucien van Impe	1971-83	1	3	3	2	1	32
Miguel Induráin	1991-5	5	-	-	-	-	30
Raymond Poulidor	1962-76	-	3	5	-	-	27
Greg LeMond	1984-90	3	1	1	-	-	25
Louison Bobet	1948-55	3	-	1	1	-	23
Bernard Thévenet	1971-7	2	1	-	1	-	18

Giro d'Italia

After the Tour de France, the Tour of Italy (Giro d'Italia) is the second most prestigious of the Continental tours. It was first held in 1909; until 1950, when Switzerland's Hugo Koblet won, all winners had been Italian.

Winners:

1909	Luigi Ganna (Ita)		1950	Hugo Koblet (Swi)
1910-11	Carlo Galleti (Ita)		1951	Fiorenzo Magni (Ita)
1912	Team Atala *(team race only)*		1952-3	Fausto Coppi (Ita)
1913	Carlo Oriani (Ita)		1954	Carlo Clerici (Swi)
1914	Alfonso Calzolari (Ita)		1955	Fiorenzo Magni (Ita)
1919	Constante Girardengo (Ita)		1956	Charly Gaul (Lux)
1920	Gaetano Belloni (Ita)		1957	Gastone Nencini (Ita)
1921-2	Giovanni Brunero (Ita)		1958	Ercole Baldini (Ita)
1923	Constante Girardengo (Ita)		1959	Charly Gaul (Lux)
1924	Giuseppe Enrici (Ita)		1960	Jacques Anquetil (Fra)
1925	Alfredo Binda (Ita)		1961	Arnaldo Pambianco (Ita)
1926	Giovanni Brunero (Ita)		1962-3	Franco Balmanion (Ita)
1927-9	Alfredo Binda (Ita)		1964	Jacques Anquetil (Fra)
1930	Luigi Marchisio (Ita)		1965	Vittorio Adorni (Ita)
1931	Francesco Camusso (Ita)		1966	Gianni Motta (Ita)
1932	Antonio Pesenti (Ita)		1967	Felice Gimondi (Ita)
1933	Alfredo Binda (Ita)		1968	Eddy Merckx (Bel)
1934	Learco Guerra (Ita)		1969	Felice Gimondi (Ita)
1935	Vasco Bergamaschi (Ita)		1970	Eddy Merckx (Bel)
1936-7	Gino Bartali (Ita)		1971	Gosta Petterson (Swe)
1938-9	Giovanni Valetti (Ita)		1972-4	Eddy Merckx (Bel)
1940	Fausto Coppi (Ita)		1975	Fausto Bertoglio (Ita)
1941-5	*Not held*		1976	Felice Gimondi (Ita)
1946	Gino Bartali (Ita)		1977	Michel Pollentier (Bel)
1947	Fausto Coppi (Ita)		1978	Johan De Muynck (Bel)
1948	Fiorenzo Magni (Ita)		1979	Giuseppe Saronni (Ita)
1949	Fausto Coppi (Ita)		1980	Bernard Hinault (Fra)
			1981	Giovani Battaglin (Ita)
			1982	Bernard Hinault (Fra)
			1983	Giuseppe Saronni (Ita)

1984	Francesco Moser (Ita)
1985	Bernard Hinault (Fra)
1986	Roberto Visentini (Ita)
1987	Stephen Roche (Ire)
1988	Andy Hampsten (USA)
1989	Laurent Fignon (Fra)
1990	Gianni Bugno (Ita)
1991	Franco Chioccioli (Ita)
1992-3	Miguel Induráin (Spa)
1994	Yevgeniy Berzin (Rus)
1995	Tony Rominger (Swz)
1996	Pavel Tonkov (Rus)
1997	Ivan Gotti (Ita)
1998	Marco Pantani (Ita)

Most wins: 5 Binda, Coppi, Merckx

Vuelta a España

The Tour of Spain is the third major tour of the Continental season. It was first held in 1935, and has been held annually from 1955.

Winners:

1935-6	Gustave Deloor (Bel)
1941-2	Julian Berrendero (Spa)
1945	Delio Rodriguez (Spa)
1946	Dalmacio Langarica (Spa)
1947	Edward Van Dyck (Bel)
1948	Bernardo Ruiz (Spa)
1950	Emilio Rodriguez (Spa)
1955	Jean Dotto (Fra)
1956	Angelo Conterno (Ita)
1957	Jesus Loreno (Spa)
1958	Jean Stablisnki (Fra)
1959	Antonio Suarez (Spa)
1960	Frans De Mulder (Bel)
1961	Angelo Soler (Spa)
1962	Rudi Altig (Ger)
1963	Jacques Anquetil (Fra)
1964	Raymond Poulidor (Fra)
1965	Rolf Wolfshohl (FRG)
1966	Francesco Gabica (Spa)
1967	Jan Janssen (Hol)
1968	Felice Gimondi (Ita)
1969	Roger Pingeon (Fra)
1970	Luis Ocaña (Spa)
1971	Ferdinand Bracke (Bel)
1972	José Manuel Fuente (Spa)
1973	Eddy Merckx (Bel)
1974	José Manuel Fuente (Spa)
1975	Agust. Tamames (Spa)
1976	José Pesarrodona (Spa)
1977	Freddie Maertens (Bel)
1978	Bernard Hinault (Fra)
1979	Joop Zoetemelk (Hol)
1980	Faustino Ruperez (Spa)
1981	Giovani Battaglin (Ita)

1982	Marino Lejaretta (Spa)
1983	Bernard Hinault (Fra)
1984	Eric Caritoux (Fra)
1985	Pedro Delgado (Spa)
1986	Alvaro Pino (Spa)
1987	Luis Herrera (Col)
1988	Sean Kelly (Ire)
1989	Pedro Delgado (Spa)
1990	Marco Giovannetti (Ita)
1991	Melchior Mauri (Spa)
1992-4	Tony Rominger (Swi)
1995	Laurent Jalabert (Fra)
1996-7	Alex Zülle (Swi)

Most wins: 3 Rominger

Most stage wins: 40 Delio Rodriguez (Spa); 18 Rik van Looy (Bel); 16 Sean Kelly (Ire)

Most stage wins in one year: 13 Freddy Maertens (Bel) 1977

Continental Classics

Milan–San Remo

First held in 1907, this race is known as the Primavera in Italy. The first major classic of the season, it is the longest unpaced race of all the classics (initially at 281km, and now about 290km).

Winners from 1980:

1980	Pierino Gavazzi (Ita)
1981	Alfons De Wolf (Bel)
1982	Marc Gomez (Fra)
1983	Giuseppe Saronni (Ita)
1984	Francesco Moser (Ita)
1985	Hennie Kuiper (Hol)
1986	Sean Kelly (Ire)
1987	Erich Mächler (Swi)
1988-9	Laurent Fignon (Fra)
1990	Gianni Bugno (Ita)
1991	Claudio Chiappucci (Ita)
1992	Sean Kelly (Ire)
1993	Maurizio Fondriest (Ita)
1994	Giorgio Furlan (Ita)
1995	Laurent Jalabert (Fra)
1996	Gabriele Colombo (Ita)
1997-8	Erik Zabel (Ger)

Most wins: 7 Merckx 1966-7, 1969, 1971-2, 1975-6; 6 Costante Girardengo (Ita) 1918, 1921, 1923, 1925-6, 1928

Tour of Flanders

Held since 1913 around Ghent, Belgium. A major feature of the race is climbing over steep cobbled roads, notably the Koppenberg from 1975 to 1987.

Winners from 1980:

1980	Michel Pollentier (Bel)
1981	Hennie Kuiper (Hol)
1982	René Martens (Bel)
1983	Jan Raas (Hol)
1984	Johan Lammerts (Hol)
1985	Eric Vanderaerden (Bel)
1986	Adri Van der Poel (Bel)
1987	Claude Criquielion (Bel)
1988	Eddy Planckaert (Bel)
1989	Edwig Van Hooydonck (Bel)
1990	Moreno Argentin (Ita)
1991	Edwig Van Hooydonck (Bel)
1992	Jacky Durand (Fra)
1993	Johan Museeuw (Bel)
1994	Giovanni Bugno (Ita)
1995	Johan Museeuw (Bel)
1996	Michele Bartoli (Ita)
1997	Rolf Sorensen (Den)
1998	Johan Museeuw (Bel)

Most wins: 3 Achiel Buysse (Bel) 1940-1, 1943, Fiorenzo Magni (Ita) 1949-51, Leman

Paris-Roubaix

Regarded as the toughest one-day race in the world, hence its nickname, 'The Hell of the North'. The latter stages of the race are over farm tracks and cobbled roads. *c.*260km. First held in 1896.

Winners from 1981:

1981	Bernard Hinault (Fra)
1982	Jan Raas (Bel)
1983	Hennie Kuiper (Hol)
1984	Sean Kelly (Ire)
1985	Marc Madiot (Fra)
1986	Sean Kelly (Ire)
1987	Eric Vanderaerden (Bel)
1988	Dirk De Mol (Bel)
1989	Jean-Marie Wampers (Bel)
1990	Eddy Planckaert (Bel)
1991	Marc Madiot (Fra)
1992-3	Gilbert Duclos-Lassalle (Fra)
1994	Andrey Tchmil (Mol)
1995	Franco Ballerini (Ita)
1996	Johan Museeuw (Bel)
1997	Frédéric Guesdon (Fra)
1998	Franco Ballerini (Ita)

Most wins: 4 De Vlaeminck; 3 Octave Lapize (Fra) 1909-11, Gaston Rebry (Bel) 1931, 1934-5, Rik Van Looy (Bel) 1961-2, 1965, Merckx 1968, 1970, 1973, Moser

Flèche Wallonne

Staged around the hilly Ardennes district of Belgium since 1936, recently a little over 200km around Huy after many years of different routes.

Winners from 1980:

1980	Giuseppe Saronni (Ita)
1981	Daniël Willems (Bel)
1982	Mario Beccia (Bel)
1983	Bernard Hinault (Fra)
1984	Kim Andersen (Den)
1985	Claude Criquielion (Bel)
1986	Laurent Fignon (Fra)
1987	Jean Claude Leclercq (Fra)
1988	Rolf Golz (FRG)
1989	Claude Criquelion (Bel)
1990-1	Moreno Argentin (Ita)
1992	Giorgio Furlan (Ita)
1993	Maurizio Fondriest (Ita)
1994	Moreno Argentin (Ita)
1995	Laurent Jalabert (Fra)
1996	Lance Armstrong (USA)
1997	Laurent Jalabert (Fra)
1998	Bo Hamburger (Den)

Most wins: 3 Marcel Kint (Bel) 1943-5, Merckx 1967, 1970, 1972, Argentin

Liège-Bastogne-Liège

First held in 1892, this is the oldest of the Belgian classics and recognized as one the toughest, although shorter than some, at about 250km. Until 1912 it was for amateurs only. Like the Flèche Wallonne, it takes place around the Ardennes district.

Winners from 1980:

1980	Bernard Hinault (Fra)
1981	Josef Fuchs (Swi)★
1982	Silvano Contini (Ita)
1983	Steven Rooks (Hol)
1984	Sean Kelly (Ire)
1985-7	Moreno Argentin (Ita)
1988	Adri Van der Poel (Bel)
1989	Sean Kelly (Ire)
1990	Eric Van Lancker (Bel)
1991	Moreno Argentin (Ita)
1992	Dirk De Wolf (Bel)
1993	Rolf Sorensen (Den)
1994	Yevgeniy Berzin (Rus)
1995	Mauro Gianetti (Swi)
1996	Pascal Richard (Swi)
1997-8	Michele Bartoli (Ita)

★ Original winner J Van de Velde (Hol) disqualified on a positive drugs test.

Most wins: 5 Merckx 1969, 1971-3, 1975; 4 Argentin; 3 Léon Houa (Bel) 1892-4, Alphonse Scheppers (Bel) 1929, 1931, 1935, Alfred Debruyne (Bel) 1956, 1958-9

Paris-Brussels

First held in 1893, but not again until 1906, when professionals were allowed to compete. The race was discontinued in 1966 and replaced on the Classics list by the Frankfurt Grand Prix, but it returned in 1973.

Winners from 1980:

1980	Pierino Gavazzi (Ita)
1981	Roger De Vlaeminck (Bel)
1982	Jaak Hanegraaf (Hol)
1983	Tommy Primm (Swe)
1984	Eric Vanderaerden (Bel)
1985	Adri Van der Poel (Bel)
1986	Guido Bontempi (Ita)
1987	Wim Arras (Bel)
1988	Rolf Golz (Ger)
1989	Jelle Nijdam (Hol)
1990	Franco Ballerini (Ita)
1991	Brian Holm (Den)
1992	Rolf Sorensen (Den)
1993	Francis Moreau (Fra)
1994	Rolf Sorensen (Den)
1995	Frank Vandenbroucke (Bel)
1996	Andrea Tafi (Ita)
1997	Alessandro Bertolini (Ita)

Most wins: 3 Octave Lapize (Fra) 1911-3, Felix Sellier (Bel) 1922-4

Tour of Lombardy

First held in 1905, the Tour of Lombardy, an autumn classic, traditionally marks the end of the road-racing season on the continent. It is often referred to as 'The Race of the Falling Leaves'.

Winners from 1980:

1980	Alfons De Wolf (Bel)
1981	Hennie Kuiper (Hol)
1982	Giuseppe Saronni (Ita)
1983	Sean Kelly (Ire)
1984	Bernard Hinault (Fra)
1985	Sean Kelly (Ire)
1986	Gianbattista Baroncelli (Ita)
1987	Moreno Argentin (Ita)
1988	Charly Mottet (Fra)
1989	Tony Rominger (Swi)
1990	Gilles Delion (Fra)
1991	Sean Kelly (Ire)
1992	Tony Rominger (Swi)

1993	Pascal Richard (Swi)
1994	Vladislav Bobrik (Rus)
1995	Johan Musseeuw (Bel)
1996	Andrea Tafi (Ita)
1997	Laurent Jalabert (Fra)

Most wins: 5 Fausto Coppi (Ita) 1946-9, 1954; 4 Alfredo Binda (Ita) 1925-7, 1931; 3 Costante Girardengo (Ita) 1919, 1921-2, Gino Bartali (Ita) 1936, 1939-40

Grand Prix des Nations

Regarded as the time-trialists' unofficial world championship, this has been the only time trial in the World Cup. The venue for the race has varied over the years but it was always held in France from the first in 1932 until a move to Pisa in Italy in 1991.

Winners from 1980:

1980	Jean-Luc Vandenbroucke (Bel)
1981	Daniël Gisiger (Swi)
1982	Bernard Hinault (Fra)
1983	Daniël Gisiger (Swi)
1984	Bernard Hinault (Fra)
1985	Charly Mottet (Fra)
1986	Sean Kelly (Ire)
1987-8	Charly Mottet (Fra)
1989	Laurent Fignon (Fra)
1990	Thomas Wegmüller (Swi)
1991	Tony Rominger (Swi)
1992	Johan Bruyneel (Bel)
1993	Armand de las Cuevas (Fra)
1994	Tony Rominger (Swi)
1995	*Cancelled*
1996	Chris Boardman (UK)
1997	Uwe Peschel (Ger)

Most wins: 9 Jacques Anquetil (Fra) 1953-8, 1961, 1965-6; 5 Hinault; 3 Antonin Magne (Fra) 1934-6

Paris-Nice

An gruelling early-season stage race, in which the riders cover more than 1100km in six days. The 1998 winner was Franck Vandenbroucke (Bel).

Most wins: 7 Sean Kelly (Ire) 1982-8; 5 Jacques Anquetil (Fra) 1957, 1961, 1963, 1965-6; 3 Eddy Merckx (Bel) 1969-71, Joop Zoetemelk (Hol) 1974-5, 1979, Laurent Jalabert (Fra) 1995-7

Classic Riders

The riders to have had most wins in the Classic races: Milan – San Remo (MR), Tour of Flanders (Fl), Paris-Roubaix (PR), Flèche Wallonne (FW), Liège-Bastogne-Liège (LB), Paris-Brussels (PB), Tour of Lombardy (TL) and Bordeaux-Paris (BP), the Grand Prix des Nations (GN), the World Road Race Championship (WC), and the three prestigious Continental tours: Tour de France (Fr), Tour of Italy (It), Tour of Spain (Sp).

Name	MR	Fl	PR	FW	LB	PB	TL	BP	GN	WC	Fr	It	Sp	Total
Eddy Merckx	7	2	3	3	5	1	2	-	1	3	5	5	1	38
Bernard Hinault	-	-	1	2	2	-	2	-	5	1	5	3	2	23
Fausto Coppi	3	-	1	1	-	-	5	-	2	1	2	5	-	20
Jacques Anquetil	-	-	-	-	1	-	-	1	9	-	5	2	1	19
Alfredo Binda	2	-	-	-	-	-	4	-	-	3	-	5	-	14
Roger De Vlaeminck	3	1	4	1	1	1	3	-	-	-	-	-	-	14
Rik van Looy	1	2	3	1	1	2	1	-	-	2	-	-	-	13
Gino Bartali	4	-	-	-	-	-	3	-	-	-	2	3	-	12
Felice Gimondi	1	-	1	-	-	1	2	-	2	1	1	2	1	12
Rik van Steenbergen	1	2	2	2	-	1	-	-	-	3	-	-	-	11
Sean Kelly	2	-	2	-	2	-	3	-	1	-	-	-	1	11
Herman van Springel	-	-	-	-	-	-	1	7	2	-	-	-	-	10
Louison Bobet	1	1	1	-	-	-	1	1	1	1	3	-	-	10
Moreno Argentin	-	1	-	3	4	-	1	-	-	1	-	-	-	10

World Cup

The World Cup, sponsored by Perrier, was introduced in 1989. Riders annually score points in 10–12 major races, including six classics.
Winners:

1989	Sean Kelly (Ire)		1993	Maurizio Fondriest (Ita)
1990	Gianni Bugno (Ita)		1994	Gianluca Bortolani (Ita)
1991	Maurizio Fondriest (Ita)		1995-6	Johan Museeuw (Bel)
1992	Olaf Ludwig (Ger)		1997	Michele Bartoli (Ita)

World Speed Records

From 1 Jan 1993 the list of records accepted by the UCI was drastically reduced, with no distinction as previously for professionals and amateurs, for open-air or indoor tracks, or for low or high altitude. The records now accepted by the UCI are as follows:

Men

	min:sec			
1km unpaced standing start	1:00.613A	Shane Kelly (Aus)	Bogotá	26 Sep 1995
4km unpaced standing start	4:11.114	Chris Boardman (UK)	Manchester	29 Aug 1996
4km team unpaced standing start	4:00.958	Italy	Manchester	31 Aug 1996
		(Adler Capelli, Cristiano Citto, Andrea Collinelli, Mauro Trentino)		
200 metres unpaced flying start	9.865	Curtis Harnett (Can)	Bogotá	28 Sep 1995
500 metres unpaced flying start	26.649	Aleksandr Kirichenko (USSR)	Moscow	29 Oct 1988

Women

500 metres unpaced standing start	33.438	Galina Yenyukhina (Rus)	Moscow	29 Apr 1993
3km unpaced standing start	3:30.974	Marion Clignet (Fra))	Manchester	31 Aug 1996
200 metres unpaced flying start	10.831	Olga Slyusareva (Rus)	Moscow	25 Apr 1993
500 metres unpaced flying start	29.655	Erika Salumäe (USSR/Est)	Moscow	6 Aug 1987

1-hour record

The classic speed record is for 1 hour.

Men

km

38.220	Jules Dubois (Fra)	Paris	31 Oct 1894
39.240	Oscar van den Eynde (Bel)	Paris	30 Jul 1897
40.781	Willie Hamilton (USA)	Denver	9 Jul 1898
41.110	Lucien Petot-Bretor (Fra)	Paris	24 Aug 1905
41.520	Marcel Berthet (Fra)	Paris	20 Jun 1907
42.360	Oscar Egg (Swi)	Paris	22 Aug 1912
42.741	Marcel Berthet (Fra)	Paris	7 Aug 1913
43.525	Oscar Egg (Swi)	Paris	21 Aug 1913
43.775	Marcel Berthet (Fra)	Paris	20 Sep 1913
44.247	Oscar Egg (Swi)	Paris	18 Jun 1914
44.588	Jan Van Hout (Hol)	Roermond	25 Aug 1933
44.777	Maurice Richard (Fra)	Milan	14 Oct 1935
45.090	Giuseppe Olmo (Ita)	Milan	31 Oct 1935
45.398	Maurice Richard (Fra)	Milan	14 Oct 1936
45.558	Frans Slaats (Hol)	Milan	29 Sep 1937
45.767	Maurice Archambaud (Fra)	Milan	3 Nov 1937
45.871	Fausto Coppi (Ita)	Milan	7 Nov 1942
46.159	Jacques Anquetil (Fra)	Milan	29 Jun 1956
46.393	Ercole Baldini (Ita)	Milan	19 Sep 1956
46.923	Roger Rivière (Fra)	Milan	18 Sep 1957
47.346	Roger Rivière (Fra)	Milan	23 Sep 1958
47.493u	Jacques Anquetil (Fra)	Milan	27 Sep 1967
48.093	Ferdi Bracke (Bel)	Rome	30 Oct 1967
48.653A	Ole Ritter (Den)	Mexico City	6 Dec 1968
49.431A	Eddy Merckx (Bel)	Mexico City	25 Oct 1972
50.808A	Francesco Moser (Ita)	Mexico City	19 Jan 1984
51.151A	Francesco Moser (Ita)	Mexico City	23 Jan 1984
51.596	Graeme Obree (UK)	Hamar	17 Jul 1993
52.270	Chris Boardman (UK)	Bordeaux	28 Jul 1993
52.713	Graeme Obree (UK)	Bordeaux	27 Apr 1994
53.040	Miguel Induráin (Spa)	Bordeaux	2 Sep 1994
53.832	Tony Rominger (Swz)	Bordeaux	22 Oct 1994
55.291	Tony Rominger (Swz)	Bordeaux	6 Nov 1994
56.375	Chris Boardman (UK)	Manchester	5 Sep 1996

Women

km

41.347	Elsy Jacobs (Lux)	Milan	9 Nov 1958
41.471A	Maria Cressari (Ita)	Mexico City	25 Nov 1972
43.082	Cornelia Van Oosten (Hol)	Munich	16 Sep 1978
44.770A	Jeannie Longo (Fra)	Col. Springs	21 Sep 1986
43.587	Jeannie Longo (Fra)	Milan	30 Sep 1986
46.352A	Jeannie Longo (Fra)	Mexico City	1 Oct 1989
47.112	Catherine Marsal (Fra)	Bordeaux	29 Apr 1995
47.411	Yvonne McGregor (UK)	Manchester	17 Jun 1995
48.159A	Jeanne Longo (Fra)	Mexico City	26 Oct 1996

u unratified, A altitude over 1000m.

Mountain Biking

World Championships

Men's cross-country

1990	Ted Overend (USA)
1991	John Tomac (USA)
1992-4	Henrik Djemis (Den)
1995	Bart Brentjens (Hol)

1996	Jerôme Chiotti (Fra
1997	Hubert Pallhuber (Ita))

Men's downhill

1990	Greg Herbold (USA)
1991	Albert Iten (Swi)

1992	Dave Cullinan (USA)
1993	Mike King (USA)
1994	François Gachet (Fra)
1995-7	Nicolas Vouilloz (Fra)

Women's cross-country

1990	Julie Furtado (USA)
1991	Ruthie Matthes (USA)
1992	Silvia Fürst (Swi)
1993	Paola Pezzo (Ita)
1994-6	Alison Sydor (Can)
1997	Paola Pezzo (Ita)

Women's downhill

1990	Cindy Devine (Can)
1991	Giovanna Bonazzi (Ita)
1992	Julie Furtado (USA)
1993	Giovanna Bonazzi (Ita)
1994	Missy Giove (USA)
1995	Leigh Donovan (USA)
1996-7	Anne-Caroline Chausson (Fra)

Olympic Games

Mountain bike cross-country races were held for the first time at the 1996 Games. Bart Jan Brentjens (Hol) won the men's event, and Paola Pezzo (Ita) the women's.

Cyclo-Cross

Bicycle racing on a cross-country course probably originated in France c 1900-10 and championship races were staged in Europe from the 1920s. The British Cyclo-Cross Association was formed in 1954. A standard course is usually of 16-24 km over testing terrain.

World Championships

From 1967 to 1993 the Championships were split into amateur and professional categories.

Open and professional champions

1950	Jean Robic (Fra)
1951-3	Roger Rondeaux (Fra)
1954-8	André Dufraisse (Fra)
1959	Renato Longo (Ita)
1960-1	Rolf Wolfshohl (FRG)
1962	Renato Longo (Ita)
1963	Rolf Wolfshohl (FRG)
1964-5	Renato Longo (Ita)
1966	Eric De Vlaeminck (Bel)
1967	Renato Longo (Ita)
1968-73	Eric De Vlaeminck (Bel)
1974	Albert Van Damme (Bel)
1975	Roger De Vlaeminck (Bel)
1976-9	Albert Zweifel (Swi)
1980	Roland Liboton (Bel)
1981	Johannes Stamsnijder (Hol)
1982-4	Roland Liboton (Bel)
1985	Klaus-Peter Thaler (FRG)
1986	Albert Zweifel (Swi)
1987	Klaus-Peter Thaler (FRG)
1988	Pascal Richard (Swi)
1989	Danny De Bie (Bel)
1990	Henk Baars (Hol)
1991	Radomir Simunek (Cs)
1992	Mike Kluge (Ger)
1993	Dominique Arnould (Fra)
1994	Paul Herijgers (Bel)
1995	Dieter Runkel (Swi)
1996	Adri van der Poel (Hol)
1997	Daniele Pontoni (Ita)
1998	Mario De Clercq (Bel)

Most wins: 7 Eric De Vlaeminck; 5 André Dufraisse, Renato Longo

Amateur champions

1967	Michel Pelchat (Fra)
1968	Roger De Vlaeminck (Bel)
1969	René De Clercq (Bel)
1970-1	Robert Vermeire (Bel)
1972	Norbert De Deckere (Bel)
1973	Klaus-Peter Thaler (FRG)
1974-5	Robert Vermeire (Bel)
1976	Klaus-Peter Thaler (FRG)
1977	Robert Vermeire (Bel)
1978	Roland Liboton (Bel)
1979	Vito Di Tano (Ita)
1980	Fritz Saladin (Swi)
1981-2	Milos Fisera (Cs)
1983-4	Radomir Simunek (Cs)
1985	Mike Kluge (FRG)

1986	Vito Di Tano (Ita)
1987	Mike Kluge (FRG)
1988	Karel Camrda (Cs)
1989	Ondrej Glajza (Cs)
1990	Andreas Brüsser (Swz)
1991	Thomas Frischknecht (Swz)
1992	Daniele Pontoni (Ita)
1993	Henrik Djernis (Den)

Most wins: 5 Robert Vermeire

Team

Amateur from 1979 to 1993, now Open.

1979	Poland
1980	Switzerland
1981	Italy
1982-4	Czechoslovakia
1985	Switzerland
1986	Belgium
1987	Czechoslovakia
1988	Switzerland
1989	Czechoslovakia
1990-2	Switzerland
1993	France
1994	Belgium
1995	Switzerland
1996	Italy
1997	Switzerland

Darts

Darts, or Dartes, were first used as a means of self-defence in battles in Ireland in the 16th century. The Pilgrim Fathers played darts aboard the *Mayflower* on their way to discovering the New World in 1620. The modern game, however, dates from 1896 when Brian Gamlin of Bury, Lancashire, devised the present numbering system. The National Darts Association was formed in 1924 and the British Darts Organization (BDO) in 1973. Darts has developed into a popular television sport, with more than 6 million people playing in Britain alone.

In 1992, dissatisfied with the BDO, many of the world's top players formed the World Darts Council (WDC), which introduced its own World Championship. Agreement between the WDC and BDO was reached in 1997, and the WDC name changed to the Professional Darts Council (PDC).

BDO World Professional Championship

The World Professional Championship, sponsored by Embassy, was instituted by the BDO at the Heart of the Midlands Nightclub, Nottingham in 1978. Between 1979 and 1985 the tournaments were held at Jollees Nightclub, Stoke-on-Trent, and from 1986 at the Lakeside Country Club, Frimley Green, Surrey.
(1977 played over the best of 21 legs, 1978-82 best of 9, 1983 best of 11, 1984 best of 13, from 1985 best of 11)

Year	Winner	Runner-up	Score
1978	Leighton Rees (Wal)	John Lowe (Eng)	11–7
1979	John Lowe (Eng)	Leighton Rees (Wal)	5–0
1980	Eric Bristow (Eng)	Bobby George (Eng)	5–3
1981	Eric Bristow (Eng)	John Lowe (Eng)	5–3
1982	Jocky Wilson (Sco)	John Lowe (Eng)	5–3
1983	Keith Deller (Eng)	Eric Bristow (Eng)	6–5
1984	Eric Bristow (Eng)	Dave Whitcombe (Eng)	7–1
1985	Eric Bristow (Eng)	John Lowe (Eng)	6–2
1986	Eric Bristow (Eng)	Dave Whitcombe (Eng)	6–0
1987	John Lowe (Eng)	Eric Bristow (Eng)	6–4
1988	Bob Anderson (Eng)	John Lowe (Eng)	6–4
1989	Jocky Wilson (Sco)	Eric Bristow (Eng)	6–4
1990	Phil Taylor (Eng)	Eric Bristow (Eng)	6–1
1991	Dennis Priestley (Eng)	Eric Bristow (Eng)	6–0
1992	Phil Taylor (Eng)	Mike Gregory (Eng)	6–5
1993	John Lowe (Eng)	Alan Warriner (Eng)	6–3
1994	John Part (Can)	Bobby George (Eng)	6–0
1995	Richie Burnett (Wal)	Raymond Barneveld (Hol)	6–3
1996	Steve Beaton (Eng)	Richie Burnett (Wal)	6–3
1997	Les Wallace (Sco)	Marshall James (Wal)	6–3
1998	Raymond Barneveld (Hol)	Richie Burnett (Wal)	6–5

WDC World Championships

The first championships, sponsored by Skol and organized by the breakaway group of top players, was played at Purfleet, Surrey, ending on 1 Jan 1994.

Year	Winner	Runner-up	Score
1993/4	Dennis Priestley (Eng)	Phil Taylor (Eng)	6–1
1994/5	Phil Taylor (Eng)	Rod Harrington (Eng)	6–2
1995/6	Phil Taylor (Eng)	Dennis Priestley (Eng)	6–4
1996/7	Phil Taylor (Eng)	Dennis Priestley (Eng)	6–3
1997/8	Phil Taylor (Eng)	Dennis Priestley (Eng)	6–0

World Masters

The first World Masters took place at the West Centre Hotel, Fulham in 1974. Now sponsored by Winmau.

Winners:

1974	Cliff Inglis (Eng)
1975	Alan Evans (Wal)
1976	John Lowe (Eng)
1977	Eric Bristow (Eng)
1978	Ronnie Davis (Eng)
1979	Eric Bristow (Eng)
1980	John Lowe (Eng)
1981	Eric Bristow (Eng)
1982	Dave Whitcombe (Eng)
1983-4	Eric Bristow (Eng)
1985	Dave Whitcombe (Eng)
1986-8	Bob Anderson (Eng)
1989	Peter Evison (Eng)
1990	Phil Taylor (Eng)
1991	Rod Harrington (Eng)
1992	Dennis Priestley (Eng)
1993	Steve Beaton (Eng)
1994/5	Richie Burnett (Wal)
1995/6	Eric Clarijs (Bel)
1996/7	Colin Monk (Eng)
1997/8	Graham Hunt (Aus)

World Cup

The winning nation in this biennial event, first held at Wembley in 1977, is the team with the most points from singles, pairs and fours competition. The women's competition was introduced in 1983.

Team winners

9	England	1979, 1981, 1983, 1985, 1987, 1989, 1991, 1993, 1995
2	Wales	1977, 1997

Individual title

1977	Leighton Rees (Wal)
1979	Nicky Virachkul (USA)
1981	John Lowe (Eng)
1983	Eric Bristow (Eng)
1985	Eric Bristow (Eng)
1987	Eric Bristow (Eng)
1989	Eric Bristow (Eng)
1991	John Lowe (Eng)
1993	Roland Scholten (Hol)
1995	Martin Adams (Eng)

1997   Raymond Barneveld (Hol)
Most winning teams: 7 John
    Lowe, Eric Bristow (both
    England)

World Matchplay

Held annually 1984-8 and reintroduced by the WDC in 1994.

Winners:

1984	John Lowe (Eng)
1985	Eric Bristow (Eng)
1986	Mike Gregory (Eng)
1987	Bob Anderson (Eng)
1988	Eric Bristow (Eng)
1994	Larry Butler (USA
1995	Phil Taylor (Eng)
1996	Peter Evison (Eng)
1997	Phil Taylor (Eng)

Women's World Cup

Team

4	England	1983, 1985, 1989, 1995
3	USA	1987, 1993, 1997
1	New Zealand 1991	

Individual

1983	Sandy Reitan (USA)
1985	Linda Batten (UK)
1987	Valerie Maycum (Hol)
1989	Eva Grisby (USA)
1991	Jill MacDonald (NZ)
1993	Stacy Bromberg (USA)
1995	Mandy Solomons (Eng)
1997	Noeline Gear (NZ)

Women's World Masters

1982	Ann-Marie Davies (Wal)
1983	Sonja Ralphs (Eng)
1984	Kathy Wones (Eng)
1985	Lilian Barnett (NZ)
1986	Kathy Wones (Eng)
1987	Ann Thomas (Wal)
1988-9	Mandy Solomons (Eng)
1990	Rhian Speed (UK)
1991	Sandy Reitan (USA)
1992	Leanne Maddock (Wal)
1993	Mandy Solomons (Eng)
1994	Deta Hedman (Eng)
1995	Sharon Colclough (Eng)
1996	Sharon Douglas (Sco)
1997	Mandy Solomons (Eng)

Equestrian Sports

The earliest known show jumping competition was in Ireland when the Royal Dublin Society held its first 'Horse Show' on 15 Apr 1864. The Société Hippique Française was founded in 1865 and held its first Concours Hippique in Paris in 1866. The first event in England was at the Agricultural Hall, London in 1869.

Dressage competition derived from the exercises taught at 16th century Italian and French horsemanship academies, while the three-day event developed from cavalry endurance rides. One of the earliest known three-day event competitions was a ride from Vienna to Berlin in 1892.

World championships at six different equestrian disciplines – show jumping, three-day eventing, dressage, carriage driving, endurance riding and vaulting – were first combined at the first World Equestrian Games held in Stockholm in 1990; the second event was held at The Hague in 1994.

International governing body: Fédération Equestre Internationale (FEI), Avenue Mon-Repos, Case Postale 157, CH-100 Lausanne 5, Switzerland. Tel: (41) 21 312 5656. Fax: (41) 21 312 8677. President: HRH the Infanta Dona Pilar de Borbon, Secretary General: Dr Bo Helander. Founded in Brussels in 1921, initially with 8 member nations. 116 member nations in 1998.

Women riders' name changes

Single name	*Married surname*
Jane Bullen	Holderness-Roddam
Marion Coakes	Mould
Jean Goodwin	Davenport
Virginia Holgate	Leng
Janou Lefèbvre	Tissou
Lucinda Prior-Palmer	Green
Lorna Sutherland	Clarke
Sheila Willcox	Waddington
Alison Westwood	Dawes

Show Jumping

Olympic Games

Although not connected with events staged with the World Fair, the three days of international competition staged by the Société Hippique Française in Paris in 1900, with jumping, high jump and long jump events, are now regarded as the first Olympic show jumping event. Two equestrian events were planned for 1908, but were not held due to a paucity of entries, and show

jumping was officially introduced in 1912. The 1956 competition took place in Stockholm, Sweden, because of quarantine restrictions in force in Australia at the time.

Winners:

Individual

	Rider	*Horse*
1900	Aimé Haegeman (Bel)	Benton II
1912	Jean Cariou (Fra)	Mignon
1920	Tommaso Lequio (Ita)	Trebecco
1924	Alphonse Gemuseus (Swi)	Lucette
1928	Frantisek Ventura (Cs)	Eliot
1932	Takeichi Nishi (Jap)	Uranus
1936	Kürt Hasse (Ger)	Tora
1948	Humberto Mariles Cortés (Mex)	Arete
1952	Pierre Jonquères d'Oriola (Fra)	Ali Baba
1956	Hans Günter Winkler (Ger)	Halla
1960	Raimondo d'Inzeo (Ita)	Posillipo
1964	Pierre Jonquères d'Oriola (Fra)	Lutteur B
1968	William Steinkraus (USA)	Snowbound
1972	Graziano Mancinelli (Ita)	Ambassador
1976	Alwin Schockemöhle (FRG)	Warwick Rex

1980	Jan Kowalczyk (Pol)	Artemor
1984	Joe Fargis (USA)	Touch of Class
1988	Pierre Durand (Fra)	Jappeloup
1992	Ludger Beerbaum (Ger)	Classic Touch
1996	Ullrich Kirchhoff (Ger)	Jus de Pommes

Team

7	Germany	Ger 1936, FRG 1956, 1960, 1964, 1972, 1988, Ger 1996
3	Sweden	1912, 1920, 1924
1	Spain 1928, Mexico 1948, Great Britain 1952, Canada 1968, France 1976, USSR 1980, USA 1984, Netherlands 1992

No medals awarded 1932 – event not decided, as no nation completed the course with three riders.

Most gold medals

5 Hans Günter Winkler (FRG) team 1956, 1960, 1964, 1972, individual 1956

Most medals

7 Hans Günter Winkler 5 gold, team silver 1976, team bronze 1968

6 Raimondo d'Inzeo (Ita) 1 gold (individual 1960), 2 silver (team and individual 1956), 3 bronze team 1960, 1964, 1972)

6 Piero d'Inzeo (Ita) 2 silver, 4 bronze (individual silver 1960, bronze 1960, 1 team silver and 3 team bronze as above, for younger brother Raimondo)

World Championships

Instituted in 1953, the championships are now held every four years. In the individual final each rider has to ride not only his own horse but also those of the other finallists. In 1965, 1970 and 1974, women had a separate competition on their own horses only, but now compete equally with their male counterparts. A team competition was introduced in 1978.
Winners:

Individual – men

	Rider	*Horse*
1953	Francisco Goyoago (Spa)	Quorum
1954	Hans Günter Winkler (FRG)	Halla
1955	Hans Günter Winkler (FRG)	Halla
1956	Raimondo d'Inzeo (Ita)	Merano
1960	Raimondo d'Inzeo (Ita)	Gowran Girl
1966	Pierre Jonquères d'Oriola (Fra)	Pomone B
1970	David Broome (UK)	Beethoven
1974	Hartwig Steenken (FRG)	Simona
1978	Gerd Wiltfang (FRG)	Roman
1982	Norbert Koof (FRG)	Fire II
1986	Gail Greenhough (Can)	Mr T
1990	Eric Navet (Fra)	Quito de Baussy
1994	Franke Sloothaak (Ger)	San Patrignano Weihaiwej

Individual – women (up to 1974)

| 1965 | Marion Coakes (UK) | Stroller |

| 1970 | Janou Lefèbvre (Fra) | Rocket |
| 1974 | Janou Tissot (née Lefèbvre) (Fra) | Rocket |

Team

| 3 | France 1982, 1986, 1990 |
| 1 | Great Britain 1978, USA 1986, Germany 1994 |

Volvo World Cup

Instituted by the FEI in 1979 and contested over a series of primarily indoor competitions held between October and April with an annual final.
Winners:

1979	Hugo Simon (Aut)	Gladstone
1980	Conrad Homfeld (USA)	Balbuco
1981	Michael Matz (USA)	Jet Run
1982	Melanie Smith (USA)	Calypso
1983	Norman Dello Joio (USA)	I Love You
1984	Mario Deslauriers (Can)	Aramis
1985	Conrad Homfeld (USA)	Abdullah
1986	Leslie Burr-Lenehan (USA)	McLain
1987	Katharine Burdsall (USA)	The Natural
1988-9	Ian Millar (Can)	Big Ben
1990-1	John Whitaker (UK)	Milton
1992	Thomas Fruhmann (Aut)	Bockmann's Genius
1993	Ludger Beerbaum (Ger)	Ratinoz
1994	Jos Lansink (Hol)	Bollvorm's Libero
1995	Nick Skelton (UK)	Everest Dollar Girl
1996-7	Hugo Simon (Aut)	E T
1998	Rodrigo Pessoa (Bra)	Baloubet de Rouet

Nations Cup

The President's Cup was introduced by the FEI in 1965 for Nations Cup teams. The performances by national teams of four at selected meetings count towards the Cup, with different countries staging just one Nations Cup meeting, which must be at its official International Horse Show. Renamed the Prince Philip Trophy in 1985, to mark his 21st year in office as FEI President, and the Gucci Trophy from 1987.
Winning nations:

15	Great Britain	1965, 1967, 1970, 1972-4, 1977-9, 1983, 1985-6, 1989, 1991, 1996
8	Germany/FRG	1969, 1971, 1975-6, 1981-2, 1984, 1994
5	France	1980, 1987-8, 1990, 1992, 1995
3	USA	1966, 1968, 1997

European Championships

Inaugurated in 1957, and staged biennially from 1963, men and women had separate competitions (and were allowed to ride two horses) until 1975, when the FEI introduced a team event as well as an individual competition open to both men and women. In 1957 and 1959 they were conducted with a change-horse final, as per the World Championships, but that was then abandoned.

Winners (with first horses prior to 1975):

Men

	Rider	Horse
1957	Hans Günter Winkler (FRG)	Sonnenglanz
1958	Fritz Thiedemann (FRG)	Meteor
1959	Piero d'Inzeo (Ita)	Uruguay
1961	David Broome (UK)	Sunsalve
1962	David Barker (UK)	Mister Softee
1963	Graziano Mancinelli (Ita)	Rockette
1965	Hermann Schridde (FRG)	Dozent
1966	Nelson Pessoa (Bra)	Gran Geste
1967	David Broome (UK)	Mister Softee
1969	David Broome (UK)	Mister Softee
1971	Hartwig Steenken (FRG)	Simona
1973	Paddy McMahon (UK)	Pennwood Forge Mill
1975	Alwin Schockemöhle (FRG)	Warwick
1977	Johan Heins (Hol)	Seven Valleys
1979	Gerhard Wiltfang (FRG)	Roman
1981	Paul Schockemöhle (FRG)	Deister
1983	Paul Schockemöhle (FRG)	Deister
1985	Paul Schockemöhle (FRG)	Deister
1987	Pierre Durand (Fra)	Jappeloup
1989	John Whitaker (UK)	Next Milton
1991	Eric Navet (Fra)	Quito de Baussy*
1993	Willi Melliger (Swi)	Quinta C
1995	Peter Charles (Ire)	La Ina
1997	Ludger Beerbaum (Ger)	Ratina

* Horse later failed drugs test.

Team

4	Great Britain	1979, 1985, 1987, 1989
3	Switzerland	1983, 1993, 1995
3	Germany	FRG 1975, 1981; GER 1997
2	Netherlands	1977, 1991

Women

1957	Pat Smythe (UK)	Flanagan*
1958	Guilia Serventi (Ita)	Doly
1959	Ann Townsend (UK)	Bandit IV
1960	Susan Cohen (UK)	Clare Castle
1961	Pat Smythe (UK)	Scorchin
1962	Pat Smythe (UK)	Flanagan
1963	Pat Smythe (UK)	Flanagan
1966	Janou Lefèbvre (Fra)	Kenavo
1967	Kathy Kusner (USA)	Untouchable
1968	Anneli Drummond-Hay (UK)	Merely-a-Monarch
1969	Iris Kellett (Ire)	Morning Light
1971	Ann Moore (UK)	Psalm
1973	Ann Moore (UK)	Psalm

* Flanagan is the only horse to have won four European Championships, these three, and 1961, when he was Pat Smythe's second horse.

Royal International Horse Show

First staged as the International Horse Show in the Grand Hall at Olympia in 1907. The world's first

Nations Cup for teams was staged in 1909. The Show has been held annually at Wembley, but at Hickstead in 1993. The two most famous events are the King George V Gold Cup and the Queen Elizabeth II Cup.

King George V Gold Cup

First contested in 1911, the competition is regarded as the principal annual show jumping event for male riders. Any rider winning the event three times keeps the gold international perpetual challenge trophy, which was presented by King George V.

Post-war winners:

1947	Pierre Jonquères d'Oriola (Fra)	Marquis III
1948	Harry Llewellyn (UK)	Foxhunter
1949	Brian Butler (UK)	Tankard
1950	Harry Llewellyn (UK)	Foxhunter
1951	Kevin Barry (Ire)	Ballyneety
1952	Carlos Figueroa (Spa)	Gracieux
1953	Harry Llewellyn (UK)	Foxhunter
1954	Fritz Thiedemann (FRG)	Meteor
1955	Luigi Cartesegna (Ita)	Brando
1956	William Steinkraus (USA)	First Boy
1957	Piero d'Inzeo (Ita)	Uruguay
1958	Hugh Wiley (USA)	Master William
1959	Hugh Wiley (USA)	Nautical
1960	David Broome (UK)	Sunsalve
1961-2	Piero d'Inzeo (Ita)	The Rock
1963	Thomas Wade (Ire)	Dundrum
1964	William Steinkraus (USA)	Sinjon
1965	Hans Günter Winkler (FRG)	Fortun
1966	David Broome (UK)	Mister Softee
1967	Peter Robeson (UK)	Firecrest
1968	Hans Günter Winkler (FRG)	Enigk
1969	Ted Edgar (UK)	Uncle Max
1970	Harvey Smith (UK)	Mattie Brown
1971	Gerd Wiltfang (FRG)	Askan
1972	David Broome (UK)	Sportsman
1973	Paddy McMahon (UK)	Pennwood Forge Mill
1974	Frank Chapot (USA)	Main Spring
1975	Alwin Schockemöhle (FRG)	Rex the Robber
1976	Michael Saywell (UK)	Chain Bridge
1977	David Broome (UK)	Philco
1978	Jeff McVean (Aus)	Claret
1979	Robert Smith (UK)	Video
1980	David Bowen (UK)	Scorton
1981	David Broome (UK)	Mr Ross
1982	Michael Whitaker (UK)	Disney Way
1983	Paul Schockemöhle (FRG)	Deister
1984	Nick Skelton (UK)	St James
1985	Malcolm Pyrah (UK)	Towerlands Anglezark
1986	John Whitaker (UK)	Next Ryan's Son
1987	Malcolm Pyrah (UK)	Towerlands Anglezark
1988	Robert Smith (UK)	Brook Street Boysie
1989	Michael Whitaker (UK)	Next Didi
1990	John Whitaker (UK)	Milton
1991	David Broome (UK)	Lannegan
1992	Michael Whitaker (UK)	Midnight Madness

1993	Nick Skelton (UK)	Limited Edition
1994	Michael Whitaker (UK)	Midnight Madness
1995	Robert Splaine (Ire)	Heather Blaze
1996	Nick Skelton (UK)	Cuthleen
1997	John Whitaker (UK)	Welham
1998	Robert Smith (UK)	Mighty Blue

Most wins

Rider: 6 Broome; 4 M Whitaker; 3 Jack Talbot-
Ponsonby 1930, 1932, 1934, Llewellyn, P d'Inzeo
Horse: 3 Foxhunter 1948, 1950, 1953

Queen Elizabeth II Cup

The women's equivalent of the King George V Gold
Cup, inaugurated in 1949.
Winners:

1949	Iris Kellett (Ire)	Rusty
1950	Gill Palethorpe (UK)	Silver Cloud
1951	Iris Kellett (Ire)	Rusty
1952	Gill Rich (UK)	Quicksilver III
1953	Marie Delfosse (UK)	Fanny Rosa
1954	Josée Bonnaud (Fra)	Charleston
1955-6	Dawn Palethorpe (UK)	Earlsrath Rambler
1957	Elizabeth Anderson (UK)	Sunsalve
1958	Pat Smythe (UK)	Mr Pollard
1959	Anna Clement (FRG)	Nico
1960	Susan Cohen (UK)	Clare Castle
1961	Lady Sarah FitzAlan Howard (UK)	Oorskiet
1962	Judy Crago (UK)	Spring Fever
1963	Julie Nash (UK)	Trigger Hill
1964	Gillian Makin (UK)	Jubilant
1965	Marion Coakes (UK)	Stroller
1966	Althea Roger Smith (UK)	Havana Royal
1967	Betty Jennaway (UK)	Grey Leg
1968	Mary Chapot (USA)	White Lightning
1969	Alison Westwood (UK)	The Maverick VII
1968	A Drummond-Hay (UK)	Merely-a-Monarch
1971	Marion Mould (née Coakes) (UK)	Stroller
1972	Ann Moore (UK)	Psalm
1973	Ann Moore (UK) &	Psalm
	Alison Dawes (née Westwood)	Mr Banbury
1974	Jean Davenport (UK)	All Trumps
1975	Jean Davenport (UK)	Hang On
1976	Marion Mould (UK)	Elizabeth Ann
1977	Liz Edgar (UK)	Everest Wallaby
1978	Caroline Bradley (UK)	Marius
1979	Liz Edgar (UK)	Forever
1980	Caroline Bradley (UK)	Tigre
1981-2	Liz Edgar (UK)	Everest Forever
1983	Jean Germany (UK)	Mandingo
1984	Véronique Whitaker (UK)	Next's Jingo
1985	Sue Pountain (UK)	Ned Kelly VI
1986	Liz Edgar (UK)	Everest Rapier
1987	Gillian Greenwood (UK)	Monsanta
1988-9	Janet Hunter (UK)	Everest Lisnamarrow
1990	Emma-Jane Mac (UK)	Everest Oyster
1991	Janet Hunter (UK)	Everest Lisnamarrow
1992	Tina Cassan (UK)	Genesis

1993	Tina Cassan (UK)	Bond Xtra
1994	Di Lampard (UK)	Abbervail Dream
1995-6	Marion Hughes (Ire)	Flo Jo
1997	Lynne Bevan (UK)	Grafton Magna
1998	Di Lampard (UK)	Abbervail Dream

Most wins: 5 Edgar; 3 Mould (née Coakes)
The only horse to win the King George V Gold Cup
and the Queen Elizabeth II Cup is Sunsalve, 1957, 1960.

British Show Jumping Derby

Held annually at the All-England Jumping Centre,
Hickstead, Sussex, the first Derby was in 1961. A
Derby is contested over a course of *c*.1300m, about
500m longer than an Olympic Nations Cup course.
Winners:

1961	Seamus Hayes (Ire)	Goodbye III
1962	Pat Smythe (UK)	Flanagan
1963	Nelson Pessoa (Bra)	Gran Geste
1964	Seamus Hayes (Ire)	Goodbye III
1965	Nelson Pessoa (Bra)	Gran Geste
1966	David Broome (UK)	Mister Softee
1967	Marion Coakes (UK)	Stroller
1968	Alison Westwood (UK)	The Maverick VII
1969	Anneli Drummond-Hay (UK)	Xanthos II
•1970	Harvey Smith (UK)	Mattie Brown
1971	Harvey Smith (UK)	Mattie Brown
1972	Hendrick Snoek (FRG)	Shirokko
1973	Alison Dawes (née Westwood)	Mr Banbury
1974	Harvey Smith (UK)	Salvador
1975	Paul Darragh (Ire)	Pele
1976-9	Eddie Macken (Ire)	Boomerang
1980	Michael Whitaker (UK)	Owen Gregory
1981	Harvey Smith (UK)	Sanyo Video
1982	Paul Schockemöhle (FRG)	Deister
1983	John Whitaker (UK)	Ryan's Son
1984	John Ledingham (Ire)	Gabhran
1985	Paul Schockemöhle (FRG)	Lorenzo
1986	Paul Schockemöhle (FRG)	Deister
1987	Nick Skelton (UK)	Raffles
1988-9	Nick Skelton (UK)	Apollo
1990	Joe Turi (UK)	Vital
1991-2	Michael Whittaker (UK)	Monsanta
1993	Michael Whittaker (UK)	My Messieur
1994-5	John Ledingham (Ire)	Kilbaha
1996	Nelson Pessoa (Bra)	Vivaldi
1997	John Popely (UK)	Sight and Sound Bluebird
1998	Erik Holstein (Ire)	Ballaseyr Kalosha

Most wins: 4 Macken, Smith, M Whitaker;
3 Schockemöhle, Skelton

Jumping Records

The official high jump world record is 2.47m (8ft
1¼in) by Huasó, ridden by Capt. Alberto Larraguibel
(Chl) on 5 Feb 1949; the indoor record is 2.40m by
Franke Sloothaak (Ger) on Optibeurs Leonardi on
9 Jun 1991. The world long jump record is 8.40m
(27ft 6¾in) by Something, ridden by André Ferreira
(SAf) on 26 Apr 1975.

Three-Day Eventing

Competitors ride the same horse in a) a dressage test; b) an endurance competition of four phases: roads and track 16-20km in Games and championships, steeplechase of 3105-3450m, roads and track again, cross country of 7410-7980m; and c) a jumping test.

Olympic Games

Both individual and team competitions were first held at the 1912 Games, when it was known as 'the military' and restricted to Army officers. The current three-event pattern was established at Paris in 1924.

Winners:

Individual

1912	Axel Nordlander (Swe)	Lady Artist
1920	Helmer Mörner (Swe)	Germania
1924	Adolph v d Voort van Zijp (Hol)	Silver Piece
1928	Charles Pahud de Mortanges (Hol)	Marcroix
1932	Charles Pahud de Mortanges (Hol)	Marcroix
1936	Ludwig Stubbendorff (Ger)	Nurmi
1948	Bernard Chevallier (Fra)	Aiglonne
1952	Hans von Blixen-Finecke Jr (Swe)	Jubal
1956	Petrus Kastenman (Swe)	Iluster
1960	Lawrence Morgan (Aus)	Salad Days
1964	Mauro Checcoli (Ita)	Surbean
1968	Jean-Jacques Gùyon (Fra)	Pitou
1972	Richard Meade (UK)	Laurieston
1976	Edmund Coffin (USA)	Bally-Cor
1980	Federico Roman (Ita)	Rossinan
1984	Mark Todd (NZ)	Charisma
1988	Mark Todd (NZ)	Charisma
1992	Matthew Ryan (Aus)	Kibah Tic Toc
1996	Blyth Tait (NZ)	Ready Teddy

Team

4	USA	1932, 1948, 1976, 1984
3	Sweden	1912, 1920, 1952
3	Great Britain	1956, 1968, 1972
3	Australia	1960, 1992, 1996
2	Netherlands	1924, 1928
2	Germany	1936, FRG 1988
1	Italy 1964, USSR 1980	

Most gold medals: 4 Charles Pahud de Mortanges (Hol) team 1924, 1928; individual 1928, 1932 (also won team silver 1932 for a record five medals)

World Championships

Instituted in 1966; men and women have competed together at all championships.

Individual

1966	Carlos Moratorio (Arg)	Chalon
1970	Mary Gordon-Watson (UK)	Cornishman V
1974	Bruce Davidson (USA)	Irish Cap
1978	Bruce Davidson (USA)	Might Tango
1982	Lucinda Green (UK	Regal Realm

1986	Virginia Leng (UK)	Priceless
1990	Blyth Tait (NZ)	Messiah
1994	Vaughan Jefferis (NZ)	Bounce

Team wins

4	Great Britain	1970, 1982, 1986, 1994
1	Ireland 1966, USA 1974, Canada 1978, New Zealand 1990	

Most gold medals

3 Bruce Davidson individual 1974, 1978, team 1974, Virginia Leng individual 1986, team 1982, 1986

European Championships

Individual

1953	Lawrence Rook (UK)	Starlight
1954	Albert Hill (UK)	Crispin
1955	Frank Weldon (UK)	Kilbarry
1957	Sheila Willcox (UK)	High and Mighty
1959	Hans Schwarzenbach (Swi)	Burn Trout
1962	James Templar (UK)	M'Lord Connolly
1965	Marian Babirecki (Pol)	Volt
1967	Eddie Boylan (Ire)	Durlas Eile
1969	Mary Gordon-Watson (UK)	Cornishman V
1971	HRH Princess Anne (UK)	Doublet
1973	Aleksandr Yevdokimov (USSR)	Jeger
1975	Lucinda Prior-Palmer (UK)	Be Fair
1977	Lucinda Prior-Palmer (UK)	George
1979	Nils Haagensen (Den)	Monaco
1981	Hansueli Schmutz (Swi)	Oran
1983	Rachel Bayliss (UK)	Mystic Minstrel
1985	Virginia Holgate (UK)	Priceless
1987	Virginia Leng (née Holgate) (UK)	Night Cap
1989	Virginia Leng (UK)	Master Craftsman
1991	Ian Stark (UK)	Glenburnie
1993	Jean-Louis Bigot (Fra)	Twist la Beige
1995	Lucy Thompson (Ire)	Welton Romance
1997	Bettina Oversch-Boker (Ger)	Watermill Stream

Team wins

14	Great Britain	1953-5, 1957, 1967, 1969, 1971, 1977, 1981, 1985, 1987, 1989, 1991, 1995, 1997
3	USSR	1962, 1965, 1975
2	F R Germany	1959, 1973
2	Sweden	1983, 1993
1	Ireland	1979

Badminton

First held in 1949, the Badminton Horse Trials take place annually in the grounds of Badminton House in Gloucestershire, home of the Beaufort family. The attendance is around 200,000.

Winners:

1949	John Shedden (UK)	Golden Willow
1950	Tony Collings (UK)	Remus
1951	Hans Schwarzenbach (Swi)	Vae Victus

1952	Mark Darley (Ire)	Emily Little
1953	Lawrence Rook (UK)	Starlight
1954	Margaret Hough (UK)	Bambi
1955-6	Frank Weldon (UK)#	Kilbarry
1957-8	Sheila Willcox (UK)	High and Mighty
1959	Sheila Waddington (née Wilcox) (UK)	Airs and Graces
1960	Bill Roycroft (Aus)	Our Solo
1961	Lawrence Morgan (Aus)	Salad Days
1962	Anneli Drummond-Hay (UK)	Merely-a-Monarch
1963	Susan Fleet (UK)★	Gladiator
1964	James Templer (UK)	M'Lord Connolly
1965	Eddie Boylan (Ire)	Durlas Eile
1966	*Not held*	
1967	Celia Ross-Taylor (UK)	Jonathan
1968	Jane Bullen (UK)	Our Nobby
1969	Richard Walker (UK)	Pasha
1970	Richard Meade (UK)	The Poacher
1971-2	Mark Phillips (UK)	Great Ovation
1973	Lucinda Prior-Palmer (UK)	Be Fair
1974	Mark Phillips (UK)	Columbus
1975	*Cancelled after dressage*	
1976	Lucinda Prior-Palmer (UK)	Wideawake
1977	Lucinda Prior-Palmer (UK)	George
1978	Jane Holderness-Roddam (née Bullen) (UK)	Warrior
1979	Lucinda Prior-Palmer (UK)	Killaire
1980	Mark Todd (NZ)	Southern Comfort
1981	Mark Phillips (UK)	Lincoln
1982	Richard Meade (UK)	Speculator III
1983	Lucinda Green (née Prior-Palmer) (UK)	Regal Realm
1984	Lucinda Green (UK)	Beagle Bay
1985	Virginia Holgate (UK)	Priceless
1986	Ian Stark (UK)	Sir Wattie
1987	*Not held*	
1988	Ian Stark (UK)	Sir Wattie
1989	Virginia Leng (née Holgate) (UK)	Master Craftsman
1990	Nicola McIrvine (UK)	Middle Road
1991	Rodney Powell (UK)	The Irishman
1992	Mary Thomson (UK)	King William
1993	Virginia Leng (UK)	Houdini
1994	Mark Todd (NZ)	Horton Point
1995	Bruce Davidson (USA)	Eagle Lion
1996	Mark Todd (NZ)	Bertie Blunt
1997	David O'Connor (USA)	Custom Made
1998	Christopher Bartle (UK)	Word Perfect II

Held at Windsor 1955.

★ Reduced to a one-day event because of the weather.

Most wins: 6 Green (née Prior-Palmer); 4 Phillips; 3 Waddington (née Willcox), Leng (née Holgate), Todd

Burghley Horse Trials

Held each September on the estate surrounding Burghley House in Lincolnshire, this is the major event of the autumn trials season. Burghley House was the home of the 1928 Olympic athletics gold medallist, David Burghley, the Marquess of Exeter.

Winners:

1968	Anneli Drummond-Hay (UK)	Merely-a-Monarch
1963	Harry Freeman-Jackson (Ire)	St Finbar
1964	Richard Meade (UK)	Barberry
1965	Jeremy Beale (UK)	Victoria Bridge
1967	Lorna Sutherland (UK)	Popadom
1968	Sheila Willcox (UK)	Fair and Square
1969	Gillian Watson (UK)	Shaitan
1970	Judy Bradwell (UK)	Don Camillo
1972	Janet Hodgson (UK)	Larkspur
1973	Mark Phillips (UK)	Maid Marion
1975	Aly Pattinson (UK)	Carawich
1976	Jane Holderness-Roddam (UK)	Warrior
1977	Lucinda Prior-Palmer (UK)	George
1978	Lorna Clarke (UK	Greco
1979	Andrew Hoy (Aus)	Davy
1980	Richard Walker (UK)	John of Gaunt
1981	Lucinda Prior-Palmer (UK)	Beagle Bay
1982	Richard Walker (UK)	Ryan's Cross
1983	Virginia Holgate (UK)	Priceless
1984	Virginia Holgate (UK)	Night Cap
1986	Virginia Leng (née Holgate) (UK)	Murphy Himself
1987	Mark Todd (NZ)	Wilson Fair
1988	Jane Thelwall (UK)	King's Jester
1990	Mark Todd (NZ)	Face the Music
1991	Mark Todd (NZ)	Welton Greylag
1992	Charlotte Hollingsworth (UK)	The Cool Customer
1993	Stephen Bradley (USA)	Sassy Reason
1994	Willim Fox-Pitt (UK)	Chaka
1995	Andrew Nicholson (UK)	Buckley Province
1996	Mary King (UK)	Star Appeal
1997	Mark Todd (NZ)	Broadcast News

1962, 1971, 1985, 1989 *see* European Championship;
1966, 1974 *see* World Championship

Most wins: 4 Todd; 3 Leng (née Holgate)

Dressage

Olympic Games

The individual competition was included in the 1912 Games, but a team competition was not introduced until 1928.

Individual

1912	Carl Bonde (Swe)	Emperor
1920	Janne Lundblad (Swe)	Uno
1924	Ernst Linder (Swe)	Piccolomini

1928	Carl von Langen (Ger)	Draufgänger
1932	Xavier Lesage (Fra)	Taine
1936	Heinz Pollay (Ger)	Kronos
1948	Hans Moser (Swi)	Hummer
1952	Henri St Cyr (Swe)	Master Rufus
1956	Henri St Cyr (Swe)	Juli
1960	Sergey Filatov (USSR)	Absent
1964	Henri Chammartin (Swi)	Woermann
1968	Ivan Kizimov (USSR)	Ichor
1972	Liselott Linsenhoff (FRG)	Piaff
1976	Christine Stückelberger (Swi)	Granat
1980	Elisabeth Theurer (Aut)	Mon Cherie
1984	Reiner Klimke (FRG)	Ahlerich
1988	Nicole Uphoff (FRG)	Rembrandt
1992	Nicole Uphoff (Ger)	Rembrandt
1996	Isabelle Werth (Ger)	Gigolo

Team

9	Germany/FRG	1928, 1936, 1964, 1992, 1996; FRG: 1968, 1976, 1984, 1988
2	France	1932, 1948
2	Sweden	1952, 1956, USSR 1972, 1980

Not held 1960.

Most gold medals: 6 Reiner Klimke (FRG) team gold 1964, 1968, 1976, 1984, 1988, individual 1984; 4 Henri St Cyr (Swe) team 1952, 1956; individual 1952, 1956

Most medals: 8 Klimke, six gold, individual bronze 1968, 1976

World Championships

Inaugurated 1966.
Winners:

Individual

1966	Josef Neckermann (FRG)	Mariano
1970	Yelena Petuchkova (USSR)	Pepel
1974	Reiner Klimke (FRG)	Mehmed
1978	Christine Stückelberger (Swi)	Granat
1982	Reiner Klimke (FRG)	Ahlerich
1986	Anne Grethe Jensen (Den)	Marzog
1990	Nicole Uphoff (FRG)	Rembrandt
1994	Isabell Werth (Ger)	Gigolo

Freestyle

| 1994 | Anky van Grunsven (Hol) | Olympic Bonfire |

Team

| 7 | Germany | FRG 1966, 1974, 1978, 1982, 1986, 1990; GER 1994 |
| 1 | USSR | 1970 |

Most gold medals: 6 Reiner Klimke, 2 individual, 4 team 1966, 1974, 1982, 1986

FEI World Cup

First held in 1986.
Winners:

| 1986 | Anne Grethe Jensen (Den) | Marzog |

1987-8	Christine Stückelberger (Swi)	Gauguin de Lully
	(Swi)	
1989	Margrit Otto-Crepin (Fra)	Corlandus
1990	Sven Rothenberger (FRG)	Andiamo
1991	Kyra Kyrklund (Fin)	Matador
1992	Isabell Werth (Ger)	Fabienne
1993-4	Monica Theodorescu	Ganimedes Tecrent
	(Ger)	
1995-7	Anky van Grunsven (Hol)	Bonfire

European Championships

Inaugurated 1963.
Winners:

Individual

1963	Henri Chammartin (Swi)	Wolfdietrich
1965	Henri Chammartin (Swi)	Wolfdietrich
1967	Reiner Klimke (FRG)	Dux
1969	Liselott Linsenhoff (FRG)	Piaff
1971	Liselott Linsenhoff (FRG)	Piaff
1973	Reiner Klimke (FRG)	Mehmed
1975	Christine Stückelberger (Swi)	Granat
1977	Christine Stückelberger (Swi)	Granat
1979	Elisabeth Theurer (Aut)	Mon Cherie
1981	Uwe Schulten-Baumer (FRG)	Madras
1983	Anne Grethe Jensen (Den)	Marzog
1985	Reiner Klimke (FRG)	Ahlerich
1987	Margrit Otto-Crepin (Fra)	Corlandus
1989	Nicole Uphoff (FRG)	Rembrandt
1991	Isabell Werth (Ger)	Gigolo
1993	Isabell Werth (Ger)	Gigolo
1995	Isabell Werth (Ger)	Gigolo
1997	Isabell Werth (Ger)	Gigolo

Team

| 16 | FRG/Germany | 1965, 1967, 1969, 1971, 1973, 1975, 1977, 1979, 1981, 1983, 1985, 1987, 1989, 1991, 1993, 1995, 1997 |
| 1 | Great Britain | 1963 |

Carriage Driving

Rules for driving events were established by the FEI in 1970. Combined driving for teams of four horses or for pairs consists of a) presentation and dressage; b) an endurance marathon of 23-27km; and c) obstacle driving.

World Championships

Instituted in 1972 and subsequently held every two years.

Individual

1972	Auguste Dubey (Swi)
1974	Sándor Fülöp (Hun)
1976	Imre Abonyi (Hun)
1978	György Bárdos (Hun)
1980	György Bárdos (Hun)

1982	Tjeerd Velstra (Hol)
1984	László Juhász (Hun)
1986	Tjeerd Velstra (Hol)
1988	Ijsbrand Chardon (Hol)
1990	Tómas Eriksson (Swe)*
1992	Ijsbrand Chardon (Hol)
1994	Michael Freund (Ger)
1996	Felix Brasseur (Bel)

Team

3	Netherlands	1982, 1986, 1988
3	Great Britain	1972, 1974, 1980
3	Hungary	1976, 1978, 1984
2	Germany	1992, 1994
1	Sweden 1990*, Belgium 1996	

* Original winner Ad Aarts (Hol) lost his title after his horse Pablo failed a dope test. The Netherlands also lost their team title.

Members of three winning teams: György Bárdos and Sándor Fülöp (Hun), Ijsbrand Chardon (Hol)

World Pairs

An open FEI Pairs Championship was held in Paris in 1983. Its success led to the introduction of the World Pair Driving Championship, first held in 1985 at Sandringham, England. This site was offered by HRH Prince Philip, then the FEI president and himself a successful Four-in-Hand driver.
Winners:

Team		**Individual**
1983	Netherlands	Paul Gregory (UK)
1985	Switzerland	Ekkert Meinecke (FRG)
1987	F R Germany	László Kecskerneti (Hun)
1989	Hungary	Udo Hochgeschorz (Can)
1991	USA	Werner Ullrich (Swz)
1993	Austria	Georg Moser (Aut)
1995	France	Mieke Van Tergouw (Hol)
1997	Great Britain	Zoltán Lazar (Hun)

Endurance Riding

World Championships

Instituted in 1986 and subsequently held every two years.

Individual

1986	Casandra Schuler (US)	Skiko's Omar
1988	Becky Hart (USA)	Grand Sultan
1990	Becky Hart (USA)	Grand Sultan
1992	Becky Hart (USA)	Grand Sultan
1994	Valerie Kanavy (USA)	Pieraz
1996	Daniella Kanavy (USA)	Pieraz

Team

2 Great Britain 1986, 1990, France 1992, 1994, USA 1988, 1996

Vaulting

World Championships

Instituted in 1986, and subsequently held every two years.

Individual – men

1986	Dietmar Ott (FRG)
1988	Christoph Lensing (FRG)
1990	Michael Lehner (FRG)
1992	Christoph Lensing (Ger)
1994	Thomas Fiskbaek (Den)
1996	Christoph Lensing (Ger)

Individual – women

1986	Silke Bernhard (FRG)
1988	Silke Bernhard (FRG)
1990	Silke Bernhard (FRG)
1992	Barbara Strobel (Ger)
1994	Tanja Benedetto (Ger)
1996	Tanja Benedetto (Ger)

Team

| 4 | FRG/GER | 1986, 1988, 1992, 1996 |
| 2 | Switzerland | 1990, 1994 |

Fencing

Fencing, the sport of fighting with a sword, is one of man's oldest pastimes, obviously related to the use of swords in war or single combat. There is evidence of swordsmanship in Egypt as early as 1360BC. Fencing was widespread in the Middle Ages, and the rapier had been developed as the principal weapon by the end of the 16th century.

Modern weapons are the épée, foil and sabre. With the épée (weighing 770 grams) the conditions closely follow those that once related to duelling and the whole body is a target area. With the lighter weapons, for the foil (maximum weight 500 grams) the target area is the metallic jacket covering the top half of the body, and for the sabre (500 grams) the area is above the waist, including the head. For the two latter weapons, a hit must follow prescribed movements – the 'phrase'.

International governing body: Fédération Internationale d'Escrime (FIE), Avenue Mon Repos 24, Case Postale 7243, 1002 Lausanne, Switzerland. President: René Roch, Secretary General: Mario Favia. Founded in Paris in 1913. 96 member nations.

Olympic Games

Fencing has been included at all Olympic Games, and these tournaments count as world championships in Olympic years. At the Games between 1896 and 1906, in addition to the competitions, of which the winners are shown below, there were also events for Fencing Masters, at which these professionals competed against the other contestants. Women first competed in 1924 (with the foil); electronic scoring was introduced for the épée in 1936 and for the foil in 1956. *Winners:*

Men's individual

	Foil	Épée	Sabre
1896	Emile Gravelotte (Fra)	*Not held*	Jean Georgiadis (Gre)
1900	Emile Coste (Fra)	Ramón Fonst (Cub)	Georges de la Falaise (Fra)
1904	Ramón Fonst (Cub)	Ramón Fonst (Cub)	Manuel Diaz (Cub)
1906	Georges Dillon-Kavanagh (Fra)	Georges de la Falaise (Fra)	Jean Georgiadis (Gre)
1908	*Not held*	Gaston Alibert (Fra)	Jenö Fuchs (Hun)
1912	Nedo Nadi (Ita)	Paul Anspach (Bel)	Jenö Fuchs (Hun)
1920	Nedo Nadi (Ita)	Armand Massard (Fra)	Nedo Nadi (Ita)
1924	Roger Ducret (Fra)	Charles Delporte (Bel)	Sándor Posta (Hun)
1928	Lucien Gaudin (Fra)	Lucien Gaudin (Fra)	Odön Tersztyanszky (Hun)
1932	Gustavo Marzi (Ita)	Giancarlo Cornaggia-Medici (Ita)	György Piller (Hun)
1936	Giulio Gaudini (Ita)	Franco Riccardi (Ita)	Endre Kabos (Hun)
1948	Jean Buhan (Fra)	Luigi Cantone (Ita)	Aladár Gerevich (Hun)
1952	Christian d'Oriola (Fra)	Edoardo Mangiarotti (Ita)	Pál Kovács (Hun)
1956	Christian d'Oriola (Fra)	Carlo Pavesi (Ita)	Rudolf Kárpáti (Hun)
1960	Viktor Zhdanovich (USSR)	Giuseppe Delfino (Ita)	Rudolf Kárpáti (Hun)
1964	Egon Franke (Pol)	Grigoriy Kriss (USSR)	Tibor Pézsa (Hun)
1968	Ion Drimba (Rom)	Gyözö Kulcsár (Hun)	Jerzy Pawlowski (Pol)
1972	Witold Woyda (Pol)	Csaba Fenyvesi (Hun)	Viktor Sidiak (USSR)
1976	Fabio Dal Zotto (Ita)	Alexander Pusch (FRG)	Viktor Krovopuskov (USSR)
1980	Vladimir Smirnov (USSR)	Johan Harmenberg (Swe)	Viktor Krovopuskov (USSR)
1984	Mauro Numa (Ita)	Philippe Boisse (Fra)	Jean François Lamour (Fra)
1988	Stefano Cerioni (Ita)	Arnd Schmitt (FRG)	Jean François Lamour (Fra)
1992	Philippe Omnès (Fra)	Eric Srecki (Fra)	Bence Szabó (Hun)
1996	Alessandro Puccini (Ita)	Aleksandr Beketov (Rus)	Stanislav Pozdynakov (Rus)

Men's team

Wins:

Foil

6	France	1924, 1932, 1948, 1952, 1968, 1980
5	Italy	1920, 1928, 1936, 1956, 1984
3	USSR	1960, 1964, 1988
2	Germany	1976 (FRG), 1992
1	Cuba 1904, Poland 1972, Russia 1996	

Épée

7	France	1906, 1908, 1924, 1932, 1948, 1980, 1988
7	Italy	1920, 1928, 1936, 1952, 1956, 1960, 1996
3	Hungary	1964, 1968, 1972
2	Germany	1984 (FRG), 1992
1	Belgium 1912, Sweden 1976	

Sabre

10	Hungary	1908, 1912, 1928, 1932, 1936, 1948, 1952, 1956, 1960, 1988
5	USSR/CIS	1964, 1968, 1976, 1980, 1992 (CIS)
4	Italy	1920, 1924, 1972, 1984
1	Germany 1906, Russia 1996	

Women's individual

Foil

1924	Ellen Osiier (Den)
1928	Helene Mayer (Ger)
1932	Ellen Preis (Aut)
1936	Ilona Elek (Hun)
1948	Ilona Elek (Hun)
1952	Irene Camber (Ita)
1956	Gillian Sheen (UK)
1960	Heidi Schmid (FRG)
1964	Ildikó Ujlaki-Rejtö (Hun)
1968	Yelena Novikova (USSR)
1972	Antonella Ragno-Lonzi (Ita)
1976	Ildikó Schwarczenberger (Hun)
1980	Pascale Trinquet (Fra)
1984	Luan Jujie (Chn)
1988	Anja Fichtel (FRG)
1992	Giovanna Trillini (Ita)
1996	Laura Badea (Rom)

Épée

1996   Laura Flessel (Fra)

Women's foil team

Wins:

4	USSR	1960, 1968, 1972, 1976
2	F R Germany	1984, 1988
1	Hungary 1964, France 1980, Italy 1992	

Women's épée team

Wins:

1	France	1996

Most Olympic medals

Men

(G – Gold, S – Silver, B – Bronze; individual/team)

	Name	G	S	B	Years
13	Edoardo Mangiarotti (Ita)	1/5	1/4	2/-	1936-60
10	Aladár Gerevich (Hun)	1/6	1/-	1/1	1932-60
9	Giulio Gaudini (Ita)	1/2	1/3	2/-	1928-36
8	Roger Ducret (Fra)	1/2	2/2	1/-	1920-28
8	Philippe Cattiau (Fra)	-/3	2/2	-/1	1920-36
7	Pál Kovács (Hun)	1/5	-/-	1/-	1936-60

Others with five or more including four gold medals:

6	Nedo Nadi (Ita)★	3/3	-/-	-/-	1912-20
6	Christian d'Oriola (Fra)	2/2	1/1	-/-	1948-56
6	Rudolf Kárpáti (Hun)	2/4	-/-	-/-	1948-60
6	Lucien Gaudin (Fra)	2/2	-/2	-/-	1920-28
6	Giuseppe Delfino (Ita)	1/3	1/1	-/-	1952-64
6	Gyözö Kulcsár (Hun)	1/3	-/-	2/-	1964-76
6	Viktor Sidiak (USSR)	1/3	-/1	1/-	1968-80
5	Ramón Fonst (Cub)	3/1	1/-	-/-	1900-04

★ Nadi won a record five gold medals at one Games in 1920.

Women

7	Ildikó Sagi-Ujlaki-Rejtö (Hun)	1/1	-/3	1/1	1960-76
6	Yelena Byelova (USSR) (née Novikova)	1/3	-/1	1/-	1968-80

World Championships

Held annually except in Olympic years (*see* above). From 1921 to 1935 they were styled as European Championships.

Winners:

Men

	Foil	Épée	Sabre
1921	-	Lucien Gaudin (Fra)	-
1922	-	Raoul Herde (Nor)	Adrianus de Jong (Hol)
1923	-	Wouter Brouwer (Hol)	Adrianus de Jong (Hol)
1925	-	-	János Garay (Hun)
1926	Giorgio Chiavacci (Ita)	Georges Tainturier (Fra)	Sándor Gambos (Hun)
1927	Oreste Puliti (Ita)	Georges Buchard (Fra)	Sándor Gambos (Hun)
1929	Oreste Puliti (Ita)	Philippe Cattiau (Fra)	Gyula Glykais (Hun)
1930	Giulio Gaudini (Ita)	Philippe Cattiau (Fra)	György Piller (Hun)
1931	René Lemoine (Fra)	Georges Buchard (Fra)	György Piller (Hun)
1933	Gioacchino Guaragna (Ita)	Georges Buchard (Fra)	Endre Kabos (Hun)
1934	Giulio Gaudini (Ita)	Pál Dunay (Hun)	Endre Kabos (Hun)
1935	shared by four men	Hans Drakenberg (Swe)	Aladár Gerevich (Hun)
1937	Gustavo Marzi (Ita)	Bernard Schmetz (Fra)	Pál Kovács (Hun)
1938	Gioacchino Guaragna (Ita)	Michel Pécheux (Fra)	Aldo Montano (Ita)

1947	Christian d'Oriola (Fra)	Edouard Artigas (Fra)	Aldo Montano (Ita)
1949	Christian d'Oriola (Fra)	Dario Mangiarotti (Ita)	Gastone Daré (Fra)
1950	Renzo Nostino (Ita)	Mogens Luchow (Den)	Jean Levavasseur (Fra)
1951	Manlio Di Rosa (Ita)	Edoardo Mangiarotti (Ita)	Aladár Gerevich (Hun)
1953	Christian d'Oriola (Fra)	József Sákovics (Hun)	Pál Kovács (Hun)
1954	Christian d'Oriola (Fra)	Edoardo Mangiarotti (Ita)	Rudolf Kárpáti (Hun)
1955	Jozsef Gyuricza (Hun)	Giorgio Anglesio (Ita)	Aladár Gerevich (Hun)
1957	Mihaly Fülöp (Hun)	Armand Mouyal (Fra)	Jerzy Pawlowski (Pol)
1958	Giancarlo Bergamini (Ita)	Bill Hoskyns (UK)	Yakov Rylsky (USSR)
1959	Allan Jay (UK)	Bruno Khabarov (USSR)	Rudolf Kárpáti (Hun)
1961	Ryszard Parulski (Pol)	Jack Guittet (Fra)	Yakov Rylsky (USSR)
1962	German Sveshnikov (USSR)	István Kausz (Hun)	Zoltán Horváth (Hun)
1963	Jean-Claude Magnan (Fra)	Roland Losert (Aut)	Yakov Rylsky (USSR)
1965	Jean-Claude Magnan (Fra)	Zoltán Nemere (Hun)	Jerzy Pawlowski (Pol)
1966	German Sveshnikov (USSR)	Aleksey Nikanchikov (USSR)	Jerzy Pawlowski (Pol)
1967	Viktor Putyatin (USSR)	Aleksey Nikanchikov (USSR)	Mark Rakita (USSR)
1969	Friedrich Wessel (FRG)	Bogdan Andrzejewski (Pol)	Viktor Sidiak (USSR)
1970	Friedrich Wessel (FRG)	Aleksey Nikanchikov (USSR)	Tibor Pézsa (Hun)
1971	Vasiliy Stankovich (USSR)	Grigoriy Kriss (USSR)	Michele Maffei (Ita)
1973	Christian Noël (Fra)	Rolf Edling (Swe)	Mario Aldo Monttano (Ita)
1974	Aleksandr Romankov (USSR)	Rolf Edling (Swe)	Mario Aldo Monttano (Ita)
1975	Christian Noël (Fra)	Alexander Pusch (FRG)	Vladimir Nazlimov (USSR)
1977	Aleksandr Romankov (USSR)	Johan Harmenberg (Swe)	Pál Gerevich (Hun)
1978	Didier Flament (Fra)	Alexander Pusch (FRG)	Viktor Krovopuskov (USSR)
1979	Aleksandr Romankov (USSR)	Philippe Riboud (Fra)	Vladimir Nazlimov (USSR)
1981	Vladimir Smirnov (USSR)	Zoltán Szekely (Hun)	Mariusz Wodke (Pol)
1982	Aleksandr Romankov (USSR)	Jenö Pap (Hun)	Viktor Krovopuskov (USSR)
1983	Aleksandr Romankov (USSR)	Ellmar Bormann (FRG)	Vasiliy Etropolski (Bul)
1985	Mauro Numa (Ita)	Philippe Boisse (Fra)	György Nébald (Hun)
1986	Andrea Borella (Ita)	Philippe Riboud (Fra)	Sergey Mindirgassov (USSR)
1987	Mathias Gey (FRG)	Volker Fischer (FRG)	Jean François Lamour (Fra)
1989	Alexander Koch (FRG)	Manuel Pereira (Spa)	Grigoriy Kirienko (USSR)
1990	Philippe Omnès (Fra)	Thomas Gerull (FRG)	György Nébald (Hun)
1991	Ingo Weissenborn (Ger)	Andrey Shuvalov (USSR)	Grigoriy Kirienko (USSR)
1993	Alexander Koch (Ger)	Pavel Kolobkov (Rus)	Grigoriy Kirienko (Rus)
1994	Rolando Tucker (Cub)	Pavel Kolobkov (Rus)	Felix Becker (Ger)
1995	Dmitriy Shevchenko (Rus)	Eric Srecki (Fra)	Grigoriy Kirienko (Rus)
1997	Sergey Golubitskiy (Ukr)	Eric Srecki (Fra)	Stanislav Pozdnyakov (Rus)

Most wins: 5 Romankov (USSR); 4 d'Oriola (Fra), Kirienko (Rus); 3 Buchard (Fra), Nikanchikov (USSR)

Team foil

Wins:

16	Italy	1929-31, 1933-5, 1937-8, 1949-50, 1954-5, 1985-6, 1990, 1994
14	USSR	1959, 1961-3, 1965-6, 1969-70, 1973-4, 1979, 1981-2, 1989
7	France	1947, 1951, 1953, 1958, 1971, 1975, 1997
4	FRG/Germany	1977, 1983, 1987, 1993
2	Cuba	1991, 1995
1	Hungary 1957, Romania 1967, Poland 1978	

Team épée

Wins:

13	Italy	1931, 1933, 1937, 1949-50, 1953-5, 1957-8, 1989-90, 1993
11	France	1934-5, 1938, 1947, 1951, 1962, 1965-6, 1982-3, 1994
7	USSR	1961, 1967, 1969, 1979, 1981, 1987, 1991
4	Hungary	1959, 1970-1, 1978
4	Germany	FRG 1973, 1985-6; Ger 1995
3	Sweden	1974-5, 1977
1	Belgium 1930, Poland 1963, Cuba 1997	

Team sabre

Wins:

19	Hungary	1930-1, 1933-5, 1937, 1951, 1953-5, 1957-8, 1966, 1973, 1978, 1981-2, 1991, 1993
15	USSR	1965, 1967, 1969-71, 1974-5, 1977, 1979, 1983, 1985-7, 1989-90
5	Italy	1938, 1947, 1949-50, 1995
4	Poland	1959, 1961-3
1	Russia 1994, France 1997	

Women

Foil

1929	Helene Mayer (Ger)
1930	Jenny Addams (Bel)
1931	Helene Mayer (Ger)
1933	Gwen Neligan (UK)
1934	Ilona Elek (Hun)
1935	Ilona Elek (Hun)
1937	Helene Mayer (Ger)
1938	Marie Sediva (Cs)
1947	Ellen Müller-Preiss (Aut)
1949	Ellen Müller-Preiss (Aut)
1950	Ellen Müller-Preiss (Aut) & Renée Garilhe (Fra)
1951	Ilona Elek (Hun)
1953	Irene Camber (Ita)
1954	Karen Lachman (Den)
1955	Lidia Dömölki (Hun)
1957	Aleksandra Zabelina (USSR)
1958	Valentina Kiselyeva (USSR)
1959	Yelina Yefimova (USSR)
1961	Heidi Schmid (FRG)
1962	Olga Szabo-Orban (Rom)
1963	Ildikó Rejtö (Hun)
1965	Galina Gorokhova (USSR)
1966	Tatyana Samusenko (USSR)
1967	Aleksandra Zabelina (USSR)
1969	Yelena Novikova (USSR)
1970	Galina Gorokhova (USSR)
1971	Marie-Chantal Demaille (Fra)
1973	Valentina Nikonova (USSR)
1974	Ildikó Bóbis (Hun)
1975	Ecaterina Stahl (Rom)
1977	Valentina Sidorova (USSR)
1978	Valentina Sidorova (USSR)
1979	Cornelia Hanisch (FRG)
1981	Cornelia Hanisch (FRG)
1982	Naila Giliazova (USSR)
1983	Dorina Vaccaroni (Ita)
1985	Cornelia Hanisch (FRG)
1986	Anja Fichtel (FRG)
1987	Elisabeta Tufan (Rom)
1989	Olga Velichko (USSR)
1990	Anja Fichtel (FRG)
1991	Giovanna Trillini (Ita)
1993	Francesca Bortolozzi (Ita)
1994	Reka Szabo-Lazar (Rom)
1995	Laura Badea (Rom)
1997	Giovanna Trillini (Ita)

Most wins: 3 Mayer, Elek, Müller-Preiss, Hanisch

Épée

1989	Anja Straub (Swi)
1990	Taime Chappe (Cub)
1991-2	Marianne Horváth (Hun)
1993	Oksana Yermakova (Est)
1994	Laura Chiesa (Ita)
1995	Joanna Jakimiuk (Pol)
1997	Miraide García (Cub)

Team foil

Wins:

15	USSR 1956, 1958, 1961, 1963, 1965-6, 1970-1, 1974-5, 1977-9, 1981, 1986
13	Hungary 1933-5, 1937, 1952-5, 1959, 1962, 1967, 1973, 1987
7	Italy 1957, 1982-3, 1990-1, 1995, 1997
4	FRG/Germany 1936, 1985, 1989, 1993
3	Denmark 1932, 1947-8
2	France 1950-1
2	Romania 1969, 1994

Team épée

6	Hungary 1989, 1991-3, 1995, 1997
1	F R Germany 1990, Spain 1994

Fives (Eton)

The game originated at Eton College in 1840, when courts were built incorporating features of the area where a handball game had been played before (first recorded in 1825). The courts had a distinctive built-in buttress, which had been used by boys playing against the outside of the chapel.

Amateur Championship

Played, as doubles, annually for the Kinnaird Cup. First held in 1928.

Most wins by one pair

10	Brian Matthews & John Reynolds 1981-90
8	Anthony Hughes and Arthur Campbell 1958, 1965-8, 1971, 1973, 1975
3	Howard Fabian & John Webb 1937, 1939, 1948
3	Peter May & John May 1951-3
3	Jimmy Biggs & Jim Wallis 1961-2, 1964
3	Robin Mason & Andrew Mole 1993-5

Reynolds also won with Manuel de Souza-Girao in 1991; Hughes also won in 1963 with David Guilford.

Other recent winners

1992	Mark Moore & Gary Baker
1996-7	Edward Wass & James Halstead
1998	Robin Mason & Jonathan Mole

Fives (Rugby)

This court game was first played around 1850. The court differs from that used for Eton Fives in that there is no buttress. The Rugby Fives Association was formed in 1927. It drew up a standard set of rules in 1930 and in the following year established the standard court dimensions – 28ft (8.54m) long and 18ft (5.49m) wide).

National Singles Championship

Contested annually for the Jesters' Club Cup from 1932, except in 1940-7. Wayne Enstone has dominated in recent years.

Most wins

22 Wayne Enstone 1973-8, 1980-95
 4 John Pretlove 1953, 1955-6, 1958
 4 Eric Marsh 1960-3
 3 Philip Malt 1933-5

Other recent winners

1979 David Hebden, 1996 Neil Roberts, 1997 Ian Fuller

National Doubles Championship

Contested annually for the Cyriax Cup, first in 1926, then annually 1930-9 and from 1947.

Most wins

13 Wayne Enstone 1975-9 (with John East), 1986 (with Steve Ashton), 1991-7 (with Neil Roberts)
11 Ian Fuller & David Hebden 1980-5, 1987-90
 7 John Pretlove 1952, 1954, 1956-9, 1961 (4 with Dennis Silk 1956-9)
 7 David Gardner 1960, 1965-6, 1970-2, 1974
 5 John East 1975-9

Football

The Chinese played a form of football, *Tsu chu* (meaning 'to kick a ball of stuffed leather'), over 2500 years ago. Other versions may have been played in various parts of the world, but much of the game's development took place in England. In an early reference to the sport, in 1314, Edward II issued a prohibition on the game to stop the excessive noise that people were making hustling over footballs in the streets of London. Three subsequent British monarchs also banned the sport, for one reason or another, until it became organized in the 19th century. The first rules were drawn up at Cambridge University in 1848 and there were various modifications over the next decades. The Sheffield club, the oldest club still in existence, was formed in 1855, and the Football Association was founded in London in 1863. The sport grew rapidly in popularity world-wide.

International governing body: Fédération Internationale de Football Association (FIFA), Case Postale 85, CH-8030 Zürich, Switzerland. Tel: (41) 1 384 9595, Fax: (41) 1 384 9696. President: Joseph 'Sepp' Blatter. Formed in Paris in 1904. 203 member nations.

World Cup

The first World Cup tournament for the Jules Rimet Trophy (named after the president of FIFA) was held in Uruguay in 1930, contested by 13 nations. A qualifying tournament was introduced in 1934, and the competition has been staged every four years since, with the exception of the war years. Brazil won the trophy outright in 1970 following their third win, and teams now compete for the FIFA World Cup. A record 152 nations contested the 1998 tournament in Continental groups, from which 32 (as opposed to 24 in 1994) qualified for the final stage. Hosts France and holders Brazil automically went through, and the remaining places were allocated as follows: Europe 14, Africa 5, South America 4, Asia/Oceania 4, Central and North America 3. Hosting of the 2002 tournament will be shared by Japan and South Korea.

Finals

(Goal-scorers are shown beneath each team)

Year	Winners		Runners-up		Venue	Attendance
1930	**Uruguay** Dorado, Cea, Iriarte, Castro	4	**Argentina** Peucelle, Stabile	2	Montevideo, Uruguay	90,000
1934	**Italy** Orsi, Schiavio	2	**Czechoslovakia** Puc	1★	Rome, Italy	55,000
1938	**Italy** Colaussi 2, Piola 2	4	**Hungary** Titkos, Sarosi	2	Paris, France	50,000
1950	**Uruguay** Schiaffino, Ghiggia	2	**Brazil** Friaca	1#	Rio de Janeiro, Brazil	199,854
1954	**F R Germany** Rahn 2, Morlock	3	**Hungary** Puskas, Czibor	2	Berne, Switzerland	55,000
1958	**Brazil** Vava 2, Pele 2, Zagalo	5	**Sweden** Liedholm, Simonsson	2	Stockholm, Sweden	49,737
1962	**Brazil** Amarildo, Zito, Vava	3	**Czechoslovakia** Masopust	1	Santiago, Chile	69,068
1966	**England** Hurst 3, Peters	4	**F R Germany** Haller, Weber	2★	Wembley, England	93,000
1970	**Brazil** Pele, Gerson, Jairzinho, C Alberto	4	**Italy** Boninsegna	1	Mexico City, Mexico	110,000
1974	**F R Germany** Breitner (pen), Muller	2	**Netherlands** Neeskens (pen)	1	Munich, F R Germany	77,833
1978	**Argentina** Kempes 2, Bertoni	3	**Netherlands** Nanninga	1★	Buenos Aires, Argentina	77,000
1982	**Italy** Rossi, Tardelli, Altobelli	3	**F R Germany** Breitner	1	Madrid, Spain	92,000
1986	**Argentina** Brown, Valdano, Burruchaga	3	**F R Germany** Rummenigge, Völler	2	Mexico City, Mexico	114,580
1990	**F R Germany** Brehme (pen)	1	**Argentina**	0	Rome, Italy	73,603
1994	**Brazil** Won by Brazil 3-2 on penalties	0	**Italy**	0★	Pasadena, USA	90,000
1998	**France**	3	**Brazil**	0	Saint-Denis, France	75,000

★ After extra time, # deciding match of final pool.

Leading nations

A summary of the leading nations' records in the final stages of the World Cup, including those nations to have appeared in nine or more finals tournaments (*Apps.*) or to have won 15 or more matches. Losses on penalties included as draws.

	Wins	2nd	SF	Apps.	Played	Games Won	Drawn	Lost	Goals For	Against
Brazil	4	2	3	16	80	53	14	13	172	78
Germany (FRG)★	3	3	3	14	78	45	17	16	163	104
Italy	3	2	2	14	66	38	16	12	105	62
Argentina	2	2	–	12	57	29	10	18	100	69
Uruguay	2	–	2	9	37	15	8	14	61	52
France	1	–	3	10	41	21	6	14	86	58
England	1	–	1	10	45	20	13	12	62	42
Hungary	–	2	–	9	32	15	3	14	87	57
Sweden	–	1	3	9	38	14	9	15	62	60
Spain	–	–	1	10	40	16	10	14	61	48
Belgium	–	–	1	10	32	9	7	16	40	56
USSR/Russia★ 1994	–	–	1	8	34	16	6	12	60	40
Yugoslavia	–	–	1	8	33	14	7	12	55	42

★ Germany includes FRG 1950-90, Russia includes USSR 1958-90.

Highest score (final rounds): 10-1 Hungary v El Salvador, 15 Jun 1982; aggregate: 7-5 Austria v Switzerland, 26 Jun 1954

Highest score (qualifying rounds): 13-0 New Zealand v Fiji, 15 Aug 1981

Finals tournament records

Most appearances: 25 Lothar Matthäus (Ger) 1982-98; 21 Uwe Seeler (FRG) 1958-70, Wladyslaw Szmuda (Pol) 1974-86, Diego Maradona (Arg) 1982-94; 20 Grzegorz Lato (Pol) 1974-82

Most final tournaments: 5 Antonio Carbajal (Mex) 1950-66, Lothar Matthäus (Ger) 1982-98

Most goals in each tournament

1930	Guillermo Stabile (Arg)	8
1934	Three men	4
1938	Leonidas da Silva (Bra)	8
1950	Ademir de Menenzes (Bra)	9
1954	Sándor Kocsis (Hun)	11
1958	Just Fontaine (Fra)	13
1962	Six men	4
1966	Eusebio (Por)	9
1970	Gerd Müller (FRG)	10
1974	Gregorz Lato (Pol)	7
1978	Mario Kempes (Arg)	6
1982	Paolo Rossi (Ita)	6
1986	Gary Lineker (Eng)	6
1990	Salvatore Schillaci (Ita)	6
1994	Hristo Stoichkov (Bul)	6
	Oleg Salenko (Rus)	6
1998	Davor Suker (Cro)	6

Most goals in career

14 Gerd Müller (FRG) 1970-74; 13 Just Fontaine (Fra) 1958; 12 Pele (Bra) 1958-70; 11 Sándor Kocsis (Hun) 1954

Most goals in one game

5	Oleg Salenko (Rus) v Cameroon 1994
4	Leonidas (Bra) v Poland 1938
4	Ernst Willimowski (Pol) v Brazil 1938,
4	Gustav Wetterström (Swe) v Cuba 1938
4	Juan Schiaffino (Uru) v Bolivia 1950
4	Ademir (Bra) v Sweden 1950
4	Sándor Kocsis (Hun) v F R Germany 1954
4	Just Fontaine (Fra) v F R Germany 1958
4	Eusebio (Por) v North Korea 1966
4	Emilio Butragueño (Spa) v Denmark 1986

Golden Ball award

Selected at each World Cup from 1982 by a panel of international journalists.

1982	Paolo Rossi (Ita)
1986	Diego Maradona (Arg)
1990	Toto Schillaci (Ita)
1994	Romario (Bra)

World Cup 1998

The biggest event on the world sporting calendar for 1998 was undoubtedly FRANCE 98, the World Cup of Football. There was unprecedented media coverage, and undoubtedly huge interest around the world, even if not *everybody*, as the football zealots would have one believe, was tuned in!

Thirty-two nations, the largest ever assembly for the Finals Tournament, played in France in June and July. These plus Brazil, the holders, and France, the hosts, had qualified from area qualifying competitions in which 152 nations had taken part: 5 qualified from 36 in the African groups, 3 from 36 in the Asian, with a further place determined on a play-off between the fourth Asian nation and the winner from 10 teams in the Oceanian group, 3 from 12 in the Central & North American, 14 from 49 in the European, and 4 from 9 in the South American.

After the first round group of round-robin matches, the top 16 nations engaged in a knock-out competition, which resulted in the 'dream' final, between the perennial favourites and holders, Brazil, and the host nation, France, in the Stade de France in the northern Parisian suburb of Saint-Denis.

The final was unexpectedly one-sided with France becoming the sixth host nation to win from 16 tournaments. Their victory came against an uncharacteristically lacklustre Brazilian team, whose star player, Ronaldo, was only declared fit to play just prior to the start.

While there were many excellent games, there was less to excite the uncommitted follower of sport than in previous World Cups, no team reaching the heights of, for instance, the majestic Brazilians of the past. The 'golden goal' concept was introduced – whereby if scores were level at the end of full time, the first nation to score in extra time won the match. However the admittedly exciting but, to many, unsatisfactory method of determining the result on a penalty shoot-out led to the exclusion of England, Italy and Holland in the knock-out stages.

Group A

Jun 10	Saint-Denis	**Brazil**	2	**Scotland**	1
		César Sampaio, Boyd (og)		Collins	
Jun 10	Montpellier	**Morocco**	2	**Norway**	2
		Hadji, Hadda		Chippo (og), Eggen	
Jun 16	Bordeaux	**Scotland**	1	**Norway**	1
		Burley		H Flo	

Jun 16	Nantes	**Brazil**	3	**Morocco**	0
		Ronaldo, Rivaldo, Bebeto			
Jun 23	St Etienne	**Morocco**	3	**Scotland**	0
		Bassir 2, Hadda			
Jun 23	Marseilles	**Norway**	2	**Brazil**	1
		T Flo, Rekdal		Bebeto	

1. Brazil 6 pts   2. Norway 5   3. Morocco 4   4. Scotland 1

Group B

Jun 11	Bordeaux	**Chile**	2	**Italy**	2
		Salas (2)		Vieri, R Baggio	
Jun 11	Toulouse	**Austria**	1	**Cameroon**	1
		Polster		Njanka	
Jun 17	St Etienne	**Chile**	1	**Austria**	1
		Salas		Vastic	
Jun 17	Montpellier	**Italy**	3	**Cameroon**	0
		Di Biagio, Vieri 2			
Jun 23	Saint-Denis	**Italy**	2	**Austria**	1
		Vieri, R Baggio		Herzog	
Jun 23	Nantes	**Chile**	1	**Cameroon**	1
		Sierra		Mboma	

1. Italy 7 pts   2. Chile 3   3. Austria 2   4. Cameroon 2

Group C

Jun 12	Lens	**Denmark**	1	**Saudi Arabia**	0
		Rieper			
Jun 12	Marseilles	**France**	3	**South Africa**	0
		Dugarry, Issa (og), Henry			
Jun 18	Toulouse	**South Africa**	1	**Denmark**	1
		McCarthy		Nielsen	
Jun 18	Saint-Denis	**France**	4	**Saudi Arabia**	0
		Henry 2, Trezeguet, Lizarazu			
Jun 24	Lyons	**France**	2	**Denmark**	1
		Djorkaeff, Petit		M Laudrup	
Jun 24	Bordeaux	**South Africa**	2	**Saudi Arabia**	2
		Bartlett 2		Al-Jaber, Al-Thynayan	

1. France 9 pts   2. Denmark 5   3. South Africa 2   4. Saudi Arabia 1

Group D

Jun 12	Montpellier	**Bulgaria**	0	**Paraguay**	0
Jun 13	Nantes	**Nigeria**	3	**Spain**	2
		Adepoju, Zubizaretta (og), Oliseh		Hierro, Raul	
Jun 19	Paris (PP)	**Nigeria**	1	**Bulgaria**	0
		Ikpeba			
Jun 19	St Etienne	**Spain**	0	**Pargauay**	0
Jun 24	Lens	**Spain**	6	**Bulgaria**	1
		Hierro, Luis Enrique,		Kostadinov	
		Morientes 2, Kiko 2			
Jun 24	Toulouse	**Paraguay**	3	**Nigeria**	1
		Ayala, Benitez, Cardozo		Oruma	

1. Nigeria 6 pts   2. Paraguay 5   3. Spain 4   4. Bulgaria 1

Group E

Jun 13	Lyons	**Mexico**	3	**South Korea**	2
		Pelaez, Hernández 2		Ha Seok-ju	
Jun 13	Saint-Denis	**Belgium**	0	**Holland**	0
Jun 20	Bordeaux	**Belgium**	2	**Mexico**	2
		Wilmots 2		García Aspe, Blanco	
Jun 20	Marseilles	**Holland**	5	**South Korea**	0
		Cocu, Overmars, Bergkamp,			
		van Hooijdonk, R de Boer			

Jun 25	Paris (PP)	**Belgium**	1	**South Korea**	1
		Nilis		Yoo Sang-Chul	
Jun 25	St Etienne	**Holland**	2	**Mexico**	2
		Cocu, R de Boer		Pelaez, Hernández	

1. Holland 5 pts   2. Mexico 5   3. Belgium 3   4. South Korea 1

Group F

Jun 14	St Etienne	**Yugoslavia**	1	**Iran**	0
		Mihajlovic			
Jun 15	Paris (PP)	**Germany**	2	**United States**	0
		Möller, Klinsmann			
Jun 21	Lens	**Germany**	2	**Yugoslavia**	2
		Tarnat, Bierhoff		Stankovic, Stojkovic	
Jun 21	Lyons	**Iran**	2	**United States**	1
		Estili, Mahdavikia		McBride	
Jun 25	Montpellier	**Germany**	2	**Iran**	0
		Bierhoff, Klinsmann			
Jun 25	Nantes	**Yugoslavia**	1	**United States**	0
		Komljenovic			

1. Germany 7 pts   2. Yugoslavia 7   3. Iran 3   4. USA 0

Group G

Jun 15	Marseilles	**England**	2	**Tunisia**	0
		Shearer, Scholes			
Jun 15	Lyons	**Romania**	1	**Colombia**	0
		Ilie			
Jun 22	Montpellier	**Colombia**	1	**Tunisia**	0
		Preciado			
Jun 22	Toulouse	**Romania**	2	**England**	1
		Moldovan, Petrescu		Owen	
Jun 26	Saint-Denis	**Romania**	1	**Tunisia**	1
		Moldovan		Souayah	
Jun 26	Lens	**England**	2	**Colombia**	0
		Anderton, Beckham			

1. Romania 7 pts   2. England 6   3. Colombia 3   4. Tunisia 1

Group H

Jun 14	Toulouse	**Argentina**	1	**Japan**	0
		Batistuta			
Jun 14	Lens	**Croatia**	3	**Jamaica**	1
		Stanic, Prosinecki, Suker		Earle	
Jun 20	Nantes	**Croatia**	1	**Japan**	0
		Suker			
Jun 21	Paris (PP)	**Argentina**	5	**Jamaica**	0
		Ortega 2, Batistuta 3			
Jun 26	Lyons	**Jamaica**	2	**Japan**	1
		Whitmore 2		Nakayama	
Jun 26	Bordeaux	**Argentina**	1	**Croatia**	0
		Pineda			

1. Argentina 9 pts   2. Croatia 6   3. Jamaica 3   4. Japan 0

Second Round

Jun 27	Marseilles	**Italy**	1	**Norway**	0
		Vieri			
Jun 27	Paris (PP)	**Brazil**	4	**Chile**	1
		César Sampaio 2, Ronaldo 2		Salas	
Jun 28	Lens	**France**	1*	**Paraguay**	0
		Blanc (G)			
Jun 28	Saint-Denis	**Denmark**	4	**Nigeria**	1
		Moller, B Laudrup, Sand, Helveg		Babangida	
Jun 29	Montpellier	**Germany**	2	**Mexico**	1

		Klinsmann, Bierhoff		Hernández	
Jun 29	Toulouse	**Holland**	2	**Yugoslavia**	1
		Bergkamp, Davids		Komljenovic	
Jun 30	Bordeaux	**Croatia**	1	**Romania**	0
		Suker			
Jun 30	St Etienne	**Argentina**	2★	**England**	2
		Batistuta, Zanetti		Shearer, Owen	
		Argentina won 4-3 on penalties			

Quarter Finals

Jul 3	Saint-Denis	**France**	0★	**Italy**	0
		France won 4-3 on penalties			
Jul 3	Nantes	**Brazil**	3	**Denmark**	2
		Bebeto, Rivaldo 2		Jørgensen, B Laudrup	
Jul 4	Lyons	**Croatia**	3	**Germany**	0
		Jarni, Vlaovic, Suker			
Jul 4	Marseilles	**Holland**	2	**Argentina**	1
		Kluivert, Bergkamp		López	

Semi Finals

Jul 7	Marseilles	**Brazil**	1	**Holland**	1
		Ronaldo		Kluivert	
		Brazil won 4-2 on penalties			
Jul 8	Saint-Denis	**France**	2	**Croatia**	1
		Thuram 2		Suker	

Third Place play-off

Jul 11	Paris (PP)	**Croatia**	2	**Holland**	1
		Prosinecki, Suker		Zenden	

Final

Jul 12	Saint-Denis	**France**	3	**Brazil**	0
		Zidane 2, Petit			

G = golden goal; ★ won by 'golden goal' in extra time; og = own goal.
Paris venues: Stade de France, Saint-Denis; (PP) = Parc des Princes
Overall top goal scorers: 6 Davor Suker (Cro); 5 Christian Vieri (Ita), Gabriel Batistuta (Arg); 4 Marcelo Salas (Chi), Luis Hernández (Mex), Ronaldo (Bra)

Olympic Games

Soccer was unofficially played in the first modern Olympics in 1896. It was included in the Paris Games four years later but some sources still regard it as having been an unofficial competition then, and in 1904 and 1906. It has been an official sport at all Olympics from 1908, except for 1932 in Los Angeles, when it was not staged. Because of the strength of the so-called 'non-professional' Eastern-bloc nations, FIFA ruled that all players who had competed in the 1982 World Cup could not compete in the Los Angeles Olympics two years later. As it transpired, the ban had no effect on the eastern European nations because of their boycott of the Games. A record 126 nations took part in the qualifying tournament for the 1992 Games, when the competition was restricted to players under the age of 23.

Finals

Year	Winner	Runner-up
1900	Upton Park FC (UK) 4	UFSA (Fra) 0
1904	Galt FC, Ontario (Can) 7	Christian Brothers College (USA) 2
1906	Denmark 5	Smyrna (Gre) 2
1908	Great Britain 2	Denmark 0
1912	Great Britain 4	Denmark 2
1920	Belgium 2	Czechoslovakia 0#
1924	Uruguay 3	Switzerland 0
1928	Uruguay 2	Argentina 1
	(replayed after 1-1 draw)	
1936	Italy 2	Austria 1★
1948	Sweden 3	Yugoslavia 1
1952	Hungary 2	Yugoslavia 0

1956	USSR 2	Yugoslavia 0
1960	Yugoslavia 3	Denmark 1
1964	Hungary 2	Czechoslovakia 1
1968	Hungary 4	Bulgaria 1
1972	Poland 2	Hungary 1
1976	GDR 3	Poland 1
1980	Czechoslovakia 1	GDR 0
1984	France 2	Brazil 0
1988	USSR 2	Brazil 1★
1992	Spain 3	Poland 2
1996	Nigeria 3	Argentina 2

★ After extra time.

Czechoslovakia were disqualified after walking off the pitch as a protest against refereeing decisions. Spain were awarded the silver medal.

Leading medal-winning nations
(G – Gold, S – Silver, B – Bronze)

Total		G	S	B	Total		G	S	B	
5	Hungary	3	1	1	3	Poland	1	2	-	**Biggest win:** 17-1 Denmark
5	USSR	2	-	3	3	GDR	1	1	1	v France 'A' 1908
5	Denmark	1	3	1	3	Sweden	1	-	2	**Most goals in an Olympic**
5	Yugoslavia	1	3	1	3	Netherlands	-	-	3	**tournament:** 12 Ferenc Bene
3	Great Britain	3	-	-	3	Brazil	-	2	1	(Hun) 1964

European Championship

Held every four years, the championship is played over a two-year period. Originally called the European Nations Cup, it took its present name in 1968. Competing nations compete for the Henri Delaunay Cup, named after the former General Secretary of the Union of European Football Associations (UEFA).

Finals

Year	Winners		Runners-up		Venue	Attendance
1960	**USSR** Metreveli, Ponedelnik	2	**Yugoslavia** Galic	1★	Paris, France	17,966
1964	**Spain** Pereda, Marcellino	2	**USSR** Khusainov	1	Madrid, Spain	105,000
1968	**Italy** Domenghini	1	**Yugoslavia** Dzajic	1★	Rome, Italy	85,000
Replay	**Italy** Riva, Anastasi	2	**Yugoslavia**	0	Rome, Italy	50,000
1972	**F R Germany** G Müller 2, Wimmer	3	**USSR**	0	Brussels, Belgium	43,437
1976	**Czechoslovakia** Svehlik, Dobiás (Czechoslovakia won 5-4 on penalties)	2	**F R Germany** D Müller, Hölzenbein	2★	Belgrade, Yugoslavia	45,000
1980	**F R Germany** Hrubesch 2	2	**Belgium** Van der Eycken	1	Rome, ITA	47,864
1984	**France** Platini, Bellone	2	**Spain**	0	Paris, FRA	47,000
1988	**Netherlands** Gullit, van Basten	2	**USSR**	0	Munich, GER	72,308
1992	**Denmark** Jensen, Vilfort	2	**Germany**	0	Gothenburg, SWE	37,800
1996	**Germany** Bierhoff 2	2	**Czech Republic** Berger (pen)	1★	Wembley, ENG	76,000

★ After extra time.
Most wins: 3 FRG/Germany
Most finals: 5 FRG/Germany; 4 USSR

European Champion Clubs' Cup

Popularly known as the European Cup, this is an annual knock-out competition for the league champions of all UEFA-affiliated countries. It was first held in 1955/6, shortly after the formation of UEFA, and was the idea of Gabriel Hanot, the soccer editor of the French daily newspaper *L'Equipe*. From the 1991/2 season the competition structure was modified so that the top eight teams take part in the Champions League, with home and away matches between teams in two groups of four, the winners of each group meeting in the final.

Finals

Year	Winners		Runners-up		Venue	Attendance
1956	**Real Madrid**	4	**Stade de Reims**	3	Paris	38,000
	Rial 2, Di Stéfano, Marquitos		Leblond, Templin, Hidalgo			
1957	**Real Madrid**	2	**Fiorentina**	0	Madrid	124,000
	Di Stéfano (pen), Gento					
1958	**Real Madrid**	3	**AC Milan**	2*	Brussels	67,000
	Di Stéfano, Rial, Gento		Schiaffino, Grillo			
1959	**Real Madrid**	2	**Stade de Reims**	0	Stuttgart	80,000
	Mateos, Di Stéfano					
1960	**Real Madrid**	7	**Eintracht Frankfurt**	3	Glasgow	127,621
	Puskas 4, Di Stéfano 3		Stein 2, Kress			
1961	**Benfica**	3	**Barcelona**	2	Berne	27,000
	Aguas, Coluna, Ramallets (og)		Kocsis, Czibor			
1962	**Benfica**	5	**Real Madrid**	3	Amsterdam	65,000
	Eusebio 2 (1 pen), Aguas,		Puskas 3			
	Cavem, Coluna					
1963	**AC Milan**	2	**Benfica**	1	London	45,000
	Altafini 2		Eusebio			
1964	**Internazionale Milan**	3	**Real Madrid**	1	Vienna	72,000
	Mazzola 2, Milani		Felo			
1965	**Internazionale Milan**	1	**Benfica**	0	Milan	80,000
	Jair					
1966	**Real Madrid**	2	**Partizan Belgrade**	1	Brussels	55,000
	Amancio, Serena		Vasovic			
1967	**Glasgow Celtic**	2	**Internazionale Milan**	1	Lisbon	54,000
	Gemmell, Chalmers		Mazzola (pen)			
1968	**Manchester United**	4	**Benfica**	1*	London	100,000
	Charlton 2, Best, Kidd		Graca			
1969	**AC Milan**	4	**Ajax**	1	Madrid	31,000
	Prati 3, Sormani		Vasovic (pen)			
1970	**Feyenoord**	2	**Glasgow Celtic**	1*	Milan	53,000
	Israel, Kindvall		Gemmell			
1971	**Ajax**	2	**Panathinaikos**	0	London	83,000
	van Dijk, Haan					
1972	**Ajax**	2	**Internazionale Milan**	0	Rotterdam	61,000
	Cruyff 2					
1973	**Ajax**	1	**Juventus**	0	Belgrade	89,000
	Rep					
1974	**Bayern München**	1	**Atlético Madrid**	1*	Brussels	65,000
	Schwarzenbeck		Luis			
Replay	**Bayern München**	4	**Atlético Madrid**	0	Brussels	23,000
	Hoeness 2, Müller 2					
1975	**Bayern München**	2	**Leeds United**	0	Paris	48,000
	Roth, Müller					
1976	**Bayern München**	1	**St Etienne**	0	Glasgow	54,864
	Roth					
1977	**Liverpool**	3	**Borussia Mönchengladbach**	1	Rome	52,000
	McDermott, Smith, Neal (pen)		Simonsen			

Year	Winners		Runners-up		Venue	Attendance
1978	**Liverpool** Dalglish	1	**FC Bruges**	0	London	92,000
1979	**Nottingham Forest** Francis	1	**Malmö FF**	0	Munich	57,000
1980	**Nottingham Forest** Robertson	1	**Hamburger SV**	0	Madrid	50,000
1981	**Liverpool** A Kennedy	1	**Real Madrid**	0	Paris	48,360
1982	**Aston Villa** Withe	1	**Bayern München**	0	Rotterdam	46,000
1983	**Hamburger SV** Magath	1	**Juventus**	0	Athens	75,000
1984 .	**Liverpool** Neal (Liverpool won 4-2 on penalties)	1	**AS Roma** Pruzzo	1★	Rome	69,693
1985	**Juventus** Platini (pen)	1	**Liverpool**	0	Brussels	58,000
1986	**Steaua Bucuresti** (Steaua won 2-0 on penalties)	0	**Barcelona**	0★	Seville	70,000
1987	**FC Porto** Madjer, Juary	2	**Bayern München** Kögl	1	Vienna	56,000
1988	**PSV Eindhoven** (Eindhoven won 6-5 on penalties)	0	**Benfica**	0★	Stuttgart	55,000
1989	**AC Milan** Gullit 2, van Basten 2	4	**Steaua Bucuresti**	0	Barcelona	97,000
1990	**AC Milan** Rijkaard	1	**Benfica**	0	Vienna	57,500
1991	**Crvena Zvezda Beograd** (Beograd won 5-3 on penalties)	0	**Marseille**	0★	Bari	50,000
1992	**Barcelona** R Koeman	1	**Sampdoria**	0★	Wembley	70,827
1993	**Marseille** Boli (Marseille subsequently stripped of title)	1	**AC Milan**	0	Munich	64,400
1994	**AC Milan** Massaro 2, Savicevic, Desailly	4	**Barcelona**	0	Athens	75,000
1995	**Ajax** Kluivert	1	**AC Milan**	0	Vienna	49,730
1996	**Juventus** Ravanelli (Juventus won 4-2 on penalties)	1	**Ajax** Litmanen	1	Rome	67,000
1997	**Borussia Dortmund** Riedle 2, Ricken 1	3	**Juventus** Del Piero	1	München	59,000
1998	**Real Madrid** Mijatovic	1	**Juventus**	0	Amsterdam	47,500

★ After extra time.

Biggest win: 12-2 Feyenoord v Reykjavik (1st round) 17 Sep 1969

Biggest win in a final: 7-3 Real Madrid v Eintracht 18 May 1960

Biggest win (aggregate): 18-0 (8-0 & 10-0) Benfica v Stade Dudelange (preliminary round) Sep & Oct 1965

European Cup-Winners' Cup

The Cup-Winners' Cup is open to winners of domestic senior cup competitions in UEFA-affiliated countries. The first final in 1961 was over two legs, but all subsequent finals have been played as a single game.

Finals

Year	Winners		Runners-up		Venue	Attendance
1961	**Fiorentina** Milani 2	2	**Glasgow Rangers**	0	Glasgow	80,000

Year	Winners		Runners-up		Venue	Attendance
1961	**Fiorentina** Milani, Hamrin (Fiorentina won 4-1 on aggregate)	2	**Glasgow Rangers** Scott	1	Florence	50,000
1962	**Atlético Madrid** Peiro	1	**Fiorentina** Hamrin	1	Glasgow	27,289
Replay	**Atlético Madrid** Jones, Mendonca, Peiro	3	**Fiorentina**	0	Stuttgart	38,120
1963	**Tottenham Hotspur** Greaves 2, Dyson 2, White	5	**Atlético Madrid** Collar (pen)	1	Rotterdam	49,143
1964	**Sporting Lisbon** Figueiredo 2, Dansky (og)	3	**MTK Budapest** Sándor 2, Kuti	3*	Brussels	3,208
Replay	**Sporting Lisbon** Morais	1	**MTK Budapest**	0	Antwerp	19,924
1965	**West Ham United** Sealey 2	2	**München 1860**	0	London	97,974
1966	**Borussia Dortmund** Held, Libuda	2	**Liverpool** Hunt	1*	Glasgow	41,657
1967	**Bayern München** Roth	1	**Glasgow Rangers**	0*	Nuremberg	69,480
1968	**AC Milan** Hamrin 2	2	**Hamburger SV**	0	Rotterdam	53,276
1969	**Slovan Bratislava** Cvetler, Hrivnak, Jan Capkovich	3	**Barcelona** Zaldua, Rexach	2	Basel	19,478
1970	**Manchester City** Young, Lee (pen)	2	**Gornik Zabrze** Oslizlo	1	Vienna	7,968
1971	**Chelsea** Osgood	1	**Real Madrid** Zoco	1*	Athens	42,000
Replay	**Chelsea** Dempsey, Osgood	2	**Real Madrid** Fleitas	1	Athens	35,000
1972	**Glasgow Rangers** Johnston 2, Stein	3	**Dynamo Moscow** Yestrekov, Makovikov	2	Barcelona	24,701
1973	**AC Milan** Chiarugi	1	**Leeds United**	0	Thessaloniki	45,000
1974	**FC Magdeburg** Lanzi (og), Seguin	2	**AC Milan**	0	Rotterdam	4,641
1975	**Dynamo Kiev** Onischenko 2, Blokhin	3	**Ferencvaros**	0	Basel	10,897
1976	**Anderlecht** Rensenbrink 2 (1 pen) van der Elst 2	4	**West Ham United** Holland, Robson	2	Brussels	58,000
1977	**Hamburger SV** Volkert (pen), Magath	2	**Anderlecht**	0	Amsterdam	66,000
1978	**Anderlecht** Rensenbrink 2, van Binst 2	4	**FK Austria**	0	Paris	48,679
1979	**Barcelona** Sánchez, Asensi, Rexach, Krankl	4	**Fortuna Düsseldorf** Seel 2, K Allofs	3*	Basel	58,000
1980	**Valencia** (Valencia won 5-4 on penalties)	0	**Arsenal**	0*	Brussels	35,000
1981	**Dynamo Tbilisi** Gutsayev, Daraselia	2	**Carl Zeiss Jena** Hoppe	1	Düsseldorf	9,000
1982	**Barcelona** Simonsen, Quini	2	**Standard Liège** Vandermissen	1	Barcelona	100,000
1983	**Aberdeen** Black, Hewitt	2	**Real Madrid** Juanito (pen)	1*	Gothenburg	17,804
1984	**Juventus** Vignola, Boniek	2	**FC Porto** Sousa	1	Basel	60,000

Year	Winners		Runners-up		Venue	Attendance
1985	**Everton**	3	**SK Rapid Wien**	1	Rotterdam	50,000
	Gray, Steven, Sheedy		Krankl			
1986	**Dynamo Kiev**	3	**Atlético Madrid**	0	Lyon	39,300
	Zavarov, Blokhin, Yevtushenko					
1987	**Ajax Amsterdam**	1	**Lokomotiv Leipzig**	0	Athens	35,000
	van Basten					
1988	**KV Mechelen**	1	**Ajax Amsterdam**	0	Strasbourg	39,446
	den Boer					
1989	**Barcelona**	2	**Sampdoria**	0	Berne	45,000
	Salinas, Recarte					
1990	**Sampdoria**	2	**RSC Anderlecht**	0★	Gothenburg	20,103
	Vialli 2					
1991	**Manchester United**	2	**Barcelona**	1	Rotterdam	45,000
	Hughes 2		R Koeman			
1992	**Werder Bremen**	2	**Monaco**	0	Lisbon	16,000
	Allofs, Rufer					
1993	**Parma**	3	**Antwerp**	1	Wembley	37,393
	Minotti, Melli, Cuoghi		Seveneyns			
1994	**Arsenal**	1	**Parma**	0	Copenhagen	33,765
	Smith					
1995	**Real Zaragoza**	2	**Arsenal**	1★	Paris	42,224
	Esnaider, Nayim		Hartson			
1996	**Paris St Germain**	1	**Rapid Vienna**	0	Brussels	37,500
	N'Gotty					
1997	**Barcelona**	1	**Paris St Germain**	0	Rotterdam	40,000
	Ronaldo					
1998	**Chelsea**	1	**VfB Stuttgart**	0	Stockholm	30,216
	Zola					

★ After extra time.

Biggest win: 16-1 Sporting Lisbon v Apoel Nicosia (1st round) 13 Nov 1963
Biggest win (final): 5-1 Tottenham Hotspur v Atlético Madrid 15 May 1963
Biggest win (aggregate): 21-0 (8-0 & 13-0) Chelsea v Jeunesse Hautcharage (1st round) 15 & 29 Sep 1971

UEFA Cup

Initially intended, when established in 1955, as a tournament for European cities that sponsored international trade fairs, hence the competition's original name – the International Industries Fairs Inter-Cities Cup, commonly known as the Fairs Cup. The first tournament took three years to complete. The second Fairs Cup predominantly involved club sides and from 1960/1 the competition became an annual event. It became known as the European Fairs Cup in 1966 and in 1971 the UEFA Cup. The competition is open to leading sides not eligible for the other two main European competitions. The final was played over two legs on a home and away basis to 1997, changing to a single final in 1998. The matches are shown in the order in which they were played:

Finals

Year	Home team		Away team		Attendance
1958	**London**	2	**Barcelona**	2	45,466
	Greaves, Langley (pen)		Tejada, Martinez		
	Barcelona	6	**London**	0	62,000
	Suárez 2, Evaristo 2, Martinez, Verges				
	(Barcelona won 8-2 on aggregate)				
1960	**Birmingham City**	0	**Barcelona**	0	40,500
	Barcelona	4	**Birmingham City**	1	70,000
	Czibor 2, Martinez, Coll		Hooper		
	(Barcelona won 4-1 on aggregate)				
1961	**Birmingham City**	2	**AS Roma**	2	21,005
	Hellawell, Orritt		Manfredini 2		

Year	Home team		Away team		Attendance
1961	**AS Roma**	2	**Birmingham City**	0	60,000
	Farmer (og), Pestrin				
	(AS Roma won 4-2 on aggregate)				
1962	**Valencia**	6	**Barcelona**	2	65,000
	Guillot 3, Yosu 2, H Nunez		Kocsis 2		
	Barcelona	1	**Valencia**	1	60,000
	Kocsis		Guillot		
	(Valencia won 7-3 on aggregate)				
1963	**Dinamo Zagreb**	1	**Valencia**	2	40,000
	Zambata		Waldo, Urtiaga		
	Valencia	2	**Dinamo Zagreb**	0	55,000
	Mano, Nunez				
	(Valencia won 4-1 on aggregate)				
1964	**Real Zaragoza**	2	**Valencia**	1	50,000
	Villa, Marcelino		Urtiaga		
	(Played over one leg, at Barcelona)				
1965	**Ferencvaros**	1	**Juventus**	0	25,000
	Fenyvesi				
	(Played over one leg, at Turin)				
1966	**Barcelona**	0	**Real Zaragoza**	1	70,000
			Canario		
	Real Zaragoza	2	**Barcelona**	4*	70,000
	Marcelino 2		Pujol 3, Zaballa		
	(Barcelona won 4-3 on aggregate)				
1967	**Dinamo Zagreb**	2	**Leeds United**	0	40,000
	Cercek 2				
	Leeds United	0	**Dinamo Zagreb**	0	35,604
	(Dinamo Zagreb won 2-0 on aggregate)				
1968	**Leeds United**	1	**Ferencvaros**	0	25,368
	Jones				
	Ferencvaros	0	**Leeds United**	0	76,000
	(Leeds United won 1-0 on aggregate)				
1969	**Newcastle United**	3	**Ujpest Dozsa**	0	60,000
	Moncur 2, Scott				
	Ujpest Dozsa	2	**Newcastle United**	3	37,000
	Bene, Gorocs		Moncur, Arentoft, Foggon		
	(Newcastle United won 6-2 on aggregate)				
1970	**RSC Anderlecht**	3	**Arsenal**	1	37,000
	Mulder 2, Devrindt		Kennedy		
	Arsenal	3	**RSC Anderlecht**	0	51,612
	Kelly, Radford, Sammels				
	(Arsenal won 4-3 on aggregate)				
1971	**Juventus**	0	**Leeds United**	0	40,000
	(abandoned after 51 min, waterlogged pitch)				
Replay	**Juventus**	2	**Leeds United**	2	42,000
	Bettega, Capello		Madeley, Bates		
	Leeds United	1	**Juventus**	1	42,483
	Clarke		Anastasi		
	(Leeds United won on the away-goals rule)				
1972	**Wolverhampton W.**	1	**Tottenham Hotspur**	2	38,362
	McCalliog		Chivers 2		
	Tottenham Hotspur	1	**Wolverhampton W**	1	54,303
	Mullery		Wagstaffe		
	(Tottenham Hotspur won 3-2 on aggregate)				
1973	**Liverpool**	0	**Borussia Mönchengladbach**	0	44,967
	(abandoned after 27 min, waterlogged pitch)				

Year	Home team		Away team		Attendance
Replay	**Liverpool**	3	**Borussia Mönchengladbach**	0	41,169
	Keegan 2, Lloyd				
	Borussia Mönchengladbach	2	**Liverpool**	0	35,000
	Heynckes 2				
	(Liverpool won 3-2 on aggregate)				
1974	**Tottenham Hotspur**	2	**Feyenoord**	2	46,281
	England, van Daele (og)		van Hanegem, de Jong		
	Feyenoord	2	**Tottenham Hotspur**	0	59,317
	Rijsbergen, Ressel				
	(Feyenoord won 4-2 on aggregate)				
1975	**Borussia Mönchengladbach**	0	**Twente Enschede**	0	42,368
	Twente Enschede	1	**Borussia Mönchengladbach**	5	21,767
	Drost		Heynckes 3, Simonsen 2 (1 pen)		
	(Borussia Mönchengladbach won 5-1 on aggregate)				
1976	**Liverpool**	3	**FC Bruges**	2	49,981
	Kennedy, Case, Keegan (pen)		Lambert, Cools		
	FC Bruges	1	**Liverpool**	1	32,000
	Lambert (pen)		Keegan		
	(Liverpool won 4-3 on aggregate)				
1977	**Juventus**	1	**Athletic Bilbao**	0	75,000
	Tardelli				
	Athletic Bilbao	2	**Juventus**	1	43,000
	Irureta, Carlos		Bettega		
	(Juventus won on the away-goals rule)				
1978	**SEC Bastia**	0	**PSV Eindhoven**	0	15,000
	PSV Eindhoven	3	**SEC Bastia**	0	27,000
	W van der Kerkhof, Deykers, van der Kuijlen				
	(Eindhoven won 3-0 on aggregate)				
1979	**Crvena Zvezda Beograd**	1	**Borussia Mönchengladbach**	1	87,500
	Sestic		Juristic (og)		
	Borussia Mönchengladbach	1	**Crvena Zvezda Beograd**	0	45,000
	Simonsen (pen)				
	(Borussia Mönchengladbach won 2-1 on aggregate)				
1980	**Borussia Mönchengladbach**	3	**Eintracht Frankfurt**	2	25,000
	Kulik 2, Matthäus		Karger, Holzenbein		
	Eintracht Frankfurt	1	**Borussia Mönchengladbach**	0	60,000
	Schaub				
	(Eintracht won on the away-goals rule)				
1981	**Ipswich Town**	3	**AZ 67 Alkmaar**	0	27,532
	Wark (pen), Thijssen, Mariner				
	AZ 67 Alkmaar	4	**Ipswich Town**	2	28,500
	Welzl, Metgod, Tol, Jonker		Thijssen, Wark		
	(Ipswich Town won 5-4 on aggregate)				
1982	**IFK Göteborg**	1	**Hamburger SV**	0	42,548
	Tord Holmgren				
	Hamburger SV	0	**IFK Göteborg**	3	60,000
	(Göteborg won 4-0 on aggregate)		Corneliusson, Nilsson, Fredriksson (pen)		
1983	**RSC Anderlecht**	1	**Benfica**	0	60,000
	Brylle				
	Benfica	1	**RSC Anderlecht**	1	80,000
	Sheu		Lozano		
	(Anderlecht won 2-1 on aggregate)				
1984	**RSC Anderlecht**	1	**Tottenham Hotspur**	1	40,000
	Olsen		Miller		
	Tottenham Hotspur	1	**RSC Anderlecht**	1*	46,205
	Roberts		Czerniatynski		
	(Tottenham Hotspur won 4-3 on penalties)				

Year	Home team		Away team		Attendance
1985	**Videoton SC**	0	**Real Madrid**	3	30,000
			Michel, Santillana, Juanito		
	Real Madrid	0	**Videoton SC**	1	90,000
			Majer		
	(Real Madrid won 3-1 on aggregate)				
1986	**Real Madrid**	5	**FC Köln**	1	80,000
	Valdano 2, Sánchez, Gordillo, Santillana		K Allofs		
	FC Köln	2	**Real Madrid**	0	15,000
	Bein, Geilenkirchen				
	(Real Madrid won 5-3 on aggregate)				
1987	**IFK Göteborg**	1	**Dundee United**	0	50,023
	Pettersson				
	Dundee United	1	**IFK Göteborg**	1	20,911
	Clark		Nilsson		
	(Göteborg won 2-1 on aggregate)				
1988	**Español**	3	**Bayer Leverkusen**	0	42,000
	Losada 2, Soler				
	Bayer Leverkusen	3	**Español**	0*	22,000
	Tita, Goetz, Cha-Bum Kun				
	(Leverkusen won 3-2 on penalties)				
1989	**Napoli**	2	**Stuttgart**	1	83,000
	Maradona (pen), Careca		Gaudino		
	Stuttgart	3	**Napoli**	3	67,000
	Klinsmann, O Schmaler, Gaudino		Alemao, Ferrara, Careca		
	(Napoli won 5-4 on aggregate)				
1990	**Juventus**	3	**Fiorentina**	1	45,000
	Galia, Casiraghi, De Agostini		Buso		
	Fiorentina	0	**Juventus**	0	32,000
	(Juventus won 3-1 on aggregate)				
1991	**Internazionale Milan**	2	**AS Roma**	0	68,887
	Matthäus (pen), Berti				
	AS Roma	1	**Internazionale Milan**	0	70,901
	Rizzitelli				
	(Inter won 2-1 on aggregate)				
1992	**Torino**	2	**Ajax**	2	65,377
	Casagrande 2		W Jonk, Pettersson		
	Ajax	0	**Torino**	0	40,000
	(Ajax won on away goals)				
1993	**Borussia Dortmund**	1	**Juventus**	3	37,000
	Rummenigge		D Baggio, R Baggio 2		
	Juventus	3	**Borussia Dortmund**	0	70,000
	D Baggio 2, Möller				
	(Juventus won 6-1 on aggregate)				
1994	**Salzburg**	0	**Internazionale Milan**	1	40,000
			Berti		
	Internazionale Milan	1	**Salzburg**	0	80,000
	Jonk				
	(Inter Milan won 2-0 on aggregate)				
1995	**Parma**	1	**Juventus**	0	26,350
	D Baggio				
	Juventus	1	**Parma**	1	80,750
	Vialli		D Baggio		
	(Parma won 2-1 on aggregate)				
1996	**Bayern München**	2	**Bordeaux**	0	62,000
	Helmer, Scholl				
	Bayern München	3	**Bordeaux**	1	36,000
	Scholl, Kostadinov, Klinsmann		Dutuel		

Year	Home team		Away team		Attendance
1997	**Schalke 04**	1	**Internazionale Milan**	0	56,824
	Wilmots				
	Internazionale Milan	1	**Schalke 04**	0★	81,670
	Zamorano				
	(Schalke 04 won 4–1 on penalties)				
1998	**Internazionale**	3	**Lazio**	0	47,000
	Zamorano, Zanetti, Ronaldo				

★ After extra time.

Biggest win: 13–0 Cologne v Union Luxembourg (1st round) 5 Oct 1965
Biggest win (final/aggregate): 8–2 (2–2 & 6–0) Barcelona v London 5 Mar & 1 May 1958
Biggest win (aggregate): 21–0 (9–0 & 12–0) Feyenoord v US Rumelange (1st round) 13 & 27 Sep 1972

Europe's Leading Teams

The following teams have won four or more major European tournaments *(Ch = Champion's Cup, CW = Cup-Winners' Cup, UEFA = Fairs/UEFA Cup):*

Total		Ch	CW	UEFA	Total		Ch	CW	UEFA
9	Real Madrid	7	–	2	6	Ajax	4	1	1
8	Barcelona	1	4	3	6	Juventus	2	1	3
7	AC Milan	5	2	–	5	Bayern München	3	1	1
6	Liverpool	4	–	2	5	Internazionale Milan	2	–	5

European Super Cup

After Ajax won the European Cup for the second successive year in 1972, the Dutch newspaper *De Telegraaf* suggested they play the winners of the Cup-Winners' Cup for a Super Cup. They beat Glasgow Rangers over two legs and became the first winners of this new event, which was not officially recognized by UEFA until 1974. There was no competition in 1981 and 1985. In 1984, 1986 and 1991, the cup was decided on one match.

Year	Winners	Runners-up	Result(s)
1972	Ajax★	Glasgow Rangers	3–1, 3–2
1973	Ajax★	AC Milan	0–1, 6–0
1974#	Bayern München★	FC Magdeburg	3–2, 2–1
1975	Dynamo Kiev	Bayern München★	1–0, 2–0
1976	Anderlecht	Bayern München★	1–2, 4–1
1977	Liverpool★	Hamburger SV	1–1, 6–0
1978	RSC Anderlecht	Liverpool★	3–1, 1–2
1979	Nottingham Forest★	Barcelona	1–0, 1–1
1980	Valencia	Nottingham Forest★	1–2, 1–0
	(Valencia won on the away-goals rule)		
1982	Aston Villa★	Barcelona	0–1, 3–0
1983	Aberdeen	Hamburger SV★	0–0, 2–0
1984	Juventus	Liverpool★	2–0
1986	Steaua Bucuresti★	Dynamo Kiev	1–0
1987	FC Porto★	Ajax	1–0, 1–0
1988	KV Mechelen	PSV Eindhoven★	3–0, 0–1
1989	AC Milan★	Barcelona	1–1, 1–0
1990	AC Milan★	Sampdoria	1–1, 2–0
1991	Manchester United	Crvena Zvezda Beograd★	1–0
1992	Barcelona★	Werder Bremen	1–1, 2–1
1994	Parma	AC Milan★	0–1, 2–0
1995	AC Milan★	Arsenal	0–0, 2–0
1996	Ajax★	Zaragoza	1–1, 4–0
1997	Juventus★	Paris St Germain	6–1, 3–1

★ Indicates European Cup holders.
The two scheduled clubs, Bayern München and Magdeburg, were drawn together in the second round of the 1974/5 European Champions Cup. It was decided that the results of that match would also settle that season's Super Cup.

Copa América

In 1910 an Argentine national side, composed mainly of British exiles, suggested a tournament against Uruguay and Chile. This was the forerunner of the South American Championship, which was inaugurated in 1916, the year of the formation of the South American Football Confederation. Organization has left a lot to be desired over the years and the popularity of the event diminished considerably in the 1960s, particularly after the introduction of the Copa Libertadores (*see* South American Cup), when club soccer began to be regarded in some countries as more important than the international game. The championship was revived in 1975, after a gap of eight years, and is now played as the Copa América, with the ten competing nations split into two groups, and then the top two from each group playing off. Held every four years 1975-87 and now every two years.

Winners:

14	Argentina	1921, 1925, 1927, 1929, 1937, 1941★, 1945★, 1946★, 1947, 1955, 1957, 1959, 1991, 1993
14	Uruguay	1916-7, 1920, 1923-4, 1926, 1935★, 1942, 1956★, 1959★,1967, 1983, 1987, 1995
5	Brazil	1919, 1922, 1949, 1989, 1997
2	Peru	1939, 1975
2	Paraguay	1953, 1979
1	Bolivia	1963

★ Extraordinary tournament.

South American Cup

First contested in 1960 as the South American Champion's Club Cup. Like the European Cup, it was open to national league champions of countries affiliated to the South American Confederation. In 1965 league runners-up were also allowed to enter the competition and, that year, its name was changed to the Copa Libertadores de América.

Winners:

1960-1	Peñarol (Uru)	1979	Olimpia (Par)	1989	Nacional Medellín (Col)
1962-3	Santos (Bra)	1980	Nacional Montevideo (Uru)	1990	Olimpia (Par)
1964-5	Independiente (Arg)	1981	Flamengo (Bra)	1991	Colo Colo (Chl)
1966	Peñarol (Uru)	1982	Peñarol (Uru)	1992-3	São Paulo (Bra)
1967	Racing Club (Arg)	1983	Gremio (Bra)	1994	Vélez Sársfield (Arg)
1968-70	Estudiantes (Arg)	1984	Independiente (Arg)	1995	Gremio (Bra)
1971	Nacional Montevideo (Uru)	1985	Argentinos Juniors (Arg)	1996	River Plate (Arg)
1972-5	Independiente (Arg)	1986	River Plate (Arg)	1997	Cruzeiro (Bra)
1976	Cruzeiro (Bra)	1987	Peñarol (Uru)	**Most wins:** 7 Independiente;
1977-8	Boca Juniors (Arg)	1988	Nacional Montevideo (Uru)	5 Peñarol; 3 Estudiantes, Nacional (Uru)

World Club Championship

The World Club Championship was first held in 1960 as a meeting between the winners of the European Champion Club's Cup and the Copa Libertadores. The two competing teams played each other on a home-and-away basis (with the exception of 1973) but since 1980 the winners have been decided by one match (for the Intercontinental Cup), played in Tokyo. There were no championship matches in 1975 and 1978. During the 1970s many of the matches became very physical, and on five occasions the European Cup holders refused to take part; their places were taken by the runners-up. Prior to 1969, if both sides won a match each, a third match was played to decide the winner.

Year	Winners	Runners-up	Result(s)	Play-off
1960	Real Madrid (Spa)	Peñarol (Uru)	0-0, 5-1	
1961	Peñarol (Uru)	Benfica (Por)	0-1, 5-0	2-1
1962	Santos (Bra)	Benfica (Por)	3-2, 5-2	
1963	Santos (Bra)	AC Milan (Ita)	2-4, 4-2	1-0
1964	Internazionale Milan (Ita)	Independiente (Arg)	0-1, 2-0	1-0
1965	Internazionale Milan (Ita)	Independiente (Arg)	3-0, 0-0	
1966	Peñarol (Uru)	Real Madrid (Spa)	2-0, 2-0	
1967	Racing Club (Arg)	Celtic (Sco)	0-1, 2-1	1-0
1968	Estudiantes (Arg)	Manchester United (Eng)	1-0, 1-1	
1969	AC Milan (Ita)	Estudiantes (Arg)	3-0, 1-2	

1970	Feyenoord (Hol)	Estudiantes (Arg)	2-2, 1-0
1971	Nacional Montevideo (Uru)	Panathinaikos (Gre)	1-1, 2-1
1972	Ajax (Hol)	Independiente (Arg)	1-1, 3-0
1973	Independiente (Arg)	Juventus (Ita)	1-0
1974	Atlético Madrid (Spa)	Independiente (Arg)	0-1, 2-0
1976	Bayern München (FRG)	Cruzeiro (Bra)	2-0, 0-0
1977	Boca Juniors (Arg)	Borussia Mönchengladbach (FRG)	2-2, 3-0
1979	Olimpia (Par)	Malmö (Swe)	1-0, 2-1
1980	Nacional Montevideo (Uru)	Nottingham Forest (Eng)	1-0
1981	Flamengo (Bra)	Liverpool (Eng)	3-0
1982	Peñarol (Uru)	Aston Villa (Eng)	2-0
1983	Gremio (Bra)	Hamburger SV (FRG)	2-1
1984	Independiente (Arg)	Liverpool (Eng)	1-0
1985	Juventus (Ita)	Argentinos Juniors (Arg)	2-2
	(Juventus won 4-2 on penalties)		
1986	River Plate (Arg)	Steaua Bucuresti (Rom)	1-0
1987	FC Porto (Por)	Peñarol (Uru)	2-1
1988	Nacional (Uru)	PSV Eindhoven (Hol)	2-2
	(Nacional won 7-6 on penalties)		
1989	AC Milan (Ita)	Atletico Medellín (Col)	1-0
1990	AC Milan (Ita)	Olimpia Asuncion (Par)	3-0
1991	Crvena Zvezda Beograd (Yug)	Colo Colo (Chl)	3-0
1992	São Paulo (Bra)	Barcelona (Spa)	2-1
1993	São Paulo (Bra)	AC Milan (Ita)	3-2
1994	Vélez Sársfield (Arg)	AC Milan (Ita)	2-0
1995	Ajax (Hol)	Gremio (Bra)	0-0
	(Ajax won 4-3 on penalties)		
1996	Juventus (Ita)	River Plate (Arg)	1-0
1997	Borussia Dortmund (Ger)	Cruzeiro Belo Horizonte (Bra)	2-0

Most wins: 3 Peñarol, Nacional, AC Milan
European wins 15, South American wins 20
No European team has won a match in South America. Real Madrid (1960), Internazionale Milan (1965), Feyenoord (1970), Ajax (1972) and Bayern München (1976) all managed to draw.
Biggest attendance: 150,000 Santos v AC Milan (2nd leg 1963) at Rio de Janeiro

African Nations Cup

First contested in the Sudan in 1957, and now held biennially.
Winners:

4	Egypt	1957, 1959, 1986, 1998
4	Ghana	1963, 1965, 1978, 1982
2	Zaïre	1968, 1974
2	Nigeria	1980, 1994
2	Cameroon	1984, 1988
1	Ethiopia 1962, Sudan 1970, Congo 1972, Morocco 1976, Algeria 1990, Ivory Coast 1992, South Africa 1996	

International Caps

England's Billy Wright was the first player to reach the milestone of making 100 senior international appearances. His 100th match was against Scotland at Wembley on 11 April 1959. Since then, many players have passed the 100 mark. There are variances over the definition of an international match, but a FIFA list showed that Majid Abdullah of Saudi Arabia has made the most appearances with 147 in 1978-94, followed by Thomas Ravelli (Swe) 138 in 1981-97. The most by a British player is 126 Peter Shilton (Eng) 1970-90.

Most Expensive Transfers

World-wide

£22 million	Denilson, São Paulo to Réal Belis August 1997
£18 million	Ronaldo, Barcelona to Internazionale, July 1997
£16.1 million	Rivaldo, Deportivo La Coruña to Barcelona, August 1997
£15 million	Alan Shearer, Blackburn Rovers to Newcastle United, July 1996
£13.2 million	Ronaldo, PSV Eindhoven at Barcelona, July 1996

Other expensive transfers involving British players

£8.5 million	Stan Collymore, Nottingham Forest to Liverpool, June 1995
£7 million	Andy Cole, Newcastle United to Manchester United, Jan 1995
£7 million	Paul Ince, Manchester United to Internazionale Milano, June 1995
£6.5 million	David Platt, Bari to Juventus, May 1992

Individual Goal-Scoring Records for First-Class Matches

Most goals in one game

World record: 16 Stephan Stanis (Racing Club Lens v Aubry-Asturies) 13 Dec 1942

International: 10 Sofus Nielsen (Denmark v France) 1908 Olympics, Gottfried Fuchs (Germany v Russia) 1912 Olympics

British international record: 6 Joe Bambrick (Northern Ireland v Wales) 1 Feb 1930

World Cup: 5 Oleg Salenko (Russia v Cameroon) 28 June 1994

Major European competition: 6 Lothar Emmerich (Borussia Dortmund v Floriana) Cup-Winners' Cup 1st round 13 Oct 1965

FA Cup (proper): 9 Ted MacDougall (Bournemouth v Margate) 1st round 20 Nov 1971

FA Cup (preliminary round): 10 Chris Marron (South Shields v Radcliffe) 20 Sep 1947

Football League Cup: 6 Frankie Bunn (Oldham Athletic v Scarborough) 25 Oct 1989

Football League: 10 Joe Payne (Luton Town v Bristol Rovers) Div 3S 13 Apr 1936

Scottish Cup: 13 John Petrie (Arbroath v Bon Accord) Cup 5 Sep 1885

Scottish League: 8 Jimmy McGrory (Celtic v Dunfermline Athletic) Div 1 14 Jan 1928

Most goals in a career

World record: 1329 Artur Friedenreich (Germania, CA Ipiranga, Americano, CA Paulistano, São Paulo, Flamengo) 1909-35

Full internationals: 97 Pele (Bra) 1957-70

British record: 49 Bobby Charlton (Eng) 1958-70

World Cup: 14 Gerd Müller (FRG) 1970-74

European Cup: 49 Alfredo di Stéfano (Real Madrid) 1955-64

Football League: 434 Arthur Rowley (West Bromwich Albion, Fulham, Leicester, Shrewsbury Town) 1946-65

Scottish League: 410 Jimmy McGrory (Celtic, Clydebank) 1922-38

Hat-tricks (3 goals) in major finals

World Cup: Geoff Hurst (England v F R Germany) 30 Jul 1966

European Championship and European Cup-Winners' Cup: none

European Cup: Ferenc Puskas (4 goals) (Real Madrid v Eintracht) 18 May 1960, Alfredo di Stéfano (Real Madrid v Eintracht) 18 May 1960, Ferenc Puskas (Real Madrid v Benfica) 2 May 1962, Pierino Prati (AC Milan v Ajax) 28 May 1969

UEFA/Fairs Cup: Vicente Guillot (Valencia v Barcelona) 8 Sep 1962, Luis Pujol (Barcelona v Real Zaragoza) 21 Sep 1966, Jupp Heynckes (Borussia Mönchengladbach v Twente Enschede) 21 May 1975

FA Cup: William Townley (Blackburn Rovers v Sheffield Wednesday) 29 Mar 1890, Jimmy Logan (Notts County v Bolton Wanderers) 31 Mar 1894, Stan Mortensen (Blackpool v Bolton Wanderers) 2 May 1953

Football League/Milk/Littlewoods Cup: none

Scottish FA Cup: Jimmy Quinn (Celtic v Rangers) 16 Apr 1904, Dixie Deans (Celtic v Hibernian) 6 May 1972

Scottish League Cup: Davie Duncan (East Fife v Falkirk) 1 Nov 1948, Willie Bauld (Hearts v Motherwell) 23 Oct 1954, John McPhail (Celtic v Rangers) 19 Oct 1957, Jim Forrest (4 g) (Rangers v Morton) 26 Oct 1963, Bobby Lennox (Celtic v Hibernian) 5 Apr 1969, Dixie Deans (Celtic v Hibernian) 26 Oct 1974, Joe Harper (Hibernian v Celtic) 26 Oct 1974, Ally McCoist (Rangers v Celtic) 25 Mar 1984

Most hat-tricks in a career: 92 Pele 1956-77

Most hat-tricks in a career (British): 37 Dixie Dean 1924-39

British (Home) International Championship

The oldest international championship in the world, contested annually from 1883/4 until 1983/4 by the four home countries of England, Scotland, Wales and Northern Ireland (formerly Ireland). Each country played each other once with two points for a win and one for a draw. The title was shared if points were equal until 1979/80 when goal difference was used in case of a tie. Following a decline in interest, this Home International Championship ended after the 1983/4 season. In 1955/6 all four nations shared the title with three points each; the championship was not completed in 1980/1.

Outright wins:

34	England	1888, 1891-3, 1895, 1898-9, 1901, 1904-5, 1909, 1911, 1913, 1930, 1932, 1938, 1947-8, 1950, 1954-5,

24	Scotland	1957, 1961, 1965-6, 1968-9, 1971, 1973, 1975, 1978-9, 1982-3 1884-5, 1887, 1889, 1894, 1896-7, 1900, 1902, 1910, 1921-3, 1925-6, 1929, 1936, 1949, 1951, 1962-3, 1967, 1976-7
7	Wales	1907, 1920, 1924, 1928, 1933-4, 1937
3	N Ireland	1914 (Ireland), 1980, 1984

Football League

The Football League was the brainchild of William McGregor of Aston Villa who called the first meeting of interested clubs to the Anderton's Hotel, Fleet Street, London on 22 March 1888. The first formal meeting took place less than a month later on 17 April at the Royal Hotel, Manchester, when 12 members, all from the Midlands and the north of England, agreed to form the Football League. The first matches were played the following September. A Second Division was formed in 1892 when most members of the old Football Alliance joined the League. A Third Division was added in 1920 and when 20 northern clubs joined the League in 1921 this division was split into two sections, Northern and Southern. The complement of 92 clubs was reached in 1950 and in 1958 the geographically divided Third Divisions were split into Third and Fourth Divisions. In 1991 the number of members rose to 93 before Aldershot and Maidstone left the League in 1992.

First Division champions

Season	Champions	Pts
1888/9	Preston North End	40
1889/90	Preston North End	33
1890/1	Everton	29
1891/2	Sunderland	42
1892/3	Sunderland	48
1893/4	Aston Villa	44
1894/5	Sunderland	47
1895/6	Aston Villa	45
1896/7	Aston Villa	47
1897/8	Sheffield United	42
1898/9	Aston Villa	45
1899/00	Aston Villa	50
1900/1	Liverpool	45
1901/2	Sunderland	44
1902/3	Sheffield Wednesday	42
1903/4	Sheffield Wednesday	47
1904/5	Newcastle United	48
1905/6	Liverpool	51
1906/7	Newcastle United	51
1907/8	Manchester United	52
1908/9	Newcastle United	53
1909/10	Aston Villa	53
1910/1	Manchester United	52
1911/2	Blackburn Rovers	49
1912/3	Sunderland	54
1913/4	Blackburn Rovers	51
1914/5	Everton	46
1919/20	West Bromwich Albion	60
1920/1	Burnley	59
1921/2	Liverpool	57
1922/3	Liverpool	60
1923/4	Huddersfield Town	57
1924/5	Huddersfield Town	58
1925/6	Huddersfield Town	57
1926/7	Newcastle United	56
1927/8	Everton	53
1928/9	Sheffield Wednesday	52
1929/30	Sheffield Wednesday	60
1930/1	Arsenal	66
1931/2	Everton	56
1932/3	Arsenal	58
1933/4	Arsenal	59
1934/5	Arsenal	58
1935/6	Sunderland	56
1936/7	Manchester City	57
1937/8	Arsenal	52
1938/9	Everton	59
1946/7	Liverpool	57
1947/8	Arsenal	59
1948/9	Portsmouth	58
1949/50	Portsmouth	56
1950/1	Tottenham Hotspur	60
1951/2	Manchester United	57
1952/3	Arsenal	54
1953/4	Wolverhampton Wanderers	57
1954/5	Chelsea	52
1955/6	Manchester United	60
1956/7	Manchester United	64
1957/8	Wolverhampton Wanderers	64
1958/9	Wolverhampton Wanderers	61
1959/60	Burnley	55
1960/1	Tottenham Hotspur	66
1961/2	Ipswich Town	56
1962/3	Everton	61
1963/4	Liverpool	57
1964/5	Manchester United	61
1965/6	Liverpool	61
1966/7	Manchester United	60
1967/8	Manchester City	58
1968/9	Leeds United	67
1969/70	Everton	66
1970/1	Arsenal	65
1971/2	Derby County	58
1972/3	Liverpool	60
1973/4	Leeds United	62
1974/5	Derby County	53
1975/6	Liverpool	60
1976/7	Liverpool	57
1977/8	Nottingham Forest	64
1978/9	Liverpool	68
1979/80	Liverpool	60

1980/1	Aston Villa	60
1981/2	Liverpool	87
1982/3	Liverpool	82
1983/4	Liverpool	80
1984/5	Everton	90
1985/6	Liverpool	88
1986/7	Everton	86
1987/8	Liverpool	90
1988/9	Arsenal	76
1989/90	Liverpool	79
1990/1	Arsenal	83
1991/2	Leeds United	82

Maximum points available: 44 1888/9 to 1890/1, 52 1891/2, 60 1892/3 to 1897/8, 68 1898/9 to 1904/5, 76 1905/6 to 1914/5, 84 1919/20 to 1980/1, 126 1981/2 to 1986/7, 120 1987/8, 114 1988/9 to 1990/1, 126 1991/2

FA Premier League

The top 22 clubs from the Football League Division One formed the FA Premier League from 1992/3, with the Football League of three divisions succeeding the previous Divisions 2-4. From 1995/6 the Premier League was reduced to 20 clubs.
Winners:

1992/3	Manchester United	84
1993/4	Manchester United	92
1994/5	Blackburn Rovers	89
1995/6	Manchester United	82
1996/7	Manchester United	75
1997/8	Arsenal	78

Most League titles

Div 1/Premier: 18 Liverpool; 11 Manchester United (inc 4 Premier), Arsenal (inc 1 Premier); 9 Everton; 7 Aston Villa
Division 2: 6 Leicester City, Manchester City

Champions of most divisions

Wolverhampton Wanderers have uniquely been champions of Divisions 1, 2, 3, 4 and 3N (one win at each of the last three). Burnley have been champions of Divisions 1, 2, 3 and 4.

Clubs that have been champions of Divisions 1, 2 and 3 (including 3N or 3S)

Aston Villa, Blackburn R, Wolverhampton W, Preston North End, Derby County, Ipswich Town, Nottingham Forest, Sunderland
  Grimsby Town have been champions of Divisions 2, 3, 4 and 3N
  Huddersfield Town and Sheffield United have also been champions of Divisions 1 and 4

Highest scores

13-0	Stockport County v Halifax Town 6 Jan 1934 Div 3N
13-0	Newcastle United v Newport County 5 Oct 1946 Div 2
13-4	Tranmere Rovers v Oldham Athletic 26 Dec 1935 Div 3N
12-0	West Bromwich Albion v Darwen 4 Apr 1892 Div 1
12-0	Small Heath (later Birmingham City) v Walsall Town Swifts 17 Dec 1892 Div 2
12-0	Darwen v Walsall 26 Dec 1896 Div 2
12-0	Arsenal v Loughborough Town 12 Mar 1900 Div 2
12-0	Small Heath (later Birmingham City) v Doncaster Rovers 11 Apr 1903 Div 2
12-0	Nottingham Forest v Leicester Fosse 21 Apr 1909 Div 1
12-0	Chester v York City 1 Feb 1936 Div 3N
12-0	Luton Town v Bristol Rovers 13 Apr 1936 Div 3S
11-0	Oldham Athletic v Southport 26 Dec 1962 Div 4
10-0	Gillingham v Chesterfield 5 Sep 1987 Div 3

Most individual goals in a game

10	Joe Payne, Luton Town v Bristol Rovers 13 Apr 1936 Div 3S
9	Robert Bell, Tranmere Rovers v Oldham Athletic 26 Dec 1935 Div 3N
7	Arthur Whitehurst, Bradford City v Tranmere Rovers 6 Mar 1929 Div 3N
7	Ted Drake, Arsenal v Aston Villa 14 Dec 1935 Div 1
7	Ted Harston, Mansfield Town v Hartlepool United 23 Jan 1937 Div 3N
7	Eric Gemmell, Oldham Athletic v Chester 19 Jan 1952 Div 3N
7	Tommy Briggs, Blackburn Rovers v Bristol Rovers 5 Feb 1955 Div 2
7	Neville Coleman, Stoke City v Lincoln City 23 Feb 1957 Div 2

Most individual goals in a season

Div 1	60 Dixie Dean, Everton 1927-8
Div 2	59 George Camsell, Middlesbrough 1926-7
Div 3S	55 Joe Payne, Luton Town 1936-7
Div 3N	55 Ted Harston, Mansfield Town 1936-7
Div 4	52 Terry Bly, Peterborough United 1960-1

FA Cup

The idea for the Football Association Challenge Cup came from the secretary of the Football Association Charles Alcock, who put forward his plans at a meeting attended by 12 clubs on 18 October 1871. The following 15 teams entered the first competition: Wanderers, Harrow Chequers, Clapham Rovers, Upton Park, Crystal Palace, Hitchin, Maidenhead, Great Marlow, Barnes, Civil Service, Royal Engineers, Reigate Priory, Donington School, Hampstead Heathens, Queen's Park (Glasgow). Contested annually on a knock-out basis. Sponsored by Littlewoods Pools from 1994/5 to 1997/8.

The original trophy was made in 1872 by Messrs Martin, Hall & Co at a cost of about £20. This Cup was stolen in 1895 from a football outfitter's shop in Birmingham, where it was being displayed after Aston Villa's victory, and never recovered. A second trophy, an exact replica of the original, was then used until 1910, when it was presented to Lord Kinnaird in recognition of his 21 years as president of the FA. The present trophy was made (for 50 guineas) in 1911 by Fattorini and Sons of Bradford, Yorkshire. It is made of silver, standing on a base of ebony.

Year	Winners		Runners-up		Venue	Attendance
1872	**Wanderers** Betts	1	**Royal Engineers**	0	Kennington Oval	2,000
1873	**Wanderers** Kinnaird, Wollaston	2	**Oxford University**	0	Lillie Bridge	3,000
1874	**Oxford University** Mackarness, Patton	2	**Royal Engineers**	0	Kennington Oval	2,000
1875	**Royal Engineers** Renny-Tailyour	1	**Old Etonians** Bonsor	1★	Kennington Oval	3,000
Replay	**Royal Engineers** Renny-Tailyour, Stafford	2	**Old Etonians**	0	Kennington Oval	3,000
1876	**Wanderers** Edwards	1	**Old Etonians** Bonsor	1	Kennington Oval	3,000
Replay	**Wanderers** Hughes 2, Wollaston	3	**Old Etonians**	0	Kennington Oval	3,500
1877	**Wanderers** Lindsay, Kenrick	2	**Oxford University** Kinnaird (og)	1★	Kennington Oval	3,000
1878	**Wanderers** Kenrick 2, Kinnaird	3	**Royal Engineers** unknown	1	Kennington Oval	4,500
1879	**Old Etonians** Clerke	1	**Clapham Rovers**	0	Kennington Oval	5,000
1880	**Clapham Rovers** Lloyd-Jones	1	**Oxford University**	0	Kennington Oval	6,000
1881	**Old Carthusians** Wyngard, Parry, Todd	3	**Old Etonians**	0	Kennington Oval	4,500
1882	**Old Etonians** Macauley	1	**Blackburn Rovers**	0	Kennington Oval	6,500
1883	**Blackburn Olympic** Matthews, Crossley	2	**Old Etonians** Goodhart	1★	Kennington Oval	8,000
1884	**Blackburn Rovers** Sowerbutts, Forrest	2	**Queen's Park** Christie	1	Kennington Oval	4,000
1885	**Blackburn Rovers** Forrest, Brown	2	**Queen's Park**	0	Kennington Oval	12,500
1886	**Blackburn Rovers**	0	**West Bromwich Albion**	0	Kennington Oval	15,000
Replay	**Blackburn Rovers** Brown, Sowerbutts	2	**West Bromwich Albion**	0	Derby (Racecourse Ground)	12,000
1887	**Aston Villa** Hunter, Hodgetts	2	**West Bromwich Albion**	0	Kennington Oval	15,500
1888	**West Bromwich Albion** Woodhall, Bayliss	2	**Preston North End** Dewhurst	1	Kennington Oval	19,000
1889	**Preston North End** Dewhurst, Ross, Thomson	3	**Wolverhampton W**	0	Kennington Oval	22,000
1890	**Blackburn Rovers** Townley 3, Walton John Southworth, Lofthouse	6	**Sheffield Wednesday** Bennett	1	Kennington Oval	20,000

Year	Winners		Runners-up		Venue	Attendance
1891	**Blackburn Rovers**	3	**Notts County**	1	Kennington Oval	23,000
	Southworth, Dewar, Townley		Oswald			
1892	**West Bromwich Albion**	3	**Aston Villa**	0	Kennington Oval	32,810
	Nicholls, Geddes, Reynolds					
1893	**Wolverhampton W**	1	**Everton**	0	Fallowfield	45,000
	Allen					
1894	**Notts County**	4	**Bolton Wanderers**	1	Everton	37,000
	Logan 3, Watson		Cassidy			
1895	**Aston Villa**	1	**West Bromwich Albion**	0	Crystal Palace	42,560
	Devey					
1896	**Sheffield Wednesday**	2	**Wolverhampton W**	1	Crystal Palace	48,836
	Spiksley 2		Black			
1897	**Aston Villa**	3	**Everton**	2	Crystal Palace	65,891
	Devey, Campbell, Crabtree		Bell, Hartley			
1898	**Nottingham Forest**	3	**Derby County**	1	Crystal Palace	62,017
	Capes 2, McPherson		Bloomer			
1899	**Sheffield United**	4	**Derby County**	1	Crystal Palace	73,833
	Bennett, Priest, Beers, Almond		Boag			
1900	**Bury**	4	**Southampton**	0	Crystal Palace	68,945
	McLuckie 2, Wood, Plant					
1901	**Tottenham Hotspur**	2	**Sheffield United**	2	Crystal Palace	110,820
	Brown 2		Bennett, Priest			
Replay	**Tottenham Hotspur**	3	**Sheffield United**	1	Bolton	20,470
	Cameron, Smith, Brown		Priest			
1902	**Sheffield United**	1	**Southampton**	1	Crystal Palace	76,914
	Common		Wood			
Replay	**Sheffield United**	2	**Southampton**	1	Crystal Palace	33,068
	Hedley, Barnes		Brown			
1903	**Bury**	6	**Derby County**	0	Crystal Palace	63,102
	Leeming 2, Ross, Sagar, Plant, Wood					
1904	**Manchester City**	1	**Bolton Wanderers**	0	Crystal Palace	61,374
	Meredith					
1905	**Aston Villa**	2	**Newcastle United**	0	Crystal Palace	101,117
	Hampton 2					
1906	**Everton**	1	**Newcastle United**	0	Crystal Palace	75,609
	Young					
1907	**Sheffield Wednesday**	2	**Everton**	1	Crystal Palace	84,584
	Stewart, Simpson		Sharp			
1908	**Wolverhampton W**	3	**Newcastle United**	1	Crystal Palace	74,967
	Hunt, Hedley, Harrison		Howie			
1909	**Manchester United**	1	**Bristol City**	0	Crystal Palace	71,401
	A Turnbull					
1910	**Newcastle United**	1	**Barnsley**	1	Crystal Palace	77,747
	Rutherford		Tufnell			
Replay	**Newcastle United**	2	**Barnsley**	0	Everton	69,000
	Shepherd 2 (1 pen)					
1911	**Bradford City**	0	**Newcastle United**	0	Crystal Palace	69,098
Replay	**Bradford City**	1	**Newcastle United**	0	Old Trafford	58,000
	Spiers					
1912	**Barnsley**	0	**West Bromwich Albion**	0	Crystal Palace	54,556
Replay	**Barnsley**	1	**West Bromwich Albion**	0★	Bramall Lane	38,555
	Tufnell					
1913	**Aston Villa**	1	**Sunderland**	0	Crystal Palace	120,081
	Barber					
1914	**Burnley**	1	**Liverpool**	0	Crystal Palace	72,778
	Freeman					

Year	Winners		Runners-up		Venue	Attendance
1915	**Sheffield United**	3	**Chelsea**	0	Old Trafford	49,557
	Simmons, Kitchen, Fazackerley					
1920	**Aston Villa**	1	**Huddersfield Town**	0*	Stamford Bridge	50,018
	Kirton					
1921	**Tottenham Hotspur**	1	**Wolverhampton W**	0	Stamford Bridge	72,805
	Dimmock					
1922	**Huddersfield Town**	1	**Preston North End**	0	Stamford Bridge	53,000
	Smith (pen)					
1923	**Bolton Wanderers**	2	**West Ham United**	0	Wembley	126,047
	Jack, J R Smith					
1924	**Newcastle United**	2	**Aston Villa**	0	Wembley	91,695
	Harris, Seymour					
1925	**Sheffield United**	1	**Cardiff City**	0	Wembley	91,763
	Tunstall					
1926	**Bolton Wanderers**	1	**Manchester City**	0	Wembley	91,447
	Jack					
1927	**Cardiff City**	1	**Arsenal**	0	Wembley	91,206
	Ferguson					
1928	**Blackburn Rovers**	3	**Huddersfield Town**	1	Wembley	92,041
	Roscamp 2, McLean		Jackson			
1929	**Bolton Wanderers**	2	**Portsmouth**	0	Wembley	92,576
	Butler, Blackmore					
1930	**Arsenal**	2	**Huddersfield Town**	0	Wembley	92,488
	James, Lambert					
1931	**West Bromwich Albion**	2	**Birmingham**	1	Wembley	92,406
	W G Richardson 2		Bradford			
1932	**Newcastle United**	2	**Arsenal**	1	Wembley	92,298
	Allen 2		John			
1933	**Everton**	3	**Manchester City**	0	Wembley	92,950
	Stein, Dean, Dunn					
1934	**Manchester City**	2	**Portsmouth**	1	Wembley	93,258
	Tilson 2		Rutherford			
1935	**Sheffield Wednesday**	4	**West Bromwich Albion**	2	Wembley	93,204
	Rimmer 2, Hooper, Palethorpe		Boyes, Sandford			
1936	**Arsenal**	1	**Sheffield United**	0	Wembley	93,384
	Drake					
1937	**Sunderland**	3	**Preston North End**	1	Wembley	93,495
	Gurney, Carter, Burbanks		F O'Donnell			
1938	**Preston North End**	1	**Huddersfield Town**	0*	Wembley	93,497
	Mutch (pen)					
1939	**Portsmouth**	4	**Wolverhampton W**	1	Wembley	99,370
	Parker 2, Barlow, Anderson		Dorsett			
1946	**Derby County**	4	**Charlton Athletic**	1*	Wembley	98,215
	Stamps 2, Doherty, H Turner (og)		H Turner			
1947	**Charlton Athletic**	1	**Burnley**	0*	Wembley	99,000
	Duffy					
1948	**Manchester United**	4	**Blackpool**	2	Wembley	99,000
	Rowley 2, Pearson, Anderson		Shimwell (pen), Mortensen			
1949	**Wolverhampton W**	3	**Leicester City**	1	Wembley	99,500
	Pye 2, Smyth		Griffiths			
1950	**Arsenal**	2	**Liverpool**	0	Wembley	100,000
	Lewis 2					
1951	**Newcastle United**	2	**Blackpool**	0	Wembley	100,000
	Milburn 2					
1952	**Newcastle United**	1	**Arsenal**	0	Wembley	100,000
	G Robledo					

Year	Winners		Runners-up		Venue	Attendance
1953	**Blackpool** Mortensen 3, Perry	4	**Bolton Wanderers** Lofthouse, Moir, Bell	3	Wembley	100,000
1954	**West Bromwich Albion** Allen 2 (1 pen), Griffin	3	**Preston North End** Morrison, Wayman	2	Wembley	100,000
1955	**Newcastle United** Milburn, Mitchell, Hannah	3	**Manchester City** Johnstone	1	Wembley	100,000
1956	**Manchester City** Hayes, Dyson, Johnstone	3	**Birmingham City** Kinsey	1	Wembley	100,000
1957	**Aston Villa** McParland 2	2	**Manchester United** Taylor	1	Wembley	100,000
1958	**Bolton Wanderers** Lofthouse 2	2	**Manchester United**	0	Wembley	100,000
1959	**Nottingham Forest** Dwight, Wilson	2	**Luton Town** Pacey	1	Wembley	100,000
1960	**Wolverhampton W** McGrath (og), Deeley 2	3	**Blackburn Rovers**	0	Wembley	100,000
1961	**Tottenham Hotspur** Smith, Dyson	2	**Leicester City**	0	Wembley	100,000
1962	**Tottenham Hotspur** Greaves, Smith, Blanchflower (pen)	3	**Burnley** Robson	1	Wembley	100,000
1963	**Manchester United** Herd 2, Law	3	**Leicester City** Keyworth	1	Wembley	100,000
1964	**West Ham United** Sissons, Hurst, Boyce	3	**Preston North End** Holden, Dawson	2	Wembley	100,000
1965	**Liverpool** Hunt, St John	2	**Leeds United** Bremner	1*	Wembley	100,000
1966	**Everton** Trebilcock 2, Temple	3	**Sheffield Wednesday** McCalliog, Ford	2	Wembley	100,000
1967	**Tottenham Hotspur** Robertson, Saul	2	**Chelsea** Tambling	1	Wembley	100,000
1968	**West Bromwich Albion** Astle	1	**Everton**	0*	Wembley	100,000
1969	**Manchester City** Young	1	**Leicester City**	0	Wembley	100,000
1970	**Chelsea** Houseman, Hutchinson	2	**Leeds United** Charlton, Jones	2*	Wembley	100,000
Replay	**Chelsea** Osgood, Webb	2	**Leeds United** Jones	1*	Old Trafford	62,078
1971	**Arsenal** Kelly, George	2	**Liverpool** Heighway	1*	Wembley	100,000
1972	**Leeds United** Clarke	1	**Arsenal**	0	Wembley	100,000
1973	**Sunderland** Porterfield	1	**Leeds United**	0	Wembley	100,000
1974	**Liverpool** Keegan 2, Heighway	3	**Newcastle United**	0	Wembley	100,000
1975	**West Ham United** A Taylor 2	2	**Fulham**	0	Wembley	100,000
1976	**Southampton** Stokes	1	**Manchester United**	0	Wembley	100,000
1977	**Manchester United** Pearson, J Greenhoff	2	**Liverpool** Case	1	Wembley	100,000
1978	**Ipswich Town** Osborne	1	**Arsenal**	0	Wembley	100,000

Year	Winners		Runners-up		Venue	Attendance
1979	**Arsenal**	3	**Manchester United**	2	Wembley	100,000
	Talbot, Stapleton, Sunderland		McQueen, McIlroy			
1980	**West Ham United**	1	**Arsenal**	0	Wembley	100,000
	Brooking					
1981	**Tottenham Hotspur**	1	**Manchester City**	1*	Wembley	100,000
	Hutchison (og)		Hutchison			
Replay	**Tottenham Hotspur**	3	**Manchester City**	2	Wembley	92,000
	Villa 2, Crooks		Mackenzie, Reeves (pen)			
1982	**Tottenham Hotspur**	1	**Queen's Park Rangers**	1*	Wembley	100,000
	Hoddle		Fenwick			
Replay	**Tottenham Hotspur**	1	**Queen's Park Rangers**	0	Wembley	90,000
	Hoddle (pen)					
1983	**Manchester United**	2	**Brighton & Hove Albion**	2*	Wembley	100,000
	Stapleton, Wilkins		Smith, Stevens			
Replay	**Manchester United**	4	**Brighton & Hove Albion**	0	Wembley	92,000
	Robson 2, Whiteside, Muhren (pen)					
1984	**Everton**	2	**Watford**	0	Wembley	100,000
	Sharp, Gray					
1985	**Manchester United**	1	**Everton**	0*	Wembley	100,000
	Whiteside					
1986	**Liverpool**	3	**Everton**	1	Wembley	98,000
	Rush 2, Johnston		Lineker			
1987	**Coventry City**	3	**Tottenham Hotspur**	2*	Wembley	98,000
	Bennett, Houchen, Mabbutt (og)		C Allen, Mabbutt			
1988	**Wimbledon**	1	**Liverpool**	0	Wembley	98,203
	Sanchez					
1989	**Liverpool**	3	**Everton**	2*	Wembley	82,800
	Rush 2, Aldridge		McCall 2			
1990	**Manchester United**	3	**Crystal Palace**	3*	Wembley	80,000
	Hughes 2, Pemberton (og)		I Wright 2, O'Reilly			
Replay	**Manchester United**	1	**Crystal Palace**	0	Wembley	80,000
	Martin					
1991	**Tottenham Hotspur**	2	**Nottingham Forest**	1*	Wembley	80,000
	Stewart, Walker (og)		Pearce			
1992	**Liverpool**	2	**Sunderland**	0	Wembley	79,544
	Thomas, I Rush					
1993	**Arsenal**	1	**Sheffield Wednesday**	1*	Wembley	79,347
	Wright		Hirst			
Replay	**Arsenal**	2	**Sheffield Wednesday**	1*	Wembley	62,267
	Wright, Linighan		Waddle			
1994	**Manchester United**	4	**Chelsea**	0	Wembley	79,634
	Cantona (2 pen), Hughes, McClair					
1995	**Everton**	1	**Manchester United**	0	Wembley	79,592
	Rideout					
1996	**Manchester United**	1	**Liverpool**	0	Wembley	79,007
	Cantona					
1997	**Chelsea**	2	**Middlesbrough**	0	Wembley	79,160
	Di Matteo, Newton					
1998	**Arsenal**	2	**Newcastle United**	0	Wembley	79,183
	Overmars, Anelka					

* After extra time.

Most wins: 9 Manchester United, 8 Tottenham Hotspur, 7 Aston Villa, Arsenal; 6 Blackburn Rovers, Newcastle United

Most winners' medals: 5 James Forrest (Blackburn Rovers) 1884-86, 1890-1, Hon. Arthur Kinnaird (Wanderers) 1873, 1877-8 (Old Etonians) 1879, 1882, Charles Wollaston (Wanderers) 1872-3, 1876-8

Biggest win: 26-0 Preston North End v Hyde United (1st round) 15 Oct 1887

Biggest win (final): 6-0 Bury v Derby County 18 Apr 1903

Second Division finalists

The following clubs from the 2nd division (formed 1892/3) of the Football League have reached the FA Cup final:

1894	Notts County*
1904	Bolton Wanderers
1908	Wolverhampton Wanderers*
1910	Barnsley
1912	Barnsley*
1920	Huddersfield Town
1921	Wolverhampton Wanderers
1923	West Ham United
1931	West Bromwich Albion*
1936	Sheffield United
1947	Burnley
1949	Leicester City
1964	Preston North End
1973	Sunderland*
1975	Fulham
1976	Southampton*
1980	West Ham United*
1982	Queen's Park Rangers
1992	Sunderland

* Winners.

No club from the 3rd or 4th divisions has reached the FA Cup final; however, since the formation of the League, non-league clubs Southampton 1900 and 1902, and Tottenham Hotspur 1901* have achieved this.

English League Cup

Instituted as the Football League Cup in 1960/1, it was not until the 1969/70 season that all 92 Football League teams took part. All finals up to 1966 were played on a two-leg basis, but since then they have been played at Wembley Stadium. With sponsorship from the Milk Marketing Board in 1982 the Cup's name was changed to the Milk Cup, from 1986 to 1990 it was the Littlewoods Cup, in 1991-2 the Rumbelows Cup, from 1993-8 the Coca-Cola Cup and, with new sponsorship from Bass, it is to be the Worthington's Cup from 1998/9.

Year	Winners		Runners-up		Venue	Attendance
1961	**Rotherham United** Webster, Kirkman	2	**Aston Villa**	0		12,226
	Aston Villa O'Neill, Burrows, McParland (Aston Villa won 3-2 on aggregate)	3	**Rotherham United**	0*		31,202
1962	**Rochdale**	0	**Norwich City** Lythgoe 2, Punton	3		11,123
	Norwich City Hill (Norwich City won 4-0 on aggregate)	1	**Rochdale**	0		19,708
1963	**Birmingham City** Leek 2, Bloomfield	3	**Aston Villa** Thomson	1		31,850
	Aston Villa (Birmingham City won 3-1 on aggregate)	0	**Birmingham City**	0		37,920
1964	**Stoke City** Bebbington	1	**Leicester City** Gibson	1		22,309
	Leicester City Stringfellow, Gibson, Riley (Leicester City won 4-3 on aggregate)	3	**Stoke City** Viollet, Kinnell	2		25,372
1965	**Chelsea** Tambling, McCreadie, Venables (pen)	3	**Leicester City** Appleton, Goodfellow	2		20,690
	Leicester City (Chelsea won 3-2 on aggregate)	0	**Chelsea**	0		26,958
1966	**West Ham United** Moore, Byrne	2	**West Bromwich Albion** Astle	1		28,341
	West Bromwich Albion Kaye, Brown, Clark, Williams (West Bromwich Albion won 5-3 on aggregate)	4	**West Ham United** Peters	1		31,925
1967	**Queen's Park Rangers** R Morgan, Marsh, Lazarus	3	**West Bromwich Albion** Clark 2	2	Wembley	97,952
1968	**Leeds United** Cooper	1	**Arsenal**	0	Wembley	97,887
1969	**Swindon Town** Rogers 2, Smart	3	**Arsenal** Gould	1	Wembley	98,189

Year	Winners		Runners-up		Venue	Attendance
1970	**Manchester City**	2	**West Bromwich Albion**	1	Wembley	97,963
	Doyle, Pardoe		Astle			
1971	**Tottenham Hotspur**	2	**Aston Villa**	0	Wembley	100,000
	Chivers 2					
1972	**Stoke City**	2	**Chelsea**	1	Wembley	100,000
	Conroy, Eastham		Osgood			
1973	**Tottenham Hotspur**	1	**Norwich City**	0	Wembley	100,000
	Coates					
1974	**Wolverhampton W**	2	**Manchester City**	1	Wembley	100,000
	Hibbitt, Richards		Bell			
1975	**Aston Villa**	1	**Norwich City**	0	Wembley	100,000
	Graydon					
1976	**Manchester City**	2	**Newcastle United**	1	Wembley	100,000
	Barnes, Tueart		Gowling			
1977	**Aston Villa**	0	**Everton**	0	Wembley	100,000
Replay	**Aston Villa**	1	**Everton**	1*	Hillsborough	55,000
	Kenyon (og)		Latchford			
Replay	**Aston Villa**	3	**Everton**	2*	Old Trafford	54,749
	Little 2, Nicholl		Latchford, Lyons			
1978	**Nottingham Forest**	0	**Liverpool**	0*	Wembley	100,000
Replay	**Nottingham Forest**	1	**Liverpool**	0	Old Trafford	54,375
	Robertson (pen)					
1979	**Nottingham Forest**	3	**Southampton**	2	Wembley	100,000
	Birtles 2, Woodcock		Peach, Holmes			
1980	**Wolverhampton W**	1	**Nottingham Forest**	0	Wembley	100,000
	Gray					
1981	**Liverpool**	1	**West Ham United**	1*	Wembley	100,000
	A Kennedy		Stewart (pen)			
Replay	**Liverpool**	2	**West Ham United**	1	Villa Park	36,693
	Dalglish, Hansen		Goddard			
1982	**Liverpool**	3	**Tottenham Hotspur**	1*	Wembley	100,000
	Whelan 2, Rush		Archibald			
1983	**Liverpool**	2	**Manchester United**	1*	Wembley	100,000
	Kennedy, Whelan		Whiteside			
1984	**Liverpool**	0	**Everton**	0*	Wembley	100,000
Replay	**Liverpool**	1	**Everton**	0	Maine Road	52,089
	Souness					
1985	**Norwich City**	1	**Sunderland**	0	Wembley	100,000
	Chisholm (og)					
1986	**Oxford United**	3	**Queen's Park Rangers**	0	Wembley	90,396
	Hebberd, Houghton, Charles					
1987	**Arsenal**	2	**Liverpool**	1	Wembley	96,000
	Nicholas 2		Rush			
1988	**Luton Town**	3	**Arsenal**	2	Wembley	95,732
	B Stein 2, Wilson		Hayes, Smith			
1989	**Nottingham Forest**	3	**Luton Town**	1	Wembley	76,130
	Clough 2 (1 pen), Webb		Harford			
1990	**Nottingham Forest**	1	**Oldham**	0	Wembley	74,343
	Jemson					
1991	**Sheffield Wednesday**	1	**Manchester United**	0	Wembley	80,000
	Sheridan					
1992	**Manchester United**	1	**Nottingham Forest**	0	Wembley	76,810
	McClair					
1993	**Arsenal**	2	**Sheffield Wednesday**	1	Wembley	74,007
	Merson, Morrow		Harkes			
1994	**Aston Villa**	3	**Manchester United**	1	Wembley	77,231
	Atkinson, Saunders 2 (1 pen)		Hughes			

Year	Winners		Runners-up		Venue	Attendance
1995	**Liverpool**	2	**Bolton Wanderers**	1	Wembley	75,595
	McManaman 2		Thompson			
1996	**Aston Villa**	3	**Leeds United**	0	Wembley	77,056
	Milosevic, Taylor, Yorke					
1997	**Middlesbrough**	1	**Leicester City**	1*	Wembley	76,757
	Ravanelli		Heskey			
Replay	**Leicester City**	1	**Middlesbrough**	0*	Hillsborough	39,428
	Claridge					
1998	**Chelsea**	2	**Middlesbrough**	0*	Wembley	77,698
	Sinclair, Di Matteo					

* After extra time.

Most wins: 5 Liverpool, Aston Villa; 4 Nottingham Forest

Most winners' medals: 5 Ian Rush; 4 Phil Neal, Alan Kennedy, Kenny Dalglish, Sammy Lee, Graeme Souness (all Liverpool)

Biggest win: 10-0 West Ham United v Bury (2nd round, 2nd leg) 25 Oct 1983, 10-0 Liverpool v Fulham (2nd round, 1st leg) 23 Sep 1986

Biggest win (final): 4-1 West Bromwich Albion v West Ham United (2nd leg) 23 Mar 1966

Second Division finalists

The following clubs from the 2nd division of the Football League have reached the English League Cup final:

1961	Rotherham United
1962	Norwich City*
1975	Aston Villa*, Norwich City
1981	West Ham United
1990	Oldham Athletic
1991	Sheffield Wednesday*

Third and Fourth Division finalists

1962	Rochdale (4)
1967	Queen's Park Rangers* (3)
1969	Swindon Town* (3)
1971	Aston Villa (3)

* Winners.

Leading English Football League Clubs

This table shows the leading English clubs (to the end of the 1997/8 season), detailing their honours and (for fun) awarding points as follows:

Football League Division 1 (now Premier League) 1st – 12, 2nd – 10, 3rd – 8; Division 2 champions (Division 1 from 1993) – 1 point

FA Cup: W – winners 10, RU – runners-up – 8, SF – losing semi-finalists 4

Football League Cup: W – winners 8, RU – runners-up 4, SF – losing semi-finalists 2

Club	FL Div 1/P			Div 2/1	FA Cup			FL Cup			Points
	1st	*2nd*	*3rd*	*1st*	*W*	*RU*	*SF*	*W*	*RU*	*SF*	
Liverpool	18	10	4	4	4	6	10	5	2	3	534
Manchester United	11	12	3	2	9	5	7	1	3	3	462
Everton	9	7	7	1	5	7	11	–	2	1	395
Arsenal	11	3	5	–	7	6	6	2	3	4	380
Aston Villa	7	10	2	2	7	2	9	5	2	3	378
Tottenham Hotspur	2	4	8	2	8	1	6	2	1	5	272
Sunderland	6	5	8	2	2	2	7	–	1	1	258
Wolverhampton Wanderers	3	5	6	2	4	4	6	2	–	1	246
Sheffield Wednesday	4	1	7	5	3	3	10	1	1	1	222
Newcastle United	4	2	3	2	6	6	2	–	1	–	214
Manchester City	2	3	3	6	4	4	2	2	1	2	188
West Bromwich Albion	1	2	1	2	5	5	9	1	2	1	186
Blackburn Rovers	3	1	3	1	6	2	8	–	–	2	183
Preston North End	2	6	2	3	2	5	3	–	–	–	175
Nottingham Forest	1	2	4	2	2	1	9	4	2	–	170
Leeds United	3	5	1	3	1	3	4	1	1	3	165
Derby County	2	3	4	4	1	3	9	–	–	1	162
Huddersfield Town	3	3	3	1	1	4	2	–	–	1	143
Chelsea	1	–	3	2	2	3	8	2	1	3	140
Burnley	2	2	5	2	1	2	5	–	–	3	138
Bolton Wanderers	–	–	3	3	4	3	5	–	1	1	117

Club	FL Div 1/P			Div 2/1	FA Cup			FL Cup			Points
	1st	2nd	3rd	1st	W	RU	SF	W	RU	SF	
Sheffield United	1	2	-	1	4	2	6	-	-	-	113
Leicester City	-	1	1	6	-	4	4	2	1	-	92
Ipswich Town	1	2	3	3	1	-	2	-	-	2	81
West Ham United	-	-	1	2	3	1	2	-	2	5	74
Southampton	-	1	-	-	1	2	7	-	1	1	70
Portsmouth	2	-	1	-	1	2	2	-	-	-	66

Scottish Football League

The Scottish League was formed in 1890, two years after the Football League. A second division was added in 1893 and the biggest re-organization in the League since its formation came in 1975/6, when it was completely re-structured. The leading ten teams formed a new Premier Division while the remaining teams were divided into Divisions 1 and 2. The number of teams in the Premier Division was increased to twelve in 1986/7, but reduced back to ten from 1988/9, then twelve 1991/2 and ten again in 1994/5, when there were also ten clubs in each of Divisions 1, 2 and 3.

First Division/Premier Division champions

Season	Champions	Pts	Max	Season	Champions	Pts	Max
1890/1	Dumbarton	29	36	1928/9	Rangers	67	76
	& Rangers	29	36	1929/30	Rangers	60	76
1891/2	Dumbarton	37	44	1930/1	Rangers	60	76
1892/3	Celtic	29	36	1931/2	Motherwell	66	76
1893/4	Celtic	29	36	1932/3	Rangers	62	76
1894/5	Hearts	31	36	1933/4	Rangers	66	76
1895/6	Celtic	30	36	1934/5	Rangers	55	76
1896/7	Hearts	28	36	1935/6	Celtic	66	76
1897/8	Celtic	33	36	1936/7	Rangers	61	76
1898/9	Rangers	36	36	1937/8	Celtic	61	76
1899/00	Rangers	32	36	1938/9	Rangers	59	76
1900/1	Rangers	35	40	1946/7	Rangers	46	68
1901/2	Rangers	28	36	1947/8	Hibernian	48	68
1902/3	Hibernian	37	44	1948/9	Rangers	46	68
1903/4	Third Lanark	43	52	1949/50	Rangers	50	68
1904/5	Celtic	41	52	1950/1	Hibernian	48	68
1905/6	Celtic	49	60	1951/2	Hibernian	45	68
1906/7	Celtic	55	68	1952/3	Rangers	43	68
1907/8	Celtic	55	68	1953/4	Celtic	43	68
1908/9	Celtic	51	68	1954/5	Aberdeen	49	68
1909/10	Celtic	54	68	1955/6	Rangers	52	68
1910/1	Rangers	52	68	1956/7	Rangers	55	68
1911/2	Rangers	51	68	1957/8	Hearts	62	68
1912/3	Rangers	53	68	1958/9	Rangers	50	68
1913/4	Celtic	65	76	1959/60	Hearts	54	68
1914/5	Celtic	65	76	1960/1	Rangers	51	68
1915/6	Celtic	67	76	1961/2	Dundee	54	68
1916/7	Celtic	64	76	1962/3	Rangers	57	68
1917/8	Rangers	56	68	1963/4	Rangers	55	68
1918/9	Celtic	58	68	1964/5	Kilmarnock	50	68
1919/20	Rangers	71	84	1965/6	Celtic	57	68
1920/1	Rangers	76	84	1966/7	Celtic	58	68
1921/2	Celtic	67	84	1967/8	Celtic	63	68
1922/3	Rangers	55	76	1968/9	Celtic	54	68
1923/4	Rangers	59	76	1969/70	Celtic	57	68
1924/5	Rangers	60	76	1970/1	Celtic	56	68
1925/6	Celtic	58	76	1971/2	Celtic	60	68
1926/7	Rangers	56	76	1972/3	Celtic	57	68
1927/8	Rangers	60	76	1973/4	Celtic	53	68

Season	Champions	Pts	Max
1974/5	Rangers	56	68
1975/6	Rangers	54	72
1976/7	Celtic	55	72
1977/8	Rangers	55	72
1978/9	Celtic	48	72
1979/80	Aberdeen	48	72
1980/1	Celtic	56	72
1981/2	Celtic	55	72
1982/3	Dundee Utd	56	72
1983/4	Aberdeen	57	72
1984/5	Aberdeen	59	72
1985/6	Celtic	50	72
1986/7	Rangers	69	88
1987/8	Celtic	72	88
1988/9	Rangers	56	72
1989/90	Rangers	51	72
1990/1	Rangers	55	72
1991/2	Rangers	72	88
1992/3	Rangers	73	88
1993/4	Rangers	58	88
1994/5	Rangers	69	108
1995/6	Rangers	87	108
1996/7	Rangers	80	108
1997/8	Celtic	74	108

Most wins: 47 Rangers, 36 Celtic, 4 Aberdeen, Hearts, Hibernian

Biggest win: 13-2 East Fife v Edinburgh City 11 Dec 1937 Div 2

Biggest win (Division 1 or Premier Division): 11-0 Celtic v Dundee 26 Oct 1895

Most individual goals in a match

8   Owen McNally (Div 2, Arthurlie v Armadale) 1 Oct 1927

8   Jimmy McGrory (Div 1, Celtic v Dunfermline Athletic) 14 Jan 1928

8   Jim Dyet (Div 2, King's Park v Forfar Athletic) 2 Jan 1930

8   John Calder (Div 2, Morton v Raith Rovers) 18 Mar 1936

Most individual goals in a season

66   Jim Smith (Div 2 Ayr United) 1927/8

53   Robert Skinner (Div 2 Dunfermline Athletic) 1925/6

52   Bill McFadyen (Div 1 Motherwell) 1931/2

50   Jimmy McGrory (Div 1 Celtic) 1935/6

Scottish FA Cup

When Queen's Park called a meeting of clubs on 13 March 1873 it was with the intention of organizing a cup competition, similar to the FA Cup. Eight clubs attended that first meeting and Queen's Park's wishes were granted but, at the same meeting it was also decided to form the Scottish Football Association. The new cup competition was called the Scottish Football Association Cup. It is now sponsored by Tennents.

The venue of the final has been Hampden Park, except for: Hamilton Crescent 1876-7, Cathkin Park 1880, 1882, 1886; Kinning Park 1881, Ibrox Park 1890, 1892-3, 1895, 1900-1, 1906, 1910-12, 1914, 1924, 1997; Logie Green 1896, Celtic Park 1902-3, 1913, 1921.

Year	Winners	Runners-up	Attendance
1874	Queen's Park 2	Clydesdale 0	3,500
1875	Queen's Park 3	Renton 0	7,000
1876	Queen's Park 1	Third Lanark 1	10,000
Replay	Queen's Park 2	Third Lanark 0	6,000
1877	Vale of Leven 0	Rangers 0	10,000
Replay	Vale of Leven 1	Rangers 1	15,000
Replay	Vale of Leven 3	Rangers 2	12,000
1878	Vale of Leven 1	Third Lanark 0	5,000
1879	Vale of Leven 1	Rangers 1	9,000
	Vale of Leven awarded trophy as Rangers refused to appear for the replay		
1880	Queen's Park 3	Thornlibank 0	4,000
1881	Queen's Park 2	Dumbarton 1	15,000
	Replayed due to spectator invasion of pitch		
Replay	Queen's Park 3	Dumbarton 1	7,000
1882	Queen's Park 2	Dumbarton 2	12,500
Replay	Queen's Park 4	Dumbarton 1	14,000
1883	Dumbarton 2	Vale of Leven 2	9,000
Replay	Dumbarton 2	Vale of Leven 1	12,000
1884	Queen's Park awarded cup as Vale of Leven failed to appear		
1885	Renton 0	Vale of Leven 0	2,500
Replay	Renton 3	Vale of Leven 1	3,500

Year	Winners	Runners-up	Attendance
1886	Queen's Park 3	Renton 1	7,000
1887	Hibernian 2	Dumbarton 1	12,000
1888	Renton 6	Cambuslang 1	11,000
1889	Third Lanark 3	Celtic 1	18,000
	Game declared void due to snowstorm		
Replay	Third Lanark 2	Celtic 1	13,000
1890	Queen's Park 1	Vale of Leven 1	11,000
Replay	Queen's Park 2	Vale of Leven 1	14,000
1891	Hearts 1	Dumbarton 0	10,836
1892	Celtic 1	Queen's Park 0	40,000
	Replayed due to spectator disruption		
Replay	Celtic 5	Queen's Park 1	26,000
1893	Queen's Park 0	Celtic 1	18,771
	Replayed due to frosty pitch		
Replay	Queen's Park 2	Celtic 1	13,239
1894	Rangers 3	Celtic 1	17,000
1895	St Bernard's 2	Renton 1	15,000
1896	Hearts 3	Hibernian 1	17,034
1897	Rangers 5	Dumbarton 1	14,000
1898	Rangers 2	Kilmarnock 0	13,000
1899	Celtic 2	Rangers 0	25,000
1900	Celtic 4	Queen's Park 3	15,000
1901	Hearts 4	Celtic 3	12,000
1902	Hibernian 1	Celtic 0	16,000
1903	Rangers 1	Hearts 1	40,000
Replay	Rangers 0	Hearts 0	35,000
Replay	Rangers 2	Hearts 0	32,000
1904	Celtic 3	Rangers 2	65,000
1905	Third Lanark 0	Rangers 0	54,000
Replay	Third Lanark 3	Rangers 1	55,000
1906	Hearts 1	Third Lanark 0	25,000
1907	Celtic 3	Hearts 0	50,000
1908	Celtic 5	St Mirren 1	55,000
1909	Celtic 2	Rangers 2	70,000
Replay	Celtic 1	Rangers 1	61,000
	Owing to a riot, cup withheld after the two drawn games		
1910	Dundee 2	Clyde 2	62,300
Replay	Dundee 0	Clyde 0	24,500
Replay	Dundee 2	Clyde 1	25,400
1911	Celtic 0	Hamilton A 0	45,000
Replay	Celtic 2	Hamilton A 0	24,700
1912	Celtic 2	Clyde 0	46,000
1913	Falkirk 2	Raith Rovers 0	45,000
1914	Celtic 0	Hibernian 0	56,000
Replay	Celtic 4	Hibernian 1	40,000
1920	Kilmarnock 3	Albion Rovers 2	95,000
1921	Partick Thistle 1	Rangers 0	28,300
1922	Morton 1	Rangers 0	75,000
1923	Celtic 1	Hibernian 0	80,100
1924	Airdrieonians 2	Hibernian 0	59,218
1925	Celtic 2	Dundee 1	75,137
1926	St Mirren 2	Celtic 0	98,620
1927	Celtic 3	East Fife 1	80,070
1928	Rangers 4	Celtic 0	118,115
1929	Kilmarnock 2	Rangers 0	114,708
1930	Rangers 0	Partick Thistle 0	107,475

Year	Winners	Runners-up	Attendance
Replay	Rangers 2	Partick Thistle 1	103,686
1931	Celtic 2	Motherwell 2	105,000
Replay	Celtic 4	Motherwell 2	98,579
1932	Rangers 1	Kilmarnock 1	111,982
Replay	Rangers 3	Kilmarnock 0	104,965
1933	Celtic 1	Motherwell 0	102,339
1934	Rangers 5	St Mirren 0	113,403
1935	Rangers 2	Hamilton A 1	87,286
1936	Rangers 1	Third Lanark 0	88,859
1937	Celtic 2	Aberdeen 1	147,365
1938	East Fife 1	Kilmarnock 1	80,091
Replay	East Fife 4	Kilmarnock 2	92,716
1939	Clyde 4	Motherwell 0	94,799
1947	Aberdeen 2	Hibernian 1	82,140
1948	Rangers 1	Morton 1	129,176
Replay	Rangers 1	Morton 0	133,570
1949	Rangers 4	Clyde 1	108,435
1950	Rangers 3	East Fife 0	118,262
1951	Celtic 1	Motherwell 0	131,943
1952	Motherwell 4	Dundee 0	136,274
1953	Rangers 1	Aberdeen 1	129,681
Replay	Rangers 1	Aberdeen 0	112,619
1954	Celtic 2	Aberdeen 1	129,926
1955	Clyde 1	Celtic 1	106,111
Replay	Clyde 1	Celtic 0	68,735
1956	Hearts 3	Celtic 1	133,339
1957	Falkirk 1	Kilmarnock 1	83,000
Replay	Falkirk 2	Kilmarnock 1	79,785
1958	Clyde 1	Hibernian 0	95,124
1959	St Mirren 3	Aberdeen 1	108,591
1960	Rangers 2	Kilmarnock 0	108,017
1961	Dunfermline A 0	Celtic 0	113,618
Replay	Dunfermline A 2	Celtic 0	87,866
1962	Rangers 2	St Mirren 0	126,930
1963	Rangers 1	Celtic 1	129,527
Replay	Rangers 3	Celtic 0	120,263
1964	Rangers 3	Dundee 1	120,982
1965	Celtic 3	Dunfermline A 2	108,800
1966	Rangers 0	Celtic 0	126,552
Replay	Rangers 1	Celtic 0	98,202
1967	Celtic 2	Aberdeen 0	127,117
1968	Dunfermline A 3	Hearts 1	56,366
1969	Celtic 4	Rangers 0	132,874
1970	Aberdeen 3	Celtic 1	108,434
1971	Celtic 1	Rangers 1	120,092
Replay	Celtic 2	Rangers 1	103,332
1972	Celtic 6	Hibernian 1	106,102
1973	Rangers 3	Celtic 2	122,714
1974	Celtic 3	Dundee United 0	75,959
1975	Celtic 3	Airdrieonians 1	75,457
1976	Rangers 3	Hearts 1	85,354
1977	Celtic 1	Rangers 0	54,252
1978	Rangers 2	Aberdeen 1	61,563
1979	Rangers 0	Hibernian 0	50,610
Replay	Rangers 0	Hibernian 0	33,506
Replay	Rangers 3	Hibernian 2	30,602

Year	Winners	Runners-up	Attendance
1980	Celtic 1	Rangers 0★	70,303
1981	Rangers 0	Dundee United 0	55,000
Replay	Rangers 4	Dundee United 1	43,009
1982	Aberdeen 4	Rangers 1★	53,788
1983	Aberdeen 1	Rangers 0★	62,979
1984	Aberdeen 2	Celtic 1★	58,900
1985	Celtic 2	Dundee United 1	60,346
1986	Aberdeen 3	Hearts 0	62,841
1987	St Mirren 1	Dundee United 0★	51,792
1988	Celtic 2	Dundee United 1	74,000
1989	Celtic 1	Rangers 0	72,069
1990	Aberdeen 0	Celtic 0★	60,493
	Aberdeen won 9-8 on penalties		
1991	Motherwell 4	Dundee United 3★	57,319
1992	Rangers 2	Airdrieonians 1	44,045
1993	Rangers 2	Aberdeen 1	50,715
1994	Dundee United 1	Rangers 0	38,000
1995	Celtic 1	Airdrie 0	36,915
1996	Rangers 5	Hearts 0	37,730
1997	Kilmarnock 1	Falkirk 0	48,953
1998	Hearts 2	Rangers 1	48,946

★ After extra time.

Most wins: 30 Celtic; 27 Rangers; 10 Queen's Park
Biggest win: 36-0 Arbroath v Bon Accord (1st round) 5 Sep 1885
Biggest win (final): 6-1 Renton v Cambuslang 4 Feb 1888, 6-1 Celtic v Hibernian 6 May 1972
Most individual goals in one match: 13 John Petrie (Arbroath v Bon Accord) 1st round 12 Sep 1885
Most winner's medals: 8 Charles Campbell (Queen's Park) 1874-6, 1880-2, 1884, 1886

Scottish League Cup

The Scottish League Cup was first contested in 1946/7, replacing the Southern League Cup that had been played during the war. Prior to 1977/8 the teams were split into eight or nine groups, with the winners going through to a knock-out competition. The Cup became known as the Skol Cup in 1984/5 and as the Coca-Cola Cup from 1994/5. All finals have been at Hampden Park, unless stated otherwise.

Year	Winners	Runners-up	Year	Winners	Runners-up
1946/7	Rangers 4	Aberdeen 0	1965/6	Celtic 2	Rangers 1
1947/8	East Fife 1	Falkirk 1★	1966/7	Celtic 1	Rangers 0
Replay	East Fife 4	Falkirk 1	1967/8	Celtic 5	Dundee 3
1948/9	Rangers 2	Raith Rovers 0	1968/9	Celtic 6	Hibernian 2
1949/50	East Fife 3	Dunfermline A 0	1969/70	Celtic 1	St Johnstone 0
1950/1	Motherwell 3	Hibernian 0	1970/1	Rangers 1	Celtic 0
1951/2	Dundee 3	Rangers 2	1971/2	Partick Thistle 4	Celtic 1
1952/3	Dundee 2	Kilmarnock 0	1972/3	Hibernian 2	Celtic 1
1953/4	East Fife 3	Partick Thistle 2	1973/4	Dundee 1	Celtic 0
1954/5	Hearts 4	Motherwell 2	1974/5	Celtic 6	Hibernian 3
1955/6	Aberdeen 2	St Mirren 1	1975/6	Rangers 1	Celtic 0
1956/7	Celtic 0	Partick Thistle 0★	1976/7	Aberdeen 2	Celtic 1
Replay	Celtic 3	Partick Thistle 0	1977/8	Rangers 2	Celtic 1
1957/8	Celtic 7	Rangers 1	1978/9	Rangers 2	Aberdeen 1
1958/9	Hearts 5	Partick Thistle 1	1979/80	Dundee United 0	Aberdeen 0
1959/60	Hearts 2	Third Lanark 1	Replay	Dundee United 3	Aberdeen 0#
1960/1	Rangers 2	Kilmarnock 0	1980/1	Dundee United 3	Dundee 0#
1961/2	Rangers 1	Hearts 1★	1981/2	Rangers 2	Dundee United 1
Replay	Rangers 3	Hearts 1	1982/3	Celtic 2	Rangers 1
1962/3	Hearts 1	Kilmarnock 0	1983/4	Rangers 3	Celtic 2★
1963/4	Rangers 5	Morton 0	1984/5	Rangers 1	Dundee United 0
1964/5	Rangers 2	Celtic 1	1985/6	Aberdeen 3	Hibernian 0

Year	Winners	Runners-up
1986/7	Rangers 2	Celtic 1
1987/8	Rangers 3	Aberdeen 3*
	(Rangers won 5-3 on penalties)	
1988/9	Rangers 3	Aberdeen 2
1989/90	Aberdeen 2	Rangers 1*
1990/1	Rangers 2	Celtic 1*
1991/2	Hibernian 2	Dunfermline 0
1992/3	Rangers 2	Aberdeen 1
1993/4	Rangers 2	Hibernian 1
1994/5	Raith Rovers 2	Celtic 2*
	(Raith Rovers won 6-5 on penalties)	
1995/6	Aberdeen 2	Dundee 0
1996/7	Rangers 4	Hearts 3
1997/8	Celtic 3	Dundee United 0

* After extra time.
\# Played at Dens Park, Dundee.
Biggest win (final): 7-1 Celtic v Rangers
   19 Oct 1957

Most successful Scottish clubs

Wins		League	Cup	Lg.Cup
94	Rangers	47	27	20
76	Celtic	36	30	10
17	Aberdeen	4	7	6
14	Hearts	4	6	4
10	Queen's Park	-	10	-

German League

The first club entirely devoted to football was SC Germania Hamburg, formed in 1887. Regional leagues were set up from 1898 and the Deutscher Fussball-Bund was formed in 1900. Two years later it decided to invite the winners of the regional leagues to take part in end-of-season play-offs to determine the national champions. This system remained until 1963, when the West Germans became the last European country to institute a single national league.

League Champions

Named German League to 1944, FRG Champions 1948-63, and Bundesliga from 1964.

14	Bayern München	1932, 1969, 1972-4, 1980-1, 1985-7, 1989-90, 1994, 1997
9	1.FC Nürnberg	1920-1, 1924-5, 1927, 1936, 1948, 1961, 1968
7	FC Schalke 04	1934-5, 1937, 1939-40, 1942, 1958
6	Hamburger SV	1923, 1928, 1960, 1979, 1982-3
5	Borussia Dortmund	1956-7, 1963, 1995-6
5	Borussia Mönchengladbach	1970-1, 1975-7
4	VfB Stuttgart	1950, 1952, 1984, 1992
4	1.FC Kaiserslautern	1951, 1953, 1991, 1998

3	VfB Leipzig	1903, 1906, 1913
3	SPVGG Fürth	1914, 1926, 1929
3	1.FC Köln	1962, 1964, 1978
3	Werder Bremen	1965, 1988, 1993
2	Viktoria Berlin	1908, 1911
2	Hannover 96	1938, 1954
2	Hertha BSC Berlin	1930-1
2	Dresdner SC	1943-4
1	Union 92 Berlin 1905, SC Freiburg 1907, Phönix Karlsruhe 1909, Karlsruher FV 1910, Holstein Kiel 1912, Fortuna Düsseldorf 1933, Rapid Wien 1941, VfR Mannheim 1949, Rot-Weiss Essen 1955, Eintracht Frankfurt 1959, TSV München 1860 1966, Eintracht Braunschweig 1967	

German Cup finals

9	Bayern München	1957, 1966-7, 1969, 1971, 1982, 1984, 1986, 1998
4	1.FC Köln	1968, 1977-8, 1983
4	Eintracht Frankfurt	1974-5, 1981, 1988
3	1.FC Nürnberg	1935, 1939, 1962
3	VfB Stuttgart	1954, 1958, 1997
3	Borussia Mönchengladbach	1960, 1973, 1995
3	Werder Bremen	1961, 1991, 1994
3	Hamburger SV	1963, 1976, 1987
2	FC Schalke 04	1937, 1972
2	Borussia Dortmund	1965, 1989
2	1.FC Kaiserslautern	1990, 1996
2	Dresdner SC	1940-1
2	TSV München 1860	1942, 1964
2	Karlsruher FC	1955-6
2	Fortuna Düsseldorf	1979-80
1	VfB Leipzig 1936, Rapid Wien 1938, First Vienna FC 1943, Rot-Weiss Essen 1953, Schwarz-Weiss Essen 1959, Kickers Offenbach 1970, Bayer Uerdingen 1985, Hannover 96 1992, Bayer Leverkusen 1993	

Italian League

The Italian League was founded in 1898, when just three games were played. It was called Seric A from 1930.

Wins:

25	Juventus	1905, 1926, 1931-5, 1950, 1952, 1958, 1960-1, 1967, 1972-3, 1975, 1977-8, 1981-2, 1984, 1986, 1995, 1997-8
15	AC Milan	1901, 1906-7, 1951, 1955, 1957, 1959, 1962, 1968, 1979, 1988, 1992-4, 1996

13	Internazionale Milano	1910, 1920, 1930, 1938, 1940, 1953-4, 1963, 1965-6, 1971, 1980, 1989 (Ambrosiana-Inter 1929-46)
9	Genoa	1898-1900, 1902-4, 1915, 1923-4
8	Torino	1927-8, 1943, 1946-9, 1976
7	Pro Vercelli	1908-09, 1911-13, 1921, 1922
7	Bologna	1925, 1929, 1936-7, 1939, 1941, 1964
2	Roma	1942, 1983
2	Florentina	1956, 1969
2	Napoli	1987, 1990
1	Casale 1914, Novese 1922, Cagliari 1970, Lazio 1974, Hellas Verona 1985, Sampdoria 1991	

Italian Cup

First contested in 1922, then again 1936-43, and annually from 1958, although on a league basis in 1968-70. *Wins:*

9	Juventus	1938, 1942, 1959-60, 1965, 1979, 1983, 1990, 1995
6	Roma	1964, 1969, 1980-1, 1984, 1986
5	Torino	1936, 1943, 1968, 1971, 1993
5	Florentina	1940, 1961, 1966, 1975, 1996
4	AC Milan	1967, 1972-3, 1977
4	Sampdoria	1985, 1988-9, 1994
3	Napoli	1962, 1976, 1987
2	Internazionale Milano	1978, 1982
1	Vado 1922, Genoa 1937, Ambrosiana-Inter 1939, Venezia 1941, Lazio 1958, Atalanta 1963, Bologna 1974, Parma 1992, Vicenza 1997	

Awards

World Footballer of the Year

Elected annually by *World Soccer* from 1982.
Winners:

1982	Paolo Rossi (Ita, Juventus)
1983	Zico (Bra, Udinese)
1984-5	Michel Platini (Fra, Juventus)
1986	Diego Maradona (Arg, Napoli)
1987	Ruud Gullit (Hol, AC Milan)
1988	Marco Van Basten (Hol, AC Milan)
1989	Ruud Gullit (Hol, AC Milan)
1990	Lothar Matthäus (FRG, Internazionale Milan)
1991	Jean-Pierre Papin (Fra, Marseille)
1992	Marco Van Basten (Hol, AC Milan)
1993	Roberto Baggio (Ita, Juventus)
1994	Paulo Maldini (Ita, AC Milan)
1995	Gianluca Vialli (Ita, Juventus)
1996-7	Ronaldo (Bra, Barcelona)

FIFA World Footballer of the Year

Presented by FIFA, the European Sports Management Association and Adidas, and selected annually by national team coaches from around the world.

1991	Lothar Matthäus (Ger, Internazionale Milan)
1992	Marco Van Basten (Hol, AC Milan)
1993	Roberto Baggio (Ita, Juventus)
1994	Romario (Bra, Barcelona)
1995	George Weah (Lib, Paris St Germain, AC Milan)
1996-7	Ronaldo (Bra, Barcelona, Internazionale Milan)

European Footballer of the Year

Le Ballon D'Or (the Golden Ball) is awarded each year by the French newspaper *France Football* from a poll of journalists in UEFA-affiliated countries. *Winners:*

1956	Stanley Matthews (UK, Blackpool)
1957	Alfredo di Stéfano (Spa, Real Madrid)
1958	Raymond Kopa (Fra, Real Madrid)
1959	Alfredo di Stéfano (Spa, Real Madrid)
1960	Luis Suárez (Spa, Barcelona)
1961	Omar Sivori (Ita, Juventus)
1962	Josef Masopust (Cs, Dukla Praha)
1963	Lev Yashin (USSR, Dynamo Moscow)
1964	Denis Law (UK, Manchester United)
1965	Eusébio (Por, Benfica)
1966	Bobby Charlton (UK, Manchester United)
1967	Florian Albert (Hun, Ferencváros)
1968	George Best (UK, Manchester United)
1969	Gianni Rivera (Ita, AC Milan)
1970	Gerd Müller (FRG, Bayern München)
1971	Johan Cruyff (Hol, Ajax)
1972	Franz Beckenbauer (FRG, Bayern München)
1973-4	Johan Cruyff (Hol, Barcelona)
1975	Oleg Blokhin (USSR, Dynamo Kiev)
1976	Franz Beckenbauer (FRG, Bayern München)
1977	Allan Simonsen (Den, Borussia Mönchengladbach)
1978-9	Kevin Keegan (UK, Hamburger SV)
1980-1	Karl-Heinz Rummenigge (FRG, Bayern München)
1982	Paolo Rossi (Ita, Juventus)
1983-5	Michel Platini (Fra, Juventus)
1986	Igor Belanov (USSR, Dynamo Kiev)
1987	Ruud Gullit (Hol, AC Milan)
1988-9	Marco Van Basten (Hol, AC Milan)
1990	Lothar Matthäus (FRG, Internazionale Milan)
1991	Jean-Pierre Papin (Fra, Marseille)
1992	Marco Van Basten (Hol, AC Milan)
1993	Roberto Baggio (Ita, Juventus)
1994	Hristo Stoichkov (Bul, Barcelona)

1995	George Weah (Lib, Paris-SG, AC Milan)		1994	Alan Shearer (Blackburn Rovers)
1996	Matthias Sammer (Ger, Borussia Dortmund)		1995	Jürgen Klinsmann (Tottenham Hotspur, Ger)
1997	Ronaldo (Bra, Internazionale Milan)		1996	Eric Cantona (Manchester United, Fra)

Most wins: 3 Cruyff, Platini, Van Basten

Football Writers' Player of the Year

The Football Writers' Association was founded in 1947 and since 1947/8 its members have voted for their Player of the Year.

Winners:

1948	Stanley Matthews (Blackpool)
1949	Johnny Carey (Manchester United)
1950	Joe Mercer (Arsenal)
1951	Harry Johnston (Blackpool)
1952	Billy Wright (Wolverhampton Wanderers)
1953	Nat Lofthouse (Bolton Wanderers)
1954	Tom Finney (Preston North End)
1955	Don Revie (Manchester City)
1956	Bert Trautmann (Manchester City, FRG)
1957	Tom Finney (Preston North End)
1958	Danny Blanchflower (Tottenham Hotspur)
1959	Syd Owen (Luton Town)
1960	Bill Slater (Wolverhampton Wanderers)
1961	Danny Blanchflower (Tottenham Hotspur)
1962	Jimmy Adamson (Burnley)
1963	Stanley Matthews (Stoke City)
1964	Bobby Moore (West Ham United)
1965	Bobby Collins (Leeds United)
1966	Bobby Charlton (Manchester United)
1967	Jackie Charlton (Leeds United)
1968	George Best (Manchester United)
1969	Tony Book (Manchester City) & Dave Mackay (Derby County)
1970	Billy Bremner (Leeds United)
1971	Frank McLintock (Arsenal)
1972	Gordon Banks (Stoke City)
1973	Pat Jennings (Tottenham Hotspur)
1974	Ian Callaghan (Liverpool)
1975	Alan Mullery (Fulham)
1976	Kevin Keegan (Liverpool)
1977	Emlyn Hughes (Liverpool)
1978	Kenny Burns (Nottingham Forest)
1979	Kenny Dalglish (Liverpool)
1980	Terry McDermott (Liverpool)
1981	Frans Thijssen (Ipswich Town, Hol)
1982	Steve Perryman (Tottenham Hotspur)
1983	Kenny Dalglish (Liverpool)
1984	Ian Rush (Liverpool)
1985	Neville Southall (Everton)
1986	Gary Lineker (Everton)
1987	Clive Allen (Tottenham Hotspur)
1988	John Barnes (Liverpool)
1989	Steve Nicol (Liverpool)
1990	John Barnes (Liverpool)
1991	Gordon Strachan (Leeds United)
1992	Gary Lineker (Tottenham Hotspur)
1993	Chris Waddle (Sheffield Wednesday)

1994	Alan Shearer (Blackburn Rovers)
1995	Jürgen Klinsmann (Tottenham Hotspur, Ger)
1996	Eric Cantona (Manchester United, Fra)
1997	Gianfranco Zola (Chelsea, Ita)
1998	Denis Bergkamp (Arsenal, Hol)

Most wins: 2 Finney, Blanchflower, Matthews, Dalglish, Barnes, Lineker

Most wins (clubs): 10 Liverpool; 7 Tottenham Hotspur

Winners never to win a full international cap: Bert Trautmann (1956), Jimmy Adamson (1962), Tony Book (1969)

Winners while with a Second Division club: Stanley Matthews (1963), Dave Mackay (1969), Alan Mullery (1975)

Professional Footballers' Association Player of the Year

The professional players have voted annually each March since 1974 for their Player of the Year. A Young Player award is also presented, as well as a Merit Award.

Winners:

1974	Norman Hunter (Leeds United)
1975	Colin Todd (Derby County)
1976	Pat Jennings (Tottenham Hotspur)
1977	Andy Gray (Aston Villa)
1978	Peter Shilton (Nottingham Forest)
1979	Liam Brady (Arsenal)
1980	Terry McDermott (Liverpool)
1981	John Wark (Ipswich Town)
1982	Kevin Keegan (Southampton)
1983	Kenny Dalglish (Liverpool)
1984	Ian Rush (Liverpool)
1985	Peter Reid (Everton)
1986	Gary Lineker (Everton)
1987	Clive Allen (Tottenham Hotspur)
1988	John Barnes (Liverpool)
1989	Mark Hughes (Manchester United)
1990	David Platt (Aston Villa)
1991	Mark Hughes (Manchester United)
1992	Gary Pallister (Manchester United)
1993	Paul McGrath (Aston Villa)
1994	Eric Cantona (Manchester United, Fra)
1995	Alan Shearer (Blackburn Rovers)
1996	Les Ferdinand (Newcastle United)
1997	Alan Shearer (Newcastle United)
1998	Denis Bergkamp (Arsenal, Hol)

Scottish Footballer Player of the Year

Awarded annually by the Scottish PFA.

Winners:

1965	Billy McNeill (Celtic)
1966	John Greig (Rangers)
1967	Ronnie Simpson (Celtic)
1968	Gordon Wallace (Raith Rovers)
1969	Bobby Murdoch (Celtic)
1970	Pat Stanton (Hibernian)

1971	Martin Buchan (Aberdeen)	1985	Hamish McAlpine (Dundee United)
1972	Dave Smith (Rangers)	1986	Sandy Jardine (Hearts)
1973	George Connelly (Celtic)	1987	Brian McClair (Celtic)
1974	Scotland World Cup squad	1988	Paul McStay (Celtic)
1975	Sandy Jardine (Rangers)	1989	Richard Gough (Rangers)
1976	John Greig (Rangers)	1990	Alex McLeish (Aberdeen)
1977	Danny McGrain (Celtic)	1991	Maurice Malpas (Dundee United)
1978	Derek Johnstone (Rangers)	1992	Ally McCoist (Rangers)
1979	Andy Ritchie (Morton)	1993	Andy Goram (Rangers)
1980	Gordon Strachan (Aberdeen)	1994	Mark Hateley (Rangers)
1981	Alan Rough (Partick Thistle)	1995	Brian Laudrup (Rangers, Den)
1982	Paul Sturrock (Dundee United)	1996	Paul Gascoigne (Rangers, Eng)
1983	Charlie Nicholas (Celtic)	1997	Brian Laudrup (Rangers, Den)
1984	Willie Miller (Aberdeen)	1998	Craig Burley (Celtic)

Women's Soccer

The first recorded women's football match was played in England in 1895, with the first international played between England and France in 1920. The Women's Football Association (WFA), formed in England in 1969, was affiliated to the FA in 1983. The FA Women's Premier League has ten teams in each of three divisions: National, Northern and Southern.

World Championships

After a qualifying tournament, the first-ever women's World Championships were contested by teams in China in 1991 from 12 nations.
Results of finals:

| 1991 | USA 2 | Norway 1 |
| 1995 | Norway 2 | Germany 0 |

European Championships

First held in 1983/4.
Winners:

4	Germany (FRG)
	FRG 1989, 1991; Ger 1995,
	1997
2	Norway
	1987, 1993
1	Sweden
	1984

Olympic Games

First held in 1996, when the USA were the winners.

English Champions

Year	FA Cup	National League	League Cup
1992/3	Arsenal	Arsenal	Arsenal
1993/4	Doncaster Belles	Doncaster Belles	Arsenal
1994/5	Arsenal	Arsenal	Wimbledon
1995/6	Croydon	Croydon	Wembley
1996/7	Millwall Lionesses	Arsenal	Millwall Lionesses
1997/8	Arsenal	Everton	Arsenal

Gaelic Football

A 15-a-side game, Gaelic football, the most popular sport in Ireland with about 250,000 players, has common features with soccer, rugby and Australian Rules football. The first reference to a game resembling Gaelic football was in 1712 when a match between Meath and Louth took place at Slane. The rules were standardized following the formation of the Gaelic Athletic Association, the governing body in Ireland for handball, hurling and rounders as well as for Gaelic football, in 1884. The number of players per team was fixed at 21 in 1884, but reduced to 17 in 1892 and to 15 in 1913.

Governing body: Gaelic Athletic Association (GAA), Croke Park, Dublin 3. Tel: (353) 1 836-3222, Fax: (353) 1 836-6420. President: Joe McDonagh, Director General: Liam Mulvihill. Founded 1884.

All-Ireland Championships

The sport's principal championship, an inter-county event; the final is played at Dublin's Croke Park on the third Sunday in September each year for the Sam Maguire Cup. Held annually from 1887, except for 1888 when it was unfinished.

Most wins:

31	Kerry	1903-4, 1909, 1913-4, 1924, 1926, 1929-32, 1937, 1939-41, 1946, 1953, 1955, 1959, 1962, 1969-70, 1975, 1978-81, 1984-6, 1997
22	Dublin	1891-2, 1894, 1897-9, 1901-2, 1906-8, 1921-3, 1942, 1958, 1963, 1974, 1976-7, 1983, 1995
7	Galway	1925, 1934, 1938, 1956, 1964-6
6	Cork	1890, 1911, 1945, 1973, 1989-90
6	Meath	1949, 1954, 1967, 1987-8, 1996
5	Wexford	1893, 1915-8
5	Cavan	1933, 1935, 1947-8, 1952
5	Down	1960-1, 1968, 1991, 1994
4	Tipperary	1889, 1895, 1900, 1920
4	Kildare	1905, 1919, 1927-8
3	Louth	1910, 1912, 1957
3	Mayo	1936, 1950-1
3	Offaly	1971-2, 1982
2	Limerick	1887, 1896
2	Roscommon	1943-4
1	Donegal	1992
1	Derry	1993

Most appearances in final: 46 Kerry, 34 Dublin
Highest team score in a final: 27 Dublin (5 goals, 12 points) beat Armagh 15 (3, 6) in 1977
Highest aggregate score in a final: 45 Cork (26) beat Galway (19) in 1973.
Most individual appearances: 10, including a record 8 wins by the Kerry players Pat Spillane, Paudie O'Shea, Denis 'Ogie' Moran, Ger Power and Mike Sheehy 1975-86.
Highest attendance: 90,556 in 1961

Gliding

There is some evidence of the use of gliders in Ancient Egypt about four thousand years ago, and the ability to float in the air like a bird has long captured man's imagination. Gliding (or soaring) as a sport began to gain popular appeal in the 1930s in Europe and the USA.

International governing body: Fédération Aéronautique Internationale (FAI), 93 boulevard du Montparnasse, 75006 Paris, France. Tel: (33) 1 49 54 3892, Fax: (33) 1 49 54 3888. President: Eilif Ness, Secretary General: Max Bishop. The FAI is to relocate to Lausanne, Switzerland. Founded 1905. 78 member nations (and 12 associate) in 1998.

Records

A wide variety of world records are maintained for single-seater and for multi-seater gliders, for both men and women pilots. There are also records for motor gliders.

Single-seaters – open class
(Category: Record, Pilot, Glider, Venue, Date)
Straight distance: 1460.8km Hans-Werner Grosse (FRG), ASW-12, Lübeck, FRG to Biarritz, France, 25 Apr 1972
Straight distance to a declared goal: 1383km Gérard Herbaud & Jean-Noël Herbaud (Fra), ASH 25, Vinon, France to Fès, Morocco 17 Apr 1992
Out and return distance: 1646.68km Tom Knauff (USA), Nimbus 3, Williamsport to Knoxville, USA, 25 Apr 1983
Triangular course distance: 1400.19km Klaus Holighaus (Ger), Nimbus 4M, Hendrik Verwoerd Dam, South Africa, 7 Jan 1993

Height gain: 12,894m Paul Bikle (USA), Schweizer SGS 1-23E, Lancaster, USA, 25 Feb 1961
Absolute altitude: 14,938m Robert Harris (USA), Grob G102, California City, USA, 17 Feb 1986
Speed over triangular course:

100km	217.41km/h James Payne (USA), Discus A, California City, USA, 4 Mar 1997
300km	176.99km/h Beat Bünzli (Swz), DG-400, Bitterwasser, Namibia, 14 Nov 1985
500km	171.10km/h Hans-Werner Grosse & Jörg Hacker (FRG), ASH 25T, Mount Newman Aerodrome, Western Australia, 31 Dec 1990
750km	161.33km/h Hans-Werner Grosse & Karin Grosse (FRG), ASH 25, Alice Springs, Australia, 10 Jan 1988
1000km	169.72km/h Helmut Fischer (Ger), Ventus, Hendrik Verwoerd Dam, South Africa, 5 Jan 1995
1250km	143.46km/h Hans-Werner Grosse & Hans-Heinrich Kohlmeier (FRG), ASH 25, Alice Springs, Australia, 10 Jan 1987

Women's single-seaters – open class

Straight distance: 949.70km Karla Karel (UK), LS-3, Tocumwal Aerodrome, Australia, 20 Jan 1980

Straight distance to declared goal: 951.43km Joann Shaw (USA), Nimbus 2, Hobbs, NM, USA, 2 Jul 1990

Out and return distance: 1127.68km Doris Grove (USA), Nimbus 2, Lockhaven, USA, 28 Sep 1981

Triangular course distance: 928.29km Hana Zejdová (Cze), LAK 12, Tocumwal Aerodrome, Australia, 20 Jan 1997

Height gain: 10,212m Yvonne Loader (NZ), Nimbus 2, Omarama, New Zealand, 12 Jan 1988

Absolute altitude: 12,637m Sabrina Jackintell (USA), Grob Astir GS, Colorado Springs, USA, 14 Feb 1979

Speed over triangular course:

100km	151.12km/h Joann Shaw (USA), Nimbus 3, Hobbs, NM, USA, 17 Jul 1997
300km	143.90km/h Susan Beatty (SAf), ASW 20 B, Vryburg, South Africa, 26 Dec 1990
500km	135.38km/h Hana Zejdová (Cze) & Masako Ishikawa (Jap), Nimbus 4 DM, Tocumwal, Australia, 2 Jan 1997
750km	131.39km/h Hana Zejdová (Cze) & Elisabeth Ashby (Aus), Nimbus 4 DM, Tocumwal, Australia, 5 Jan 1997

World Championships

First held in 1937 and now staged biennially. *Winners:*

Open category

1937	Heini Dittmar (Ger)
1948	Per Persson (Swe)
1950	Billy Nilsson (Swe)
1952	Philip Wills (UK)
1954	Gérard Pierre (Fra)
1956	Paul MacCready (USA)
1958	Ernst Haase (FRG)
1960	Rudolf Hossinger (Arg)
1963	Eduard Makula (Pol)
1965	Jan Wroblewski (Pol)
1968	Harro Wödl (Aut)
1970	George Moffat (USA)
1972	Göran Ax (Swe)
1974	George Moffat (USA)
1976	George Lee (UK)
1978	George Lee (UK)
1981	George Lee (UK)
1983	Ingo Renner (Aus)
1985	Ingo Renner (Aus)
1987	Ingo Renner (Aus)
1989	Claude Lopitaux (Fra)
1991	Janusz Centka (Pol)
1993	Janusz Centka (Pol)
1995	Ray Lynskey (NZ)
1997	Gérhard Therm (Fra)

Two-seater

1952	Luis Juez & J Ara (Spa)
1954	Z Rain & P Komac (Yug)
1956	Nick Goodhart & Frank Foster (UK)

Standard class

1958	Adam Witek (Pol)
1960	Heinz Huth (FRG)
1963	Heinz Huth (FRG)
1965	Francois Henry (Fra)
1968	A J Smith (USA)
1970	Helmut Reichmann (FRG)
1972	Jan Wroblewski (Pol)
1974	Helmut Reichmann (FRG)
1976	Ingo Renner (Aus)
1978	Baer Selen (Hol)
1981	Marc Schroeder (Fra)
1983	Stig Oye (Den)
1985	Leonardo Brigliadori (Ita)
1987	Markku Kuittinen (Fin)
1989	Jacques Aboulin (Fra)
1991	Baer Selen (Hol)
1993	Andy Davis (UK)
1995	Markku Kuittinen (Fin)
1997	Jean-Marc Calliard (Fra)

15 metres class

1978	Helmut Reichmann (FRG)
1981	Göran Ax (Swe)
1983	Kees Musters (Hol)
1985	Doug Jacobs (USA)
1987	Brian Speckley (UK)
1989	Bruno Gartenbrink (FRG)
1991	Bradley Edwards (Aus)
1993	Gilbert Gerbaud & Éric Napoleon (Fra)
1995	Éric Napoleon (Fra)
1997	Werner Meuser (Ger)

Most titles: 4 Renner; 3 Reichmann, Lee

Golf

The exact origins of golf are uncertain. The Chinese played a form of the game 1800 years ago, and the French, Dutch and Belgians played something resembling it in the middle ages. Scotland must, however, be regarded as the home of golf. The game was banned in 1457 but golf was later played by Scottish royalty such as James IV and Mary. The world's first golf club, the Honourable Company of Edinburgh golfers, was founded in 1744. The ruling body of the sport, in the eyes of most countries, is the Royal & Ancient, situated at St Andrews. The Society of St Andrews Golfers, the forerunner of the R&A, played its first game of golf over the famous St Andrews links on 14 May 1754. The United States Golf Association (USGA) was founded in 1894.

Governing bodies: Royal & Ancient Golf Club of St Andrews, Golf Place St Andrews, Fife, Scotland KY16 9JD.
Tel: 01334 472112, Fax: 01334 477580. Secretary: Michael Bonallack.
World Golf Association, formed in 1989 with the purpose of gaining Olympic status for the sport.
World Amateur Golf Council (WAGC), David B Fay, Golf House, PO Box 708, Far Hills, NJ 07931-0708, USA.
Tel: (1) 908 234 2300, Fax: (1) 908 234 9687.

British Open

The Open first took place at Prestwick on 17 October 1860 with eight competitors playing over three 12-hole rounds. Prestwick hosted the first twelve Opens and all subsequent championships have been played over seaside links. The original prize was a Championship Belt but this was won outright by Tom Morris junior in 1870 and there was no event the following year. When it resumed in 1872 the prize was the silver claret jug that is still awarded to the champion today. Played over 36 holes 1860-91 and thereafter over 72 holes. Prize money (totalling £10) was introduced in 1863. The total grew, at first steadily and in recent years rapidly: some landmarks were £110 in 1892, £500 1931, £1000 1946, £5000 1959, £10,000 1965, £50,000 1972, £200,000 1980, £651,000 1987, £900,000 1991, £1,400,000 1996. The winner received £300,000 in 1998.

Winners:

		Score	Venue
1860	Willie Park, Sr (UK)	174	Prestwick
1861	Tom Morris, Sr (UK)	163	Prestwick
1862	Tom Morris, Sr (UK)	163	Prestwick
1863	Willie Park, Sr (UK)	168	Prestwick
1864	Tom Morris, Sr (UK)	167	Prestwick
1865	Andrew Strath (UK)	162	Prestwick
1866	Willie Park, Sr (UK)	169	Prestwick
1867	Tom Morris, Sr (UK)	170	Prestwick
1868	Tom Morris, Jr (UK)	157	Prestwick
1869	Tom Morris, Jr (UK)	154	Prestwick
1870	Tom Morris, Jr (UK)	149	Prestwick
1872	Tom Morris, Jr (UK)	166	Prestwick
1873	Tom Kidd (UK)	179	St Andrews
1874	Mungo Park (UK)	159	Musselburgh
1875	Willie Park, Sr (UK)	166	Prestwick
1876	Bob Martin (UK)	176	St Andrews
1877	Jamie Anderson (UK)	160	Musselburgh
1878	Jamie Anderson (UK)	157	Prestwick
1879	Jamie Anderson (UK)	169	St Andrews
1880	Robert Ferguson (UK)	162	Musselburgh
1881	Robert Ferguson (UK)	170	Prestwick
1882	Robert Ferguson (UK)	171	St Andrews
1883	Willie Fernie (UK)	158*	Musselburgh
1884	Jack Simpson (UK)	160	Prestwick
1885	Bob Martin (UK)	171	St Andrews
1886	David Brown (UK)	157	Musselburgh
1887	Willie Park, Jr (UK)	161	Prestwick
1888	Jack Burns (UK)	171	St Andrews
1889	Willie Park, Jr (UK)	155*	Musselburgh
1890	John Ball (UK)#	164	Prestwick
1891	Hugh Kirkaldy (UK)	166	St Andrews
1892	Harold H Hilton (UK)#	305	Muirfield
1893	William Auchterlonie (UK)	322	Prestwick
1894	John H Taylor (UK)	326	Sandwich
1895	John H Taylor (UK)	322	St Andrews
1896	Harry Vardon (UK)	316*	Muirfield
1897	Harold H Hilton (UK)#	314	Hoylake
1898	Harry Vardon (UK)	307	Prestwick
1899	Harry Vardon (UK)	310	Sandwich
1900	John H Taylor (UK)	309	St Andrews
1901	James Braid (UK)	309	Muirfield
1902	Sandy Herd (UK)	307	Hoylake
1903	Harry Vardon (UK)	300	Prestwick
1904	Jack White (UK)	296	Sandwich
1905	James Braid (UK)	318	St Andrews
1906	James Braid (UK)	300	Muirfield
1907	Arnaud Massy (Fra)	312	Hoylake
1908	James Braid (UK)	291	Prestwick
1909	John H Taylor (UK)	295	Deal
1910	James Braid (UK)	299	St Andrews
1911	Harry Vardon (UK)	303	Sandwich
1912	Edward Ray (UK)	295	Muirfield
1913	John H Taylor (UK)	304	Hoylake
1914	Harry Vardon (UK)	306	Prestwick
1920	George Duncan (UK)	303	Deal
1921	Jock Hutchinson (USA)	296*	St Andrews
1922	Walter Hagen (USA)	300	Sandwich
1923	Arthur Havers (UK)	295	Troon
1924	Walter Hagen (USA)	301	Hoylake
1925	Jim Barnes (USA)	300	Prestwick
1926	Bobby Jones (USA)#	291	Royal Lytham
1927	Bobby Jones (USA)#	285	St Andrews
1928	Walter Hagen (USA)	292	Sandwich
1929	Walter Hagen (USA)	292	Muirfield
1930	Bobby Jones (USA)#	291	Hoylake
1931	Tommy Armour (USA)	296	Carnoustie
1932	Gene Sarazen (USA)	283	Prince's
1933	Densmore Shute (USA)	292*	St Andrews
1934	Henry Cotton (UK)	283	Sandwich
1935	Alfred Perry (UK)	283	Muirfield
1936	Alfred Padgham (UK)	287	Hoylake
1937	Henry Cotton (UK)	290	Carnoustie
1938	Reg Whitcombe (UK)	295	Sandwich
1939	Dick Burton (UK)	290	St Andrews
1946	Sam Snead (USA)	290	St Andrews
1947	Fred Daly (UK)	293	Hoylake
1948	Henry Cotton (UK)	284	Muirfield
1949	Bobby Locke (SAf)	283*	Sandwich
1950	Bobby Locke (SAf)	279	Troon
1951	Max Faulkner (UK)	285	Portrush
1952	Bobby Locke (SAf)	287	Royal Lytham

1953	Ben Hogan (USA)	282	Carnoustie
1954	Peter Thomson (Aus)	283	Royal Birkdale
1955	Peter Thomson (Aus)	281	St Andrews
1956	Peter Thomson (Aus)	286	Hoylake
1957	Bobby Locke (SAf)	279	St Andrews
1958	Peter Thomson (Aus)	278★	Royal Lytham
1959	Gary Player (SAf)	284	Muirfield
1960	Kel Nagle (Aus)	278	St Andrews
1961	Arnold Palmer (USA)	284	Royal Birkdale
1962	Arnold Palmer (USA)	276	Troon
1963	Bob Charles (NZ)	277★	Royal Lytham
1964	Tony Lema (USA)	279	St Andrews
1965	Peter Thomson (Aus)	285	Royal Birkdale
1966	Jack Nicklaus (USA)	282	Muirfield
1967	Roberto de Vicenzo (Arg)	278	Hoylake
1968	Gary Player (SAf)	289	Carnoustie
1969	Tony Jacklin (UK)	280	Royal Lytham
1970	Jack Nicklaus (USA)	283★	St Andrews
1971	Lee Trevino (USA)	278	Royal Birkdale
1972	Lee Trevino (USA)	278	Muirfield
1973	Tom Weiskopf (USA)	276	Troon
1974	Gary Player (SAf)	282	Royal Lytham
1975	Tom Watson (USA)	279★	Carnoustie
1976	Johnny Miller (USA)	279	Royal Birkdale
1977	Tom Watson (USA)	268	Turnberry
1978	Jack Nicklaus (USA)	281	St Andrews
1979	Seve Ballesteros (Spa)	283	Royal Lytham
1980	Tom Watson (USA)	271	Muirfield
1981	Bill Rogers (USA)	276	Sandwich
1982	Tom Watson (USA)	284	Troon
1983	Tom Watson (USA)	275	Royal Birkdale
1984	Seve Ballesteros (Spa)	276	St Andrews
1985	Sandy Lyle (UK)	282	Sandwich
1986	Greg Norman (Aus)	280	Turnberry
1987	Nick Faldo (UK)	279	Muirfield
1988	Seve Ballesteros (Spa)	273	Royal Lytham
1989	Mark Calcavecchia (USA)	275★	Troon
1990	Nick Faldo (UK)	270	St Andrews
1991	Ian Baker-Finch (Aus)	272	Royal Birkdale
1992	Nick Faldo (UK)	272	Muirfield
1993	Greg Norman (Aus)	267	Sandwich
1994	Nick Price (Zim)	268	Turnberry
1995	John Daly (USA)	282★	St Andrews
1996	Tom Lehmann (USA)	271	Royal Lytham
1997	Justin Leonard (USA)	272	Troon
1998	Mark O'Meara (USA)	280★	Royal Birkdale

★ After play-off, # amateur champion.

Most wins: 6 Vardon; 5 Braid, Taylor, Thomson, Watson

Most top 3 placings: 13 Nicklaus (record 7 times runner-up); 12 Vardon, Taylor; 11 Braid

Most top 6 placings: 18 Taylor; 17 Nicklaus; 16 Vardon, Braid; 12 Thomson

US Open

First played on a 9-hole course at Newport, Rhode Island on 4 Oct 1895, when English-born Horace Rawlins won, collecting a cheque for $150 (from a total of $335). Now played over 72 holes (36 in 1895-7). Prize money reached $1200 in 1916, $5000 1929, $15,000 1950, $131,690 1965, $506,184 1983, $1 million 1990, $2 million 1995.

Winners (all USA unless stated otherwise):

		Score	Venue
1895	Horace Rawlins	173	Newport
1896	James Foulis	152	Shinnecock Hills
1897	Joe Lloyd	162	Chicago
1898	Fred Herd	328	Myopia Hunt
1899	Willie Smith	315	Baltimore
1900	Harry Vardon (UK)	313	Chicago
1901	Willie Anderson	331★	Myopia Hunt
1902	Laurie Auchterlonie	307	Garden City
1903	Willie Anderson	307★	Baltusrol
1904	Willie Anderson	303	Glen View
1905	Willie Anderson	314	Myopia Hunt
1906	Alex Smith	295	Onwentsia
1907	Alex Ross	302	Philadelphia
1908	Fred McLeod	322★	Myopia Hunt
1909	George Sargent	290	Englewood
1910	Alex Smith	298★	Philadelphia
1911	John McDermott	307★	Chicago
1912	John McDermott	294	Buffalo
1913	Francis Ouimet#	304★	Brookline
1914	Walter Hagen	290	Midlothian
1915	Jerome Travers#	297	Baltusrol
1916	Charles Evans, Jr#	286	Minikahda
1919	Walter Hagen	301★	Brae Burn
1920	Edward Ray (UK)	295	Inverness
1921	Jim Barnes	289	Columbia
1922	Gene Sarazen	288	Skokie
1923	Bobby Jones#	296★	Inwood
1924	Cyril Walker	297	Oakland Hills
1925	Willie Macfarlane	291★	Worcester
1926	Bobby Jones#	293	Scioto
1927	Tommy Armour	301★	Oakmont
1928	Johnny Farrell	294★	Olympia Fields
1929	Bobby Jones#	294★	Winged Foot
1930	Bobby Jones#	287	Interlachen
1931	Billy Burke	292★	Inverness
1932	Gene Sarazen	286	Fresh Meadow
1933	Johnny Goodman#	287	North Shore
1934	Olin Dutra	293	Merion
1935	Sam Parks, Jr	299	Oakmont
1936	Tony Manero	282	Baltusrol
1937	Ralph Guldahl	281	Oakland Hills
1938	Ralph Guldahl	284	Cherry Hills
1939	Byron Nelson	284★	Philadelphia
1940	Lawson Little	287★	Canterbury
1941	Craig Wood	284	Colonial
1946	Lloyd Mangrum	284★	Canterbury

1947	Lew Worsham	282*	St Louis
1948	Ben Hogan	276	Riviera
1949	Cary Middlecoff	286	Medinah
1950	Ben Hogan	287*	Merion
1951	Ben Hogan	287	Oakland Hills
1952	Julius Boros	281	Northwood
1953	Ben Hogan	283	Oakmont
1954	Ed Furgol	284	Baltusrol
1955	Jack Fleck	287*	Olympic
1956	Cary Middlecoff	281	Oak Hill
1957	Dick Mayer	282*	Inverness
1958	Tommy Bolt	283	Southern Hills
1959	Billy Casper	282	Winged Foot
1960	Arnold Palmer	280	Cherry Hills
1961	Gene Littler	281	Oakland Hills
1962	Jack Nicklaus	283*	Oakmont
1963	Julius Boros	293*	Brookline
1964	Ken Venturi	278	Congressional
1965	Gary Player (SAf)	282*	Bellerive
1966	Billy Casper	278*	Olympic
1967	Jack Nicklaus	275	Baltusrol
1968	Lee Trevino	275	Oak Hill
1969	Orville Moody	281	Champions
1970	Tony Jacklin (UK)	281	Hazeltine
1971	Lee Trevino	280*	Merion
1972	Jack Nicklaus	290	Pebble Beach
1973	Johnny Miller	279	Oakmont
1974	Hale Irwin	287*	Winged Foot
1975	Lou Graham	287	Medinah
1976	Jerry Pate	277	Atlanta
1977	Hubert Green	278	Southern Hills
1978	Andy North	285	Cherry Hills
1979	Hale Irwin	284	Inverness
1980	Jack Nicklaus	272	Baltusrol
1981	David Graham (Aus)	273	Merion
1982	Tom Watson	282	Pebble Beach
1983	Larry Nelson	280	Oakmont
1984	Fuzzy Zoeller	276*	Winged Foot
1985	Andy North	279	Oakland Hills
1986	Raymond Floyd	279	Shinnecock Hills
1987	Scott Simpson	277	Olympic Club
1988	Curtis Strange	278	Brookline
1989	Curtis Strange	278	Oak Hill
1990	Hale Irwin	280*	Medinah
1991	Payne Stewart	282*	Hazeltine
1992	Tom Kite	285	Monterey
1993	Lee Janzen	272	Ballustrol
1994	Ernie Els (SAf)	279*	Oakmont
1995	Corey Pavin	280	Shinnecock Hills
1996	Steve Jones	278	Oakland Hills
1997	Ernie Els (SAf)	276	Bethesda
1998	Lee Janzen	280	Olympic Club

* After play-off, # amateur champion.

Most wins: 4 Anderson, Jones, Hogan, Nicklaus

Most top 3 placings: 9 Nicklaus; 7 Hogan, Sarazen; 6 Anderson, Palmer

Most top 6 placings: 12 Hogan; 11 Anderson, Hagan, Sarazen, Palmer, Nicklaus

US Masters

Held annually at the Augusta National Golf Club in Georgia from 1934. Both the course and the tournament were the idea of the legendary golfer Bobby Jones. Entry to the Masters is by invitation only and the winner is presented with a coveted green jacket. Contested over 72 holes of stroke-play.

Winners (all USA unless stated otherwise):

1934	Horton Smith	284
1935	Gene Sarazen	282*
1936	Horton Smith	285
1937	Byron Nelson	283
1938	Henry Picard	285
1939	Ralph Guldahl	279
1940	Jimmy Demaret	280
1941	Craig Wood	280
1942	Byron Nelson	280*
1946	Herman Keiser	282
1947	Jimmy Demaret	281
1948	Claude Harmon	279
1949	Sam Snead	282
1950	Jimmy Demaret	283
1951	Ben Hogan	280
1952	Sam Snead	286
1953	Ben Hogan	274
1954	Sam Snead	289*
1955	Cary Middlecoff	279
1956	Jack Burke, Jr	289
1957	Doug Ford	282
1958	Arnold Palmer	284
1959	Art Wall, Jr	284
1960	Arnold Palmer	282*
1961	Gary Player (SAf)	280
1962	Arnold Palmer	280*
1963	Jack Nicklaus	286
1964	Arnold Palmer	276
1965	Jack Nicklaus	271
1966	Jack Nicklaus	288*
1967	Gay Brewer	280
1968	Bob Goalby	277
1969	George Archer	281
1970	Billy Casper	279*
1971	Charles Coody	279
1972	Jack Nicklaus	286
1973	Tommy Aaron	283
1974	Gary Player (SAf)	278
1975	Jack Nicklaus	276
1976	Raymond Floyd	271
1977	Tom Watson	276
1978	Gary Player (SAf)	277
1979	Fuzzy Zoeller	280*
1980	Seve Ballesteros (Spa)	275
1981	Tom Watson	280
1982	Craig Stadler	284*
1983	Seve Ballesteros (Spa)	280

1984	Ben Crenshaw	277
1985	Bernhard Langer (FRG)	282
1986	Jack Nicklaus	279
1987	Larry Mize	285★
1988	Sandy Lyle (UK)	281
1989	Nick Faldo (UK)	283★
1990	Nick Faldo (UK)	278★
1991	Ian Woosnam (UK)	277
1992	Fred Couples	275
1993	Bernhard Langer (Ger)	277

1994	José-Maria Olazábal (Spa)	279
1995	Ben Crenshaw	274
1996	Nick Faldo (UK)	276
1997	Tiger Woods	270
1998	Mark O'Meara	279

★ After play-off.

Most wins: 6 Nicklaus; 4 Palmer

Most top 5 placings: 15 Nicklaus; 9 Snead, Hogan, Palmer

US PGA Championship

First held in 1916, this was a matchplay event until 1958, when it became a stroke-play competition over four rounds. Entry is based on qualification from the Professional Golfers' Association (PGA) tour; it has been the least publicized of the four Majors.

Winners (all USA unless stated otherwise):

		Score	Venue
1916	Jim Barnes	1 up	Siwanoy
1919	Jim Barnes	6 & 5	Engineers
1920	Jock Hutchison	1 up	Flossmoor
1921	Walter Hagen	3 & 2	Inwood
1922	Gene Sarazen	4 & 3	Oakmont
1923	Gene Sarazen	at 38th	Pelham
1924	Walter Hagen	2 up	French Lick
1925	Walter Hagen	6 & 5	Olympia Fields
1926	Walter Hagen	5 & 3	Salisbury
1927	Walter Hagen	1 up	Cedar Crest
1928	Leo Diegel	6 & 5	Five Farms
1929	Leo Diegel	6 & 4	Hill Crest
1930	Tommy Armour	1 up	Fresh Meadow
1931	Tom Creavy	2 & 1	Wannamoisett
1932	Olin Dutra	4 & 3	Keller
1933	Gene Sarazen	5 & 4	Blue Mound
1934	Paul Runyan	at 38th	Park
1935	Johnny Revolta	5 & 4	Twin Hills
1936	Densmore Shute	3 & 2	Pinehurst
1937	Densmore Shute	at 37th	Pittsburgh
1938	Paul Runyan	8 & 7	Shawnee
1939	Henry Picard	at 37th	Pomonok
1940	Byron Nelson	1 up	Hershey
1941	Vic Ghezzi	at 38th	Cherry Hills
1942	Sam Snead	2 & 1	Sea View
1944	Bob Hamilton	1 up	Manito
1945	Byron Nelson	4 & 3	Morraine
1946	Ben Hogan	6 & 4	Portland
1947	Jim Ferrier	2 & 1	Plum Hollow
1948	Ben Hogan	7 & 6	Norwood Hills
1949	Sam Snead	3 & 2	Hermitage
1950	Chandler Harper	4 & 3	Scioto
1951	Sam Snead	7 & 6	Oakmont
1952	Jim Turnesa	1 up	Big Spring
1953	Walter Burkemo	2 & 1	Birmingham
1954	Chick Harbert	4 & 3	Keller
1955	Doug Ford	4 & 3	Meadowbrook
1956	Jack Burke	3 & 2	Blue Hill
1957	Lionel Hebert	2 & 1	Miami Valley
1958	Dow Finsterwald	276	Llanerch
1959	Bob Rosburg	277	Minneapolis
1960	Jay Hebert	281	Firestone
1961	Jerry Barber	277★	Olympia Fields
1962	Gary Player (SAf)	278	Aronomink
1963	Jack Nicklaus	279	Dallas
1964	Bobby Nichols	271	Columbus
1965	Dave Marr	280	Laurel Valley
1966	Al Geiberger	280	Firestone
1967	Don January	281★	Columbine
1968	Julius Boros	281	Pecan Valley
1969	Raymond Floyd	276	NCR, Dayton
1970	Dave Stockton	279	Southern Hills
1971	Jack Nicklaus	281	PGA National
1972	Gary Player (SAf)	281	Oakland Hills
1973	Jack Nicklaus	277	Canterbury
1974	Lee Trevino	276	Tanglewood
1975	Jack Nicklaus	276	Firestone
1976	Dave Stockton	281	Congressional
1977	Lanny Wadkins	282★	Pebble Beach
1978	John Mahaffey	276★	Oakmont
1979	David Graham (Aus)	272★	Oakland Hills
1980	Jack Nicklaus	274	Oak Hill
1981	Larry Nelson	273	Atlanta
1982	Raymond Floyd	272	Southern Hills
1983	Hal Sutton	274	Riviera
1984	Lee Trevino	273	Shoal Creek
1985	Hubert Green	278	Cherry Hills
1986	Bob Tway	276	Toledo
1987	Larry Nelson	287★	Palm Beach
1988	Jeff Sluman	272	Oak Tree
1989	Payne Stewart	276	Kemper Lakes
1990	Wayne Grady (Aus)	282	Shoal Creek
1991	John Daly	276	Crooked Stick
1992	Nick Price (Zim)	278	St Louis
1993	Paul Azinger	272★	Toledo
1994	Nick Price (Zim)	269	Southern Hills
1995	Steve Elkington (Aus)	267★	Riviera CC
1996	Mark Brooks	277	Valhalla
1997	Davis Love III	269	Winged Foot

★ After play-off.

Most wins: 5 Hagen, Nicklaus; 3 Sarazen, Snead

The Majors – Records

Lowest four-round total

The Open	267	Greg Norman 1993
US Open	272	Jack Nicklaus 1980
	272	Lee Janzen 1993
US PGA	267	Steve Elkington 1995
	267	Colin Montgomerie (UK) 1995
US Masters	270	Tiger Woods 1997

Lowest single round

The Open	63	Mark Hayes (USA) 2nd Rd 1977
	63	Isao Aoki (Jap) 3rd Rd 1980
	63	Greg Norman (Aus) 2nd Rd 1986
	63	Paul Broadhurst (UK) 3rd Rd 1990
	63	Jodie Mudd (USA) 4th Rd 1991
	63	Nick Faldo (UK) 2nd Rd 1993
	63	Payne Stewart (USA) 4th Rd 1993
US Open	63	Johnny Miller (USA) 4th Rd 1973
	63	Tom Weiskopf (USA) 1st Rd 1980
	63	Jack Nicklaus (USA) 1st Rd 1980
US PGA	63	Bruce Crampton (Aus) 2nd Rd 1975
	63	Raymond Floyd (USA) 1st Rd 1982
	63	Gary Player (SAf) 2nd Rd 1984
	63	Vijay Singh (Fiji) 3rd Rd 1993
	63	Michael Bradley (USA) 1st Rd 1995
	63	Brad Faxon (USA) 4th Rd 1995
US Masters	63	Nick Price (SAf) 3rd Rd 1986
	63	Greg Norman (Aus) 1st Rd 1996

Oldest winners

The Open	46yr 99d	Tom Morris, Sr 1867
US Open	45yr 15d	Hale Irwin 1990
US PGA	48yr 140d	Julius Boros 1968
US Masters	46yr 82d	Jack Nicklaus 1986

Youngest winners

The Open	17yr 249d	Tom Morris, Jr 1868
US Open	19yr 318d	John McDermott 1911
US PGA	20yr 173d	Gene Sarazen 1922
US Masters	21yr 104d	Tiger Woods 1997

Most wins in Majors

(A – British Open, B – US Open, C – US PGA, D – US Masters)

		A	B	C	D
18	Jack Nicklaus	3	4	5	6
11	Walter Hagen	4	2	5	-
9	Ben Hogan	1	4	2	2
9	Gary Player	3	1	2	3
8	Tom Watson	5	1	-	2
7	Harry Vardon	6	1	-	-
7	Bobby Jones	3	4	-	-
7	Gene Sarazen	1	2	3	1
7	Sam Snead	1	-	3	3
7	Arnold Palmer	2	1	-	4

When he won the Masters in 1935 Gene Sarazen became the first man to have won all four Majors.

No man has won all four in one year, but in 1953 Ben Hogan won three (British Open, US Open and Masters); he did not contest the PGA. In 1986 Greg Norman led going into the final round of all four, but won only one – the British Open.

Jack Nicklaus also won two US Amateur titles and Bobby Jones won five US Amateur and one British Amateur. Jones uniquely won the Open and Amateur Championships of the USA and Britain in one year, 1930.

World Matchplay Championship

An annual end-of-season knock-out competition held at Wentworth, Surrey. The number of entrants was originally eight but has since been increased to 12 (16 in 1977-8). Each match consists of two rounds, one in the morning and one in the afternoon. Sponsored by Piccadilly 1964-76, Colgate 1977-8, Suntory 1979-91, Toyota from 1992.

Year	Winner	Runner-up	Score
1964	Arnold Palmer (USA)	Neil Coles (UK)	2 & 1
1965	Gary Player (SAf)	Peter Thomson (Aus)	3 & 2
1966	Gary Player (SAf)	Jack Nicklaus (USA)	6 & 4
1967	Arnold Palmer (USA)	Peter Thomson (Aus)	1 up
1968	Gary Player (SAf)	Bob Charles (NZ)	1 up
1969	Bob Charles (NZ)	Gene Littler (USA)	at 37th
1970	Jack Nicklaus (USA)	Lee Trevino (USA)	2 & 1
1971	Gary Player (SAf)	Jack Nicklaus (USA)	5 & 4
1972	Tom Weiskopf (USA)	Lee Trevino (USA)	4 & 3
1973	Gary Player (SAf)	Graham Marsh (Aus)	at 40th
1974	Hale Irwin (USA)	Gary Player (SAf)	3 & 1
1975	Hale Irwin (USA)	Al Geiberger (USA)	4 & 2
1976	David Graham (Aus)	Hale Irwin (USA)	at 38th
1977	Graham Marsh (Aus)	Raymond Floyd (USA)	5 & 3
1978	Isao Aoki (Jap)	Simon Owen (NZ)	3 & 2
1979	Bill Rogers (USA)	Isao Aoki (Jap)	1 up

1980	Greg Norman (Aus)	Sandy Lyle (UK)	1 up
1981	Seve Ballesteros (Spa)	Ben Crenshaw (USA)	1 up
1982	Seve Ballesteros (Spa)	Sandy Lyle (UK)	at 37th
1983	Greg Norman (Aus)	Nick Faldo (UK)	3 & 2
1984	Seve Ballesteros (Spa)	Bernhard Langer (FRG)	2 & 1
1985	Seve Ballesteros (Spa)	Bernhard Langer (FRG)	6 & 5
1986	Greg Norman (Aus)	Sandy Lyle (UK)	2 & 1
1987	Ian Woosnam (UK)	Sandy Lyle (UK)	1 up
1988	Sandy Lyle (UK)	Nick Faldo (UK)	2 & 1
1989	Nick Faldo (UK)	Ian Woosnam (UK)	1 up
1990	Ian Woosnam (UK)	Mark McNulty (Zim)	4 & 2
1991	Seve Ballesteros (Spa)	Nick Price (Zim)	3 & 2
1992	Nick Faldo (UK)	Jeff Sluman (USA)	8 & 7
1993	Corey Pavin (USA	Nick Faldo (UK)	1 up
1994	Ernie Els (SAf)	Colin Montgomery (UK)	4 & 2
1995	Ernie Els (SAf)	Steve Elkington (Aus)	2 & 1
1996	Ernie Els (SAf)	Vijay Singh (Fiji)	3 & 2
1997	Vijay Singh (Fiji)	Ernie Els (SAf)	1 hole

Most wins: 5 Player, Ballesteros; 3 Norman
Biggest winning margin: 11 & 9 Tom Watson (USA) v Dale Hayes (SAf) 1st round 1979

Volvo PGA Championship

The PGA Closed Championships, restricted to British and Irish golfers, was instituted in 1955. Both 'closed' and 'open' championships were held in 1968, but from 1969 it has been an open championship on the PGA tour. Not played 1970-1, it is now sponsored by Volvo and has been played at Wentworth each year from 1984.

Winners from 1972:

1972	Tony Jacklin (UK)	279
1973	Peter Oosterhuis (UK)	280
1974	Maurice Bembridge (UK)	278
1975	Arnold Palmer (USA)	285
1976	Neil Coles (UK)	280
1977	Manuel Pinero (Spa)	283
1978	Nick Faldo (UK)	278
1979	Vicente Fernández (Arg)	288
1980	Nick Faldo (UK)	283
1981	Nick Faldo (UK)	274
1982	Tony Jacklin (UK)	284
1983	Seve Ballesteros (Spa)	278
1984	Howard Clark (UK)	204 (3 rounds)
1985	Paul Way (UK)	282
1986	Rodger Davis (Aus)	281
1987	Bernard Langer (Ger)	270
1988	Ian Woosnam (UK)	274
1989	Nick Faldo (UK)	272
1990	Mike Harwood (Aus)	271
1991	Seve Ballesteros (Spa)	271
1992	Tony Johnstone (Zim)	272
1993	Bernard Langer (Ger)	274
1994	José Maria Olazábal (Spa)	271
1995	Bernard Langer (Ger)	279
1996	Constantino Rocca (Ita)	274
1997	Ian Woosnam (UK)	275
1998	Colin Montgomerie (UK)	274

Tournament Players' Championship

Introduced into the US tour at Atlanta in 1974, with the intention of being a fifth Major, a status it has not really achieved, although its prize money has been among the highest on the PGA tour. Open only to players who have won official PGA tour events in the previous year. From 1977 it has been played on the TPC's own course at Sawgrass, Ponte Vedra, Florida.

Winners (all USA unless stated otherwise):

1974	Jack Nicklaus	272
1975	Al Geiberger	270
1976	Jack Nicklaus	269
1977	Mark Hayes	289
1978	Jack Nicklaus	289
1979	Lanny Wadkins	283
1980	Lee Trevino	278
1981	Raymond Floyd	285
1982	Jerrry Pate	280
1983	Hal Sutton	283
1984	Fred Couples	277
1985	Calvin Peete	274
1986	John Mahaffey	275
1987	Sandy Lyle (UK)	274
1988	Mark McCumber	273
1989	Tom Kite	279
1990	Jodie Mudd	278
1991	Steve Elkington (Aus)	276
1992	Davis Love III	273
1993	Nick Price (Zim)	270
1994	Greg Norman (Aus)	264
1995	Lee Janzen	283
1996	Fred Couples (USA)	270
1997	Steve Elkington (Aus)	272
1998	Justin Leonard	278

Johnny Walker World Championship

First held at the Tryall Golf Club, Montego Bay, Jamaica in 1991, when total prize money was a world-record $2,550,000, including $525,000 for first place. Those figures were increased to $2.7 million and $550,000 respectively from 1992.

Winners:

1991	Fred Couples (USA)	281	1993	Larry Mize (USA)	266	1995 Fred Couples (USA)	279★
1992	Nick Faldo (UK)	274★	1994	Ernie Els (SAf)	268		

★ After play-off.

World Cup

The World Cup was the idea of American industrialist Jay Hopkins, who saw the need for an international team competition for male professionals, other than for those of Great Britain and the United States.

Contested annually over 72 holes of stroke-play by two-man teams. Interest in the competition diminished in the 1980s and it was not played in 1981 or 1986.

Year	Winning team		Leading individual	
1953	Argentina (Roberto de Vicenzo & Antonio Cerda)	287★	Antonio Cerda (Arg)	140★
1954	Australia (Peter Thomson & Kel Nagle)	556	Stan Leonard (Can)	275
1955	USA (Ed Furgol & Chick Harbert)	560	Ed Furgol (USA)	279
1956	USA (Ben Hogan & Sam Snead)	567	Ben Hogan (USA)	277
1957	Japan (Torakichi Nakamura & Koichi Ono)	557	Torakichi Nakamura (Jap)	274
1958	Ireland (Harry Bradshaw & Christy O'Connor)	579	Angel Miguel (Spa)	286
	Miguel beat Harry Bradshaw (Ire) in a play-off for leading individual			
1959	Australia (Kel Nagle & Peter Thomson)	563	Stan Leonard (Can)	275
1960	USA (Arnold Palmer & Sam Snead)	565	Flory Van Donck (Bel)	279
1961	USA (Jimmy Demaret & Sam Snead)	560	Sam Snead (USA)	272
1962	USA (Arnold Palmer & Sam Snead)	557	Roberto de Vicenzo (Arg)	276
1963	USA (Jack Nicklaus & Arnold Palmer)	482★	Jack Nicklaus (USA)	237★
1964	USA (Jack Nicklaus & Arnold Palmer)	554	Jack Nicklaus (USA)	276
1965	South Africa (Harold Henning & Gary Player)	571	Gary Player (SAf)	281
1966	USA (Jack Nicklaus & Arnold Palmer)	548	George Knudson (Can)	272
1967	USA (Jack Nicklaus & Arnold Palmer)	557	Arnold Palmer (USA)	276
1968	Canada (Al Balding & George Knudson)	569	Al Balding (Can)	274
1969	USA (Orville Moody & Lee Trevino)	552	Lee Trevino (USA)	275
1970	Australia (Bruce Devlin & David Graham)	544	Roberto de Vicenzo (Arg)	269
1971	USA (Jack Nicklaus & Lee Trevino)	555	Jack Nicklaus (USA)	271
1972	Taiwan (Hsieh Min-nan & Lu Liang-huan)	438★	Hsieh Min-nan (Tai)	217★
1973	USA (Johnny Miller & Jack Nicklaus)	558	Johnny Miller (USA)	277
1974	South Africa (Bobby Cole & Dale Hayes)	554	Bobby Cole (SAf)	271
1975	USA (Lou Graham & Johnny Miller)	554	Johnny Miller (USA)	275
1976	Spain (Severiano Ballesteros & Manuel Pincro)	574	Ernesto Pérez Acosta (Mex)	282
1977	Spain (Severiano Ballesteros & Antonio Garrido)	591	Gary Player (SAf)	289
1978	USA (John Mahaffey & Andy North)	564	John Mahaffey (USA)	281
1979	USA (John Mahaffey & Hale Irwin)	575	Hale Irwin (USA)	285
1980	Canada (Dan Halldorson & Jim Nelford)	572	Sandy Lyle (Sco)	282
1982	Spain (José-Maria Canizares & Manuel Pinero)	563	Manuel Pinero (Spa)	281
1983	USA (Rex Caldwell & John Cook)	565	Dave Barr (Can)	276
1984	Spain (José-Maria Canizares & José Rivero)	414★	José-Maria Canizares (Spa)	205★
1985	Canada (Dan Halldorson & Dave Barr)	559	Howard Clark (Eng)	272
1987	Wales (Ian Woosnam & David Llewellyn)	574	Ian Woosnam (Wal)	274
1988	USA (Ben Crenshaw & Mark McCumber)	560	Ben Crenshaw (USA)	275
1989	Australia (Peter Fowler & Wayne Grady)	278★	Peter Fowler (Aus)	137★
1990	Germany (Bernhard Langer & Torsten Giedeon)	556	Payne Stewart (USA)	271
1991	Sweden (Anders Forsbrand & Per-Ulrik Johansson)	563	Ian Woosnam (Wal)	273
1992	USA (Fred Couples, Davis Love III)	548	Brett Ogle (Aus)	270★
1993	USA (Fred Couples, Davis Love III)	556	Bernhard Langer (Ger)	272

1994	USA (Fred Couples, Davis Love III)	536	Fred Couples (USA)	265
1995	USA (Fred Couples, Davis Love III)	543	Davis Love III (USA)	267
	Love beat Hisayuki Sasaki (Jap) in a play–off for leading individual			
1996	South Africa (Ernie Els, Wayne Westner)	547	Ernie Els (SAf)	272
1997	Ireland (Paul McGinley, Padraig Harrington)	545	Colin Montgomerie (Sco)	266

* Played over 36 holes in 1953, 63 holes in 1963, 54 holes in 1972 and 1984. Rain reduced play to 36 holes in 1989.

Most team wins: 21 USA
Most team wins by individuals: 6 Nicklaus, Palmer
Most individual titles: 3 Nicklaus

Ryder Cup

The Ryder Cup started as a result of the efforts of wealthy businessman Samuel Ryder. It was launched in 1927, the year after a successful match between Great Britain and the United States at Wentworth. Opposing the USA in this biennial match have been Great Britain 1927-71, Great Britain and Ireland 1973-77, and Europe from 1979, with the venue alternating between continents. The current format is for four foursomes and four fourball matches on each of the first two days, and 12 singles on the third and final day.

Year	Venue	Winners	Score
1927	Worcester, Massachusetts	USA	9.5-2.5
1929	Moortown, Yorkshire	GB	7-5
1931	Scioto, Ohio	USA	9-3
1933	Southport & Ainsdale, Lancashire	GB	6.5-5.5
1935	Ridgewood, New Jersey	USA	9-3
1937	Southport & Ainsdale, Lancashire	USA	8-4
1947	Portland, Oregan	USA	11-1
1949	Ganton, Yorkshire	USA	7-5
1951	Pinehurst, North Carolina	USA	9.5-2.5
1953	Wentworth, Surrey	USA	6.5-5.5
1955	Thunderbird G & CC, California	USA	8-4
1957	Lindrick, Yorkshire	GB	7.5-4.5
1959	Eldorado CC, California	USA	8.5-3.5
1961	Royal Lytham, Lancashire	USA	14.5 -9.5
1963	Atlanta, Georgia	USA	23-9
1965	Royal Birkdale, Lancashire	USA	19.5-12.5
1967	Houston, Texas	USA	23.5-8.5
1969	Royal Birkdale, Lancashire	Drawn	16-16
1971	St Louis, Missouri	USA	18.5-13.5
1973	Muirfield, Scotland	USA	19-13
1975	Laurel Valley, Pennsylvania	USA	21-11
1977	Royal Lytham, Lancs.	USA	12.5-7.5
1979	Greenbrier, West Virginia	USA	17-11
1981	Walton Heath, Surrey	USA	18.5-9.5
1983	PGA National, Florida	USA	14.5-13.5
1985	The Belfry, Sutton Coldfield	Europe	16.5-11.5
1987	Muirfield Village, Ohio	Europe	15-13
1989	The Belfry, Sutton Coldfield	Drawn	14-14
1991	Kiawah Island, SouthCarolina	USA	14.5-13.5
1993	The Belfry, Sutton Coldfield	USA	15-13
1995	Oak Hill CC, New York	Europe	14.5-13.5
1997	Valderrama, Spain	Europe	14.5-13.5

Most wins: 23 United States
Oldest players: 51yr 22d Ray Floyd (USA) 1993, 50yr 66d Edward Ray (GB) 1927
Youngest player: 20yr 59d Nick Faldo (GB&I) 1977

Leading players' records

(20 or more matches or 10 wins; Pts = points as 1 for win, 0.5 for halved match.)

Name	Years	Cups	Pl	W	L	H	Pts
GB/GB & Ireland/Europe							
Nick Faldo	1977–97	11	46	23	19	4	25
Severiano Ballesteros	1979–95	8	37	20	12	5	22.5
Bernhard Langer	1981–97	9	38	18	15	5	20.5
Tony Jacklin	1967–79	7	35	13	14	8	17
Ian Woosnam	1983–97	8	31	14	12	5	16.5
José-Maria Olazábal	1987–97	5	25	14	8	4	16
Peter Oosterhuis	1971–81	6	28	14	11	3	15.5
Bernard Gallacher	1969–83	8	31	13	13	5	15.5
Neil Coles	1961–77	8	40	12	21	7	15.5
Christy O'Connor	1955–73	10	35	11	20	4	13
Peter Alliss	1953–69	8	30	10	15	5	12.5
Colin Montgomerie	1991–97	4	18	9	6	3	11.5
Brian Barnes	1969–79	6	26	11	14	1	11.5
Brian Huggett	1963–75	6	24	8	10	6	11
Sam Torrance	1981–95	8	27	7	15	5	9.5
Bernard Hunt	1953–69	8	28	6	16	6	9
Mark James	1977–95	7	24	8	15	1	8.5
United States							
Billy Casper	1961–75	8	37	20	10	7	23.5
Arnold Palmer	1961–73	6	32	22	8	2	23
Lanny Wadkins	1977–93	8	33	20	11	2	21
Lee Trevino	1969–81	6	30	17	7	6	20
Jack Nicklaus	1969–81	6	28	17	8	3	18.5
Gene Littler	1961–75	7	27	14	5	8	18
Tom Kite	1979–93	7	28	15	9	4	17
Hale Irwin	1975–91	5	20	13	5	2	14
Raymond Floyd	1969–93	8	31	12	16	3	13.5
Sam Snead*	1937–59	7	13	10	2	1	10.5
Tom Watson	1977–89	4	15	10	4	1	10.5
Fred Couples	1989–97	5	20	7	9	4	9
Curtis Strange	1983–95	5	20	6	12	2	7

* Snead was also selected for 1939 and 1941 teams when the match was not contested.

Alfred Dunhill Cup

Knock-out tournament for international teams of three professionals. Played at St Andrews, Scotland.

Finals:

1985	Australia 3	USA 0	
1986	Australia 3	Japan 0	
1987	England 2	Scotland 1	
1988	Ireland 2	Australia 1	
1989	USA 3	Japan 2	
1990	Ireland 3.5	England 2.5	
1991	Sweden 2	South Africa 1	
1992	England 2.5	Scotland 0.5	
1993	USA 2	England 1	
1994	Canada 2	USA 1	
1995	Scotland 2	Zimbabwe 1	
1996	USA 2	New Zealand 1	
1997	South Africa 2	Sweden 1	

President's Cup

Inaugurated in 1994 and contested by teams from the USA and from non-European international players. All 12 in each team contest singles with two sets of five fourballs and foursomes. The USA won the first match 20-12.

Leading Annual Money-Winners

European tour

Year	Golfer	Earnings (£)
1961	Bernard Hunt (UK)	4,492
1962	Peter Thomson (Aus)	5,764
1963	Bernard Hunt (UK)	7,209
1964	Neil Coles (UK)	7,890
1965	Peter Thomson (Aus)	7,011
1966	Bruce Devlin (Aus)	13,205
1967	Gay Brewer (USA)	20,235

Year	Golfer	Earnings
1968	Gay Brewer (USA)	£23,107
1969	Billy Casper (USA)	23,483
1970	Christy O'Connor (Ire)	31,532
1971	Gary Player (SAf)	11,281
1972	Bob Charles (NZ)	18,538
1973	Tony Jacklin (UK)	24,839
1974	Peter Oosterhuis (UK)	32,127
1975	Dale Hayes (SAf)	20,507
1976	Seve Ballesteros (Spa)	39,504
1977	Seve Ballesteros (Spa)	46,436
1978	Scve Ballesteros (Spa)	54,348
1979	Sandy Lyle (UK)	49,233
1980	Greg Norman (Aus)	74,829
1981	Bernhard Langer (FRG)	95,991
1982	Sandy Lyle (UK)	86,141
1983	Nick Faldo (UK)	140,761
1984	Bernhard Langer (FRG)	160,883
1985	Sandy Lyle (UK)	199,020
1986	Seve Ballesteros (Spa)	259,275
1987	Ian Woosnam (UK)	439,075
1988	Seve Ballesteros (Spa)	502,000
1989	Ronan Rafferty (Ire)	465,981
1990	Ian Woosnam (UK)	574,166
1991	Seve Ballesteros (Spa)	545,353
1992	Nick Faldo (UK)	708,522
1993	Colin Montgomerie (UK)	613,682
1994	Colin Montgomerie (UK)	762,719
1995	Colin Montgomerie (UK)	835,051
1996	Colin Montgomerie (UK)	875,146
1997	Colin Montgomerie (UK)	798,948

Woosnam's total world-wide earnings in 1987 were a record £1,042,662; Bernard Langer (Ger) won $2,185,358 world-wide in 1991, and Faldo £1,558,978 in 1992.

USA tour

Winners (all USA unless stated otherwise):

Year	Golfer	Earnings ($US)
1934	Paul Runyan	6,767
1935	Johnny Revolta	9,543
1936	Horton Smith	7,682
1937	Harry Cooper	14,138
1938	Sam Snead	19,534
1939	Henry Picard	10,303
1940	Ben Hogan	10,655
1941	Ben Hogan	18,358
1942	Ben Hogan	13,143
1943	*Statistics not compiled*	
1944	Byron Nelson	37,967★
1945	Byron Nelson	63,335★
1946	Ben Hogan	42,556
1947	Jimmy Demaret	27,936
1948	Ben Hogan	32,112
1949	Sam Snead	31,593
1950	Sam Snead	35,758
1951	Lloyd Mangrum	26,088
1952	Julius Boros	37,032
1953	Lew Worsham	34,002
1954	Bob Toski	65,819
1955	Julius Boros	63,121
1956	Ted Kroll	72,835
1957	Dick Mayer	65,835
1958	Arnold Palmer	42,607
1959	Art Wall, Jr	53,167
1960	Arnold Palmer	75,262
1961	Gary Player (SAf)	64,450
1962	Arnold Palmer	81,448
1963	Arnold Palmer	128,230
1964	Jack Nicklaus	113,284
1965	Jack Nicklaus	140,752
1966	Billy Casper	121,944
1967	Jack Nicklaus	188,998
1968	Billy Casper	205,168
1969	Frank Beard	164,707
1970	Lee Trevino	157,037
1971	Jack Nicklaus	244,490
1972	Jack Nicklaus	320,542
1973	Jack Nicklaus	308,362
1974	Johnny Miller	353,021
1975	Jack Nicklaus	298,149
1976	Jack Nicklaus	266,438
1977	Tom Watson	310,653
1978	Tom Watson	362,428
1979	Tom Watson	462,636
1980	Tom Watson	530,808
1981	Tom Kite	375,698
1982	Craig Stadler	446,462
1983	Hal Sutton	426,668
1984	Tom Watson	476,260
1985	Curtis Strange	542,321
1986	Greg Norman (Aus)	653,296
1987	Curtis Strange	925,941
1988	Curtis Strange	1,147,644
1989	Tom Kite	1,395,278
1990	Greg Norman (Aus)	1,165,477
1991	Corey Pavin	979,430
1992	Fred Couples	1,344,188
1993	Nick Price (Zim)	1,478,557
1994	Nick Price (Zim)	1,499,927
1995	Greg Norman (Aus)	1,654,959
1996	Tom Lehmann	1,780,159
1997	Tiger Woods	2,066,833

★ Nelson received War Bonds.

Most times leading: 8 Nicklaus

Harry Vardon Trophy

European tour

Awarded annually from 1937 to the leading player in the Order of Merit. The first winner was Charles Whitcombe.

Most wins:

5 Severiano Ballesteros (Spa) 1976-8, 1986, 1988
5 Colin Montgomerie (UK) 1993-7

4	Peter Oosterhuis (UK)	1971–4
3	Bobby Locke (SAf)	1946, 1950, 1954
3	Bernard Hunt (UK)	1958, 1960, 1965
3	Sandy Lyle (UK)	1979–80, 1985

USA tour

Awarded annually from 1937 (except 1942–6) by the USPGA to the player who has the lowest stroke average in PGA tournaments in that year.

Most wins:

5	Billy Casper	1960, 1963, 1965–6, 1968
5	Lee Trevino	1970–2, 1974, 1980
4	Sam Snead	1938, 1949–50, 1955
4	Arnold Palmer	1961–2, 1964, 1967
3	Ben Hogan	1940–1, 1948
3	Tom Watson	1977–9
3	Greg Norman (Aus)	1989–90, 1994

All-Time Earnings

European tour

	Amount (£)	Wins	Years
Bernhard Langer (Ger)	6,041,241	38	1976–97
Colin Montgomerie (UK)	5,993,655	15	1987–97
Ian Woosnam (UK)	5,384,285	32	1978–97
Nick Faldo (UK)	5,072,682	29	1976–96
Severiano Ballesteros (Spa)	4,495,588	54	1974–97
Sam Torrance (UK)	3,995,736	20	1971–97
José-Maria Olazábal (Spa)	3,525,995	16	1986–97
Mark McNulty (Zim)	3,122,039	15	1978–97
Barry Lane (UK)	2,814,057	5	1982–97
Mark James (UK)	2,804,779	17	1976–97
Ronan Rafferty (UK)	2,684,824	7	1981–97
Constantino Rocca (Ita)	2,618,725	4	1983–97
Sandy Lyle (UK)	2,521,705	19	1977–96

USA tour

	Amount ($US)	Wins	Years
Greg Norman (Aus)	11,910,518	18	1983–97
Tom Kite (USA)	10,286,177	19	1972–97
Fred Couples (USA)	8,835,487	13	1980–97
Nick Price (Zim)	8,794,431	15	1983–97
Mark O'Meara (USA)	8,506,774	14	1981–97
Davis Love III (USA	8,470,982	12	1986–97
Payne Stewart (USA)	8,465,062	9	1981–97
Tom Watson (USA)	8,307,277	33	1971–97
Corey Pavin (USA)	8,130,356	14	1984–97
Scott Hoch (USA)	7,899,250	8	1980–97
Mark Calcavecchia (USA)	7,612,931	8	1981–97
Paul Azinger (USA)	7,451,410	11	1981–97
Curtis Strange (USA)	7,147,752	17	1977–97
Ben Crenshaw (USA)	7,064,604	19	1973–97
Craig Stadler (USA)	6,870,877	12	1976–97
Jay Haas (USA)	6,390,645	9	1980–97
Steve Elkington (Aus)	6,328,138	8	1987–97
David Frost (SAf)	6,299,819	10	1985–97
Lanny Wadkins (USA)	6,249,812	21	1971–97
John Cook (USA)	6,109,117	9	1980–97

Chip Beck (USA)	5,994,624	4	1979–97
Hale Irwin (USA)	5,902,306	20	1968–97
Bruce Lietzke (USA)	5,880,803	13	1974–97

Most tournament wins: 81 Sam Snead (1937–65); 70 Jack Nicklaus; 63 Ben Hogan; 60 Arnold Palmer; 52 Byron Nelson; 51 Billy Casper; 40 Walter Hagen, Cary Middlecoff; 38 Gene Sarazen; 36 Lloyd Mangrum

Records

European tour

Most wins in a season: 7 Norman Von Nida (Aus) 1947, Flory Van Donck (Bel) 1953

Most consecutive wins: 4 Alf Padgham (UK) 1935–6, Severiano Ballesteros (Spa) 1986

Lowest score (72 holes): 258 David Llewellyn (UK) 1988 Biarritz Open, Ian Woosnam (UK) Monte Carlo Open 1990

Lowest score (18 holes): 60 Baldovino Dassu (Ita) 1971 Swiss Open, David Llewellyn (UK) 1988 Biarritz Open, Ian Woosnam (UK) Monte Carlo Open 1990, Paul Curry (UK) 1992 Scottish Open, Jamie Spence 1992 European Masters, Johan Ryström (Swe) and Darren Clarke (UK) Monte Carlo Open 1992, Bernhard Langer (Ger) German Masters 1997.

Oldest winner: 58yr Sandy Herd (UK) 1926 News of the World

Youngest winner: 18yr 290d Dale Hayes (SAf) 1971 Spanish Open

US PGA tour

Most wins in a season: 18 Byron Nelson (USA) 1945

Most consecutive wins: 11 Byron Nelson 1945

Lowest score (72 holes): 257 Mike Souchak (USA) 1955 Texas Open

Lowest score (18 holes): 59 Al Geiberger (USA) 1977 Memphis Classic, Chip Beck (USA) 1991 Las Vegas Invitational

Oldest winner: 52yr 312d Sam Snead 1965 Greater Greensboro Open

Youngest winner: 19yr 10m John McDermott (USA) 1911 US Open

US Senior PGA tour

Most career wins: 27 Lee Trevino (USA) 1989–96

Highest career earnings: $7,449,561 Lee Trevino (USA), $7,244,675 Bob Charles (NZ), $7,126,797 Jim Colbert (USA)

Highest season earnings: $2,343,364 Hale Irwin (USA) 1997

Sony World Rankings

Introduced in 1986 in an attempt to rank players on their achievements world-wide.

Top-ranked players:

Bernhard Langer (Ger)	1986, 1992
Greg Norman (Aus)	1986–9, 1990, 1994–5, 1995–7
Nick Faldo (UK)	1990–1, 1992–4
Seve Ballesteros (Spa)	1986, 1989
Ian Woosnam (UK)	1991–2
Fred Couples (USA)	1992
Nick Price (Zim)	1994–5
Tom Lehman (USA)	1997
Tiger Woods (USA)	1997–8, 1998
Ernie Els (SAf)	1997, 1998

Men's Amateur Golf

US Amateur Championship

Although unofficial US Amateur Championships had been held previously, the first official championship was at Newport, Rhode Island in 1895. The inaugural US Open was also held during the same week, and at the same venue.

The Amateur Championship was originally a matchplay competition, changed to stroke-play in 1965, and reverted to matchplay in 1973.

Recent winners (all USA):

1977	John Fought
1978	John Cook
1979	Mark O'Meara
1980	Hal Sutton
1981	Nathaniel Crosby
1982–3	Jay Sigel
1984	Scott Verplank
1985	Sam Randolph
1986	Buddy Alexander
1987	Bill Mayfair
1988	Eric Meeks
1989	Chris Patton
1990	Phil Mickelson
1991	Mitch Voges
1992	Justin Leonard
1993	John Harris
1994–6	Tiger Woods
1997	Matt Kuchar

Most wins: 5 Bobby Jones 1924–5, 1927–8, 1930; 4 Jerome Travers 1907–8, 1912–3; 3 Walter Travis 1900–01, 1903; Woods

Lowest score (stroke-play): 279 Lanny Wadkins 1970

Biggest winning margin – final (matchplay): 12 & 11 Charles Blair Macdonald 1895

British Amateur Championship

In 1885 Thomas Owen Potter of Hoylake organized the first British Amateur Championship at his home course – eight years after the Royal & Ancient showed little interest in running such a competition. Since 1886, however, the championships have been run by the R&A. It has always been a knock-out matchplay competition and since 1983 all competitors have to play two medal rounds to reduce the field to 64.

Recent winners:

1977–8	Peter McEvoy (UK)
1979	Jay Sigel (USA)
1980	Duncan Evans (UK)
1981	Phillipe Ploujoux (Fra)
1982	Martin Thompson (UK)
1983	Andrew Parkin (UK)
1984	José-Maria Olazabal (Spa)
1985	Garth McGimpsey (UK)
1986	David Curry (UK)
1987	Paul Mayo (UK)
1988	Christian Hardin (Swe)
1989	Stephen Dodd (UK)
1990	Rolf Muntz (Hol)
1991	Gary Wolstenholme (UK)
1992	Stephen Dundas (UK)
1993	Iain Pyman (UK)
1994	Lee James (UK)
1995	Gordon Sherry (UK)
1996	Warren Bladon (UK)
1997	Craig Watson (UK)
1998	Sergio García (Spa)

Most wins: 8 John Ball (UK) 1888, 1890, 1892, 1894, 1899, 1907, 1910, 1912; 5 Michael Bonallack (UK) 1961, 1965, 1968–70; 4 Harold Hilton (UK) 1900–1, 1911, 1913; 3 Joe Carr (Ire) 1953, 1958, 1960

Biggest winning margin (final): 14 & 13 W Lawson Little (USA) beat Jack Wallace (UK) 1934

Walker Cup

Following the success of an international match between amateur teams from the USA and Great Britain at Hoylake in 1921, the first official series of Walker Cup matches took place the following year. The trophy was donated by George Herbert Walker, a former president of the USA Golf Association. It is a biennial event, held alternately in the British Isles (Great Britain and Ireland playing from 1981) and the USA.

Year	Venue	Winners	Score
1922	Long Island, New York	USA	8–4
1923	St Andrews, Scotland	USA	6.5–5.5

1924	Garden City, New York	USA	9–3
1926	St Andrews, Scotland	USA	6.5-5.5
1928	Chicago GC, Illinois	USA	11–1
1930	Royal St George's, Sandwich	USA	10–2
1932	Brookline, Massachusetts	USA	9.5-2.5
1934	St Andrews, Scotland	USA	9.5-2.5
1936	Pine Valley, New Jersey	USA	10.5-1.5
1938	St Andrews, Scotland	GB	7.5-4.5
1947	St Andrews, Scotland	USA	8–4
1949	Winged Foot, New York	USA	10–2
1951	Royal Birkdale, Southport	USA	7.5-4.5
1953	Kittansett, Massachusetts	USA	9–3
1955	St Andrews, Scotland	USA	10–2
1957	Minikhada, Minnesota	USA	8.5-3.5
1959	Muirfield, Scotland	USA	9–3
1961	Seattle, Washington	USA	11–1
1963	Turnberry, Scotland	USA	14-10
1965	Baltimore, Maryland	Drawn	12-12
1967	Royal St George's, Sandwich	USA	15–9
1969	Milwaukee, Wisconsin	USA	13-11
1971	St Andrews, Scotland	GB	13-11
1973	Brookline, Massachusetts	USA	14-10
1975	St Andrews, Scotland	USA	15.5-8.5
1977	Shinnecock Hills, New York	USA	16–8
1979	Muirfield, Scotland	USA	15.5-8.5
1981	Cypress Point, California	USA	15–9
1983	Royal Liverpool, Hoylake	USA	13.5-10.5
1985	Pine Valley, Philadelphia	USA	13 -11
1987	Sunningdale, Berkshire	USA	16.5-7.5
1989	Peachtree, Georgia	GB & I	12.5-11.5
1991	Portmarnock, Ireland	USA	14-10
1993	Interlachen, Minneapolis	USA	19-5
1995	Royal Porthcawl, Wales	GB & I	14-10
1997	Quaker Ridge, New York	USA	18-6

Most wins: 31 USA
Most appearances: 10 Joe Carr (GB) 1947-67

Leading players' records

Golfers who have played 15 or more matches or who have won 10 or more matches. Some men were also selected on other occasions, but these records include only those Cups in which they actually played.

Pts = points as 1 for win, 0.5 for halved match.

Name	Years	Cups	Pl	W	L	H	Pts
GB/GB & Ireland							
Michael Bonnallack	1959-73	8	25	8	14	3	9.5
Peter McEvoy	1977-89	5	18	5	11	2	6
Joe Carr	1947-67	10	20	5	14	1	5.5
United States							
Jay Sigel	1977-93	9	33	18	10	5	20.5
William Campbell	1951-75	7	18	11	4	3	12.5
William Patton	1955-65	5	14	11	3	0	11
Francis Ouimet	1922-34	7	16	9	5	2	10
Bob Lewis, Jr	1981-7	4	14	10	4	0	10

World Amateur Team Championship

An international team competition for four-man teams, held biennially from 1958 for the Eisenhower Trophy, named after the former USA President Dwight D Eisenhower, a great golfing enthusiast. The best three scores by members of the four-man teams, each playing four rounds of stroke-play, determines the result.

Year	Winning team	Score	Leading individual	Score
1958	Australia	918	Bruce Devlin (Aus)	301
			Reid Jack (Sco)	301
			Bill Hyndman (USA)	301
1960	USA	834	Jack Nicklaus (USA)	269
1962	USA	854	Gary Cowan (Can)	280
1964	GB & Ireland	895	Hsieh Min-nan (Tai)	294
1966	Australia	877	Ronnie Shade (UK)	281
1968	USA	868	Michael Bonallack (UK)	286
			Vinnie Giles (USA)	286
1970	USA	854	Victor Regalado (Mex)	280
1972	USA	865	Tony Gresham (Aus)	285
1974	USA	888	Jerry Pate (USA)	294
			Jaime Gonzalez (Bra)	294
1976	GB & Ireland	892	Ian Hutcheon (UK)	293
			Chen Tze-ming (Tai)	293
1978	USA	873	Bob Clampett (USA)	287
1980	USA	848	Hal Sutton (USA)	276
1982	USA	859	Luis Carbonetti (Arg)	284
1984	Japan	870	Luis Carbonetti (Arg)	286
1986	Canada	838	Eduardo Herrera (Col)	275
1988	GB & Ireland	882	Peter McEvoy (GB)	284
1990	Sweden	879	Mathias Grönberg (Swe)	286
1992	New Zealand	823	Philip Tataurangi (NZ)	271
1994	USA	838	Allen Doyle (USA)	277
1996	Australia	838	Kalle Aitala (Fin)	276

Most wins: 10 USA

Women's Golf

The Women's Professional Golf Association (WPGA) was formed in the USA in 1944 and re-formed in 1948 as the LPGA, replacing 'Women's' by 'Ladies'.

Women's Majors

The four Majors in US women's golf are: *A* – US Women's Open, first held 1946; *B* – LPGA Championship, inaugurated 1955; *C* – Nabisco Dinah Shore, Major status from 1983; *D* – Du Maurier Classic, Major status from 1979. The Western Open (*E*) and Titleholders Championship (*F*) both used to be Majors.

Most wins (since formation of the US LPGA in 1950; all USA unless stated otherwise):

		A	B	C	D	E	F
12	Mickey Wright	4	4	–	–	2	2
8	Betsy Rawls	4	2	–	–	–	2
7	Patty Berg	–	–	–	–	3	4
6	Louise Suggs	1	1	–	–	3	1
6	Kathy Whitworth	–	3	–	–	2	1
6	Pat Bradley	1	1	1	3	–	–
6	Patty Sheehan	2	3	1	–	–	–
6	Betsy King	2	1	3	–	–	–
5	Mildred Zaharias	2	–	–	–	2	1
5	Amy Alcott	1	–	3	1	–	–
4	Susie Berning	3	–	–	–	–	1
4	Donna Caponi	2	2	–	–	–	–
4	Sandra Haynie	1	2	–	1	–	–
4	Nancy Lopez	–	3	1	–	–	–
4	Hollis Stacey	3	–	–	1	–	–
4	Laura Davies (UK)	1	2	–	1	–	–

US Women's Open

First held in 1946 at Spokane, Washington at matchplay; from 1947 over 72 holes of stroke-play annually on different courses.
Winners (all USA unless stated otherwise):

		Score
1946	Patty Berg	5 & 4
1947	Betty Jameson	295
1948	Mildred Zaharias	300
1949	Louise Suggs	291
1950	Mildred Zaharias	291
1951	Betsy Rawls	293
1952	Louise Suggs	284
1953	Betsy Rawls	302
1954	Mildred Zaharias	291
1955	Fay Crocker	299
1956	Kathy Cornelius	302
1957	Betsy Rawls	299
1958	Mickey Wright	290
1959	Mickey Wright	287
1960	Betsy Rawls	292
1961	Mickey Wright	293
1962	Murle Lindstrom	301
1963	Mary Mills	289
1964	Mickey Wright	290
1965	Carol Mann	290
1966	Sandra Spuzich	297
1967	Catherine Lacoste (Fra, amateur)	294
1968	Susie Berning	289
1969	Donna Caponi	294
1970	Donna Caponi	287
1971	JoAnne Carner	288
1972	Susie Berning	299
1973	Susie Berning	290
1974	Sandra Haynie	295
1975	Sandra Palmer	295
1976	JoAnne Carner	292
1977	Hollis Stacy	292
1978	Hollis Stacy	289
1979	Jerilyn Britz	284
1980	Amy Alcott	280
1981	Pat Bradley	279
1982	Janet Alex	283
1983	Jan Stephenson (Aus)	290
1985	Kathy Baker	280
1986	Jane Geddes	287
1987	Laura Davies (UK)	285
1988	Liselotte Neumann (Swi)	277
1989	Betsy King	278
1990	Betsy King	284
1991	Meg Mallon	283
1992	Patty Sheehan	280★
1993	Lauri Merten	280
1994	Patty Sheehan	277
1995	Annika Sörenstam (Swe)	278
1996	Annika Sörenstam (Swe)	272
1997	Alison Nicholas (UK)	274
1998	Pak Se-ri (SKo)	290★

★ After play-off.
Most wins: 4 Wright, Rawls
Lowest aggregate: 272 Sörenstam 1996
Lowest round: 65 Sally Little (SAf) 4th 1978, Judy Dickinson 3rd 1985, Ayako Okamoto (Jap) 4th 1989
Biggest margin of victory: 14 strokes Louise Suggs 1949
Oldest winner: Fay Crocker 40yr 11m 1955
Youngest winner: Catherine Lacoste 22yr 5d 1967

US LPGA Championship

First held in 1955 at matchplay, and subsequently over 72 holes of stroke-play. Sponsored by Mazda from 1987, McDonalds 1994.
Winners (all USA unless stated otherwise):

1955	Beverly Hanson	4 & 3
1956	Marlene Hagge	291
1957	Louise Suggs	285
1958	Mickey Wright	288
1959	Betsy Rawls	288
1960	Mickey Wright	292
1961	Mickey Wright	287
1962	Judy Kimball	282
1963	Mickey Wright	294
1964	Mary Mills	278
1965	Sandra Haynie	279
1966	Gloria Ehret	282
1967	Kathy Whitworth	284
1968	Sandra Post	294
1969	Betsy Rawls	293
1970	Shirley Englehorn	285
1971	Kathy Whitworth	288
1972	Kathy Ahem	293
1973	Mary Mills	288
1974	Sandra Haynie	288
1975	Kathy Whitworth	288
1976	Betty Burfeindt	287
1977	Chako Higuchi	279
1978	Nancy Lopez	275
1979	Donna Caponi	279
1980	Sally Little (SAf)	285
1981	Donna Caponi	280
1982	Jan Stephenson (Aus)	279
1983	Patty Sheehan	279
1984	Patty Sheehan	272
1985	Nancy Lopez	273
1986	Pat Bradley	277
1987	Jane Geddes	275
1988	Sherri Turner	281
1989	Nancy Lopez	274
1990	Beth Daniel	280
1991	Meg Mallon	274
1992	Betsy King	267
1993	Patty Sheehan	276
1994	Laura Davies (UK)	279
1995	Kelley Robbins	274
1996#	Laura Davies (UK)	213
1997	Chris Johnson (USA)	281★
1998	Pak Se-ri (SKo)	273

Reduced to 54 holes, ★ after play-off.
Most wins: 4 Wright
Lowest round: 63 Patty Sheahan 1984 King's Island, Ohio
Biggest margin of victory: 11 strokes Betsy King 1992 Bethesda, Maryland
Lowest aggregate: 267 (68, 66, 67, 66) (17 under par) Betsy King 1992 Bethesda, Maryland, the first time a woman has had four rounds in the 60s in a US Major

Nabisco Dinah Shore

Inaugurated 1972 as the Colgate-Dinah Shore, with Nabisco taking over as sponsors in 1983, when it was given Major status.
Winners (all USA unless stated otherwise):

1972	Jane Blalock	213
1973	Mickey Wright	284
1974	Jo Ann Prentice	289★
1975	Sandra Palmer	283
1976	Judy Rankin	285
1977	Kathy Whitworth	289
1978	Sandra Post	283★
1979	Sandra Post	276
1980	Donna Caponi	275
1981	Nancy Lopez	277
1982	Sally Little (SAf)	278
1983	Amy Alcott	282
1984	Juli Inkster	280★
1985	Alice Miller	275
1986	Pat Bradley	280
1987	Betsy King	283★
1988	Amy Alcott	274
1989	Juli Inkster	279
1990	Betsy King	283

1991	Amy Alcott	273
1992	Dottie Mochrie	279★
1993	Helen Alfredsson (Swe)	284
1994	Donna Andrews	276
1995	Nanci Bowen	285
1996	Patti Sheehan	281
1997	Betsy King	276
1998	Pat Hurst	282

★ After play-off.

Du Maurier Classic

First held in 1973 as the La Canadienne, and known as the Peter Jackson Classic 1974-82. Granted Major status in 1979. *Winners from 1979 (all USA unless stated otherwise):*

1979	Amy Alcott	285
1980	Pat Bradley	277
1981	Jan Stephenson (Aus)	278
1982	Sandra Haynie	280
1983	Hollis Stacy	277
1984	Juli Inkster	279
1985	Pat Bradley	278
1986	Pat Bradley	276★
1987	Jody Rosenthal	272
1988	Sally Little	279
1989	Tammie Green	279
1990	Cathy Johnston	276
1991	Mancy Scranton	279
1992	Sherri Steinhauer	277
1993	Brandie Burton	277★
1994	Martha Nause	279

1995	Jenny Lidback (Peru)	280
1996	Laura Davies (UK)	277
1997	Colleen Walker	278

★ After play-off.

British Women's Open Championship

Contested annually at stroke-play from 1976, except for 1983. *Winners:*

1976	Jennifer Lee Smith (UK)	299
1977	Vivien Saunders (UK)	306
1978	Janet Melville (UK)	310
1979	Alison Sheard (SAf)	301
1980	Debbie Massey (USA)	294
1981	Debbie Massey (USA)	295
1982	Marta Figeuras-Dotti (Spa)	296
1984	Ayako Okamoto (Jap)	289
1985	Betsy King (USA)	300
1986	Laura Davies (UK)	283
1987	Alison Nicholas (UK)	296
1988	Corinne Dibnah (Aus)	295
1989	Jane Geddes (USA)	274
1990	Helen Alfredsson (Swe)	288
1991	Penny Grice-Whittaker	284
1992★	Patty Sheehan (USA)	207
1993	Karen Lunn (Aus)	275
1994	Liselotte Neumann (Swe)	280
1995	Karrie Webb (Aus)	278
1996	Emilee Klein (USA)	277

| 1997 | Karrie Webb (Aus) | 269 |

★ Match restricted to 54 holes due to weather. Sheehan was the first to win US and British Opens in the same year.

US LPGA Tournament Records

Lowest score – 72 holes: 268 Nancy Lopez 1985 Henredon Classic, Willow Creek GC, NC
Lowest score – 18 holes: 62 Mickey Wright 1964 Tall City Open, Hogan Park CC, Texas; 62 Vicki Fergon 1984 San Jose Classic, Almaden G&CC; Laura Davies (UK) 1991 Rail Charity Golf Classic, Springfield, Illinois; 62 Hollis Stacy 1992 Safeco Classic, Meridian Valley CC, Seattle
Most consecutive wins: 4 Mickey Wright 1962 and in 1963, Kathy Whitworth 1969. Nancy Lopez won five successive tournaments 1978
Most wins in a season: 13 Mickey Wright 1963
Oldest winner: 46yr 163d JoAnne Carner 1985 Safeco Classic
Youngest winner: 18yr 14d Marlene Hagge 1952 Sarasota Open

Leading Career Money-Winners

All-time leading money-winners on the US LPGA circuit, as at end of 1997 (all USA unless stated otherwise):

	Amount ($US)	Wins	Years
Betsy King	5,972,161	31	1977-97
Pat Bradley	5,539,184	31	1974-97
Patty Sheehan	5,310,390	35	1980-97
Beth Daniel	5,207,208	32	1979-97
Nancy Lopez	4,976,021	48	1977-97
Dottie Mochrie/Pepper	3,966,317	14	1988-97
Laura Davies (UK)	3,594,229	15	1988-97
Jane Geddes	3,277,366	11	1983-97
Amy Alcott	3,261,344	29	1975-97
Rosie Jones	3,260,255	7	1982-97
Juli Inkster	3,058,805	15	1983-97
Meg Mallon	3,046,591	8	1987-97
JoAnne Carner	2,899,051	42	1970-97
Tammie Green	2,789,031	6	1984-97
Ayoko Okamoto (Jap)	2,743,174	17	1981-97
Annika Sörenstam (Swe)	2,679,084	10	1993-97
Liselotte Neumann (Swe)	2,666,345	10	1988-97
Colleen Walker	2,647,189	7	1982-97

Earnings of the winner of the most tournaments (due to the huge increase in prize money in recent years):

Kathy Whitworth	1,731,770	88	1959-95

Progressive record for the amount won in a season from $20,000 to over $200,000

1956	Marlene Hagge	$20,235
1959	Betsy Rawls	26,774
1963	Mickey Wright	31,269
1966	Kathy Whitworth	33,517
1968	Kathy Whitworth	48,379
1972	Kathy Whitworth	65,063
1973	Kathy Whitworth	82,854
1974	JoAnne Carner	87,094
1975	Sandra Palmer	94,805
1976	Judy Rankin	150,734
1978	Nancy Lopez	189,813
1979	Nancy Lopez	215,987

Yearly leaders from 1980

1980	Beth Daniel	$231,000
1981	Beth Daniel	206,978
1982	JoAnne Carner	310,399
1983	JoAnne Carner	291,404
1984	Betsy King	266,771
1985	Nancy Lopez	416,472
1986	Pat Bradley	492,021
1987	Ayoko Okomoto (Jap)	466,034
1988	Sherru Turner	350,851
1989	Betsy King	654,132
1990	Beth Daniel	863,578
1991	Pat Bradley	763,118
1992	Dottie Mochrie	693,355
1993	Betsy King	595,992
1994	Laura Davies (UK)	687,201
1995	Annika Sörenstam (Swe)	666,533
1996	Karrie Webb (Aus)	1,002,000
1997	Annika Sörenstam (Swe)	1,236,789

Most seasons as leading money-winner

8 Kathy Whitworth 1965-8, 1970-3; 4 Mildred
'Babe' Zaharias 1948-51, Mickey Wright 1961-4

Most LPGA tournament wins

88 Kathy Whitworth; 82 Mickey Wright; 57 Patty
Berg (including 13 pre-LPGA); 55 Betsy Rawls;
50 Louise Suggs; 48 Nancy Lopez; 42 Sandra
Haynie, JoAnne Carner; 38 Carol Mann; 35 Patty
Sheehan; 32 Beth Daniel; 31 Mildred 'Babe'
Zaharias, Pat Bradley, Betsy King

Women's PGA European Tour

Leading money-winners from the formalization of
the WPGA tour in 1979.

Year	Top money-winner	£
1979	Alison Sheard (UK)	4,965
1980	Muriel Thomson (UK)	8,008
1981	Jenny Lee Smith (UK)	13,519
1982	Jenny Lee Smith (UK)	12,551
1983	Beverly Huke (UK)	9,226
1984	Dale Reid (UK)	28,239
1985	Laura Davies (UK)	21,736
1986	Laura Davies (UK)	37,500
1987	Dale Reid (UK)	53,815
1988	Marie-Laure de Lorenzi (Fra)	99,360
1989	Marie-Laure de Lorenzi (Fra)	77,534
1990	Trish Johnson (UK)	83,403
1991	Corinne Dibnah (Aus)	89,058
1992	Laura Davies (UK)	66,333
1993	Karen Lunn (Aus)	66,266
1994	Liselotte Neumann (Swe)	102,750
1995	Annika Sörenstam (Swe)	130,324
1996	Laura Davies (UK)	110,880
1997	Alison Nicholas (UK)	94,589

Order of Merit winners: same as the leading
money-winner, except Catherine Panton (UK)
1979, Muriel Thomson (UK) 1983

Solheim Cup

The first team competition between women's teams
from the United States and Europe, along the lines of
the Ryder Cup for men, was staged in 1990.
Winners:

Year	Venue	Winners	Score
1990	Orlando, Florida	USA	11.5-4.5
1992	Dalmahoy, Scotland	Europe	11.5-6.5
1994	The Greenbrier, West Virginia	USA	13-7
1996	St Pierre, Chepstow, Wals	USA	17-11

Leading players' records

Name	Years	Cups	Pl	W	L	H	Pts
Laura Davies (E)	1990-6	4	14	9	5	0	9
Dottie Pepper (US)	1990-6	4	13	8	4	1	8.5
Beth Daniel (US)	1990-6	4	12	7	3	2	8
Betsy King (US)	1990-6	4	12	7	4	1	7.5

Sunrise Cup

The first women's professional team championship
was staged at the Sunrise Golf and Country Club
near Taipei, Taiwan in 1992. Contested by teams
of two over 54 holes.

Winners: 1992 Sweden (Helen Alfredsson, Liselotte
Neumann) 445

Best individual: 219 Neumann, Trish Johnson (Eng)

Women's Amateur Golf

British Women's Open Amateur Championship

First held in 1893 and contested annually at matchplay.
Recent winners:

1977	Angela Uzielli (UK)	
1978	Edwina Kennedy (Aus)	
1979	Maureen Madill (Ire)	
1980	Anne Sander (USA)	
1981	Belle Robertson (UK)	
1982	Katrina Douglas (UK)	
1983	Jill Thornhill (UK)	
1984	Jody Rosenthal (USA)	
1985	Lilian Behan (Ire)	
1986	Marnie McGuire (NZ)	
1987	Janet Collingham (UK)	
1988	Joanne Furby (UK)	
1989	Helen Dobson (UK)	
1990	Julie Hall (UK)	
1991	Valérie Michaud (Fra)	
1992	Pernille Pedersen (Den)	
1993	Catriona Lambert (UK)	
1994	Emma Duggleby (UK)	
1995	Julie Hall (UK)	
1996	Kelli Kuehne (USA)	
1997	Alison Rose (UK)	
1998	K Rostron (UK)	

Most wins: 4 Cecil Leitch 1914, 1920-1, 1926; 4 Joyce Wethered 1922, 1924-5, 1929; 3 Lady Margaret Scott 1893-5, May Hezlet 1899, 1902, 1907, Enid Wilson 1931-3, Jesse Valentine (née Anderson) 1937, 1955, 1958

Most finals: 6 Leitch, also runner-up 1922, 1925

Biggest winning margin in final: 9 & 7 Joyce Wethered beat Cecil Leitch 1922

Oldest winner: Belle Robertson 45yr 56d 1981.

Youngest winner: May Hezlet 17yr 7d 1899.

US Women's Amateur Championship

Held at stroke-play in 1895, and annually at matchplay from 1896, except for the war years of 1917-8, and 1942-5.

Most wins: 6 Glenna Vare (née Collett) 1922, 1925, 1928-30, 1935; 5 JoAnne Carner (née Gunderson) 1957, 1960, 1962, 1966, 1968; 3 Beatrix Hoyt 1896-8, Margaret Curtis 1907, 1911-12, Alexa Stirling 1916, 1919-20, Dorothy Campbell Hurd 1909-10, 1924, Virginia van Wie 1932-4, Anne Quast (later Decker, Welts, Sander) 1958, 1961, 1963, Juli Inkster 1980-2

Biggest winning margin in final: 14 & 13 Anne Quast beat Phyllis Preuss 1961

Oldest winner: Dorothy Campbell Hurd, 41yr 4m 1924

Youngest winner: Laura Baugh 16yr 82d 1971

Women's World Amateur Team Championship

Contested biennially from 1964 by teams of three for the Espirito Santo Trophy.

Wins:

12	USA	1966, 1968, 1970, 1972, 1974, 1976, 1980, 1982, 1984, 1988, 1990, 1994
2	Spain	1986, 1992
1	France 1964, Australia 1978, South Korea 1996	

Lowest aggregate total (72 holes): 569 USA 1994

Lowest individual aggregate: 278 Wendy Ward (USA) 1994

Lowest individual round: 65 Pak Se-ri (SKo) 1994

Curtis Cup

A biennial team competition between amateur women's teams from the United States, and Great Britain and Ireland. It was first held at Wentworth in 1932 and is named after American sisters Margaret and Harriot Curtis.

Year	Venue	Winners	Score	Year	Venue	Winners	Score
1932	Wentworth, Surrey	USA	5.5-3.5	1974	San Francisco, California	USA	13-5
1934	Chevy Chase, Maryland	USA	6.5-2.5	1976	Royal Lytham, Lancashire	USA	11.5-6.5
1936	Gleneagles, Scotland	Drawn	4.5-4.5	1978	Apawamis, New York	USA	12-6
1938	Essex, Massachusetts	USA	5.5-3.5	1980	St Pierre, Chepstow	USA	13-5
1948	Royal Birkdale, Southport	USA	6.5-2.5	1982	Denver, Colorado	USA	14.5-3.5
1950	Buffalo CC, New York	USA	7.5-1.5	1984	Muirfield, Scotland	USA	9.5-8.5
1952	Muirfield, Scotland	GB&I	5-4	1986	Prairie Dunes, Kansas	GB&I	13-5
1954	Merion, Pennsylvania	USA	6-3	1988	Royal St George's, Sandwich	GB&I	11-7
1956	Prince's, Sandwich	GB&I	5-4	1990	Somerset Hills, New Jersey	USA	14-4
1958	Brae Burn, Massachusetts	Drawn	4.5-4.5	1992	Royal Liverpool, Hoylake	GB&I	10-8
1960	Lindrick, Sheffield	USA	6.5-2.5	1994	Chattanooga, Tennessee	Drawn	9-9
1962	Broadmoor, Colorado Springs	USA	8-1	1996	Killarney, Ireland	GB&I	11.5-6.5
1964	Royal Porthcawl, Wales	USA	10.5-7.5				
1966	Hot Springs, Virginia	USA	13-5				
1968	Royal County Down, Ireland	USA	10.5-7.5				
1970	Brae Burn, Massachusetts	USA	11.5-6.5				
1972	Western Gailes, Scotland	USA	10-8				

Most wins: 20 USA

Most appearances: 9 Mary McKenna (GB&I) 1970-86, Carol Semple Thompson (USA); 8 Anne Sander (USA)

Leading players' records

Golfers who have played 20 or more matches or won 10 or more. (Pts = points as 1 for win, 0.5 for halved.)

Name	Years	Cups	Pl	W	L	H	Pts
GB/GB & Ireland							
Mary McKenna	1970-86	9	30	10	16	4	12
Belle Robertson	1960-86	7	24	5	12	7	8.5
United States							
Carol Semple Thompson	1974-96	9	27	15	7	4	17
Anne Quast Sander	1958-90	8	22	11	7	4	13
Phyllis Preuss	1962-70	5	15	10	4	1	10.5

Gymnastics

There were *gymnasia* in most ancient Greek cities, and gymnastic activities were included in the original Olympic Games. Modern techniques, however, were developed in Germany towards the latter part of the 18th century, and the first teacher of modern gymnastics was Johann Friedrich Simon at Basedow's School, Dessau, in 1776. Friedrich Jahn, who founded the Turnverein in Berlin in 1811, is regarded as the father figure of modern gymnastics. In Britain the Amateur Gymnastics Association was formed in 1888.

International governing body: Fédération Internationale de Gymnastique (FIG), Rue des Oeuches 10, Case Postale 359, CH-2740 Moutier 1, Switzerland. Tel: (41) 32 936666, Fax: (41) 32 936671. President: Bruno Grandi, Secretary General: Norbert Bueche. Formed in 1891. 124 member nations in 1996.

Apparatus

Men

Parallel bars: two bars of round cross section, 350cm long, set 42-52cm apart, and supported 195cm above the floor on uprights fixed to a broad stable base

Horizontal bar: bar 240cm long and 2.8cm in diameter, supported 275 cm above the ground by an upright at each end and braced with wires

Pommel horse: similar to vaulting horse; 115 cm high, 35cm wide, 163cm long, but with two raised handles (pommels) 40-45cm apart at the centre

Rings: two rigid rings 18cm in diameter suspended 250cm from the floor by two wires 50cm apart attached to a frame, braced with wires, 575cm high

Horse vault: horse is 163cm long 135cm high, springboard is 120cm long, placed in line with the long side of the horse

Men and women

Floor exercises: on a 12m square

Women

Asymmetrical bars: two horizontal bars 350cm long, arranged parallel to one another at different heights – lower 140-160 cm and upper 235- 240 cm above the floor – supported by an upright at each end; the two frames are placed 43cm apart

Beam: rigid beam of wood 5m long 10cm wide mounted horizontally at 120cm above the floor

Horse vault: horse is 163cm long and 35cm wide, 120cm high, springboard as for men's vault

Rhythmic sportive gymnastics

In this women's sport the disciplines are characterized by the handling of skipping ropes, hoops, clubs, ribbons and balls to musical accompaniment. The IGF recognized rhythmic gymnastics in 1962, world championships were first held in 1963 and the sport was added to the Olympics in 1984.

Olympic Games

Gymnastics was included in the first Modern Olympics of 1896. A women's competition was first included in 1928.

Winners:

Men

Team

5	Japan	1960, 1964, 1968, 1972, 1976
5	USSR/CIS	1952, 1956, 1980, 1988, 1992
4	Italy	1912, 1920, 1924, 1932,
2	USA	1904 (TG Philadelphia), 1984
1	Norway 1906, Sweden 1908, Switzerland 1928, Germany 1936, Finland 1948, Russia 1996	

Combined exercises

1900	Gustave Sandras (Fra)
1904	Julius Lenhart (Aut)#
1906	Pierre Payssé (Fra)★
1908	Alberto Braglia (Ita)
1912	Alberto Braglia (Ita)
1920	Giorgio Zampori (Ita)
1924	Leon Stukelj (Yug)
1928	Georges Miez (Sui)
1932	Romeo Neri (Ita)
1936	Alfred Schwarzmann (Ger)
1948	Veikko Huhtanen (Fin)
1952	Viktor Chukarin (USSR)
1956	Viktor Chukarin (USSR)
1960	Boris Shakhlin (USSR)
1964	Yukio Endo (Jap)
1968	Sawao Kato (Jap)
1972	Sawao Kato (Jap)
1976	Nikolay Andrianov (USSR)
1980	Aleksandr Ditiatin (USSR)
1984	Koji Gushiken (Jap)
1988	Vladimir Artemov (USSR)
1992	Vitaliy Scherbo (CIS/Blr)
1996	Li Xiaoshuang (Chn)

★ Won two competitions in 1906: 5 events and 6 events.

\# Member of USA Philadelphia Club, who won team event.

Floor exercises

1932	István Pelle (Hun)
1936	Georges Miez (Swi)
1948	Ferenc Pataki (Hun)
1952	William Thoresson (Swe)
1956	Valentin Muratov (USSR)
1960	Nobuyuki Aihara (Jap)
1964	Franco Menichelli (Ita)
1968	Sawao Kato (Jap)
1972	Nikolay Andrianov (USSR)
1976	Nikolay Andrianov (USSR)
1980	Roland Brückner (GDR)
1984	Li Ning (Chn)
1988	Sergey Kharikov (USSR)
1992	Li Xiaoshuang (Chn)
1996	Ioannis Melissanidis (Gre)

Parallel bars

1896	Alfred Flatow (Ger)
1904	George Eyser (USA)
1924	August Güttinger (Swi)
1928	Ladislav Vácha (Cs)
1932	Romeo Neri (Ita)
1936	Konrad Frey (Ger)
1948	Michael Reusch (Swi)
1952	Hans Eugster (Swi)
1956	Viktor Chukarin (USSR)
1960	Boris Shakhlin (USSR)
1964	Yukio Endo (Jap)
1968	Akinori Nakayama (Jap)
1972	Sawao Kato (Jap)
1976	Sawao Kato (Jap)
1980	Aleksandr Tkachev (USSR)
1984	Bart Conner (USA)
1988	Vladimir Artemov (USSR)
1992	Vitaliy Scherbo (CIS/Blr)
1996	Rustam Sharipov (Ukr)

Pommel horse

1896	Louis Zutter (Swi)
1904	Anton Heida (USA)
1924	Josef Wilhelm (Swi)
1928	Hermann Hänggi (Swi)
1932	István Pelle (Hun)
1936	Konrad Frey (Ger)
1948	Paavo Aaltonen (Fin), Veikko Huhtanen (Fin) & Ilmari Savolainen (Fin)
1952	Viktor Chukarin (USSR)
1956	Boris Shakhlin (USSR)
1960	Eugen Ekman (Fin) & Boris Shakhlin (USSR)
1964	Miroslav Cerar (Yug)
1968	Miroslav Cerar (Yug)
1972	Viktor Klimenko (USSR)
1976	Zoltán Magyar (Hun)
1980	Zoltán Magyar (Hun)
1984	Li Ning (Chn) & Peter Vidmar (USA)
1988	Dmitriy Bilozerchev (USSR), Zsolt Borkai (Hun) & Lyubomir Gueraskov (Bul)
1992	Vitaliy Scherbo (CIS/Blr) & Pae Gil-su (NKo)
1996	Li Donghua (Swi)

Rings

1896	Ioannis Mitropoulos (Gre)
1904	Hermann Glass (USA)
1924	Francesco Martino (Ita)
1928	Leon Stukelj (Yug)
1932	George Gulack (USA)
1936	Alois Hudec (Cs)
1948	Karl Frei (Swi)
1952	Grant Shaginyan (USSR)
1956	Albert Azaryan (USSR)
1960	Albert Azaryan (USSR)
1964	Takuji Hayata (Jap)
1968	Akinori Nakayama (Jap)
1972	Akinori Nakayama (Jap)
1976	Nikolay Andrianov (USSR)
1980	Aleksandr Ditiatin (USSR)
1984	Koji Gushiken (Jap) & Li Ning (Chn)
1988	Holger Behrendt (GDR) & Dmitriy Bilozerchev (USSR)
1992	Vitaliy Scherbo (CIS/Blr)
1996	Yuri Chechi (Ita)

Horizontal bar

1896	Hermann Weingärtner (Ger)
1904	Anton Heida (USA) & Edward Hennig (USA)
1924	Leon Stukelj (Yug)
1928	Georges Miez (Swi)
1932	Dallas Bixler (USA)
1936	Aleksanteri Saarvala (Fin)
1948	Josef Stalder (Swi)
1952	Jack Günthard (Swi)
1956	Takashi Ono (Jap)
1960	Takashi Ono (Jap)
1964	Boris Shakhlin (USSR)
1968	Mikhail Voronin (USSR) & Akinori Nakayama (Jap)
1972	Mitsuo Tsukahara (Jap)
1976	Mitsuo Tsukahara (Jap)
1980	Stoyan Deltchev (Bul)
1984	Shinji Morisue (Jap)
1988	Vladimir Artemov (USSR) & Valeriy Lyukin (USSR)
1992	Trent Dimas (USA)
1996	Andreas Wecker (Ger)

Horse vault

1896	Carl Schuhmann (Ger)
1904	Anton Heida (USA) & George Eyser (USA)
1924	Frank Kriz (USA)
1928	Eugen Mack (Swi)
1932	Savino Guglielmetti (Ita)
1936	Alfred Schwarzmann (Ger)
1948	Paavo Aaltonen (Fin)
1952	Viktor Chukarin (USSR)
1956	Helmuth Bantz (Ger) & Valentin Muratov (USSR)
1960	Takashi Ono (Jap) & Boris Shakhlin (USSR)
1964	Haruhiro Yamashita (Jap)
1968	Mikhail Voronin (USSR)
1972	Klaus Köste (GDR)
1976	Nikolay Andrianov (USSR)
1980	Nikolay Andrianov (USSR)
1984	Lou Yun (Chn)
1988	Lou Yun (Chn)
1992	Vitaliy Scherbo (CIS/Blr)
1996	Aleksey Nemov (Rus)

Women

Team

10	USSR/CIS 1952, 1956, 1960, 1964, 1968, 1972, 1976, 1980, 1988, 1992
1	Netherlands 1928, Germany 1936, Czechoslovakia 1948, Romania 1984, USA 1996

Combined exercises

1952	Maria Gorokhovskaya (USSR)
1956	Larisa Latynina (USSR)
1960	Larisa Latynina (USSR)
1964	Vera Cáslavská (Cs)
1968	Vera Cáslavská (Cs)
1972	Lyudmila Tourischeva (USSR)
1976	Nadia Comaneci (Rom)
1980	Yelena Davydova (USSR)
1984	Mary Lou Retton (USA)
1988	Yelena Shushunova (USSR)
1992	Tatyana Gutsu (CIS/Ukr)
1996	Lilia Podkopayeva (Ukr)

Asymmetrical bars

1952	Margit Korondi (Hun)
1956	Agnes Keleti (Hun)
1960	Polina Astakhova (USSR)
1964	Polina Astakhova (USSR)
1968	Vera Cáslavská (Cs)
1972	Karin Janz (GDR)
1976	Nadia Comaneci (Rom)
1980	Maxi Gnauck (GDR)
1984	Ma Yanhong (Chn) & Julianne McNamara (USA)
1988	Daniela Silivas (Rom)
1992	Li Lu (Chn)
1996	Svetlana Chorkina (Rus)

Balance beam

1952	Nina Bocharova (USSR)
1956	Agnes Keleti (Hun)
1960	Eva Bosáková (Cs)
1964	Vera Cáslavská (Cs)
1968	Natalya Kuchinskaya (USSR)
1972	Olga Korbut (USSR)
1976	Nadia Comaneci (Rom)
1980	Nadia Comaneci (Rom)
1984	Simona Pauca (Rom) & Ecaterina Szabo (Rom)
1988	Daniela Silivas (Rom)
1992	Tatyana Lysenko (CIS/Ukr)
1996	Shannon Miller (USA)

Floor exercises

1952	Agnes Keleti (Hun)
1956	Larisa Latynina (USSR) & Agnes Keleti (Hun)
1960	Larisa Latynina (USSR)
1964	Larisa Latynina (USSR)
1968	Larisa Petrik (USSR) & Vera Cáslavská (Cs)
1972	Olga Korbut (USSR)
1976	Nelli Kim (USSR)
1980	Nelli Kim (USSR) & Nadia Comaneci (Rom)
1984	Ecaterina Szabo (Rom)
1988	Daniela Silivas (Rom)
1992	Lavinia Milosovici (Rom)
1996	Lilia Podkopayeva (Ukr)

Horse vault

1952	Yekaterina Kalinchuk (USSR)
1956	Larisa Latynina (USSR)
1960	Margarita Nikolayeva (USSR)
1964	Vera Cáslavská (Cs)
1968	Vera Cáslavská (Cs)

1972	Karin Janz (GDR)
1976	Nelli Kim (USSR)
1980	Natalya Shaposhnikova (USSR)
1984	Ecaterina Szabo (Rom)
1988	Svetlana Boginskaya (USSR)
1992	Lavinia Milosovici (Rom) & Henrietta Ónodi (Hun)
1996	Simona Amonar (Rom)

Rhythmic gymnastics

1984	Lori Fung (Can)
1988	Marina Lobach (USSR)
1992	Aleksandra Timoschenko (CIS/Ukr)
1996	Yekaterina Serebryanskaya (Ukr)

Team – rhythmic gymnastics

1996	Spain

Discontinued events (men)

Parallel bars (team)

1896	Germany

Horizontal bars (team)

1896	Germany

Rope-climbing

1896	Nicolaos Andriakopoulos (Gre)
1904	George Eyser (USA)

1906	Georgios Aliprantis (Gre)
1924	Bedrich Supcik (Cs)
1932	Raymond Bass (USA)

Club-swinging

1904	Edward Hennig (USA)
1932	George Roth (USA)

Seven-event competition

1904	Anton Heida (USA)

Nine-event competition

1904	Adolf Spinnler (Swi)

Triathlon (100 yards, long jump, shot)

1904	Max Emmerich (USA)

Sidehorse vault

1924	Albert Séguin (Fra)

Tumbling

1932	Rowland Wolfe (USA)

Swedish event (team)

1912	Sweden
1920	Sweden

Free system (team)

1912	Norway
1920	Denmark

Women – portable apparatus (team)

1952	Sweden
1956	Hungary

Most Olympic medals

(G – Gold, S – Silver, B – Bronze)

Total	Gymnast	G	S	B	Years
Men:					
15	Nikolay Andrianov (USSR)	7	5	3	1972-80
13	Boris Shakhlin (USSR)	7	4	2	1956-64
13	Takashi Ono (Jap)	5	4	4	1956-64
12	Sawao Kato (Jap)	8	3	1	1968-76
11	Viktor Chukarin (USSR)	7	3	1	1952-6
10	Akinori Nakayama (Jap)	6	2	2	1968-72
10	Aleksandr Ditiatin (USSR)	3	6	1	1976-80
10	Vitaliy Scherbo* (CIS/Blr)	6	–	4	1992-6
9	Mitsuo Tsukahara (Jap)	5	1	3	1968-76
9	Elizo Kenmotsu (Jap)	3	3	3	1968-76
9	Mikhail Voronin (USSR)	2	6	1	1968-72
9	Yuriy Titov (USSR)	1	5	3	1956-64

Also 4 gold medals: Georges Miesz (Swi), Anton Heida (USA), Yukio Endo (Jap), Giorgio Zampori (Ita), Valentin Muratov (USSR), Vladimir Artemov (USSR)

* Vitaliy Shcherbo won a record 6 gold medals at one Games 1992.

Total	Gymnast	G	S	B	Years
Women:					
18	Larisa Latynina (USSR)	9	5	4	1956-64
11	Vera Cáslavská (Cs)	7	4	0	1964-8

10	Agnes Kaleti (Hun)	5	3	2	1952-6
10	Polina Astakhova (USSR)	5	2	3	1956-64
9	Nadia Comaneci (Rom)	5	3	1	1976-80
9	Lyudmila Tourischeva (USSR)	4	3	2	1968-76

Also 4 gold medals: Olga Korbut (USSR), Nelli Kim (USSR)

World Championships

First held for men at Antwerp in 1903 and every two years until 1913. They were re-introduced in 1922 and held every four years, with the Olympic champions also being the world champions. They were biennial 1979-93, and since then have again been held annually.

The first women's championships were held in 1934. Team championships, separate from the individual events, were held in 1994.

Winners:

Men

Team

8	USSR	1954, 1958, 1979, 1981, 1985, 1987, 1989, 1991
7	Czechoslovakia	1907, 1911, 1913, 1922, 1926, 1930, 1938
5	Japan	1962, 1966, 1970, 1974, 1978
4	China	1983, 1994-5, 1997
3	France	1903, 1905, 1909
2	Switzerland	1934, 1950

There was no team competition in 1934.

All-around

1903	Joseph Martinez (Fra/Alg)
1905	Marcel Lalu (Fra)
1907	Josef Cada (Bohemia)
1909	Marco Torrès (Fra)
1911	Ferdinand Steiner (Bohemia)
1913	Marco Torrès (Fra)
1922	Peter Sumi (Yug) & Frantisek Pechacek (Bohemia)
1926	Peter Sumi (Yug)
1930	Josip Primozic (Yug)
1934	Eugen Mack (Swi)
1938	Jan Gajdos (Cs)
1950	Walter Lehmann (Swi)
1954	Viktor Chukarin (USSR) & Valentin Muratov (USSR)
1958	Boris Shakhlin (USSR)
1962	Yuriy Titov (USSR)
1966	Mikhail Voronin (USSR)
1970	Eizo Kenmotsu (Jap)
1974	Shigeru Kasamatsu (Jap)
1978	Nikolay Andrianov (USSR)
1979	Aleksandr Ditiatin (USSR)
1981	Yuriy Korolev (USSR)
1983	Dmitriy Bilozerchev (USSR)
1985	Yuriy Korolev (USSR)
1987	Dmitriy Bilozerchev (USSR)
1989	Igor Korobchinskiy (USSR)
1991	Grigoriy Misutin (USSR)
1993	Vitaliy Scherbo (Blr)
1994	Ivan Ivankov (Blr)
1995	Li Xiaoshuang (Chn)
1997	Ivan Ivankov (Blr)

Floor exercises

1913	Giorgio Zampori (Ita) & V Rabic (Bohemia)
1930	Josip Primozic (Yug)
1934	Georges Miesz (Swi)
1938	Jan Gajdos (Cs)
1950	Josef Stadler (Swi)
1954	Valentin Muratov (USSR) & Masao Takemoto (Jap)
1958	Masao Takemoto (Jap)
1962	Nobuyuki Aihara (Jap) & Yukio Endo (Jap)
1966	Akinori Nakayama (Jap)
1970	Akinori Nakayama (Jap)
1974	Shigeru Kasamatsu (Jap)
1978	Kurt Thomas (USA)
1979	Kurt Thomas (USA) & Roland Brückner (GDR)
1981	Yuriy Korolev (USSR) & Li Yuejiu (Chn)
1983	Tong Fei (Chn)
1985	Tong Fei (Chn)
1987	Lou Yun (Chn)
1989	Igor Korobchinskiy (USSR)
1991	Igor Korobchinskiy (USSR)
1993	Grigoriy Misutin (Ukr)
1994-5	Vitaliy Scherbo (Blr)
1997	Aleksey Nemov (Rus)

Horizontal bar

1903	Joseph Martinez (Fra/Alg) & Pierre Payssé (Fra)
1905	Marcel Lalu (Fra)
1907	Georges Charmoille (Fra) & Frantisek Erben (Bohemia)
1909	Joseph Martinez (Fra), Josef Cada (Bohemia) & Frantisek Erben (Fra)
1911	Josef Cada (Bohemia
1913	Josef Cada (Bohemia)
1922	Miroslav Klinger (Cs)
1926	Leon Stukelj (Yug)
1930	István Pelle (Hun)
1934	Ernst Winter (Ger)
1938	Michael Reusch (Swi)
1950	Paavo Aaltonen (Fin)
1954	Valentin Muratov (USSR)
1958	Boris Shakhlin (USSR)
1962	Takashi Ono (Jap)
1966	Akinori Nakayama (Jap)
1970	Eizo Kenmotsu (Jap)
1974	Eberhard Gienger (FRG)
1978	Shigeru Kasamatsu (Jap)
1979	Kurt Thomas (USA)
1981	Aleksandr Tkachev (USSR)
1983	Dmitriy Bilozerchev (USSR)
1985	Tong Fei (Chn)
1987	Dmitriy Bilozerchev (USSR)
1989	Li Chunyang (Chn)
1991	Li Chunyang (Chn) & Ralf Büchner (Ger)
1993	Sergey Kharkov (Rus)
1994	Vitaliy Scherbo (Blr)
1995	Andreas Wecker (Ger)
1997	Jani Tanskanen (Fin)

Parallel bars

1903	Joseph Martinez (Fra) & Francois Hentges (Lux)
1905	Joseph Martinez (Fra/Alg)
1907	Jos Lux (Fra)

1909	Joseph Martinez (Fra/Alg)	1979	Aleksandr Ditiatin (USSR)	**Pommel horse**
1911	Giorgio Zampori (Ita)	1981	Ralf-Peter Hemmann	1911 Osvaldo Palazzi (Ita)
1913	Giorgio Zampori (Ita) &		(GDR)	1913 Giorgio Zampori (Ita),

1909   Joseph Martinez (Fra/Alg)
1911   Giorgio Zampori (Ita)
1913   Giorgio Zampori (Ita) &
          Guido Boni (Ita)
1922   Leon Stukelj (Yug), Stane
          Derganc (Yug), N Jindrich
          (Cs), Miroslav Klinger
          (Cs) & Vlado Simoncic
          (Yug)
1926   Ladislav Vácha (Cs)
1930   Josip Primozic (Yug)
1934   Eugen Mack (Swi)
1938   Michael Reusch (Swi)
1950   Hans Eugster (Swi)
1954   Viktor Chukarin (USSR)
1958   Boris Shakhlin (USSR)
1962   Miroslav Cerar (Yug)
1966   Sergey Diomidov (USSR)
1970   Akinori Nakayama (Jap)
1974   Eizo Kenmotsu (Jap)
1978   Eizo Kenmotsu (Jap)
1979   Bart Conner (USA)
1981   Aleksandr Ditiatin (USSR)
          & Koji Gushiken (Jap)
1983   Vladimir Artemov (USSR)
          & Lou Yun (Chn)
1985   Silvio Kroll (GDR) &
          Valentin Mogilnyi (USSR)
1987   Vladimir Artemov (USSR)
1989   Li Jing (Chn) & Vladimir
          Artemov (USSR)
1991   Li Jing (Chn)
1993   Vitaliy Scherbo (Blr)
1994   Huang Liping (Chn)
1995   Vitaliy Scherbo (Blr)
1997   Zhang Jinjing (Chn)

Horse vault

1903   G De Jaeghere (Fra), Jos
          Lux (Fra) & N Thysen
          (Hol)
1905   G De Jaeghere (Fra)
1907   Frantisek Erben (Bohemia)
1913   Karel Stary (Bohemia),
          Ben Sadoun (Fra),
          Osvaldo Palazzi (Ita) &
          Stane Vidmar (Yug)
1934   Eugen Mack (Swi)
1938   Eugen Mack (Swi)
1950   Ernst Gebendinger (Swi)
1954   Leo Sotornik (Cs)
1958   Yuriy Titov (USSR)
1962   Premysel Krbec (Cs)
1966   Haruhiro Matsuda (Jap)
1970   Mitsuo Tsukahara (Jap)
1974   Shigeru Kasamatsu (Jap)
1978   Junichi Shimizu (Jap)

1979   Aleksandr Ditiatin (USSR)
1981   Ralf-Peter Hemmann
          (GDR)
1983   Artur Akopian (USSR)
1985   Yuriy Korolev (USSR)
1987   Silvio Kroll (GDR) & Lou
          Yun (Chn)
1989   Jörg Behrendt (GDR)
1991   Yu Ok-yul (SKo)
1993-4 Vitaliy Scherbo (Blr)
1995   Grigoriy Misutin (Ukr) &
          Aleksey Nemov (Rus)
1997   Sergey Fedorchenko (Kaz)

Rings

1903   Joseph Martinez (Fra/Alg)
          & Jos Lux (Lux)
1909   Guido Romano (Ita) &
          Marco Torres (Fra)
1911   Ferdinand Steiner
          (Bohemia), Dominique
          Follacci (Fra) & Pietro
          Bianchi (Ita)
1913   Laurent Grech (Fra),
          Marco Torres (Fra), Guido
          Boni (Ita), Giorgio
          Zampori (Ita)
1922   Laurent Karasek (Cs), Josef
          Maly (Cs), Leon Stukelj
          (Yug) & Peter Sumi (Yug)
1926   Leon Stukelj (Yug)
1930   Emanuel Löffler (Cs)
1934   Alois Hudec (Cs)
1938   Alois Hudec (Cs)
1950   Walter Lehmann (Swi)
1954   Albert Azarian (USSR)
1958   Albert Azarian (USSR)
1962   Yuriy Titov (USSR)
1966   Mikhail Voronin (USSR)
1970   Akinori Nakayama (Jap)
1974   Nikolay Andrianov
          (USSR) & Dan Grecu
          (Rom)
1978   Nikolay Andrianov
          (USSR)
1979   Aleksandr Ditiatin (USSR)
1981   Aleksandr Ditiatin (USSR)
1983   Dmitriy Bilozerchev
          (USSR) & Koji Gushiken
          (Jap)
1985   Li Ning (Chn) & Yuriy
          Korolev (USSR)
1987   Yuriy Korolev (USSR)
1989   Andreas Aguilar (FRG)
1991   Grigoriy Misutin (USSR)
1993-5 Yuri Chechi (Ita)
1997   Yuri Chechi (Ita)

Pommel horse

1911   Osvaldo Palazzi (Ita)
1913   Giorgio Zampori (Ita),
          N Aubrey (Fra) &
          Osvaldo Palazzi (Ita)
1922   Miroslav Klinger (Cs),
          N Jindrich (Cs) & Leon
          Stukelj (Yug)
1926   Jan Karafiát (Cs)
1930   Josip Primozic (Yug)
1934   Eugène Mack (Swi)
1938   Michael Reusch (Swi) &
          Vratislav Petracek (Cs)
1950   Josef Stalder (Swi)
1954   Grant Chaginyan (USSR)
1958   Boris Shakhlin (USSR)
1962   Miroslav Cerar (Yug)
1966   Miroslav Cerar (Yug)
1970   Miroslav Cerar (Yug)
1974   Zoltán Magyar (Hun)
1978   Zoltán Magyar (Hun)
1979   Zoltán Magyar (Hun)
1981   Michael Nikolay (GDR)
          & Li Xiaoping (Chn)
1983   Dmitriy Bilozerchev
          (USSR)
1985   Valentin Mogilnyi (USSR)
1987   Dmitriy Bilozerchev
          (USSR) & Zsolt Borkai
          (Hun)
1989   Valentin Mogilnyi (USSR)
1991   Valeriy Belenkiy (USSR)
1993   Gil Su-pae (NKo)
1994   Marius Urzica (Rom)
1995   Li Donghua (Swi)
1997   Waleri Belenki (Ger)

Women

Team

11   USSR
          1954, 1958, 1962, 1970,
          1974, 1978, 1981, 1983,
          1985, 1989, 1991
5   Romania
          1979, 1987, 1994-5, 1997
3   Czechoslovakia
          1934, 1938, 1966
1   Sweden
          1950

All-around

1934   Vlasta Dekanová (Cs)
1938   Vlasta Dekanová (Cs)
1950   Helena Rakoczy (Pol)
1954   Galina Roudiko (USSR)
1958   Larisa Latynina (USSR)
1962   Larisa Latynina (USSR)
1966   Vera Cáslavská (Cs)

1970	Lyudmila Tourischeva (USSR)
1974	Lyudmila Tourischeva (USSR)
1978	Yelena Mukhina (USSR)
1979	Nelli Kim (USSR)
1981	Olga Bicherova (USSR)
1983	Natalya Yurchenko (USSR)
1985	Oksana Omelianchik (USSR) & Yelena Shushunova (USSR)
1987	Aurelia Dobre (Rom)
1989	Svetlana Boginskaya (USSR)
1991	Kim Zmeskal (USA)
1993-4	Shannon Miller (USA)
1995	Lilia Podkopayeva (Ukr)
1997	Svetlana Chorkina (Rus)

Parallel bars

| 1938 | Vlasta Dekanová (Cs) |

Horse vault

1938	Matylda Pálfyová (Cs) & Marta Majowska (Pol)
1950	Helena Rakoczy (Pol)
1954	Tamara Manina (USSR) & Anna Petersson (Swe)
1958	Larisa Latynina (USSR)
1962	Vera Cáslavská (Cs)
1966	Vera Cáslavská (Cs)
1970	Erika Zuchold (GDR)
1974	Olga Korbut (USSR)
1978	Nelli Kim (USSR)
1979	Dumitrata Turner (Rom)
1981	Maxi Gnauck (GDR)
1983	Boriana Stoyanova (Bul)
1985	Yelena Shushunova (USSR)
1987	Yelena Shushunova (USSR)
1989	Olessia Dudnik (USSR)
1991	Lavinia Milosovici (Rom)
1993	Yelena Piskun (Blr)
1994	Gina Gogean (Rom)
1995	Lilia Podkopayeva (Ukr)
1997	Simona Amanar (Rom)

Balance beam

1938	Vlasta Dekanová (Cs)
1950	Helena Rakoczy (Pol)
1954	Keiko Tanaka (Jap)
1958	Larisa Latynina (USSR)
1962	Eva Bosáková (Cs)
1966	Natalya Kuchinskaya (USSR)
1970	Erika Zuchold (GDR)

1974	Lyudmila Tourischeva (USSR)
1978	Nadia Comaneci (Rom)
1979	Vera Cerna (Cs)
1981	Maxi Gnauck (GDR)
1983	Olga Mostepanova (USSR)
1985	Daniela Silivas (Rom)
1987	Aurelia Dobre (Rom)
1989	Daniela Silivas (Rom)
1991	Svetlana Boginskaya (USSR)
1993	Lavinia Milosovici (Rom)
1994	Shannon Miller (USA)
1995	Mo Huilan (Chn)
1997	Gina Gogean (Rom)

Floor exercises

1938	Matylda Pálfyová (Cs)
1950	Helena Rakoczy (Pol)
1954	Tamara Manina (USSR)
1958	Eva Bosáková (Cs)
1962	Larisa Latynina (USSR)
1966	Natalya Kuchinskaya (USSR)
1970	Lyudmila Tourischeva (USSR)
1974	Lyudmila Tourischeva (USSR)
1978	Nelli Kim (USSR) & Yelena Mukhina (USSR)
1979	Emilia Eberle (Rom)
1981	Natalya Ilyenko (USSR)
1983	Ecaterina Szabo (Rom)
1985	Oksana Omelianchik (USSR)
1987	Yelena Shushunova (USSR) & Daniela Silivas (Rom)
1989	Daniela Silivas (Rom) & Svetlana Boginskaya (USSR)
1991	Cristina Bontas (Rom) & Oksana Chusovitina (USSR)
1993	Shannon Miller (USA)
1994	Dina Kochetkova (Rus)
1995	Gina Gogean (Rom)
1997	Gina Gogean (Rom)

Asymmetrical bars

1950	Gertchen Kolar (Aut) & Anna Pettersson (Swe)
1954	Agnes Kaleti (Hun)
1958	Larisa Latynina (USSR)
1962	Irina Pervuschina (USSR)
1966	Natalya Kuchinskaya (USSR)

1970	Karin Janz (GDR)
1974	Annelore Zinke (GDR)
1978	Marcia Frederick (USA)
1979	Ma Yanhong (Chn) & Maxi Gnauck (GDR)
1981	Maxi Gnauck (GDR)
1983	Maxi Gnauck (GDR)
1985	Gabriela Fahnrich (GDR)
1987	Daniela Silivas (Rom) & Dörte Thümmler (GDR)
1989	Fan Di (Chn) & Daniela Silivas (Rom)
1991	Kim Gwang-suk (NKo)
1993	Shannon Miller (USA)
1994	Li Luo (Chn)
1995	Svetlana Chorkina (Rus)
1997	Svetlana Chorkina (Rus)

Most Medals

Most Olympic and World Championship golds

Men

13	Vitaliy Scherbo (Blr) 1992-5
10	Boris Shakhlin (USSR) 1956-64
9	Leon Stukelj (Yug) 1922-8
9	Akinori Nakayama (Jap) 1966-72
9	Nikolay Andrianov (USSR) 1972-80
9	Dmitriy Bilozerchev (USSR) 1983-8
7	Joseph Martinez (Fra) 1903-9
6	Eugen Mack (Swi) 1928-38
6	Yuriy Korolev (USSR) 1981-7
6	Vladimir Artemov (USSR) 1983-9

Women

12	Larisa Latynina (USSR) 1956-64
10	Vera Cáslavská (Cs) 1962-8
9	Daniela Silivas (Rom) 1985-9
6	Lyudmila Tourischeva (USSR) 1968-76
6	Nadia Comaneci (Rom) 1976-80
6	Nelli Kim (USSR) 1976-80
6	Maxi Gnauck (GDR) 1979-83

World Championships only

Men

Most gold medals – individual:
8 Vitaliy Scherbo; 7 Dmitriy Bilozerchev; 6 Yuriy Korolev; 5 Eugen Mack, Akinori Nakayama, Aleksandr Ditiatin (USSR)

Most medals: 12 Eizo Kenmotsu (Jap); 10 Akinori Nakayama, Boris Shakhlin, Nikolay Andrianov

Women

Most gold medals – individual: 6 Daniela Silivas; 5 Larisa Latynina, Lyudmila Tourischeva, Shannon Miller (USA)

Most medals: 9 Larisa Latynina, Lyudmila Tourischeva, Eva Bosáková (Cs)

World Individual Event Championships

Held for the first time in Paris in 1992.
1992 winners:

Men

Floor exercises: Igor Korobchinskiy (Rus)

Horizontal bar: Grigoriy Misutin (CIS)

Parallel bars: Li Jing (Chn) & Aleksey Voropayev (CIS)

Horse vault: Yu Ok-yul (SKo)

Rings: Vitaliy Scherbo (Blr)

Pommel horse: Gil Su-pae (NKo) & Vitaliy Shcherbo (Blr)

Women

Horse vault: Henrietta Ónodi (Hun)

Balance beam: Kim Zmeskal (USA)

Floor exercises: Kim Zmeskal (USA)

Asymmetrical bars: Lavinia Milosevici (Rom)

World Cup

First held 1975.
Overall champions:

Men

1975	Nikolay Andrianov (USSR)
1977	Nikolay Andrianov (USSR) & Vladimir Markelov (USSR)
1978	Aleksandr Ditiatin (USSR)
1979	Aleksandr Ditiatin (USSR)
1980	Bogdan Makuts (USSR)
1982	Li Ning (Chn)
1986	Yuriy Korolev (USSR) & Li Ning (Chn)
1990	Valeriy Belenky (SU)

Women

1975	Lyudmila Tourischeva (USSR)
1977	Mariya Filatova (USSR
1978	Mariya Filatova (USSR)
1979-80	Stella Zakharova (USSR)
1982	Olga Bicherova (USSR) & Natalya Yurchenko (USSR)
1986	Yelena Shushunova (USSR)
1990	Tatyana Lisenko (USSR)

European Championships

First held 1955.
Overall champions:

	Men	Women
1955	Boris Shakhlin (USSR)	-
1957	Joachim Blume (Spa)	Larisa Latynina (USSR)
1959	Yuriy Titov (USSR)	Natalie Kot (Pol)
1961	Miroslav Cerar (Yug)	Larisa Latynina (USSR)
1963	Miroslav Cerar (Yug)	Mirjana Bilic (Yug)
1965	Franco Menichelli (Ita)	Vera Cáslavská (Cs)
1967	Mikhail Voronin (USSR)	Vera Cáslavská (Cs)
1969	Mikhail Voronin (USSR)	Karin Janz (GDR)
1971	Viktor Klimenko (USSR)	Lyudmila Tourischeva (USSR) & Tamara Lazakovich (USSR)
1973	Viktor Klimenko (USSR)	Lyudmila Tourischeva (USSR)
1975	Nikolay Andrianov (USSR)	Nadia Comaneci (Rom)
1977	Vladimir Markelov (USSR)	Nadia Comaneci (Rom)
1979	Stoyan Deltchev (Bul)	Nadia Comaneci (Rom)
1981	Aleksandr Tkachev (USSR)	Maxi Gnauck (GDR)
1983	Dmitriy Bilozerchev (USSR)	Olga Bicherova (USSR)
1985	Dmitriy Bilozerchev (USSR)	Yelena Shushunova (USSR)
1987	Valeriy Lyukin (USSR)	Daniela Silivas (Rom)
1989	Igor Korobchinskiy (USSR)	Svetlana Boginskaya (USSR)
1990	Valentin Mogilnyi (USSR)	Svetlana Boginskaya (USSR)
1992	Igor Korobchinskiy (Rus)	Tatyana Gutsu (Ukr)
1994	Ivan Ivankov (Blr)	Gina Gogean (Rom)
1996	Ivan Ivankov (Blr)	Lilia Podkopayeva (Ukr)
1998	Aleksey Bondarenko (Rus)	Svetlana Khorkina (Rus)

Rhythmic Sportive Gymnastics World Champions

All-around team winners

9	Bulgaria	1969, 1971, 1981, 1983, 1985, 1987, 1989, 1993, 1995-6
5	USSR	1967, 1973, 1977, 1979
3	Russia	1992, 1994, 1997
1	Italy 1975, Spain 1991, Belarus 1998	

Individual overall winners

1963	Lyudmila Savinkova (USSR)
1965	Hana Micechová (Cs)
1967	Yelena Karpukhina (USSR)
1969	Maria Gigova (Bul)
1971	Maria Gigova (Bul)
1973	Maria Gigova (Bul) & Galina Shugarova (USSR)
1975	Carmen Rischer (FRG)
1977	Irina Deryugina (USSR)
1979	Irina Deryugina (USSR)
1981	Anelia Ralenkova (Bul)
1983	Diliana Georgieva (Bul)
1985	Diliana Georgieva (Bul)
1987	Bianka Panova (Bul)★
1989	Aleksandra Timoschenko (USSR)
1991	Oksana Skaldina (USSR)
1992	Oksana Kostina (Rus)
1993-4	Maria Petrova (Bul)
1995	Maria Petrova (Bul) & Yekaterina Serebryanskaya (Ukr)
1997	Yelena Vitrichenko (Ukr)

* In 1987 Bianka Panova won all four disciplines, all with maximum scores, a unprecedented achievement. In 1991 Aleksandra Timoshenko also won all four individual titles, although she had been second to Skaldina in the preceding overall event.

Rhythmic Sportive Gymnastics World Cup

	Individual overall winners	Team
1983	Lilia Ignatova (Bul)	USSR
1986	Lilia Ignatova (Bul)	Bulgaria
1990	Oksana Skaldina (USSR)	USSR

Handball

The modern game, similar to Association football, with hands used instead of feet, was first played in Germany around 1895. The first international match was played at Halle/Salle on 3 Sep 1925 when Austria beat Germany 6-3. Germany has long been a stronghold of the game, which was introduced to the Olympic Games at Berlin in 1936 as an 11-a-side outdoor game. When re-introduced in 1972, again in Germany (Munich), it was as an indoor 7-a-side game; this version of the game has been predominant since 1952. The indoor court is 40m long by 20m wide; the goals are 2m high and 3m wide.

Prior to 1928 the International Amateur Athletic Federation looked after the interests of handball, but in that year the International Amateur Handball Federation (FIHA) was founded with Avery Brundage (USA), later the President of the IOC, as its first president.

International governing body: International Handball Federation (IHF), PO Box 312, CH-4020 Basel, Switzerland. Tel: (41) 61 272 1300, Fax: (41) 61 272 1344. President: Erwin Lanc, Managing Director: Frank Birkefeld. Founded in 1946, replacing the FIHA. 138 member federations (and 4 provisional) by 1998.

Olympic Games

Played outdoors with 11-a-side in 1936, indoors with 7-a-side from 1972 (men) and 1976 (women).
Winners:

	Men	Women
1936	Germany	-
1972	Yugoslavia	-
1976	USSR	USSR
1980	GDR	USSR
1984	Yugoslavia	Yugoslavia
1988	USSR	South Korea
1992	CIS	South Korea
1996	Croatia	Denmark

World Championships

First held outdoors in 1938 for men and in 1949 for women. Men's nations are now divided into three groups – A, B and C; the women are in two - A and B.
Winners:

Men outdoors (11-a-side)

1938	Germany
1948	Sweden
1952	F R Germany
1955	F R Germany
1959	Germany
1963	GDR
1966	F R Germany

Men indoors (A group) (7-a-side)

1938	Germany
1954	Sweden
1958	Sweden
1961	Romania
1964	Romania
1967	Czechoslovakia
1970	Romania
1974	Romania
1978	F R Germany
1982	USSR
1986	Yugoslavia
1990	Sweden
1993	Russia
1995	France
1997	Russia

Women outdoors (11-a-side)

1949	Hungary
1956	Romania
1960	Romania

Women indoors (A group) (7-a-side)

1957	Czechoslovakia (played outdoors)
1962	Romania (played outdoors)
1965	Hungary
1971	GDR
1973	Yugoslavia
1975	GDR
1979	GDR
1982	USSR

1986	USSR
1990	USSR
1993	Germany
1997	Denmark

European Cup

Contested by national champions. First held in 1957 (men), 1961 (women).
Winners:

Men

1957	Stadtmannschaft Prague (Cs)
1959	RIK Göteborg (Swe)
1961-2	Frischauf Göppingen (FRG)
1963	Dukla Prague (Cs)
1965	Dinamo Bucharest (Rom)
1966	DHfK Leipzig (GDR)
1967	Vfl Gummersbach (FRG)
1968	Steaua Bucharest (Rom)
1970-1	Vfl Gummersbach (FRG)
1972	Partizan Bjelovar (Yug)
1973	MAI Moscow (USSR)
1974	Vfl Gummersbach (FRG)
1975	ASK Vorwärts Frankfurt/Oder (GDR)
1976	Borac Banjalukar (Yug)
1977	Steaua Bucharest (Rom)
1978	SC Magdeburg (GDR)
1979-80	TV Grosswallstadt (FRG)
1981	SC Magdeburg (GDR)

1982	Honved SE, Budapest (Hun)
1983	VfL Gummersbach (FRG)
1984	Dukla Prague (Cs)
1985-6	Metaloplastika Sabac (Yug)
1987	SKA Minsk (USSR)
1988	CSKA Moscow (USSR)
1989-90	SKA Minsk (USSR)
1991	FC Barcelona (Spa)
1992-3	RK/Badel Zagreb (Cro)
1994	TEKA Santander (Spa)
1995	Elgorriaga Bidasoa (Spa)
1996-8	FC Barcelona (Spa)

Most wins: 5 Vfl Gummersbach

Women

1961	Stiinta Bucharest (Rom)
1962	Spartak Prague (Cs)
1963	Trud Moscow (USSR)
1964	Rapid Bucharest (Rom)
1965	HG København (Den)
1966	SC Leipzig (GDR)
1967-8	Zalgiris Kaunas (USSR)
1970-3	Spartak Kiev (USSR)
1974	SC Leipzig (GDR)
1975	Spartak Kiev (USSR)
1976	Radnicki Belgrad (Yug)
1977	Spartak Kiev (USSR)
1978	TSC Berlin (GDR)
1979	Spartak Kiev (USSR)
1980	RK Radnicki Belgrad (Yug)
1981	Spartak Kiev (USSR)
1982	Vasas SC, Budapest (Hun)
1983	Spartak Kiev (USSR)
1984	Radnicki Belgrad (Yug)
1985-8	Spartak Kiev (USSR)
1989-90	Hypobank Sudstadt (Aut)
1991	TV Lützellinden (Ger)
1992-5	Hypobank Südstadt Wien (Aut) (Hypo Niederösterreich)
1996	Podravka Koprivnica (Cro)
1997	Valencia (Spa)
1998	Nieder Österreich (Aut)

Most wins: 13 Spartak Kiev

European Cup-Winners' Cup

First held 1976 (men), 1977 (women).
Winners:

Men

1976	Balonmano Granollers (Spa)
1977	MAI Moskva (USSR)
1978-9	VfL Gummersbach (FRG)
1980	Calpisa Alicante (Spa)
1981	TuS Nettelstedt (FRG)
1982	SC Empor Rostock (GDR)
1983	SKA Minsk (USSR)
1984-6	FC Barcelona (Spa)
1987	CSKA Moscow (USSR)
1988	SKA Minsk (USSR)
1989	Tusam Essen (FRG)
1990	Teka Santander (Spa)
1991	Bidasoa Irun (Spa)
1992	Bramac Veszpram (Hun)
1993	Olympique Marseille Vitrolles (Fra)
1994-5	FC Barcelona (Spa)
1996	TBV Lemgo (Ger)
1997	Bidasoa Irun (Spa)
1998	Caja Santander (Spa)

Most wins: 4 FC Barcelona

Women

1977	TSC Berlin (GDR)
1978	Ferencvarosi Budapest (Hun)
1979	TSC Berlin (GDR)
1980	Iskra Partizanske (Cs)
1981	Spartacus Budapest (Hun)
1982-3	RK Osiejek (Yug)
1984	Dalma Split (Yug)
1985	Budocnost Titograd (Yug)
1986	Radnicki Belgrad (Yug)
1987-8	Kuban Krasnodar (USSR)
1989	Stiinta Bacau (Rom)
1990	Rostelmach Rostov (USSR)
1991-2	Radnicki Belgrad (Yug)
1993	TV Lützellinden (Ger)
1994	TUS Walle Bremen (Ger)
1995	Dunsferr (Hun)
1996	TV Lützellinden (Ger)
1997	Rostov (Rus)
1998	Ikast FS (Den)

Most wins: 3 Kuban Krasnodar

IHF Cup

First held in 1982.
Winners:

Men

1982	Vfl Gummersbach (FRG)
1983	IL Saporozhye (USSR)
1984	TV Grosswallstadt (FRG)
1985	Minaur Baia Mare (Rom)
1986	Raba Vasas Etö Györ (Hun)
1987	Granitas Kaunas (USSR)
1988	Minaur Baia Mare (Rom)
1989	Türu Düsseldorf (FRG)
1990	Kuban Krasnodar (USSR)
1991	Borac Banja-Luka (Yug)
1992	SG Wallau-Massenheim (Ger)
1993	Teka Santander (Spa)
1994	Alzira Avidesa (Spa)
1995	Granollers (Spa)
1996	Balomanon Granollers (Spa)
1997	SG Flensburg-Handewitt (Ger)
1998	THW Kiel (Ger)

Women

1982	IHK Tresnjevka, Zagreb (Yug)
1983	Automobilist Baku (USSR)
1984	Chimistul Vilcea (Rom)
1985	ASK Vorwärts Frankfurt/Oder (GDR)
1986	SC Leipzig (GDR)
1987	Budocnost Titograd (Yug)
1988	Egle Vilnius (USSR)
1989	Chimistul Vilcea (Rom)
1990	ASK Vorwärts Frankfurt (GDR)
1991	Lokomotive Zagreb (Yug)
1992	SC Leipzig (Ger)
1993	Rapid Bucuresti (Rom)
1994	HK Viborg (Den)
1995-6	Debrecen (Hun)
1997	Olimpija Ljubljana (Slo)
1998	Dunaferr SE (Hun)

In 1983 Vfl Gummersbach (FRG) recorded a unique achievement, winning all possible competitions in one year – the FRG national championship and cup, the European Champions Cup and the IHF Super Cup (contested by the winners of the two European Cup competitions).

Record

Highest score in an international match: USSR beat Afghanistan 86-2 in the 'Friendly Army Tournament' at Miskolc, Hungary August 1981

Court Handball

Handball played against walls or in a court is a game of ancient Celtic origin. It has been particularly prominent in Ireland and the USA, and the first-ever international match was between the champions of these nations in 1887, when Phil Casey (USA) beat Bernard McQuade (Ire). In Ireland and Australia the court is 60ft (18.3m) long and 30ft (9.1m) wide, but a smaller court of 40ft (12m) long and 20ft (6.1m) wide is used in North America.

The first US Championships under the suspices of the AAU were held in 1919 at four-wall singles and doubles. The United States Handball Association (USHA) was founded in 1951.

World Four-Wall Championships

1984	Merv Deckert (Can)
1986	Vern Roberts (USA)
1988	Naty Alvarado (USA)
1991	Pancho Monreal (USA)
1994	David Chapman (USA)
1997	John Bike Jr (USA)

US National Championships

First held in 1919.

Most wins:

National four-wall men's singles: 11 Naty Alvarado 1977, 1979-80, 1982-7, 1990

National four-wall men's doubles: 8 Marty Decatur 1962-3, 1965, 1967-8, 1975, 1978-9 (the first five with Jim Jacobs)

National four-wall women's singles: 6 Rosemary Bellini 1980-2, 1984, 1987-8, Anna Engele 1990-1, 1993-6

National three-wall men's singles: 9 Vic Hershkowitz 1960-8

National three-wall women's singles: 8 Rosemary Bellini 1984-91

Hang Gliding

An elementary form of hang glider is reputed to have been used by the monk Eilmer, to fly from the top of Malmesbury Abbey, Wiltshire. The first modern pioneer of hang gliding was Otto Lilienthal in Germany in the 1890s. Duration and distance records have increased substantially in recent years as pilots have utilized optimum conditions and improved designs of glider.

International governing body: FIA (*see* Gliding).

Men's World Championships

An unofficial world championship was held in 1975, won by David Cronk (USA), with the first official championships taking place the following year at Kössen in Austria.

Winners:

Team

1976	Austria
1979	France
1981	Great Britain
1983	Australia
1985	Great Britain
1988	Australia
1989	Great Britain
1991	Great Britain
1993	USA
1995	Austria
1998	Austria

Individual

1976	Class I – Standard: Christian Steinbach (Aut)
	Class II – High-Aspect Ratio: Terry Dolore (NZ)
	Class III – Open: Ken Battle (Aus)
1979	Class I – Weight Shift: Josef Guggenmos (FRG)
	Class II – Movable Surfaces: Rex Miller (USA)
1981	Class I – Weight Shift: Pepe Lopes (Bra)
	Class II – Movable Surfaces: Graeme Bird (NZ)
1983	Steve Moyes (Aus)
1985	John Pendry (UK)
1988	Rick Duncan (Aus)
1989	Robbie Whittall (UK)
1991	Tomás Schanek (Cs)
1993	Tomás Schanek (Cs)
1995	Tomás Schanek (Cs)
1998	Guido Gehrman (Ger)

Women's World Championships

Held separately from the men's, first in 1987.

Winners:

Team

1987	UK
1991	France
1993-4	Switzerland
1996	Germany

Individual

1987	Judy Leden (UK)
1991	Judy Leden (UK)
1993	Françoise Dieuzeide (Fra)
1994	Annelise Müller (Swi)
1996	Kari Castle (USA)

World Records

As officially recognized by the FAI.

(Category: Record, Pilot, Glider, Venue, Date)

Men – FAI Class O-1 – flex-wing hang gliders

Straight line distance	495.0km Larry Tudor (USA), Rock Springs, USA, 1 Jul 1994
Height gain	4343m Larry Tudor (USA), Horseshoe Meadows, USA, 4 Aug 1985

Distance via a single turn point   412.6km Mark Gibson (USA), Horseshoe Meadows, USA, 31 Jul 1992
Declared goal distance   488.2km Larry Tudor (USA), Hobbs, New Mexico to Elkart, Kansas, USA,
                                   3 Jul 1990
Out and return distance   310.3km Geoffrey Loyns (UK) & Larry Tudor (USA), Horseshoe Meadows,
                                   USA, 26 Jun 1988
Distance over triangular course   205.0km Jo Bathman (Ger), Schmittenhöhe, Austria, 17 Jun 1996

Men – FAI Class O-2 – rigid-wing hang gliders

Straight line distance   230.2km William Woodruff (USA), Lone Pine, CA, USA 26 Jun 1993
Height gain   3820m Rainer Scholl (FRG), Horseshoe Meadows, USA 5 Aug 1985

Women – FAI Class O-1 – flex-wing hang gliders

Straight line distance   335.8km Kari Castle (USA), Horseshoe Meadows, USA, 22 Jul 1991
Height gain   3970m Judy Leden (UK), Karuman, South Africa, 1 Dec 1992
Distance via a single turn point   292.1km Kari Castle (USA), Hobbs, New Mexico, USA, 1 Jul 1990
Declared goal distance   212.5km Liavan Mallin (Ire), Horseshoe Meadows, USA, 13 Jul 1989
Out and return distance   132.0km Tøve Buås-Hansen (Nor), Gunter, USA, 6 Jul 1989
Distance over triangular course   167.2km Nichola Hamilton (UK), 2 Jan 1997

Paragliding records FAI Class O-3

Men

Straight line distance   283.9km Alex Louw (SAf), Kuruman, South Africa, 31 Dec 1993
Height gain   4526m Rob Whittal (UK), Brandvlei, South Africa, 6 Jan 1993
Declared goal distance   250.2km Alex Louw (SAf), 18 Dec 1994
Distance over triangular course   165.9km Pierre Bouilloux (Fra), 9 Jul 1995

Women

Straight line distance   285km Kat Thurston (UK), Kuruman, South Africa, 25 Dec 1995
Height gain   4325m Kat Thurston (UK), Kuruman, South Africa, 1 Jan 1996
Declared goal distance   166km Kat Thurston (UK), 20 Jul 1995
Distance over triangular course   50.3km Judy Leden & Sarah Fenwick (UK), Piedrahita, Spain, 20 Jul 1994

Microlight records

The Fédération Aéronautique Internationale recognizes records for microlights in their class R (sub-divisions R1 landplanes, R2 seaplanes and R4 foot-launched powered hang gliders). The following are the R1 bests:
Altitude:
  9720m Serge Zin (Fra), Saint Auban, France, 18 Sep 1994
Distance in a straight line without landing:
  1369.0km Bernard d'Otreppe (Bel), Fréjus La Palud, France, 6 Sep 1988
Distance over a closed circuit without landing:
  1071.2km Michel Serane (Fra), Besançon-Thise, France, 5 Aug 1991
Speed over a straight 15/25km course:
  168.55km/h Serge Ferrari (Fra), Belley-Peyrieu, France, 29 Jun 1995
Speed over 50km closed circuit without landing:
  157.44km/h Serge Ferrari (Fra), Belley-Peyrieu, France, 30 Jun 1995
Speed over 100km closed circuit without landing:
  163.61km/h Serge Ferrari (Fra), Belleville sur Saône, France, 10 Oct 1995

R1 Multiplace records (where better than solo)

Speed over a straight 15/25km course:
  194.50km/h Philippe Zen & Rodolphe de Frayssinet (Fra), Belley-Peyrieu, France, 1 Jun 1994
Speed over 50km closed circuit without landing:
  163.02km/h Philippe Zen & Patrick Durand (Fra), Belley-Peyrieu, France, 4 Jun 1994

Harness Racing

A form of racing in which horses trot or pace while being driven in a light two-wheeled cart, or 'sulky'. Pacers have a lateral gait, moving their fore and hind legs in unison on one side and then the other, whereas trotters have a diagonal gait, bringing their off-fore and near-hind legs together in unison, followed by their near-fore and off-hind legs. Standardbred horses (which race up to a certain standard of speed) are raced, not thoroughbreds, as in horse racing. Race tracks have a dirt surface, are oval in shape, and half a mile to a mile in circumference.

Trotting races were first held in the Netherlands in 1554, and the sulky first appeared in harness racing in 1829. The sport became very popular in the USA in the 19th century, and the National Trotting Association was founded, originally as the National Association for the Promotion of the Interests of the Trotting Turf in 1870. It brought much-needed controls to a sport threatened by gambling corruption.

(*In references to earnings and prize money, $ denotes $US.*)

1-Mile Records

Trotting record: 1:51.0 Pine Chip (driver John Campbell) at Lexington, Kentucky, 1 Oct 1994

Trotting race record: 1:51.8 Beat the Wheel (driver Cat Manzi) at Meadowlands, East Rutherford, NJ, 7 Jul 1994

Pacing record: 1:48.4 Matt's Scooter (driver Michel Lachance) at Lexington, Kentucky, 23 Sep 1988

Pacing race record: 1:49.4 Artsplace (driver Catello Manzi) at Meadowlands, East Rutherford, NJ, 20 Aug 1992

Hambletonian Stakes

The most famous race in North America is the Hambletonian Stakes, run annually for three-year-olds. It was first staged at Syracuse, New York in 1926; then at Syracuse, Lexington, and the New York tracks of Yonkers and Goshen, Du Quoin, Illinois 1956-80 and at Meadowlands, East Rutherford, NJ from 1981. The horse Hambletonian, born in 1849, although only an ordinary racer, had a notable influence on the breeding of American trotters.

Winners since 1970:

Year	Horse	Driver
1970	Timothy T	John Simpson, Jr
1971	Speedy Crown	Howard Beissinger
1972	Super Bowl	Stanley Dancer
1973	Flirth	Ralph Baldwin
1974	Christopher T	Bill Haughton
1975	Bonefish	Stanley Dancer
1976	Steve Lobell	Bill Haughton
1977	Green Speed	Bill Haughton
1978	Speedy Somolli	Howard Beissinger
1979	Legend Hanover	George Sholty
1980	Burgomeister	Bill Haughton
1981	Shiaway St Pat	Ray Remmen
1982	Speed Bowl	Tommy Haughton
1983	Duenna	Stanley Dancer
1984	Historic Freight	Ben Webster
1985	Prakas	Bill O'Donnell
1986	Nuclear Kosmos	Ulf Thoresen
1987	Mack Lobell	John Campbell
1988	Armbro Goal	John Campbell
1989	Park Avenue Joe★	Ron Wables
	Probe★	Bill Fahy
1990	Harmonious	John Campbell
1991	Giant Victory	Jack Moiseyev
1992	Alf Palema	Mickey McNichol
1993	American Winner	Ron Pierce
1994	Victory Dream	Mike LaChance
1995	Tagliabue	John Campbell
1996	Continentalvictory	Mike LaChance
1997	Malabar Man	Mal Burroughs

★ Tied.

Race record: 1:53 1/5 American Winner 1993

The prize purse first passed $100,000 with $117,118 in 1953, when the winner was Helicopter; $200,000 in 1975 when it was $232,192; $500,000 in 1981 when it was $838,000; and a million dollars in 1983 at $1,080,000. A record $1,380,000 was paid in 1992.

The Little Brown Jug

Pacing's three-year-old classic has been held annually at Delaware, Ohio from 1946. The name honours a great 19th-century pacer.

Winners from 1970:

Year	Horse	Driver
1970	Most Happy Fella	Stanley Dancer
1971	Nansemond	Herve Filion
1972	Strike Out	Keith Waples
1973	Melvin's Woe	Joe O'Brien
1974	Ambro Omaha	Bill Haughton
1975	Seatrain	Ben Webster
1976	Keystone Ore	Stanley Dancer
1977	Governor Skipper	John Chapman
1978	Happy Escort	Bill Popfinger
1979	Hot Hitter	Herve Filion
1980	Niatross	Clint Galbraith
1981	Fan Hanover (*filly*)	Glen Garnsey
1982	Merger	John Campbell
1983	Ralph Hanover	Ron Waples
1984	Colt Forty Six	Chris Boring
1985	Nihilator	Bill O'Donnell
1986	Barbery Spur	Bill O'Donnell
1987	Jaguar Spur	Dick Stillings
1988	B J Scoot	Bill Fahy
1989	Goalie Jeff	Michel LaChance
1990	Beach Towel	Ray Remmen
1991	Precious Bunny	Jack Moiseyev
1992	Fake Left	Ron Waples
1993	Life Sign	John Campbell
1994	Magical Mike	Michel LaChance
1995	Nick's Fantasy	John Campbell
1996	Armbro Operative	Michel LaChance
1997	Western Dreamer	Michel LaChance

Race record: 1:52 Life Sign 1993

Leading Drivers and Horses

Most wins in a year

(Progressive record)

210	Robert G Farrington	1961
312	Robert G Farrington	1964
407	Herve Filion	1968
486	Herve Filion	1970
543	Herve Filion	1971
605	Herve Filion	1972
637	Herve Filion	1974
770	Michel LaChance	1986
798	Herve Filion	1988
814	Herve Filion	1989
843	Walter Case, Jr	1992

Top all-time money-winners (to end of 1997)

Driver	Winnings ($US)	Races (position on all-time list)	
John Campbell	155,377,361	7579	(5)
Michel LaChance	100,417,010	7986	(2)
Bill O'Donnell	90,505,187	5159	(23)
Herve Filion	85,044,328	14,783	(1)
Jack Moiseyev	69,207,541	7113	(8)
Ron Waples	66,685,462	6399	(11)
Douglas Brown	66,104,866	6943	(9)
Catello Manzi	64,744,781	7618	(4)
Dave Magee	54,939,852	7833	(3)
Steve Condren	51,238,687	4564	(34)
Carmine Abbatiello	50,291,158	7167	(7)
In top ten by races won:			
Eddie Davis	31,890,807	6592	(10)
Walter Case, Jr	28,197,404	7214	(6)

The first driver to win $1 million in a year was Stanley Dancer, $1,051,538 in 1964; $2 million was first passed by Herve Filion with $2,473,265 in 1972 and $10 million in 1985.

Top money-winners from 1980

Year	Driver	Winnings ($US)
1980	John Campbell	3,732,306
1981	Bill O'Donnell	4,065,608
1982	Bill O'Donnell	5,755,067
1983	John Campbell	6,104,082
1984	Bill O'Donnell	9,059,184
1985	Bill O'Donnell	10,207,372
1986	John Campbell	9,515,055
1987	John Campbell	10,186,495
1988	John Campbell	11,148,565
1989	John Campbell	9,738,450
1990	John Campbell	11,620,878
1991	Jack Moiseyev	9,568,468
1992	John Campbell	8,202,108
1993	John Campbell	9,926,482
1994	John Campbell	9,834,139
1995	John Campbell	9,469,797
1996	Michel LaChance	8,408,231
1997	Michel LaChance	9,215,388

Most years as top money-winning driver from 1948

12	John Campbell	1979-80, 1983, 1986-90, 1992-5
12	Bill Haughton	1952-9, 1963, 1965, 1967-8
7	Herve Filion	1970-4, 1976-7

Top money-winning trotter: $5,506,443 Peace Corps 1988-93

Top money-winning pacer: $3,225,653 Nihilator 1984-5

First to win $1 million in a year and current record

Pacer: Niatross $1,414,313 in 1980; first over $2 million: Beach Towel $2,091,860 in 1990; record: $2,264,714 Cam's Card Shark 1994

Trotter: Joie De Vie $1,007,705 in 1983; record: $1,878,798 Mack Lobell in 1987

Largest-ever purse

$2,161,000 for the Woodrow Wilson two-year-old race for pacers at Meadowlands, New Jersey on 16 Aug 1984. The winner, Nihilator, driven by Bill O'Donnell, earned a record $1,080,500.

Harness Horse of the Year

Chosen annually by the US Trotting Association and the US Harness Writers Association.

Most wins

3 Bret Hanover 1964-6, Nevele Pride 1967-9; 2 Scott Frost 1955-6, Adios Butler 1960-1, Albatross 1971-2, Niatross 1980-1, Cam Fella 1982-3, Mack Lobell 1987-8

Recent winners

1989 Matt's Scooter, 1990 Beach Towel, 1991 Precious Bunny, 1992 Artsplace, 1993 Staying Together, 1994 Cam's Card Shark, 1995 C R Kay Suzie, 1996 Continentalvictory, 1997 Malabar Man

Hockey

Stick and ball games date back some 4000 years, with modern hockey, which is played by teams of 11-a-side, becoming established in the 19th century. The sport's first governing body was an English Hockey Association, formed in London in 1875. The current English men's governing body, the Hockey Association, was founded in 1886 and the All-England Women's Hockey Association in 1895, a year after the Irish Ladies' Hockey Union.

The sport was long dominated by India and Pakistan, who won every Olympic tournament from 1928 to

1968. From then, however, success has been more widespread, with the amazing result at the 1986 World Cup of India and Pakistan in 11th and 12th places.

International governing body: Fédération Internationale de Hockey (FIH), 1 Avenue des Arts, BP 5, B-1210 Bruxelles, Belgium. Tel: (32) 2 219 4537, Fax: (32) 2 219 2761. President: Juan Angel Calzado, Executive Director: Hans Bertels. Formed in 1924. 119 member nations (and 4 associate) in 1998. A separate body, the International Federation of Women's Hockey Association (IFWHA), governed women's hockey until both men's and women's games were united under the auspices of the FIH in 1982.

Olympic Games

Men's winners

England	1908, 1920
India	1928, 1932, 1936, 1948, 1952, 1956, 1964, 1980
Pakistan	1960, 1968, 1984
Germany	1972 (FRG), 1992
New Zealand	1976
Great Britain	1988
Netherlands	1996

Highest score: India beat USA 24-1 at Los Angeles 1932

Most gold medals: 3 Richard Allen 1928-36, Dhyan Chand 1928-36, Randhir Singh Gentle 1948-56, Leslie Claudius 1948-56, Ranganandan Francis 1948-56, Udham Singh 1952-64 (all India). Claudius and Udham Singh also won silver medals in 1960.

Women's winners

Zimbabwe	1980
Netherlands	1984
Australia	1988, 1996
Spain	1992

FIH World Cup

First contested in 1971 for men, 1972 for women. Now held every four years.
Winners:

Men

Pakistan	1971, 1978, 1982, 1994
Netherlands	1973, 1990, 1998
India	1975
Australia	1986

Women

Netherlands	1972, 1974, 1978, 1983, 1986, 1990
F R Germany	1976, 1981
Australia	1994, 1998

Women's World Championships

Thrice organized by the IFWHA.
Winners:

Netherlands	1971, 1979
England	1975

Men's Champions' Trophy

First held in Lahore, Pakistan in 1978, contested annually by the leading six men's teams.
Winners:

7	Germany	FRG 1986-8, Ger 1991-2, 1995, 1997
5	Australia	1983-5, 1989-90
3	Netherlands	1981-2, 1996
2	Pakistan	1978, 1980

Women's Champions' Trophy

First contested in 1987.
Winners:

Australia	1991, 1993, 1995, 1997
Netherlands	1987
South Korea	1989

European Championships

Contested by national teams at four-yearly intervals. First contested for men in 1970, and for women in 1984.
Winners:

Men

Germany	1970, 1978 (FRG), 1991, 1995
Netherlands	1983, 1987
Spain	1974

Women

Netherlands	1984, 1987, 1995
England	1991

European Cup for Club Champions

First held unofficially in 1969 and 1970, and officially from 1971.
Winners:

Men

1969-70	Club Egara de Tarrasa (Spa)
1971-5	SC Frankfurt 1880 (FRG)
1976-8	Southgate (Eng)
1979	Klein Zwitserland (Hol)
1980	Slough (Eng)
1981	Klein Zwitserland (Hol)
1982-3	Dynamo Alma-Ata (USSR)
1984	TG 1846 Frankenthal (FRG)
1985	Atletico Tarrasa (Spa)
1986	Kampong, Utrecht (Hol)
1987	Bloemendaal (Hol)

1988-95	Uhlenhorst Mülheim (FRG/Ger)
1996	SV Kampong (Hol)
1997	HGC Wassenaar (Hol)
1998	Athletic Terrassa (Spa)

Women

1974	Harvestehuder Hamburg (FRG)
1975-82	Amsterdam (Hol)
1983-7	HGC Wassenaar (Hol)
1988-90	Amsterdam (Hol)
1991	HGC Wassenaar (Hol)
1992	Amsterdam (Hol)
1993	Rüsselsheimer (Ger)
1994	HGC Wassenaar (Hol)
1995	SV Kampong (Hol)
1996	Donchanka (Rus)
1997	Berliner (Ger)
1998	Rüsselsheimer (Ger)

European Cup-Winners' Cup

Men's event first held in 1990. Contested by winners of national cup competitions, or, if none held, league runners-up. Women's event first held in 1991.
Winners:

Men

1990	Hounslow (Eng)
1991	Kampong (Hol)
1992-3	HGC Wassenaar (Hol)
1994	Atletico Tarrasa (Spa)
1995	Harvestehuder Hamburg (Ger)
1996	Durkheimer (Ger)
1997	Gladbacher (Ger)
1998	Den Bosch (Hol)

Women

1991	Rhythm Grodno (USSR)
1992	Sutton Coldfield (Eng)
1993	HGC Wassenaar (Hol)
1994	Bayer Leverkusen (Ger)
1995	Rüsselsheimer RK (Ger)
1996	Hightown (Eng)
1997	Berliner (Ger)
1998	Amsterdam (Hol)

European Indoor Cup

First contested in 1974, the men's event has been won every time contested by Germany (FRG) 1974, 1976, 1980, 1984, 1988, 1991, 1994, 1997.

The women's cup was won by Germany 1974, 1977, 1981, 1984, 1987, 1990 and 1993, and England in 1996.

English Men's National Club Champions

Winners of the knock-out competition for the Hockey Association Cup. From 1993 sponsored by the Royal Bank of Scotland.
Winners:

1972-3	Hounslow
1974-5	Southgate
1976	Nottingham
1977	Slough
1978	Guildford
1979-81	Slough
1982	Southgate
1983	Neston
1984	East Grinstead
1985-8	Southgate
1989	Hounslow
1990	Havant
1991-3	Hounslow
1994	Teddington
1995	Guildford
1996	Old Loughtonians
1997	Teddington
1998	Cannock

Men's English National Inter-League

First held in 1975, and contested by the winners of all the major English leagues for the Poundstretcher League Cup from 1989.
Winners:

1975	Bedfordshire Eagles
1976	Slough
1977-8	Southgate
1979	Isca
1980-3	Slough
1984	Neston
1985-6	East Grinstead
1987	Slough
1988	Southgate
1989	Hounslow

1990	Havant
1991	Hounslow
1992	Harleston

Men's National League

Winners:

1993	Hounslow
1994	Havant
1995	Teddington
1996	Cannock
1997	Reading
1998	Cannock

National Women's Club Champions

From 1992 for the AEWHA (now EHA) Cup.

1977-8	Chelsea CPE
1979	Chelmsford
1980	Norton
1981	Sutton Coldfield
1982-3	Slough
1984	Sheffield
1985	Ipswich
1986	Slough
1987-9	Ealing
1990-1	Sutton Coldfield
1992	Hightown
1993	Leicester
1994	Slough
1995	Hightown
1996	Ipswich
1997	Hightown
1998	Clifton

National Women's League

Sponsored by Typhoo, and inaugurated in 1989/90.
Winners:

1990-2	Slough
1993	Ipswich
1994	Leicester
1995	Slough
1996	Hightown
1997-8	Slough

Horse Racing

The Ancient Egyptians are believed to have participated in horse racing more than 3000 years ago, and the sport was certainly a part of the ancient Olympic Games. Smithfield in London staged the first regular race meetings in the 12th century and Britain's oldest racecourse, on the Roodee at Chester, staged its first meeting on 9 February 1540. The Jockey Club was formed in 1750, and in 1752 the earliest recorded steeplechase took place in Co. Cork, Ireland.

Flat Racing

English Classics

Five races run from April to September each year for three-year-olds.

1000 Guineas

The first classic of the English season, for fillies only, carrying 9 stone. Raced over 1 mile at Newmarket, and first run in 1814. Sponsored by General Accident 1984-92, Madagans 1993-5, Pertemps 1996-7, Sagitta 1998.

Post-war winners:

Year	Winner	Jockey
1946	Hypericum	Doug Smith
1947	Imprudence	Rae Johnstone
1948	Queenpot	Gordon Richards
1949	Musidora	Edgar Britt
1950	Camaree	Rae Johnstone
1951	Belle of All	Gordon Richards
1952	Zabara	Ken Gethin
1953	Happy Laughter	Manny Mercer
1954	Festoon	Scobie Breasley
1955	Meld	Harry Carr
1956	Honeylight	Edgar Britt
1957	Rose Royal II	Charlie Smirke
1958	Bella Paola	Serge Boullenger
1959	Petite Etoile	Doug Smith
1960	Never Too Late	Roger Poincelet
1961	Sweet Solera	Bill Rickaby
1962	Abermaid	Bill Williamson
1963	Hula Dancer	Roger Poincelet
1964	Pourparler	Garnie Bougoure
1965	Night Off	Bill Williamson
1966	Glad Rags	Paul Cook
1967	Fleet	George Moore
1968	Caergwrle	Sandy Barclay
1969	Full Dress II	Ron Hutchinson
1970	Humble Duty	Lester Piggott
1971	Altesse Royale	Yves Saint-Martin
1972	Waterloo	Eddie Hide
1973	Mysterious	Geoff Lewis
1974	Highclere	Joe Mercer
1975	Nocturnal Spree	Johnny Roe
1976	Flying Water	Yves Saint-Martin
1977	Mrs McArdy	Eddie Hide
1978	Enstone Spark	Ernie Johnson
1979	One in a Million	Joe Mercer
1980	Quick as Lightning	Brian Rouse
1981	Fairy Footsteps	Lester Piggott
1982	On the House	John Reid
1983	Ma Biche	Freddie Head
1984	Pebbles	Philip Robinson
1985	Oh So Sharp	Steve Cauthen
1986	Midway Lady	Ray Cochrane
1987	Miesque	Freddie Head
1988	Ravinella	Gary Moore
1989	Musical Bliss	Walter Swinburn
1990	Salsabil	Willie Carson
1991	Shadayid	Willie Carson
1992	Hatoof	Walter Swinburn
1993	Sayyedati	Walter Swinburn
1994	Las Meninas	Jimmy Reid
1995	Harayir	Richard Hills
1996	Bosra Sham	Pat Eddery
1997	Sleepytime	Kieren Fallon
1998	Cape Verdi	Frankie Dettori

Most wins – jockey:
7 George Fordham – 1859 Mayonaise, 1861 Nemesis, 1865 Siberia, 1868 Formosa, 1869 Scottish Queen, 1881 Thebais, 1883 Hauteur

6 Frank Buckle – 1818 Corinne, 1820 Rowena, 1821 Zeal, 1822 Whizgig, 1823 Zinc, 1827 Arab

5 Jem Robinson – 1824 Cobweb, 1828 Zoe, 1830 Charlotte West, 1841 Potentia, 1844 Sorella

5 John Barnham Day – 1826 Problem, 1834 May-day, 1836 Destiny, 1837 Chapeau d'Espagne, 1840 Crucifix

Most wins – trainer: 9 Robert Robson – 1818 Corinne, 1819 Catgut, 1820 Rowena, 1821 Zeal, 1822 Whizgig, 1823 Zinc, 1825 Tontine, 1826 Problem, 1827 Arab

Most wins – owner: 8 4th Duke of Grafton – 1819 Catgut, 1820 Rowena, 1821 Zeal, 1822 Whizgig, 1823 Zinc, 1825 Tontine, 1826 Problem, 1827 Arab

Fastest time: 1 min 36.71 sec Las Meninas 1994

Biggest winning margin: 20 lengths Mayonaise 1859

2000 Guineas

First run at Newmarket in 1809, the other early-season Classic. Run over 1 mile; colts carry 9 stone, and fillies (rarely entered) 8st 9lb. Seven fillies have won the race, the last being Garden Path in 1944. Sponsored by General Accident 1984-92, Madagans 1993-5, Pertemps 1996-7, Sagitta 1998.

Post-war winners:

Year	Winner	Jockey
1946	Happy Knight	Tommy Weston
1947	Tudor Minstrel	Gordon Richards

1948	My Babu	Charlie Smirke
1949	Nimbus	Charlie Elliott
1950	Palestine	Charlie Smirke
1951	Ki Ming	Scobie Breasley
1952	Thunderhead II	Roger Poincelet
1953	Nearula	Edgar Britt
1954	Darius	Manny Mercer
1955	Our Babu	Doug Smith
1956	Gilles de Retz	Frank Barlow
1957	Crepello	Lester Piggott
1958	Pall Mall	Doug Smith
1959	Taboun	George Moore
1960	Martial	Ron Hutchinson
1961	Rockavon	Norman Stirk
1962	Privy Councillor	Bill Rickaby
1963	Only for Life	Jimmy Lindley
1964	Baldric II	Bill Pyers
1965	Niksar	Duncan Keith
1966	Kashmir II	Jimmy Lindley
1967	Royal Palace	George Moore
1968	Sir Ivor	Lester Piggott
1969	Right Tack	Geoff Lewis
1970	Nijinsky	Lester Piggott
1971	Brigadier Gerard	Joe Mercer
1972	High Top	Willie Carson
1973	Mon Fils	Frankie Durr
1974	Nonoalco	Yves Saint-Martin
1975	Bolkonski	Gianfranco Dettori
1976	Wollow	Gianfranco Dettori
1977	Nebbiolo	Gabriel Curran
1978	Roland Gardens	Frankie Durr
1979	Tap on Wood	Steve Cauthen
1980	Known Fact	Willie Carson
1981	To-Agori-Mou	Greville Starkey
1982	Zino	Freddie Head
1983	Lomond	Pat Eddery
1984	El Gran Senor	Pat Eddery
1985	Shadeed	Lester Piggott
1986	Dancing Brave	Greville Starkey
1987	Don't Forget Me	Willie Carson
1988	Doyoun	Walter Swinburn
1989	Nashwan	Willie Carson
1990	Tirol	Michael Kinane
1991	Mystiko	Michael Roberts
1992	Rodrigo de Triano	Lester Piggott
1993	Zafonic	Pat Eddery
1994	Mister Baileys	Jason Weaver
1995	Pennekamp	Thierry Jarnet
1996	Mark of Esteem	Frankie Dettori
1997	Entrepreneur	Michael Kinane
1998	King of Kings	Michael Kinane

Most wins – jockey:

9 Jem Robinson – 1825 Enamel, 1828 Cadland, 1831 Riddlesworth, 1833 Clearwell, 1834 Glencoe, 1835 Ibrahim, 1836 Bay Middleton, 1847 Conyngham, 1848 Flatchatcher

6 John Osborne – 1857 Vedette, 1869 Pretender, 1871 Bothwell, 1872 Prince Charlie, 1875 Camballo, 1888 Ayrshire

5 Frank Buckle – 1810 Hephestion, 1820 Pindarrie, 1821 Reginald, 1822 Pastille, 1827 Turcoman

5 Charlie Elliott – 1923 Ellangowan, 1928 Flamingo, 1940 Djebel, 1941 Lambert Simnel, 1949 Nimbus

5 Lester Piggott – 1957, 1968, 1970, 1985, 1992

Most wins – trainer: 7 John Scott 1842 Meteor, 1843 Cotherstone, 1849 Nunnykirk, 1853 West Australian, 1856 Fazzoletto, 1860 The Wizard, 1862 The Marquis

Most wins – owner: 5 4th Duke of Grafton – 1820 Pindarrie, 1821 Reginald, 1822 Pastille, 1826 Dervise, 1827 Turcoman; 5th Earl of Jersey – 1831 Riddlesworth, 1834 Glencoe, 1835 Ibrahim, 1836 Bay Middleton, 1837 Achmet

Fastest time: 1 min 35.08 sec Mister Baileys 1994

Biggest winning margin: 8 lengths Tudor Minstrel 1947

The Derby

The greatest of the Classics is raced each June over 1 mile 4 furlongs at Epsom Downs, except for 1915-8 and 1940-5, when the race was run at Newmarket. It was sponsored by Ever Ready 1984-94 and Vodafone 1995-8. Colts carry 9 stone, and fillies, if entered, 8st 9lb.

Winners (denotes fillies):*

Year	Winner	Jockey
1780	Diomed	Sam Arnull
1781	Young Eclipse	Charles Hindley
1782	Assassin	Sam Arnull
1783	Saltram	Charles Hindley
1784	Sergeant	John Arnull
1785	Aimwell	Charles Hindley
1786	Noble	J White
1787	Sir Peter Teazle	Sam Arnull
1788	Sir Thomas	William South
1789	Skyscraper	Sam Chifney, Sr
1790	Rhadamanthus	John Arnull
1791	Eager	Matt Stephenson
1792	John Bull	Frank Buckle
1793	Waxy	Bill Clift
1794	Daedalus	Frank Buckle
1795	Spread Eagle	Anthony Wheatley
1796	Didelot	John Arnull
1797	(Un-named colt)	John Singleton
1798	Sir Harry	Sam Arnull
1799	Archduke	John Arnull
1800	Champion	Bill Clift
1801	Eleanor*	John Saunders
1802	Tyrant	Frank Buckle
1803	Ditto	Bill Clift
1804	Hannibal	Bill Arnull
1805	Cardinal Beaufort	Denni Fitzpatrick
1806	Paris	John Shepherd
1807	Election	John Arnull

Year	Winner	Jockey	Year	Winner	Jockey
1808	Pan	Frank Collinson	1865	Gladiateur	Harry Grimshaw
1809	Pope	Tom Goodison	1866	Lord Lyon	Harry Custance
1810	Whalebone	Bill Clift	1867	Hermit	John Daley
1811	Phantom	Frank Buckle	1868	Blue Gown	John Wells
1812	Octavius	Bill Arnull	1869	Pretender	John Osborne
1813	Smolensko	Tom Goodison	1870	Kingcraft	Tom French
1814	Blucher	Bill Arnull	1871	Favonius	Tom French
1815	Whisker	Tom Goodison	1872	Cremorne	Charlie Maidment
1816	Prince Leopold	Will Wheatley	1873	Doncaster	Fred Webb
1817	Azor	Jem Robinson	1874	George Frederick	Harry Custance
1818	Sam	Sam Chifney, Jr	1875	Galopin	Jack Morris
1819	Tiresias	Bill Clift	1876	Kisber	Charlie Maidment
1820	Sailor	Sam Chifney, Jr	1877	Silvio	Fred Archer
1821	Gustavus	Sam Day	1878	Sefton	Harry Constable
1822	Moses	Tom Goodison	1879	Sir Bevys	George Fordham
1823	Emilius	Frank Buckle	1880	Bend Or	Fred Archer
1824	Cedric	Jem Robinson	1881	Iroquois	Fred Archer
1825	Middleton	Jem Robinson	1882	Shotover★	Tom Cannon
1826	Lapdog	George Dockeray	1883	St Blaise	Charlie Wood
1827	Mameluke	Jem Robinson	1884	St Gatien	Charlie Wood
1828	Cadland	Jem Robinson		Harvester (dead heat)	Sam Loates
1829	Frederick	John Forth	1885	Melton	Fred Archer
1830	Priam	Sam Day	1886	Ormonde	Fred Archer
1831	Spaniel	Will Wheatley	1887	Merry Hampton	Jack Watts
1832	St Giles	Bill Scott	1888	Ayrshire	Fred Barrett
1833	Dangerous	Jem Chapple	1889	Donovan	Tommy Loates
1834	Plenipotentiary	Patrick Conolly	1890	Sainfoin	Jack Watts
1835	Mundig	Bill Scott	1891	Common	George Barrett
1836	Bay Middleton	Jem Robinson	1892	Sir Hugo	Fred Allsopp
1837	Phosphorus	George Edwards	1893	Isinglass	Tommy Loates
1838	Amato	Jim Chapple	1894	Ladas	Jack Watts
1839	Bloomsbury	Sim Templeman	1895	Sir Visto	Sam Loates
1840	Little Wonder	William MacDonald	1896	Persimmon	Jack Watts
1841	Coronation	Patrick Conolly	1897	Galtee More	Charlie Wood
1842	Attila	Bill Scott	1898	Jeddah	Otto Madden
1843	Cotherstone	Bill Scott	1899	Flying Fox	Morny Cannon
1844	Orlando	Nat Flatman	1900	Diamond Jubilee	Herbert Jones
1845	The Merry Monarch	Foster Bell	1901	Volodyovski	Lester Reiff
1846	Pyrrhus the First	Sam Day	1902	Ard Patrick	Skeets Martin
1847	Cossack	Sim Templeman	1903	Rock Sand	Danny Maher
1848	Surplice	Sim Templeman	1904	St Amant	Kempton Cannon
1849	The Flying Dutchman	Charlie Marlow	1905	Cicero	Danny Maher
1850	Voltigeur	Job Marson	1906	Spearmint	Danny Maher
1851	Teddington	Job Marson	1907	Orby	Johnny Reiff
1852	Daniel O'Rourke	Frank Butler	1908	Signorinetta★	Billy Bullock
1853	West Australian	Frank Butler	1909	Minoru	Herbert Jones
1854	Andover	Alfred Day	1910	Lemberg	Bernard Dillon
1855	Wild Dayrell	Robert Sherwood	1911	Sunstar	George Stern
1856	Ellington	Tom Aldcroft	1912	Tagalie★	Johnny Reiff
1857	Blink Bonny★	Jack Charlton	1913	Aboyeur	Edwin Piper
1858	Beadsman	John Wells	1914	Durbar II	Matt MacGee
1859	Musjid	John Wells	1915	Pommern	Steve Donoghue
1860	Thormanby	Harry Custance	1916	Fifinella★	Joe Childs
1861	Kettledrum	Ralph Bullock	1917	Gay Crusader	Steve Donaghue
1862	Caractacus	John Parsons	1918	Gainsborough	Joe Childs
1863	Macaroni	Tom Challoner	1919	Grand Parade	Fred Templeman
1864	Blair Athol	Jim Snowden	1920	Spion Kop	Frank O'Neill

Year	Winner	Jockey	Year	Winner	Jockey
1921	Humorist	Steve Donoghue	1978	Shirley Heights	Greville Starkey
1922	Captain Cuttle	Steve Donoghue	1979	Troy	Willie Carson
1923	Papyrus	Steve Donoghue	1980	Henbit	Willie Carson
1924	Sansovino	Tommy Weston	1981	Shergar	Walter Swinburn
1925	Manna	Steve Donoghue	1982	Golden Fleece	Pat Eddery
1926	Coronach	Joe Childs	1983	Teenoso	Lester Piggott
1927	Call Boy	Charlie Elliott	1984	Secreto	Christy Roche
1928	Fellstead	Harry Wragg	1985	Slip Anchor	Steve Cauthen
1929	Trigo	Joe Marshall	1986	Shahrastani	Walter Swinburn
1930	Blenheim	Harry Wragg	1987	Reference Point	Steve Cauthen
1931	Cameronian	Freddie Fox	1988	Kahyasi	Ray Cochrane
1932	April the Fifth	Fred Lane	1989	Nashwan	Willie Carson
1933	Hyperion	Tommy Weston	1990	Quest for Fame	Pat Eddery
1934	Windsor Lad	Charlie Smirke	1991	Generous	Alan Munro
1935	Bahram	Freddie Fox	1992	Dr Devious	John Reid
1936	Mahmoud	Charlie Smirke	1993	Commander in Chief	Michael Kinane
1937	Mid-day Sun	Michael Beary	1994	Erhaab	Willie Carson
1938	Bois Roussel	Charlie Elliott	1995	Lammtarra	Walter Swinburn
1939	Blue Peter	Eph Smith	1996	Shaamit	Michael Hills
1940	Pont l'Eveque	Sam Wragg	1997	Benny the Dip	Willie Ryan
1941	Owen Tudor	Billy Nevett	1998	High-Rise	Olivier Peslier
1942	Watling Street	Harry Wragg			
1943	Straight Deal	Tommy Carey			
1944	Ocean Swell	Billy Nevett			
1945	Dante	Billy Nevett			
1946	Airborne	Tommy Lowrey			
1947	Pearl Diver	George Bridgland			
1948	My Love	Rae Johnstone			
1949	Nimbus	Charlie Elliott			
1950	Galcador	Rae Johnstone			
1951	Arctic Prince	Charlie Spares			
1952	Tulyar	Charlie Smirke			
1953	Pinza	Gordon Richards			
1954	Never Say Die	Lester Piggott			
1955	Phil Drake	Freddie Palmer			
1956	Lavandin	Rae Johnstone			
1957	Crepello	Lester Piggott			
1958	Hard Ridden	Charlie Smirke			
1959	Parthia	Harry Carr			
1960	St Paddy	Lester Piggott			
1961	Psidium	Roger Poincelet			
1962	Larkspur	Neville Sellwood			
1963	Relko	Yves Saint-Martin			
1964	Santa Claus	Scobie Breasley			
1965	Sea Bird II	Pat Glennon			
1966	Charlottown	Scobie Breasley			
1967	Royal Palace	George Moore			
1968	Sir Ivor	Lester Piggott			
1969	Blakeney	Ernie Johnson			
1970	Nijinsky	Lester Piggott			
1971	Mill Reef	Geoff Lewis			
1972	Roberto	Lester Piggott			
1973	Morston	Eddie Hide			
1974	Snow Knight	Brian Taylor			
1975	Grundy	Pat Eddery			
1976	Empery	Lester Piggott			
1977	The Minstrel	Lester Piggott			

Most wins – jockey: 9 Lester Piggott; 6 Jem Robinson, Steve Donoghue; 5 John Arnull, Bill Clift, Frank Buckle, Fred Archer; 4 Sam Arnull, Tom Goodison, Bill Scott, Jack Watts, Charlie Smirke, Willie Carson

Most wins – trainer: 7 Robert Robson 1793, 1802, 1809-10, 1815, 1817, 1823; John Porter 1868, 1882-3, 1886, 1890-1, 1899; Fred Darling 1922, 1925-6, 1931, 1938, 1940-1

Most wins – owner: 5 3rd Earl of Egremont 1782, 1804, 1806-7, 1826; HH Aga Khan III 1930, 1935-6, 1948 (half-share), 1952. 4 John Bowes 1835, 1843, 1852-3; Sir Joseph Hawley 1851, 1858-9, 1868; 1st Duke of Westminster 1880, 1882, 1886, 1899; Sir Victor Sassoon 1953, 1957-8, 1960

Fastest time: 2 min 32.31 sec Lammtarra 1995

Biggest winning margin: 10 lengths Shergar 1981

The Oaks

Raced at Epsom, over 1 mile 4 furlongs for fillies only, all of whom carry 9 stone. It was raced at Newmarket during both World Wars. From 1984-92 the race was sponsored by Gold Seal, 1993-4 Energizer, 1995-8 Vodafone. Named after the Epsom home of the 12th Earl of Derby, the first race was in 1779.

Post-war winners:

Year	Winner	Jockey
1946	Steady Aim	Harry Wragg
1947	Imprudence	Rae Johnstone
1948	Masaka	Billy Nevett
1949	Musidora	Edgar Britt
1950	Asmena	Rae Johnstone
1951	Neasham Belle	Stan Clayton
1952	Frieze	Edgar Britt
1953	Ambiguity	Joe Mercer

Year	Winner	Jockey
1954	Sun Cap	Rae Johnstone
1955	Meld	Harry Carr
1956	Sicarelle	Freddie Palmer
1957	Carrozza	Lester Piggott
1958	Bella Paola	Max Garcia
1959	Petite Etoile	Lester Piggott
1960	Never Too Late	Roger Poincelet
1961	Sweet Solera	Bill Rickaby
1962	Monade	Yves Saint-Martin
1963	Noblesse	Garnie Bougoure
1964	Homeward Bound	Greville Starkey
1965	Long Look	Jack Purtell
1966	Valoris	Lester Piggott
1967	Pia	Eddie Hide
1968	La Lagune	Gérard Thiboeuf
1969	Sleeping Partner	John Gorton
1970	Lupe	Sandy Barclay
1971	Altesse Royale	Geoff Lewis
1972	Ginevra	Tony Murray
1973	Mysterious	Geoff Lewis
1974	Polygamy	Pat Eddery
1975	Juliette Marny	Lester Piggott
1976	Pawneese	Yves Saint-Martin
1977	Dunfermline	Willie Carson
1978	Fair Salinia	Greville Starkey
1979	Scintillate	Pat Eddery
1980	Bireme	Willie Carson
1981	Blue Wind	Lester Piggott
1982	Time Charter	Billy Newnes
1983	Sun Princess	Willie Carson
1984	Circus Plume	Lester Piggott
1985	Oh So Sharp	Steve Cauthen
1986	Midway Lady	Ray Cochrane
1987	Unite	Walter Swinburn
1988	Diminuendo	Steve Cauthen
1989★	Snow Bride	Steve Cauthen
1990	Salsabil	Willie Carson
1991	Jet Ski Lady	Christy Roche
1992	User Friendly	George Duffield
1993	Intrepidity	Michael Roberts
1994	Ballanchine	Frankie Dettori
1995	Moonshell	Frankie Dettori
1996	Lady Carla	Pat Eddery
1997	Reams of Verse	Kieren Fallon
1998	Shahtoush	Michael Kinane

★ Aliysa, ridden by Walter Swinburn, won the race, but on 20 Nov 1990 it was announced that the horse had been disqualified due to the presence of camphor in a post-race urine test.

Most wins – jockey: 9 Frank Buckle – 1797 Niké, 1798 Bellisimma, 1799 Bellina, 1802 Scotia, 1803 Theophania, 1805 Meteora, 1817 Neva, 1818 Corinne, 1823 Zinc; 6 Frank Butler – 1843 Poison, 1844 The Princess, 1849 Lady Evelyn, 1850 Rhedycina, 1851 Irish, 1852 Songstress; 6 Piggott – as above

Most wins – trainer: 12 Robert Robson – 1802 Scotia, 1804 Pelisse, 1805 Meteora, 1807 Briseis, 1808 Morel, 1809 Maid of Orleans, 1813 Music, 1815 Minuet, 1818 Corinne, 1822 Pastille, 1823 Zinc, 1825 Wings

Most wins – owner: 6 4th Duke of Grafton – 1813 Music, 1815 Minuet, 1822 Pastille, 1823 Zinc, 1828 Turquoise, 1831 Oxygen

Fastest time: 2 min 34.19 sec Intrepidity 1993

Biggest winning margin: 12 lengths Sun Princess 1983

St Leger

The oldest of the five Classics, first held in 1776. It is run over a distance of 1 mile 6 furlongs 132 yards at Doncaster. Both colts and fillies enter; colts carry 9 stone, fillies 8st 11lb. In wartime the race was held at Newmarket (1915-8 and 1942-4), Thirsk (1940), Manchester (1941) and York (1945). Sponsored by Holsten Pils 1984-8, Coalite 1991-3, Teleconnection 1994, Pertemps 1995-7. The 1989 race was moved to Ayr, the first time an English classic had been held in Scotland, due to damage to the Doncaster track.

Post-war winners (★ denotes fillies):

Year	Winner	Jockey
1946	Airborne	Tommy Lowrey
1947	Sayajirao	Edgar Britt
1948	Black Tarquin	Edgar Britt
1949	Ridge Wood	Michael Beary
1950	Scratch II	Rae Johnstone
1951	Talma II	Rae Johnstone
1952	Tulyar	Charlie Smirke
1953	Premonition	Eph Smith
1954	Never Say Die	Charlie Smirke
1955	Meld★	Harry Carr
1956	Cambremer	Freddie Palmer
1957	Ballymoss	Tommy Burns
1958	Alcide	Harry Carr
1959	Cantelo★	Eddie Hide
1960	St Paddy	Lester Piggott
1961	Aurelius	Lester Piggott
1962	Hethersett	Harry Carr
1963	Ragusa	Garnie Bougoure
1964	Indiana	Jimmy Lindley
1965	Provoke	Joe Mercer
1966	Sodium	Frankie Durr
1967	Ribocco	Lester Piggott
1968	Ribero	Lester Piggott
1969	Intermezzo	Ron Hutchinson
1970	Nijinsky	Lester Piggott
1971	Athens Wood	Lester Piggott
1972	Boucher	Lester Piggott
1973	Peleid	Frankie Durr
1974	Bustino	Joe Mercer
1975	Bruni	Tony Murray
1976	Crow	Yves Saint-Martin
1977	Dunfermline★	Willie Carson

1978	Julio Mariner	Eddie Hide
1979	Son of Love	Alain Lequeux
1980	Light Cavalry	Joe Mercer
1981	Cut Above	Joe Mercer
1982	Touching Wood	Paul Cook
1983	Sun Princess★	Willie Carson
1984	Commanche Run	Lester Piggott
1985	Oh So Sharp★	Steve Cauthen
1986	Moon Madness	Pat Eddery
1987	Reference Point	Steve Cauthen
1988	Minster Son	Willie Carson
1989	Michelozzo	Steve Cauthen
1990	Snurge	Richard Quinn
1991	Toulon	Pat Eddery
1992	User Friendly★	George Duffield
1993	Bob's Return	Philip Robinson
1994	Moonax	Pat Eddery
1995	Classic Cliche	Frankie Dettori
1996	Shantou	Frankie Dettori
1997	Silver Patriarch	Pat Eddery

Most wins – jockey: 9 Bill Scott – 1821 Jack Spigot, 1825 Memnon, 1828 The Colonel, 1829 Rowton, 1838 Don John, 1839 Charles the Twelfth, 1840 Launcelot, 1841 Satirist, 1846 Sir Tatton Sykes; 8 John Jackson – 1791 Young Traveller, 1794 Beningbrough, 1796 Ambrosia, 1798 Symmetry, 1805 Staveley, 1813 Altisidora, 1815 Filho da Puta, 1822 Theodore; 8 Piggott, as above

Most wins – trainer: 16 John Scott – 1827 Matilda, 1828 The Colonel, 1829 Rowton, 1832 Margrave, 1834 Touchstone, 1838 Don John, 1839 Charles the Twelfth, 1840 Launcelot, 1841 Satirist, 1845 The Baron, 1851 Newminster, 1853 West Australian, 1856 Warlock, 1857 Imperieuse, 1859 Gamester, 1862 The Marquis

Most wins – owner: 7 9th Duke of Hamilton – 1786 Paragon, 1787 Spadille, 1788 Young Flora, 1792 Tartar, 1808 Petronius, 1809 Ashton, 1814 William

Fastest time: 3 min 1.6 sec Coronach 1926, Windsor Lad 1934

Biggest winning margin: 12 lengths Never Say Die 1954

Classics Records

Triple Crown (2000 Guineas, Derby and St Leger)

Winners:

West Australian 1853, Gladiateur 1865, Lord Lyon 1866, Ormonde 1866, Common 1891, Isinglass 1893, Galtee More 1897, Flying Fox 1899, Diamond Jubilee 1900, Rock Sand 1903, Pommern 1915, Gay Crusader 1917, Gainsborough 1918, Bahram 1935, Nijinsky 1970

Fillies Triple Crown (1000 Guineas, Oaks and St Leger)

Winners:

Hannah 1871, Apology 1874, La Flèche 1892, Pretty Polly 1904, Sun Chariot 1942, Meld 1955, Oh So Sharp 1985

Four Classics (except the Derby) won by: Formosa 1868, Sceptre 1902

Leading jockeys at the five Classics

	Total	Derby	Oaks	2000	1000	Leger	Years
Lester Piggott	30	9	6	5	2	8	1954–92
Frank Buckle	27	5	9	5	6	2	1792–1827
Jem Robinson	24	6	2	9	5	2	1817–48
Fred Archer	21	5	4	4	2	6	1874–86
Bill Scott	19	4	3	3	–	9	1821–46
Jack Watts	19	4	4	2	4	5	1883–97
Willie Carson	17	4	4	4	2	3	1972–94
John Barham Day	16	–	5	4	5	2	1826–41
George Fordham	16	1	5	3	7	–	1859–83
Joe Childs	15	3	4	2	2	4	1912–33
Frank Butler	14	2	6	2	2	2	1843–53
Steve Donoghue	14	6	2	3	1	2	1915–37
Charlie Elliott	14	3	2	5	4	–	1923–49
Gordon Richards	14	1	2	3	3	5	1930–53

Leading trainers at the five Classics

John Scott	40	5	8	7	4	16	1827–63
Robert Robson	34	7	12	6	9	–	1793–1827
Mat Dawson	28	6	5	5	6	6	1853–95
John Porter	23	7	3	5	2	6	1868–1900
Alec Taylor	21	3	8	4	1	5	1905–27
Fred Darling	19	7	2	5	2	3	1916–47
Noel Murless	19	3	5	2	6	3	1948–73

Leading owners at the five Classics

	Total	Derby	Oaks	2000	1000	Leger	Years
4th Duke of Grafton	20	1	6	5	8	–	1813-31
17th Earl of Derby	20	3	2	2	7	6	1910-45
HH Aga Khan III	17	5	2	3	1	6	1924-57
6th Viscount Falmouth	16	2	4	3	4	3	1862-83

Group One Races in England

Pattern racing was introduced into Europe in 1971, with the major races classified into Groups 1, 2 and 3. The following are the leading Group One races showing winning horses and jockeys (with recent results, mostly from 1980).

Coronation Cup

Raced at Epsom each year, at the Derby meeting. It is run over 1 mile 4 furlongs. First run 1902 to celebrate the Coronation of King Edward VII. Raced at Newbury 1915-6, Newmarket 1941, 1943-5. Sponsored by Ever Ready 1993-4, Vodafone 1995-8.

Year	Winner	Jockey
1980	Sea Chimes	Lester Piggott
1981	Master Willie	Phillip Waldron
1982	Easter Sun	Bruce Raymond
1983	Be My Native	Lester Piggott
1984	Time Charter	Steve Cauthen
1985	Rainbow Quest	Pat Eddery
1986	Saint Estephe	Pat Eddery
1987	Triptych	Tony Cruz
1988	Triptych	Steve Cauthen
1989	Sherriff's Star	Ray Cochrane
1990	In the Wings	Cash Asmussen
1991	In the Groove	Steve Cauthen
1992	Saddler's Hall	Walter Swinburn
1993	Opera House	Michael Roberts
1994	Apple Tree	Thierry Jarnet
1995	Sunshack	Pat Eddery
1996	Swain	Frankie Dettori
1997	Singspiel	Frankie Dettori
1998	Silver Patriarch	Pat Eddery

Most wins: 2 Pretty Polly 1905-6, The White Knight 1907-8, Petite Etoile 1960-1, Triptych

St James's Palace Stakes

For 3-year-olds at the Royal Ascot meeting over 1 mile; first run in 1834.

1980	Posse	Pat Eddery
1981	To-Agori-Mou	Greville Starkey
1982	Dara Monarch	Michael Kinane
1983	Horage	Steve Cauthen
1984	Chief Singer	Ray Cochrane
1985	Bairn	Lester Piggott
1986	Sure Blade	Brent Thomson
1987	Half a Year	Ray Cochrane
1988	Persian Heights	Pat Eddery
1989	Shaadi	Walter Swinburn
1990	Shavian	Steve Cauthen
1991	Marju	Willie Carson
1992	Brief Truce	Michael Kinane
1993	Kingmambo	Cash Asmussen
1994	Grand Lodge	Michael Kinane
1995	Bahri	Willie Carson
1996	Bijou D'Inde	Jason Weaver
1997	Starborough	Frankie Dettori
1998	Dr Fong	Kieren Fallon

Coronation Stakes

For 3-year-old fillies at the Royal Ascot meeting over 1 mile; first run in 1840, celebrating, a little belatedly, the coronation of Queen Victoria in 1837.

1980	Cairn Rouge	Tony Murray
1981	Tolmi	Eddie Hide
1982	Chalon	Lester Piggott
1983	Flame of Tara	Declan Gillespie
1984	Katies	Philip Robinson
1985	Al Bahathri	Tony Murray
1986	Sonic Lady	Walter Swinburn
1987	Milligram	Walter Swinburn
1988	Magic of Life	Pat Eddery
1989	Golden Opinion	Cash Asmussen
1990	Chimes of Freedom	Steve Cauthen
1991	Kooyonga	Warren O'Connor
1992	Marling	Walter Swinburn
1993	Gold Splash	Gérald Mosse
1994	Kissing Cousin	Michael Kinane
1995	Ridgewood Pearl	John Murtagh
1996	Shake the Yoke	Olivier Peslier
1997	Rebecca Sharp	Michael Hills
1998	Exclusive	Walter Swinburn

Ascot Gold Cup

The highlight of the Royal Ascot meeting, the Gold Cup has been contested since 1807. It is the premier long-distance race on the flat, run over 2 miles 4 furlongs. Between 1845-53 it was run as the Emperor's Plate in honour of the Tsar of Russia. Held at Newmarket in 1917-8 (as the Newmarket Gold Cup), and in 1941-4.

1980	Le Moss	Joe Mercer
1981	Ardross	Lester Piggott
1982	Ardross	Lester Piggott
1983	Little Wolf	Willie Carson
1984	Gildoran	Steve Cauthen
1985	Gildoran	Brent Thomson
1986	Longboat	Willie Carson
1987	Paean	Steve Cauthen

1988	Sadeem	Greville Starkey
1989	Sadeem	Willie Carson
1990	Ashal	Richard Hills
1991	Indian Queen	Walter Swinburn
1992	Drum Taps	Frankie Dettori
1993	Drum Taps	Frankie Dettori
1994	Arcadian Heights	Michael Hills
1995	Double Trigger	Jason Weaver
1996	Classic Cliché	Michael Kinane
1997	Celeric	Pat Eddery
1998	Kayf Tara	Frankie Dettori

Most wins: 3 Sagaro

Eclipse Stakes

Named after the great horse Eclipse and first run in 1886. Raced over 1 mile 2 furlongs at Sandown Park each July. Run at Ascot 1946, Kempton Park 1973. Sponsored by Benson & Hedges 1974-5, and Coral since then.

1980	Ela-Mana-Mou	Willie Carson
1981	Master Willie	Phillip Waldron
1982	Kalaglow	Greville Starkey
1983	Solford	Pat Eddery
1984	Sadlers Wells	Pat Eddery
1985	Pebbles	Steve Cauthen
1986	Dancing Brave	Greville Starkey
1987-8	Mtoto	Michael Roberts
1989	Nashwan	Willie Carson
1990	Elmaamul	Willie Carson
1991	Environment Friend	George Duffield
1992	Kooyonga	Warren O'Connor
1993	Opera House	Michael Kinane
1994	Ezzoud	Walter Swinburn
1995	Halling	Walter Swinburn
1996	Halling	John Reid
1997	Pilsudski	Michael Kinane
1998	Daylami	Frankie Dettori

Most wins: 2 Buchan 1919-20, Polyphontes 1924-5, Mtoto, Halling

July Cup

Run at Newmarket over 6 furlongs. First run 1876. Sponsored by William Hill 1978-86, Norcros 1987-8, Carroll Foundation 1989-94, Darley 1996-7.

1980	Moorestyle	Lester Piggott
1981	Marwell	Walter Swinburn
1982	Sharpo	Pat Eddery
1983	Habibti	Willie Carson
1984	Chief Singer	Ray Cochrane
1985	Never So Bold	Steve Cauthen
1986	Green Desert	Walter Swinburn
1987	Ajdal	Walter Swinburn
1988	Soviet Star	Cash Asmussen
1989	Cadeaux Genereux	Paul Eddery
1990	Royal Academy	John Reid
1991	Polish Patriot	Ray Cochrane
1992	Mr Brooks	Lester Piggott
1993	Hamas	Willie Carson

1994	Owington	Paul Eddery
1995	Lake Coniston	Pat Eddery
1996	Anabaa	Freddie Head
1997	Compton Place	Seb Sanders
1998	Elnadim	Richard Hills

Most wins: 3 Sundridge 1902-4

King George VI & Queen Elizabeth Diamond Stakes

First run in 1951 as the King George VI & Queen Elizabeth Festival of Britain Stakes. It became the King George VI & Queen Elizabeth Stakes in 1952 and the word 'Diamond' was added in 1975. Raced over 1 mile 4 furlongs at Ascot, it is one of the leading weight-for-age races in Europe.

1951	Supreme Court	Charlie Elliott
1952	Tulyar	Charlie Smirke
1953	Pinza	Gordon Richards
1954	Aureole	Eph Smith
1955	Vimy	Roger Poincelet
1956	Ribot	Enrico Camici
1957	Montaval	Freddie Palmer
1958	Ballymoss	Scobie Breasley
1959	Alcide	Willie Carr
1960	Aggressor	Jimmy Lindley
1961	Right Royal V	Roger Poincelet
1962	Match III	Yves Saint-Martin
1963	Ragusa	Georges Bougoure
1964	Nasram II	Bill Pyers
1965	Meadow Court	Lester Piggott
1966	Aunt Edith	Lester Piggott
1967	Busted	George Moore
1968	Royal Palace	Sandy Barclay
1969	Park Top	Lester Piggott
1970	Nijinsky	Lester Piggott
1971	Mill Reef	Geoff Lewis
1972	Brigadier Gerard	Joe Mercer
1973	Dahlia	Bill Pyers
1974	Dahlia	Lester Piggott
1975	Grundy	Pat Eddery
1976	Pawneese	Yves Saint-Martin
1977	The Minstrel	Lester Piggott
1978	Ile de Bourbon	John Reid
1979	Troy	Willie Carson
1980	Ela-Mana-Mou	Willie Carson
1981	Shergar	Walter Swinburn
1982	Kalaglow	Greville Starkey
1983	Time Charter	Joe Mercer
1984	Teenoso	Lester Piggott
1985	Petoski	Willie Carson
1986	Dancing Brave	Pat Eddery
1987	Reference Point	Steve Cauthen
1988	Mtoto	Michael Roberts
1989	Nashwan	Willie Carson
1990	Belmez	Michael Kinane
1991	Generous	Alan Munro
1992	St Jovite	Stephen Craine

1993	Opera House	Michael Roberts
1994	King's Theatre	Michael Kinane
1995	Lammtarra	Frankie Dettori
1996	Pentire	Michael Hills
1997	Swain	John Reid
1998	Swain	Frankie Dettori

Most wins: 2 Dahlia, Swain

Sussex Stakes

Raced over 1 mile at Goodwood. Sponsored from 1985 by the Swettenham Stud (headed by Robert Sangster). First run in 1841 as a race for 2-year-olds over 6 furlongs. For 3-year-olds 1878-59, 3- & 4-year-olds 1960-74, 3-year-old upwards since 1975.

1980	Posse	Pat Eddery
1981	King's Lake	Pat Eddery
1982	On the House	John Reid
1983	Noalcoholic	George Duffield
1984	Chief Singer	Ray Cochrane
1985	Rousillon	Greville Starkey
1986	Sonic Lady	Walter Swinburn
1987	Soviet Star	Greville Starkey
1988	Warning	Pat Eddery
1989	Zilzal	Walter Swinburn
1990	Distant Relative	Willie Carson
1991	Second Set	Frankie Dettori
1992	Marling	Pat Eddery
1993	Bigstone	Dominic Boeuf
1994	Distant View	Pat Eddery
1995	Sayyedati	Brett Doyle
1996	First Island	Michael Hills
1997	Ali-Royal	Kieren Fallon
1998	Among Men	Michael Kinane

Juddmonte International Stakes

Inaugurated in 1972, known as the Benson & Hedges Gold Cup until 1985, the Matchmaker International 1986-7, becoming the International Stakes in 1988. The principal race of the three-day August meeting at York, it is run over 1 mile 2 furlongs.

1980	Master Willie	Phillip Waldron
1981	Beldale Flutter	Pat Eddery
1982	Assert	Pat Eddery
1983	Caerleon	Pat Eddery
1984	Cormorant Wood	Steve Cauthen
1985	Commanche Run	Lester Piggott
1986	Shardari	Walter Swinburn
1987	Triptych	Steve Cauthen
1988	Persian Heights	Pat Eddery
1989	Ile de Chypre	Tony Clark
1990	In the Groove	Steve Cauthen
1991	Terimon	Michael Roberts
1992	Rodrigo de Triano	Lester Piggott
1993-4	Ezzoud	Walter Swinburn
1995-6	Halling	Walter Swinburn
1997	Singspiel	Frankie Dettori
1998	One So Wonderful	Pat Eddery

Yorkshire Oaks

Held at York over 1 mile 4 furlongs. First run in 1849. For 3-year-old fillies, but from 1994 also for older horses. Now sponsored by Aston Upthorpe.

1980	Shoot a Line	Lester Piggott
1981	Condessa	Declan Gillespie
1982	Awaasif	Lester Piggott
1983	Sun Princess	Willie Carson
1984	Circus Plume	Willie Carson
1985	Sally Brown	Walter Swinburn
1986	Untold	Greville Starkey
1987	Bint Pasha	Richard Quinn
1988	Diminuendo	Steve Cauthen
1989	Roseate Tern	Willie Carson
1990	Hellenic	Willie Carson
1991	Magnificent Star	Tony Cruz
1992	User Friendly	George Duffield
1993	Only Royale	Ray Cochrane
1994	Only Royale	Frankie Dettori
1995	Pure Grain	John Reid
1996	Key Change	Johnny Murtagh
1997	My Emma	Darryl Holland
1998	Catchas Catchcan	Kieren Fallon

Nunthorpe Stakes

Run over 5 furlongs at York for 2-year-olds and up. First run 1903, run at Newmarket 1942-4, and as the William Hill Sprint Championship 1976-89, then the Keeneland Nunthorpe Stakes.

1980-2	Sharpo	Pat Eddery
1983	Habibti	Willie Carson
1984	Committed	Brent Thomson
1985	Never So Bold	Steve Cauthen
1986	Last Tycoon	Yves Saint-Martin
1987	Ajdal	Walter Swinburn
1988	Handsome Sailor	Michael Hills
1989	Cadeaux Genereaux	Pat Eddery
1990	Dayjur	Willie Carson
1991	Sheikh Albadou	Pat Eddery
1992	Lyric Fantasy	Michael Roberts
1993	Lochsong	Frankie Dettori
1994	Piccolo	John Reid
1995	So Factual	Frankie Dettori
1996	Pivotal	George Duffield
1997	Coastal Bluff	Kevin Darley
	Ya Malak (*dead heat*)	Alex Greaves
1998	Lochangel	Frankie Dettori

Haydock Park Sprint Cup

Run over 6 furlongs at Haydock Park for 2-year-olds and up. First run 1966 as the Vernons November Sprint Cup. Vernons Sprint Cup 1968-88, Ladbroke Sprint Cup 1989-91. Sponsored by Hazlewood Foods 1993. Group One since 1988.

1988	Dowsing	Pat Eddery
1989	Danehill	Pat Eddery
1990	Dayjur	Willie Carson
1991	Polar Falcon	Cash Asmussen
1992	Sheikh Albadou	Bruce Raymond
1993	Wolfhound	Michael Roberts

1994	Lavinia Fontana	Jason Weaver
1995	Cherokee Rose	Cash Asmussen
1996	Iktamal	Willie Ryan
1997	Royal Applause	Michael Hills

Fillies Mile

Run over 1 mile by fillies at Ascot in September.
First run 1973 as the Green Shield Stakes, with various sponsors since.

1990	Shamshir	Frankie Dettori
1991	Culture Vulture	Tommy Quinn
1992	Ivanka	Michael Roberts
1993	Fairy Heights	Cash Asmussen
1994	Aqaarid	Willie Carson
1995	Bosra Sham	Pat Eddery
1996	Reams of Verse	Michael Kinane
1997	Glorosio	Frankie Dettori

Queen Elizabeth II Stakes

Raced over 1 mile at Ascot. First run 1955, Group 2 pre-1987.

1987	Milligram	Pat Eddery
1988	Warning	Pat Eddery
1989	Zilzal	Walter Swinburn
1990	Markofdistinction	Frankie Dettori
1991	Selkirk	Ray Cochrane
1992	Lahib	Willie Carson
1993	Bigstone	Pat Eddery
1994	Maroof	Richard Hills
1995	Bahri	Willie Carson
1996	Mark of Esteem	Frankie Dettori
1997	Air Express	Olivier Peslier

Cheveley Park Stakes

Run over the last 6 furlongs of the Bunbury Mile at Newmarket by 2-year-old fillies. First run in 1870. Sponsored by William Hill 1973-83, Tattersalls 1985-92, Shadwell Stud from 1993.

1980	Marwell	Lester Piggott
1981	Woodstream	Pat Eddery
1982	Ma Biche	Freddie Head
1983	Desirable	Steve Cauthen
1984	Park Appeal	Declan Gillespie
1985	Embla	Angel Cordero
1986	Minstrella	John Reid
1987	Ravinella	Gary Moore
1988	Pass the Peace	Richard Quinn
1989	Dead Certain	Cash Asmussen
1990	Capricciosa	John Reid
1991	Marling	Walter Swinburn
1992	Sayyedati	Walter Swinburn
1993	Prophecy	Pat Eddery
1994	Gay Gallanta	Pat Eddery
1995	Blue Duster	Michael Kinane
1996	Pas de Response	Freddie Head
1997	Embassy	Kieron Fallon

Middle Park Stakes

A 6-furlong sprint for 2-year-olds run at Newmarket. First run in 1866 as the Middle Park Plate. Became Middle Park Stakes 1922. Run at Nottingham 1940. Sponsored by Tattersalls 1986-9, Newgate Stud from 1990.

1980	Mattaboy	Lester Piggott
1981	Cajun	Lester Piggott
1982	Diesis	Lester Piggott
1983	Creag-an-Sgor	Steve Cauthen
1984	Bassenthwaite	Pat Eddery
1985	Stalker	Joe Mercer
1986	Mister Majestic	Ray Cochrane
1987	Gallic League	Steve Cauthen
1988	Mon Tresor	Michael Roberts
1989	Balla Cove	Steve Cauthen
1990	Lycius	Cash Asmussen
1991	Rodrigo de Triano	Willie Carson
1992	Zieten	Steve Cauthen
1993	First Trump	Michael Hills
1994	Fard	Willie Carson
1995	Royal Applause	Walter Swinburn
1996	Bahamian Bounty	Frankie Dettori
1997	Hayil	Richard Hills

Champion Stakes

Run at Newmarket over 1 mile 2 furlongs. First run in 1877. Dubai Champion Stakes from 1982.

1980	Cairn Rouge	Tony Murray
1981	Vayrann	Yves Saint-Martin
1982	Time Charter	Billy Newnes
1983	Cormorant Wood	Steve Cauthen
1984	Palace Music	Yves Saint-Martin
1985	Pebbles	Pat Eddery
1986	Triptych	Tony Cruz
1987	Triptych	Tony Cruz
1988	Indian Skimmer	Michael Roberts
1989	Legal Case	Ray Cochrane
1990	In the Groove	Steve Cauthen
1991	Tel Quel	Thierry Jarnet
1992	Rodrigo de Triano	Lester Piggott
1993	Hatoof	Walter Swinburn
1994	Dernier Empereur	Sylvain Guillot
1995	Spectrum	John Reid
1996	Bosra Sham	Pat Eddery
1997	Pilsudski	Michael Kinane

Most wins: 2 Lemberg 1910-1, Orpheus 1920-1, Fairway 1928-9, Wychwood Abbot 1935-6, Hippius 1940-1, Dynamite 1951-2, Brigadier Gerard 1971-2, Triptych 1986-7

Dewhurst Stakes

An end-of-season race for 2-year-olds at Newmarket, over 7 furlongs. It was first run in 1875 and was sponsored by William Hill 1973-86, then Three Chimneys. Named the Generous Dewhurst Stakes from 1994.

| 1980 | Storm Bird | Pat Eddery |
| 1981 | Wind and Wuthering | Philip Waldron |

1982	Diesis	Lester Piggott
1983	El Gran Senor	Pat Eddery
1984	Kala Dancer	Geoff Baxter
1985	Huntingdale	Michael Hills
1986	Ajdal	Walter Swinburn
1987	*Cancelled*	
1988	Prince of Dance	Willie Carson
	Scenic (*dead heat*)	Michael Hills
1989	Dashing Blade	John Matthias
1990	Generous	Richard Quinn
1991	Dr Devious	Willie Carson
1992	Zafonic	Pat Eddery
1993	Grand Lodge	Pat Eddery
1994	Pennekamp	Thierry Jarnet
1995	Alhaath	Willie Crason
1996	In Command	Michael Hills
1997	Xaar	Olivier Peslier

Racing Post Trophy

Run over 1 mile at Doncaster for 2-year-olds. Run as the Timeform Gold Cup 1961-4, Observer Gold Cup 1965-75, William Hill Futurity 1976-88.

1980	Beldale Flutter	Pat Eddery
1981	Count Pahlen	Geoff Baxter
1982	Dunbeath	Lester Piggott
1983	Alphabatim	Greville Starkey
1984	Lanfranco	Lester Piggott
1985	Bakharoff	Greville Starkey
1986	Reference Point	Pat Eddery
1987	Emmson	Willie Carson
1988	Al Hareb	Willie Carson
1989	Be My Chief	Steve Cauthen
1990	Peter Davies	Steve Cauthen
1991	Seattle Rhyme	Cash Asmussen
1992	Armiger	Pat Eddery
1993	King's Theatre	Willie Ryan
1994	Celtic Swing	Kevin Darley
1995	Beauchamp King	John Reid
1996	Medaaly	Gary Hind
1997	Saratoga Springs	Michael Kinane

Irish Classics

All Irish Classics are run at the Curragh, in County Kildare. The distances of all five races are the same as those of their English counterparts.
Winners since 1970:

Irish 2000 Guineas

First run 1921. Now sponsored by Hibernia Foods.

1970	Decies	Lester Piggott
1971	King's Company	Freddie Head
1972	Ballymore	Christy Roche
1973	Sharp Edge	Joe Mercer
1974	Furry Glen	George McGrath
1975	Grundy	Pat Eddery
1976	Northern Treasure	Gabriel Curran

1977	Pampapaul	Franco Dettori
1978	Jaazeiro	Lester Piggott
1979	Dickens Hill	Tony Murray
1980	Nikoli	Christy Roche
1981	King's Lake	Pat Eddery
1982	Dara Monarch	Michael Kinane
1983	Wassl	Tony Murray
1984	Sadlers Wells	George McGrath
1985	Triptych	Christy Roche
1986	Flash of Steel	Michael Kinane
1987	Don't Forget Me	Willie Carson
1988	Prince of Birds	Declan Gillespie
1989	Shaadi	Walter Swinburn
1990	Tirol	Pat Eddery
1991	Fourstars Allstar	Mike Smith
1992	Rodrigo de Triano	Lester Piggott
1993	Barathea	Michael Roberts
1994	Turtle Island	John Reid
1995	Spectrum	John Reid
1996	Spinning World	Cash Asmussen
1997	Desert King	Christy Roche
1998	Desert Prince	Olivier Peslier

Irish 1000 Guineas

First run 1922. Now sponsored by Airlie/Coolmore.

1970	Black Satin	Ron Hutchinson
1971	Favoletta	Lester Piggott
1972	Pidget	Walter Swinburn, Sr
1973	Cloonagh	Greville Starkey
1974	Gaily	Ron Hutchinson
1975	Miralla	Ryan Parnell
1976	Sarah Siddons	Christy Roche
1977	Lady Capulet	Tom Murphy
1978	More So	Christy Roche
1979	Godetia	Lester Piggott
1980	Cairn Rouge	Tony Murray
1981	Arctique Royale	Gabriel Curran
1982	Prince's Polly	Walter Swinburn
1983	L'Attrayante	Alain Badel
1984	Katies	Philip Robinson
1985	Al Bahathri	Tony Murray
1986	Sonic Lady	Walter Swinburn
1987	Forest Flower	Tony Ives
1988	Trusted Partner	Michael Kinane
1989	Ensconce	Ray Cochrane
1990	In the Groove	Steve Cauthen
1991	Kooyonga	Willie Carson
1992	Marling	Walter Swinburn
1993	Nicer	Michael Hills
1994	Mehthaaf	Willie Carson
1995	Ridgewood Pearl	Christy Roche
1996	Matiya	Willie Carson
1997	Classic Park	Stephen Craine
1998	Tarascon	Jamie Spencer

Irish Derby

First run 1866 at 1 mile 6 furlongs, reduced to
1 mile 4 furlongs in 1872. Now sponsored by
Budweiser.

1970	Nijinsky	Liam Ward
1971	Irish Ball	Fredo Gilbert
1972	Steel Pulse	Bill Williamson
1973	Weaver's Hall	George McGrath
1974	English Prince	Yves Saint-Martin
1975	Grundy	Pat Eddery
1976	Malacate	Philippe Paquet
1977	The Minstrel	Lester Piggott
1978	Shirley Heights	Greville Starkey
1979	Troy	Willie Carson
1980	Tyrnavos	Tony Murray
1981	Shergar	Lester Piggott
1982	Assert	Christy Roche
1983	Shareef Dancer	Walter Swinburn
1984	El Gran Senor	Pat Eddery
1985	Law Society	Pat Eddery
1986	Shahrastani	Walter Swinburn
1987	Sir Harry Lewis	Steve Cauthen
1988	Kahyasi	Ray Cochrane
1989	Old Vic	Steve Cauthen
1990	Salsabil★	Willie Carson
1991	Generous	Alan Munro
1992	St Jovite	Christy Roche
1993	Commander in Chief	Pat Eddery
1994	Balanchine★	Frankie Dettori
1995	Winged Love	Olivier Peslier
1996	Zagreb	Pat Shanahan
1997	Desert King	Christy Roche
1998	Dream Well	Cash Asmussen

★ Salsabil and Balanchine were the first fillies to win
the race since 1900.

Irish Oaks

First run in 1895. Now sponsored by Kildangan Stud.

1970	Santa Tina	Lester Piggott
1971	Altesse Royale	Geoff Lewis
1972	Regal Exception	Maurice Philipperon
1973	Dahlia	Bill Pyers
1974	Dibidale	Willie Carson
1975	Juliette Marny	Lester Piggott
1976	Lagunette	Philippe Paquet
1977	Olwyn	John Lynch
1978	Fair Salinia	Greville Starkey
1979	Godetia	Lester Piggott
1980	Shoot a Line	Willie Carson
1981	Blue Wind	Walter Swinburn
1982	Swiftfoot	Willie Carson
1983	Give Thanks	Declan Gillespie
1984	Princess Pati	Pat Shanahan
1985	Helen Street	Willie Carson
1986	Colorspin	Pat Eddery
1987	Unite	Walter Swinburn
1988	Diminuendo	Steve Cauthen
	Melodist (*dead heat*)	Walter Swinburn

1989	Alydaress	Michael Kinane
1990	Knight's Baroness	Richard Quinn
1991	Possessive Dancer	Steve Cauthen
1992	User Friendly	George Duffield
1993	Wemyss Bight	Pat Eddery
1994	Bolas	Pat Eddery
1995	Pure Grain	John Reid
1996	Dance Design	Michael Kinane
1997	Ebadeyla	John Murtagh
1998	Winona	John Murtagh

Irish St Leger

First run in 1915. Now sponsored by Jefferson Smurfit
and from 1983 open to older horses as weight-for-age.

1970	Allangrange	George McGrath
1971	Parnell	Alan Simpson
1972	Pidget	Thomas Burns
1973	Conor Pass	Peter Jarman
1974	Mistigri	Christy Roche
1975	Caucasus	Lester Piggott
1976	Meneval	Lester Piggott
1977	Transworld	Thomas Murphy
1978	M-Lolshan	Brian Taylor
1979	Niniski	Willie Carson
1980	Gonzales	Raymond Carroll
1981	Protection Racket	Brian Taylor
1982	Touching Wood	Paul Cook
1983	Mountain Lodge	Declan Gillespie
1984	Opale	Darrell McHargue
1985	Leading Counsel	Pat Eddery
1986	Authaal	Christy Roche
1987	Eurobird	Cash Asmussen
1988	Dark Lomond	Declan Gillespie
1989	Petite Ile	Ron Quinton
1990	Ibn Bey	Richard Quinn
1991	Turgeon	Tony Cruz
1992	Mashaallah	Steve Cauthen
1993-4	Vintage Crop	Michael Kinane
1995	Strategic Choice	Richard Quinn
1996-7	Oscar Schindler	Stephen Craine

French Classics

Poule d'Essai des Pouliches

The equivalent of the 1000 Guineas, run at Longchamp
over 1600 metres (1 mile). First run 1883. Held at Le
Tremblay 1943, Maisons-Laffitte 1944-5.
Winners since 1970:

1970	Pampered Miss	Maurice Philipperon
1971	Bold Fascinator	Bill Williamson
1972	Mata Hari	Jean Cruguet
1973	Allez France	Yves Saint-Martin
1974	Dumka	Alain Lequeux
1975	Ivanjica	Freddie Head
1976	Riverqueen	Freddie Head
1977	Madelia	Yves Saint-Martin
1978	Dancing Maid	Freddie Head
1979	Three Troikas	Freddie Head

1980	Aryenne	Maurice Philipperon
1981	Ukraine Girl	Pat Eddery
1982	River Lady	Lester Piggott
1983	L'Attrayante	Alain Badel
1984	Masarika	Yves Saint-Martin
1985	Silvermine	Freddie Head
1986	Baiser Volé	Guy Guignard
1987	Miesque	Freddie Head
1988	Ravinella	Gary Moore
1989	Pearl Bracelet	Alfred Gilbert
1990	Houseproud	Pat Eddery
1991	Danseuse Du Soir	Dominic Boeuf
1992	Culture Vulture	Richard Quinn
1993	Madelein's Dream	Cash Asmussen
1994	East of the Moon	Cash Asmussen
1995	Matiara	Freddie Head
1996	Ta Rib	Willie Carson
1997	Always Loyal	Freddie Head
1998	Zalaiyki	Gérald Mosse

Poule d'Essai des Poulains

Also run at Longchamp over 1600 metres, the equivalent of the 2000 Guineas. First run 1883. Run at Auteuil 1940, Le Tremblay 1943, Maisons-Laffitte 1944-5.

Winners since 1970:

1970	Caro	Bill Williamson
1971	Zug	Jean-Claude Desaint
1972	Riverman	Jean-Claude Desaint
1973	Kalamoun	Henri Samani
1974	Moulines	Maurice Philipperon
1975	Green Dancer	Freddie Head
1976	Red Lord	Freddie Head
1977	Blushing Groom	Henri Samani
1978	Nishapour	Henri Samani
1979	Irish River	Maurice Philipperon
1980	In Fijar	Georges Doleuze
1981	Recitation	Greville Starkey
1982	Melyno	Yves Saint-Martin
1983	L'Emigrant	Cash Asmussen
1984	Siberian Express	Fredo Gibert
1985	No Pass No Sale	Yves Saint-Martin
1986	Fast Topaze	Cash Asmussen
1987	Soviet Star	Greville Starkey
1988	Blushing John	Freddie Head
1989	Kendor	Maurice Philliperon
1990	Linamix	Freddie Head
1991	Hector Protector	Freddie Head
1992	Shanghai	Freddie Head
1993	Kingmambo	Cash Asmussen
1994	Green Tune	Olivier Doleuze
1995	Vettori	Frankie Dettori
1996	Ashkalani	Gérald Mosse
1997	Daylami	Gérald Mosse
1998	Victory Note	John Reid

Prix du Jockey Club

The French Derby, first run in 1836. Raced over 2400 metres (1 mile 4 furlongs) at Chantilly. Raced at Longchamp 1919-20, 1941-2, 1945-7, Auteuil 1940, Le Tremblay 1943-4.

Winners since 1970:

1970	Sassafras	Yves Saint-Martin
1971	Rheffic	Bill Pyers
1972	Hard to Beat	Lester Piggott
1973	Roi Lear	Freddie Head
1974	Caracolero	Philippe Paquet
1975	Val de L'Orme	Freddie Head
1976	Youth	Freddie Head
1977	Crystal Palace	Gérard Dubroeucq
1978	Acamas	Yves Saint-Martin
1979	Top Ville	Yves Saint-Martin
1980	Policeman	Willie Carson
1981	Bikala	Serge Gorli
1982	Assert	Christy Roche
1983	Caerleon	Pat Eddery
1984	Darshaan	Yves Saint-Martin
1985	Mouktar	Yves Saint-Martin
1986	Bering	Gary Moore
1987	Natroun	Yves Saint-Martin
1988	Hours After	Pat Eddery
1989	Old Vic	Steve Cauthen
1990	Sanglamore	Pat Eddery
1991	Suave Dancer	Cash Asmussen
1992	Polytain	Frankie Dettori
1993	Hernando	Cash Asmussen
1994	Celtic Arms	Gérald Mosse
1995	Celtic Swing	Kevin Darley
1996	Ragmar	Gérald Mosse
1997	Peintre Célèbre	Olivier Peslier
1998	Dream Well	Cash Asmussen

Prix de Diane Hermès

The equivalent of the Oaks. It is run over 2100 metres (c.1 mile 2 furlongs) at Chantilly. Prix de Diane 1843-1976, Prix de Diane Revlon 1977-81, Prix de Diane Hermès since. Raced at Longchamp 1919-20, 1941-2, 1945-7, Le Tremblay 1943-4. No race 1975.

Winners since 1970:

1970	Sweet Mimosa	Bill Williamson
1971	Pistol Packer	Freddie Head
1972	Rescousse	Yves Saint-Martin
1973	Allez France	Yves Saint-Martin
1974	Highclere	Joe Mercer
1976	Pawneese	Yves Saint-Martin
1977	Madelia	Yves Saint-Martin
1978	Reine de Saba	Freddie Head
1979	Dunette	Georges Doleuze
1980	Mrs Penny	Lester Piggott
1981	Madam Gay	Lester Piggott
1982	Harbour	Freddie Head
1983	Escaline	Gary Moore
1984	Northern Trick	Cash Asmussen

1985	Lypharita	Lester Piggott
1986	Lacovia	Freddie Head
1987	Indian Skimmer	Steve Cauthen
1988	Restless Kara	Gérard Mosse
1989	Lady in Silver	Tony Cruz
1990	Rafha	Willie Carson
1991	Caerlina	Eric Legrix
1992	Jolypha	Pat Eddery
1993	Shemaka	Gérald Mosse
1994	East of the Moon	Cash Asmussen
1995	Carling	Thierry Thulliez
1996	Sil Sila	Cash Asmussen
1997	Vereva	Gérald Mosse
1998	Zainta	Gérard Mosse

Prix Royal Oak

Run over 3100 metres (*c*.1 mile 7 furlongs) at
Longchamp. Roughly the equivalent of the St Leger,
it was open only to 3-year-olds until 1978; since then
it has been open to 3-year-olds and upwards. First run
1869. Run at Le Tremblay 1943-4.

Winners since 1970:

1970	Sassafras	Yves Saint-Martin
1971	Bourbon	Freddie Head
1972	Pleben	Marcel Depalmas
1973	Lady Berry	Marcel Depalmas
1974	Busiris	Freddie Head
1975	Henri Le Balafre	Henri Samani
1976	Exceller	Georges Dubroecq
1977	Rex Magan	Philippe Paquet
1978	Brave Johnny	Henri Samani
1979	Niniski	Willie Carson
1980	Gold River	Freddie Head
1981	Ardross	Lester Piggott
1982	Denel	Yves Saint-Martin
1983	Old Country	Pat Eddery
1984	Agent Double	Freddie Head
1985	Mersey	Jean-Luc Kessas
1986	El Cuite	Steve Cauthen
1987	Royal Gait	Alfred Gilbert
1988	Star Lift	Cash Asmussen
1989	Top Sunrise	Freddie Head
1990	Braashee	Michael Roberts
	Indian Queen (*dead heat*)	Walter Swinburn
1991	Turgeon	Tony Cruz
1992	Assessor	Richard Quinn
1993	Mashaallah	Frankie Dettori
1994	Moonax	Pat Eddery
1995	Sunshack	Thierry Jarnet
1996	Red Roses Story	V Vion
1997	Ebadiyla	Gérald Mosse

Prix de l'Arc de Triomphe

Europe's most prestigious race. It is run over 2400
metres (*c*.1 mile 4 furlongs) at Longchamp on the
first Sunday in October. It was first run in 1920.
The 1943-4 races were at Le Tremblay over 2300
metres (*c*.1 mile 3 furlongs).

Winners:

1920	Comrade	Frank Bullock
1921	Ksar	George Stern
1922	Ksar	Frank Bullock
1923	Parth	Frank O'Neill
1924	Massine	Fred Sharpe
1925	Priori	Marcel Allemand
1926	Biribi	Domingo Torterolo
1927	Mon Talisman	Charles Semblat
1928	Kantar	Arthur Esling
1929	Ortello	Paolo Caprioli
1930	Motrico	Marcel Fruhinsholtz
1931	Pearl Cap	Charles Semblat
1932	Motrico	Charles Semblat
1933	Crapom	Paolo Caprioli
1934	Brantôme	Charles Bouillon
1935	Samos	Wally Sibbritt
1936	Corrida	Charlie Elliott
1937	Corrida	Charlie Elliott
1938	Eclair au Chocolat	Charles Bouillon
1941	La Pacha	Paul Francolon
1942	Djebel	Jacko Doyasbère
1943	Verso II	Guy Duforez
1944	Ardan	Jacko Doyasbère
1945	Nikellora	Rae Johnstone
1946	Caracalla	Charlie Elliott
1947	Le Paillon	Fernand Rochetti
1948	Migoli	Charlie Smirke
1949	Coronation	Roger Poincelet
1950	Tantième	Jacko Doyasbère
1951	Tantième	Jacko Doyasbère
1952	Nuccio	Roger Poincelet
1953	La Sorellina	Maurice Larraun
1954	Sica Boy	Rae Johnstone
1955	Ribot	Enrico Camici
1956	Ribot	Enrico Camici
1957	Oroso	Serge Boullenger
1958	Ballymoss	Scobie Breasley
1959	Saint Crespin	George Moore
1960	Puissant Chef	Max Garcia
1961	Molvedo	Enrico Camici
1962	Soltikoff	Marcel Depalmas
1963	Exbury	Jean Deforge
1964	Prince Royal II	Roger Poincelet
1965	Sea Bird II	Pat Glennon
1966	Bon Mot	Freddie Head
1967	Topyo	Bill Pyers
1968	Vaguely Noble	Bill Williamson
1969	Levmoss	Bill Williamson
1970	Sassafras	Yves Saint-Martin
1971	Mill Reef	Geoff Lewis

1972	San San	Freddie Head
1973	Rheingold	Lester Piggott
1974	Allez France	Yves Saint-Martin
1975	Star Appeal	Greville Starkey
1976	Ivanjica	Freddie Head
1977	Alleged	Lester Piggott
1978	Alleged	Lester Piggott
1979	Three Troikas	Freddie Head
1980	Detroit	Pat Eddery
1981	Gold River	Gary Moore
1982	Akiyda	Yves Saint-Martin
1983	All Along	Walter Swinburn
1984	Sagace	Yves Saint-Martin
1985	Rainbow Quest	Pat Eddery
1986	Dancing Brave	Pat Eddery
1987	Trempolino	Pat Eddery
1988	Tony Bin	John Reid
1989	Carroll House	Michael Kinane
1990	Saumarez	Gerald Mosse
1991	Suave Dancer	Cash Asmussen
1992	Subotica	Thierry Jarnet
1993	Urban Sea	Eric Saint-Martin
1994	Carnegie	Thierry Jarnet
1995	Lammtarra	Frankie Dettori
1996	Helissio	Olivier Peslier
1997	Peintre Célèbre	Olivier Peslier

Most wins – horse: 2 Ksar, Motrico, Corrida, Tantième, Ribot, Alleged

Most wins – jockey: 4 Jacko Doyasbère, Freddie Head, Yves Saint-Martin, Pat Eddery

Most wins – trainer: 4 Charles Semblat 1942, 1944, 1946, 1949; Alec Head 1952, 1959, 1976, 1981; François Mathet 1950-1, 1970, 1982; André Fabre 1987, 1992, 1994, 1997

Most wins – owner: 6 Marcel Boussac 1936-7, 1942, 1944, 1946, 1949

Fastest winning time: 2 min 24.6 sec Peintre Célèbre 1997

Greatest winning margin: 6 lengths Ribot 1956, Sea Bird II 1965

Champion Jockeys (Flat)

The position of champion jockey on the flat in Britain is determined on most winners each year. *Champions since 1900:*

Year	Champion	No. of winners
1900	Lester Reiff	143
1901	Otto Madden	130
1902	Willie Lane	170
1903	Otto Madden	154
1904	Otto Madden	161
1905	Elijah Wheatley	124
1906	Billy Higgs	149
1907	Billy Higgs	146
1908	Danny Maher	139
1909	Frank Wootton	165
1910	Frank Wootton	137
1911	Frank Wootton	187
1912	Frank Wootton	118
1913	Danny Maher	115
1914	Steve Donoghue	129
1915	Steve Donoghue	62
1916	Steve Donoghue	43
1917	Steve Donoghue	42
1918	Steve Donoghue	66
1919	Steve Donoghue	129
1920	Steve Donoghue	143
1921	Steve Donoghue	141
1922	Steve Donoghue	102
1923	Steve Donoghue	89
	Charlie Elliott	89
1924	Charlie Elliott	106
1925	Gordon Richards	118
1926	Tommy Weston	95
1927	Gordon Richards	164
1928	Gordon Richards	148
1929	Gordon Richards	135
1930	Freddy Fox	129
1931	Gordon Richards	145
1932	Gordon Richards	190
1933	Gordon Richards	259
1934	Gordon Richards	212
1935	Gordon Richards	217
1936	Gordon Richards	174
1937	Gordon Richards	216
1938	Gordon Richards	200
1939	Gordon Richards	155
1940	Gordon Richards	68
1941	Harry Wragg	71
1942	Gordon Richards	67
1943	Gordon Richards	65
1944	Gordon Richards	88
1945	Gordon Richards	104
1946	Gordon Richards	212
1947	Gordon Richards	269
1948	Gordon Richards	224
1949	Gordon Richards	261
1950	Gordon Richards	201
1951	Gordon Richards	227
1952	Gordon Richards	231
1953	Gordon Richards	191
1954	Doug Smith	129
1955	Doug Smith	168
1956	Doug Smith	155
1957	Scobie Breasley	173
1958	Doug Smith	165
1959	Doug Smith	157
1960	Lester Piggott	170
1961	Scobie Breasley	171
1962	Scobie Breasley	179
1963	Scobie Breasley	176
1964	Lester Piggott	140
1965	Lester Piggott	166

1966	Lester Piggott	191
1967	Lester Piggott	117
1968	Lester Piggott	139
1969	Lester Piggott	163
1970	Lester Piggott	162
1971	Lester Piggott	162
1972	Willie Carson	132
1973	Willie Carson	163
1974	Pat Eddery	148
1975	Pat Eddery	164
1976	Pat Eddery	162
1977	Pat Eddery	176
1978	Willie Carson	182
1979	Joe Mercer	164
1980	Willie Carson	165
1981	Lester Piggott	179
1982	Lester Piggott	188
1983	Willie Carson	159
1984	Steve Cauthen	130
1985	Steve Cauthen	195
1986	Pat Eddery	177
1987	Steve Cauthen	197
1988	Pat Eddery	183
1989	Pat Eddery	171
1990	Pat Eddery	209
1991	Pat Eddery	165
1992	Michael Roberts	206
1993	Pat Eddery	169
1994	Frankie Dettori	233
1995	Frankie Dettori	216
1996	Pat Eddery	186
1997	Kieren Fallon	196

Most times champion

26	Gordon Richards	
14	George Fordham	1855-63, 1865, 1867-9, 1871*
13	Fred Archer	1874-86
13	Elnathan Flatman	1840-52
11	Lester Piggott	
10	Steve Donoghue	

* Shared title.

Progressive records of most wins in a season since 1840

1840	Elnathan Flatman	50
1841	Elnathan Flatman	68
1845	Elnathan Flatman	81
1846	Elnathan Flatman	81
1847	Elnathan Flatman	89
1848	Elnathan Flatman	104
1856	George Fordham	108
1859	George Fordham	118
1860	George Fordham	146
1862	George Fordham	166
1875	Fred Archer	172
1876	Fred Archer	207
1877	Fred Archer	218

1878	Fred Archer	229
1883	Fred Archer	232
1884	Fred Archer	241
1885	Fred Archer	246
1933	Gordon Richards	259
1947	Gordon Richards	269

Michael Roberts had a record 1068 rides in a season in 1992.

Most career wins in Britain

Wins	Jockey	Years
4870	Gordon Richards	1921-54
4513	Lester Piggott	1948-95
4000	Pat Eddery	1969-97
3828	Willie Carson	1962-96
3111	Doug Smith	1931-67
2810	Joe Mercer	1950-85
2748	Fred Archer	1870-86
2591	Edward Hide	1951-85
2587	George Fordham	1850-84
2313	Eph Smith	1930-65
2161	Scobie Breasley	1950-68
2067	Bill Nevett	1924-56

Leading Trainers since 1945

1945	Walter Earl	£29,557
1946	Frank Butters	56,140
1947	Fred Darling	65,313
1948	Noel Murless	66,542
1949	Frank Butters	71,721
1950	Charles Semblat (Fra)	57,044
1951	Jack Jarvis	56,397
1952	Marcus Marsh	92,093
1953	Jack Jarvis	71,546
1954	Cecil Boyd-Rochfort	65,326
1955	Cecil Boyd-Rochfort	74,424
1956	Charles Elsey	61,621
1957	Noel Murless	116,898
1958	Cecil Boyd-Rochfort	84,186
1959	Noel Murless	145,727
1960	Noel Murless	118,327
1961	Noel Murless	95,972
1962	Dick Hern	70,206
1963	Paddy Prendergast (Ire)	125,294
1964	Paddy Prendergast (Ire)	128,102
1965	Paddy Prendergast (Ire)	75,323
1966	Vincent O'Brien (Ire)	123,848
1967	Noel Murless	256,899
1968	Noel Murless	141,508
1969	Arthur Budgett	105,349
1970	Noel Murless	199,524
1971	Ian Balding	157,488
1972	Dick Hern	206,767
1973	Noel Murless	132,984
1974	Peter Walwyn	206,784
1975	Peter Walwyn	382,527
1976	Henry Cecil	261,301

Year	Trainer	£		Year	Owner	£
1977	Vincent O'Brien (Ire)	439,124		1974	Nelson Bunker Hunt	£147,217
1978	Henry Cecil	382,301		1975	Dr Carlo Vittadini	209,492
1979	Henry Cecil	683,971		1976	Daniel Wildenstein	244,500
1980	Dick Hern	831,964		1977	Robert Sangster	348,023
1981	Michael Stoute	723,786		1978	Robert Sangster	160,406
1982	Henry Cecil	872,614		1979	Sir Michael Sobell	339,751
1983	Dick Hern	549,598		1980	Simon Weinstock	236,332
1984	Henry Cecil	551,939		1981	HH Aga Khan IV	441,654
1985	Henry Cecil	1,148,206		1982	Robert Sangster	397,749
1986	Michael Stoute	1,266,807		1983	Robert Sangster	464,488
1987	Henry Cecil	1,882,116		1984	Robert Sangster	395,901
1988	Henry Cecil	1,186,110		1985	Sheikh Mohammad	1,132,987
1989	Michael Stoute	2,000,465		1986	Sheikh Mohammad	830,121
1990	Henry Cecil	1,927,735		1987	Sheikh Mohammad	1,232,240
1991	Paul Cole	1,510,929		1988	Sheikh Mohammad	1,143,343
1992	Richard Hannon	1,780,014		1989	Sheikh Mohammad	2,097,405
1993	Richard Hannon	1,969,789		1990	Hamdam Al-Maktoum	1,536,815
1994	Michael Stoute	1,914,079		1991	Sheikh Mohammad	1,836,590
1995	John Dunlop	2,018,491		1992	Sheikh Mohammad	1,917,136
1996	Saeed bin Suroor	1,962,598		1993	Sheikh Mohammad	2,603,693
1997	Michael Stoute	2,140,949		1994	Sheikh Mohammad	2,683,384
				1995	Hamdam Al-Maktoum	2,596,289
				1996	Godolphin	1,852,813
				1997	Sheikh Mohammad	1,480,859

Most times leading trainer (since 1896): 12 Alec Taylor 1907, 1909-10, 1914, 1917-23, 1925; 9 Henry Cecil, Noel Murless; 8 Frank Butters 1927-8, 1932, 1934-5, 1944, 1946, 1949; 6 Fred Darling 1926, 1933, 1940-2, 1947

Most times leading owner (since 1882): 13 HH Aga Khan III 1924, 1929-30, 1932, 1934-5, 1937, 1944, 1946-9, 1952; 10 Sheikh Mohammad; 6 17th Earl of Derby 1923, 1927-8, 1933, 1938, 1945; 5 Robert Sangster

Leading Owners since 1945

Year	Owner	£
1945	17th Earl of Derby	£25,067
1946	HH Aga Khan III	24,118
1947	HH Aga Khan III	44,020
1948	HH Aga Khan III	46,393
1949	HH Aga Khan III	68,916
1950	Marcel Boussac	57,044
1951	Marcel Boussac	39,339
1952	HH Aga Khan III	92,518
1953	Sir Victor Sassoon	58,579
1954	HM The Queen	40,993
1955	Lady Zia Wernher	46,345
1956	Major Lionel Holliday	39,327
1957	HM The Queen	62,211
1958	John McShain	63,264
1959	Prince Aly Khan	100,668
1960	Sir Victor Sassoon	90,069
1961	Major Lionel Holliday	39,227
1962	Major Lionel Holliday	70,206
1963	Jim Mullion	68,882
1964	Mrs Howell Jackson	98,270
1965	Jean Ternynck	65,301
1966	Lady Zia Wernher	78,075
1967	Jim Joel	120,925
1968	Raymond Guest	97,075
1969	David Robinson	92,553
1970	Charles Engelhard	182,059
1971	Paul Mellon	138,786
1972	Mrs Jean Hislop	155,190
1973	Nelson Bunker Hunt	124,771

Leading Money-Winners – Season by Season

The leading horses in terms of first-prize money won each season in Britain since 1945:

Year	Horse	£
1945	Sun Stream	£13,685
1946	Airborne	20,345
1947	Migoli	17,215
1948	Black Tarquin	21,423
1949	Nimbus	30,236
1950	Palestine	21,583
1951	Supreme Court	36,016
1952	Tulyar	75,173
1953	Pinza	44,101
1954	Never Say Die	30,332
1955	Meld	42,562
1956	Ribot	23,727
1957	Crepello	32,257
1958	Ballymoss	38,686
1959	Petite Etoile	55,487
1960	St Paddy	71,256
1961	Sweet Solera	36,988
1962	Hethersett	38,497
1963	Ragusa	66,011
1964	Santa Claus	72,067
1965	Sea Bird II	65,301
1966	Charlottown	78,075

1967	Royal Palace	£92,998
1968	Sir Ivor	97,075
1969	Blakeney	63,108
1970	Nijinsky	159,681
1971	Mill Reef	121,913
1972	Brigadier Gerard	151,213
1973	Dahlia	79,230
1974	Dahlia	120,771
1975	Grundy	188,375
1976	Wollow	166,389
1977	The Minstrel	201,184
1978	Ile de Bourbon	136,012
1979	Troy	310,359
1980	Ela-Mana-Mou	236,332
1981	Shergar	295,654
1982	Kalaglow	242,304
1983	Sun Princess	221,356
1984	Secreto (USA)	227,680
1985	Oh So Sharp	311,576
1986	Dancing Brave	423,601
1987	Reference Point	683,029
1988	Mtoto	412,002
1989	Nashwan	772,045
1990	In the Groove	475,524
1991	Generous	631,945
1992	Rodrigo de Triano	494,764
1993	Commander in Chief	877,391
1994	Erhaab	582,588
1995	Lammtarra	783,260
1997	Benny the Dip	778,943

All 3-year olds except Ribot, Ballymoss, Brigadier Gerard, Dahlia (1974), Kalaglow.

International Classification

The official Handicappers in Britain, Ireland and France have jointly compiled International Classifications each year from 1977. Racing in Italy and Germany was added from 1985. These ratings are now produced for six categories: colts and fillies each at 2-year-old and 3-year-old, and older male and older female.

Highest rating overall each year:

1977	Alleged (Ire) 3-y-o 138
1978	Alleged (Ire) 4-y-o 140
1979	Three Troikas* (Fra) 3-y-o 137
1980	Moorestyle (UK) 3-y-o 131
1981	Shergar (UK) 3-y-o 140
1982	Golden Fleece (Ire) 3-y-o 134
1983	Shareef Dancer (UK) 3-y-o 133
1984	El Gran Senor (Ire) 3-y-o 138
1985	Slip Anchor (UK) 3-y-o 135
1986	Dancing Brave (UK) 3-y-o 141
1987	Reference Point (UK) 3-y-o 135
1988	Warning (UK) 3-y-o 133
1989	Old Vic (Ire) 3-y-o 134
	Zilzal (Fra) 3-y-o 134
1990	Dayjur (UK) 3-y-o 133

1991	Generous (UK) 3-y-o 137
1992	St Jovite (Ire) 3-y-o 135
1993	Zafonic (UK) 3-y-o 130
1994	Celtic Swing (UK) 2-y-o 130
	Ballanchine* (Fra) 3-y-o 130
1995	Lammtarra (UK) 3-y-o 130
	in USA: Cigar 5-y-o 132
1996	Helissio (Fra) 3-y-o 134
	in USA: Cigar 5-y-o 135
1997	Peintre Célèbre (Fra) 3-y-o 137

* Fillies.

National Hunt Racing, Steeplechasing and Hurdling

Grand National

The most famous steeplechase in the world has been run annually at Aintree, Liverpool since 1847 with the exception of the war years. It was held at Gatwick in 1916-8. It was run at Aintree as the Grand Liverpool Steeple Chase 1839-42 and as the Liverpool and National Steeple Chase 1843-6. The current course takes in 30 fences over two circuits and is 4 miles 4 furlongs long. The race is now sponsored by Martell. Also shown below are the winners of a preceding steeplechase run at a course in Maghull, some four miles from the present site at Aintree, in 1836-8.

Winners (amateur riders are given their titles, e.g. Mr, Capt.):

Year	Winner	Jockey	Weight (st-lb)
1836	The Duke	–	–
1837	The Duke	Mr Potts	12-0
1838	Sir William	Tom Oliver	12-0
1839	Lottery	Jem Mason	12-0
1840	Jerry	Mr B Bretherton	12-0
1841	Charity	H N Powell	12-0
1842	Gay Lad	Tom Oliver	12-0
1843	Vanguard	Tom Oliver	11-10
1844	Discount	H Crickmere	10-12
1845	Cureall	Bill Loft	11-5
1846	Pioneer	W Taylor	11-12
1847	Matthew	Denny Wynne	10-6
1848	Chandler	Capt. Josey Little	11-12
1849	Peter Simple	Tom Cunningham	11-0
1850	Abd-el-Kader	Chris Green	9-12
1851	Abd-el-Kader	T Abbott	10-4
1852	Miss Mowbray	Mr Alec Goodman	10-4
1853	Peter Simple	Tom Oliver	10-10
1854	Bourton	J Tasker	11-12
1855	Wanderer	J Hanlon	9-8
1856	Freetrader	George Stevens	9-6
1857	Emigrant	Charlie Boyce	9-10
1858	Little Charley	William Archer	10-7
1859	Half Caste	Chris Green	9-7

1860	Anatis	Mr Tommy Pickernell	9-10	1917	Ballymacad	Ted Driscoll	9-12
1861	Jealousy	Joe Kendall	9-12	1918	Poethlyn	Ernie Piggott	11-6
1862	Huntsman	Harry Lamplugh	11-0	1919	Poethlyn	Ernie Piggott	12-7
1863	Emblem	George Stevens	10-10	1920	Troytown	Mr Jack Anthony	11-9
1864	Emblematic	George Stevens	10-6	1921	Shaun Spadah	Dick Rees	11-7
1865	Alcibiade	Capt. Bee Coventry	11-4	1922	Music Hall	Bilbie Rees	11-8
1866	Salamnader	Mr Alec Goodman	10-7	1923	Sergeant Murphy	Capt. Tuppy Bennett	11-3
1867	Cortolvin	John Page	11-13	1924	Master Robert	Bob Trudgill	10-5
1868	The Lamb	Mr George Ede	10-7	1925	Double Chance	Major Jack Wilson	10-9
1869	The Colonel	George Stevens	10-7	1926	Jack Horner	Billy Watkinson	10-5
1870	The Colonel	George Stevens	11-12	1927	Sprig	Ted Leader	12-4
1871	The Lamb	Mr Tommy Pickernell	11-4	1928	Tipperary Tim	Mr Bill Dutton	10-0
1872	Casse Tête	John Page	10-0	1929	Gregalach	Bob Everett	11-4
1873	Disturbance	Mr Maunsell Richardson	11-11	1930	Shaun Goilin	Tommy Cullinan	11-0
1874	Reugny	Mr Maunsell Richardson	10-12	1931	Grakle	Bob Lyall	11-7
1875	Pathfinder	Mr Tommy Pickernell	10-11	1932	Forbra	Jim Hamey	10-7
1876	Regal	Joe Cannon	11-3	1933	Kellsboro' Jack	Dudley Williams	11-9
1877	Austerlitz	Mr Fred Hobson	10-8	1934	Golden Miller	Gerry Wilson	12-2
1878	Shifnal	Jack Jones	10-12	1935	Reynoldstown	Mr Frank Furlong	11-4
1879	The Liberator	Mr Garrett Moore	11-4	1936	Reynoldstown	Mr Fulke Walwyn	12-2
1880	Empress	Mr Tommy Beasley	10-7	1937	Royal Mail	Evan Williams	11-13
1881	Woodbrook	Mr Tommy Beasley	11-3	1938	Battleship	Bruce Hobbs	11-6
1882	Seaman	Lord Manners	11-6	1939	Workman	Tim Hyde	10-6
1883	Zoëdone	Count Graf Karl Kinsky	11-0	1940	Bogskar	Mervyn Jones	10-4
1884	Voluptuary	Mr Ted Wilson	10-5	1946	Lovely Cottage	Capt. Bobby Petre	10-8
1885	Roquefort	Mr Ted Wilson	11-0	1947	Caughoo	Eddie Dempsey	10-0
1886	Old Joe	Tom Skelton	10-9	1948	Sheila's Cottage	Arthur Thompson	10-7
1887	Gamecock	Bill Daniels	11-0	1949	Russian Hero	Leo McMorrow	10-8
1888	Playfair	George Mawson	10-7	1950	Freebooter	Jimmy Power	11-11
1889	Frigate	Mr Tommy Beasley	11-5	1951	Nickel Coin	Johnny Bullock	10-1
1890	Ilex	Arthur Nightingall	10-5	1952	Teal	Arthur Thompson	10-12
1891	Come Away	Mr Harry Beasley	11-12	1953	Early Mist	Bryan Marshall	11-2
1892	Father O'Flynn	Capt. Roddy Owen	10-5	1954	Royal Tan	Bryan Marshall	11-7
1893	Cloister	Bill Dollery	12-7	1955	Quare Times	Pat Taaffe	11-0
1894	Why Not	Arthur Nightingall	11-3	1956	E S B	Dave Dick	11-3
1895	Wild Man from Borneo	Mr Joe Widger	10-1	1957	Sundew	Fred Winter	11-7
1896	The Soarer	Mr David Campbell	9-13	1958	Mr What	Arthur Freeman	10-6
1897	Manifesto	Terry Kavanagh	11-3	1959	Oxo	Michael Scudamore	10-13
1898	Drogheda	John Gourley	10-12	1960	Merryman II	Gerry Scott	10-12
1899	Manifesto	George Williamson	12-7	1961	Nicolaus Silver	Bobby Beasley	10-1
1900	Ambush II	Algy Anthony	11-3	1962	Kilmore	Fred Winter	10-4
1901	Grudon	Arthur Nightingall	10-0	1963	Ayala	Pat Buckley	10-0
1902	Shannon Lass	David Read	10-1	1964	Team Spirit	Willie Robinson	10-3
1903	Drumcree	Percy Woodland	11-3	1965	Jay Trump	Mr Tommy Smith	11-5
1904	Moifaa	Arthur Birch	10-7	1966	Anglo	Tim Norman	10-0
1905	Kirkland	Tich Mason	11-5	1967	Foinavon	John Buckingham	10-0
1906	Ascetic's Silver	Hon. Aubrey Hastings	10-9	1968	Red Alligator	Brian Fletcher	10-0
1907	Eremon	Alf Newey	10-1	1969	Highland Wedding	Eddie Harty	10-4
1908	Rubio	Henry Bletsoe	10-5	1970	Gay Trip	Pat Taaffe	11-5
1909	Lutteur III	George Parfrement	10-11	1971	Specify	John Cook	10-13
1910	Jenkinstown	Bob Chadwick	10-5	1972	Well To Do	Graham Thorner	10-1
1911	Glenside	Mr Jack Anthony	10-3	1973	Red Rum	Brian Fletcher	10-5
1912	Jerry M	Ernie Piggott	12-7	1974	Red Rum	Brian Fletcher	12-0
1913	Covertcoat	Percy Woodland	11-6	1975	L'Escargot	Tommy Carberry	11-3
1914	Sunloch	William Smith	9-7	1976	Rag Trade	John Burke	10-12
1915	Ally Sloper	Mr Jack Anthony	10-6	1977	Red Rum	Tommy Stack	11-8
1916	Vermouth	John Reardon	11-10	1978	Lucius	Bob Davies	10-9

Year	Winner	Jockey	Weight
1979	Rubstic	Maurice Barnes	10-0
1980	Ben Nevis	Mr Charlie Fenwick	10-12
1981	Aldaniti	Bob Champion	10-13
1982	Grittar	Mr Dick Saunders	11-5
1983	Corbière	Ben De Haan	11-4
1984	Hallo Dandy	Neale Doughty	10-2
1985	Last Suspect	Hywel Davies	10-5
1986	West Tip	Richard Dunwoody	10-11
1987	Maori Venture	Steve Knight	10-13
1988	Rhyme 'N' Reason	Brendan Powell	10-11
1989	Little Polveir	Jimmy Frost	10-3
1990	Mr Frisk	Mr Marcus Armytage	10-6
1991	Seagram	Nigel Hawke	10-6
1992	Party Politics	Carl Llewellyn	10-7
1993	*Race void after false start*		
1994	Miinnehoma	Richard Dunwoody	10-8
1995	Royal Athlete	Jason Titley	10-6
1996	Rough Quest	Mick Fitzgerald	10-7
1997	Lord Gyllene	Tony Dobbin	10-0
1998	Earth Summit	Carl Llewellyn	10-5

Most wins – horse: 3 Red Rum; 2 Abd-el-Kader, Peter Simple, The Colonel, The Lamb, Manifesto, Reynoldstown, Poethlyn

Most wins – jockey: 5 George Stevens; 4 Tom Oliver; 3 Mr Tommy Pickernell, Mr Tommy Beasley, Arthur Nightingall, Ernie Piggott, Mr Jack Anthony, Brian Fletcher

Most wins – trainer: 4 Fred Rimell 1956, 1961, 1970, 1976; 4 Aubrey Hastings 1906, 1915, 1917,★ 1924; 3 William Holman 1856, 1858, 1860; 3 William Moore 1894, 1896, 1899; 3 Tom Coulthwaite 1907, 1910, 1931; 3 Vincent O'Brien 1953-5; 3 Neville Crump 1948, 1952, 1960; 3 Donald McCain 1973-4, 1977; 3 Tim Forster 1972, 1980, 1985;

★ Gatwick race.

Most wins – owner: 3 James Machell 1873-4, 1876; Sir Charles Assheton-Smith 1893, 1912-3; Noel Le Mare 1973-4, 1977

Fastest winning time: 8 min 47.8 sec Mr Frisk 1990

Record field: 66 in 1927

Richest prize money: £212,569 in 1997

Cheltenham Gold Cup

First held in 1924, the Cheltenham Gold Cup is the most prestigious race on the National Hunt calendar in Britain. The course has varied over the years but is now 3 miles 2 furlongs 110 yards over 22 fences. Since 1980 the race has been sponsored by the Horserace Totalisator Board. There was no race in 1931, 1937, 1943-4. All horses now carry 12 stone.

Year	Winner	Jockey
1924	Red Splash	Dick Rees
1925	Ballinode	Ted Leader
1926	Koko	Tim Hamey
1927	Thrown In	Mr Hugh Grosvenor
1928	Patron Saint	Dick Rees
1929	Easter Hero	Dick Rees
1930	Easter Hero	Tommy Cullinan
1932	Golden Miller	Ted Leader
1933	Golden Miller	Billy Stott
1934	Golden Miller	Gerry Wilson
1935	Golden Miller	Gerry Wilson
1936	Golden Miller	Evan Williams
1938	Morse Code	Danny Morgan
1939	Brendan's Cottage	George Owen
1940	Roman Hackle	Evan Williams
1941	Poet Prince	Roger Burford
1942	Médoc II	Frenchie Nicholson
1945	Red Rower	Davy Jones
1946	Prince Regent	Tim Hyde
1947	Fortina	Mr Dick Black
1948	Cottage Rake	Aubrey Brabazon
1949	Cottage Rake	Aubrey Brabazon
1950	Cottage Rake	Aubrey Brabazon
1951	Silver Fame	Martin Molony
1952	Mont Tremblant	Dave Dick
1953	Knock Hard	Tim Molony
1954	Four Ten	Tommy Cusack
1955	Gay Donald	Tony Grantham
1956	Limber Hill	Jimmy Power
1957	Linwell	Michael Scudamore
1958	Kerstin	Stan Hayhurst
1959	Roddy Owen	Bobby Beasley
1960	Pas Seul	Bill Rees
1961	Saffron Tartan	Fred Winter
1962	Mandarin	Fred Winter
1963	Mill House	Willie Robinson
1964	Arkle	Pat Taaffe
1965	Arkle	Pat Taaffe
1966	Arkle	Pat Taaffe
1967	Woodland Venture	Terry Biddlecombe
1968	Fort Leney	Pat Taaffe
1969	What a Myth	Paul Kelleway
1970	L'Escargot	Tommy Carberry
1971	L'Escargot	Tommy Carberry
1972	Glencaraig Lady	Frank Berry
1973	The Dikler	Ron Barry
1974	Captain Christy	Bobby Beasley
1975	Ten Up	Tommy Carberry
1976	Royal Frolic	John Burke
1977	Davy Lad	Dessie Hughes
1978	Midnight Court	John Francome
1979	Alverton	Jonjo O'Neill
1980	Master Smudge	Richard Hoare
1981	Little Owl	Mr Jim Wilson
1982	Silver Buck	Robert Earnshaw
1983	Bregawn	Graham Bradley
1984	Burrough Hill Lad	Phil Tuck
1985	Forgive 'N' Forget	Martin Dwyer
1986	Dawn Run	Jonjo O'Neill
1987	The Thinker	Ridley Lamb
1988	Charter Party	Richard Dunwoody
1989	Desert Orchid	Simon Sherwood

1990	Norton's Coin	Graham McCourt
1991	Garrison Savannah	Mark Pitman
1992	Cool Ground	Adrian Maguire
1993	Jodami	Mark Dwyer
1994	The Fellow	Adam Kondrat
1995	Master Oats	Norman Williamson
1996	Imperial Call	Conor O'Dwyer
1997	Mr Mulligan	Tony McCoy
1998	Cool Dawn	Andrew Thornton

Most wins – horse: 5 Golden Miller; 3 Cottage Rake, Arkle; 2 Easter Hero, L'Escargot

Most wins – jockey: 4 Pat Taafe; 3 Dick Rees, Aubrey Brabazon, Tommy Carberry

Most wins – trainer: 5 Tom Dreaper 1946, 1964-6, 1968; 4 Basil Briscoe 1932-5, Vincent O'Brien 1948-50, 1953, Fulke Walwyn 1952, 1962-3, 1973

Most wins – owner: 7 Miss Dorothy Paget 1932-6, 1940, 1952; 4 Anne, Duchess of Westminster 1964-6, 1975; 3 Frank Vickerman 1948-50

Fastest winning time: 6 min 23.4 sec Silver Fame 1951

Most placings by a horse: 6 Golden Miller (5 wins, 2nd 1938); 4 The Dikler (won 1972, 2nd 1973, 3rd 1971-2)

Champion Hurdle

The leading race in England for hurdlers, the Champion Hurdle was inaugurated in 1927. It is raced at Cheltenham during the Spring Festival meeting and is now over 2 miles 110 yards. The race was sponsored by Waterford Crystal 1978-92 and by Smurfit from 1993. There was no race in 1931, 1943-4. The current weights are 11st 6lb for 4-year-olds, 12st for older horses with a 5lb allowance for mares.

Year	Winner	Jockey
1927	Blaris	George Duller
1928	Brown Jack	Bilbie Rees
1929	Royal Falcon	Dick Rees
1930	Brown Tony	Tommy Cullinan
1932	Insurance	Ted Leader
1933	Insurance	Billy Stott
1934	Chenango	Danny Morgan
1935	Lion Courage	Gerry Wilson
1936	Victor Norman	Frenchie Nicholson
1937	Free Fare	Georges Pellerin
1938	Our Hope	Capt. Perry Harding
1939	African Sister	Keith Piggott
1940	Solford	Sean Magee
1941	Seneca	Ron Smyth
1942	Forestation	Ron Smyth
1945	Brains Trust	Fred Rimell
1946	Distel	Bobby O'Ryan
1947	National Spirit	Danny Morgan
1948	National Spirit	Ron Smyth
1949	Hatton's Grace	Aubrey Brabazon
1950	Hatton's Grace	Aubrey Brabazon
1951	Hatton's Grace	Tim Molony
1952	Sir Ken	Tim Molony
1953	Sir Ken	Tim Molony
1954	Sir Ken	Tim Molony
1955	Clair Soleil	Fred Winter
1956	Doorknocker	Harry Sprague
1957	Merry Deal	Grenville Underwood
1958	Bandalore	George Slack
1959	Fare Time	Fred Winter
1960	Another Flash	Bobby Beasley
1961	Eborneezer	Fred Winter
1962	Anzio	Willie Robinson
1963	Winning Fair	Mr Alan Lillingston
1964	Magic Court	Pat McCarron
1965	Kirriemuir	Willie Robinson
1966	Salmon Spray	Johnny Haine
1967	Saucy Kit	Roy Edwards
1968	Persian War	Jimmy Uttley
1969	Persian War	Jimmy Uttley
1970	Persian War	Jimmy Uttley
1971	Bula	Paul Kelleway
1972	Bula	Paul Kelleway
1973	Comedy of Errors	Bill Smith
1974	Lanzarote	Richard Pitman
1975	Comedy of Errors	Ken White
1976	Night Nurse	Paddy Broderick
1977	Night Nurse	Paddy Broderick
1978	Monksfield	Tommy Kinane
1979	Monksfield	Dessie Hughes
1980	Sea Pigeon	Jonjo O'Neill
1981	Sea Pigeon	John Francome
1982	For Auction	Mr Colin Magnier
1983	Gaye Brief	Richard Linley
1984	Dawn Run	Jonjo O'Neill
1985	See You Then	Steve Smith-Eccles
1986	See You Then	Steve Smith-Eccles
1987	See You Then	Steve Smith-Eccles
1988	Celtic Shot	Peter Scudamore
1989	Beech Road	Richard Guest
1990	Kribensis	Richard Dunwoody
1991	Morley Street	Jimmy Frost
1992	Royal Gait	Graham McCourt
1993	Granville Again	Peter Scudamore
1994	Flakey Dove	Mark Dwyer
1995	Alderbrook	Norman Williamson
1996	Collier Bay	Graham Bradley
1997	Make a Stand	Tony McCoy
1998	Istabraq	Charlie Swan

Most wins – horse: 3 Hatton's Grace, Sir Ken, Persian War, See You Then

Most wins – jockey: 4 Tim Moloney; 3 Ron Smyth, Fred Winter, Jimmy Uttley, Steve Smith-Eccles

Most wins – trainer: 5 Peter Easterby 1967, 1976-7, 1980-1; 4 Vic Smyth 1941-2, 1947-8, Fred Winter 1971-2, 1974, 1988; 3 Vincent O'Brien 1949-51, Willie Stephenson 1952-4, Ryan Price 1955, 1959, 1961, Colin Davies 1968-70, Nicky Henderson 1985-7

Most wins – owner: 4 Miss Dorothy Paget 1932-3, 1940, 1946; 3 Mrs Moya Keogh 1949-51, Maurice Kingsley 1952-4, Henry Alper 1968-70, Stype Wood Stud Ltd 1985-7

Fastest winning time: 3 min 48.4 sec Make a Stand 1997

Other Principal National Hunt Races

Whitbread Gold Cup

The Whitbread Gold Cup has a special place in British National Hunt racing – when inaugurated, in 1957, it was the first race to attract major commercial sponsorship. Run at Sandown Park over 3 miles 5 furlongs 18 yards. The 1973 race was at Newcastle.

Year	Winner	Jockey	Weight (st-lb)
1957	Much Obliged	Henry East	10-12
1958	Taxidermist	Hon. John Lawrence	10-8
1959	Done Up	Harry Sprague	10-13
1960	Plummers Plain	Ron Harrison	10-0
1961	Pas Seul	Dave Dick	12-0
1962	Frenchman's Cove	Stan Mellor	11-3
1963	Hoodwinked	Paddy Buckley	10-9
1964	Dormant	Paddy Buckley	9-7
1965	Arkle	Pat Taaffe	12-7
1966	What a Myth	Paul Kelleway	9-8
1967	Mill House	David Nicholson	11-11
1968	Larbawn	Macer Gifford	10-9
1969	Larbawn	Josh Gifford	11-4
1970	Royal Toss	Richard Pitman	10-0
1971	Titus Oates	Ron Barry	11-13
1972	Grey Sombrero	Willie Shoemark	9-10
1973	Charlie Potheen	Ron Barry	12-0
1974	The Dikler	Ron Barry	11-13
1975	April Seventh	Stephen Knight	9-13
1976	Otter Way	John King	10-10
1977	Andy Pandy	John Burke	10-12
1978	Strombolus	Tommy Stack	10-0
1979	Diamond Edge	Bill Smith	11-11
1980	Royal Mail	Phillip Blacker	11-5
1981	Diamond Edge	Bill Smith	11-7
1982	Shady Deal	Richard Rowe	10-0
1983	Drumlargan	Mr Frank Codd	10-10
1984	Special Cargo	Kevin Mooney	11-2
1985	By the Way	Robert Earnshaw	10-0
1986	Plundering	Simon Sherwood	10-6
1987	Lean Ar Aghaidh	Guy Landau	9-10
1988	Desert Orchid	Simon Sherwood	11-11
1989	Brown Windsor	Mark Bowlby	10-0
1990	Mr Frisk	Mr Marcus Armytage	10-5
1991	Docklands Express	Anthony Tory	10-3
1992	Topsham Bay	Hywel Davies	10-0
1993	Topsham Bay	Richard Dunwoody	10-0
1994	Ushers Island	Charlie Swan	10-0
1995	Cache Fleur	Richard Dunwoody	9-10
1996	Life of a Lord	Charlie Swan	11-10

| 1997 | Harwell Lad | Mr Rupert Nuttall | 10-0 |
| 1998 | Call it a Day | Adrian Maguire | 10-10 |

Mackeson/Murphy's Gold Cup

Held annually over 2 miles 4 furlongs at Cheltenham since 1960, except for 1976 when it was run at Haydock Park. Its name changed in 1996 to the Murphy's Gold Cup.

Year	Winner	Jockey	Weight (st-lb)
1960	Fortria	Pat Taaffe	12-8
1961	Scottish Memories	Chris Finnegan	10-7
1962	Fortria	Pat Taaffe	12-0
1963	Richard of Bordeaux	Bobby Beasley	10-5
1964	Super Flash	Stan Mellor	10-5
1965	Dunkirk	Bill Rees	12-7
1966	Pawnbroker	Paddy Broderick	11-9
1967	Charlie Worcester	Josh Gifford	10-11
1968	Jupiter Boy	Eddie Harty	10-3
1969	Gay Trip	Terry Biddlecombe	11-5
1970	Chatham	Ken White	10-3
1971	Gay Trip	Terry Biddlecombe	11-3
1972	Red Candle	Jim Fox	10-0
1973	Skymas	Tommy Murphy	10-5
1974	Bruslie	Andy Turnell	10-7
1975	Clear Cut	Dennis Greaves	10-9
1976	Cancello	Dennis Atkins	11-1
1977	Bachelor's Hall	Martin O'Halloran	10-6
1978	Bawnogues	Craig Smith	10-7
1979	Man Alive	Ron Barry	10-9
1980	Bright Highway	Gerry Newman	11-1
1981	Henry Kissinger	Paul Barton	10-13
1982	Fifty Dollars More	Richard Linley	11-0
1983	Pounentes	Neale Doughty	10-6
1984	Half Free	Richard Linley	11-10
1985	Half Free	Richard Linley	11-10
1986	Very Promising	Richard Dunwoody	11-13
1987	Beau Ranger	Mark Perrett	10-2
1988	Pegwell Bay	Peter Scudamore	11-2
1989	Joint Sovereignty	Graham McCourt	10-4
1990	Multum in Parvo	Norman Williamson	10-2
1991	Another Coral	Richard Dunwoody	10-0
1992	Tipping Tim	Carl Llewellyn	10-10
1993	Bradbury Star	Declan Murphy	11-8
1994	Bradbury Star	Philip Hide	12-0
1995	Dublin Flyer	Brendan Powell	11-8
1996	Challenger Du Lac	Richard Dunwoody	10-2
1997	Swnor El Betrutti	Jamie Osborne	10-0

Hennessy Cognac Gold Cup (England)

Run at Newbury over 3 miles 2 furlongs 82 yards. Inaugurated in 1957, and run at Cheltenham 1957-9.

Year	Winner	Jockey	Weight (st-lb)
1957	Mandarin	Gerry Madden	11-0
1958	Taxidermist	John Lawrence	11-1
1959	Kerstin	Stan Hayhurst	11-10

1960	Knucklecracker	Derek Ancil	11-1
1961	Mandarin	Willie Robinson	11-5
1962	Springbok	Gerry Scott	10-8
1963	Mill House	Willie Robinson	12-0
1964	Arkle	Pat Taaffe	12-7
1965	Arkle	Pat Taaffe	12-7
1966	Stalbridge Colonist	Stan Mellor	10-2
1967	Rondetto	Jeff King	10-1
1968	Man of the West	Willie Robinson	10-0
1969	Spanish Steps	John Cooke	11-6
1970	Border Mask	David Mould	11-1
1971	Bighorn	David Cartwright	10-11
1972	Charlie Potheen	Richard Pitman	11-4
1973	Red Candle	Jim Fox	10-4
1974	Royal Marshall II	Graham Thorner	10-0
1975	April Seventh	Andy Turnell	11-2
1976	Zeta's Son	Ian Watkinson	10-9
1977	Bachelor's Hall	Martin O'Halloran	10-10
1978	Approaching	Bob Champion	10-6
1979	Fighting Fit	Richard Linley	11-7
1980	Bright Highway	Gerry Newman	11-6
1981	Diamond Edge	Bill Smith	11-10
1982	Bregawn	Graham Bradley	11-10
1983	Brown Chamberlin	John Francome	11-8
1984	Burrough Hill Lad	John Francome	12-0
1985	Galway Blaze	Mark Dwyer	10-0
1986	Broadheath	Paul Nicholls	10-5
1987	Playschool	Paul Nicholls	10-8
1988	Strands of Gold	Peter Scudamore	10-0
1989	Ghofar	Hywel Davies	10-0
1990	Arctic Call	Jamie Osborne	11-0
1991	Chatam	Peter Scudamore	10-6
1992	Sibton Abbey	Adrian Maguire	10-0
1993	Cogent	Dan Fortt	10-8
1994	One Man	Tony Dobbin	10-0
1995	Couldn't be Better	Dean Gallagher	10-8
1996	Coome Hill	Jamie Osborne	10-0
1997	Suny Bay	Graham Bradley	11-8

King George VI Chase

This traditional Boxing Day fixture over 3 miles at Kempton Park, first run in 1947, brings together a small, but quality field of steeplechasers. Not held due to bad weather in 1961-2, 1967-8, 1970, 1981 and 1995.

Year	Winner	Jockey	Weight (st-lb)
1947	Rowland Roy	Bryan Marshall	11-13
1948	Cottage Rake	Aubrey Brabazon	12-6
1949	Finnure	Dick Francis	11-10
1950	Manicou	Bryan Marshall	11-8
1951	Statecraft	Anthony Grantham	11-11
1952	Halloween	Fred Winter	11-13
1953	Galloway Braes	Robert Morrow	12-6
1954	Halloween	Fred Winter	12-10
1955	Limber Hill	James Power	11-13
1956	Rose Park	Michael Scudamore	11-7

1957	Mandarin	Gerry Madden	12-0
1958	Lochroe	Arthur Freeman	11-7
1959	Mandarin	Gerry Madden	11-5
1960	Saffron Tartan	Fred Winter	11-7
1963	Mill House	Willie Robinson	12-0
1964	Frenchman's Cove	Stan Mellor	11-7
1965	Arkle	Pat Taaffe	12-0
1966	Dormant	John King	11-0
1969	Titus Oates	Stan Mellor	11-10
1971	The Dikler	Barry Brogan	11-7
1972	Pendil	Richard Pitman	12-0
1972	Pendil	Richard Pitman	12-0
1974	Captain Christy	Bobby Coonan	12-0
1975	Captain Christy	Gerry Newman	12-0
1976	Royal Marshall	Graham Thorner	11-7
1977	Bachelor's Hall	Martin O'Halloran	11-7
1978	Gay Spartan	Tommy Carmody	11-10
1979	Silver Buck	Tommy Carmody	11-10
1980	Silver Buck	Tommy Carmody	11-10
1982	Wayward Lad	John Francome	11-10
1983	Wayward Lad	Robert Earnshaw	11-10
1984	Burrough Hill Lad	John Francome	11-10
1985	Wayward Lad	Graham Bradley	11-10
1986	Desert Orchid	Colin Brown	11-10
1987	Nupsala	Andre Pommier	11-10
1988	Desert Orchid	Simon Sherwood	11-10
1989	Desert Orchid	Richard Dunwoody	11-10
1990	Desert Orchid	Richard Dunwoody	11-10
1991	The Fellow	Adam Kondrat	11-10
1992	The Fellow	Adam Kondrat	11-10
1993	Barton Bank	Adrian Maguire	11-10
1994	Algan	Philippe Chevalier	11-10
1995*	One Man	Richard Dunwoody	11-10
1996	One Man	Richard Dunwoody	11-10
1997	See More Business	Andrew Thornton	11-10

* Actually run at Sandown Park January 1996.

Hennessy Cognac Gold Cup (Ireland)

Ireland's richest steeplechase, first run at Leopardstown in 1987 over 3 miles. Originally the Vincent O'Brien Irish Gold Cup.

1987	Forgive 'N' Forget	Mark Dwyer
1988	Playschool	Paul Nicholls
1989	Carvill's Hill	Ken Morgan
1990	Nick the Brief	Michael Lynch
1991	Nick the Brief	Robert Supple
1992	Carvill's Hill	Peter Scudamore
1993-4	Jodami	Mark Dwyer
1996*	Imperial Call	Conor O'Dwyer
1997	Danoli	Tommy Treacy
1998	Dorans Pride	Richard Dunwoody

* January.

Champion Jockeys (National Hunt)

Prior to the 1925/6 season the championship was decided by winners in a calendar year. Since then it has been based on the most winners over the season.

Leading jockeys since 1944/5:

Year	Champion	Winners
1944/5	Frenchie Nicholson	15
	Fred Rimell	15
1945/6	Fred Rimell	54
1946/7	Jack Dowdeswell	58
1947/8	Bryan Marshall	66
1948/9	Tim Molony	60
1949/50	Tim Molony	95
1950/1	Tim Molony	83
1951/2	Tim Molony	99
1952/3	Fred Winter	121
1953/4	Dick Francis	76
1954/5	Tim Molony	67
1955/6	Fred Winter	74
1956/7	Fred Winter	80
1957/8	Fred Winter	82
1958/9	Tim Brookshaw	83
1959/60	Stan Mellor	68
1960/1	Stan Mellor	118
1961/2	Stan Mellor	80
1962/3	Josh Gifford	70
1963/4	Josh Gifford	94
1964/5	Terry Biddlecombe	114
1965/6	Terry Biddlecombe	102
1966/7	Josh Gifford	122
1967/8	Josh Gifford	82
1968/9	Terry Biddlecombe	77
	Bob Davies	77
1969/70	Bob Davies	91
1970/1	Graham Thorner	74
1971/2	Bob Davies	89
1972/3	Ron Barry	125
1973/4	Ron Barry	94
1974/5	Tommy Stack	82
1975/6	John Francome	96
1976/7	Tommy Stack	97
1977/8	Jonjo O'Neill	149
1978/9	John Francome	95
1979/80	Jonjo O'Neill	115
1980/1	John Francome	105
1981/2	John Francome	120
	Peter Scudamore	120
1982/3	John Francome	106
1983/4	John Francome	131
1984/5	John Francome	101
1985/6	Peter Scudamore	91
1986/7	Peter Scudamore	123
1987/8	Peter Scudamore	132
1988/9	Peter Scudamore	221
1989/90	Peter Scudamore	170
1990/1	Peter Scudamore	141
1991/2	Peter Scudamore	175
1992/3	Richard Dunwoody	173
1993/4	Richard Dunwoody	198
1994/5	Richard Dunwoody	160
1995/6	Tony McCoy	175
1996/7	Tony McCoy	190
1997/8	Tony McCoy	222+

Most times champion (since 1900): 8 Scudamore (inc. one shared); 7 Gerry Wilson 1932/3-1937/8, 1940/1, Francome; 6 Tich Mason 1901-2, 1904-7; 5 Bilbie Rees 1920-1, 1924-5, 1926/7; Billy Stott 1927/8-1931/2, Tim Moloney

Progressive record of most wins in a season/year (since 1900)

1900	Mr H S Sidney	53
1901	Tich Mason	58
1902	Tich Mason	67
1905	Tich Mason	73
1911	Bill Payne	76
1912	Ivor Anthony	78
1922	Jack Anthony	78
1924	Bilbie Rees	108
1952/3	Fred Winter	121
1966/7	Josh Gifford	122
1972/3	Ron Barry	125
1977/8	Jonjo O'Neill	149
1988/9	Peter Scudamore	221
1997/8	Tony McCoy	222+

Most wins in a National Hunt career

Jockey	Wins	Years
Peter Scudamore	1680	1978-95
Richard Dunwoody	1479	1983-97
John Francome	1138	1970-85
Stan Mellor	1035	1952-72
Fred Winter	923	1939-64
Bob Davies	911	1966-82
Terry Biddlecombe	908	1958-74
Jonjo O'Neill	885	1972-86
Steve Smith-Eccles	866	1974-95
Ron Barry	823	1961-83

USA

Triple Crown

In common with the English Classics, the three races that make up the American Triple Crown – the Kentucky Derby, the Preakness Stakes and the Belmont Stakes – are for 3-year-olds only.

Kentucky Derby

Raced annually on the first Saturday in May at Churchill Downs, Louisville over 1 mile 2 furlongs. First run in 1875, and at a distance of 1 mile 4 furlongs 1879-95.

Winners since 1970:

Year	Winnner	Jockey
1970	Dust Commander	Mike Manganello
1971	Canonero	Gustavo Avila
1972	Riva Ridge	Ron Turcotte
1973	Secretariat	Ron Turcotte
1974	Cannonade	Angel Cordero, Jr
1975	Foolish Pleasure	Jacinto Vasquez
1976	Bold Forbes	Angel Cordero, Jr
1977	Seattle Slew	Jean Cruguet
1978	Affirmed	Steve Cauthen
1979	Spectacular Bid	Ron Franklin
1980	Genuine Risk★	Jacinto Vasquez
1981	Pleasant Colony	Jorge Velasquez
1982	Gato Del Sol	Eddie Delahoussaye
1983	Sunny's Halo	Eddie Delahoussaye
1984	Swale	Laffit Pincay, Jr
1985	Spend a Buck	Angel Cordero, Jr
1986	Ferdinand	Billie Shoemaker
1987	Alysheba	Chris McCarron
1988	Winning Colors★	Gary Stevens
1989	Sunday Silence	Pat Valenzuela
1990	Unbridled	Craig Perret
1991	Strike the Gold	Chris Antley
1992	Lil E Tee	Pat Day
1993	Sea Hero	Jerry Bailey
1994	Go for Gin	Chris McCarron
1995	Thunder Gulch	Gary Stevens
1996	Grindstone	Jerry Bailey
1997	Silver Charm	Gary Stevens
1998	Real Quiet	Kent Desormeaux

★ Fillies.

Most wins – jockey: 5 Eddie Arcaro 1938, 1941, 1945, 1948, 1952; Bill Hartack 1957, 1960, 1962, 1964, 1969

Most wins – trainer: 6 Ben Jones 1938, 1941, 1944, 1948-9, 1952

Most wins – owner: 8 Calumet Farm 1941, 1944, 1948-9, 1952, 1957-8, 1968

Fastest time: 1 min 59.4 sec Secretariat 1973

Preakness Stakes

Raced at Pimlico, Baltimore, Maryland over 1 mile 1.5 furlongs (1 mile 4 furlongs 1873-88, and at distances between 1 mile 70 yards and 1 mile 2 furlongs 1889-1925).

Winners since 1970:

1970	Personality	Eddie Belmonte
1971	Canonero	Gustavo Avila
1972	Bee Bee Bee	Eddie Nelson
1973	Secretariat	Ron Turcotte
1974	Little Current	Miguel Rivera
1975	Master Derby	Darrell McHargue
1976	Elocutionist	John Lively
1977	Seattle Slew	Jean Cruguet
1978	Affirmed	Steve Cauthen
1979	Spectacular Bid	Ron Franklin
1980	Codex	Angel Cordero, Jr
1981	Pleasant Colony	Jorge Velasquez
1982	Aloma's Ruler	Jack Kaenel
1983	Deputed Testamony	Don Miller, Jr
1984	Gate Dancer	Angel Cordero, Jr
1985	Tank's Prospect	Pat Day
1986	Snow Chief	Alex Solis
1987	Alysheba	Chris McCarron
1988	Risen Star	Eddie Delahoussaye
1989	Sunday Silence	Pat Valenzuela
1990	Summer Squall	Pat Day
1991	Hansel	Jerry Bailey
1992	Pine Bluff	Chris McCarron
1993	Prairie Bayou	Mike Smith
1994	Tabasco Cat	Pat Day
1995	Timber Country	Pat Day
1996	Louis Quatorze	Pat Day
1997	Silver Charm	Gary Stevens
1998	Real Quiet	Kent Desormeaux

Most wins – jockey: 6 Eddie Arcaro 1941, 1948, 1950-1, 1955, 1957

Most wins – trainer: 7 Robert Wyndham Walden 1875, 1878-82, 1888

Most wins – owner: 5 George Lorillard 1878-82

Fastest time: 1 min 53.2 sec Tank's Prospect 1985

Belmont Stakes

The oldest of the three Triple Crown races, first run in 1867 at Jerome Park. The race moved to Morris Park in 1889 and to Belmont Park, New York in 1890. Raced at 1 mile 5 furlongs 1867-73, at shorter distances 1890-25, and the current distance of 1 mile 4 furlongs in 1874-89, and from 1926.

Winners since 1970·

1970	Echelon	John Rotz
1971	Pass Catcher	Walter Blum
1972	Riva Ridge	Ron Turcotte
1973	Secretariat	Ron Turcotte
1974	Little Current	Miguel Rivera
1975	Avatar	Billie Shoemaker
1976	Bold Forbes	Angel Cordero, Jr
1977	Seattle Slew	Jean Cruguet
1978	Affirmed	Steve Cauthen
1979	Coastal	Ruben Hernandez
1980	Temperence Hill	Eddie Maple
1981	Summing	George Martens
1982	Conquistador Cielo	Laffit Pincay, Jr
1983	Caveat	Laffit Pincay, Jr
1984	Swale	Laffit Pincay, Jr
1985	Creme Fraiche	Eddie Maple
1986	Danzig Connection	Chris McCarron
1987	Bet Twice	Craig Perrett
1988	Risen Star	Eddie Delahoussaye
1989	Easy Goer	Pat Day
1990	Go and Go	Michael Kinane
1991	Hansel	Jenny Bailey
1992	A P Indy	Eddie Delahoussaye

1993	Colonial Affair	Julie Krone*
1994	Tabasco Cat	Pat Day
1995	Thunder Gulch	Gary Stevens
1996	Editor's Note	Rene Douglas
1997	Touch Gold	Chris McCarron
1998	Victory Gallop	Gary Stevens

* Krone became the first woman jockey to ride the winner of a Triple Crown race.

Most wins – jockey: 6 Jimmy McLaughlin 1882-4, 1886-8; Eddie Arcaro 1941-2, 1945, 1948, 1952, 1955

Most wins – trainer: 8 James Rowe, Sr 1883-4, 1901, 1904, 1907-8, 1910, 1913

Most wins – owner: 5 Dwyer Bros 1883-4, 1886-8; James R Keene 1901, 1904, 1907-8, 1910; William Woodward, Sr (Belair Stud) 1930, 1932, 1935-6, 1939

Fastest time: 2 min 24.0 sec Secretariat 1973 (won by a record 31 lengths)

Horses to win all legs of the Triple Crown

1919 Sir Barton, 1930 Gallant Fox, 1935 Omaha, 1937 War Admiral, 1941 Whirlaway, 1943 Count Fleet, 1946 Assault, 1948 Citation, 1973 Secretariat, 1977 Seattle Slew, 1978 Affirmed

Jockeys to have ridden most Triple Crown winners:

17 Eddie Arcaro; 11 Bill Shoemaker; 9 Bill Hartack, Earl Sande; 8 Jim McLaughlin, Pat Day

Trainers of most Triple Crown winners:

13 Sunny Jim Fitzsimmons; 12 R W Walden; 11 James Rowe, Sr; 10 D Wayne Lukas; 9 Max Hirsch, Ben A Jones

Breeders' Cup

The Breeders' Cup programme was founded in 1984, administered by breeders with the aim of stimulating throughbred racing in North America. The series offers more than $20 million annually, $10 million in the seven races run on the Breeders' Cup Event Day each October/November. The top purse, $3 million, is for the Breeders' Cup Classic ($1.35m to the winning owner). The purse for the Breeders' Cup Turf is $2 million, and the other races are each for $1 million. Various venues in the USA (and Canada 1996) have been used, from the first meeting at Hollywood Park in 1984. Distances shown are those run currently.

Winners:

Breeders' Cup Sprint (6 furlongs)

1984	Ellio	Craig Perret
1985	Precisionist	Chris McCarron
1986	Smile	Jacinto Vasquez
1987	Very Subtle	Pat Valenzuela
1988	Gulch	Angel Cordero
1989	Dancing Spree	Angel Cordero
1990	Safely Kept	Craig Perret
1991	Skeikh Albadou	Pat Eddery
1992	Thirty Slews	Eddie Delahoussaye
1993	Cardmania	Eddie Delahoussaye
1994	Cherokee Run	Mike Smith
1995	Desert Stormer	Kent Desormeaux
1996	Li De Justice	Corey Nakatani
1997	Elmhurst	Corey Nakatani

Breeders' Cup Juvenile Fillies (1 mile 110 yards)

1984	Outstandingly	Walter Guerra
1985	Twilight Ridge	Jorge Velasquez
1986	Brave Raj	Pat Valenzuela
1987	Epitome	Pat Day
1988	Open Mind	Angel Cordero
1989	Go for Wand	Randy Romero
1990	Meadow Star	José Santos
1991	Pleasant Stage	Eddie Delahoussaye
1992	Eliza	Pat Valenzuela
1993	Phone Chatter	Laffit Pincay, Jr
1994	Flanders	Pat Day
1995	My Flag	Jerry Bailey
1996	Storm Song	Craig Perret
1997	Countess Diana	Shane Sellers

Breeders' Cup Distaff (1 mile 1 furlong)

1984	Princess Rooney	Eddie Delahoussaye
1985	Life's Magic	Angel Cordero, Jr
1986	Lady's Secret	Pat Day
1987	Sacahuista	Randy Romero
1988	Personal Ensign	Randy Romero
1989	Bayakoa	Laffit Pincay, Jr
1990	Bayakoa	Laffit Pincay, Jr
1991	Dance Smartly	Pat Day
1992	Paseana	Chris McCarron
1993	Hollywood Wildcat	Eddie Delahoussaye
1994	One Dreamer	Gary Stevens
1995	Inside Information	Mike Smith
1996	Jewel Princess	Corey Nakatani
1997	Ajina	Mike Smith

Breeders' Cup Mile

1984	Royal Heroine	Fernando Toro
1985	Cozzene	Walter Guerra
1986	Last Tycoon	Yves Saint-Martin
1987	Miesque	Freddy Head
1988	Miesque	Freddy Head
1989	Steinlen	José Santos
1990	Royal Academy	Lester Piggott
1991	Opening Verse	Pat Valenzuela
1992	Lure	Mike Smith
1993	Lure	Mike Smith
1994	Barathea	Frankie Dettori
1995	Ridgewood Pearl	John Murtagh
1996	Da Hoss	Gary Stevens
1997	Spinning World	Cash Asmussen

Breeders' Cup Juvenile (1 mile 110 yards)

1984	Chief's Crown	Don MacBeth
1985	Tasso	Laffit Pincay, Jr
1986	Capote	Laffit Pincay, Jr

1987	Success Express	José Santos
1988	Is it True?	Laffit Pincay, Jr
1989	Rhythm	Craig Perret
1990	Fly So Free	José Santos
1991	Arazi	Pat Valenzuela
1992	Gilded Time	Chris McCarron
1993	Brocco	Gary Stevens
1994	Timber Country	Pat Day
1995	Unbridled's Song	Mike Smith
1996	Boston Harbour	Jerry Bailey
1997	Favorite Trick	Pat Day

Breeders' Cup Turf (1 mile 4 furlongs)

1984	Lashkari	Yves Saint-Martin
1985	Pebbles	Pat Eddery
1986	Manila	José Santos
1987	Theatrical	Pat Day
1988	Great Communicator	Ray Sibille
1989	Prized	Eddie Delahoussaye
1990	In the Wings	Gary Stevens
1991	Miss Alleged	Eric Legrix
1992	Fraise	Pat Valenzuela
1993	Kotashaan	Kent Desormeaux
1994	Tikkanen	Mike Smith
1995	Northern Spur	Chris McCarron
1996	Pilsudski	Walter Swinburn
1997	Chief Bearhart	José Santos

Breeders' Cup Classic (1 mile 2 furlongs)

1984	Wild Again	Pat Day
1985	Proud Truth	Jorge Velasquez
1986	Skywalker	Laffit Pincay, Jr
1987	Ferdinand	Billie Shoemaker
1988	Alysheba	Chris McCarron
1989	Sunday Silence	Chris McCarron
1990	Unbridled	Pat Day
1991	Black Tie Affair	Jerry Bailey
1992	A P Indy	Eddie Delahoussaye
1993	Arcangues	Jerry Bailey
1994	Concern	Jerry Bailey
1995	Cigar	Jerry Bailey
1996	Alphabet Soup	Chris McCarron
1997	Skip Away	Mike Smith

Most wins – jockeys: 9 Day; 8 Smith; 7 Pincay, Delahoussaye; 6 Bailey, McCarron, Santos, Valenzuela; 4 Cordero

Most wins – trainer: 13 D.Wayne Lukas; 7 Shug McGaughey

Leading Money-Winners

Annual US leading money-winning horses (from 1946)

Year	Leading horse	Money ($US)
1946	Assault	424,195
1947	Armed	376,325
1948	Citation	709,470
1949	Ponder	321,825

1950	Noor	346,940
1951	Counterpoint	250,525
1952	Crafty Admiral	277,255
1953	Native Dancer	513,425
1954	Determine	328,700
1955	Nashua	752,550
1956	Needles	440,850
1957	Round Table	600,383
1958	Round Table	662,780
1959	Sword Dancer	537,004
1960	Bally Ache	455,045
1961	Carry Back	565,349
1962	Never Bend	402,969
1963	Candy Spots	604,481
1964	Gun Bow	580,100
1965	Buckpasser	568,096
1966	Buckpasser	669,078
1967	Damascus	817,941
1968	Forward Pass	546,674
1969	Arts and Letters	555,604
1970	Personality	444,049
1971	Riva Ridge	503,263
1972	Droll Roll	471,633
1973	Secretariat	860,404
1974	Chris Evert	551,063
1975	Foolish Pleasure	716,278
1976	Forego	491,701
1977	Seattle Slew	641,370
1978	Affirmed	901,541
1979	Spectacular Bid	1,279,334
1980	Temperance Hill	1,130,452
1981	John Henry	1,148,800
1982	Perrault	1,197,400
1983	All Along	2,138,963
1984	Slew O'Gold	2,627,944
1985	Spend A Buck	3,552,704
1986	Snow Chief	1,875,200
1987	Alysheba	2,511,156
1988	Alysheba	3,808,600
1989	Sunday Silence	4,578,454
1990	Unbridled	3,718,149
1991	Dance Smartly	2,876,821
1992	A P Indy	2,622,560
1993	Kotashaan (Fra)	2,619,014
1994	Paradise Creek	2,610,187
1995	Cigar	4,819,800
1996	Cigar	4,230,000
1997	Skip Away	4,089,000

Most won in a year: $4,578,454 by Sunday Silence 1989

Annual US leading money-winning jockeys

1946	Ted Atkinson	$1,036,825
1947	Doug Dodson	1,429,949
1948	Eddie Arcaro	1,686,230
1949	Steve Brooks	1,316,817
1950	Eddie Arcaro	1,410,160

1951	Billie Shoemaker	$1,329,890
1952	Eddie Arcaro	1,859,591
1953	Billie Shoemaker	1,784,187
1954	Billie Shoemaker	1,876,760
1955	Eddie Arcaro	1,864,796
1956	Bill Hartack	2,343,955
1957	Bill Hartack	3,060,501
1958	Billie Shoemaker	2,961,693
1959	Billie Shoemaker	2,843,133
1960	Billie Shoemaker	2,123,961
1961	Billie Shoemaker	2,690,819
1962	Billie Shoemaker	2,916,844
1963	Billie Shoemaker	2,526,925
1964	Billie Shoemaker	2,649,553
1965	Braulio Baeza	2,582,702
1966	Braulio Baeza	2,951,022
1967	Braulio Baeza	3,088,888
1968	Braulio Baeza	2,835,108
1969	Jorge Velasquez	2,542,315
1970	Laffit Pincay, Jr	2,626,526
1971	Laffit Pincay, Jr	3,784,377
1972	Laffit Pincay, Jr	3,225,827
1973	Laffit Pincay, Jr	4,093,492
1974	Laffit Pincay, Jr	4,251,060
1975	Braulio Baeza	3,695,198
1976	Angel Cordero, Jr	4,709,500
1977	Steve Cauthen	6,151,750
1978	Darrel McHargue	6,029,885
1979	Laffit Pincay, Jr	8,913,535
1980	Chris McCarron	7,663,300
1981	Chris McCarron	8,397,604
1982	Angel Cordero, Jr	9,483,590
1983	Angel Cordero, Jr	10,116,697
1984	Chris McCarron	12,045,813
1985	Laffit Pincay	13,353,299
1986	José Santos	11,329,297
1987	José Santos	12,375,433
1988	José Santos	14,877,298
1989	José Santos	13,838,389
1990	Gary Stevens	13,881,198
1991	Chris McCarron	14,441,083
1992	Kent Desormeaux	14,193,006
1993	Mike Smith	14,024,815
1994	Mike Smith	15,979,820
1995	Jerry Bailey	16,311,876
1996	Jerry Bailey	19,465,376
1997	Jerry Bailey	18,238,173

Total career earnings – horses

	$US	Years
Cigar	9,999,815	1993-6
Skip Away	8,300,000	1995-8
Alysheba	6,679,242	1986-8
John Henry	6,597,947	1977-84
Best Pal	5,668,245	1990-6

Total career earnings – jockeys

	$US	Wins	Years
Chris McCarron	203,438,047	6338	1974-96
Laffit Pincay	194,212,231	8497	1966-96
Angel Cordero, Jr	164,561,227	7057	1960-92
Pat Day	174,639,847	6821	1972-96
Eddie Delahoussaye	156,024,892	5709	1970-96
Gary Stevens	144,691,251	4050	1976-96
Jerry Bailey	135,342,143	3888	1972-96
Jorge Velasquez	125,235,150	6778	1965-96
Bill Shoemaker	123,375,524	8833	1949-90
Other jockeys with over 6000 winners:			
David Gall	22,791,959	6997	1957-96
Sandy Hawley	87,052,722	6402	1968-96
Larry Snyder	47,207,289	6388	1953-94
Carl Gambardella	29,389,041	6349	1956-94
Johnny Longden	24,665,800	6032	1926-66

Trainers

Greatest season's earnings: $17,842,358 D Wayne Lukas in 1988 from 318 winners

Greatest career earnings: $178,073,034 D Wayne Lukas 1977-96

Most Wins

Most wins in a year

Wins	Jockey	Year	Rides
598	Kent Desormeaux	1989	2312
546	Chris McCarron	1974	2199
515	Sandy Hawley	1973	1925
487	Steve Cauthen	1977	2075
485	Billie Shoemaker	1953	1683

Most wins in a year: 496 Jack Van Berg 1976
Most wins in a career: 7200 Dale Baird 1962-97
Most wins in stakes races: 746+ D Wayne Lukas

Eclipse Awards

From 1971 the annual polls conducted by the Throughbred Racing Association, the *Daily Racing Form* and the National Turf Writers' Association have been combined to determine the recipients of the Eclipse Awards.

Overall horse of the year

1971	Ack Ack
1972-3	Secretariat
1974-6	Forego
1977	Seattle Slew
1978-9	Affirmed
1980	Spectacular Bid
1981	John Henry
1982	Conquistador Cielo
1983	All Along
1984	John Henry
1985	Spend a Buck
1986	Lady's Secret
1987	Ferdinand

1988	Alysheba		1974	Think Big	Harry White
1989	Sunday Silence		1975	Think Big	Harry White
1990	Criminal Type		1976	Van der Hum	Bobby Skelton
1991	Black Tie Affair		1977	Gold and Black	John Duggan
1992	A P Indy		1978	Arwon	Harry White
1993	Kotashaan		1979	Hyperno	Harry White
1994	Holy Bull		1980	Beldale Ball	John Letts
1995	Cigar		1981	Just a Dash	Peter Cook
1996	Cigar		1982	Gurner's Lane	Mick Dittman
1997	Favorite Trick		1983	Kiwi	Jimmy Cassidi

Most wins in the Throughbred Racing Association poll prior to 1971: 5 Kelso 1960-4; 2 Challedon 1940-1, Whirlaway 1941-2, Native Dancer 1952 (tie), 1954

Other Racing Outside the UK

Australia – Melbourne Cup

The highlight of the racing season in Australia is the Melbourne Cup. Like Royal Ascot it is as much a social occasion as a race-day. Always held on the first Tuesday in November, it was inaugurated in 1861. The race is for 3-year-olds and upwards, and since 1972 has been over 3200 metres of the Flemington race-course in Victoria. Prior to then it was over the Imperial equivalent of 2 miles. Now sponsored by Fosters.

Post-war winners:

Year	Winner	Jockey
1945	Rainbird	Billy Cook
1946	Russia	Darby Munro
1947	Hiraji	Jack Purtell
1948	Rimfire	Ray Neville
1949	Foxzami	Bill Fellows
1950	Comic Court	Pat Glennon
1951	Delta	Neville Sellwood
1952	Dalray	Bill Williamson
1953	Wodalla	Jack Purtell
1954	Rising Fast	Jack Purtell
1955	Toparoa	Neville Sellwood
1956	Evening Peal	George Podmore
1957	Straight Draw	Noel McGrowdie
1958	Baystone	Mel Schumacher
1959	Macdougal	Pat Glennon
1960	Hi Jinx	Bill Smith
1961	Lord Fury	Roy Selkrig
1962	Even Stevens	Les Coles
1963	Gatum Gatum	Jim Johnson
1964	Polo Prince	Ron Taylor
1965	Light Fingers	Roy Higgins
1966	Galilee	John Miller
1967	Red Handed	Roy Higgins
1968	Rain Lover	Jim Johnson
1969	Rain Lover	Jim Johnson
1970	Baghdad Note	Midge Didham
1971	Silver Knight	Bruce Marshall
1972	Piping Lane	John Letts
1973	Gala Supreme	Frank Reys

1984	Black Knight	Peter Cook
1985	What a Nuisance	Pat Hyland
1986	At Talaq	Michael Clarke
1987	Kensei	Larry Olsen
1988	Empire Rose	Tony Allan
1989	Tawrrific	Shane Dye
1990	Kingston Rule	Darren Beadman
1991	Let's Elope	Stephen King
1992	Subzero	Greg Hall
1993	Vintage Crop (Ire)	Michael Kinane
1994	Jeune	Wayne Harris
1995	Doriemus	Damien Oliver
1996	Saintly	Darren Beadman
1997	Might and Power	Jim Cassidy

Most wins – jockey: 4 Bobby Lewis (The Victory 1902, Patrobas 1915, Artilleryman 1919, Trivalve 1927), Harry White

Most wins – trainer: 10 Bart Cummings 1965-7, 1974-5, 1977, 1979, 1990-1, 1996

Most wins – horse: 2 Archer 1861-2, Peter Pan 1932, 1934, Rain Lover 1968-9, Think Big 1974-5

Fastest winning time: 3 min 16.3 sec Kingston Rule 1990

Japan

Japan Cup

The Japan Cup, run each November in Tokyo over 1 mile 4 furlongs, was in the early 1990s the world's richest race.

Winners:

Year	Winner	Jockey
1981	Mairzy Doates	Cash Asmussen
1982	Half Ired	Don Macbeth
1983	Stanerra	Brian Rouse
1984	Katsuragi Ace	Katsuiti Nishiura
1985	Symboli Rudolf	Yukio Okabe
1986	Jupiter Island (UK)	Pat Eddery
1987	Le Glorieux	Alain Lequeux
1988	Pay the Butler (USA)	Chris McCarron
1989	Horlicks	Lance O'Sullivan
1990	Better Loosen Up (Aus)	Michael Clarke
1991	Golden Pheasant (USA)	Gary Stevens
1992	Tokai Teio	Yukio Okabe
1993	Legacy World	Hiroshi Kawachi
1994	Marvellous Crown	Katsumi Minai
1995	Lando (Ger)	Michael Roberts
1996	Singspiel (UK)	Frankie Dettori
1997	Pilsudski (UK)	Michael Kinane

Dubai

Dubai World Cup

When first run, in 1996, this became the world's richest race, worth $4 million, with $2.4 million to the winner. It is run on a dirt course over 1 mile 2 furlongs.

Winners:

Year	Winner	Jockey
1996	Cigar (USA)	Jerry Bailey
1997	Singspiel (UK)	Jerry Bailey
1998	Silver Charm (USA)	Gary Stevens

Hurling

Played at 15-a-side with stick and ball, hurling, the second most popular traditional sport in Ireland, is of great antiquity. It was included in the Tailteann Games (instituted 1829BC). It survived despite a medieval prohibition, being outlawed by the statute of Kilkenny in 1367. The Irish Hurling Union was founded in 1879 and rules were standardized following the formation of the Gaelic Athletic Association in 1884.

All-Ireland Championships

The final of this inter-county event takes place during September each year at Croke Park, Dublin; the winning team receives the Liam McCarthy Cup. Contested annually from 1887, with the exception of the unfinished championship of 1888.

Wins:

27	Cork	1890, 1892-4, 1902-3, 1919, 1926, 1928-9, 1931,1941-4, 1946, 1952-4, 1966, 1970, 1976-8, 1984, 1986, 1990
25	Kilkenny	1904-5, 1907, 1909, 1911-3, 1922, 1932-3, 1935, 1939, 1947, 1957, 1963, 1967, 1969, 1972, 1974-5, 1979, 1982-3, 1992-3
24	Tipperary	1887, 1895-6, 1898-1900, 1906, 1908, 1916, 1925, 1930, 1937, 1945, 1949-51, 1958, 1961-2, 1964-5, 1971, 1989, 1991
7	Limerick	1897, 1918, 1921, 1934, 1936, 1940, 1973
6	Dublin	1889, 1917, 1920, 1924, 1927, 1938
6	Wexford	1910, 1955-6, 1960, 1968, 1996
4	Galway	1923, 1980, 1987-8
3	Offaly	1981, 1985, 1994
3	Clare	1914, 1995, 1997
2	Waterford	1948, 1959
1	Kerry 1891, London Irish 1901, Laois 1915	

Highest team score in a final: Tipperary 41 (4 goals, 29 points) Antrim 18 (3, 9) in 1989
Highest aggregate score in a final: 64 Cork 39 (6, 21) beat Wexford 25 (5, 10) in 1970
Most individual appearances: 10 Christy Ring (Cork and Munster) 1941-54, John Doyle (Tipperary) 1949-65, each with 8 wins; 10 Frank Cummins (Kilkenny) 1969-83, with 7 wins
Highest individual score: 19 (5 goals, 4 points) Michael Ahearne (Cork) 1928; 18 (2 goals, 12 points) Nicholas English (Tipperary) 1989
Highest attendance: 84,856 in 1954

Winners of All-Ireland medals in Gaelic football and hurling

Jack Lynch (Cork) hurling 1941-4, 1946; football 1945
Ray Cummins (Cork) hurling 1971-2, 1977; football 1971, 1973
Jimmy Barry Murphy (Cork) hurling 1976-8, 1983, 1986; football 1973-4
Brian Murphy (Cork) hurling 1978, 1981; football 1973, 1976
Liam Currans (Offaly) hurling 1981; football 1982
Teddy Mccarthy (Cork) hurling and football 1990 (first to do so in the same year)

Ice Hockey

Played by 6-a-side teams with stick and puck. It probably derives from bandy (qv), played on ice-covered pitches; the puck probably arrived in Canada in the 1850s, and the game has for a long time been the major sport in that country. The first rules were drawn up by W F Robertson and R F Smith, students at McGill University, Montreal in 1879. The Ontario Hockey Association was formed in 1887.

Governing bodies: International Ice Hockey Federation (IIHF), Parkring 11, CH-8002 Zürich, Switzerland. Tel: (41) 1 289 8600, Fax: (41) 1 289 8622. President: Dr René Fasel, General Secretary: Jan-Åke Edvinsson. Founded in 1908 by Belgium, Bohemia, England, France and Switzerland. 53 member nations (and 2 associate) in 1998.

National Hockey League (NHL), 1251 Avenue of the Americas 47th Floor, New York, NY 100020-1198, USA. Tel: (1) 212 789 2000. Commissioner: Gary Bettman.

Olympic Games

An Olympic sport from 1920, ice hockey was contested at the summer Games of 1920, but thereafter at the Winter Olympics. A women's event was added in 1998, when the USA won.

Wins:

8	USSR	1956, 1964, 1968, 1972, 1976, 1984, 1988, 1992 (CIS)
6	Canada	1920, 1924, 1928, 1932, 1948, 1952
2	USA	1960, 1980
1	Great Britain 1936, Sweden 1994, Czech Republic 1998	

Most gold medals by an individual: 3 by the USSR players Vitaliy Davidov, Anatoliy Firssov, Viktor Kuzkin and Aleksandr Ragulin 1964-72; also Vladislav Tretyak 1972-84, Andrey Khomutov 1984-92.

Men's World Championships

Held annually from 1930, except for the war years and in 1980. In Olympic years up to 1968 those championships were also recognized as the world championships.

Most wins:

22	USSR	1954, 1956, 1963-71, 1973-5, 1978-9, 1981-3, 1986, 1989-90
21	Canada	1920, 1924, 1928, 1930-2, 1934-5, 1937-9, 1948, 1950-2, 1955, 1958-9, 1961, 1994, 1997
6	Czechoslovakia	1947, 1949, 1972, 1976-7, 1985
6	Sweden	1953, 1957, 1962, 1987, 1991-2, 1998
2	USA	1933, 1960
1	Great Britain 1936, Russia 1993, Finland 1995, Czech Republic 1996	

Highest score in a world championship match: Australia 58 New Zealand 0 at Perth, 14 Mar 1987

Women's World Championships

First held in 1990.

Winners:

4	Canada	1990, 1992, 1994, 1997

World Cup

Men's competition first held in 1996.

Winners:

1	USA	1996

Men's European Championships

Held annually, first in 1910. In recent years held concurrently with World Championships, but not from 1980 in Olympic years. Abandoned after 1991.

Champions:

29	USSR	1954-6, 1958-60, 1963-70, 1973-5, 1978-83, 1985-7, 1989-91
15	Czechoslovakia	Bohemia: 1911-2, 1914 Cs: 1922, 1925, 1929, 1933, 1947-9, 1961, 1971-2, 1976-7
9	Sweden	1921, 1923, 1928, 1932, 1951-3, 1957, 1962
4	Great Britain	1910, 1936-8
4	Switzerland	1926, 1935, 1939, 1950
2	Austria	1927, 1931
2	Germany	1930, 1934
1	Belgium 1913, France 1924	

Women's European Championships

First held 1989.

Winners:

Finland	1989, 1991, 1993, 1995
Sweden	1996

IIHF Canada Cup/World Cup

First held in 1979, the Canada Cup was contested by the world's six best teams. Last held in 1991, it has now been renamed the World Cup. This was first held in 1996, when, with the leading NHL players in the teams, the USA beat Canada 2 matches to 1 in the finals.

Winners:

Canada	1979, 1984, 1987, 1991
USSR	1981
USA	1996

National Hockey League (NHL)

Founded in 1917 in Montreal, succeeding the
National Hockey Association. It is now contested by
26 teams, 6 from Canada and 20 from the USA,
divided into two divisions within two conferences:
Central and Pacific in the Western Conference;
Northeast and Atlantic in the Eastern Conference.
The top teams play off annually for the Stanley Cup,
which was first presented in 1893 by Lord Stanley of
Preston, then Governor-General of Canada. From
1894 it was contested by amateur teams for the
Canadian Championship. From 1910 it became the
award for the winners of the professional league
play-offs, under NHL control from 1918.

There were two contests in 1896 and 1907; in
1919 the series was unfinished due to an influenza
outbreak.

Stanley Cup

(Year given is that of second half of season)

Wins:

24	Montreal Canadiens	1916, 1924, 1930-1, 1944, 1946, 1953, 1956-60, 1965-6, 1968-9, 1971, 1973, 1976-9, 1986, 1993
13	Toronto Maple Leafs	1918 (Toronto Arenas), 1922 (Toronto St Patricks), 1932, 1942, 1945, 1947-9, 1951, 1962-4, 1967
8	Detroit Red Wings	1936-7, 1943, 1950, 1952, 1954-5, 1997
6	Ottawa Senators	1909, 1911, 1920-1, 1923, 1927
5	Boston Bruins	1929, 1939, 1941, 1970, 1972
5	Edmonton Oilers	1984-5, 1987-8, 1990
4	Montreal Victorias	1895, 1896 (Dec), 1897-8
4	Montreal Wanderers	1906-8, 1910
4	New York Islanders	1980-3
4	New York Rangers	1928, 1933, 1940, 1994
3	Montreal AAA	1893-4, 1902
3	Ottawa Silver Seven	1903-5
3	Chicago Black Hawks	1934, 1938, 1961
2	Winnipeg Victorias	1896 (Feb), 1901
2	Québec Bulldogs	1912-3
2	Montreal Maroons	1926, 1935
2	Philadelphia Flyers	1974-5
2	Montreal Shamrocks	1899, 1900
2	Pittsburgh Penguins	1991-2
1	Kenora Thistles 1907 (Jan), Toronto Ontarios 1914, Vancouver Millionaires 1915, Seattle Metropolitans 1917, Victoria Cougars 1925, Calgary Flames 1989, New Jersey Devils 1995, Colorado Avalanche 1996	

Most finals: 32 Montreal Canadiens; 21 Toronto
Maple Leafs; 20 Detroit Red Wings; 17 Boston
Bruins

Conn Smythe Trophy

Awarded annually from 1965 for the most valuable
player in the play-offs.

Winners from 1980:

1980	Bryan Trottier (NY Islanders)
1981	Butch Goring (NY Islanders)
1982	Mike Bossy (NY Islanders)
1983	Billy Smith (NY Islanders)
1984	Mark Messier (Edmonton)
1985	Wayne Gretzky (Edmonton)
1986	Patrick Roy (Montreal)
1987	Ron Hextall (Philadelphia)
1988	Wayne Gretzky (Edmonton)
1989	Al MacInnis (Calgary)
1990	Bill Ranford (Edmonton)
1991-2	Mario Lemieux (Pittsburgh)
1993	Patrick Roy (Montreal)
1994	Brian Leetch (New York)
1995	Claude Lemieux (New Jersey)
1996	Joe Sakic (Colorado)
1997	Mike Vernon (Detroit)

Players to win twice: Bobby Orr (Boston) 1970,
1972, Bernie Parent (Philadelphia) 1974-5,
Gretzky, M Lemieux

NHL scoring leaders (career)

For regular season games, not including play-offs.

Name	Goals	Assists	Pts	Games	Years
Wayne Gretzky	885	1910	2795	1417	1979-98
Gordie Howe	801	1049	1850	1767	1946-71
Marcel Dionne	731	1040	1771	1348	1971-89
Phil Esposito	717	873	1590	1282	1963-81
Mark Messier	575	977	1552	1272	1979-97
Mario Lemieux	613	881	1494	745	1984-97
Stan Mitika	541	926	1467	1394	1958-80
Paul Coffey	381	1063	1444	1211	1980-97
Ron Francis	428	1006	1434	1247	1981-98
Bryan Trottier	524	901	1425	1279	1975-94
Dale Hawerchuk	518	891	1409	1188	1981-97
Steve Yzerman	563	846	1409	1098	1983-98
Jari Kurri	596	780	1376	1181	1980-97
John Bucyk	556	813	1369	1540	1955-78
Ray Bourque	362	1001	1363	1290	1979-97
Guy Lafleur	560	793	1353	1126	1971-92
Denis Savard	473	865	1338	1196	1980-97

Other players with more than 600 goals:

Mike Gartner	696	612	1308	1372	1979-97
Bobby Hull	610	560	1170	1063	1957-80

NHL scoring records (season)

Goals: 92 Wayne Gretzky (Edmonton Oilers) 1981/2

Assists: 163 Wayne Gretzky (Edmonton Oilers)
1985/6

Points: 215 Wayne Gretzky (Edmonton Oilers)
1985/6

NHL points: 132 Montreal Canadiens 1976/7
(80 games, won 60, lost 8, tied 12)

Team goals: 446 Edmonton Oilers 1983/4
Team assists: 737 Edmonton Oilers 1985/6
Team points: 1182 Edmonton Oilers 1983/4

NHL scoring records (game)

Goals: 7 Joe Malone for Québec Bulldogs v Toronto
St Patrick's, 31 Jan 1920

Assists: 7 Billy Taylor for Detroit Red Wings
v Chicago Black Hawks, 16 Mar 1947, Wayne
Gretzky for Edmonton Oilers v Washington,
15 Feb 1980, Wayne Gretzky for Edmonton Oilers
v Chicago, 11 Dec 1985, Wayne Gretzky for
Edmonton Oilers v Québec, 14 Feb 1986

Points: 10 Darryl Sittler (6 goals 4 assists) for Toronto
Maple Leafs v Boston Bruins, 7 Feb 1976

Play-off game: 8 (3g/5a) Patrik Sundström for New
Jersey Devils v Washington, 22 Apr 1988; 8 (5g/3a)
Mario Lemieux for Pittsburgh v Philadelphia,
25 Apr 1989.

Team goals: 16 Montreal Canadiens beat Québec
Bulldogs 16-3, Québec City, 3 Nov 1920

Team aggregate: 21 Montreal Canadiens beat
Toronto St Patrick's 14-7, Montreal, 10 Jan 1930,
21 Edmonton Oilers beat Chicago Black Hawks
12-9, Chicago 11 Dec 1985

Most play-off points

382	Wayne Gretzky (record 122 goals, 260 assists)
295	Mark Messier (109 G, 186 A)
233	Jari Kurri (106 G, 127 A)
214	Glenn Anderson (93 G, 121 A)
195	Paul Coffey (59 G, 136 A)
184	Bryan Trottier (71 G, 113 A)
176	Jean Béliveau (79G, 97A)
175	Denis Savard (66G, 109A)

Wayne Gretzky

Gretzky has been scoring at a record pace since he
entered the NHL. On 15 Oct 1989 he passed Gordie
Howe's NHL scoring record of 1850 points (taking
10 years to Howe's 26 to reach this figure), and on 23
Mar 1994 Howe's career record of 801 goals. Gretzky's
season-by-season record in regular season games – for
Edmonton Oilers until 1987/8, Los Angeles Kings
1988-96, St Louis Blues 1996, New York Rangers
from 1996 – is phenomenal.

Season	Goals	Assists	Points
1979/80	51	86	137
1980/1	55	109	164
1981/2	92	120	212
1982/3	71	125	196
1983/4	87	118	205
1984/5	73	135	208
1985/6	52	163	215
1986/7	62	121	183
1987/8	40	109	149
1988/9	54	114	168
1989/90	40	102	142
1990/1	41	122	163
1991/2	31	90	121
1992/3	16	49	65
1993/4	38	92	130
1994/5	11	37	48
1995/6	23	79	102
1996/7	25	72	97
1997/8	23	67	90

Hart Trophy

Awarded annually from the 1923/4 season by the
Professional Hockey Writers Association as the Most
Valuable Player award of the NHL. Named after
Cecil Hart, former manager-coach of the Montreal
Canadiens.

Most wins: 9 Wayne Gretzky (Edmonton) 1980-7,
1989; 6 Gordie Howe (Detroit) 1952-3, 1957-8,
1960, 1963; 3 Eddie Shore (Boston) 1933, 1936,
1938, Bobby Orr (Boston) 1970-2, Bobby Clarke
(Philadelphia) 1973, 1975-6, Mario Lemieux
(Pittsburgh) 1988, 1993, 1996

Other winners since 1970: 1974 Phil Esposito
(Boston), 1977-8 Guy Lafleur (Montreal), 1979
Bryan Trottier (NY Islanders), 1990 Mark Messier
(Edmonton), 1991 Brett Hull (St Louis), 1992 Mark
Messier (New York), 1994 Sergey Fedorov (Detroit
Red Wings), 1995 Eric Lindros (Philadelphia), 1997
Dominik Hasek (Buffalo Sabres)

Art Ross Trophy

For the NHL season's leading scorer annually from
1947/8.

Most wins: 10 Wayne Gretzky (Edmonton)
1981-7, 1990-1, 1994; 6 Gordie Howe (Detroit)
1951-4, 1957, 1963, Mario Lemieux (Pittsburgh)
1988-9, 1992-3, 1996-7; 5 Phil Esposito (Boston)
1969, 1971-4; 4 Stan Mikita (Chicago) 1964-5,
1967-8; 3 Bobby Hull (Chicago) 1960, 1962,
1966, Guy Lafleur (Montreal Can) 1976-8

Other winners from 1980: 1970 & 1975 Bobby
Orr (Boston), 1979 Bryan Trottier (NY Islanders),
1980 Marcel Dionne (Los Angeles), 1995 & 1998
Jaromir Jagr (Pittsburgh)

James Norris Memorial Trophy

Awarded annually from the 1953/4 season to the
league's leading defenceman.

Most wins: 8 Bobby Orr (Boston) 1968-75;
7 Doug Harvey (Montreal/NY Rangers) 1955-8,
1960-2; 4 Ray Bourque (Boston) 1987-8, 1990-1;
3 Pierre Pilote (Chicago) 1963-5, Denis Potvin
(NY Islanders) 1976, 1978-9, Paul Coffey
(Edmonton/Detroit) 1985-6, 1995, Chris Chelios
(Montreal/Chicago) 1989, 1993, 1996.

Other winners from 1980: 1980 Larry Robinson
(Montreal), 1981 Randy Carlyle (Pittsburgh),
1982 Doug Wilson (Chicago), 1983-4 Rod
Langway (Washington), 1992 Brian Leetch (New
York), 1994 Ray Bourque (Boston), 1997 Brian
Leetch (New York Rangers)

World Hockey Association

Contested for seven seasons from 1972/3 to 1978/9 as a 12-team rival of the NHL.
Winners:

1973	NE Whalers
1974-5	Houston Aeros
1976	Winnipeg Jets
1977	Québec Nordiques
1978-9	Winnipeg Jets

Adding WHA points to NHL points, leading scorers: 2905 Wayne Gretzky (931 G/1974 A);
2358 Gordie Howe (975/1383); 1808 Bobby Hull (913/895)

Ice Skating

Skating in a primitive form is over 2000 years old, but probably first became popular on frozen canals in the Netherlands some 300 years ago. The Dutch were the main exponents of speed skating over the next 200 years, although the first recorded race was in the Fens, England in 1763. Figure skating originated in Britain and the first known skating club was the Edinburgh Skating Club, formed c.1742. The earliest artificial rink – the surface of which was not of ice – was opened in Baker Street, London, in 1842. The first artificial ice rink was opened at the Glaciarium, London in 1876, three years before the foundation of the National Skating Association of Great Britain.

Ice skating is divided into two disciplines – figure skating, on rinks of 60 x 30m, and speed skating.
International governing body: International Skating Union (ISU), Chemin de Primerose 2, 1007
Lausanne, Switzerland. Tel: (41) 21 612 6666, Fax: (41) 21 612 6677. President: Ottavio Cinquanta,
General Secretary: Fredi Schmid. Founded in 1892.

Figure Skating

(Note that, in pairs and ice dance competitions, the convention is to list the woman's name first.)

Olympic Games

Ice skating was first included at the Olympic Games in 1908 in London, where events were held at Prince's Rink. The sport was included again in 1920 and at all Winter Games from 1924.
Winners:

	Men	**Women**
1908	Ulrich Salchow (Swe)	Madge Syers (née Cave) (UK)
1908	Nikolay Panin (USSR)	
	(special figures competition)	
1920	Gillis Grafström (Swe)	Magda Julin-Mauroy (Swe)
1924	Gillis Grafström (Swe)	Herma Planck-Szabó (Aut)
1928	Gillis Grafström (Swe)	Sonja Henie (Nor)
1932	Karl Schäfer (Aut)	Sonja Henie (Nor)
1936	Karl Schäfer (Aut)	Sonja Henie (Nor)
1948	Richard Button (USA)	Barbara Ann Scott (Can)
1952	Richard Button (USA)	Jeannette Altwegg (UK)
1956	Hayes Alan Jenkins (USA)	Tenley Albright (USA)
1960	David Jenkins (USA)	Carol Heiss (USA)
1964	Manfred Schnelldorfer (FRG)	Sjoukje Dijkstra (Hol)
1968	Wolfgang Schwarz (Aut)	Peggy Fleming (USA)
1972	Ondrej Nepela (Cs)	Beatrix Schuba (Aut)
1976	John Curry (UK)	Dorothy Hamill (USA)
1980	Robin Cousins (UK)	Anett Pötzsch (GDR)
1984	Scott Hamilton (USA)	Katarina Witt (GDR)
1988	Brian Boitano (USA)	Katarina Witt (GDR)
1992	Viktor Petrenko (CIS/Ukr)	Kristi Yamaguchi (USA)
1994	Aleksey Urmanov (Rus)	Oksana Bayul (Ukr)
1998	Ilya Kulik (Rus)	Tara Lipinski (USA)

Pairs

1908	Anna Hübler & Heinrich Burger (Ger)
1920	Ludowika Jakobsson & Walter Jakobsson (Fin)
1924	Helene Engelmann & Alfred Berger (Aut)
1928	Andrée Joly & Pierre Brunet (Fra)
1932	Andrée Brunet (née Joly) & Pierre Brunet (Fra)
1936	Maxi Herber & Ernst Baier (Ger)
1948	Micheline Lannoy & Pierre Baugniet (Bel)
1952	Ria Falk & Paul Falk (FRG)
1956	Elisabeth Schwarz & Kurt Oppelt (Aut)
1960	Barbara Wagner & Robert Paul (Can)
1964	Lyudmila Belousova & Oleg Protopopov (USSR)
1968	Lyudmila Belousova & Oleg Protopopov (USSR)
1972	Irina Rodnina & Aleksey Ulanov (USSR)
1976	Irina Rodnina & Aleksandr Zaitsev (USSR)
1980	Irina Rodnina & Aleksandr Zaitsev (USSR)
1984	Yelena Valova & Oleg Vasilyev (USSR)
1988	Yekaterina Gordeyeva & Sergey Grinkov (USSR)
1992	Natalya Mishkutienok & Artur Dmitriyev (CIS/Rus)
1994	Yekaterina Gordeyeva & Sergey Grinkov (Rus)
1998	Oksana Kazakova & Artur Dmitriyev (Rus)

Ice dance

1976	Lyudmila Pakhomova & Aleksandr Gorshkov (USSR)
1980	Natalya Linichuk & Gennadiy Karponosov (USSR)
1984	Jayne Torvill & Christopher Dean (UK)
1988	Natalya Bestemianova & Andrey Bukin (USSR)
1992	Marina Klimova & Sergey Ponomarenko (CIS)
1994	Oksana Gritschuk & Yevgeniy Platov (Rus)
1998	Oksana Gritschuk & Yevgeniy Platov (Rus)

Olympic medals

Most gold medals: 3 Gillis Grafström, Sonja Henie, Irina Rodnina

Most medals: 4 Gillis Grafström, who also won a silver in 1932.

Oldest gold medallist: 38yr 80d Walter Jakobsson, pairs 1920

Youngest gold medallist: 15yr 128d Maxi Herber, pairs 1936

Best marks: Jayne Torvill and Christopher Dean were awarded a maximum nine sixes for artistic impression, and three sixes for technical merit, in the 1984 ice dancing free dance section

World Championships

Held annually, first in St Petersburg (now Leningrad) in 1896. The 1961 championships were cancelled after all members of the US team were killed in a plane crash.
Winners:

Men

1896	Gilbert Fuchs (Ger)
1897	Gustav Hügel (Aut)
1898	Henning Grenander (Swe)
1899-	
1900	Gustav Hügel (Aut)
1901-5	Ulrich Salchow (Swe)
1906	Gilbert Fuchs (Ger)
1907-11	Ulrich Salchow (Swe)
1912-3	Fritz Kachler (Aut)
1914	Gösta Sandahl (Swe)
1922	Gillis Grafström (Swe)
1923	Fritz Kachler (Aut)
1924	Gillis Grafström (Swe)
1925-8	Willy Böckl (Aut)
1929	Gillis Grafström (Swe)
1930-6	Karl Schäfer (Aut)
1937-8	Felix Kaspar (Aut)
1939	Graham Sharp (UK)
1947	Hans Gerschwiler (Swi)
1948-52	Richard Button (USA)
1953-6	Hayes Alan Jenkins (USA)
1957-9	David Jenkins (USA)
1960	Alain Giletti (Fra)
1962	Donald Jackson (Can)
1963	Donald McPherson (Can)
1964	Manfred Schnelldorfer (FRG)
1965	Alain Calmat (Fra)
1966-8	Emmerich Danzer (Aut)
1969-70	Tim Wood (USA)
1971-3	Ondrej Nepela (Cs)
1974	Jan Hoffmann (GDR)
1975	Sergey Volkov (USSR)
1976	John Curry (UK)
1977	Vladimir Kovalyev (USSR)
1978	Charles Tickner (USA)
1979	Vladimir Kovalyev (USSR)
1980	Jan Hoffmann (GDR)
1981-4	Scott Hamilton (USA)
1985	Aleksandr Fadeyev (USSR)
1986	Brian Boitano (USA)
1987	Brian Orser (Can)
1988	Brian Boitano (USA)
1989-91	Kurt Browning (Can)
1992	Viktor Petrenko (CIS/Ukr)
1993	Kurt Browning (Can)
1994-5	Elvis Stojko (Can)
1996	Todd Eldredge (USA)
1997	Elvis Stojko (Can)
1998	Aleksey Yagudin (Rus)

Most wins: 10 Ulrich Salchow; 7 Karl Schäfer; 5 Richard Button

Women

1906-7	Madge Syers (UK)
1908-11	Lily Kronberger (Hun)
1912-4	Opika von Méray Horvath (Hun)
1922-4	Herma Planck (née Szabó) (Aut)
1925-6	Herma Jaross (formerly Planck-Szabó) (Aut)
1927-36	Sonja Henie (Nor)
1937	Cecilia Colledge (UK)
1938-9	Megan Taylor (UK)
1947-8	Barbara Ann Scott (Can)
1949-50	Alena Vrzánová (Cs)
1951	Jeannette Altwegg (UK)
1952	Jacqueline du Bief (Fra)
1953	Tenley Albright (USA)
1954	Gundi Busch (FRG)
1955	Tenley Albright (USA)
1956-60	Carol Heiss (USA)
1962-4	Sjoukje Dijkstra (Hol)
1965	Petra Burka (Can)
1966-8	Peggy Fleming (USA)
1969-70	Gabriele Seyfert (GDR)
1971-2	Beatrix Schuba (Aut)
1973	Karen Magnussen (Can)
1974	Christine Errath (GDR)
1975	Dianne De Leeuw (Hol)
1976	Dorothy Hamill (USA)
1977	Linda Fratianne (USA)
1978	Anett Pötzsch (GDR)
1979	Linda Fratianne (USA)
1980	Anett Pötzsch (GDR)
1981	Denise Biellmann (Swi)
1982	Elaine Zayak (USA)
1983	Rosalynn Sumners (USA)
1984-5	Katarina Witt (GDR)
1986	Debbie Thomas (USA)
1987-8	Katarina Witt (GDR)
1989	Midori Ito (Jap)
1990	Jill Trenary (USA)
1991-2	Kristi Yamaguchi (USA)
1993	Oksana Bayul (Ukr)
1994	Yuka Sato (Jap)
1995	Lu Chen (Chn)
1996	Michelle Kwan (USA)
1997	Tara Lipinski (USA)
1998	Michelle Kwan (USA)

Most wins: 10 Sonja Henie; 5 Carol Heiss

Pairs

1908	Anna Hübler & Heinrich Burger (Ger)
1909	Phyllis Johnson & James Johnson (UK)
1910	Anna Hübler & Heinrich Burger (Ger)
1911	Ludowika Eilers & Walter Jakobsson (Fin)
1912	Phyllis Johnson & James Johnson (UK)
1913	Helene Engelmann & Karl Mejstrick (Aut)
1914	Ludowika Eilers & Walter Jakobsson (Fin)
1922	Helene Engelmann & Alfred Berger (Aut)
1923	Ludowika Jakobsson (née Eilers) & Walter Jakobsson (Fin)
1924	Helene Engelmann & Alfred Berger (Aut)
1925	Herma Jaross & Ludwig Wrede (Aut)
1926	Andrée Joly & Pierre Brunet (Fra)
1927	Herma Jaross & Ludwig Wrede (Aut)
1928	Andrée Joly & Pierre Brunet (Fra)
1929	Lilly Scholz & Otto Kaiser (Aut)
1930	Andrée Brunet (née Joly) & Pierre Brunet (Fra)
1931	Emilia Rotter & László Szollás (Hun)
1932	Andrée Brunet & Pierre Brunet (Fra)
1933-5	Emilie Rotter & László Szollás(Hun)
1936-9	Maxi Herber & Ernst Baier (Ger)
1947-8	Micheline Lannoy & Pierre Baugniet (Bel)
1949	Andrea Kékesy & Ede Király (Hun)
1950	Karol Kennedy & Peter Kennedy (USA)
1951-2	Ria Falk (née Baran) & Paul Falk (FRG)
1953	Jennifer Nicks & John Nicks (UK)
1954-5	Frances Dafoe & Norris Bowden (Can)
1956	Elisabeth Schwarz & Kurt Oppelt (Aut)
1957-60	Barbara Wagner & Robert Paul (Can)
1962	Maria Jelinek & Otto Jelinek (Can)
1963-4	Marika Kilius & Hans-Jürgen Bäumler (FRG)
1965-8	Lyudmila Belousova & Oleg Protopopov (USSR)
1969-72	Irina Rodnina & Aleksey Ulanov (USSR)
1973-8	Irina Rodnina & Aleksandr Zaitsev (USSR)
1979	Tai Babilonia & Randy Gardner (USA)
1980	Marina Tcherkasova & Sergey Shakrai (USSR)
1981	Irina Vorobyeva & Igor Lissovsky (USSR)
1982	Sabine Baess & Tassilo Thierbach (GDR)
1983	Yelena Valova & Oleg Vasilyev (USSR)
1984	Barbara Underhill & Paul Martini (Can)
1985	Yelena Valova & Oleg Vasilyev (USSR)
1986-7	Yekaterina Gordeyeva & Sergey Grinkov (USSR)
1988	Yelena Valova & Oleg Vasilyev (USSR)
1989-90	Yekaterina Gordeyeva & Sergey Grinkov (USSR)
1991-2	Natalya Mishkutienok & Artur Dmitriyev (CIS/Rus)
1993	Isabelle Braseur & Lloyd Eisler (Can)
1994	Yevgeniya Shishkova & Vadim Naumov (Rus)
1995	Radka Kovács & Rene Novotny (Cze)
1996	Marina Yeltsova & Andrey Bushkov (Rus)
1997	Mandy Wötzel & Ingo Steuer (Ger)
1998	Yelena Berezhnaya & Anton Sikharulidze (Rus)

Most wins: 10 Irina Rodnina; 6 Aleksandr Zaitsev. The only skater to win both singles and pairs world titles in the same year was Herma Jaross (née Stark, then Planck, then Jaross, then Stark) in 1925.

Ice dance

Although the first official world ice dance championships were in 1952, unofficial championships were
staged in 1950 and 1951.

1950	Lois Waring & Michael McGean (USA)
1951	Jean Westwood & Lawrence Demmy (UK)
1952-5	Jean Westwood & Lawrence Demmy (UK)
1956	Pamela Weight & Paul Thomas (UK)
1957-8	June Markham & Courtney Jones (UK)
1959-60	Doreen Denny & Courtney Jones (UK)
1962-5	Eva Románová & Pavel Roman (Cs)
1966-9	Diana Towler & Bernard Ford (UK)
1970-4	Lyudmila Pakhomova & Aleksandr Gorshkov (USSR)
1975	Irina Moiseyeva & Andrey Minenkov (USSR)
1976	Lyudmila Pakhomova & Aleksandr Gorshkov (USSR)
1977	Irina Moiseyeva & Andrey Minenkov (USSR)
1978-9	Natalya Linichuk & Gennadiy Karponosov (USSR)
1980	Krisztina Regoczy & András Sallay (Hun)
1981-4	Jayne Torvill & Christopher Dean (UK)
1985-8	Natalya Bestemianova & Andrey Bukin (USSR)
1989-90	Marina Klimova & Sergey Ponomarenko (USSR)
1991	Isabelle & Paul Duchesnay (Fra)
1992	Marina Klimova & Sergey Ponomarenko (CIS)
1993	Maia Usova & Aleksandr Zhulin (Rus)
1994-7	Oksana Gritschuk & Yevgeniy Platov (Rus)
1998	Anzhelika Krylova & Oleg Ovsyannikov (Rus)

Most wins: 6 Lyudmila Pakhomova & Aleksandr
Gorshkov

Best marks: Jayne Torvill and Christopher Dean
were awarded 29 maximum sixes for ice dancing
at the 1984 World Championships – seven in
the compulsory dances, a perfect set of nine for
artistic impression in both the set pattern and free
dance sections, and a further four for technical
merit in the latter.

Champions Series

First held in 1996, unifying five hitherto indepen-
dent contests into a World Cup-style series. These,
together with the 1996 World and European
Championships, became the first ISU events to
award prize money.

Winners:

	Men	Women
1996	Aleksey Urmanov (Rus)	Michelle Kwan (USA)
1997	Elvis Stojko (Can)	Tara Lipinski (USA)
1998	Ilya Kulik (Rus)	Tara Lipinski (USA)

Pairs

1996	Yevgeniya Shishkova & Vadim Naumov (Rus)
1997	Mandy Wötzel & Ingo Steuer (Ger)
1998	Yelena Berezhnaya & Anton Sikharulidze (Rus)

Ice dance

1996	Oksana Grichuk & Yevgeniy Platov (Rus)
1997	Shae-Lynn Bourne & Victor Kraatz (Can)
1998	Oksana Grichuk & Yevgeniy Platov (Rus)

Speed Skating

A standard outdoor speed skating circuit is 400m, with
two lanes. The speed skaters race in pairs, the lanes
crossing on the straights on either side of the track.
Indoor speed skating is conducted on short tracks, the
standard length being 111.12m, which can be laid out
on a 60 x 30m skating or ice hockey rink.

Olympic Games

Held at each Olympic Games from 1924 (for men)
and 1960 (for women). Women's races were also
staged as demonstration events in 1932.
Winners:

Men

500 metres

1924	Charles Jewtraw (USA) 44.0
1928	Bernt Eversen (Nor) &
	Clas Thunberg (Fin) 43.4
1932	John Shea (USA) 43.4
1936	Ivar Ballangrud (Nor) 43.4
1948	Finn Helgesen (Nor) 43.1
1952	Kenneth Henry (USA) 43.2
1956	Yevgeniy Grishin (USSR) 40.2
1960	Yevgeniy Grishin (USSR) 40.2
1964	Terry McDermott (USA) 40.1
1968	Erhard Keller (FRG) 40.3
1972	Erhard Keller (FRG) 39.44
1976	Yevgeniy Kulikov (USSR) 39.17
1980	Eric Heiden (USA) 38.03
1984	Sergey Fokichev (USSR) 38.19
1988	Uwe-Jens Mey (GDR) 36.45
1992	Uwe-Jens Mey (Ger) 37.14
1994	Aleksandr Golubev (Rus) 36.33
1998	Hiroyasu Shimizu (Jap) 35.76 & 35.59

1000 metres

1976	Peter Mueller (USA) 1:19.32
1980	Eric Heiden (USA) 1:15.18
1984	Gaetan Boucher (Can) 1:15.80
1988	Nikolay Gulyayev (USSR) 1:13.03
1992	Olaf Zinke (Ger) 1:14.85
1994	Dan Jansen (USA) 1:12.43
1998	Ids Postma (Hol) 1:10.64

1500 metres

1924	Clas Thunberg (Fin) 2:20.8
1928	Clas Thunberg (Fin) 2:21.1

1932	John Shea (USA) 2:57.5
1936	Charles Mathiesen (Nor) 2:19.2
1948	Sverre Farstad (Nor) 2:17.6
1952	Hjalmar Andersen (Nor) 2:20.4
1956	Yevgeniy Grischin (USSR) & Yuriy Mikhailov (USSR) 2:08.6
1960	Roald Aas (Nor) & Yevgeniy Grischin (USSR) 2:10.4
1964	Ants Antson (USSR) 2:10.3
1968	Cornelis Verkerk (Hol) 2:03.4
1972	Ard Schenk (Hol) 2:02.96
1976	Jan Egil Storholt (Nor) 1:59.38
1980	Eric Heiden (USA) 1:55.44
1984	Gaetan Boucher (Can) 1:58.36
1988	André Hoffmann (GDR) 1:52.06
1992	Johann Olav Koss (Nor) 1:54.81
1994	Johann Olav Koss (Nor) 1:51.29
1998	Ådne Søndrål (Nor) 1:47.87

5000 metres

1924	Clas Thunberg (Fin) 8:39.0
1928	Ivar Ballangrud (Nor) 8:50.5
1932	Irving Jaffee (USA) 9:40.8
1936	Ivar Ballangrud (Nor) 8:19.6
1948	Reidar Liaklev (Nor) 8:29.4
1952	Hjalmar Andersen (Nor) 8:10.6
1956	Boris Schilkov (USSR) 7:48.7
1960	Viktor Kositschkin (USSR) 7:51.3
1964	Knut Johannesen (Nor) 7:38.4
1968	Anton Maier (Nor) 7.22.4
1972	Ard Schenk (Hol) 7:23.61
1976	Sten Stensen (Nor) 7:24.48
1980	Eric Heiden (USA) 7:02.29
1984	Tomas Gustafsson (Swe) 7:12.28
1988	Tomas Gustafsson (Swe) 6:44.63
1992	Geir Karlstad (Nor) 6:59.97
1994	Johann Olav Koss (Nor) 6:34.96
1998	Gianni Romme (Hol) 6:22.20

10,000 metres

1924	Julius Skutnabb (Fin) 18:04.8
1928	*Event cancelled after five races*
1932	Irving Jaffee (USA) 19:13.6
1936	Ivar Ballangrud (Nor) 17:24.3
1948	Åke Seyffarth (Swe) 17:26.3
1952	Hjalmar Andersen (Nor) 16:45.8
1956	Sigvard Ericsson (Swe) 16:35.9
1960	Knut Johannesen (Nor) 15:46.6
1964	Jonny Nilsson (Swe) 15:50.1
1968	Johnny Höglin (Swe) 15:23.6
1972	Ard Schenk (Hol) 15:01.35
1976	Piet Kleine (Hol) 14:50.59
1980	Eric Heiden (USA) 14:28.13
1984	Igor Malkov (USSR) 14:39.90
1988	Tomas Gustafsson (Swe) 13:48.20
1992	Bart Veldkamp (Hol) 14:12.12
1994	Johann Olav Koss (Nor) 13:30.55
1998	Gianni Romme (Hol) 13:15.33

All-round (aggregate)

1924	Clas Thunberg (Fin)

Women

500 metres

1960	Helga Haase (GDR) 45.9
1964	Lidiya Skoblikova (USSR) 45.0
1968	Lyudmila Titova (USSR) 46.1
1972	Anne Henning (USA) 43.33
1976	Sheila Young (USA) 42.76
1980	Karin Enke (GDR) 41.78
1984	Christa Rothenburger (GDR) 41.02
1988	Bonnie Blair (USA) 39.10
1992	Bonnie Blair (USA) 40.33
1994	Bonnie Blair (USA) 39.25
1998	Catriona LeMay-Doan (Can) 38.39 & 38.21

1000 metres

1960	Klara Guseva (USSR) 1:34.1
1964	Lidiya Skoblikova (USSR) 1:33.2
1968	Carolina Geijssen (Hol) 1:32.6
1972	Monika Pflug (FRG) 1:31.40
1976	Tatyana Averina (USSR) 1:28.43
1980	Natalya Petruseva (USSR) 1:24.10
1984	Karin Enke (GDR) 1:21.61
1988	Christa Rothenburger (GDR) 1:17.65
1992	Bonnie Blair (USA) 1:21.90
1994	Bonnie Blair (USA) 1:18.74
1998	Marianne Timmer (Hol) 1:16.51

1500 metres

1960	Lidiya Skoblikova (USSR) 2:25.2
1964	Lidiya Skoblikova (USSR) 2:22.6
1968	Kaija Mustonen (Fin) 2:22.4
1972	Dianne Holum (USA) 2:20.85
1976	Galina Stepanskaya (USSR) 2:16.58
1980	Annie Borckink (Hol) 2:10.95
1984	Karin Enke (GDR) 2:03.42
1988	Yvonne van Gennip (Hol) 2:00.68
1992	Jacqueline Börner (Ger) 2:05.87
1994	Emese Hunyady (Aut) 2:02.19
1998	Marianne Timmer (Hol) 1:57.58

3000 metres

1960	Lidiya Skoblikova (USSR) 5:14.3
1964	Lidiya Skoblikova (USSR) 5:14.9
1968	Johanna Schut (Hol) 4:56.2
1972	Christina Baas-Kaiser (Hol) 4:52.14
1976	Tatyana Averina (USSR) 4:45.19
1980	Björg Eva Jensen (Nor) 4:32.13
1984	Andrea Schöne (GDR) 4:27.79
1988	Yvonne van Gennip (Hol) 4:11.94
1992	Gunda Niemann (Ger) 4:19.90
1994	Svetlana Bazhanova (Rus) 4:17.43
1998	Gunda Niemann-Stirnemann (Ger) 4:07.29

5000 metres

1988	Yvonne van Gennip (Hol) 7:14.13
1992	Gunda Niemann (Ger) 7:31.57

1994   Claudia Pechstein (Ger) 7:14.37
1998   Claudia Pechstein (Ger) 6:59.61

Most Olympic medals

(G – Gold, S – Silver, B – Bronze)

Men

		G	S	B
7	Clas Thunberg (Nor)	5	1	1
7	Ivar Ballangrud (Nor)	4	2	1
6	Roald Larsen (Nor)	-	2	4
5	Eric Heiden (USA)	5	-	-
5	Yevgeniy Grischin (USSR)	4	1	
5	Johann Olav Koss (Nor)	4	1	-
5	Knut Johannesen (Nor)	2	2	1
5	Rintje Ritsma (Hol)	-	2	3

Women

8	Karin Enke/Kania (GDR)	3	4	1
8	Gunda Niemann-Stirnemann (Ger)	3	4	1
7	Andrea Schöne/Ehrig (GDR)	1	5	1
6	Lidiya Skoblikova (USSR)	6	-	-
6	Bonnie Blair (USA)	5	-	1
5	Claudia Pechstein (Ger)	2	1	2

Eric Heiden, uniquely, won all five gold medals at one Games (1980).

World Championships

Held annually, first at Amsterdam in 1889. Officially recognized by the ISU from 1893.

Champions:

Men – overall

Contested over four distances: 500m, 1000m, 5000m and 10,000m. Titles not awarded 1889–90, 1894, 1902-3, 1906-7.

1891	Joseph Donoghue (USA)
1893	Jaap Eden (Hol)
1895-6	Jaap Eden (Hol)
1897	Jack McCulloch (Can)
1898-9	Peder Østlund (Nor)
1900	Edvard Engelsaas (Nor)
1901	Franz Frederik Wathen (Fin)
1904	Sigurd Mathisen (Nor)
1905	Coen de Koning (Hol)
1908-9	Oscar Mathisen (Nor)
1910-1	Nikolay Strunnikov (Rus)
1912-4	Oscar Mathisen (Nor)
1922	Harald Ström (Nor)
1923	Clas Thunberg (Fin)
1924	Roald Larsen (Nor)
1925	Clas Thunberg (Fin)
1926	Ivar Ballangrud (Nor)
1927	Bernt Evensen (Nor)
1928-9	Clas Thunberg (Fin)
1930	Michael Staksrud (Nor)
1931	Clas Thunberg (Fin)
1932	Ivar Ballangrud (Nor)
1933	Hans Engnestangen (Nor)
1934	Bernt Evensen (Nor)
1935	Michael Staksrud (Nor)
1936	Ivar Ballangrud (Nor)
1937	Michael Staksrud (Nor)
1938	Ivar Ballangrud (Nor)
1939	Birger Wasenius (Fin)
1947	Lauri Parkkinen (Fin)
1948	Odd Lundberg (Nor)
1949	Kornel Pajor (Hun)
1950-2	Hjalmar Andersen (Nor)
1953	Oleg Goncharenko (USSR)
1954	Boris Schilkov (USSR)
1955	Sigvard Ericsson (Swe)
1956	Oleg Goncharenko (USSR)
1957	Knut Johannesen (Nor)
1958	Oleg Goncharenko (USSR)
1959	Juhani Järvinen (Fin)
1960	Boris Stenin (USSR)
1961	Henk van der Grift (Hol)
1962	Viktor Kosichkin (USSR)
1963	Jonny Nilsson (Swe)
1964	Knut Johannesen (Nor)
1965	Per Ivar Moe (Nor)
1966-7	Cornelis Verkerk (Hol)
1968	Anton Maier (Nor)
1969	Dag Fornaess (Nor)
1970-2	Ard Schenk (Hol)
1973	Göran Claesen (Swe)
1974	Sten Stensen (Nor)
1975	Harm Kuipers (Hol)
1976	Piet Kleine (Hol)
1977-9	Eric Heiden (USA)
1980	Hilbert van der Duim (Hol)
1981	Amund Sjøbrend (Nor)
1982	Hilbert van der Duim (Hol)
1983	Rolf Falk-Larssen (Nor)
1984	Oleg Bozyiev (USSR)
1985-6	Hein Vergeer (Hol)
1987	Nikolay Gulyayev (USSR)
1988	Eric Flaim (USA)
1989	Leo Visser (Hol)
1990-1	Johann Olav Koss (Nor)
1992	Roberto Sighel (Ita)
1993	Falko Zandstra (Hol)
1994	Johann Olav Koss (Nor)
1995-6	Rintje Ritsma (Hol)
1997-8	Ids Postma (Hol)

Most wins: 5 Mathisen, Thunberg

Women – overall

Contested over four distances: 500m, 1000m, 1500m and 3000m.

1936	Kit Klein (USA)
1937-8	Laila Schou Nilsen (Nor)
1939	Vernä Lesche (Fin)
1947	Vernä Lesche (Fin)
1948-50	Maria Isakova (USSR)
1951	Eevi Huttunen (Fin)
1952	Lidiya Selikhova (USSR)
1953	Khalida Schegoleyeva (USSR)
1954	Lidiya Selikhova (USSR)
1955	Rimma Zhukova (USSR)

1956	Sofiya Kondakova (USSR)
1957-8	Inga Artamonova (USSR)
1959	Tamara Rylova (USSR)
1960-1	Valentina Stenina (USSR)
1962	Inga Artamonova (USSR)
1963-4	Lidiya Skoblikova (USSR)
1965	Inga Artamonova (USSR)
1966	Valentina Stenina (USSR)
1967-8	Christina Kaiser (Hol)
1969	Lasma Kauniste (USSR)
1970	Atje Keulen-Deelstra (Hol)
1971	Nina Statkevich (USSR)
1972-4	Atje Keulen-Deelstra (Hol)
1975	Karin Kessow (GDR)
1976	Sylvia Burka (Can)
1977	Vera Bryndzey (USSR)
1978	Tatyana Averina (USSR)
1979	Beth Heiden (USA)
1980-1	Natalya Petruseva (USSR)
1982	Karin Enke (then Busch) (GDR)
1983	Andrea Schöne (GDR)
1984	Karin Enke (GDR)
1985	Andrea Schöne (GDR)
1986-8	Karin Kania (née Enke) (GDR)
1989	Constanze Moser (GDR)
1990	Jacqueline Börner (GDR)
1991-3	Gunda Niemann (née Kleeman) (Ger)
1994	Emese Hunyady (Aut)
1995-8	Gunda Niemann (-Stirnemann) (Ger)

Most wins: 7 Niemann; 5 Kania; 4 Artamonova, Keulen-Deelstra

World Sprint Championships

First held in 1970. Both men's and women's championships are contested over two distances: 500m and 1000m.

Champions:

Men – overall

1970	Valeriy Muratov (USSR)
1971	Erhard Keller (FRG)
1972	Leo Linkovesi (Fin)
1973	Valeriy Muratov (USSR)
1974	Per Bjørang (Nor)
1975	Aleksandr Safranov (USSR)
1976	Johan Granath (Swe)
1977-80	Eric Heiden (USA)
1981	Frode Rømming (Nor)
1982	Sergey Khlebnikov (USSR)
1983	Akira Kuroiwa (Jap)
1984	Gaetan Boucher (Can)
1985-6	Igor Zhelezovskiy (USSR)
1987	Akira Kuroiwa (Jap)
1988	Dan Jansen (USA)
1989	Igor Zhelezovskiy (USSR)
1990	Ki Tae-bae (SKo)
1991-3	Igor Zhelezovskiy (USSR/Blr)
1994	Dan Jansen (USA)

1995	Kim Yoon-man (SKo)
1996-7	Sergey Klevchenya (Rus)
1998	Jan Bos (Hol)

Most wins: 6 Zhelezovskiy; 4 Heiden

Women – overall

1970	Lyudmila Titova (USSR)
1971	Ruth Schleiermacher (GDR)
1972	Monika Pflug (FRG)
1973	Sheila Young (USA)
1974	Leah Poulos (USA)
1975-6	Sheila Young (USA)
1977	Sylvia Burka (Can)
1978	Lyubov Sadchikova (USSR)
1979	Leah Muller (née Poulos) (USA)
1980-1	Karin Enke (GDR)
1982	Natalya Petruseva (USSR)
1983-4	Karin Enke (GDR)
1985	Christa Rothenburger (GDR)
1986-7	Karin Kania (née Enke) (GDR)
1988	Christa Rothenburger (GDR)
1989	Bonnie Blair (USA)
1990	Angela Hauck (GDR)
1991	Monique Garbrecht (Ger)
1992-3	Ye Qiaobo (Chn)
1994-5	Bonnie Blair (USA)
1996	Christine Witty (USA)
1997	Franziska Schenk (Ger)
1998	Catriona LeMay-Doan (Can)

Most wins: 6 Kania

World Cup

Contested over a series of events during the winter, annually from the 1985/6 season.

Winners:

Men

500 metres

1986	Dan Jansen (USA)
1987	Nick Thometz (USA)
1988-91	Uwe-Jens Mey (GDR)
1992-4	Dan Jansen (USA)
1995	Hiroyasu Shimizu (Jap)
1996	Manabu Horii (Jap)
1997	Hiroyasu Shimizu (Jap)
1998	Jeremy Wotherspoon (Can)

1000 metres

1986	Dan Jansen (USA)
1987	Nick Thometz (USA)
1988	Dan Jansen (USA)
1989-90	Uwe-Jens Mey (GDR)
1991-3	Igor Zhelezovskiy (USSR/Blr)
1994	Dan Jansen (USA)
1995	Yukinori Miyabe (Jap)
1996	Ådne Søndrål (Nor)
1997	Manabu Horii (Jap)
1998	Jeremy Wotherspoon (Can)

1500 metres

1986	Michael Hadschieff (Aut)
1987	Hans Magnusson (Swe)
1988	André Hoffmann (GDR)
1989	Eric Flaim (USA)
1990-1	Johann Olav Koss (Nor)
1992	Falko Zandstra (Hol)
1993	Rintje Ritsma (Hol)
1994	Falko Zandstra (Hol)
1995	Neal Marshal (Can)
1996	Hiroyaki Noake (Jap)
1997	Rintje Ritsma (Hol)
1998	Ids Postma (Hol)

5000 and 10,000 metres

1986	Dave Silk (USA)
1987	Geir Karlstad (Nor)
1988	Tomas Gustafsson (Swe)
1989	Gerard Kemkers (Hol)
1990	Bart Veldkamp (Hol)
1991	Johann Olav Koss (Nor)
1992	Geir Karlstad (Nor)
1993	Bart Veldkamp (Hol)
1994	Johann Olav Koss (Nor)
1995-7	Rintje Ritsma (Hol)
1998	Gianni Romme (Hol)

Women

500 metres

1986	Christa Rothenburger (GDR)
1987	Bonnie Blair (USA)
1988	Christa Rothenburger (GDR)
1989	Christa Luding (née Rothenburger) (GDR)
1990	Angela Hauck (GDR) and Bonnie Blair (USA)
1991	Kyoko Shimazaki (Jap)
1992	Bonnie Blair (USA)

1993	Ye Qiaobo (Chn)
1994-5	Bonnie Blair (USA)
1996	Svetlana Zhurova (Rus)
1997	Xue Ruihong (Chn)
1998	Catriona LeMay-Doan (Can)

1000 metres

1986	Karin Kania (GDR)
1987	Bonnie Blair (USA)
1988	Christa Rothenburger (GDR)
1989-90	Angela Hauck (GDR)
1991	Monique Garbrecht (Ger)
1992-5	Bonnie Blair (USA)
1996	Christine Witty (USA)
1997	Franziska Schenk (Ger)
1998	Catriona LeMay-Doan (Can)

1500 metres

1986	Annette Carlén (Swe)
1987	Yvonne van Gennip (Hol)
1988	Bonnie Blair (USA)
1989	Constanze Moser (GDR)
1990	Jacqueline Börner (GDR)
1991-3	Gunda Kleeman/Niemann (Ger)
1994	Emese Hunyady (Aut)
1995-8	Gunda Niemann (-Stirnemann) (Ger)

3000 metres (and 5000 metres from 1989)

1986	Andrea Ehrig (GDR)
1987	Yvonne van Gennip (Hol)
1988	Gabi Zange (GDR)
1989	Heike Schalling (GDR)
1990	Gunda Kleeman (GDR)
1991	Heike Warnicke (née Schalling) (Ger)
1992-6	Gunda Niemann (Ger)
1997	Tonny de Jong (Hol)
1998	Gunda Niemann (-Stirnemann) (Ger)

Speed Skating World Records

Men

	min:sec	Name	Venue	Date
500 metres	34.82	Hiroyasu Shimizu (Jap)	Calgary	28 Mar 1998
1000 metres	1:09.60	Sylvain Bouchard (Can)	Calgary	29 Mar 1998
1500 metres	1:46.43	Ådne Søndrål (Nor)	Calgary	28 Mar 1998
3000 metres	3:48.91	Bart Veldkamp (Hol)	Calgary	21 Mar 1998
5000 metres	6:21.49	Gianni Romme (Hol)	Calgary	27 Mar 1998
10,000 metres	13:08.71	Gianni Romme (Hol)	Calgary	29 Mar 1998
Sprint points	141.995	Jeremy Wotherspoon (Can) (500m 35.50, 1000m 1:10.76, 500m 35.77, 1000m 1:10.69)	Calgary	22-23 Nov 1997
Points	153.767	Carl Verheijen (Hol) (500m 38.46, 3000m 3:49.97, 1500m 1:50.93, 5000m 6:40.03)	Calgary	20-21 Mar 1998
Overall points	153.367	Ids Postma (500m 36.48, 5000m 6:33.09, 1500m 1:48.85, 10,000m 13:45.91)	Heerenveen	13-15 Mar 1998

Women

500 metres	37.55	Catriona LeMay Doan (Can)	Calgary	29 Dec 1997
1000 metres	1:14.96	Chris Witty (USA)	Calgary	28 Mar 1998

	min:sec	Name	Venue	Date
1500 metres	1:56.95	Anni Friesinger (Ger)	Calgary	29 Mar 1998
3000 metres	4:01.67	Gunda Niemann-Stiernemann (Ger) (née Kleeman)	Calgary	27 Mar 1998
5000 metres	6:58.63	Gunda Niemann-Stiernemann (Ger)	Calgary	28 Mar 1998
Sprint points	151.690	Catriona LeMay Doan (Can) (500m 37.90, 1000m 1:16.07, 500m 37.90, 1000m 1:15.71)	Calgary	29 Dec 1997
Points	163.315	Marianne Timmer (Hol) (500m 39.30, 1500m 2:00.27, 1000m 1:18.22, 3000m 4:28.89)	Calgary	15-16 Mar 1998
Overall points	163.020	Gunda Niemann-Stiernemann (Ger) (500m 40.57, 3000m 1:58.69, 1500m 4:05.08, 5000m 7:00.41)	Heerenveen	13-15 Mar 1998

Short-Track Speed Skating

Short-track speed skating is held indoors on an oval track of 111.12m circumference, with four to six skaters in a race. Championships are contested over four distances: 500m, 1000m, 1500m and 3000m.

Olympic Games

After being a demonstration sport at the 1988 Olympic Games, short-track racing was added to the Games in 1992, with the programme being expanded in 1994.

Winners:

Men

	500 metres	1000 metres	5000 metres relay
1992	*Not held*	Kim Ki-hoon (SKo) 1:30.76	South Korea 7:14.02
1994	Chae Ji-hoon (SKo) 43.45	Kim Ki-hoon (SKo) 1:34.57	Italy 7:11.74
1998	Takafumi Nishitani (Jap) 42.862	Kim Dong-sung (SKo) 1:32.375	Canada 7:06.075

Women

	500 metres	1000 metres	5000 metres relay
1992	Cathy Turner (USA) 47.04	*Not held*	Canada 4:36.62
1994	Cathy Turner (USA) 45.98	Chun Lee-kyung (SKo) 1:36.87	South Korea 4:26.64
1998	Annie Perreault (Can) 46.568	Chun Lee-kyung (SKo) 1:42.776	South Korea 4:16.260

Most gold medals

Men: 3 Kim Kee-hoon (SKo) 1000m 1992 & 1994, relay 1992
Women: 4 Chun Lee-kyung (SKo) 1000m and relay 1994 & 1998

World Championships

World Championships were held unofficially 1978-80 and officially recognized by the ISU from 1981.

Winners:

Men

1978	Jim Lynch (Aus)
1979	Hiroshi Toda (Jap)
1980	Gaetan Boucher (Can)
1981	Benoit Baril (Can)
1982	Guy Daigneault (Can)
1983	Louis Grenier (Can)
1984	Guy Daigneault (Can)
1985	Toshinobu Kawai (Jap)
1986	Tatsuyoshi Isihara (Jap)
1987	Michel Daignault (Can) & Toshinobu Kawai (Jap)
1988	Paul van der Velde (Hol)
1989	Michel Daignault (Can)
1990	Lee Joon-ho (SKo)
1991	Wilfred O'Reilly (UK)
1992	Kim Ki-hoon (SKo)
1993-4	Marc Gagnon (Can)
1995	Chae Ji-hoon (Sko)
1996	Marc Gagnon (Can)
1997	Kim Dong-sung (SKo)
1998	Kai Feng (Chn)

Women

1978	Sarah Docter (USA)
1979	Sylvie Daigle (Can)
1980	Miyoshi Kato (Jap)
1981	Miyoshi Kato (Jap)
1982	Maryse Perreault (Can)
1983	Sylvie Daigle (Can)
1984	Mariko Kinoshita (Jap)
1985	Eiko Shishii (Jap)
1986	Bonnie Blair (USA)
1987	Eiko Shishii (Jap)
1988-90	Sylvie Daigle (Can)
1991	Nathalie Lambert (Can)
1992	Kim So-hee (SKo)
1993-4	Nathalie Lambert (Can)
1995-7	Chun Lee-kyung (SKo)
1998	Wang Chenlu (Chn)

Most wins: 4 Daigle

World Team Championships

First held in 1991, these are separate from the individual World Championships.
Winners:

Men		**Women**	
South Korea	1992, 1994, 1997	South Korea	1992, 1995-7
Canada	1995-6, 1998	Canada	1991, 1994
Japan	1991	Italy	1993
Italy	1993	China	1998

Short-Track Speed Skating World Records

Men

	min:sec	*Name*	*Venue*	*Date*
500 metres	41.938	Nicola Francheschina (Ita)	Bormio	29 Mar 1998
1000 metres	1:28.230	Marc Gagnon (Can)	Seoul	4 Apr 1997
1500 metres	2:15.50	Kai Feng (Chn)	Groningen	11 Nov 1997
3000 metres	4:53.43	Lee Seug-chan (SKo)	Beijing	23 Nov 1997
5000 metres relay	7:00.042	South Korea	Nagano	30 Mar 1997
		(Kim Sun-tae, Lee Jun-hwan,		
		Kim Dong-sung, Lee Ho-eung)		

Women

500 metres	44.867	Isabelle Charest (Can)	Nagano	29 Mar 1997
1000 metres	1:31.991	Yang Yang (Chn)	Nagano	21 Feb 1998
1500 metres	2:25.17	Kim Yun-mi (SKo)	Harbin	2 Dec 1995
3000 metres	5:02.19	Chun Lee-kyung (SKo)	Gjövik	19 Mar 1995
3000 metres relay	4:16.260	China	Nagano	17 Feb 1998
		(Chun Lee-kyung, Won Hye-kyung,		
		Kim Sun-mi, An Sang-mi)		

Judo

The combat sport of judo developed from Japanese martial arts, especially from several different schools of *ju-jitsu*. Dr Jigoro Kano devised the modern sport from these, and in 1882 founded the Kodokan judo training school at Shitaya. Efficiency classes in judo are divided into pupil (*kyu*) and master (*dan*) grades. The highest possible grade is 12th Dan, awarded only to Jigoro Kano, the only *Shihan* (or 'doctor'). The next highest is the red belt representing 10th Dan, which has been awarded to fifteen men.

Belt colours for Dan grades: 1st-5th Dan – black, 6th-8th Dan – red and white, 9th-11th Dan – red, 12th Dan – white.

The first judo club in Europe was The Budokwai, founded in London in 1918. The first All-Japan Championships were held in 1930, the first European championships in 1951, and the first World Championships in 1956. Competitions are held at various weight limits; note that these changed in 1979 and again in 1998.

International governing body: International Judo Federation (IJF), 21st Fl Doosang Bldg, 101-1 Ulchiro ik1, Chungku, Seoul, Korea. President: Park Yong-sung. Formed in 1951. 175 member nations in 1998.

Olympic Games

When the Olympic Games were held in Tokyo in 1964, judo was added to the Olympic programme, initially at three weight categories. Judo was not included in 1968, but from 1972 has been on the programme at all Games. Women's judo was staged as a demonstration sport at Seoul in 1988 and became a medal sport in 1992.
Winners:

Men

Open		**Over 95kg**		**Over 93kg**	
1964	Anton Geesink (Hol)	1980	Angelo Parisi (Fra)	1964	Isao Inokuma (Jap)
1972	Willem Ruska (Hol)	1984	Hitoshi Saito (Jap)	1972	Willem Ruska (Hol)
1976	Haruki Uemura (Jap)	1988	Hitoshi Saito (Jap)	1976	Sergey Novikov (USSR)
1980	Dietmar Lorenz (GDR)	1992	David Khakkaleichvili		
1984	Yasuhiro Yamashita (Jap)		(CIS/Geo)		
		1996	David Douillet (Fra)		

Under 95kg

1980	Robert Van de Walle (Bel)
1984	Ha Hyoung-zoo (SKo)
1988	Aurelio Miguel (Bra)
1992	Antal Kovács (Hun)
1996	Pawel Nastula (Pol)

Under 93kg

1972	Shota Chochoshvili (USSR)
1976	Kazuhiro Ninomiya (Jap)

Under 86kg

1980	Jürg Röthlisberger (Swi)
1984	Peter Seisenbacher (Aut)
1988	Peter Seisenbacher (Aut)
1992	Waldemar Legien (Pol)
1996	Jeon Ki-young (Kor)

Under 80kg

1964	Isao Okano (Jap)
1972	Shinobu Sekine (Jap)
1976	Isamu Sonoda (Jap)

Under 78kg

1980	Shota Khabareli (USSR)
1984	Frank Wieneke (FRG)
1988	Waldemar Legien (Pol)
1992	Hidehiko Yoshida (Jap)
1996	Djamel Bouras (Fra)

Under 71kg

1980	Ezio Gamba (Ita)
1984	Ahn Byeong-kuen (SKo)
1988	Marc Alexandre (Fra)
1992	Toshihiko Koga (Jap)
1996	Kenzo Nakamura (Jap)

Under 70kg

1964	Takehide Nakatani (Jap)
1972	Toyokazu Nomura (Jap)
1976	Vladimir Nevzorov (USSR)

Under 65kg

1980	Nikolay Solodukhin (USSR)
1984	Yoshiyuki Matsuoka (Jap)
1988	Lee Kyung-keun (SKo)
1992	Rogerio Sampalo (Bra)
1996	Udo Quellmatz (Ger)

Under 63kg

1972	Takao Kawaguchi (Jap)
1976	Héctor Rodriguez (Cub)

Under 60kg

1980	Thierry Rey (Fra)
1984	Shinji Hosokawa (Jap)
1988	Kim Jae-yup (SKo)
1992	Nazim Gusseinov (CIS/Aze)
1996	Tadahiro Nomura (Jap)

Most titles

2 Ruska, Saito, Seisenbacher, Legien

Women

Over 72kg

1988	Angelique Seriese (Hol)
1992	Zhuang Xiaoyan (Chn)
1996	Sun Fuming (Chn)

Under 72kg

1988	Ingrid Berghmans (Hol)
1992	Kim Mi-jung (SKo)
1996	Ulla Werbrouck (Bel)

Under 66kg

1988	Hikari Sasaki (Jap)
1992	Odalis Reve (Cub)
1996	Cho Min-sun (SKo)

Under 61kg

1988	Diane Bell (UK)
1992	Catherine Fleury (Fra)
1996	Yuko Emoto (Jap)

Under 56kg

1988	Suzanne Williams (Aus)
1992	Miriam Blasco (Spa)
1996	Driulis González (Cub)

Under 52kg

1988	Sharon Rendle (UK)
1992	Almudena Munoz (Spa)
1996	Marie-Claire Restoux (Fra)

Under 48kg

1988	Li Zhongyun (Chn)
1992	Cécile Nowak (Fra)
1996	Sun Kye (NKo)

World Championships

World Championships were first held in 1956, and split into weight categories from 1965. Women's World Championships were first held in 1980. Championships are now biennial.

Men

Open

1956	Shokichi Natsui (Jap)
1958	Koji Sone (Jap)
1961	Anton Geesink (Hol)
1965	Isao Inokuma (Jap)
1967	Matsuo Matsunaga (Jap)
1969	Masatoshi Shinomaki (Jap)
1971	Masatoshi Shinomaki (Jap)
1973	Kazuhiro Ninomiya (Jap)
1975	Haruki Uemura (Jap)
1979	Sumio Endo (Jap)
1981	Yasuhiro Yamashita (Jap)
1983	Hitoshi Saito (Jap)
1985	Yoshimi Masaki (Jap)
1987	Naoya Ogawa (Jap)
1989	Naoya Ogawa (Jap)
1991	Naoya Ogawa (Jap)
1993	Rafael Kubacki (Pol)
1995	David Douillet (Fra)
1997	Rafael Kubacki (Pol)

Over 95kg

1979	Yasuhiro Yamashita (Jap)
1981	Yasuhiro Yamashita (Jap)
1983	Yasuhiro Yamashita (Jap)
1985	Cho Yong-chul (SKo)
1987	Grigoriy Vertichev (USSR)
1989	Naoya Ogawa (Jap)
1991	Sergey Kosorotov (USSR)
1993	David Douillet (Fra)
1995	David Douillet (Fra)
1997	David Douillet (Fra)

Over 93kg

1965	Anton Geesink (Hol)
1967	Willem Ruska (Hol)
1969	Shuji Suma (Jap)
1971	Willem Ruska (Hol)
1973	Chonufuhe Tagaki (Jap)
1975	Sumio Endo (Jap)

Under 95kg

1979	Tengiz Khubuluri (USSR)
1981	Tengiz Khubuluri (USSR)
1983	Valeriy Divisenko (USSR)
1985	Hitoshi Sugai (Jap)
1987	Hitoshi Sugai (Jap)
1989	Koba Kurtanidze (USSR)
1991	Stéphane Traineau (Fra)
1993	Antal Kovács (Hun)
1995	Pawel Nastula (Pol)
1997	Pawel Nastula (Pol)

Under 93kg

1967	Nobuyuki Sato (Jap)
1969	Fumio Sasahara (Jap)
1971	Fumio Sasahara (Jap)
1973	Nobuyuki Sato (Jap)
1975	Jean-Luc Rouge (Fra)

Under 86kg

1979	Detlef Ultsch (GDR)
1981	Bernard Tchoullouyan (Fra)
1983	Detlef Ultsch (GDR)
1985	Peter Seisenbacher (Aut)
1987	Fabien Canu (Fra)
1989	Fabien Canu (Fra)
1991	Hirotaka Okada (Jap)
1993	Yoshiro Nakamura (Jap)
1995	Jeon Ki-young (SKo)
1997	Jeon Ki-young (SKo)

Under 80kg

1965	Isao Okano (Jap)
1967	Eiji Maruki (Jap)
1969	Isamu Sonoda (Jap)
1971	Shozo Fujii (Jap)
1973	Shozo Fujii (Jap)
1975	Shozo Fujii (Jap)

Under 78kg

1979	Shozo Fujii (Jap)
1981	Neil Adams (UK)
1983	Nobutoshi Hikage (Jap)
1985	Nobutoshi Hikage (Jap)
1987	Hirotaka Okada (Jap)
1989	Kim Byung-ju (SKo)
1991	Daniel Lascau (Ger)
1993	Chun Ki-young (SKo)
1995	Toshihiko Koga (Jap)
1997	Cho In-chul (SKo)

Under 71kg

1979	Kyoto Katsuki (Jap)
1981	Park Chong-hak (SKo)
1983	Hidetoshi Nakanishi (Jap)
1985	Ahn Byeong-kuen (SKo)
1987	Mike Swain (USA)
1989	Toshihiko Koga (Jap)
1991	Toshihiko Koga (Jap)
1993	Yung Chung-hoon (SKo)
1995	Daisuke Hideshima (Jap)
1997	Kenzo Nakamura (Jap)

Under 70kg

1967	Hiroshi Minatoya (Jap)
1969	Hiroshi Minatoya (Jap)
1971	Hizashi Tsuzawa (Jap)
1973	Kazutoyo Nomura (Jap)
1975	Vladimir Nevzorov (USSR)

Under 65kg

1979	Nikolay Soludukhin (USSR)
1981	Katsuhiko Kashiwazaki (Jap)
1983	Nikolay Soludukhin (USSR)
1985	Yuriy Sokolov (USSR)
1987	Yosuke Yamamoto (Jap)
1989	Drago Becanovic (Yug)
1991	Udo Quellmalz (Ger)
1993	Yukimasa Nakamura (Jap)
1995	Udo Quellmalz (Ger)
1997	Kim Hyuk (SKo)

Under 63kg

1965	Hirofumi Matsuda (Jap)
1967	Takosumi Shigeoka (Jap)
1969	Yoshio Sonoda (Jap)
1971	Takao Kawaguchi (Jap)
1973	Yoshiharu Minami (Jap)
1975	Yoshiharu Minami (Jap)

Under 60kg

1979	Thierry Ray (Fra)
1981	Yasuhiko Moriwaki (Jap)
1983	Khazret Tletseri (USSR)
1985	Shinji Hosokawa (Jap)
1987	Kim Jae-yup (SKo)
1989	Amiran Totikashvili (USSR)

1991	Tadanori Koshino (Jap)
1993	Ryuji Sonoda (Jap)
1995	Nikolay Oyeguin (Rus)
1997	Tadahiro Nomura (Jap)

Most titles
4 Yashiro Yamashita, Shozo Fujii, Naoya Ogawa, David Douillet

Women

Open

1980	Ingrid Berghmans (Bel)
1982	Ingrid Berghmans (Bel)
1984	Ingrid Berghmans (Bel)
1986	Ingrid Berghmans (Bel)
1987	Gao Fengliang (Chn)
1989	Estella Rodriguez (Cub)
1991	Zhuang Xiaoyan (Chn)
1993	Beata Maksymow (Pol)
1995	Monique van der Lee (Hol)
1997	Daina Beltran (Cub)

Over 72kg

1980	Margarita de Cal (Ita)
1982	Natalina Lupino (Fra)
1984	Maria-Teresa Motta (Ita)
1986	Gao Fengliang (Chn)
1987	Gao Fengliang (Chn)
1989	Gao Fengliang (Chn)
1991	Moon Ji-yoon (SKo)
1993	Johanna Hagn (Ger)
1995	Angelique Seriese (Hol)
1997	Christine Cicot (Fra)

Under 72kg

1980	Jocelyne Triadou (Fra)
1982	Barbara Classen (FRG)
1984	Ingrid Berghmans (Bel)
1986	Irene de Kok (Hol)
1987	Irene de Kok (Hol)
1989	Ingrid Berghmans (Bel)
1991	Kim Mi-jung (SKo)
1993	Leng Chunhui (Chn)
1995	Castellano Luna (Cub)
1997	Noriko Anno (Jap)

Under 66kg

1980	Edith Simon (Aut)
1982	Brigitte Deydier (Fra)
1984	Brigitte Deydier (Fra)
1986	Brigitte Deydier (Fra)
1987	Alexandra Schreiber (FRG)
1989	Emanuela Pierantozzi (Ita)
1991	Emanuela Pierantozzi (Ita)
1993	Cho Min-sun (SKo)
1995	Cho Min-sun (SKo)
1997	Kate Howey (UK)

Under 61kg

1980	Anita Staps (Hol)
1982	Martine Rothier (Fra)
1984	Natasha Hernandez (Ven)

1986	Diane Bell (UK)
1987	Diane Bell (UK)
1989	Catherine Fleury (Fra)
1991	Fraucke Eickoff (Ger)
1993	Gella van de Cavaye (Bel)
1995	Jung Sung-sook (SKo)
1997	Séverine Vandenhende (Fra)

Under 56kg

1980	Gerda Winklbauer (Aut)
1982	Béatrice Rodriguez (Fra)
1984	Ann-Maria Burns (USA)
1986	Ann Hughes (UK)
1987	Catherine Arnaud (Fra)
1989	Catherine Arnaud (Fra)
1991	Miriam Blasco (Spa)
1993	Nicola Fairbrother (UK)
1995	Drulys González (Cub)
1997	Isabel Fernández (Spa))

Under 52kg

1980	Edith Hrovat (Aut)
1982	Loretta Doyle (UK)
1984	Kaori Yamaguchi (Jap)
1986	Dominique Brun (Fra)
1987	Sharon Rendle (UK)
1989	Sharon Rendle (UK)
1991	Alessandra Giungi (Ita)
1993	Legna Verdecia (Cub)
1995	Marie-Claire Restoux (Fra)
1997	Marie-Claire Restoux (Fra)

Under 48kg

1980	Jane Bridge (UK)
1982	Karen Briggs (UK)
1984	Karen Briggs (UK)
1986	Karen Briggs (UK)
1987	Li Zhangyun (Chn)
1989	Karen Briggs (UK)
1991	Cécile Nowak (Fra)
1993	Ryoko Tamura (Jap)
1995	Ryoko Tamura (Jap)
1997	Ryoko Tamura (Jap)

Most titles
6 Berghmans; 4 Briggs, Gao Fengliang; 3 Deydier, Tamura

Men's World Cup

A team event, first held in 1994, when the winners were France.

Women's World Cup

A team event, first held in 1997, when the winners were Cuba.

Karate

Karate is a martial art that developed in Japan. Its name originated as recently as the 1930s, but its techniques were devised from the 6th-century Chinese art of Shaolin boxing, *kempo*. This developed around 1500 in Okinawa into 'Tang Hand', whereby the island's inhabitants fought bare-handed against armed Japanese oppressors. Tang Hand was introduced to Japan in the 1920s by Funakoshi Gichin, who adopted the word *karate* for the art, meaning 'empty hand'. The style he practised became known as *Shotokan*, and this is now one of five major styles in Japan, the others being *Wado-ryu*, *Gojo-ryu*, *Shito-ryu* and *Kyokushinkai*. Each places a different emphasis on technique, speed and power.

Karate spread to the Western world from the 1950s, and the All-Japan Karate-do Organization (FAJKO), founded in 1964, staged the first multi-style World Championships in 1970. Following this, the World Union of Karate-do Organizations was created.

International governing body: World Karate Federation (WKF) or Fédération Mondiale de Karaté (FMK), 122 rue de la Tombe, Issoire, 75014 Paris, France. Tel: (33) 1 4395 4200, Fax: (33) 1 4543 8984. President: Jacques Delcourt, Secretary General: George Yerolimpos. Over 160 member federations.

World Championships

First held in Tokyo in 1970, when there were team and individual championships. Women first competed in 1980. *Kumite* championships are now staged at different weight categories and there are also *Kata* (or sequence) events, whereby contestants do not fight each other but are marked for their routines.
Winners:

Men

Team

1970	Japan
1972	France
1975	Great Britain
1977	Netherlands
1980	Spain
1982	Great Britain
1984	Great Britain
1986	Great Britain
1988	Great Britain
1990	Great Britain
1992	Spain
1994	France
1996	France

Kumite – no weight limit

1970	Kouji Wada (Jap)
1972	L.Watanabe-Taske (Bra)
1975	Kazusada Murakami (Jap)
1977	Otti Roethoff (Hol)

Kumite – under 60kg

1980	Ricardo Abad (Spa)
1982	Jukka-Pekka Väyrinen (Fin)
1984	Dirk Betzien (FRG)
1986	Hideto Nakano (Jap)
1988	Abdu Shaher (UK)
1990	Stewin Widar Rönning (Nor)
1992	Veysel Bugur (Tur)
1994	Damien Dovy (Fra)
1996	David Luque (Spa)

Kumite – under 65kg

1980	Toshiaki Maeda (Jap)
1982	Yuichi Suzuki (Jap)
1984	Ramon Malavé (Swe)
1986	Eizou Kondo (Jap)
1988	Tim Stephens (UK)
1990	Toshikatsu Azumi (Jap)
1992	Jesús Juan Rubio (Spa)
1994	Teruchika Ito (Jap)
1996	Mahdi Amouzadeh (Irn)

Kumite – under 70kg

1980	Damian Gonzales (Spa)
1982	Seiji Nishimura (Jap)
1984	Jim Collins (UK)
1986	Thierry Masci (Fra)
1988	Thierry Masci (Fra)
1990	Haldun Alagas (Tur)
1992	Willie Thomas (UK)
1994	Shisua Shiina (Jap)
1996	A Gubachyev (Rus)

Kumite – under 75kg

1980	Sadao Tajima (Jap)
1982	Javier Gomez (Swi)
1984	Toon Stelling (Hol)
1986	Kenneth Leeuwin (Hol)
1988	Kyo Hayashi (Jap)
1990	Hideo Tamaru (Jap)
1992	Wayne Otto (UK)
1994	Daniel Devigli (Aut)
1996	Wayne Otto (UK)

Kumite – under 80kg

1980	Tokey Hill (USA)
1982	Pat McKay (UK)
1984	Pat McKay (UK)
1986	Jacques Tapol (Fra)
1988	Dudley Josepa (Hol)
1990	José Manuel Egea (Spa)
1992	José Manuel Egea (Spa)
1994	David Benetello (Ita)
1996	Gilles Cherdieu (Fra)

Kumite – over 80kg

1980	Jean-Luc Montana (Fra)
1982	Jeff Thompson (UK)
1984	Jerome Atkinson (UK)
1986	Vic Charles (UK)
1988	Emmanuel Pinda (Fra)
1990	Marc Pyrée (Fra)
1992	B Peakall (Aus)
1994	Alain Le Hetet (Fra)
1996	Yasumasa Shimizu (Jpn)

Kumite – open

1980	Ricciardi (Ita)
1982	Hsiao Murase (Jap)
1984	Emmanuel Pinda (Fra)
1986	Karl Daggfeldt (Swe)
1992	Hiroshi Hayashi (Jap)
1994	Manabu Takanouchi (Jap)
1996	P Alderson (UK)

Sanbon shobu

1988	José Manuel Egea (Spa)
1990	Wayne Otto (UK)

Ippon shobu

1988	Claudio Guazzaroni (Ita)
1990	Giovanni Tramontini (Fra)

Individual *Kata*

1977	Keiji Okada (Jap)
1980	Keiji Okada (Jap)
1982	Masashi Koyama (Jap)
1984	Tsuguo Sakumoto (Jap)
1986	Tsuguo Sakumoto (Jap)
1988	Tsuguo Sakumoto (Jap)
1990	Tomojuki Aihara (Jap)
1992	Luis-Maria Sanz (Spa)
1994	Michaël Milon (Fra)
1996	Michaël Milon (Fra)

Team *Kata*

1986	Japan
1988	Japan
1990	Italy
1992	Japan
1994	Japan
1996	Japan

Women

Kumite – under 53kg

1982	Sophie Berger (Fra)
1984	Sophie Berger (Fra)
1986	Johanna Kauri (Fin)
1988	Yuko Hasama (Jap)
1990	Yuko Hasama (Jap)
1992	C Machin (Aus)
1994	Sari Laine (Fin)
1996	Teresia Larsson (Swe)

Kumite – under 60kg

1982	Yukari Yamakawa (Jap)
1984	Tomoko Kinishi (Jap)
1986	Ritva Virelius (Fin)
1988	Akimi Kimura (Jap)
1990	Monique Amghar (Fra)
1992	Mollie Samuels (UK)
1994	Mayumi Baba (Jap)
1996	Jillian Toney (UK)

Kumite – over 60kg

1982	Guus van Mourik (Hol)
1984	Guus van Mourik (Hol)
1986	Guus van Mourik (Hol)
1988	Guus van Mourik (Hol)
1990	Catherine Belrhiti (Fra)
1992	Catherine Belrhiti (Fra)
1994	Sandra Louw (SAf)
1996	Patricia Duggin (UK)

Open

1996	Ivonne Senff (Ant)

Individual *Kata*

1980	Suzuko Okamura (Jap)
1982	Mie Nakayama (Jap)
1984	Mie Nakayama (Jap)
1986	Mie Nakayama (Jap)
1988	Yuki Mimura (Jap)
1990	Yuki Mimura (Jap)
1992	Yuki Mimura (Jap)
1994	Hisami Yokoyama (Jap)
1996	Yuki Mimura (Jap)

Team *Kata*

1986	Taiwan
1988	Japan
1990	Japan
1992	Japan
1994	Japan
1996	Japan

Team Kumite

1994	Spain
1996	Great Britain

Kendo

The Japanese martial art of swordsmanship, which was practised by the warrior class, the samurai. The earliest known reference to such arts in Japan was in 789 AD. Kendo is now practised with *shiani*, or bamboo swords. **International governing body:** International Kendo Federation (IKF), NTT Bldg. 3-2-13, Kudan-Kita, Chiyoda-ku, Tokyo, Japan, Tel: (81) 3 3234 6271, Fax: (81) 3 3234 6007. President: Jiro Kageyama, General Secretary: Hiroshi Onuma.

World Championships

First held in 1970.
Winners:

Men

1970	Mitsuru Kobayashi (Jap)
1973	Tatsushi Sakuragi (Jap)
1976	Eijo Yoko (Jap)
1979	Hironori Yamada (Jap)
1982	Minoru Makita (Jap)
1985	Kunishide Koda (Jap)
1988	Isawu Okido (Jap)
1991	S Muto (Jap)
1994	H Takahashi (Jap)
1997	Masahiro Miyazaki (Jap)

Japan has won the team title at all ten championships.

Women

1994	A Horibe (HK)
1997	Mike Kimura (Jap) (3rd Dan)
	Sumi Takashima (Jap)
	(2nd Dan)

Women's team

1994	South Korea
1997	Japan

Korfball

Korfball is played indoors on a pitch of 40 x 20m (or outdoors up to 60 x 30m) by mixed teams of four men and four women. Related to basketball, handball and netball, Korfball is a passing game, using a ball of 68-71 cm circumference, shooting into a cylindrical basket on a 3.5m high post. Its origins can be traced back to the game developed in 1902 in Amsterdam, Netherlands, by schoolteacher Nico Broekhuysen, who was inspired by a game that he had played in Nääs, Sweden. The sport was demonstrated at the Olympic Games of 1920 and 1928. The sport has grown from an Amsterdam school activity into an international sport.
International governing body: International Korfball Federation, PO Box 1000, 3980 da Bunnik, Netherlands. Tel: (31) 30656 6354, Fax: (31) 30657 0468. President: Bob de Die, Secretary General: Dr Jan Fransoo. Founded in 1933 as the Fédération Internationale de Korfball (FIK) by the Dutch and Belgian Associations. Current name taken in 1982. From just four member nations in 1970, the membership reached 35 in 1998.

World Championships

The first World Championships were held in 1978 to celebrate the 75th anniversary of the founding of the Royal Netherlands Korfball Association (KNKV). Eight nations took part at the first two championships, with 12 subsequently.

Winners:

Netherlands   1978, 1984, 1987, 1995
Belgium   1991

Lacrosse

The name *la crosse*, the French word for a crozier or staff, was given by French settlers in North America to a game played there by Indians. Known by them as 'baggataway', it took place on a very large pitch, some 500m long, and the *crosse* or racket was a staff curved at one end into a rough circle into which a net was fitted. The sport was introduced to Britain in 1867 by a party of Caughnawaga Indians.

The first non-Indian club was the Montreal Lacrosse Club, founded in 1839, and the first national body was the National Lacrosse Association, formed in Canada in 1867. Women were first reported to have played lacrosse in 1886 and the All-England Women's Lacrosse Association was formed in 1912.

The women's game has evolved from the men's game and there are now considerable differences in the rules. Men's lacrosse is played by teams of 10-a-side while the women's is principally 12-a-side, although a major variant is the 6-a-side game.

International governing body: International Federation of Amateur Lacrosse (IFAL). Founded in 1928.

Men's Lacrosse

World Championships

First held in 1967 in Toronto.

Winners:

USA   1967, 1974, 1982, 1986, 1990, 1994, 1998
Canada   1978

The USA also won the pre-Olympic tournament in 1984. Their only loss at this level was 16-17 to Canada in the 1978 final, after extra time to decide the only drawn game at world level.

Olympic Games

Lacrosse was played at two Olympic Games, when the winners were: 1904 Shamrock (Can), 1908 Canada. It was also a demonstration sport in 1928, 1932 and 1948.

Women's Lacrosse

World Championships/World Cup

First held in 1969 as the World Championships, becoming the World Cup in 1982.

Winners:

5   USA   1974, 1982, 1989, 1993, 1997
1   Great Britain 1965, Canada 1978, Australia 1986

Modern Pentathlon

This is the five-sport discipline of cross-country riding, épée fencing, pistol shooting (at 25m), swimming (300m) and cross-country running (4000m). It has been included at every Olympic Games from 1912, and has been known as the 'military pentathlon'. For many years the sport was dominated by members of the armed forces, who were best able to pursue such diverse activities. Military lore explains the origin of the sport: a messenger has to travel across country on horseback, fighting his way through with sword and pistol; he then has to swim across a river, before finishing his journey on foot.

Each event is scored on points, determined either against the other competitors or against scoring tables. Note that the points scores given in the lists of champions are not necessarily comparable. Prior to 1954 the scoring was on the basis of places at each event.

International governing body: L'Union Internationale de Pentathlon Moderne (UIPM), Stade Louis II Entrée E, 13 avenue des Castelans, MC 98000, Monaco. Tel: (377) 9777 8555, Fax: (377) 9777 8550. President: Klaus Schormann, Secretary General: Joël Bouzou. Founded in 1948. 85 member nations in 1998. In 1960, biathlon (cross-country skiing and shooting) joined the Union to form the umbrella organization the UIPMB.

Olympic Games

Held as a five-day event 1912-80, over three to four days 1984-92. At Atlanta 1996 the competition was a one-day event for a group of 32 men who qualified from pre-Olympic events. A women's competition is to be included at the 2000 Olympic Games. *Winners:*

Individual

1912	Gösta Lilliehöök (Swe)	27
1920	Gustaf Dyrssen (Swe)	18
1924	Bo Lindman (Swe)	18
1928	Sven Thofelt (Swe)	47
1932	Johan Oxenstierna (Swe)	32
1936	Gotthard Handrick (Ger)	31.5
1948	Willie Grut (Swe)	16
1952	Lars Hall (Swe)	32
1956	Lars Hall (Swe)	4843
1960	Ferenc Németh (Hun)	5024
1964	Ferenc Török (Hun)	5116
1968	Björn Ferm (Swe)	4964
1972	András Balczó (Hun)	5412
1976	Janusz Pyciak-Peciak (Pol)	5520
1980	Anatoliy Starostin (USSR)	5568
1984	Daniele Masala (Ita)	5469
1988	János Martinek (Hun)	5404
1992	Arkadiusz Skrzypaszek (Pol)	5559
1996	Aleksandr Parygin (Kaz)	5551

Team

(First held 1952, and not in 1996.)

Hungary	1952, 1960, 1968, 1988
USSR	1956, 1964, 1972, 1980
Great Britain	1976
Italy	1984
Poland	1992

Most gold medals: 3 András Balczó (Hun) individual 1972, team 1960 and 1968
Most medals: 7 Pavel Lednev (USSR) individual 2nd 1976, 3rd 1968, 1972, 1980, team 1st 1972, 1980, 2nd 1968
Greatest margin of victory: Probably by Willie Grut in 1948, winning three events and being placed 5th and 8th in the other two. On the present scoring system: 77 points András Balczó in 1972 over Boris Onischenko (USSR). (Four years later Onischenko was disqualified for using an illegal fencing weapon, which registered hits when no contact had occurred.)

Men's World Championships

Held annually from 1949 with the exception of Olympic years.
Winners:

Individual

Year	Name & country	Points
1949	Tage Bjurefelt (Swe)	19
1950	Lars Hall (Swe)	19
1951	Lars Hall (Swe)	22
1953	Gábor Benedek (Hun)	22
1954	Björn Thofelt (Swe)	4634.5
1955	Konstantin Salnikov (USSR)	4453.5
1957	Igor Novikov (USSR)	4769
1958	Igor Novikov (USSR)	4924
1959	Igor Novikov (USSR)	4847
1961	Igor Novikov (USSR)	5217
1962	Eduards Dobnikov (USSR)	4647
1963	András Balczó (Hun)	5267
1965	András Balczó (Hun)	5302
1966	András Balczó (Hun)	5217
1967	András Balczó (Hun)	5056
1969	András Balczó (Hun)	5515
1970	Péter Kelemen (Hun)	5220
1971	Boris Onischenko (USSR)	5206
1973	Pavel Lednev (USSR)	5413
1974	Pavel Lednev (USSR)	5302
1975	Pavel Lednev (USSR)	5056
1977	Janusz Pyciak-Peciak (Pol)	5485
1978	Pavel Lednev (USSR)	5498
1979	Robert Nieman (USA)	5483
1981	Janusz Pyciak-Peciak (Pol)	5662
1982	Daniele Masala (Ita)	5680
1983	Anatoliy Starostin (USSR)	5506
1985	Attila Mizsér (Hun)	5525
1986	Carlo Massullo (Ita)	5463★
1987	Joël Bouzou (Fra)	5462
1989	László Fábián (Hun)	5654
1990	Gianluca Tiberti (Ita)	5441
1991	Arkadiusz Skrzypaszek (Pol)	5498
1993	Richard Phelps (UK)	5755
1994	Dmitriy Svatkovskiy (Rus)	5543
1995	Dmitriy Svatkovskiy (Rus)	5583
1997	Sébastien Deleigne (Fra)	5575

★ The original winner was Anatoliy Starostin (USSR) 5563, but he and 14 others were subsequently disqualified for illegal drugs use. The USSR also lost their women's team title.

Team

14	USSR	1957-9, 1961-2, 1969, 1971, 1973-4, 1982-3, 1985, 1990-1
11	Hungary	1954-5, 1963, 1965-7, 1970, 1975, 1987, 1989, 1997
4	Sweden	1949-51, 1953
3	Poland	1977-8, 1981
2	Italy	1986,1995
1	USA 1979, France 1994	

Relay

First held as a one-day event for three-man teams, in 1989

4	Hungary	1989, 1991, 1993-4
3	Poland	1992, 1995-6
1	USSR 1994, USA 1997	

Most titles: 13 András Balczó (Hun) six individual, seven team including Olympics 1960-72

Women's World Championships

First held in London in 1981.
Winners:

Individual

Year	Name	Points
1981	Anne Ahlgren (Swe)	4975
1982	Wendy Norman (UK)	5311
1983	Lynn Chernobrywy (Can)	5328
1984	Svetlana Yakovleva (USSR)	5481
1985	Barbara Kotowska (Pol)	5336
1986	Irina Kiselyeva (USSR)	5323
1987	Irina Kiselyeva (USSR)	5406
1988	Dorota Idzi (Pol)	5308
1989	Lori Norwood (USA)	5315
1990	Eva Fjellerup (Den)	5478
1991	Eva Fjellerup (Den)	5286
1992	Iwona Kowalewska (Pol)	5491
1993	Eva Fjellerup (Den)	5543
1994	Eva Fjellerup (Den)	5590
1995	Kerstin Danielsson (Swe)	5524
1996	Janna Chubenok Dolgacheva (Blr)	5446
1997	Yelizaveta Suvorova (Rus)	5240

Team

7	Poland	1985, 1988-92, 1995
3	Great Britain	1981-3
2	USSR	1984, 1987
2	Italy	1994, 1997
1	France 1986, Russia 1996	

Team relay

4	Poland	1991, 1992, 1994-5
1	Russia 1993, Italy 1997	

Women's World Cup

This event preceded the world championships.
Winners:

1978	Wendy Skipwith (UK)
1979	Kathy Taylor (UK)
1980	Wendy Norman (UK)

Team winners: Great Britain 1978-80

Motor Cycling

The first recorded motor-cycle race took place on 20 September 1896, when eight competitors took part in a race from Paris to Nantes and back. The course covered 152km (139 miles) and was won by M Chevalier on a Michelin-Dion tricycle in 4hr 10 min 37 sec. The first race for two-wheeled motor cycles was held over 1 mile of an oval track at Sheen House, Richmond, Surrey on 29 Nov, 1897. The race was won by Charles Jarrott, riding a Fournier, in a time of 2 min 8 sec. The Auto-Cycle Union (ACU), founded in 1903, is the governing body of the sport in Britain.

International governing body: Fédération Internationale Motocycliste (FIM), 11 route Suisse, CH-1295, Mies, Switzerland. Tel: (41) 22 950 9500, Fax: (41) 22 950 9501. President: Av. Francesco Zerbi, Chief Executive Officer: Guy Maitre. Formed in 1904 under the title Fédération Internationale des Clubs Motorcyclistes. The FIM had 79 member nations in 1998.

World Championships

World Championships were instituted by the FIM in 1949 for 125, 250, 350 and 500*cc* classes, as well as for sidecars. The 50*cc* class was introduced in 1962 but was discontinued in 1983 to make way for the larger 80*cc* class. In 1977-9 a Formula 750 class was contested. The 350*cc* class was discontinued at the end of the 1982 season.

Winners (and bike manufacturers):

50cc

1962	Ernst Degner (FRG)	Suzuki	1972	Angel Nieto (Spa)	Derbi
1963-4	Hugh Anderson (NZ)	Suzuki	1973	Jan de Vries (Hol)	Kreidler
1965	Ralph Bryans (Ire)	Honda	1974	Henk van Kessel (Hol)	Kreidler
1966-8	Hans-Georg Anscheidt (FRG)	Suzuki	1975	Angel Nieto (Spa)	Kreidler
1969-70	Angel Nieto (Spa)	Derbi	1976-7	Angel Nieto (Spa)	Bultaco
1971	Jan de Vries (Hol)	Kreidler	1978	Ricardo Tormo (Spa)	Bultaco

1979-80	Eugenio Lazzarini (Ita)	Kreidler
1981	Ricardo Tormo (Spa)	Bultaco
1982	Stefan Dörflinger (Swi)	MBA
1983	Stefan Dörflinger (Swi)	Krauser Kreidler

80cc

1984	Stefan Dörflinger (Swi)	Zundapp
1985	Stefan Dörflinger (Swi)	Krauser
1986-8	Jorge Martinez (Spa)	Derbi
1989	Manuel Herreros (Spa)	Derbi

125cc

1949	Nello Pagani (Ita)	Mondial
1950	Bruno Ruffo (Ita)	Mondial
1951	Carlo Ubbiali (Ita)	Mondial
1952	Cecil Sandford (UK)	MV
1953	Werner Haas (FRG)	NSU
1954	Rupert Hollaus (Aut)	NSU
1955-6	Carlo Ubbiali (Ita)	MV
1957	Tarquinio Provini (Ita)	Mondial
1958-60	Carlo Ubbiali (Ita)	MV
1961	Tom Phillis (Aus)	Honda
1962	Luigi Taveri (Swi)	Honda
1963	Hugh Anderson (NZ)	Suzuki
1964	Luigi Taveri (Swi)	Honda
1965	Hugh Anderson (NZ)	Suzuki
1966	Luigi Taveri (Swi)	Honda
1967	Bill Ivy (UK)	Yamaha
1968	Phil Read (UK)	Yamaha
1969	Dave Simmonds (UK)	Kawasaki
1970	Dieter Braun (FRG)	Suzuki
1971-2	Angel Nieto (Spa)	Derbi
1973-4	Kent Andersson (Swe)	Yamaha
1975	Paolo Pileri (Ita)	Morbidelli
1976-7	Pier-Paolo Bianchi (Ita)	Morbidelli
1978	Eugenio Lazzarini (Ita)	MBA
1979	Angel Nieto (Spa)	Morbidelli
1980	Pier-Paolo Bianchi (Ita)	MBA
1981	Angel Nieto (Spa)	Minarelli
1982-4	Angel Nieto (Spa)	Garelli
1985	Fausto Gresini(Ita)	Garelli
1986	Luca Cadalora (Ita)	Garelli
1987	Fausto Gresini (Ita)	Garelli
1988	Jorge Martinez (Spa)	Derbi
1989	Alex Criville (Spa)	Cobas
1990-1	Loris Capirossi (Ita)	Honda
1992	Alessandro Gramigni (Ita)	Aprilia
1993	Dirk Raudies (Ger)	Honda
1994	Kazuto Sakata (Jap)	Aprilia
1995-6	Haruchiko Aoki (Jap)	Honda
1997	Valentino Rossi (Ita)	Honda

250cc

1949	Bruno Ruffo (Ita)	Guzzi
1950	Dario Ambrosini (Ita)	Benelli
1951	Bruno Ruffo (Ita)	Guzzi
1952	Enrico Lorenzetti (Ita)	Guzzi
1953-4	Werner Haas (FRG)	NSU

1955	Herman Müller (FRG)	NSU
1956	Carlo Ubbiali (Ita)	MV
1957	Cecil Sandford (UK)	Mondial
1958	Tarquinio Provini (Ita)	MV
1959-60	Carlo Ubbiali (Ita)	MV
1961	Mike Hailwood (UK)	Honda
1962-3	Jim Redman (Rho)	Honda
1964-5	Phil Read (UK)	Yamaha
1966-7	Mike Hailwood (UK)	Honda
1968	Phil Read (UK)	Yamaha
1969	Kel Caruthers (Aus)	Benelli
1970	Rod Gould (UK)	Yamaha
1971	Phil Read (UK)	Yamaha
1972	Jarno Saarinen (Fin)	Yamaha
1973	Dieter Braun (FRG)	Yamaha
1974-6	Walter Villa (Ita)	Harley-Davidson
1977	Mario Lega (Ita)	Morbidelli
1978-9	Kork Ballington (SAf)	Kawasaki
1980-1	Anton Mang (FRG)	Kawasaki
1982	Jean-Louis Tournadre (Fra)	Yamaha
1983	Carlos Lavado (Ven)	Yamaha
1984	Christian Sarron (Fra)	Yamaha
1985	Freddie Spencer (USA)	Honda
1986	Carlos Lavado (Ven)	Yamaha
1987	Anton Mang (FRG)	Honda
1988-9	Sito Pons (Spa)	Honda
1990	John Kocinski (USA)	Yamaha
1991-2	Luca Cadalora (Ita)	Honda
1993	Tetsuya Harada (Jap)	Yamaha
1994-6	Massimiliano Biaggi (Ita)	Aprilia
1997	Massimiliano Biaggi (Ita)	Honda

350cc

1949	Freddie Frith (UK)	Velocette
1950	Bob Foster (UK)	Velocette
1951-2	Geoff Duke (UK)	Norton
1953-4	Fergus Anderson (UK)	Guzzi
1955-6	Bill Lomas (UK)	Guzzi
1957	Keith Campbell (Aus)	Guzzi
1958-60	John Surtees (UK)	MV
1961	Gary Hocking (Rho)	MV
1962-5	Jim Redman (Rho)	Honda
1966-7	Mike Hailwood (UK)	Honda
1968-73	Giacomo Agostini (Ita)	MV
1974	Giacomo Agostini (Ita)	Yamaha
1975	Johnny Cecotto (Ven)	Yamaha
1976	Walter Villa (Ita)	Harley-Davidson
1977	Takazumi Katayama (Jap)	Yamaha
1978-9	Kork Ballington (SAf)	Kawasaki
1980	Jon Ekerold (SAf)	Yamaha
1981-2	Anton Mang (FRG)	Kawasaki

500cc

1949	Leslie Graham (UK)	AJS
1950	Umberto Masetti (Ita)	Gilera
1951	Geoff Duke (UK)	Norton
1952	Umberto Masetti (Ita)	Gilera
1953-55	Geoff Duke (UK)	Gilera

1956	John Surtees (UK)	MV	1954	Wilhelm Noll (FRG)	BMW
1957	Libero Liberati (Ita)	Gilera	1955	Wilhelm Faust (FRG)	BMW
1958–60	John Surtees (UK)	MV	1956	Wilhelm Noll (FRG)	BMW
1961	Gary Hocking (Rho)	MV	1957	Fritz Hillebrand (FRG)	BMW
1962–65	Mike Hailwood (UK)	MV	1958–9	Walter Schneider (FRG)	BMW
1966–72	Giacomo Agostini (Ita)	MV	1960	Helmut Fath (FRG)	BMW
1973–4	Phil Read (UK)	MV	1961–4	Max Deubel (FRG)	BMW
1975	Giacomo Agostini (Ita)	Yamaha	1965–6	Fritz Scheidegger (Swi)	BMW
1976–7	Barry Sheene (UK)	Suzuki	1967	Klaus Enders (FRG)	BMW
1978–80	Kenny Roberts (USA)	Yamaha	1968	Helmut Fath (FRG)	URS
1981	Marco Lucchinelli (Ita)	Suzuki	1969–70	Klaus Enders (FRG)	BMW
1982	Franco Uncini (Ita)	Suzuki	1971	Horst Owesle (FRG)	Munch
1983	Freddie Spencer (USA)	Honda	1972–3	Klaus Enders (FRG)	BMW
1984	Eddie Lawson (USA)	Yamaha	1974	Klaus Enders (FRG)	Busch BMW
1985	Freddie Spencer (USA)	Honda	1975	Rolf Steinhausen (FRG)	Konig
1986	Eddie Lawson (USA)	Yamaha	1976	Rolf Steinhausen (FRG)	Busch Konig
1987	Wayne Gardner (Aus)	Honda	1977	George O'Dell (UK)	Yamaha
1988	Eddie Lawson (USA)	Yamaha	1978–9	Rolf Biland (Swi)	Yamaha
1989	Eddie Lawson (USA)	Honda	1980	Jock Taylor (UK)	Yamaha
1990–2	Wayne Rainey (USA)	Yamaha	1981	Rolf Biland (Swi)	Yamaha
1993	Kevin Schwantz (USA)	Suzuki	1982	Werner Schwärzel (FRG)	Yamaha
1994–7	Michael Doohan (Aus)	Honda	1983	Rolf Biland (Swi)	Yamaha
			1984–6	Egbert Streuer (Hol)	Yamaha

750cc

			1987–9	Steve Webster (UK)	Yamaha
1977	Steve Baker (USA)	Yamaha	1990	Alain Michel (Fra)	Krauser
1978	Johnny Cecotto (Ven)	Yamaha	1991	Steve Webster (UK)	Krauser
1979	Patrick Pons (Fra)	Yamaha	1992–3	Rolf Biland (Swi)	Krauser

Sidecar

			1994	Rolf Biland (Swi)	Swiss Auto
1949–51	Eric Oliver (UK)	Norton	1995–6	Darren Dixon (UK)	Windle-ADM
1952	Cyril Smith (UK)	Norton	1997	Steve Webster (UK)	LCR-ADM
1953	Eric Oliver (UK)	Norton			

Most titles (solo)

Total	Rider	50cc	80	125	250	350	500	750	F1	Years
15	Giacomo Agostini (Ita)	–	–	–	–	7	8	–	–	1966–75
13	Angel Nieto (Spa)	6	–	7	–	–	–	–	–	1969–84
10	Mike Hailwood (UK)	–	–	–	3	2	4	–	1	1961–78
9	Carlo Ubbiali (Ita)	–	–	6	3	–	–	–	–	1951–60
8	Phil Read (UK)	–	–	1	4	–	2	–	1	1964–77
7	John Surtees (UK)	–	–	–	–	3	4	–	–	1956–60
6	Geoff Duke (UK)	–	–	–	–	2	4	–	–	1951–5
6	Jim Redman (Rho)	–	–	–	2	4	–	–	–	1962–5

Mike Hailwood and Phil Read are the only riders to have won world titles in four classes.

Most titles in each class

50cc   6 Angel Nieto
80cc   3 Jorge Martinez
125cc   7 Angel Nieto; 6 Carlo Ubbiali
250cc   4 Phil Read, Massimiliano Biaggi
350cc   7 Giacomo Agostini; 4 Jim Redman
500cc   8 Giacomo Agostini; 4 Geoff Duke, Mike Hailwood, John Surtees, Eddie Lawson
Sidecar 7 Rolf Biland; 6 Klaus Enders; 4 Max Deubel, Eric Oliver, Steve Webster

Most Grand Prix wins

122   Giacomo Agostini (350cc – 54, 500cc – 68)
90   Angel Nieto (50cc – 27, 80cc – 1, 125cc – 62)
79   Rolf Biland (all sidecar)

76   Mike Hailwood (125cc – 2, 250cc – 21, 350cc – 16, 500cc – 37)
52   Phil Read (125cc – 10, 250cc – 27, 350cc – 4, 500cc – 11)

Hailwood, Read, Jim Redman (Rho) and Charles Mortimer (UK) are the only riders to have won Grands Prix in four different classes.

Most wins at 500cc

68 Agostini; 46 Michael Doohan (Aus); 37 Hailwood; 32 Eddie Lawson (USA); 25 Kevin Schwantz (USA); 24 Wayne Rainey (Aus); 22 Geoff Duke (UK), Kenny Roberts (USA), John Surtees (UK); 20 Freddie Spencer (USA); 19 Barry Sheene (UK); 18 Wayne Gardner (Aus)

Most wins in other classes

50cc	27 Angel Nieto (Spa)
80cc	21 Jorge Martinez (Spa)
125cc	62 Angel Nieto (Spa)
250cc	33 Anton Mang (FRG); 29 Massimiliano Biaggi (Ita)
350cc	54 Giacomo Agostini (Ita)
Sidecar	79 Rolf Biland (Swi)

Fastest race: 1977 Belgian GP at Spa-Francorchamps, won by Barry Sheene (UK) on a 495cc Suzuki at an average speed of 217.37km/h (135.07 mph)

World Manufacturers' Championships

Most wins

40 Honda	50cc:	1965-6
	125cc:	1961-2, 1964, 1966, 1990-1, 1993, 1995-6
	250cc:	1961-3, 1966-7, 1985-9, 1991-2, 1997
	350cc:	1962-7
	500cc:	1966, 1983-5, 1987, 1989, 1994-7
37 MV Augusta	125cc:	1952-3, 1955-6, 1958-60
	250cc:	1955-6, 1958-60
	350cc:	1958-61, 1968-72,
	500cc:	1956, 1958-65, 1967-73
31 Yamaha	125cc:	1967-8, 1973-4
	250cc:	1964-5, 1968, 1970-4, 1977, 1982-4, 1990, 1993
	350cc:	1973-7, 1980
	500cc:	1974-5, 1986, 1988, 1990-2
16 Suzuki	50cc:	1962-4, 1967-8
	125cc:	1963, 1965, 1970
	500cc:	1976-82, 1993

Most wins – sidecar

19 BMW 1955-73

World Endurance Championship

Inaugurated in 1980, replacing the FIM Coupe d'Endurance.

Winners (and bike manufacturers):

1980	Marc Fontan & Hervé Moineau (Fra)	Honda
1981	Jean Lafond & Raymond Roche (Fra)	Kawasaki
1982	Jean-Claude Chemarin (Fra) & Jacques Cornu (Swi)	Kawasaki
1983	Richard Hubin (Bel) & Hervé Moineau (Fra)	Suzuki
1984-5	Gérard Coudray & Patrick Igoa (Fra)	Honda
1986	Patrick Igoa (Fra)	Honda
1987	Hervé Moineau (Fra)	Suzuki
1988	Hervé Moineau (Fra) & Thierry Crine (Fra)	Suzuki
1989-90	Alex Vieira (Fra)	Honda
1991	Alex Vieira (Fra)	Kawasaki
1992	Carl Fogarty & Terry Rymer (UK)	Kawasaki

1990	Eric Geboers (Bel)	Honda
1991-2	Georges Jobé (Bel)	Honda
1993	Jacky Martens (Bel)	Husqvarna
1994	Marcus Hansson (Swe)	Honda
1995	Joel Smets (Bel)	Husaberg
1996	Shayne King (NZ)	KTM
1997	Joel Smets (Bel)	Husaberg

250cc

1962-3	Torsten Hallman (Swe)	Husqvarna
1964	Joël Robert (Bel)	CZ
1965	Viktor Arbekov (USSR)	CZ
1966-7	Torsten Hallman (Swe)	Husqvarna
1968-9	Joël Robert (Bel)	CZ
1970-2	Joël Robert (Bel)	Suzuki
1973	Håkan Andersson (Swe)	Yamaha
1974	Gennadiy Moisseyev (USSR)	KTM
1975	Harry Everts (Bel)	Puch
1976	Heikki Mikkola (Fin)	Husqvarna
1977-8	Gennadiy Moisseyev (USSR)	KTM
1979	Håkan Carlqvist (Swe)	Husqvarna
1980	Georges Jobe (Bel)	Suzuki
1981	Neil Hudson (UK)	Yamaha
1982	Danny la Porte (USA)	Yamaha
1983	Georges Jobé (Bel)	Suzuki
1984-5	Heinz Kinigadner (Aut)	KTM
1986	Jacky Vimond (Fra)	Yamaha
1987	Eric Geboers (Bel)	Honda
1988-9	Jean-Michel Bayle (Fra)	Honda
1990	Alessandro Puzar (Ita)	Suzuki
1991	Trampas Parker (USA)	Honda
1992	Donny Schmit (USA)	Yamaha
1993	Greg Albertyn (SAf)	Honda
1994	Greg Albertyn (SAf)	Suzuki
1995	Stefan Everts (Bel)	Kawasaki
1996-7	Stefan Everts (Bel)	Honda

125cc

1975-7	Gaston Rahier (Bel)	Suzuki
1978	Akira Watanabe (Jap)	Suzuki
1979-81	Harry Everts (Bel)	Suzuki
1982-3	Eric Geboers (Bel)	Suzuki
1984	Michèle Rinaldi (Ita)	Suzuki
1985	Pekka Vehkonen (Fin)	Cagira
1986	Dave Strijbos (Hol)	Cagira
1987-8	John Van Den Berg (Hol)	Yamaha
1989	Trampas Parker (USA)	KTM
1990	Donny Schmit (USA)	Suzuki
1991	Stefan Everts (Bel)	Suzuki
1992	Greg Albertyn (SAf)	Honda
1993	Pedro Tragter (Hol)	Suzuki
1994	Bobby Moore (USA)	Yamaha
1995	Alessandro Puzar (Ita)	Honda
1996	Sébastien Tortelli (Fra)	Kawasaki
1997	Alessandro Chiodi (Ita)	Yamaha

Sidecar

1980	Reinhardt Bohler (FRG)	Yamaha
1981	Tom van Heugten (Hol)	Yamaha Wasp
1982-3	Erik Bollhalder (Swi)	Yamaha
1984-7	Hans Bachtöld (Swi)	EML Jumbo
1988	Christoph Hüsser (Lie)	KTM
1989	Christoph Hüsser (Lie)	KU 71
1990	Benny Janssen (Hol)	EML Honda
1991-2	Eimbert Timmermans (Hol)	Kawasaki
1993-6	Andreas Fuhrer (Swi)	VMC
1997	Kristers Sergis (Lat)	KTM EML

Most world titles: 6 (all 250cc) Joël Robert (Bel) 1964, 1968-72

Moto-Cross des Nations

1947-75 for five-man teams (best three to score). 1976-84 four-man teams, at 500cc. From 1985 the Coupe des Nations, Trophée des Nations, and Moto-Cross des Nations have been merged into one three-class (500, 250 and 125cc) competition.
Wins:

16	Great Britain	1947, 1949-50, 1952-4, 1956-7,1959-60, 1963-7, 1994
14	USA	1981-93, 1996
11	Belgium	1948, 1951, 1969, 1972-3, 1976-7, 1979-80, 1995, 1997
7	Sweden	1955, 1958, 1961-2, 1970-1, 1974
2	USSR	1968, 1978
1	Czechoslovakia	1975

Trophée des Nations

1961-75 for five-man teams (best three to score). From 1976-84 four-man teams, at 250cc. Merged with the above event in 1985. In 1965 there was no result, and the meeting was declared null and void.
Wins:

11	Belgium	1969-78, 1980
5	Sweden	1963-4, 1966-8
4	USA	1981-4
3	Great Britain	1961-2, 1965
1	USSR	1979

Coupe des Nations

At 125cc.
Winners:
Italy 1982, Belgium 1983, Netherlands 1984

Trials

Trials Riding – manipulating the bike around a predetermined course containing many obstacles and natural hazards – has been practised since the early days of motor cycling. The famous Scottish Six Days Trial, based around Edinburgh, was introduced in 1909, and the first International Six Days Trial took place in 1913. A World Championship was introduced in 1975.

World Champions

Winners (and bike manufacturers):

1975	Martin Lampkin (UK)	Bultaco	1988	Thierry Michaud (Fra)	Fantic
1976-8	Yrjö Vesterinen (Fin)	Bultaco	1989-91	Jordi Tarrès (Spa)	Beta
1979	Bernie Schreiber (USA)	Bultaco	1992	Tommi Ahvala (Fin)	Aprilia
1980	Ulf Karlsson (Swe)	Montesa	1993-5	Jordi Tarrès (Spa)	Gas-Gas
1981	Gilles Burgat (Fra)	SWM	1996	Marc Colomer (Spa)	Montesa
1982-4	Eddy Lejeune (Bel)	Honda	1997	Doug Lampkin (UK)	Beta
1985-6	Thierry Michaud (Fra)	Fantic			
1987	Jordi Tarrès (Spa)	Beta			

Most titles: 7 Tarrès; 3 Vesterinen, Lejeune, Michaud

Motor Racing

Following the birth of the motor car in the 19th century, it was inevitable that man would soon start racing. The first race involving motorized vehicles is believed to have been the La Vélocipède race of 31km (19.3 miles) in Paris on 20 April 1887, won by Count Jules Felix Philippe Albert de Dion de Malfiance driving a de Dion steam quadricycle. There is a claim, however, that an earlier race took place in the United States in 1878, from Green Bay to Madison, Wisconsin, won by an Oshkosk steamer. The first 'real' motor car race was on 11-14 June 1895, over 1178km (732 miles) from Paris to Bordeaux and back. Grand Prix racing started with the 1906 French Grand Prix, and the World Drivers' Championship was instituted in 1950.

International goverrning body: Fédération Internationale de l'Automobile (FIA), 8 place de la Concorde, 75008 Paris, France. Tel: (33) 1 4312 4455, Fax: (33) 1 4312 4466. General Secretary: Jacques Sarrut.

Originally founded as the Association Internationale des Automobiles Clubs Reconnus in 1904, changing its name to FIA in 1946. 149 national member motor clubs.

Formula One

World Championship Grand Prix Races

The FIA took a decision in 1949 to inaugurate a World Championship for Drivers in 1950. At the first race, at Silverstone on 13 May 1950, the Italian Giuseppe Farina won the British Grand Prix. A Constructors' Championship was instituted in 1958. From 1950 to 1960 the Indianapolis 500 formed part of the Championship.

The following is a list of winners of all World Championship Grand Prix races, with notes on the origins of the Grand Prix races in pre-World Championhip days. Note that some events are staged annually, but others have been staged irregularly as part of the World Championhip series, which has had 16-17 Formula One races annually in recent years.

Argentine Grand Prix

The inaugural Buenos Aires Grand Prix was run in 1947.

Winners, at Buenos Aires:

1953	Alberto Ascari (Ita)	Ferrari
1954	Juan Manuel Fangio (Arg)	Maserati
1955	Juan Manuel Fangio (Arg)	Mercedes-Benz
1956	Juan Manuel Fangio (Arg)	Ferrari
	& Luigi Musso (Arg) (*shared drive*)	
1957	Juan Manuel Fangio (Arg)	Maserati
1958	Stirling Moss (UK)	Cooper
1960	Bruce McLaren (NZ)	Cooper

1972	Jackie Stewart (UK)	Tyrrell
1973	Emerson Fittipaldi (Bra)	Lotus
1974	Denny Hulme (NZ)	McLaren
1975	Emerson Fittipaldi (Bra)	McLaren
1977	Jody Scheckter (SAf)	Wolf
1978	Mario Andretti (USA)	Lotus
1979	Jacques Laffite (Fra)	Ligier
1980	Alan Jones (Aus)	Williams
1981	Nelson Piquet (Bra)	Brabham
1995-6	Damon Hill (UK)	Williams
1997	Jacques Villeneuve (Can)	Williams
1998	Michael Schumacher (Ger)	Ferrari

Australian Grand Prix

The first Australian Grand Prix was held at Phillip Island, Victoria in 1928.

Winners, at Adelaide 1985-95; at Melbourne 1996-8:

1985	Keke Rosberg (Fin)	Williams
1986	Alain Prost (Fra)	McLaren
1987	Gerhard Berger (Aut)	Ferrari
1988	Alain Prost (Fra)	McLaren
1989	Thierry Boutsen (Fra)	Williams
1990	Nelson Piquet (Bra)	Benetton
1991	Ayrton Senna (Bra)	McLaren
1992	Gerhard Berger (Aut)	McLaren
1993	Ayrton Senna (Bra)	McLaren
1994	Nigel Mansell (UK)	Williams
1995-6	Damon Hill (UK)	Williams
1997	David Coulthard (UK)	McLaren
1998	Mika Hakkinen (Fin)	McLaren

Austrian Grand Prix

Winners, at Zeltweg 1964, 1997-8; at Österreichring 1970-87:

1964	Lorenzo Bandini (Ita)	Ferrari
1970	Jacky Ickx (Bel)	Ferrari
1971	Jo Siffert (Swi)	BRM
1972	Emerson Fittipaldi (Bra)	Lotus
1973	Ronnie Peterson (Swe)	Lotus
1974	Carlos Reutemann (Arg)	Brabham
1975	Vittorio Brambilla (Ita)	March
1976	John Watson (UK)	Penske
1977	Alan Jones (Aus)	Shadow
1978	Ronnie Peterson (Swe)	Lotus
1979	Alan Jones (Aus)	Williams
1980	Jean-Pierre Jabouille (Fra)	Renault
1981	Jacques Laffite (Fra)	Ligier
1982	Elio de Angelis (Ita)	Lotus
1983	Alain Prost (Fra)	Renault
1984	Niki Lauda (Aut)	McLaren
1985-6	Alain Prost (Fra)	McLaren
1987	Nigel Mansell (UK)	Williams
1997	Jacques Villeneuve (Can)	Williams
1998	Mika Hakkinen (Fin)	McLaren

Belgian Grand Prix

The Belgian GP was first raced in 1925.
Winners, at Spa-Francorchamps 1950-6, 1958, 1960-8, 1970, 1983, 1985-98; at Nivelles 1972, 1974; at Zolder 1973, 1975-82, 1984:

1950	Juan Manuel Fangio (Arg)	Alfa-Romeo
1951	Giuseppe Farina (Ita)	Alfa-Romeo
1952-3	Alberto Ascari (Ita)	Ferrari
1954	Juan Manuel Fangio (Arg)	Maserati
1955	Juan Manuel Fangio (Arg)	Mercedes-Benz
1956	Peter Collins (UK)	Ferrari
1958	Tony Brooks (UK)	Vanwall
1960	Jack Brabham (Aus)	Cooper
1961	Phil Hill (USA)	Ferrari
1962-5	Jim Clark (UK)	Lotus
1966	John Surtees (UK)	Ferrari
1967	Dan Gurney (USA)	Eagle
1968	Bruce McLaren (NZ)	McLaren
1970	Pedro Rodriguez (Mex)	BRM
1972	Emerson Fittipaldi (Bra)	Lotus
1973	Jackie Stewart (UK)	Tyrrell
1974	Emerson Fittipaldi (Bra)	McLaren
1975-6	Niki Lauda (Aut)	Ferrari
1977	Gunnar Nilsson (Swe)	Lotus
1978	Mario Andretti (USA)	Lotus
1979	Jody Scheckter (SAf)	Ferrari
1980	Didier Pironi (Fra)	Ligier
1981	Carlos Reutemann (Arg)	Williams
1982	John Watson (UK)	McLaren
1983	Alain Prost (Fra)	Renault
1984	Michele Alboreto (Ita)	Ferrari
1985	Ayrton Senna (Bra)	Lotus
1986	Nigel Mansell (UK)	Williams

1987	Alain Prost (Fra)	McLaren
1988-91	Ayrton Senna (Bra)	McLaren
1992	Michael Schumacher (Ger)	Benetton
1993-4	Damon Hill (UK)	Williams
1995	Michael Schumacher (Ger)	Benetton
1996-7	Michael Schumacher (Ger)	Ferrari

Brazilian Grand Prix

Winners, at Interlagos, São Paulo 1973-7, 1979-80, 1990-8; at Rio de Janeiro 1978, 1981-9:

1973	Emerson Fittipaldi (Bra)	Lotus
1974	Emerson Fittipaldi (Bra)	McLaren
1975	Carlos Pace (Bra)	Brabham
1976	Niki Lauda (Aut)	Ferrari
1977-8	Carlos Reutemann (Arg)	Ferrari
1979	Jacques Laffite (Fra)	Ligier
1980	René Arnoux (Fra)	Renault
1981	Carlos Reutemann (Arg)	Williams
1982	Alain Prost (Fra)	Renault
1983	Nelson Piquet (Bra)	Brabham
1984-5	Alain Prost (Fra)	McLaren
1986	Nelson Piquet (Bra)	Williams
1987-8	Alain Prost (Fra)	McLaren
1989	Nigel Mansell (UK)	Ferrari
1990	Alain Prost (Fra)	Ferrari
1991	Ayrton Senna (Bra)	McLaren
1992	Nigel Mansell (UK)	Williams
1993	Ayrton Senna (Bra)	McLaren
1994-5	Michael Schumacher (Ger)	Benetton
1996	Damon Hill (UK)	Williams
1997	Jacques Villeneuve (Can)	Williams
1998	Mika Hakkinen (Fin)	McLaren

British Grand Prix

The RAC Grand Prix was raced at Brooklands in 1926-7 and at Donington 1935-9, with the name British Grand Prix first used at Silverstone in 1948.
Winners, at Silverstone 1950-4, 1956, 1958, 1960 and uneven years from 1963-87, then annually from 1988; at Aintree 1955, 1957, 1959, 1961-2; at Brands Hatch, even years from 1964-86:

1950	Giuseppe Farina (Ita)	Alfa-Romeo
1951	José Froilan González (Arg)	Ferrari
1952-3	Alberto Ascari (Ita)	Ferrari
1954	José Froilan González (Arg)	Ferrari
1955	Stirling Moss (UK)	Mercedes-Benz
1956	Juan Manuel Fangio (Arg)	Ferrari
1957	Stirling Moss (UK) & Tony Brooks (UK)	Vanwall
1958	Peter Collins (UK)	Ferrari
1959-60	Jack Brabham (Aus)	Cooper
1961	Wolfgang von Trips (FRG)	Ferrari
1962-5	Jim Clark (UK)	Lotus
1966	Jack Brabham (Aus)	Brabham
1967	Jim Clark (UK)	Lotus
1968	Jo Siffert (Swi)	Lotus
1969	Jackie Stewart (UK)	Matra
1970	Jochen Rindt (Aut)	Lotus

1971	Jackie Stewart (UK)	Tyrrell
1972	Emerson Fittipaldi (Bra)	Lotus
1973	Peter Revson (USA)	McLaren
1974	Jody Scheckter (SAf)	Tyrrell
1975	Emerson Fittipaldi (Bra)	McLaren
1976	Niki Lauda (Aut)	Ferrari
1977	James Hunt (UK)	McLaren
1978	Carlos Reutemann (Arg)	Ferrari
1979	Clay Regazzoni (Swi)	Williams
1980	Alan Jones (Aus)	Williams
1981	John Watson (UK)	McLaren
1982	Niki Lauda (Aut)	McLaren
1983	Alain Prost (Fra)	Renault
1984	Niki Lauda (Aut)	McLaren
1985	Alain Prost (Fra)	McLaren
1986-7	Nigel Mansell (UK)	Williams
1988	Ayrton Senna (Bra)	McLaren
1989	Alain Prost (Fra)	McLaren
1990	Alain Prost (Fra)	Ferrari
1991-2	Nigel Mansell (UK)	Williams
1993	Alain Prost (Fra)	Williams
1994	Damon Hill (UK)	Williams
1995	Johnny Herbert (UK)	Benetton
1996-7	Jacques Villeneuve (Can)	Williams
1998	Michael Schumacher (Ger)	Ferrari

Canadian Grand Prix

Winners, at Mosport 1967, 1969, 1971-7; at Mont Tremblant 1968, 1970; at Montreal 1978-86, 1988-98:

1967	Jack Brabham (Aus)	Brabham
1968	Denny Hulme (NZ)	McLaren
1969	Jacky Ickx (Bel)	Brabham
1970	Jacky Ickx (Bel)	Ferrari
1971-2	Jackie Stewart (UK)	Tyrrell
1973	Peter Revson (USA)	McLaren
1974	Emerson Fittipaldi (Bra)	McLaren
1976	James Hunt (UK)	McLaren
1977	Jody Scheckter (SAf)	Wolf
1978	Gilles Villeneuve (Can)	Ferrari
1979-80	Alan Jones (Aus)	Williams
1981	Jacques Laffite (Fra)	Ligier
1982	Nelson Piquet (Bra)	Brabham
1983	René Arnoux (Fra)	Ferrari
1984	Nelson Piquet (Bra)	Brabham
1985	Michele Alboreto (Ita)	Ferrari
1986	Nigel Mansell (UK)	Williams
1988	Ayrton Senna (Bra)	McLaren
1989	Thierry Boutsen (Bel)	Williams
1990	Ayrton Senna (Bra)	McLaren
1991	Nelson Piquet (Bra)	Benetton
1992	Gerhard Berger (Aut)	McLaren
1993	Alain Prost (Fra)	Williams
1994	Michael Schumacher (Ger)	Benetton
1995	Jean Alesi (Fra)	Ferrari
1996	Damon Hill (UK)	Williams
1997-8	Michael Schumacher (Ger)	Ferrari

Dutch Grand Prix

First held in 1948.

Winners, at Zandvoort:

1952-3	Alberto Ascari (Ita)	Ferrari
1955	Juan Manuel Fangio (Arg)	Mercedes-Benz
1958	Stirling Moss (UK)	Vanwall
1959	Jo Bonnier (Swe)	BRM
1960	Jack Brabham (Aus)	Cooper
1961	Wolfgang von Trips (FRG)	Ferrari
1962	Graham Hill (UK)	BRM
1963-5	Jim Clark (UK)	Lotus
1966	Jack Brabham (Aus)	Brabham
1967	Jim Clark (UK)	Lotus
1968-9	Jackie Stewart (UK)	Matra
1970	Jochen Rindt (Aut)	Lotus
1971	Jacky Ickx (Bel)	Ferrari
1973	Jackie Stewart (UK)	Tyrrell
1974	Niki Lauda (Aut)	Ferrari
1975	James Hunt (UK)	Hesketh
1976	James Hunt (UK)	McLaren
1977	Niki Lauda (Aut)	Ferrari
1978	Mario Andretti (USA)	Lotus
1979	Alan Jones (Aus)	Williams
1980	Nelson Piquet (Bra)	Brabham
1981	Alain Prost (Fra)	Renault
1982	Didier Pironi (Fra)	Ferrari
1983	René Arnoux (Fra)	Ferrari
1984	Alain Prost (Fra)	McLaren
1985	Niki Lauda (Aut)	McLaren

European Grand Prix

In the early years of the World Championships, from the British Grand Prix of 1950, one Grand Prix each year was designated 'European Grand Prix'. In 1983-5 and 1993-4 it was held as a separate race.

Winners, at Brands Hatch 1983, 1985; at New Nürburgring 1984, 1995-6; at Donington Park 1993; at Jerez 1994, 1997:

1983	Nelson Piquet (Bra)	Brabham
1984	Alain Prost (Fra)	McLaren
1985	Nigel Mansell (UK)	Williams
1993	Ayrton Senna (Bra)	McLaren
1994-5	Michael Schumacher (Ger)	Benetton
1996-7	Jacques Villeneuve (Can)	Williams

French Grand Prix

The oldest Grand Prix, the French dates from 1906, when it took place at Le Mans.

Winners, at Rheims 1950-1, 1953-4, 1956, 1958-61, 1963, 1966; at Rouen-les Essarts 1952, 1957, 1962, 1964, 1968; Clermont-Ferrand 1965, 1969-70, 1972; at Le Mans 1967, Paul Ricard 1971, 1973, 1975-6, 1978, 1980, 1982-3, 1985-9; at Dijon Prenois 1974, 1977, 1979, 1981, 1984; at Magny Cours 1991-8:

| 1950 | Juan Manuel Fangio (Arg) | Alfa-Romeo |
| 1951 | Juan Manuel Fangio (Arg) & Luigi Fagioli (Ita) | Alfa-Romeo |

1952	Alberto Ascari (Ita)	Ferrari
1953	Mike Hawthorn (UK)	Ferrari
1954	Juan Manuel Fangio (Arg)	Mercedes-Benz
1956	Peter Collins (UK)	Ferrari
1957	Juan Manuel Fangio (Arg)	Maserati
1958	Mike Hawthorn (UK)	Ferrari
1959	Tony Brooks (UK)	Ferrari
1960	Jack Brabham (Aus)	Cooper
1961	Giancarlo Baghetti (Ita)	Ferrari
1962	Dan Gurney (USA)	Porsche
1963	Jim Clark (UK)	Lotus
1964	Dan Gurney (USA)	Brabham
1965	Jim Clark (UK)	Lotus
1966-7	Jack Brabham (Aus)	Brabham
1968	Jacky Ickx (Bel)	Ferrari
1969	Jackie Stewart (UK)	Matra
1970	Jochen Rindt (Aut)	Lotus
1971-2	Jackie Stewart (UK)	Tyrrell
1973-4	Ronnie Peterson (Swe)	Lotus
1975	Niki Lauda (Aut)	Ferrari
1976	James Hunt (UK)	McLaren
1977-8	Mario Andretti (USA)	Lotus
1979	Jean-Pierre Jabouille (Fra)	Renault
1980	Alan Jones (Aus)	Williams
1981	Alain Prost (Fra)	Renault
1982	René Arnoux (Fra)	Renault
1983	Alain Prost (Fra)	Renault
1984	Niki Lauda (Aut)	McLaren
1985	Nelson Piquet (Bra)	Brabham
1986-7	Nigel Mansell (UK)	Williams
1988-9	Alain Prost (Fra)	McLaren
1990	Alain Prost (Fra)	Ferrari
1991-2	Nigel Mansell (UK)	Williams
1993	Alain Prost (Fra)	Williams
1994-5	Michael Schumacher (Ger)	Benetton
1996	Damon Hill (UK)	Williams
1997-8	Michael Schumacher (Ger)	Ferrari

German Grand Prix

The first German Grand Prix was held at Avus in 1926.
Winners, at Nürburgring 1951-4, 1956-8, 1961-9, 1971-6; at Avus 1959; at Hockenheim 1970, 1977-84, 1986-98; at New Nürburgring 1985:

1951-2	Alberto Ascari (Ita)	Ferrari
1953	Giuseppe Farina (Ita)	Ferrari
1954	Juan Manuel Fangio (Arg)	Mercedes-Benz
1956	Juan Manuel Fangio (Arg)	Ferrari
1957	Juan Manuel Fangio (Arg)	Maserati
1958	Tony Brooks (UK)	Vanwall
1959	Tony Brooks (UK)	Ferrari
1961	Stirling Moss (UK)	Lotus
1962	Graham Hill (UK)	BRM
1963-4	John Surtees (UK)	Ferrari
1965	Jim Clark (UK)	Lotus
1966	Jack Brabham (Aus)	Brabham
1967	Denny Hulme (NZ)	Brabham

1968	Jackie Stewart (UK)	Matra
1969	Jacky Ickx (Bel)	Brabham
1970	Jochen Rindt (Aut)	Lotus
1971	Jackie Stewart (UK)	Tyrrell
1972	Jacky Ickx (Bel)	Ferrari
1973	Jackie Stewart (UK)	Tyrrell
1974	Clay Regazzoni (Swi)	Ferrari
1975	Carlos Reutemann (Arg)	Brabham
1976	James Hunt (UK)	McLaren
1977	Niki Lauda (Aut)	Ferrari
1978	Mario Andretti (USA)	Lotus
1979	Alan Jones (Aus)	Williams
1980	Jacques Laffite (Fra)	Ligier
1981	Nelson Piquet (Bra)	Brabham
1982	Patrick Tambay (Fra)	Ferrari
1983	René Arnoux (Fra)	Ferrari
1984	Alain Prost (Fra)	McLaren
1985	Michele Alboreto (Ita)	Ferrari
1986-7	Nelson Piquet (Bra)	Williams
1988-90	Ayrton Senna (Bra)	McLaren
1991-2	Nigel Mansell (UK)	Williams
1993	Alain Prost (Fra)	Williams
1994	Gerhard Berger (Aut)	Ferrari
1995	Michael Schumacher (Ger)	Benetton
1996	Damon Hill (UK)	Williams
1997	Gerhard Berger (Aut)	Benetton

Hungarian Grand Prix

Winners, at Budapest:

1986-7	Nelson Piquet (Bra)	Williams
1988	Ayrton Senna (Bra)	McLaren
1989	Nigel Mansell (UK)	Ferrari
1990	Thierry Boutsen (Bel)	Williams
1991-2	Ayrton Senna (Bra)	McLaren
1993	Damon Hill (UK)	Williams
1994	Michael Schumacher (Ger)	Benetton
1995	Damon Hill (UK)	Williams
1996-7	Jacques Villeneuve (Can)	Williams

Italian Grand Prix

The first Italian Grand Prix was raced at Brescia in 1921, with Monza staging the race from 1922.
Winners, at Monza 1950-79, 1981-9, 1991-8; at Imola 1980:

1950	Giuseppe Farina (Ita)	Alfa-Romeo
1951-2	Alberto Ascari (Ita)	Ferrari
1953	Juan Manuel Fangio (Arg)	Maserati
1954-5	Juan Manuel Fangio (Arg)	Mercedes-Benz
1956	Stirling Moss (UK)	Maserati
1957	Stirling Moss (UK)	Vanwall
1958	Tony Brooks (UK)	Vanwall
1959	Stirling Moss (UK)	Cooper
1960-1	Phil Hill (USA)	Ferrari
1962	Graham Hill (UK)	BRM
1963	Jim Clark (UK)	Lotus
1964	John Surtees (UK)	Ferrari
1965	Jackie Stewart (UK)	BRM
1966	Lodovico Scarfiotti (Ita)	Ferrari

1967	John Surtees (UK)	Honda
1968	Denny Hulme (NZ)	McLaren
1969	Jackie Stewart (UK)	Matra
1970	Clay Regazzoni (Swi)	Ferrari
1971	Peter Gethin (UK)	BRM
1972	Emerson Fittipaldi (Bra)	Lotus
1973-4	Ronnie Peterson (Swe)	Lotus
1975	Clay Regazzoni (Swi)	Ferrari
1976	Ronnie Peterson (Swe)	March
1977	Mario Andretti (USA)	Lotus
1978	Niki Lauda (Aut)	Brabham
1979	Jody Scheckter (SAf)	Ferrari
1980	Nelson Piquet (Bra)	Brabham
1981	Alain Prost (Fra)	Renault
1982	René Arnoux (Fra)	Renault
1983	Nelson Piquet (Bra)	Brabham
1984	Niki Lauda (Aut)	McLaren
1985	Alain Prost (Fra)	McLaren
1986-7	Nelson Piquet (Bra)	Williams
1988	Gerhard Berger (Aut)	Ferrari
1989	Alain Prost (Fra)	McLaren
1990	Ayrton Senna (Bra)	McLaren
1991	Nigel Mansell (UK)	Williams
1992	Ayrton Senna (Bra)	McLaren
1993-4	Damon Hill (UK)	Williams
1995	Johnny Herbert (UK)	Benetton
1996	Michael Schumacher (Ger)	Ferrari
1997	David Coulthard (UK)	McLaren

Japanese Grand Prix

Winners, at Fuji 1976-7; at Suzuka 1987-98:

1976	Mario Andretti (USA)	Lotus
1977	James Hunt (UK)	McLaren
1987	Gerhard Berger (Aut)	Ferrari
1988	Ayrton Senna (Bra)	McLaren
1989	Alessandro Nannini (Ita)	Benetton
1990	Nelson Piquet (Bra)	Benetton
1991	Gerhard Berger (Aut)	McLaren
1992	Riccardo Patrese (Ita)	Williams
1993	Ayrton Senna (Bra)	McLaren
1994	Damon Hill (UK)	Williams
1995	Michael Schumacher (Ger)	Benetton
1996	Damon Hill (UK)	Williams
1997	Michael Schumacher (Ger)	Ferrari

Las Vegas Grand Prix

Winners, at Caesar's Palace:

| 1981 | Alan Jones (Aus) | Williams |
| 1982 | Michele Alboreto (Ita) | Tyrrell |

Luxembourg Grand Prix

First held in 1997.

Winner, at Nürburgring (Germany):

| 1997 | Jacques Villeneuve (Can) | Williams |

Mexican Grand Prix

First held in 1962 and granted World Championhip status a year later.

Winners, at Mexico City:

1963	Jim Clark (UK)	Lotus
1964	Dan Gurney (USA)	Brabham
1965	Richie Ginther (USA)	Honda
1966	John Surtees (UK)	Cooper
1967	Jim Clark (UK)	Lotus
1968	Graham Hill (UK)	Lotus
1969	Denny Hulme (NZ)	McLaren
1970	Jacky Ickx (Bel)	Ferrari
1986	Gerhard Berger (Aut)	Benetton
1987	Nigel Mansell (UK)	Williams
1988	Alain Prost (Fra)	McLaren
1989	Ayrton Senna (Bra)	McLaren
1990	Alain Prost (Fra)	Ferrari
1991	Riccardo Patrese (Ita)	Williams
1992	Nigel Mansell (UK)	Williams

Monaco Grand Prix

First held in 1929.

Winners, at Monte Carlo:

1950	Juan Manuel Fangio (Arg)	Alfa-Romeo
1955	Maurice Trintignant (Fra)	Ferrari
1956	Stirling Moss (UK)	Maserati
1957	Juan Manuel Fangio (Arg)	Maserati
1958	Maurice Trintignant (Fra)	Cooper
1959	Jack Brabham (Aus)	Cooper
1960-1	Stirling Moss (UK)	Lotus
1962	Bruce McLaren (NZ)	Cooper
1963-5	Graham Hill (UK)	BRM
1966	Jackie Stewart (UK)	BRM
1967	Denny Hulme (NZ)	Brabham
1968-9	Graham Hill (UK)	Lotus
1970	Jochen Rindt (Aut)	Lotus
1971	Jackie Stewart (UK)	Tyrrell
1972	Jean-Pierre Beltoise (Fra)	BRM
1973	Jackie Stewart (UK)	Tyrrell
1974	Ronnie Peterson (Swe)	Lotus
1975-6	Niki Lauda (Aut)	Ferrari
1977	Jody Scheckter (SAf)	Wolf
1978	Patrick Depailler (Fra)	Tyrrell
1979	Jody Scheckter (SAf)	Ferrari
1980	Carlos Reutemann (Arg)	Williams
1981	Gilles Villeneuve (Can)	Ferrari
1982	Riccardo Patrese (Ita)	Brabham
1983	Keke Rosberg (Fin)	Williams
1984-6	Alain Prost (Fra)	McLaren
1987	Ayrton Senna (Bra)	Lotus
1988	Alain Prost (Fra)	McLaren
1989-93	Ayrton Senna (Bra)	McLaren
1994-5	Michael Schumacher (Ger)	Benetton
1996	Olivier Panis (Fra)	Ligier
1997	Michael Schumacher (Ger)	Ferrari
1998	Mika Hakkinen (Fin)	McLaren

Moroccan Grand Prix
First held in 1925.
Winner, at Ain Diab, Casablanca:

1958	Stirling Moss (UK)	Vanwall

Pacific Grand Prix
First held in 1994.
Winner, at Aida, Japan:

1994–5	Michael Schumacher (Ger)	Benetton

Pescara Grand Prix
First held in 1924.
Winner, at Circuit Pescara:

1957	Stirling Moss (UK)	Vanwall

Portuguese Grand Prix
First held for sports cars in 1951.
Winners, at Oporto 1958, 1960; at Monsanto 1959; at Estoril 1984-98:

1958	Stirling Moss (UK)	Vanwall
1959	Stirling Moss (UK)	Cooper
1960	Jack Brabham (Aus)	Cooper
1984	Alain Prost (Fra)	McLaren
1985	Ayrton Senna (Bra)	Lotus
1986	Nigel Mansell (UK)	Williams
1987–8	Alain Prost (Fra)	McLaren
1989	Gerhard Berger (Aut)	Ferrari
1990	Nigel Mansell (UK)	Ferrari
1991	Riccardo Patrese (Ita)	Williams
1992	Nigel Mansell (UK)	Williams
1993	Michael Schumacher (Ger)	Benetton
1994	Damon Hill (UK)	Williams
1995	David Coulthard (UK)	Williams
1996	Jacques Villeneuve (Can)	Williams

San Marino Grand Prix
Held at Imola, where the 1980 Italian GP was run.
Winners, at Imola:

1981	Nelson Piquet (Bra)	Brabham
1982	Didier Pironi (Fra)	Ferrari
1983	Patrick Tambay (Fra)	Ferrari
1984	Alain Prost (Fra)	McLaren
1985	Elio de Angelis (Ita)	Lotus
1986	Alain Prost (Fra)	McLaren
1987	Nigel Mansell (UK)	Williams
1988–9	Ayrton Senna (Bra)	McLaren
1990	Riccardo Patrese (Ita)	Williams
1991	Ayrton Senna (Bra)	McLaren
1992	Nigel Mansell (UK)	Williams
1993	Alain Prost (Fra)	Williams
1994	Michael Schumacher (Ger)	Benetton
1995–6	Damon Hill (UK)	Williams
1997	Heinz-Harald Frentzen (Ger)	Williams
1998	David Coulthard (UK)	McLaren

South African Grand Prix
First raced at East London in 1934.
Winners, at East London 1962-3, 1965; at Kyalami 1967-80, 1982-5, 1991-3:

1962	Graham Hill (UK)	BRM
1963	Jim Clark (UK)	Lotus
1965	Jim Clark (UK)	Lotus
1967	Pedro Rodriguez (Mex)	Cooper
1968	Jim Clark (UK)	Lotus
1969	Jackie Stewart (UK)	Matra
1970	Jack Brabham (Aus)	Brabham
1971	Mario Andretti (USA)	Ferrari
1972	Denny Hulme (NZ)	McLaren
1973	Jackie Stewart (UK)	Tyrrell
1974	Carlos Reutemann (Arg)	Brabham
1975	Jody Scheckter (SAf)	Tyrrell
1976-7	Niki Lauda (Aut)	Ferrari
1978	Ronnie Peterson (Swe)	Lotus
1979	Gilles Villeneuve (Can)	Ferrari
1980	René Arnoux (Fra)	Renault
1982	Alain Prost (Fra)	Renault
1983	Riccardo Patrese (Ita)	Brabham
1984	Niki Lauda (Aut)	McLaren
1985	Nigel Mansell (UK)	Williams
1992	Nigel Mansell (UK)	Williams
1993	Alain Prost (Fra)	Williams

Spanish Grand Prix
The first Spanish Grand Prix was at Guadarrama in 1913.
Winners, at Pedralbes 1951, 1954; at Jarama 1968, 1970, 1972, 1974, 1976-9, 1981; at Montjuïc Park 1969, 1971, 1973, 1975; at Jerez de la Frontera 1986-90; at Catalunya, Barcelona 1991-8:

1951	Juan Manuel Fangio (Arg)	Alfa-Romeo
1954	Mike Hawthorn (UK)	Ferrari
1968	Graham Hill (UK)	Lotus
1969	Jackie Stewart (UK)	Matra
1970	Jackie Stewart (UK)	March
1971	Jackie Stewart (UK)	Tyrrell
1972-3	Emerson Fittipaldi (Bra)	Lotus
1974	Niki Lauda (Aut)	Ferrari
1975	Jochen Mass (FRG)	McLaren
1976	James Hunt (UK)	McLaren
1977-8	Mario Andretti (USA)	Lotus
1979	Patrick Depailler (Fra)	Ligier
1981	Gilles Villeneuve (Can)	Ferrari
1986	Ayrton Senna (Bra)	Lotus
1987	Nigel Mansell (UK)	Williams
1988	Alain Prost (Fra)	McLaren
1989	Ayrton Senna (Bra)	McLaren
1990	Alain Prost (Fra)	Ferrari
1991-2	Nigel Mansell (UK)	Williams
1993	Alain Prost (Fra)	Williams
1994	Damon Hill (UK)	Williams
1995	Michael Schumacher (Ger)	Benetton
1996	Michael Schumacher (Ger)	Ferrari
1997	Jacques Villeneuve (Can)	Williams
1998	Mika Hakkinen (Fin)	McLaren

Swedish Grand Prix

First held in 1955-7 for sports cars.

Winners, at Anderstorp:

1973	Denny Hulme (NZ)	McLaren
1974	Jody Scheckter (SAf)	Tyrrell
1975	Niki Lauda (Aut)	Ferrari
1976	Jody Scheckter (SAf)	Tyrrell
1977	Jacques Lafitte (Fra)	Ligier
1978	Niki Lauda (Aut)	Brabham

Swiss Grand Prix

First held at Bremgarten, Berne in 1934.

Winners, at Bremgarten 1950-4; at Dijon (France) 1982:

1950	Giuseppe Farina (Ita)	Alfa-Romeo
1951	Juan Manuel Fangio (Arg)	Alfa-Romeo
1952	Piero Taruffi (Ita)	Ferrari
1953	Alberto Ascari (Ita)	Ferrari
1954	Juan Manuel Fangio (Arg)	Mercedes-Benz
1982	Keke Rosberg (Fin)	Williams

United States Grand Prix

The first US Grand Prix was a sports-car race in 1958.

Winners, at Sebring 1959; at Riverside 1960; at Watkins Glen 1961-80; at Detroit 1987-8; at Phoenix 1989-91:

1959	Bruce McLaren (NZ)	Cooper
1960	Stirling Moss (UK)	Lotus
1961	Innes Ireland (UK)	Lotus
1962	Jim Clark (UK)	Lotus
1963-5	Graham Hill (UK)	BRM
1966-7	Jim Clark (UK)	Lotus
1968	Jackie Stewart (UK)	Matra
1969	Jochen Rindt (Aut)	Lotus
1970	Emerson Fittipaldi (Bra)	Lotus
1971	François Cevert (Fra)	Tyrrell
1972	Jackie Stewart (UK)	Tyrrell
1973	Ronnie Peterson (Swe)	Lotus
1974	Carlos Reutemann (Arg)	Brabham
1975	Niki Lauda (Aut)	Ferrari
1976-7	James Hunt (UK)	McLaren
1978	Carlos Reutemann (Arg)	Ferrari
1979	Gilles Villeneuve (Can)	Ferrari
1980	Alan Jones (Aus)	Williams
1987	Ayrton Senna (Bra)	Lotus
1988	Ayrton Senna (Bra)	McLaren
1989	Alain Prost (Fra)	McLaren
1990-1	Ayrton Senna (Bra)	McLaren

United States Grand Prix (East)

Winners, at Detroit:

1982	John Watson (UK)	McLaren
1983	Michele Alboreto (Ita)	Tyrrell
1984	Nelson Piquet (Bra)	Brabham
1985	Keke Rosberg (Fin)	Williams
1986	Ayrton Senna (Bra)	Lotus

United States Grand Prix (West)

Winners, at Long Beach 1976-8; at Fir Park, Dallas 1984:

1976	Clay Regazzoni (Swi)	Ferrari
1977	Mario Andretti (USA)	Lotus
1978	Carlos Reutemann (Arg)	Ferrari
1979	Gilles Villeneuve (Can)	Ferrari
1980	Nelson Piquet (Fra)	Brabham
1981	Alan Jones (Aus)	Williams
1982	Niki Lauda (Aut)	McLaren
1983	John Watson (UK)	McLaren
1984	Keke Rosberg (Fin)	Williams

World Champions and Runners-Up

Points allocated – 1950-9: 1st 8, 2nd 6, 3rd 4, 4th 3, 5th 2; fastest lap 1; 1960: 8-6-4-3-2-1 for 1st to 6th; 1961-90: 9-6-4-3-2-1 for 1st to 6th; 1992- 10-6-4-3-2-1 for 1st to 6th.

Year	Winner	Points	Runner-up	Points
1950	Giuseppe Farina (Ita)	30	Juan Manuel Fangio (Arg)	27
1951	Juan Manuel Fangio (Arg)	31	Alberto Ascari (Ita)	25
1952	Alberto Ascari (Ita)	36	Giuseppe Farina (Ita)	24
1953	Alberto Ascari (Ita)	34.5	Juan Manuel Fangio (Arg)	28
1954	Juan Manuel Fangio (Arg)	42	José Froilán González (Arg)	25.14
1955	Juan Manuel Fangio (Arg)	40	Stirling Moss (UK)	23
1956	Juan Manuel Fangio (Arg)	30	Stirling Moss (UK)	27
1957	Juan Manuel Fangio (Arg)	40	Stirling Moss (UK)	25
1958	Mike Hawthorn (UK)	42	Stirling Moss (UK)	41
1959	Jack Brabham (Aus)	31	Tony Brooks (UK)	27
1960	Jack Brabham (Aus)	43	Bruce McLaren (NZ)	34
1961	Phil Hill (USA)	34	Wolfgang von Trips (FRG)	33
1962	Graham Hill (UK)	42	Jim Clark (UK)	30
1963	Jim Clark (UK)	54	Graham Hill (UK) & Richie Ginther (USA)	29
1964	John Surtees (UK)	40	Graham Hill (UK)	39
1965	Jim Clark (UK)	54	Graham Hill (UK)	40

Year	Winner	Points	Runner-up	Points
1966	Jack Brabham (Aus)	42	John Surtees (UK)	28
1967	Denny Hulme (NZ)	51	Jack Brabham (Aus)	46
1968	Graham Hill (UK)	48	Jackie Stewart (UK)	36
1969	Jackie Stewart (UK)	63	Jacky Ickx (Bel)	37
1970	Jochen Rindt (Aut)	45	Jacky Ickx (Bel)	40
1971	Jackie Stewart (UK)	62	Ronnie Peterson (Swe)	33
1972	Emerson Fittipaldi (Bra)	61	Jackie Stewart (UK)	45
1973	Jackie Stewart (UK)	71	Emerson Fittipaldi (Bra)	55
1974	Emerson Fittipaldi (Bra)	55	Clay Regazzoni (Swi)	52
1975	Niki Lauda (Aut)	64.5	Emerson Fittipaldi (Bra)	45
1976	James Hunt (UK)	69	Niki Lauda (Aut)	68
1977	Niki Lauda (Aut)	72	Jody Scheckter (SAf)	55
1978	Mario Andretti (USA)	64	Ronnie Peterson (Swe)	51
1979	Jody Scheckter (SAf)	51	Gilles Villeneuve (Can)	47
1980	Alan Jones (Aus)	67	Nelson Piquet (Bra)	54
1981	Nelson Piquet (Bra)	50	Carlos Reutemann (Arg)	49
1982	Keke Rosberg (Fin)	44	John Watson (UK) & Didier Pironi (Fra)	39
1983	Nelson Piquet (Bra)	59	Alain Prost (Fra)	57
1984	Niki Lauda (Aut)	72	Alain Prost (Fra)	71.5
1985	Alain Prost (Fra)	73	Michele Alboreto (Ita)	53
1986	Alain Prost (Fra)	72	Nigel Mansell (UK)	70
1987	Nelson Piquet (Bra)	73	Nigel Mansell (UK)	61
1988	Ayrton Senna (Bra)	90	Alain Prost (Fra)	87
1989	Alain Prost (Fra)	76	Ayrton Senna (Bra)	60
1990	Ayrton Senna (Bra)	78	Alain Prost (Fra)	71
1991	Ayrton Senna (Bra)	96	Nigel Mansell (UK)	72
1992	Nigel Mansell (UK)	108	Riccardo Patrese (Ita)	56
1993	Alain Prost (Fra)	99	Ayrton Senna (Bra)	73
1994	Michael Schumacher (Ger)	92	Damon Hill (UK)	91
1995	Michael Schumacher (Ger)	102	Damon Hill (UK)	69
1996	Damon Hill (UK)	97	Jacques Villeneuve (Can)	78
1997★	Jacques Villeneuve (Can)	81	Heinz-Harald Frentzen (Ger)	42

★ Michael Schumacher (Ger) was stripped of 2nd place (78 points) after he was determined to have deliberately rammed his Ferrari into Villenuve's Williams at the final Grand Prix of 1997.

Most Grand Prix Wins in a Career (to end 1997)

Points – 9 for 1st (10 from 1991), 6 for 2nd, 4 for 3rd, 3 for 4th, 2 for 5th, 1 for 6th – include those that were deducted in some years, when a driver had more qualifying races than those counted.

Wins	Driver	Career	Races	Points	Av. pts	Poles	Champs
51	Alain Prost (Fra)	1980-93	199	798.5	4.0	33	4
41	Ayrton Senna (Bra)	1985-94	161	614	3.9	65	3
31	Nigel Mansell (UK)	1980-95	187	482	2.6	32	1
27★	Michael Schumacher (Ger)	1991-7	102	440★	4.3	17	2
27	Jackie Stewart (UK)	1965-73	99	360	3.6	17	3
25	Jim Clark (UK)	1960-8	72	274	3.8	33	2
25	Niki Lauda (Aut)	1971-85	171	420.5	2.5	24	3
24	Juan Manuel Fangio (Arg)	1950-8	51	277.14	5.4	28	5
23	Nelson Piquet (Bra)	1978-91	204	485.5	2.4	24	3
21	Damon Hill (UK)	1992-7	84	333	4.0	20	1
16	Stirling Moss (UK)	1951-61	66	186.64	2.8	16	–
14	Graham Hill (UK)	1958-75	176	289	1.6	13	2
14	Jack Brabham (Aus)	1955-70	126	261	2.1	13	3
14	Emerson Fittipaldi (Bra)	1970-80	144	281	2.0	6	2
13	Alberto Ascari (Ita)	1951-5	31	140.64	4.5	14	2
12	Mario Andretti (USA)	1968-82	128	180	1.4	18	1
12	Carlos Reutemann (Arg)	1972-82	146	310	2.1	6	–

Wins	Driver	Career	Races	Points	Av. pts	Poles	Champs
12	Alan Jones (Aus)	1975–86	116	206	1.8	6	1
11	Jacques Villeneuve (Can)	1996–7	33	159	4.8	13	1
10	James Hunt (UK)	1973–9	92	179	1.9	14	1
10	Ronnie Peterson (Swe)	1970–8	123	206	1.7	14	–
10	Jody Scheckter (SAf)	1972–80	112	255	2.3	3	1
9	Gerhard Berger (Aut)	1984–97	210	385	1.8	10	–
8	Denny Hulme (NZ)	1965–74	112	248	2.2	1	1
7	Jackie Ickx (Bel)	1966–79	116	181	1.6	13	–
7	René Arnoux (Fra)	1978–89	149	179	1.2	18	–
Others to average more than 2.8 points per drive:							
5	Giuseppe Farina (Ita)	1950–5	33	127.33	3.9	5	1
3	Mike Hawthorn (UK)	1953–8	45	127.64	2.8	4	1
Others with over 200 points:							
6	Riccardo Patrese (Ita)	1977–93	256	281	1.1	8	–
6	Jacques Laffite (Fra)	1974–86	176	228	1.3	7	–
5	Clay Regazzoni (Sui)	1970–80	132	212	1.6	6	–
1	Jean Alesi (Fra)	1989–97	135	225	1.7	2	–

* Schumacher's total includes 78 points with 5 wins from 16 races in 1997 (see above).

Most wins in a season: 9 Mansell 1992, Schumacher 1995; 8 Senna 1988, Schumacher 1994, Hill 1996; 7 Clark 1963, Prost 1984, 1988, Senna 1991, Prost 1993; 6 Ascari 1952, Fangio 1954, Clark 1965, Stewart 1969 & 1971, Hunt 1976, Andretti 1978, Mansell 1987, Senna 1989 & 1990, Hill 1994

Most successive wins: 9 Ascari 1952-3; 5 Brabham 1960, Clark 1965, Mansell 1992

Most pole positions in a season: 14 Mansell 1992

Oldest GP driver: 55yr 292d Louis Chiron (Mon) 1955 Monaco GP

Oldest GP winner: 53yr 22d Luigi Fagioli (Ita) 1951 French GP

Oldest GP points scorer: 53yr 248d Phillipe Etancelin (Fra) 1950 Italian GP (5th)

Oldest world champion: 46yr 41d Juan Manuel Fangio (Arg) 1957

Youngest GP driver: 19yr 182d Mike Thackwell (NZ) 1980 Canadian GP

Youngest GP winner: 22yr 80d Troy Ruttman (USA) 1952 Indianapolis 500 (a championship race that year), 22yr 104 days Bruce McLaren (NZ) 1959 US GP

Youngest GP points scorer: 20yr 113d Ricardo Rodriguez (Mex) 1962 Belgian GP (4th)

Youngest world champion: 25yr 273d Emerson Fittipaldi (Bra) 1972

Constructors' Championship

Year	Constructor	Points	Year	Constructor	Points
1958	Vanwall	48	1979	Ferrari	113
1959	Cooper-Climax	40	1980	Williams-Ford	120
1960	Cooper-Climax	48	1981	Williams-Ford	95
1961	Ferrari	45	1982	Ferrari	74
1962	BRM	42	1983	Ferrari	89
1963	Lotus-Climax	54	1984	McLaren-TAG-Porsche	143
1964	Ferrari	45	1985	McLaren-TAG-Porsche	90
1965	Lotus-Climax	54	1986	Williams-Honda	141
1966	Brabham-Repco	42	1987	Williams-Honda	137
1967	Brabham-Repco	63	1988	McLaren-Honda	199
1968	Lotus-Ford	62	1989	McLaren-Honda	141
1969	Matra-Ford	66	1990	McLaren-Honda	110
1970	Lotus-Ford	59	1991	McLaren-Honda	139
1971	Tyrrell-Ford	73	1992	Williams-Renault	164
1972	Lotus-Ford	61	1993	Williams-Renault	168
1973	Lotus-Ford	92	1994	Williams-Renault	118
1974	McLaren-Ford	73	1995	Benetton-Renault	137
1975	Ferrari	72	1996	Williams-Renault	175
1976	Ferrari	83	1997	William-Renault	123
1977	Ferrari	95			
1978	Lotus-Ford	86			

Most wins: 8 Ferrari, Williams; 7 Lotus, McLaren

Most Grand Prix wins

113	Ferrari	1951-97
107	McLaren	1968-97
103	Williams	1979-97
79	Lotus	1960-87
35	Brabham	1964-85
26	Benetton	1986-95
23	Tyrrell	1971-83
17	BRM	1959-72
16	Cooper	1958-67
15	Renault	1979-83
10	Alfa-Romeo	1950-51

Most wins by make of engine

174	Ford
111	Ferrari
94	Renault
72	Honda
40	Climax
26	Porsche
18	BRM

12	Alfa-Romeo
12	Mercedes
11	Maserati

Most wins in a season:
15 McLaren 1988; 12 McLaren 1984, Williams 1996; 11 Benetton 1995; 10 McLaren 1989, Williams 1992; 9 Williams 1987 & 1993; 8 Lotus 1978, McLaren 1991, Benetton 1994

Most successive wins: 14 Ferrari 1952-3; 11 McLaren-Honda 1988; 9 Alfa-Romeo 1950-1; 8 McLaren-Porsche 1984-5

Fastest average speed: 242.62km/h (150.75 mph) 1971 Italian GP at Monza, won by Peter Gethin (UK) in a BRM

Slowest winning average speed: 98.68km/h (61.33 mph) 1950 Monaco GP, Monte Carlo, won

by Juan Manuel Fangio (Arg) in an Alfa-Romeo

Fastest lap: 247.02km/h (153.49 mph) Henri Pescarolo (Fra) March-Ford, 1971 Italian GP, Monza.

Qualifying lap record: 258.803km/h (160.817 mph) Keke Rosberg (Fin) Williams-Honda, 1985 British GP at Silverstone.

Longest circuit: 25.57km (15.89 miles) Pescara, Italy (1957 Pescara GP)

Shortest circuit: 3.14km (1.95 miles) Monte Carlo, France (1955-72 Monaco GP)

Formula Two, Formula Three and Formula 3000

Formula Two was introduced in 1947 to enable young drivers to gain experience for the step up to Formula One. Formula Three was created in the early 1950s for much the same reason. A European Formula Two championship was introduced in 1967 and a Formula Three championship followed in 1975. Both were discontinued in 1984, making way for the new European Formula 3000 Championship, later renamed the FIA Formula 3000 International Championship. Formula Three remains popular in Britain and championships have existed in various forms since 1966, when Harry Stiller won the Les Leston Championship. It was not until the introduction of the Vandervell British Formula Three Championship in 1979 that the event became unified. In 1992 the British Formula 3000 Championship was renamed F2.

European Formula Two Champions

1967	Jacky Ickx (Bel)
1968	Jean-Pierre Beltoise (Fra)
1969	Johnny Servoz-Gavin (Fra)
1970	Clay Regazzoni (Swi)
1971	Ronnie Peterson (Swe)
1972	Mike Hailwood (UK)
1973	Jean-Pierre Jarier (Fra)
1974	Patrick Depailler (Fra)
1975	Jacques Laffite (Fra)
1976	Jean-Pierre Jabouille (Fra)
1977	René Arnoux (Fra)
1978	Bruno Giacomelli (Ita)
1979	Marc Surer (Swi)
1980	Brian Henton (UK)
1981	Geoff Lees (UK)
1982	Corrado Fabi (Ita)
1983	Jonathan Palmer (UK)
1984	Mike Thackwell (NZ)

Most race wins: 12 Jochen Rindt (Aut); 11 Bruno Giacomelli (Ita); 9 Mike Thackwell (NZ); 7 Jean-Pierre Jarier (Fra), Jacques Laffite (Fra)

FIA Formula 3000 Champions

1985	Christian Danner (FRG)
1986	Ivan Capelli (Ita)
1987	Stefano Modena (Ita)
1988	Roberto Moreno (Bra)
1989	Jean Alesi (Fra)
1990	Eric Comas (Fra)
1991	Christian Fittipaldi (Bra)
1992	Luca Badoer (Ita)
1993	Olivier Panis (Fra)
1994	Jules Boullion (Fra)
1995	Vincenzo Sospiri (Ita)
1996	Jörg Müller (Ger)
1997	Ricardo Zonta (Bra)

Sports Car Racing

Le Mans

The most famous of all sports-car races, the Le Mans 24-hour race was inaugurated on 26-27 May 1923, and won by André Lagache and René Leonard in a 3-litre Chenard & Walcker. The original Le Mans circuit at Sarthe, France, measured 17.26km (10.73 miles) but the present circuit is 13.64km (8.48 miles).

Post-war winners:

Year	Drivers	Car	Av. speed (km/h)
1949	Luigi Chinetti (Ita), Lord Peter Selsdon (UK)	Ferrari	132.418
1950	Louis Rosier, Jean-Louis Rosier (Fra)	Talbot-Lago	144.379
1951	Peter Walker, Peter Whitehead (UK)	Jaguar	150.466
1952	Hermann Lang, Karl Riess (FRG)	Mercedes-Benz	155.574
1953	Tony Rolt, Duncan Hamilton (UK)	Jaguar	170.335
1954	Froilan Gonzalez (Arg), Maurice Trintignant (Fra)	Ferrari	164.386
1955	Mike Hawthorn, Ivor Bueb (UK)	Jaguar	172.308
1956	Ron Flockhart, Ninian Sanderson (UK)	Jaguar	168.120
1957	Ron Flockhart, Ivor Bueb (UK)	Jaguar	183.216
1958	Olivier Gendebien (Bel), Phil Hill (USA)	Ferrari	170.912
1959	Carroll Shelby, Roy Salvadori (UK)	Aston Martin	181.162
1960	Olivier Gendebien, Paul Frère (Bel)	Ferrari	175.729
1961	Olivier Gendebien (Bel), Phil Hill (USA)	Ferrari	186.526
1962	Olivier Gendebien (Bel), Phil Hill (USA)	Ferrari	185.467
1963	Ludovico Scarfiotti, Lorenzo Bandini (Ita)	Ferrari	190.071
1964	Jean Guichet (Fra), Nino Vaccarella (Ita)	Ferrari	195.638
1965	Jochen Rindt (Aut), Masten Gregory (USA)	Ferrari	194.879
1966	Chris Amon, Bruce McLaren (NZ)	Ford	201.795
1967	Dan Gurney, A J Foyt (USA)	Ford	218.033
1968	Pedro Rodriguez (Mex), Lucien Bianchi (Bel)	Ford	185.536
1969	Jacky Ickx (Bel), Jackie Oliver (UK)	Ford	208.250
1970	Hans Herrmann (FRG), Richard Attwood (UK)	Porsche	191.992
1971	Helmut Marko (Aut), Gijs van Lennep (Hol)	Porsche	222.304
1972	Henri Pescarolo (Fra), Graham Hill (UK)	Matra-Simca	195.472
1973	Henri Pescarolo, Gérard Larrousse (Fra)	Matra-Simca	202.250
1974	Henri Pescarolo, Gérard Larrousse (Fra)	Matra-Simca	191.940
1975	Jacky Ickx (Bel), Derek Bell (UK)	Mirage-Ford	191.480
1976	Jacky Ickx (Bel), Gijs van Lennep (Hol)	Porsche	198.750
1977	Jacky Ickx (Bel), Jürgen Barth (FRG), Hurley Haywood (USA)	Porsche	194.802
1978	Jean-Pierre Jaussaud, Didier Pironi (Fra)	Renault Alpine	210.190
1979	Klaus Ludwig (FRG), Bill and Don Whittington (USA)	Porsche	173.900
1980	Jean-Pierre Jaussaud, Jean Rondeau (Fra)	Rondeau-Ford	192.000
1981	Jacky Ickx (Bel), Derek Bell (UK)	Porsche	201.060
1982	Jacky Ickx (Bel), Derek Bell (UK)	Porsche	204.128
1983	Vern Schuppan (Aut), Hurley Haywood (USA), Al Holbert (USA)	Porsche	210.330
1984	Klaus Ludwig (FRG), Henri Pescarolo (Fra)	Porsche	204.180
1985	Klaus Ludwig (FRG), Paulo Barillo (Ita), 'John Winter' (FRG)	Porsche	212.021
1986	Hans Stück (FRG), Derek Bell (UK), Al Holbert (USA)	Porsche	203.197
1987	Hans Stück (FRG), Derek Bell (UK), Al Holbert (USA)	Porsche	199.657
1988	Jan Lammers (Hol), Johnny Dumfries (UK), Andy Wallace (UK)	Jaguar	221.630
1989	Jochen Mass (FRG), Manuel Reuter (FRG), Stanley Dickens (Swe)	Mercedes	219.991
1990	John Nielsen (Den), Martin Brundle (UK), Price Cobb (USA)	Jaguar	204.070
1991	Johnny Herbert (UK), Bertrand Gachot (Bel), Volker Wendler (Ger)	Mazda	206.530
1992	Derek Warwick (UK), Mark Blundell (UK), Yannick Dalmas (Fra)	Peugeot	199.342
1993	Geoff Brabham (Aus), Cristophe Bouchut (Fra), Éric Hélary (Fra)	Peugeot	213.358
1994	Yannick Dalmas (Fra), Hurley Haywood (USA), Mauro Baldi (Ita)	Dauer Porsche	195.265
1995	Yannick Dalmas (Fra), J J Lehto (Fin), Masanori Sekiya (Jap)	McLaren	168.992
1996	Manuel Reuter (Ger), Davey Jones (USA), Alexander Wurz (Aut)	TWR Porsche	200.600
1997	Michele Alboreto (Ita), Stefan Johansson (Swe), Tom Kristensen (Den)	TWR Porsche	204.186
1998	Allan McNish (UK), Laurent Aiello (Fra), Stéphane Oretlli (Fra)	Porsche	199.324

Most wins: 6 Ickx; 5 Bell; 4 Gendebien, Pescarolo; 3 Woolf Barnato (UK) 1928-30, Luigi Chinetti (Ita/USA) 1932, 1934, 1949, Hill, Holbert, Ludwig
Most successful combinations: 3 wins Olivier Gendebien & Phil Hill, and Jacky Ickx & Derek Bell
Fastest winning speed: 222.304 km/h Helmut Marko & Gijs van Lennep 1971
Greatest distance covered: 5333.72km (3314.22 miles) Helmut Marko & Gijs van Lennep 1971
Record for current circuit: 5331.998km (3313.24 miles) Jan Lammers/Johnny Dumfries & Andy Wallace 1988
Most successful cars: 15 wins Porsche; 9 Ferrari; 7 Jaguar

World Sports-Car Championship

The format, and car specification, have changed many times since the introduction of this championship in 1953. Between 1953-61 it was known as the Sports-Car World Championship, with the title going to the leading manufacturer. A Speed World Challenge was contested in 1962-3 and an International Championship for Makes from 1964-71, with new regulations from 1968; this was a championship for competition sports cars and prototypes. With the distinction between competition and prototypes disappearing, a new World Championship for Makes was introduced in 1972, with a separate World Championship for Sports Cars in 1976-7. In 1981, a championship for drivers was introduced for the first time, becoming known as the World Endurance Championship 1982-5. The name was changed again in 1986, to the World Sports-Prototype Championship, for both cars and drivers, and back to World Sports-Car Championship 1991-2. From 1985 the constructors' championship was for teams. FISA declared that the series would be terminated after the 1992 season.

Winners:

Drivers

1981	Bob Garretson (USA)
1982-3	Jacky Ickx (Bel)
1984	Stefan Bellof (FRG)
1985-6	Derek Bell (UK) & Hans-Joachim Stück (FRG)
1987	Raul Boesel (Bra)
1988	Martin Brundle (UK)
1989	Jean-Louis Schlesser (Fra)
1990	Mauro Baldi (Ita) & Jean-Louis Schlesser (Fra)
1991	Teo Fabi (Ita)
1992	Derek Warwick (UK) & Yannick Dalmas (Fra)

Cars

1953-4	Ferrari
1955	Mercedes-Benz
1956-8	Ferrari
1959	Aston Martin
1960-5	Ferrari
1966	Ford
1967	Ferrari
1968	Ford
1969-71	Porsche
1972	Ferrari
1973-4	Matra-Simca
1975	Alfa-Romeo

1976-9	Porsche
1980	Lancia
1981-4	Porsche
1985	Rothmans-Porsche
1986	Brun Motorsport
1987-8	Silk Cut Jaguar
1989-90	Sauber Mercedes
1991	Silk Cut Jaguar
1992	Peugeot Talbot Special

Sports cars

| 1976 | Porsche |
| 1977 | Alfa-Romeo |

US Motor Racing

Indianapolis 500

The Indianapolis 500 forms part of the US Memorial Day celebrations at the end of May each year. The race is held at the Indianapolis Raceway, Indiana, over 200 laps of the 2.5-mile oval-shaped circuit. The first race, on 30 May 1911, was won by Ray Harroun in a Marmon Wasp. From 1950 to 1960 the race formed part of the World Drivers' Championship, but very few European drivers competed in it.

The Borg-Warner Trophy has been awarded to the winner annually from 1936. It was introduced by Captain Eddie Rickenbacker, then owner of the Indianapolis Motor Speedway, and replaced the Wheeler-Shebler Trophy, presented from 1911 to 1935. The trophy, made of 80lb of sterling silver, cost $10,000 originally and is now priceless. It displays the faces of all winners of the race from 1911. Winners personally keep a sterling silver miniature of the trophy, which is 5ft 9in high, and also has a new base of 1ft 6in high.

Winners since 1950 (all US unless otherwise stated):

Year	Winner	Manufacturer	Av. speed (mph)
1950	Johnny Parsons	Kurtis Kraft-Offenhauser	124.002
1951	Lee Wallard	Kurtis Kraft-Offenhauser	126.244
1952	Troy Ruttmann	Kuzna-Offenhauser	128.922
1953	Bill Vukovich	Kurtis Kraft 500A-Offenhauser	128.740
1954	Bill Vukovich	Kurtis Kraft 500A-Offenhauser	130.840

Year	Winner	Manufacturer	Av. speed (mph)
1955	Bob Sweikert	Kurtis Kraft 500C-Offenhauser	128.209
1956	Pat Flaherty	Watson-Offenhauser	128.490
1957	Sam Hanks	Epperly-Offenhauser	135.601
1958	Jimmy Bryan	Epperly-Offenhauser	133.791
1959	Rodger Ward	Watson-Offenhauser	135.857
1960	Jim Rathmann	Watson-Offenhauser	138.767
1961	A J Foyt	Watson-Offenhauser	139.130
1962	Rodger Ward	Watson-Offenhauser	140.293
1963	Parnelli Jones	Watson-Offenhauser	143.137
1964	A J Foyt	Watson-Offenhauser	147.350
1965	Jim Clark (UK)	Lotus-Ford	150.686
1966	Graham Hill (UK)	Lola-Ford	144.317
1967	A J Foyt	Coyote-Ford	151.207
1968	Bobby Unser	Eagle-Offenhauser	152.882
1969	Mario Andretti	Hawk-Ford	156.867
1970	Al Unser	P J Colt-Ford	155.749
1971	Al Unser	P J Colt-Ford	157.735
1972	Mark Donohue	McLaren-Offenhauser	162.962
1973	Gordon Johncock	Eagle-Offenhauser	159.036
1974	Johnny Rutherford	McLaren-Offenhauser	158.589
1975	Bobby Unser	Eagle-Offenhauser	149.213
1976	Johnny Rutherford	McLaren-Offenhauser	148.725
1977	A J Foyt	Coyote-Ford	161.331
1978	Al Unser	Lola-Cosworth	161.363
1979	Rick Mears	Penske-Cosworth	158.899
1980	Johnny Rutherford	Chaparral-Cosworth	142.862
1981	Bobby Unser	Penske-Cosworth	139.085
1982	Gordon Johncock	Wildcat-Cosworth	162.062
1983	Tom Sneva	March-Cosworth	162.117
1984	Rick Mears	March-Cosworth	163.621
1985	Danny Sullivan	March-Cosworth	152.982
1986	Bobby Rahal	March-Cosworth	170.722
1987	Al Unser	March-Cosworth	162.175
1988	Rick Mears	Penske-Chevrolet	144.809
1989	Emerson Fittipaldi (Bra)	Penske-Chevrolet	167.581
1990	Arie Luyendyk (Hol)	Lola-Chevrolet	185.981
1991	Rick Mears	Penske-Chevrolet	176.457
1992	Al Unser, Jr	Penske-Chevrolet	134.477
1993	Emerson Fittipaldi (Bra)	Penske-Chevrolet	157.207
1994	Al Unser, Jr	Penske-Mercedes	160.872
1995	Jacques Villeneuve (Can)	Reynard-Ford	153.616
1996	Buddy Lazier	Reynard-Ford	147.956
1997	Arie Luyendyk (Hol)	G-Force Olds Aurora	144.984
1998	Eddy Cheever	Dallara Aurora	145.155

Most wins: 4 A J Foyt, Al Unser, Rick Mears; 3 Louis Meyer 1928, 1933, 1936, Mauri Rose 1941,
    1947, 1948, Bobby Unser, Johnny Rutherford

Fastest winning speed: 185.981 mph (299.299km/h) Arie Luyendyk (Hol) in a Lola-Chevrolet, 1990

Qualifying record speed for four laps: 236.986 mph (381.392km/h) Arie Luyendyk in a Reynard-Ford
    1996, including single lap qualifying record of 237.498 mph (382.205km/h)

Closest finish: 0.043 sec Al Unser, Jr over Scott Goodyear 1992

Record prize money: $8,612,450 in 1997, of which winner received $1,568,150

Indy Car Racing

Indy Car racing (on oval speedways) has been in existence since 1909. Between 1909-55 the season-long championship was known as the AAA National Championship. It then became the United States Auto Club (USAC) National Championship. CART (Championship Auto Racing Teams, Inc.) was founded in 1978 by Roger Penske and U E 'Pat' Patrick, in a break away from the USAC. CART had its own series of races in 1979, and after a short-lived joint venture between CART and USAC in 1980, CART produced its own National Championship series. It now sanctions all Indy Car racing (the PPG Indy Car World Series), except the Indianapolis 500, which is still governed by the USAC.

National Championship results

AAA National Championship (1909-55)

Most wins: 3 Earl Cooper 1913, 1915, 1917, Louie Meyer 1928-9, 1933, Ted Horn 1946-8

USAC National Championship

1956-7	Jimmy Bryan
1958	Tony Bettenhausen, Sr
1959	Rodger Ward
1960-1	A J Foyt
1962	Rodger Ward
1963-4	A J Foyt
1965-6	Mario Andretti
1967	A J Foyt
1968	Bobby Unser
1969	Mario Andretti
1970	Al Unser
1971-2	Joe Leonard
1973	Roger McCluskey
1974	Bobby Unser
1975	A J Foyt
1976	Gordon Johncock
1977-8	Tom Sneva
1979	A J Foyt

PPG Indy Car World Series

1979	Rick Mears
1980	Johnny Rutherford
1981-2	Rick Mears
1983	Al Unser
1984	Mario Andretti
1985	Al Unser
1986-7	Bobby Rahal
1988	Danny Sullivan
1989	Emerson Fittipaldi
1990	Al Unser, Jr
1991	Michael Andretti
1992	Bobby Rahal
1993	Nigel Mansell (UK)
1994	Al Unser, Jr
1995	Jacques Villeneuve (Can)
1996	Jimmy Vasser
1997	Alex Zanardi (Ita)

Most championships: 7 A J Foyt, Jr; 4 Mario Andretti

Most wins in a season: 10 A J Foyt, Jr 1964, Al Unser 1970

Most wins in career: 67 A J Foyt, Jr 1960-81 (whole career 1957-93); 52 Mario Andretti; 39 Al Unser; 37 Michael Andretti; 35 Bobby Unser; 31 Al Unser, Jr; 29 Rick Mears; 27 Johnny Rutherford

Season's money record: $3,535,813 Al Unser, Jr 1994

Indy Car career earnings leaders (at end 1997)

Al Unser, Jr	$18,342,156
Bobby Rahal	15,900,258
Michael Andretti	14,704,619
Emerson Fittipaldi (Bra)	14,293,625
Mario Andretti	11,552,154
Rick Mears	11,050,807
Danny Sullivan	8,844,126
Arie Luyendyk (Hol)	7,732,188
Raul Boesel	6,971,887
Al Unser Sr	6,740,843
Jimmy Vassar	6,554,954

NASCAR Championship Winston Cup

The National Association for Stock Car Auto Racing, Inc. (NASCAR) was the brainchild of Virginian Bill France who formed the Association in 1947. The first race sanctioned by NASCAR was over the Daytona Beach course on 15 February 1948. Early races were either over dirt tracks or beach circuits.

Today they are run over enclosed circuits and NASCAR races are now among the most popular in the United States. The Winston Cup series was started in 1949 and was known as the Grand National series. It became the Winston Cup in 1970 following sponsorship by the R J Reynolds Tobacco Company.

Winners:

1949	Red Byron
1950	Bill Rexford
1951	Herb Thomas
1952	Tim Flock
1953	Herb Thomas
1954	Lee Petty
1955	Tim Flock
1956-7	Buck Baker
1958-9	Lee Petty
1960	Rex White
1961	Ned Jarrett
1962-3	Joe Weatherley
1964	Richard Petty
1965	Ned Jarrett
1966	David Pearson
1967	Richard Petty
1968-9	David Pearson
1970	Bobby Isaac
1971-2	Richard Petty
1973	Benny Parsons
1974-5	Richard Petty
1976-8	Cale Yarborough
1979	Richard Petty
1980	Dale Earnhardt
1981-2	Darrell Waltrip
1983	Bobby Allison
1984	Terry Labonte
1985	Darrell Waltrip
1986-7	Dale Earnhardt
1988	Bill Elliott
1989	Rusty Wallace
1990-1	Dale Earnhardt
1992	Alan Kulwicki
1993-4	Dale Earnhardt
1995	Jeff Gordon
1996	Terry Labonte
1997	Jeff Gordon

Most titles: 7 Richard Petty, Dale Earnhardt

				Season's money record:
Dale Earnhardt	$31,861,203	Darrell Waltrip	16,493,653	$4,201,227 Jeff Gordon 1997
Bill Elliott	18,399,264	Mark Martin	15,576,824	**Most Winston Cup race wins:**
Terry Labonte	17,426,907	Ricky Rudd	13,976,595	200 Richard Petty; 105 David
Jeff Gordon	17,413,094	Dale Jarrett	12,008,814	Pearson; 84 Bobby Allison,
Rusty Wallace	16,972,082	Geoff Bodine	11,926,626	Darrell Waltrip; 83 Cale
				Yarborough; 70 Dale Earnhardt

Daytona 500

The Daytona 500, held at the Daytona International Speedway every February, is one of NASCAR's top events.

Winners:

Year	Winner	Car	Average speed	
1959	Lee Petty	Oldsmobile	218.05km/h	*135.52 mph*
1960	Junior Johnson	Chevrolet	200.71km/h	*124.74 mph*
1961	Marvin Panch	Pontiac	240./1km/h	*149.60 mph*
1962	Fireball Roberts	Pontiac	245.42km/h	*152.53 mph*
1963	Tiny Lund	Ford	243.88km/h	*151.57 mph*
1964	Richard Petty	Plymouth	248.32km/h	*154.33 mph*
1965	Fred Lorenzen	Ford	227.74km/h	*141.54 mph*
1966	Richard Petty	Plymouth	258.45km/h	*160.63 mph*
1967	Mario Andretti	Ford	236.41km/h	*146.93 mph*
1968	Cale Yarborough	Mercury	230.49km/h	*143.25 mph*
1969	LeeRoy Yarborough	Ford	254.14km/h	*157.95 mph*
1970	Pete Hamilton	Plymouth	240.71km/h	*149.60 mph*
1971	Richard Petty	Plymouth	232.44km/h	*144.46 mph*
1972	A J Foyt	Mercury	259.93km/h	*161.55 mph*
1973	Richard Petty	Dodge	252.95km/h	*157.21 mph*
1974	Richard Petty	Dodge	226.69km/h	*140.89 mph*
1975	Benny Parsons	Chevrolet	247.22km/h	*153.65 mph*
1976	David Pearson	Mercury	244.86km/h	*152.18 mph*
1977	Cale Yarborough	Chevrolet	246.53km/h	*153.22 mph*
1978	Bobby Allison	Ford	257.01km/h	*159.73 mph*
1979	Richard Petty	Oldsmobile	231.66km/h	*143.98 mph*
1980	Buddy Baker	Oldsmobile	285.76km/h	*177.60 mph*
1981	Richard Petty	Buick	272.97km/h	*169.65 mph*
1982	Bobby Allison	Buick	247.77km/h	*153.99 mph*
1983	Cale Yarborough	Pontiac	250.97km/h	*155.98 mph*
1984	Cale Yarborough	Chevrolet	242.94km/h	*150.99 mph*
1985	Bill Elliott	Ford	277.18km/h	*172.27 mph*
1986	Geoff Bodine	Chevrolet	238.33km/h	*148.12 mph*
1987	Bill Elliott	Ford	283.60km/h	*176.26 mph*
1988	Bobby Allison	Buick	221.29km/h	*137.53 mph*
1989	Darrell Waltrip	Chevrolet	238.88km/h	*148.47 mph*
1990	Derrike Cope	Chevrolet	266.76km/h	*165.76 mph*
1991	Ernie Irvan	Chevrolet	238.42km/h	*148.15 mph*
1992	Davey Allison	Ford	257.90km/h	*160.256 mph*
1993	Dale Jarrett	Chevrolet	252.993km/h	*157.207 mph*
1994	Sterling Marlin	Chevrolet	252.556km/h	*156.931 mph*
1995	Sterling Marlin	Chevrolet	228.054km/h	*141.710 mph*
1996	Dale Jarrett	Ford	248.328km/h	*154.308 mph*
1997	Jeff Gordon	Chrevolet	238.651km/h	*148.295 mph*

Most wins: 7 Richard Petty; 4 Cale Yarborough; 3 Bobby Allison

Drag Racing

In this form of motor racing, two cars (or bikes) race each other over a distance of a quarter of a mile (402.3m). The sport was developed in the 1930s in the USA. The sport's governing body in the USA, the National Hot Rod Association (NHRA), was founded in 1950.

Records

The lowest elapsed time recorded by a piston-engined dragster from a standing start to 440 yards is 4.445 seconds by Larry Dixon (USA) at Englishtown, New Jersey on 19 May 1995. The highest terminal velocity at the end of a 440 yards run is 318.69 mph (5012.87km/h) by Kenny Bernstein (USA) at Topeka, Kansas on 12 Oct 1996.

NHRA Winston Series

Each year drivers collect points in a series of races throughout North America, culminating in the annual Winston Finals. The élite competition is the Top Fuel class.

Recent winners:

1980	Shirley Muldowney
1981	Jeb Allen
1982	Shirley Muldowney
1983	Gary Beck
1984	Joe Amato
1985-6	Don Garlits
1987	Dick LaHaie
1988	Joe Amato
1989	Gary Ormsby
1990-2	Joe Amato
1993	Eddie Hill
1994-5	Scott Kalita
1996	Kenny Bernstein
1997	Gary Scelzi

Most titles in Pro Stock: 10 Bob Glidden 1974-5, 1978-80, 1985-9; 4 Lee Shepherd 1981-4

Most titles in Funny Car: 8 John Force 1990-1, 1993-7; 4 Don Prudhomme 1975-8, Kenny Bernstein 1985-8

Rallying

The first long-distance rally was from Peking, China, to Paris between 10 June-10 August 1907. It was won by Prince Scipione Borghese (Ita) driving an Itala. Since then many famous long-distance races have been staged, the most famous being the Monte Carlo Rally, instituted in 1911. The RAC International Rally of Great Britain (now known as the Lombard-RAC Rally) was first held in 1927, but it did not gain recognition as an international event by the FIA until 1951.

Monte Carlo Rally

Winners (and their vehicles):

1911	Henri Rougier (Fra)	Turcat-Mery
1912	Julius Beutler (Ger)	Berliet
1924	Jean Ledure (Fra)	Bignan
1925	François Repusseau (Fra)	Renault 40 CV
1926	Hon. Victor Bruce & W J Brunell (UK)	AC Bristol
1927	Lefebvre & Despeux (Fra)	Amilcar
1928	Jacques Bignan (Fra)	Fiat
1929	Dr Sprenger van Eijk (Hol)	Graham-Paige
1930	Hector Petit (Fra)	Licorne
1931	Donald Healey (UK)	Invicta
1932-3	M Vasselle (Fra)	Hotchkiss
1934	Gas & Jean Trevoux (Fra)	Hotchkiss
1935	Christian Lahaye & R Quatresous (Fra)	Renault Nervasport
1936	Ion Zamfirescu & Christea (Rom)	Ford
1937	René le Begue & J Quinlin (Fra)	Delahaye
1938	G Bakker Schut & Karel Ton (Hol)	Ford
1939	Jean Trevoux & M Lesurque (Fra)	Hotchkiss
1949	Jean Trevoux & M Lesurque (Fra)	Hotchkiss
1950	Marcel Becquart & H Secret (Fra)	Hotchkiss
1951	Jean Trevoux & Roger Crovetto (Fra)	Delahaye
1952	Sidney Allard & Guy Warburton (UK)	Allard P2
1953	Maurice Gatsonides (Hol) & P Worledge (UK)	Ford Zephyr

1954	Louis Chiron (Fra) & Giro Basadonna (Spa)	Lancia-Aurelia
1955	Per Malling & Gunnar Fadum (Nor)	Sunbeam-Talbot
1956	Ronnie Adams & Frank Bigger (Ire)	Jaguar Mk VII
1957	*No race due to Suez crisis*	
1958	Guy Monraisse & Jacques Feret (Fra)	Renault Dauphine
1959	Paul Coltelloni & Pierre Alexandre (Fra)	Citroen ID19
1960	Walter Schock & Ralf Moll (Ger)	Mercedes 220SE
1961	Maurice Martin & Roger Bateau (Fra)	Panhard PL17
1962	Erik Carlsson & Gunnar Häggbom (Swe)	Saab 96
1963	Erik Carlsson & Gunnar Palm (Swe)	Saab 96
1964	Paddy Hopkirk & Henry Liddon (UK)	Mini-Cooper 'S'
1965	Timo Mäkinen (Fin) & Paul Easter (UK)	Mini-Cooper 'S'
1966	Pauli Toivonen & Ensio Mikander (Fin)	Citroen DS21
1967	Rauno Aaltonen (Fin) & Henry Liddon (UK)	Mini-Cooper 'S'
1968	Vic Elford & David Stone (UK)	Porsche 911T
1969-70	Björn Waldegård & Lars Helmer (Swe)	Porsche 911
1971	Ove Andersson (Swe) & David Stone (UK)	Alpine Renault A110
1972	Sandro Munari & Mario Manucci (Ita)	Lancia Fulvia
1973	Jean-Claude Andruet (Fra) & 'Biche' (Michèle Petit)	Alpine Renault A110
1974	*No race due to fuel crisis*	
1975	Sandro Munari & Mario Manucci (Ita)	Lancia Stratos
1976	Sandro Munari & Silvio Maiga (Ita)	Lancia Stratos
1977	Sandro Munari & Mario Manucci (Ita)	Lancia Stratos
1978	Jean-Pierre Nicolas & Vincent Laverne (Fra)	Porsche Carrera 911
1979	Bernard Darniche & Alain Mahe (Fra)	Lancia Stratos
1980	Walter Röhrl & Christian Geistdörfer (FRG)	Fiat Abarth 131
1981	Jean Ragnotti & Jean-Marc André (Fra)	Renault 5 Turbo
1982-3	Walter Röhrl & Christian Geistdörfer (FRG)	Opel Ascona
1984	Walter Röhrl & Christian Geistdörfer (FRG)	Audi Quattro
1985	Ari Vatanen (Fin) & Terry Harryman (UK)	Peugeot 205 Turbo 16
1986	Henri Toivonen (Fin) & Sergio Cresto (Ita)	Lancia Delta S4
1987	Massimo Biasion & Tiziano Siviero (Ita)	Lancia Delta HF4
1988	Bruno Saby & Jean-Francois Fauchille (Fra)	Lancia Delta HF4
1989	Massimo Biasion & Tiziano Siviero (Ita)	Lancia Delta Integrale
1990	Didier Auriol & Bernard Occelli (Fra)	Lancia Delta Integrale 16
1991	Carlos Sainz & Luis Moya (Spa)	Toyoya Celica GT4
1992	Didier Auriol & Bernard Occelli (Fra)	Lancia HF Integrale
1993	Didier Auriol & Bernard Occelli (Fra)	Toyota Celica
1994	François Delecour & Daniel Grataloup (Fra)	Ford Escort
1995	Carlos Sainz & Luis Moya (Spa)	Subaru Impreza
1996	Patrick Bernardini & Bernard Occelli (Fra)	Ford Escort
1997	Piero Liatti & Fabrizia Pons (Ita)	Subaru Impreza
1998	Carlos Sainz & Luis Moya (Spa)	Toyota Corolla

Most wins: 4 Munari, Röhrl
Most successful co-driver: 4 wins Geistdörfer

RAC Rally

Winners since 1951:

1951	Ian Appleyard & Pat Appleyard (UK)	Jaguar XK120
1952	Godfrey Imhof & Mrs B Fleming (UK)	Allard Cadillac J2
1953	Ian Appleyard & Pat Appleyard (UK)	Jaguar XK120
1954	Johnny Wallwork & J H Brooks (UK)	Triumph TR2
1955	James Ray & Brian Horrocks (UK)	Standard Ten
1956	Lyndon Sims, R Jones & Tony Ambrose (UK)	Aston Martin DB2
1957	*Not held due to Suez crisis*	
1958	Peter Harper & Bill Deane (UK)	Sunbeam Rapier II
1959	Gerald Burgess & Sam Croft-Pearson(UK)	Ford Zephyr

1960	Erik Carlsson (Swe) & Stuart Turner (UK)	Saab 96
1961	Erik Carlsson (Swe) & John Brown (UK)	Saab 96
1962	Erik Carlsson (Swe) & David Stone (UK)	Saab 96
1963	Tom Trana & Sune Lindström (Swe)	Volvo PV544
1964	Tom Trana & Gunnar Thermaenius (Swe)	Volvo 122S
1965	Rauno Aaltonen (Fin) & Tony Ambrose (UK)	BMC Mini-Cooper 'S'
1966	Bengt Soderström & Gunnar Palm (Swe)	Ford Cortina Lotus
1967	*Not held due to foot and mouth outbreak*	
1968	Simo Lampinen (Fin) & John Davenport (UK)	Saab 96 V4
1969-70	Harry Kallström (Fin) & Gunnar Häggbom (Swe)	Lancia Fulvia HF
1971	Stig Blomqvist & Arne Hertz (Swe)	Saab 96 V4
1972	Roger Clark & Tony Mason (UK)	Ford Escort RS
1973-5	Timo Mäkinen (Fin) & Henry Liddon (UK)	Ford Escort RS
1976	Roger Clark & Stuart Pegg (UK)	Ford Escort RS
1977	Björn Waldegård & Hans Thorszelius (Swe)	Ford Escort RS
1978-9	Hannu Mikkola (Fin) & Arne Hertz (Swe)	Ford Escort RS
1980	Henri Toivonen (Fin) & Paul White (UK)	Talbot Sunbeam Lotus
1981-2	Hannu Mikkola (Fin) & Arne Hertz (Swe)	Audi Quattro A1 & A2
1983	Stig Blomqvist & Björn Cederberg (Swe)	Audi Quattro A2
1984	Ari Vatanen (Fin) & Terry Harryman (UK)	Peugeot 205 Turbo 16
1985	Henri Toivonen (Fin) & Neil Wilson (UK)	Lancia Delta S4
1986	Timo Salonen (Fin) & Seppo Harjanne (Fin)	Peugeot 205 Turbo 16E2
1987	Juha Kankkunen & Jiro Piironen (Fin)	Lancia Delta 4WD
1988	Markku Alén & Ilkka Kivimäki (Fin)	Lancia Delta HF Integrale
1989	Pentti Airikkala (Fin) & Ronan McNamee (Ire)	Mitsubishi Galant VR-4
1990	Carlos Sainz & Luis Moya (Spa)	Toyoya Celica GT4
1991	Juha Kankkunen & Juha Piironen (Fin)	Lancia Delta HF Integrale
1992	Carlos Sainz & Luis Moya (Spa)	Toyoya Celica GT-Four
1993	Juha Kankkunen (Fin) & Nicky Grist (UK)	Toyota Celica Turbo
1994 -5	Colin McRae & Derek Ringer (UK)	Subaru Impreza
1996	Armin Schwarz (Ger) & Denis Giraudet (Fra)	Toyota Celica
1997	Colin McRae & Nicky Grist (UK)	Subaru Impreza

Most wins: 4 Mikkola; 3 Carlsson, Mäkinen, Kankkunen, McRae

Most successful co-drivers: 5 wins Hertz; 3 Liddon

World Rally Championships

A World Championship for makes of car was inaugurated in 1968 and a driver's championship, known as the FIA Cup for Drivers was instituted in 1977; it became the official World Drivers' Championship in 1979. A championship for co-drivers was introduced in 1981.

Winners

Makes

1968	Ford (GB)
1969	Ford (Europe)
1970	Porsche
1971	Alpine-Renault
1972	Lancia
1973	Alpine-Renault
1974-6	Lancia
1977-8	Fiat
1979	Ford
1980	Fiat
1981	Talbot
1982	Audi
1983	Lancia
1984	Audi
1985-6	Peugeot
1987-92	Lancia
1993-4	Toyota
1995-7	Subaru

Drivers

1977	Sandro Munari (Ita)
1978	Markku Alén (Fin)
1979	Björn Waldegård (Swe)
1980	Walter Röhrl (FRG)
1981	Ari Vatanen (Fin)
1982	Walter Röhrl (FRG)
1983	Hannu Mikkola (Fin)
1984	Stig Blomqvist (Swe)
1985	Timo Salonen (Fin)
1986-7	Juha Kankkunen (Fin)
1988-9	Mikki Biasion (Ita)

1990	Carlos Sainz (Spa)
1991	Juha Kankkunen (Fin)
1992	Carlos Sainz (Spa)
1993	Juha Kankkunen (Fin)
1994	Didier Auriol (Fra)
1995	Colin McRae (UK)
1996-7	Tommi Mäkinen (Fin)

Most event wins (1973-97):
21 Kankkunen; 20 Alén, Sainz; 18 Mikkola; 17 Biasion, Auriol; 16 Waldegård (19); 14 Röhrl; 13 McRae; 11 Blomqvist (14 from 1970), Salonen; 10 Tommi Mäkinen, Vatanen

Most wins in a season: 6 Auriol 1992

Netball

Invented in the USA in 1891, netball is a women's 7-a-side game, developed from basketball. The first national association was that of New Zealand in 1924, followed by England in 1926.

International governing body: International Federation of Netball Associations (IFNA), Birmingham Sports Centre, 201 Balsall Heath Road, Highgate, Birmingham B12 9DL. Tel: 0121 446 4451, Fax: 0121 440 2408. President: Anne Taylor, Executive Officer: Anne Steele. Formed in 1960. 40 member nations.

World Championships

First held in 1963.

Winners:

1963	Australia
1967	New Zealand
1971	Australia
1975	Australia
1979	Australia, New Zealand, Trinidad & Tobago
1983	Australia
1987	New Zealand
1991	Australia
1995	Australia

Olympic Games

The first Olympic Games of the modern era were staged in Athens, Greece, from 6-15 April 1896. The driving force behind their revival was Pierre de Fredi, Baron de Coubertin, who was born in Paris in 1863. He believed in the Greek athletic ideal of perfection of mind and body, and his energies were devoted to achieving his dream of reintroducing the Olympic Games, which had been staged for more than a thousand years before their prohibition in AD 394. In 1889, de Coubertin was commissioned by the French government to form a universal sports association and he visited other European nations to gather information. He made public his views on 25 November 1892 at the Sorbonne in Paris. This led to the formation of the International Olympic Committee in 1894, and thence to the staging of the Olympic Games, which were opened in Athens on Easter Monday 1896.

International Olympic Committee, Château de Vidy, C.P. 356, 1007 Lausanne, Switzerland. Tel: (41) 21 621 6111, Fax: (41) 21 621 6216. President: Juan Antonio Samaranch. All 197 member nations of the IOC competed at the 1996 Summer Games in Atlanta.

Venues of Summer Games

1896	Athens
1900	Paris
1904	St Louis
1906	Athens*
1908	London
1912	Stockholm
1920	Antwerp
1924	Paris
1928	Amsterdam
1932	Los Angeles
1936	Berlin
1948	London
1952	Helsinki
1956	Melbourne
1960	Rome
1964	Tokyo
1968	Mexico City
1972	Munich
1976	Montreal
1980	Moscow
1984	Los Angeles
1988	Seoul
1992	Barcelona
1996	Atlanta#
2000	Sydney
2004	Athens

* Intercalated Games held to celebrate the tenth anniversary of the 1896 Games. (Results from these 1906 Games have been included in the records in this book.)

Record participation: 10,310 competitors (6797 men, 3513 women), from 197 nations.

Venues of Winter Games

1924	Chamonix
1928	St Moritz
1932	Lake Placid
1936	Garmisch-Partenkirchen
1948	St Moritz
1952	Oslo
1956	Cortina d'Ampezzo
1960	Squaw Valley
1964	Innsbruck
1968	Grenoble
1972	Sapporo
1976	Innsbruck
1980	Lake Placid
1984	Sarajevo
1988	Calgary
1992	Albertville
1994	Lillehammer
1998	Nagano
2002	Salt Lake City

From 1994 the Winter Games have been held in the middle of the four-year cycle of the Summer Games.

The record participation has been 2176 (1389 men and 787 women) in 1998 with a record 72 nations.

Olympic Records

(See individual sports for champions at all events.)

Most medals

18   Larisa Latynina (USSR) gymnastics 1956-64
15   Nikolay Andrianov (USSR) gymnastics 1972-80
13   Eduardo Mangaiorotti (Ita) fencing 1936-60
13   Takashi Ono (Jap) gymnastics 1952-64
13   Boris Shakhlin (USSR) gymnastics 1956-64
12   Sawao Kato (Jap) gymnastics 1968-76
12   Paavo Nurmi (Fin) athletics 1920-28

Most gold medals

10   Ray Ewry (USA) athletics 1900-08
 9   Larisa Latynina (USSR) gymnastics 1956-64
 9   Paavo Nurmi (Fin) athletics 1920-28
 9   Mark Spitz (USA) swimming 1968-72
 9   Carl Lewis (USA) athletics 1984-96
 8   Sawao Kato (Jap) gymnastics 1968-76
 8   Matt Biondi (USA) swimming 1984-92
 8   Bjørn Dæhlie (Nor) Nordic skiing 1992-8

Most silver medals

 6   Shirley Babashoff (USA) swimming 1972-76
 6   Aleksandr Dityatin (USSR) gymnastics 1976-80
 6   Mikhail Voronin (USSR) gymnastics 1968-72

Most bronze medals

 6   Heikki Savolainen (Fin) gymnastics 1928-52

Most games winning medals

 6   Aladár Gerevich (Hun) fencing 1932-60

Most Games

Men

 9   Hubert Raudaschl (Aut) yachting 1964-96
 8   Raimondo d'Inzeo (Ita) equestrian 1948-76
 8   Piero d'Inzeo (Ita) equestrian 1948-76
 8   Paul Elvstrøm (Den) yachting 1948-60, 1968-72, 1984-8
 8   Durwood Knowles (UK/Bah) yachting 1948-72, 1988
 7   Ivan Ossier (Den) fencing 1908-32, 1948
 7   Rainer Klimke (FRG) equestrian 1960-76, 1984-8
 7   Michael Plumb (USA) equestrian 1960-76, 1984, 1992

Women

 7   Kerstin Palm (Swe) fencing 1964-88

Longest span of appearances

40 years Ivan Ossier (Den) fencing 1908-48, Magnus Konow (Nor) yachting 1908-48, Durwood Knowles (UK/Bah) yachting 1948-88, Paul Elvstrøm (Den) yachting 1948-88

Youngest gold medallists

The unknown French boy who coxed the winning Dutch rowing pair in 1900 was probably aged 7-10 years.

13yr 83d Kim Yoon-mi (SKo) women's short-track speed skating 1994 (youngest at Winter Games)
13yr 267d Marjorie Gestring (USA) women's diving 1936
14yr12d Giorgio Cesana (Ita) men's rowing 1906

Youngest medallists

10yr 215d Dimitrios Loundras (Gre) bronze men's gymnastics 1896
11yr 302d Luigina Giavotti (Ita) silver women's gymnastics 1928
12yr 24d Inge Sörensen (Den) bronze women's swimming 1936

Oldest gold medallists

64yr 257d Oscar Swahn (Swe) shooting 1912
64yr 2d Galen Spencer (USA) archery 1904
63yr 244d Robert Williams (USA) archery 1904

Oldest medallists

72yr 279d Oscar Swahn (Swe) silver shooting 1920
68yr 194d Samuel Duvall (USA) silver archery 1904
66yr 154d Louis Noverraz (Swi) silver yachting 1968

Oldest medallists at Winter Games

Gold: 48yr 357d Jay O'Brien(USA) bobsleigh 1932
Oldest medallist (of any colour): 49yr 278d Max Houben (Bel) bobsleigh 1948

The only man to win a gold medal in both Summer and Winter Games is Edward Eagan (USA): boxing 1920 and bobsleigh 1932.

The first woman to win a medal at both Summer and Winter Games was Christa Luding (née Rothenburger). She won speed skating gold at 500m in 1984 and 1000m in 1988 as well as the silver for 500m in 1988; in the 1988 Summer Games she won the silver medal at sprint cycling.

Olympic Medal-Winners at Summer Games 1896-1996 (including 1906)

Nation	G	S	B	Total
USA	833	634	548	2015
USSR/CIS	485	395	354	1234
Germany/FRG★	207	245	264	716
United Kingdom	177	233	225	635
France	176	181	205	562
Sweden	134	152	173	459
Italy	166	136	142	444
Hungary	142	128	155	425
GDR	153	130	127	410
Australia	87	85	122	294
Finland	99	80	132	292
Japan	93	89	98	280
Romania	63	77	99	239
Poland	50	67	110	227
Canada	49	77	91	217
Netherlands	49	57	81	187
Bulgaria	43	76	63	182
Switzerland	46	68	60	174
China	52	63	49	164

Nation	G	S	B	Total	Nation	G	S	B	Total
Czechoslovakia/Cze#	53	53	53	160	Lithuania	1	–	2	3
Denmark	39	60	57	156	Israel	–	1	2	3
Belgium	37	50	49	136	Malaysia	–	1	2	3
South Korea	38	42	46	126	Armenia	1	1	–	2
Norway	46	40	38	124	Costa Rica	1	1	–	2
Greece	28	42	44	114	Luxembourg	1	1	–	2
Cuba	45	33	31	109	Syria	1	1	–	2
Yugoslavia	27	31	32	90	Surinam	1	–	1	2
Austria	19	31	34	84	Tanzania	–	2	–	2
New Zealand	30	12	29	71	Cameroon	–	1	1	2
Russia	26	25	19	70	Haiti	–	1	1	2
Spain	22	25	17	64	Iceland	–	1	1	2
Turkey	30	16	13	59	Moldova	–	1	1	2
South Africa	19	18	21	58	Uzbekistan	–	1	1	2
Brazil	12	13	29	54	Zambia	–	1	1	2
Argentina	13	21	16	50					
Kenya	14	17	16	47					
Mexico	9	13	19	41					
Iran	5	13	18	36					
Jamaica	5	16	11	32					
North Korea	8	6	12	26					
Ukraine	9	2	12	23					
Estonia	7	6	10	23					
Ireland	8	5	6	19					
Egypt	6	6	6	18					
Ethiopia	8	1	7	16					
India	8	3	4	15					
Portugal	3	4	8	15					
Belarus	1	6	8	15					
Nigeria	2	5	7	14					
Mongolia	–	5	9	14					
Morocco	4	2	5	11					
Kazakhstan	3	4	4	11					
Indonesia	3	4	3	10					
Pakistan	3	3	4	10					
Uruguay	2	1	6	9					
Trinidad & Tobago	1	2	6	9					
Philippines	–	2	7	9					
Venezuela	1	2	5	8					
Chile	–	6	2	8					
Algeria	3	–	4	7					
Latvia	–	5	2	7					
Croatia	2	2	2	6					
Uganda	1	3	2	6					
Tunisia	1	2	3	6					
Thailand	1	1	4	6					
Colombia	–	2	4	6					
Puerto Rico	–	1	5	6					
Taiwan	–	3	2	5					
Peru	1	3	–	4					
Bahamas	1	1	2	4					
Namibia	–	4	–	4					
Lebanon	–	2	2	4					
Slovenia	–	2	2	4					
Ghana	–	1	3	4					
Slovakia	1	1	1	3					

★ Germany 1896-1952 and 1992-6 and including 200 medals by FRG 1956-88. See also GDR. Medals won by the combined German teams of 1956, 1960 and 1964 have been allocated to FRG or GDR according to the athlete's origin.

Czechoslovakia includes Bohemia and Czech Republic. Medals won in 1896, 1900 and 1904 by mixed teams from two countries have been included for both.

2 bronze: Georgia, Panama

1 gold: Burundi, Ecuador, Hong Kong, Zimbabwe

1 silver: Azerbaijan, Ivory Coast, Netherlands Antilles, Sénegal, Singapore, Sri Lanka, Tonga, Virgin Islands

1 bronze: Barbados, Bermuda, Djibouti, Dominican Republic, Guyana, Iraq, Mozambique, Niger Republic, Qatar

114 nations in all.

Olympic Medal-Winners at Winter Games (to 1998)

Nation	G	S	B	Total
Norway	83	87	69	239
USSR/CIS#	87	63	67	217
USA	59	59	41	159
Germany/FRG★	57	53	45	155
Austria	39	53	53	145
Finland	38	49	48	135
GDR★	39	36	35	110
Sweden	39	28	35	102
Switzerland	29	31	32	92
Canada	25	25	29	79
Italy	27	27	23	77
Netherlands	19	23	19	61
France	18	17	26	61
Russia	21	14	7	42
Japan	8	9	12	29
Czechoslovakia#	2	8	16	26
United Kingdom	7	4	13	24
South Korea	9	3	4	16
China	–	10	4	14
Liechtenstein	2	2	5	9

Nation	G	S	B	Total
Hungary	-	2	4	6
Kazakhstan	1	2	2	5
Belgium	1	1	3	5
Poland	1	1	2	4
Yugoslavia	-	3	1	4
Belarus	-	2	2	4
Czech Republic#	1	1	1	3
Ukraine	1	1	1	3
Slovenia	-	-	3	3
Bulgaria	1	-	1	3
Spain	1	-	1	2
Luxembourg	-	2	-	2
North Korea	-	1	1	2
Australia	-	-	2	2

Separate republics from 1994.
* Germany to 1952 and 1992, Federal Republic of Germany 1956-88. GDR 1956-88 tallied separately. Medals won by the combined German teams of 1956, 1960 and 1964 have been allocated to FRG or GDR according to the athlete's origin.
1 gold: Uzbekistan
1 silver: New Zealand, Denmark
1 bronze: Romania
   Liechtenstein is the only nation to have won medals at the Winter Games but not at the Summer event.

Orienteering

Cross-country running with the aid of map and compass, orienteering was invented by Major Ernst Killander in 1918 in Sweden. That country's national federation, the Svenska Orienteringsförbundet, was formed in 1938.
International governing body: International Orienteering Federation (IOF), Radiokatu 20, FI-00093 SLU, Finland. Tel: (358) 9 3481 3112, Fax: (358) 9 3481 3113. President: Sue Harvey, Secretary General: Barbro Rönnberg. Founded in 1961. 41 member nations (9 associate) in 1998.

World Championships

First held in 1966 and staged biennially, with short event titles being added in 1991. The long event is at 17.5km, short at 5.8km for men; the distances for women are 10.5km and 5.5km respectively.
Winners:

	Men	Women
1966	Åge Hadler (Nor)	Ulla Lindkvist (Swe)
1968	Karl Johansson (Swe)	Ulla Lindkvist (Swe)
1970	Stig Berge (Nor)	Ingrid Hadler (Nor)
1972	Åge Hadler (Nor)	Sarolta Monspart (Hun)
1974	Bernt Frilen (Swe)	Mona Norgaard (Den)
1976	Egil Johansen (Nor)	Liisa Veijalainen (Fin)
1978	Egil Johansen (Nor)	Anne Berit Eid (Nor)
1979	Øyvin Thon (Nor)	Outi Borgenstrom (Fin)
1981	Øyvin Thon (Nor)	Annichen Kringstad (Swe)
1983	Morten Berglia (Nor)	Annichen Kringstad (Swe)
1985	Kari Sallinen (Fin)	Annichen Kringstad (Swe)
1987	Kent Olsson (Swe)	Arja Hannus (Swe)
1989	Petter Thoresen (Nor)	Marita Skogum (Swe)
1991	Jörgen Mårtensson (Swe)	Katalin Olah (Hun)
1993	Allan Mogensen (Den)	Marita Skogum (Swe)
1995	Jörgen Mårtensson (Swe)	Marie-Luce Romanens (Swz)
1997	Petter Thoresen (Nor)	Hanne Staff (Nor)

	Men's short event	Women's short event
1991	Petr Kazak (Cs)	Jana Cieslarová (Cs)
1993	Petter Thoresen (Nor)	Anna Bogren (Swe)
1995	Yuriy Omelchenko (Ukr)	Katalin Oláh (Hun)
1997	Janne Salmi (Fin)	Lucie Böhm (Aut)

Men's relay

Norway	1970, 1978, 1981, 1983, 1985, 1987, 1989
Sweden	1966, 1968, 1972, 1974, 1976, 1979
Switzerland	1991, 1993, 1995
Denmark	1997

Women's relay

Sweden   1966, 1970, 1974, 1976, 1981, 1983, 1985, 1989, 1991, 1993, 1997
Finland   1972, 1978, 1979, 1995
Norway   1968, 1987

World Cup

A biennial event introduced in 1988 and held over a series of races.
Overall winners:

	Men	Women
1988	Øyvin Thon (Nor)	Ragnhild Bratberg (Nor)
1990	Havard Tveite (Nor)	Ragnhild Bente-Andersen (Nor)
1992	Joakim Ingelssen (Swe)	Marita Skogum (Swe)
1994	Petter Thoresen (Nor)	Marlena Jansson (Swe)
1996	Johan Ivarsson (Swe)	Gunilla Svärd (Swe)

Ski Orienteering World Championships

First held in 1975 and now contested biennially over the classic distance (c.20km), and from 1988 over
a short distance, or as a sprint event (7-9 km) as well.
Winners:

Classic

	Men	Women
1975	Olavi Svanberg (Fin)	Sinikka Kukkonen (Fin)
1977	Örjan Svahn (Swe)	Marianne Bogestedt (Swe)
1980	Pertti Tikka (Fin)	Mirja Puhakka (Fin)
1982	Olavi Svanberg (Fin)	Arja Hannus (Swe)
1984	Anssi Juutilainen (Fin)	Mirja Puhakka (Fin)
1986	Claes Berglund (Swe)	Ragnhild Bratberg (Nor)
1988	Anssi Juutilainen (Fin)	Virpi Juutilainen (Fin)
1990	Anders Björkman (Swe)	Ragnhild Bratberg (Nor)
1992	Vidar Benjaminsen (Nor)	Annika Zell (Swe)
1994	Nicolo Corradini (Ita)	Pepa Miloucheva (Bul)
1996	Nicolo Corradini (Ita)	Annika Zell (Swe)
1998	Viktor Korchagin (Rus)	Liisa Antilla (Fin)

Sprint

	Men	Women
1988	Hannu Koponen (Fin)	Ragnhild Bratberg (Nor)
1990	Anssi Juutilainen (Fin)	Ragnhild Bratberg (Nor)
1992	Vidar Benjaminsen (Nor)	Arja Hannus (Swe)
1994	Nicolo Corradini (Ita) &	
	Ivan Kuzmin (Rus)	Virpi Juutilainen (Fin)
1996	Björn Lans (Swe)	Arja Noolioja (Fin)
1998	Raino Pesu (Fin)	Anika Zell (Swe)

Men's relay

Sweden   1977. 1980, 1982, 1984, 1990, 1996
Finland   1975, 1988, 1992
Norway   1986, 1994

Women's relay

Sweden   1982, 1984, 1992, 1994, 1996
Finland   1975, 1977, 1980, 1988, 1990
Norway   1986

Pelota

Pelota is the generic name for a number of court games that are played, usually with gloves or baskets, although originally with the hands. *Longue paume* was introduced into France from Italy in the 13th century, and this developed into real tennis (qv), for a long time the French national game. Although the game languished in the 17th century, it survived in the Basque country, which straddles France and Spain on the Atlantic coast, and it is there that the current game of Pelote Basque was developed. The Fédération Française de Pelote Basque was formed in 1921 and the Federación Internacional de Pelota Vasca was founded in 1929 in Spain, where the sport is known as pelota.

In the Basque country the traditional courts are known as *trinquete*, while in Latin America and the rest of Spain the courts are usually of the *fronton* (enclosed stadium) variety. This type of court is known in Basque as *jai-alai*, and this is the name of the game itself in the USA and Latin America.

The *chistera*, attached to the player's arm and used to propel the ball at great speed, was developed from a wicker fruit-basket in the 1860s. Claims that pelota is the fastest of all ball games are reinforced by the fact that a ball by José Ramon Areitio at Newport, Rhode Island in 1979. was measured electronically at 302km/h.

International governing body: Federación Internacional de Pelota Vasca (FIPV), Palacio de Urdanibia, Apdo. de Correos 468, 20300 Irun, Spain. Tel: (34) 943 610006, Fax: (34) 943 610044. President: Enrique Gaytan de Ayala, General Director: José Iraundegui. Founded 1929. 21 full and 25 associate member nations in 1998.

World Championships

The FIVP stages World Championships every four years, the first of which was in 1952 for a variety of events, including long- and short-court and trinquete-court games. The most successful pair have been Roberto Elias and Juan Labat (Arg), who won the Trinquete Share in 1952, 1958, 1962 and 1966. Labat won seven world titles in all.

The most wins in the long-court game of Cesta Punta is three by Hamuy (Mex), with different partners, 1958, 1962 and 1966.

Olympic Games

Pelota was played as a demonstration sport at the Olympic Games in 1924, 1968 and 1992.

Pétanque

Also known as 'boules', pétanque is derived from the ancient French game of *Jeu Provençal*. It differs in that, in the latter, the bowls are delivered from a short run-up, whereas in pétanque they are delivered from a stationary position. The steel bowls (or boules) have a diameter of 7-8cm and weigh 620-800g.

International governing bodies: Confédération Mondiale Sports Boules (CMSB), Stade Bouliste Rainier III, rue de l'Industrie, MC 98000, Monaco. Tel: (377) 9315 8724, Fax: (377) 9315 8217. President: Alphonse Lagier-Bruno, General Secretary: Denis Ravera. Founded 1985. 71 member nations in 1998.

Fédération Internationale de Pétanque et Jeu Provençal (FIPJP), 13 rue Trigovine, F-13002, Marseille, France. Tel: (33) 9191 8517, Fax: (33) 9362 3579. President: Henri Bernard, Secretary-General: Claude Azema. Founded 1945, originally as the Fédération Française de Pétanque et Jeu Provençal (FFPJP), becoming the FIPJP in 1958. 43 member nations.

Men's World Championships

First held in 1959. Contested by teams of three.
Wins:

16	France	1959, 1961, 1963, 1972, 1974, 1976-7, 1985, 1988-9, 1991-6
4	Switzerland	1965-6, 1973, 1980
3	Italy	1975, 1978-9
3	Morocco	1984, 1987, 1990
3	Tunisia	1983, 1986, 1997
1	Algeria 1964, Spain 1971, Belgium 1981, Monaco 1982	

Women's World Championships

Held biennially from 1988.
Winners:

2	Thailand	1988, 1990
2	France	1992, 1994
1	Spain	1996

Polo

A 4-a-side stick and ball game played on horseback, polo originated in Central Asia. Its origins can be traced to around 3100BC, when it was played as Sagol Kangjei in Manipur State, India. It is also claimed to be of Persian origin, having been played as Pulu c.525BC. The British picked up the game in India in the 1850s, and the earliest polo club of the modern era was the Cachar Club, founded in Assam in 1859. The game was first played in England in 1869 by the 10th Hussars, and in the USA in 1876. The Hurlingham Polo Association, Hurlingham, London, first staged a match in 1874 and the club committee drew up the first set of English rules a year later.

Polo is played on the largest pitch of any game, with maximum length of 300 yards (274m) and width of 200 yards (182m) without boards, or 160 yards (146m) with boards.

International governing body: Federation of International Polo (FIP), 269 South Beverly Drive, Suite 364, Beverly Hills, CA 90212, USA. Tel: (1) 310 557 9259, Fax: (1) 310 472 5220. President: Glen Holden. Founded 1983. 47 member nations in 1998.

High-goal players

Polo games are often contested on a handicap basis, each player being awarded a handicap measured in goals up to a maximum of ten, attained by the world's best players. In the history of the game, 55 players have been awarded this handicap. A high-goal player is one with a handicap of five, so a high-goal team rates at 20 or more. Two matches have been played between two 40-goal teams, that is, with all players having the highest handicap: the first was at Palermo, Buenos Aires, Argentina between El Trébol and Venado Tuerto in 1975; the second was contested by Mexican and Argentinian players at the Empire Polo Club, Indio, California, USA on 16 December 1990, with Westbury beating River Plate 8-7.

The highest handicap ever attained by a woman is five, by Claire Tomlinson in 1986.

World Championships

Contested in 1989 in West Berlin, when the USA beat Great Britain 7-6 in the final; 3rd Argentina, 4th Chile.

Westchester Cup

The first international match was between Great Britain and the United States at Newport, Rhode Island in 1886 for an international trophy given by the Westchester Club. Last contested in 1939, the series was revived in 1988 when the USA beat Australasia.

Winners:

Great Britain	1886, 1900, 1902, 1914, 1997
United States	1909, 1911, 1913, 1921, 1924, 1927, 1930, 1936, 1939, 1988, 1992

Cup of the Americas

Contested by Argentina and the USA. The USA won the first two matches in 1928 and 1932, and Argentina all subsequent contests: 1936, 1950, 1966, 1969, 1979, 1980 and 1988.

Olympic Games

Polo has been included at five Olympic Games.
Winners:

1900	Foxhunters (UK/USA)
1908	Roehampton (UK)
1920	Great Britain
1924	Argentina
1936	Argentina

Champion Cup

Britain's premier tournament from its inception in 1876 to 1939, when it was last played at Hurlingham, London. The teams with most wins were Freebooters 9, and Sussex 8

British Open Championship

Played annually for the Cowdray Park Gold Cup (now the Veuve Clicquot Gold Cup) at Cowdray Park, Midhurst, Sussex; this competition replaced the Champion Cup.
Winners:

Los Indios	1956
Windsor Park	1957, 1966, 1969
Cowdray Park	1958, 1961-2
Casarejo	1959-60
La Vulci	1963
Jersey Lilies	1964-5
Woolmer's Park	1967
Pimms	1968, 1971-2
Boca Raton	1970
Stowell Park	1973-4, 1976, 1978, 1980
Greenhill Farm	1975
Foxcote	1977
Songhai	1979
Falcons	1981, 1983
Southfield	1982, 1984
Maple Leafs	1985
Tramontana	1986-9, 1991
Hildon	1990
Black Bears	1992
Alcatel	1993
Ellerston	1994 (Black), 1995 (White), 1998
C S Brooks	1996
Labegarce	1997

Most wins: 5 Stowell Park, Tramontana
Most wins by individual: 9 Carlos Gracida (Mex)

Powerboating

Powerboat racing started in about 1900, and there are now a large number of categories of boats that race either on inland waters or offshore. A petrol engine was first fitted in a boat by Jean Lenoir on the River Seine in 1865.

International governing body: Union Internationale Motonautique (UIM), Stade Louis II Entrée H, 1 Avenue des Castelans, MC 98000, Monaco. Tel: (377) 9205 2522, Fax: (377) 9205 2523. President: Ralf Fröhling, Secretary-General: Régine Vandekerckhove. Founded 1922, 61 member nations (and 5 associate) in 1998.

Harmsworth Trophy

This perpetual trophy was presented by Sir Alfred Harmsworth (later Lord Northcliffe) in 1903. The race for the trophy was for many years the world's most prestigious powerboating event.

Winners (to 1961):

Year	Boat	Driver	Speed (km/h)
1903	Napier I (Eng)	Dorothy Levitt	31.43
1904	Trefle-A-Quatre (Fra)	Emile Thubron	42.86
1905	Napier II (Eng)	Lord Montague	41.89
1906	Yarrow-Napier (Eng)	Lionel de Rothschild	24.91
1907	Dixie I (USA)	E J Schroeder	51.14
1908	Dixie II (USA)	E J Schroeder	50.45
1910	Dixie III (USA)	F K Burnham	58.00
1911	Dixie IV (USA)	F K Burnham	64.82
1912	Maple Leaf IV (Eng)	Tommy Sopwith	69.49
1913	Maple Leaf IV (Eng)	Tommy Sopwith	92.46
1920	Miss America I (USA)	Garfield Wood	98.99
1921	Miss America II (USA)	Garfield Wood	96.16
1926	Miss America V (USA)	Garfield Wood	98.359
1928	Miss America VII (USA)	Garfield Wood	95.474
1929	Miss America VIII (USA)	Garfield Wood	121.163
1930	Miss America IX (USA)	Garfield Wood	124.294
1932	Miss America X (USA)	Garfield Wood	126.315
1933	Miss America X (USA)	Garfield Wood	139.915
1949	Skip-A-Long (USA)	Stanley Dollar	151.737
1950	Slo-Mo-Shun IV (USA)	Stanley Sayres	162.029
1956	Shanty I (USA)	William Waggoner, Jr	144.439
1959	Miss Supertest III (Can)	Bob Hayward	160.595
1960	Miss Supertest III (Can)	Bob Hayward	185.852
1961	Miss Supertest III (Can)	Bob Hayward	158.066

The series lapsed, but was revised under a new formula in 1977 as the Harmsworth British & Commonwealth Trophy for Motorboats.

Winners (from 1977):

Year	Boat	Driver
1977-8	Limit-Up (Eng)	Michael Doxford & Tim Powell
1979	Uno-Mint-Jewellery (Eng)	Derek Pobjoy

From 1980 to 1983 the Harmsworth Trophy was awarded on points for a series of offshore races.

Winning drivers:

1980	Bill Elswick & Paul Clauser (USA)
1981	Paul Clauser (USA)
1982	Al Copeland & B Sirios (USA)
1983	George Morales (USA)

The Harmsworth trophy was then contested by 2-boat national teams at Formula Two for outboard engines.

Winners:

1985	Jonathan Jones, Mark Wilson & John Hill (UK)
1986	Bill Seebold, Jr (USA)

Not contested in 1987 and 1988; in 1989 the trophy was returned to world offshore competition and won by Stefano Casiraghi (Ita).

American Powerboat Association Gold Cup

The American Powerboat Association was formed in 1903, and held its first Gold Cup race on the Hudson River in 1904, when the winner was Standard, piloted by C C Riotto at an average speed of 39km/h.

Winners (with average speed) from 1970:

Year	Boat	Driver	km/h	mph
1970	Miss Budweiser	Dean Chenoweth	101.848	163.908
1971	Miss Madison	Jim McCormick	101.522	163.384
1972	Atlas Van Lines	Bill Muncey	103.547	166.643
1973	Miss Budweiser	Dean Chenoweth	104.046	167.446
1974	Pay 'N' Pak	George Henley	112.056	180.337
1975	Pay 'N' Pak	George Henley	113.350	182.419
1976	Miss US	Tom d'Eath	108.021	173.843
1977	Atlas Van Lines	Bill Muncey	114.849	184.832
1978	Atlas Van Lines	Bill Muncey	104.448	167.330
1979	Atlas Van Lines	Bill Muncey	107.892	173.631
1980	Miss Budweiser	Dean Chenoweth	108.459	174.543
1981	Miss Budweiser	Dean Chenoweth	117.815	189.600
1982	Atlas Van Lines	Chip Hanauer	120.081	193.246
1983	Atlas Van Lines	Chip Hanauer	118.506	190.712
1984	Atlas Van Lines	Chip Hanauer	130.866	210.603
1985	Miller American	Chip Hanauer	121.612	195.710
1986	Miller American	Chip Hanauer	116.886	188.105
1987	Miller American	Chip Hanauer	127.745	205.580
1988	Circus Circus	Chip Hanauer	128.406	206.644
1989	Miss Budweiser	Tom D'Eath	131.388	211.443
1990	Miss Budweiser	Tom D'Eath	143.176	230.413
1991	Winston Eagle	Mark Tate	137.771	221.715
1992	Miss Budweiser	Chip Hanauer	136.282	219.319
1993	Miss Budweiser	Chip Hanauer	141.296	227.388
1994	Smokin' Joe Camel	Mark Tate	145.260	233.773
1995	Miss Budweiser	Chip Hanauer	149.160	240.050
1996	PICO American Dream	Dave Villwock	149.328	240.314
1997	Miss Budweiser	Dave Villwock	129.366	208.189
1998	Miss Budweiser	Dave Villwock	140.309	225.799

Most wins (pilot): 10 Chip Hanauer; 8 Bill Muncey 1956-7, 1961-2, 1972, 1977-9; 5 Garfield Wood 1917-21

Olympic Games

Motorboating was included in the 1908 Olympic Games. Emile Thubron (Fra) won Class A in his boat Camille; Thomas Thornycroft, Bernard Redwood and Captain Field-Richards won Classes B and C in their boat Gyrinus.

World Champions

Formula One
Currently 2000cc.

1981	Renato Molinari (Ita)
1982	Roger Jenkins (UK)
1983	Renato Molinari (Ita)
1984	Renato Molinari (Ita)
1985	Bob Spalding (UK)
1986	Gene Thibodaux (USA)
1987	Ben Robertson (USA) *(just one race)*
1990	John Hill (UK)
1991	Jonathan Jones (UK)
1992	Fabricio Bocca (Ita)
1993-6	Guido Cappellini (Ita)
1997	Scott Gilman (USA)

Formula Two (Formula Grand Prix) World Champions

Inland circuit championships.

1982-3	Michael Werner (FRG)
1984-5	John Hill (UK)
1986	Jonathan Jones (UK) & Buck Thornton (USA)
1987	Bill Seebold (USA)
1988	Chris Bush (USA)
1989	Jonathan Jones (UK)

Offshore Class 1 World Champions

For 16-litre engines. On points for a worldwide series of races 1964-76 and from 1992; for a single or two races 1977-91

1966	Jim Wynne (USA)
1967	Don Aronow (USA)
1968	Vincenzo Balestrieri (Ita)
1969	Don Aronow (USA)
1970	Vincenzo Balestrieri (Ita)
1971	William Wishnick (USA)
1972	Bobby Rautboard (USA)
1973-4	Carlo Bonomi (Ita)
1975	Franz Wallace (Bra)
1976	Tom Gentry (USA)
1977	Betty Cook (USA)
1978	Francesco Cosentino (Ita)
1979	Betty Cook (USA)
1980	Michael Maynard (USA)
1981	Jerry Jacoby (USA)
1982	Renato della Valle (Ita)
1983	Tony Garcia (USA)
1984	Alberto Petri (Ita)
1985	Anthony Roberts (USA)
1986	Antonio Giofredi (Ita)
1987	Steve Curtis (UK)
1988	Fabio Buzzi (Ita)
1989	Stefano Casiraghi (Ita)
1990	*Not held*
1991	Angelo Spelta (Ita)
1992	Walter Ragazzi (Ita)
1993	Khalsan Harib (UAE)
1994	Norberto Feretti (Ita)
1995	Saeed Al Tayer & Felix Serralles (UAE)
1996	Saeed Al Tayer (UAE)
1997	Laith Pharaon

Speed Records

The UIM recognizes a large number of speed records for different categories of boats. The fastest speed recognized for an outboard-powered boat is 285.83km/h in a Lauterbach hull powered by a Chevrolet engine, driven in class E by P R Knight on Lake Ruataniwha, New Zealand, 1986. The fastest speed recorded for a diesel (compression ignition) boat is 218.248km/h by the hydroplane Iveco World Leader powered by an Aifo-Fiat engine, driven by Carlo Bonomi at Venice, Italy on 4 Apr 1985.

Powerlifting

Among the many different lifts that have been practised by weight-lifters and incorporated in tests of strength, powerlifting now recognizes the squat, bench press and dead lift, all performed two-handed. The competitor is allowed three attempts at each lift and the best successful attempt on each lift is totalled. There are eleven weight categories for men and ten for women.

The sport of powerlifting was first contested at national level in Great Britain in 1958. The first US Championships were held in 1964.

International governing body: International Powerlifting Federation (IPF), PO Box 6007, S-129 06, Hagersten, Sweden. President: Grahame Fong, Secretary General: Arnold Boström. Founded in 1972. 71 member nations in 1998.

World Championships

First held for men as unofficial championships in 1971 and officially in 1973, and for women in 1980. *Champions from 1980 (figures represent total of three lifts in kg):*

Men

52kg

1980	Hideaki Inaba (Jap) 567.5
1981	Hideaki Inaba (Jap) 560
1982	Hideaki Inaba (Jap) 552.5
1983	Hideaki Inaba (Jap) 565
1984	Chuck Dunbar (USA) 532.5
1985	Hideaki Inaba (Jap) 562.5
1986	Hideaki Inaba (Jap) 577.5
1987	Hideaki Inaba (Jap) 587.5
1988	Hideaki Inaba (Jap) 560
1989	Hideaki Inaba (Jap) 560
1990	Hideaki Inaba (Jap) 560
1991	Hideaki Inaba (Jap) 545
1992	Sergey Zhuravlev (Rus) 550
1993	Andrzej Stanaszek (Pol) 567.5
1994	Andrzej Stanaszek (Pol) 577.5
1995	Andrzej Stanaszek (Pol) 567.5
1996	Andrzej Stanaszek (Pol) 570
1997	Andrzej Stanaszek (Pol) 580

56kg

1980	Precious McKenzie (NZ) 587.5
1981	Hiroyuki Isagawa (Jap) 577.5
1982	Lamar Gant (USA) 590
1983	Lamar Gant (USA) 575
1984	Lamar Gant (USA) 580
1985	Hiroyuki Isagawa (Jap) 562.5
1986	Hiroyuki Isagawa (Jap) 572.5
1987	Gerrard McNamara (Ire) 550
1988	Hiroyuki Isagawa (Jap) 585
1989	Hiroyuki Isagawa (Jap) 600
1990	Gary Simes (UK) 567.5
1991	Hiroyuki Isagawa (Jap) 602.5
1992	Denis Thios (Ina) 580
1993	Denis Thios (Ina) 605
1994	Hiroyuki Isagawa (Jap) 592.5
1995	Konstantin Pavlov (Rus) 597.5
1996	Konstantin Pavlov (Rus) 622.5
1997	Hu Chun-Hsiung (Tai) 625

60kg

1980	Lamar Gant (USA) 705
1981	Lamar Gant (USA) 625
1982	Kullervo Lampela (Fin) 582.5
1983	Göran Henrysson (Swe) 605
1984	Göran Henrysson (Swe) 600

1985	Göran Henrysson (Swe) 605		1983	Mike Bridges (USA) 807.5
1986	Lamar Gant (USA) 647.5		1984	Ed Coan (USA) 875
1987	Lamar Gant (USA) 677.5		1985	Jarmo Virtanen (Fin) 842.5
1988	Lamar Gant (USA) 675		1986	Jarmo Virtanen (Fin) 850
1989	Lamar Gant (USA) 650		1987	Gene Bell (USA) 822.5
1990	Lamar Gant (USA) 647.5		1988	Hannu Malinen (Fin) 750
1991	Gerard Tromp (Hol) 615		1989	Jarmo Virtanen (Fin) 827.5
1992	Gerald McNamara (Ire) 650		1990	Jarmo Virtanen (Fin) 832.5
1993	Talambanua Nanda (Ina) 630		1991	Aleksandr Lekomtyev (USSR) 790
1994	Wim Elyn (Bel) 645		1992	Jarmo Virtanen (Fin) 832.5
1995	Wim Elyn (Bel) 657.5		1993	Jarmo Virtanen (Fin) 850
1996	Sutrisno (Ina) 702.5		1994	Walter Thomas (USA) 807.5
1997	Lee Yung-Chang (Tai) 642.5		1995	Jarmo Virtanen (Fin) 827.5
			1996	Roman Szymkowiak (Pol) 792.5
			1997	Sergey Mor (Rus) 810

67.5kg

1980	Rickey Crain (USA) 730			
1981	Joe Bradley (USA) 732.5		**90kg**	
1982	Stefan Nentis (Swe) 697.5		1980	Vince Anello (USA) 867.5
1983	Bob Wahl (USA) 705		1981	Walter Thomas (USA) 930
1984	Dan Austin (USA) 722.5		1982	Walter Thomas (USA) 857.5
1985	Eddie Pengelly (UK) 667.5		1983	Kenneth Mattsson (Swe) 872.5
1986	Dan Austin (USA) 712.5		1984	Dennis Wright (USA) 840
1987	Dan Austin (USA) 717.5		1985	David Caldwell (UK) 832.5
1988	Dan Austin (USA) 717.5		1986	Jari Tahtinen (Fin) 822.5
1989	Dan Austin (USA) 690		1987	Sly Anderson (USA) 830
1990	Dan Austin (USA) 730		1988	Gene Bell (USA) 860
1991	Dan Austin (USA) 742.5		1989	George Herring (USA) 855
1992	Dan Austin (USA) 695		1990	George Herring (USA) 835
1993	Aleksey Sivokon (Kzk) 750		1991	Sly Anderson (USA) 835
1994	Aleksey Sivokon (Kzk) 765		1992	Sly Anderson (USA) 862.5
1995	Jan Wilczynski (Pol) 682.5		1993	Gene Bell (USA) 870
1996	Wade Hooper (USA) 730		1994	Frank Schramm (Ger) 882.5
1997	Aleksey Sivokon (Kzk) 772.5		1995	Janne Toivanen (Fin) 862.5
			1996	Gene Bell (USA) 882.5
			1997	Gene Bell (USA) 862.5

75kg

1980	Rick Gaugler (USA) 787.5		**100kg**	
1981	Steve Alexander (USA) 752.5		1980	Mark Dimiduk (USA) 922.5
1982	Rickey Crain (USA) 772.5		1981	Jim Cash (USA) 922.5
1983	Rickey Crain (USA) 762.5		1982	Kenneth Mattsson (Swe) 880
1984	Gene Bell (USA) 762.5		1983	Fred Hatfield (USA) 920
1985	Eric Coppin (Bel) 765		1984	Tony Stevens (UK) 915
1986	Rick Crilly (Can) 732.5		1985	Tony Stevens (UK) 907.5
1987	Jarmo Virtanen (Fin) 802.5		1986	Tony Stevens (UK) 882.5
1988	Jarmo Virtanen (Fin) 792.5		1987	Conny Nilsson (Swe) 847.5
1989	Ausby Alexander (USA) 752.5		1988	Ed Coan (USA) 972.5
1990	Ausby Alexander (USA) 770		1989	Ed Coan (USA) 1015
1991	Dave Ricks (USA) 782.5		1990	Juha Hyttinen (Fin) 887.5
1992	Dave Ricks (USA) 755		1991	George Harring (USA) 905
1993	Dave Ricks (USA) 750		1992	Brian Reynolds (UK) 872.5
1994	Dave Ricks (USA) 807.5		1993	Ed Coan (USA) 1017.5
1995	Sirayutin Bazayev (Ukr) 782.5		1994	Ed Coan (USA) 1035
1996	Dan Austin (USA) 785		1995	Ed Coan (USA) 1000
1997	Sirayutin Bazayev (Ukr) 787.5		1996	Janne Toivanen (Fin) 912.5
			1997	Oleksey Soloviov (Ukr) 932.5

82.5kg

1980	Bill West (UK) 777.5
1981	Mike Bridges (USA) 945
1982	Mike Bridges (USA) 845

110kg

1980	John Kuc (USA) 1000
1981	Reijo Kiviranta (Fin) 920
1982	Hannu Saarelainen (Fin) 887.5
1983	Steve Wilson (USA) 910
1984	Dave Jacoby (USA) 935
1985	Dave Jacoby (USA) 907.5
1986	Fred Hatfield (USA) 902.5
1987	Dave Jacoby (USA) 910
1988	Dave Jacoby (USA) 902.5
1989	John Neighbour (UK) 925
1990	Aarre Käpypä (Fin) 920
1991	Guon Sigurjonsson (Ice) 907.5
1992	Dave Jacoby (USA) 935
1993	Andrey Mustrikov (Rus) 912.5
	(after Philip Farmer (USA) 962.5 *disqualified*)
1994	Kirk Karwoski (USA) 980
1995	Derek Pomana (NZ) 935
1996	Derek Pomana (NZ) 962.5
1997	Derek Pomana (NZ) 967.5

125 kg

1981	Ernie Hackett (USA) 962.5
1982	John Gamble (USA) 907.5
1983	Lars Norén (Swe) 890
1984	Ab Wolders (Hol) 945
1985	Tom Henderson (USA) 935
1986	Lars Norén (Swe) 942.5
1987	John Neighbour (UK) 922.5
1988	Kyösti Vilmi (Fin) 930
1989	Kyösti Vilmi (Fin) 930
1990	Kyösti Vilmi (Fin) 970
1991	Kirk Karwoski (USA) 942.5
1992	Kirk Karwoski (USA) 980
1993	Kirk Karwoski (USA) 977.5
1994	Viktor Naleykin (Ukr) 960
1995	Kirk Karwoski (USA) 1000
1996	Kirk Karwoski (USA) 1020
1997	Sturla Davidsen (Nor) 987.5

Over 125kg

1980	Doyle Kenady (USA) 1000 (*over 110kg*)
1981	Paul Wrenn (USA) 1027.5
1982	Tom Maggee (Can) 942.5
1983	Bill Kazmaier (USA) 975
1984	Lee Moran (USA) 977.5
1985	George Hechter (USA) 947.5
1986	Mike Hall (USA) 980
1987	Lars Norén (Swe) 1077.5
1988	Oders Wilson (USA) 1012.5
1989	Mike Hall (USA) 952.5
1990	Jean-Pierre Brulois (Fra) 972.5
1991	Hjalti Arnason (Ice) 957.5
1992	Luiz Farnettani (Bra) 975
1993	Hans Zerhoch (Ger) 985
1994	Karl Saliger (Aut) 1000
1995	Yuriy Spinov (Ukr) 990
1996	Yuriy Spinov (Ukr) 997.5
1997	Viktor Naleykin (Ukr) 995

Women

44kg

1980	Joan Fruth (USA) 275
1981	Donna Wicker (USA) 287.5
1982	Ginger Lord (USA) 300
1983	Cheryl Jones (USA) 317.5
1984	Cheryl Jones (USA) 347.5
1985	Cheryl Jones (USA) 350
1986	Judy Gedney (USA) 322.5
1987	Anna-Liisa Prinkkala (Fin) 332.5
1988	Hisako Yoshida (Jap) 335
1989	Anna-Liisa Prinkkala (Fin) 340
1990	Anna-Liisa Prinkkala (Fin) 347.5
1991	Helen Wolsey (UK) 350
1992	Helen Wolsey (UK) 337.5
1993	Nathalie Janot (Fra) 365
1994	Anna-Liisa Prinkkala (Fin) 362.5
1995	Raja Koskinen (Fin) 365
1996	Svetlana Tesleva (Rus) 375
1997	Svetlana Tesleva (Rus) 377.5

48kg

1980	Sue Roberts (Aus) 330
1981	Terry Dillard (USA) 340
1982	Terry Dillard (USA) 347.5
1983	Diana Rowell (USA) 355
1984	Majik Jones (USA) 390
1985	Bernadette Plouviez (Bel) 345
1986	Marie Vassart (Bel) 350
1987	Vuokko Viitasaari (Fin) 352.5
1988	Irma Ruler (Hol) 360
1989	Claudine Cognac (Fra) 352.5
1990	Claudine Cognac (Fra) 372.5
1991	Malou Thill (Lux) 357.5
1992	Claudine Cognac (Fra) 375
1993	Claudine Cognac (Fra) 382.5
1994	Vuokko Viitasaari (Fin) 370
1995	Yelena Yamskikh (Rus) 395
1996	Yelena Yamskikh (Rus) 412.5
1997	Yelena Yamskikh (Rus) 402.5

52kg

1980	Terry Dillard (USA) 347.5
1981	Sue Roberts (Aus) 370
1982	Sue Jordan (Aus) 365
1983	Kali Bogias (Can) 390
1984	Kali Bogias (Can) 392.5
1985	Sisi Dolman (Hol) 400
1986	Sisi Dolman (Hol) 400
1987	Mary Jeffrey (USA) 420
1988	Sisi Dolman (Hol) 410
1989	Sisi Dolman (Hol) 422.5
1990	Sisi Dolman (Hol) 400
1991	Sisi Dolman (Hol) 415

1992	Mary Jeffrey (USA) 435	
1993	Gema Cristóbal (Spa) 405	
1994	Ingeborg Marx (Bel) 410	
1995	Nadezhda Mir (Kzk) 417.5	
1996	Oksana Belova (Rus) 465	
1997	Oksana Belova (Rus) 457.5	

56kg

1980	Sue Elwyn (USA) 330
1981	Gayla Crain (USA) 395
1982	Julie Thomas (USA) 365
1983	Juli Thomas (USA) 440
1984	Vicky Steenrod (USA) 475
1985	Tina van Duyn-Woodley (Hol) 415
1986	Felecia Johnson (USA) 407.5
1987	Joy Burt (Can) 427.5
1988	Mary Jeffrey (USA) 440
1989	Mary Jeffrey (USA) 445
1989	Mary Jeffrey (USA) 447.5
1991	Carrie Graffam (USA) 442.5
1992	Joy Burt (Can) 470
1993	Carrie Graffam-Boudreau (USA) 500
1994	Nadezhda Mir (Kaz) 427.5
1995	Carrie Boudreau (USA) 517.5
1996	Carrie Boudreau (USA) 500
1997	Carrie Boudreau (USA) 495

60kg

1980	Karen Gajda (USA) 405
1981	Eileen Todaro (USA) 387.5
1982	Ruth Shafer (USA) 450
1983	Ruth Shafer (USA) 500
1984	Diane Frantz (USA) 435
1985	Vicky Steenrod (USA) 502.5
1986	Rita Bass (UK) 420
1987	Vicky Steenrod (USA) 487.5
1988	Silvana Bollmann (FRG) 445
1989	Judith Auerbach (USA) 427.5
1990	Rachel Mathias (USA) 417.5
1991	Ingjerd Pytte (Nor) 420
1992	Marion Hammang (Lux) 440
1993	Beate Amdahl (Nor) 482.5
1994	Beate Amdahl (Nor) 492.5
1995	Eriko Himeno (Jap) 475
1996	Bettina Altizer (USA) 487.5
1997	Marina Kudinova (Rus) 522.5

67.5kg

1980	Jennifer Reid (USA) 405
1981	Jennifer Weyland (USA) 467.5
1982	Angie Ross (USA) 435
1983	Linda Miller (Aus) 435
1984	Ruth Shafer (USA) 552.5
1985	Ruth Shafer (USA) 427.5
1986	Heidi Wittesch (Aus) 470
1987	Deborah McElroy (USA) 490
1988	Jackie Pierce (USA) 497.5
1989	Silvana Bollmann (FRG) 502.5

1990	Jackie Pierce (USA) 515
1991	Yekaterina Tanakova (USSR) 490
1992	Yekaterina Tanakova (Rus) 497.5
1993	Yekaterina Tanakova (Rus) 535
1994	Yekaterina Tanakova (Rus) 535
1995	Lisa Sjöstrand (Swe) 532.5
1996	Lisa Sjöstrand (Swe) 560
1997	Lisa Sjöstrand (Swe) 570

75kg

1980	Beverley Francis (Aus) 460
1981	Judith Oakes (UK) 462.5
1982	Beverley Francis (Aus) 497.5
1983	Pamela Matthews (Aus) 487.5
1984	Deborah McElroy-Patton (USA) 475
1985	Heidi Wittesch (Aus) 470
1986	Deborah Patton (USA) 462.5
1987	Terry Byland (USA) 477.5
1988	Heidi Wittesch (Aus) 522.5
1989	Liz Odendaal (Hol) 577.5
1990	Liz Odendaal (Hol) 552.5
1991	Cathy Millen (NZ) 602.5
1992	Sara Robertson (USA) 512.5
1993	Tammy Dainde (USA) 540
1994	Yelena Suchoruk (Ukr) 577.5
1995	Yelena Suchoruk (Ukr) 605
1996	Vicky Steenrod (USA) 580
1997	Marina Zhguleva (Rus) 580

82.5kg

1980	Vicky Gagne (USA) 450
1981	Beverley Francis (Aus) 575
1982	Judith Oakes (UK) 502.5
1983	Beverley Francis (Aus) 577.5
1984	Beverley Francis (Aus) 557.5
1985	Beverley Francis (Aus) 565
1986	Juanita Trujillo (USA) 537.5
1987	Maggie Sandoval (USA) 522.5
1988	Judith Oakes (UK) 542.5
1989	Heidi Wittesch (Aus) 520
1990	Cathy Millen (NZ) 562.5
1991	Shelby Corson (USA) 477.5
1992	Monika Norberg (Swe) 465
1993	Natalya Rumyantseva (Rus) 532.5
1994	Natalya Rumyantseva (Rus) 575
1995	Natalya Rumyantseva (Rus) 557.5
1996	Natalya Rumyantseva (Rus) 575
1997	Natalya Rumyantseva (Rus) 597.5

Over 82.5kg

1980	Ann Turbyne (USA) 502.5
1981	Wanda Sander (USA) 550

90kg

1982	Rebecca Waibler (FRG) 475
1983	Gael Mulhall (Aus) 525
1984	Annette Bohach (USA) 500
1985	Tore Eriksen (Nor) 465
1986	Lorraine Costango (USA) 550

1987	Jacqueline Pepper (UK) 462.5
1988	Lorraine Costanzo (USA) 605
1989	Heike Buch (FRG) 555
1990	Ulrike Herchenhein (FRG) 532.5
1991	Susanne Tjernell-Formgren (Swe) 485
1992	Cathy Millen (NZ) 622.5
1993	Cathy Millen (NZ) 655
1994	Cathy Millen (NZ) 682.5
1995	Alla Korshunova (Rus) 552.5
1996	Alla Korshunova (Rus) 580
1997	Alla Korshunova (Rus) 587.5

Over 90kg

1982	Annie McElroy (USA) 502.5
1983	Wanda Sander (USA) 522.5
1984	Annie McElroy (USA) 485
1985	Annie McElroy (USA) 527.5
1986	Annie McElroy (USA) 527.5
1987	Lorraine Costanzo (USA) 622.5
1988	Myrtle Augee (UK) 557.5
1989	Ulrike Herchenhein (FRG) 555
1900	Sylvia Iskin (Fra) 510
1991	Sylvia Iskin (Fra) 552.5
1992	Juanita Trujillo (USA) 560
1993	Ulrike Herchenhein (Ger) 610
1994	Ulrike Herchenhein (Ger) 630
1995	Chao Chen-yen (Tai) 590
1996	Chao Chen-yen (Tai) 617.5
1997	Katrina Robertson (Aus) 647.5

Most world titles

Men

17	Hideaki Inaba (Jap) 52kg 1974-83, 1985-91
15	Lamar Gant (USA) 56kg 1975-7, 1979, 1982-4; 60kg 1978, 1980-1, 1986-90
9	Dan Austin (USA) 67.5kg 1984, 1986-92; 75kg 1996
8	Larry Pacifico (USA) 90kg 1976; 100kg 1974-5, 1977-9; 110kg 1972-3
8	Jarmo Virtanen (Fin) 75kg 1987-8; 82.5kg 1985-6, 1989-90, 1992-3

Women

6	Beverley Francis (Aus) 75kg 1980, 1982; 82.5kg 1981, 1983-5
6	Sisi Dolman (Hol) 52kg 1985-6, 1988-91

World Records

Men

Class	Weight lifted (kg)	Name
Squat		
52kg	277.5	Andrzej Stanaszek (Pol) 1997
56kg	287.5	Magnus Karlsson (Swe) 1996
60kg	295.5	Magnus Karlsson (Swe) 1994
67.5kg	303	Wade Hooper (USA) 1997
75kg	328	Ausby Alexander (USA) 1989
82.5kg	379.5	Mike Bridges (USA) 1982
90kg	375	Fred Hatfield (USA) 1980
100kg	423	Ed Coan (USA) 1994
110kg	415	Kirk Karwoski (USA) 1994
125kg	455	Kirk Karwoski (USA) 1995
125+kg	447.5	Shane Hamman (USA) 1994
Bench press		
52kg	177.5	Andrzej Stanaszek (Pol) 1994
56kg	187.5	Magnus Karlsson (Swe) 1996
60kg	185	Magnus Karlsson (Swe) 1997
67.5kg	200.5	Aleksey Sivokon (Kzk) 1997
75kg	217.5	James Rouse (USA) 1980
82.5kg	240	Mike Bridges (USA) 1981
90kg	255	Mike McDonald (USA) 1980
100kg	261.5	Mike McDonald (USA) 1977
110kg	270	Jeffrey Magruder (USA) 1982
125kg	278.5	Tom Hardman (USA) 1982
125+kg	322.5	James Henderson (USA) 1997
Dead lift		
52kg	256	Sajeeva Bhaskaran (Ind) 1993
56kg	289.5	Lamar Gant (USA) 1982
60kg	310	Lamar Gant (USA) 1988
67.5kg	316	Daniel Austin (USA) 1991
75kg	337.5	Daniel Austin (USA) 1994
82.5kg	357.5	Veli Kumpuniemi (Fin) 1980
90kg	372.5	Walter Thomas (USA) 1982
100kg	390	Ed Coan (USA) 1993
110kg	395	John Kuc (USA) 1980
125kg	387.5	Lars Norén (Swe) 1987
125+kg	406	Lars Norén (Swe) 1988
Total		
52kg	592.5	Andrzej Stanaszek (Pol) 1996
56kg	637.5	Hu Chun-Hsiung (Tai) 1997
60kg	707.5	Joe Bradley (USA) 1982
67.5kg	795	Aleksey Sivokon (Kzk) 1997
75kg	850	Rick Gaugler (USA) 1982
82.5kg	952.5	Mike Bridges (USA) 1982
90kg	937.5	Mike Bridges (USA) 1980
100kg	1035	Ed Coan (USA) 1994
110kg	1000	John Kuc (USA) 1980
125kg	1045	Kirk Karwoski (USA) 1995
125+kg	1100	Bill Kazmaier (USA) 1981

Women

Squat		
44kg	162.5	Raija Koskinen (Fin) 1998
48kg	171	Raija Koskinen (Fin) 1997
52kg	182.5	Oksana Belova (Rus) 1997
56kg	191.5	Carrie Boudreau (USA) 1995
60kg	210	Beate Amdahl (Nor) 1994
67.5kg	230	Ruth Shafer (USA) 1984
75kg	245	Anne Stiklestad (Nor) 1997
82.5kg	242.5	Anne Stiklestad (Nor) 1997
90kg	260	Cathy Millen (NZ) 1994
90+kg	277.5	Juanita Trujillo (USA) 1994

Bench press

44kg	85	Svetlana Tesleva (Rus) 1996
48kg	100	Marlina (Ina) 1997
52kg	107.5	Anna Olsson (Swe) 1997
56kg	122.5	Valentina Nelyubova (Rus) 1997
60kg	118	Helena Heiniluoma (Fin) 1996
67.5kg	120	Vicky Steenrod (USA) 1990
75kg	145.5	Marina Zhguleva (Rus) 1997
82.5kg	151	Natalya Rumyantseva (Rus) 1997
90kg	162.5	Cathy Millen (NZ) 1994
90+kg	175	Chao Chen-yeh (Tai) 1997

Dead lift

44kg	165.5	Anna-Liisa Prinkkala (Fin) 1998
48kg	182.5	Majik Jones (USA) 1984
52kg	197.5	Diana Rowell (USA) 1984
56kg	222.5	Carrie Boudreau (USA) 1995
60kg	213.5	Ingeborg Marx (Bel) 1997

67.5kg	244	Ruth Shafer (USA) 1984
75kg	252.5	Yelena Sukhoruk (Ukr) 1995
82.5kg	257.5	Cathy Millen (NZ) 1993
90kg	260	Cathy Millen (NZ) 1994
90+kg	262.5	Katherine Robertson (Aus) 1997

Total

44kg	397.5	Raija Koskinen (Fin) 1997
48kg	415	Yelena Ramskikh (Rus) 1997
52kg	475	Oksana Belova (Rus) 1997
56kg	522.5	Carrie Boudreau (USA) 1995
60kg	525	Ingborg Marx (Bel) 1997
67.5kg	572.5	Lisa Sjöstrand (Swe) 1997
75kg	605	Yelena Sukhoruk (Ukr) 1995
82.5kg	637.5	Cathy Millen (NZ) 1993
90kg	682.5	Cathy Millen (NZ) 1994
90+kg	657.5	Lee Chia-Sui (Tai) 1997

Racquetball

Two versions of the game exist. The original game from which both versions derive was invented in 1949 by Joe Sobek at the Greenwich YMCA, Connecticut, USA. He called the game Paddle Rackets, and used a tennis racket with half the handle sawn off.

Racquetball (US spelling) uses handball courts 40 x 20ft (12.2 x 6.1m). In the USA the International Racquetball Association was founded in 1968 by Bob Kendler (USA). Its name was changed in 1980 to the American Amateur Racquetball Association (AARA). The sport now has more than ten million players in the USA.

International governing body: International Racquetball Federation (IRF), 1685 West Uintah, Colorado Springs, Colorado 80904-2921, USA. Tel: (1) 719 635 5396, Fax: (1) 719 635 0685. President: Han van der Heijden, Secretary General: Luke St Onge. Founded in 1979. 91 member nations in 1998.

World Championships

The IRF has staged World Championships biennially since 1982 at men's and women's singles and doubles, and mixed doubles.

Winners:

	Men singles	Women singles
1982	Ed Andrews (USA)	Cindy Baxter (USA)
1984	Ross Horney (Can)	Mary Dee (USA)
1986	Egan Inoue (USA)	Cindy Baxter (USA)
1988	Andy Roberts (USA)	Heather Stupp (Can)
1990	Egan Inoue (USA)	Heather Stupp (Can)
1992	Chris Cole (USA)	Michelle Gould (USA)
1994	Sherman Greenfeld (Can)	Michelle Gould (USA)
1996	Todd O'Neil (USA)	Michelle Gould (USA)

Most titles: 3 Michelle Gould, Doug Ganim (USA) men's doubles 1988, 1990, 1992

The USA have been overall team champions at all eight championships, except in 1986 when they tied with Canada. Canada won the men's team title in 1986 and 1988, but the other six men's and all women's team titles went to the USA.

Racketball

Racketball (British spelling), played on a squash court 32 x 21ft (9.75 x 6.4m), was introduced in 1976, by Ian Wright, at Bexley SRC, Kent. The game uses a less bouncy ball than that used in the larger American courts. The British Racketball Association (BRA) was formed in 1984 and staged inaugural British National Championships in the same year.

Rackets

A racket and ball game for two or four players, derived, like other such games, from various forms of handball games played in the Middle Ages. In England it was often played against walls of buildings, especially those of the Fleet Prison, London, in the 18th century. One inmate, Robert Mackay, claimed the first world title in 1820. The first closed court was built in 1853 at the Prince's Club, Hans Place, London.

Governing body: Tennis & Rackets Association, c/o The Queen's Club, Palliser Road, West Kensington, London W14 9EQ. Tel: 0171 386 3448, Fax: 0171 385 7424. Chairman: Charles Swallow, Chief Executive: Brig. A D Myrtle. Formed in 1907.

World Champions

Determined on a challenge basis.

1820	Robert Mackay (UK)
1825-34	Thomas Pittman (UK)
1834-8	John Pittman (UK)
1838-40	John Lamb (UK)
1840-6	*Vacant*
1846-60	John Mitchell (UK)
1860	Francis Erwood (UK)
1862-3	Sir William Hart-Dyke (UK)
1863-6	Henry Gray (UK)
1866-75	William Gray (UK)
1876-8	H B Fairs (UK)
1878-87	Joseph Gray (UK)
1887-	
1902	Peter Latham (UK)
1903-11	J Jamsetji (Ind)
1911-3	Charles Williams (UK)
1913-28	Jock Soutar (USA)
1929-35	Charles Williams (UK)
1937-47	David Milford (UK)
1947-54	James Dear (UK)
1954-71	Geoffrey Atkins (UK)
1972-3	William Surtees (USA)
1973-4	Howard Angus (UK)
1975-81	William Surtees (USA)
1981-4	John Prenn (UK)
1984-6	William Boone (UK)
1986-8	John Prenn (UK)
1988-	James Male (UK)

World Doubles Championships

Held over two legs, first in 1990.
Winners:

1990	James Male & John Prenn (UK)
1992	Neil Smith & Shannon Hazell (UK)
1993	Neil Smith & Shannon Hazell (UK)
1995	Rupert Owen-Browne (UK) & K Nemec (Can)
1996	Neil Smith & Shannon Hazell (UK)
1998	Neil Smith & Shannon Hazell (UK)

British Amateur Championships

Held annually, first in 1888 at singles and in 1890 at doubles.
Winners:

Men's singles (from 1969)

1969	Charles Swallow
1970-1	Martin Smith
1972-5	Howard Angus
1976	William Boone
1977	Charles Hue Williams
1978	William Boone
1979-80	John Prenn
1981	William Boone
1982-3	John Prenn
1984-5	William Boone
1986	James Male★

1987	William Boone
1988	James Male (Jan)
1989-90	William Boone
1991	James Male★
1992	John Prenn★
1993	James Male★
1994	William Boone ★
1995-8	James Male★

★ December the previous year.

Most wins:

9	Edgar M Baerlein 1903, 1905, 1908-11, 1920-1, 1923
9	William Boone
8	Henry K Foster 1894-1900, 1904
8	James Male
7	David Milford 1930, 1935-8, 1950-1
5	John Thompson 1954-5, 1957-9
5	John Prenn

Men's doubles (from 1969)

1969-71	Richard Gracey & Martin Smith
1972-3	Howard Angus & Charles Hue Williams
1974	Geofrey Atkins & Charles Hue Williams
1975-7	William Boone & Tom Pugh
1978-9	Howard Angus & Andrew Milne
1980-4	William Boone & Randall Crawley (6 wins)
1985	John Prenn & Charles Hue Williams
1986	William Boone & Randall Crawley
1987	James Male & Rupert Owen-Browne
1988-91	James Male & John Prenn
1992	William Boone & Tim Cockroft
1993	James Male & John Prenn
1994	William Boone & Tim Cockroft
1995	James Male & John Prenn
1996	William Boone & Tim Cockroft
1997	Tim Cockroft & Rupert Owen-Browne
1998	William Boone & James Male

Most wins by the same pair: 10 David Milford & John Thompson 1948, 1950-2, 1954-9

Most wins by individuals with various partners

13	William Boone
11	David Milford also in 1938
11	John Thompson also in 1966
8	Harry Foster 1893-4, 1896-1900, 1903
8	Lord Aberdare (formerly the Hon. C N Bruce) 1921, 1924-8, 1930, 1934
8	James Male

British Open Championships

Held irregularly for the Sheppard Cup 1929-71 on a challenge basis. From 1971 there has been an annual championship, held first as the Louis Roederer Open Invitation Tournament.

Sheppard Cup champions

1929-30	Cyril Simpson
1932	Lord Aberdare
1933	Ian Akers-Douglas
1934	Albert Cooper

1936	David Milford
1946	James Dear
1951	James Dear
1954	Geoffrey Atkins
1959	John Thompson
1960	James Dear
1961	Geoffrey Atkins
1964	Geoffrey Atkins
1967	James Leonard
1970	Charles Swallow
1971	Martin Smith
1971	Howard Angus

Open singles

Winners:

1971-3	Howard Angus
1974	William Surtees
1975-6	Howard Angus
1977	John Prenn
1978	Howard Angus
1979	William Boone
1980-3	John Prenn
1984	William Boone
1985	John Prenn
1986	William Boone

1987-9	James Male
1990	Neil Smith
1991	James Male
1992	Shannon Hazell
1993-4	Neil Smith
1995	William Boone
1996	James Male
1997-8	William Boone

Open doubles

First held 1981.
Winners:

1981-5	William Boone & Randall Crawley
1986-90	John Prenn & James Male
1991-2	Neil Smith & Shannon Hazell
1993	John Prenn & James Male
1994-6	William Boone & Tim Cockroft
1997	William Boone & Peter Brake
1998	James Male & M Hue Williams

Olympic Games

Rackets was included in the 1908 Olympics, when gold medals were won at singles by Evan Noel (UK) and doubles by Vane Pennel and John Jacob Astor (UK).

Real Tennis

An indoor racket and ball game, which was first played as *jeu de paume* in France in monastery cloisters in the 11th century. From the Middle Ages it was played by royalty, particularly by several Kings of France, where the game was extremely popular around 1600. It spread to other parts of Europe and was played by Henry VII and Henry VIII of England, but declined considerably in popularity in the 17th and 18th centuries.
Governing body: Tennis & Rackets Association (*see* Rackets).

World Champions

Frenchman Clergé, winner in 1740, is the first-recorded world champion for any sport. The World Championship is determined on a challenge basis.
Winners:

Men's singles

*c.*1740-50	Clergé (Fra)
1765-85	Raymond Masson (Fra)
1785-1816	Joseph Barcellon (Fra)
1816-9	Marchesio (Ita)
1819-29	Philip Cox (UK)
1829-62	Edmond Barre (Fra)
1862-71	Edmund Tomkins (UK)
1871-85	George Lambert (UK)
1885-90	Tom Pettitt (USA)
1890-95	Charles Saunders (UK)
1895-1905	Peter Latham (UK)
1905-7	Cecil Fairs (UK)
1907-8	Peter Latham (UK)
1908-12	Cecil Fairs (UK)
1912-4	Fred Covey (UK)
1914-6	Jay Gould (USA)
1916-28	Fred Covey (UK)
1928-54	Pierre Etchebaster (Fra)
1955-7	James Dear (UK)

1957-9	Albert Johnson (UK)
1959-69	Northrup Knox (USA)
1969-72	G H 'Pete' Bostwick (USA)
1972-5	Jimmy Bostwick (USA)
1976-81	Howard Angus (UK)
1981-7	Chris Ronaldson (UK)
1987-94	Wayne Davies (Aus)
1994-	Robert Fahey (Aus)

Women's singles

First played in 1985.

1985	Judy Clarke (Aus)
1987	Judy Clarke (Aus)
1989	Penny Fellows (UK)
1991	Penny Lumley (née Fellows) (UK)
1993	Sally Jones (UK)
1995	Penny Lumley (UK)
1997	Penny Lumley (UK)

Women's doubles

First played in 1985.

1985	Judy Clarke & Annie Link (Aus)
1987	Lesley Ronaldson & Katrina Allen (UK)
1989	Alex Warren-Piper & Melissa Briggs (UK)
1991	Sally Jones & Alex Garside (née Warren-Piper) (UK)
1993	Charlotte Cornwallis & Penny Lumley (UK)
1995	Sally Jones & Sue Haswell

Olympic Games

The sport was included once in the Olympic Games, in 1908, when the men's title was won by Jay Gould (USA).

British Amateur Championships

Held annually, first in 1888 at singles and in 1920 at doubles. All winners from UK unless stated.

Singles

Winners from 1965:

1965	David Warburg
1966-80	Howard Angus
1981	Alan Lovell
1982	Howard Angus
1983-6	Alan Lovell
1987-9	Julian Snow
1990	James Male
1991-8	Julian Snow

Most wins:

16	Howard Angus 1966-80, 1982
13	Edgar M Baerlein 1912, 1914, 1919-27, 1929-30
11	Julian Snow
9	Eustace Miles 1899-1903, 1905-6, 1909-10

Doubles

Winners from 1967:

1967-70	Howard Angus & David Warburg
1972-4	Howard Angus & David Warburg
1975	John Clench & Alan Lovell
1976	Howard Angus & David Warburg
1977-9	Alan Lovell & Andrew Windham
1980	Howard Angus & Richard Cooper
1981	Alan Lovell & Michael Dean
1982	Peter Seabrook & John Ward
1983-6	Alan Lovell & Michael Dean
1987	Julian Snow & James Male
1988	Alan Lovell & Michael Dean
1989-90	James Male (UK) & Michael Happell (Aus)
1991-3	Julian Snow & Michael McMurragh
1994	James Acheson-Gray & Nigel Pendrigh
1995	Julian Snow & Michael McMurragh
1996	Julian Snow (UK) & Sam Howe (USA)
1997-8	Julian Snow & James Acheson-Gray

Most wins by the same pair:

8	Howard Angus & David Warburg 1967-70, 1972-4, 1976
7	Edgar M Baerlein & Lowther Lees 1929-31, 1934-7

Most wins by individuals with various partners:

11	Edgar M Baerlein 1920-2, 1925, 1929-31, 1934-7
10	Lowther Lees 1926, 1928-31, 1934-7, 1946
10	Alan Lovell 1975, 1977-9, 1981, 1983-6, 1988

British Open Championships

The open championship, on a challenge basis for the Prince's Club Shield (to 1976).

Winners (all UK unless stated):

1931	Edgar Baerlein
1931	Ernest Ratcliffe
1932	Jack Groom
1934-5	Lowther Lees
1938	James Dear
1950	Ronald Hughes
1951	James Dear
1956	James Dear
1962	Ronald Hughes
1967-8	Frank Willis
1970	Howard Angus
1972	Howard Angus
1975-6	Howard Angus

Men's open singles

1965	Ronald Hughes
1966-7	Frank Willis
1968	Howard Angus
1969	Frank Willis
1970	Howard Angus
1970	
(Nov)	Frank Willis
1971	Norwood Cripps
1972	Frank Willis
1973	Norwood Cripps
1974	Howard Angus
1975	Chris Ennis
1976-7	Howard Angus
1978	Chris Ronaldson
1979	Howard Angus
1980-5	Chris Ronaldson *(two in 1980)*
1986-91	Lachlan Deuchar (Aus)
1992-4	Julian Snow
1995	Robert Fahey (Aus)
1996	Mike Gooding
1997	Chris Bray

Most wins: 8 Ronaldson, Angus; 6 Deuchar

Men's open doubles

First held in 1971.

1971	Ronald Hughes & Norwood Cripps
1972	Frank Willis & Chris Ennis
1973-5	Charles Swallow & Norwood Cripps
1976	Frank Willis & David Cull
1977-80	Norwood Cripps & Alan Lovell *(5 wins, two in 1977)*
1981	Chris Ronaldson & Michael Dean
1982	Norwood Cripps & Alan Lovell
1983	Chris Ronaldson & Michael Dean
1984-90	Wayne Davies & Lachlan Deuchar (Aus)
1991	Chris Bray & Mike Gooding
1992	Lachlan Deuchar & Wayne Davies (Aus)
1993-4	Chris Bray & Mike Gooding

1995	Robert Fahey & Frank Filippeli (Aus)
1996	Chris Bray (UK) & Mike Happell (Aus)
1997	Julian Snow & James Male

Women's open singles

First held in 1978.

1978	Anna Moore
1979-81	Lesley Ronaldson
1982	Judy Clarke (Aus)
1983-6	Katrina Allen
1986	
(Nov)	Lesley Ronaldson
1987	Sally Jones
1988	Penny Fellows
1989	Sally Jones
1990	Alex Warren-Piper

1991	Penny Fellows
1992	Charlotte Cornwallis
1993	Penny Lumley (née Fellows)
1994	Alex Garside
1995-7	Penny Lumley

Women's open doubles

1989	Sally Jones & Alex Warren-Piper
1990	Alex Warren-Piper & Melissa Briggs
1991	Penny Fellows & Alex Garside
	(née Warren-Piper)
1992-3	Sally Grant (née Jones) & Alex Garside
1994	Fiona Deuchar & Mandy Happell (Aus)
1995	Sally Jones & Sue Haswell
1995-7	Penny Lumley & Sue Haswell

Rodeo

Rodeo was developed from the 18th-century fiestas of the early days of the North American cattle industry. Demonstrating ranching skills has now become a highly competitive activity in the professional rodeos held in the USA, Canada and Mexico.

A bronc-riding competition for prize money was held in Deer Trail, Colorado, USA, in 1869, and claims to be the first rodeo held before paying spectators are many. The earliest-documented organized competition was the West of the Pecos Rodeo at Pecos, Texas, first held in 1883.

Standard rodeo events are: bareback riding, saddle bronc riding, bull riding, calf roping and steer wrestling, with the three additional events of team roping, barrel racing and single-steer roping also often contested. In the first three riding events the object is to stay on for a minimum of eight seconds; in the others the object is to complete the task in the shortest time.

Governing body: Professional Rodeo Cowboys Association (PRCA), 101 Pro Rodeo Drive, Colorado Springs, CO 80919, USA. Tel: (1) 719 593 8840. Commissioner: Lewis Cryer. Originally formed in 1936, and known as the Cowboys Turtles Association until 1945, then the Rodeo Cowboys Association, taking the PRCA name in 1974.

National Finals Rodeo

Each December the PRCA and Women's Professional Rodeo Association (WPRA) stage the National Finals Rodeo (NFR), which is the culmination of the season's rodeo events. The top 15 money-earning cowboys in each of six PRCA events and the top 15 WPRA barrel racers compete at the Finals. The first NFR was in 1959 in Dallas, Texas. Oklahoma City, Oklahoma hosted the Finals for 20 years before the event was moved to Las Vegas, Nevada in 1985.

Most wins

Saddle bronc riding: 6 Casey Tibbs 1949, 1951-4, 1959

Bareback bronc riding: 5 Joe Alexander 1971-5, Bruce Ford 1979-80, 1982-3, 1987

Bull riding: 8 Donnie Gay 1974-7, 1979-81, 1984; 7 Jim Shoulders 1951, 1954-9

Calf roping: 8 Dean Oliver 1955, 1958, 1960-4, 1969, Roy Cooper 1976-8, 1980-4

Steer wrestling: 6 Homer Pettigrew 1940, 1942-5, 1948

Team roping: 7 Jake Barnes & Clay O'Brien Cooper 1985-9, 1992, 1994

Steer roping: 11 Guy Allen 1977, 1980, 1982, 1984, 1989, 1991-6

Women's barrel racing: 10 Charmayne Rodman/James 1984-93

All events: 16 Jim Shoulders 1949-59

All-Around Cowboy World Champions

Title won annually by the cowboy who has won the most money in two or more different events.

Winners (with money won in $US):

1947	Todd Whatley	–
1948	Gerald Roberts	21,766
1949	Jim Shoulders	21,496
1950	Bill Linderman	30,715
1951	Casey Tibbs	29,104
1952	Harry Tompkins	30,934
1953	Bill Linderman	33,674
1954	Buck Rutherford	40,404
1955	Casey Tibbs	42,065
1956	Jim Shoulders	43,381
1957	Jim Shoulders	33,299
1958	Jim Shoulders	33,212
1959	Jim Shoulders	32,905
1960	Harry Tompkins	32,522

1961	Benny Reynolds	31,309
1962	Tom Nesmith	32,611
1963	Dean Oliver	31,329
1964	Dean Oliver	31,150
1965	Dean Oliver	33,163
1966	Larry Mahan	40,358
1967	Larry Mahan	51,996
1968	Larry Mahan	49,129
1969	Larry Mahan	57,726
1970	Larry Mahan	41,493
1971	Phil Lyne	49,245
1972	Phil Lyne	60,852
1973	Larry Mahan	64,447
1974	Tom Ferguson	66,929
1975	Leo Camarillo & Tom Ferguson	50,300
1976	Tom Ferguson	87,908
1977	Tom Ferguson	76,730
1978	Tom Ferguson	103,734
1979	Tom Ferguson	96,272
1980	Paul Tierney	105,568
1981	Jimmie Cooper	105,862

1982	Chris Lybbert	123,709
1983	Roy Cooper	153,391
1984	Dee Pickett	122,618
1985	Lewis Feild	130,347
1986	Lewis Feild	166,042
1987	Lewis Feild	144,334
1988	Dave Appleton	121,546
1989	Ty Murray	134,806
1990	Ty Murray	213,772
1991	Ty Murray	244,231
1992	Ty Murray	225,992
1993	Ty Murray	297,896
1994	Ty Murray	246,170
1995	Joe Beaver	141,753
1996	Joe Beaver	166,103
1997	Dan Mortensen	184,559

Most wins: 6 Mahan, Ferguson, Murray

Leading money-winners (career)

$1,804,320	Roy Cooper 1975–97
$1,511,541	Joe Beaver 1985–97
$1,509,987	Ty Murray 1988–97

Roller Hockey

An adaptation of hockey and ice hockey, played as a five-a-side game on roller skates was first known in Europe as rink hockey. The Amateur Rink Hockey Association was formed in Britain, originally c.1898, taking this name in 1908. The first European Championships were held at Herne Bay, England, in 1926.

International governing bodies: Fédération Internationale de Roller Skating (FIRS), 80 Rambla Catalunya (Piso 1), 08008 Barcelona, Spain.

Committee of International Roller Hockey (CIRH), José A D'Assa Castel Branco, Praca José Fortuna 121, P-1000 Lisboa, Portugal. Tel (351): 155 6753, Fax (351): 153 2689.

World Championships

First held in 1936. A biennial tournament, the World Group A Championship was transferred to odd years from 1989.
Wins:

14	Portugal	1947-50, 1952, 1956, 1958, 1960, 1962, 1968, 1974, 1982, 1991, 1993
10	Spain	1951, 1954-5, 1964, 1966, 1970, 1972, 1976, 1980, 1989
4	Italy	1953, 1986, 1988, 1997
3	Argentina	1978, 1984, 1995
2	England	1936, 1939

Women's World Championships

First held in October 1992.
Wins:

| 2 | Spain | 1994, 1996 |
| 1 | Canada | 1992 |

Olympic Games

Roller hockey was staged as a demonstration sport at the 1992 Olympic Games, with Argentina the winners.

European Championships

Preceded the world championships, with which it was amalgamated from 1936 to 1957. A women's European championship was held unofficially in 1989, and officially from 1991.
Wins:

Men

19	Portugal	1947-50, 1952, 1956, 1959, 1961, 1963, 1965, 1967, 1971, 1973, 1975, 1977, 1987, 1992, 1994, 1996
12	England	1926-32, 1934, 1936-9
9	Spain	1951, 1954-5, 1957, 1969, 1979, 1981, 1983, 1985
3	Italy	1953, 1990-1

Women

| 2 | Italy | 1991, 1993 |
| 1 | Netherlands 1989, Spain 1995, Portugal 1997 | |

In-Line World Championships

First held in 1995.
Wins:
USA 1995, 1996, 1997, 1998

Roller Skating

The first-ever roller skate was invented by Joseph Merlin of Belgium. He demonstrated it in 1760, but it was not a success. The modern four-wheeled roller skate was introduced by James Plympton in the USA in 1863. At first it was used by ice skaters for practice, but its use soon developed into a sport in its own right. The first roller rink in the USA was opened by Plympton in 1866 at Newport, Rhode Island. In Britain the National Skating Association assumed control of roller skating in 1893 and staged the first national championships the following year.

In 1937 the first world championships were held for speed skating (at Monza) and in the same year European championships for figure skating were introduced (at Stuttgart).

International governing body: Fédération Internationale de Roller Skating (FIRS), 80 Rambla Catalunya (Piso 1), 08008 Barcelona, Spain. Tel: (34) 93 487 5348, Fax: (34) 93 487 6916. President: Isidro Oliveras, Secretary General: Roberto Marotta. Founded in 1924 as the Fédération Internationale de Patinage à Roulettes (FIPR). 58 member nations.

World Figure Skating Championships

First held in 1947.
Winners:

Combined figures and free skating

Men

1947	Donald Mounce (USA)
1949	Karl Peter (Swi)
1951-2	Freimut Stein (FRG)
1955-6	Franz Ningel (FRG)
1958-9	Karl-Heinz Losch (FRG)
1961-2	Karl-Heinz Losch (FRG)
1965	Hans Dahmen (FRG)
1966	Karl-Heinz Losch (FRG)
1967	Hans Dahmen (FRG)
1968	Jack Courtney (USA)
1970-2	Michael Obrecht (FRG)
1973	Randy Dayney (USA)
1974	Michael Obrecht (FRG)
1975	Leonardo Lienhard (Swi)
1976-8	Thomas Nieder (FRG)
1979-82	Michael Butzke (GDR)
1983	Joachim Helmle (FRG)
1984-5	Michele Biserni (Ita)
1986	Michele Tolomini (Ita)
1987-9	Sandro Guerra (Ita)
1990	Samo Kokorovec (Ita)
1991-2	Sandro Guerra (Ita)
1993	Samo Kokorovec (Ita)
1994	Lee Taylor (UK)
1995	Jayson Sutcliffe (USA)
1996	Francesco Cerisola (Ita)
1997	Mauro Mazzoni (Ita)

Most wins: 5 Losch, Guerra

Women

1947	Ursula Wehrli (Swi)
1949	Franca Rio (Ita)
1951	Franca Rio (Ita)
1952	Lotte Cadenbach (FRG)
1955	Helene Kienzle (FRG)
1956	Rita Blumenberg (FRG)
1958	Marika Kilius (FRG)
1959	Ute Kitz (FRG)
1961	Marlies Fahse (FRG)
1962	Fränzi Schmidt (Swi)
1965-8	Astrid Bader (FRG)
1970	Christine Kreutzfeldt (FRG)
1971-2	Petra Häusler (FRG)
1973-5	Sigrid Mullenbach (FRG)
1976-8	Natalie Dunn (USA)
1979-81	Petra Schneider (née Ernert) (FRG)
1982-4	Claudia Bruppacher (FRG)
1985-7	Chiara Sartori (Ita)
1988-92	Rafaella Del Vinaccio (Ita)
1993-5	Letizia Tinghi (Ita)
1996	Giusy Locane (Ita)
1997	Sandra Tomassini (Ita)

Most wins: 5 Del Vinaccio; 4 Bader

Pairs

1947	Fernand Leemans & Elvire Collin (Bel)
1949	Ken Byrne & Jean Phethean (UK)
1951	Paul Falk & Ria Baran (FRG)
1952	Günther Koch & Sigrid Knake (FRG)
1955-6	Günther Koch & Sigrid Knake (FRG)
1958	Werner Mensching & Rita Blumenberg (FRG)
1959	Dieter Fingerle & Susu Schneider (FRG)
1961-2	Walther Hoffman & Maria Ludolph (FRG)
1965-7	Dieter Fingerle & Uta Keller (FRG)
1968	Jack Courtney & Sheryl Trueman (USA)
1970-2	Ronald Robovitsky & Gail Robovitsky (USA)
1973	Louis Stovel & Vicki Handyside (USA)
1974	Ron Sabo & Susan McDonald (USA)
1975-6	Ron Sabo & Darlene Waters (USA)
1977	Ray Chapatta & Karen Mejia (USA)
1978	Pat Jones & Rooie Coleman (USA)
1979	Ray Chapatta & Karen Mejia (USA)
1980-2	Paul Price & Tina Kniesley (USA)
1983-6	John Arishita & Tammy Jeru (USA)
1987-8	Fabio Trevisani & Monica Mezzadri (Ita)
1989	David DeMotte & Nicky Armstrong (USA)
1990-1	Larry McGrew & Tammy Jeru (USA)
1992-3	Patrick Venerucci & Maura Ferri (Ita)
1994-7	Patrick Venerucci & Beatrice Palazzi-Rossi (Ita)

Most wins: 6 Tammy Jeru, Patrick Venerucci
World titles won on both ice and rollers: Ria and Paul Falk – roller pairs 1951, ice pairs 1951-2; Marika Kilius – roller 1958, ice pairs 1963-4.

Dance

1947	Fred Ludwig & Barbara Gallagher (USA)
1949	Ken Byrne & Jean Phethean (UK)
1952	Ted Ellis & Marion Mercer (UK)
1955	Karl-Heinz Beyer & Marga Schäfer (FRG)
1956	Günther Koch & Sigrid Knake (FRG)
1958	Sydney Cooper & Patricia Cooper (UK)
1959	Peter Kwiet & Rita Paucka (FRG)
1961	Peter Kwiet & Rita Kwiet (née Paucka) (FRG)
1962	Brian Colclough & Patricia Colclough (UK)
1965	Brian Colclough & Patricia Colclough (UK)
1966-7	Hans-Jürgen Schamberger & Martha Schamberger (FRG)
1968	Donald Rudalawicz & Rita Smith (USA)
1970-1	Richard Horne & Jane Pankey (USA)
1972	Tom Straker & Bonnie Lambert (USA)
1973	James Stephens & Jane Puracchio (USA)
1974	Udo Donsdorf & Christine Henke (FRG)
1975-6	Kerry Cavazzi & Jane Puracchio (USA)
1977-9	Dan Littel & Florence Arsenault (USA)
1980	Torsten Carels & Gabriele Achenbach (GDR)
1981-2	Mark Howard & Cindy Smith (USA)
1983-4	David Golub & Angela Famiano (USA)
1985	Martin Hauss & Andrea Steudte (FRG)
1986	Scott Myers & Anna Danks (USA)
1987	Rolf Ferando & Lori Walsh (USA)
1988	Peter Wulf & Michaela Mitzlaff (FRG)
1989-91	Greg Goody & Jodee Viola (USA)
1992-3	Doug Wait & Deanna Monahan (USA)
1994	Timothy Patten & Lisa Friday (USA)
1995	Kyoko Harada & Trey Knight (USA)
1996-7	Axel Haber & Swantje Gebauer (Ger)

World Speed Skating Championships

First contested in 1937 for men and 1953 for women. Held on track or road, men's and women's events at distances from 300m to 10,000m.

Most titles won (track/road)
Men: 15 Giuseppe Cantarella (Ita) 7/8 1964-80, Giuseppe Cruciani (Ita) 8/7 1978-83
Women: 19 Alberta Vianello (Ita) 8/11 1953-65, Annie Lambrechts (Bel) 1/17 1964-81

World Speed Skating Records

Men

Track

	min:sec	
300m	25.248	Oscar Galliazzo (Ita) 1987
500m	41.233	Giuseppe De Persio (Ita) 1980
1000m	1:23.09	Guillermo Botero (Col) 1988
1500m	2:07.770	Giuseppe De Persio (Ita) 1980
2000m	2:54.56	Roland Klöss (FRG) 1988
3000m	4:21.764	Giuseppe De Persio (Ita) 1980
5000m	7:34.938	Marco Giupponi (Ita) 1987
10,000m	15:14.876	Oscar Galliazzo (Ita) 1987
15,000m	23:07.868	Oscar Galliazzo (Ita) 1987
20,000m	30:52.792	Paolo Bomben (Ita) 1987
30,000m	47:42.820	Tommaso Rossi (Ita) 1987
50,000m	1hr 20:17.736	Tommaso Rossi (Ita) 1987

Road – where superior to track times

300m	24.41	Ippolito Sanfratello (Ita) 1996
500m	40.33	Alessio Gagggioli (Ita) 1996
1000m	1:22.124	Patrizio Sarto (Ita) 1987
2000m	2:51.333	Giuseppe De Persio (Ita) 1987
5000m	7:19.39	Brayden Jones (Aus) 1996
10,000m	14:25.51	Arnauld Gicquel (Ita) 1996

Women

Track

	min:sec	
300m	26.986	Simona De Cesaris (Ita) 1987
500m	44.404	Simona De Cesaris (Ita) 1987
1000m	1:27.60	Barbara Fischer (FRG) 1988
1500m	2:14.644	Marisa Canafoglia (Ita) 1987
2000m	3:02.25	Nicola Malmström (FRG) 1988
3000m	4:38.464	Marisa Canafoglia (Ita) 1987
5000m	7:48.508	Marisa Canafoglia (Ita) 1987
10,000m	15:58.022	Marisa Canafoglia (Ita) 1987
15,000m	26:18.290	Francesca Monteverde (Ita) 1987
20,000m	32:53.970	Annie Lambrechts (Bel) 1985
30,000m	49:15.906	Annie Lambrechts (Bel) 1985
50,000m	1hr 21:26.942	Annie Lambrechts (Bel) 1985

Road – where superior to track times

300m	26.794	Marisa Canafoglia (Ita) 1987
1500m	2:14.122	Marisa Canafoglia (Ita) 1987
15,000m	26:02.624	Patrizia Biagini (Ita) 1987

Rowing

Rowing originates from ancient times, and there are several references to it in Greek and Roman literature. Races were held for many years on the River Thames in London, and in 1715 Irish comedian Thomas Doggett instituted his famous race for Thames watermen. There were many races at Walton in 1768, but the first known regatta was on the Thames at Ranelagh Gardens, Putney in 1775. The Belgian Federation of Rowing Clubs staged a 'European Championship', with just one category of boat, the sculling outrigger, in 1890; the winner over the 2800m course was Edouard Lescrauwaet (Bel). FISA held their first official European Championships in 1893.

International governing body: Fédération Internationale des Sociétés d'Aviron (FISA), Av. de Cour 135, Case Postale 18, 1000 Lausanne 3, Switzerland. Tel: (41) 12 617 8373, Fax: (41) 21 617 8375. President: Denis Oswald, Executive Director: Matt Smith. Founded 1892. 103 member nations in 1998.

Olympic Games

The first Olympic rowing competition was on the River Seine over a 1750m course in 1900, but in more recent times rowing courses have been on still waters. The standard length is now 2000m, but the course measured 2 miles (3219m) in 1904, 1.5 miles (2414m) in 1908, and 1883m in 1948. Weather and water conditions affect the times recorded.

Winners:

Men

Single sculls

1900	Henri Barrelet (Fra)	7:35.6
1904	Frank Greer (USA)	10:08.5
1906	Gaston Delaplane (Fra)	5:53.4
1908	Harry Blackstaffe (UK)	9:26.0
1912	William Kinnear (UK)	7:47.6
1920	John Kelly Snr (USA)	7:35.0
1924	Jack Beresford Jr (UK)	7:49.2
1928	Henry Pearce (Aus)	7:11.0
1932	Henry Pearce (Aus)	7:44.4
1936	Gustav Schäfer (Ger)	8:21.5
1948	Mervyn Wood (Aus)	7:24.4
1952	Yuriy Tyukalov (USSR)	8:12.8
1956	Vyacheslav Ivanov (USSR)	8:02.5
1960	Vyacheslav Ivanov (USSR)	7:13.96
1964	Vyacheslav Ivanov (USSR)	8:22.51
1968	Henri Jan Wienese (Hol)	7:47.80
1972	Yuriy Malishev (USSR)	7:10.12
1976	Pertti Karppinen (Fin)	7:29.03
1980	Pertti Karppinen (Fin)	7:09.61
1984	Pertti Karpinnen (Fin)	7:00.24
1988	Thomas Lange (GDR)	6:49.86
1992	Thomas Lange (Ger)	6:51.40
1996	Xeno Müller (Swi)	6:44.85

Double sculls

1904	John Mulcahy & William Varley (USA) 10:03.2
1920	Paul Costello & John Kelly Snr (USA) 7:09.0
1924	Paul Costello & John Kelly Snr (USA) 7:45.0
1928	Paul Costello & Charles McIlvaine (USA) 6:41.4
1932	William Garrett Gilmore & Kenneth Myers (USA) 7:17.4
1936	Jack Beresford & Leslie Southwood (UK) 7:20.8
1948	Richard Burnell & Herbert Bushnell (UK) 6:51.3
1952	Tranquilo Capozzo & Eduardo Guerrero (Arg) 7:32.2
1956	Aleksandr Berkutov & Yuriy Tyukalov (USSR) 7:24.0
1960	Václav Kozák & Pavel Schmidt (Cs) 6:47.50

1964	Boris Dubrovsky & Oleg Tyurin (USSR) 7:10.66
1968	Anatoliy Sass & Aleksandr Timoshinin (USSR) 6:51.82
1972	Gennadiy Korshikov & Aleksandr Timoshinin (USSR) 7:01.77
1976	Alf Hansen & Frank Hansen (Nor) 7:13.20
1980	Joachim Dreifke & Klaus Kröppelien (GDR) 6:24.33
1984	Bradley Lewis & Paul Enquist (USA) 6:36.87
1988	Ronald Florjin & Nicolaas Rienks (Hol) 6:21.13
1992	Peter Antonie & Mark Hawkins (Aus) 6:17.72
1996	Davide Tizzano & Agostino Abbagnale (Ita) 6:16.98

Coxless pairs

1904	Robert Farnam & Joseph Ryan (USA) 10:57.0
1908	John Fenning & Gordon Thomson (UK) 9:41.0
1924	Antonie Beijnen & Wilhelm Rösingh (Hol) 8:19.4
1928	Kurt Moeschter & Bruno Müller (Ger) 7:06.4
1932	Lewis Clive & Arthur Edwards (UK) 8:00.0
1936	Willie Eichorn & Hugo Strauss (Ger) 8:16.1
1948	George Laurie & John Wilson (UK) 7:21.1
1952	Charles Logg & Thomas Price (USA) 8:20.7
1956	James Fifer & Duvall Hecht (USA) 7:55.4
1960	Valentin Boreyko & Oleg Golovanov (USSR) 7:02.01
1964	George Hungerford & Roger Jackson (Can) 7:32.94
1968	Heinz-Jürgen Bothe & Jörg Lucke (GDR) 7:26.56
1972	Siegfried Brietzke & Wolfgang Mager (GDR) 6:53.16
1976	Bernd Landvoigt & Jörg Landvoigt (GDR) 7:23.31
1980	Bernd Landvoigt & Jörg Landvoigt (GDR) 6:48.01
1984	Petru Iosub & Valer Toma (Rom) 6:45.39
1988	Andrew Holmes & Steven Redgrave (UK) 6:36.84
1992	Matthew Pinsent & Steven Redgrave (UK) 6:27.72
1996	Matthew Pinsent & Steven Redgrave (UK) 6:20.09

Coxed pairs

(Coxes' names omitted.)

1900	François Brandt & Roelof Klein (Hol) 7:34.2	
1906	Enrico Bruna & Emilio Fontanella (Ita) 4:23.0 (1000m)	
1906	Enrico Bruna & Emilio Fontanella (Ita) 7:32.4 (1609m)	
1920	Ercole Olgeni & Giovanni Scatturin (Ita) 7:56.0	
1924	Edouard Candeveau & Alfred Felber (Swi) 8:39.0	
1928	Hans Schöchlin & Karl Schöchlin (Swi) 7:42.6	
1932	Joseph Schauers & Charles Kieffer (USA) 8:25.8	
1936	Gerhard Gustmann & Herbert Adamski (Ger) 8:36.9	
1948	Finn Pedersen & Tage Henriksen (Den) 8:00.5	
1952	Raymond Salles & Gaston Mercier (Fra) 8:28.6	
1956	Arthur Ayrault & Conn Findlay (USA) 8:26.1	
1960	Bernhard Knubel & Heinz Renneberg (FRG) 7:29.14	
1964	Edward Ferry & Conn Findlay (USA) 8:21.23	
1968	Primo Baran & Renzo Sambo (Ita) 8:04.81	
1972	Wolfgang Gunkel & Jörg Lucke (GDR) 7:17.25	
1976	Harald Jährling & Freidrich-Wilhelm Ulrich (GDR) 7:58.99	
1980	Harald Jährling & Freidrich-Wilhlem Ulrich (GDR) 7:02.54	
1984	Carmine & Giuseppe Abbagnale (Ita) 7:05.99	
1988	Carmine & Giuseppe Abbagnale (Ita) 6:58.79	
1992	Greg & Jonny Searle (UK) 6:49.83	

Lightweight double sculls

1996	Markus Gier & Michael Gier (Swi) 6:23.47	

Quadruple sculls

1976	GDR	6:18.65
1980	GDR	5:49.81
1984	F R Germany	5:57.55
1988	Italy	5:53.37
1992	Germany	5:45.17
1996	Germany	5:56.93

Coxless fours

1904	Century BC, St Louis (USA)	9:53.8
1908	Magdalen College, Oxford (UK)	8:34.0
1924	Great Britain	7:08.6
1928	Great Britain	6:36.0
1932	Great Britain	6:58.2
1936	Germany	7:01.8
1948	Italy	6:39.0
1952	Yugoslavia	7:16.0
1956	Canada	7:08.8
1960	USA	6:26.26
1964	Denmark	6:59.30
1968	GDR	6:39.18
1972	GDR	6:24.27
1976	GDR	6:37.42
1980	GDR	6:08.17
1984	New Zealand	6:03.48
1988	GDR	6:03.11
1992	Australia	5:55.04
1996	Australia	6:06.37

Coxed fours

1900★	Germania RC, Hamburg (Ger)	5:59.0
1900★	Cercle de l'Aviron (Fra)	7:11.0
1906	Italy	8:13.0
1912	Germany	6:59.4
1920	Switzerland	6:54.0
1924	Switzerland	7:18.4
1928	Italy	6:47.8
1932	Germany	7:19.0
1936	Germany	7:16.2
1948	USA	6:50.3
1952	Czechoslovakia	7:33.4
1956	Italy	7:19.4
1960	F R Germany	6:39.12
1964	F R Germany	7:00.44
1968	New Zealand	6:45.62
1972	F R Germany	6:31.85
1976	USSR	6:40.22
1980	GDR	6:14.51
1984	Great Britain	6:18.64
1988	GDR	6:10.74
1992	Romania	5:59.37

★ Two finals were held in 1900.

Eights

1900	Vesper BC (USA)	6:09.8
1904	Vesper BC (USA)	7:50.0
1908	Leander Club (UK)	7:52.0
1912	Leander Club (UK)	6:15.0
1920	USA	6:02.6
1924	USA	6:33.4
1928	USA	6:03.2
1932	USA	6:37.6
1936	USA	6:25.4
1948	USA	5:56.7
1952	USA	6:25.9
1956	USA	6:35.2
1960	Germany	5:57.18
1964	USA	6:18.23
1968	F R Germany	6:07.00
1972	New Zealand	6:08.94
1976	GDR	5:58.29

1980	GDR	5:49.05
1984	Canada	5:41.32
1988	F R Germany	5:46.05
1992	Canada	5:29.53
1996	Netherlands	5:42.74

Lightweight coxed fours

1996	Denmark	6:09.58

Women

Women rowed over 1000m 1976-84, and 2000m 1988-96.

Single sculls

1976	Christine Scheiblich (GDR)	4:05.56
1980	Sanda Toma (Rom)	3:40.69
1984	Valeria Racila (Rom)	3:40,68
1988	Jutta Behrendt (GDR)	7:47.19
1992	Elisabeta Lipa (Rom)	7:25.54
1996	Yekaterina Khodotovich (Blr)	7:32.21

Double sculls

1976	Svetla Otzetova & Zdravka Yordanova (Bul) 3:44.36
1980	Yelena Khlopsteva & Larisa Popova (USSR) 3:16.27
1984	Marioara Popescu & Elisabeta Oleniuc (Rom) 3:26.75
1988	Birgit Peter & Martina Schröter (GDR) 7:00.48
1992	Kerstin Köppen & Kathrin Boron (Ger) 6:49.00
1996	Marnie McBean & Kathleen Heddle (Can) 6:56.84

Coxless pairs

1976	Stoyanka Grouitcheva & Siika Kelbetcheva (Bul) 4:01.22
1980	Cornelia Klier & Ute Steindorf (GDR) 3:30.49
1984	Rodica Arba & Elena Horvat (Rom) 3:32.60
1988	Rodica Arba & Olga Homeghi (Rom) 7:28.13
1992	Marnie McBean & Kathleen Heddle (Can) 7:06.22
1996	Megan Still & Kate Slatter (Aus) 7:01.39

Lightweight double sculls

1996	Constanta Burcica & Camelia Macoviciuc (Rom) 7:12.78

Quadruple sculls

1976	GDR	3:29.99
1980	GDR	3:15.32
1984	Romania	3:14.11
1988	GDR	6:21.06
1992	Germany	6:20.18
1996	Germany	6:27.44

Coxed fours

1976	GDR	3:45.08
1980	GDR	3:19.27
1984	Romania	3:19.30
1988	GDR	6:56.00

Coxless fours

1992	Canada	6:30.85

Eights

1976	GDR	3:33.32
1980	GDR	3:03.32
1984	USA	2:59.80
1988	GDR	6:15.17
1992	Canada	6:02.62
1996	Romania	6:19.73

Discontinued events (men)

76-man naval rowing boats (2000 metres)

1906	Varese (Ita)	10:45.0

17-man naval rowing (3000 metres)

1906	Poros (Gre)	16:35.0

Coxed fours inriggers

1912	Denmark	7:47.0

Most Olympic gold medals

4	Steven Redgrave (UK) 4+ 1984; 2- 1988, 1992, 1996
3	John B Kelly (USA) 1x 1920; 2x 1920, 1924
3	Paul Costello (USA) 2x 1920, 1924, 1928
3	Jack Beresford, Jr (UK) 1x 1924; 4+ 1932; 2x 1936
3	Vyacheslav Ivanov (USSR) 1x 1956, 1960, 1964
3	Siegfried Brietzke (GDR) 2- 1972; 4- 1976, 1980
3	Pertti Karpinnen (Fin) 1x 1976, 1980, 1984

Key: 1x single sculls, 2x double sculls, 4x quadruple sculls, 2- coxless pairs, 2+ coxed pairs, 4- coxless fours, 4+ coxed fours, 8+ eights

Most Olympic medals

5 (3 gold, 2 silver) Jack Beresford, Jr 1920-36 (at five different Games)

Oldest Olympic medallist: Robert Zimonyi, also a winner, at 46yr 180d; coxed the US eights, 1964

Oldest oarsman to win a gold medal: Guy Nickalls (UK) at 42yr 170d, in the eights, 1908 The youngest Olympic medallist at any sport is an unknown French boy who coxed the winning Dutch pair in 1900; he was believed to have been between seven and ten years of age.

World Championships

The first World Championships were held at Lucerne in 1962. Women's events were first included in 1974. *Winners:*

Men

Single sculls

1962	Vyacheslav Ivanov (USSR)
1966	Don Spero (USA)
1970	Alberto Demiddi (Arg)
1974	Wolfgang Hönig (GDR)
1975	Peter-Michael Kolbe (FRG)
1977	Joachim Dreifke (GDR)
1978	Peter-Michael Kolbe (FRG)
1979	Pertti Karppinen (Fin)
1981	Peter-Michael Kolbe (FRG)
1982	Rüdiger Reiche (GDR)
1983	Peter-Michael Kolbe (FRG)
1985	Pertti Karppinen (Fin)
1986	Peter-Michael Kolbe (FRG)
1987	Thomas Lange (GDR)
1989	Thomas Lange (GDR)
1990	Yuriy Yaanson (USSR)
1991	Thomas Lange (Ger)
1993	Derek Porter (Can)
1994	André Willms (Ger)
1995	Iztok Cop (Slo)
1997	Jamie Koven (USA)

Double sculls

1962	René Duhamel & Bernard Monnereau (Fra)
1966	Melchior Bürgin & Martin Studach (Swi)
1970	Jörgen Engelbrecht & Niels Secher (Den)
1974	Christof Kreuziger & Hans-Ulrich Schmied (GDR)
1975	Alf Hansen & Frank Hansen (Nor)
1977	Chris Baillieu & Michael Hart (UK)
1978-9	Alf Hansen & Frank Hansen (Nor)
1981	Klaus Kröppelien & Joachim Dreifke (GDR)
1982	Alf Hansen & Rolf Thorsen (Nor)
1983	Thomas Lange & Uwe Heppner (GDR)
1985	Thomas Lange & Uwe Heppner (GDR)
1986	Alberto Belgori & Igor Pescialli (Ita)
1987	Vasil Radeyev & Danatyl Yordanov (Bul)
1989	Lars Bjønness & Rol Bent Thorsen (Nor)
1990	Christophe Zerbst & Arnold Jonke (Aut)
1991	Henk-Jan Zwolle & Nicolaas Rienks (Hol)
1993	Yves Lamarque & Samuel Barathay (Fra)
1994	Ralf Thorsen & Lars Bjønness (Nor)
1995	Lars Christensen & Martin Halabo-Hansen (Den)
1997	Stephan Volkert & Andreas Hajek (Ger)

Coxless pairs

1962	Dieter Bender & Günther Zumkeller (FRG)
1966	Peter Gorny & Werner Klatt (GDR)
1970	Peter Gorny & Werner Klatt (GDR)
1974-5	Bernd Landvoigt & Jörg Landvoigt (GDR)
1977	Vitaliy Yeliseyev & Aleksandr Kulagin (USSR)
1978-9	Bernd Landvoigt & Jörg Landvoigt (GDR)
1981	Yuriy Pimenov & Nikolay Pimenov (USSR)
1982	Magnus Grepperud & Sverre Loken (Nor)
1983	Carl Ertel & Ulf Sauerbrey (GDR)
1985-6	Nikolay Pimenov & Yuriy Pimenov (USSR)
1987	Andrew Holmes & Steven Redgrave (UK)
1989-90	Thomas Jung & Uwe Kellner (GDR)
1991	Steven Redgrave & Matthew Pinsent (UK)
1993-5	Steven Redgrave & Matthew Pinsent (UK)
1997	Michel Andrieux & Jean-Christophe Rolland (Fra)

Coxed pairs

1962	F R Germany
1966	Netherlands
1970	Romania
1974	USSR
1975	GDR
1977	Bulgaria
1978	GDR
1979	GDR
1981	Italy
1982	Italy
1983	GDR
1985	Italy
1986	Great Britain
1987	Italy
1989-91	Italy
1993	Great Britain
1994	Croatia
1995	Italy
1996	France
1997	USA

Coxless fours

1962	F R Germany
1966	GDR
1970	GDR
1974-5	GDR
1977	GDR
1978	USSR
1979	GDR
1981	USSR
1982	Switzerland
1983	F R Germany
1985	F R Germany
1986	USA
1987	GDR
1989	GDR
1990-1	Australia
1993	France
1994	Italy
1995	Italy
1997	UK

Coxed fours

1962	F R Germany
1966	GDR
1970	F R Germany
1974	GDR
1975	USSR
1977-9	GDR
1981-2	GDR
1983	New Zealand
1985	USSR
1986-7	GDR
1989	Romania
1990	GDR
1991	Germany
1993-4	Romania
1995	USA
1996	Romania
1997	France

Quadruple sculls

1974-5	GDR
1977-9	GDR
1981-2	GDR
1983	F R Germany
1985	Canada
1986-7	USSR
1989	Romania
1990	USSR
1991	USSR
1993	Germany
1994-5	Italy
1997	Italy

Eights

1962	F R Germany
1966	F R Germany
1970	GDR
1974	USA
1975	GDR
1977-9	GDR
1981	USSR
1982-3	New Zealand
1985	USSR
1986	Australia
1987	USA
1989-90	F R Germany
1991	Germany
1993	Germany
1994	USA
1995	Germany
1997	USA

Women

Single sculls

1974-5	Christine Scheiblich (GDR)
1977	Christine Scheiblich (GDR)
1978	Christine Hahn (née Scheiblich) (GDR)
1979	Sanda Toma (Rom)
1981	Sanda Toma (Rom)
1982	Irina Fetissova (USSR)
1983	Jutta Hampe (GDR)
1985	Cornelia Linse (GDR)
1986	Jutta Hampe (GDR)
1987	Magdalena Georgeyeva (Bul)
1989	Elisabeta Lipa (Rom)
1990	Birgit Peter (GDR)
1991	Silken Laumann (Can)
1993	Jana Thieme (Ger)
1994	Trine Hansen (Den)
1995	Maria Brandin (Swe)
1997	Yekaterina Khodotovich (Bul)

Double sculls

1974-5	Yelena Antonova & Galina Yermoleyeva (USSR)
1977	Anke Borchmann & Roswietha Zobelt (GDR)
1978	Svetla Otzetova & Zdravka Yordanova (Bul)
1979	Cornelia Linse & Heidi Westphal (GDR)
1981	Margarita Kokarevitha & Antonina Makhina (USSR)
1982	Yelena Braticko & Antonina Makhina (USSR)
1983	Jutta Scheck & Martina Schröter (GDR)
1985	Sylvia Schurabe & Martina Schröter (GDR)
1986	Sylvia Schurabe & Beate Schramm (GDR)
1987	Steska Madina & Violeta Ninova (Bul)
1989	Jana Sorgers & Beate Schramm (GDR)
1990-1	Kathrin Boron & Beate Schramm (GDR/Ger)
1993-4	Philippa Baker & Brenda Lawson (NZ)
1995	Marnie McBean & Kathleen Heddle (Can)
1997	Meike Evers & Kathrin Boron (Ger)

Coxless pairs

1974	Marilena Ghita & Cornelia Neascu (Rom)
1975	Sabine Dähne & Angelika Noack (GDR)
1977	Sabine Dähne & Angelika Noack (GDR)
1978-9	Cornelia Bugel & Ute Steindorf (GDR)
1981	Sigrid Anders & Iris Rudolph (GDR)
1982-3	Silvia Fröhlich & Marita Sandig (GDR)
1985	Rodica Arba & Elena Florea (Rom)
1986-7	Rodica Arba & Olga Homeghi (Rom)
1989	Kathrin Haaker & Judith Zeidler (GDR)
1990	Stefanie Werremeier & Ingeburg Althoff (FRG)
1991	Marnie McBean & Kathleen Heddle (Can)
1993-4	Hélène Cortin & Christine Gossé (Fra)
1995	Megan Still & Kate Slatter (Aus)
1997	Emma Robinson & Alison Korn (Can)

Quadruple sculls

1974-5	GDR
1977	GDR
1978	Bulgaria
1979	GDR
1981-2	USSR
1983	USSR

1985-7	GDR
1989-90	GDR
1991	Germany
1993	China
1994-5	Germany
1997	Germany

Coxed fours

1974-5	GDR
1977-8	GDR
1979	USSR
1981-2	USSR
1983	GDR
1985	GDR
1986-7	Romania

Coxless fours

1986	USA
1989	GDR
1990	Romania
1991	Canada
1993	China
1994	Netherlands
1995	USA
1996	USA
1997	UK

Eights

1974-5	GDR
1977	GDR
1978-9	USSR
1981-3	USSR
1985-6	USSR
1987	Romania
1989-90	Romania
1991	Canada
1993	Romania
1994	Germany
1995	USA
1997	Romania

Lightweight World Champions

Men

Single sculls

1974	William Belden (USA)
1975	Reto Wyss (Swi)
1976	Raimund Haberl (Aut)
1977	Reto Wyss (Swi)
1978	José Antonio Montosa (Spa)
1979	William Belden (USA)
1980	Christian Georg Wahrlich (FRG)
1981	Scott Roop (USA)
1982	Raimund Haberl (Aut)
1983-4	Bjarne Eltang (Den)
1985	Ruggero Verroca (Ita)
1986	Peter Antonie (Aus)

1987	Willem Van Belleghem (Bel)
1988	Alwin Otten (FRG)
1989-90	Frans Goebel (Hol)
1991	Niall O'Toole (Ire)
1992	Jens Mohr Ernst (Den)
1993-5	Peter Haining (UK)
1996-7	Karsten Nielsen (Den)

Lightweight double sculls

1978-9	Pal Bornick & Arne Gilje (Nor)
1980-4	Francesco Esposito & Ruggero Verroca (Ita)
1985	Luc Crispon & Thierry Renault (Fra)
1986	Carl Smith & Allan Whitwell (UK)
1987	Enrico Gandola & Giovanni Calabrese (Ita)
1988	Enrico Gandola & Francesco Esposito (Ita)
1989	Christoph Schmölzer & Walter Rantasa (Aut)
1990	Steve Peterson & Robert Dreher (USA)
1991	Kai Von Warburg & Michael Buchheit (Ger)
1992-3	Gary Lynagh & Bruce Hick (Aus)
1994	Francesco Esposito & Michelangelo Crispi (Ita)
1995	Michael Gier & Markus Gier (Swi)
1997	Tomasz Kucharski & Robert Sycz (Pol)

Coxless pairs

1993	Fernando Climent & Fernando Molina (Spa)
1994	Leonardo Pettinari & Carlo Gaddi (Ita)
1995	Carlo Grande & Pasquale Marigliano (Ita)
1996	Thomas Ebert & Bo Svendsen (Den)
1997	Mathias Binder & Benedikt Schmidt (Swi)

Coxless fours

1974	Australia
1975-7	France
1978	Switzerland
1979	United Kingdom
1980-1	Australia
1982	Italy
1983	Spain
1984	Spain
1985	F R Germany
1986	Italy
1987	F R Germany
1988	Italy
1989-90	F R Germany
1991-2	United Kingdom
1993	USA
1994	Denmark
1995	Italy
1997	Denmark

Quadruple sculls

1989	F R Germany
1990	Italy
1991	Australia
1992	Italy
1993-5	Austria
1996-7	Italy

Eights

1974	USA
1975-6	F R Germany
1977-8	United Kingdom
1979	Spain
1980	United Kingdom
1981	Denmark
1982	Italy
1983	Spain
1984	Denmark
1985-91	Italy
1992	Denmark
1993	Canada
1994	United Kingdom
1995	Denmark
1996	Germany
1997	Australia

Women

Single sculls

1985	Adair Ferguson (Aus)
1986	Maria Sava (Rom)
1987	Magdalena Georgieva (Bul)
1988-9	Kris Karlson (USA)
1990	Mette Bloch Jensen (Den)
1991	Philippa Baker (NZ)
1992	Mette Bloch Jensen (Den)
1993	Michele Darvill (Can)
1994	Constanta Pipota (Rom)
1995	Rebecca Joyce (Aus)
1996	Constanta Burcica (Rom)
1997	Sarah Garner (USA)

Coxless pairs

1987	Rodica Arba & Olga Homeghi (Rom)
1996	Christine Smith & Ellen Munzner (USA)
1997	Eliza Blair & Justine Joyce (Aus)

Double sculls

1985	Lin Clark & Beryl Crockford (UK)
1986	Chris Ernst & Cary Beth Sands (USA)
1987	Stefka Madina & Violeta Ninova (Bul)
1988	Laurien Vermuist & Ellen Meliesie (Hol)
1989	Cary Beth Sands & Kris Karlson (USA)
1990	Ulla Jensen & Regitze Siggaard (Den)
1991-2	Christiane Weber & Claudia Waldi (Ger)
1993-5	Colleen Miller & Wendy Wiebe (Can)
1997	Michelle Darvill & Angelika Brand (Ger)

Coxed fours

1985	F R Germany
1986	USA
1987	Romania

Coxless fours

1988	China
1989	China
1990	Canada

1991	China
1992	Australia
1993	United Kingdom
1994-5	USA
1996	China

Quadruple sculls

1997	Germany

Most Gold Medals in World Championships and Olympic Games

Men

11   Steven Redgrave (UK) 4+ 1984; 2- 1987-8, 1991, 1992-6; 2+ 1986; 4- 1997

9   Giuseppe & Carmine Abbagnale and their cox Giuseppe Di Capua (Ita) 2+ 1981-2, 1984-5, 1987-91

7   Thomas Lange (GDR) 1x 1987-9, 1991-2; 2x 1983, 1985

6   Bernd & Jörg Landvoigt (GDR) 2- 1974-80

6   Joachim Dreifke (GDR) 1x 1977; 2x 1980-1; 4x 1974, 1978-9

6   Karl-Heinz Bussert (GDR) 4x 1976-9, 1981-2

6   Ulrich Diessner (GDR) 4+ 1977-80, 1982; 2+ 1983

6   Siegfried Brietzke & Wolfgang Mager (GDR) 2- 1972; 4- 1974-7, 1979

5   Pertti Karppinen (Fin) 1x 1976, 1979-80, 1984-5

5   Peter-Michael Kolbe (FRG) 1x 1975, 1978, 1981, 1983, 1986

5   Andreas Decker & Stefan Sempler (GDR) 4- 1974-7, 1979

5   Ulrich Karnatz (GDR) 8+ 1975-9

5   Gottfried Döhn (GDR) 4+ 1977-8, 1980; 8+ 1975-6

5   Alf Hansen (Nor) 2x 1975-6, 1978-9, 1982 (first four with his brother Frank)

5   Martin Winter (GDR) 4x 1977-8, 1980-2

5   Uwe Heppner (GDR) 2x 1983, 1985; 4x 1980-2

5   Andreas Gregor (GDR) cox 2+ 1983; 4+ 1977-8, 1980, 1982

5   Thomas Greiner (GDR) 4+ 1982; 2+ 1983; 4- 1987-9

Lightweight – men

9   Francesco Esposito (Ita) 2x 1980-4 (all with Verroca), 1988 (with Enrico Gandola), 1994 (with Michelangelo Crispi), 4x 1990, 1992

7   Andrea Re & Fabrizio Ravasi (Ita) 8+ 1985-91

6   Ruggero Verroca (Ita) 1x 1985; 2x 1980-4

Women

7   Yelena Tereshina (USSR) 8+ 1978-9, 1981-3, 1985-6

6   Jutta Behrendt (née Hampe) 1x 1983, 1986, 1988; 4x 1985, 1987, 1989

6   Birgit Peter (GDR/Ger) 1x 1990; 4x 1985-8, 1992

5   Christine Hahn (née Schieblich) 1x 1974-8
5   Angelika Noack (GDR) 2- 1975, 1977; 4+ 1974, 1978, 1980
5   Beate Schramm (GDR/Ger) 2x 1986, 1988-91
Key: 1x single sculls, 2x double sculls, 4x quadruple sculls, 2- coxless pairs, 2+ coxed pairs, 4- coxless fours, 4+ coxed fours, 8+ eights

World Sculls Cup

Introduced for men's and women's single sculls over a series of races during a season from 1990 to 1995.
Winners:

	Men	Women
1990	Vaclav Chalupa (Cs)	Birgit Peter (GDR)
1991	Vaclav Chalupa (Cs)	Silken Laumann (Can)
1992	Thomas Lange (Ger)	Beate Schramm (Ger)
1993	Vaclav Chalupa (Cze)	Annelies Bredael (Bel)
1994	Xeno Müller (Swi)	Marnie McBean (Can)
1995	Juri Jaanson (Est)	Trine Hansen (Den)

World Cup

FISA introduced a World Cup based on three regattas – Munich, Paris and Lucerne – in 1997, when the winners were Germany.

University Boat Race

The Boat Race between the Universities of Oxford and Cambridge is rowed annually on the River Thames in London, from Putney to Mortlake over a distance of 6.779km (4 miles 374 yards). It was first contested on 10 June 1829 from Hambledon Lock to Henley Bridge. From 1836 to 1842 it was rowed from Westminster to Putney, and in 1846, 1856 and 1863 from Mortlake to Putney; on all other occasions the present course has been used. Outrigged eights were first used in 1846.

To 1998 Cambridge leads in the series of 144 races, with 75 wins to Oxford's 68. There were two races in 1849 and on 24 March 1877 there was the only dead heat in the race's history.

Cambridge wins: 1836, 1839-41, 1845-6, 1849, 1856, 1858, 1860, 1870-4, 1876, 1879, 1884, 1886-9, 1899-1900, 1902-4, 1906-8, 1914, 1920-2, 1924-36, 1939, 1947-51, 1953, 1955-8, 1961-2, 1964, 1968-73, 1975, 1986, 1993-8

Oxford wins: 1829, 1842, 1849, 1852, 1854, 1857, 1859, 1861-9, 1875, 1878, 1880-3, 1885, 1890-8, 1901, 1905, 1909-13, 1923, 1937-8, 1946, 1952, 1954, 1959-60, 1963, 1965-7, 1974, 1976-85, 1987-92

Race record time: 16 min 19 sec Cambridge 28 Mar 1998, an average speed of 24.93km/h (15.49 mph)

Greatest margin: 20 lengths Cambridge 1900, apart from sinkings

Most successful individual: Boris Rankov (Oxford) rowed in six winning boats 1978-83

Most successful coach: Daniel Topolski, of Oxford's ten successive wins 1976-85

Heaviest competitor: Chris Heathcote (Oxford, 1990) 110kg (243lb)

Heaviest crew: Cambridge 1998, average weight 94.8kg (209lb)

Tallest competitor: Ethan Ayer (USA, Cambridge, 1996-7) 2.05m (6ft 8¾in)

Youngest competitor: Matthew Brittin (Cambridge, 1987) 18yr 208d

Oldest rower: Donald McDonald (Oxford, 1987) 31yr

Oldest cox: Andy Probert (Cambridge) 38yr 1992
The first woman to take part was Susan Brown, who coxed the winning Oxford boats of 1981-2.

Henley Royal Regatta

Inaugurated in 1839. The course has varied slightly, but has been about 1 mile 550 yards (2112m).

Diamond Sculls

Instituted in 1884, the Diamond Challenge Sculls at Henley is regarded as the Blue Riband of amateur sculling.
Winners since 1970:

1970	Jochen Meissner (FRG)
1971	Alberto Demiddi (Arg)
1972	Aleksandr Timoshin (USSR)
1973-5	Sean Drea (Ire)
1976	Edward Hale (Aus)
1977-8	Tim Crooks (UK)
1979	Hugh Matheson (UK)
1980	Riccardo Ibarra (Arg)
1981-2	Chris Baillieu (UK)
1983	Steven Redgrave (UK)
1984	Chris Baillieu (UK)
1985	Steven Redgrave (UK)
1986	Bjarne Eltang (Den)
1987	Peter Michael Kolbe (FRG)
1988	Hamish McGlashan (Aus)
1989	Vaclav Chalupa (Cs)
1990	Eric Verdonk (NZ)
1991	Win Van Belleghem (Bel)
1992	Rorie Henderson (UK)
1993	Thomas Lange (Ger)
1994	Xeno Müller (Swi)
1995	Juri Jaanson (Est)
1996	Merlin Vervoorn (Hol)
1997	Greg Searle (UK)
1998	Jamie Koven (USA)

Most wins: 6 Stuart Mackenzie 1957-62, Guy Nickalls (1888-91, 1893-4); 5 A A Casamajor 1855-8, 1861, J Lowndes 1879-83; 4 Jack Beresford, Jr 1920, 1924-6; 3 A C Dicker 1873-5, Frederick Kelly 1902-3, 1905, Drea, Baillieu

Record time: 7 min 23 sec Vaclav Chalupa, 2 Jul 1989

Grand Challenge Cup

The oldest of all the Henley races, dating back to the first Regatta in 1839. It is the world's premier open event for eights.

Winners since 1970:

1970	ASK Rostock (GDR)
1971	Tideway Scullers (UK)
1972	WMF Moscow (USSR)
1973-4	Trud Kolomna (USSR)
1975	Leander/Thames Tradesmen (UK)
1976	Thames Tradesmen (UK)
1977	University of Washington (USA)
1978	Trakia Club (Bul)
1979	Thames Tradesmen (UK)
1980	Charles River RA (USA)
1981	Oxford University/Thames Tradesmen (UK)
1982	Leander/London RC(UK)
1983	London RC/University of London (UK)
1984	Leander/London RC (UK)
1985	Harvard University (USA)
1986	Nautilus (UK)
1987	Soviet Army (USSR)
1988	Leander/University of London RC (UK)
1989-90	Hansa Dortmund RC (FRG)
1991	Leander/Star (UK)
1992	University of London (UK)
1993	Dortmund (Ger)
1994	Charles River and San Diego (USA)
1995	San Diego (USA)
1996	Imperial College & Queen's Tower (UK)
1997	Australian & NSW Institutes of Sport (Aus)
1998	Hansa Dortmund/Berlin RC (Ger)

Most wins: 27 Leander Club 1840, 1875, 1880, 1891-4, 1896, 1898-1901,1903-5, 1913, 1922, 1924-6, 1929, 1932, 1934, 1946, 1949, 1952-3

Most winning teams: 7 Guy Nickalls 1920-2, 1924-6, 1929

Record time: 5 min 58 sec Hansa Dortmund RC 2 Jul 1989

Steve Redgrave has a record 17 wins at Henley to 1998, including the Diamond Sculls in 1983 and 1985, and a record seven wins in the Silver Goblets and Nickalls' Cup (coxless pairs).

The Nickalls family – Guy, his brother Vivian, and Guy's son, Guy Oliver – have 43 Henley wins between them.

Rugby League

When the Rugby Union refused permission for players of northern clubs to receive broken time for loss of wages while playing matches, 22 clubs formed their own breakaway union; following a meeting at the George Hotel, Huddersfield, Yorkshire, in 1895, the Northern Union was formed. The number of players per side was reduced from 15 to 13 in 1906 and the new union's name was changed to the Northern Rugby League in 1922. The word 'Northern' was dropped in 1980.

Governing body: Rugby Football League, Red Hall, Red Hall Lane, Leeds LS17 8NB. Tel: 0113 232 9111, Fax: 0113 232 3838. Chairman: Sir Rodney Walker, Chief Executive: J N Tunnicliffe.

World Cup/International Championship

Inaugurated in France in 1954, when Great Britain, France, New Zealand and Australia played each other on a round-robin basis. In 1975, when the competition was renamed the International Championship, England and Wales replaced Great Britain and the competition was played at different venues worldwide. The World Cup was discontinued after the 1977 championship but was revived in 1985, when one match from each test series was designated a World Cup game, with the leading two nations playing off in the final in 1988.

	Winners	Venue
1954	Great Britain	France
1957	Australia	Australia
1960	Great Britain	England
1968	Australia	Australia/New Zealand
1970	Australia	England
1972	Great Britain	France
1975	Australia	World-wide
1977	Australia	Australia/New Zealand
1988	Australia	New Zealand (*final*)
1992	Australia	Great Britain (*final*)
1995	Australia	England

Most wins: 8 Australia

Highest score: Australia 86 South Africa 6 at Gateshead, England 10 Oct 1995

Super League World Club Championship

Launched in November 1996, and contested by 12 teams from Europe and 10 from Australia (including Auckland, New Zealand). The top teams from four pools play off for finals, the first of which was in October 1997.

Results of finals:

1997   Brisbane Broncos 36   Hunter Mariners 12

Challenge Cup

Rugby League's premier knock-out tournament in England, the first final was at Leeds in 1897. The first Wembley final was in 1929 and since 1933 the London stadium has been the final's permanent venue, with the exception of the war years. Now the Silk Cut Challenge Cup.

Results of finals:

1897	Batley	10	St Helens	3
1898	Batley	7	Bradford	0
1899	Oldham	19	Hunslet	9
1900	Swinton	16	Salford	8
1901	Batley	6	Warrington	0
1902	Broughton Rangers	25	Salford	0
1903	Halifax	7	Salford	0
1904	Halifax	8	Warrington	3
1905	Warrington	6	Hull K R	0
1906	Bradford	5	Salford	0
1907	Warrington	17	Oldham	3
1908	Hunslet	14	Hull	0
1909	Wakefield Trinity	17	Hull	0
1910	Leeds	7	Hull	7
Replay	Leeds	26	Hull	12
1911	Broughton Rangers	4	Wigan	0
1912	Dewsbury	8	Oldham	5
1913	Huddersfield	9	Warrington	5
1914	Hull	6	Wakefield Trinity	0
1915	Huddersfield	37	St Helens	3
1920	Huddersfield	21	Wigan	10
1921	Leigh	13	Halifax	0
1922	Rochdale Hornets	10	Hull	9
1923	Leeds	28	Hull	3
1924	Wigan	21	Oldham	4
1925	Oldham	16	Hull K R	3
1926	Swinton	9	Oldham	3
1927	Oldham	26	Swinton	7
1928	Swinton	5	Warrington	3
1929	Wigan	13	Dewsbury	2
1930	Widnes	10	St Helens	3
1931	Halifax	22	York	8
1932	Leeds	11	Swinton	8
1933	Huddersfield	21	Warrington	17
1934	Hunslet	11	Widnes	5
1935	Castleford	11	Huddersfield	8
1936	Leeds	18	Warrington	2
1937	Widnes	18	Keighley	5
1938	Salford	7	Barrow	4
1939	Halifax	20	Salford	3
1940	*Not held*			
1941	Leeds	19	Halifax	2
1942	Leeds	15	Halifax	10
1943★	Dewsbury	16	Leeds	9
	Dewsbury	0	Leeds	6
1944★	Bradford Northern	0	Wigan	3
	Bradford Northern	8	Wigan	0
1945★	Huddersfield	7	Bradford Northern	4
	Huddersfield	6	Bradford Northern	5
1946	Wakefield Trinity	13	Wigan	12
1947	Bradford Northern	8	Leeds	4

1948	Wigan	8	Bradford Northern	3
1949	Bradford Northern	12	Halifax	0
1950	Warrington	19	Widnes	0
1951	Wigan	10	Barrow	0
1952	Workington Town	18	Featherstone Rovers	10
1953	Huddersfield	15	St Helens	10
1954	Warrington	4	Halifax	4
Replay	Warrington	8	Halifax	4
1955	Barrow	21	Workington Town	12
1956	St Helens	13	Halifax	2
1957	Leeds	9	Barrow	7
1958	Wigan	13	Workington Town	9
1959	Wigan	30	Hull	13
1960	Wakefield Trinity	38	Hull	5
1961	St Helens	12	Wigan	6
1962	Wakefield Trinity	12	Huddersfield	6
1963	Wakefield Trinity	25	Wigan	10
1964	Widnes	13	Hull K R	5
1965	Wigan	20	Hunslet	16
1966	St Helens	21	Wigan	2
1967	Featherstone Rovers	17	Barrow	12
1968	Leeds	11	Wakefield Trinity	10
1969	Castleford	11	Salford	6
1970	Castleford	7	Wigan	2
1971	Leigh	24	Leeds	7
1972	St Helens	16	Leeds	13
1973	Featherstone Rovers	33	Bradford Northern	14
1974	Warrington	24	Featherstone Rovers	9
1975	Widnes	14	Warrington	7
1976	St Helens	20	Widnes	5
1977	Leeds	16	Widnes	7
1978	Leeds	14	St Helens	12
1979	Widnes	12	Wakefield Trinity	3
1980	Hull K R	10	Hull	5
1981	Widnes	18	Hull K R	9
1982	Hull	14	Widnes	14
Replay	Hull	18	Widnes	9
1983	Featherstone Rovers	14	Hull	12
1984	Widnes	19	Wigan	6
1985	Wigan	28	Hull	24
1986	Castleford	15	Hull K R	14
1987	Halifax	19	St Helens	18
1988	Wigan	32	Halifax	12
1989	Wigan	27	St Helens	0
1990	Wigan	36	Warrington	14
1991	Wigan	13	St Helens	8
1992	Wigan	28	Castleford	12
1993	Wigan	20	Widnes	14
1994	Wigan	26	Leeds	16
1995	Wigan	30	Leeds	10
1996	St Helens	40	Bradford Bulls	32
1997	St Helens	32	Bradford Bulls	22
1998	Sheffield Eagles	17	Wigan Warriors	8

* In 1943-5, the competition was held over two legs, with the winner determined on aggregate.

Most wins: 16 Wigan; 10 Leeds; 7 Widnes, St Helens; 6 Huddersfield; 5 Wakefield Trinity, Warrington, Halifax

Most finals: 27 Wigan; 17 Leeds; 15 St Helens; 13 Warrington, Widnes
Highest score and record aggregate (final): St Helens 40 Bradford Bulls 32 on 27 Apr 1996
Most wins by a player: 9 Shaun Edwards 1985, 1988-95 (all for Wigan; also played on losing side in 1984);
   7 Andy Gregory 1981, 1984, 1988-92 (for Wigan, from 8 finals, also played 1982 for Widnes), Denis Betts
   (Wigan) 1989-95
Most points in a final: 20 Neil Fox, Wakefield 1960

Lance Todd Award

The Lance Todd Award goes to the Man of the Match in the Challenge Cup Final, decided by a panel of rugby-league writers. The trophy is named after former New Zealand international Lance Todd who played for Wigan and later managed Salford. The first award was made in 1946.

Recent winners:

1976	Geoff Pimblett (St Helens)
1977	Steve Pitchford (Leeds)
1978	George Nicholls (St Helens)
1979	Dave Topliss (Wakefield Trinity)
1980	Brian Lockwood (Hull K R)
1981	Mick Burke (Widnes)
1982	Eddie Cunningham (Widnes)
1983	David Hobbs (Featherstone Rovers)
1984	Joe Lydon (Widnes)
1985	Brett Kenny (Wigan)
1986	Bob Beardmore (Castleford)
1987	Graham Eadie (Halifax)
1988	Andy Gregory (Wigan)
1989	Ellery Hanley (Wigan)
1990	Andy Gregory (Wigan)
1991	Dennis Betts (Wigan)
1992	Martin Offiah (Wigan)
1993	Dean Bell (Wigan)
1994	Martin Offiah (Wigan)
1995	Jason Robinson (Wigan)
1996	Robbie Paul (Bradford Bulls)
1997	Tommy Martyn (St Helens)
1998	Mark Aston (Sheffield Eagles)

Warrington's Gerry Helme (1950 and 1954), Andy Gregory and Martin Offiah are the only players to have won the award twice.

European Super League

The Stones Super League of three divisions was initiated in 1996, to be played during the summer months.

Premier League winners:

1996	St Helens
1997	Bradford Bulls

Premiership Trophy

The Premiership Trophy competition replaced the Championship Play-off, and was first contested at the end of the 1974/5 season. It is a knock-out competition involving the top eight clubs in the first division with the champions playing the 8th club, the 2nd club playing the 7th, and so on. The highest-placed club has home advantage, and the final is played at a neutral venue. A 2nd Division Premiership was launched in 1987. Both Premiership finals are now played at Old Trafford, the home of Manchester United FC. A new system of play-offs from the Super League was introduced in 1998.

Winners (figures in brackets indicates final league positions):

1975	Leeds (3)
1976	St Helens (5)
1977	St Helens (2)
1978	Bradford Northern (2)
1979	Leeds (4)
1980	Widnes (2)
1981	Hull K R (3)
1982	Widnes (3)
1983	Widnes (5)
1984	Hull Kingston Rovers (1)
1985	St Helens (2)
1986	Warrington (4)
1987	Wigan (1)
1988	Widnes (1)
1989	Widnes (1)
1990	Widnes (3)
1991	Hull (3)
1992	Wigan (1)
1993	St Helens (2)
1994	Wigan (1)
1995	Wigan (1)
1996	Wigan (2)
1997	Wigan (4)

Most wins: 6 Widnes, Wigan; 4 St Helens
Highest score (final): Wigan 69 Leeds 12 at Old
   Trafford, Manchester 21 May 1995
Most appearances (final): 8 (6 wins, 2 losses)
   Martin Offiah (Widnes 1988-91, Wigan 1992-5);
   6 (all wins) Mike O'Neill (Widnes 1980,1982-3,
   1988-90)

Harry Sunderland Trophy

Named after former Australian team manager, broadcaster and journalist Harry Sunderland, this award is made to the Man of the Match in the Premiership Final (formerly the Championship Play-off). It was first awarded in 1965.

Recent winners:

1976	George Nicholls (St Helens)
1977	Geoff Pimblett (St Helens)
1978	Bob Haigh (Bradford Northern)
1979	Kevin Dick (Leeds)
1980	Mal Aspey (Widnes)

1981	Len Casey (Hull K R)
1982	Mick Burke (Widnes)
1983	Tony Myler (Widnes)
1984	John Dorahy (Hull K R)
1985	Harry Pinner (St Helens)
1986	Les Boyd (Warrington)
1987	Joe Lydon (Wigan)
1988	David Hulme (Widnes)
1989	Alan Tait (Widnes)
1990	Alan Tait (Widnes)
1991	Greg Mackey (Hull)
1992	Andy Platt (Wigan)
1993	Chris Joynt (St Helens)
1994	Sam Panapa (Wigan)
1995	Kris Radlinski (Wigan)
1996-7	Andrew Farrell (Wigan)

Alan Tait and Andrew Farrell are the only players to have won the trophy more than once.

League Championship

Twenty-two clubs formed the original Northern Union in 1895/6, won by Manningham. The 'league' then split into Yorkshire and Lancashire Senior Competitions until 1901/2 when 14 clubs broke away to form the Northern Rugby League. Two divisions were formed the following season. In 1905/6 the two divisions were merged into one and that is how they stayed (except in the war years) until 1962/3, when two divisions were re-introduced. That lasted just two years, but returned in 1973/4. In 1991/2 and 1992/3 there were three divisions and from 1993/4 two divisions of 16 clubs. From 1995/6 a Super League of 12 clubs was formed, also with First and Second Divisions.

The title 'Rugby Football League' was adopted in 1922. Because not all clubs played each other twice, or at all in some cases, a Championship Play-off, involving the top four teams, was introduced in 1906/7. This remained unaltered (except during the war years) until 1962, when two divisions were re-introduced. On the return to one division in 1964/5, the play-off involved the top 16 teams. It was scrapped at the end of the 1972/3 season.

Championship play-off wins

9	Wigan	1909, 1922, 1926, 1934, 1946-7, 1950, 1952, 1960
7	Huddersfield	1912-3, 1915, 1929-30, 1949, 1962
6	St Helens	1932, 1953, 1959, 1966, 1970-1
5	Hull	1920-1, 1936, 1956, 1958
4	Salford	1914, 1933, 1937, 1939
4	Swinton	1927-8, 1931, 1935
3	Leeds	1961, 1969, 1972
3	Oldham	1910-1, 1957
3	Warrington	1948, 1954-5
2	Halifax	1907, 1965
2	Hull K R	1923, 1925

2	Hunslet	1908, 1938
2	Wakefield Trinity 1967-8
1	Batley 1924, Dewsbury 1973, Leigh 1906, Workington Town 1951

Division One Champions 1974-95

(Year given is that of second half of season.)

1974	Salford
1975	St Helens
1976	Salford
1977	Featherstone Rovers
1978	Widnes
1979	Hull K R
1980-1	Bradford Northern
1982	Leigh
1983	Hull
1984-5	Hull K R
1986	Halifax
1987	Wigan
1988-9	Widnes
1990-5	Wigan

Super League

| 1995/6 | Wigan |
| 1997 | Bradford Bulls |

Knock-Out Trophy

The knock-out competition was first held in 1971/2. It was originally known as the Player's No.6 Trophy, and then the John Player Trophy until 1983, when it was renamed the John Player Special Trophy. It became the Regal Trophy 1989-96, after which it was discontinued.

Winners:

1972	Halifax
1973	Leeds
1974	Warrington
1975	Bradford Northern
1976	Widnes
1977	Castleford
1978	Warrington
1979	Widnes
1980	Bradford Northern
1981	Warrington
1982	Hull
1983	Wigan
1984	Leeds
1985	Hull K R
1986-7	Wigan
1988	St Helens
1989-90	Wigan
1991	Warrington
1992	Widnes
1993	Wigan
1994	Castleford
1995-6	Wigan

Most wins: 8 Wigan; 4 Warrington; 3 Widnes; 2 Bradford Northern, Leeds

Highest aggregate (final): Wigan 40 Warrington 10 at Huddersfield on 28 Jan 1995

Most appearances (final): 6 Mick Adams, Keith Elwell, Eric Hughes (all Widnes) 1975-6, 1978-80, 1984

County Cups

Both the Lancashire and Yorkshire County Challenge Cup competitions were first held in 1905/6 and became early-season knock-out competitions. Discontinued in 1993/4.

Wins:

(Years given indicate first half of season, although in a few cases the final was played early in the following year.)

Lancashire Cup

21	Wigan	1905, 1908-09, 1912, 1922, 1928, 1938, 1946-51, 1966, 1971, 1973, 1985-8, 1992
11	St Helens	1926, 1953, 1960-4, 1967-8, 1984, 1991
9	Oldham	1907, 1910, 1913, 1919, 1924, 1933, 1956-8
9	Warrington	1921, 1929, 1932, 1937, 1959, 1965, 1980, 1982, 1989
7	Widnes	1945, 1974-6, 1978-9, 1990
5	Salford	1931, 1934-6, 1972
4	Swinton	1925, 1927, 1939, 1969
4	Leigh	1952, 1955, 1970, 1981
3	Rochdale Hornets	1911, 1914, 1918
2	Broughton Rangers	1906, 1920
2	St Helens Recs	1923, 1930
2	Barrow	1954, 1983
1	Workington Town	1977

Yorkshire Cup

17	Leeds	1921, 1928, 1930, 1932, 1934-5, 1937, 1958, 1968, 1970, 1972-3, 1975-6, 1979-80, 1988
12	Huddersfield	1909, 1911, 1913-4, 1918-9, 1926, 1931, 1938, 1950, 1952, 1957
11	Bradford Northern	1940-1, 1943, 1945, 1948-9, 1953, 1965, 1978, 1987, 1989
10	Wakefield Trinity	1910, 1924, 1946-7, 1951, 1956, 1960-1, 1964, 1992
7	Hull K R	1920, 1929, 1966-7, 1971, 1974, 1985
5	Halifax	1908, 1944, 1954-5, 1963
5	Hull	1923, 1969, 1982-4
5	Castleford	1977, 1981, 1986, 1990-1
3	Hunslet	1905, 1907, 1962
3	York	1922, 1933, 1936
3	Dewsbury	1925, 1927, 1942
2	Featherstone R	1939, 1959
1	Bradford 1906, Batley 1912	

County Leagues

With the introduction of two divisions in 1902/3 the Lancashire and Yorkshire Senior competitions were scrapped, but they re-appeared in 1907/8 as the Lancashire and Yorkshire Leagues. Club's results in the normal league, against teams from their own county, counted towards the appropriate County League. Both leagues were abandoned in 1970.

Most wins Lancashire League: 18 Wigan 1909, 1911-5, 1921, 1923-4, 1926, 1941, 1946-7, 1950, 1952, 1959, 1962, 1970

Most wins Yorkshire League: 15 Leeds 1902, 1928, 1931, 1934-5, 1937-8, 1951, 1955, 1957, 1961, 1967-70

Top Teams

Wins in major competitions by teams currently playing in the League.

(In the final column is a points tally based on: Challenge Cup 5, Super League 4, Premiership/Championship 4, Regal/John Player Trophy 4, Division One title 2, Lancashire or Yorkshire Cup 1.)

	Chall Cup	Champ P-off	Prem Trphy	Div 2 Prem	KO Trophy	Floodlit Final	C'ty Cup	C'ty Lge	Div 1	Div 2	Points
Wigan	16	9	6	–	8	1	21	18	8	–	209
Leeds	10	3	2	–	2	1	17	15	–	–	95
St Helens	6	6+1	4	–	1	2	11	8	1	1	91
Widnes	7	–	6	–	3	1	7	1	3	–	84
Huddersfield Barracudas	6	7	–	–	–	–	12	11	–	1	70
Warrington	5	3	1	–	4	–	9	8	–	–	66
Bradford Northern/Bulls	4	1 SL	1	–	2	–	12	5	3	1	54
Halifax	5	2	–	–	1	–	5	6	2	–	46
Hull	2	5	1	–	1	1	5	4	1	2	45
Wakefield Trinity	5	2	–	–	–	–	10	7	–	1	43
Swinton	3	4	–	1	–	–	4	5	2	1	39
Hull Kingston Rovers	1	2	2	–	1	1	7	2	3	1	38
Oldham	3	3	–	2	–	–	9	7	1	3	38
Castleford	4	–	–	–	2	4	5	3	–	–	33

	Chall Cup	Champ P-off	Prem Trphy	Div 2 Prem	KO Trophy	Floodlit Final	C'ty Cup	C'ty Lge	Div 1	Div 2	Points
Salford	1	4	-	2	-	1	5	5	2	-	30
Hunslet	2	2	-	-	-	-	3	3	-	2	21
Batley	3	1	-	-	-	-	1	2	-	-	20
Leigh	2	1	-	-	-	2	4	-	1	3	20
Featherstone Rovers	3	-	-	1	-	-	2	-	1	2	19
Dewsbury	2	1	-	-	-	-	3	1	-	1	17
Workington Town	1	1	-	1	-	-	1	-	-	1	10
Rochdale Hornets	1	-	-	-	-	-	3	1	-	-	8
Barrow	1	-	-	-	-	-	2	-	-	2	7
Sheffield Eagles	1	-	-	-	-	-	-	-	-	-	5
Ryedale York	-	-	-	-	-	-	3	-	-	1	3

Man of Steel

The RFL personality judged to have made the greatest impact on the season. Sponsored by Trumans Steel 1977-83, Greenall Whitley 1984-9, Stones Bitter from 1990.

Winners:

1977	David Ward (Leeds)
1978	George Nicholls (St Helens)
1979	Doug Laughton (Widnes)
1980	George Fairbairn (Wigan)
1981	Ken Kelly (Warrington)
1982	Mick Morgan (Carlisle)
1983	Allan Agar (Featherstone R)
1984	Joe Lydon (Widnes)
1985	Ellery Hanley (Bradford N)
1986	Gavin Miller (Hull KR)
1987	Ellery Hanley (Wigan)
1988	Martin Offiah (Widmes)
1989	Ellery Hanley (Wigan)
1990	Shaun Edwards (Wigan)
1991	Garry Schofield (Leeds)
1992	Dean Bell (Wigan)
1993	Andy Platt (Wigan)
1994	Jonathan Davies (Warrington)
1995	Denis Betts (Wigan)
1996	Andy Farrell (Wigan)
1997	James Lowes (Bradford Bulls)

Australian Grand Final

The principal competition in Australia was the Sydney Premiership (sometimes referred to as the New South Wales Premiership), culminating in the Grand Final each year. To 1995 the winning team received the Winfield Cup, but the competition has been the Australian Rugby League Optus Cup from 1996. The first Grand Final was in 1908.

Most wins

20	South Sydney	1908-9, 1914, 1918, 1925-9, 1931-2, 1950-1, 1953-5, 1967-8, 1970-1
15	St George	1941, 1949, 1956-66, 1977, 1979
11	Balmain	1915-7, 1919-20, 1924, 1939, 1944, 1946-7, 1969
11	Eastern Suburbs	1911-3, 1923, 1935-7, 1940, 1945, 1974-5
6	Canterbury-Bankstown	1938, 1942, 1980, 1984-5, 1988
6	Manly-Warringah	1972-3, 1976, 1978, 1987, 1996
4	Western Suburbs	1930, 1934, 1948, 1952
4	Parramatta	1981-3, 1986
3	Canberra	1989-90, 1994
2	North Sydney	1921-2
2	Brisbana Broncos	1992-3
1	Penrith 1991, Sydney Bulldogs 1995, Newcastle Knights 1997	

State of Origin Series

The annual series of matches between New South Wales and Queensland began in 1980, taking the current format of a 3-match series from 1982. From then to 1997 Queensland and New South Wales have won 8 series each.

World Club Challenge

Contested by the winners of the Challenge Cup Final and the Australian Grand Final winners. Sponsored by Fosters Lager.

1987	Wigan 8 Manly-Warringah 2
1989	Widnes 30 Canberra 18
1991	Wigan 21 Penrith 4
1992	Brisbane Broncos 22 Wigan 8
1994	Wigan 20 Brisbane Broncos 14

Records

All matches

Biggest win: Huddersfield 142 Blackpool Gladiators 4 (Regal Trophy first round) 26 Nov 1994

Most tries in a match: 11 George West (Hull K R) v Brookland Rovers (Challenge Cup) 4 Mar 1905

Most goals in a match: 22 Jim Sullivan for Wigan v Flimby & Fothergill (Challenge Cup) 14 Feb 1925

Most points in a match: 53 (10 goals, 11 tries) George West (Hull K R)

Internationals

Most appearances: 60 Jim Sullivan (Wigan) Wales, GB & Other Nationalities, 1921-39

Most tries: 45 Mick Sullivan (Huddersfield, Wigan, St Helens, York) GB & England 1954-63

Most goals (points): 160 (329) Jim Sullivan

Biggest win: Australia 86 South Africa 6 at Gateshead 10 Oct 1995

Individual points: 32 Andrew Johns for Australia v Fiji at Newcastle 12 Jul 1996, Bobby Goulding for Great Britain (72) v Fiji (4) at Nadi, Fiji 5 Oct 1996

Season

Most tries: 80 Albert Rosenfeld (Huddersfield) 1913/4

Most goals: 221 David Watkins (Salford) 1972/3

Most points: 496 (194 goals, 36 tries) Lewis Jones (Leeds) 1956/7

Career

Most tries: 796 Brian Bevan (Warrington & Blackpool Borough) 1946-64

Most goals: 2867 Jim Sullivan (Wigan) 1921-46

Most points: 6220 (2575 goals, 358 tries, 4 drop goals) Neil Fox (Wakefield Trinity, Bradford Northern, Hull K R, York, Bramley, Huddersfield) 1956-79

Most senior appearances: 928 Jim Sullivan (Wigan) 1921-46

Most consecutive club appearances: 239 Keith Elwell (Widnes) May 1977- Sep 1982

Most consecutive games scoring points: 92 David Watkins (Salford) Aug 1972-Apr 1974

Test Match Records (to 1 May 1998)

	P	W	D	L
Great Britain				
v Australia	114	54	4	56
v France	59	42	3	14
v New Zealand	85	51	3	31
v Papua New Guinea	8	7	0	1
Australia				
v France	43	28	3	12
v New Zealand	77	52	1	24
France				
v New Zealand	37	10	4	23
v Papua New Guinea	1	0	0	1
New Zealand				
v Papua New Guinea	11	10	0	1

The above table includes the Super League Tests between Australia (won 2) and Great Britain (won 1) in November 1997.

World Sevens

Held at Sydney in 1994, when the winners were Manly-Warringah (Aus).

Rugby Union

Legend has it that the game of Rugby Union had its beginnings at Rugby School, when pupil William Webb Ellis picked up the ball during a game of football in November 1823, and ran with it. The new 'handling' code of football developed and was played at Cambridge University in 1839. The first rugby club was formed at Guy's Hospital in 1843 and the Rugby Football Union (RFU) was founded in January 1871.

International governing bodies: International Rugby Football Board (IRFB), Huguenot House, 35/38 St Stephen's Green, Dublin 2, Ireland. Tel: (353) 1 662 5444, Fax: (353) 1 676 9334. Chairman: Vernon Pugh, Chief Executive Officer: Stephen Baines. Founded in 1886. 83 member nations in 1998.

Fédération Internationale de Rugby Amateur (FIRA), 7 Cité d'Antin, F-75009, Paris, France. Tel: (33) 1 4874 8475, Fax: (33) 1 4526 1919. General Secretary: Albert Ferrasse. Founded in 1934. Membership reached 76 nations in 1997.

Changing values of points scored

(Con − conversion, Pen − penalty goal, DG − drop goal, GM − goal from mark)

Year	Try	Con	Pen	DG	GM
1890	1	2	2	3	3
1892	2	3	3	4	4
1894	3	2	3	4	4
1905	3	2	3	4	3
1948	3	2	3	3	3
1971	4	2	3	3	3
1978	4	2	3	3	-
1992	5	2	3	3	-

World Cup

The inaugural World Cup was contested in Australia and New Zealand in 1987 by 16 national teams. The second was played in Britain and France in 1991, and the third in South Africa in 1995.

Results of finals:
1987 New Zealand 29 France 9
1991 Australia 12 England 6
1995 South Africa 15 New Zealand 12

Highest team score: New Zealand 145 Japan 17 at Bloemfontein on 4 Jun 1995

Most points in a match by an individual
(con – conversion, pen – penalty goal)
45 Simon Culhane (1 try, 20 con), for New Zealand (145) v Japan (17), Bloemfontein 4 Jun 1995
44 Gavin Hastings (4 tries, 2 pen, 9 con), for Scotland (89) v Ivory Coast (0), Rustenberg 26 May 1995
31 Gavin Hastings (1 try, 8 pen, 1 con), for Scotland (41) v Tonga (5), Pretoria 30 May 1995
30 Didier Camberabero (3 tries, 9 con), for France (70) v Zimbabwe (12), Auckland 2 Jun 1987
Most tries in a match: 6 Marc Ellis, for New Zealand v Japan, Bloemfontein 4 Jun 1995

Highest points-scorers
1987 Grant Fox (NZ) 126 pts in 6 games
1991 Roger Keyes (Ire) 68 pts in 4 games
1995 Thierry Lacroix (Fra) 112 ps in 6 games
Gavin Hastings (Sco) 104 pts in 4 games
1987-95 227 Hastings
195 Michael Lynagh (Aus)
170 Fox

Scorers of most tries
1987 6 Craig Green (NZ), John Kirwan (NZ)
1991 6 David Campese (Aus), Jean-Baptiste Lafond
1995 7 Marc Ellis NZ), Jonah Lomu (NZ)
1987-95 11 Rory Underwood (Eng)
10 Campese
Most appearances: Sean Fitzpatrick (NZ) 17

International Championships

Five Nations

This international championship was first contested by England, Ireland, Scotland and Wales in 1884. France made it a 'Five Nations' tournament when they joined in 1910. Each country plays each other once during each season's championship. The championships of 1885, 1888-9, 1897-8 and 1972 were not completed, for various reasons.

Winners (outright/shared wins):

22/11	Wales	1893, 1900, 1902, 1905, 1906,★ 1908-9, 1911, 1920,★ 1922, 1931, 1932,★ 1936, 1939,★ 1947,★ 1950, 1952, 1954-5,★ 1956, 1964,★ 1965-6, 1969, 1970,★ 1971, 1973,★ 1975-6, 1978-9, 1988,★ 1994
22/9	England	1883-4, 1886,★ 1890,★ 1892, 1910, 1912,★ 1913-4, 1921, 1923-4, 1928, 1930, 1932,★ 1934, 1937, 1939,★ 1947,★ 1953, 1954,★ 1957-8, 1960,★ 1963, 1973,★ 1980, 1991-2, 1995-6
13/8	Scotland	1886,★ 1887, 1890,★ 1891, 1895, 1901, 1903-4, 1907, 1920,★ 1925, 1926-7,★ 1929, 1933, 1938, 1964,★ 1973,★ 1984, 1986,★ 1990
12/8	France	1954,★ 1955,★ 1959, 1960,★ 1961-2, 1967-8, 1970,★ 1973,★ 1977, 1981, 1983,★ 1986,★ 1987, 1988,★ 1989, 1993, 1997-8
10/8	Ireland	1894, 1896, 1899, 1906★, 1912,★ 1926-7,★ 1932,★ 1935, 1939,★ 1948-9, 1951, 1973,★ 1974, 1982, 1983,★ 1985

★ Denotes shared win.
There was a quintuple tie in 1973.

Five Nations Grand Slam
A Grand Slam is achieved by winning against each of the other four countries during one season's championship.
Number of Grand Slams won:
11 England 1913-4, 1921, 1923-4, 1928, 1957, 1980, 1991-2, 1995
8 Wales 1908-9,★ 1911, 1950, 1952, 1971, 1976, 1978
5 France 1968, 1977, 1981, 1987, 1998
3 Scotland 1925, 1984, 1990
1 Ireland 1948
★ Not including France, who were yet to enter.

Five Nations Triple Crown
The Triple Crown is achieved by winning against the other three 'home countries' in one season's championship.
Triple Crowns won:
20 England 1883-4, 1892, 1913-4, 1921, 1923-4, 1928, 1934, 1937, 1954, 1957, 1960, 1980, 1991-2, 1995, 1997-8
17 Wales 1893, 1900, 1902, 1905, 1908-9, 1911, 1950, 1952, 1965, 1969, 1971, 1976-9, 1988
10 Scotland 1891, 1895, 1901, 1903, 1907, 1925, 1933, 1938, 1984, 1990
6 Ireland 1894, 1899, 1948-9, 1982, 1985

Five Nations records

Team

Highest score: England 60 Wales 26 at Twickenham 21 Feb 1998
Most points in a season: 146 England 1998
Most tries in a season: 21 Wales 1909-10

Individual

(con – conversion, DG – drop goal, pen – penalty goal)
Most points in a season:
  67 (3 tries, 3 pen, 11 con) Jonathan Webb (Eng) 1992
  66 (1 try, 1 DG, 10 pen, 14 con) Paul Grayson (Eng) 1998
  60 (18 pen, 3 con) Simon Hodgkinson (Eng) 1991
  56 (13 pen, 6 con, 1 try) Gavin Hastings (Sco) 1995
Most tries in a season: 8 Cyril Lowe (Eng) 1913-14, Ian Smith (Sco) 1924-5
Most conversions in a season: 14 Paul Grayson (Eng) 1998
Most penalty goals in a season: 18 Simon Hodgkinson (Eng) 1991
Most points in a match: 24 Sébastien Viers, for France v Ireland, Paris 21 Mar 1992 (2 tries, 2 pen, 5 con);
  24 Rob Andrew, for England v Scotland, Twickenham 18 Mar 1995 (7 pen, 1 DG)
Most goals in a match: 9 (8 con, 1 pen) William Bancroft, for Wales v France 1 Jan 1910
Most tries in a match: 5 George Lindsay, for Scotland v Wales 26 Feb 1887, Douglas 'Daniel' Lambert,
  for England v France 5 Jan 1907

International Records

Team statistics

The playing records between major rugby-playing nations at 20 Jul 1998.
(First figure – wins, second figure – draws.)

	ARG	AUS	BI	ENG	FIJ	FRA	IRE	NZ	ROM	SCO	SAF	WAL
Argentina	–	4/1	–	2/2	0/0	4/1	0/0	0/1	3/0	3/0	0/0	1/1
Australia	8/1	–	2/-	14/1	12/1	12/2	11/0	28/5	1/0	11/0	12/0	11/0
British Isles	–	8/0	–	–	0/0	–	–	6/5	–	–	14/6	–
England	6/2	8/1	–	–	5/1	40/7	65/8	4/1	3/0	59/17	4/1	44/12
Fiji	1/0	2/1	1/0	0/1	–	0/0	0/0	0/0	0/0	1/0	–	0/0
France	27/1	13/2	–	28/7	4/0	–	42/5	8/0	34/2	35/3	5/5	32/3
Ireland	2/0	6/0	–	38/8	3/0	25/5	–	0/1	2/1	45/6	1/1	37/6
New Zealand	12/1	73/5	24/5	17/1	4/0	24/0	13/1	–	1/0	18/2	24/3	14/0
Romania	0/0	–	–	0/0	1/0	8/2	0/1	0/0	–	2/0	–	2/0
Scotland	3/0	7/0	–	39/17	3/0	32/3	59/6	0/2	6/0	–	3/0	44/2
South Africa	6/0	26/0	20/6	10/1	1/0	18/5	10/1	22/3	1/0	7/0	–	10/1
Wales	2/1	8/0	–	48/12	5/0	38/3	59/6	3/0	4/0	56/2	0/1	–

Calcutta Cup

The annual England – Scotland games are played for the Calcutta Cup, named because it was made in India from the rupees left in the bank by the disbanded Calcutta Club in 1876.

Bledisloe Cup

Contested by New Zealand and Australia, the Bledisloe Cup was instigated in 1931 by Lord Bledisloe, the Governor-General of New Zealand. To the end of 1997 New Zealand had 62 wins, Australia 22, and 4 games were drawn.

Individual records

Leading cap-winners.
(British Lions (BL) appearances in brackets; as at 6 Jul 1998.)

111		Philippe Sella (Fra) 1982-95
101		David Campese (Aus) 1982-96
93		Serge Blanco (Fra) 1980-91
91	(6)	Rory Underwood (Eng) 1984-96
91		Sean Fitzpatrick (NZ) 1986-97
81	(12)	Mike Gibson (Ire) 1964-79
80	(17)	Willie John McBride (Ire) 1962-75
78	(6)	Ieuan Evans (Wal) 1987-98
76	(5)	Rob Andrew (Eng) 1985-97
73	(1)	Will Carling (Eng) 1988-97
73		Ian Jones (NZ) 1990-8
72		Michael Lynagh (Aus) 1984-95

69		Philippe Saint-André (Fra) 1990-7	63		Michel Crauste (Fra) 1957-66
69		Roland Bertranne (Fra) 1971-81	63		Benoit Dauga (Fra) 1964-72
69	(5)	Brian Moore (Eng) 1987-95	63		Nick Farr-Jones (Aus) 1984-93
67	(6)	Gavin Hastings (Sco) 1986-95	63		John Kirwan (NZ) 1984-94
67	(2)	Scott Hastings (Sco) 1986-97	63		Cuesta-Silva (Arg)
65	(4)	Fergus Slattery (Ire) 1970-84	63	(10)	Gareth Edwards (Wal) 1967-78
65	(7)	Peter Winterbottom (Eng) 1982-93	63	(8)	John P R Williams (Wal) 1969-81
64		Jean-Luc Sadourny (Fra) 1991-8			Also 77 Lungu (Rom); 70 Dinu (Rom); 69 Dimitru
64	(2)	Jason Leonard (Eng) 1990-8			(Rom)

Leading points-scorers

Name	Points	Matches	Av. per match	Year
Michael Lynagh (Aus)	911	72	12.7	1984-95
Gavin Hastings (Sco/BL)	755	67	11.3	1986-95
Grant Fox (NZ)	645	46	14.0	1985-93
Neil Jenkins (Wal)	631	60	10.5	1991-8
Diego Dominguez (Ita)	609	43	14.2	1991-8
Hugo Porta (Arg)	530	33	10.0	1972-90
Stefano Bettarello (Ita)	483	55	8.8	1979-88
Rob Andrew (Eng/BL)	407	76	5.4	1985-97
Andrew Mehrtens (NZ)	388	25	15.5	1995-8
Thierry Lacroix (Fra)	367	43	8.5	1989-97
Didier Camberabero (Fra)	354	36	9.8	1985-93
Naas Botha (SAf)	312	28	11.1	1980-92
Michael Kiernan (Ire)	308	43	7.2	1982-91
Paul Thorburn (Wal)	301	37	8.1	1985-91
Andy Irvine (Sco/BL)	301	60	5.0	1972-82
More than 200 points and average over 10:				
Simon Hodgkinson (Eng)	203	14	14.5	1989-91
Paul McLean (Aus)	260	22	11.8	1979-82

Most points in a major international match

30 Rob Andrew for England v Canada, at Twickenham 10 Dec 1994; *see also* World Cup records.

Leading try-scorers

Tries		Matches	
64	David Campese (Aus)	101	1982-96
50	Rory Underwood (Eng/BL)	91	1984-96
38	Serge Blanco (Fra)	93	1980-91
35	John Kirwan (NZ)	63	1984-94
34	Ieuan Evans (Wal/BL)	78	1987-97
33	Philippe Saint-André (Fra)	69	1990-7
30	Philippe Sella (Fra)	111	1982-95
28	Jeff Wilson (NZ)	36	1993-8
25	Tim Horan (Aus)	54	1989-98
24	Ian Smith (Sco)	32	1924-33
23	Christian Darrouy (Fra)	40	1957-67
23	Gerald Davies (Wal/BL)	51	1966-78

Most for other nations

South Africa: 21 Joost van der Westhuizen 1993-8
Ireland: 15 George Stephenson 1920-30

Most dropped goals

24	Hugo Porta (Arg) 1972-90
23	Rob Andrew (Eng/BL) 1985-95
18	Naas Botha (SAf) 1980-92
17	Stefano Betterello (Ita) 1979-91
15	Jean-Patrick Lescarboura (Fra) 1982-90

Most successful captains

44 wins in 55 games: Will Carling (Eng) 1988-96
41 wins in 51 games: Sean Fitzpatrick (NZ) 1992-7
23 wins in 36 games: Nick Farr-Jones (Aus) 1984-92
22 wins in 30 games: Wilson Whineray (NZ) 1958-65

Other Records (All Matches)

Biggest winning margin: Hong Kong 154 Singapore 13, at Kuala Lumpur on 27 Oct 1994 in the Asian Championships, with Ashley Billington scoring a record 10 tries and James McKee kicking a record 17 conversions

Highest score in an International Tour match: Western Samoa 128 Marlborough 0, at Blenheim, New Zealand on 8 Jul 1993

Most team points scored in a season: 1917 by Neath (Wales) in 1988/9

Most team tries in a season: 345 Neath 1988/9

Individual career points: 7337 Dusty Hare (Nottingham, Leicester, England, British Lions, and other representative matches) 1971-89

World Cup Sevens

First contested in 1993 by 24 teams at Murrayfield, Edinburgh, and then combined with the Hong Kong Sevens in 1997.

Winners:

1993   England
1997   Fiji

Hong Kong Sevens

Now sponsored by Cathay Pacific and the Hong Kong Bank, the first Hong Kong International Sevens was held in 1976, with 12 teams taking part. Long regarded as the most prestigious Sevens tournament in the world.

Wins:

8	Fiji	1977-8, 1980, 1984, 1990-2, 1997
6	New Zealand	1986-7, 1989, 1994-6
5	Australia	1979, 1982-3, 1985, 1988
1	Cantabrians 1976, Barbarians 1981, Western Samoa 1993

British Lions

The British Lions went on their first Tour in 1888, when they played a total of 35 matches in Australia and New Zealand. Since then there have been a further 21 Lions tours.

(Complete record of all matches on each tour, with matches played, won, drawn and lost, with total points for and against.)

Year	Country	P	W	D	L	F	A	Tour captain
1888	Australia	16	14	2	0	210	65	Robert Seddon (Eng)★
	New Zealand	19	13	4	2	82	33	
1891	South Africa	19	19	0	0	224	3	Bill MacLagan (Sco)
1896	South Africa	21	19	1	1	310	45	John Hammond (Eng)#
1899	Australia	21	18	0	3	333	90	Rev Matthew Mullineaux (Eng)#
1903	South Africa	22	11	3	8	231	138	Mark Morrison (Sco)
1904	Australia	14	14	0	0	265	51	Darky Bedell-Sivright (Sco)
	New Zealand	5	2	1	2	22	33	
1908	Australia	9	7	0	2	139	48	Arthur Harding (Wal)
	New Zealand	17	9	1	7	184	153	
1910	South Africa	24	13	3	8	290	236	Dr Tom Smyth (Ire)
1924	South Africa	21	9	3	9	175	155	Dr Ronald Cove-Smith (Eng)
1930	New Zealand	21	15	0	6	420	205	Doug Prentice (Eng)
	Australia	7	5	0	2	204	113	
1938	South Africa	23	17	0	6	407	272	Sam Walker (Ire)
1950	New Zealand	23	17	1	5	420	162	
	Australia	6	5	0	1	150	52	Karl Mullen (Ire)
1955	South Africa	24	18	1	5	418	271	Robin Thompson (Ire)
1959	Australia	6	5	0	1	174	70	Ronnie Dawson (Ire)
	New Zealand	25	20	0	5	582	266	
1962	South Africa	24	15	4	5	351	208	Arthur Smith (Sco)
1966	Australia	8	7	1	0	202	48	Michael Campbell-Lamerton (Sco)
	New Zealand	25	15	2	8	300	281	
1968	South Africa	20	15	1	4	377	181	Tom Kiernan (Ire)
1971	Australia	2	1	0	1	25	27	John Dawes (Wal)
	New Zealand	24	22	1	1	555	204	
1974	South Africa	22	21	1	0	729	207	Willie John McBride (Ire)
1977	New Zealand	25	21	0	4	596	295	Phil Bennett (Wal)
	Fiji	1	0	0	1	21	25	
1980	South Africa	18	15	0	3	401	244	Billy Beaumont (Eng)
1983	New Zealand	18	12	0	6	478	276	Cieran Fitzgerald (Ire)
1989	Australia	12	11	0	1	360	192	Finlay Calder (Sco)
1993	New Zealand	13	7	0	6	314	285	Gavin Hastings (Sco)
1997	South Africa	13	11	0	2	480	278	Martin Johnson (Eng)

★ Seddon drowned in an accident on the Hunter River, NSW, during the tour. He was replaced by Andrew Stoddart (Eng), who also went on to captain England at cricket, the only man to achieve this double distinction.
Neither Mullineaux nor Hammond ever played international rugby for their home country.

Test summary

British Lions	P	W	D	L
v Australia	17	14	0	3
v New Zealand	35	25	3	7
v South Africa	43	16	6	21

British Lions records

Biggest test win: 31-0 v Australia at Brisbane 4 Jun 1966

Biggest test defeat: 6-38 v New Zealand at Auckland 16 Jul 1983

Most caps: 17 Willie John McBride (Ire) 1962-74

Most internationals as captain: 6 Ronnie Dawson (Ire) 1959

Most points in internationals: 66 Gavin Hastings (Sco) 1989-93 (7 games)

Most points in one international: 18 Tony Ward (Ire) v South Africa at Cape Town 31 May 1980, Gavin Hastings (Sco) v New Zealand at Christchurch 12 Jun 1993

Most tries in internationals: 6 Tony O'Reilly (Ire) 1955-9

Most tries in one international: 8 players have each scored two tries, most recently Gavin Hastings (Sco) v Australia in 1989

Most points on a tour: 188 Barry John (Wal) 1971, in Australia and New Zealand

Most tries on a tour: 22 Tony O'Reilly (Ire) 1959, in Australia and New Zealand

Most points in a tour match: 37 Alan Old (Eng) v South Western Districts at Mossel Bay, South Africa 29 May 1974

Most tries in a tour match: 6 David Duckham (Eng) v West Coast-Buller at Greymouth, NZ 17 Jun 1971; J J Williams (Wal) v South Western Districts at Mossel Bay, South Africa 29 May 1974

Varsity Match

The first match between the Universities of Oxford and Cambridge took place at The Parks, Oxford on 10 February 1872. It has been contested annually ever since, with the exception of the First World War years. During the Second World War, a special series of matches was played. Cambridge staged the second match in 1873, the Oval 1874-80, Blackheath 1881-7, Queen's Club 1888-1921, and Twickenham thereafter. The years quoted are for the second half of the season, although the match has been played in December since 1995.

Wins:

55 Cambridge 1873, 1877, 1880, 1886-9, 1892, 1896,1899-1900, 1905-6, 1913-14, 1920, 1923, 1926-9, 1935, 1937, 1939, 1946, 1948, 1953, 1955, 1957, 1959, 1961-4, 1968-9, 1973-7, 1979, 1981-5, 1988, 1990, 1992-3, 1995-8

48 Oxford 1872, 1876, 1878, 1882-5, 1890, 1894, 1897-8, 1901-2, 1904, 1907-8, 1910-2, 1921-2, 1924-5, 1930, 1932-4, 1938, 1947, 1949-52, 1956, 1958, 1960, 1965, 1967, 1970-2, 1978, 1980, 1986-7, 1989, 1991, 1994

13 Drawn 1874-5, 1879, 1881, 1891, 1893, 1895, 1903, 1909, 1931, 1936, 1954, 1966

Between 1940-5 a total of 12 matches were played in the wartime series. Wins: 9 Cambridge 1941 (2), 1942 (2), 1943 (3), 1944, 1945; 2 Oxford 1940, 1944; 1 drawn 1945.

English County Championship

The English County Championship was introduced in 1889 when, after an unbeaten season, Yorkshire were declared the champions by the Rugby Union. The current system, the fifth, divides the counties into Northern Midland, London and South-western divisions, with a promotion and relegation system. The leading four counties play off in semi-finals to decide the participants in the final. From 1994 the event was downgraded, with the exclusion of players from the 1st and 2nd Divisions of the Courage Clubs Championship. Not held 1915-9, 1940-6.

Winners:

16	Lancashire	1891, 1935, 1938, 1947-9, 1955, 1969, 1973, 1977, 1980, 1982, 1988, 1990, 1992-3
16	Gloucestershire	1910, 1913, 1920-2, 1930-2, 1937, 1972, 1974-6, 1983-4, 1996
12	Yorkshire	1889-90, 1892-6, 1926, 1928, 1953, 1987, 1994
10	Warwickshire	1939, 1958-60, 1962-5, 1986, 1995
8	Durham	1900, 1902-3, 1905, 1907,★ 1909, 1967,★ 1989
8	Middlesex	1929, 1952, 1954, 1956, 1966, 1968, 1979, 1985
7	Devon	1899, 1901, 1906, 1907,★ 1911-2, 1957
3	Kent	1897, 1904, 1927
3	Cheshire	1950, 1961, 1998
2	Cornwall	1908, 1991
2	Northumberland	1898, 1981
2	Hampshire	1933, 1936
2	East Midlands	1934, 1951
2	Surrey	1967,★ 1971
1	Midlands 1914, Cumberland 1924, Leicestershire 1925, Staffordshire 1970, North Midlands 1978, Cumbria 1997	

★ Shared title.

John Player Special/Pilkington/ Tetley's Bitter Cup

The RFU knock-out competition for English club sides was inaugurated in the 1971/2 season and has been held annually since. Sponsored by John Player 1971/2 to 1987/8, Pilkington 1988/9 to 1996/7, and Tetley's Bitter from 1997/8. The final is played at Twickenham.

Finals:

1972	Gloucester 17 Moseley 6
1973	Coventry 27 Bristol 15
1974	Coventry 26 London Scottish 6
1975	Bedford 28 Rosslyn Park 12
1976	Gosforth 23 Rosslyn Park 14
1977	Gosforth 27 Waterloo 11
1978	Gloucester 6 Leicester 3
1979	Leicester 15 Moseley 12
1980	Leicester 21 London Irish 9
1981	Leicester 22 Gosforth 15
1982	Gloucester 12 Moseley 12★ *(shared)*
1983	Bristol 28 Leicester 22
1984	Bath 10 Bristol 9
1985	Bath 24 London Welsh 15
1986	Bath 25 Wasps 17
1987	Bath 19 Wasps 12
1988	Harlequins 28 Bristol 22
1989	Bath 10 Leicester 6
1990	Bath 48 Gloucester 6
1991	Harlequins 25 Northampton 13★
1992	Bath 15 Harlequins 12★
1993	Leicester 23 Harlequins 16
1994	Bath 21 Leicester 9
1995	Bath 36 Wasps 16
1996	Bath 16 Leicester 15
1997	Leicester 9 Sale 3
1998	Saracens 48 Wasps 18

★ After extra time.

Most wins: 10 Bath; 4 Leicester; 3 Gloucester

Clubs' Championship/Premiership

The RFU approved a plan in 1985 for the leading English clubs to form into two divisions known as Merit Tables 'A' and 'B'. Selected matches throughout the season were designated Merit Table matches, and an end-of-season league table was drawn up. A third Merit Table, C, was added in 1986/7. There soon followed an extensive series of leagues sponsored by Courage.

Winners of Merit Table A 1985/6 and 1986/7, Division One of the Courage League to 1996/7 and the Allied Dunbar Premiership 1997/8:

1985/6	Gloucester
1986/7	Bath
1987/8	Leicester
1988/9	Bath
1989/90	Wasps
1990/1	Bath

1991/2	Bath
1992/3	Bath
1993/4	Bath
1994/5	Leicester
1995/6	Bath
1996/7	Wasps
1997/8	Newcastle Falcons

Welsh Cup

The Welsh Rugby Union Challenge Cup has been contested annually since the 1971/2 season. All finals have been in Cardiff, at the Arms Park, now the National Stadium. Formerly the Schweppes Cup, the competition was renamed the Swalec Cup from 1992/3.

Finals:

1972	Neath 15 Llanelli 9
1973	Llanelli 30 Cardiff 7
1974	Llanelli 12 Aberavon 10
1975	Llanelli 15 Aberavon 6
1976	Llanelli 15 Swansea 4
1977	Newport 16 Cardiff 15
1978	Swansea 13 Newport 9
1979	Bridgend 18 Pontypridd 12
1980	Bridgend 15 Swansea 9
1981	Cardiff 14 Bridgend 6
1982	Cardiff 12★ Bridgend 12
1983	Pontypool 18 Swansea 6
1984	Cardiff 24 Neath 19
1985	Llanelli 15 Cardiff 14
1986	Cardiff 28 Newport 21
1987	Cardiff 16 Swansea 15#
1988	Llanelli 28 Neath 13
1989	Neath 14 Llanelli 13
1990	Neath 16 Bridgend 10
1991	Llanelli 24 Pontypool 9
1992	Llanelli 16 Swansea 7
1993	Llanelli 21 Neath 18
1994	Cardiff 15 Llanelli 8
1995	Swansea 17 Pontypridd 12
1996	Pontypridd 29 Neath 22
1997	Cardiff 33 Swansea 26
1998	Llanelli 19 Ebbw Vale 12

★ Won on most tries.
After extra time.

Most wins: 10 Llanelli, 7 Cardiff

Welsh League

Sponsored by Heineken and introduced in 1990/1.

Premier Division winners:

1990/1	Neath
1991/2	Swansea
1992/3	Llanelli
1993/4	Swansea
1994/5	Cardiff
1995/6	Neath
1996/7	Pontypridd
1997/8	Swansea

Scottish Club Championship

The premier club competition in Scotland was instituted 1974. Formerly the McEwans League, and now the SRU Tennent's Premiership. There are currently seven divisions.

Division One winners (year given is second half of the season):

1974–8	Hawick
1979	Heriot's FP
1980	Gala
1982	Hawick
1983	Gala
1984–7	Hawick
1988–9	Kelso
1990	Melrose
1991	Boroughmuir
1992–4	Melrose
1995	Stirling County
1996–7	Melrose
1998	Heriot's FP

Most wins: 10 Hawick; 6 Melrose

Tennants Cup Final

First played 1996.

1996	Hawick 17 Watsonians 15
1997	Melrose 31 Boroughmuir 23
1998	Glasgow 36 Kelso 14

All-Ireland League

Inaugurated in 1990.
Winners:

1991	Cork Constitution
1992	Garryowen
1993	Young Munster
1994	Garryowen
1995–8	Shannon

From 1947 Connacht, Leinster, Munster and Ulster have contested the Irish Inter-provincial Championship.

Middlesex Sevens

This leading Sevens tournament was inaugurated in 1926. The final of the knock-out tournament is played at Twickenham. The winners receive the Russell-Cargill Memorial Cup.
Winners:

13	Harlequins	1926–9, 1933, 1935, 1967, 1978, 1986–90
11	Richmond	1951 *(second team)*, 1953, 1955, 1974–80, 1983 *(first team)*
8	London Welsh	1930–1, 1956, 1968, 1971–3, 1984
7	London Scottish	1937, 1960–3, 1965, 1991
5	St Mary's Hospital	1940, 1942–4, 1946

5	Loughborough Colls	1959, 1964, 1966, 1970, 1976
4	Rosslyn Park	1947, 1950, 1954, 1981
4	Wasps	1948, 1952, 1985, 1993
3	Barbarians	1934, 1997–8
2	Blackheath	1932, 1958
2	St Luke's College	1957, 1969
1	Sale 1936, Metropolitan Police 1938, Cardiff 1939, Cambridge University 1941, Nottingham 1945, Heriot's FP 1949, Stewart's Melville FP 1982, Western Samoa 1992, Bath 1994, Leicester 1995, Wigan (RL) 1996	

French Championship

First contested in 1892.
Most titles:

14	Toulouse	1912, 1922–4, 1926–7, 1947, 1985–6, 1989, 1994–7 (and wartime 1916)
11	AS Béziers	1961, 1971–2, 1974–5, 1977–8, 1980–1, 1983–4
9	Stade Français	1893–5, 1897–8, 1901, 1903, 1908, 1998
8	SU Agen	1930, 1945, 1962, 1965–6, 1976, 1982, 1988
8	FC Lourdes	1948, 1952–3, 1956–8, 1960, 1968
7	Bordeaux	1899, 1904–7, 1909, 1911
5	Racing Club de France	1892, 1900, 1902, 1959, 1990 (and wartime 1918)
5	USA Perpignan	1921, 1925, 1938, 1944, 1955

Heineken European Cup

Contested for the first time in 1995/6 by the leading teams in Europe.
Results of finals:

1995/6	Toulouse (Fra) 21 Cardiff (Wal) 18
1996/7	Brive (Fra) 28 Leicester (Eng) 9
1997/8	Bath (Eng) 19 Brive (Fra) 18

Olympic Games

Rugby has been included in four Olympic celebrations, the first time at Paris in 1900. Three teams took part in 1900 and 1924, and played on a round-robin basis, while just two teams entered in 1908 and 1920, and the one match decided the gold medallist.
Winners:

1900	France
1908	Australia
1920	USA
1924	USA

Australia

Rugby was first played in Australia in 1829 and the first administrative body, the Southern Union, was formed in 1874. It was renamed the NSW Rugby Union in 1892. The first Australian rugby club was that of Sydney University, formed in 1864. New South Wales and Queensland are the two states where the game is predominant.

Sydney First Grade Premiership

First played in 1900.

Wins:

26	Randwick	1930, 1934, 1938, 1940, 1948, 1959, 1965-7, 1971, 1973-4, 1978-82, 1984, 1987-92, 1994, 1996
21	University	1901,★ 1904, 1919-20, 1923-4, 1926-8, 1937, 1939, 1945, 1951, 1953-5, 1961-2, 1968, 1970, 1972
9	Eastern Suburbs	1903, 1913, 1921, 1931, 1941, 1944, 1946-7, 1969
8	Glebe	1900, 1901,★ 1906-7, 1909, 1912, 1914, 1925★
7	Gordon	1949, 1952, 1956, 1958, 1976, 1993, 1995
7	Manly	1922, 1932, 1942-3, 1950, 1983, 1997
6	Northern Suburbs	1933, 1935, 1960, 1963-4, 1975
3	Newtown	1908, 1910-1
3	Parramatta	1977, 1985-6
2	Western Suburbs	1902, 1929
1	South Sydney 1905, Balmain 1925,★ Drummoyne 1936, St George 1957	

★ Shared.

New Zealand

Rugby was introduced into New Zealand in 1870 and has been the nation's top sport for a long time. The first provincial union was that of Canterbury in 1879, and the New Zealand Rugby Football Union was founded in 1892.

Ranfurly Shield

The inter-provincial championship, first held in 1904. It is not a knock-out competition, but one in which the champion state puts its title up for a challenge.

Years when the title changed hands, and champions:

1904	Wellington
1905	Auckland
1913	Taranki
1914	Wellington
1920	Southland
1921	Wellington
1922	Hawke's Bay
1927	Wairarapa
1927	Manawhenua
1927	Canterbury
1928	Wairarapa
1929	Southland
1930	Wellington
1931	Canterbury
1934	Hawke's Bay
1934	Auckland
1935	Canterbury
1935	Otago
1937	Southland
1938	Otago
1938	Southland
1947	Otago
1950	Canterbury
1950	Wairarapa
1950	South Canterbury
1950	North Auckland
1951	Waikato
1952	Auckland
1952	Waikato
1953	Wellington
1953	Canterbury
1956	Wellington
1957	Otago
1957	Taranaki
1959	Southland
1959	Auckland
1960	North Auckland
1960	Auckland
1963	Wellington
1963	Taranki
1965	Auckland
1966	Waikato
1966	Hawke's Bay
1969	Canterbury
1971	Auckland
1971	North Auckland
1972	Auckland
1972	Canterbury
1973	Marlborough
1974	South Canterbury
1974	Wellington
1974	Auckland
1976	Manawatu
1978	North Auckland
1979	Auckland
1980	Waikato
1981	Wellington
1982	Canterbury
1985	Auckland
1993	Waikato
1994	Canterbury
1995	Auckland
1996	Waikato
1996	Auckland
1997	Waikato

Most successive defences:
61 Auckland 1985-93; 25 Auckland 1960-3, Canterbury 1982-5

Record attendance: 52,000 Auckland v Canterbury at Lancaster Park 1985

New Zealand National Championship

A season-long league championship was inaugurated in 1976 involving 11 states in the First Division, with each team playing every other team once. There were also supplementary divisions enabling promotion to the first division. The format was changed in 1992 to 27 teams divided into three groups of nine, with the top four from each section playing semi-finals and a final.

Winners of First Division:

1976	Bay of Plenty
1977	Canterbury
1978	Wellington
1979	Counties
1980	Manawatu

1981	Wellington	
1982	Auckland	
1983	Canterbury	
1984-5	Auckland	
1986	Wellington	
1987-90	Auckland	
1991	Otago	
1992	Waikato	
1993-6	Auckland	
1997	Canterbury	

South Africa

Rugby in South Africa, developed from a form of football known as 'Gog's game', was first played between civilian and military teams at Green Point Common, Cape Town, in 1862. The first union to be formed was Western Province in 1883 and the South African Rugby Board was founded in 1889.

Currie Cup

Inter-provincial tournament, first held 1889. Mostly biennial to 1968, avoiding international tours, and annual since then.

Wins:

30	Western Province	1889, 1892, 1894-5, 1897-8, 1904, 1906, 1908, 1914, 1920, 1925, 1927, 1929, 1932,★ 1934,★ 1936, 1947, 1954, 1959, 1964, 1966, 1979,★ 1982-6, 1989,★ 1997
18	Northern Transvaal	1946, 1956, 1968-9, 1971,★ 1973-8, 1979,★ 1980-1, 1987-8, 1989,★ 1991
4	Natal	1990, 1992, 1995-6
8	Transvaal	1922, 1939, 1950, 1952, 1971,★ 1972, 1993-4
3	Griqualand West	1899, 1911, 1970
2	Border	1932,★ 1934★

★ Shared.

1934 competition was unfinished.

Highest score: Transvaal 99 Far North 9 at Ellis Park, Johannesburg 7 Jul 1973

Super 12 Series

Contested by the top teams from Australia, New Zealand and South Africa, first as the Super 6, then Super 10 (1993-5).

Winners:

1993	Transvaal
1994-5	Queensland
1996-7	Auckland Blues
1998	Canterbury Crusaders

Women's World Cup

Contested for the first time in 1991, when 12 national teams played in Cardiff, Wales.

Finals:

1991	USA 19 England 6
1994	England 38 USA 23
1998	New Zealand 44 USA 12

Record score: New Zealand 134 Germany 6, Amsterdam, Netherlands 1998

Sailing

The sport of yachting (or sailing) originated in the 16th and 17th centuries in the Netherlands, then the world's greatest maritime power. The first known yacht race for pleasure took place in September 1661, when Charles II challenged the Duke of York to a race over a 23-mile stretch of the River Thames from Greenwich to Gravesend. The sport became popular towards the end of the 19th century, nearly 150 years after the formation of the world's first yacht club, the Water Club of Cork, Ireland, in 1720.

International governing body: International Sailing Federation (ISAF), formerly the International Yacht Racing Union (IYRU), 27 Broadwall, Waterloo, London SE1 9PL. Fax: 0171 401 8304. President: Paul Henderson, Secretary General: Arve Sundheim.

America's Cup

Originally the 'Hundred Guinea Cup', one of the most famous of all sporting trophies, the Cup was donated by the Royal Yacht Squadron for a race around the Isle of Wight in 1851. The US schooner *America* won the race and took the trophy back to the USA. The New York Yacht Club then offered it as a challenge trophy but, despite many challenges over the years, it stayed in the USA until 1983, when it temporarily became Australian property and again in 1995, when it went to New Zealand.

Year	Winning boat	Winning skipper	Score	Challenger
1870	Magic	Andrew Comstock	–	Cambria (Eng)
1871	Columbia & Sappho	Nelson Comstock, Sam Greenwood	4-1	Livonia (Eng)
1876	Madeleine	Josephus Williams	2-0	Countess of Dufferin (Can)
1881	Mischief	Nathaniel Clock	2-0	Atalanta (Can)
1885	Puritan	Aubrey Crocker	2-0	Genesta (Eng)

Year	Winning boat	Winning skipper	Score	Challenger
1886	Mayflower	Martin Stone	2-0	Galatea (Eng)
1887	Volunteer	Henry Haff	2-0	Thistle (Sco)
1893	Vigilant	William Hansen	3-0	Valkyrie II (Eng)
1895	Defender	Henry Haff	3-0	Valkyrie III (Eng)
1899	Columbia	James Barr	3-0	Shamrock (Eng)
1901	Columbia	James Barr	3-0	Shamrock II (Eng)
1903	Reliance	James Barr	3-0	Shamrock III (Eng)
1920	Resolute	Charles Adams	3-2	Shamrock IV (Eng)
1930	Enterprise	Harold Vanderbilt	4-0	Shamrock V (Eng)
1934	Rainbow	Harold Vanderbilt	4-2	Endeavour (Eng)
1937	Ranger	Harold Vanderbilt	4-0	Endeavour II (Eng)
1958	Columbia	Briggs Cunningham	4-0	Sceptre (Eng)
1962	Weatherly	Emil Mosbacher, Jr	4-1	Gretel (Aus)
1964	Constellation	Bob Bavier, Jr	4-0	Sovereign (Eng)
1967	Intrepid	Emil Mosbacher, Jr	4-0	Dame Pattie (Aus)
1970	Intrepid	Bill Ficker	4-1	Gretel II (Aus)
1974	Courageous	Ted Hood	4-0	Southern Cross (Aus)
1977	Courageous	Ted Turner	4-0	Australia (Aus)
1980	Freedom	Dennis Conner	4-1	Australia (Aus)
1983	Australia II (Aus)	John Bertrand	4-3	Liberty (USA)
1987	Stars and Stripes	Dennis Conner	4-0	Kookaburra III (Aus)
1988	Stars and Stripes★	Dennis Conner	2-0	New Zealand (NZ)
1992	America^3	Bill Koch	4-1	Il Moro di Venezia (Ita)
1995	Black Magic (NZ)	Russell Coutts	5-0	Young America (USA)

★ *Stars and Stripes* accepted a special challenge from *New Zealand* (skippered by David Barnes) in a best-of-three series in 1988. After Conner had made a successful defence, the American Supreme Court ruled that his use of the catamaran against the New Zealand monohull had violated the Deed of Gift governing the race. However, this decision was reversed by the New York Appeals Court in 1989, and the legal battle ended in 1990 in favour of Conner.

Most times winning skipper: 3 Barr, Vanderbilt, Conner; 2 Haff, Mosbacher
Most times skipper of challenger: 3 Jim Hardy 1970, 1974, 1980

Admiral's Cup

The Royal Ocean Racing Club donated this trophy in 1957 to encourage yachtsmen from abroad to race in English waters. Contested by national three-boats teams, the biennial series of six races (five until 1987), combining inshore and offshore racing, takes place in the English Channel, at Cowes, in the Solent. The series culminates in the Fastnet Race (established in 1925), 605 miles (975km) from Cowes, round the Fastnet Rock off the south-west coast of Ireland, and back. The points system is weighted towards the offshore races.

Winners:

9	UK	1957, 1959, 1963, 1965, 1971, 1975, 1977, 1981, 1989
3	Germany	1973, 1983, 1985 (FRG); 1993
3	USA	1961, 1969, 1997
2	Australia	1967, 1979
1	New Zealand	1987, France 1991, Italy 1995

Olympic Games

Yachting did not make its Olympic debut until 1900. It should have been included in the first modern Olympics programme four years earlier, but bad weather prevented any competition. The classes of competition have varied over the years. Champions at current classes are shown first, followed by winning teams at the discontinued events.

Soling

1972	USA (Harry Melges, William Bentsen, William Allen)
1976	Denmark (Poul Jensen, Valdemar Bandolowski, Erik H Hansen)
1980	Denmark (Poul Jensen, Valdemar Bandolowski, Erik H Hansen)
1984	USA (Robert Haines Jr, Edward Trevelyan, Roderick Davis)
1988	GDR (Jochen Schümann, Thomas Flach, Bernd Jäkel)
1992	Denmark (Jesper Bonk, Steen Secher, Jesper Seier)
1996	Germany (Thomas Flach, Bernd Jaekel, Jochen Schumann)

Men

Finn – Olympic monotype

Classes: 12-foot and 18-foot (2-handed) dinghies in 1920, Meulan 1924, International 12-foot 1928, Snowbird 1932, International Olympia 1936, Firefly 1948, Finn from 1952.

1920	Franciscus Hin & Johannes Hin (Hol)
1924	Léon Huybrechts (Bel)
1928	Sven Thorell (Swe)
1932	Jacques Lebrun (Fra)
1936	Daniel Kagchelland (Hol)
1948	Paul Elvstrøm (Den)
1952	Paul Elvstrøm (Den)
1956	Paul Elvstrøm (Den)
1960	Paul Elvstrøm (Den)
1964	Willi Kuhweide (FRG)
1968	Valentin Mankin (USSR)
1972	Serge Maury (Fra)
1976	Jochen Schümann (GDR)
1980	Esko Rechardt (Fin)
1984	Russell Coutts (NZ)
1988	José-Luis Doreste (Spa)
1992	José Maria van der Ploeg (Spa)
1996	Mateusz Kusznierewicz (Pol)

470 class

1976	Frank Hübner & Harro Bode (FRG)
1980	Marcos Soares & Eduardo Penido (Bra)
1984	Luis Doreste & Roberto Molina (Spa)
1988	Thierry Peponnet & Luc Pillot (Fra)
1992	Jorge Calafat & Francisco Sánchez (Spa)
1996	Yevhin Braslevets & Igor Matviyenko (Ukr)

Flying Dutchman

Sharpie class in 1956.

1956	Peter Mander & John Cropp (NZ)
1960	Peder Lunde, Jr & Björn Bergvall (Nor)
1964	Helmer Pedersen & Earle Wells (NZ)
1968	Rodney Pattisson & Iain Macdonald-Smith (UK)
1972	Rodney Pattisson & Christopher Davies (UK)
1976	Jörg Diesch & Eckert Diesch (FRG)
1980	Alejandro Abascal & Miguel Noguer (Spa)
1984	Jonathan McKee & William Carl Buchan (USA)
1988	Jørgen Bojsen-Møller & Christian Grønberg (Den)
1992	Luis Doreste & Domingo Manrique (Spa)

Star

1932	Gilbert Gray & Andrew Libano Jr (USA)
1936	Peter Bischoff & Hans-Joachim Weise (Ger)
1948	Hilary Smart & Paul Smart (USA)
1952	Agostino Straulino & Nicolo Rode (Ita)
1956	Herbert Williams & Lawrence Low (USA)
1960	Timir Pinegin & Fyodor Shutkov (USSR)
1964	Durward Knowles & Cecil Cooke (Bah)
1968	Lowell North & Peter Barrett (USA)
1972	David Forbes & John Anderson (Aus)
1980	Valentin Mankin & Aleksandr Muzychenko (USSR)
1984	Bill Buchan & Stephen Erickson (USA)
1988	Michael McIntyre & Bryn Vaile (UK)
1992	Mark Reynolds & Hal Haenel (USA)
1996	Torben Grael & Marcelo Ferreira (Bra)

Tornado

1976	Reg White & John Osborn (UK)
1980	Alexandre Welter & Lars Björkström (Bra)
1984	Rex Sellers & Christopher Timms (NZ)
1988	Jean-Yves Le Deroff & Nicolas Hénard (Fra)
1992	Yves Loday & Nicolas Hénard (Fra)
1996	José Luis Ballester & Fernando León (Spa)

Laser

1996	Robert Scheidt (Bra)

Women

470 class

1988	Allison Jolly & Lynne Jewell (USA)
1992	Theresa Zabell & Patricia Guerra (Spa)
1996	Begona Via Dufresne & Theresa Zabell (Spa)

Europe

1992	Linda Andersen (Nor)
1996	Kristine Roug (Den)

Discontinued events (men)

Swallow

1948	Stewart Morris & David Bond (UK)

Tempest

1972	Valentin Mankin & Vitaliy Dyrdyra (USSR)
1976	John A lbrechtson & Ingvar Hansson (Swe)

Dragon

1948	Norway
1952	Norway
1956	Sweden
1960	Greece
1964	Denmark
1968	USA
1972	Australia

5.5 metres

1952	USA
1956	Sweden
1960	USA
1964	Australia
1968	Sweden

6 metres

1908	Great Britain
1912	France
1920	Norway
1924	Norway
1928	Norway
1932	Sweden

1936	Great Britain
1948	USA
1952	USA

6 metres (1907 rating)

| 1920 | Belgium |

6.5 metres

| 1920 | Netherlands |

7 metres

| 1908 | Great Britain |
| 1920 | Great Britain |

8 metres

1908	Great Britain
1912	Norway
1920	Norway

1924	Norway
1928	France
1932	USA
1936	Italy

8 metres (1907 rating)

| 1920 | Norway |

10 metres

1912	Sweden
1920	Norway (1907 rating)
	Norway (1919 rating)

12 metres

1908	Great Britain
1912	Norway
1920	Norway (1907 rating)
	Norway (1919 rating)

30 square metres

| 1920 | Sweden |

40 square metres

| 1920 | Sweden |

Tonnage categories in 1900

½ ton	France
½–1 ton	France
1–2 ton	Switzerland
2–3 ton	Great Britain
3–10 ton	France
10–20 ton	France
Open	Great Britain

Most individual gold medals:
  4 Paul Elvstrøm

Whitbread Round-the-World Race

The longest race in the world, the Whitbread was inaugurated in August 1973, and is organized by the Royal Naval Sailing Association. Held quadrennially, the distance has been 26,180 nautical miles (increased to 32,000 in 1990), starting and finishing at Portsmouth, England and rounding the Cape of Good Hope and Cape Horn. Conducted as a handicap race, with various classes. The result of the 1998 race was determined on a points basis over a series of legs.

(Handicap winner shown first, followed by the fastest yacht that year.)

Year	Winning skipper	Yacht	Time
1974	Ramon Carlin (Mex)	Sayula II	152d 9h 00m
	Chay Blyth (UK)	Great Britain II	144d 10 hr
1978	Cornelis van Rietschoten (Hol)	Flyer	136d 5hr
	Rob James (UK)	Great Britain II	134d 12hr
1982	Cornelis van Rietschoten (Hol)	Flyer II★	120d 6h 35m
1986	Lionel Pean (Fra)	L'Esprit d'Equipe	132d 0h 16m
	Pierre Fehlmann (Swi)	U B S Switzerland	117d 14h 32m
1990	Peter Blake (NZ)	Steinlager 2★	128d 9h 40m
1994	Grant Dalton (NZ)	New Zealand Endeavour	120d 5h 9m
1998	Paul Cayard (USA)	E F Language	

★ *Flyer II* and *Steinlager 2* won on both actual and corrected time.

A world record for single-handed non-stop sailing around the world was set in the Vendée Globe Challenge, 109d 8 hrs 48 mins 50 secs by Titouan Lamazou (Fra) in the 60-ft sloop *Ecureuil d'Aquitaine* from Les Sables d'Olonne, France and back, 26 Nov 1989 to 15 Mar 1990.

Single-Handed Transatlantic Race

Originally the idea of Colonel 'Blondie' Hasler (who finished second in the inaugural race), this event is held every four years from Plymouth, UK to Newport, Rhode Island, USA, approximately 3000 miles (4825km). It was named the Observer Single-Handed Transatlantic Race (OSTAR) 1960–84, and when *The Observer* was succeeded as sponsor by the Carlsberg brewing company, in 1988, it became known as C-STAR.

There is now a size limit for the boats of 18.3m (60ft), but the largest contestant was the 71.9m four-master *Club Mediterranée*, sailed to second place in 1976 by Alain Colas (Fra). Monohulls won the first three races and in 1976, but trimarans have won all the others, and the average speed of the winner has risen from 3.09 knots in 1960 to 11.23 knots in 1988.

Year	Winner	Yacht	Time
1960	Francis Chichester (UK)	Gypsy Moth III	40d 12hr 30min
1964	Éric Tabarly (Fra)	Pen Duick II	27d 3hr 56min
1968	Geoffrey Williams (UK)	Sir Thomas Lipton	25d 20hr 33min
1972	Alain Colas (Fra)	Pen Duick IV	20d 13hr 15min
1976	Éric Tabarly (Fra)	Pen Duick VI	23d 20hr 12min

1980	Phil Weld (USA)	Moxie	17d 23hr 12min
1984	Yvon Fauconnier (Fra)	Umupro Jardin V	16d 6hr 00min
1988	Philippe Poupon (Fra)	Fleury Michon	10d 9hr 15min
1992	Loïck Peyron (Fra)	Fuijicolor II	11d 1hr 35min
1996	Loïck Peyron (Fra)	Fuijicolor II	10d 10hr 5min

Boardsailing

Boardsailing (often called Windsurfing, although this is a trade name) was pioneered as a sport by Henry Hoyle Schweitzer and Jim Drake in California, USA in 1968, but its origins go back to 1958 when 12-year-old Peter Chilvers of England devised the first prototype sailboard. The sport became popular in the 1970s and a World Championship was instituted in 1973. Boardsailing was included in the Olympic Games for the first time in 1984.

Olympic Champions

Men's Windglider (Mistral 1996)

1984	Stephan van den Berg (Hol)
1988	Bruce Kendall (NZ)
1992	Franck David (Fra)
1996	Nikolaos Kaklamanakis (Gre)

Women's Windglider (Mistral 1996)

| 1992 | Barbara-Anne Kendall (NZ) |
| 1996 | Lee Lai-Shan (HK) |

Speed record

The boardsailing speed record was set by Thierry Bielak (Fra) at 45.34 knots (83.95km/h) at Saintes Maries de-la-Mer, Camargue, France 24 Apr 1993. The women's record was set by Babethe Coquelle (Fra) who achieved a speed of 40.36 knots (74.79km/h) at Tarifa, Spain 8 Jul 1995.

Speed Sailing

The highest speed reached under sail on water by any craft over a 500m timed run is 46.52 knots (86.21km/h) by Simon McKeon and Tim Daddo (Aus) in *Yellow Pages Endeavour*, a wing-masted tri-foiler at Shallow Inlet, Melbourne, Australia 26 Oct 1993.

Shinty

This 12-a-side game, played with a curved stick (the *caman*) and ball, is almost exclusive to the Scottish Highlands. The pitch is up to 170 yards (155m) long and 80 yards (73m) wide, and the goals are 10 x 12ft (3.0 x 3.65m). The ball is about the size of a tennis ball and has a thick leather covering over a cork and worsted core.

The game's origins date back more than 2000 years to the ancient game of *camanachd*, meaning 'the sport of the curved stick', and was brought to Scotland from Ireland by Celtic immigrants about 1400 years ago. The sport provided effective as battle training, and was indeed probably a crude substitute for battle between clans. The present ruling body, the Camanachd Association, was founded in 1893.

Camanachd Cup

The Camanachd Association Challenge Cup, instituted in 1896, is shinty's premier competition.

Most wins

28	Newtonmore 1907-10, 1929, 1931-2, 1936, 1947-8, 1950-1, 1955, 1957-9, 1967, 1970-2, 1975, 1977-9, 1981-2, 1985-6
20	Kyles Athletic 1904-6, 1920, 1922, 1924, 1927-8, 1935, 1956, 1962, 1965-6, 1968-9, 1974, 1976, 1980, 1983, 1994
14	Kingussie 1896, 1900, 1902-3, 1914, 1921, 1961, 1984, 1987-9, 1991, 1993, 1995

Other recent winners: 1990 Skye, 1992 Fort William

A record 11 winner's medals have been won by the Newtonmore players Johnnie Campbell, David Ritchie and Hugh Chisholm.

Highest score: Newtonmore 11 Furnace 3 1909

Shooting

The first shooting club, the Lucerne Shooting Guild (Switzerland), was formed around 1466 and the first recorded shooting match took place at Zürich in 1472. The National Rifle Association of Great Britain was formed in 1860 and the Clay Bird Shooting Association was founded in 1903. The National Rifle Association (NRA) was formed in the USA in 1871.

International governing body: Union Internationale de Tir (UIT) with the name proposed to be changed in 1998 to International Shooting Sport Federation (ISSF), Bavariaring 21, D-80336 München, Germany. Tel: (49) 89 53 1012, Fax: (49) 89 530 9481. President: Olegario Vázquez Raña, Secretary General: Horst G Schreiber. Formed in Zürich in 1907. 150 member nations in 1998.

Olympic Games

Shooting has been part of the Olympic programme since the first Games, in 1896; its early inclusion may have been as a result of the Games' founder, Baron Pierre de Coubertin, being an excellent shot. Separate events for women were first held in 1984, although they had competed alongside their male counterparts since 1968. Skeet and trap events were open to both men and women until 1992. In 1986 the ISU introduced new regulations for determining major championships and world records. The leading eight competitors at the end of the designated number of rounds take part in a final shoot-out round with the target sub-divided into tenths of a point for rifle and pistol shooting. For trap and skeet shooting each of the leading competitors has 25 extra shots. This new scoring system was introduced into the Olympic programme for the first time in 1988.

Winners, with current regulations:

Men

Free pistol

60 shots from 50 metres.

1896	Sumner Paine (USA) 442 *(from 30m)*
1900	Conrad Röderer (Swi) 503
1906	Georgios Orphanidis (Gre) 221
1912	Alfred Lane (USA) 499
1920	Karl Frederick (USA) 496
1936	Torsten Ullmann (Swe) 559
1948	Edwin Vazquez Cam (Per) 545
1952	Huelet Benner (USA) 553
1956	Pentti Linnosvuo (Fin) 556
1960	Aleksey Gushchin (USSR) 560
1964	Väinö Markkanen (Fin) 560
1968	Grigoriy Kossykh (USSR) 562
1972	Ragnar Skanåkar (Swe) 567
1976	Uwe Potteck (GDR) 573
1980	Aleksandr Melentyev (USSR) 581
1984	Xu Haifeng (Chn) 566
1988	Sorin Babii (Rom) 660 (566 + 94)
1992	Konstantin Loukachik (CIS/Blr) 658 (567 + 91)
1996	Boris Kokorev (Rus) 666.4 (570 + 96.4)

Rapid-fire pistol

Since 1948; 30 shots at five targets each at 25 metres. The shooter has 8 seconds at each target in the first round, then 6 seconds and then 4 seconds. The set of 15 shots is then repeated.

1896	Jean Phrangoudis (Gre) 344
1900	Maurice Larrouy (Fra) 58
1906	Maurice Lecoq (Fra) 250
1908	Paul van Asbroeck (Bel) 490
1912	Alfred Lane (USA) 287
1920	Guilherme Paraense (Bra) 274
1924	Henry Bailey (USA) 18
1932	Renzo Morigi (Ita) 36
1936	Cornelius van Oyen (Ger) 36
1948	Károly Takács (Hun) 580
1952	Károly Takács (Hun) 579
1956	Stefan Petrescu (Rom) 587
1960	William McMillan (USA) 587
1964	Pentti Linnosvuo (Fin) 592
1968	Józef Zapedzki (Pol) 593
1972	Józef Zapedzki (Pol) 595
1976	Norbert Klaar (GDR) 597
1980	Corneliu Ion (Rom) 596
1984	Takeo Kamachi (Jap) 595
1988	Afanasi Kuzmin (USSR) 698 (598 + 100)
1992	Ralf Schumann (Ger) 885 (594 + 105 + 96)
1996	Ralf Schumann (Ger) 698.0 (596 + 102.0)

Small-bore rifle – prone

60 shots within 1.5 hours at a target with a bullseye diameter of just 0.487in, from 50 metres.

1908	Arthur Carnell (UK) 387
1912	Frederick Hird (USA) 194
1920	Lawrence Nuesslein (USA) 391
1924	Pierre Coquelin de Lisle (Fra) 398
1932	Bertil Rönnmark (Swe) 294
1936	Willy Rögeberg (Nor) 300
1948	Arthur Cook (USA) 599
1952	Iosif Sarbu (Rom) 400
1956	Gerald Ouellette (Can) 600*
1960	Peter Kohnke (FRG) 590
1964	László Hammerl (Hun) 597
1968	Jan Kurka (Cs) 598
1972	Li Ho-jun (NKo) 599
1976	Karlheinz Smieszek (FRG) 599
1980	Károly Varga (Hun) 599
1984	Edward Etzel (USA) 599
1988	Miroslav Varga (Cs) 703.9 (600 + 103.9)
1992	Lee Eun-chul (SKo) 702.5 (597 + 105.5)
1996	Christian Klees (Ger) 704.8 (600 + 104.8)

* Record not allowed, range marginally short.

Small-bore rifle – three positions

40 shots each from kneeling, standing and prone positions at a target 50 metres away.

1952	Erling Kongshaug (Nor) 1164
1956	Anatoliy Bogdanov (USSR) 1172
1960	Viktor Shamburkin (USSR) 1149
1964	Lones Wigger (USA) 1164
1968	Bernd Klingner (FRG) 1157
1972	John Writer (USA) 1166
1976	Lanny Bassham (USA) 1162
1980	Viktor Vlasov (USSR) 1173
1984	Malcolm Cooper (UK) 1173
1988	Malcolm Cooper (UK) 1279.3 (1180 + 99.3)
1992	Grachya Petikian (CIS/Arm) 1267.4 (1169 + 98.4)
1996	Jean-Pierre Amat (Fra) 1273.9 (1175 + 98.9)

Running target

30 shots, using a .177-calibre air rifle, at a 2in 10-ring target on a simulated boar. The target does two 'runs' across a 10 metres gap, one at 2.5 seconds and one at 5 seconds.

1900	Louis Debray (Fra) 20	
1972	Yakov Zhelezniak (USSR) 569	
1976	Aleksandr Gazov (USSR) 579	
1980	Igor Sokolov (USSR) 589	
1984	Li Yuwei (Chn) 587	
1988	Tor Heiestad (Nor) 689 (591 + 98)	
1992	Michael Jakosits (Ger) 673 (580 + 93)	
1996	Yang Ling (Chn) 685.8 (585 + 100.8)	

Air rifle

60 shots from 10 metres using a .177-calibre air rifle.

1984	Philippe Heberle (Fra) 589
1988	Goran Maksimovic (Yug) 695.6 (594 + 101.6)
1992	Yuriy Fedkin (CIS/Rus) 695.3 (593 + 102.3)
1996	Artem Khadzhibekov (Rus) 695.7 (594 + 101.7)

Air pistol

60 shots from 10 metres in 1:45 hours.

1988	Taniou Kiriakov (Bul) 687.9 (585 + 102.9)
1992	Wang Yifu (Chn) 684.8 (585 + 99.8)
1996	Roberto Di Donna (Ita) 684.2 (585 + 99)

Trap

200 clay birds are released, one at a time, and at varying angles. The shooter has two shots at each clay.

1900	Roger de Barbarin (Fra) 17
1906	Gerald Merlin (UK)* 24
	Sidney Merlin (UK)# 15
1908	Walter Ewing (Can) 72
1912	James Graham (USA) 96
1920	Mark Arie (USA) 95
1924	Gyula Halasy (Hun) 98
1952	George Généreux (Can) 192
1956	Galliano Rossini (Ita) 195
1960	Ion Dumitrescu (Rom) 192
1964	Ennio Mattarelli (Ita) 198
1968	Bob Braithwaite (UK) 198
1972	Angelo Scalzone (Ita) 199
1976	Don Haldeman (USA) 190
1980	Luciano Giovanetti (Ita) 198
1984	Luciano Giovanetti (Ita) 192
1988	Dmitriy Monakov (USSR) 222 (197 + 25)
1992	Petr Hrdlicka (Cs) 219 (195 + 24)
1996	Michael Diamond (Aus) 149 (124 + 25)

* Single shot, # double shot.

Double trap

Similar to trap, but targets are thrown two at a time. Three rounds of 50 targets.

1996	Russell Mark (Aus) 189 (141 + 48)

Skeet

200 clay targets released either one or two at a time, firing from eight different 'stations'; the clays are released from towers, not at ground level, as in trap event.

1968	Yevgeniy Petrov (USSR) 198
1972	Konrad Wirnhier (FRG) 195
1976	Josef Panácek (Cs) 198
1980	Hans Kjeld Rasmussen (Den) 196
1984	Matthew Dryke (USA) 198
1988	Axel Wegner (GDR) 222 (198+24)
1992	Zhang Shan (Chn) 223 (200 + 23) (woman)
1996	Ennio Falco (Ita) 149 (125 +24)

Women

Sport pistol

60 shots at 25 metres.

1984	Linda Thom (Can) 585
1988	Nino Salukvadze (USSR) 690 (591 + 99)
1992	Marina Logvinenko (CIS/Rus) 684 (587 + 97)
1996	Li Duihong (Chn) 687.9 (589 + 98.9)

Air rifle

40 shots at 10 metres.

1984	Pat Spurgin (USA) 393
1988	Irina Chilova (USSR) 498.5 (395 + 103.5)
1992	Yeo Kab-soon (SKo) 498.2 (396 + 102.2)
1996	Renata Mauer (Pol) 497.6 (395 + 102.6)

Air pistol

40 shots at 10 metres.

1988	Jasna Sekaric (Yug) 489.5 (389 + 100.5)
1992	Marina Logvinenko (CIS/Rus) 486.4 (387 + 99.4)
1996	Olga Klochneva (Rus) 490.1 (389 + 101.1)

Small-bore standard rifle

60 shots at 10 metres.

1984	Wu Xiaoxuan (Chn) 581
1988	Silvia Sperber (FRG) 685.6 (590 + 95.6)
1992	Launi Meili (USA) 684.3 (587 + 97.3)
1996	Aleksandra Ivosek (Yug) 686.1 (587 + 99.1)

Double trap

1996	Kim Rhode (USA) 141 (108 + 33)

Discontinued events (men)

Free rifle – three positions

120 shots from 300 metres.

1896	Georgis Orphanidis (Gre) 1583
1906	Gudbrand Skatteboe (Nor) 973
1908	Albert Helgerud (Nor) 909
1912	Paul Colas (Fra) 987
1920	Morris Fisher (USA) 996
1924	Morris Fisher (USA) 95
1948	Emil Grüning (Swi) 1120
1952	Anatoliy Bogdanov (USSR) 1123
1956	Vasiliy Borissov (USSR) 1138

1960	Hubert Hammerer (Aut) 1129
1964	Gary Anderson (USA) 1153
1968	Gary Anderson (USA) 1157
1972	Lones Wigger (USA) 1155

Free rifle

1896	Pantelis Karasevdas (Gre) 2320: over 200m
1906	Marcel de Stadelhofen (Swi) 243: any position (300m)
1906	Gudbrand Skatteboe (Nor): prone (300m)
1906	Konrad Stäheli (Swi): kneeling (300m)
1906	Gudbrand Skatteboe (Nor): standing (300m)
1908	Jerry Millner (UK) 98: over 1000yd

Free rifle – team

1906	Switzerland 4596
1908	Norway 5055
1912	Sweden 5655 (at 400m, 600m, 800m)
1920	USA 4876
1924	USA 676

Military rifle

1900	Emil Kellenberger (Swi) 930: three positions (300m)
1900	Lars Madsen (Den) 305: standing (300m)
1900	Konrad Stäheli (Swi) 324: kneeling (300m)
1900	Achille Paroche (Fra) 332: prone (300m)
1906	Léon Moreaux (Fra) 187: stand or kneel (200m)
1906	Louis Richardet (Swi) 238: stand or kneel (300m)
1912	Sándor Prokopp (Hun) 97: three positions (300m)
1912	Paul Colas (Fra) 94: any position (600m)
1920	Otto Olsen (Nor) 60: prone (300m)
1920	Carl Osburn (USA) 56: standing (300m)
1920	Hugo Johansson (Swe) 59: prone (600m)

Military rifle – team

1900	Switzerland 4399: (300m)
1908	USA 2531: (200, 500, 600, 800, 900, 1000yd)
1912	USA 1687: (200, 400, 500, 600m)
1920	Denmark 266: standing (300m)
1920	USA 289: prone (300m)
1920	USA 287: prone (600m)
1920	USA 573: prone (300m, 600m)

Small-bore rifle

1908	John Fleming (UK) 24: moving target
1908	William Styles (UK) 45: disappearing target
1912	Wilhelm Carlberg (Swe) 242: disappearing

Small-bore rifle – team

1908	United Kingdom 771 (50, 100yd)
1912	Sweden 925 (25m)
1912	United Kingdom 762 (50m)
1920	USA 1899 (50m)

Live pigeon shooting

1900	Léon de Lunden (Bel) 21

Clay pigeons – team

1908	UK 407
1912	USA 532
1920	USA 547
1924	USA 363

Running deer

1908	Oscar Swahn (Swe) 25★
1908	Walter Winans (USA) 46#
1912	Alfred Swahn (Swe) 41★
1912	Åke Lundeberg (Swe) 79#
1920	Otto Olsen (Nor) 43★
1920	Ole Lilloe-Olsen (Nor) 82#
1924	John Boles (USA) 40★
1924	Ole Lilloe-Olsen (Nor) 76#

★ Single shot, # double shot.

Running deer – team

1908	Sweden 86	
1912	Sweden 151	
	Single shot	*Double shot*
1920	Norway 178	Norway 343
1924	Norway 160	United Kingdom 263

Running deer – single and double shot

1952	John Larsen (Nor) 413
1956	Vitaliy Romanenko (USSR) 441

Military revolver

1896	John Paine (USA) 442: (25m)
1906	Louis Richardet (Swi) 253: (20m)
1906	Jean Fouconnier (Fra) 219 (model 1873)

Duelling pistol

1906	Léon Moreaux (Fra) 242: over 20m
1906	Konstantinos Skarlatos (Gre) 133: over 25m

Team event

1900	Switzerland 2271
1908	USA 1914
1912	USA 1916★
1912	Sweden 1145#
1920	USA 2372★
1920	USA 1310#

★ Over 50m, # over 30 metres.

Most Olympic medals

(G - Gold, S - Silver, B – Bronze)

Shooters to have won four or more gold medals:

	Name	G	S	B	Years
11	Carl Osburn (USA)	5	4	2	1912-24
8	Konrad Stäheli (Swi)	5	2	1	1900
8	Otto Olsen (Nor)	4	3	1	1920-4

	Name	G	S	B	Years
7	Gudbrand Skatteboe (Nor)	4	3	-	1906-20
7	Willis Lee (USA)	5	1	1	1920
7	Lloyd Spooner (USA)	4	1	2	1920
7	Einer Liberg (Nor)	4	2	1	1908-24
6	Louis Richardet (Swi)	5	1	-	1900
6	Ole Lilloe-Olsen (Nor)	5	1	-	1920-4
6	Alfred Lane (USA)	5	-	1	1912-20
5	Morris Fisher (USA)	5	-	-	1920-4

Most by a woman:

5	Marina Logvinenko (CIS/Rus)	2	1	2	1992-6

Most individual gold medals: 3 Gudbrand Skatteboe (Nor) 1906
Oldest medallist: Oscar Swahn (Swe) was aged 64yr 258d when he won a gold medal in the team running deer event in 1912 to become the oldest gold medallist in Olympic history. He became the oldest-ever medallist, and indeed competitor, in 1920, when he appeared in Sweden's silver medal-winning team, again in the running deer event. He qualified for the 1924 Games, but illness prevented him competing.
Longest medal span: Ragnar Skanåker (Swe) won the gold medal at free pistol in 1972, took the silver in 1984 and 1988, and the bronze in 1992 for a record 20-year medal span.

World Records

World records, as recognized by the UIT, can only be set in certain major championships, such as the Olympic Games, World and Continental Championships, and the World Cup events.
(Figures in brackets indicate score at end of regular competition + final shoot-out round score.)

Men

Free rifle (three positions, 3 x 40 shots at 50m)	1287.9 (1186 + 101.9)	Rajmond Debevec (Slo)	1992
Free rifle (prone, 60 shots at 50m)	704.8 (600 + 104.8)	Christian Klees (Ger)	1996
Free pistol (60 shots at 50m)	675.3 (580 + 95.3)	Taniu Kiriakov (Bul)	1995
Rapid-fire pistol (60 shots at 25m)	699.7 (596 + 103.7)	Ralf Schumann (FRG)	1994
Running target (60 shots at 10m)	685.6 (585 + 100.6)	Miroslav Janus (Cze)	1995
Air rifle (60 shots at 10m)	699.4 (596+ 103.4)	Rajmond Debevec (Slo)	1990
Air pistol (60 shots at 10m)	695.1 (593 + 102.1)	Sergey Pyzhyanov (USSR)	1989
Skeet (125 targets + 25)	150 (125 + 25)	Marcello Titarelli (Ita)	1996
Trap (125 targets + 25)	150 (125 + 25)	Jan Henrik Heinrich (Ger)	1996
	150 (125 + 25)	Andrea Bellini (Ita)	1996
Double trap (150 targets + 50)	191 (143 + 48)	Joshua Lakatos (USA)	1993

Women

Standard rifle (three positions, 3 x 20 shots at 50m)	689.7 (592 + 97.7)	Vessela Letcheva (Bul)	1995
Sport pistol (60 shots at 25m)	696.2 (594 + 102.2)	Diana Jorgova (Bul)	1994
Air rifle (40 shots at 10m)	501.5 (398 + 103.5)	Vessela Letcheva (Bul)	1996
Air pistol (40 shots at 10m)	492.7 (392 + 100.7)	Jasna Sekaric (Yug)	1996
Double trap (120 targets + 40)	149 (113 + 36)	Deborah Gelisio (Ita)	1995

Skiing

The word *ski* was the Norwegian word for 'snow-shoe'. The earliest ski, recovered from a peat bog in Sweden, has been dated to *c.*2500BC. It is 1.1m long and about 20cm wide. Long skis, over 2m in length, were used in Norway about 4000 years ago, and both long and short skis have been widely used in Scandinavian countries. Two main categories of skiing have evolved – Nordic, which encompasses cross-country skiing and ski-jumping, and Alpine, which covers downhill and slalom events. More recently Freestyle skiing has also become popular.

The first ski races were held in Norway and Australia in the 1850s and 1860s, after Søndre Nordheim had developed techniques and skis in the province of Telemark in Norway. The first national governing body, formed in 1883, was that of Norway; there, public imagination was captured by the epic Greenland trek using skis of the great Norwegian explorer Fridtjof Nansen, in 1888.

The technique of Alpine skiing was pioneered by the Austrian Mathias Zdarsky at the end of the 19th century and British enthusiasts developed winter sports and races, notably in Switzerland in the 1900s.

Sir Henry Lunn was a pioneer in the provision of skiing holidays and his son Sir Arnold Lunn introduced the modern slalom event.

International governing body: Fédération Internationale de Ski (FIS), Blochenstrasse 2, CH-3653 Oberhofen/Thunersee, Switzerland. Tel: (41) 033 244 6161, Fax: (41) 033 243 5353. President: Gian-Franco Kasper. Founded in 1924 to succeed the International Skiing Commission, founded in Oslo in 1910. (*See also* Biathlon for the results of combined skiing and shooting.)

Alpine Skiing

Olympic Games

Alpine skiing events were first included at the Olympic Games in 1936.
Winners:

Men

	Slalom	Giant slalom	Downhill
1948	Edy Reinalter (Swi)	*Not held*	Henri Oreiller (Fra)
1952	Othmar Schneider (Aut)	Stein Eriksen (Nor)	Zeno Colò (Ita)
1956	Toni Sailer (Aut)	Toni Sailer (Aut)	Toni Sailer (Aut)
1960	Ernst Hinterseer (Aut)	Roger Staub (Swi)	Jean Vuarnet (Fra)
1964	Josef Stiegler (Aut)	François Bonlieu (Fra)	Egon Zimmermann (Aut)
1968	Jean-Claude Killy (Fra)	Jean-Claude Killy (Fra)	Jean-Claude Killy (Fra)
1972	Francisco Fernández Ochoa (Spa)	Gustavo Thoeni (Ita)	Bernhard Russi (Swi)
1976	Piero Gros (Ita)	Heini Hemmi (Swi)	Franz Klammer (Aut)
1980	Ingemar Stenmark (Swe)	Ingemar Stenmark (Swe)	Leonhard Stock (Aut)
1984	Phil Mahre (USA)	Max Julen (Swi)	William Johnson (USA)
1988	Alberto Tomba (Ita)	Alberto Tomba (Ita)	Pirmin Zurbriggen (Swi)
1992	Finn-Christian Jagge (Nor)	Alberto Tomba (Ita)	Patrick Ortlieb (Aut)
1994	Thomas Stangassinger (Aut)	Markus Wasmeier (Ger)	Tommy Moe (USA)
1998	Hans-Petter Buraas (Nor)	Hermann Maier (Aut)	Jean-Luc Crétier (Fra)

	Super-giant slalom	Alpine combination
		Downhill and slalom.
1988	Franck Piccard (Fra)	
1992	Kjetil André Aamodt (Nor)	1936 Franz Pfnür (Ger)
1994	Markus Wasmeier (Ger)	1948 Henri Oreiller (Fra)
1998	Hermann Maier (Aut)	1988 Hubert Strolz (Aut)
		1992 Josef Polig (Ita)
		1994 Lasse Kjus (Nor)
		1998 Mario Reiter (Aut)

Women

	Slalom	Giant slalom	Downhill
1948	Gretchen Fraser (USA)	*Not held*	Hedy Schlunegger (Swi)
1952	Andrea Mead-Lawrence (USA)	Andrea Mead-Lawrence (USA)	Trude Jochum (née Beiser) (Aut)
1956	Renée Colliard (Swi)	Ossi Reichert (FRG)	Madeleine Berthod (Swi)
1960	Anne Heggtveit (Can)	Yvonne Rüegg (Swi)	Heidi Biebl (FRG)
1964	Christine Goitschel (Fra)	Marielle Goitschel (Fra)	Christl Haas (Aut)
1968	Marielle Goitschel (Fra)	Nancy Greene (Can)	Olga Pall (Aut)
1972	Barbara Cochran (USA)	Marie-Thérèse Nadig (Swi)	Marie-Thérèse Nadig (Swi)
1976	Rosi Mittermaier (FRG)	Kathy Kreiner (Can)	Rosi Mittermaier (FRG)
1980	Hanni Wenzel (Lie)	Hanni Wenzel (Lie)	Annemarie Moser-Pröll (Aut)
1984	Paoletta Magoni (Ita)	Debbie Armstrong (USA)	Michela Figini (Swi)
1988	Vreni Schneider (Swi)	Vreni Schneider (Swi)	Marina Kiehl (FRG)
1992	Petra Kronberger (Aut)	Pernilla Wiberg (Swe)	Kerrin Lee-Gartner (Can)
1994	Vreni Schneider (Swi)	Deborah Compagnoni (Ita)	Katja Seizinger (Ger)
1998	Hilde Gerg (Ger)	Deborah Compagnoni (Ita)	Katja Seizinger (Ger)

	Super-giant slalom
1988	Sigrid Wolf (Aut)
1992	Deborah Compagnoni (Ita)
1994	Diann Roffe-Steinrotter (USA)
1998	Picabo Street (USA)

Alpine combination

Downhill and slalom.

1936	Christl Cranz (Ger)
1948	Trude Beiser (Aut)
1988	Anita Wachter (Aut)
1992	Petra Kronberger (Aut)
1994	Pernilla Wiberg (Swe)
1998	Katja Seizinger (Ger)

Most Olympic gold medals

Men: 3 Toni Sailer (Aut) 1956, Jean-Claude Killy (Fra) 1968, Alberto Tomba (Aut) 1988-92
Women: 3 Vreni Schneider (Swi) 1988-94

Most Olympic medals

Men: 5 Alberto Tomba (Ita) (3 gold, silver slalom 1992, 1994), Kjetil André Aamodt (Nor) (gold super-G 1992, silver combined, downhill 1994, bronze giant slalom 1992, super-G 1994)
Women: 5 Vreni Schneider (Swi) (3 gold, silver combined 1994, bronze giant slalom 1994), Katja Seizinger (Ger) (3 gold, bronze super-G 1992, giant slalom 1998)

World Championships

First held at downhill in 1931 at Mürren. Held annually 1931-9 and from 1995, biennially 1950-93. Up to 1980 the Olympic champions were also world champions, except in 1936 when separate championships were held. The 1995 championships were cancelled due to lack of snow.

Winners, additional to Olympic champions (in 'Most wins' ★ denotes Olympic win):

Men

Slalom

1931	David Zogg (Swi)
1932	Friedrich Daüber (Ger)
1933	Anton Seelos (Aut)
1934	Franz Pfnür (Ger)
1935	Anton Seelos (Aut)
1936	Rudi Matt (Ger)
1937	Emile Allais (Fra)
1938-9	Rudolf Rominger (Ger)
1950	Georges Schneider (Swi)
1954	Stein Eriksen (Nor)
1958	Josef Rieder (Aut)
1962	Charles Bozon (Fra)
1966	Carlo Senoner (Ita)
1970	Jean-Noël Augert (Fra)
1974	Gustavo Thoeni (Ita)
1978	Ingemar Stenmark (Swe)
1982	Ingemar Stenmark (Swe)
1985	Jonas Nilsson (Swe)
1987	Frank Wörndl (FRG)
1989	Rudolf Nierlich (Aut)
1991	Marc Girardelli (Lux)
1993	Kjetil André Aamodt (Nor)
1996	Alberto Tomba (Ita)
1997	Tom Stiansen (Nor)

Most wins: 3 Stenmark also 1980★

Giant slalom

1950	Zeno Colò (Ita)
1954	Stein Eriksen (Nor)
1958	Toni Sailer (Aut)
1962	Egon Zimmermann (Aut)
1966	Guy Périllat (Fra)
1970	Karl Schranz (Aut)
1974	Gustavo Thoeni (Ita)
1978	Ingemar Stenmark (Swe)
1982	Steve Mahre (USA)
1985	Markus Wasmaier (FRG)
1987	Pirmin Zurbriggen (Swi)
1989	Rudolf Nierlich (Aut)
1991	Rudolf Nierlich (Aut)
1993	Kjetil André Aamodt (Nor)
1996	Alberto Tomba (Ita)
1997	Michael von Grünigen (Swi)

Most wins: 2 Eriksen, Sailer, Thoeni, Stenmark (each also one ★), Nierlich

Super-giant slalom

1987	Pirmin Zurbriggen (Swi)
1989	Martin Hangl (Swi)
1991	Stefan Eberharter (Aut)
1993	*Not held*
1996-7	Atle Skårdal (Nor)

Downhill

1931	Walter Prager (Swi)
1932	Guzzi Lantschner (Aut)
1933	Walter Prager (Swi)
1934	David Zogg (Swi)
1935	Franz Zingerle (Aut)
1936	Rudolf Rominger (Swi)
1937	Emile Allais (Fra)
1938	James Couttet (Fra)
1939	Helmut Lantschner (Ger)
1950	Zeno Colò (Ita)
1954	Christian Pravda (Aut)
1958	Toni Sailer (Aut)
1962	Karl Schranz (Aut)
1966	Jean-Claude Killy (Fra)
1970	Bernhard Russi (Swi)
1974	David Zwilling (Aut)
1978	Josef Walcher (Aut)
1982	Harti Weirather (Aut)
1985	Pirmin Zurbriggen (Swi)
1987	Peter Müller (Swi)
1989	Hansjörg Tauscher (FRG)
1991	Franz Heinzer (Swi)
1993	Urs Lehmann (Swi)
1996	Patrick Ortlieb (Aut)
1997	Bruno Kernen (Swi)

Most wins: 2 Prager (Swi); 1 Colò, Sailer, Killy, Russi each also have one ★

Alpine combination

1932	Otto Furrer (Swi)
1933	Anton Seelos (Aut)
1934	David Zogg (Swi)
1935	Anton Seelos (Aut)
1936	Rudolf Rominger (Swi)
1937–8	Emile Allais (Fra)
1939	Josef Jennewein (Ger)
1954	Stein Eriksen (Nor)
1956	Toni Sailer (Aut)
1958	Toni Sailer (Aut)
1960	Guy Périllat (Fra)
1962	Karl Schranz (Aut)
1964	Ludwig Leitner (FRG)
1966	Jean-Claude Killy (Fra)
1968	Jean-Claude Killy (Fra)
1970	Bill Kidd (USA)
1972	Gustavo Thoeni (Ita)
1974	Franz Klammer (Aut)
1976	Gustavo Thoeni (Ita)
1978	Andreas Wenzel (Lie)
1980	Phil Mahre (USA)
1982	Michel Vion (Fra)
1985	Pirmin Zurbriggen (Swi)
1987	Marc Girardelli (Lux)
1989	Marc Girardelli (Lux)
1991	Stefan Eberharter (Aut)
1993	Lasse Kjus (Nor)
1996	Marc Girardelli (Lux)
1997	Kjetil André Aamodt (Nor)

Most wins: 3 Girardelli

Women

Slalom

1950	Dagmar Rom (Aut)
1954	Trude Klecker (Aut)
1958	Inger Björnbakken (Nor)
1962	Marianne Jahn (Aut)
1966	Annie Famose (Fra)
1970	Ingrid Lafforgue (Fra)
1974	Hanni Wenzel (Lie)
1978	Lea Sölkner (Aut)
1982	Erika Hess (Swi)
1985	Perrine Pelen (Fra)
1987	Erika Hess (Swi)
1989	Mateja Svet (Yug)
1991	Vreni Schneider (Swi)
1993	Karin Buder (Aut)
1996	Pernilla Wiberg (Swe)
1997	Deborah Compagnoni (Ita)

Most wins: 4 Cranz

Giant slalom

1950	Dagmar Rom (Aut)
1954	Lucienne Schmitt (Fra)
1958	Lucille Wheeler (Can)
1962	Marianne Jahn (Aut)

1966	Marielle Goitschel (Fra)
1970	Betsy Clifford (Can)
1974	Fabienne Serrat (Fra)
1978	Maria Epple (FRG)
1982	Erika Hess (Swi)
1985	Diann Roffe (USA)
1987	Vreni Schneider (Swi)
1989	Vreni Schneider (Swi)
1991	Pernilla Wiberg (Swe)
1993	Carole Merle (Fra)
1996–7	Deborah Compagnoni (Ita)

Most wins: 3 Schneider also 1988★, Compagnoni also 1998★

Super-giant slalom

1987	Maria Walliser (FRG)
1989	Ulrike Maier (Aut)
1991	Ulrike Maier (Aut)
1993	Katja Seizinger (Ger)
1996–7	Isolde Kostner (Ita)

Downhill

1950	Trude Beiser-Jochum (Aut)
1954	Ida Schöpfer (Swi)
1958	Lucille Wheeler (Can)
1962	Christl Haas (Aut)
1966	Erika Schinegger# (Aut)
1970	Annerösli Zyrd (Swi)
1974	Annemarie Moser-Pröll (Aut)
1978	Annemarie Moser-Pröll (Aut)
1982	Gerry Sorensen (Can)
1985	Michela Figini (Swi)
1987	Maria Walliser (Swi)
1989	Maria Walliser (Swi)
1991	Petra Kronberger (Aut)
1993	Kate Pace (Can)
1996	Picabo Street (USA)
1997	Hilary Lindh (USA)

Later declared to be a man; gold went to Marielle Goitschel (Fra).

Most wins: 3 Cranz, Moser-Pröll also 1980★

Alpine combination

1954	Ida Schöpfer (Swi)
1956	Madeleine Berthod (Swi)
1958	Frieda Dänzer (Swi)
1960	Anne Heggtveit (Can)
1962	Marielle Goitschel (Fra)
1964	Marielle Goitschel (Fra)
1966	Marielle Goitschel (Fra)
1968	Nancy Greene (Can)
1970	Michèle Jacot (Fra)
1972	Annemarie Pröll (Aut)
1974	Fabienne Serrat (Fra)
1976	Rosi Mittermaier (FRG)
1978	Annemarie Moser-Pröll (Aut)
1980	Hanni Wenzel (Lie)
1982	Erika Hess (Swi)

1985	Erika Hess (Swi)
1987	Erika Hess (Swi)
1989	Tamara McKinney (USA)
1991	Chantal Bournissen (Swi)
1993	Miriam Vogt (Ger)
1996	Pernilla Wiberg (Swe)
1997	Renate Götschl (Aut)

Most wins: 5 Cranz; 3 M Goitschel, Hess

Most wins at all events

Men: 7 Toni Sailer (Aut); 6 Jean-Claude Killy (Fra)
Women: 12 Christl Cranz (Ger), and the 1936 Olympic combined; 7 Marielle Goitschel; 6 Erika Hess
All four titles have been won in one year by Sailer 1956 and Killy 1968.

World Cup

Contested annually from 1967 over a series of events during the winter season. The year given is that of the second half of the season.
Winners:

Men

Overall

1967-8	Jean-Claude Killy (Fra)
1969-70	Karl Schranz (Aut)
1971-3	Gustavo Thoeni (Ita)
1974	Piero Gros (Ita)
1975	Gustavo Thoeni (Ita)
1976-8	Ingemar Stenmark (Swe)
1979	Peter Lüscher (Swi)
1980	Andreas Wenzel (Lie)
1981-3	Phil Mahre (USA)
1984	Pirmin Zurbriggen (Swi)
1985-6	Marc Girardelli (Lux)
1987-8	Pirmin Zurbriggen (Swi)
1989	Marc Girardelli (Lux)
1990	Pirmin Zurbriggen (Swi)
1991	Marc Girardelli (Lux)
1992	Paul Accola (Swi)
1993	Marc Girardelli (Lux)
1994	Kjetil André Aamodt (Nor)
1995	Alberto Tomba (Ita)
1996	Lasse Kjus (Nor)
1997	Luc Alphand (Fra)
1998	Hermann Maier (Aut)

Most wins: 5 Girardelli; 4 Thoeni, Zurbriggen; 3 Stenmark, Mahre

Slalom

1967	Jean-Claude Killy (Fra)
1968	Domeng Giovanoli (Swi)
1969	Jean-Noël Augert (Fra), Alfred Matt (Aut), Alain Penz (Fra), Patrick Russel (Fra)
1970	Patrick Russel & Alain Penz (Fra)
1971-2	Jean-Noël Augert (Fra)
1973-4	Gustavo Thoeni (Ita)

1975-81	Ingemar Stenmark (Swe)
1982	Phil Mahre (USA)
1983	Ingemar Stenmark (Swe)
1984-5	Marc Girardelli (Lux)
1986	Rok Petrovic (Yug)
1987	Bojan Krizaj (Yug)
1988	Alberto Tomba (Ita)
1989-90	Armin Bittner (FRG)
1991	Marc Girardelli (Lux)
1992	Alberto Tomba (Ita)
1993	Tomas Fogdö (Swe)
1994-5	Alberto Tomba (Ita)
1996	Sébastien Amiez (Fra)
1997-8	Thomas Sykora (Aut)

Most wins: 8 Stenmark

Giant slalom

1967-8	Jean-Claude Killy (Fra)
1969	Karl Schranz (Aut)
1970	Gustavo Thoeni (Ita)
1971	Gustavo Thoeni (Ita) & Patrick Russel (Fra)
1972	Gustavo Thoeni (Ita)
1973	Hans Hinterseer (Aut)
1974	Piero Gros (Aut)
1975-6	Ingemar Stenmark (Swe)
1977	Heini Hemmi (Swi)
1978-81	Ingemar Stenmark (Swe)
1982-3	Phil Mahre (USA)
1984	Ingemar Stenmark (Swe) & Pirmin Zurbriggen (Swi)
1985	Marc Girardelli (Lux)
1986	Joel Gaspoz (Swi)
1987	Joel Gaspoz (Swi) & Pirmin Zurbriggen (Swi)
1988	Alberto Tomba (Ita)
1989	Ole Christian Furuseth (Nor) & Pirmin Zurbriggen (Swi)
1990	Ole Christian Furuseth (Nor)
1991-2	Alberto Tomba (Ita)
1993	Kjetil André Aamodt (Nor)
1994	Christian Mayer (Aut)
1995	Alberto Tomba (Ita)
1996-7	Michael von Grünigen (Swi)
1998	Hermann Maier (Aut)

Most wins: 7 Stenmark; 4 Tomba

Super-giant slalom

1986	Markus Wasmeier (FRG)
1987-90	Pirmin Zurbriggen (Swi)
1991	Franz Heinzer (Swi)
1992	Paul Accola (Swi)
1993	Kjetil André Aamodt (Nor)
1994	Jan Einar Thorsen (Nor)
1995	Peter Runggaldier (Ita)
1996	Atle Skårdal (Nor)
1997	Luc Alphand (Fra)
1998	Hermann Maier (Aut)

Most wins: 4 Zurbriggen

Downhill

1967	Jean-Claude Killy (Fra)
1968	Gerhard Nenning (Aut)
1969	Karl Schranz (Aut)
1970	Karl Schranz (Aut) & Karl Cordin (Aut)
1971-2	Bernhard Russi (Swi)
1973-4	Roland Collombin (Swi)
1975-8	Franz Klammer (Aut)
1979-80	Peter Müller (Swi)
1981	Harti Weirather (Aut)
1982	Steve Podborski (Can) & Peter Müller (Swi)
1983	Franz Klammer (Aut)
1984	Urs Räber (Swi)
1985	Helmut Höhflehner (Aut)
1986	Peter Wirnsberger (Aut)
1987-8	Pirmin Zurbriggen (Swi)
1989	Marc Girardelli (Lux)
1990	Helmut Höhflehner (Aut)
1991-3	Franz Heinzer (Swi)
1994	Marc Girardelli (Lux)
1995-7	Luc Alphand (Fra)
1998	Andreas Schiffer (Aut)

Most wins: 5 Klammer

Women

Overall

1967-8	Nancy Greene (Can)
1969	Gertrud Gabl (Aut)
1970	Michèle Jacot (Fra)
1971-5	Annemarie Moser-Pröll (Aut)
1976	Rosi Mittermaier (FRG)
1977	Lise-Marie Morerod (Swi)
1978	Hanni Wenzel (Lie)
1979	Annemarie Moser-Pröll (Aut)
1980	Hanni Wenzel (Lie)
1981	Marie-Thérèse Nadig (Swi)
1982	Erika Hess (Swi)
1983	Tamara McKinney (USA)
1984	Erika Hess (Swi)
1985	Michela Figini (Swi)
1986-7	Maria Walliser (Swi)
1988	Michela Figini (Swi)
1989	Vreni Schneider (Swi)
1990-2	Petra Kronberger (Aut)
1993	Anita Wachter (Aut)
1994-5	Vreni Schneider (Swi)
1996	Katja Seizinger (Ger)
1997	Pernilla Wiberg (Swe)
1998	Katja Seizinger (Ger)

Most wins: 6 Moser-Pröll

Slalom

1967	Marielle Goitschel (Fra) & Annie Famose (Fra)
1968	Marielle Goitschel (Fra)
1969	Gertrud Gabl (Aut)
1970	Ingrid Lafforgue (Fra)
1971	Britt Laforgue (Fra) & Betsy Clifford (Can)
1972	Britt Laforgue (Fra)
1973	Patricia Emonet (Fra)
1974	Christa Zechmeister (FRG)
1975	Lise-Marie Morerod (Swi)
1976	Rosi Mittermaier (FRG)
1977	Lise-Marie Morerod (Swi)
1978	Hanni Wenzel (Lie)
1979	Regina Sackl (Aut)
1980	Perrine Pelen (Fra)
1981-3	Erika Hess (Swi)
1984	Tamara McKinney (USA)
1985	Erika Hess (Swi)
1986	Erika Hess (Swi) & Roswitha Steiner (Aut)
1987	Corinne Schmidhauser (Swi)
1988	Roswitha Steiner (Aut)
1989-90	Vreni Schneider (Swi)
1991	Petra Kronberger (Aut)
1992-5	Vreni Schneider (Swi)
1996	Elfi Eder (Aut)
1997	Pernilla Wiberg (Swe)
1998	Ylva Nowen (Swe)

Most wins: 6 Schneider; 5 Hess

Giant slalom

1967-8	Nancy Greene (Can)
1969	Marilyn Cochran (USA)
1970	Michèle Jacot & Françoise Macchi (Fra)
1971-2	Annemarie Moser-Pröll (Aut)
1973	Monika Kaserer (Aut)
1974	Hanni Wenzel (Lie)
1975	Annemarie Moser-Pröll (Aut)
1976-8	Lise-Marie Morerod (Swi)
1979	Christa Kinshoffer (FRG)
1980	Hanni Wenzel (Lie)
1981	Tamara McKinney (USA)
1982	Irene Epple (FRG)
1983	Tamara McKinney (USA)
1984	Erika Hess (Swi)
1985	Marina Kiehl (FRG)
1986	Vreni Schneider (Swi)
1987	Vreni Schneider (Swi)
1988	Mateja Svet (Yug)
1989	Vreni Schneider (Swi)
1990	Anita Wachter (Aut)
1991	Vreni Schneider (Swi)
1992-3	Carole Merle (Fra)
1994	Anita Wachter (Aut)
1995	Vreni Schneider (Swi)
1996	Martina Ertl (Ger)
1997	Deborah Compagnoni (Ita)
1998	Martina Ertl (Ger)

Most wins: 5 Schneider

Super-giant slalom

1986	Marina Kiehl (FRG)
1987	Maria Walliser (Swi)
1988	Michela Figini (Swi)
1989-92	Carole Merle (Fra)

1993-6	Katja Seizinger (Ger)
1997	Hilde Gerg (Ger)
1998	Katja Seizinger (Ger)

Most wins: 5 Seizinger; 4 Merle

Downhill

1967	Marielle Goitschel (Fra)
1968	Isabelle Mir (Fra) & Olga Pall (Aut)
1969	Wiltrud Drexel (Aut)
1970	Isabelle Mir (Fra)
1971-5	Annemarie Moser-Pröll (Aut)
1976-7	Brigitte Habersatter-Totschnig (Aut)
1978-9	Annemarie Moser-Pröll (Aut)
1980-1	Marie-Thérèse Nadig (Swi)
1982	Cécile Gros-Gaudenier (Fra)
1983	Doris De Agostini (Swi)
1984	Maria Walliser (Swi)
1985	Michela Figini (Swi)
1986	Maria Walliser (Swi)
1987-9	Michela Figini (Swi)
1990	Katrin Gutensohn-Knopl (FRG)
1991	Chantal Bournissen (Swi)
1992-4	Katja Seizinger (Ger)
1995-6	Picabo Street (USA)
1997	Renate Götschl (Aut)
1998	Katja Seizinger (Ger)

Most wins: 7 Moser-Pröll (Aut); 4 Figini, Seizinger

Most individual event wins

Men

86	Ingemar Stenmark (Swe) 1974-89 (46 giant slalom, 40 slalom)
50	Alberto Tomba (Ita) 1984-98 (35 slalom, 15 giant slalom)
46	Marc Girardelli (Lux) 1983-96 (16 slalom, 11 combined, 9 giant slalom, 7 super-G, 3 downhill)
40	Pirmin Zurbriggen (Swi) 1982-90 (11 downhill, 11 giant slalom, 10 combined, 6 super-G, 2 slalom)
27	Phil Mahre (USA) 1977-84
26	Franz Klammer (Aut) 1974-84 (including a record 24 downhill races)

Ingemar Stenmark won a men's record 13 World Cup races in a season, 1978/9, including a record at one discipline – 10 giant slalom.

Women

62	Annemarie Moser (Aut), 1970-9 (36 downhill, 16 giant slalom, 7 combined, 3 slalom)
54	Vreni Schneider (Sui) 1985-95 (34 slalom, 19 giant slalom, 1 combined)
36	Katja Seizinger (Ger) 1992-8
33	Hanni Wenzel (Lie) 1974-84
31	Erika Hess (Sui) 1981-6
26	Michela Figini (Sui) 1984-90

Vreni Schneider won a record 14 World Cup races in a season, including all seven slalom, 1988/9.

Next bests: 12 Jean-Claude Killy (Fra) 1966/7; 11 Marc Girardelli (Lux) 1984/5, Stenmark 1979/80, Pirmin Zurbriggen 1986/7, Alberto Tomba 1994/5

Nations' Cup

Awarded on the overall results for men and women obtained in the World Cup.
Wins:

19	Austria	1969, 1973-80, 1982, 1990-8
8	Switzerland	1981, 1983-9
5	France	1967-8, 1970-2

Nordic Skiing

Until 1985 'classical' was the only **cross-country** skiing technique, but now the faster 'skating' technique, known as 'freestyle', is also recognized, and there are events for both disciplines. At the 1992 Winter Olympics the pursuit was introduced; this consists of a classical race on the first day, over 10km for men and 5km for women, with a freestyle race on the second day, over 15km and 10km respectively, with the competitors starting according to their time difference from the first day.

Ski jumpers are judged for distance and execution. They jump from hills rated according to the expected distance from take-off to landing (e.g. 70m, 80m, 120m).

The **Nordic combined** event involves a cross-country race over 15km and jumping from a 70m hill.

Olympic Games

The first Winter Olympic Games, held at Chamonix in 1924, included Nordic skiing events, and they have been included on the programme ever since.
Winners:

Men

10 kilometres cross-country (classical)

1992	Vegard Ulvang (Nor) 27:36.0
1994	Bjørn Dæhlie (Nor) 24:20.1
1998	Bjørn Dæhlie (Nor) 27:24.5

15 kilometres cross-country (classical)

Held at 18km 1924, 1936-52, 19.7km 1928, 18.214km 1932.

1924	Thorleif Haug (Nor) 1:14:31
1928	Johan Grøttumsbraaten (Nor) 1:37:01
1932	Sven Utterström (Swe) 1:23:07
1936	Erik-August Larsson (Swe) 1:14:38
1948	Martin Lundström (Swe) 1:13:50
1952	Hallgeir Brenden (Nor) 1:01:34
1956	Hallgeir Brenden (Nor) 49:39.0
1960	Haakon Brusveen (Nor) 51:55.5
1964	Eero Mäntyranta (Fin) 50:54.1
1968	Harald Grönningen (Nor) 47:54.2
1972	Sven-Åke Lundback (Swe) 45:28.24
1976	Nikolay Bayukov (USSR) 43:58.47

1980   Thomas Wassberg (Swe) 41:57.63
1984   Gunde Svan (Swe) 41:25.6
1988   Mikhail Devyatyarov (USSR) 41:18.9

10 kilometres classical + 15 kilometres freestyle cross-country pursuit

1992   Bjørn Dæhlie (Nor) 1:05:37.9
1994   Bjørn Dæhlie (Nor) 1:00:08.8
1998   Thomas Alsgaard (Nor) 1:07:01.7

30 kilometres cross-country (classical)

1956   Veikko Hakulinen (Fin) 1:44:06.0
1960   Sixten Jernberg (Swe) 1:51:03.9
1964   Eero Mäntyranta (Fin) 1:30:50.7
1968   Franco Nones (Ita) 1:35:39.2
1972   Vyacheslav Vedenin (USSR) 1:36:31.2
1976   Sergey Savelyev (USSR) 1:30:29.38
1980   Nikolay Zimyatov (USSR) 1:27:02.80
1984   Nikolay Zimyatov (USSR) 1:28:56.3
1988   Aleksey Prokurakov (USSR) 1:24:26.3
1992   Vegard Ulvang (Nor) 1:22:27.8
1994   Thomas Alsgaard (Nor) 1:12:26.4 (*freestyle*)
1998   Mika Myllylä (Fin) 1:33:55.8

50 kilometres cross-country (freestyle)

1924   Thorleif Haug (Nor) 3:44:32
1928   Per-Erik Hedlund (Swe) 4:52:03
1932   Veli Saarinen (Fin) 4:28:00
1936   Elis Wiklund (Swe) 3:30:11
1948   Nils Karlsson (Swe) 3:47:48
1952   Veikko Hakulinen (Fin) 3:33:33
1956   Sixten Jernberg (Swe) 2:50:27
1960   Kalevi Hämäläinen (Fin) 2:59:06.3
1964   Sixten Jernberg (Swe) 2:43:52.6
1968   Ole Ellefsaeter (Nor) 2:28:45.8
1972   Pål Tyldum (Nor) 2:43:14.75
1976   Ivar Formo (Nor) 2:37:30.50
1980   Nikolay Zimyatov (USSR) 2:27:24.60
1984   Thomas Wassberg (Swe) 2:15:55.8
1988   Gunde Svan (Swe) 2:04:30.9
1992   Bjørn Dæhlie (Nor) 2:03:41.5
1994   Vladimir Smirnov (Kaz) 2:07:20.3 (*classical*)
1998   Bjørn Dæhlie (Nor) 2:05:08.2

4 x 10 kilometres cross-country relay

1936   Finland 2:41:33
1948   Sweden 2:32:08
1952   Finland 2:20:16
1956   USSR 2:15:30
1960   Finland 2:18:45.6
1964   Sweden 2:18:34.6
1968   Norway 2:08:33.5
1972   USSR 2:04:47.94
1976   Finland 2:07:59.72
1980   USSR 1:57:03.46
1984   Sweden 1:55:06.30
1988   Sweden 1:43:58.6
1992   Norway 1:39:26.0
1994   Italy 1:41:15.0
1998   Norway 1:40:55.7

Ski jumping – normal hill

90 metre hill 1992-8.

1924   Jacob Tullin Thams (Nor)
1928   Alf Andersen (Nor)
1932   Birger Ruud (Nor)
1936   Birger Ruud (Nor)
1948   Petter Hugstedt (Nor)
1952   Arnfinn Bergmann (Nor)
1956   Anti Hyvärinen (Fin)
1960   Helmut Recknagel (GDR)
1964   Viekko Kankkänen (Fin)
1968   Jiri Raska (Cs)
1972   Yukio Kasaya (Jap)
1976   Hans-Georg Aschenbach (GDR)
1980   Toni Innauer (Aut)
1984   Jens Weissflog (GDR)
1988   Matti Nykänen (Fin)
1992   Ernst Vettori (Aut)
1994   Espen Bredesen (Nor)
1998   Jani Soininen (Fin)

Ski jumping – large hill

120 metre hill 1992-4.

1964   Toralf Engan (Nor)
1968   Vladimir Byeloussov (USSR)
1972   Wojciech Fortuna (Pol)
1976   Karl Schnabl (Aut)
1980   Jouko Törmänen (Fin)
1984   Matti Nykänen (Fin)
1988   Matti Nykänen (Fin)
1992   Toni Nieminen (Fin)
1994   Jens Weissflog (Ger)
1998   Kazuyoshi Funaki (Jap)

Team ski jumping

1988   Finland
1992   Finland
1994   Germany
1998   Japan

Nordic combined – skiing and jumping

1924   Thorleif Haug (Nor)
1928   Johan Grøttumsbraaten (Nor)
1932   Johan Grøttumsbraaten (Nor)
1936   Oddbjørn Hagen (Nor)
1948   Heikki Hasu (Fin)
1952   Simon Slatvik (Nor)
1956   Sverre Stenersen (Nor)
1960   Georg Thoma (FRG)
1964   Tormod Knutsen (Nor)
1968   Franz Keller (FRG)
1972   Ulrich Wehling (GDR)
1976   Ulrich Wehling (GDR)
1980   Ulrich Wehling (GDR)
1984   Tom Sandberg (Nor)
1988   Hippolyt Kempf (Swi)
1992   Fabrice Guy (Fra)
1994   Fred Borre Lundberg (Nor)
1998   Bjarte-Engen Vik (Nor)

Team Nordic combined

1988	F R Germany
1992	Japan
1994	Japan
1998	Norway

Women

5 kilometres cross-country (classical)

1964	Klaudia Boyarskikh (USSR) 17:50.5
1968	Toini Gustafsson (Swe) 16:45.2
1972	Galina Kulakova (USSR) 17:00.50
1976	Helena Takalo (Fin) 15:48.69
1980	Raisa Smetanina (USSR) 15:06.92
1984	Marja-Liisa Hämäläinen (Fin) 17:04.0
1988	Marjo Matikainen (Fin) 15:04.0
1992	Marjat Lukkarinen (Fin) 14:13.8
1994	Lyubov Yegorova (Rus) 14:08.8
1998	Larisa Lazutina (Rus) 17:37.9

10 kilometres cross-country (classical)

1952	Lydia Wideman (Fin) 41:40.0
1956	Lyubov Kozyryeva (USSR) 38:11.0
1960	Maria Gusakova (USSR) 39:46.6
1964	Klaudia Boyarskikh (USSR) 40:24.3
1968	Toini Gustafsson (Swe) 36:46.5
1972	Galina Kulakova (USSR) 34:17.8
1976	Raisa Smetanina (USSR) 30:13.41
1980	Barbara Petzold (GDR) 30:31.54
1984	Marja-Liisa Hämäläinen (Fin) 31:44.2
1988	Vida Ventsene (USSR) 30:08.3

5 kilometres classical + 10 kilometres freestyle cross-country pursuit

1992	Lyubov Yegorova (CIS/Rus) 40:07.7
1994	Lyubov Yegorova (Rus) 41:38.9
1998	Larisa Lazutina (Rus) 46:06.9

15 kilometres cross-country (classical)

1992	Lyubov Yegorova (CIS/Rus) 42:20.8
1994	Manuela Di Centa (Ita) 39:44.5 (freestyle)
1998	Olga Danilova (Rus) 46:55.4

20 kilometres cross-country (freestyle)

1984	Marja-Liisa Hämäläinen (Fin) 1:01:45.0
1988	Tamara Tikhonova (USSR) 55:53.6

30 kilometres cross-country (freestyle)

1992	Stefania Belmondo (Ita) 1:22:30.1
1994	Manuela Di Centa (Ita) 1:25:41.6 (classical)
1998	Yuliya Shchepalova (Rus) 1:22:01.5

4 x 5 kilometres cross-country relay

1956	Finland 1:09:01.0
1960	Sweden 1:04:21.4
1964	USSR 59:20.2
1968	Norway 57:30.0
1972	USSR 48:46.15
1976	USSR 1:07:49.75
1980	GDR 1:02:11.10
1984	Norway 1:06:49.70

1988	USSR 59:51.1
1992	CIS 59:34.8
1994	Russia 57:12.5
1998	Russia 55:13.5

World Championships

After Nordic events had been included in the 1924 Olympics, the FIS organized annual competitions until 1937, when for the first time they were given official world championship status. They were held annually until 1939, but biennially post-war. Up to 1980 the Olympic Champions were also world champions.

Winners, additional to Olympic champions (in 'Most wins' ★ denotes Olympic win):

Men

10 kilometres cross-country (classical)

1991	Terje Langli (Nor)
1993	Sture Sivertsen (Nor)
1995	Vladimir Smirnov (Kaz)
1997	Björn Dæhlie (Nor)

18 kilometres cross-country

1925	Otokar Nemecky (Cs)
1927	John Lindgren (Swe)
1929	Veli Saarinen (Fin)
1930	Arne Rudstadstuen (Nor)
1931	Johan Gröttumsbraaten (Nor)
1933	Nils-Joel Englund (Swe)
1934	Sulo Nurmela (Fin)
1935	Klaes Karppinen (Fin)
1937	Lauritz Bergendahl (Nor)
1938	Pauli Pitkänen (Fin)
1939	Juho Kurikkala (Fin)
1950	Karl Erik Åström (Swe)

15 kilometres cross-country

1954	Veikko Hakulinen (Fin)
1958	Veikko Hakulinen (Fin)
1962	Assar Rönnlund (Swe)
1966	Gjermund Eggen (Nor)
1970	Lars-Göran Åslund (Swe)
1974	Magne Myrmo (Nor)
1978	Josef Luszczek (Pol)
1982	Oddvar Brå (Nor)
1985	Kari Härkänen (Fin)
1987	Marco Albarello (Ita)
1989	Gunde Svan (Swe); classical: Harri Kirvesniemi (Fin)
1991	Björn Dæhlie (Nor)

Most wins: 2 Johan Gröttumsbraaten (Nor) 1928,★ 1931, Hallgeir Brendan 1952,★ 1956,★ Hakulinen, Svan 1984★

Pursuit – 10 kilometres classical + 15 kilometres freestyle

1993	Björn Dæhlie (Nor)
1995	Vladimir Smirnov (Kaz)
1997	Björn Dæhlie (Nor)

30 kilometres cross-country
Classical; freestyle 1997.

1926	Matti Raivo (Fin)
1954	Vladimir Kusin (USSR)
1958	Kalevi Hämäläinen (Fin)
1962	Eero Mäntyranta (Fin)
1966	Eero Mäntyranta (Fin)
1970	Vyacheslav Vedenin (USSR)
1974	Thomas Magnusson (Swe)
1978	Sergey Savelyev (USSR)
1982	Thomas Eriksson (Swe)
1985	Gunde Svan (Swe)
1987	Thomas Wassberg (Swe)
1989	Vladimir Smirnov (USSR)
1991	Gunde Svan (Swe)
1993	Björn Dæhlie (Nor)
1995	Vladimir Smirnov (Kaz)
1997	Aleksey Prokurorov (Rus)

Most wins: 3 Mäntyranta also 1964*

50 kilometres cross-country

1925	Frantisek Donth (Cs)
1926	Matti Raivo (Fin)
1927	John Lindgren (Swe)
1929	Anselm Knuttila (Fin)
1930	Sven Utterström (Swe)
1931	Ole Stenen (Nor)
1933	Veli Saarinen (Fin)
1934	Elis Wiklund (Swe)
1935	Nils-Joel Englund (Swe)
1937	Pekka Niemi (Fin)
1938	Kalle Jalkanen (Fin)
1939	Lauritz Bergendahl (Nor)
1950	Gunnar Eriksson (Swe)
1954	Vladimir Kusin (USSR)
1958	Sixten Jernberg (Swe)
1962	Sixten Jernberg (Swe)
1966	Gjermund Eggen (Nor)
1970	Kalevi Oikarainen (Fin)
1974	Gerhard Grimmer (GDR)
1978	Sven-Åke Lundbäck (Swe)
1982	Thomas Wassberg (Swe)
1985	Gunde Svan (Swe)
1987	Maurilio De Zolt (Ita)
1989	Gunde Svan (Swe)
1991	Torgny Mogren (Swe)
1993	Torgny Mogren (Swe)
1995	Silvio Fauner (Ita)
1997	Mika Myllylä (Fin)

Most wins: 4 Jernberg also 1956,* 1964*

4 x 10 kilometres cross-country relay
Wins including Olympics (*):

10	Sweden	1933, 1950, 1958, 1962, 1978, 1987, 1989 and 3*
9	Finland	1934-5, 1938-9, 1954 and 4*
9	Norway	1937, 1966, 1982 tie, 1985, 1991, 1993, 1995, 1997 and 1*

5	USSR	1970, 1982 tie and 3*
1	GDR	1974

Ski jumping – normal hill (70 metres, now 90 metres)

1925	Willi Dick (Cs)
1926	Jacob Thullin Thams (Nor)
1927	Tore Edman (Swe)
1929	Sigmund Ruud (Nor)
1930	Reidar Andersen (Nor)
1931	Birger Ruud (Nor)
1933	Marcel Reymond (Swi)
1934	Kristian Johanson (Nor)
1935	Birger Ruud (Nor)
1937	Birger Ruud (Nor)
1938	Asbjörn Ruud (Nor)
1939	Joseph Bradl (Ger)
1950	Hans Bjornstad (Nor)
1954	Matti Pietikäinen (Fin)
1958	Juhanni Kärkänen (Fin)
1962	Toralf Engan (Nor)
1966	Björn Wirkola (Nor)
1970	Gariy Napalkov (USSR)
1974	Hans-Georg Aschenbach (GDR)
1978	Mathias Buse (GDR)
1982	Armin Kogler (Aut)
1985	Jens Weissflog (GDR)
1987	Jiri Parma (Cs)
1989	Jens Weissflog (GDR)
1991	Heinz Kuttin (Aut)
1993	Masahiko Harada (Jap)
1995	Takanobu Okabe (Jap)
1997	Janne Ahonen (Fin)

Most wins: 5 Birger Ruud also 2*

Ski jumping – large hill (90 metres, then 115 metres, now 120 metres)

1962	Helmut Recknagel (GDR)
1966	Björn Wirkola (Nor)
1970	Gariy Napalkov (USSR)
1974	Hans-Georg Aschenbach (GDR)
1978	Tapio Räisänen (Fin)
1982	Matti Nykänen (Fin)
1985	Per Bergerud (Nor)
1987	Andreas Felder (Aut)
1989	Jari Puikkonen (Fin)
1991	Franci Petek (Yug)
1993	Espen Bredesen (Nor)
1995	Tommy Ingebrigtsen(Nor)
1997	Masahiko Harada (Jap)

Most wins: 3 Nykänen 1982, 1984,* 1988*

Team ski jumping

Norway	1982, 1993
Finland	1984-5, 1987, 1989, 1995, 1997
Austria	1991

Nordic combined

1925	Otokar Nemecky (Cs)
1926	Johan Gröttumsbraaten (Nor)
1927	Rudolf Purkert (Cs)
1929-30	Hans Vinjarengen (Nor)
1931	Johan Gröttumsbraaten (Nor)
1933	Sven Eriksson (Swe)
1934-5	Oddbjörn Hagen (Nor)
1937	Sigurd Röen (Nor)
1938	Olaf Hoffsbakken (Nor)
1939	Gustaf Berauer (Ger)
1950	Heikki Hasu (Fin)
1954	Sverre Stenersen (Nor)
1958	Paavo Korhonen (Fin)
1962	Arne Larsen (Nor)
1966	Georg Thoma (FRG)
1970	Ladislav Rygel (Cs)
1974	Ulrich Wehling (GDR)
1978	Konrad Winkler (GDR)
1982	Tom Sandberg (Nor)
1985	Hermann Weinbuch (FRG)
1987	Torbjørn Løkken (Nor)
1989	Einar Elden (Nor)
1991	Fred-Børre Lundberg (Nor)
1993	Kenji Ogiwara (Jap)
1995	Fred Børre Lundberg (Nor)
1997	Kenji Ogiwara (Jap)

Most wins: 4 Johan Grøttumsbraaten (Nor) 1926, 1928,★ 1931, 1932,★ Wehling with 3;★ 3 Oddbjørn Hagen (Nor) 1934-5, 1936★

Team Nordic combined

1982	GDR
1984	Norway
1985	F R Germany
1987	F R Germany
1989	Norway
1991	Austria
1993	Japan
1995	Japan
1997	Norway

Women

5 kilometres cross-country

Now classical.

1962	Alevtina Kolchina (USSR)
1966	Alevtina Kolchina (USSR)
1970	Galina Kulakova (USSR)
1974	Galina Kulakova (USSR)
1978	Helena Takalo (Fin)
1982	Berit Aunli (Nor)
1985	Anette Bøe (Nor)
1987	Marjo Matikainen (Fin)
1991	Trude Dybendahl (Nor)
1993	Larisa Lazutina (Rus)
1995	Larisa Lazutina (Rus)
1997	Yelena Välbe (Rus)

Most wins: 3 Kulakova also 1972★

10 kilometres cross-country

1954	Lyubov Kozyryeva (USSR)
1958	Alevtina Kolchina (USSR)
1962	Alevtina Kolchina (USSR)
1966	Klaudia Boyarskikh (USSR)
1970	Alevtina Olyunina (USSR)
1974	Galina Kulakova (USSR)
1978	Zinaida Amosova (USSR)
1982	Berit Aunli (Nor)
1985	Anette Bøe (Nor)
1987	Anne Jahren (Nor)
1989	Yelena Välbe (USSR); *classical*: Marja-Liisa Kirvesniemi (Fin)
1991	Yelena Välbe (USSR)

Most wins: 2 Kozyryeva also 1956,★ Välbe, Koltschina, Kulakova also 1972★

15 kilometres cross-country (classical)

Freestyle 1997.

1989	Marjo Matikainen (Fin)
1991	Yelena Välbe (USSR)
1993	Yelena Välbe (Rus)
1995	Larisa Lazutina (Rus
1997	Yelena Välbe (Rus)

Pursuit – 5 kilometres classical + 10 kilometres freestyle

1993	Stefania Belmondo (Ita)
1995	Larisa Lazutina (Rus
1997	Yelena Välbe (Rus)

20 kilometres cross-country

1978	Zinaida Amosova (USSR)
1980	Veronika Hesse (GDR)
1982	Raisa Smetanina (USSR)
1985	Grete Nykkelmo (Nor)
1987	Maria-Elena Westin (Swe)

30 kilometres cross-country (freestyle)

Classical 1997.

1989	Yelena Välbe (USSR)
1991	Lyubov Yegorova (USSR)
1993	Stefania Belmondo (Ita)
1995	Yelena Välbe (Rus)
1997	Yelena Välbe (Rus)

Most wins: 3 Välbe

Cross-country relay (3 x 5km 1954-72, 4 x 5km from 1974)

Wins including Olympics (★):

12	USSR	1954, 1958, 1962, 1966, 1970, 1974, 1985, 1987 and 4★
3	Finland	1978, 1989 and 1★
3	Russia	1993, 1995, 1997
1	Sweden, Norway, GDR all ★	

Most wins at all events (individual/relay and including Olympic Games)

Men

17	(11/6)	Bjørn Dæhlie (Nor) 1991-8
11	(7/4)	Gunde Svan (Swe) 1984-91
8	(5/3)	Sixten Jernberg (Swe) 1956-64
7	(4/3)	Thomas Wassberg (Swe) 1980-8
6	(6/-)	Johan Grøttumsbraaten (Nor) 1926-32
6	(4/2)	Veikko Hakulinen (Fin) 1952-60
6	(1/5)	Klaes Karppinen (Fin) 1934-9

Women

16	(10/7)	Yelena Välbe (USSR/Rus) 1989-98
11	(6/5)	Larisa Lazutina (USSR/Rus) 1992-8
9	(5/4)	Galina Kulakova (USSR) 1970-80
8	(4/4)	Alevtina Kolchina (USSR) 1958-66
7	(3/4)	Raisa Smetanina (USSR) 1974-91

Most medals: 24 Välbe, 21 Smetanina, 18 Kulakova

Most at one Championships: 5 Marjo Matikainen 1988, Välbe 1997, Lazutina 1998*

World Ski Flying Championships

Held separately from the Nordic World Championships in 1972 and biennially from 1973.
Winners:

1972	Walter Steiner (Swi)
1973	Hans-Georg Aschenbach (GDR)
1975	Karel Kodejska (Cs)
1977	Walter Steiner (Swi)
1979	Armin Kogler (Aut)
1981	Jarri Puikkonen (Fin)
1983	Klaus Ostwald (GDR)
1985	Matti Nykänen (Fin)
1986	Andreas Felder (Aut)
1988	Gunnar Fidjestøl (Nor)
1990	Dieter Thoma (FRG)
1992	Noriaki Kasai (Jap)
1994	Jaroslav Sakala (Cze)
1996	Andreas Goldberger (Aut)
1998	Kazuyoshi Funaki (Jap)

World Cup

Contested over a series of events during the winter season.
Winners:

Men's cross-country

1979	Oddvar Brå (Nor)
1980	Juha Mieto (Fin)
1981	Aleksandr Zavialov (USSR)
1982	Bill Koch (USA)
1983	Aleksandr Zavialov (USSR)
1984	Gunde Svan (Swe)
1985	Gunde Svan (Swe)
1986	Gunde Svan (Swe)
1987	Torgny Mogren (Swe)

1988	Gunde Svan (Swe)
1989	Gunde Svan (Swe)
1990	Vegard Ulvang (Nor)
1991	Vladimir Smirnov (USSR)
1992-3	Bjørn Dæhlie (Nor)
1994	Vladimir Smirnov (Kaz)
1995-7	Bjørn Dæhlie (Nor)
1998	Thomas Alsgaard (Nor)

Women's cross-country

1979	Galina Kulakova (USSR)
1980	Not held
1981	Raisa Smetanina (USSR)
1982	Berit Aunli (Nor)
1983	Marja-Liisa Hämäläinen (Fin)
1984	Marja-Liisa Hämäläinen (Fin)
1985	Anette Bøe (Nor)
1986	Marjo Matikainen (Fin)
1987	Marjo Matikainen (Fin)
1988	Marjo Matikainen (Fin)
1989	Yelena Välbe (USSR)
1990	Larisa Lasutina (USSR)
1991-2	Yelena Välbe (USSR/Rus)
1993	Lyubov Yegorova (Rus)
1994	Manuela Di Centa (Ita)
1995	Yelena Välbe (Rus)
1996	Manuela Di Centa (Ita)
1997	Yelena Välbe (Rus)
1998	Larisa Lazutina (Rus)

Most race wins: (men) 41 Björn Dæhlie, 31 Gunde Svan; (women) 45 Yelena Välbe

Nordic combination

1983	Espen Andersen (Nor)
1984	Tom Sandberg (Nor)
1985	Geir Andersen (Nor)
1986	Hermann Weinbuch (FRG)
1987	Torbjørn Løkken (Nor)
1988	Klaus Sulzenbacher (Aut)
1989	Trond Arne Bredesen (Nor)
1990	Klaus Sulzenbacher (Aut)
1991	Fred-Børre Lundberg (Nor)
1992	Fabrice Guy (Fra)
1993-5	Kenji Ogiwara (Jap)
1996	Knut Tore Apeland (Nor)
1997	Samppa Lajunen (Fin)
1998	Bjarte Engen Vik (Nor)

Ski jumping

1980	Hubert Neuper (Aut)
1981	Armin Kogler (Aut)
1982	Armin Kogler (Aut)
1983	Matti Nykänen (Fin)
1984	Jens Weissflog (GDR)
1985	Matti Nykänen (Fin)
1986	Matti Nykänen (Fin)
1987	Vegard Opaas (Nor)

1988	Matti Nykänen (Fin)
1989	Jan Boklöv (Swe)
1990	Ari-Pekka Nikkola (Fin)
1991	Andreas Felder (Aut)
1992	Toni Nieminen (Fin)
1993	Andreas Goldberger (Aut)
1994	Espen Bredesen (Nor)
1995-6	Andreas Goldberger (Aut)
1997-8	Primoz Peterka (Slo)

Ski flying

1991	Stefan Zuend (Swi)
1992	Werner Rathmayr (Aut)
1993-4	Jaroslav Sakala (Cze)
1995-6	Andreas Goldberger (Aut)
1997	Primoz Peterka (Slo)
1998	Sven Hannawald(Ger)

Cross-country Nations' Cup (men and women)

Norway	1982-7, 1992-3, 1997-8
USSR	1981, 1989-91
Sweden	1988
Russia	1994-6

Ski jumping Nations' Cup

Austria	1981-2, 1986, 1990-3
Norway	1983, 1987, 1989, 1994
Finland	1984-5, 1988, 1995-6
Japan	1997-8

Vasalopp

The world's most famous long-distance skiing race is the Vasalopp, contested annually since 1922 over a distance of 90km. It commemorates the flight in 1521 of Gustav Vasa, later King Gustavus Eriksson, from Mora to Sälen in Sweden (85.8km). He was overtaken by speedy loyal scouts on skis and persuaded to return to lead a rebellion and become king of Sweden. Each year, about 12,000 men and women now contest this famous race, which is always run on the first Sunday in March from Sälen to Mora. The fastest recorded time is 3 hr 48 min 55 sec by Bengt Hassis (Swe) in 1986.

Most wins

8	Nils Karlsson (Swe)	1945-51, 1953
7	Janne Stefansson (Swe)	1962-6, 1968-9
4	Arthur Häggblad (Swe)	1933, 1935, 1937, 1940

Worldloppet Cup

A series of great long-distance (42-90km) races, staged in various parts of the world, annually form the Worldloppet (13 races scheduled 1994-8). The Vasalopp is the longest of the series.
Champions:

1979-80	Matti Kuosku (Swe)
1981	Sven-Åke Lundbäck (Swe)
1982-3	Lars Frykberg (Swe)
1984	Bengt Hassis (Swe)

1985	Örjan Blomqvist (Swe)
1986	Konrad Hallenbarter (Swi)
1987-8	Anders Blomqvist (Swe)
1989	Örjan Blomqvist (Swe)
1990	Konrad Hallenbarter (Swi)
1991	Håkan Westin (Swe)
1992	Erik Hansson (Swe)
1993	Håkan Westin (Swe)
1994	Alec Vanek (Cze)
1995-6	Håkan Westin (Swe)
1997	Michael Botwinov (Aut)
1998	Håkan Westin (Swe)

Women (from 1989)

1989	Ellen Holcomb (USA)
1990-2	Dorota Dziadkowiec (Pol)
1993	Beatrice Grünenfelder (Swi)
1994-6	Maria Theuri (Aut)
1997	Gudrun Pflüger (Aut)
1998	Nadezhda Shlesareva (Rus)

Freestyle Skiing

There are three activities in freestyle skiing: aerials, ballet and moguls. Aerials, incorporating two different jumps, take place on a small jumping hill at an angle of about 30°. In the moguls competitors have timed and judged runs incorporating two jumps down a 250m 30° slope covered with moguls, or hard-packed mounds of snow.

Competition originated in New Hampshire, USA in 1973, and after coming under the wing of the FIS, a World Cup circuit began in 1980.

Olympic Games

Freestyle skiing was introduced in 1992 as a medal sport for moguls and with ballet and aerials as demonstration events. Medals were awarded for both moguls and aerials in 1994.
Winners:

Men

Moguls

1992	Edgar Grospiron (Fra)
1994	Jean-Luc Brassard (Can)
1998	Johnny Moseley (USA)

Aerials

1994	Andreas Schönbächler (Swi)
1998	Eric Bergoust (USA)

Women

Moguls

1992	Donna Weinbrecht (USA)
1994	Stine Lise Hattestad (Nor)
1998	Tae Satoya (Jap)

Aerials

1994	Lina Cheryazova (Uzb)
1998	Nikki Stone (USA)

World Champions

Men

	Ballet	Moguls	Aerials
1986	Richard Schabel (FRG)	Eric Berthon (Fra)	Lloyd Langlois (Can)
1989	Hermann Reitberger (FRG)	Edgar Grospiron (Fra)	Lloyd Langlois (Can)
1991	Lane Spina (USA)	Edgar Grospiron (Fra)	Philippe Laroche (Can)
1993	Fabrice Becker (Fra)	Jean-Luc Brassard (Can)	Philippe Laroche (Can)
1995	Rune Kristiansen (Nor)	Edgar Grospiron (Fra)	Trace Worthington (USA)
1997	Fabrice Becker (Fra)	Jean-Luc Brassard (Can)	Nicolas Fontaine (Can)

Combined

1986	Alain Laroche (Can)
1989	Chris Simboli (Can)
1991	Sergey Shupletsov (USSR)
1993	Sergey Shupletsov (Rus
1995	Trace Worthington (USA)
1997	Darcy Downs (Can)

Women

	Ballet	Moguls	Aerials
1986	Jan Bucher (USA)	Mary Jo Tiampo (USA)	Maria Quintana (Cub)
1989	Jan Bucher (USA)	Raphaëlle Monod (Fra)	Catherine Lombard (Fra)
1991	Ellen Breen (USA)	Donna Weinbrecht (USA)	Vasselisa Semenchuk (USSR)
1993	Ellen Breen (USA)	Stine Lise Hattestad (Nor)	Lina Cheryazova (Uzb)
1995	Yelena Batalova (Rus)	Candice Gilg (Fra)	Nikki Stone (USA)
1997	Oksana Kushenko (Rus)	Candice Gilg (Fra)	Kristie Marshall (Aus)

Combined

1986	Connie Kissling (Swz)
1989	Melanie Palenik (USA)
1991	Maja Schmid (Swz)
1993	Katherina Kubenk (Can)
1995	Kristean Porter (USA)

World Cup

First held in 1980.

Men overall		Women overall	
1980	Greg Athans (Can)	1980-2	Marie-Claude Asselin (Can)
1981-2	Frank Beddor (USA)		
1983-5	Alain Laroche (Can)	1983-92	Conny Kissling (Swi)
1986-8	Eric Laboureix (Fra)	1993	Katherina Kubenk (Can)
1989	Chris Simboli (Can)		
1990-1	Eric Laboureix (Fra)	1994-5	Kristean Porter (USA)
1992-3	Trace Worthington (USA)	1996	Katherina Kubenk (Can)
1994	Sergey Shupletsov (Rus)	1997	Stacey Blumer (USA)
1995	Trace Worthington (USA)	1998	Nikki Stone (USA)
1996	Johnny Moseley (USA)		
1997	Darcy Downs (Can)		
1998	Fabrice Becker (Fra)		

Speed Skiing

Olympic Games

Staged at Albertville in 1992 as a demonstration sport. World records were set by the winners, who were (men) Michaël Prüfer (Fra) 229.299km/h, and (women) Tarja Mulari (Fin) 219.245km/h.

Current world records

Men: 241.448km/h Jeffrey Hamilton (USA), Vars, Hautes-Alpes 14 Apr 1995

Women: 226.700km/h Karine Dubouchet (Fra), Les Arcs, Hautes-Alpes 20 Apr 1996

Sled Dog Racing

Racing between harnessed dog teams (usually huskies) was traditionally practised by the Inuit people of the north of the North American continent, and in Scandinavia, but the first record of a formal race dates back to 1908. In that year, the All-Alaskan Sweepstakes were contested on a run of 408 miles (657km), from Nome to Candle and back.

Sled Dog Racing was a demonstration sport at the 1932 Olympic Games, with two races for twelve sled teams, seven dogs to a sled; winner on aggregate was Emile St Goddard (Can). Most races are held at comparatively short distances, such as the World Championship races, first held in 1936 at 18 miles (29km). Undoubtedly, however, the Iditarod now captures the greatest world-wide interest.

International governing bodies: International Sled Dog Racing Association (ISDRA). Formed in 1966. International Federation of Sleddog Sports (IFSS), Ms Glenda Walling, 7118 N.Beehive Road, Pocatello, ID 83701, USA. Tel: (1) 208 232 5130, Fax: (1) 208 234 1608.

Iditarod Trail

Raced annually since 1973 by dog teams, over 1158 miles (1864km) from Anchorage to Nome, Alaska. The inaugural winner Dick Wilmarth took 20 days 49 minutes and 41 seconds to complete the course, beating 33 other racers. In 1985 Libby Riddles became the first woman ever to win the race and she was followed by Susan Butcher, who was the first to win in three successive years.

Winners (all USA except where shown) with times in days hr:min:sec:

1973	Dick Wilmarth 20d 00:49:41	1987	Susan Butcher 11d 02:05:13
1974	Carl Huntington 20d 15:02:07	1988	Susan Butcher 11d 11:41:40
1975	Emmitt Peters 14d 14:43:45	1989	Joe Runyan 11d 05:24:34
1976	Gerald Riley 18d 22:58:17	1990	Susan Butcher 11d 01:53:23
1977	Rick Swenson 16d 17:27:13	1991	Rick Swenson 12d 16:34:39
1978	Rick Mackey 14d 18:52:24	1992	Martin Buser (Swi) 10d 19:36:15
1979	Rick Swenson 15d 10:37:47	1993	Jeff King 10d 15:38
1980	Joe May 14d 07:11:51	1994	Martin Buser (Swi) 10d13:02:39
1981	Rick Swenson 12:08:45:02	1995	Doug Swingley 9d 2:42:19
1982	Rick Swenson 12d 14:10:44	1996	Jeff King 9d 5:43:13
1984	Dean Osmar 12d 15:07:33	1997	Martin Buser (Swi) 9d 08:30:45
1985	Libby Riddles 18d 00:20:17	1998	Jeff King 9d 05:52:26
1986	Susan Butcher 11d 15:06:00	**Most wins:** 5 Swenson, 4 Butcher	

Snooker

Snooker was first played at Jubbulpore, India in 1875. Colonel Neville Chamberlain (not to be confused with the Prime Minister of the same name) was playing a game of Black Pool, with extra coloured balls added, with a fellow officer in the Devonshire Regiment, whom he insulted by calling him a 'snooker' after the latter missed an easy shot. A 'snooker' was then the name given to a new recruit at the Woolwich Military Academy. The name stuck and came to be used for their new game. The Billiards Association was formed in 1885 and it recognized snooker's first set of rules in 1900.

International governing bodies: *see* Billiards.

World Championship

The first world professional championship was organized in 1926-7 and was held continuously (except for the war years) until 1952 when the professional players and the governing body, the Billiards Association & Control Club, had a disagreement. A match between Horace Lindrum (Aus) and Clark McConachy (NZ) in 1952 was accorded World Championship status. The professional players, however, did not recognize this as the official championship and broke away to organize their own event, known as the Professional Matchplay Championship. This ended in 1957 and it was not until its revival, albeit on a challenge basis, in 1964 that the World Championship was held again. It became a knock-out event, similar to today's competition, in 1969.

Current sponsors Embassy started their association with the Championship in 1976 and all finals since 1977 have been played at the Crucible Theatre, Sheffield.

Winners:

1927-40	Joe Davis (Eng)
1946	Joe Davis (Eng)
1947	Walter Donaldson (Sco)
1948-9	Fred Davis (Eng)
1950	Walter Donaldson (Sco)
1951	Fred Davis (Eng)
1952	Horace Lindrum(Aus)
1952-6	Fred Davis (Eng)★
1957	John Pulman (Eng)★
1964-8	John Pulman (Eng)#
1969	John Spencer (Eng)
1970	Ray Reardon (Wal)
1971	John Spencer (Eng)
1972	Alex Higgins (NI)
1973-6	Ray Reardon (Wal)
1977	John Spencer (Eng)
1978	Ray Reardon (Wal)
1979	Terry Griffiths (Wal)
1980	Cliff Thorburn (Can)
1981	Steve Davis (Eng)
1982	Alex Higgins (NI)
1983-4	Steve Davis (Eng)
1985	Dennis Taylor (NI)
1986	Joe Johnson (Eng)
1987-9	Steve Davis (Eng)
1990	Stephen Hendry (Sco)
1991	John Parrott (Eng)
1992-6	Stephen Hendry (Sco)
1997	Ken Doherty (Ire)
1998	John Higgins (Sco)

★ Professional Matchplay Championship.
Between 1964 and 1968 John Pulman met, and beat, seven challengers: Fred Davis (3), Rex Williams (2), Freddie Van Rensburg, Eddie Charlton.

World Rankings

The World Professional Billiards & Snooker Association, representing the top players, published its first set of world rankings in 1976. Players gather world-ranking points at leading events around the world. A revised list is produced after the World Championship each year.

Top-ranked players:

1976-80	Ray Reardon (Wal)
1981	Cliff Thorburn (Can)
1982	Ray Reardon (Wal)
1983-9	Steve Davis (Eng)
1990-8	Stephen Hendry (Sco)
1998-	John Higgins (Sco)

Grand Prix

Previously known as the Professional Players Tournament, this became the Rothmans Grand Prix 1984-92 and thereafter the Skoda Grand Prix.
Winners:

1982	Ray Reardon (Wal)
1983	Tony Knowles (Eng)

1984	Dennis Taylor (NI)
1985	Steve Davis (Eng)
1986	Jimmy White (Eng)
1987	Stephen Hendry (Sco)
1988-9	Steve Davis (Eng)
1990-1	Stephen Hendry (Sco)
1992	Jimmy White (Eng)
1993	Peter Ebdon (Eng)
1994	John Higgins (Eng)
1995	Stephen Hendry (Sco)
1996	Mark Williams (Wal)
1997	Dominic Dale (Wal)

Mercantile Credit Classic

A ranking tournament from 1984. Mercantile succeeded Lada as sponsors of the Classic in 1985. Lada had succeeded the event's first sponsor, Wilsons Brewery, in 1981.
Winners:

1980 (Jan)	John Spencer (Eng)
1980 (Dec)	Steve Davis (Eng)
1982	Terry Griffiths (Wal)
1984	Steve Davis (Eng)
1985	Willie Thorne (Eng)
1986	Jimmy White (Eng)
1987-8	Steve Davis (Eng)
1989	Doug Mountjoy (Wal)
1990	Steve James (Eng)
1991	Jimmy White (Eng)
1992	Steve Davis (Eng)

United Kingdom Open/Championship

First held at Blackpool in 1977. Known as the United Kingdom Professional Championship until 1984, when it became open to overseas players. All finals since 1978 have been at the Preston Guildhall. It became the Royal Liver Assurance UK Championship from 1992.
Winners (ranking from 1984):

1977	Patsy Fagan (Ire)
1978	Doug Mountjoy (Wal)
1979	John Virgo (Eng)
1980-1	Steve Davis (Eng)
1982	Terry Griffiths (Wal)
1983	Alex Higgins (NI)
1984-7	Steve Davis (Eng)
1988	Doug Mountjoy (Wal)
1989-90	Stephen Hendry (Sco)
1991	John Parrott (Eng)
1992	Jimmy White (Eng)
1993	Ronnie O'Sullivan (Eng)
1994-6	Stephen Hendry (Sco)
1997	Ronnie O'Sullivan (Eng)

British Open

The British Open started as the British Gold Cup in 1980. Between 1981-4 it was known as the Yamaha International, and from 1985 it has been a ranking tournament with various sponsors.

Winners:

1980	Alex Higgins (NI)
1981-2	Steve Davis (Eng)
1983	Ray Reardon (Wal)
1984	Steve Davis (Eng)
1985	Silvino Francisco (SAf)
1986	Steve Davis (Eng)
1987	Jimmy White (Eng)
1988	Stephen Hendry (Sco)
1989	Tony Meo (Eng)
1990	Bob Chaperon (Can)
1991	Stephen Hendry (Sco)
1992	Jimmy White (Eng)
1993	Steve Davis (Eng)
1994	Ronnie O'Sullivan (Eng)
1995	John Higgins (Eng)
1996	Nigel Bond (Eng)
1997	Mark Williams (Wal)
1998	John Higgins (Sco)

European Open

First held in 1989 at Deauville and subsequently in various countries.

Winners:

1989-90	John Parrott (Eng)
1991	Tony Jones (Eng)
1992	Jimmy White (Eng)
1993	Steve Davis (Eng)
1993-4*	Stephen Hendry (Sco)
1996	John Parrott (Eng)
1997	John Higgins (Sco)

* Held in December.

Benson & Hedges Masters

One of the most prestigious events after the World Professional Championship, and the leading non-ranking tournament. Entry is by invitation only to 16 leading players.

Winners:

1975	John Spencer (Eng)
1976	Ray Reardon (Wal)
1977	Doug Mountjoy (Wal)
1978	Alex Higgins (NI)
1979	Perrie Mans (SAf)
1980	Terry Griffiths (Wal)
1981	Alex Higgins (NI)
1982	Steve Davis (Eng)
1983	Cliff Thorburn (Can)
1984	Jimmy White (Eng)
1985-6	Cliff Thorburn (Can)
1987	Dennis Taylor (NI)
1988	Steve Davis (Eng)
1989-93	Stephen Hendry (Sco)
1994	Alan McManus (Sco)
1995	Ronnie O'Sullivan (Eng)
1996	Stephen Hendry (Sco)
1997	Steve Davis (Eng)
1998	Mark Williams (Wal)

Benson & Hedges Irish Masters

Held annually at the Goff's Sales Ring in County Kildare as the last major event before the World Championships.

Winners:

1978	John Spencer (Eng)
1979	Doug Mountjoy (Wal)
1980-2	Terry Griffiths (Wal)
1983-4	Steve Davis (Eng)
1985-6	Jimmy White (Eng)
1987-8	Steve Davis (Eng)
1989	Alex Higgins (NI)
1990-1	Steve Davis (Eng)
1992	Stephen Hendry (Sco)
1993-4	Steve Davis (Eng)
1995	Peter Ebdon (Eng)
1996	Darren Morgan (Wal)
1997	Stephen Hendry (Sco)
1998	Ken Doherty (Ire)*

* Ronnie O'Sullivan (Eng) was stripped of his title due to a positive drugs test.

World Cup

First staged in 1979, the event was moved to the second half of the season in 1984/5 and has been held annually until 1990. Re-started in November 1996, when a record 39 nations entered.

Winners:

1979-80	Wales
1981	England
1982	Canada
1983	England
1985	All-Ireland
1986-7	All-Ireland 'A'
1988-9	England
1990	Canada
1996	Scotland

Scottish Masters

This early-season competition carries no ranking points as the field is limited to invited professionals only.

Winners:

1981	Jimmy White (Eng)
1982-4	Steve Davis (Eng)
1985-6	Cliff Thorburn (Can)
1987	Joe Johnson (Eng)
1989-90	Stephen Hendry (Sco)
1991	Mike Hallett (Eng)
1992	Neal Foulds (Eng)
1993-4	Ken Doherty (Ire)
1995	Stephen Hendry (Sco)
1996	Peter Ebdon (Eng)
1997	Nigel Bond (Eng)

World Matchplay Championship

An invitation-only event restricted to the world's top 12 players based on the previous season's performances only. It was the first snooker competition, in 1988, to offer a £100,000 first prize.

Winners:

1988	Steve Davis (Eng)
1989-90	Jimmy White (Eng)
1991	Gary Wilkinson (Eng)
1992	James Wattana (Tha)

IBSF World Amateur Championship

First held in Calcutta, India in 1963, and held biennially until 1984 when it became an annual competition. Run by the International Billiards & Snooker Federation (IBSF), which became the non-professional game's governing body in 1985. Lower-ranked professionals were allowed to compete from 1995.

Winners:

1963	Gary Owen (Eng)
1966	Gary Owen (Eng)
1968	David Taylor (Eng)
1970	Jonathan Barron (Eng)
1972	Ray Edmonds (Eng)
1974	Ray Edmonds (Eng)
1976	Doug Mountjoy (Wal)
1978	Cliff Wilson (Wal)
1980	Jimmy White (Eng)
1982	Terry Parsons (Wal)
1984	O B Agrawal (Ind)
1985-6	Paul Mifsud (Malta)
1987	Darren Morgan (Wal)
1988	James Wattana (Tha)
1989	Ken Doherty (Ire)
1990	Stephen O'Connor (Ire)
1991	Noppodon Noppachorn (Tha)
1992	Neil Mosley (Eng)
1993	Tai Pichit (Tha)
1994	Mohammed Yusuf (Pak)
1995	Sakchai Sim-ngam (Tha)
1996	Stuart Bingham (Eng)
1997	Marco Fu (HK)

Most wins: 2 Owen, Edmonds, Mifsud
Highest break: 135 Brady Gollan (Can) 1988

Breaks

In recent years the compiling of a maximum 147 break under official conditions has become more common. The first man to compile a maximum was 'Murt' O'Donoghue (NZ) at Griffiths, NSW, Australia in 1934 and the first officially ratified maximum was by Joe Davis in 1955. The first achieved in major tournaments were by John Spencer at Slough in 1979, when the table had over-sized pockets, and by Steve Davis in the 1982 Lada Classic.

Cliff Thorburn was the first to make two tournament maximums, at the 1983 Embassy World Championship and again in 1989. With his maximums at the World and UK Championships in 1995, Stephen Hendry became the first to achieve three in ranking tournaments.

The first official maximum break by an amateur was by Geet Sethi (Ind) during his national championships, on 21 February 1988.

Women's World Open Championships

The Women's Billiards Association, later the Billiards and Snooker Association, was founded in 1931, running the Women's Amateur Billiards Championship from 1931 and the Women's Amateur Snooker Championship from 1933. The first Snooker World Championship was held in 1976, in conjunction with the men's event at Middlesbrough. Women's World Championships have subsequently been staged annually from 1980, except for 1982 and 1992. The 1985-6 events were entitled Amateur Championships, while the rest were Open.

Winners:

1976	Vera Selby (Eng)
1980	Lesley McIlraith (Aus)
1981	Vera Selby (Eng)
1983	Sue Foster (Eng)
1984	Stacey Hillyard (Eng)
1985-6	Allison Fisher (Eng)
1987	Ann-Marie Farren (Eng)
1988-9	Allison Fisher (Eng)
1990	Karen Corr (Eng)
1991	Allison Fisher (Eng)
1993-4	Allison Fisher (Eng)
1995	Karen Corr (Eng)
1996★	Karen Corr (Eng)

★ Title finished in 1997.

UK Women's Championship

The UK Women's Open Championship was first held in 1986.

Winners:

1986-90	Allison Fisher
1991-2	Tessa Davidson
1993	Stacey Hillyard
1994	Karen Corr
1995	Allison Fisher
1996-8	Karen Corr

The Women's Amateur Snooker Championship was first held in 1933. The most wins is eight by Maureen Baynton (née Barrett) 1954-6, 1961-2, 1964, 1966, 1968, and five by Vera Selby 1972-5, 1979.

Snowboarding

Snowboarding evolved, principally in the USA, from the mid-1960s, giving birth to a culture similar to that of surfing. World Championships were started by the FIS in 1993 and the sport was included for the first time in the Olympic Games in 1998. The two Olympic events were the giant slalom, on a course c.1000m long and 290m downhill, run like the Alpine downhill, except that a symmetrical layout was used; and the halfpipe, on a 120m long course like a U-shaped section from a cylinder cut lengthways, in which competitors were awarded points for rotations and other mid-air manoeuvres.

International governing body: FIS (*see* Skiing).

World Championships

First held in 1993.
Winners:

Men

	Slalom	Parallel slalom	Halfpipe
1993	Alexis Parmentier (Fra)	Mosca Cla (Swi)	Terje Haakonsen (Nor)
1995	Martin Freinademetz (Aut)	Martin Freinademetz (Aut)	Terje Haakonsen (Nor)
1997	Bernd Kroshweski (Ger)	Mike Jacoby (USA)	Fabien Rohrer (Swi)

	Giant slalom	Snowboard cross
1997	Thomas Prugger (Ita)	Helmut Pramstaller (Aut)

	Combined
1993	Kevin Delany (USA)
1995	Bertrand Denervaud (Swi)
1997	Romain Retsin (Fra)

Women

	Slalom	Parallel slalom	Halfpipe
1993	Ashild Loftus (Nor)	Ashild Loftus (Nor)	Nicole Angelrath (Swi)
1995	Christine Rauter (Aut)	Michelle Taggart (USA)	Sandra Farmand (Ger)
1997	Heide Renoth (Ger)	Dag Mair Unter Der Eggen (Ita)	Anita Schwaller (Swi)

	Giant slalom	Snowboard cross
1997	Sandra Van Ert (USA)	Karine Ruby (Fra)

	Combined
1993	Michelle Taggart (USA)
1995	Sandra Farmand (Ger)
1997	Sandra Farmand (Ger)

Olympic Games

Held for the first time in 1998.

Men

	Giant slalom	Halfpipe
1998	Ross Rebagliati (Can)	Gian Simmen (Swi)

Women

	Giant slalom	Halfpipe
1998	Karine Ruby (Fra)	Nicola Thost (Ger)

Softball

Softball, invented by George Hancock of the Farragut Boat Club, Chicago, in 1887, began as an indoor version of baseball. The game was originally known as 'kitten-ball' or 'mush-ball', the name softball being introduced by Walter Hakanson in 1926. The sport gained appeal rapidly in the 1920s and 1930s and the Amateur Softball Association of America (ASA) was formed in 1933 after a national tournament contested by 55 teams was staged as part of the Century of Progress Exposition in Chicago. The ASA introduced US Championships for both men's

and women's teams that year. Played by 9-a-side teams, the game developed internationally following the formation in 1950 of the International Softball Federation. There are slow-pitch and fast-pitch versions of the game.
International governing body: International Softball Federation (ISF), 4141 NW Expressway, Suite 340, Oklahoma City, OK 73116, USA. President: Don E Porter, Secretary General: Andrew S Loechner. 101 member nations by 1998.

World Championships

World championships (fast-pitch) for women were introduced in 1965 and for men a year later.
Winners:

Men

USA	1966, 1968, 1976 *(shared)*, 1980, 1988
Canada	1972, 1976 *(shared)*, 1992
New Zealand	1976 *(shared)*, 1984

Women

USA	1974, 1978, 1986, 1994
Australia	1965
Japan	1970
New Zealand	1982

World Championship tournament records

Men

Most runs: 19 Marty Kernaghan(Can) 1988
Best average: .647 Clark Bosch (Can) 1988
Most strikeouts: 99 Kevin Herlihy (NZ) 1972

Women
Most runs: 13 Kathy Elliott (USA) 1974
Best average: .550 Tamara Bryce (Pan) 1978
Most strikeouts: 76 Joan Joyce (USA) 1974

ISF Slow-pitch Championships

First held in 1987, when the men's winners were the USA.

Olympic Games

An 8-team fast-pitch tournament for women was held in the 1996 Games and won by the USA.

Women's European Championships

Winners:

Netherlands	1979-84, 1988, 1990
Italy	1986-7, 1992
Russia	1997

Speedway

Dirt-track racing on motorcycles in the United States has been traced back to 1902, and in England the first fully documented motorcycle track races were held at Portman Road, Ipswich in 1904. Modern speedway has developed from the short-track races held at the West Maitland Agricultural Show, New South Wales in 1923. The organizer of that meeting, Johnnie Hoskins, brought the sport to Britain, where it evolved with small-diameter track racing at Droylsden, Greater Manchester in 1927. The first meeting on a cinder track took place at High Beech, Essex in the following year.

World Championships

The first World Championship for individual riders was held at Wembley, London in 1936. The team competition was introduced in 1960, and the pairs in 1970. Two pairs championships, in 1968 and 1969, had claimed the status of World Championship, but the governing body does not recognize these two events for record purposes. The Long-track Championship was inaugurated in 1971.
Winners:

Individual

1936	Lionel Van Praag (Aus)
1937	Jack Milne (USA)
1938	Bluey Wilkinson (Aus)
1949	Tommy Price (Eng)
1950	Freddie Williams (Wal)
1951-2	Jack Young (Aus)
1953	Freddie Williams (Wal)
1954	Ronnie Moore (NZ)
1955	Peter Craven (Eng)
1956	Ove Fundin (Swe)
1957-8	Barry Briggs (NZ)
1959	Ronnie Moore (NZ)
1960-1	Ove Fundin (Swe)
1962	Peter Craven (Eng)
1963	Ove Fundin (Swe)
1964	Barry Briggs (NZ)
1965	Björn Knutsson (Swe)
1966	Barry Briggs (NZ)
1967	Ove Fundin (Swe)
1968-70	Ivan Mauger (NZ)
1971	Ole Olsen (Den)
1972	Ivan Mauger (NZ)
1973	Jerzy Szczakiel (Pol)
1974	Anders Michanek (Swe)
1975	Ole Olsen (Den)
1976	Peter Collins (Eng)
1977	Ivan Mauger (NZ)
1978	Ole Olsen (Den)
1979	Ivan Mauger (NZ)
1980	Michael Lee (Eng)

1981-2	Bruce Penhall (USA)
1983	Egon Müller (FRG)
1984-5	Erik Gundersen (Den)
1986-7	Hans Nielsen (Den)
1988	Erik Gundersen (Den)
1989	Hans Nielsen (Den)
1990	Per Jonsson (Swe)
1991	Jan O Pedersen (Den)
1992	Gary Havelock (Eng)
1993	Sam Ermolenko (USA)
1994	Tony Rickardsson (Swe)
1995	Hans Nielsen (Den)
1996	Billy Hamill (USA)
1997	Greg Hancock (UK)

Most successful riders

	1st	2nd	3rd
Ivan Mauger	6	3	1
Ove Fundin	5	3	3
Barry Briggs	4	3	3
Hans Nielsen	4	5	1

Most appearances in finals: 18 Briggs 1954-70, 1972

Pairs (unofficial 1968-9)

1968	Sweden (Ove Fundin & Torbjörn Harryson)
1969	New Zealand (Ivan Mauger & Bob Andrews)
1970	New Zealand (Ronnie Moore & Ivan Mauger)
1971	Poland (Jerzy Szczakiel & Andrzej Wyglenda)
1972	England (Ray Wilson & Terry Betts)
1973	Sweden (Anders Michanek & Tommy Jansson)
1974	Sweden (Anders Michanek & Soren Sjösten)
1975	Sweden (Anders Michanek & Tommy Jansson)
1976	England (John Louis & Malcolm Simmons)
1977	England (Peter Collins & Malcolm Simmons)
1978	England (Malcolm Simmons & Gordon Kennett)
1979	Denmark (Ole Olsen & Hans Nielsen)
1980	England (David Jessup & Peter Collins)
1981	USA (Bruce Penhall & Bobby Schwartz)
1982	USA (Dennis Sigalos & Bobby Schwartz)
1983	England (Kenny Carter & Peter Collins)
1984	England (Peter Collins & Chris Morton)
1985	Denmark (Erik Gundersen & Tommy Knudsen)
1986-9	Denmark (Hans Nielsen & Erik Gundersen)
1990-1	Denmark (Hans Nielsen & Jan O.Pedersen)
1992	USA (Greg Hancock, Sam Ermolenko, Ronnie Correy)
1993	Sweden (Tony Rickardsson, Henrik Gustafsson, Per Jonsson)

Renamed as team event 1994:
1994	Sweden (Tony Rickardsson, Henrik Gustafsson)
1995	Denmark (Tommy Knudsen, Hans Nielsen, Brian Karger)
1996	Poland (Tomas Gollob, Slawomir Drabnik, Piotr Proasiewicz)
1997	Denmark (Tommy Knudsen, Hans Nielsen)

Most wins (team): 10 Denmark; 7 England; 6 Sweden

Most wins (individual): 9 Nielsen; 5 Gundersen; 4 Collins; 3 Michanek, Simmons, Knudsen

Maximum points: 30/30 was scored by the winners in 1971 and 1982

Team

(Discontinued 1994.)
Wins:

9	Great Britain/ England	1968, 1971-3 1974-5, 1977, 1980, 1989
9	Denmark	1978, 1981, 1983-8, 1991
6	Sweden	1960, 1962-4, 1967, 1970
4	Poland	1961, 1965-6, 1969
4	USA	1982, 1990, 1992-3
1	Australia 1976, New Zealand 1979	

Most wins by individual team members

9	Hans Nielsen (Den) 1978, 1981, 1983-8, 1991
7	Erik Gundersen (Den) 1981, 1983-8
6	Ove Fundin (Swe) 1960, 1962-4, 1967, 1970
5	Peter Collins (GB/Eng) 1973-5, 1977, 1980
4	Malcolm Simmons (GB/Eng) 1973-5, 1977
4	Ivan Mauger (GB/NZ) 1968, 1971-2, 1979
4	Rune Sormander (Swe) 1960, 1962-4
4	Björn Knutsson (Swe) 1960, 1962-4
4	Gote Nordin (Swe) 1962-4, 1967

Long-track

1971-2	Ivan Mauger (NZ)
1973	Ole Olsen (Den)
1974-5	Egon Müller (FRG)
1976	Ivan Mauger (NZ)
1977	Anders Michanek (Swe)
1978	Egon Müller (FRG)
1979	Alois Weisbock (FRG)
1980	Karl Maier (FRG)
1981	Michael Lee (Eng)
1982	Karl Maier (FRG)
1983	Shawn Moran (USA)
1984	Erik Gundersen (Den)
1985	Simon Wigg (Eng)
1986	Erik Gundersen (Den)
1987-8	Karl Maier (FRG)
1989-90	Simon Wigg (Eng)
1991	Gerd Riss (Ger)
1992	Marcel Gerhard (Swi)
1993-4	Simon Wigg (Eng)
1995	Kelvin Tatum (Eng)
1996	Gerd Riss (Ger)
1997	Steve Schofield (UK)

Most wins: 5 Wigg, 4 Maier, 3 Müller
Most placings in first three: 7 Müller, Maier

Most World titles

	Total	Ind.	Pairs	Team	L/T
Hans Nielsen (Den)	22	4	9	9	–
Erik Gundersen (Den)	17	3	5	7	2
Ivan Mauger (NZ)	15	6	2★	4	3
Ove Fundin (Swe)	12	5	1★	6	–
Peter Collins (Eng)	10	1	4	5	–
Ole Olsen (Den)	8	3	1	3	1
Tommy Knudsen (Den)	8	–	3	5	–
Malcolm Simmons (Eng)	7	–	3	4	–
Jan O Pedersen (Den)	7	1	2	4	–
Barry Briggs (NZ)	6	4	–	2	–

★ Including one unofficial pairs win.

British Speedway League

League racing was introduced to Britain in 1929, with a Southern League and a Northern Dirt Track League. The National League was founded in 1932. A second division was added in 1936 and there was a third division in 1947-51. From 1957 there was again only one division. A rival league, the Provincial League, came into being in 1960 and the two leagues merged in 1965 to form the British League. A second division was created in 1968. The new division was renamed the New National League in 1975, and from 1976 was known as the National League. In 1994 there were three divisions of the British League. In 1997 a new Elite League of ten clubs was formed.

Winners:

Most wins (top division)

11	Belle Vue	1933-6, 1939, 1963, 1970-2, 1982, 1993
8	Wembley	1932, 1946-7, 1949-53
7	Wimbledon	1954-6, 1958-61
5	Coventry	1968, 1978-9, 1987-8

British/Premier League Riders' Championship

1965-70	Barry Briggs (Swindon)
1971	Ivan Mauger (Belle Vue)
1972	Ole Olsen (Wolverhampton)
1973	Ivan Mauger (Exeter)
1974-5	Peter Collins (Belle Vue)
1976-8	Ole Olsen (Coventry)
1979	John Louis (Ipswich)
1980	Les Collins (Leicester)
1981-2	Kenny Carter (Halifax)
1983	Erik Gundersen (Cradley Heath)
1984	Chris Morton (Belle Vue)
1985	Erik Gundersen (Cradley Heath)
1986-7	Hans Nielsen (Oxford)
1988	Jan Pedersen (Cradley Heath)
1989	Shawn Moran (Belle Vue)
1990	Hans Nielsen (Oxford)
1991	Sam Ermolenko (Wolverhampton)
1992	Joe Screen (Belle Vue)
1993	Per Jonsson (Reading)
1994	Sam Ermolenko (Wolverhampton)
1995	Gary Havelock (Bradford)
1996	Sam Ermolenko (Sheffield)
1997	Greg Hancock (Coventry)

World Ice Speedway Championship

World championships were instituted in 1966 with an individual competition; a team competition was added in 1979.

Individual winners

1966	Gabdrahman Kadirov (USSR)
1967	Boris Samorodov (USSR)
1968-9	Gabdrahman Kadirov (USSR)
1970	Antonin Svaab (Cs)
1971-3	Gabdrahman Kadirov (USSR)
1974	Milan Spinka (Cs)
1975-8	Sergey Tarabanko (USSR)
1979-80	Anatoliy Bondarenko (USSR)
1981	Vladimir Lyubich (USSR)
1982-3	Sergey Kosakov (USSR)
1984	Erik Stenlund (Swe)
1985	Vladimir Suchov (USSR)
1986-7	Yuriy Ivanov (USSR)
1988	Erik Stenlund (Swe)
1989	Nikolay Nischenko (USSR)
1990	Jarmo Hirvasoija (Fin)
1991	Sergey Ivanov (USSR)
1992	Yuriy Ivanov (Rus)
1993	Vladimir Fadeyev (Rus)
1994	Aleksandr Balashchov (Rus)
1995	Per Olaf Serenius (Swe)
1996	Aleksandr Balashchov (Rus)
1997	Kyril Dragalin (Rus)
1998	Aleksandr Balashchov (Rus)

Team wins

12	USSR	1979-82, 1984, 1986-92
5	Russia	1993-4, 1996-8
2	Sweden	1985, 1995
1	FRG	1983

Squash

Squash rackets developed from rackets, being played with a softer ball, first at Harrow School in 1817, but it was not until the formation of the Squash Rackets Association in 1928 that the game grew in popularity world-wide. The first recognized champion was John Miskey, who won the US Amateur Championship in 1907, the year that the United States Squash Racquets Association was founded. The Women's Squash Rackets Association was founded in 1934.

International governing body: World Squash Federation (WSF), 6 Havelock Road, Hastings, East Sussex TN34 1BP. Tel 01424 429245, Fax 01424 429 250. 115 member nations in 1998 (including 49 associates). President: Susie Simcock, Chief Executive: Edward J Wallbutton.

The International Squash Rackets Federation (ISRF) was founded in 1967 and the Women's International Squash Rackets Federation in 1976. In 1992 the ISRF abandoned the name of 'rackets' and reconstituted as the WSF.

World Open Championship

First held in 1976. There were no championships in 1978 but since 1979 it has been an annual event for men, and a biennial (annual from 1990) event for women.

Winners:

Men

1976–7	Geoff Hunt (Aus)
1979–80	Geoff Hunt (Aus)
1981–5	Jahangir Khan (Pak)
1986	Ross Norman (NZ)
1987	Jansher Khan (Pak)
1988	Jahangir Khan (Pak)
1989–90	Jansher Khan (Pak)
1991	Rodney Martin (Aus)
1992–6	Jansher Khan (Pak)
1997	Rodney Eyles (Aus)

Most wins: 8 Jansher Khan; 6 Jahangir Khan; 4 Hunt

Women

1976	Heather McKay (Aus)
1979	Heather McKay (Aus)
1981	Rhonda Thorne (Aus)
1983	Vicki Cardwell (Aus)
1985	Susan Devoy (NZ)
1987	Susan Devoy (NZ)
1989	Martine Le Moignan (UK)
1990–2	Susan Devoy (NZ)
1993–5	Michelle Martin (Aus)
1996–7	Sarah Fitz-Gerald (Aus)

Most wins: 5 Devoy

Women's team

Great Britain	1979
Australia	1981, 1983, 1992, 1994, 1996
England	1985, 1987, 1989, 1990

Men's World Team Championship

Held with the World Amateur/ISRF until 1985, with professionals first admitted in 1981, and now separately.

Wins:

Australia	1967, 1969, 1971, 1973, 1989, 1991
Pakistan	1977, 1981, 1983, 1985, 1987, 1993
Great Britain	1975, 1979
England	1995, 1997

World Amateur/ISRF Championship

First held in 1967, this tournament became known as the ISRF World Championship in 1979 after the sport went open. Held every two years until 1985.

Winners:

1967	Geoff Hunt (Aus)
1969	Geoff Hunt (Aus)
1971	Geoff Hunt (Aus)
1973	Cameron Nancarrow (Aus)
1975	Kevin Shawcross (Aus)
1977	Maqsood Ahmed (Pak)
1979	Jahangir Khan (Pak)
1981	Steve Bowditch (Aus)
1983	Jahangir Khan (Pak)
1985	Jahangir Khan (Pak)

Most wins: 3 Hunt, Jahangir Khan

World Cup

Held in 1984, when Jahangir Khan (Pak) won the men' singles, and Ross Thorne & Dean Williams (Aus) won the men's doubles.

British Open Championship

First held in 1922 for women, and in 1930 for men, the British Open was regarded as the unofficial World Championship until the creation of the World Amateur Championship in 1967.

Men

1930–1	Don Butcher (UK)
1932–7	Abdelfattah Amr Bey (Egy)
1938	James Dear (UK)

1946-9	Mahmoud Karim (Egy)
1950-5	Hashim Khan (Pak)
1956	Roshan Khan (Pak)
1957	Hashim Khan (Pak)
1958-61	Azam Khan (Pak)
1962	Mohibullah Khan (Pak)
1963-6	Abdelfattah AbouTaleb (Egy)
1967-8	Jonah Barrington (UK)
1969	Geoff Hunt (Aus)
1970-3	Jonah Barrington (UK)
1974	Geoff Hunt (Aus)
1975	Qamar Zaman (Pak)
1976-81	Geoff Hunt (Aus)
1982-91	Jahangir Khan (Pak)
1992-7	Jansher Khan (Pak)
1998	Peter Nicol (UK)

Most wins: 10 Jahangir Khan; 8 Hunt; 7 Hashim Khan; 6 Amr Bey, Barrington, Jansher Khan

Women

1922	Joyce Cave (UK)
1922	Sylvia Huntsman(UK)
1923	Nancy Cave (UK)
1924	Joyce Cave (UK)
1925-6	Cecily Fenwick (UK)
1928	Joyce Cave (UK)
1929-30	Nancy Cave (UK)
1931	Cecily Fenwick (UK)
1932-4	Susan Noel (UK)
1934-9	Margot Lumb (UK)
1947-9	Joan Curry (UK)
1950-8	Janet Morgan (UK)(ten wins)
1960	Sheila Macintosh (UK)
1961	Fran Marshall (UK)
1962-5	Heather Blundell (Aus)
1966-77	Heather McKay (née Blundell) (Aus)
1978	Susan Newman (Aus)
1979	Barbara Wall (Aus)
1980-1	Vicki Hoffman (Aus)
1982-3	Vicki Cardwell (née Hoffman) (Aus)
1984-90	Susan Devoy (NZ)
1991	Lisa Opie (UK)
1992	Susan Devoy (NZ)
1993-8	Michelle Martin (Aus)

Most wins: 16 McKay (née Blundell); 10 Morgan; 8 Devoy; 6 Lumb, Martin; 4 Cardwell (née Hoffmann)

British Amateur Championship

Instituted in 1922. With the distinction between amateurs and professionals disappearing in 1979, the tournament came to an end.

Winners (all UK unless otherwise stated):

1922-3	Tommy Jameson
1924	Dugald Macpherson
1925	Victor Cazalet
1926	Jimmy Tomkinson
1927	Victor Cazalet
1928	Dugald McPherson
1929-30	Victor Cazalet
1931-3	Abdelfattah Amr Bey (Egy)
1934	Cyril Hamilton
1935-7	Abdelfattah Amr Bey (Egy)
1938	Kenneth Gandar Dower
1946-50	Norman Borrett
1951	Gavin Hildick-Smith
1952-3	Alan Fairbairn
1954	Roy Wilson
1955	Ibrahim Amin (Egy)
1956	Roy Wilson
1957-8	Nigel Broomfield
1959	Ibrahim Amin (Egy)
1960-1	Michael Oddy
1962	Ken Hiscoe (Aus)
1963-5	Aftab Jawaid (Pak)
1966-8	Jonah Barrington
1969	Geoff Hunt (Aus)
1970-1	Gogi Alauddin (Pak)
1972	Cameron Nancarrow (Aus)
1973-4	Mohibullah Khan (Pak)
1975	Kevin Shawcross (Aus)
1976	Bruce Brownlee (NZ)
1977-8	Gamal Awad (Egy)
1979	Jonathan Leslie

Most wins: 6 Amr Bey; 5 Borrett; 4 Cazalet; 3 Aftab Jawaid

Unbeaten champions

Heather McKay (née Blundell) was unbeaten in women's squash from 1962 to 1980. She won 16 British Open titles and 14 consecutive Australian Amateur titles 1960-73 before turning professional. After winning her second world title in 1979 she concentrated on a new sport – racquetball – and became the best player in Canada (to where she had moved in 1975) within a year.

When Jahangir Khan lost to Ross Norman in the World Championship final at Toulouse, France in November 1986, it was his first defeat since April 1981, when Geoff Hunt beat him in the final of the British Open.

Surfing

Surfing was a traditional Polynesian activity, which has been popular for a long time on suitable coastlines, for example, off California, Hawaii or Australia. It was developed as a sporting activity in the 1950s and 1960s, with the first professional event for women held in 1969.

International governing body: International Surfing Association (ISA), 5580 La Jolla Boulevard, Suite 145, La Jolla, CA 92037, USA. Tel: (1) 619 514 3606, Fax: (1) 619 514 3620. President: Fernando Aguerre, Executive Director: Cadu Villela. Founded 1978. 44 member nations.

World Professional Championships

First held in 1970. The Grand Prix circuit is held throughout the year at venues worldwide. It is now organized by the Association of Surfing Professionals (ASP).

Winners (year given 1983-4 is that of the first half of each May-April season):

Men

1970	Robert Young (Aus)
1971	Paul Neilsen (Aus)
1972	Jonathan Paarman (SAf)
1973	Ian Cairns (Aus)
1974	Reno Abellira (USA/Haw)
1975	Mark Richards (Aus)
1976	Peter Townend (Aus)
1977	Shaun Tomson (SAf)
1978	Wayne Bartholomew (Aus)
1979-82	Mark Richards (Aus)
1983-4	Tom Carroll (Aus)
1985-6	Tommy Curren (USA)
1987	Damien Hardman (Aus)
1988	Barton Lynch (Aus)
1989	Martin Potter (UK)
1990	Tommy Curren (USA)
1991	Damien Hardman (Aus)
1992	Kelly Slater (USA)
1993	Derek Ho (USA/Haw)
1994-7	Kelly Slater (USA)

Women

1977	Margo Oberg (Haw)
1978-9	Lyne Boyer (Haw)
1980-1	Margo Oberg (Haw)
1982	Debbie Beacham (USA)
1983	Kim Mearig (USA)
1984-6	Frieda Zamba (USA)
1987	Wendy Botha (SAf)
1988	Frieda Zamba (USA)
1989	Wendy Botha (SAf)
1990	Pam Burridge (Aus)
1991-2	Wendy Botha (Aus, ex SAf)
1993	Pauline Menczer (Aus)
1994-5	Lisa Andersen (USA)
1996	Kylie Webb (Aus)
1997	Lisa Andersen (USA)

Swimming and Diving

Although swimming may have been popular in ancient times, it was not included in the ancient Olympic Games. The earliest references to swimming races were in Japan in 36BC. In modern times competitive swimming was popularized in Britain from at least 1791.

The first national swimming association was the Metropolitan Swimming Clubs Association, later to become the Amateur Swimming Association (ASA), founded in London in 1869. The first national champion was Tom Morris, who won a one-mile race in the Thames that year.

International governing body: (for swimming, diving and water polo) Fédération Internationale de Natation Amateur (FINA), 9 ave de Beaumont, 1012 Lausanne, Switzerland. Tel: (41) 21 312 6602, Fax: (41) 21 312 6610. President: Mustapha Larfaoui, Director: Cornel Marculescu. Founded in 1908. 170 member nations in 1998.

World Records

World records for swimming were first recognized by FINA in 1908. At that time records for distances under 800m could be set in pools of any length over 25 yards, and it was possible for times to be taken in mid-course, and not just at the end of the pool. The range of distances proliferated, but was cut back in 1948 and in 1952, when records for the breaststroke and butterfly were also separated. In 1957 FINA decreed that henceforth only times set in 50-metre or 55-yard pools would be accepted and no mid-pool times would be recognized. As short-course times are quicker by about 0.7 sec. per turn, in some events it took a few years before the old records were surpassed. In 1968 Imperial distances were cut from the lists.

Records are shown for each of the currently recognized events, with the records at 15-year intervals from 1915 to 1990, and all records since then. Also listed are those swimmers to have set most records at each distance.

(* Denotes records set in short-course pools (up to 1957); y denotes record made at Imperial distance – 220yd, 440yd, or 880yd – longer equivalent to 200m, 400m and 800m respectively.)

Men's records – currently recognized events

	min sec	Name	Date
50 metres freestyle			
1990	21.98	Tom Jager (USA)	24 Mar 1990
	21.81	Tom Jager (USA)	24 Mar 1990

Most records: 5 Tom Jager (USA) 22.32–21.81 1987-90; 3 Matt Biondi (USA) 22.33–22.14 1986-8

100 metres freestyle

1915	1:01.6	Duke Kahanamoku (USA)	17 Feb 1924
1930	57.4★	Johnny Weissmuller (USA)	17 Feb 1924
1945	55.9★	Alan Ford (USA)	13 Apr 1944
1960	54.6	John Devitt (Aus)	28 Jan 1957
1975	50.59	Jim Montgomery (USA)	23 Aug 1975
1990	48.42	Matt Biondi (USA)	10 Aug 1988
	48.21	Aleksandr Popov (Rus)	18 Jun 1994

Most records: 4 Jim Montgomery (USA) 51.12–49.99 1975-6, Matt Biondi (USA) 49.24–48.42 1985-8; 3 Duke Kahanamoku (USA) 61.6–60.4 1912-20, Mark Spitz (USA) 51.9–51.22 1970-2

200 metres freestyle

1915	2:25.4y★	Charles Daniels (USA)	26 Mar 1909
1930	2:08.0★	Johnny Weissmuller (USA)	5 Apr 1927
1945	2:06.2★	Bill Smith (USA)	12 Feb 1944
1960	2:01.5	Tsuyoshi Yamanaka (Jap)	26 Jul 1959
1975	1:50.32	Bruce Furniss (USA)	21 Aug 1975
1990	1:46.69	Giorgio Lamberti (Ita)	15 Aug 1989

Most records: 9 Don Schollander (USA) 1:58.8–1:54.3 1963-8; 5 Tsuyoshi Yamanaka (Jap) 2:03.0–2:00.4 1958-61; 4 Mark Spitz (USA) 1:54.3–1:52.78 1969-72, Bruce Furniss (USA) 1:51.41–1:50.29 1975-6, Michael Gross (FRG) 1:48.28–1:47.44 1983-4

400 metres freestyle

1915	5:21.6★	Jack Hatfield (UK)	26 Sep 1912
1930	4:50.3★	Arne Borg (Swe)	11 Sep 1925
1945	4:38.5★	Bill Smith (USA)	13 May 1941
1960	4:15.9y	John Konrads (Aus)	23 Feb 1960
1975	3:53.31	Tim Shaw (USA)	20 Aug 1975
1990	3:46.95	Uwe Dassler (GDR)	23 Sep 1988
	3:46.47	Kieren Perkins (Aus)	3 Apr 1992
	3:45.00	Yevgeniy Sadoviy (Rus)	29 Jul 1992
	3:43.80	Kieren Perkins (Aus)	9 Sep 1994

Most records: 6 Vladimir Salnikov (USSR) 3:51.41–3:48.32 1979-83; 4 John Konrads (Aus) 4:25.9y–4:15.9y 1958-60, Tim Shaw (USA) 3:56.96–3:53.31 1974-5

800 metres freestyle

1915	11:25.4y	Henry Taylor (UK)	21 Jul 1906
1930	10:19.6	Jean Taris (Fra)	30 May 1930
1945	9:50.9	Bill Smith (USA)	24 Jul 1941
1960	8:59.6y	John Konrads (Aus)	10 Jan 1959
1975	8:09.60	Tim Shaw (USA)	12 Jul 1975
1990	7:50.64	Vladimir Salnikov (USSR)	4 Jul 1986
	7:47.85	Kieren Perkins (Aus)	25 Aug 1991
	7:46.60	Kieren Perkins (Aus)	16 Feb 1992
	7:46.00	Kieren Perkins (Aus)	24 Aug 1994

Most records: 7 Steve Holland (Aus) 8:17.6–8:02.91 1973-6; 4 Shozo Makino (Jap) 10:16.6–9:55.8 1931-5, Vladimir Salnikov (USSR) 7:56.43–7:50.64 1979-86

1500 metres freestyle

1915	22:00.0	George Hodgson (Can)	10 Jul 1912
1930	19:07.2	Arne Borg (Swe)	2 Sep 1927
1945	18:58.8	Tomikatsu Amano (Jap)	10 Aug 1938
1960	17:11.0y	John Konrads (Aus)	27 Feb 1960
1975	15:20.91	Tim Shaw (USA)	21 Jun 1975
1990	14:54.76	Vladimir Salnikov (USSR)	22 Feb 1983
	14:53.6	Glen Housman (Aus)	13 Dec 1989
		(unratified due to timing malfunction)	
	14:50.36	Jörg Hoffmann (Ger)	13 Jan 1991
	14:48.40	Kieren Perkins (Aus)	3 Apr 1992

| | 14:43.48 | Kieren Perkins (Aus) | 31 Jul 1992 |
| | 14:41.66 | Kieren Perkins (Aus) | 24 Aug 1994 |

Most records: 5 Arne Borg (Swe) 21:35.3–19:07.2 1923-7, Mike Burton (USA) 16:41.6–15:52.58 1966-72; 4 Steve Holland (Aus) 15:37.8–15:10.59 1973-6

4 x 100 metres freestyle

1945	3:50.8*	Yale University (USA)	18 Mar 1942
1960	3:44.4	USA	21 Jul 1959
1975	3:24.85	USA	23 Jul 1975
1990	3:16.53	USA	23 Sep 1988
	3:15.11	USA	12 Aug 1995
		(David Fox, Joe Hudepohl, Jon Olsen, Gary Hall Jr)	

4 x 200 metres freestyle relay

1945	8:51.5	Japan	11 Aug 1936
1960	8:10.2	USA	1 Sep 1960
1975	7:30.54	Long Beach SC (USA)	22 Aug 1975
1990	7:12.51	USA	21 Sep 1988
	7:11.95	CIS	27 Jul 1992
		(Dmitriy Lepikov, Vladimir Pychnenko, Venyamin Tayanovich, Yevgeniy Sadoviy)	

100 metres backstroke

1915	1:15.6*	Otto Fahr (Ger)	29 May 1912
1930	1:08.2	George Kojac (USA)	9 Aug 1928
1945	1:04.8*	Adolph Kiefer (USA)	18 Jan 1936
1960	1:01.5y	John Monckton (Aus)	15 Feb 1958
1975	56.30	Roland Matthes (GDR)	4 Sep 1972
1990	54.51	David Berkoff (USA)	24 Sep 1988
	53.93	Jeff Rouse (USA)	25 Aug 1991
	53.86	Jeff Rouse (USA)	31 Jul 1992

Most records: 8 Roland Matthes (GDR) 58.4–56.30 1967-72; 4 Warren Kealoha (USA) 1:14.8–1:11.4* 1920-6, Adolph Kiefer (USA) 1:07.0*–1:04.8# 1935-6

200 metres backstroke

1915	2:48.4*	Otto Fahr (Ger)	3 Apr 1912
1930	2:32.2*	George Kojac (USA)	16 Jun 1930
1945	2:19.3*	Adolph Kiefer (USA)	4 Mar 1944
1960	2:13.2	Tom Stock (USA)	24 Jul 1960
1975	2:01.87	Roland Matthes (GDR)	7 Sep 1973
1990	1:58.14	Igor Polyanskiy (USSR)	3 Mar 1985
	1:57.30	Martin López-Zubero (Spa)	13 Aug 1991
	1:56.57	Martin López-Zubero (Spa)	23 Nov 1991

Most records: 9 Roland Matthes (GDR) 2:07.9–2:01.87 1967-73; 4 Tom Stock (USA) 2:16.0–2:10.9 1960-2

100 metres breaststroke

1915	1:17.8	Walther Bathe (Ger)	18 Dec 1910
1930	1:14.0*	Walter Spence (USA)	28 Oct 1927
1945	1:07.3*#	Dick Hough (USA)	15 Apr 1939
1960	1:11.5	Vladimir Minashkin (USSR)	15 Sep 1957
1975	1:03.88	John Hencken (USA)	31 Aug 1974
1990	1:01.49	Adrian Moorhouse (UK)	15 Aug 1989
	1:01.49	Adrian Moorhouse (UK)	25 Jan 1990
	1:01.49	Adrian Moorhouse (UK)	26 Jul 1990
	1:01.49	Norbert Rózsa (Hun)	7 Jan 1991
	1:01.45	Norbert Rózsa (Hun)	7 Jan 1991
	1:01.29	Norbert Rózsa (Hun)	20 Aug 1991
	1:00.95	Karoly Guttler (Hun)	3 Aug 1993
	1:00.60	Frédéric Deburghgraeve (Bel)	20 Jul 1996

Most records: 7 John Hencken (USA) 1:05.68–1:03.11 1972-6; 6 Chet Jastremski (USA) 1:11.1–1:07.5 1961;
    5 Leonid Meshkov (USSR) 1:07.2*#–1:06.5*# 1949-51, Steven Lundquist (USA) 1:02.62–1:01.65 1982-4
With butterfly stroke.

200 metres breaststroke

1915	2:56.6*	Percy Courtman (UK)	28 Jul 1914
1930	2:45.0*	Yoshiyuki Tsuruta (Jap)	27 Jul 1929
1945	2:36.8*#	Alfred Nakache (Fra)	6 Jul 1941
1960	2:36.5y	Terry Gathercole (Aus)	28 Jun 1958
1975	2:18.21	John Hencken (USA)	1 Sep 1974
1990	2:11.53	Mike Barrowman (USA)	21 Jul 1990
	2:11.23	Mike Barrowman (USA)	11 Jan 1991
	2:10.60	Mike Barrowman (USA)	13 Aug 1991
	2:10.16	Mike Barrowman (USA)	29 Jul 1992

Most records: 6 Joe Verdeur (USA) 2:35.6*#–2:28.3*# 1946-50, Mike Barrowman (USA) 2:12.90–2:10.16
    1989-92; 5 John Hencken (USA) 2:22.79–2:18.21 1972-4; 4 Masaru Furukawa (Jap) 2:36.6u#– 2:31.0#u 1954-5
With butterfly stroke.
u Underwater swimming, permitted with breaststroke until 1957.

100 metres butterfly

1960	58.7	Lance Larson (USA)	24 Jul 1960
1975	54.27	Mark Spitz (USA)	31 Aug 1972
1990	52.84	Pablo Morales (USA)	24 Jun 1986
	52.32	Denis Pankratov (Rus)	23 Aug 1995
	52.27	Denis Pankratov (Rus)	24 Jul 1996
	52.15	Michael Klim (Aus)	9 Oct 1997

Most records: 7 Mark Spitz (USA) 56.3–54.27 1967-72; 6 György Tumpek (Hun) 1:04.3*–1:03.4 1953-7;
    5 Takashi Ishimoto (Jap) 1:01.5–1:00.1 1957-8

200 metres butterfly

1960	2:12.8	Mike Troy (USA)	2 Sep 1960
1975	2:00.70	Mark Spitz (USA)	28 Aug 1972
1990	1:56.24	Michael Gross (FRG)	28 Jun 1986
	1:55.69	Melvin Stewart (USA)	12 Jan 1991
	1:55.22	Denis Pankratov (Rus)	14 Jun 1995

Most records: 9 Mark Spitz (USA) 2:06.4–2:00.70 1967-72; 6 Mike Troy (USA) 2:19.0–2:12.8 1959-60;
    5 Kevin Berry (Aus) 2:12.5y–2:06.6 1962-4

200 metres individual medley

1975	2:06.08	Bruce Furniss (USA)	23 Aug 1975
1990	2:00.11	David Wharton (USA)	20 Aug 1989
	1:59.36	Tamás Darnyi (Hun)	13 Jan 1991
	1:58.16	Jani Sievinen (Fin)	11 Sep 1994

Most records: 4 Alex Baumann (Can) 2:02.78–2:01.42 1981-6

400 metres individual medley

1960	5:04.5	Dennis Rounsavelle (USA)	22 Jul 1960
1975	4:28.89	András Hargitay (Hun)	20 Aug 1974
1990	4:14.75	Tamás Darnyi (Hun)	21 Sep 1988
	4:12.36	Tamás Darnyi (Hun)	8 Jan 1991
	4:12.30	Tom Dolan (USA)	6 Sep 1994

Most records: 5 Gary Hall (USA) 4:43.3–4:30.81 1968-72; 4 Ted Stickles (USA) 5:04.3–4:51.0y 1961-2

4 x 100 metres medley relay

1960	4:05.4	USA	1 Sep 1960
1975	3:48.16	USA	4 Sep 1972
1990	3:36.93	USA	25 Sep 1988
	3:36.93	USA	31 Jul 1992
	3:34.84	USA	26 Jul 1996

(Gary Hall Jr, Mark Henderson, Jeremy Linn, Jeff Rouse)

Women's records – currently recognized events

	min sec	Name	Date

50 metres freestyle

1990	24.98	Yang Wenyi (Chn)	11 Apr 1988
	24.79	Yang Wenyi (Chn)	31 Jul 1992
	24.51	Le Jingyi (Chn)	11 Sep 1994

Most records: 4 Tamara Costache (Rom) 25.50–25.28 1986

100 metres freestyle

1915	1:16.2	Fanny Durack (Aus)	6 Feb 1915
1930	1:08.0★	Helene Madison (USA)	14 Mar 1930
1945	1:04.6★	Willy den Ouden (Hol)	27 Feb 1936
1960	1:00.2y	Dawn Fraser (Aus)	23 Feb 1960
1975	56.22	Kornelia Ender (GDR)	26 Jul 1975
1990	54.73	Kristin Otto (GDR)	19 Aug 1986
	54.48	Jenny Thompson (USA)	1 Mar 1992
	54.01	Le Jingyi (Chn)	5 Sep 1994

Most records: 11 Dawn Fraser (Aus) 1:04.5–58.9 1956-64; 10 Kornelia Ender (GDR) 58.25–55.65 1973-6

200 metres freestyle

1915	2:56.0y★	Fanny Durack (Aus)	4 Mar 1915
1930	2:34.6★	Helene Madison (USA)	6 Mar 1930
1945	2:21.7★	Ragnhild Hveger (Den)	11 Sep 1938
1960	2:11.6y	Dawn Fraser (Aus)	27 Feb 1960
1975	2:02.27	Kornelia Ender (GDR)	15 Mar 1975
1990	1:57.55	Heike Friedrich (GDR)	18 Jun 1986
	1:56.78	Franziska van Almsick (Ger)	6 Sep 1994

Most records: 4 Dawn Fraser (Aus) 2:20.7–2:11.6y 1956-60; Kornelia Ender (GDR) 2:03.22–1:59.26 1974-6

400 metres freestyle

1930	5:39.2★	Martha Norelius (USA)	27 Aug 1928
1945	5:00.1★	Ragnhild Hveger (Den)	15 Sep 1940
1960	4:44.5	Chris Von Saltza (USA)	5 Aug 1960
1975	4:14.76	Shirley Babashoff (USA)	20 Jun 1975
1990	4:03.85	Janet Evans (USA)	22 Sep 1988

Most records: 8 Ragnhild Hveger (Den) 5:14.2★–5:00.1★ 1937-40; 5 Debbie Meyer (USA) 4:32.6–4:24.3 1967-70; 4 Martha Norelius (USA) 5:51.4y–5:39.2★ 1927-8

800 metres freestyle

1930	11:41.2y★	Helene Madison (USA)	6 Jul 1930
1945	10:52.5	Ragnhild Hveger (Den)	13 Aug 1941
1960	9:55.6	Jane Cederqvist (Swe)	17 Aug 1960
1975	8:43.48	Jenny Turrall (Aus)	31 Mar 1975
1990	8:16.22	Janet Evans (USA)	20 Aug 1989

Most records: 5 Debbie Meyer (USA) 9:35.8–9:10.4 1967-8; 4 Ilsa Konrads (Aus) 10:17.7y–10:11.4y 1958-9; Petra Thümer (GDR) 8:40.68–8:35.04 1976-7

1500 metres freestyle

1930	23:44.6	Martha Norelius (USA)	28 Jul 1927
1945	20:57.0	Ragnhild Hveger (Den)	20 Aug 1941
1960	19:23.6	Jane Cederqvist (Swe)	8 Sep 1960
1975	16:33.94	Jenny Turrall (Aus)	25 Aug 1974
1990	15:52.10	Janet Evans (USA)	26 Mar 1988

Most records: 5 Jenny Turrall (Aus) 16:49.9–16:33.94 1973-4; 4 Debbie Meyer (USA) 18:11.1–17:19.9 1967-9

4 x 100 metres freestyle

1945	4:27.6	Denmark	7 Aug 1938
1960	4:08.9	USA	3 Sep 1960
1975	3:49.37	GDR	26 Jul 1975

1990	3:40.57	GDR	19 Aug 1986
	3:39.46	USA	28 Jul 1992
	3:37.91	China	7 Sep 1994

(Le Jingyi, Shan Ying, Le Ying, Lu Bin)

4 x 200 metres freestyle relay

1990	7:55.47	GDR	18 Aug 1987

(Manuela Stellmach, Astrid Strauss, Anke Möhring, Heike Friedrich)

100 metres backstroke

1930	1:20.6★	Bonnie Mealing (Aus)	27 Feb 1930
1945	1:10.9★	Cor Kint (Hol)	22 Sep 1939
1960	1:09.0	Lynn Burke (USA)	2 Sep 1960
1975	1:02.98	Ulrike Richter (GDR)	1 Sep 1974
1990	1:00.59	Ina Kleber (GDR)	24 Aug 1984
	1:00.31	Krisztina Egerszegi (Hun)	22 Aug 1991
	1:00.16	He Cihong (Chn)	10 Sep 1994

Most records: 9 Ulrike Richter (GDR) 1:05.39–1:01.51 1973-6; 4 Ria van Velsen (Hol) 1:12.3–1:10.9 1958-60, Lynn Burke (USA) 1:10.1–1:09.0 1960

200 metres backstroke

1930	2:58.2★	Eleanor Holm (USA)	1 Mar 1930
1945	2:38.8★	Cor Kint (Hol)	29 Nov 1939
1960	2:33.3	Satoko Tanaka (Jap)	23 Jul 1960
1975	2:15.46	Birgit Treiber (GDR)	25 Jul 1975
1990	2:08.60	Betsy Mitchell (USA)	27 Jun 1986
	2:06.62	Krisztina Egerszegi (Hun)	25 Aug 1991

Most records: 10 Satoko Tanaka (Jap) 2:37.1–2:28.2 1959-63; 4 Karen Muir (SAf) 2:27.1–2:23.8 1966-8

100 metres breaststroke

1930	1:26.3★	Lotte Mühe (Ger)	9 Jun 1928
1945	1:19.8★	Gisela Grass (Ger)	9 May 1943
1960	1:19.0	Ursula Küper (GDR)	14 Jul 1960
1975	1:12.28	Renate Vogel (GDR)	1 Sep 1974
1990	1:07.91	Silke Hörner (GDR)	21 Aug 1987
	1:07.69	Samantha Riley (Aus)	9 Sep 1994
	1:07.46	Penny Heyns (SAf)	4 Mar 1996
	1:07.02	Penny Heyns (SAf)	21 Jul 1996

Most records: 6 Ute Geweniger (GDR) 1:10.20–1:08.51 1980-3; 5 Catie Ball (USA) 1:15.6–1:14.2 1966-8

200 metres breaststroke

1930	3:11.2	Lotte Mühe (Ger)	15 Jul 1928
1945	2:56.0★	Maria Lenk (Bra)	8 Nov 1939
1960	2:49.5	Anita Lonsbrough (UK)	27 Aug 1960
1975	2:34.99	Karla Linke (GDR)	19 Aug 1974
1990	2:26.71	Silke Hörner (GDR)	21 Sep 1988
	2:25.92	Anita Nall (USA)	2 Mar 1992
	2:25.35	Anita Nall (USA)	2 Mar 1992
	2:24.76	Rebecca Brown (Aus)	16 Mar 1994

Most records: 4 Ada den Haan (Hol) 2:46.4★–2:51.3 1956-7, Galina Prozumenshikova (USSR) 2:47.7y–2:40.8 1964-6

100 metres butterfly

1960	1:09.1	Nancy Ramey (USA)	2 Sep 1959
1975	1:01.24	Kornelia Ender (GDR)	24 Jul 1975
1990	57.93	Mary T Meagher (USA)	16 Aug 1981

Most records: 6 Atie Voorbij (Hol) 1:13.7★–1:10.5 1955-7, Kornelia Ender (GDR) 1:03.05–1:00.13 1973-6

200 metres butterfly

1960	2:34.4	Marianne Heemskerk (Hol)	12 Jun 1960
1975	2:13.76	Rosemarie Kother (GDR)	8 Sep 1973
1990	2:05.96	Mary T Meagher (USA)	13 Aug 1981

Most records: 5 Rosemarie Kother (GDR) 2:15.45–2:11.22 1973-6, Mary T Meagher (USA) 2:09.77–2:05.96 1979-81; 4 Ada Kok (Hol) 2:25.8–2:21.0y 1965-7, Karen Moe (USA) 2:20.7–2:15.27 1970-2

200 metres individual medley

1975	2:18.83	Ulrike Tauber (GDR)	10 Jun 1975
1990	2:11.73	Ute Geweniger (GDR)	4 Jul 1981
	2:11.65	Li Lin (Chn)	30 Jul 1992
	(2:11.57	Lu Bin (Chn) *(drugs: disqualified)*	7 Oct 1994)
	2:09.72	Wu Yanyan (Chn)	17 Oct 1997

Most records: 6 Ulrike Tauber (GDR) 2:18.97–2:15.85 1974-7; 5 Claudia Kolb (USA) 2:27.8–2:23.5 1966-8

400 metres individual medley

1960	5:36.5	Donna de Varona (USA)	15 Jul 1960
1975	4:52.20	Ulrike Tauber (GDR)	7 Jun 1975
1990	4:36.10	Petra Schneider (GDR)	1 Aug 1982
	4:34.79	Chen Yan (Chn)	13 Oct 1997

Most records: 6 Donna de Varona (USA) 5:36.5–5:14.9 1960-4; 5 Claudia Kolb (USA) 5:11.7–5:04.7 1967-8; 4 Sylvia Ruuska (USSR) 5:46.6–5:40.2y 1958-9, Petra Schneider (GDR) 4:39.96–4:36.10 1980-2

4 x 100 metres medley relay

1960	4:41.1	USA	2 Sep 1960
1975	4:13.78	GDR	24 Aug 1974
1990	4:03.69	GDR	24 Aug 1984
	4:02.54	USA	30 Jul 1992
	4:01.67	China	10 Sep 1994
		(He Cihong, Dai Guohong, Liu Limin, Le Jingyi)	

Most world records at individual events

For currently recognized events

(fr = freestyle, ba = backstroke, br = breaststroke, bu = butterfly, im = individual medley)

Men

26	Mark Spitz (USA) 3 100fr, 4 200fr, 3 400fr, 7 100bu, 9 200bu 1967-72
17	Roland Matthes (GDR) 8 100ba, 9 200ba 1967-73
13	Vladimir Salnikov (USSR) 6 400fr, 4 800fr, 3 1500fr
12	John Konrads (Aus) 3 200fr, 4 400fr, 3 800fr 1958-60
12	Don Schollander (USA) 9 200fr, 3 400fr 1963-8
12	John Hencken (USA) 7 100br, 5 200br 1972-6
10	Arne Borg (Swe) 3 400fr, 2 800fr, 5 1500fr 1922-7
10	Gary Hall (USA) 1 200ba, 1 200bu, 3 200im, 5 400im 1968-72
10	Steve Holland (Aus) 6 800fr, 4 1500fr 1973-6
10	Michael Gross (FRG) 4 200fr, 1 400fr, 1 100bu, 4 200bu 1983-6

Women

23	Kornelia Ender (GDR) 10 100fr, 4 200fr, 1 100ba, 6 100bu, 2 200im 1973-6
15	Ragnhild Hveger (Den) 1 200fr, 8 400fr, 2 800fr, 3 1500fr, 1 200ba 1937-41
15	Dawn Fraser (Aus) 11 100fr, 4 200fr 1956-64
15	Debbie Meyer (USA) 1 200fr, 5 400fr, 5 800fr, 4 1500fr 1967-70
11	Claudia Kolb (USA) 5 200im, 5 400im, 1 100br 1964-8
11	Shane Gould (Aus) 2 100fr, 3 200fr, 2 400fr, 1 800fr, 2 1500fr, 1 200im 1971-2
11	Ulrike Richter (GDR) 9 100ba, 2 200ba 1973-6

Helene Madison (USA) 1930-2 and Shane Gould (Aus) 1971-2 set records at each freestyle distance: 100m, 200m, 400m, 800m and 1500m.

Including now-obsolete distances

Men: 32 Arne Borg (Swe) 1921-9
Women: 42 Ragnhild Hveger (Den) 1936-42

Olympic Games

Swimming has been held at every Olympic Games since the first, in 1896. Swimming and diving events on the current programme are listed, followed by discontinued events.

(OR denotes Olympic record.)

Men

50 metres freestyle

1988	Matt Biondi (USA) 22.14
1992	Aleksandr Popov (Rus) 21.90 OR
1996	Aleksandr Popov (Rus) 22.13

100 metres freestyle

1896	Alfréd Hajós (Hun) 1:22.2
1904	Zoltán von Halmay (Hun) 1:02.08 (100y)
1906	Charles Daniels (USA) 1:13.4
1908	Charles Daniels (USA) 1:05.6
1912	Duke Kahanamoku (USA) 1:03.4
1920	Duke Kahanamoku (USA) 1:01.4
1924	Johnny Weissmuller (USA) 59.0
1928	Johnny Weissmuller (USA) 58.6
1932	Yasuji Miyazaki (Jap) 58.2
1936	Ferenc Csik (Hun) 57.6
1948	Walter Ris (USA) 57.3
1952	Clarke Scholes (USA) 57.4
1956	Jon Henricks (Aus) 55.4
1960	John Devitt (Aus) 55.2
1964	Don Schollander (USA) 53.4
1968	Mike Wenden (Aus) 52.2
1972	Mark Spitz (USA) 51.22
1976	Jim Montgomery (USA) 49.99
1980	Jörg Woithe (GDR) 50.40
1984	Rowdy Gaines (USA) 49.80
1988	Matt Biondi (USA) 48.63 OR
1992	Aleksandr Popov (CIS/Rus) 49.02
1996	Aleksandr Popov (Rus) 48.74

200 metres freestyle

1900	Frederick Lane (Aus) 2:25.2
1904	Charles Daniels (USA) 2:44.2 (220y)
1968	Mike Wenden (Aus) 1:55.2
1972	Mark Spitz (USA) 1:52.78
1976	Bruce Furniss (USA) 1:50.29
1980	Sergey Koplyakov (USSR) 1:49.81
1984	Michael Gross (FRG) 1:47.44
1988	Duncan Armstrong (Aus) 1:47.25
1992	Yevgeniy Sadoviy (CIS/Rus) 1:46.70 OR
1996	Danyon Loader (NZ) 1:47.63

400 metres freestyle

1896	Paul Neumann (Aut) 8:12.6 (500m)
1904	Charles Daniels (USA) 6:16.2 (440y)
1906	Otto Scheff (Aut) 6:23.8
1908	Henry Taylor (UK) 5:36.8
1912	George Hodgson (Can) 5:24.4
1920	Norman Ross (USA) 5:26.8
1924	Johnny Weissmuller (USA) 5:04.2
1928	Alberto Zorilla (Arg) 5:01.6
1932	Buster Crabbe (USA) 4:48.4
1936	Jack Medica (USA) 4:44.5
1948	William Smith (USA) 4:41.0
1952	Jean Boiteux (Fra) 4:30.7
1956	Murray Rose (Aus) 4:27.3
1960	Murray Rose (Aus) 4:18.3
1964	Don Schollander (USA) 4:12.2
1968	Mike Burton (USA) 4:09.0
1972	Brad Cooper (Aus) 4:00.27
1976	Brian Goodell (USA) 3:51.93
1980	Vladimir Salnikov (USSR) 3:51.31
1984	George DiCarlo (USA) 3:51.23
1988	Uwe Dassler (GDR) 3:46.95
1992	Yevgeniy Sadoviy (CIS/Rus) 3:45.00
1996	Danyon Loader (NZ) 3:47.97

1500 metres freestyle

1896	Alfréd Hajós (Hun) 18:22.2 (1200m)
1900	John Jarvis (UK) 13:40.2 (1000m)
1904	Emil Rausch (Ger) 27:18.2 (1 mile)
1906	Henry Taylor (UK) 28:28.0
1908	Henry Taylor (UK) 22:48.4
1912	George Hodgson (Can) 22:00.0
1920	Norman Ross (USA) 22:23.2
1924	Andrew Charlton (Aus) 20:06.6
1928	Arne Borg (Swe) 19:51.8
1932	Kusuo Kitamura (Jap) 19:12.4
1936	Noboru Terada (Jap) 19:13.7
1948	James McLane (USA) 19:18.5
1952	Ford Konno (USA) 18:30.0
1956	Murray Rose (Aus) 17:58.9
1960	John Konrads (Aus) 17:19.6
1964	Bob Windle (Aus) 17:01.7
1968	Mike Burton (USA) 16:38.9
1972	Mike Burton (USA) 15:52.58
1976	Brian Goodell (USA) 15:02.40
1980	Vladimir Salnikov (USSR) 14:58.27
1984	Michael O'Brien (USA) 15:05.20
1988	Vladimir Salnikov (USSR) 15:00.40
1992	Kieren Perkins (Aus) 14:43.48 OR
1996	Kieren Perkins (Aus) 14:56.40

100 metres backstroke

1904	Walter Brack (Ger) 1:16.8 (100y)
1908	Arno Bieberstein (Ger) 1:24.6
1912	Harry Hebner (USA) 1:21.2
1920	Warren Kealoha (USA) 1:15.2
1924	Warren Kealoha (USA) 1:13.2
1928	George Kojac (USA) 1:08.2
1932	Masaji Kiyokawa (Jap) 1:08.6
1936	Adolf Kiefer (USA) 1:05.9
1948	Allen Stack (USA) 1:06.4
1952	Yoshinobu Oyakawa (USA) 1:05.4
1956	David Theile (Aus) 1:02.2
1960	David Theile (Aus) 1:01.9
1968	Roland Matthes (GDR) 58.7

1972	Roland Matthes (GDR) 56.58
1976	John Naber (USA) 55.49
1980	Bengt Baron (Swe) 56.53
1984	Rick Carey (USA) 55.79
1988	Daichi Suzuki (Jap) 55.05
1992	Mark Tewksbury (Can) 53.98 OR
1996	Jeff Rouse (USA) 54.10

200 metres backstroke

1900	Ernst Hoppenberg (Ger) 2:47.0
1964	Jed Graef (USA) 2:10.3
1968	Roland Matthes (GDR) 2:09.6
1972	Roland Matthes (GDR) 2.02.82
1976	John Naber (USA) 1:59.19
1980	Sándor Wladár (Hun) 2:01.93
1984	Rick Carey (USA) 2:00.23
1988	Igor Polyanskiy (USSR) 1:59.37
1992	Martin López-Zubero (Spa) 1:58.47 OR
1996	Brad Bridgewater (USA) 1:58.54

100 metres breaststroke

1968	Don McKenzie (USA) 1:07.7
1972	Nobutaka Taguchi (Jap) 1:04.94
1976	John Hencken (USA) 1:03.11
1980	Duncan Goodhew (UK) 1:03.34
1984	Steve Lundquist (USA) 1:01.65
1988	Adrian Moorhouse (UK) 1:02.04
1992	Nelson Diebel (USA) 1:01.50
1996	Frédéric Deburghgraeve (Bel) 1:00.65 (1:00.60 OR *in heat*)

200 metres breaststroke

1908	Frederick Holman (UK) 3:09.2
1912	Walter Bathe (Ger) 3:01.8
1920	Håken Malmroth (Swe) 3:04.4
1924	Robert Skelton (USA) 2:56.5
1928	Yoshiyuki Tsuruta (Jap) 2:48.8
1932	Yoshiyuki Tsuruta (Jap) 2:45.4
1936	Tetsuo Hamuro (Jap) 2.41.5
1948	Joseph Verdeur (USA) 2:39.3
1952	John Davies (Aus) 2:34.4
1956	Masaru Furukawa (Jap) 2:34.7
1960	William Mulliken (USA) 2:37.4
1964	Ian O'Brien (Aus) 2:27.8
1968	Felipe Munoz (Mex) 2:28.7
1972	John Hencken (USA) 2:21.55
1976	David Wilkie (UK) 2:15.11
1980	Robertas Zhulpa (USSR) 2:15.85
1984	Victor Davis (Can) 2:13.34
1988	József Szabó (Hun) 2:13.52
1992	Mike Barrowman (USA) 2:10.16 OR
1996	Norbert Rozsa (Hun) 2:12.57

100 metres butterfly

1968	Doug Russell (USA) 55.9
1972	Mark Spitz (USA) 54.27
1976	Matt Vogel (USA) 54.35
1980	Pär Arvidsson (Swe) 54.92
1984	Michael Gross (FRG) 53.08

1988	Anthony Nesty (Sur) 53.00
1992	Pablo Morales (USA) 53.32
1996	Denis Pankratov (Rus) 52.27 OR

200 metres butterfly

1956	William Yorzyk (USA) 2:19.3
1960	Mike Troy (USA) 2:12.8
1964	Kevin Berry (Aus) 2:06.6
1968	Carl Robie (USA) 2:08.7
1972	Mark Spitz (USA) 2:00.70
1976	Mike Bruner (USA) 1:59.23
1980	Sergey Fesenko (USSR) 1:59.76
1984	Jon Sieben (Aus) 1:57.04
1988	Michael Gross (FRG) 1:56.94
1992	Melvin Stewart (USA) 1:56.26 OR
1996	Denis Pankratov (Rus) 1:56.51

200 metres individual medley

1968	Charles Hickcox (USA) 2:12.0
1972	Gunnar Larsson (Swe) 2:07.17
1984	Alex Baumann (Can) 2:01.42
1988	Tamás Darnyi (Hun) 2:00.17
1992	Tamás Darnyi (Hun) 2:00.76
1996	Attila Czene (Hun) 1:59.91 OR

400 metres individual medley

1964	Richard Roth (USA) 4:45.4
1968	Charles Hickcox (USA) 4:48.4
1972	Gunnar Larsson (Swe) 4:31.98
1976	Rod Strachan (USA) 4:23.68
1980	Aleksandr Sidorenko (USSR) 4:22.89
1984	Alex Baumann (Can) 4:17.41
1988	Tamás Darnyi (Hun) 4:14.75
1992	Tamás Darnyi (Hun) 4:14.23 OR
1996	Tom Dolan (USA) 4:14.90

4 x 100 metres freestyle relay

1964	USA 3:33.2
1968	USA 3:31.7
1972	USA 3:26.42
1984	USA 3:19.03
1988	USA 3:16.53
1992	USA 3:16.74
1996	USA 3:15.41 OR

4 x 200 metres freestyle relay

1906	Hungary 16:52.4
1908	United Kingdom 10:55.6
1912	Australasia 10:11.6
1920	USA 10:04.4
1924	USA 9:53.4
1928	USA 9:36.2
1932	Japan 8:58.4
1936	Japan 8:51.5
1948	USA 8:46.0
1952	USA 8:31.1
1956	Australia 8:23.6
1960	USA 8:10.2
1964	USA 7:52.1

1968	USA 7:52.3
1972	USA 7:35.78
1976	USA 7:23.22
1980	USSR 7:23.50
1984	USA 7:15.69
1988	USA 7:12.51
1992	CIS 7:11.95 OR
1996	USA 7:14.84

4 x 100 metres medley relay

1960	USA 4:05.4
1964	USA 3:58.4
1968	USA 3:54.9
1972	USA 3:48.16
1976	USA 3:42.22
1980	Australia 3:45.70
1984	USA 3:39.30
1988	USA 3:36.93
1992	USA 3:36.93
1996	USA 3:34.84 OR

Springboard diving

1908	Albert Zürner (Ger)
1912	Paul Günther (Ger)
1920	Louis Kuehn (USA)
1924	Albert White (USA)
1928	Peter Desjardins (USA)
1932	Michael Galitzen (USA)
1936	Richard Degener (USA)
1948	Bruce Harlan (USA)
1952	David Browning (USA)
1956	Robert Clotworthy (USA)
1960	Gary Tobian (USA)
1964	Kenneth Sitzberger (USA)
1968	Bernard Wrightson (USA)
1972	Vladimir Vasin (USSR)
1976	Philip Boggs (USA)
1980	Aleksandr Portnov (USSR)
1984	Greg Louganis (USA)
1988	Greg Louganis (USA)
1992	Mark Lenzi (USA)
1996	Xiong Ni (Chn)

Highboard platform diving

1904	George Sheldon (USA)
1906	Gottlob Walz (Ger)
1908	Hjalmar Johansson (Swe)
1912	Erik Adlerz (Swe)
1920	Clarence Pinkston (USA)
1924	Albert White (USA)
1928	Peter Desjardins (USA)
1932	Harold Smith (USA)
1936	Marshall Wayne (USA)
1948	Samuel Lee (USA)
1952	Samuel Lee (USA)
1956	Joaquin Capilla (Mex)
1960	Robert Webster (USA)
1964	Robert Webster (USA)

1968	Klaus Dibiasi (Ita)
1972	Klaus Dibiasi (Ita)
1976	Klaus Dibiasi (Ita)
1980	Falk Hoffmann (GDR)
1984	Greg Louganis (USA)
1988	Greg Louganis (USA)
1992	Sun Shuwei (Chn)
1996	Dmitriy Sautin (Rus)

Women

50 metres freestyle

1988	Kristin Otto (GDR) 25.49
1992	Yang Wenyi (Chn) 24.79 OR
1996	Amy Van Dyken (USA) 24.87

100 metres freestyle

1912	Fanny Durack (Aus) 1:22.2
1920	Ethelda Bleibtrey (USA) 1:13.6
1924	Ethel Lackie (USA) 1:12.4
1928	Albina Osipowich (USA) 1:11.0
1932	Helene Madison (USA) 1:06.8
1936	Hendrika Mastenbroek (Hol) 1:05.9
1948	Greta Andersen (Den) 1:06.3
1952	Katalin Szöke (Hun) 1:06.8
1956	Dawn Fraser (Aus) 1:02.0
1960	Dawn Fraser (Aus) 1:01.2
1964	Dawn Fraser (Aus) 59.5
1968	Jan Henne (USA) 1:00.0
1972	Sandra Neilson (USA) 58.59
1976	Kornelia Ender (GDR) 55.65
1980	Barbara Krause (GDR) 54.79
1984	Nancy Hogshead (USA) & Carrie Steinseifer (USA) 55.92
1988	Kristin Otto (GDR) 54.93
1992	Zhuang Yong (Chn) 54.64
1996	Le Jingyi (Chn) 54.50

200 metres freestyle

1968	Debbie Meyer (USA) 2:10.5
1972	Shane Gould (Aus) 2:03.56
1976	Kornelia Ender (GDR) 1:59.26
1980	Barbara Krause (GDR) 1:58.33
1984	Mary Wayte (USA) 1:59.23
1988	Heike Friedrich (GDR) 1:57.65 OR
1992	Nicole Haislett (USA) 1:57.90
1996	Claudia Poll (CR) 1:58.16

400 metres freestyle

1920	Ethelda Bleibtrey (USA) 4:34.0 (300m)
1924	Martha Norelius (USA) 6:02.2
1928	Martha Norelius (USA) 5:42.8
1932	Helene Madison (USA) 5:28.5
1936	Hendrika Mastenbroek (Hol) 5:26.4
1948	Ann Curtis (USA) 5:17.8
1952	Valéria Gyenge (Hun) 5:12.1
1956	Lorraine Crapp (Aus) 4:54.6
1960	Chris Von Saltza (USA) 4:50.6
1964	Virginia Duenkel (USA) 4:43.3

1968	Debbie Meyer (USA) 4:31.8
1972	Shane Gould (Aus) 4:19.04
1976	Petra Thümer (GDR) 4:09.89
1980	Ines Diers (GDR) 4:08.76
1984	Tiffany Cohen (USA) 4:07.10
1988	Janet Evans (USA) 4:03.85 OR
1992	Dagmar Hase (Ger) 4:07.18
1996	Michelle Smith (Ire) 4:07.25

800 metres freestyle

1968	Debbie Meyer (USA) 9:24.0
1972	Keena Rothhammer (USA) 8:53.68
1976	Petra Thümer (GDR) 8:37.14
1980	Michelle Ford (Aus) 8:28.90
1984	Tiffany Cohen (USA) 8:24.95
1988	Janet Evans (USA) 8:20.20 OR
1992	Janet Evans (USA) 8:25.52
1996	Brooke Bennett (USA) 8:27.89

100 metres backstroke

1924	Sybil Bauer (USA) 1:23.2
1928	Maria Braun (Hol) 1:22.0
1932	Eleanor Holm (USA) 1:19.4
1936	Dina Senff (Hol) 1:18.9
1948	Karen Harup (Den) 1:14.4
1952	Joan Harrison (SAf) 1:14.3
1956	Judy Grinham (UK) 1:12.9
1960	Lynn Burke (USA) 1:09.3
1964	Cathy Ferguson (USA) 1:07.7
1968	Kaye Hall (USA) 1:06.2
1972	Melissa Belote (USA) 1:05.78
1976	Ulrike Richter (GDR) 1:01.83
1980	Rica Reinisch (GDR) 1:00.86
1984	Theresa Andrews (USA) 1:02.55
1988	Kristin Otto (GDR) 1:00.89
1992	Krisztina Egerszegi (Hun) 1:00.68 OR
1996	Beth Botsford (USA) 1:01.19

200 metres backstroke

1968	Pokey Watson (USA) 2:24.8
1972	Melissa Belote (USA) 2:19.19
1976	Ulrike Richter (GDR) 2:13.43
1980	Rica Reinisch (GDR) 2:11.77
1984	Jolanda de Rover (Hol) 2:12.38
1988	Krisztina Egerszegi (Hun) 2:09.29
1992	Krisztina Egerszegi (Hun) 2:07.06 OR
1996	Krisztina Egerszegi (Hun) 2:07.83

100 metres breaststroke

1968	Djurdjica Bjedov (Yug) 1:15.8
1972	Catherine Carr (USA) 1:13.58
1976	Hannelore Anke (GDR) 1:11.16
1980	Ute Geweniger (GDR) 1:10.22
1984	Petra van Staveren (Hol) 1:09.88
1988	Tania Dangalakova (Bul) 1:07.95 OR
1992	Yelena Rudkovskaya (CIS/Blr) 1:08.00
1996	Penny Heyns (SAf) 1:07.73 (1:07.02 OR *in heat*)

200 metres breaststroke

1924	Lucy Morton (UK) 3:33.2
1928	Hilde Schrader (Ger) 3:12.6
1932	Claire Dennis (Aus) 3:06.3
1936	Hideko Maehata (Jap) 3:03.6
1948	Petronella van Vliet (Hol) 2:57.2
1952	Eva Székely (Hun) 2:51.7
1956	Ursula Happe (FRG) 2:53.1
1960	Anita Lonsbrough (UK) 2:49.5
1964	Galina Prozumenshchikova (USSR) 2:46.4
1968	Sharon Wichman (USA) 2:44.4
1972	Beverley Whitfield (Aus) 2:41.71
1976	Marina Koshevaya (USSR) 2:33.35
1980	Lina Kachushite (USSR) 2:29.54
1984	Anne Ottenbrite (Can) 2:30.38
1988	Silke Hörner (GDR) 2:26.71
1992	Kyoko Iwasaki (Jap) 2:26.65
1996	Penny Heyns (SAf) 2:25.41 OR

100 metres butterfly

1956	Shelley Mann (USA) 1:11.0
1960	Carolyn Schuler (USA) 1:09.5
1964	Sharon Stouder (USA) 1:04.7
1968	Lynette McClements (Aus) 1:05.0
1972	Mayumi Aoki (Jap) 1:03.34
1976	Kornelia Ender (GDR) 1:00.13
1980	Caren Metschuck (GDR) 1:00.42
1984	Mary T Meagher (USA) 59.26
1988	Kristin Otto (GDR) 59.00
1992	Qian Hong (Chn) 58.62 OR
1996	Amy Van Dyken (USA) 59.13

200 metres butterfly

1968	Ada Kok (Hol) 2:24.7
1972	Karen Moe (USA) 2:15.57
1976	Andrea Pollack (GDR) 2:11.41
1980	Ines Geissler (GDR) 2:10.44
1984	Mary T Meagher (USA) 2:06.90 OR
1988	Kathleen Nord (GDR) 2:09.51
1992	Summer Sanders (USA) 2:08.67
1996	Susan O'Neill (Aus) 2:07.76

200 metres individual medley

1968	Claudia Kolb (USA) 2:24.7
1972	Sharon Gould (Aus) 2:23.07
1984	Tracy Caulkins (USA) 2:12.64
1988	Daniela Hunger (GDR) 2:12.59
1992	Lin Li (Chn) 2:11.65 OR
1996	Michelle Smith (Ire) 2:13.93

400 metres individual medley

1964	Donna De Varona (USA) 5:18.7
1968	Claudia Kolb (USA) 5:08.5
1972	Gail Neall (Aus) 5:02.97
1976	Ulrike Tauber (GDR) 4:42.77
1980	Petra Schneider (GDR) 4:36.29 OR
1984	Tracy Caulkins (USA) 4:39.24
1988	Janet Evans (USA) 4:37.76

| 1992 | Krisztina Egerszegi (Hun) 4:36.54 |
| 1996 | Michelle Smith (Ire) 4:39.18 |

4 x 100 metres freestyle medley

1912	United Kingdom 5:52.8
1920	USA 5:11.6
1924	USA 4:58.8
1928	USA 4:47.6
1932	USA 4:38.0
1936	Netherlands 4:36.0
1948	USA 4:29.2
1952	Hungary 4:24.4
1956	Australia 4:17.1
1960	USA 4:08.9
1964	USA 4:03.8
1968	USA 4:02.5
1972	USA 3:55.19
1976	USA 3:44.82
1980	GDR 3:42.71
1984	USA 3:43.43
1988	GDR 3:40.63
1992	USA 3:39.46
1996	USA 3:39.29 OR

4 x 200 metres freestyle medley

| 1996 | USA 7:59.87 OR |

4 x 100 metres medley relay

1960	USA 4:41.1
1964	USA 4:33.9
1968	USA 4:28.3
1972	USA 4:20.75
1976	GDR 4:07.95
1980	GDR 4:06.67
1984	USA 4:08.34
1988	GDR 4:03.74
1992	USA 4:02.54 OR
1996	USA 4:02.88

Springboard diving

1920	Aileen Riggin (USA)
1924	Elizabeth Becker (USA)
1928	Helen Meany (USA)
1932	Georgia Coleman (USA)
1936	Marjorie Gestring (USA)
1948	Victoria Draves (USA)
1952	Pat McCormick (USA)
1956	Pat McCormick (USA)
1960	Ingrid Krämer (GDR)
1964	Ingrid Engel (née Krämer) (GDR)
1968	Sue Gossick (USA)
1972	Micki King (USA)
1976	Jennifer Chandler (USA)
1980	Irina Kalinina (USSR)
1984	Sylvie Bernier (Can)
1988	Gao Min (Chn)
1992	Gao Min (Chn)
1996	Fu Mongxia (Chn)

Highboard platform diving

1912	Greta Johansson (Swe)
1920	Stefani Fryland-Clausen (Den)
1924	Caroline Smith (USA)
1928	Elizabeth Pinkston (USA)
1932	Dorothy Poynton (USA)
1936	Dorothy Hill (née Poynton) (USA)
1948	Victoria Draves (USA)
1952	Pat McCormick (USA)
1956	Pat McCormick (USA)
1960	Ingrid Krämer (GDR)
1964	Lesley Bush (USA)
1968	Milena Duchková (Cs)
1972	Ulrika Knape (Swe)
1976	Yelena Vaytsekhovskaya (USSR)
1980	Martina Jäschke (GDR)
1984	Zhou Jihong (Chn)
1988	Xu Yanmei (Chn)
1992	Fu Mingxia (Chn)
1996	Fu Mongxia (Chn)

Synchronized swimming – solo

1984	Tracie Ruiz (USA)
1988	Carolyn Waldo (Can)
1992	Sylvie Frechette (Can)★

★ Frechette was awarded the gold medal over a year later, after a judge had admitted to pressing the wrong scoring button. Her total then exceeded that of Kristen Babb-Sprague (USA), originally declared the winner, who was allowed to keep her gold medal.

Synchronized swimming – duet

1984	Candy Costie & Tracie Ruiz (USA)
1988	Michelle Cameron & Carolyn Waldo (Can)
1992	Karen & Sarah Josephson (USA)

Synchronized swimming – team

| 1996 | USA |

Discontinued events (men)

50 yards freestyle

| 1904 | Zoltán Halmay (Hun) 28.0 |

100 metres freestyle for sailors

| 1896 | Ioannis Maiokinis (Gre) 2:20.4 |

200 metres obstacle event

| 1900 | Frederick Lane (Aus) 2:38.4 |

440 yards breaststroke

| 1904 | Georg Zacharias (Ger) 7:23.6 |

400 metres breaststroke

| 1912 | Walter Bathe (Ger) 6:29.6 |
| 1920 | Håkan Malmroth (Swe) 6:31.8 |

880 yards freestyle

| 1904 | Emil Rausch (Ger) 13:11.4 |

4000 metres freestyle

| 1900 | John Jarvis (UK) 58:24.0 |

Underwater swimming

1900   Charles de Vendeville (Fra)

Plunge for distance

1904   Paul Dickey (USA) 19.05m

200 metres team swimming

1900   Germany

4 x 50 yards relay

1904   New York AC (USA)

Plain high diving

1912   Erik Adlerz (Swe)
1920   Arvid Wallman (Swe)
1924   Richmond Eve (USA)

Most Olympic gold medals

(Individual/relay)

Men

9 (4/5)   Mark Spitz (USA) 1968-72
8 (3/5)   Matt Biondi (USA) 1984-92
5 (4/1)   Charles Daniels (USA) 1904-08
5 (3/2)   Johnny Weissmuller (USA) 1924-8
5 (2/3)   Don Schollander (USA) 1964-8
4 (4/-)   Roland Matthes (GDR) 1968-72
4 (3/1)   Henry Taylor (UK) 1906-08
4 (3/1)   Murray Rose (Aus) 1956-60
4 (2/2)   John Naber (USA) 1976
4 (3/1)   Vladimir Salnikov (USSR) 1980-8
4 (4/-)   Greg Louganis (USA) 1984-8
4 (4/-)   Aleksandr Popov (Rus) 1992-6

Spitz won a record seven gold medals at one Games, in 1972.

Women

6 (4/2)   Kristin Otto (GDR) 1988
5 (5/-)   Krisztina Egerszegi (Hun) 1988-96
4 (4/-)   Pat McCormick (USA) 1952-6
4 (3/1)   Dawn Fraser (Aus) 1956-64
4 (3/1)   Kornelia Ender (GDR) 1976

Most Olympic medals

(Gold/silver/bronze)

Men

11 (9/1/1)   Mark Spitz (USA) 1968-72
11 (8/2/1)   Matt Biondi (USA) 1984-92
8 (5/1/2)   Charles Daniels (USA) 1904-08
8 (4/2/2)   Roland Matthes (GDR) 1968-72
8 (4/1/3)   Henry Taylor (UK) 1906-20

Women

8 (4/4/-)   Dawn Fraser (Aut) 1956-64
8 (4/4/-)   Kornelia Ender (GDR) 1972-6
8 (2/6/-)   Shirley Babashoff (USA) 1972-6

Youngest gold medallist

Men: 14yr 309d Kusuo Kitamura (Jap) 1500m freestyle 1932
Women: 13yr 268d Marjorie Gestring (USA) springboard diving 1936

Oldest gold medallist

Men: 34yr 186d Hjalmar Johansson (Swe) highboard diving 1908
Women: 30yr 41d Ursula Happe (FRG) 200m breaststroke 1956

Youngest medallist

Men: 14yr 10d Nils Skoglund (Swe) 2nd highboard diving 1928
Women: 12yr 24d Inge Sørensen (Den) 3rd 200m breaststroke 1936

World Championships

World Championships separate from the Olympic Games were held every four years from 1973, going biennial from 1998. Venues have been: 1973 Belgrade; 1975 Cali, Colombia; 1978 West Berlin; 1982 Guayaquil, Ecuador; 1986 Madrid; 1991 (January) Perth, Australia; 1994 Rome; 1998 Perth. Long-distance events, over 25 kilometres, were introduced in 1991.

Champions:

Men

50 metres freestyle

1986   Tom Jager (USA) 22.49
1991   Tom Jager (USA) 22.16
1994   Aleksandr Popov (Rus) 22.17
1998   Bill Pilczuk (USA) 22.29

100 metres freestyle

1973   Jim Montgomery (USA) 51.70
1975   Andrew Coan (USA) 51.25
1978   David McCagg (USA) 50.24
1982   Jörg Woithe (GDR) 50.18
1986   Matt Biondi (USA) 48.94
1991   Matt Biondi (USA) 49.18
1994   Aleksandr Popov (Rus) 49.12
1998   Aleksandr Popov (Rus) 48.93

200 metres freestyle

1973   Jim Montgomery (USA) 1:53.02
1975   Tim Shaw (USA) 1:51.04
1978   William Forrester (USA) 1:51.02
1982   Michael Gross (FRG) 1:49.84
1986   Michael Gross (FRG) 1:47.92
1991   Giorgio Lamberti (Ita) 1:47.27
1994   Antti Kasvio (Fin) 1:47.32
1998   Michael Klim (Aus) 1:47.41

400 metres freestyle

1973   Rick DeMont (USA) 3:58.18
1975   Tim Shaw (USA) 3:54.88
1978   Vladimir Salnikov (USSR) 3:51.94
1982   Vladimir Salnikov (USSR) 3:51.30
1986   Rainer Henkel (FRG) 3:50.05
1991   Jörg Hoffmann (Ger) 3:48.04
1994   Kieren Perkins (Aus) 3:43.80
1998   Ian Thorpe (Aus) 3:46.29

1500 metres freestyle

1973	Steve Holland (Aus) 15:31.85
1975	Tim Shaw (USA) 15:28.92
1978	Vladimir Salnikov (USSR) 15:03.99
1982	Vladimir Salnikov (USSR) 15:01.77
1986	Rainer Henkel (FRG) 15:05.31
1991	Jörg Hoffmann (Ger) 14:50.36
1994	Kieren Perkins (Aus) 14:50.52
1998	Grant Hackett (Aus) 14:51.70

4 x 100 metres freestyle

1973	USA 3:27.18
1975	USA 3:24.85
1978	USA 3:19.74
1982	USA 3:19.26
1986	USA 3:19.89
1991	USA 3:17.15
1994	USA 3:16.90
1998	USA 3:16.69

4 x 200 metres freestyle relay

1973	USA 7:33.22
1975	F R Germany 7:39.44
1978	USA 7:20.82
1982	USA 7:21.09
1986	GDR 7:15.91
1991	Germany 7:13.50
1994	Sweden 7:17.70
1998	Australia 7:12.48

100 metres backstroke

1973	Roland Matthes (GDR) 57.47
1975	Roland Matthes (GDR) 58.15
1978	Robert Jackson (USA) 56.36
1982	Dirk Richter (GDR) 55.95
1986	Igor Polyanski (USSR) 55.58
1991	Jeff Rouse (USA) 55.23
1994	Martin López Zubero (Spa) 55.17
1998	Lenny Krayzelburg (USA) 55.00

200 metres backstroke

1973	Roland Matthes (GDR) 2:01.87
1975	Zoltán Verraszto (Hun) 2:05.05
1978	Jesse Vassallo (USA) 2:02.16
1982	Rick Carey (USA) 2:00.82
1986	Igor Polyanski (USSR) 1:58.78
1991	Martin López Zubero (Spa) 1:59.52
1994	Vladimir Selkov (Rus) 1:57.42
1998	Lenny Krayzelburg (USA) 1:58.84

100 metres breaststroke

1973	John Hencken (USA) 1:04.02
1975	David Wilkie (UK) 1:04.26
1978	Walter Kusch (FRG) 1:03.56
1982	Steve Lundquist (USA) 1:02.75
1986	Victor Davis (Can) 1:02.71
1991	Norbert Rózsa (Hun) 1:01.45
1994	Norbert Rózsa (Hun) 1:01.24
1998	Frédéric Deburghgraeve (Bel) 1:01.34

200 metres breaststroke

1973	David Wilkie (UK) 2:19.28
1975	David Wilkie (UK) 2:18.23
1978	Nick Nevid (USA) 2:18.37
1982	Victor Davis (Can) 2:14.77
1986	József Szabó (Hun) 2:14.27
1991	Mike Barrowman (USA) 2:11.23
1994	Norbert Rózsa (Hun) 2:12.81
1998	Kurt Grote (USA) 2:13.40

100 metres butterfly

1973	Bruce Robertson (Can) 55.69
1975	Greg Jagenburg (USA) 55.63
1978	Joe Bottom (USA) 54.30
1982	Matt Gribble (USA) 53.88
1986	Pablo Morales (USA) 53.54
1991	Anthony Nesty (Sur) 53.29
1994	Rafal Szukala (Pol) 53.51
1998	Michael Klim (Aus) 52.25

200 metres butterfly

1973	Robin Backhaus (USA) 2:03.32
1975	William Forrester (USA) 2:01.95
1978	Michael Bruner (USA) 1:59.38
1982	Michael Gross (FRG) 1:58.85
1986	Michael Gross (FRG) 1:56.53
1991	Melvin Stewart (USA) 1:55.69
1994	Denis Pankratov (Rus) 1:56.54
1998	Denys Sylantyev (Ukr) 1:56.61

200 metres individual medley

1973	Gunnar Larsson (Swe) 2:08.36
1975	András Hargitay (Hun) 2:07.72
1978	Graham Smith (Can) 2:03.65
1982	Aleksey Sidorenko (USSR) 2:03.30
1986	Tamás Darnyi (Hun) 2:01.57
1991	Tamás Darnyi (Hun) 1:59.36
1994	Jani Sievinen (Fin) 1:58.16
1998	Marcel Wouda (Hol) 2:01.18

400 metres individual medley

1973	András Hargitay (Hun) 4:31.11
1975	András Hargitay (Hun) 4:32.57
1978	Jesse Vassallo (USA) 4:20.05
1982	Ricardo Prado (Bra) 4:19.78
1986	Tamás Darnyi (Hun) 4:18.98
1991	Tamás Darnyi (Hun) 4:12.36
1994	Tom Dolan (USA) 4:12.30
1994	Tom Dolan (USA) 4:14.95

4 x 100 metres medley relay

1973	USA 3:49.49
1975	USA 3:49.00
1978	USA 3:44.63
1982	USA 3:40.84
1986	USA 3:41.25
1991	USA 3:39.66
1994	USA 3:37.74
1998	Australia 3:37.98

5 kilometres river/sea swim

1998   Aleksey Akatiyev (Rus) 55:18.6

25 kilometres river/sea swim

1991   Chad Hundeby (USA) 5:01:45.78
1994   Greg Steppel (Can) 5:35:25.56
1998   Aleksey Akatiyev (Rus) 5:05:42.1

1 metre springboard diving

1991   Edwin Jongejans (Hol)
1994   Evan Stewart (Zim)
1998   Yu Zhuochng (Chn)

Springboard diving (3 metres from 1991)

1973   Phil Boggs (USA)
1975   Phil Boggs (USA)
1978   Phil Boggs (USA)
1982   Greg Louganis (USA)
1986   Greg Louganis (USA)
1991   Kent Ferguson (USA)
1994   Yu Zhuocheng (Chn)
1998   Dmitriy Sautin (Rus)

Highboard platform diving

1973   Klaus Dibiasi (Ita)
1975   Klaus Dibiasi (Ita)
1978   Greg Louganis (USA)
1982   Greg Louganis (USA)
1986   Greg Louganis (USA)
1991   Sun Shuwei (Chn)
1994   Dmitriy Sautin (Rus)
1998   Dmitriy Sautin (Rus)

Women

50 metres freestyle

1986   Tamara Costache (Rom) 25.28
1991   Zuang Yong (Chn) 25.47
1994   Le Jingyi (Chn) 24.51
1998   Amy Van Dyken (USA) 25.15

100 metres freestyle

1973   Kornelia Ender (GDR) 57.54
1975   Kornelia Ender (GDR) 56.50
1978   Barbara Krause (GDR) 55.68
1982   Birgit Meineke (GDR) 55.79
1986   Kristin Otto (GDR) 55.05
1991   Nicole Haislett (USA) 55.17
1994   Le Jingyi (Chn) 54.01
1998   Jenny Thompson (USA) 54.95

200 metres freestyle

1973   Keena Rothhammer (USA) 2:04.99
1975   Shirley Babashoff (USA) 2:02.50
1978   Cynthia Woodhead (USA) 1:58.53
1982   Annemarie Verstappen (Hol) 1:59.53
1986   Heike Friedrich (GDR) 1:58.26
1991   Hayley Lewis (Aus) 2:00.48
1994   Franziska van Almsick (Ger) 1:56.78
1998   Claudia Poll (CR) 1:58.90

400 metres freestyle

1973   Heather Greenwood (USA) 4:20.28
1975   Shirley Babashoff (USA) 4:16.87
1978   Tracey Wickham (Aus) 4:06.28
1982   Carmela Schmidt (GDR) 4:08.98
1986   Heike Friedrich (GDR) 4:07.45
1991   Janet Evans (USA) 4:08.63
1994   Yang Aihua (Chn) 4:09.64
1998   Chen Yan (Chn) 4:06.72

800 metres freestyle

1973   Novella Calligaris (Ita) 8:52.97
1975   Jenny Turrall (Aus) 8:44.75
1978   Tracey Wickham (Aus) 8:24.94
1982   Kim Lineham (USA) 8:27.48
1986   Astrid Strauss (GDR) 8:28.24
1991   Janet Evans (USA) 8:24.05
1994   Janet Evans (USA) 8:29.85
1998   Brooke Bennett (USA) 8:28.71

4 x 100 metres freestyle

1973   GDR 3:52.45
1975   GDR 3:49.37
1978   USA 3:43.43
1982   GDR 3:43.97
1986   GDR 3:40.57
1991   USA 3:43.26
1994   China 3:37.91
1998   USA 3:42.11

4 x 200 metres freestyle relay

1986   GDR 7:59.33
1991   Germany 8:02.56
1994   China 7:57.96
1998   Germany 8:01.46

100 metres backstroke

1973   Ulrike Richter (GDR) 1:05.42
1975   Ulrike Richter (GDR) 1:03.30
1978   Linda Jezek (USA) 1:02.55
1982   Kristin Otto (GDR) 1:01.30
1986   Betsy Mitchell (USA) 1:01.74
1991   Krisztina Egerszegi (Hun) 1:01.78
1994   He Cihong (Chn) 1:00.57
1998   Lea Maurer (USA) 1:01.16

200 metres backstroke

1973   Melissa Belote (USA) 2:20.52
1975   Birgit Treiber (GDR) 2:15.46
1978   Linda Jezek (USA) 2:11.93
1982   Cornelia Sirch (GDR) 2:09.91
1986   Cornelia Sirch (GDR) 2:11.37
1991   Krisztina Egerszegi (Hun) 2:09.15
1994   He Cihong (Chn) 2:07.40
1998   Rosanna Maracineanu (Fra) 2:11.26

100 metres breaststroke

1973   Renate Vogel (GDR) 1:13.74
1975   Hannelore Anke (GDR) 1:12.72

1978	Yulia Bogdanova (USSR) 1:10.31
1982	Ute Geweniger (GDR) 1:09.14
1986	Sylvia Gerasch (GDR) 1:08.11
1991	Linley Frame (Aus) 1:08.81
1994	Samantha Riley (Aus) 1:07.69
1998	Kristy Kowal (USA) 1:08.42

200 metres breaststroke

1973	Renate Vogel (GDR) 2:40.01
1975	Hannelore Anke (GDR) 2:37.25
1978	Lina Kachushite (USSR) 2:31.42
1982	Svetlana Varganova (USSR) 2:28.82
1986	Silke Horner (GDR) 2:27.40
1991	Yelena Volkova (USSR) 2:29,53
1994	Samantha Riley (Aus) 2:26.87
1998	Agnés Kovács (Hun) 2:25.45

100 metres butterfly

1973	Kornelia Ender (GDR) 1:02.53
1975	Kornelia Ender (GDR) 1:01.24
1978	Mary-Joan Pennington (USA) 1:00.20
1982	Mary T Meagher (USA) 59.41
1986	Kornelia Gressler (GDR) 59.51
1991	Qian Hong (Chn) 59.68
1994	Liu Limin (Chn) 58.98
1998	Jenny Thompson (USA) 58.46

200 metres butterfly

1973	Rosemarie Kother (GDR) 2:13.76
1975	Rosemarie Kother (GDR) 2:13.82
1978	Tracy Caulkins (USA) 2:09.87
1982	Ines Geissler (GDR) 2:08.66
1986	Mary T Meagher (USA) 2:08.41
1991	Summer Sanders (USA) 2:09.24
1994	Liu Limin (Chn) 2:07.25
1998	Susie O'Neill (Aus) 2:07.93

200 metres individual medley

1973	Angela Hübner (GDR) 2:20.51
1975	Kathy Heddy (USA) 2:19.80
1978	Tracy Caulkins (USA) 2:14.07
1982	Petra Schneider (GDR) 2:11.79
1986	Kristin Otto (GDR) 2:15.56
1991	Lin Li (Chn) 2:13.40
1994	Lu Bin (Chn) 2:12.34
1998	Wu Yanyan (Chn) 2:10.88

400 metres individual medley

1973	Gudrun Wegner (GDR) 4:57.31
1975	Ulrike Tauber (GDR) 4:52.76
1978	Tracy Caulkins (USA) 4:40.83
1982	Petra Schneider (GDR) 4:36.10
1986	Kathleen Nord (GDR) 4:43.75
1991	Lin Li (Chn) 4:41.45
1994	Dai Guohong (Chn) 4:39.14
1998	Chen Yan (Chn) 4:36.66

4 x 100 metres medley relay

1973	GDR 4:16.84
1975	GDR 4:14.74
1978	USA 4:08.21
1982	GDR 4:05.88
1986	GDR 4:04.82
1991	USA 4:06.51
1994	China 4:01.67
1998	USA 4:01.93

5 kilometres river/sea swim

1998	Erica Rose (USA) 59:23.5

25 kilometres river/sea swim

1991	Shelley Taylor-Smith (Aus) 5:21:05.53
1994	Melissa Cunningham (Aus) 5:48:25.04
1998	Tobie Smith (USA) 5:31:20

1 metre springboard diving

1991	Gao Min (Chn)
1994	Chen Lixia (Chn)
1998	Irina Lashko (Rus)

Springboard diving (3 metres from 1991)

1973	Christine Kohler (GDR)
1975	Irina Kalinina (USSR)
1978	Irina Kalinina (USSR)
1982	Megan Neyer (USA)
1986	Gao Min (Chn)
1991	Gao Min (Chn)
1994	Tan Shuping (Chn)
1998	Yuliya Pakhalina (Rus)

Highboard platform diving

1973	Ulrike Knape (Swe)
1975	Janet Ely (USA)
1978	Irina Kalinina (USSR)
1982	Wendy Wyland (USA)
1986	Lin Chen (Chn)
1991	Fu Mingxia (Chn)
1994	Fu Mingxia (Chn)
1994	Fu Mingxia (Chn)
1998	Olena Zhupyna (Ukr)

Synchronized 3 metres springboard diving

1998	Irina Lashko & Yuliya Pakhalina (Rus)

Synchronized platform diving

1998	Olena Zhupyna & Svilana Serbina (Ukr)

Synchronized swimming – solo

1973	Teresa Andersen (USA)
1975	Gail Buzonas (USA)
1978	Helen Vanderburg (Can)
1982	Tracie Ruiz (USA)
1986	Carolyn Waldo (Can)
1991	Sylvie Frechette (Can)
1994	Becky Dyroen Lancer (USA)
1998	Olga Sedakova (Rus)

Synchronized swimming – duet

1973	Teresa Andersen & Gail Johnson (USA)
1975	Robin Curren & Amanda Norrish (USA)
1978	Michele Calkins & Helen Vanderburg (Can)
1982	Kelly Kryczka & Sharon Hambrook (Can)
1986	Carolyn Waldo & Michelle Cameron (Can)
1991	Karen & Sarah Josephson (USA)
1994	Becky Dyroen Lancer & Jill Sudduth (USA)
1998	Olga Sedakova & Olga Brusnikova (Rus)

Synchronized swimming – team

1973	USA
1975	USA
1978	USA
1982	Canada
1986	Canada
1991	USA
1994	USA
1998	Russia

Most gold medals

(Individual/relay)

Men

6	(2/4)	Jim Montgomery (USA) 1973-5
5	(5/0)	Greg Louganis (USA) 1978-86
5	(4/1)	Michael Gross (FRG) 1982-90
5	(0/5)	Rowdy Gaines (USA) 1978-82

Women

8	(4/4)	Kornelia Ender (GDR) 1973-5
7	(3/4)	Kristin Otto (GDR) 1982-6

Most medals

(Gold/silver/bronze)

Men

13	(5/5/3)	Michael Gross (FRG) 1982-90
11	(5/3/3)	Matt Biondi (USA) 1986-90
8	(5/3/0)	Rowdy Gaines (USA) 1978-82
7	(4/2/1)	Michael Klim (Aus) 1998

Women

10	(8/2/0)	Kornelia Ender (GDR) 1973-5
9	(7/2/0)	Kristin Otto (GDR) 1982-6
9	(2/5/2)	Mary T Meagher (USA) 1982-6

Most medals at one Championships

(Gold/silver/bronze)

Men

7	(3/1/3)	Matt Biondi (USA) 1986

Women

6	(5/1/0)	Tracy Caulkins (USA) 1978
6	(4/2/0)	Kristin Otto (GDR) 1986
6	(1/3/2)	Mary T Meagher (USA) 1986

World Cup

Held as a team competition in 1979 only, when the USA won both men's and women's events. Now contested at individual events at a series of short-course meetings.

World Cup – Diving

First held in 1979, a biennial team competition.
Winners:

China	1981, 1983, 1985, 1989, 1991, 1997
USA	1987

European Championships

First held in Budapest in 1926, and subsequently in 1927, 1931, 1934, 1938, 1947, at four-yearly intervals 1950-74, in 1977 and biennially from 1981.
Winners since 1983 and swimmers to have won a particular event twice:

Men

50 metres freestyle

1987	Jörg Woithe (GDR) 22.66
1989	Vladimir Tkachenko (USSR) 22.64
1991	Nils Rudolph (Ger) 22.73
1993	Aleksandr Popov (Rus) 22.27
1995	Aleksandr Popov (Rus) 22.25
1997	Aleksandr Popov (Rus) 22.30

100 metres freestyle

1983	Per Johansson (Swe) 50.20
1985	Stéphane Caron (Fra) 50.20
1987	Sven Lodziewski (GDR) 49.79
1989	Giorgio Lamberti (Ita) 49.24
1991	Aleksandr Popov (USSR) 49.18
1993	Aleksandr Popov (Rus) 49.15
1995	Aleksandr Popov (Rus) 49.10
1997	Aleksandr Popov (Rus) 49.09

Most wins: 4 Popov; 2 Istvan Barany (Hun) 1926, 1931, Alex Jany (Fra) 1947, 1950, Peter Nocke (FRG) 1974, 1977, Per Johansson (Swe) 1981, 1983

200 metres freestyle

1983	Michael Gross (FRG) 1:47.87
1985	Michael Gross (FRG) 1:47.95
1987	Anders Holmertz (Swe) 1:48.44
1989	Giorgio Lamberti (Ita) 1:46.69
1991	Artur Wojdat (Pol) 1:48.10
1993	Antti Kasvio (Fin) 1:47.11
1995	Jani Sievinen (Fin) 1:48.98
1997	Paul Palmer (UK) 1:48.85

Most wins: 2 Peter Nocke (FRG) 1974, 1977, Gross

400 metres freestyle

1983	Vladimir Salnikov (USSR) 3:49.80
1985	Uwe Dassler (GDR) 3:51.52
1987	Uwe Dassler (GDR) 3:48.95
1989	Artur Wojdat (Pol) 3:47.78
1991	Yevgeniy Sadovyi (USSR) 3:49.02
1993	Antti Kasvio (Fin) 3:47.81
1995	Steffen Zessner (Ger) 3:50.35
1997	Emiliano Brembilla (Ita) 3:45.96

Most wins: 2 Arne Borg (Swe) 1926-7, Alex Jany (Fra) 1947, 1950, Dassler

1500 metres freestyle

1983	Vladimir Salnikov (USSR)	15:08.84
1985	Uwe Dassler (GDR)	15:08.56
1987	Rainer Henkel (FRG)	15:02.23
1989	Jörg Hoffmann (GDR)	15:01.52
1991	Jörg Hoffmann (Ger)	15:02.57
1993	Jörg Hoffmann (Ger)	15:13.31
1995	Jörg Hoffmann (Ger)	15:11.25
1997	Emiliano Brembilla (Ita)	14:58.65

Most wins: 4 Hoffmann; 3 Vladimir Salnikov (USSR) 1977, 1981, 1983; 2 Arne Borg (Swe) 1926-7

4 x 100 metres freestyle relay

1983	USSR 3:20.88
1985	FRG 3:22.18
1987	GDR 3:19.17
1989	FRG 3:19.68
1991	USSR 3:17.11
1993	Russia 3:18.80
1995	Russia 3:18.84
1997	Russia 3:16.85

4 x 200 metres freestyle relay

1983	FRG 7:20.40
1985	FRG 7:19.23
1987	FRG 7:13.10
1989	Italy 7:15.39
1991	USSR 7:15.96
1993	Russia 7:15.84
1995	Germany 7:18.22
1997	UK 7:17.56

100 metres backstroke

1983	Dirk Richter (GDR)	56.10
1985	Igor Polyanskiy (USSR)	55.24
1987	Sergey Zabolotnov (USSR)	56.06
1989	Martin López-Zubero (Spa)	56.44
1991	Martin López-Zubero (Spa)	55.30
1993	Martin López-Zubero (Spa)	55.03
1995	Vladimir Selkov (Rus)	55.48
1997	Martin López-Zubero (Spa)	55.71

Most wins: 4 López-Zubero; 2 Roland Matthes (GDR) 1970, 1974

200 metres backstroke

1983	Sergey Zabolotnov (USSR)	2:01.00
1985	Igor Polyanskiy (USSR)	1:58.50
1987	Sergey Zabolotnov (USSR)	1:59.35
1989	Stefano Battistelli (Ita)	1:59.96
1991	Martin López-Zubero (Spa)	1:58.66
1993	Vladimir Selkov (Rus)	1:58.09
1995	Vladimir Selkov (Rus)	1:58.48
1997	Vladimir Selkov (Rus)	1:59.21

Most wins: 3 Selkov; 2 Roland Matthes (GDR) 1970, 1974, Zabolotnov

100 metres breaststroke

1983	Robertas Zhulpa (USSR)	1:03.32
1985	Adrian Moorhouse (UK)	1:02.99
1987	Adrian Moorhouse (UK)	1:02.13
1989	Adrian Moorhouse (UK)	1:01.71 (1:01.49 ht)
1991	Norbert Rózsa (Hun)	1:01.49 (1:01.29 ht)
1993	Karoly Guttler (Hun)	1:01.04 (1:00.95 ht)
1995	Frédéric Deburghgraeve (Bel)	1:01.12
1997	Aleksandr Gukov (Rus)	1:02.17

Most wins: 3 Moorhouse; 2 Nikolay Pankin (USSR) 1970, 1974

200 metres breaststroke

1983	Adrian Moorhouse (UK)	2:17.49
1985	Dmitriy Volkov (USSR)	2:19.53
1987	József Szabó (Hun)	2:13.87
1989	Nick Gillingham (UK)	2:12.90
1991	Nick Gillingham (UK)	2:12.55
1993	Nick Gillingham (UK)	2:12.49
1995	Andrey Korneyev (Rus)	2:12.62
1997	Aleksandr Gukov (Rus)	2:13.90

Most wins: 3 Gillingham; 2 Erich Rademacher (Ger) 1926-7, Georgiy Prokopenko (USSR) 1962, 1966

100 metres butterfly

1983	Michael Gross (FRG)	54.00
1985	Michael Gross (FRG)	54.02
1987	Andrew Jameson (UK)	53.62
1989	Rafal Szukala (Pol)	54.47
1991	Vladislav Kulikov (USSR)	54.22
1993	Rafal Szukala (Pol)	53.41
1995	Denis Pankratov (Rus)	52.32
1997	Lars Frölander (Swe)	52.85

Most wins: 2 Roger Pyttel (GDR) 1974, 1977, Gross

200 metres butterfly

1983	Michael Gross (FRG)	1:57.05
1985	Michael Gross (FRG)	1:56.65
1987	Michael Gross (FRG)	1:57.59
1989	Tamás Darnyi (Hun)	1:58.87
1991	Franck Esposito (Fra)	1:59.59
1993	Denis Pankratov (Rus)	1:56.25
1995	Denis Pankratov (Rus)	1:56.34
1997	Franck Esposito (Fra)	1:57.24

Most wins: 4 Gross 1981 and as above; 2 Valentin Kuzmin (USSR) 1962, 1966, Pankratov, Esposito

200 metres individual medley

1983	Giovanni Franceshi (Ita)	2:02.48
1985	Tamás Darnyi (Hun)	2:03.23
1987	Tamás Darnyi (Hun)	2:00.56
1989	Tamás Darnyi (Hun)	2:01.03
1991	Lars Sørensen (Den)	2:02.63
1993	Jani Sievinen (Fin)	1:59.50
1995	Jani Sievinen (Fin)	1:58.61
1997	Marcel Wouda (Hol)	2:00.77

Most wins: 3 Darnyi; 2 Sievinen

400 metres individual medley

1983	Giovanni Franceshi (Ita)	4:20.41
1985	Tamás Darnyi (Hun)	4:20.70
1987	Tamás Darnyi (Hun)	4:15.42

1989	Tamás Darnyi (Hun) 4:15.25
1991	Luca Sacchi (Ita) 4:17.81
1993	Tamás Darnyi (Hun) 4:15.24
1995	Jani Sievinen (Fin) 4:14.75
1997	Marcel Wouda (Hol) 4:15.38

Most wins: 4 Darnyi; 2 Sergey Fesenko (USSR) 1977, 1981

4 x 100 metres medley relay

1983	USSR 3:43.99
1985	FRG 3:43.59
1987	USSR 3:41.51
1989	USSR 3:41.44
1991	USSR 3:40.68
1993	. Russia 3:38.90
1995	Russia 3:38.11
1997	Russia 3:39.67

5 kilometres long distance

| 1995 | Aleksey Akatiyev (Rus) 55:00.30 |
| 1995 | Aleksey Akatiyev (Rus) 56:07 |

25 kilometres long distance

| 1995 | Christof Wandrotsch (Ger) 5:11:36.30 |
| 1997 | Aleksey Akatiyev (Rus) 5:05:00 |

Springboard diving (3 metres)

1983	Petar Georgiev (Bul)
1985	Nikolay Droschin (USSR)
1987	Albin Killat (FRG)
1989	Albin Killat (FRG)
1991	Albin Killat (FRG)
1993	Jan Hempel (Ger)
1995	Dmitriy Sautin (Rus)
1997	Dmitriy Sautin (Rus)

Most wins: 3 Killat; 2 Sautin, Ewald Riebschlager (Ger) 1927, 1932

1 metre springboard diving

1989	Edwin Jongejans (Hol)
1991	Andrey Semeniyk (USSR)
1993	Peter Böhler (Ger)
1995	Edwin Jongejans (Hol)
1997	Andreas Weis (Ger)

Highboard diving

1983	David Ambarzumyan (USSR)
1985	Thomas Knuths (GDR)
1987	Georgiy Chogovadze (USSR)
1989	Georgiy Chogovadze (USSR)
1991	Vladimir Timoshinin (USSR)
1993	Dmitriy Sautin (Rus)
1995	Vladimir Timoshinin (Rus)
1997	Jan Hempel (Ger)

Most wins: 2 Hans Luber (Ger) 1926-7, Brian Phelps (UK) 1958, 1962, Klaus Dibiasi (Ita) 1966, 1974, Chogovadze, Timoshinin

Synchronized 3 metres springboard diving

| 1997 | Holger Schlepps & Alexander Mesch (Ger) |

Synchronized highboard diving

| 1997 | Jan Hempel & Michael Kühne (Ger) |

Women

50 metres freestyle

1987	Tamara Costache (Rom) 25.50
1989	Catherine Plewinski (Fra) 25.63
1991	Simone Osygus (Ger) 25.80
1993	Franziska van Almsick (Ger) 25.23
1995	Linda Olofsson (Swe) 25.76
1997	Natalya Mescheryakova (Rus) 25.31

100 metres freestyle

1983	Birgit Meineke (GDR) 55.18
1985	Heike Friedrich (GDR) 55.71
1987	Kristin Otto (GDR) 55.38
1989	Katrin Meissner (GDR) 55.38
1991	Catherine Plewinski (Fra) 56.20
1993	Franziska van Almsick (Ger) 54.57
1995	Franziska van Almsick (Ger) 55.34
1997	Sandra Volker (Ger) 55.38

Most wins: 2 van Almsick

200 metres freestyle

1983	Birgit Meineke (GDR) 1:59.45
1985	Heike Friedrich (GDR) 1:59.55
1987	Heike Friedrich (GDR) 1:58.24
1989	Manuela Stellmach (GDR) 1:58.93
1991	Mette Jacobsen (Den) 2:00.29
1993	Franziska van Almsick (Ger) 1:57.97
1995	Kerstin Kielgass (Ger) 2:00.56
1997	Michelle de Bruin (née Smith) (Ire) 1.59.93

Most wins: 2 Friedrich

400 metres freestyle

1983	Astrid Strauss (GDR) 4:08.07
1985	Astrid Strauss (GDR) 4:09.22
1987	Heike Friedrich (GDR) 4:06.39
1989	Anke Möhring (GDR) 4:05.84
1991	Irene Dalby (Nor) 4:11.63
1993	Dagmar Hase (Ger) 4:10.47
1995	Franziska van Almsick (Ger) 4:08.37
1997	Dagmar Hase (Ger) 4:09.58

Most wins: 2 Marie Braun (Hol) 1927, 1931, Strauss, Hase

800 metres freestyle

1983	Astrid Strauss (GDR) 8:32.12
1985	Astrid Strauss (GDR) 8:32.45
1987	Anke Möhring (GDR) 8:19.53
1989	Anke Möhring (GDR) 8:23.99
1991	Irene Dalby (Nor) 8:32.08
1993	Jana Henke (Ger) 8:32.47
1995	Julia Jung (Ger) 8:36.08
1997	Kerstin Kielgass (Ger) 8:34.41

Most wins: 2 Strauss, Möhring

4 x 100 metres freestyle

1983	GDR	3:44.72
1985	GDR	3:44.48
1987	GDR	3:42.58
1989	GDR	3:42.46
1991	Netherlands	3:45.36
1993	Germany	3:41.69
1995	Germany	3:43.89
1997	Germany	3:41.49

4 x 200 metres freestyle relay

1983	GDR	8:02.27
1985	GDR	8:03.82
1987	GDR	7:55.47
1989	GDR	7:58.54
1991	Denmark	8:05.90
1993	Germany	8:03.13
1995	Germany	8:06.11
1997	Germany	8:03.59

100 metres backstroke

1982	Ina Kleber (GDR)	1:01.79
1985	Birte Weigang (GDR)	1:02.16
1987	Kristin Otto (GDR)	1:01.86
1989	Kristin Otto (GDR)	1:01.86
1991	Krisztina Egerszegi (Hun)	1:00.31
1993	Krisztina Egerszegi (Hun)	1:00.83
1995	Mette Jacobsen (Den)	1:02.46
1997	Antje Buschschulte (Ger)	1:01.74

Most wins: 2 Kleber 1981, 1983, Otto, Egerszegi

200 metres backstroke

1983	Cornelia Sirch (GDR)	2:12.05
1985	Cornelia Sirch (GDR)	2:10.89
1987	Cornelia Sirch (GDR)	2:10.20
1989	Dagmar Hase (GDR)	2:12.46
1991	Krisztina Egerszegi (Hun)	2:06.62
1993	Krisztina Egerszegi (Hun)	2:09.12
1995	Krisztina Egerszegi (Hun)	2:07.24
1997	Cathleen Rund (Ger)	2:11.56

Most wins: 3 Sirch, Egerszegi

100 metres breaststroke

1983	Ute Geweniger (GDR)	1:08.51
1985	Sylvia Gerasch (GDR)	1:08.62
1987	Silke Hörner (GDR)	1:07.91
1989	Susanne Börnicke (GDR)	1:09.55
1991	Yelena Rudkovskaya (USSR)	1:09.05
1993	Sylvia Gerasch (Ger)	1:10.65
1995	Brigitte Bécue (Bel)	1:09.30
1997	Agnes Kovács (Hun)	1:08.08

Most wins: 2 Geweniger 1981, 1983, Gerasch

200 metres breaststroke

1983	Ute Geweniger (GDR)	2:30.64
1985	Tamara Bogomilova (Bul)	2:28.57
1987	Silke Hörner (GDR)	2:27.49
1989	Susanne Börnicke (GDR)	2:27.77
1991	Yelena Rudkovskaya (USSR)	2:29.50

1993	Brigitte Bécue (Bel)	2:31.18
1995	Brigitte Bécue (Bel)	2:27.66
1997	Agnes Kovács (Hun)	2:24.90

Most wins: 2 Galina Prozumeshikova/Stepanova (USSR) 1966, 1970, Geweniger 1981, 1983, Bécue

100 metres butterfly

1983	Ines Geissler (GDR)	1:00.31
1985	Kornelia Gressler (GDR)	59.46
1987	Kristin Otto (GDR)	59.52
1989	Catherine Plewinski (Fra)	59.08
1991	Catherine Plewinski (Fra)	1:00.32
1993	Catherine Plewinski (Fra)	1:00.13
1995	Mette Jacobsen (Den)	1:00.64
1997	Mette Jacobsen (Den)	59.64

Most wins: 3 Plewinski; 2 Ada Kok (Hol) 1962, 1966, Jacobsen

200 metres butterfly

1983	Cornelia Polit (GDR)	2:07.82
1985	Jacqueline Alex (GDR)	2:11.78
1987	Kathleen Nord (GDR)	2:08.85
1989	Kathleen Nord (GDR)	2:09.33
1991	Mette Jacobsen (Den)	2:12.87
1993	Krisztina Egerszegi (Hun)	2:10.71
1995	Michelle Smith (Ire)	2:11.60
1997	Maria Palaez (Spa)	2:10.25

Most wins: 2 Nord

200 metres individual medley

1983	Ute Geweniger (GDR)	2:13.07
1985	Kathleen Nord (GDR)	2:16.07
1987	Cornelia Sirch (GDR)	2:15.04
1989	Daniela Hunger (GDR)	2:13.26
1991	Daniela Hunger (Ger)	2:15.53
1993	Daniela Hunger (Ger)	2:15.33
1995	Michelle Smith (Ire)	2:15.27
1997	Oksana Verevka (Rus)	2:14.74

Most wins: 3 Hunger; 2 Ulrike Tauber (GDR) 1974, 1977, Geweniger 1981 (2:12.64 rec), 1983

400 metres individual medley

1983	Kathleen Nord (GDR)	4:39.95
1985	Kathleen Nord (GDR)	4:47.08
1987	Noemi Lung (Rom)	4:40.21
1989	Daniela Hunger (GDR)	4:41.82
1991	Krisztina Egerszegi (Hun)	4:39.78
1993	Krisztina Egerszegi (Hun)	4:39.55
1995	Krisztina Egerszegi (Hun)	4:40.33
1997	Michelle de Bruin (Hol)	4:42.08

Record: 1981 Petra Schneider (GDR) 4:39.30

Most wins: 3 Egerszegi; 2 Ulrike Tauber (GDR) 1974, 1977, Nord

4 x 100 metres medley relay

1983	GDR	4:05.79
1985	GDR	4:06.93
1987	GDR	4:04.05
1989	GDR	4:07.40

1991   USSR 4:08.55
1993   Germany 4:06.91
1995   Germany 4:09.97
1997   Germany 4:07.73

5 kilometres long distance

1995   Rita Kovács (Hun) 1:00:38.30
1997   Peggy Busche (Ger) 1:00:51

25 kilometres long distance

1995   Peggy Busche (Ger) 5:32:36.40
1997   Rita Kovács (Hun) 5:21:58

Springboard diving (3 metres)

1983   Brita Baldus (GDR)
1985   Zhanna Tsirulnikova (USSR)
1987   Daphne Jongejans (Hol)
1989   Marina Babkova (USSR)
1991   Irina Lashko (USSR)
1993   Brita Baldus (Ger)
1995   Vera Ilyina (Rus)
1997   Yuliya Pakhalina (Rus)
Most wins: 2 Olga Jensch (née Jordan) (Ger) 1931, 1934, Mady Moreau (Fra) 1947, 1950, Baldus

1 metre springboard diving

1989   Irina Lashko (USSR)
1991   Brita Baldus (Ger)
1993   Simona Koch (Ger)
1995   Vera Ilyina (Rus)
1997   Vera Ilyina (Rus)

Highboard diving

1983   Alla Lobankina (USSR)
1985   Anzyela Stasyulevich (USSR)
1987   Yelena Miroshina (USSR)
1989   Ute Wetzig (GDR)
1991   Yelena Miroshina (USSR)
1993   Svetlana Khokhlova (Rus)
1995   Ute Wetzig (Ger)
1997   Olga Kristoferova (Rus)
Most wins: 2 Nicole Pelissard (Fra) 1947, 1950

Synchronized 3 metres springboard diving

1997   Claudia Bückner & Conny Schmalfuss (Ger)

Synchronized highboard diving

1997   Ute Wetzig & Anke Piper (Ger)

Synchronized swimming – solo

1983   Carolyn Wilson (UK)
1985   Carolyn Wilson (UK)
1987   Muriel Hermine (Fra)
1989   Khristina Falasinidi (USSR)
1991   Olga Sedakova (USSR)
1993   Olga Sedakova (Rus)
1995   Olga Sedakova (Rus)
1997   Olga Sedakova (Rus)
Most wins: 4 Sedakova; 2 Wilson

Synchronized swimming – duet

1983   Carolyn Wilson & Amanda Dodd (UK)
1985   Eva-Maria Edinger & Alexandra Worisch (Aut)
1987   Muriel Hermine & Karine Schuler (Fra)
1989   Karine Schuler & Marianne Aeschbacher (Fra)
1991   Anna Kozlova & Olga Sedakova (USSR)
1993   Anna Kozlova & Olga Sedakova (Rus)
1995   Yelena Azarova & Mariya Kisselyova (Rus)
1997   Olga Brosnikina & Mariya Kisselyova (Rus)

Synchronized swimming – team

1983   UK
1985   France
1987   France
1989   France
1991   Russia
1993   Russia
1995   Russia
1997   Russia

Most gold medals

(Individual/relay)

Men

15   (7/8)   Aleksandr Popov (Rus) 1991-7
13   (8/5)   Michael Gross (FRG) 1981-5

Michael Gross won three individual events in both 1983 and 1985; in 1985 he also swam on three winning FRG relay teams, for a record six golds at one Championships. With 13 gold medals, four silvers and a bronze, he had a record 18 medals in the four Championships 1981-7.

Women

11   (4/7)   Heike Friedrich (GDR) 1985-9
9   (4/5)   Kristin Otto (GDR) 1983-9
9   (8/1)   Krisztina Egerszegi (Hun) 1991-5
                (including a record four individual
                events in 1993)
8   (7/1)   Ute Geweniger (GDR) 1981-3

A women's record six gold medals at one Championships was won by Franziska van Almsick (Ger) in 1993 (three individual, three relay). Five have been won by three women: two individual and three relay by Birgit Meineke (GDR) in 1983 and Heike Friedrich in 1985; three individual and two relay by Kristin Otto (GDR) in 1987.

Others to have won three individual events at one Championships: Arne Borg (Swe) 1927, Ian Black (UK) 1958, Gunnar Larsson (Swe) 1970, Ute Geweniger (GDR) 1981, Tamás Darnyi (Hun) 1987, Jani Sievinen (Fin) 1995.

World Short-Course Championships

These biennial championships, in a 25m pool, were first staged at Palma de Mallorca, Spain in December 1993. *Winners:*

Men

50 metres freestyle

1993   Mark Foster (UK) 21.84
1995   Francisco Sánchez (Ven) 21.80
1997   Francisco Sánchez (Ven) 21.80

100 metres freestyle

1993   Fernando Scherer (Bra) 48.38
1995   Fernando Scherer (Bra) 47.97
1997   Francisco Sánchez (Ven) 47.86

200 metres freestyle

1993   Antti Kasvio (Fin) 1:45.21
1995   Gustavo Borges (Bra) 1:45.55
1997   Gustavo Borges (Bra) 1:45.45

400 metres freestyle

1993   Daniel Kowalski (Aus) 3:42.95
1995   Daniel Kowalski (Aus) 3:45.14
1997   Jacob Carstensen (Den) 3:43.44

1500 metres freestyle

1993   Daniel Kowalski (Aus) 14:42.04
1995   Daniel Kowalski (Aus) 14:48.51
1997   Grant Hackett (Aus) 4:39.54

4 x 100 metres freestyle relay

1993   Brazil 3:12.11
1995   Brazil 3:12.42
1997   Germany 3:14.08

4 x 200 metres freestyle relay

1993   Sweden 7:05.92
1995   Australia 7:07.97
1997   Australia 7:02.74

100 metres backstroke

1993   Tripp Schwenk (USA) 52.98
1995   Rodolfo Falcon (Cub) 53.12
1997   Neisser Bent (Cub) 52.77

200 metres backstroke

1993   Tripp Schwenk (USA) 1:54.19
1995   Rodolfo Falcon (Cub) 1:55.16
1997   Neisser Bent (Cub) 1:54.21

100 metres breaststroke

1993   Philip Rogers (Aus) 59.56
1995   Maren Warnecke (Ger) 58.89
1997   Patrik Isaksson (Swe) 59.99

200 metres breaststroke

1993   Nick Gillingham (UK) 2:07.91
1995   Wang Yiwu (Chn) 2:11.11
1997   Aleksandr Gukov (Rus) 2:09.25

100 metres butterfly

1993   Milos Milosevic (Cro) 52.79
1995   Scott Miller (Aus) 52.38
1997   Lars Frölander (Swe) 51.95

200 metres butterfly

1993   Franck Esposito (Fra) 1:55.42
1995   Scott Goodman (Aus) 1:54.7
1997   James Hickman (UK) 1:55.55

200 metres individual medley

1993   Christian Keller (Ger) 1:56.80
1995   Matthew Dunn (Aus) 1:56.06
1997   Matthew Dunn (Aus) 1:57.16

400 metres individual medley

1993   Curtis Myden (Can) 4:10.41
1995   Matthew Dunn (Aus) 4:08.02
1997   Matthew Dunn (Aus) 4:6.89

4 x 100 metres medley relay

1993   USA 3:32.57
1995   New Zealand 3:35.69
1997   Australia 3:30.66

Women

50 metres freestyle

1993   Le Jingyi (Chn) 24.23
1995   Le Jingyi (Chn) 24.62
1997   Sandra Volker (Ger) 24.70

100 metres freestyle

1993   Le Jingyi (Chn) 53.01
1995   Le Jingyi (Chn) 53.23
1997   Jenny Thompson (USA) 53.46

200 metres freestyle

1993   Karen Pickering (UK) 1:56.25
1995   Claudia Poll (CR) 1:55.42
1997   Claudia Poll (CR) 1:57.90

400 metres freestyle

1993   Janet Evans (USA) 4:05.64
1995   Claudia Poll (CR) 4:05.15
1997   Claudia Poll (CR) 4:00.03

800 metres freestyle

1993   Janet Evans (USA) 8:22.43
1995   Sarah Hardcastle (UK) 8:26.46
1997   Natasha Bowron (Aus) 8:26.45

4 x 100 metres freestyle relay

1993   China 3:35.97
1995   China 3:37.00
1997   China 3:34.55

4 x 200 metres freestyle relay

1993   China 7:52.45
1995   Canada 7:58.25
1997   China 7:51.92

100 metres backstroke

1993	Angel Martino (USA) 58.50
1995	Misty Hyman (USA) 1:00.21
1997	Lu Donghua (Chn) 59.75

200 metres backstroke

1993	He Cihong (Chn) 2:06.09
1995	Mette Jacobsen (Den) 2:08.18
1997	Chen Yan (Chn) 2:07.50

100 metres breaststroke

1993	Dai Guohong (Chn) 1:06.58
1995	Samantha Riley (Aus) 1:05.70
1997	Kristy Ellem (Aus) 1:08.27

200 metres breaststroke

1993	Dai Guohong (Chn) 2:21.99
1995	Samantha Riley (Aus) 2:20.85
1997	Kristy Ellem (Aus) 2:22.68

100 metres butterfly

1993	Susan O'Neill (Aus) 59.19
1995	Liu Limin (Chn) 58.68
1997	Jenny Thompson (USA) 57.79

200 metres butterfly

1993	Liu Limin (Chn) 2:08.51
1995	Susan O'Neill (Aus) 2:06.18
1997	Liu Limin (Chn) 2:07.20

200 metres individual medley

1993	Allison Wagner (USA) 2:07.79
1995	Elli Overton (Aus) 2:11.87
1997	Louise Karlsson (Swe) 2:11.19

400 metres individual medley

1993	Dai Guohong (Chn) 4:29.00
1995	Joanne Malar (Can) 4:36.40
1997	Emma Johnson (Aus) 4:35.18

4 x 100 metres medley relay

1993	China 3:57.73
1995	Australia 4:00.46
1997	China 3:57.83

In 1993 Dai Guohong won four gold medals, setting world records in each event, including the medley relay, and one silver (200m individual medley).

World Short-Course Records (in 25 metres Pools)

Event	min:sec	Name	Venue	Date
Men				
50m freestyle	21.50	Aleksandr Popov (Rus)	Desenzano	13 Mar 1994
100m freestyle	46.74	Aleksandr Popov (Rus)	Gelsenkirchen	19 Mar 1994
200m freestyle	1:43.64	Giorgio Lamberti (Ita)	Bonn	11 Feb 1990
400m freestyle	3:40.46	Danyon Loader (NZ)	Sheffield	11 Feb 1995
800m freestyle	7:34.90	Kieren Perkins (Aus)	Sydney	25 Jul 1993
1500m freestyle	14:26.52	Kieren Perkins (Aus)	Auckland	14 Jul 1993
4 x 50m freestyle	1:27.62	Sweden	Stavanger	3 Dec 1994
4 x 100m freestyle	3:12.11	Brazil	Palma de Mallorca	5 Dec 1993
4 x 200m freestyle	7:02.74	Australia	Gothenburg	18 Apr 1997
50m backstroke	24.25	Chris Renaud (Can)	St Catherine's	1 Mar 1997
100m backstroke	51.43	Jeff Rouse (USA)	Sheffield	12 Apr 1993
200m backstroke	1:52.51	Martin López-Zubero (Spa)	Gainesville	11 Apr 1991
50m breaststroke	26.97	Mark Warnecke (Ger)	Paris	8 Feb 1997
	26.97	Mark Warnecke (Ger)	Paris	28 Mar 1998
100m breaststroke	59.02	Frédéric Deburghgraeve (Bel)	Bastogne	17 Feb 1996
200m breaststroke	2:07.66	Ryan Mitchell (Aus)	Melbourne	21 Dec 1996
50m butterfly	23.35	Denis Pankratov (Rus)	Paris	8 Feb 1997
100m butterfly	51.78	Denis Pankratov (Rus)	Paris	9 Feb 1997
200m butterfly	1:51.76	James Hickman (UK)	Paris	28 Mar 1998
100m individual medley	53.10	Jani Sievinen (Fin)	Malmö	30 Jan 1996
200m individual medley	1:54.65	Jani Sievinen (Fin)	Kuopio	21 Jan 1994
400m individual medley	4:05.41	Marcel Wonda (Hol)	Paris	8 Feb 1997
4 x 50m medley	1:36.69	Auburn Aquatics (USA)	Auburn	9 Apr 1996
	1:38.04u	Germany	Stavanger	4 Dec 1994
4 x 100m medley	3:30.66	Australia	Gothenburg	17 Apr 1997
Women				
50m freestyle	24.23	Le Jingyi (Chn)	Palma de Mallorca	3 Dec 1993
100m freestyle	53.01	Le Jingyi (Chn)	Palma de Mallorca	2 Dec 1993
200m freestyle	1:54.17	Claudia Poll (CR)	Gothenburg	17 Apr 1997
400m freestyle	4:00.03	Claudia Poll (CR)	Gothenburg	19 Apr 1997

800m freestyle	8:15.34	Astrid Strauss (GDR)	Bonn	6 Feb 1987
1500m freestyle	15:43.31	Petra Schneider (GDR)	Gainesville	10 Jan 1982
4 x 50m freestyle	1:40.63	Germany	Espoo	22 Nov 1992
4 x 100m freestyle	3:34.55	China	Gothenburg	19 Apr 1997
4 x 200m freestyle	7:51.92	China	Gothenburg	17 Apr 1997
50m backstroke	27.64	Bai Xiunju (Chn)	Desenzano	12 Mar 1994
100m backstroke	58.50	Angel Martino (USA)	Palma de Mallorca	2 Dec 1995
200m backstroke	2:06.09	He Cihong (Chn)	Palma de Mallorca	5 Dec 1993
50m breaststroke	30.77	Han Xue (Chn)	Gelsenkirchen	2 Feb 1997
100m breaststroke	1:05.70	Samantha Riley (Aus)	Rio de Janeiro	2 Dec 1995
200m breaststroke	2:20.85	Samantha Riley (Aus)	Rio de Janeiro	1 Dec 1995
50m butterfly	26.55	Misty Hyman (USA)	Gothenburg	19 Apr 1997
100m butterfly	57.79	Jenny Thompson (USA)	Gothenburg	19 Apr 1997
200m butterfly	2:05.65	Mary T Meagher (USA)	Gainesville	2 Jan 1981
100m individual medley	1:00.60	Hu Xiaowen (Chn)	Beijing	26 Feb 1998
200m individual medley	2:07.79	Allison Wagner (USA)	Palma de Mallorca	5 Dec 1993
400m individual medley	4:29.00	Dai Guohong (Chn)	Palma de Mallorca	2 Dec 1993
4 x 50m medley	1:51.79	Germany	Rostock	15 Dec 1996
4 x 100m medley	3:57.73	China	Palma de Mallorca	5 Dec 1993

Table Tennis

The origins of table tennis are uncertain, but sports-goods manufacturers were selling equipment for the game in England in the 1880s. The use of a celluloid table-tennis ball was pioneered by James Gibb. This ball, called 'Gossima', was manufactured by J Jacques & Son, and it was probably Jacques who conceived the onomatopoeic name 'Ping Pong', by which the game was popularly known in the early part of the 20th century. The use of pimpled rubber stuck on to the wooden bat was introduced at around this time. A Ping Pong Association was formed in 1902, when the craze for the game was at a peak. This organization was renamed the Table Tennis Association, but became defunct, before being re-constituted as the English Table Tennis Association in 1927.

International governing body: International Table Tennis Federation (ITTF), 53 London Road, St Leonards-on-Sea, East Sussex TN37 6AY, UK. Tel: 01424 721414, Fax: 01424 431871. President: Xu Yinsheng, Deputy President and Chief Executive Officer: Adham Sharara. Founded 1926. 180 member nations in 1998.

World Championships

European Championships were contested in December 1926, when the ITTF was first formed, and the event was retrospectively designated as the World Championships. Subsequent championships were contested annually until 1957, except for the war years, and biennially from 1959.

(Two results are shown for 1933, and none for 1934, as the 1933/4 tournament was held in December 1933.)

Men's team

The Swaythling Cup, the trophy for the men's team championship, was given in 1926 by Lady Swaythling, mother of the Hon. Ivor Montagu, the first President of the ITTF. Matches are played over the best of nine singles, by teams of three.

Wins:

12	Hungary	1926, 1928 31, 1933 (2), 1935, 1938, 1949, 1952, 1979
12	China	1961, 1963, 1965, 1971, 1975, 1977, 1981, 1983, 1985, 1987, 1995, 1997
7	Japan	1954-7, 1959, 1967, 1969
6	Czechoslovakia	1932, 1939, 1947-8, 1950-1
4	Sweden	1973, 1989, 1991, 1993
1	Austria 1936, USA 1937, England 1953	

Women's team

The Marcel Corbillon Cup was presented in 1934 by M Corbillon, President of the French Table Tennis Association, to be awarded to the winners of the women's team event. Matches are contested as the best of four singles and a doubles.

Wins:

12	China	1965, 1975, 1977, 1979, 1981, 1983, 1985, 1987, 1989, 1993, 1995, 1997
8	Japan	1952, 1954, 1957, 1959, 1961, 1963, 1967, 1971
5	Romania	1950-1, 1953, 1955-6
3	Czechoslovakia	1935-6, 1938
2	Germany	1933, 1939
2	USA	1937, 1949
2	England	1947-8
2	Korea	1973 (South), 1991 (North & South)
1	USSR	1969

Men's singles

The St Bride Vase for the men's singles was presented in 1929 by the St Bride Institute Table Tennis Club, London, in recognition of the title won in 1929 by Fred Perry, later triple Wimbledon champion at lawn tennis.

Winners:

1926	Roland Jacobi (Hun)
1928	Zoltán Mechlovits (Hun)
1929	Fred Perry (Eng)
1930	Viktor Barna (Hun)
1931	Miklós Szabados (Hun)
1932-5	Viktor Barna (Hun)
1936	Stanislav Kolár (Cs)
1937	Richard Bergmann (Aut)
1938	Bohumil Vána (Cs)
1939	Richard Bergmann (Aut)
1947	Bohumil Vána (Cs)
1948	Richard Bergmann (Eng)
1949	Johnny Leach (Eng)
1950	Richard Bergmann (Eng)
1951	Johnny Leach (Eng)
1952	Hiroji Satoh (Jap)
1953	Ferenc Sidó (Hun)
1954	Ichiro Ogimura (Jap)
1955	Toshiaki Tanaka (Jap)
1956	Ichiro Ogimura (Jap)
1957	Toshiaki Tanaka (Jap)
1959	Jung Kuo-tuan (Chn)
1961	Chuang Tse-tung (Chn)
1963	Chuang Tse-tung (Chn)
1965	Chuang Tse-tung (Chn)
1967	Nobuhiko Hasegawa (Jap)
1969	Shigeo Ito (Jap)
1971	Stellan Bengtsson (Swe)
1973	Hsi En-ting (Chn)
1975	István Jónyer (Hun)
1977	Mitsuru Kohno (Jap)
1979	Seiji Ono (Jap)
1981	Guo Yuehua (Chn)
1983	Guo Yuehua (Chn)
1985	Jiang Jialiang (Chn)
1987	Jiang Jialiang (Chn)
1989	Jan-Ove Waldner (Swe)
1991	Jörgen Persson (Swe)
1993	Jean-Philippe Gatien (Fra)
1995	Kong Linghui (Chn)
1997	Jan-Ove Waldner (Swe)

Most wins: 5 Barna; 4 Bergmann

Women's singles

The G Geist Prize, awarded to the winner of the women's singles, was donated in 1931 by Dr Gaspar Geist, President of the Hungarian Association.

Winners:

1926	Mária Mednyánszky (Hun)
1928-31	Mária Mednyánszky (Hun)
1932-3	Anna Sipos (Hun)
1933	Marie Kettnerová (Cs)
1935	Marie Kettnerová (Cs)
1936	Ruth Aarons (USA)
1937	Ruth Aarons (USA) & Trudi Pritzi (Aut)★
1938	Trudi Pritzi (Aut)
1939	Vlasta Depetrisová (Cs)
1947-9	Gizi Farkas (Hun)
1950-5	Angelica Rozeanu (Rom)
1956	Tomi Okawa (Jap)
1957	Fujie Eguchi (Jap)
1959	Kimiyo Matsuzaki (Jap)
1961	Chiu Chung-hui (Chn)
1963	Kimiyo Matsuzaki (Jap)
1965	Naoko Fukazu (Jap)
1967	Sachiko Morisawa (Jap)
1969	Toshiko Kowada (Jap)
1971	Lin Hui-ching (Chn)
1973	Hu Yu-lan (Chn)
1975	Pak Yung-sun (NKo)
1977	Pak Yung-sun (NKo)
1979	Ge Xinai (Chn)
1981	Tong Ling (Chn)
1983	Cao Yanhua (Chn)
1985	Cao Yanhua (Chn)
1987	He Zhili (Chn)
1989	Qiao Hong (Chn)
1991	Deng Yaping (Chn)
1993	Hyun Jung-hwa (SKo)
1995	Deng Yaping (Chn)
1997	Deng Yaping (Chn)

★ Title left vacant; these were the finalists.

Most wins: 6 Angelica Rozeanu; 5 Mária Mednyánszky

Men's doubles

Contested for the Iran Cup, presented by the Shah of Iran in Paris in 1947.

Winners:

1926	Roland Jacobi & Daniel Pécsi (Hun)
1928	Alfred Liebster & Robert Thum (Aut)
1929-32	Viktor Barna & Miklós Szabados (Hun)
1933	Viktor Barna & Sándor Glancz (Hun)
1933	Viktor Barna & Miklós Szabados (Hun)
1935	Viktor Barna & Miklós Szabados (Hun)
1936-7	Robert Blattner & James McClure (USA)
1938	James McClure & Sol Schiff (USA)
1939	Viktor Barna & Richard Bergmann (Eng)
1947	Adolf Slár & Bohumil Vána (Cs)
1948	Ladislav Stipek & Bohumil Vána (Cs)
1949	Ivan Andreadis & Frantisek Tokár (Cs)
1950	Ferenc Sidó & Ferenc Soós (Hun)
1951	Ivan Andreadis & Bohumil Vána (Cs)
1952	Norikazu Fujii & Tadaski Hayashi (Jap)
1953	József Kóczián & Ferenc Sidó (Hun)
1954	Zarko Dolinar & Vilim Harangozo (Yug)
1955	Ivan Andreadis & Ladislav Stipek (Cs)
1956	Ichiro Ogimura & Yoshio Tomita (Jap)

1957	Ivan Andreadis & Ladislav Stipek (Cs)
1959	Teruo Murakami & Ichiro Ogimura (Jap)
1961	Nobuyo Hoshino & Koji Kimura (Jap)
1963	Chang Shih-lin & Wang Chih-liang (Chn)
1965	Chuang Tse-tung & Hsu Yin-sheng (Chn)
1967	Hans Alser & Kjell Johansson (Swe)
1969	Hans Alser & Kjell Johansson (Swe)
1971	István Jonyer & Tibor Klampar (Hun)
1973	Stellan Bengtsson & Kjell Johansson (Swe)
1975	Gábor Gergely & István Jónyer (Hun)
1977	Li Zhenshi & Liang Geliang (Chn)
1979	Dragutin Surbek & Anton Stipancic (Yug)
1981	Cai Zhenhua & Li Zhenshi (Chn)
1983	Dragutin Surbek & Zoran Kalinic (Yug)
1985	Mikael Applegren & Ulf Carlsson (Swe)
1987	Chen Longcan & Wei Qinguang (Chn)
1989	Jörg Rosskopf & Steffen Fetzner (FRG)
1991	Peter Karlsson & Thomas von Scheele (Swe)
1993	Wang Tao & Lu Lin (Chn)
1995	Wang Tao & Lu Lin (Chn)
1997	Kong Linghui & Liu Guoliang (Chn)

Most wins: 8 Viktor Barna; 6 Miklós Szabados

Women's doubles

Contested for the W J Pope Trophy, presented in 1948 by Mr Pope, Honorary Secretary of the ITTF 1947-50.
Winners:

1928	Erika Flamm (Aut) & Mária Mednyánszky (Hun)
1929	Erika Metzger & Mona Rüster (Ger)
1930-5	Mária Mednyánszky & Anna Sipos (Hun)
1936	Marie Kettnerová & Marie Smídová (Cs)
1937-8	Vlasta Depetrisová & Vera Votrubcová (Cs)
1939	Hilde Bussmann & Trudi Pritzi (Ger)
1947	Gizi Farkas (Hun) & Trudi Pritzi (Aut)
1948	Margaret Franks & Vera Thomas (Eng)
1949	Helen Elliot (Sco) & Gizi Farkas (Hun)
1950	Dora Beregi (Eng) & Helen Elliot (Sco)
1951	Diane Rowe & Rosalind Rowe (Eng)
1952	Shizuki Narahara & Tomi Nishimura (Jap)
1953	Gizi Farkas (Hun) & Angelica Rozeanu (Rom)
1954	Diane Rowe & Rosalind Rowe (Eng)
1955-6	Angelica Rozeanu & Ella Zeller (Rom)
1957	Livia Mosoczy & Agnes Simon (Hun)
1959	Taeko Namba & Kazuko Yamaizumi (Jap)
1961	Maria Alexandru & Geta Pitica (Rom)
1963	Kimiyo Matsuzaki & Masako Seki (Jap)
1965	Cheng Min-chih & Lin Hui-ching (Chn)
1967	Saeko Hirota & Sachiko Morisawa (Jap)
1969	Svetlana Grinberg & Zoya Rudnova (USSR)
1971	Cheng Min-chih & Lin Hui-ching (Chn)
1973	Maria Alexandru (Rom) & Miho Hamada (Jap)
1975	Maria Alexandru (Rom) & Shoko Takashima (Jap)
1977	Pak Yong-ok (NKo) & Yang Yin (Chn)
1979	Zhang Li & Zhang Deying (Chn)
1981	Zhang Deying & Cao Yanhua (Chn)

1983	Shen Jianping & Dai Lili (Chn)
1985	Dai Lili & Geng Lijuan (Chn)
1987	Yang Young-Ja & Hyun Jung-hwa (SKo)
1989	Deng Yaping & Qiao Hong (Chn)
1991	Chen Zhie & Gao Jun (Chn)
1993	Liu Wei & Qiao Yunping (Chn)
1995	Deng Yaping & Qiao Hong (Chn)
1997	Deng Yaping & Yang Ying (Chn)

Most wins: 7 Mária Mednyánszky; 6 Anna Sipos

Mixed doubles

Contested for the Heydusek Prize, presented in 1948 by Zdenek Heydusek, Secretary of the Czechoslovak Association.
Winners:

1927-8	Zoltán Mechlovits & Mária Mednyánszky (Hun)
1929	István Kelen & Anna Sipos (Hun)
1930-1	Miklós Szabados & Mária Mednyánszky (Hun)
1932	Viktor Barna & Anna Sipos (Hun)
1933	István Kelen & Mária Mednyánszky (Hun)
1933	Miklós Szabados & Mária Mednyánszky (Hun)
1935	Viktor Barna & Anna Sipos (Hun)
1936	Miloslav Hamr & Trude Kleinová (Cs)
1937	Bohumil Vána & Vera Votrubcová (Cs)
1938	Lászlo Béllak (Hun) & Wendy Woodhead (Eng)
1939	Bohumil Vána & Vera Votrubcová (Cs)
1947	Ferenc Soós & Gizi Farkas (Hun)
1948	Richard Miles & Thelma Thall (USA)
1949-50	Ferenc Sidó & Gizi Farkas (Hun)
1951	Bohumil Vána (Cs) & Angelica Rozeanu (Rom)
1952-3	Ferenc Sidó (Hun) & Angelica Rozeanu (Rom)
1954	Ivan Andreadis (Cs) & Gizi Farkas (Hun)
1955	Kálmán Szepesi & Eva Kóczián (Hun)
1956	Erwin Klein & Leah Neuberger (USA)
1957	Ichiro Ogimura & Fujie Eguchi (Jap)
1959	Ichiro Ogimura & Fujie Eguchi (Jap)
1961	Ichiro Ogimura & Kimiyo Matsuzaki (Jap)
1963	Koji Kimura & Kazuko Ito (Jap)
1965	Koji Kimura & Masako Seki (Jap)
1967	Nobuhiko Hasegawa & Noriko Yamanaka (Jap)
1969	Nobuhiko Hasegawa & Yasuka Kono (Jap)
1971	Chang Shih-ling & Lin Hui-ching (Chn)
1973	Liang Geliang & Li Li (Chn)
1975	Stanislav Gomozkov & Tatyana Ferdman (USSR)
1977	Jacques Secretin & Claude Bergeret (Fra)
1979	Liang Geliang & Ge Xinai (Chn)
1981	Xie Saike & Huang Junqun (Chn)
1983	Guo Yuehua & Ni Xialian (Chn)
1985	Cai Zhenhua & Cao Yanhua (Chn)

1987	Hui Jun & Geng Lijuan (Chn)
1989	Yoo Nam-kyu & Hyun Jung-hwa (SKo)
1991	Wang Tao & Liu Wei (Chn)
1993	Wang Tao & Liu Wei (Chn)
1995	Wang Tao & Liu Wei (Chn)
1997	Wu Na & Liu Guoliang (Chn)

Most wins: 6 Mária Mednyánszky

Most individual world titles overall

Men: 15 Viktor Barna (Hun/Eng); 10 Miklós Szabados (Hun)

Women: 18 Mária Mednyánszky (-Klucsik) (Hun); 12 Angelica Rozeanu (Rom); 11 Anna Sipos (Hun); 10 Gizi Farkas (Hun)

Olympic Games

The sport was added to the Games in 1988.
Winners:

Men

Singles

1988	Yoo Nam-kyu (SKo)
1992	Jan-Ove Waldner (Swe)
1996	Liu Guiliang (Chn)

Doubles

1988	Chen Longcan & Wei Qingguang (Chn)
1992	Lu Lin & Wang Tao (Chn)
1996	Kong Linhui & Lui Guiliang (Chn)

Women

Singles

1988	Chen Jing (Chn)
1992	Deng Yaping (Chn)
1996	Deng Yaping (Chn)

Doubles

1988	Hyun Jung-hwa & Yang Young-ja (SKo)
1992	Deng Yaping & Qiao Hong (Chn)
1996	Deng Yaping & Qiao Hong (Chn)

World Cup

Held annually from 1980 for men and from 1996 for women.
Winners:

Men

Singles

1980	Guo Yuehua (Chn)
1981	Tibor Klampar (Hun)
1982	Guo Yuehua (Chn)
1983	Mikael Appelgren (Swe)
1984	Jiang Jialiang (Chn)
1985	Chen Xinhua (Chn)
1986	Chen Longcan (Chn)
1987	Yi Teng (Chn)
1988	Andrzej Grubba (Pol)
1989	Ma Wenge (Chn)

1990	Jan-Ove Waldner (Swe)
1991	Jörgen Persson (Swe)
1992	Ma Wenge (Chn)
1993	Zoran Primorac (Cro)
1994	Jean-Philippe Gatien (Fra)
1995	Kong Linghui (Chn)
1996	Liu Guiliang (Chn)
1997	Zoran Primorac (Cro)

Doubles

| 1990 | Yoo Nam-kyu & Kim Taek-soo (SKo) |
| 1992 | Kim Taek-soo & Yoo Nam-kyu (SKo) |

Women

Singles

| 1996 | Deng Yaping (Chn) |
| 1997 | Wang Nan (Chn) |

Doubles

| 1990 | Hyun Jung-hwa & Hong Cha-ok (SKo) |
| 1992 | Deng Yaping & QiaoHong (Chn) |

World Team Cup

	Men	Women
1990	Sweden	China
1991	China	China
1994	China	Russia
1995	S Korea	China

European Championships

Biennial from 1958.
Winners:

Men

Singles

1958	Zoltán Berczik (Hun)
1960	Zoltán Berczik (Hun)
1962	Hans Alser (Swe)
1964	Kjell Johansson (Swe)
1966	Kjell Johansson (Swe)
1968	Dragutin Surbek (Yug)
1970	Hans Alser (Swe)
1972	Stellan Bengtsson (Swe)
1974	Milan Orlowski (Cs)
1976	Jacques Secretin (Fra)
1978	Gábor Gergely (Hun)
1980	John Hilton (UK)
1982	Mikael Appelgren (Swe)
1984	Ulf Bengtsson (Swe)
1986	Jörgen Persson (Swe)
1988	Mikael Appelgren (Swe)
1990	Mikael Appelgren (Swe)
1992	Jörg Rosskopf (Ger)
1994	Jean-Michel Saive (Bel)
1996	Jan-Ove Waldner (Swe)
1998	Vladimir Samsonov (Blr)

Team

12	Sweden	1964, 1966, 1968, 1970, 1972, 1974, 1980, 1986, 1988, 1990, 1992, 1996
4	Hungary	1958, 1960, 1978, 1982
3	France	1984, 1994, 1998
2	Yugoslavia	1962, 1976

Women

Singles

1958	Eva Kóczián (Hun)
1960	Eva Kóczián (Hun)
1962	Agnes Simon (FRG)
1964	Eva Földi (née Kóczián) (Hun)
1966	Maria Alexandru (Rom)
1968	Ilona Vostová (Cs)
1970	Zoya Rudnova (USSR)
1972	Zoya Rudnova (USSR)
1974	Judit Magos (Hun)
1976	Jill Hammersley (UK)
1978	Judit Magos (Hun)
1980	Valentina Popova (USSR)
1982	Bettina Vriesekoop (Hol)
1984	Valentina Popova (USSR)
1986	Csilla Bátorfi (Hun)
1988	Flyura Bulatova (USSR)
1990	Daniela Guergelcheva (Bul)
1992	Bettine Vriesekoop (Hol)
1994	Marie Svensson (Swe)
1996	Nicole Struse (Ger)
1998	Ni Xia Lian (Lux)

Team

7	Hungary	1960, 1966, 1972, 1978, 1982, 1986, 1990
6	USSR	1970, 1974, 1976, 1980, 1984, 1988
4	Germany	1962, 1968 (FRG), 1994, 1998
2	England	1958, 1964
1	Romania 1992, Russia 1994

English Open Championships

Instituted in 1921 this is the longest-established national championship and has attracted many of the world's best players. Held annually to 1980, and biennially since then.

Most titles

Men's singles: 6 Richard Bergmann (Aut/Eng) 1939-40, 1948, 1950, 1952, 1954; 5 Viktor Barna (Hun) 1933-5, 1937-8

Women's singles: 6 Maria Alexandru (Rom) 1963-4, 1970-2, 1974

Men's doubles: 7 Viktor Barna 1931, 1933-5, 1938-9, 1949

Women's doubles: 12 Diane Rowe (Eng) 1950-6, 1960, 1962-5 (first 6 with her twin Rosalind)

Mixed doubles: 8 Viktor Barna 1933-6, 1938, 1940, 1951, 1953

All events – men: 20 Viktor Barna

All events – women: 17 Diane Rowe (and singles 1962, mixed 1952, 1954, 1956, 1960)

Taekwondo

Taekwondo is a martial art in which all activities are based on a defensive spirit. It was developed over 20 centuries in Korea, being officially recognized as part of Korean tradition and culture in 1955. Thereafter the sport spread internationally, with world championships first held in 1973. Taekwondo was played as an official sport at the 1983 Pan-American Games and at the 1984 Asian Games, and was a demonstration sport at the 1988 and 1992 Olympic Games. There are eight weight categories ranging from fin to heavyweight.

International governing body: World Taekwondo Federation (WTF), 635 Yuksamdong, Kangnamku, Seoul 135-080, Korea. Tel: (82) 2 566 2505, Fax: (82) 2 553 4728. President: Dr Lim Un-yong. Founded 1978, 143 member nations.

World Championships

These biennial championships were first held in Seoul in 1973, when they were organized by the Korea Taekwondo Association. Women's events were first staged unofficially in 1983, and have been included in the official programme from 1987. A record 82 nations contested the men's events and 54 nations the women's in 1993.

Champions at each weight category:

Men

Fin – 50kg

1975	Whang Soo-yong (SKo)
1977	Song Ki-yul (SKo)
1979	Lee Seung-kyung (SKo)
1982	José Cedeno (Ecu)
1983	Kwang Yeon-wang (SKo)
1985	Lee Sun-jang (SKo)
1987	Lim Sung-wook (SKo)
1989	Kwon Tae-ho (SKo)
1991	Salim Gergely (Den)
1993	Chin Seung-tae (SKo)
1995	Chin Seung-tae (SKo)
1997	Juan Antonio Ramos (Spa)

Fly – 54kg

1975	Han You-keun (SKo)
1977	Ha Suk-kwang (SKo)
1979	Yang Ki-mo (SKo)
1982	Jeon Woong-hwan (SKo)
1983	Ko Jeong-ho (SKo)
1985	Kim Yeong-sik (SKo)
1987	Kang Chang-mo (SKo)
1989	Kim Chul-ho (SKo)
1991	Kim Chul-ho (SKo)
1993	Javier Argudo (Spa)
1995	Cihat Kutluca (Tur)
1997	Chin Seung-tae (SKo)

Bantam – 58kg

1975	Son Tae-whan (SKo)
1977	Kim Chong-ki (SKo)
1979	Kim Chong-ki (SKo)
1982	Kim Chong-ki (SKo)
1983	Han Hong-sik (SKo)
1985	Yoo Myung-sik (SKo)
1987	Yoo Myung-sik (SKo)
1989	Ham Jun (SKo)
1991	Angel Alonso (Spa)
1993	Kim In-kyoung (SKo)
1995	Chang Dae-soon (NKo)
1997	Hsiung Huang-Chin (Tai)

Feather – 64kg

1975	Lee Gyeo-sung (SKo)
1977	Park Chung-ho (SKo)
1979	Yim Dai-taik (SKo)
1982	Jang Myeong-sam (SKo)
1983	Lee Jae-bong (SKo)
1985	Han Jae-koo (SKo)
1987	Lee Chian-hsiang (Tai)
1989	Jang Hyuk (SKo)
1991	Jang Hyuk (SKo)
1993	Kim Byong-cheol (SKo)
1995	Kim Byung-uk (SKo)
1997	Kim In-dong (SKo)

Light – 70kg

1973	Lee Ki-hyung (SKo)
1975	You Young-hab (SKo)
1977	Hwang Ming Der (Tai)
1979	Park Oh-sung (SKo)
1982	Park Oh-sung (SKo)
1983	Han Jae-ku (SKo)
1985	Park Bong-kwon (SKo)
1987	Yang Dae-seung (SKo)
1989	Yang Dae-seung (SKo)
1991	Yang Dae-seung (SKo)
1993	Park Se-jin (SKo)
1995	Aziz Acharki (Ger)
1997	Tamer Abdel Moneim (Egy)

Welter – 76kg

1975	Song Hur (SKo)
1977	You Young-hab (SKo)
1979	Oscar Mendiola (Mex)
1982	Park Cheon-jae (SKo)
1983	Yilmaz Helvacioglu (Tur)
1985	Chung Kook-hyun (SKo)
1987	Chung Kook-hyun (SKo)
1989	Lee Hyun-suk (SKo)
1991	Park Yong-woong (SKo)
1993	Lim Young-ho (SKo)
1995	José Marquez (Spa)
1997	José Marquez (Spa)

Light-middle

1979	Rainer Müller (FRG)
1982	Chung Kook-hyun (SKo)
1983	Chung Kook-hyun (SKo)

Middle – 83kg

1975	Yang Young-kwan (SKo)
1977	Song Hur (SKo)
1979	Kim Sang-chun (SKo)
1982	Kim Sang-chun (SKo)
1983	Lee Dong-joon (SKo)
1985	Lee Dong-joon (SKo)
1987	Lee Kye-haeng (SKo)
1989	Jeong Yong-suk (SKo)
1991	Yoon Soon-cheul (SKo)
1993	Michael Meloui (Fra)
1995	Lee Dong-wan (SKo)
1997	Lee Dong-wan (SKo)

Light-heavy

1979	Chung Chan (SKo)
1982	Ha Yong-seong (SKo)
1983	Fargas Inreno (Spa)

Heavy – over 83kg

1973	Kim Jeong-tae (SKo)
1975	Choi Jeong-do (SKo)
1977	Ahn Jang-shik (SKo)
1979	Sjef Vos (Hol)
1982	Dirk Jung (FRG)
1983	Jang Seung-hwa (SKo)
1985	Hendrik Meijer (Hol)
1987	Michael Arndt (FRG)
1989	Amr Khairy Mahmoud (Egy)
1991	Tonny Sorensen (Den)
1993	Kim Je-kyoung (SKo)
1995	Kim Je-kyoung (SKo)
1997	Kim Je-kyoung (SKo)

Most wins: 4 Chung Kook-hyun; 3 Kim Chong-ki, Yang Dae-seung, Kim Je-kyoung, Chin Seung-tae

Women

Fin – 43kg

1987	Jang Ei-suk (SKo)
1989	Chin Yu-fang (Tai)
1991	Elisabeth Delgado (Spa)
1993	Isabel Cruzado (Spa)
1995	Chun Chin-kuang (Tai)
1997	Yang So-Hee (SKo)

Fly – 47kg

1987	Pai Yun-yao (Tai)
1989	Weon Sun-jin (SKo)
1991	Tan Arzu (Tur)

1993	You Su-mi (SKo)
1995	Hamide Bickin (Tur)
1997	Ju Chi-su (SKo)

Bantam – 51kg

1987	Tennur Yerlhsu (Tur)
1989	Jung Nam-suk (SKo)
1991	Park Dong-seon (SKo)
1993	Tang Hui-wen (Tai)
1995	Sun Jin-won (NKo)
1997	Hwang Eun-suk (SKo)

Feather – 55kg

1987	Kim So-young (SKo)
1989	Kim So-young (SKo)
1991	Tung Ya-ling (Tai)
1993	Lee Seung-min (SKo)
1995	Lee Seung-min (SKo)
1997	Jang Jae-eun (SKo)

Light – 60kg

1987	Lee Eun-young (SKo)
1989	Lee Eun-young (SKo)
1991	Jeong Eun-ok (Kor)
1993	Jesús Santolaria (Spa)
1995	Park Kyung-suk (SKo)
1997	Kang Hae-eun (SKo)

Welter – 65kg

1987	Coral Bistuer (Spa)
1989	Anita Silsby (USA)
1991	Arlene Limas (USA)
1993	Kim Mi-young (SKo)
1995	Cho Hyang-mi (SKo)
1997	Cho Hyang-mi (SKo)

Middle – 70kg

1987	Margaretha de Jongh (Hol)
1989	Lydia Zele (USA)
1991	Yang In-deok (SKo)
1993	Park Eun-sun (SKo)
1995	Ruiz Ireana (Spa)
1997	Woo Eun-joung (SKo)

Heavy – over 70kg

1987	Lynette Love (USA)
1989	Jung Wan-sook (SKo)
1991	Lynette Love (USA)
1993	Jung Myung-suk (SKo)
1995	Jung Myung-suk (SKo)
1997	Jung Myung-suk (SKo)

Most wins: 3 Jung Myung-suk

Olympic Games

Included in the Olympic programme as a demonstration sport in 1988 and 1992, Taekwondo becomes a medal sport at the 2000 Games with four categories each for men and women.
Winners:

Men

	50kg	**54kg**	**58kg**
1988	Kwon Tae-ho (SKo)	Ha Tae-kyung (SKo)	Ji Yong-suk (SKo)
1992	Gergely Salim (Den)	Arlindo Couvela (Ven)	William Cordova (Mex)

	64kg	**70kg**	**76kg**
1988	Chang Myung-sam (SKo)	Park Bong-kwon (SKo)	Chung Kook-hyun (SKo)
1992	Kim Byong-cheol (SKo)	José Santolaria (Spa)	Ha Tae-kyoung (SKo)

	83kg	**83+kg**	
1988	Lee Kye-haeng (SKo)	Jimmy Kim (USA)	
1992	Herbert Perez (USA)	Kim Je-kyoung (SKo)	

Women

	43kg	**47kg**	**51kg**
1988	Chin Yu-fang (Tai)	Choo Nan-yool (SKo)	Chen Yi-an (Tai)
1992	Lo Yueh-ying (Tai)	Elisabet Delgado (Spa)	Hwang Eun-suk (SKo)

	55kg	**60kg**	**65kg**
1988	Annemette Christensen (Den)	Dana Hee (USA)	Arlene Limas (USA)
1992	Tung Ya-ling (Tai)	Chen Yi-an (Tai)	Elena Benitez (Spa)

	70kg	**70+kg**	
1988	Kim Hyun-hee (SKo)	Lynette Love (USA)	
1992	Lee Sun-hee (SKo)	Coral Astrid Bistuer (Spa)	

Tennis

Lawn tennis evolved from real tennis and, while accounts of various forms of 'field tennis' were recorded in the 18th century, a Major Wingfield is regarded as the real 'father' of the game as it is known today. He showed off his new game, which he called 'Sphairistike', at a Christmas party at a country house at Nantclwyd, Wales, in 1873, and patented it in 1874. The Marylebone Cricket Club was responsible for revising Wingfield's initial rules and in 1877 the All England Croquet Club added 'Lawn Tennis' to its title.

International governing body: International Tennis Federation (ITF), Bank Lane, Roehampton, London SW15 5XZ. Tel: 0181 878 6464, Fax: 0181 392 4747. President: Brian Tobin. Founded as the International Lawn Tennis Federation in Paris in 1913 with 12 founding member nations. Membership reached 196 nations in 1997.

Maiden names/married names of women players

	Maiden name	Married name		Maiden name	Married name
Chris	Evert	Lloyd, then Mill	Billie Jean	Moffitt	King
Mary	Bevis	Hawton	Sarah	Palfrey	Fabyan, then
Blanche	Bingley	Hillyard			Cooke
Molly	Bjurstedt	Mallory	Margaret	Osborne	Du Pont
Mary	Carter	Reitano	Vera	Puzejová	Suková
Charlotte	Cooper	Sterry	Peggy	Saunders	Michel
Thelma	Coyne	Long	Larisa	Savchenko	Neiland
Evonne	Goolagong	Cawley	Elizabeth	Sayers	Smyllie
Helen	Gourlay	Cawley	Gail	Sherriff	Chanfreau, then
Karen	Hantze	Susman			Lovera
Ann	Haydon	Jones	Margaret	Smith	Court
Hazel	Hotchkiss	Wightman	Judy	Tegart	Dalton
Dorothea	Lambert-Chambers	Douglass	Helen	Wills	Moody
Kathleen	McKane	Godfree	Nancye	Wynne	Bolton
Kerry	Melville	Reid			

Wimbledon Championships

The All-England Championships, held on grass courts at Wimbledon, London, are regarded as the most prestigious championships in the world. They were first held in 1877 and, until 1922, were organized on a challenge-round basis, in which the defending champion met the winner of an all-comers tournament in the final. The tournament became Open in 1968, when, from a prize money total of £26,150, the men's singles champion received £2000. In 1998 the corresponding figures were £7,207,590 and £435,000.

Winners:

Men's singles

1877	Spencer Gore (UK)
1878	Frank Hadow (UK)
1879-80	Rev. John Hartley (UK)
1881-6	William Renshaw (UK)
l887	Herbert Lawford (UK)
1888	Ernest Renshaw (UK)
1889	William Renshaw (UK)
1890	Willoughby Hamilton (UK)
1891-2	Wilfred Baddeley (UK)
1893-4	Joshua Pim (UK)
1895	Wilfred Baddeley (UK)
1896	Harold Mahoney (UK)
1897-	
1900	Reginald Doherty (UK)
1901	Arthur Gore (UK)
1902-6	Laurence Doherty (UK)
1907	Norman Brookes (Aus)
1908-9	Arthur Gore (UK)
1910-3	Tony Wilding (NZ)
1914	Norman Brookes (Aus)
1919	Gerald Patterson (Aus)
1920-1	Bill Tilden (USA)
1922	Gerald Patterson (Aus)
1923	William Johnston (USA)
1924	Jean Borotra (Fra)
1925	René Lacoste (Fra)
1926	Jean Borotra (Fra)
1927	Henri Cochet (Fra)
1928	René Lacoste (Fra)
1929	Henri Cochet (Fra)
1930	Bill Tilden (USA)
1932	Ellsworth Vines (USA)
1933	Jack Crawford (Aus)
1934-6	Fred Perry (UK)
1937-8	Donald Budge (USA)
1939	Bobby Riggs (USA)
1946	Yvon Petra (Fra)
1947	Jack Kramer (USA)
1948	Bob Falkenburg (USA)
1949	Ted Schroeder (USA)
1950	Budge Patty (USA)
1951	Dick Savitt (USA)
1952	Frank Sedgman (Aus)
1953	Vic Seixas (USA)
1954	Jaroslav Drobny (Egy)
1955	Tony Trabert (USA)
1956-7	Lew Hoad (Aus)
1958	Ashley Cooper (Aus)
1959	Alex Olmedo (USA)
1960	Neale Fraser (Aus)
1961-2	Rod Laver (Aus)
1963	Chuck McKinley (USA)
1964-5	Roy Emerson (Aus)
1966	Manuel Santana (Spa)
1967	John Newcombe (Aus)
1968-9	Rod Laver (Aus)
1970-1	John Newcombe (Aus)
1972	Stan Smith (USA)
1973	Jan Kodes (Cs)
1974	Jimmy Connors (USA)
1975	Arthur Ashe (USA)
1976-80	Björn Borg (Swe)
1981	John McEnroe (USA)
1982	Jimmy Connors (USA)
1983-4	John McEnroe (USA)
1985-6	Boris Becker (FRG)
1987	Pat Cash (Aus)
1988	Stefan Edberg (Swe)
1989	Boris Becker (FRG)
1990	Stefan Edberg (Swe)
1991	Michael Stich (Ger)
1992	Andre Agassi (USA)
1993-5	Pete Sampras (USA)
1996	Richard Krajicek (Hol)
1997-8	Pete Sampras (USA)

Most wins: (pre-1922) 7 William Renshaw; (post-1922) 5 Borg, Sampras

Women's singles

1884-5	Maud Watson (UK)
1886	Blanche Bingley (UK)
1887-8	Lottie Dod (UK)
1889	Blanche Hillyard (UK)
1890	Helena Rice (UK)
1891-3	Lottie Dod (UK)
1894	Blanche Hillyard (UK)
1895-6	Charlotte Cooper (UK)
1897	Blanche Hillyard (UK)
1898	Charlotte Cooper (UK)
1899-	
1900	Blanche Hillyard (UK)
1901	Charlotte Sterry (UK)
1902	Muriel Robb (UK)
1903-4	Dorothea Douglass (UK)
1905	May Sutton (USA)
1906	Dorothea Douglass (UK)
1907	May Sutton (USA)
1908	Charlotte Sterry (UK)
1909	Dora Boothby (UK)

1910-1	Dorothea Lambert Chambers (UK)
1912	Ethel Larcombe (UK)
1913-4	Dorothea Lambert Chambers (UK)
1919-23	Suzanne Lenglen (Fra)
1924	Kathleen McKane (UK)
1925	Suzanne Lenglen (Fra)
1926	Kathleen Godfree (UK)
1927-9	Helen Wills (USA)
1930	Helen Moody (USA)
1931	Cilly Aussem (Ger)
1932-3	Helen Moody (USA)
1934	Dorothy Round (UK)
1935	Helen Moody (USA)
1936	Helen Jacobs (USA)
1937	Dorothy Round (UK)
1938	Helen Moody (USA)
1939	Alice Marble (USA)
1946	Pauline Betz (USA)
1947	Margaret Osborne (USA)
1948-50	Louise Brough (USA)
1951	Doris Hart (USA)
1952-4	Maureen Connolly (USA)
1955	Louise Brough (USA)
1956	Shirley Fry (USA)
1957-8	Althea Gibson (USA)
1959-60	Maria Bueno (Bra)
1961	Angela Mortimer (UK)
1962	Karen Susman (USA)
1963	Margaret Smith (Aus)
1964	Maria Bueno (Bra)
1965	Margaret Smith (Aus)
1966-8	Billie Jean King (USA)
1969	Ann Jones (UK)
1970	Margaret Court (Aus)
1971	Evonne Goolagong (Aus)
1972-3	Billie Jean King (USA)
1974	Chris Evert (USA)
1975	Billie Jean King (USA)
1976	Chris Evert (USA)
1977	Virginia Wade (UK)
1978-9	Martina Navrátilová (Cs)
1980	Evonne Cawley (Aus)
1981	Chris Evert Lloyd (USA)
1982-7	Martina Navrátilová (USA)
1988-9	Steffi Graf (FRG)
1990	Martina Navrátilová (USA)
1991-3	Steffi Graf (Ger)
1994	Conchita Martínez (Spa)
1995-6	Steffi Graf (Ger)
1997	Martina Hingis (Swi)
1998	Jana Novotná (Cze)

Most wins: (pre-1922) 7 Lambert Chambers (née Douglass); (post-1922) 9 Navrátilová; 8 Moody (née Wills); 7 Graf

Men's doubles

1879	L R Erskine & Herbert Lawford (UK)
1880-1	Ernest Renshaw & William Renshaw (UK)
1882	Rev. John Hartley & R T Richardson (UK)
1883	Charles Grinstead & CharlesWelldon (UK)
1884-6	Ernest & William Renshaw (UK)
1887	Patrick Bowes-Lyon & Herbert Wilberforce (UK)
1888-9	Ernest & William Renshaw (UK)
1890	Joshua Pim & Frank Stoker (UK)
1891	Herbert Baddeley & Wilfred Baddeley (UK)
1892	Harry Barlow & Ernest Lewis (UK)
1893	Joshua Pim & Frank Stoker (UK)
1894-6	Herbert Baddeley & Wilfred Baddeley (UK)
1897-	
1901	Laurence & Reginald Doherty (UK)
1902	Frank Riseley & Sidney Smith (UK)
1903-5	Laurence & Reginald Doherty (UK)
1906	Frank Riseley & Sidney Smith (UK)
1907	Norman Brookes (Aus) & Anthony Wilding (NZ)
1908	Major Ritchie (UK) & Anthony Wilding (NZ)
1909	Arthur Gore & Roper Barrett (UK)
1910	Major Ritchie (UK) & Anthony Wilding (NZ)
1911	Max Decugis & André Gobert (Fra)
1912-3	Charles Dixon & Roper Barrett (UK)
1914	Norman Brookes (Aus) & Anthony Wilding (NZ)
1919	Pat O'Hara Wood & Ronald Thomas (Aus)
1920	Charles Garland & Richard Williams (USA)
1921	Randolph Lycett & Max Woosnam (UK)
1922	James Anderson (Aus) & Randolph Lycett (UK)
1923	Leslie Godfree & Randolph Lycett (UK)
1924	Frank Hunter & Vincent Richards (USA)
1925	Jean Borotra & René Lacoste (Fra)
1926	Jacques Brugnon & Henri Cochet (Fra)
1927	Frank Hunter & William Tilden (USA)
1928	Jacques Brugnon & Henri Cochet (Fra)
1929-30	William Allison & John Van Ryn (USA)
1931	George Lott & John Van Ryn (USA)
1932-3	Jean Borotra & Jacques Brugnon (Fra)
1934	George Lott & Lester Stoefen (USA)
1935	Jack Crawford & Adrian Quist (Aus)
1936	Pat Hughes & Raymond Tuckey (UK)
1937-8	Don Budge & Gene Mako (USA)
1939	Ellwood Cooke & Bobby Riggs (USA)
1946	Tom Brown & Jack Kramer (USA)
1947	Bob Falkenburg & Jack Kramer (USA)
1948	John Bromwich & Frank Sedgman (Aus)
1949	Ricardo Gonzales & Frank Parker (USA)
1950	John Bromwich & Adrian Quist (Aus)
1951-2	Ken McGregor & Frank Sedgman (Aus)
1953	Lew Hoad & Ken Rosewall (Aus)
1954	Rex Hartwig & Mervyn Rose (Aus))
1955	Rex Hartwig & Lew Hoad (Aus)
1956	Lew Hoad & Ken Rosewall (Aus)

1957	Gardnar Mulloy & Budge Patty (USA)
1958	Sven Davidson & Ulf Schmidt (Swe)
1959	Roy Emerson & Neale Fraser (Aus)
1960	Rafael Osuna (Mex) & Dennis Ralston (USA)
1961	Roy Emerson & Neale Fraser (Aus)
1962	Bob Hewitt & Fred Stolle (Aus)
1963	Rafael Osuna & Antonio Palafox (Mex)
1964	Bob Hewitt & Fred Stolle (Aus)
1965	John Newcombe & Tony Roche (Aus)
1966	Ken Fletcher & John Newcombe (Aus)
1967	Bob Hewitt & Frew McMillan (SAf)
1968-70	John Newcombe & Tony Roche (Aus)
1971	Roy Emerson & Rod Laver (Aus)
1972	Bob Hewitt & Frew McMillan (SAf)
1973	Jimmy Connors (USA) & Ilie Nastase (Rom)
1974	John Newcombe & Tony Roche (Aus)
1975	Vitas Gerulaitis & Sandy Mayer (USA)
1976	Brian Gottfried (USA) & Raúl Ramirez (Mex)
1977	Ross Case & Geoff Masters (Aus)
1978	Bob Hewitt & Frew McMillan (SAf)
1979	Peter Fleming & John McEnroe (USA)
1980	Peter McNamara & Paul McNamee (Aus)
1981	Peter Fleming & John McEnroe (USA)
1982	Peter McNamara & Paul McNamee (Aus)
1983-4	Peter Fleming & John McEnroe (USA)
1985	Heinz Günthardt (Swi) & Balázs Taróczy (Hun)
1986	Joakim Nyström & Mats Wilander (Swe)
1987-8	Ken Flach & Robert Seguso (USA)
1989	John Fitzgerald (Aus) & Anders Järryd (Swe)
1990	Rick Leach & Jim Pugh (USA)
1991	John Fitzgerald (Aus) & Anders Järryd (Swe)
1992	John McEnroe (USA) & Michael Stich (Ger)
1993-7	Todd Woodbridge & Mark Woodforde (Aus)
1998	Jacco Eltingh & Paul Haarhuis (Hol)

Most wins: 8 Laurence & Reginald Doherty

Women's doubles

1913	Winifred McNair & Dora Boothby (UK)
1914	Agnes Morton (UK) & Elizabeth Ryan (USA)
1919-23	Suzanne Lenglen (Fra) & Elizabeth Ryan (USA)
1924	Hazel Wightman & Helen Wills (USA)
1925	Suzanne Lenglen (Fra) & Elizabeth Ryan (USA)
1926	Mary Browne & Elizabeth Ryan (USA)
1927	Helen Wills & Elizabeth Ryan (USA)
1928	Peggy Saunders & Phyllis Watson (UK)
1929	Peggy Michell & Phyllis Watson (UK)
1930	Helen Moody (née Wills) & Elizabeth Ryan (USA)
1931	Dorothy Barron & Phyllis Mudford (UK)
1932	Doris Metaxa (Fra) & Josane Sigart (Bel)
1933-4	Simone Mathieu (Fra) & Elizabeth Ryan (USA)
1935-6	Freda James & Kay Stammers (UK)
1937	Simone Mathieu (Fra) & Billie Yorke (UK)

1938-9	Sarah Fabyan & Alice Marble (USA)
1946	Louise Brough & Margaret Osborne (USA)
1947	Doris Hart & Pat Todd (USA)
1948-50	Louise Brough & Margaret Du Pont (USA)
1951-3	Shirley Fry & Doris Hart (USA)
1954	Louise Brough & Margaret Du Pont (USA)
1955	Angela Mortimer & Anne Shilcock (UK)
1956	Angela Buxton (UK) & Althea Gibson (USA)
1957	Althea Gibson & Darlene Hard (USA)
1958	Maria Bueno (Bra) & Althea Gibson (USA)
1959	Jean Arth & Darlene Hard (USA)
1960	Maria Bueno (Bra) & Darlene Hard (USA)
1961	Karen Hantze & Billie Jean Moffitt (USA)
1962	Billie Jean Moffitt & Karen Susman (USA)
1963	Maria Bueno (Bra) & Darlene Hard (USA)
1964	Margaret Smith & Lesley Turner (Aus)
1965	Maria Bueno (Bra) & Billie Jean Moffitt (USA)
1966	Maria Bueno (Bra) & Nancy Richey (USA)
1967-8	Rosemary Casals & Billie Jean King (USA)
1969	Margaret Court & Judy Tegart (Aus)
1970-1	Rosemary Casals & Billie Jean King (USA)
1972	Billie Jean King (USA) & Betty Stove (Hol)
1973	Rosemary Casals & Billie Jean King (USA)
1974	Evonne Goolagong (Aus) & Peggy Michel (USA)
1975	Ann Kiyomura (USA) & Kazuko Sawamatsu (Jap)
1976	Chris Evert (USA) & Martina Navrátilová (Cs)
1977	Helen Cawley (Aus) & Joanne Russell (USA)
1978	Kerry Reid & Wendy Turnbull (Aus)
1979	Billie Jean King (USA) & Martina Navrátilová (Cs)
1980	Kathy Jordan & Anne Smith (USA)
1981-4	Martina Navrátilová & Pam Shriver (USA)
1985	Kathy Jordan (USA) & Elizabeth Smylie (Aus)
1986	Martina Navrátilová & Pam Shriver (USA)
1987	Claudia Kohde-Kilsch (FRG) & Helena Sukova (Cs)
1988	Steffi Graf (FRG) & Gabriela Sabatini (Arg)
1989-90	Jana Novotná & Helena Suková (Cs)
1991	Larisa Savchenko & Natalya Zvereva (USSR)
1992-4	Gigi Fernandez (USA) & Natalya Zvereva (Blr)
1995	Jana Novotná & Arantxa Sánchez (Spa)
1996	Martina Hingis (Swi) & Helena Suková (Cze)
1997	Gigi Fernandez (USA) & Natalya Zvereva (Blr)
1998	Martina Hingis (Swi) & Jana Novotná (Cze)

Most wins: 12 Ryan

Mixed doubles

1913	Hope Crisp & Agnes Tuckey (UK)
1914	Cecil Parke & Ethel Larcombe (UK)
1919	Randolph Lycett (UK) & Elizabeth Ryan (USA)
1920	Gerald Patterson (Aus) & Suzanne Lenglen (Fra)

1921	Randolph Lycett (UK) & Elizabeth Ryan (USA)	1967	Owen Davidson (Aus) & Billie Jean King (USA)
1922	Pat O'Hara Wood (USA) & Suzanne Lenglen (Fra)	1968	Ken Fletcher & Margaret Court (Aus)
1923	Randolph Lycett (UK) & Elizabeth Ryan (USA)	1969	Fred Stolle (Aus) & Ann Jones (UK)
		1970	Ilie Nastase (Rom) & Rosemary Casals (USA)
1924	Brian Gilbert & Kathleen McKane (UK)	1971	Owen Davidson (Aus) & Billie Jean King (USA)
1925	Jean Borotra & Suzanne Lenglen (Fra)	1972	Ilie Nastase (Rom) & Rosemary Casals (USA)
1926	Leslie Godfree & Kathleen Godfree (UK)	1973-4	Owen Davidson (Aus) & Billie Jean King (USA)
1927	Frank Hunter & Elizabeth Ryan (USA)		
1928	Pat Spence (SAf) & Elizabeth Ryan (USA)	1975	Marty Riessen (USA) & Margaret Court (Aus)
1929	Frank Hunter & Helen Wills (USA)	1976	Tony Roche (Aus) & Françoise Durr (Fra)
1930	Jack Crawford (Aus) & Elizabeth Ryan (USA)	1977	Bob Hewitt & Greer Stevens (SAf)
		1978	Frew McMillan (SAf) & Betty Stove (Hol)
1931	George Lott & Anna Harper (USA)	1979	Bob Hewitt & Greer Stevens (SAf)
1932	Enrique Maier (Spa) & Elizabeth Ryan (USA)	1980	John Austin & Tracy Austin (USA)
1933	Gottfried von Cramm & Hilda Krahwinkel (Ger)	1981	Frew McMillan (SAf) & Betty Stove (Hol)
		1982	Kevin Curren (SAf) & Anne Smith (USA)
1934	Ryuki Miki (Jap) & Dorothy Round (UK)	1983-4	John Lloyd (UK) & Wendy Turnbull (Aus)
1935-6	Fred Perry & Dorothy Round (UK)	1985	Paul McNamee (Aus) & Martina Navrátilová (USA)
1937-8	Don Budge & Alice Marble (USA)		
1939	Bobby Riggs & Alice Marble (USA)	1986	Ken Flach & Kathy Jordan (USA)
1946	Tom Brown & Louise Brough (USA)	1987	Jeremy Bates & Jo Durie (UK)
1947-8	John Bromwich (Aus) & Louise Brough (USA)	1988	Sherwood Stewart & Zina Garrison (USA)
1949	Eric Sturgess & Sheila Summers (SAf)	1989	Jim Pugh (USA) & Jana Novotná (Cs)
1950	Eric Sturgess (SAf) & Louise Brough (USA)	1990	Rick Leach & Zina Garrison (USA)
1951-2	Frank Sedgman (Aus) & Doris Hart (USA)	1991	John Fitzgerald & Elizabeth Smylie (Aus)
1953-5	Vic Seixas & Doris Hart (USA)	1992	Cyril Suk (CS) & Larisa Savchenko (Lat)
1956	Vic Seixas & Shirley Fry (USA)	1993	Mark Woodforde (Aus) & Martina Navrátilová (USA)
1957	Mervyn Rose (Aus) & Darlene Hard (USA)		
1958	Bob Howe & Lorraine Coghlan (Aus)	1994	Todd Woodbridge (Aus) & Helena Suková (Cs)
1959-60	Rod Laver (Aus) & Darlene Hard (USA)		
1961	Fred Stolle & Lesley Turner (Aus)	1995	Jonathan Stark & Martina Navrátilová (USA)
1962	Neale Fraser (Aus) & Margaret Du Pont (USA)	1996-7	Cyril Suk & Helena Suková (Cze)
1963	Ken Fletcher & Margaret Smith (Aus)	1998	Max Mirnyi (Blr) & Serena Williams (USA)
1964	Fred Stolle & Lesley Turner (Aus)	**Most wins:** (men) 4 Seixas, Davidson, Fletcher;	
1965-6	Ken Fletcher & Margaret Smith (Aus)	(women) 7 Ryan	

Most Wimbledon titles

	Total	Singles	Doubles	Mixed	Years
Billie Jean King (USA)	20	6	10	4	1961-79
Elizabeth Ryan (USA)	19	-	12	7	1914-34
Martina Navrátilová (Cs/USA)	19	9	7	3	1976-95
Suzanne Lenglen (Fra)	15	6	6	3	1919-25
Laurence Doherty (UK)	13	5	8	-	1897-1905
Louise Brough (USA)	13	4	5	4	1946-55

Most successful singles players

The following list shows leading players, from the abolition of the challenge round in 1922, scored on the following points basis: 8 for winning the tournament, 4 for losing finalists, 2 for losing semi-finalists and 1 for losing quarter-finalists.

Points	Name	Won	F	SF	QF	Years
Men						
46	Björn Borg	5	1	-	2	1973-81
45	Jimmy Connors	2	4	5	3	1972-87
45	Boris Becker	3	4	2	1	1985-94
42	Pete Sampras	5	-	1	-	1992-8
41	Rod Laver	4	2	-	1	1959-71

Points	Name	Won	F	SF	QF	Years
39	John McEnroe	3	2	3	1	1977-92
33	Jean Borotra	2	3	2	1	1924-31
29	John Newcombe	3	1	–	1	1966-74
27	Henri Cochet	2	1	3	1	1925-33
27	Fred Perry	3	–	1	1	1931-6
27	Stefan Edberg	2	1	3	1	1987-93
24	Jaroslav Drobny	1	2	3	2	1946-55
23	Roy Emerson	2	–	1	5	1959-70
20	Don Budge	2	–	2	–	1935-8

Bill Tilden had two wins 1920-1 in challenge-round days plus 14 points (1 win, 2 sf) 1927-30.

Most semi-finals: 11 Connors

Women

Points	Name	Won	F	SF	QF	Years
97	Martina Navrátilová	9	3	5	3	1975-94
75	Billie Jean Moffitt/King	6	3	5	5	1962-83
68	Helen Wills/Moody	8	1	–	–	1924-38
66	Chris Evert	3	7	7	–	1972-89
62	Steffi Graf	7	1	1	–	1987-96
51	Louise Brough	4	3	3	1	1946-57
41	Margaret Smith/Court	3	2	4	1	1961-75
36	Maria Bueno	3	2		4	1958-68
35	Helen Jacobs	1	5	2	3	1929-39
28	Doris Hart	1	3	3	2	1946-55
27	Evonne Goolagong/Cawley	2	3	3	1	1971-80
26★	Suzanne Lenglen	3	–	1	–	1922-5
26	Ann Haydon/Jones	1	1	6	2	1958-69
24	Dorothy Round	2	1	–	4	1931-7
24	Maureen Connolly	3	–	–	–	1952-4
23	Kitty McKane/Godfree	2	1	1	1	1923-7
23	Margaret Osborne/Du Pont	1	2	2	3	1946-58
20	Virginia Wade	1	–	3	6	1967-83

★ Also three wins 1919-21.

Most appearances in finals: 12 Navrátilová; 10 Evert; 9 King

Most semi-finals: 17 Evert; Navrátilová; 14 King

Most successful players in challenge-round days (pre-1922)

(W = wins, RU = times as runner-up, losing in challenge-round final, AC = wins in all-comers tournament)

	W	RU	AC
Men			
William Renshaw	7	1	2
Laurence Doherty	5	1	2
Reginald Doherty	4	1	1
Tony Wilding	4	1	1
Arthur Wentworth Gore	3	3	4
Wilfred Baddeley	3	3	3
Herbert Lawford	1	5	5
Women			
Dorothea Lambert Chambers	7	4	4
Blanche Hillyard	6	6	8
Charlotte Sterry	5	5	6
Lottie Dod	5	–	2

US Championships

An American championship, open to all-comers, was held at Staten Island in September 1880 and won by Englishman O E Woodhouse. The first official US Championships were in 1881, following the formation of the US National Lawn Tennis Association. These were contested annually by amateurs until 1969, the year after the sport went Open. In 1968 and 1969 there were two Championships – Amateur and Open events. Since 1970 there has only been an Open competition. Played at Flushing Meadow, New York since 1978, previously at various venues, notably the West Side Club, Forest Hills, New York for the singles 1915-6 and 1924-77.

Winners:

Men's singles

Played on a challenge-round basis
1884-1911.

1881-7	Richard Sears (USA)
1888-9	Henry Slocum Jr (USA)
1890-2	Oliver Campbell (USA)
1893-4	Robert Wrenn (USA)
1895	Fred Hovey (USA)
1896-7	Robert Wrenn (USA)
1898-	
1900	Malcolm Whitman (USA)
1901-2	William Larned (USA)
1903	Laurence Doherty (UK)
1904	Holcombe Ward (USA)
1905	Beals Wright (USA)
1906	William Clothier (USA)
1907-11	William Larned (USA)
1912-3	Maurice McLoughlin (USA)
1914	Norris Williams (USA)
1915	William Johnston (USA)
1916	Norris Williams (USA)
1917-8	Lindley Murray (USA)
1919	William Johnston (USA)
1920-5	Bill Tilden (USA)
1926-7	René Lacoste (Fra)
1928	Henri Cochet (Fra)
1929	Bill Tilden (USA)
1930	John Doeg (USA)
1931-2	Ellsworth Vines (USA)
1933-4	Fred Perry (UK)
1935	Wilmer Allison (USA)
1936	Fred Perry (UK)
1937-8	Donald Budge (USA)
1939	Bobby Riggs (USA)
1940	Donald McNeil (USA)
1941	Bobby Riggs (USA)
1942	Ted Schroeder (USA
1943	Joseph Hunt (USA)
1944-5	Frank Parker (USA)
1946-7	Jack Kramer (USA)
1948-9	Ricardo Gonzales (USA)
1950	Arthur Larsen (USA)
1951-2	Frank Sedgman (Aus)
1953	Tony Trabert (USA)
1954	Vic Seixas (USA)
1955	Tony Trabert (USA)
1956	Ken Rosewall (Aus)
1957	Malcolm Anderson (Aus)
1958	Ashley Cooper (Aus)
1959-60	Neale Fraser (Aus)
1961	Roy Emerson (Aus)
1962	Rod Laver (Aus)
1963	Raphael Osuna (Mex)
1964	Roy Emerson (Aus)
1965	Manuel Santana (Spa)
1966	Fred Stolle (Aus)
1967	John Newcombe (Aus)
1968	Arthur Ashe (USA)
Open	Arthur Ashe (USA)
1969	Stan Smith (USA)
Open	Rod Laver (Aus)
1970	Ken Rosewall (Aus)
1971	Stan Smith (USA)
1972	Ilie Nastase (Rom)
1973	John Newcombe (Aus)
1974	Jimmy Connors (USA)
1975	Manuel Orantes (Spa)
1976	Jimmy Connors (USA)
1977	Guillermo Vilas (Arg)
1978	Jimmy Connors (USA)
1979-81	John McEnroe (USA)
1982-3	Jimmy Connors (USA)
1984	John McEnroe (USA)
1985-7	Ivan Lendl (Cs)
1988	Mats Wilander (Swe)
1989	Boris Becker (FRG)
1990	Pete Sampras (USA)
1991-2	Stefan Edberg (Swe)
1993	Pete Sampras (USA)
1994	Andre Agassi (USA)
1995-6	Pete Sampras (USA)
1997	Patrick Rafter (Aus)

Most wins: 7 Sears, Larned, Tilden

Women's singles

Played on a challenge-round basis
1887-1918.

1887	Ellen Hansell (USA)
1888-9	Bertha Townsend (USA)
1890	Ellen Roosevelt (USA)
1891-2	Mabel Cahill (USA)
1893	Aline Terry (USA)
1894	Helen Helwig (USA)
1895	Juliette Atkinson (USA)
1896	Elisabeth Moore (USA)
1897-8	Juliette Atkinson (USA)
1899	Marion Jones (USA)
1900	Myrtle McAteer (USA)
1901	Elisabeth Moore (USA)
1902	Marion Jones (USA)
1903	Elisabeth Moore (USA)
1904	May Sutton (USA)
1905	Elisabeth Moore (USA)
1906	Helen Homans (USA)
1907	Evelyn Sears (USA)
1908	Maud Bargar-Wallach (USA)
1909-11	Hazel Hotchkiss (USA)
1912-4	Mary Browne (USA)
1915-8	Molla Bjurstedt (USA)
1919	Hazel Wightman (née Hotchkiss) (USA)
1920-2	Molla Mallory (née Bjurstedt) (USA)
1923-5	Helen Wills (USA)
1926	Molla Mallory (USA)
1927-9	Helen Wills (USA)
1930	Betty Nuthall (UK)
1931	Helen Moody (née Wills)
1932-5	Helen Jacobs (USA)
1936	Alice Marble (USA)
1937	Anita Lizana (Chl)
1938-40	Alice Marble (USA)
1941	Sarah Cooke (USA)
1942-4	Pauline Betz (USA)
1945	Sarah Cooke (USA)
1946	Pauline Betz (USA)
1947	Louise Brough (USA)
1948-50	Margaret Du Pont (USA)
1951-3	Maureen Connolly (USA)
1954-5	Doris Hart (USA)
1956	Shirley Fry (USA)
1957-8	Althea Gibson (USA)
1959	Maria Bueno (Bra)
1960-1	Darlene Hard (USA)
1962	Margaret Smith (Aus)
1963-4	Maria Bueno (Bra)
1965	Margaret Smith (Aus)
1966	Maria Bueno (Bra)
1967	Billie Jean King (USA)
1968	Margaret Court (Aus)
Open	Virginia Wade (UK)
1969	Margaret Court (Aus)
Open	Margaret Court (Aus)
1970	Margaret Court (Aus)
1971-2	Billie Jean King (USA)
1973	Margaret Court (Aus)
1974	Billie Jean King (USA)
1975-8	Chris Evert (USA)
1979	Tracy Austin (USA)
1980	Chris Evert Lloyd (USA)
1981	Tracy Austin (USA)
1982	Chris Evert Lloyd (USA)
1983-4	Martina Navrátilová (USA)
1985	Hanna Mandlíková (Cs)
1986-7	Martina Navrátilová (USA)
1988-9	Steffi Graf (FRG)
1990	Gabriela Sabatini (Arg)
1991-2	Monica Seles (Yug)
1993	Steffi Graf (Ger)
1994	Arantxa Sánchez (Spa)
1995-6	Steffi Graf (Ger)
1997	Martina Hingis (Swi)

Most wins: 7 Bjurstedt/Mallory, Wills/Moody

Winners from 1946:

Men's doubles

1946	Gardnar Mulloy & William Talbert (USA)
1947	Jack Kramer & Ted Schroeder (USA)
1948	Gardnar Mulloy & William Talbert (USA)
1949	John Bromwich & William Sidwell (Aus)
1950	John Bromwich & Frank Sedgman (Aus)
1951	Ken McGregor & Frank Sedgman (Aus)
1952	Mervin Rose (Aus) & Vic Seixas (USA)
1953	Rex Hartwig & Mervyn Rose (Aus)
1954	Vic Seixas & Tony Trabert (USA)
1955	Kosei Kano & Atsushi Miyagi (Jap)
1956	Lew Hoad & Ken Rosewall (Aus)
1957	Ashley Cooper & Neale Fraser (Aus)
1958	Alex Olmedo & Ham Richardson (USA)
1959-60	Roy Emerson & Neale Fraser (Aus)
1961	Charles McKinley & Dennis Ralston (USA)
1962	Antonio Palafox & Rafael Osuna (Mex)
1963-4	Charles McKinley & Dennis Ralston (USA)
1965-6	Roy Emerson & Fred Stolle (Aus)
1967	John Newcombe & Tony Roche (Aus)
1968	Bob Lutz & Stan Smith (USA)
Open	Bob Lutz & Stan Smith (USA)
1969	Dick Crealy & Allan Stone (Aus)
Open	Ken Rosewall & Fred Stolle (Aus)
1970	Pierre Barthes (Fra) & Nikki Pilic (Yug)
1971	John Newcombe (Aus) & Roger Taylor (UK)
1972	Cliff Drysdale (SAf) & Roger Taylor (UK)
1973	Owen Davidson & John Newcombe (Aus)
1974	Bob Lutz & Stan Smith (USA)
1975	Jimmy Connors (USA) & Ilie Nastase (Rom)
1976	Tom Okker (Hol) & Marty Riessen (USA)
1977	Bob Hewitt & Frew McMillan (SAf)
1978	Bob Lutz & Stan Smith (USA)
1979	Peter Fleming & John McEnroe (USA)
1980	Bob Lutz & Stan Smith (USA)
1981	Peter Fleming & John McEnroe (USA)
1982	Kevin Curren (SAf) & Steve Denton (USA)
1983	Peter Fleming & John McEnroe (USA)
1984	John Fitzgerald (Aus) & Tomás Smid (Cs)
1985	Ken Flach & Robert Seguso (USA)
1986	Andrés Gómez (Ecu) & Slobodan Zivojinovic (Yug)
1987	Stefan Edberg & Anders Järryd (Swe)
1988	Sergio Casal & Emilio Sánchez (Spa)
1989	John McEnroe (USA) & Mark Woodforde (Aus)
1990	Pieter Aldrich & Danie Visser (SAf)
1991	John Fitzgerald (Aus) & Anders Järryd (Swe)
1992	Jim Grabb & Richey Reneberg (USA)
1993	Ken Flach & Rick Leach (USA)
1994	Jacco Eltingh & Paul Haarhuis (Hol)
1995-6	Todd Woodbridge & Mark Woodforde (Aus)
1997	Yevgeniy Kafelnikov (Rus) & Daniel Vacek (Cze)

Most wins by one pair: 5 Richard Sears & James Dwight 1882-4, 1886-7

Most wins by player: 6 Richard Sears (also won with Joseph Clark 1885), Holcombe Ward 1899-1901 (with Dwight Davis), 1904-6 (with Beals Wright); 5 Bill Tilden 1918, 1921-2 (with Vincent Richards), 1923 (with Brian Norton), 1927 (with Francis Hunter), Vincent Richards, also with Norris Williams 1925-6, George Lott, Jr 1928 (with John Hennessy), 1929-30 (with John Doeg), 1933-4 (with Lester Stoefen)

Women's doubles

1942-50	Louise Brough & Margaret Osborne (USA)
1951-4	Shirley Fry & Doris Hart (USA)
1955-7	Louise Brough & Margaret Du Pont (USA)
1958-9	Jean Arth & Darlene Hard (USA)
1960	Maria Bueno (Bra) & Darlene Hard (USA)
1961	Darlene Hard (USA) & Lesley Turner (Aus)
1962	Maria Bueno (Bra) & Darlene Hard (USA)
1963	Robyn Ebbern & Margaret Smith (Aus)
1964	Karen Susman & Billie Jean Moffitt (USA)
1965	Nancy Richey & Carole Graebner (USA)
1966	Maria Bueno (Bra) & Nancy Richey (USA)
1967	Rosemary Casals & Billie Jean King (USA)
1968	Maria Bueno (Bra) & Margaret Court (Aus)
Open	Maria Bueno (Bra) & Margaret Court (Aus)
1969	Margaret Court (Aus) & Virginia Wade (UK)
Open	Françoise Durr (Fra) & Darlene Hard (USA)
1970	Margaret Court & Judy Dalton (Aus)
1971	Rosemary Casals (USA) & Judy Dalton (Aus)
1972	Françoise Durr (Fra) & Betty Stove (Hol)
1973	Margaret Court (Aus) & Virginia Wade (UK)
1974	Rosemary Casals & Billie Jean King (USA)
1975	Margaret Court (Aus) & Virginia Wade (UK)
1976	Linda Boshoff & Ilana Kloss (SAf)
1977	Martina Navrátilová (Cs) & Betty Stove (Hol)
1978	Billie Jean King (USA) & Martina Navrátilová (Cs)
1979	Betty Stove (Hol) & Wendy Turnbull (Aus)
1980	Billie Jean King (USA) & Martina Navrátilová (Cs)
1981	Kathy Jordan & Anne Smith (USA)
1982	Rosemary Casals (USA) & Wendy Turnbull (Aus)
1983-4	Martina Navrátilová & Pam Shriver (USA)
1985	Claudia Kohde-Kilsch (FRG) & Helena Suková (Cs)
1986-7	Martina Navrátilová & Pam Shriver (USA)
1988	Gigi Fernandez & Robin White (USA)
1989	Martina Navrátilová (USA) & Hana Mandlíková (Aus)
1990	Martina Navrátilová & Gigi Fernandez (USA)
1991	Pam Shriver (USA) & Natalya Zvereva (USSR)
1992	Gigi Fernandez (USA) & Natalya Zvereva (Blr)

1993	Arantxa Sánchez (Spa) & Helena Suková (Cze)
1994	Arantxa Sánchez (Spa) & Jana Novotná (Cze)
1995-6	Gigi Fernandez (USA) & Natalya Zvereva (Blr)
1997	Lindsay Davenport (USA) & Jana Novotná (Cze)

Most wins by one pair: 12 Brough & Du Pont (née Osborne)

Most wins by player: 13 Du Pont also 1941 (with Sarah Cooke); 12 Brough; 9 Navrátilová; 7 Juliette Atkinson 1894-5 (with Helen Helwig), 1896 (with Elisabeth Moore), 1897-8 (with Kathleen Atkinson), 1901 (with Myrtle McAteer), 1902 (with Marion Jones), Smith/Court; 6 Hazel Wightman (née Hotchkiss) 1909-10 (with Edith Rotch), 1911, 1915 (with Eleonora Sears), 1924, 1928 (with Helen Wills)

Mixed doubles

1943-6	William Talbert & Margaret Osborne (USA)
1947	John Bromwich (Aus) & Louise Brough (USA)
1948	Tom Brown & Louise Brough (USA)
1949	Eric Sturgess (SAf) & Louise Brough (USA)
1950	Ken McGregor (Aus) & Margaret Du Pont (USA)
1951-2	Frank Sedgman (Aus) & Doris Hart (USA)
1953-5	Vic Seixas & Doris Hart (USA)
1956	Ken Rosewall (Aus) & Margaret Du Pont (USA)
1957	Kurt Nielsen (Den) & Althea Gibson (USA)
1958-60	Neale Fraser (Aus) & Margaret Du Pont (USA)
1961	Robert Mark & Margaret Smith (Aus)
1962	Fred Stolle & Margaret Smith (Aus)
1963	Ken Fletcher & Margaret Smith (Aus)
1964	John Newcombe & Margaret Smith (Aus)
1965	Fred Stolle & Margaret Smith (Aus)
1966	Owen Davidson (Aus) & Donna Fales (USA)
1967	Owen Davidson (Aus) & Billie Jean King (USA)
1968	Peter Curtis (UK) & Mary-Ann Eisel (USA)
1969	Paul Sullivan & Patty Hogan (USA)
Open	Marty Riessen (USA) & Margaret Court (née Smith) (Aus)
1970	Marty Riessen (USA) & Margaret Court (Aus)
1971	Owen Davidson (Aus) & Billie Jean King (USA)
1972	Marty Riessen (USA) & Margaret Court (Aus)
1973	Owen Davidson (Aus) & Billie Jean King (USA)
1974	Geoff Masters (Aus) & Pam Teeguarden (USA)
1975	Dick Stockton & Rosemary Casals (USA)
1976	Phil Dent (Aus) & Billie Jean King (USA)
1977-8	Frew McMillan (SAf) & Betty Stove (Hol)

1979	Bob Hewitt & Greer Stevens (SAf)
1980	Marty Riessen & Wendy Turnbull (USA)
1981-2	Kevin Curren (SAf) & Anne Smith (USA)
1983	John Fitzgerald & Elizabeth Sayers (Aus)
1984	Tom Gullikson (USA) & Manuela Maleeva (Bul)
1985	Heinz Günthardt (Swi) & Martina Navrátilová (USA)
1986	Sergio Casal (Spa) & Raffaella Reggi (Ita)
1987	Emilio Sánchez (Spa) & Martina Navrátilová (USA)
1988	Jim Pugh (USA) & Jana Novotná (Cs)
1989	Shelby Cannon & Robin White (USA)
1990	Todd Woodbridge & Elizabeth Smylie (Aus)
1991	Tom Nijssen & Manon Bollegraf (Hol)
1992	Mark Woodforde & Nicole Provis (Aus)
1993	Todd Woodbridge (Aus) & Helena Suková (Cze)
1994	Patrick Galbraith (USA) & Elna Reinach (SAf)
1995	Matt Lucena & Meredith McGrath (USA)
1996	Patrick Galbraith & Lisa Raymond (USA)
1997	Rick Leach (USA) & Manon Bollegraf (Hol)

Most wins by one pair: 4 William Talbert & Margaret Osborne 1943-6

Most wins by woman player: 9 Osborne/Du Pont; 8 Smith/Court; 6 Hazel Wightman (née Hotchkiss) 1909, 1910 (with Joseph Carpenter), 1911, 1915 (with Harry Johnson), 1918 (with Irving Wright), 1920 (with Wallace Johnson),

Most wins by man player: 4 Edwin Fischer 1894-6, 1898; Wallace Johnson 1907, 1909, 1911, 1920, Bill Tilden 1913-4, 1922-3, William Talbert 1943-6, Davidson, Riessen

French Open

The French Championships were first held in 1891. Until 1925 they were open only to members of French clubs, but thereafter became a fully international event. They have always been held on clay courts, and at the Stade Roland Garros since 1928. Prize money totalled 57 million francs in 1997.
Winners from 1925:

Men's singles

1925	René Lacoste (Fra)
1926	Henri Cochet (Fra)
1927	René Lacoste (Fra)
1928	Henri Cochet (Fra)
1929	René Lacoste (Fra)
1930	Henri Cochet (Fra)
1931	Jean Borotra (Fra)
1932	Henri Cochet (Fra)
1933	Jack Crawford (Aus)
1934	Gottfried Von Cramm (Ger)
1935	Fred Perry (UK)
1936	Gottfried Von Cramm (Ger)

1937	Henner Henkel (Ger)	
1938	Donald Budge (USA)	
1939	Donald McNeill (USA)	
1946	Marcel Bernard (Fra)	
1947	József Asboth (Hun)	
1948-9	Frank Parker (USA)	
1950	Budge Patty (USA)	
1951-2	Jaroslav Drobny (Egy)	
1953	Ken Rosewall (Aus)	
1954-5	Tony Trabert (USA)	
1956	Lew Hoad (Aus)	
1957	Sven Davidson (Swe)	
1958	Mervyn Rose (Aus)	
1959-60	Nicola Pietrangeli (Ita)	
1961	Manuel Santana (Spa)	
1962	Rod Laver (Aus)	
1963	Roy Emerson(Aus)	
1964	Manuel Santana (Spa)	
1965	Fred Stolle (Aus)	
1966	Tony Roche (Aus)	
1967	Roy Emerson (Aus)	
1968	Ken Rosewall (Aus)	
1969	Rod Laver (Aus)	
1970-1	Jan Kodes (Cs)	
1972	Andrés Gimeno (Spa)	
1973	Ilie Nastase (Rom)	
1974-5	Björn Borg (Swe)	
1976	Adriano Panatta (Ita)	
1977	Guillermo Vilas (Arg)	
1978-81	Björn Borg (Swe)	
1982	Mats Wilander (Swe)	
1983	Yannick Noah (Fra)	
1984	Ivan Lendl (Cs)	
1985	Mats Wilander (Swe)	
1986-7	Ivan Lendl (Cs)	

1988	Mats Wilander (Swe)
1989	Michael Chang (USA)
1990	Andrés Gómez (Ecu)
1991-2	Jim Courier (USA)
1993-4	Sergi Bruguera (Spa)
1995	Thomas Muster (Aut)
1996	Yevgeniy Kafelnikov (Rus)
1997	Gustavo Kuerten (Bra)
1998	Carlos Moyà (Spa)

Most wins: 6 Borg

Women's singles

1925-6	Suzanne Lenglen (Fra)
1927	Kea Bouman (Hol)
1928-30	Helen Wills Moody (USA)
1931	Cilly Aussem (Ger)
1932	Helen Moody (USA)
1933-4	Margaret Scriven (UK)
1935-7	Hilde Sperling (Ger)
1938-9	Simone Mathieu (Fra)
1946	Margaret Osborne (USA)
1947	Pat Todd (USA)
1948	Nelly Landry (Fra)
1949	Margaret Du Pont (née Osborne) (USA)
1950	Doris Hart (USA)
1951	Shirley Fry (USA)
1952	Doris Hart (USA)
1953-4	Maureen Connolly (USA)
1955	Angela Mortimer (UK)
1956	Althea Gibson (USA)
1957	Shirley Bloomer (UK)
1958	Zsuzsi Körmöczy (Hun)
1959	Christine Truman (UK)
1960	Darlene Hard (USA)

1961	Ann Haydon (UK)
1962	Margaret Smith (Aus)
1963	Lesley Turner (Aus)
1964	Margaret Smith (Aus)
1965	Lesley Turner (Aus)
1966	Ann Jones (UK)
1967	Françoise Durr (Fra)
1968	Nancy Richey (USA)
1969	Margaret Court (née Smith) (Aus)
1970	Margaret Court (Aus)
1971	Evonne Goolagong (Aus)
1972	Billie Jean King (USA)
1973	Margaret Court (Aus)
1974-5	Chris Evert (USA)
1976	Sue Barker (UK)
1977	Mimi Jausovec (Yug)
1978	Virginia Ruzici (Rom)
1979-80	Chris Evert Lloyd (USA)
1981	Hana Mandlíková (Cs)
1982	Martina Navrátilová (USA)
1983	Chris Evert Lloyd (USA)
1984	Martina Navrátilová (USA)
1985-6	Chris Evert Lloyd (USA)
1987-8	Steffi Graf (FRG)
1989	Arantxa Sánchez (Spa)
1990-2	Monica Seles (Yug)
1993	Steffi Graf (Ger)
1994	Arantxa Sánchez (Spa)
1995-6	Steffi Graf (Ger)
1997	Iva Majoli (Cro)
1998	Arantxa Sánchez (Spa)

Most wins: 7 Evert Lloyd

Winners from 1946:

Men's doubles

1946	Marcel Bernard & Yvon Petra (Fra)
1947	Eustace Fannin & Eric Sturgess (SAf)
1948	Lennart Bergelin (Swe) & Jaroslav Drobny (Cs)
1949	Richard Gonzales & Frank Parker (USA)
1950	William Talbert & Tony Trabert (USA)
1951-2	Ken McGregor & Frank Sedgman (Aus)
1953	Lew Hoad & Ken Rosewall (Aus)
1954-5	Vic Seixas & Tony Trabert (USA)
1956	Don Candy (Aus) & Robert Perry (USA)
1957	Mal Anderson & Ashley Cooper (Aus)
1958	Ashley Cooper & Neale Fraser (Aus)
1959	Nicola Pietrangeli & Orlando Sirola (Ita)
1960	Roy Emerson & Neale Fraser (Aus)
1961	Roy Emerson & Rod Laver (Aus)
1962	Roy Emerson & Neale Fraser (Aus)
1963	Roy Emerson (Aus) & Manuel Santana (Spa)
1964	Roy Emerson & Ken Fletcher (Aus)

1965	Roy Emerson & Fred Stolle (Aus)
1966	Clark Graebner & Dennis Ralston (USA)
1967	John Newcombe & Tony Roche (Aus)
1968	Ken Rosewall & Fred Stolle (Aus)
1969	John Newcombe & Tony Roche (Aus)
1970	Ilie Nastase & Ion Tiriac (Rom)
1971	Arthur Ashe & Marty Riessen (USA)
1972	Bob Hewitt & Frew McMillan (SAf)
1973	John Newcombe (Aus) & Tom Okker (Hol)
1974	Dick Crealy (Aus) & Onny Parun (NZ)
1975	Brian Gottfried (USA) & Raúl Ramirez (Mex)
1976	Fred McNair & Sherwood Stewart (USA)
1977	Brian Gottfried (USA) & Raúl Ramirez (Mex)
1978	Gene Mayer & Hank Pfister (USA)
1979	Sandy Mayer & Gene Mayer (USA)
1980	Victor Amaya & Hank Pfister (USA)
1981	Heinz Günthardt (Swi) & Balázs Taróczy (Hun)
1982	Sherwood Stewart & Ferdi Taygan (USA)

1983	Anders Järryd & Hans Simonsson (Swe)
1984	Henri Leconte & Yannick Noah (Fra)
1985	Mark Edmondson & Kim Warwick (Aus)
1986	John Fitzgerald (Aus) & Tomás Smid (Cs)
1987	Anders Järryd (Swe) & Robert Seguso (USA)
1988	Andrés Gómez (Ecu) & Emilio Sánchez (Spa)
1989	Jim Grabb & Patrick McEnroe (USA)
1990	Sergio Casal & Emilio Sánchez (Spa)
1991	John Fitzgerald (Aus) & Anders Järryd (Swe)
1992	Jakob Hlasek & Marc Rosset (Swi)
1993	Luke Jensen & Murphy Jensen (USA)
1994	Byron Black (Zim) & Jonathan Stark (USA)
1995	Jacco Eltingh & Paul Haarhuis (Hol)
1996-7	Yevgeniy Kafelnikov (Rus) & Daniel Vacek (Cze)
1998	Jacco Eltingh & Paul Haarhuis (Hol)

Most wins: 6 Emerson; 5 Jean Borotra, 1925, 1928, 1929 (with René Lacoste), 1934 (with Brugnon), 1936 (with Marcel Bernard), Jacques Brugnon 1927, 1928, 1930, 1932 (with Henri Cochet), 1934 (with Borotra)

Women's doubles

1946-7	Louise Brough & Margaret Osborne (USA)
1948	Doris Hart & Pat Todd (USA)
1949	Louise Brough & Margaret Du Pont (née Osborne) (USA)
1950-3	Shirley Fry & Doris Hart (USA)
1954	Maureen Connolly (USA) & Nell Hopman (Aus)
1955	Beverley Fleitz & Darlene Hard (USA)
1956	Angela Buxton (UK) & Althea Gibson (USA)
1957	Shirley Bloomer (UK) & Darlene Hard (USA)
1958	Yola Ramirez & Rosa Reyes (Mex)
1959	Sandra Reynolds & Renée Schuurman (SAf)
1960	Maria Bueno (Bra) & Darlene Hard (USA)
1961	Sandra Reynolds & Renée Schuurman (SAf)
1962	Sandra Price (née Reynolds) & Renée Schuurman (SAf)
1963	Ann Jones (UK) & Renée Schuurman (SAf)
1964-5	Margaret Smith & Lesley Turner (Aus)
1966	Margaret Smith & Judy Tegart (Aus)
1967	Françoise Durr (Fra) & Gail Sheriff (Aus)
1968-9	Françoise Durr (Fra) & Ann Jones (UK)
1970-1	Françoise Durr & Gail Chanfreau (Fra)
1972	Billie Jean King (USA) & Betty Stove (Hol)
1973	Margaret Court (Aus) & Virginia Wade (UK)
1974	Chris Evert (USA) & Olga Morozova (USSR)
1975	Chris Evert (USA) & Martina Navrátilová (Cs)
1976	Fiorella Bonicelli (Uru) & Gail Lovera (Fra)
1977	Regina Marsikova (Cs) & Pam Teeguarden (USA)
1978	Mimi Jausovec (Yug) & Virginia Ruzici (Rom)
1979	Betty Stove (Hol) & Wendy Turnbull (Aus)
1980	Kathy Jordan & Anne Smith (USA)
1981	Ros Fairbank & Tanya Harford (SAf)

1982	Martina Navrátilová & Anne Smith (USA)
1983	Ros Fairbank (SAf) & Candy Reynolds (USA)
1984-5	Martina Navrátilová & Pam Shriver (USA)
1986	Martina Navrátilová (USA) & Andrea Temesvári (Hun)
1987-8	Martina Navrátilová & Pam Shriver (USA)
1989	Larisa Savchenko & Natalya Zvereva (USSR)
1990	Jana Novotná & Helena Suková (Cs)
1991	Gigi Fernandez (USA) & Jana Novotná (Cs)
1992-5	Gigi Fernandez (USA) & Natalya Zvereva (Blr)
1996	Lindsay Davenport & Mary Joe Fernandez (USA)
1997	Gigi Fernandez (USA) & Natalya Zvereva (Blr)
1998	Martina Hingis (Swi) & Jana Novotná (Cze)

Most wins: 7 Navrátilová; 6 Simone Mathieu (Fra) 1933-4 (with Elizabeth Ryan), 1936-8 (with Billie Yorke), Zvereva, G Fernandez

Mixed doubles

1946	Budge Patty & Pauline Betz (USA)
1947	Eric Sturgess & Sheila Summers (SAf)
1948	Jaroslav Drobny (Cs) & Pat Todd (USA)
1949	Eric Sturgess & Sheila Summers (SAf)
1950	Enrique Morea (Arg) & Barbara Scofield (USA)
1951-2	Frank Sedgman (Aus) & Doris Hart (USA)
1953	Vic Seixas & Doris Hart (USA)
1954	Lew Hoad (Aus) & Maureen Connolly (USA)
1955	Gordon Forbes (SAf) & Darlene Hard (USA)
1956	Luis Ayala (Chl) & Thelma Long (Aus)
1957	Jan Javorsky & Vera Puzejová (Cs)
1958	Nicola Pietrangeli (Ita) & Shirley Bloomer (UK)
1959	Billy Knight (UK) & Yola Ramirez (Mex)
1960	Bob Howe (Aus) & Maria Bueno (Bra)
1961	Rod Laver (Aus) & Darlene Hard (USA)
1962	Bob Howe (Aus) & Renée Schuurman (SAf)
1963-5	Ken Fletcher & Margaret Smith (Aus)
1966	Frew McMillan & Annette Van Zyl (SAf)
1967	Owen Davidson (Aus) & Billie Jean King (USA)
1968	Jean-Claude Barclay & Françoise Durr (Fra)
1969	Marty Riessen (USA) & Margaret Court (née Smith) (Aus)
1970	Bob Hewitt (SAf) & Billie Jean King (USA)
1971	Jean-Claude Barclay & Françoise Durr (Fra)
1972	Kim Warwick & Evonne Goolagong (Aus)
1973	Jean-Claude Barclay & Françoise Durr (Fra)
1974	Ivan Molina (Col) & Martina Navrátilová (Cs)
1975	Thomaz Koch (Bra) & Fiorella Bonicelli Uru)
1976	Kim Warwick (Aus) & Ilana Kloss (SAf)
1977	John McEnroe & Mary Carillo (USA)
1978	Pavel Slozil & Renata Tomanova (Cs)
1979	Bob Hewitt (SAf) & Wendy Turnbull (Aus)
1980	Bill Martin & Anne Smith (USA)

1981	Jimmy Arias & Andrea Jaeger (USA)	1992	Todd Woodbridge (Aus) & Arantxa Sánchez
1982	John Lloyd (UK) & Wendy Turnbull (Aus)		(Spa)
1983	Eliot Teltscher & Barbara Jordan (USA)	1993	Andrey Olkhovskiy & Yevgeniya Maniokova
1984	Dick Stockton & Anne Smith (USA)		(Rus)
1985	Heinz Günthardt (Swi) & Martina	1994	Menno Oosting & Kristie Boogert (Hol)
	Navrátilová (USA)	1995	Mark Woodforde (Aus) & Larisa Neiland
1986	Ken Flach & Kathy Jordan (USA)		(Lat)
1987	Emilio Sánchez (Spa) & Pam Shriver (USA)	1996	Javier Frana & Patricia Tarabini (Arg)
1988	Jorge Lozano (Mex) & Lori McNeill (USA)	1997	Mahesh Bhupathi (Ind) & Rika Hiraki (Jap)
1989	Tom Nijssen & Manon Bollegraf (Hol)	1998	Justin Gimelstob & Venus Williams (USA)
1990	Jorge Lozano (Mex) & Arantxa Sánchez (Spa)	**Most wins:** (men) 3 Fletcher, Barclay; (women)	
1991	Cyril Suk & Helena Suková (Cs)	4 Smith/Court	

Most French titles

	Total	Singles	Doubles	Mixed	Years
Margaret Smith/Court (Aus)	13	5	4	4	1962-73
Martina Navrátilová (Cs/USA)	11	2	7	2	1974-88
Simone Mathieu (Fra)	10	2	6	2	1933-9
Doris Hart (USA)	10	2	5	3	1948-53
Henri Cochet (Fra)	9	4	3	2	1926-30
Françoise Durr (Fra)	9	1	5	3	1967-73
Chris Evert Lloyd (USA)	9	7	2	–	1974-86

Australian Championships

The first Australasian championships were held in 1905, and it was not until 1925 that the title changed to its present style. New Zealand twice hosted the championship, in 1906 (Christchurch) and 1912 (Hastings) and each of the five major Australian cities staged the tournament before it settled at Melbourne – 1927-87 at Kooyong and from 1988 at the National Tennis Centre, Flinders Park, now known as Melbourne Park, where the main court has a moveable roof. The championships were held on grass up to 1987, but thereafter on a rubberized cement composition court. There were two championships in 1977 because the event was moved from early-season (January) to December. It reverted to a January date in 1987, which meant there was no tournament in 1986.

Post-war winners:

Men's singles

1946	John Bromwich (Aus)
1947	Dinny Pails (Aus)
1948	Adrian Quist (Aus)
1949-50	Frank Sedgman (Aus)
1951	Dick Savitt (USA)
1952	Ken McGregor (Aus)
1953	Ken Rosewall (Aus)
1954	Mervyn Rose (Aus)
1955	Ken Rosewall (Aus)
1956	Lew Hoad (Aus)
1957-8	Ashley Cooper (Aus)
1959	Alex Olmedo (USA)
1960	Rod Laver (Aus)
1961	Roy Emerson (Aus)
1962	Rod Laver (Aus)
1963-7	Roy Emerson (Aus)
1968	Bill Bowrey (Aus)
1969	Rod Laver (Aus)
1970	Arthur Ashe (USA)
1971-2	Ken Rosewall (Aus)
1973	John Newcombe (Aus)
1974	Jimmy Connors (USA)
1975	John Newcombe (Aus)
1976	Mark Edmondson (Aus)
1977	Roscoe Tanner (USA)
1977	Vitas Gerulaitis (USA)
1978-9	Guillermo Vilas (Arg)
1980	Brian Teacher (USA)
1981-2	Johan Kriek (SAf)
1983-4	Mats Wilander (Swe)
1985	Stefan Edberg (Swe)
1987	Stefan Edberg (Swe)
1988	Mats Wilander (Swe)
1989-90	Ivan Lendl (Cs)
1991	Boris Becker (Ger)
1992-3	Jim Courier (USA)
1994	Pete Sampras (USA)
1995	Andre Agassi (USA)
1996	Boris Becker (Ger)
1997	Pete Sampras (USA)
1998	Petr Korda (Cze)

Most wins: 6 Emerson; 4 Jack Crawford (Aus) 1931-3, 1935, Rosewall

Women's singles

1946-8	Nancye Bolton (Aus)
1949	Doris Hart (USA)
1950	Louise Brough (USA)
1951	Nancye Bolton (Aus)
1952	Thelma Long (Aus)
1953	Maureen Connolly (USA)
1954	Thelma Long (Aus)
1955	Beryl Penrose (Aus)
1956	Mary Carter (Aus)
1957	Shirley Fry (USA)
1958	Angela Mortimer (UK)
1959	Mary Reitano (Aus)
1960-6	Margaret Smith (Aus)
1967	Nancy Richey (USA)
1968	Billie Jean King (USA)
1969	Margaret Court (née Smith) (Aus)
1970-1	Margaret Court (Aus)
1972	Virginia Wade (UK)
1973	Margaret Court (Aus)
1974-5	Evonne Goolagong (Aus)

1976	Evonne Cawley (née Goolagong) (Aus)
1977	Kerry Reid (Aus)
1977	Evonne Cawley (Aus)
1978	Christine O'Neill (Aus)
1979	Barbara Jordan (USA)
1980	Hana Mandlíková (Cs)
1981	Martina Navrátilová (USA)
1982	Chris Evert Lloyd (USA)
1983	Martina Navrátilová (USA)
1984	Chris Evert Lloyd (USA)
1985	Martina Navrátilová (USA)
1987	Hana Mandlíková (Cs)
1988-90	Steffi Graf (FRG)
1991-3	Monica Seles (Yug)
1994	Steffi Graf (Ger)
1995	Mary Pierce (Fra)
1996	Monica Seles (USA)
1997-8	Martina Hingis (Swi)

Most wins: 11 Smith/Court; 6 Nancye Bolton (née Wynne) 1937, 1940, 1946-8, 1951; 5 Daphne Akhurst 1925-6, 1928-30

Men's doubles

1946-50	John Bromwich & Adrian Quist (Aus)
1951-2	Ken McGregor & Frank Sedgman (Aus)
1953	Lew Hoad & Ken Rosewall (Aus)
1954	Rex Hartwig & Mervyn Rose (Aus)
1955	Vic Seixas & Tony Trabert (USA)
1956	Lew Hoad & Ken Rosewall (Aus)
1957	Neale Fraser & Lew Hoad (Aus)
1958	Ashley Cooper & Neale Fraser (Aus)
1959-61	Rod Laver & Robert Mark (Aus)
1962	Roy Emerson & Neale Fraser (Aus)
1963-4	Bob Hewitt & Fred Stolle (Aus)
1965	John Newcombe & Tony Roche (Aus)
1966	Roy Emerson & Fred Stolle (Aus)
1967	John Newcombe & Tony Roche (Aus)
1968	Dick Crealy & Allan Stone (Aus)
1969	Roy Emerson & Rod Laver (Aus)
1970	Bob Lutz & Stan Smith (USA)
1971	John Newcombe & Tony Roche (Aus)
1972	Owen Davidson & Ken Rosewall (Aus)
1973	Mal Anderson & John Newcombe (Aus)
1974	Ross Case & Geoff Masters (Aus)
1975	John Alexander & Phil Dent (Aus)
1976	John Newcombe & Tony Roche (Aus)
1977	Arthur Ashe (USA) & Tony Roche (Aus)
1977	Ray Ruffels & Allan Stone (Aus)
1978	Wojtek Fibak (Pol) & Kim Warwick (Aus)
1979	Peter McNamara & Paul McNamee (Aus)
1980-1	Mark Edmondson & Kim Warwick (Aus)
1982	John Alexander & John Fitzgerald (Aus)
1983	Mark Edmonson & Paul McNamee (Aus)
1984	Mark Edmondson (Aus) & Sherwood Stewart (USA)
1985	Paul Annacone (USA) & Christo Van Rensburg (SAf)

1987	Stefan Edberg & Anders Järryd (Swe)
1988-9	Rick Leach & Jim Pugh (USA)
1990	Pieter Aldrich & Dannie Visser (SAf)
1991	Scott Davis & David Pate (Aus)
1992	Todd Woodbridge & Mark Woodforde (Aus)
1993	Dannie Visser (SAf) & Laurie Warder (Aus)
1994	Jacco Eltingh & Paul Haarhuis (Hol)
1995	Richey Reneburg & Jared Palmer (USA)
1996	Stefan Edberg (Swe) & Petr Korda (Cze)
1997	Todd Woodbridge & Mark Woodforde (Aus)
1998	Jonas Bjorkman (Swe) & Jacco Eltingh (Hol)

Most wins by one pair: 8 John Bromwich & Adrian Quist 1938-40, 1946-50

Most wins by player: 10 Adrian Quist 1936-7 (with Don Turnbull), and 8 with John Bromwich

Women's doubles

1946	Mary Bevis & Joyce Fitch (Aus)
1947-9	Nancye Bolton & Thelma Long (Aus)
1950	Louise Brough & Doris Hart (USA)
1951-2	Nancye Bolton & Thelma Long (Aus)
1953	Maureen Connolly & Julie Sampson (USA)
1954	Mary Hawton (née Bevis) & Beryl Penrose (Aus)
1955	Mary Hawton & Beryl Penrose (Aus)
1956	Mary Hawton & Thelma Long (Aus)
1957	Shirley Fry & Althea Gibson (USA)
1958	Mary Hawton & Thelma Long (Aus)
1959	Sandra Reynolds & Renée Schuurman (SAf)
1960	Maria Bueno (Bra) & Christine Truman (UK)
1961	Mary Reitano & Margaret Smith (Aus)
1962-3	Robyn Ebbern & Margaret Smith (Aus)
1964	Judy Tegart & Lesley Turner (Aus)
1965	Margaret Smith & Lesley Turner (Aus)
1966	Carole Graebner & Nancy Richey (USA)
1967	Judy Tegart & Lesley Turner (Aus)
1968	Karen Krantzcke & Kerry Melville (Aus)
1969	Margaret Court (née Smith) & Judy Tegart (Aus)
1970	Margaret Court & Judy Dalton (née Tegart) (Aus)
1971	Margaret Court & Evonne Goolagong (Aus)
1972	Helen Gourlay & Kerry Harris (Aus)
1973	Margaret Court (Aus) & Virginia Wade (UK)
1974-5	Evonne Goolagong (Aus) & Peggy Michel (USA)
1976	Evonne Cawley (née Goolagong) & Helen Gourlay (Aus)
1977	Diane Fromholtz & Helen Gourlay (Aus)
1977★	Evonne Cawley & Helen Cawley (Aus) & Ramona Guerrant (USA) & Kerry Reid (née Melville) (Aus)
1978	Betsy Nagelsen (USA) & Renata Tomanova (Cs)
1979	Judith Chaloner (NZ) & Dianne Evers (Aus)
1980	Betsy Nagelsen (USA) & Martina Navrátilová (Cs)

1981	Kathy Jordan & Anne Smith (USA)
1982-5	Martina Navrátilová & Pam Shriver (USA)
1987-9	Martina Navrátilová & Pam Shriver (USA)
1990	Helena Suková & Jana Novotná (Cs)
1991	Patti Fendick & Mary Jo Fernandez (USA)
1992	Arantxa Sánchez (Spa) & Helena Suková (Cs)
1993-4	Gigi Fernandez (USA) & Natalya Zvereva (Blr)
1995	Jana Novotná (Cze) & Arantxa Sánchez (Spa)
1996	Chanda Rubin (USA) & Arantxa Sánchez (Spa)
1997	Martina Hingis (Swi) & Natalya Zvereva (Blr)
1998	Martina Hingis (Swi) & Mirjana Lucic (Cro)

* Shared title, final not played.

Most wins by one pair: 10 Nancye Bolton (née Wynne) & Thelma Long (née Coyne) 1936-40, 1947-9, 1951-2; 7 Navrátilová & Shriver

Most wins by player: 12 Thelma Long, also 1956, 1958 (with Mary Hawton); 10 Bolton; 8 Smith/Court, Navrátilová; 7 Shriver

Mixed doubles

1946-8	Colin Long & Nancye Bolton (Aus)
1949-50	Frank Sedgman (Aus) & Doris Hart (USA)
1951-2	George Worthington & Thelma Long (Aus)
1953	Rex Hartwig (Aus) & Julie Sampson (USA)
1954	Rex Hartwig & Thelma Long (Aus)
1955	George Worthington & Thelma Long (Aus)
1956	Neale Fraser & Beryl Penrose (Aus)
1957	Mal Anderson & Fay Muller (Aus)
1958	Bob Howe & Mary Hawton (Aus)
1959	Robert Mark (Aus) & Sandra Reynolds (SAf)
1960	Trevor Fancutt (SAf) & Jan Lehane (Aus)
1961	Bob Hewitt & Jan Lehane (Aus)
1962	Fred Stolle & Lesley Turner (Aus)
1963-4	Ken Fletcher & Margaret Smith (Aus)
1965*	John Newcombe & Margaret Smith (Aus) & Owen Davidson & Robyn Ebbern (Aus)
1966	Tony Roche & Judy Tegart (Aus)
1967	Owen Davidson & Lesley Turner (Aus)
1968	Dick Crealy (Aus) & Billie Jean King (USA)
1969*	Marty Riessen (USA) & Margaret Court (née Smith) (Aus) & Fred Stolle (Aus) & Ann Jones (UK)
1970-86	*Not held*
1987	Sherwood Stewart & Zina Garrison (USA)
1988-89	Jim Pugh (USA) & Jana Novotná (Cs)
1990	Jim Pugh (USA) & Natalya Zvereva (USSR)
1991	Jeremy Bates & Jo Durie (UK)
1992	Mark Woodforde & Nicole Provis (Aus)
1993	Todd Woodbridge (Aus) & Arantxa Sánchez (Spa)
1994	Andrey Olkhovskiy (Rus) & Larisa Neiland (Lat)
1995	Rick Leach (USA) & Natalya Zvereva (Blr)
1996	Mark Woodforde (Aus) & Larisa Neiland (Lat)
1997	Rick Leach (USA) & Manon Bollegraf (Hol)
1998	Justin Gimelstob & Venus Williams (USA)

* Shared title, final not played.

Most wins by one pair: 4 Harry Hopman & Nell Hopman (née Hall) 1930, 1936-7, 1939, Colin Long & Nancye Bolton (née Wynne) 1940, 1946-8

Most Australian titles

	Total	Singles	Doubles	Mixed	Years
Margaret Court (Aus)	21	11	8	2	1960-73
Nancye Bolton (Aus)	20	6	10	4	1936-51
Thelma Long (Aus)	18	2	12	4	1936-58
Daphne Akhurst (Aus)	13	5	4	4	1924-30
Adrian Quist (Aus)	13	3	10	–	1936-50
Best record by a non-Australian:					
Martina Navrátilová	11	3	8	–	1980-89

All-Time Greats

A summary of the most titles won by players in the four Grand Slam events – Wimbledon, US Open, French Championship and Australian Championship, first for each tournament and then analysed by singles and doubles.

	Total	Wimb.	US	French	Aus.	Singles	Doubles	Mixed
Margaret Court (Aus)*	66	10	22	13	21	26	21	19
Martina Navrátilová (Cs/USA)	56	19	15	11	11	18	31	7
Billie Jean King (USA)	39	20	13	4	2	12	16	11
Margaret Du Pont (USA)	37	7	25	5	–	6	21	10
Louis Brough (USA)	35	13	17	3	2	6	21	8
Doris Hart (USA)	35	10	11	10	4	6	14	15
Helen Wills-Moody (USA)	31	12	13	6	–	19	9	3
Roy Emerson (Aus)	28	5	6	8	9	12	16	–
Elizabeth Ryan (USA)	26	19	3	4	–	–	17	9

	Total	Wimb.	US	French	Aus.	Singles	Doubles	Mixed
John Newcombe (Aus) ★	25	9	6	3	7	7	17	1
Frank Sedgman (Aus)	22	6	6	4	6	5	9	8
Steffi Graf (Ger)	22	8	5	5	4	21	1	–
Pam Shriver (USA)	22	5	5	5	7	–	21	1

★ Court's totals include both US Amateur and Open Championships 1968-9. Not included are the undecided Australian mixed doubles finals, two for Court, one for Newcombe.

Most Grand Slam doubles wins by one pair: 20 Louise Brough & Margaret Du Pont 1942-57, Martina Navrátilová & Pam Shriver 1981-9

Grand Slam Records

The Grand Slam is achieved by simultaneously holding the title of each of the four major tournaments – Wimbledon, and the US, Australian and French Championships. More precisely, the Grand Slam is all four titles in one calendar year. The following players have held all four titles at once.
(Single years indicates all four titles won in one year.)

Men's singles
Donald Budge (USA) 1937/8, 1938
Rod Laver (Aus) 1962 and 1969

Women's singles
Maureen Connolly (USA) 1952/3, 1953
Margaret Court (Aus) 1969/70, 1970, 1970/1
Martina Navrátilová (USA) 1983/4
Steffi Graf (FRG/Ger) 1988, 1988/9, 1993/4
The first three each won six successive Grand Slam tournaments; Graf won five in 1988/9.

Men's doubles
Frank Sedgman (Aus) 1950/1, 1951, 1951/2
Ken McGregor (Aus) 1951, 1951/2
Jacco Eltingh & Paul Haarhuis (Hol) 1997/8

Women's doubles
Louise Brough (USA) 1949/50
Maria Bueno (Bra) 1960
Martina Navrátilová (USA) 1983/4, 1984, 1984/5, 1985/6, 1986/7
Pam Shriver (USA) 1983/4, 1984, 1984/5, 1986/7
Navrátilová and Shriver won a record eight successive Grand Slam tournaments together 1983-5.

Mixed doubles
Margaret Smith (Aus) 1962/3, 1963, 1963/4
Ken Fletcher (Aus) 1963, 1963/4
Owen Davidson (Aus) 1966/7, 1967
Billie Jean King (USA) 1967/8

Davis Cup

The American player Dwight F Davis donated a cup in 1900 to be contested by national teams. Until 1971 the winning nation accepted a challenge from the country that came out on top of a knock-out competition. Since 1972 the entire competition has been on a knock-out basis, with countries divided into zonal groups with promotion and relegation into the World Group of 16 nations who play off for the Davis Cup. There was no competition in 1901 and 1910, or during the war years. Each match is contested over two pairs of singles and a doubles. Currently sponsored by NEC.

Finals	Winners	Runners-up	Score
1900	USA	British Isles	3-0
1902	USA	British Isles	3-2
1903	British Isles	USA	4-1
1904	British Isles	Belgium	5-0
1905	British Isles	USA	5-0
1906	British Isles	USA	5-0
1907	Australasia	British Isles	3-2
1908	Australasia	USA	3-2
1909	Australasia	USA	5-0
1911	Australasia	USA	5-0
1912	British Isles	Australasia	3-2
1913	USA	British Isles	3-2
1914	Australasia	USA	3-2
1919	Australasia	British Isles	4-1
1920	USA	Australasia	5-0
1921	USA	Japan	5-0
1922	USA	Australasia	4-1
1923	USA	Australia	4-1
1924	USA	Australia	5-0
1925	USA	France	5-0
1926	USA	France	4-1
1927	France	USA	3-2
1928	France	USA	4-1
1929	France	USA	3-2
1930	France	USA	4-1
1931	France	Great Britain	3-2
1932	France	USA	3-2
1933	Great Britain	France	3-2
1934	Great Britain	USA	4-1
1935	Great Britain	USA	5-0
1936	Great Britain	Australia	3-2
1937	USA	Great Britain	4-1
1938	USA	Australia	3-2

Finals	Winners	Runners-up	Score	Finals	Winners	Runners-up	Score
1939	Australia	USA	3-2	1975	Sweden	Czechoslovakia	3-2
1946	USA	Australia	5-0	1976	Italy	Chile	4-1
1947	USA	Australia	4-1	1977	Australia	Italy	3-1
1948	USA	Australia	5-0	1978	USA	Great Britain	4-1
1949	USA	Australia	4-1	1979	USA	Italy	5-0
1950	Australia	USA	4-1	1980	Czechoslovakia	Italy	4-1
1951	Australia	USA	3-2	1981	USA	Argentina	3-1
1952	Australia	USA	4-1	1982	USA	France	4-1
1953	Australia	USA	3-2	1983	Australia	Sweden	3-2
1954	USA	Australia	3-2	1984	Sweden	USA	4-1
1955	Australia	USA	5-0	1985	Sweden	F R Germany	3-2
1956	Australia	USA	5-0	1986	Australia	Sweden	3-2
1957	Australia	USA	3-2	1987	Sweden	India	5-0
1958	USA	Australia	3-2	1988	F R Germany	Sweden	4-1
1959	Australia	USA	3-2	1989	F R Germany	Sweden	3-2
1960	Australia	Italy	4-1	1990	USA	Australia	3-2
1961	Australia	Italy	5-0	1991	France	USA	3-1
1962	Australia	Mexico	5-0	1992	USA	Switzerland	3-1
1963	USA	Australia	3-2	1993	Germany	Australia	4-1
1964	Australia	USA	3-2	1994	Sweden	Russia	4-1
1965	Australia	Spain	4-1	1995	USA	Russia	3-2
1966	Australia	India	4-1	1996	France	Sweden	3-2
1967	Australia	Spain	4-1	1997	Sweden	USA	5-0
1968	USA	Australia	4-1				
1969	USA	Romania	5-0				
1970	USA	F R Germany	5-0				
1971	USA	Romania	3-2				
1972	USA	Romania	3-2				
1973	Australia	USA	5-0				
1974	South Africa	India	w/o				

Wins: 31 USA; 26 Australia/Australasia; 9 British Isles/Great Britain; 8 France; 6 Sweden; 3 Germany; 1 Czechoslovakia, Italy, South Africa

Most times played for winning team: 8 Roy Emerson (Aus) 1959-62, 1964-7; 7 Bill Tilden (USA) 1920-6

Most Davis Cup appearances

(Singles and doubles figures show wins/matches played.)

	Rubbers	Wins	Singles	Doubles	Win %	Years
Nicola Pietrangeli (Ita)	164	120	78/110	42/54	73.1	1954-72
Ilie Nastase (Rom)	146	109	74/96	35/50	74.7	1966-85
Manuel Santana (Spa)	120	92	69/86	23/34	76.7	1958-73
Jacques Brichant (Bel)	120	71	52/79	19/41	59.2	1949-65
Thomaz Koch (Bra)	118	74	46/78	28/40	62.7	1962-81
Best win percentage of those to have played more than 100 matches:						
Gottfried von Cramm (Ger)	101	82	58/68	24/33	81.2	1932-53
Most appearances and most wins for Great Britain:						
Mike Sangster	65	43	29/48	14/17	66.2	1960-8
Bobby Wilson	61	41	16/28	25/33	67.9	1955-68
Fred Perry	52	45	34/38	11/14	86.5	1931-6

Best records in Davis Cup finals/challenge rounds (10 or more wins)

Bill Tilden (USA)	28	21	17/22	4/6	75.0	1920-30
Roy Emerson (Aus)	18	15	11/12	4/6	83.3	1959-67
Norman Brookes (Aus)	22	15	9/14	6/8	68.2	1907-20
Henri Cochet (Fra)	20	14	11/14	3/6	70.0	1926-33
Stan Smith (USA)	16	12	6/8	6/8	75.0	1968-79
William Johnston (USA)	16	13	11/14	2/2	81.2	1920-7
Laurence Doherty (UK)	12	12*	7/7	4/4	100.0	1902-06
John McEnroe (USA)	14	12	9/10	3/4	85.7	1978-92
Rod Laver (Aus)	12	10	8/10	2/2	83.3	1959-73

* Including a walk-over.

Wightman Cup

The former American player Hazel Wightman (née Hotchkiss) donated a trophy in 1920 to be contested by national female teams. However, none showed any interest until 1923 when the USA and Great Britain played for the trophy. Since then, all Wightman Cup matches have been between these two nations, over five singles and two doubles. In 1990, with the decline in British tennis standards, and after four 7-0 US wins in the previous five matches, a decision was taken to suspend the event.
Wins:

51	USA	1923, 1926-7, 1929, 1931-9, 1946-57, 1959, 1961-7, 1969-73, 1976-7, 1979-89
10	Great Britain	1924-5, 1928, 1930, 1958, 1960, 1968, 1974-5, 1978

The United States 'whitewashed' Great Britain 14 times by inflicting a 7-0 defeat upon them: 1923, 1946-7, 1949-50, 1952-4,* 1977, 1979, 1981, 1985-6, 1988-9. Great Britain's best results were 6-1 wins in 1924 and 1974.
* In 1954 the USA won all six matches played.

Federation Cup/Fed Cup

An international women's team competition played on a knock-out basis at one venue each year. The Federation Cup was held from 1963 to 1994 as a knock-out competition at one venue, all the contests having two singles and a doubles. From 1995 the competition, renamed the Fed Cup, had a new format. In 1997, a record 98 nations competed in groups: eight in each of the World Group and Group 1 followed by teams split into continental zones. The group matches (quarter-finals) are followed by semi-finals and finals at different dates and venues.
Wins:

15	USA	1963, 1966-7, 1969, 1976-82, 1986, 1989-90, 1996
7	Australia	1964-5, 1968, 1970-1, 1973-4
5	Czechoslovakia	1975, 1983-5, 1988
4	Spain	1991, 1993-5
2	Germany	1987 (FRG), 1992
1	South Africa 1972, France 1997	

Chris Evert Lloyd won her first 29 singles in the competition 1977-86. Margaret Court won all her 20 singles matches (and 15/20 in doubles) for Australia 1963-71.

World Team Cup

Formerly known as the Nations Cup, this is an eight-nation men's team event. First held in Kingston, Jamaica, in 1975, it was not held the next two years but was revived in 1977.
Winners:

5	USA	1975, 1982, 1984-5, 1993
4	Spain	1978, 1983, 1992, 1997

3	Sweden	1988, 1991, 1995
2	Czechoslovakia	1981, 1987
2	Germany	1989 (FRG), 1994
1	Australia 1979, Argentina 1980, France 1986, Yugoslavia 1990, Switzerland 1996	

Men's Grand Prix Masters – ATP Championships

Prior to 1990, throughout the season various tournaments counted towards the Masters, with points gained according to performances and based on the stature of the tournament. At the end of the season the leading 16 players played off for the Masters singles title, and eight pairs for the doubles title. There was no event in 1977 because the date of the final was switched from December to the following January. There were two tournaments in 1986 because there was a reversion to a December final. From 1990 the event was replaced by the ATP Tour World Championship (*see* below).
Winners:

Singles

1970	Stan Smith (USA)
1971-3	Ilie Nastase (Rom)
1974	Guillermo Vilas (Arg)
1975	Ilie Nastase (Rom)
1976	Manuel Orantes (Spa)
1978	Jimmy Connors (USA)
1979	John McEnroe (USA)
1980-1	Björn Borg (Swe)
1982-3	Ivan Lendl (Cs)
1984-5	John McEnroe (USA)
1986-7	Ivan Lendl (Cs)
1988	Boris Becker (FRG)
1989	Stefan Edberg (Swe)

Most wins: 4 Nastase, Lendl
Jimmy Connors qualified for the play-offs for a record 14 years 1972-85.

Doubles

1970	Arthur Ashe & Stan Smith (USA)
1971-4	*Not held*
1975	Juan Gisbert & Manuel Orantes (Spa)
1976	Fred McNair & Sherwood Stewart (USA)
1978	Bob Hewitt & Frew McMillan (SAf)
1979-85	Peter Fleming & John McEnroe (USA)
1986	Stefan Edberg & Anders Järryd (Swe) (2 *wins*)
1987	Miloslav Mecir & Tomás Smid (Cs)
1988	Rick Leach & Jim Pugh (USA)
1989	Patrick McEnroe & Jim Grabb (USA)

Most wins: 7 Peter Fleming & John McEnroe

ATP Tour Championships Final

Contested annually in Germany each November from 1990, at Frankfurt 1990-5 and Hannover 1996-7.
Winners:

1990	Andre Agassi (USA)
1991	Pete Sampras (USA)
1992	Boris Becker (Ger)

1993	Michael Stich (Ger)
1994	Pete Sampras (USA)
1995	Boris Becker (Ger)
1996-7	Pete Sampras (USA)

ATP World Doubles

Winners:
1990	Guy Forget (Fra) & Jakob Hlasek (Swi)
1991	John Fitzgerald (Aus) & Anders Järryd (Swe)
1992	Todd Woodbridge & Mark Woodforde (Aus)
1993	Jacco Eltingh & Paul Haarhuis (Hol)
1994	Jan Apell & Jonas Bjorkman (Swe)
1995	Grant Connell (Can) & Patrick Galbraith (USA)
1996	Todd Woodbridge & Mark Woodforde (Aus)
1997	Rick Leach & Jonathan Stark (USA)

Women's International Series

As with the men, the women have had an international championship played after a season-long series of tournaments.

Winners (see also Virginia Slims/Avon Series below):

Singles
1977-8	Chris Evert (USA)
1979*	Martina Navrátilová (Cs)
1980*	Tracy Austin (USA)
1981	Tracy Austin (USA)
1982	Martina Navrátilová (USA)
1983*	Martina Navrátilová (USA)
1984*	Martina Navrátilová (USA)

Doubles
1977	Françoise Durr (Fra) & Virginia Wade (UK)
1978	Billie Jean King (USA) & Martina Navrátilová (Cs)
1979*	Billie Jean King (USA) & Martina Navrátilová (Cs)
1980*	Rosemary Casals (USA) & Wendy Turnbull (Aus)
1981	Martina Navrátilová (Cs) & Pam Shriver (USA)
1982	Martina Navrátilová & Pam Shriver (USA)
1983*	Martina Navrátilová & Pam Shriver (USA)
1984*	Martina Navrátilová & Pam Shriver (USA)

* Played the following year.

WTA Tour Championships

From 1971 there was an annual series of Virginia Slims tournaments, with a Championships as the climax. Avon Products took over the sponsorship 1979-82, with Virginia Slims back again in 1983 when their initial series ran for 15 months to March 1984. From 1983 the Virginia Slims final, now the Chase Championship, has been the one women's match played over the best of five sets.

Winners:

Singles
1971	Billie Jean King (USA)
1972-3	Chris Evert (USA)
1974	Evonne Goolagong (Aus)
1975	Chris Evert (USA)
1976	Evonne Cawley (née Goolagong) (Aus)
1977	Chris Evert (USA)
1978-9	Martina Navrátilová (Cs)
1980	Tracy Austin (USA)
1981	Martina Navrátilová (Cs)
1982	Sylvia Hanika (FRG)
1983-5*	Martina Navrátilová (USA)
1986	Martina Navrátilová (USA)
1987	Steffi Graf (FRG)
1988	Gabriela Sabatini (Arg)
1989	Steffi Graf (FRG)
1990-2	Monica Seles (Yug)
1993	Steffi Graf (Ger)
1994	Gabriela Sabatini (Arg)
1995-6	Steffi Graf (Ger)
1997	Jana Novotná (Cze)

Doubles
Not staged each year.
1971	Rosemary Casals & Bille Jean King (USA)
1973	Rosemary Casals (USA) & Margaret Court (Aus)
1974	Rosemary Casals & Billlie Jean King (USA)
1979	Françoise Durr (Fra) & Betty Stove (Hol)
1980	Billie Jean King (USA) & Martina Navrátilová (Cs)
1981	Martina Navrátilová (Cs) & Pam Shriver (USA)
1982	Martina Navrátilová & Pam Shriver (USA)
1984*	Martina Navrátilová & Pam Shriver (USA)
1985*	Hana Mandlíková (Cs) & Wendy Turnbull (Aus)
1986-9	Martina Navrátilová & Pam Shriver (USA)
1990	Kathy Jordan (USA) & Liz Smylie (Aus)
1991	Martina Navrátilová & Pam Shriver (USA)
1992	Arantxa Sánchez (Spa) & Helena Suková (Cs)
1993-4	Gigi Fernandez (USA) & Natalya Zvereva (Blr)
1995	Jana Novotná (Cze) & Arantxa Sánchez (Spa)
1996	Lindsay Davenport & Mary Joe Fernandez (USA)
1997	Lindsay Davenport (USA) & Jana Novotná (Cze)

* Played the following year.

World Championship Tennis

World Championship Tennis Incorporated (WCT) was founded in 1967 to promote professional tennis. Following a series of qualifying tournaments, a finals tournament was held annually for men from 1971.
Winners:

Singles

1971-2	Ken Rosewall (Aus)
1973	Stan Smith (USA)
1974	John Newcombe (Aus)
1975	Arthur Ashe (USA)
1976	Björn Borg (Swe)
1977	Jimmy Connors (USA)
1978	Vitas Gerulaitis (USA)
1979	John McEnroe (USA)
1980	Jimmy Connors (USA)
1981	John McEnroe (USA)
1982	Ivan Lendl (Cs)
1983-4	John McEnroe (USA)
1985	Ivan Lendl (Cs)
1986	Anders Järryd (Swe)
1987	Miloslav Mecir (Cs)
1988	Boris Becker (FRG)
1989	John McEnroe (USA)

Doubles

Introduced in 1973.

1973	Bob Lutz & Stan Smith (USA)
1974	Bob Hewitt & Frew McMillan (SAf)
1975	Brian Gottfried (USA) & Raúl Ramirez (Mex)
1976	Wojtek Fibak (Pol) & Tom Okker (Hol)
1977	Vijay Amritraj (Ind) & Dick Stockton (USA)
1978	Wojtek Fibak (Pol) & Tom Okker (Hol)
1979	Peter Fleming & John McEnroe (USA)
1980	Brian Gottfried (USA) & Raúl Ramirez (Mex)
1981	Peter McNamara & Paul McNamee (Aus)
1982-3	Heinz Günthardt (Swi) & Balázs Taróczy (Hun)
1984	Pavel Slozil & Tomás Smid (Cs)
1985	Ken Flach & Robert Seguso (USA)
1986	Heinz Günthardt (Swi) & Balázs Taróczy (Hun)
1986*	Stefan Edberg & Anders Järryd (Swe)
1990	Rick Leach & Jim Pugh (USA)

* Brought forward from January to December.

Grand Slam Cup

Played each December in Munich, contested by the leading players in the Grand Slam events of the previous year. In 1990-2 and in 1997 the winner received $2 million, by far the biggest prize given to a tennis player, and the runner-up took $1 million. Sponsored by Compaq.
Winners:

1990	Pete Sampras (USA)
1991	David Wheaton (USA)

1992	Michael Stich (Ger)
1993	Petr Korda (Cze)
1994	Magnus Larsson (Swe)
1995	Goran Ivanisevic (Cro)
1996	Boris Becker (Ger)
1997	Pete Sampras (USA)

ITF World Champions

A panel of former champions annually decides the International Tennis Federation's World Champions. The award for individuals was inaugurated in 1978, and an award for doubles was introduced in 1996.
Winners:

Men's singles

1978-80	Björn Borg (Swe)
1981	John McEnroe (USA)
1982	Jimmy Connors (USA)
1983-4	John McEnroe (USA)
1985-7	Ivan Lendl (Cs)
1988	Mats Wilander (Swe)
1989	Boris Becker (FRG)
1990	Ivan Lendl (Cs)
1991	Stefan Edberg (Swe)
1992	Jim Courier (USA)
1993-7	Pete Sampras (USA)

Women's singles

1978	Chris Evert (USA)
1979	Martina Navrátilová (Cs)
1980-1	Chris Evert Lloyd (USA)
1982-6	Martina Navrátilová (USA)
1987-90	Steffi Graf (FRG)
1991-2	Monica Seles (Yug)
1993	Steffi Graf (Ger)
1994	Arantxa Sánchez (Spa)
1995-6	Steffi Graf (Ger)
1997	Martina Hingis (Swi)

Men's doubles

1996-7	Todd Woodbridge & Mark Woodforde (Aus)

Women's doubles

1996	Lindsay Davenport & Mary Joe Fernandez (USA)
1997	Lindsay Davenport (USA) & Jana Novotná (Cze)

Top Money-Winners

The following players have won the most prize money. *(At end Nov 1997.)*

Men

Pete Sampras	$32,060,658
Boris Becker	24,515,647
Ivan Lendl	21,262,417
Stefan Edberg	20,630,941
Michael Chang	16,286,739
Goran Ivanisevic	16,206,537

Jim Courier	$13,322,569
Andre Agassi	13,206,463
Michael Stich	12,628,890
John McEnroe	12,539,622
Thomas Muster	11,640,654
Sergi Bruguera	10,748,349
Yevgeniy Kafelnikov	9,604,741
Petr Korda	9,039,709
Jimmy Connors	8,641,040

Women

Martina Navrátilová	20,344,061
Steffi Graf	20,076,565
Arantxa Sánchez Vicario	12,523,488
Monica Seles	9,874,510
Chris Evert	8,896,195
Gabriela Sabatini	8,785,850
Jana Novotná	8,257,780
Conchita Martínez	6,877,810
Helena Suková	6,308,521
Natalya Zvereva	6,082,686
Pam Shriver	5,460,566
Martina Hingis	4,948,617
Mary Joe Fernandez	4,903,886
Zina Garrison-Jackson	4,587,816
Gigi Fernandez	4,590,816

ATP Number-One Players

The ATP has produced ranking lists of male tennis players weekly from 23 August 1973.

No.1-ranking players, with number of weeks at No.1, at 27 Jul 1998:

Name	Weeks	Years
Ilie Nastase (Rom)	40	1973-4
John Newcombe (Aus)	8	1974
Jimmy Connors (USA)	268	1974-83
Bjorn Borg (Swe)	109	1977-81
John McEnroe (USA)	170	1980-5
Ivan Lendl (Cs)	270	1983-90
Mats Wilander (Swe)	20	1988-9
Stefan Edberg (Swe)	66	1990-2
Boris Becker (Ger)	12	1991
Jim Courier (USA)	55	1992-3
Pete Sampras (USA)	233	1993-8
Andre Agassi (USA)	30	1995-6
Thomas Muster (Swi)	5	1996
Marcelo Rios (Chi)	4	1998

Longest span continuously at No.1: Jimmy Connors 160 weeks (29 Jul 74–16 Aug 77); Ivan Lendl 157 weeks (9 Sep 85–5 Sep 88)

Professional Tour Records

Men

Most singles titles in career: 109 Jimmy Connors (USA) 1972-89; 94 Ivan Lendl (Cs/USA)
Most singles titles in season: 15 Jimmy Connors

1977, Guillermo Vilas (Arg) 1977, Ivan Lendl (Cs) 1982
Most consecutive match wins: 46 Guillermo Vilas 1977-8
Most doubles titles in career: 78 Tom Okker (Hol) 1968-79; 77 John McEnroe (USA) 1976-92
Most doubles titles in season: 17 John McEnroe 1979
Most career titles (singles & doubles): 154 John McEnroe 1976-92
Highest winnings in a season: $6,498,311 Pete Sampras (USA) 1995

Women

Most singles titles in career: 167 Martina Navrátílová (Cs/USA) 1975-94; 157 Chris Evert (USA) 1972-88; 103 Steffi Graf (Ger); 88 Evonne Cawley (Aus)
Most singles titles in year: 16 Martina Navrátílová 1983, Chris Evert 1974, 1975
Most consecutive match wins: 74 Martina Navrátílová 1984
Most doubles titles in career: 165 Martina Navrátílová 1975-94
Most doubles titles by one partnership: 79 Martina Navrátílová & Pam Shriver (USA)
Weeks ranked at No.1: 374 Steffi Graf 1987-97; 331 Martina Navrátílová; 262 Chris Evert; 178 Monica Seles (Yug/USA), including 65 as joint No.1 when injured; 40 Martina Hingis; 22 Tracy Austin; 12 Arantxa Sánchez
Most consecutive weeks at No.1: 186 Steffi Graf 17 Aug 1987–10 Mar 1991
Highest winnings in a season: $3,400,196 Martina Hingis (Swi) 1997

Olympic Games

Lawn tennis was included in the Olympic Games from 1896 to 1924 and as a demonstration sport in 1968. Following the staging of an international tournament at the 1984 Games, at which the singles winners were Stefan Edberg (Swe) and Steffi Graf (FRG), tennis was re-introduced to the Olympics in 1988.
Champions (a) outdoor (b) indoor:

Men's singles

1896	John Boland (UK/Ire)
1900	Hugh Doherty (UK)
1904	Beals Wright (USA)
1906	Max Decugis (Fra)
1908	Josiah Ritchie (UK) (a)
	Arthur Gore (UK) (b)
1912	Charles Winslow (SAf) (a)
	André Gobert (Fra) (b)
1920	Louis Raymond (SAf)
1924	Vince Richards (USA)
1988	Miloslav Mecir (Cs)

1992	Marc Rosset (Swi)
1996	Andre Agassi (USA)

Women's singles

1900	Charlotte Cooper (UK)
1906	Esmée Simiriotou (Gre)
1908	Dorothea Lambert Chambers (UK) (a)
	Gwendoline Eastlake-Smith (UK) (b)
1912	Marguerite Broquedis (Fra) (a)
	Edith Hannam (UK) (b)
1920	Suzanne Lenglen (Fra)
1924	Helen Wills (USA)
1988	Steffi Graf (FRG)
1992	Jennifer Capriati (USA)
1996	Lindsay Davenport (USA)

Men's doubles

1896	John Boland (Ire) & Fritz Traun (Ger)
1900	Reginald & Hugh Doherty (UK)
1904	Beals Wright & Edgar Leonard (USA)
1906	Max Decugis & Maurice Germot (Fra)
1908	George Hillyard & Reginald Doherty (UK) (a)
	Arthur Gore & Herbert Roper Barrett (UK) (b)
1912	Charles Winslow & Harold Kitson (SAf) (a)
	André Gobert & Maurice Germot (Fra) (b)

1920	Oswald Turnbull & Max Woosnam (UK)
1924	Vince Richards & Frank Hunter (UK)
1988	Ken Flach & Robert Seguso (USA)
1992	Boris Becker & Michael Stich (Ger)
1996	Todd Woodbridge & Mark Woodforde (Aus)

Women's doubles

1920	Winifred McNair & Kathleen McKane (UK)
1924	Hazel Wightman & Helen Wills (USA)
1988	Pam Shriver & Zina Garrison (USA)
1992	Gigi Fernandez & Mary Joe Fernandez (USA)
1996	Gigi Fernandez & Mary Joe Fernandez (USA)

Mixed doubles

1900	Reginald Doherty & Charlotte Cooper (UK)
1906	Max and Marie Decugis (Fra)
1912	Heinrich Schomburgk & Dora König (Ger) (a)
	Percy Dixon & Edith Hannam (UK) (b)
1920	Max Decugis & Suzanne Lenglen (Fra)
1924	Norris Williams & Hazel Wightman (USA)

Most medals: 6 Max Decugis (Fra) a record 4 gold, 1 silver and 1 bronze 1900-20; 5 Kathleen McKane (UK) 1 gold, 2 silver, 2 bronze, 1920-4

Trampolining

Trampolining has formed part of circus acts for many years but it only started to attract interest as a sport after the design of trampolines similar to modern-day ones, by George Nissen in the United States in 1936. The first official trampolining tournament took place in the United States in 1947. The sport is scheduled to be added to the Olympics programme in 2000.

International governing body: Fédération Internationale de Trampoline (FIT), Rue des Ceuches 10, Case Postale 359, CH-2740 Moutier 1, Switzerland. Tel: (41) 32 494 6415, Fax: (41) 32 494 6419. President: Ron Froelich, Secretary General: André F Gueisbuhler. Founded in 1964. 44 member nations.

World Championships

Instituted in 1964, these Championships have been held biennially since 1968.

Winners:

Men

Individual

1964	Danny Millman (USA)
1965	George Irwin (USA)
1966	Wayne Miller (USA)
1967-8	Dave Jacobs (USA)
1970	Wayne Miller (USA)
1972	Paul Luxon (UK)
1974	Richard Tisson (Fra)
1976	Richard Tisson (Fra) & Yevgeniy Yanes (USSR)
1978	Yevgeniy Yanes (USSR)
1980	Stewart Matthews (UK)
1982	Carl Furrer (UK)
1984	Lionel Pioline (Fra)
1986	Lionel Pioline (Fra)
1988	Vadim Krasnochapka (USSR)

1990	Aleksandr Moskalenko (USSR)
1992	Aleksandr Moskalenko (Rus)
1994	Aleksandr Moskalenko (Rus)
1996	Dmitriy Polyarush (Blr)

Synchronized pairs

1965	Gary Irwin & Frank Smith (USA)
1966	Wayne Miller & David Jacobs (USA)
1967	Hartmut Riehler & Kurt Treiter (FRG)
1968	Klaus Forster & Michael Budenberg (FRG)
1970	Don Waters & Gary Smith (USA)
1972	Paul Luxon & Robert Hughes (UK)
1974	Robet Nealy & Jim Cartledge (USA)
1976	Yevgeniy Yakovenko & Yevgeniy Yanes (USSR)
1978	Yevgeniy Yanes & Vladimir Zhadoyev (USSR)
1980	Stewart Matthews & Carl Furrer (UK)
1982	Stuart Ransom & Mark Calderon (USA)
1984	Igor Bogachev & Vadim Krasnochapka (USSR)
1986	Igor Bogachev & Vadim Krasnochapka (USSR)
1988	Igor Bogachev & Vadim Krasnochapka (USSR)
1990	Dmitriy Polyarush & Sergey Nestrelyai (USSR)
1992	Aleksandr Danilchenko & Aleksandr Moskalenko (Rus)

1994	Aleksandr Danilchenko & Aleksandr Moskalenko (Rus)
1996	Sergey Voronin & Aleksandr Kossov (Rus)

Team
Wins:

USSR	1984, 1988, 1990, 1992
France	1982, 1996
F R Germany	1986
Belarus	1994

Tumbling

1965	Frank Schmitz (USA)
1966	Frank Fortier (USA)
1976	Jim Bertz (USA)
1978	Jim Bertz (USA)
1980	Kevin Eckberg (USA)
1982	Steve Elliott (USA)
1984	Steve Elliott (USA)
1986	Jerry Hardy (USA)
1988	Pascal Eouzan (Fra)
1990	Pascal Eouzan (Fra)
1992	Jon Beck (USA)
1994	Adrian Sienkiewicz (Pol)
1996	Rayshine Harris (USA)

Double mini trampoline

1976	Ron Merriott (USA)
1978	Stuart Ransom (USA)
1980	Derrick Lotz (SAf)
1982	Brett Austine (Aus)
1984	Brett Austine (Aus)
1986	Brett Austine (Aus)
1988	Adrian Wareham (Aus)
1990	Adrian Wareham (Aus)
1992	Jorge Pereira (Por)
1994	Jorge Pereira (Por)
1996	Chris Mitruk (Can) & Jim Wallace (Aus)

Team tumbling
Wins:

USA	1986, 1992, 1994, 1996
France	1988, 1990,

Women

Individual

1964-8	Judy Wills (USA)
1970	Renee Ransom (USA)
1972	Alexandra Nicholson (USA)
1974	Alexandra Nicholson (USA)
1976	Svetlana Levina (USSR)
1978	Tatyana Anisimova (USSR)
1980	Ruth Keller (Swi)
1982	Ruth Keller (Swi)
1984	Sue Shotton (UK)
1986	Tatyana Lushina (USSR)
1988	Rusadan Khoperia (USSR)
1990	Yelena Merkulova (USSR)
1992	Yelena Merkulova (Rus)
1994	Irina Karaveyeva (Rus)
1996	Tatyana Kovalyeva (Rus)

Most wins: 5 Judy Wills

Synchronized pairs

1966-7	Judy Wills & Nancy Smith (USA)
1968	Ute Czech & Agathe Jarosch (FRG)
1970	Jennifer Liebenberg & Lucia Odendaal (SAf)
1972	Marilyn Stieg & Bobby Grant (USA)
1974	Ute Scheile & Petra Wenzel (FRG)
1976	Svetlana Levina & Olga Starikova (USSR)
1978	Ute Luxon & Ute Scheile (FRG)
1980	Gabriele Bahr & Beate Kruswicki (FRG)
1982	Jacqueline de Ruiter & Marjo van Dierman (Hol)
1984	Kirsty McDonald & Sue Shotton (UK)
1986	Tatyana Lushina & Yelena Merkulova (USSR)
1988	Yelena Kolomeets & Rusadan Khoperia (USSR)
1990	Tatyana Lushina & Yelena Merkulova (USSR)
1992	Andrea Holmes & Lorraine Lyon (UK)
1994	Hiltrud Roewe & Tina Ludwig (Ger)
1996	Yelena Movchan & Oksana Tsygulyeva (Ukr)

Team
Wins:

USSR	1986, 1988, 1990
Great Britain	1984, 1992
F R Germany	1982
Russia	1994, 1996

Tumbling

1965-6	Judy Wills (USA)
1976	Tracey Long (USA)
1978	Nancy Quattrochi (USA)
1980	Tracy Contour (USA)
1982	Jill Hollembeak (USA)
1984	Jill Hollembeak (USA)
1986	Jill Hollembeak (USA)
1988	Megan Cunningham (USA)
1990	Chrystel Robert (Fra)
1992	Chrystel Robert (Fra)
1994	Chrystel Robert (Fra)
1996	Chrystel Robert (Fra)

Double mini trampoline

1976	Leigh Hennessy (USA)
1978	Leigh Hennessy (USA)
1980	Beth Fairchild (USA)
1982	Christine Tough (Can)
1984	Gabi Dreier (FRG)
1986	Bettina Lehmann (FRG)
1988	Elizabeth Jensen (Aus)
1990	Lisa Neuman-Morris (Aus)
1992	Kylie Walker (NZ)
1994	Kylie Walker (NZ)
1996	Jennifer Sans (USA)

Team tumbling
Wins:

France	1990, 1992, 1994, 1996
USA	1986, 1988

World Cup

Originally held annually from 1980, but now bienially.

Most titles at each discipline
Men's individual: 3 Carl Furrer (UK) 1980-1, 1983
Women's individual: 5 Andrea Holmes (UK) 1984-5, 1987, 1991, 1994; 3 Sue Shotton (UK) 1981, 1983, 1986
Men's synchronized pairs: 2 John Hansen & Anders Christiansen (Den) 1982, 1985, Lionel Pioline & Daniel Pean (Fra) 1983-4
Women's synchronized pairs: 3 Gabriel Bahr & Beate Kruswicki (FRG) 1983-5

Triathlon

The triathlon combines long-distance swimming, cycling and running. A group of Americans first established the sport in 1974. Their efforts led to the first Hawaii 'Ironman', contested by 15 intrepid sportsmen, of whom 12 finished, on 18 February 1978. The growth in popularity of the event is indicated by the numbers of contestants in the 'Ironman': 15 took part in its first two years, then 108 in 1980, 326 in 1981, 580 and 850 in the two held in 1982, and 1000 in 1984.

After earlier abortive attempts to found a world-wide governing body, L'Union Internationale de Triathlon (UIT) was founded in 1988, and staged the first official World Championships at Avignon, France on 6 August 1989. The sport is being added to the Olympic Games in 2000.

International governing body: International Triathlon Union (ITU), 1154 West 24th Street, N Vancouver V7P 2J2, Canada. President: Les McDonald, Secretary-General: Phillip Coles. Founded 1989. 120 member nations by 1998.

World Championships

The first official championships were contested by national teams of five men and five women over the internationally regulated 'Olympic' distances of 1.5km swim, 40km cycle ride and 10km run. Actually, the swimming event was held in the River Rhône, and the distance was extended to compensate for the flow, but at 2.2km it was over-estimated.
Winners:

	Individual	Team
Men		
1989	Mark Allen (USA) 1:58:46	USA
1990	Greg Welch (Aus) 1:51:37	AUS
1991	Miles Stewart (Aus) 1:48:20	USA
1992	Simon Lessing (UK) 1:49:04	CAN
1993	Spencer Smith (UK) 1:51.20	UK
1994	Spencer Smith (UK) 1:51.04	AUS
1995	Simon Lessing (UK) 1:48:29	
1996	Simon Lessing (UK) 1:39:50	AUS
1997	Chris McCormack (Aus) 1:48:29	
Women		
1989	Erin Baker (NZ) 2:10:01	USA
1990	Karen Smyers (USA) 2:03:33	USA
1991	Jo-Anne Richie (Can) 2:02:04	CAN
1992	Michellie Jones (Aus) 2:02:07	AUS
1993	Michellie Jones (Aus) 2:07:41	AUS
1994	Emma Carney (Aus) 2:03:19	AUS
1995	Karen Smyers (USA) 2:05:02	
1996	Jackie Gallagher (Aus) 1:50:52	AUS
1997	Emma Carney (Aus) 1:59:22	

World Long-Distance Championships

First held in 1994. Distances: 1994-5 4km swim, 120km cycle, 32km run; 1996 1.9km, 90km, 21.6km.

Men		
1994	Rob Barel (Hol) 5:59:47	GER
1995	Simon Lessing (UK) 5:46:17	FRA
1996	Greg Welch (Aus) 3:47:05	AUS
1997	Luc Van Lierde (Bel) 5:35:44	
Women		
1994	Isabelle Mouthon (Fra) 6:41:50	FRA
1995	Jenny Rose (NZ) 6:28:06	GER
1996	Karen Smyers (USA) 4:11:00	USA
1997	Ines Estedt (Ger) 6:12:04	

Hawaii Ironman

Contestants first swim 2.4 miles (3.8km), then cycle 112 miles (180km) and finally run a full marathon of 26 miles 385 yards (42.195km). The 1978-80 course was in Oahu, and from 1981 it has been in Kona, Hawaii.
Winners:

Men	
1978	Gordon Haller (USA) 11:46:58
1979	Tom Warren (USA) 11:15:56
1980	Dave Scott (USA) 9:24:33
1981	John Howard (USA) 9:38:29
1982 (Feb)	Scott Tinley (USA) 9:19:41
1982 (Oct)	Dave Scott (USA) 9:08:23

1983	Dave Scott (USA) 9:05:57
1984	Dave Scott (USA) 8:54:30
1985	Scott Tinley (USA) 8:50:54
1986	Dave Scott (USA) 8:28:37
1987	Dave Scott (USA) 8:34:13
1988	Scott Molina (USA) 8:31:00
1989	Mark Allen (USA) 8:09:16
1990	Mark Allen (USA) 8:28:17
1991	Mark Allen (USA) 8:18:32
1992	Mark Allen (USA) 8:09:08
1993	Mark Allen (USA) 8:07:45
1994	Greg Welch (Aus) 8:20:27
1995	Mark Allen (USA) 8:20:34
1996	Luc Van Lierde (Bel) 8:04:08
1997	Thomas Hellriegel (Ger) 8:33:01

Women

1979	Lyn Lemaire (USA) 12:55:38
1980	Robin Beck (USA) 11:21:24
1981	Linda Sweeney (USA) 12:00:32
1982 (Feb)	Kathleen McCartney (USA) 11:09:40
1982 (Oct)	Julie Leach (USA) 10:54:08
1983	Sylviane Puntous (Can) 10:43:36
1984	Sylviane Puntous (Can) 10:25:13
1985	Joanne Ernst (USA) 10:25:22
1986	Paula Newby-Fraser (Zim) 9:49:14*
1987	Erin Baker (NZ) 9:35:25
1988	Paula Newby-Fraser (Zim) 9:01:01
1989	Paula Newby-Fraser (Zim) 9:00:56
1990	Erin Baker (NZ) 9:13:42
1991	Paula Newby-Fraser (Zim) 9:07:52
1992	Paula Newby-Fraser (Zim) 8:55:28
1993	Paula Newby-Fraser (Zim) 8:58:23
1994	Paula Newby-Fraser (Zim) 9:20:14
1995	Karen Smyers (USA) 9:16:46
1996	Paula Newby-Fraser (Zim) 9:06:49
1997	Heather Fuhr (USA) 9:31:43

* Sylviane Puntous (Can) was disqualified after finishing in 9:47:49.

Fastest times ever recorded over Ironman distances

Men: 7:55:27 Luc Van Lierde (Bel) at Roth, Germany on 12 Jul 1997
Women: 8:55:00 Paula Newby-Fraser (Zim) at Roth, Germany on 12 Jul 1992

European Championships

Contested from 1985 at Ironman and also at shorter distances, as follows: middle distance – 2.5km swim, 80km cycle, 20km run; and Olympic distance (as for World Championship, *see* above).

Men – long distance

1984	Klaus Klaeren (FRG) 6:03:04
1985	Gregor Stam (Hol) 8:56:55
1986	Scott Tinley (USA) 8:27:46
European	Magnus Lönnqvist (Fin) 8:40:11
1987	Axel Koenders (Hol) 8:36:22
1988	Not held
1989	Axel Koenders (Hol) 8:26:58
1991	Ben van Zelst (Hol) 8:25:30
1992	Jos Everts (Hol) 8:06:12
1993	Philippe Lie (Fra) 10:08:01
1995	Matthias Klumpp (Ger) 8:06:05
1997	Peter Sandvang (Den) 8:19:31

Women – long distance

1984	Sarah Springman (UK) 6:56:34
1985	Erin Baker (NZ) 9:26:30
European	Sarah Springman (UK) 10:18:53
1986	Erin Baker (NZ) 9:27:36
European	Sarah Springman (UK) 9:59:49
1987	Sarah Coope (UK) 9:48:17
1989	Sarah Coope (UK) 9:33:20
1991	Thea Sybesma (Hol) 9:18:04
1992	Paula Newby-Fraser (Zim) 8:55:00
1993	Anne-Marie Rouchon (Fra) 11:37:51
1995	Ines Estedt (Ger) 8:56:05
1997	Karin Jørgensen (Den) 9:49:26

Men – middle distance

1985	Peter Zijerveld (Hol) 4:10:05
1986	Rob Barel (Hol) 3:54:31
1987	Glenn Cook (UK) 3:57:19
1988	Rob Barel (Hol) 3:44:50
1990	Karl Blondeel (Bel) 4:02:25
1992	Glen Cook (UK) 3:37:58
1994	Rob Barel (Hol) 3:48:19

Women – middle distance

1985	Lieve Paulus (Bel) 4:45:19
1986	Sarah Coope (UK) 4:32:13
1987	Sarah Coope (UK) 4:28:38
1988	Sarah Coope (UK) 4:15:42
1990	Isabelle Mouthon (Fra) 4:29:04
1992	Jeannine de Ruysscher (Bel) 4:05:19
1994	Isabelle Mouthon (Fra) 4:17:45

Men – Olympic distance

1985	Rob Barel (Hol) 2:37:42
1986	Rob Barel (Hol) 1:59:50
1987	Rob Barel (Hol) 1:58:12
1988	Rob Barel (Hol) 1:50:23
1989	Yves Cordier (Fra) 2:02:08
1990	Fons Hamblock (Bel) 1:50:29
1991	Simon Lessing (UK) 1:53:25
1992	Spencer Smith (UK) 1:48:37
1993	Simon Lessing (UK) 1:54:04
1994	Simon Lessing (UK) 1:50:38
1995	Rainer Müller (Ger) 1:46:24
1996	Luc Van Lierde (Bel) 1:42:32
1997	Spencer Smith (UK) 2:00:13
1998	Andrew Johns (UK) 1:51:09

Women – Olympic distance

1985	Erin Baker (NZ) 2:51:18	
European	Alexandra Kremer (FRG) 3:06:02	
1986	Lieve Paulus (Bel) 2:17:10	
1987	Sarah Coope (UK) 2:17:03	
1988	Sarah Springman (UK) 2:04:53	
1989	Simone Mortier (Fra) 2:16:59	
1990	Thea Sybesma (Hol) 2:04:01	
1991	Isabelle Mouthon (Fra) 2:07:53	
1992	Sonja Krolik (Ger) 2:02:47	
1993	Sabine Westhoff (Ger) 2:08:59	
1994	Sonja Krolik (Ger) 2:02:51	
1995	Isabelle Mouthon (Fra) 1:59:33	
1996	Suzanne Nielsen (Den) 1:59:30	
1997	Natascha Badmann (Swi) 2:13:34	
1998	Wieke Hoogzaad (Hol) 2:04:31	

'World Championship' Triathlon, Nice

Contested annually from 1982, over a 3.2km swim, 120km cycle, and 32km run 1982-7. In 1988 the swim distance was changed to 4000m.
Winners:

Men

1982	Mark Allen (USA) 6:33:52
1983	Mark Allen (USA) 6:04:51
1984	Mark Allen (USA) 6:05:23
1985	Mark Allen (USA) 5:53:13
1986	Mark Allen (USA) 5:46:10
1987	Richard Wells (NZ) 5:59:53
1988	Rob Barel (Hol) 6:05:06
1989	Mark Allen (USA) 5:54:31
1990	Mark Allen (USA) 5:50:52
1991	Mark Allen (USA) 5:54:12
1992	Mark Allen (USA) 5:59:43
1993	Mark Allen (USA) 6:05:59

Women

1982	Lyn Brooks (USA) 7:40:44
1983	Linda Buchanan (USA) 7:06:03
1984	Colleen Cannon (USA) 7:05:15
1985	Erin Baker (NZ) 6:37:21
1986	Linda Buchanan (USA) 6:50:56★

1987	Kirsten Hanssen (USA) 6:54:27
1988	Erin Baker (NZ) 6:27:06
1989	Paula Newby-Fraser (Zim) 6:49:43
1990	Paula Newby-Fraser (Zim) 6:36:19
1991	Paula Newby-Fraser (Zim) 6:40:33
1992	Paula Newby-Fraser (Zim) 6:43:41
1993	Isabelle Mouthon (Fra) 6:44:36

★ Erin Baker (NZ) was disqualified, after finishing in 6:40:26.

World Cup

A world-wide series was first held over 11 events in 1991.
Winners:

Men

1991	Leandro Macedo (Bra)
1992-5	Brad Beven (Aus)
1996	Miles Stewart (Aus)
1997	Chris McCormack (Aus)

Women

1991	Karen Smyers (USA)
1992	Melissa Mantak (USA)
1993	Jo-Anne Richie (Can)
1994	Jenny Rose (NZ)
1995-7	Emma Carney (Aus)

Duathlon World Championships

10km run, 40km cycle, 5km run.
Winners:

Year	Men	Women
1990	Ken Souza (USA)	Thea Sijbesma (Hol)
1991	Matthew Brick (NZ)	Erin Backer (NZ)
1992	Matthew Brick (NZ)	Jenny Alcorn (Aus)
1993	Greg Welch (Aus)	Carol Montgomery (Can)
1994	Normann Stadler (Ger)	Irma Heeren (Hol)
1995	Oscar Galindez (Arg)	Natascha Badmann (Swi)
1996	Andrew Noble (Aus)	Jackie Gallagher (Aus)
1997	Jonathan Hall (Aus)	Irma Heeren (Hol)

Duathlon long-distance World Championship

First held in 1997, with an 8.5km run, 150km cycle, 30km run, when Urs Dellsperger (Swi) won the men's event, and Natascha Badmann (Swi) the women's.

Tug-of-War

The term 'tug-of-war' is thought to have originated in England in the 19th century. Such a trial of strength and skill, involving two teams of eight pulling against each other on opposite ends of a long thick rope, is believed to be of great antiquity.

The first rules were framed by the New York AC in 1879 and the sport was included in the Olympic Games from 1900 to 1920. In Britain, tug-of-war was administered by the Amateur Athletic Association, and championships were held in conjunction with the AAA until 1970. A separate organization, the Tug-of-War Association, was formed in 1958.

International governing body: Tug-of-War International Federation (TWIF), de Lepelaar 8, 2751 CW Moerkapelle, Netherlands. Tel: (31) 1 608 879 2868, Fax: (31) 1 608 879 2103. President: J A P Koren, Secretary General: Glen Johnson. Founded 1960. 28 member nations (and 6 associate) in 1998.

Olympic Games

Winners:

1900	Sweden/Denmark
1904	Milwaukee AC (USA)
1906	Germany
1908	City Police (UK)
1912	Sweden
1920	Great Britain

World Championships

European Championships for men were first held in 1965, and these were followed by World Championships for men in 1975 and for women in 1986. World Championships are now held biennially. There are different categories depending on the total weight of the team.

World champions:

Men

720kg

England	1975-8, 1980, 1982
Ireland	1984, 1986, 1988, 1990
Switzerland	1985, 1992
Netherlands	1994, 1996

680kg

Switzerland	1990, 1994, 1996

640kg

England	1975-6, 1978, 1980, 1986, 1988
Ireland	1982, 1984, 1990
Switzerland	1985, 1992, 1994, 1996

560kg

Switzerland	1982, 1985, 1990
England	1984, 1988, 1993
Ireland	1986
Spain	1992, 1994, 1996

Catchweight (no weight specification)

England	1984

Women

520kg

Sweden	1986, 1988, 1994
Switzerland	1990
Netherlands	1992, 1996

560kg

Sweden	1986, 1988, 1990, 1992, 1994

World Indoor Championships

First held in 1991.
Winners:

Men

560kg

England	1991, 1993, 1997
Spain	1995

600kg

Spain	1991, 1995
Ireland	1993

640kg

England	1991, 1993, 1997
Spain	1995

680kg

England	1991, 1993, 1997
Ireland	1995

Women

480kg

Spain	1991, 1995, 1997
Netherlands	1993

520kg

Netherlands	1991, 1993, 1995
England	1997

Volleyball

The game was invented, originally as 'Mintonette', in 1895 by William G Morgan, director of physical training at the YMCA, Holyoke, Massachusets, USA. His aim was to provide a more recreational, non-contact game than basketball, which had been invented just four years earlier by James Naismith, whom Morgan had met while he was a student at Springfield YMCA. The number of players per side was fixed at six in 1918.

Volleyball was first played at an international games at the 1913 Far Eastern Games in Manila, Philippines. World championships were first held in 1949, and the game was introduced to the Olympics in 1964. It is now one of the most widely practised games in the world.

International governing body: International Volleyball Federation (FIVB), 12 Avenue de la Gare, 1001 Lausanne, Switzerland. Tel: (44) 21 320 8932, Fax: (41) 21 320 8865. President: Dr Reuben Hernández Acosta. Formed in 1947. 214 member nations in 1998.

Olympic Games

Held for men and women at all Olympics from 1964.
Winners:

Year	Men	Women
1964	USSR	Japan
1968	USSR	USSR
1972	Japan	USSR
1976	Poland	Japan
1980	USSR	USSR
1984	USA	China
1988	USA	USSR
1992	Brazil	Cuba
1996	Netherlands	Cuba

Most medals

Men: 2 gold, 1 bronze Yuriy Poyarkov (USSR) 1964-72; 1 gold, 1 silver, 1 bronze Katsutoshi Nekoda (Jap) 1964-72

Women: 2 gold, 2 silver Inna Ryskal (USSR) 1964-76

World Champions

First held 1949, then every four years from 1952.

Men

6	USSR	1949, 1952, 1960, 1962, 1978, 1982
2	Czechoslovakia	1956, 1966
2	Italy	1990, 1994
1	GDR 1970, Poland 1974, USA 1986	

Women

5	USSR	1952, 1956, 1960, 1970, 1990
3	Japan	1962, 1967, 1974
2	China	1982, 1986
2	Cuba	1978, 1994

World Cup

Held every four years from 1965 (men) and 1973 (women).
Wins:

Men

4	USSR	1965, 1977, 1981, 1991
1	GDR 1969, USA 1985, Cuba 1989, Italy 1995	

Women

3	Cuba	1989, 1991, 1995
2	China	1981, 1985
1	USSR 1973, Japan 1977	

World League

First held in 1990, as an eight-team, two-division, 12-match per team series, culminating in a final. Expanded to 10 countries in 1991.
Winners.

6	Italy	1990-2, 1994-5, 1997
1	Brazil 1993, Netherlands 1996	

Women's World Grand Prix

Contested by the world's top eight teams; introduced in 1993.
Winners:

2	Brazil	1994, 1996
1	Cuba 1993, USA 1995, Russia 1997	

European Championships

First held in 1948 for men and 1949 for women. Now held biennially.
Wins:

Men

12	USSR	1950-1, 1967, 1971, 1975, 1977, 1979, 1981, 1983, 1985, 1987, 1991
3	Czechoslovakia	1948, 1955, 1958
3	Italy	1989, 1993, 1995
1	Romania 1963, Netherlands 1997	

Women

13	USSR	1949-51, 1958, 1963, 1967, 1971, 1975, 1977, 1979, 1983, 1985, 1989, 1991
2	Russia	1993, 1997
1	Czechoslovakia 1955, Bulgaria 1981, GDR 1987, Netherlands 1995	

Beach Volleyball

In professional beach volleyball, teams play 2-a-side on a sand court the same size as that used for indoor volleyball. The sport originated in California, with the first game at Santa Monica in 1930 and the first official tournament at State Beach in 1948. The Association of Volleyball Professionals (AVP) was formed in 1981 and the AVP/Miller Lite Tour started that year. The women's association, the WPVA, was formed in 1986.

Olympic Games

Beach volleyball first became a part of the Olympic programme in 1996, when Karch Kiraly & Kent Steffes (USA) won the men's event, and Jackie Silva & Sandra Pires (Bra) won the women's.

World Championships

The first official world championships were contested in 1997, when Pará de Souza & Guillerme Marques (Bra) won the men's event, and Jackie Silva & Sandra Pires (Bra) won the women's.

World Championships Series

Men: 1995/6 Franco Nieto & Roberto Lopez (Bra)
Women: 1995/6 Jackie Silva & Sandra Pires (Bra)

Water Polo

Played by teams of 7-a-side (from squads of 11). Originally known as 'football in the water' it was developed in Britain from 1869. The first rules were drafted in 1876 and the sport was first given official recognition by the Amateur Swimming Association in Great Britain in 1885. It has been an Olympic event since 1900, and came under the aegis of FINA after swimming's governing body was founded in 1908. The first women's international competition was in 1978. Women's water polo is being added to the Olympic programme in 2000.
International governing body: FINA (*see* Swimming).

Olympic Games

The first two winning teams were club sides: Osborne Swimming Club, Manchester, representing Great Britain in 1900, and New York AC in 1904.
Wins:

6	Hungary	1932, 1936, 1952, 1956, 1964, 1976
4	Great Britain	1900, 1908, 1912, 1920
3	Yugoslavia	1968, 1984, 1988
3	Italy	1948, 1960, 1992
2	USSR	1972, 1980
1	USA (New York AC) 1904, France 1924, Germany 1928, Spain 1996	

Individuals to have won three gold medals:
George Wilkinson (UK) 1900-12, Paul Radmilovic & Charles Smith (UK) 1908-20, Deszö Gyarmati & György Kárpáti (Hun) 1952-64.
Gyarmati won most medals, adding silver in 1948 and bronze in 1960.

World Championships

First held at the world swimming championships in 1973. Held separately in 1991.
Winners:

Men		**Women**	
1973	Hungary	1986	Australia
1975	USSR	1991	Netherlands
1978	Italy	1994	Hungary
1982	USSR		
1986	Yugoslavia		
1991	Yugoslavia		
1994	Italy		
1998	Spain		

FINA World Cup

First held in 1979.
Wins:

Men

2	Hungary	1979, 1995
2	USSR	1981, 1983
2	Yugoslavia	1987, 1989
2	USA	1991, 1997
1	F R Germany 1985, Italy 1993	

Women (unofficial until 1989)

5	Netherlands	1988, 1989, 1991, 1993, 1997
1	USA 1979, Canada 1981, Australia 1995	

European Champions

Men

11	Hungary	1926-7, 1931, 1934, 1938, 1954, 1958, 1962, 1974, 1977, 1997
5	USSR	1966, 1970, 1983, 1985, 1987
3	Italy	1947, 1993, 1995
2	F R Germany	1981, 1989
1	Netherlands 1950, Yugoslavia 1991	

Women

3	Netherlands	1985, 1987, 1989, 1993
2	Italy	1995, 1997
1	Hungary	1991

Water-Skiing

Water-skiing, as practised today, was pioneered in the 1920s, particularly by Ralph Samuelson on Lake Pepin, Minnesota, USA. The sport's origins, however, can be traced back hundreds of years to people walking on planks and aquaplaning. The development of the motor boat to tow skiers was clearly the key factor in the sport's growth. World championships were instituted in 1949.

International governing body: International Water Ski Federation (IWSF), Altopiano 55/4, P. Marconi BO, 40044, Italy. Tel: (39) 5184 5285, Fax: (39) 5184 5806. President: Andrès Botero, Secretary General: Tognala Graziano. Formerly the World Water Ski Union (WWSU), first formed as the Union Internationale de Ski Nautique in Geneva in 1946.

World Championships

First held at Juan Les Pins, France in 1949 and now staged biennially.
Winners:

	Men's overall	**Women's overall**
1949	Christian Jourdan (Fra) & Guy de Clercq (Bel)	Willa Worthington (USA)
1950	Dick Pope, Jr (USA)	Willa McGuire★ (USA)
1953	Alfredo Mendoza (USA)	Leah Marie Rawls (USA)
1955	Alfredo Mendoza (USA)	Willa McGuire★ (USA)

	Men's overall	Women's overall
1957	Joe Cash (USA)	Marina Doria (Swi)
1959	Chuck Stearns (USA)	Vickie Van Hook (USA)
1961	Bruno Zaccardi (Ita)	Sylvie Hulsemann (Lux)
1963	Billy Spencer (USA)	Jeanette Brown (USA)
1965	Roland Hillier (USA)	Liz Allan (USA)
1967	Mike Suyderhoud (USA)	Jeanette Stewart-Wood (UK)
1969	Mike Suyderhoud (USA)	Liz Allan (USA)
1971	George Athans (Can)	Christy Weir (USA)
1973	George Athans (Can)	Lisa St John (USA)
1975	Carlos Suarez (Ven)	Liz Shetter (née Allan) (USA)
1977	Mike Hazelwood (UK)	Cindy Todd (USA)
1979	Joel McClintock (Can)	Cindy Todd (USA)
1981	Sammy Duvall (USA)	Karin Roberge (USA)
1983	Sammy Duvall (USA)	Ana Maria Carrasco (Ven)
1985	Sammy Duvall (USA)	Karen Neville (Aus)
1987	Sammy Duvall (USA)	Deena Brush (USA)
1989	Patrice Martin (Fra)	Deena Mapple (née Brush)
1991	Patrice Martin (Fra)	Karen Neville (Aus)
1993	Patrice Martin (Fra)	Natalya Rumyantseva (Rus)
1995	Patrice Martin (Fra)	Judy Messer (Can)
1997	Patrice Martin (Fra)	Yelena Milakova (Rus)

	Men's slalom	Men's tricks	Men's jumping
1949	Christian Jourdan (Fra)	Pierre Gouin (Fra)	Guy de Clercq (Bel)
1950	Dick Pope, Jr (USA)	Jack Andresen (USA)	Guy de Clercq (Bel)
1953	Charles Blackwell (Can)	Warren Witherall (USA)	Alfredo Mendoza (USA)
1955	Alfredo Mendoza (USA)	Scotty Scott (USA)	Alfredo Mendoza (USA)
1957	Joe Cash (USA)	Mike Amsbury (USA)	Joe Mueller (USA)
1959	Chuck Stearns (USA)	Philippe Logut (Fra)	Buster McCalla (USA)
1961	Jimmy Jackson (USA)	Jean Marie Muller (Fra)	Larry Penacho (USA)
1963	Billy Spencer (USA)	Billy Spencer (USA)	Jimmy Jackson (USA)
1965	Roland Hillier (USA)	Ken White (USA)	Larry Penacho (USA)
1967	Tito Antunano (Mex)	Alan Kempton (USA)	Alan Kempton (USA)
1969	Victor Palomo (Spa)	Bruce Cockburn (Aus)	Wayne Grimditch (USA)
1971	Mike Suyderhoud (USA)	Ricky McCormick (USA)	Mike Suyderhoud (USA)
1973	George Athans (Can)	Wayne Grimditch (USA)	Ricky McCormick (USA)
1975	Roby Zucchi (Ita)	Wayne Grimditch (USA)	Ricky McCormick (USA)
1977	Bob LaPoint (USA)	Carlos Suarez (Ven)	Mike Suyderhoud (USA)
1979	Bob LaPoint (USA)	Patrice Martin (Fra)	Mike Hazelwood (UK)
1981	Andy Mapple (UK)	Cory Pickos (USA)	Mike Hazelwood (UK)
1983	Bob LaPoint (USA)	Cory Pickos (USA)	Sammy Duvall (USA)
1985	Bob LaPoint (USA)	Patrice Martin (Fra)	Geoff Carrington (Aus)
1987	Bob LaPoint (USA)	Patrice Martin (Fra)	Sammy Duvall (USA)
1989	Andy Mapple (UK)	Aymeric Benet (Fra)	Geoff Carrington (Aus)
1991	Lucky Lowe (USA)	Patrice Martin (Fra)	Bruce Neville (Aus)
1993	Glen Thurley (Aus)	Tory Baggiano (USA)	Andrea Alessi (Ita)
1995	Andy Mapple (UK)	Aymeric Benet (Fra)	Bruce Neville (Aus)
1997	Andy Mapple (UK)	Kyle Peterson (USA)	Jaret Llewellyn (Can)

	Women's slalom	Women's tricks	Women's jumping
1949	Willa Worthington (USA)	Madeleine Boutellier (Fra)	Willa Worthington (USA)
1950	Evie Wolford (USA)	Willa McGuire★ (USA)	Johnette Kirkpatrick (USA)
1953	Evie Wolford (USA)	Leah Marie Rawls (USA)	Sandra Swaney (USA)
1955	Willa McGuire★ (USA)	Marina Doria (Swi)	Willa McGuire★ (USA)
1957	Marina Doria (Swi)	Marina Doria (Swi)	Nancie Rideout (USA)
1959	Vickie Van Hook (USA)	Piera Castelvetri (Ita)	Nancie Rideout (USA)
1961	Janelle Kirkley (USA)	Sylvie Hulsemann (Lux)	Renate Hansluvka (Aut)

1963	Jeanette Brown (USA)	Guyonne Dalle (Fra)	Renate Hansluvka (Aut)
1965	Barbara Cooper-Clack (USA)	Dany Duflot (Fra)	Liz Allan (USA)
1967	Liz Allan (USA)	Dany Duflot (Fra)	Jeanette Stewart-Wood (UK)
1969	Liz Allan (USA)	Liz Allan (USA)	Liz Allan (USA)
1971	Christy Freeman (USA)	Willi Stahle (Hol)	Christy Weir (USA)
1973	Sylvie Maurial (Fra)	Maria Victoria Carrasco (Ven)	Liz Shetter (née Allan) (USA)
1975	Liz Shetter (USA)	Maria Victoria Carrasco (Ven)	Liz Shetter (USA)
1977	Cindy Todd (USA)	Maria Victoria Carrasco (Ven)	Linda Giddens (USA)
1979	Pattsie Messner (USA)	Natalya Rumyantseva (USSR)	Cindy Todd (USA)
1981	Cindy Todd (USA)	Ana Maria Carrasco (Ven)	Deena Brush (USA)
1983	Cindy Todd (USA)	Natalya Ponomaryeva★ (USSR)	Cindy Todd (USA)
1985	Camille Duvall (USA)	Judy McClintock (Can)	Deena Brush (USA)
1987	Kim Laskoff (USA)	Natalya Ponomaryeva★ (USSR)	Deena Brush (USA)
1989	Kim Laskoff (USA)	Tawn Larsen (USA)	Deena Mapple (née Brush) (USA)
1991	Helena Kjellander (Swe)	Tawn Larsen (USA)	Sheri Stone (USA)
1993	Helena Kjellander (Swe)	Britt Larsen (USA)	Kim De Macedo (Can)
1995	Helena Kjellander (Swe)	Tawn Larsen (USA)	Brenda Nichols (USA)
1997	Helena Kjellander (Swe)	Britt Larsen (USA)	Yelena Milakova (Rus)

★ McGuire née Worthington, Ponomaryeva née Rumyantseva.

Most individual wins

Overall – men: 5 Martin, 4 Duvall
Overall – women: 3 Worthington/McGuire, Allan/Shetter
Individual and overall – men: 9 Martin; 6 Duvall; 5 LaPoint, Suyderhoud
Individual and overall – women: 11 Allan/Shetter; 8 Worthington/McGuire; 7 Todd; 6 Brush/Mapple
   Liz Allan is the only water-skier to have won all four titles in one year, 1969.

Team

Title won by the USA at all 17 championships 1957–89; Canada 1991, 1993; France 1995, 1997.

European Champions

Held annually since 1947.
Overall champions:

Men

1947	Claude de Clercq (Bel)
1948	Jean-Pierre Mussat (Fra)
1949	Christian Jourdan (Fra) & Guy de Clercq (Bel)
1950-2	Claude de Clercq (Bel)
1953	Guy Vermeersch (Bel)
1954	Marc Flachard (Fra)
1955	Simon Khoury (Leb)
1956	Franco Carraro (Ita)
1957	Jean Marie Muller (Fra)
1958	Maxime Vazeille (Fra)
1959-61	Bruno Zaccardi (Ita)
1962-3	Maxime Vazeille (Fra)
1964	Mario Pozzini (Ita)
1965	Jean-Jacques Pottier (Fra)
1966	Bruno Zaccardi (Ita)
1967	Jean Michel Jamin (Fra)
1968	Roby Zucchi (Ita)
1969	Jean-Yves Parpette (Fra)
1970-1	Roby Zucchi (Ita)
1972	Paul Seaton (UK)
1973	Lars Björk (Swe)
1974-5	Paul Seaton (UK)
1976-7	Mike Hazelwood (UK)
1978-83	Mike Hazelwood (UK)
1984-5	Patrice Martin (Fra)
1986	Mike Hazelwood (UK)
1987-91	Andrea Alessi (Ita)
1992-4	Patrice Martin (Fra)
1995	Andrea Alessi (Ita)
1996-7	Patrice Martin (Fra)

Women

1947	Maggy Savard (Fra)
1948	Monique Girod (Swz)
1949	Madeleine Boutellier (Fra) & Maggie Wuarin (Bel)
1951-2	Jacqueline Marcour (Fra)
1953-6	Marina Doria (Swi)
1957	Jacqueline Keller (Fra)
1958-60	Piera Castelvetri (Ita)
1961	Sylvie Hulsemann (Lux)
1962-3	Renate Hansluvka (Aut)
1964	Dany Duflot (Fra)
1965	Renate Hansluvka (Aut)
1966	Sylvie Hulsemann (Lux)
1967	Jeanette Stewart-Wood (UK)
1968	Sylvie Hulsemann (Lux)
1969	Eliane Borter (Swz)
1970-1	Sylvie Maurial (Fra)
1972	Willi Stahle (Hol)

1973	Sylvie Maurial (Fra)
1974-5	Willi Stahle (Hol)
1976-7	Chantal Escot-Amade (Fra)
1978-9	Anita Carlman (Swe)
1980	Marlon van Dijk (Hol)
1981	Anita Carlman (Swe)
1982	Natalya Rumyantseva (USSR)
1983	Anita Carlman (Swe)
1984	Natalya Ponomaryeva (née Rumyantseva) (USSR)
1985	Helena Kjellander (Swe)
1986	Philippa Roberts (UK)
1987	Natalya Rumyantseva (USSR)
1988	Helena Kjellander (Swe)
1989	Natalya Rumyantseva (USSR)
1990	Philippa Roberts (UK)
1991	Olga Pavlova (USSR)
1992-4	Natalya Rumyantseva (Rus)
1995-6	Angela Andriopoulos (Gre)
1997	Olga Pavlova (Blr)

Most wins

Men: 9 Hazelwood; 5 Alessi, Martin; 4 de Clercq, Zaccardi

Women: 7 Rumyantseva; 4 Doria, Carlman

World Cup

For men's teams, first held 1980.
Wins:

2	Great Britain	1980, 1984
2	USA	1982, 1986
1	France	1988

European Cup

For men's teams, first held 1980.
Wins:

5	Great Britain	1983, 1987-9, 1991, 1993
3	Italy	1980, 1986, 1995
2	Sweden	1984-5
1	France 1982, USSR 1990	

World Records

Men

Slalom	1 buoy on a 9.75m line Jeff Rodgers (USA), Trophy Lakes, USA 1 Sep 1997
Tricks	11,680 pts Cory Pickos (USA)
Jump	68.2m John Swanson (USA) 15 Sep 1997

Women

Slalom	2.25 buoys on a 10.75m line Susi Graham (Can), Santa Rosa, Florida, USA 25 Sep 1994
Tricks	8580 pts Tawn Larsen (USA), Groveland, Florida, USA 4 Jul 1992
Jump	47.5m Deena Mapple (USA), Charlotte, N Carolina, USA 9 Jul 1988

World Barefoot Water-Skiing Championships

The first person reported to water-ski barefoot was Dick Pope, Jr in Florida in 1947. World barefoot championships, which have been dominated by Australians, were first held in 1978; events are wake slalom, tricks, start methods (not in 1988), and jump. *Overall winners:*

Individual

Year	Men	Women
1978	Brett Wing (Aus)	Colleen Wilkinson (Aus)
1980	Brett Wing (Aus)★	Kim Lampard (Aus)
1982	Brett Wing (Aus)	Kim Lampard (Aus)
1985	Mike Seipel (USA)	Kim Lampard (Aus)
1986	Mike Seipel (USA)	Kim Lampard (Aus)
1988	Rick Powell (USA)	Lori Powell (USA)
1990	Rick Powell (USA)	Jennifer Calleri (USA)
1992	Ron Scarpa (USA)	Jennifer Calleri (USA)
1994	John Penney (Aus)	Jennifer Calleri (USA)
1996	Ron Scarpa (USA)	Jennifer Calleri (USA)
1998	Ron Scarpa (USA)	Sharon Dodgson (Aus)

★ Brett Wing won all five titles in 1980.

Team

6	USA	1988, 1990, 1992, 1994, 1996, 1998
5	Australia	1978, 1980, 1982, 1984, 1986

Barefoot world jump records

Men: 27.5m Richard Mainwaring (UK) 1994
Women: 16.6m Sharon Stekelenburg (Aus) 1991

World Ski-Racing Championships

Winners:

Individual

Year	Men	Women
1979	Wayne Ritchie (Aus)	Bronwyn Wright (Aus)
1981	Danny Bertels (Bel)	Liz Hobbs (UK)
1984	Danny Bertels (Bel)	Liz Hobbs (UK)
1985	Mark Pickering (Aus)	Debbie Nordblad (USA)
1988	Stephen Moore (UK)	Tanya Williams (Aus)
1989	Ian Dipple (Aus)	Marsha Fitzgerald (USA)
1991	Paul Robertson (Aus)	Debbie Nordblad (USA)
1993	Kirk Book (USA)	Leanne Brown (Aus)
1995	Stefano Gregorio (Ita)	Leanne Brown (Aus)
1997	Wayne Mawer (Aus)	Leanne Brown (Aus)

Team

6	Australia	1979, 1981, 1985, 1991, 1995, 1997
5	USA	1979, 1984, 1988, 1989, 1993

In 1986 Stephen Moore (UK) won the inaugural ski-racing World Cup, winning all three races. The World Cup and the World Championships now take place in alternate years.

Speed Records

The fastest speed recorded on water skis is 230.26km/h by Christopher Massey (Aus) on the Hawkesbury River, NSW, Australia in 1983.

The official barefoot speed record over a quarter-mile course is 192.08km/h by Scott Pelaton (USA) at Chowchilla, California, USA in 1983. The fastest by a woman is 118.56km/h by Karen Toms (Aus) on the Hawkesbury River, NSW, Australia in 1984.

Weightlifting

Strength testing by the lifting of heavy weights is an ancient sport and competitions for lifting weights of stone were included in the ancient Olympic Games. Just five years after a world championship competition was held in 1891, weightlifting was included in the first of the modern Olympic Games. The events were for one-arm and two-arm lifts. During the couple of centuries preceding that, professional strongmen had demonstrated awesome feats of strength, but some of the advertised weights may be doubted.

Modern weightlifting, as included on the Olympic programme, is a combination of strength and skill. There are two standard lifts: the snatch, which is a one-movement lift from the floor to an extended-arm position above the head; and the jerk, a two-movement lift, the 'clean', from floor to shoulders, and then the 'jerk', from the shoulders to a fully extended-arm position above the head. Competitors have up to three attempts at each weight, and three referees determine whether lifts are correct. Until 1972 the press was also included as a standard lift, but it was then dropped due to the difficulties involved in judging it. There are ten bodyweight categories for lifters.

International governing body: International Weightlifting Federation (IWF), Hold u.1, 1054 Budapest, Hungary. Tel: (36) 1 353 0530, Fax: (36) 1 453 0199. President: Gottfried Schödl, General Secretary: Dr Tamás Aján. Founded in 1920 as the Fédération Haltérophile Internationale. 162 member nations by 1998.

Men's Weightlifting

World and Olympic Champions

Although the IWF first ran World Championships at Tallinn, Estonia in 1922, it has subsequently recognized the results from championships held in Vienna, Austria from 1898 to 1920. Championships were held again in 1923, but not again until 1937 and 1938. They have been held annually from 1946 (except for 1967), and the Olympic Games have been recognized as the official Championships during those years.

Olympic Games weightlifting was contested at one-hand jerk and two-hand jerk with no weight categories in 1896, 1904 and 1906. Weight categories were introduced at the 1920 Olympic Games and have increased in number over the years. From 1920 to 1946 there were five: 60kg, 67.5kg, 75kg, 82.5kg, over 82.5kg. Further additions were: 56kg in 1947, 90kg in 1951, 52kg and 110kg in 1969, 100kg in 1977, with the super-heavyweights now over 110kg. The heavyweight class was thus over 82.5kg until 1950, over 90kg until 1968, and at the 110kg limit when the super-heavyweight class was introduced in 1969.

New weight categories were introduced on 1 Jan 1993, and a fresh start was made for world records. This was felt to be appropriate in order to distance the sport from past accusations of drug-taking by participants.

At the 1920 Olympics three lifts were totalled, with one-hand snatch added to the one- and two-handed jerk. In 1924 two additional lifts were added: the two-hands press and the snatch. From 1928 to 1972 the results were decided on the aggregate of press, snatch and jerk, and from the 1973 World Championships on snatch and jerk. (* Denotes Olympic title throughout lists.)

Most World and Olympic titles 1896-1924

6   Josef Grafl (Aut) 67.5+kg 1910; 80+kg 1908-11, 1913

4   Josef Steinbach (Aut) overall 1904, 1905, 80+kg 1905; one-hand jerk 1906*

4   Leopold Hennermüller (Aut) 67.5kg 1910, 80kg 1911 (twice), 1913

4   Emil Kliment (Aut) 60kg 1910, 1911 (twice), 1913

World and Olympic Champions from 1928

Olympic Games 1964 to 1984 were also recognized as World Championships; 1988 was not. 1928-72 three lifts, since 1973 two lifts.

(Weight totals are shown in kilograms.)

52kg (formerly flyweight)

1969	Vladimir Krishchisin (USSR) 337.5
1970	Sandor Holczreiter (Hun) 342.5
1971	Zygmunt Smalcerz (Pol) 340
1972*	Zygmunt Smalcerz (Pol) 337.5
1973	Mohammad Nassiri (Irn) 240
1974	Mohammad Nassiri (Irn) 232.5
1975	Zygmunt Smalcerz (Pol) 237.5
1976*	Aleksandr Voronin (USSR) 242.5
1977	Aleksandr Voronin (USSR) 247.5
1978	Kanybek Osmonalyev (USSR) 240
1979	Kanybek Osmonalyev (USSR) 242.5

1980★	Kanybek Osmonalyev (USSR)	245
1981	Kanybek Osmonalyev (USSR)	247.5
1982	Stefan Leletko (Pol)	250
1983	Neno Terziiski (Bul)	260
1984★	Zeng Guoqiang (Chn)	235
1985	Sevdalin Marinov (Bul)	252.5
1986	Sevdalin Marinov (Bul)	257.5
1987	Sevdalin Marinov (Bul)	262.5
1988★	Sevdalin Marinov (Bul)	270
1989	Ivan Ivanov (Bul)	272.5
1990	Ivan Ivanov (Bul)	265
1991	Ivan Ivanov (Bul)	272.5
1992★	Ivan Ivanov (Bul)	265

54kg

1993	Ivan Ivanov (Bul)	277.5
1994	Halil Mutlu (Tur)	290
1995	Zhang Xiangsen (Chn)	285
1996★	Halil Mutlu (Tur)	287.5
1997	Lan Shizhang (Chn)	287.5

56kg (formerly bantamweight)

1947	Joseph de Pietro (USA)	300
1948★	Joseph de Pietro (USA)	307.5
1949	Mahmoud Namdjou (Irn)	315
1950	Mahmoud Namdjou (Irn)	310
1951	Mahmoud Namdjou (Irn)	317.5
1952★	Ivan Udodov (USSR)	315
1953	Ivan Udodov (USSR)	315
1954	Bakir Farhutdinov (USSR)	315
1955	Vladimir Stogov (USSR)	335
1956★	Charles Vinci (USA)	342.5
1957	Vladimir Stogov (USSR)	345
1958	Vladimir Stogov (USSR)	342.5
1959	Vladimir Stogov (USSR)	332.5
1960★	Charles Vinci (USA)	345
1961	Vladimir Stogov (USSR)	345
1962	Yoshinobu Miyake (Jap)	352.5
1963	Aleksey Vakhonin (USSR)	345
1964★	Aleksey Vakhonin (USSR)	357.5
1965	Imre Földi (Hun)	360
1966	Aleksey Vakhonin (USSR)	362.5
1968★	Mohammad Nassiri (Irn)	367.5
1969	Mohammad Nassiri (Irn)	360
1970	Mohammad Nassiri (Irn)	362.5
1971	Gennadiy Chetin (USSR)	370
1972★	Imre Földi (Hun)	377.5
1973	Atanas Kirov (USSR)	257.5
1974	Atanas Kirov (USSR)	255
1975	Atanas Kirov (USSR)	255
1976★	Norair Nurikyan (Bul)	262.5
1977	Jiro Hosotani (Jap)	252.5
1978	Daniel Nunez (Cub)	260
1979	Anton Kodiabashev (Bul)	267.5
1980★	Daniel Nunez (Cub)	275
1981	Anton Kodiabashev (Bul)	272.5
1982	Anton Kodiabashev (Bul)	280
1983	Oksen Mirzoyan (USSR)	292.5

1984★	Wu Shude (Chn)	267.5
1985	Neno Terziiski (Bul)	280
1986	Mitko Grablev (Bul)	290
1987	Neno Terziiski (Bul)	287.5
1988★	Oksen Mirzoyan (USSR)	292.5#
1989	Hafiz Suleimanov (USSR)	287.5
1990	Liu Shoubin (Chn)	285
1991	Chun Byung-kwan (SKo)	295
1992★	Chun Byung-kwan (SKo)	287.5

Mitko Grablev (Bul) scored 297.5, but was disqualified after a drugs test.

59kg

1993	Nikolay Peshalov (Bul)	305
1994	Nikolay Peshalov (Bul)	302.5
1995	Leonidas Sabanis (Gre)	302
1996★	Tang Ningsheng (Chn)	387.5
1997	Stefan Georgiev (Bul)	295

60kg (formerly featherweight)

1928★	Franz Andrysek (Aut)	287.5
1932★	Raymond Suvigny (Fra)	287.5
1936★	Anthony Terlazzo (USA)	312.5
1937	Georg Liebsch (Ger)	297.5
1938	Georg Liebsch (Ger)	305
1946	Arvid Andersson (Swe)	320
1947	Robert Higgins (USA)	310
1948★	Mahmoud Fayad (Egy)	332.5
1949	Mahmoud Fayad (Egy)	332.5
1950	Mahmoud Fayad (Egy)	327.5
1951	Sayed Gouda (Egy)	310
1952★	Rafael Chimiskyan (USSR)	337.5
1953	Nikolay Saksonov (USSR)	337.5
1954	Rafael Chimiskyan (USSR)	350
1955	Rafael Chimiskyan (USSR)	350
1956★	Isaac Berger (USA)	352.5
1957	Yevgeniy Minayev (USSR)	362.5
1958	Isaac Berger (USA)	372.5
1959	Marian Zielinski (Pol)	365
1960★	Yevgeniy Minayev (USSR)	372.5
1961	Isaac Berger (USA)	367.5
1962	Yevgeniy Minayev (USSR)	362.5
1963	Yoshinobu Miyake (Jap)	375
1964★	Yoshinobu Miyake (Jap)	397.5
1965	Yoshinobu Miyake (Jap)	385
1966	Yoshinobu Miyake (Jap)	387.5
1968★	Yoshinobu Miyake (Jap)	392.5
1969	Yoshiyuki Miyake (Jap)	385
1970	Mieczyslaw Nowak (Pol)	392.5
1971	Yoshiyuki Miyake (Jap)	387.5
1972★	Norair Nurikyan (Bul)	402.5
1973	Dito Shanidze (USSR)	272.5
1974	Georgi Todorov (Bul)	280
1975	Georgi Todorov (Bul)	285
1976★	Nikolay Kolesnikov (USSR)	285
1977	Nikolay Kolesnikov (USSR)	280
1978	Nikolay Kolesnikov (USSR)	270
1979	Marek Severyn (USSR)	290

1980★	Viktor Mazin (USSR) 290
1981	Beloslav Manolov (Bul) 302.5
1982	Yurik Sarkisyan (USSR) 302.5
1983	Yurik Sarkisyan (USSR) 312.5
1984★	Chen Weiqiang (Chn) 282.5
1985	Neum Shalamanov (Bul) 322.5
1986	Neum Shalamanov (Bul) 335
1987	Stefan Topurov (Bul) 315
1988★	Naim Suleymanoglü (Tur) 342.5#
1989	Naim Suleymanoglü (Tur) 317.5#
1990	Nikolai Peshalov (Bul) 297.5
1991	Naim Suleymanoglü (Tur) 310
1992★	Naim Suleymanoglü (Tur) 320

Born Naim Suleimanov, then known by a Bulgarian version of his name – Naum Shalamanov – and, after being given political asylum, used Turkish name Naim Suleymanoglü.

64kg

1993	Naim Suleymanoglü (Tur) 322.5
1994	Naim Suleymanoglü (Tur) 330
1995	Naim Suleymanoglü (Tur) 327.5
1996★	Naim Suleymanoglü (Tur) 335
1997	Xiao Jiangang (Chn) 317.5

67.5kg (formerly lightweight)

1928★	Kurt Helbig (Ger) 322.5
	& Hans Haas (Aut) 322.5
1932★	René Duverger (Fra) 325
1936★	Anwar Mohammad Mesbah (Egy) 342.5
	& Robert Fein (Aut) 342.5
1937	Anthony Terlazzo (USA) 357.5
1938	Anthony Terlazzo (USA) 350
1946	Stanley Stanczyk (USA) 367.5
1947	Peter George (USA) 352.5
1948★	Ibrahim Shams (Egy) 360
1949	Ibrahim Shams (Egy) 352.5
1950	Joseph Pitman (USA) 352.5
1951	Ibrahim Shams (Egy) 342.5
1952★	Tommy Kono (USA) 362.5
1953	Peter George (USA) 370
1954	Dmitriy Ivanov (USSR) 367.5
1955	Nikolay Kostilyev (USSR) 382.5
1956★	Igor Rybak (USSR) 380
1957	Viktor Bushuyev (USSR) 380
1958	Viktor Bushuyev (USSR) 390
1959	Viktor Bushuyev (USSR) 385
1960★	Viktor Bushuyev (USSR) 397.5
1961	Waldemar Baszanowski (Pol) 402.5
1962	Vladimir Kaplunov (USSR) 415
1963	Marian Zielinski (Pol) 417.5
1964★	Waldemar Baszanowski (Pol) 432.5
1965	Waldemar Baszanowski (Pol) 427.5
1966	Yevgeniy Katsura (USSR) 437.5
1968★	Waldemar Baszanowski (Pol) 437.5
1969	Waldemar Baszanowski (Pol) 445
1970	Zbigniew Kaczmarek (Pol) 440
1971	Zbigniew Kaczmarek (Pol) 440

1972★	Mukharbi Kirzhinov (USSR) 460
1973	Mukharbi Kirzhinov (USSR) 305
1974	Pyotr Korol (USSR) 305
1975	Pyotr Korol (USSR) 312.5
1976★	Pyotr Korol (USSR) 305
1977	Roberto Urrutia (Cub) 315
1978	Yanko Rusev (Bul) 310
1979	Yanko Rusev (Bul) 332.5
1980★	Yanko Rusev (Bul) 342.5
1981	Joachim Kunz (GDR) 340
1982	Piotr Mandra (Pol) 325
1983	Joachim Kunz (GDR) 340
1984★	Yao Jingyuan (Chn) 320
1985	Mikhail Petrov (Bul) 335
1986	Mikhail Petrov (Bul) 342.5
1987	Mikhail Petrov (Bul) 350
1988★	Joachim Kunz (GDR) 340#
1989	Israil Militosian (USSR) 347.5
1990	Kim Myong-nam (NKo) 342.5
1991	Yoto Yotov (Bul) 345
1992★	Israil Militosian (CIS/Arm) 337.5

Angel Guenchev (Bul) scored 362.5, but was disqualified after a drugs test.

70kg

1993	Yoto Yotov (Bul) 342.5
1994	Fedail Guler (Tur) 350
1995	Zhan Xugang (Chn) 347.5
1996★	Zhan Xugang (Chn) 357.5
1997	Zlatan Vanev (Bul) 355

75kg (formerly middleweight)

1928★	Roger Francois (Fra) 335
1932★	Rudolf Ismayr (Ger) 345
1936★	Khadr El Touni (Egy) 387.5
1937	John Terpak (USA) 352.5
1938	Adolf Wagner (Ger) 367.5
1946	Khadr El Touni (Egy) 377.5
1947	Stanley Stanczyk (USA) 405
1948★	Frank Spellman (USA) 390
1949	Khadr El Touni (Egy) 397.5
1950	Khadr El Touni (Egy) 400
1951	Peter George (USA) 395
1952★	Peter George (USA) 400
1953	Tommy Kono (USA) 407.5
1954	Peter George (USA) 405
1955	Peter George (USA) 405
1956★	Fyodor Bogdanovskiy (USSR) 420
1957	Tommy Kono (USA) 420
1958	Tommy Kono (USA) 430
1959	Tommy Kono (USA) 425
1960★	Aleksandr Kurinov (USSR) 437.5
1961	Aleksandr Kurinov (USSR) 435
1962	Aleksandr Kurinov (USSR) 422.5
1963	Aleksandr Kurinov (USSR) 437.5
1964★	Hans Zdrazila (Cs) 445
1965	Viktor Kurentsov (USSR) 437.5
1966	Viktor Kurentsov (USSR) 450

1968★	Viktor Kurentsov (USSR) 475
1969	Viktor Kurentsov (USSR) 467.5
1970	Viktor Kurentsov (USSR) 462.5
1971	Vladimir Kanygin (USSR) 477.5
1972★	Yordan Bikov (Bul) 485
1973	Nedelcho Kolev (Bul) 337.5
1974	Nedelcho Kolev (Bul) 335
1975	Peter Wenzel (GDR) 335
1976★	Yordan Mitkov (Bul) 335
1977	Yurik Vardanyan (USSR) 345
1978	Roberto Urrutia (Cub) 347.5
1979	Roberto Urrutia (Cub) 345
1980★	Asen Zlatev (Bul) 360
1981	Yanko Rusev (Bul) 360
1982	Yanko Rusev (Bul) 365
1983	Alexander Varbanov (Bul) 370
1984★	Karl-Heinz Radschinsky (FRG) 340
1985	Alexander Varbanov (Bul) 370
1986	Alexander Varbanov (Bul) 377.5
1987	Borislav Guidikov (Bul) 375
1988★	Borislav Guidikov (Bul) 375
1989	Altjamurat Orazdurdyev (USSR) 362.5
1990	Fyodor Kassapu (USSR) 360
1991	Pablo Lara (Cub) 355
1992★	Fyodor Kassapu (CIS/Mol) 357.5

76kg

1993	Altjamurat Orazdurdyev (Tkm) 362.5
1994	Pablo Lara (Cub) 365
1995	Pablo Lara (Cub) 367.5
1996★	Pablo Lara (Cub) 367.5
1997	Yoto Yotov (Bul) 367.5

82.5kg (formerly light-heavyweight)

1928★	Said Nosseir (Egy) 355
1932★	Louis Hostin (Fra) 365
1936★	Louis Hostin (Fra) 372.5
1937	Fritz Haller (Aut) 375
1938	John Davis (USA) 387.5
1946	Grigoriy Novak (USSR) 425
1947	John Terpak (USA) 387.5
1948★	Stanley Stanczyk (USA) 417.5
1949	Stanley Stanczyk (USA) 412.5
1950	Stanley Stanczyk (USA) 420
1951	Stanley Stanczyk (USA) 402.5
1952★	Trofim Lomakin (USSR) 417.5
1953	Arkadiy Vorobyev (USSR) 430
1954	Tommy Kono (USA) 435
1955	Tommy Kono (USA) 435
1956★	Tommy Kono (USA) 447.5
1957	Trofim Lomakin (USSR) 450
1958	Trofim Lomakin (USSR) 440
1959	Rudolf Plyukfelder (USSR) 457.5
1960★	Ireneusz Palinski (Pol) 442.5
1961	Rudolf Plyukfelder (USSR) 450
1962	Gyözö Veres (Hun) 460
1963	Gyözö Veres (Hun) 477.5
1964★	Rudolf Plyukfelder (USSR) 475

1965	Norbert Osimek (Pol) 472.5
1966	Vladimir Belyayev (USSR) 485
1968★	Boris Selitskiy (USSR) 485
1969	Masashi Ohuchi (Jap) 487.5
1970	Gennadiy Ivanchenko (USSR) 505
1971	Boris Pavlov (USSR) 495
1972★	Leif Jensen (Nor) 507.5
1973	Vladimir Rizhenkov (USSR) 350
1974	Trendafil Stoychev (Bul) 350
1975	Valeriy Shariy (USSR) 357.5
1976★	Valeriy Shariy (USSR) 365
1977	Gennadiy Bessonov (USSR) 352.5
1978	Yurik Vardanyan (USSR) 377.5
1979	Yurik Vardanyan (USSR) 370
1980★	Yurik Vardanyan (USSR) 400
1981	Yurik Vardanyan (USSR) 392.5
1982	Asen Zlatev (Bul) 400
1983	Yurik Vardanyan (USSR) 392.5
1984★	Petre Becheru (Rom) 355
1985	Yurik Vardanyan (USSR) 397.5
1986	Asen Zlatev (Bul) 405
1987	László Barsi (Hun) 390
1988★	Israil Arsamakov (USSR) 377.5
1989	Kiril Kounev (Bul) 385
1990	Altjamurat Orazdurdyev (USSR) 377.5
1991	Ivan Samadov (USSR) 367.5
1992★	Pyrros Dimas (Gre) 370

83kg

1993	Pyrros Dimas (Gre) 377.5
1994	Marc Huster (Ger) 382.5
1995	Pyrros Dimas (Gre) 385
1996★	Pyrros Dimas (Gre) 392.5
1997	Andrzej Cofalik (Pol) 380

90kg (formerly middle-heavyweight)

1951	Norbert Schemansky (USA) 427.5
1952★	Norbert Schemansky (USA) 445
1953	Norbert Schemansky (USA) 442.5
1954	Arkadiy Vorobyev (USSR) 460
1955	Arkadiy Vorobyev (USSR) 455
1956★	Arkadiy Vorobyev (USSR) 462.5
1957	Arkadiy Vorobyev (USSR) 470
1958	Arkadiy Vorobyev (USSR) 465
1959	Louis Martin (UK) 445
1960★	Arkadiy Vorobyev (USSR) 472.5
1961	Ireneusz Palinski (Pol) 475
1962	Louis Martin (UK) 480
1963	Louis Martin (UK) 480
1964★	Vladimir Golovanov (USSR) 487.5
1965	Louis Martin (UK) 487.5
1966	Geza Toth (Hun) 487.5
1968★	Kaarlo Kangasniemi (Fin) 517.5
1969	Kaarlo Kangasniemi (Fin) 515
1970	Vasiliy Kolotov (USSR) 537.5
1971	David Rigert (USSR) 542.5
1972★	Andon Nikolov (Bul) 525
1973	David Rigert (USSR) 365

1974	David Rigert (USSR) 387.5
1975	David Rigert (USSR) 377.5
1976*	David Rigert (USSR) 382.5
1977	Sergey Poltoratskiy (USSR) 375
1978	Rolf Milser (FRG) 377.5
1979	Gennadiy Bessonov (USSR) 380
1980*	Peter Baczako (Hun) 377.5
1981	Blagoi Blagoyev (Bul) 405
1982	Blagoi Blagoyev (Bul) 415
1983	Blagoi Blagoyev (Bul) 417.5
1984*	Nicu Vlad (Rom) 392.5
1985	Anatoliy Khrapatiy (USSR) 395
	& Viktor Solodov (USSR) 395
1986	Anatoliy Khrapatiy (USSR) 412.5
1987	Anatoliy Khrapatiy (USSR) 417.5
1988*	Anatoliy Khrapatiy (USSR) 412.5
1989	Anatoliy Khrapatiy (USSR) 415
1990	Anatoliy Khrapatiy (USSR) 397.5
1991	Sergey Syrtsov (USSR) 410
1992*	Kakhi Kakhiashvili (CIS/Geo) 412.5

91kg

1993	Ivan Chakarov (Bul) 407.5
1994	Aleksey Petrov (Rus) 412.5
1995	Aleksey Petrov (Rus) 410
1996*	Aleksey Petrov (Rus) 402.5
1997	Vadim Vacartchiuk (Mol) 387.5

99kg

1993	Viktor Tregubov (Rus) 407.5
1994	Sergey Syrtsov (Rus) 417.5
1995	Kakhi Kakiashvilis (Gre) 410
1996*	Kakhi Kakiashvilis (Gre) 420

100kg

1977	Anatoliy Kozlov (USSR) 367.5
1978	David Rigert (USSR) 390
1979	Pavel Sirchin (USSR) 385
1980*	Otto Zaremba (Cs) 395
1981	Viktor Sots (USSR) 407.5
1982	Viktor Sots (USSR) 422.5
1983	Pavel Kuznyetsov (USSR) 422.5
1984*	Rolf Milser (FRG) 385
1985	Sandor Szanyi (Hun) 415
1986	Nicu Vlad (Rom) 437.5
1987	Pavel Kuznyetsov (USSR) 422.5
1988*	Pavel Kuznyetsov (USSR) 425
1989	Petar Stefanov (Bul) 415
1990	Nicu Vlad (Rom) 412.5
1991	Igor Sadykov (USSR) 415
1992*	Viktor Tregubov (CIS/Rus) 420

108kg

1993	Timur Taimazov (Ukr) 420
1994	Timur Taimazov (Ukr) 435
1995	Igor Rozarenov (Ukr) 417.5
1996*	Timur Taimazov (Ukr) 430
1997	Martin Tesovic (Svk) 400

110kg (formerly heavyweight)

1969	Robert Bednarski (USA) 555
1970	Jan Talts (USSR) 565
1971	Yuriy Kozin (USSR) 552.5
1972*	Jan Talts (USSR) 580
1973	Pavel Pervushin (USSR) 385
1974	Valeriy Ustyuzhin (USSR) 380
1975	Valentin Khristov (Bul) 417.5
1976*	Yuriy Zaitsev (USSR) 385
1977	Valentin Khristov (Bul) 405
1978	Yuriy Zaitsev (USSR) 402.5
1979	Sergey Arakelov (USSR) 410
1980*	Leonid Taranenko (USSR) 422.5
1981	Valeriy Kravchuk (USSR) 415
1982	Sergey Arakelov (USSR) 427.5
1983	Vyacheslav Klokov (USSR) 440
1984*	Norberto Oberburger (Ita) 390
1985	Yuriy Zakharevich (USSR) 422.5
1986	Yuriy Zakharevich (USSR) 447.5
1987	Yuriy Zakharevich (USSR) 445
1988*	Yuriy Zakharevich (USSR) 455
1989	Stefan Botev (Bul) 427.5
1990	Stefan Botev (Bul) 440
1991	Artur Akoyev (USSR) 427.5
1992*	Ronny Weller (Ger) 432.5

82.5+kg – heavyweight

1928*	Josef Strassberger (Ger) 372.5
1932*	Jaroslav Skobla (Cs) 380
1936*	Josef Manger (Aut) 410
1937	Josef Manger (Ger) 420
1938	Josef Manger (Ger) 410
1946	John Davis (USA) 435
1947	John Davis (USA) 455
1948*	John Davis (USA) 452.5
1949	John Davis (USA) 442.5
1950	John Davis (USA) 462.5

90+kg – heavyweight

1951	John Davis (USA) 432.5
1952*	John Davis (USA) 460
1953	Douglas Hepburn (Can) 467.5
1954	Norbert Schemansky (USA) 487.5
1955	Paul Anderson (USA) 512.5
1956*	Paul Anderson (USA) 500
1957	Aleksey Medvedev (USSR) 500
1958	Aleksey Medvedev (USSR) 485
1959	Yuriy Vlasov (USSR) 500
1960*	Yuriy Vlasov (USSR) 537.5
1961	Yuriy Vlasov (USSR) 525
1962	Yuriy Vlasov (USSR) 540
1963	Yuriy Vlasov (USSR) 557.5
1964*	Leonid Zhabotinskiy (USSR) 572.5
1965	Leonid Zhabotinskiy (USSR) 552.5
1966	Leonid Zhabotinskiy (USSR) 567.5
1968*	Leonid Zhabotinskiy (USSR) 572.5

110+kg (formerly super-heavyweight)

1969	Joseph Dube (USA)	577.5
1970	Vasiliy Alekseyev (USSR)	612.5
1971	Vasiliy Alekseyev (USSR)	635
1972★	Vasiliy Alekseyev (USSR)	640
1973	Vasiliy Alekseyev (USSR)	402.5
1974	Vasiliy Alekseyev (USSR)	425
1975	Vasiliy Alekseyev (USSR)	427.5
1976★	Vasiliy Alekseyev (USSR)	440
1977	Vasiliy Alekseyev (USSR)	430
1978	Jürgen Heuser (GDR)	417.5
1979	Sultan Rakhmanov (USSR)	430
1980★	Sultan Rakhmanov (USSR)	440
1981	Anatoliy Pisarenko (USSR)	425
1982	Anatoliy Pisarenko (USSR)	445
1983	Anatoliy Pisarenko (USSR)	450
1984★	Dean Lukin (Aus)	412.5
1985	Antonio Krastev (Bul)	437.5
1986	Antonio Krastev (Bul)	460
1987	Aleksandr Kurlovich (USSR)	472.5
1988★	Aleksandr Kurlovich (USSR)	462.5
1989	Aleksandr Kurlovich (USSR)	460
1990	Leonid Taranenko (USSR)	450
1991	Aleksandr Kurlovich (USSR)	455
1992★	Aleksandr Kurlovich (CIS/Blr)	450

108+kg

1993	Ronny Weller (Ger)	442.5
1994	Aleksandr Kurlovich (Blr)	457.5
1995	Andrey Chemerkin (Rus)	442.5
1996★	Andrey Chemerkin (Rus)	457.5
1997	Andrey Chemerkin (Rus)	462.5

Most titles

Olympic Games

Naim Suleymanoglü (Bul/Tur) is the only man to have won three gold medals. The most medals is four by Norbert Schemansky (USA) gold 90kg 1952, silver 82+kg 1948, bronze 90+kg 1960, 1964.

World and Olympic

10	Naim Suleymanoglü (Bul/Tur)	1985-96
8	John Davis (USA)	1938-52
8	Tommy Kono (USA)	1952-9
8	Vasiliy Alekseyev (USSR)	1970-7
7	Arkadiy Vorobyev (USSR)	1953-60
7	Yurik Vardanyan (USSR)	1977-85
6	Stanley Stanczyk (Pol)	1946-51
6	Peter George (USA)	1947-55
6	Yoshinobu Miyake (Jap)	1962-8
6	David Rigert (USSR)	1971-8
6	Anatoliy Khrapatiy (USSR)	1985-90
6	Aleksandr Kurlovich (USSR/Blr)	1987-94

World Championships

World Championships medals are awarded for each lift. *Winners of the most gold medals overall (P – press, S – snatch, J – jerk, T – total):*

No.	Name	P	S	J	T
22	Naim Suleymanoglü (Bul/Tur)	–	8	7	7
22	Vasiliy Alekseyev (USSR)	2	5	7	8
20	Yurik Vardanyan (USSR)	–	6	7	7
17	David Rigert (USSR)	1	5	5	6
15	Yanko Rusev (Bul)	–	5	5	5

World Cup

Awarded on a points basis to the best lifter from a world-wide series of events, who attended an annual gala 1980-92.

Year	World Cup winner	Gala winner
1980	György Szalai (Hun)	János Sólyomvári (Hun)
1981	Yanko Rusev (Bul)	Blagoi Blagoyev (Bul)
1982	Blagoi Blagoyev (Bul)	Blagoi Blagoyev (Bul)
1983	Blagoi Blagoyev (Bul)	Yurik Sarkisian (USSR)
1984	Naim Suleimanov (Bul)	Naim Suleimanov (Bul)
1985	Neum Shalamanov (Tur)#	Neum Shalamanov (Tur)#
1986	Neum Shalamanov (Tur)#	Asen Zlatev (Bul)
1987	Mikhail Petrov (Bul)	Mikhail Petrov (Bul)
1988	Stefan Botev (Bul)	Stefan Botev (Bul)
1989	Liu Shoubin (Chn)	Liu Shoubin (Chn)
1990	Ivan Ivanov (Bul)	Ivan Ivanov (Bul)
1991	Yoto Yotov (Bul)	Ivan Ivanov (Bul)
1992	Kakhi Kakhiashvili (Geo)	Liu Weiguo (Chn)
1993	*Not held*	
1994	Aleksandr Kurlovich (Blr)	

Formerly Naim Suleimanov.

World Records

World records can be set only at events pre-elected by the IWF and at which anti-doping controls are carried out. These are the final records at the new categories set and records accepted from 1 Jan 1993 to the end of 1997. From 1 Jan 1998 a new set of weight categories was introduced: 56, 62, 69, 77, 85, 94, 105 and over 105kg. *(u denotes unratified.)*

Class	Lift	kg	Name and country	Date
54kg	Snatch	132.5	Halil Mutlu (Tur)	1996
	Jerk	160.5	Lan Shizhang (Chn)	1997
		162.5u	Lan Shizhang (Chn)	1997
	Total	290	Halil Mutlu (Tur)	1994
59kg	Snatch	140	Hafiz Suleymanoglü (Tur)	1995
		142.5u	Shi Zhiyoung (Chn)	1997
	Jerk	170	Nikolai Peshalov (Bul)	1995
		172.5u	La Maosheng (Chn)	1997
	Total	307.5	Tang Ningsheng (Chn)	1996
64kg	Snatch	150	Wang Guohua (Chn)	1997
	Jerk	187.5	Valerios Leonidis (Gre)	1996
	Total	335	Naim Suleymanoglü (Tur)	1996
70kg	Snatch	163	Wang Jianhui (Chn)	1997
	Jerk	195	Zhan Xugang (Chn)	1997
		200u	Zhan Xugang (Chn)	1997
	Total	357.5	Zhan Xugang (Chn)	1996
		360u	Zhan Xugang (Chn)	1997
76kg	Snatch	170	Ruslan Savchenko (Ukr)	1993
	Jerk	208	Pablo Lara (Cub)	1996
	Total	372.5	Pablo Lara (Cub)	1996
83kg	Snatch	180	Pyrros Dimas (Gre)	1996
	Jerk	214	Zhang Yong (Chn)	1997
	Total	392.5	Pyrros Dimas (Gre)	1996
91kg	Snatch	187.5	Aleksey Petrov (Rus)	1996
	Jerk	228.5	Kakhi Kakiashvilis (Gre)	1995
	Total	412.5	Aleksey Petrov (Rus)	1994
99kg	Snatch	192.5	Sergey Syrtsov (Rus)	1994
	Jerk	235	Kakhi Kakiasvilis (Gre)	1996
	Total	420	Kakhi Kakiasvilis (Gre)	1996
108kg	Snatch	200	Timur Taimazov (Ukr)	1994
		200.5u	Cui Wenhua (Chn)	1997
	Jerk	236	Timur Taimazov (Ukr)	1996
	Total	435	Timur Taimazov (Ukr)	1994
108+kg	Snatch	205	Aleksandr Kurlovich (Blr)	1994
	Jerk	262.5	Andrey Chemerkin (Rus)	1997
	Total	462.5	Andrey Chemerkin (Rus)	1997

Super-heavyweight jerk record

Showing the record at the end of each decade.

161.5	Charles Rigoulet (Fra)	1925
167.5	Arnold Luhäär (Estonia)	1937
177.5	John Davis (USA)	1948
197.5	Juri Vlasov (USSR)	1959
220.5	Robert Bednarski (USA)	1968
256	Vasiliy Alexeyev (USSR)	1977
266	Leonid Taranenko (USSR)	1988

The most recent record has not yet been surpassed by any of the new set of records that came into force in 1993.

Most improvements

31	Vasiliy Alexeyev (USSR) 221.5kg 1970–256kg 1977
9	Juri Vlasov (USSR) 197.5kg 1959–215.5kg 1964
6	Norbert Schemansky (USA) 185kg 1952–192.5kg 1954
6	Leonid Zhabotinsky (USSR) 213kg 1964–220kg 1968

Women's Weightlifting

World Records

World records at weight categories from 1 Jan 1993 to the end of 1997. From 1 Jan 1998 the weight categories are 48, 53, 58, 63, 69, 75 and over 75kg.

(u denotes unratified.)

Class	Lift	kg	Name and country	Date
46kg	Snatch	81	Guan Hong (Chn)	1995
		85u	Xing Feng (Chn)	1997
	Jerk	105.5	Xing Feng (Chn)	1997
		117.5u	Xing Feng (Chn)	1997
	Total	185	Guan Hong (Chn)	1996
		202.5u	Xing Feng (Chn)	1997
50kg	Snatch	88	Jiang Baoyu (Chn)	1995
		95u	Li Zhou (Chn)	1997
	Jerk	110.5	Liu Xiuhua (Chn)	1994
		122.5u	Li Zhou (Chn)	1997
	Total	197.5	Liu Xiuhua (Chn)	1994
		217.5u	Li Zhou (Chn)	1997
54kg	Snatch	93.5	Yang Xia (Chn)	1997
		100u	Yang Xia (Chn)	1997
	Jerk	117.5	Meng Xianjuan (Chn)	1997
		132.5u	Yang Xia (Chn)	1997
	Total	202.5	Zhang Juhua (Chn)	1994
		232.5u	Yang Xia (Chn)	1997
59kg	Snatch	100	Zou Feie (Chn)	1997
		112.5u	Chen Yanqing (Chn)	1997
	Jerk	125	Khassaraporn (Tai)	1997
		137.5u	Chen Yanqing (Chn)	1997
	Total	220	Chen Xiaomin (Chn)	1994
		250u	Chen Yanqing (Chn)	1997
64kg	Snatch	107.5	Chen Xiaomin (Chn)	1997
		122.5u	Lei Li (Chn)	1997
	Jerk	131	Chen Yanqing (Chn)	1997
		137.5u	Lei Li (Chn)	1997
	Total	235	Li Hongyun (Chn)	1994
		260u	Lei Li (Chn)	1997
70kg	Snatch	105.5	Xiang Fenglan (Chn)	1997
		120u	Sun Tianni (Chn)	1997
	Jerk	130.5	Xiang Fenglan (Chn)	1997
		152.5u	Sun Tianni (Chn)	1997
	Total	235	Xiang Fenglan (Chn)	1997
		272.5u	Sun Tianni (Chn)	1997
76kg	Snatch	110	Aysel Ozgur (Tur)	1997
		125u	Yue Pingtian (Chn)	1997
	Jerk	140.5	Hua Ju (Chn)	1997
		155u	Yue Pingtian (Chn)	1997
	Total	247.5	Hua Ju (Chn)	1997
		280u	Yue Pingtian (Chn)	1997
83kg	Snatch	117.5	Tang Weifang (Chn)	1997
		137.5u	Wei Xiangying (Chn)	1997
	Jerk	142.5★	Tang Weifang (Chn)	1997
		155u	Wei Xiangying (Chn)	1997
	Total	260★	Tang Weifang (Chn)	1997
		292.5u	Wei Xiangying (Chn)	1997

83+kg	Snatch	112.5	Wang Yanmei (Chn)	1997
		137.5u	Ding Meiyuan (Chn)	1997
	Jerk	155	Li Yajuan (Chn)	1993
		170u	Ding Meiyuan (Chn)	1997
	Total	260	Li Yajuan (Chn)	1993
		307.5u	Ding Meiyuan (Chn)	1997

* Derya Acigoz (Tur) scored 147.5 at the jerk in 1997 but was disqualified after a drugs test; her total score was 262.5. Chinese women surpassed all the world records at the Chinese National Games in 1997, but these could not be ratified as this meeting was not a world or area championships at which world records can be set.

World Cup Gala

Women were invited to take part from 1991.

1991   Sun Caiyun (Chn) (also won World Cup)
1992   Milena Trendafilova (Bul)
1994   Xing Shuwen (Chn)

World Championships

World Championships have been held annually since the first, in 1987 at Daytona Beach, Florida, USA.
Winners:

44kg

1987   Cai Jun (Chn) 145
1988   Xing Fen (Chn) 147.5
1989   Xing Fen (Chn) 165
1990   Wu Xiangmei (Chn) 152.5
1991   Xing Fen (Chn) 162.5
1992   Guan Hong (Chn) 175

46kg

1993   Chu Nan-mei (Tai) 152.5
1994   Yun Yanhong (Chn) 180
1995   Guan Hong (Chn) 180
1996   Guan Hong (Chn) 172.5
1997   Liu Ling (Chn) 175

48kg

1987   Huang Xiaoyu (Chn) 170
1988   Huang Xiaoyu (Chn) 165
1989   Huang Xiaoyu (Chn) 172.5
1990   Cai Jun (Chn) 165
1991   Izabela Rifatova (Bul) 170
1992   Liu Xiuhua (Chn) 187.5

50kg

1993   Liu Xiuhua (Chn) 187.5
1994   Robin Byrd (USA) 175
1995   Liu Xiuhua (Chn) 187.5
1996   Liu Xiuhua (Chn) 185
1997   Winarii (Ina) 185

52kg

1987   Yan Zangqun (Chn) 157.5
1988   Peng Liping (Chn) 175
1989   Peng Liping (Chn) 185
1990   Liao Shuping (Chn) 177.5
1991   Peng Liping (Chn) 187.5
1992   Peng Liping (Chn) 202.5

54kg

1993   Chen Xiaoming (Chn) 200
1994   Kamami Maleswari* (Ind) 197.5
1995   Kamami Maleswari (Ind) 202.5
1996   Zhang Xixiang (Chn) 197.5
1997   Meng Xianjuan (Chn) 200.5

* Original winner Wang Shen (Chn) 197.5, disqualified after drugs test.

56kg

1987   Cui Aihong (Chn) 160
1988   Ma Na (Chn) 180
1989   Xing Liwei (Chn) 180
1990   Wu Haiqing (Chn) 190
1991   Sun Caiyan (Chn) 192.5
1992   Sun Caiyan (Chn) 210

59kg

1993   Sun Caiyan (Chn) 217.5
1994   Zou Feie (Chn) 220
1995   Chen Xiaomin (Chn) 215
1996   Chen Xiaomin (Chn) 207.5
1997   Hamid Patmawati (Ina) 212.5

60kg

1987   Zeng Xinling (Chn) 180
1988   Jing Yang (Chn) 195
1989   Ma Na (Chn) 202.5
1990   Maria Christoforidi (Gre) 197.5
1991   Han Lixia (Chn) 197.5
1992   Li Hongyun (Chn) 222.5

64kg

1993   Li Hongyun (Chn) 220
1994   Li Hongyun (Chn) 235
1995   Chen Jun-Lien (Tai) 212.5
1996   Li Hongyun (Chn) 225
1997   Chen Yanqing (Chn) 230

67.5kg

1987   Gao Lijuan (Chn) 180
1988   Guo Qiuxiang (Chn) 210
1989   Guo Qiuxiang (Chn) 220
1990   Wang Genying (Chn) 212.5
1991   Lei Li (Chn) 210
1992   Gao Lijuan (Chn) 222.5

70kg

1993   Milena Trendafilova (Bul) 220
1994   Zhou Meihong (Chn) 222.5

1995	Tang Weifang (Chn) 225
1996	Tang Weifang (Chn) 222.5
1997	Xiang Fenglan (Chn) 235

75kg

1987	Li Hongling (Chn) 210
1988	Li Hongling (Chn) 212.5
1989	Milena Trendafilova (Bul) 220
1990	Milena Trendafilova (Bul) 237.5
1991	Zhang Xiaoli (Chn) 242.5
1992	Hua Ju (Chn) 237.5

76kg

1993	Hua Ju (Chn) 230
1994	Panagiota Antonopoulou (Gre) 220
1995	Li Yan (Chn) 227.5
1996	Li Yan (Chn) 225
1997	Hua Ju (Chn) 247.5

82.5kg

1987	Karyn Marshall (USA) 220
1988	Li Yanxia (Chn) 215
1989	Li Hongling (Chn) 240
1990	Maria Urrutia (Col) 230
1991	Li Hongling (Chn) 240
1992	Zhang Xiaoli (Chn) 252.5

83kg

1993	Chen Shu-chih (Tai) 230
1994	Maria Urrutia (Col) 237.5
1995	Chen Shu-chih (Tai) 240
1996	Wei Xiangying (Chn) 242.5
1997	Tang Weifang* (Chn) 260

* Original winner Derya Acigoz (Tur) 262.5, disqualified after drugs test.

82.5+kg

1987	Han Changmei (Chn) 210
1988	Han Changmei (Chn) 232.5
1989	Han Changmei (Chn) 242.5
1990	Li Yajuan (Chn) 245
1991	Li Yajuan (Chn) 255
1992	Li Yajuan (Chn) 265

83+kg

1993	Li Yajuan (Chn) 260
1994	Karolina Lundahl* (Fin) 230
1995	Erika Takacs (Hun) 232.5
1996	Wan Ni (Chn) 240
1997	Ma Runmei (Chn) 252.5

* Original winner Li Dan (Chn) 242.5, disqualified after drugs test.

Most overall titles: 4 Peng Liping, Li Hingling, Li Yajuan, Liu Xiuhua, Li Hongyun

Most gold medals (snatch, jerk and total):
13 Li Hongyun; 12 Milena Trendafilova, Peng Liping Mária Takács (Hun) won 22 silver and 6 bronze medals (from 30 possible) at all 10 World Championships 1987-96.

Wrestling

Wrestling was part of the ancient Olympics, and wall drawings from nearly 6000 years ago depict it taking place long before then. The sport was included in the first modern Olympics, in 1896.

The two forms of Wrestling at international level are Freestyle and Greco-Roman. The principal difference is that use of the legs is completely prohibited in the Greco-Roman style. Holds below the waist are also prohibited in this style of wrestling.

International governing body: Fédération Internationale des Luttes Associées (FILA), Avenue Juste-Olivier 17, CH-1006 Lausanne, Switzerland. Tel: (41) 21 312 8426, Fax: (41) 21 323 6073. President: Milan Ercegan. Founded 1912. 135 member nations in 1996.

Olympic Games

A heavyweight division of Greco-Roman wrestling was included in the first modern Olympics. Freestyle wrestling was introduced in 1904.
Winners:

Freestyle

48kg – light-flyweight

1904	Robert Curry (USA)
1972	Roman Dmitriyev (USSR)
1976	Hasan Isaev (Bul)
1980	Claudio Pollio (Ita)
1984	Robert Weaver (USA)
1988	Takashi Kobayashi (Jap)
1992	Kim Il (NKo)
1996	Kim Il (NKo)

52kg – flyweight
Limit 115lb/52.16kg in 1904

1904	George Mehnert (USA)
1948	Lennart Viitala (Fin)
1952	Hasan Gemici (Tur)
1956	Mirian Tsalkalamanidze (USSR)
1960	Ahmet Bilek (Tur)
1964	Yoshikatsu Yoshida (Jap)
1968	Shigeo Nakata (Jap)
1972	Kiyomi Kato (Jap)
1976	Yuji Takada (Jap)
1980	Anatoliy Beloglazov (USSR)
1984	Saban Trstena (Yug)
1988	Mitsuru Sato (Jap)
1992	Li Hak-son (NKo)
1996	Valentin Jordanov (Bul)

57kg – bantamweight
Limit 125lb/56.70kg 1904, 119lb/54kg 1908, 56kg 1924-36

| 1904 | Isidor Niflot (USA) |
| 1908 | George Mehnert (USA) |

1924	Kustaa Pihlajamäki (Fin)		1964	Enyu Valtschev (Bul)★
1928	Kaarlo Mäkinen (Fin)		1968	Abdollah Movahed Ardabili (Irn)
1932	Robert Pearce (USA)		1972	Dan Gable (USA)
1936	Odön Zombori (Hun)		1976	Pavel Pinigin (USSR)
1948	Nasuh Akar (Tur)		1980	Saipulla Absaidov (USSR)
1952	Shohachi Ishii (Jap)		1984	You In-tak (SKo)
1956	Mustafa Dagistanli (Tur)		1988	Arsen Fadzeyev (USSR)
1960	Terrence McCann (USA)		1992	Arsen Fadzeyev (CIS/Rus)
1964	Yojiro Uetake (Jap)		1996	Vadim Bogiyev (Rus)
1968	Yojiro Uetake (Jap)			★ Competed as Dimov in 1960.
1972	Hideaki Yanagida (Jap)			
1976	Vladimir Yumin (USSR)			

74kg – welterweight

Limit 158lb/71.67kg 1904, 72kg 1924-36, 73kg 1948-60, 78kg 1964-8

1980	Sergey Beloglazov (USSR)
1984	Hideaki Tomiyama (Jap)
1988	Sergey Beloglazov (USSR)
1992	Alejandro Puerto (Cub)
1996	Kendall Cross (USA)

62kg – featherweight

Limit 135lb/61.24kg 1904, 133lb/60.3kg 1908, 60kg 1920, 61kg 1924-36, 63kg 1964-8

1904	Benjamin Bradshaw (USA)
1908	George Dole (USA)
1920	Charles Ackerly (USA)
1924	Robin Reed (USA)
1928	Allie Morrison (USA)
1932	Hermanni Pihlajamäki (Fin)
1936	Kustaa Pihlajamäki (Fin)
1948	Gazanfer Bilge (Tur)
1952	Bayram Sit (Tur)
1956	Shozo Sasahara (Jap)
1960	Mustafa Dagistanli (Tur)
1964	Osamu Watanabe (Jap)
1968	Masaakı Kaneko (Jap)
1972	Zagalav Abdu lbekov (USSR)
1976	Yang Jung-mo (SKo)
1980	Magomedgasan Abushev (USSR)
1984	Randy Lewis (USA)
1988	John Smith (USA)
1992	John Smith (USA)
1996	Tom Brands (USA)

68kg – lightweight

Limit 145lb/65.77kg 1904, 146.75lb/66.6kg 1908, 67.5kg 1920, 66kg 1924-36, 67kg 1948-60, 70kg 1964-8

1904	Otto Roehm (USA)
1908	George de Relwyskow (UK)
1920	Kalle Anttila (Fin)
1924	Russell Vis (USA)
1928	Osväld Käpp (Est)
1932	Charles Pacôme (Fra)
1936	Károly Kárpáti (Hun)
1948	Celal Atik (Tur)
1952	Olle Anderberg (Swe)
1956	Emamali Habibi (Irn)
1960	Shelby Wilson (USA)

74kg – welterweight

Limit 158lb/71.67kg 1904, 72kg 1924-36, 73kg 1948-60, 78kg 1964-8

1904	Charles Erickson (USA)
1924	Hermann Gehri (Swi)
1928	Arvo Haavisto (Fin)
1932	Jack Van Bebber (USA)
1936	Frank Lewis (USA)
1948	Yasar Dogu (Tur)
1952	William Smith (USA)
1956	Mitsuo Ikeda (Jap)
1960	Douglas Blubaugh (USA)
1964	Ismail Ogan (Tur)
1968	Mahmut Atalay (Tur)
1972	Wayne Wells (USA)
1976	Jiichiro Date (Jap)
1980	Valentin Raitchev (Bul)
1984	David Schultz (USA)
1988	Ken Monday (USA)
1992	Park Jang-soon (SKo)
1996	Buvaysa Saytyev (Rus)

82kg – middleweight

Limit 161lb/73kg 1908, 165lb/75kg 1920, 79kg 1924-60, 87kg 1964-8

1908	Stanley Bacon (UK)
1920	Eino Leino (Fin)
1924	Fritz Hagmann (Swi)
1928	Ernst Kyburz (Swi)
1932	Ivar Johansson (Swe)
1936	Emile Poilvé (Fra)
1948	Glen Brand (USA)
1952	David Tsimakuridze (USSR)
1956	Nikolai Stanchev (Bul)
1960	Hasan Güngör (Tur)
1964	Prodan Gardschev (Bul)
1968	Boris Gurevich (USSR)
1972	Levan Tediashvili (USSR)
1976	John Peterson (USA)
1980	Ismail Abilov (Bul)
1984	Mark Schultz (USA)
1988	Han Myung-woo (SKo)
1992	Kevin Jackson (USA)
1996	Kahdzhimurad Magomedov (Rus)

90kg – light-heavyweight

Limit 82.5kg 1920, 87kg 1924-60, 97kg 1964-8

1920	Anders Larsson (Swe)
1924	John Spellman (USA)
1928	Thure Sjöstedt (Swe)
1932	Peter Mehringer (USA)
1936	Knut Fridell (Swe)
1948	Henry Wittenberg (USA)
1952	Wiking Palm (Swe)
1956	Gholam Reza Takhti (Irn)
1960	Ismet Atli (Tur)
1964	Aleksandr Medved (USSR)
1968	Ahmet Ayik (Tur)
1972	Ben Peterson (USA)
1976	Levan Tediashvili (USSR)
1980	Sanasar Oganesyan (USSR)
1984	Ed Banach (USA)
1988	Makharbek Khadartsev (USSR)
1992	Makharbek Khadartsev (CIS/Rus)
1996	Rasull Khadem Azghadi (Irn)

100kg – heavyweight

Limit over 158lb/71.60kg 1904, over 73kg 1908, over 82.5kg 1920, over 87kg 1924-60, over 97kg 1964-8

1904	Bernhuff Hansen (USA)
1908	George O'Kelly (UK)
1920	Robert Roth (Swi)
1924	Harry Steel (USA)
1928	Johan Richthoff (Swe)
1932	Johan Richthoff (Swe)
1936	Kristjan Palusalu (Est)
1948	Gyula Bóbis (Hun)
1952	Arsen Mekokishvili (USSR)
1956	Hamit Kaplan (Tur)
1960	Wilfried Dietrich (FRG)
1964	Aleksandr Ivanitskiy (USSR)
1968	Aleksandr Medved (USSR)
1972	Ivan Yarygin (USSR)
1976	Ivan Yarygin (USSR)
1980	Ilya Mate (USSR)
1984	Lou Banach (USA)
1988	Vasile Puscasu (Rom)
1992	Leri Khabelov (CIS/Geo)
1996	Kurt Angle (USA)

100+kg – super-heavyweight

1972	Aleksandr Medved (USSR
1976	Soslan Andiyev (USSR)
1980	Soslan Andiyev (USSR)
1984	Bruce Baumgartner (USA)
1988	David Gobedzhishviliy (USSR)
1992	Bruce Baumgartner (USA)
1996	Mahmut Demir (Tur)

Greco-Roman

48kg – light-flyweight

1972	Gheorghe Berceanu (Rom)
1976	Aleksey Schumakov (USSR)
1980	Zaksylik Ushkempirov (USSR)
1984	Vincenzo Maenza (Ita)
1988	Vincenzo Maenza (Ita)
1992	Oleg Kucherenko (CIS/Ukr)
1996	Sim Kwon-ho (SKo)

52kg – flyweight

1948	Pietro Lombardi (Ita)
1952	Boris Gurevich (USSR)
1956	Nikolay Solovyov (USSR)
1960	Dumitru Pirvulescu (Rom)
1964	Tsutomu Hanahara (Jap)
1968	Petar Kirov (Bul)
1972	Petar Kirov (Bul)
1976	Vitaliy Konstantinov (USSR)
1980	Vakhtang Blagidze (USSR)
1984	Atsuji Miyahara (Jap)
1988	Jon Rønningen (Nor)
1992	Jon Rønningen (Nor)
1996	Armen Nazaryan (Arm)

57kg – bantamweight

Limit 58kg 1924-8, 56kg 1932-6

1924	Eduard Pütsep (Est)
1928	Kurt Leucht (Ger)
1932	Jakob Brendel (Ger)
1936	Márton Lörincz (Hun)
1948	Kurt Pettersén (Swe)
1952	Imre Hódos (Hun)
1956	Konstantin Vyrupayev (USSR)
1960	Oleg Karavayev (USSR)
1964	Masamitsu Ichiguchi (Jap)
1968	János Varga (Hun)
1972	Rustem Kazakov (USSR)
1976	Pertti Ukkola (Fin)
1980	Shamil Serikov (USSR)
1984	Pasquale Passarelli (FRG)
1988	András Sike (Hun)
1992	An Han-bong (SKo)
1996	Yuriy Melnichenko (Kaz)

62kg – featherweight

Limit 60kg 1912-20, 62kg 1924-8, 1948-60, 61kg 1932-6, 63kg 1964-8

1912	Kaarlo Koskelo (Fin)
1920	Oskari Friman (Fin)
1924	Kalle Anttila (Fin)
1928	Voldemar Väli (Est)
1932	Giovanni Gozzi (Ita)
1936	Yasar Erkan (Tur)
1948	Mehmet Oktav (Tur)
1952	Yakov Punkin (USSR)
1956	Rauno Mäkinen (Fin)

1960	Müzahir Sille (Tur)
1964	Imre Polyák (Hun)
1968	Roman Rurua (USSR)
1972	Georgi Markov (Bul)
1976	Kazimierz Lipién (Pol)
1980	Stylianos Migiakis (Gre)
1984	Kim Weon-kee (SKo)
1988	Kamandar Madzhidov (USSR)
1992	Akif Pirim (Tur)
1996	Wlodzimierz Zawadzki (Pol)

68kg – lightweight

Limit 75kg 1906, 66.6kg 1908, 67.5kg 1912-28, 66kg 1932-6, 67kg 1948-60, 70kg 1964-8

1906	Rudolf Watzl (Aut)
1908	Enrico Porro (Ita)
1912	Eemil Väre (Fin)
1920	Eemil Väre (Fin)
1924	Oskari Friman (Fin)
1928	Lajos Keresztes (Hun)
1932	Erik Malmberg (Swe)
1936	Lauri Koskela (Fin)
1948	Gustaf Freij (Swe)
1952	Schazam Safin (USSR)
1956	Kyösti Lehtonen (Fin)
1960	Avtandil Koridze (USSR)
1964	Kazim Ayvaz (Tur)
1968	Munji Mumemura (Jap)
1972	Shamil Khisamutdinov (USSR)
1976	Suren Na lbandyan (USSR)
1980	Stefan Rusu (Rom)
1984	Vlado Lisjak (Yug)
1988	Levon Dzhulfalakyan (USSR)
1992	Attila Repka (Hun)
1996	Ryszrad Wolny (Pol)

74kg – welterweight

Limit 72kg 1932-36, 73kg 1948-60, 78kg 1964-8

1932	Ivar Johansson (Swe)
1936	Rudolf Svedberg (Swe)
1948	Gösta Andersson (Swe)
1952	Miklós Szilvási (Hun)
1956	Mithat Bayrak (Tur)
1960	Mithat Bayrak (Tur)
1964	Anatoliy Kolesov (USSR)
1968	Rudolf Vesper (GDR)
1970	Vitezslav Mácha (Cs)
1976	Anatoliy Bykov (USSR)
1980	Ferenc Kocsis (Hun)
1984	Jouko Salomaki (Fin)
1988	Kim Young-nam (SKo)
1992	Mnatsakan Iskandarian (CIS/Arm)
1996	Feliberto Ascuy (Cub)

82kg – middleweight

Limit 85kg 1906, 73kg 1908, 75kg 1912-28, 79kg 1932-60, 87kg 1964-8

1906	Verner Weckman (Fin)
1908	Frithiof Mårtensson (Fin)
1912	Claes Johansson (Swe)
1920	Carl Westergren (Swe)
1924	Edvard Westerlund (Fin)
1928	Väinö Kokkinen (Fin)
1932	Väinö Kokkinen (Fin)
1936	Ivar Johansson (Swe)
1948	Axel Grönberg (Swe)
1952	Axel Grönberg (Swe)
1956	Givy Kartoziya (USSR)
1960	Dimiter Dobrev (Bul)
1964	Branislav Simic (Yug)
1968	Lothar Metz (GDR)
1972	Csaba Hegedüs (Hun)
1976	Momir Petkovic (Yug)
1980	Gennadiy Korban (USSR)
1984	Ion Draica (Rom)
1988	Mikhail Mamiashvili (USSR)
1992	Péter Farkas (Hun)
1996	Hamza Yerlikaya (Tur)

90kg – light-heavyweight

Limit 93kg 1908, 82.5kg 1912-28, 87kg 1932-60, 97kg 1964-8

1908	Verner Weckman (Fin)
1912	*No winner*★
1920	Claes Johansson (Swe)
1924	Carl Westergren (Swe)
1928	Ibrahim Moustafa (Egy)
1932	Rudolf Svensson (Swe)
1936	Axel Cadier (Swe)
1948	Karl-Eric Nilsson (Swe)
1952	Kelpo Gröndahl (Fin)
1956	Valentin Nikolayev (USSR)
1960	Tevfik Kis (Tur)
1964	Boyan Radev (Bul)
1968	Boyan Radev (Bul)
1972	Valeriy Rezantsev (USSR)
1976	Valeriy Rezantsev (USSR)
1980	Norbert Növényi (Hun)
1984	Steven Fraser (USA)
1988	Atanas Komchev (Bul)
1992	Maik Bullmann (Ger)
1996	Vyacheslav Oleynyk (Ukr)

★ Anders Ahlgren (Swe) and Ivan Böhling (Fin) fought out a draw after nine hours.

100kg – heavyweight

Limit open 1896, over 85kg 1906, over 93kg 1908, over 82.5kg 1912-28, over 81kg 1932-60, over 91kg 1964-8

1896	Carl Schuhmann (Ger)
1906	Søren Jensen (Den)
1908	Richárd Weisz (Hun)

1912	Yrjö Saarela (Fin)
1920	Adolf Lindfors (Fin)
1924	Henri Deglane (Fra)
1928	Rudolf Svensson (Swe)
1932	Carl Westergren (Swe)
1936	Kristjan Palusalu (Est)
1948	Ahmet Kirecci (Tur)
1952	Johannes Kotkas (USSR)
1956	Anatoliy Parfenov (USSR)
1960	Ivan Bogdan (USSR)
1964	István Kozma (Hun)
1968	István Kozma (Hun)
1972	Nicolae Martinescu (Rom)
1976	Nikolay Balboshin (USSR)
1980	Georgi Raikov (Bul)
1984	Vasile Andrei (Rom)
1988	Andrzej Wronski (Pol)
1992	Héctor Milian (Cub)
1996	Andrzej Wronski (Pol)

130kg (100+kg) – super-heavyweight

1972	Anatoliy Roschin (USSR)
1976	Aleksandr Kolchinsky (USSR)
1980	Aleksandr Kolchinsky (USSR)
1984	Jeffrey Blatnick (USA)
1988	Aleksandr Karelin (USSR)
1992	Aleksandr Karelin (CIS/Rus)
1996	Aleksandr Karelin (Rus)

Discontinued event – 3-class winner

1906	Søren Marinus Jensen (Den)

World Championships

Unofficial World Championships for Greco-Roman wrestling were held at Vienna in 1904, with further such championships held on 14 occasions (including five in 1911!) prior to the first official World Championships, held in Helsinki in 1921. There was a further Greco-Roman World Championship in 1922 but no more until 1950; since then they have been held regularly, and now take place annually in non-Olympic years. The first Freestyle championships were held at Helsinki in 1951. Olympic champions are automatically world champions in Olympic years. The current weight limits have been standard since 1969, and variations are shown for each category. Note that those results shown for 1953 were unofficial.
Winners since 1950:

Freestyle

48kg – light-flyweight

1969-71	Ebrahim Javadi (Irn)
1973	Roman Dmitriyev (USSR)
1974-5	Hasan Isaev (Murselov) (Bul)
1977	Anatoliy Beloglazov (USSR)
1978-9	Sergey Kornilayev (USSR)
1981-2	Sergey Kornilayev (USSR)

1983	Kim Chol-hwan (SKo)
1985	Kim Chol-hwan (SKo)
1986-7	Li Yae-sik (NKo)
1989	Kim Jong-shin (SKo)
1990	Aldo Martinez (Cub)
1991	Vugar Orudzhev (USSR)
1993-4	Alexis Vila (Cub)
1995	Vugar Orudzhev (Rus)

52kg – flyweight

1951	Ali Yücel (Tur)
1953	Georgiy Saydov (USSR)
1954	Hüseyin Akbas (Tur)
1957	Mehmet Kartal (Tur)
1959	Ali Aliyev (USSR)
1961-2	Ali Aliyev (USSR)
1963	Kemal Yanilmaz (Tur)
1965	Yoshikatsu Yoshida (Jap)
1966	Jang Chang-sun (SKo)
1967	Shigeo Nakata (Jap)
1969	Richard Sanders (USA)
1970	Ali Riza (Tur)
1971	Mohamad Ghorbani (Irn)
1973	Ebrahim Javadi (Irn)
1974-5	Yuji Takada (Jap)
1977	Yuji Takada (Jap)
1978	Anatoliy Beloglazov (USSR)
1979	Yuji Takada (Jap)
1981	Toshio Asakura (Jap)
1982	Hartmut Reich (GDR)
1983	Valentin Jordanov (Bul)
1985	Valentin Jordanov (Bul)
1986	Kim Yong-sik (NKo)
1987	Valentin Jordanov (Bul)
1989	Valentin Jordanov (Bul)
1990	Majid Torkan (Irn)
1991	Larry 'Zeke' Jones (USA)
1993-5	Valentin Jordanov (Bul)

54kg

1997	Quintana García (Cub)

57kg – bantamweight

1951	Nasuh Akar (Tur)
1953	Hüseyin Akbas (Tur)
1954	Mustafa Dagistanli (Tur)
1957	Hüseyin Akbas (Tur)
1959	Hüseyin Akbas (Tur)
1961	Mohamad Saifpour Sabadi (Irn)
1962	Hüseyin Akbas (Tur)
1963	Aidyn Ibragimov (USSR)
1965	Tomiaki Fukada (Jap)
1966-7	Ali Aliyev (USSR)
1969	Tamadichi Tanaka (Jap)
1970-1	Hideaki Yanagida (Jap)
1973	Mohsen Farahvashi (Irn)
1974	Vladimir Yumin (USSR)
1975	Masao Arai (Jap)

1977	Tadashi Sasaki (Jap)	1957	Alimbek Bestayev (USSR)	1990	Rahmat Sofiyadi (Bul)
1978-9	Hideaki Tomiyama (Jap)	1959	Viktor Sinyavskiy (USSR)	1991	Amir Khadem (Irn)
1981	Sergey Beloglazov (USSR)	1961	Mohamad-Ali Sanatkaram	1993	Park Jang-soon (SKo)
1982	Anatoliy Beloglazov		(Irn)	1994	Turan Ceylan (Tur)
	(USSR)	1962	Enyu Valtschev (Bul)	1995	Buvaysa Saytyev (Rus)

1983   Sergey Beloglazov (USSR)
1985-7 Sergey Beloglazov (USSR)
1989   Kim Sik-seung (NKo)
1990   Alejandro Puerto (Cub)
1991   Sergey Smal (USSR)
1993   Terry Brands (USA)
1994   Alejandro Puerto (Cub)
1995   Terry Brands (USA)

58kg
1997   Ramil Islamov (Uzb)

62kg – featherweight
Limit 63kg 1962-7
1951   Haydar Zafer (Tur)
1953   Norair Musyegyan (USSR)
1954   Shozo Sasahara (Jap)
1957   Mustafa Dagistanli (Tur)
1959   Mustafa Dagistanli (Tur)
1961   Vladimir Rubashvili (USSR)
1962-3 Osamu Watanabe (Jap)
1965   Mohamad Saifpour Sabadi (Irn)
1966-7 Masaki Kaneko (Jap)
1969   Takeo Morita (Jap)
1970   Shamseddin Seyed-Abassy (Irn)
1971   Zagalav Abdu lbekov (USSR)
1973   Zagalav Abdu lbekov (USSR)
1974-5 Zeveg Oidov (Mgl)
1977-9 Vladimir Yumin (USSR)
1981   Simeon Sjeterev (Bul)
1982   Sergeiy Beloglazov(USSR)
1983   Viktor Alekseyev (USSR)
1985   Viktor Alekseyev (USSR)
1986   Hasar Isayev (USSR)
1987   John Smith (USA)
1989-91 John Smith (USA)
1993   Tom Brands (USA)
1994   Magomed Azizov (Rus)
1995   Elbrus Tedeyev (Ukr)

63kg
1997   Haji Kenari Abbas (Irn)

68kg – lightweight
Limit 67kg 1951-61, 70kg 1962-7
1951   Olle Anderberg (Swe)
1953   Viktor Sinyavskiy (USSR)
1954   Djahanbakte Tovfighe (Irn)

1963   Iwao Horiuchi (Jap)
1965-7 Abdollah Movahed (Irn)
1969-70 Abdollah Movahed (Irn)
1971   Dan Gable (USA)
1973   Lloyd Keaser (USA)
1974   Nasrulla Nasrullayev (USSR)
1975   Pavel Pinigın (USSR)
1977-8 Pavel Pinigin (USSR)
1979   Mikhail Kharachura (USSR)
1981   Saipulla Absaidov (USSR)
1982   Mikhail Kharachura (USSR)
1983   Arsen Fadzeyev (USSR)
1985-7 Arsen Fadzeyev (USSR)
1989   Boris Budayev (USSR)
1990-1 Arsen Fadzeyev (USSR)
1993   Akbar Fallah (Irn)
1994   Alexander Leipold (Ger)
1995   Araik Gevorkian (Arm)

69kg
1997   Araik Gevorkian (Arm)

74kg – welterweight
Limit 73kg 1951-61, 78kg 1962-7
1951   Celál Atik (Tur)
1953   Ismail Ogan (Tur)
1954   Vakhtang Balavadze (USSR)
1957   Vakhtang Balavadze (USSR)
1959   Emamali Habibi (Irn)
1961-2 Emamali Habibi (Irn)
1963   Guliko Sagaradze (USSR)
1965   Guliko Sagaradze (USSR)
1966   Mahmut Atalay (Tur)
1967   Daniel Robin (Fra)
1969   Zarbeg Beriashvili (USSR)
1970   Wayne Wells (USA)
1971   Yuriy Gusov (USSR)
1973   Mansour Barzegar (Irn)
1974-5 Ruslan Ashuraliyev (USSR)
1977   Stan Dziedzic (USA)
1978-9 Leroy Kemp (USA)
1981   Martin Knosp (FRG)
1982   Leroy Kemp (USA)
1983   Dave Schultz (USA)
1985-6 Raúl Cascaret (Cub)
1987   Adlan Vareyev (USSR)
1989   Ken Monday (USA)

76kg
1997   Alexander Leipold (Ger)

82kg – middleweight
Limit 79kg 1951-61, 87kg 1962-7
1951   Haydar Zafer (Tur)
1953   Hasan Güngör (Tur)
1954   Abbas Zandi (Irn)
1957   Nabi Sorouri (Irn)
1959   Georgiy Chirtladze (USSR)
1961-2 Mansour Mehdizadeh (Irn)
1963   Prodan Gardschev (Bul)
1965   Mansour Mehdizadeh (Irn)
1966   Prodan Gardschev (Bul)
1967   Boris Gurevich (USSR)
1969   Fred Fozzard (USA)
1970   Yuriy Shakhmuradov (USSR)
1971   Levan Tediashvili (USSR)
1973   Vasiliy Sulzhin (USSR)
1974   Viktor Novozhilov (USSR)
1975   Adolf Seger (FRG)
1977   Adolf Seger (FRG)
1978   Magomed Aratsilov (USSR)
1979   István Kovács (Hun)
1981   Chris Campbell (USA)
1982-3 Tejmuraj Dzogolyev (USSR)
1985   Mark Schultz (USA)
1986   Vladimir Modosyan (USSR)
1987   Mark Schultz (USA)
1989   Elmadi Zhabraylov (USSR)
1990   Jozef Lohyna (Cs)
1991   Kevin Jackson (USA)
1993   Sabahattin Öztürk (Tur)
1994   Elmadi Zhabraylov (Mol)
1995   Kevin Jackson (USA)

85kg
1997   Leslie Gutches (USA)

90kg – light-heavyweight
Limit 87kg 1951-61, 97kg 1962-7
1951   Yasar Dogu (Tur)
1953   Anatoliy Albul (USSR)
1954   August Englas (USSR)
1957   Petro Sirakov (Bul)
1959   Golam Reza Takhti (Irn)

1961	Golam Reza Takhti (Irn)
1962-3	Aleksandr Medved (USSR)
1965	Ahmet Ayik (Tur)
1966	Aleksandr Medved (USSR)
1967	Ahmet Ayik (Tur)
1969	Boris Gurevich (USSR)
1970	Gennadiy Strakhov (USSR)
1971	Rusi Petrov (Bul)
1973-5	Levan Tediashvili (USSR)
1977	Anatoliy Prokopchuk (USSR)
1978	Uwe Neupert (GDR)
1979	Khasan Ortsyev (USSR)
1981	Sanasar Oganesyan (USSR)
1982	Uwe Neupert (GDR)
1983	Piotr Nanev (USSR)
1985	Bill Sherr (USA)
1986-7	Makharbek Khadartsev (USSR)
1989-91	Makharbek Khadartsev (USSR)
1993	Abbas Jadidi (Irn)
1994-5	Rasull Khadem Azghadi (Irn)

97kg

1997	Kuamagame Kuramagomedov (Rus)

100kg – heavyweight

Limit over 87kg 1951-61, over 97kg 1962-7

1951	Bertil Antonsson (Swe)
1953	Lyutvi Akhmedov (Bul)
1954	Arsen Mekokishvili (USSR)
1957	Hamit Kaplan (Tur)
1959	Lyutvi Ahmedov (Bul)
1961	Wilfried Dietrich (FRG)
1962-3	Aleksandr Ivanitskiy (USSR)
1965-6	Aleksandr Ivanitskiy (USSR)
1967	Aleksandr Medved (USSR)
1969	Shota Lomidze (USSR)
1970	Vladimir Gulyutkin (USSR)
1971	Shota Lomidze (USSR)
1973	Ivan Yarygin (USSR)
1974	Vladimir Gulyutkin (USSR)
1975	Khorloo Baianmunkh (Mgl)
1977	Aslanbek Bisultanov (USSR)
1978	Harald Büttner (GDR)

1979	Ilya Mate (USSR)
1981	Roland Gehrke (GDR)
1982	Ilya Mate (USSR)
1983	Aslan Khadartzev (USSR)
1985	Leri Khabelov (USSR)
1986	Aslan Khadartzev (USSR)
1987	Leri Khabelov (USSR)
1989	Akhmed Atanov (USSR)
1990-1	Leri Khabelov (USSR)
1993	Leri Khabelov (Rus)
1994	Aravat Sabejev (Ger)
1995	Kurt Angle (USA)

100+kg – super-heavyweight (now 130kg)

1969-71	Aleksandr Medved (USSR)
1973	Soslan Andiyev (USSR)
1974	Ladislav Simon (Rom)
1975	Soslan Andiyev (USSR)
1977	Soslan Andiyev (USSR)
1979	Salman Khasimikov (USSR)
1981-3	Salman Khasimikov (USSR)
1985	David Gobedzhishviliy (USSR)
1986	Bruce Baumgartner (USA)
1987	Aslan Khadartzev (USSR)
1989	Ali Reza Soleimani (Irn)
1990	David Gobedzhishviliy (USSR)
1991	Andreas Schröder (Ger)
1993	Bruce Baumgartner (USA)
1994	Mahmut Demir (Tur)
1995	Bruce Baumgartner (USA)
1997	Zekeriya Güçlü (Tur)

Greco-Roman

48kg – light-flyweight

1969-70	Gheorghe Berceanu (Rom)
1971	Vladimir Zubkov (USSR)
1973-5	Vladimir Zubkov (USSR)
1977	Aleksey Shumakov (USSR)
1978	Constantin Alexandru (Rom)
1981	Zaksylik Ushkempirov (USSR)
1982	Temur Kazarashvili (USSR)
1983	Bratan Tsenov (Bul)
1985-7	Magyatdin Allakhverdyev (USSR)
1989-90	Oleg Kucherenko (USSR)
1991	Goon Duk-young (SKo)
1993-4	Wilber Sánchez (Cub)
1995	Sim Kwon-ho (SKo)

52kg – flyweight

1950	Bengt Johansson (Swe)
1953	Boris Gurevich (USSR)
1955	Ignazio Fabra (Ita)
1958	Boris Gurevich (USSR)
1961	Armais Sayadov (USSR)
1962	Sergey Rybalko (USSR)
1963	Borivoje Vukov (Yug)
1965	Sergey Rybalko (USSR)
1966	Angel Kerezov (Bul)
1967	Vladimir Bakulin (USSR)
1969	Aluzadeh Firuz (Irn)
1970-1	Petar Kirov (Bul)
1973	Nicu Ginga (Rom)
1974	Peter Kirov (USSR)
1975	Vitaliy Konstantinov (USSR)
1977	Nicu Ginga (Rom)
1978	Vakhtang Blagidze (USSR)
1979	Lajos Rácz (Hun)
1981	Vakhtang Blagidze (USSR)
1982-3	Benyur Pashayan (USSR)
1985	Jan Rønningen (Nor)
1986	Sergey Dyudyayev (USSR)
1987	Pedro Roque (Cub)
1989-90	Aleksandr Ignatenko (USSR)
1991	Raúl Martínez (Cub)
1993	Raúl Martínez (Cub)
1994	Alfred Ter-Mkrtschyan (Ger)
1995	Samuel Danielyan (Rus)

54kg

1997	Ercan Yildiz (Tur)

57kg – bantamweight

1950	Ali Mahmoud Hassan (Egy)
1953	Artyem Teryan (USSR)
1955	Vladimir Stashevich (USSR)
1958	Oleg Karavayev (USSR)
1961	Oleg Karavayev (USSR)
1962	Masamitsu Ichiguchi (Jap)
1963	János Varga (Hun)
1965	Ion Cernea (Rom)
1966	Fritz Stange (FRG)
1967	Ion Baciu (Rom)
1969	Rustem Kazakov (USSR)
1970	János Varga (Hun)
1971	Rustem Kazakov (USSR)
1973	Jozef Lipien (Pol)
1974-5	Farhat Mustafin (USSR)
1977	Pertti Ukkola (Fin)
1978-9	Shamil Serikov (USSR)

1981	Pasquale Passarelli (FRG)
1982	Piotr Michalik (Pol)
1983	Masaki Eto (Jap)
1985	Stojan Balov (Bul)
1986	Emil Ivanov (Bul)
1987	Patrice Mourier (Fra)
1989	Emil Ivanov (Bul)
1990-1	Rifat Yildiz (Ger)
1993	Agazi Manukjan (Arm)
1994	Yuriy Melnichenko (Kzk)
1995	Dennis Hall (USA)

58kg

| 1997 | Yuriy Melnichenko (Kzk) |

62kg – featherweight

Limit 63kg 1962-7

1950	Olle Anderberg (Swe)
1953	Olle Anderberg (Swe)
1955	Imre Polyák (Hun)
1958	Imre Polyák (Hun)
1961	Hamid Mustafa (Egy)
1962	Imre Polyák (Hun)
1963	Gennadiy Sapunov (USSR)
1965	Yuriy Grigoryev (USSR)
1966-7	Roman Rurua (USSR)
1969	Roman Rurua (USSR)
1970	Hideo Fujimoto (Jap)
1971	Georgi Markov (Bul)
1973-4	Kazimierz Lipien (Pol)
1975	Nelson Davidyan (USSR)
1977	Lászlo Réczi (Hun)
1978	Boris Kramarenko (USSR)
1979	István Tóth (Hun)
1981	István Tóth (Hun)
1982	Ryszard Swicrad (Pol)
1983	Hannu Lahtinen (Fin)
1985	Zhivko Vangelov (Bul)
1986	Kamandar Madzhidov (USSR)
1987	Zhivko Vangelov (Bul)
1989	Kamandar Madzhidov (USSR)
1990	Mario Oliveras (Cub)
1991	Sergey Martynov (USSR)
1993-5	Sergey Martynov (Rus)

63kg

| 1997 | Seref Eroglu (Tur) |

68kg – lightweight

Limit 67kg 1950-61, 70kg 1962-7

1950	József Gál (Hun)
1953	Gustav Freij (Swe)
1955	Grigoriy Gamarnik (USSR)
1958	Riza Dogan (Tur)
1961	Avtandil Koridze (USSR)

1962	Kazim Ayvaz (Tur)
1963	Stevan Horvat (Yug)
1965	Gennadiy Supanov (USSR)
1966	Stevan Horvat (Yug)
1967	Eero Tapio (Fin)
1969	Simion Popescu (Rom)
1970	Roman Rurua (USSR)
1971	Sreten Damjanovic (Yug)
1973	Shamil Khisamutdinov (USSR)
1974	Nelson Davidyan (USSR)
1975	Shamil Khisamutdinov (USSR)
1977	Heinz-Helmut Wehling (GDR)
1978	Stefan Rusu (Rom)
1979	Andrzej Supron (Pol)
1981-2	Gennadiy Yermilov (USSR)
1983	Tapio Sipilä (Fin)
1985	Stefan Negrisan (Rom)
1986	Levon Dzhulfalakyan (USSR)
1987	Aslautdin Abeyev (USSR)
1989	Claudio Passarelli (FRG)
1990-1	Islam Duguchiyev (USSR)
1993-4	Islam Duguchiyev (Rus)
1995	Rustam Adzhy (Ukr)

69kg

| 1997 | Son Sang-pil (SKo) |

74kg – welterweight

Limit 73kg 1950-61, 78kg 1962-7

1950	Matti Simanainen (Fin)
1953	Gurgen Chatvorjan (USSR)
1955	Vladimir Maneyev (USSR)
1958	Kazim Ayvaz (Tur)
1961	Valeriu Bularca (Rom)
1962-3	Anatoliy Kolesov (USSR)
1965	Anatoliy Kolesov (USSR)
1966-7	Viktor Igumenov (USSR)
1969-71	Viktor Igumenov (USSR)
1973	Ivan Kolev (Bul)
1974	Viteslav Mácha (Cs)
1975	Anatoliy Bykov (USSR)
1977	Viteslav Mácha (Cs)
1978	Arif Niftulayev (USSR)
1979	Ferenc Kocsis (Hun)
1981	Aleksandr Kudryavtsev (USSR)
1982	Stefan Rusu (Rom)
1983	Mikhail Mamiashvili (USSR)
1985-6	Mikhail Mamiashvili (USSR)

1987	Jouko Salomäki (Fin)
1989	Daulet Turlykhanov (USSR)
1990-1	Mnatsakan Iskamdarian (USSR)
1993	Nestor Almanza (Cub)
1994	Mnatsakan Iskamdarian (Rus)
1995	Yvon Riemer (Fra)

76kg

| 1997 | Marko Yii-Hannuksela (Fin) |

82kg – middleweight

Limit 79kg 1950-61, 97kg 1962-7

1950	Axel Gronberg (Swe)
1953	Givy Kartoziya (USSR)
1955	Givy Kartoziya (USSR)
1958	Riza Dogan (Tur)
1961	Vasiliy Zenin (USSR)
1962-3	Tevfik Kis (Tur)
1965	Roman Bogdanov (USSR)
1966	Valentin Olenik (USSR)
1967	László Sillai (Hun)
1969	Petar Krumov (Bul)
1970	Anatoliy Nazarenko (USSR)
1971	Csaba Hegedüs (Hun)
1973	Leonid Liberman (USSR)
1974-5	Anatoliy Nazarenko (USSR)
1977	Vlademir Cheboskarov (USSR)
1978	Ion Draica (Rom)
1979	Gennadiy Korban (USSR)
1981	Gennadiy Korban (USSR)
1982-3	Temur Abkhasava (USSR)
1985	Bogdan Daras (Pol)
1986	*No medal awarded* ⋆
1987	Tibor Komaromi (Hun)
1989	Tibor Komaromi (Hun)
1990-1	Péter Farkas (Hun)
1993	Hamza Yerlikaya (Tur)
1994	Thomas Zander (Ger)
1995	Hamza Yerlikaya (Tur)

⋆ Bogdan Karas (Pol) & Tibor Komaromi (Hun) both disqualified.

86kg

| 1997 | Sergey Tschvir (Rus) |

90kg – light-heavyweight

Limit 87kg 1950-61, 97kg 1962-7

1950	Muharrem Candas (Tur)
1953	August Englas (USSR)
1955	Valentin Nikolayev (USSR)
1958	Rostom Abashidze (USSR)

1961	György Gurics (Hun)	
1962-3	Rostom Abashidze (USSR)	
1965	Valeriy Anisimov (USSR)	
1966	Boyan Radev (Bul)	
1967	Nikolay Yakovenko (USSR)	
1969	Aleksandr Yurkevich (USSR)	
1970-1	Valeriy Rezantsev (USSR)	
1973-5	Valeriy Rezantsev (USSR)	
1977	Frank Andersson (Swe)	
1978	Stojan Nikolov (Bul)	
1979	Frank Andersson (Swe)	
1981	Igor Kanygin (USSR)	
1982	Frank Andersson (Swe)	
1983	Igor Kanygin (USSR)	
1985	Michael Houk (USA)	
1986	Andrzej Malina (Pol)	
1987	Vladimir Popov (USSR)	
1989-91	Maik Bullmann (GDR)	
1993-4	Gogi Koguashvili (Rus)	
1995	Hakki Basar (Tur)	

97kg

1997	Gogi Koguashvili (Rus)

100kg – heavyweight
Limit over 87kg 1950-61, over 97kg 1962-7

1950	Bertil Antonsson (Swe)
1953	Bertil Antonsson (Swe)
1955	Aleksandr Mazur (USSR)
1958	Ivan Bogdan (USSR)
1961	Ivan Bogdan (USSR)
1962	István Kozma (Hun)
1963	Anatoliy Rochin (USSR)
1965	Nikolay Shmakov (USSR)
1966-7	István Kozma (Hun)
1969	Nikolay Yakovenko (USSR)
1970-1	Per Svensson (Swe)
1973-4	Nikolay Balboshin (USSR)
1975	Kamen Lozanov (Bul)
1977-9	Nikolay Balboshin (USSR)
1981	Mikhail Saladze (USSR)
1982	Roman Wroclawski (Pol)
1983	Andrej Dmitrov (Bul)
1985	Andrej Dmitrov (Bul)
1986	Tamás Gáspár (Hun)
1987	Guram Gedekhauri (USSR)
1989	Gerhard Himmel (FRG)

1990	Sergey Demiashkyevich (USSR)
1991	Héctor Milian (Cub)
1993	Mikael Ljungberg (Swe)
1994	Andrzej Wronski (Pol)
1995	Mikael Ljungberg (Swe)

100+kg – super-heavyweight (now 130kg)

1969-70	Anatoliy Roshin (USSR)
1971	Alexandr Tomov (Bul)
1973-5	Alexandr Tomov (Bul)
1977	Nikolai Dinev (Bul)
1978	Aleksandr Kolinchskiy (USSR)
1979	Alexandr Tomov (Bul)
1981	Refik Memisevic (Yug)
1982	Nikolai Dinev (Bul)
1983	Yevgeniy Artioshin (USSR)
1985	Igor Rostozotskiy (USSR)
1986	Tomas Johansson (Swe)
1987	Igor Rostorotskiy (USSR)
1989-91	Aleksandr Karelin (USSR)
1993-5	Aleksandr Karelin (Rus)
1997	Aleksandr Karelin (Rus)

Most World and Olympic Titles

10	Aleksandr Medved (USSR) Free: 97kg 1962-4, 1966; over 97kg 1967-8, over 100kg 1969-72
10	Aleksandr Karelin (Rus) GR: 130kg 1988-97
8	Sergey Beloglazov (USSR) Free: 57kg 1980-1, 1983, 1985-8; 62kg 1982
8	Arsen Fadzeyev (USSR) Free: 68kg 1983, 1985-8, 1990-2
8	Valentin Jordanov (Bul) Free: 52kg 1983, 1985, 1987, 1989, 1993-6
7	Valeriy Rezantsev (USSR) GR: 90kg 1970-6
7	Makharbek Khadartsev (USSR) Free: 90kg 1986-92
6	Abdollah Movahed (Irn) Free: 70/68kg 1965-70
6	Levan Tediashvili (USSR) Free: 82kg 1971-2; 90kg 1973-6
6	Nikolay Ba lboshin (USSR) GR: 100kg 1973-4, 1976, 1977-9
6	Soslan Andiyev (USSR) Free: over 100kg 1973, 1975-8, 1980
6	John Smith (USA) Free: 62kg 1987-92
6	Leri Khabelov (USSR) Free: 100kg 1985, 1987, 1990-3
5	Ali Aliev (USSR) Free: 52kg 1959, 1961-2; 57kg 1966-7
5	Aleksandr Ivanitskiy (USSR) Free: over 97kg 1962-6
5	István Kozma (Hun) GR: over 97kg 1962, 1964, 1966-8
5	Viktor Igumenov (USSR) GR: 78kg 1966-7; 74kg 1969-71
5	Roman Rurua (USSR) GR: 63/62kg 1966-69; 68kg 1970
5	Petar Kirov (Bul) GR: 52kg 1968, 1970-2, 1974
5	Alexandr Tomov (Bul) GR: over 100kg 1971, 1973-5, 1979
5	Yuji Takada (Jap) Free: 52kg 1974-7, 1979

Commonwealth Games

The Commonwealth Games are multi-sport competitions, held every four years and contested by representatives of the nations of the British Commonwealth. They were first staged as the British Empire Games at Hamilton, Canada, opening on 16 August 1930. The eleven nations participating were Australia, Bermuda, British Guiana, Canada, England, Ireland, Newfoundland, New Zealand, Scotland, South Africa and Wales. Six sports were included, but there were women's events only in Swimming. Women first competed in Athletics in 1934.

The idea of staging such an event was first put forward by Yorkshireman the Rev. J Astley Cooper, in the magazine *Greater Britain* in 1891. The first Inter-Empire Sports meeting was held at Crystal Palace, London in 1911, forming part of the celebrations for the Coronation of King George V. Competitors from Britain, Canada, Australia and New Zealand contested four sports – athletics (five events), heavyweight boxing, swimming (two events) and middleweight wrestling. Canada won four gold medals, Britain three, and Australia two.

The Games became the British Empire and Commonwealth Games in 1954, and simply the British Commonwealth Games in 1970; also in this year the Games went metric for distances and weights.

Prior to 1998, ten sports were held at each Games – athletics and swimming, and eight others selected from 15 recognized sports; there were also two demonstration sports. The recognized sports yet to be included officially at any Games are canoeing, table tennis and yachting. Judo was included for the first time in 1990. In 1998 the range of sports was expanded to 15, with the inclusion for the first time of squash and tenpin bowling, and the three team sports of cricket, hockey and rugby union.

Governing body: Commonwealth Games Federation, 1st Floor, Walkden House, 3-10 Melton Street, London NW1 2 EB. Tel: 0171 383 5596, Fax: 0171 383 5506. President: Michael Fennell, General Secretary: David M Dixon. Founded 1934.

Venues

1930	Hamilton, Canada
1934	London, England
1938	Sydney, Australia
1950	Auckland, New Zealand
1954	Vancouver, Canada
1958	Cardiff, Wales
1962	Perth, Australia
1966	Kingston, Jamaica
1970	Edinburgh, Scotland
1974	Christchurch, New Zealand
1978	Edmonton, Canada
1982	Brisbane, Australia
1986	Edinburgh, Scotland
1990	Auckland, New Zealand
1994	Victoria, Canada
1998	Kuala Lumpur, Malaysia

Archery

Men: 1982 Mark Blenkarne (Eng) 2446
Women: 1982 Neroli Fairhall (NZ) 2373

Athletics

Imperial distances run 1930 to 1966. Where known, fully automatic times are given as per the current regulations (original official hand times may have differed).
(w = wind-assisted)

Men

100 yards

1930	Percy Williams (Can) 9.9
1934	Arthur Sweeney (Eng) 10.0
1938	Cyril Holmes (Eng) 9.7
1950	John Treloar (Aus) 9.7
1954	Mike Agostini (Tri) 9.6
1958	Keith Gardner (Jam) 9.66
1962	Seraphino Antao (Ken) 9.50
1966	Harry Jerome (Can) 9.41

100 metres

1970	Don Quarrie (Jam) 10.24w
1974	Don Quarrie (Jam) 10.38
1978	Don Quarrie (Jam) 10.03w
1982	Allan Wells (Sco) 10.05w
1986	Ben Johnson (Can) 10.07
1990	Linford Christie (Eng) 9.93w
1994	Linford Christie (Eng) 9.91

220 yards

1930	Stanley Engelhart (Eng) 21.8
1934	Arthur Sweeney (Eng) 21.9
1938	Cyril Holmes (Eng) 21.2
1950	John Treloar (Aus) 21.5
1954	Donald Jowett (NZ) 21.5
1958	Tom Robinson (Bah) 21.08
1962	Seraphino Antao (Ken) 21.28
1966	Stanley Allotey (Gha) 20.65

200 metres

1970	Don Quarrie (Jam) 20.56
1974	Don Quarrie (Jam) 20.73
1978	Allan Wells (Sco) 20.12w
1982	Allan Wells (Sco) & Mike McFarlane (Eng) 20.43
1986	Atlee Mahorn (Can) 20.31w
1990	Marcus Adam (Eng) 20.10w
1994	Frank Fredericks (Nam) 19.97

440 yards

1930	Alex Wilson (Can) 48.8
1934	Godfrey Rampling (Eng) 48.0
1938	Bill Roberts (Eng) 47.9
1950	Edwin Carr (Aus) 47.9
1954	Kevan Gosper (Aus) 47.2
1958	Milkha Singh (Ind) 46.71
1962	George Kerr (Jam) 46.74
1966	Wendell Mottley (Tri) 45.08

400 metres

1970	Charles Asati (Ken) 45.01
1974	Charles Asati (Ken) 46.04
1978	Rick Mitchell (Aus) 46.34
1982	Bert Cameron (Jam) 45.89
1986	Roger Black (Eng) 45.57
1990	Darren Clark (Aus) 44.60
1994	Charles Gitonga (Ken) 45.00

880 yards

1930	Thomas Hampson (Eng) 1:52.4
1934	Phil Edwards (Guy) 1:54.2
1938	Vernon Boot (NZ) 1:51.2
1950	John Parlett (Eng) 1:53.1
1954	Derek Johnson (Eng) 1:50.7
1958	Herb Elliott (Aus) 1:49.32
1962	Peter Snell (NZ) 1:47.64
1966	Noel Clough (Aus) 1:46.9

800 metres

1970	Robert Ouko (Ken) 1:46.89
1974	John Kipkurgat (Ken) 1:43.85
1978	Mike Boit (Ken) 1:46.39
1982	Peter Bourke (Aus) 1:45.18
1986	Steve Cram (Eng) 1:43.22
1990	Sammy Tirop (Ken) 1:45.98
1994	Patrick Konchellah (Ken)1:45.18

1 mile (1609.35 metres)

1930	Reg Thomas (Eng) 4:14.0
1934	Jack Lovelock (NZ) 4:12.8
1938	Jim Alford (Wal) 4:11.6
1950	William Parnell (Can) 4:11.0
1954	Roger Bannister (Eng) 3:58.8
1958	Herb Elliott (Aus) 3:59.03
1962	Peter Snell (NZ) 4:04.58
1966	Kipchoge Keino (Ken) 3:55.34

1500 metres

1970	Kipchoge Keino (Ken) 3:36.6
1974	Filbert Bayi (Tan) 3:32.16
1978	David Moorcroft (Eng) 3:35.48
1982	Steve Cram (Eng) 3:42.37
1986	Steve Cram (Eng) 3:50.87
1990	Peter Elliott (Eng) 3:33.39
1994	Reuben Chesang (Ken) 3:36.70

3 miles

1930	Stan Tomlin (Eng) 14:27.4
1934	Walter Beavers (Eng) 14:32.6
1938	Cecil Matthews (NZ) 13:59.6
1950	Len Eyre (Eng) 14:23.6
1954	Chris Chataway (Eng) 13:35.2
1958	Murray Halberg (NZ) 13:14.96
1962	Murray Halberg (NZ) 13:34.15
1966	Kipchoge Keino (Ken) 12:57.4

5000 metres

1970	Ian Stewart (Sco) 13:22.8
1974	Ben Jipcho (Ken) 13:14.4
1978	Henry Rono (Ken) 13:23.04
1982	David Moorcroft (Eng) 13:33.00
1986	Steve Ovett (Eng) 13:24.11
1990	Andrew Lloyd (Aus) 13:24.86
1994	Rob Denmark (Eng) 13:23.00

6 miles

1930	John Savidan (NZ) 30:49.6
1934	Arthur Penny (Eng) 31:00.6
1938	Cecil Matthews (NZ) 30:14.5
1950	Harold Nelson (NZ) 30:29.6
1954	Peter Driver (Eng) 29:09.4
1958	David Power (Aus) 28:48.16
1962	Bruce Kidd (Can) 28:26.13
1966	Naftali Temu (Ken) 27:14.21

10,000 metres

1970	Lachie Stewart (Sco) 28:11.71
1974	Richard Tayler (NZ) 27:46.4
1978	Brendan Foster (Eng) 28:13.65
1982	Gidamis Shahanga (Tan) 28:10.15
1986	Jonathan Solly (Eng) 27:57.42
1990	Eamonn Martin (Eng) 28:08.57
1994	Lameck Aguta (Ken) 28:38.22

Marathon (26 miles 385 yards; 42.195km)

1930	Duncan McLeod Wright (Sco) 2:43:43
1934	Harold Webster (Can) 2:40:36
1938	Johannes Coleman (SAf) 2:30:49.8
1950	Jack Holden (Eng) 2:32:57
1954	Joseph McGhee (Sco) 2:39:36
1958	David Power (Aus) 2:22:45.6
1962	Brian Kilby (Eng) 2:21:17
1966	Jim Alder (Sco) 2:22:07.8
1970	Ron Hill (Eng) 2:09:28
1974	Ian Thompson (Eng) 2:09:12
1978	Gidamis Shahanga (Tan) 2:15:39.8
1982	Rob de Castella (Aus) 2:09:18
1986	Rob de Castella (Aus) 2:10:15
1990	Douglas Wakiihuri (Ken) 2:10:27
1994	Steve Moneghetti (Aus) 2:11:49

3000 metres steeplechase

Held over 8 laps in 1930 and at 2 miles in 1934.

1930	George Bailey (Eng) 9:52.0
1934	Stanley Scarsbrook (Eng) 10:23.4
1962	Trevor Vincent (Aus) 8:43.4
1966	Peter Welsh (NZ) 8:29.44
1970	Tony Manning (Aus) 8:26.2

1974	Ben Jipcho (Ken) 8:20.8
1978	Henry Rono (Ken) 8:26.54
1982	Julius Korir (Ken) 8:23.94
1986	Graeme Fell (Can) 8:24.49
1990	Julius Kariuki (Ken) 8:20.64
1994	Johnstone Kipkoech (Ken) 8:14.72

120 yards hurdles

1930	Lord Burghley (Eng) 14.6
1934	Don Finlay (Eng) 15.2
1938	Tom Lavery (SAf) 14.0w
1950	Peter Gardner (Aus) 14.3
1954	Keith Gardner (Jam) 14.2
1958	Keith Gardner (Jam) 14.20w
1962	Ghulam Raziq (Pak) 14.34
1966	David Hemery (Eng) 14.1

110 metres hurdles

1970	David Hemery (Eng) 13.66w
1974	Fatwel Kimaiyo (Ken) 13.69
1978	Berwyn Price (Wal) 13.70w
1982	Mark McKoy (Can) 13.37
1986	Mark McKoy (Can) 13.31w
1990	Colin Jackson (Wal) 13.08
1994	Colin Jackson (Wal) 13.08

440 yards hurdles

1930	Lord Burghley (Eng) 54.4
1934	Alan Hunter (Sco) 55.2
1938	John Loaring (Can) 52.9
1950	Duncan White (Sri) 52.5
1954	David Lean (Aus) 52.4
1958	Gerhardus Potgieter (SAf) 49.73
1962	Ken Roche (Aus) 51.5
1966	Ken Roche (Aus) 50.95

400 metres hurdles

1970	John Sherwood (Eng) 50.03
1974	Alan Pascoe (Eng) 48.83
1978	Daniel Kimaiyo (Ken) 49.48
1982	Garry Brown (Aus) 49.37
1986	Phil Beattie (NI) 49.60
1990	Kriss Akabusi (Eng) 48.89
1994	Samuel Matete (Zim) 48.67

4 x 110 yards relay

1930	Canada 42.2
1934	England 42.2
1938	Canada 41.6
1950	Australia 42.2
1954	Canada 41.3
1958	England 40.72
1962	England 40.62
1966	Ghana 39.8

4 x 100 metres relay

1970	Jamaica 39.46
1974	Australia 39.31
1978	Scotland 39.24
1982	Nigeria 39.15
1986	Canada 39.15
1990	England 38.67
1994	Canada 38.39

4 x 440 yards relay

1930	England 3:19.4
1934	England 3:16.8
1938	Canada 3:16.9
1950	Australia 3:17.8
1954	England 3:11.2
1958	South Africa 3:08.21
1962	Jamaica 3:10.2
1966	Trinidad & Tobago 3:02.8

4 x 400 metres relay

1970	Kenya 3:03.63
1974	Kenya 3:04.4
1978	Kenya 3:03.54
1982	England 3:05.45
1986	England 3:07.19
1990	Kenya 3:02.48
1994	England 3:02.14

High jump

1930	Johannes Viljoen (SAf) 1.90
1934	Edwin Thacker (SAf) 1.90
1938	Edwin Thacker (SAf) 1.96
1950	John Winter (Aus) 1.98
1954	Emmanuel Ifeajuna (Nig) 2.03
1958	Ernest Haisley (Jam) 2.06
1962	Percy Hobson (Aus) 2.11
1966	Lawrie Peckham (Aus) 2.08
1970	Lawrie Peckham (Aus) 2.14
1974	Gordon Windeyer (Aus) 2.16
1978	Claude Ferragne (Can) 2.20
1982	Milt Ottey (Can) 2.31
1986	Milt Ottey (Can) 2.30
1990	Nick Saunders (Ber) 2.36
1994	Tim Forsyth (Aus) 2.32

Pole vault

1930	Victor Pickard (Can) 3.73
1934	Sylvanus Apps (Can) 3.81 (3.88 *jump-off*)
1938	Andries du Plessis (SAf) 4.11
1950	Tim Anderson (Eng) 3.97
1954	Geoff Elliott (Eng) 4.26
1958	Geoff Elliott (Eng) 4.16
1962	Trevor Bickle (Aus) 4.49
1966	Trevor Bickle (Aus) 4.80
1970	Mike Bull (NI) 5.10
1974	Don Baird (Aus) 5.05
1978	Bruce Simpson (Can) 5.10
1982	Ray Boyd (Aus) 5.20
1986	Andrew Ashurst (Eng) 5.20
1990	Simon Arkell (Aus) 5.35
1994	Nick Winter (Wal) 5.40

Long jump

1930	Leonard Hutton (Can)	7.20
1934	Sam Richardson (Can)	7.17
1938	Harold Brown (Can)	7.43
1950	Neville Price (SAf)	7.31
1954	Ken Wilmshurst (Eng)	7.54
1958	Paul Foreman (Jam)	7.47
1962	Michael Ahey (Gha)	8.05w
1966	Lynn Davies (Wal)	7.99
1970	Lynn Davies (Wal)	8.06w
1974	Alan Lerwill (Eng)	7.94
1978	Roy Mitchell (Eng)	8.06
1982	Gary Honey (Aus)	8.13
1986	Gary Honey (Aus)	8.08
1990	Yusuf Alli (Nig)	8.39w
1994	Obinna Eregbu (Nig)	8.05w (8.22q)

Triple jump

1930	Gordon Smallacombe (Can)	14.76
1934	Jack Metcalfe (Aus)	15.63
1938	Jack Metcalfe (Aus)	15.49
1950	Brian Oliver (Aus)	15.61
1954	Ken Wilmshurst (Eng)	15.28
1958	Ian Tomlinson (Aus)	15.74
1962	Ian Tomlinson (Aus)	16.20
1966	Samuel Igun (Nig)	16.40
1970	Phil May (Aus)	16.72
1974	Joshua Owusu (Gha)	16.50
1978	Keith Connor (Eng)	17.21
1982	Keith Connor (Eng)	17.81w
1986	John Herbert (Eng)	17.27w
1990	Marios Hadjiandreou (Cyp)	16.95
1994	Julian Golley (Eng)	17.03

Shot

1930	Hendrik Hart (SAf)	14.58
1934	Hendrik Hart (SAf)	14.67
1938	Louis Fouche (SAf)	14.48
1950	Maitaika Tuicakau (Fij)	14.64
1954	John Savidge (Eng)	16.77
1958	Arthur Rowe (Eng)	17.57
1962	Martyn Lucking (Eng)	18.08
1966	David Steen (Can)	18.79
1970	David Steen (Can)	19.21
1974	Geoff Capes (Eng)	20.74
1978	Geoff Capes (Eng)	19.77
1982	Bruno Pauletto (Can)	19.55
1986	Billy Cole (Eng)	18.16
1990	Simon Williams (Eng)	18.54
1994	Matthew Simson (Eng)	19.49

Discus

1930	Hendrik Hart (SAf)	41.44
1934	Hendrik Hart (SAf)	41.54
1938	Eric Coy (Can)	44.76
1950	Ian Reed (Aus)	47.72
1954	Stephanus du Plessis (SAf)	51.70
1958	Stephanus du Plessis (SAf)	55.94

1962	Warwick Selvey (Aus)	56.48
1966	Les Mills (NZ)	56.18
1970	George Puce (Can)	59.02
1974	Robin Tait (NZ)	63.08
1978	Borys Chambul (Can)	59.70
1982	Brad Cooper (Bah)	64.04
1986	Raymond Lazdins (Can)	58.86
1990	Adewale Olokoju (Nig)	62.62
1994	Werner Reiterer (Aus)	62.76

Hammer

1930	Malcolm Nokes (Eng)	47.12
1934	Malcolm Nokes (Eng)	48.24
1938	George Sutherland (Can)	48.70
1950	Duncan Clark (Sco)	49.94
1954	Mohammad Iqbal (Pak)	55.38
1958	Mike Ellis (Eng)	62.90
1962	Howard Payne (Eng)	61.64
1966	Howard Payne (Eng)	61.98
1970	Howard Payne (Eng)	67.80
1974	Ian Chipchase (Eng)	69.56
1978	Peter Farmer (Aus)	71.10
1982	Robert Weir (Eng)	75.08
1986	David Smith (Eng)	74.06
1990	Sean Carlin (Aus)	75.66
1994	Sean Carlin (Aus)	73.48

Javelin

1930	Stanley Lay (NZ)	63.12
1934	Robert Dixon (Can)	60.02
1938	James Courtwright (Can)	62.80
1950	Leo Roininen (Can)	57.10
1954	James Achurch (Aus)	68.52
1958	Colin Smith (Eng)	71.28
1962	Alfred Mitchell (Aus)	78.10
1966	John FitzSimons (Eng)	79.78
1970	David Travis (Eng)	79.50
1974	Charles Clover (Eng)	84.92
1978	Phil Olsen (Can)	84.00
1982	Michael O'Rourke (NZ)	89.48
1986	David Ottley (Eng)	80.62
1990	Steve Backley (Eng)	86.02
1994	Steve Backley (Eng)	82.74

Decathlon

(All scored on the 1984 scoring tables.)

1966	Roy Williams (NZ)	7133
1970	Geoff Smith (Aus)	7420
1974	Mike Bull (NI)	7363
1978	Daley Thompson (Eng)	8470w
1982	Daley Thompson (Eng)	8424
1986	Daley Thompson (Eng)	8663
1990	Mike Smith (Can)	8525
1994	Mike Smith (Can)	8326

20 miles road walk

1966	Ron Wallwork (Eng)	2:44:42.8
1970	Noel Freeman (Aus)	2:33:33
1974	John Warhurst (Eng)	2:35:23.0

30 kilometres road walk

1978	Ollie Flynn (Eng)	2:22:03.7
1982	Steve Barry (Wal)	2:10:16
1986	Simon Baker (Aus)	2:07:47
1990	Guillaume LeBlanc (Can)	2:08:28
1994	Nick A'Hern (Aus)	2:07:53

Women

100 yards

1934	Eileen Hiscock (Eng)	11.3
1938	Decima Norman (Aus)	11.1
1950	Marjorie Jackson (Aus)	10.8
1954	Marjorie Jackson (Aus)	10.7
1958	Marlene Willard (Aus)	10.70
1962	Dorothy Hyman (Eng)	11.2
1966	Dianne Burge (Aus)	10.6

100 metres

1970	Raelene Boyle (Aus)	11.26w
1974	Raelene Boyle (Aus)	11.27
1978	Sonia Lannaman (Eng)	11.27w
1982	Angella Taylor (Can)	11.00
1986	Heather Oakes (Eng)	11.20w
1990	Merlene Ottey (Jam)	11.02w
1994	Mary Onyali (Nig)	11.06

220 yards

1934	Eileen Hiscock (Eng)	25.0
1938	Decima Norman (Aus)	24.7
1950	Marjorie Jackson (Aus)	24.3
1954	Marjorie Nelson (née Jackson) (Aus)	24.0
1958	Marlene Willard (Aus)	23.65
1962	Dorothy Hyman (Eng)	24.00
1966	Dianne Burge (Aus)	23.73

200 metres

1970	Raelene Boyle (Aus)	22.75w
1974	Raelene Boyle (Aus)	22.50
1978	Denise Boyd (Aus)	22.82w
1982	Merlene Ottey (Jam)	22.19w
1986	Angella Issajenko (Can)	22.91w
1990	Merlene Ottey (Jam)	22.76
1994	Cathy Freeman (Aus)	22.25

440 yards

1966	Judy Pollock (Aus)	53.0

400 metres

1970	Marilyn Neufville (Jam)	51.02
1974	Yvonne Saunders (Can)	51.67
1978	Donna Hartley (Eng)	51.69
1982	Raelene Boyle (Aus)	51.26
1986	Debbie Flintoff (Aus)	51.29
1990	Fatima Yusuf (Nig)	51.08
1994	Cathy Freeman (Aus)	50.38

880 yards

1934	Gladys Lunn (Eng)	2:19.4
1962	Dixie Willis (Aus)	2:03.85
1966	Abigail Hoffman (Can)	2:04.3

800 metres

1970	Rosemary Stirling (Sco)	2:06.24
1974	Charlene Rendina (Aus)	2:01.1
1978	Judy Peckham (Aus)	2:02.82
1982	Kirsty McDermott (Wal)	2:01.31
1986	Kirsty Wade (Wal)	2:00.94
1990	Diane Edwards (Eng)	2:00.25
1994	Inez Turner (Jam)	2:01.74

1500 metres

1970	Rita Ridley (Eng)	4:18.8
1974	Glenda Reiser (Can)	4:07.8
1978	Mary Stewart (Eng)	4:06.34
1982	Christina Boxer (Eng)	4:08.28
1986	Kirsty Wade (Wal)	4:10.91
1990	Angela Chalmers (Can)	4:08.41
1994	Kelly Holmes (Eng)	4:08.86

3000 metres

1978	Paula Fudge (Eng)	9:12.95
1982	Anne Audain (NZ)	8:45.53
1986	Lynn Williams (Can)	8:54.29
1990	Angela Chalmers (Can)	8:38.38
1994	Angela Chalmers (Can)	8:32.17

10,000 metres

1986	Liz Lynch (Sco)	31:41.42
1990	Liz McColgan (née Lynch) (Sco)	32:23.56
1994	Yvonne Murray (Sco)	31:56.97

Marathon

1986	Lisa Martin (Aus)	2:26:07
1990	Lisa Martin (Aus)	2:25:28
1994	Carole Rouillard (Can)	2:30:41

80 metres hurdles

1934	Marjorie Clark (SAf)	11.8
1938	Barbara Burke (SAf)	11.7
1950	Shirley Strickland (Aus)	11.6
1954	Edna Maskell (Zam)	10.9
1958	Norma Thrower (Aus)	10.72w
1962	Pam Kilborn (Aus)	11.07
1966	Pam Kilborn (Aus)	10.9

100 metres hurdles

1970	Pam Kilborn (Aus)	13.27
1974	Judy Vernon (Eng)	13.45
1978	Lorna Boothe (Eng)	12.98w
1982	Shirley Strong (Eng)	12.78w
1986	Sally Gunnell (Eng)	13.29
1990	Kay Morley (Wal)	12.91
1994	Michelle Freeman (Jam)	13.12

400 metres hurdles

1982	Debbie Flintoff (Aus)	55.89
1986	Debbie Flintoff (Aus)	54.94
1990	Sally Gunnell (Eng)	55.38
1994	Sally Gunnell (Eng)	54.51

Sprint relay – 2 x 220 yards, 2 x 110 yards

1934	Canada 1:14.4
1938	Australia 1:15.2
1950	Australia 1:13.4

4 x 110 yards relay

1954	Australia 46.8
1958	England 45.37
1962	Australia 46.71
1966	Australia 45.3

4 x 100 metres relay

1970	Australia 44.14
1974	Australia 43.51
1978	England 43.70
1982	England 43.15
1986	England 43.39
1990	Australia 43.87
1994	Nigeria 42.99

4 x 400 metres relay

1974	England 3:29.2
1978	England 3:27.19
1982	Canada 3:27.70
1986	Canada 3:28.92
1990	England 3:28.08
1994	England 3:27.06

High jump

1934	Marjorie Clark (SAf) 1.60
1938	Dorothy Odam (Eng) 1.60
1950	Dorothy Tyler (née Odam) (Eng) 1.60
1954	Thelma Hopkins (NI) 1.67
1958	Michele Mason (Aus) 1.70
1962	Robyn Woodhouse (Aus) 1.78
1966	Michele Brown (née Mason) (Aus) 1.73
1970	Debbie Brill (Can) 1.78
1974	Barbara Lawton (Eng) 1.84
1978	Katrina Gibbs (Aus) 1.93
1982	Debbie Brill (Can) 1.88
1986	Christine Stanton (Aus) 1.92
1990	Tania Murray (NZ) 1.88
1994	Alison Inverarity (Aus) 1.94

Long jump

1934	Phyllis Bartholomew (Eng) 5.47
1938	Decima Norman (Aus) 5.80
1950	Yvette Williams (NZ) 5.90
1954	Yvette Williams (NZ) 6.08
1958	Sheila Hoskin (Eng) 6.02
1962	Pam Kilborn (Aus) 6.27
1966	Mary Rand (Eng) 6.36
1970	Sheila Sherwood (Eng) 6.73
1974	Modupe Oshikoya (Nig) 6.46
1978	Sue Reeve (Eng) 6.59
1982	Shonel Ferguson (Bah) 6.91w
1986	Joyce Oladapo (Eng) 6.43
1990	Jane Flemming (Aus) 6.78
1994	Nicole Boegman (Aus) 6.82w

Shot

1954	Yvette Williams (NZ) 13.96
1958	Valerie Sloper (NZ) 15.54
1962	Valerie Young (née Sloper) (NZ) 15.23
1966	Valerie Young (NZ) 16.50
1970	Mary Peters (NI) 15.93
1974	Jane Haist (Can) 16.12
1978	Gael Mulhall (Aus) 17.31
1982	Judy Oakes (Eng) 17.92
1986	Gael Martin (Aus) 19.00
1990	Myrtle Augee (Eng) 18.48
1994	Judy Oakes (Eng) 18.16

Discus

1954	Yvette Williams (NZ) 45.02
1958	Suzanne Allday (Eng) 45.91
1962	Valerie Young (NZ) 50.20
1966	Valerie Young (NZ) 49.78
1970	Rosemary Payne (Sco) 54.46
1974	Jane Haist (Can) 55.52
1978	Carmen Ionescu (Can) 62.16
1982	Margaret Ritchie (Sco) 62.98
1986	Gael Martin (Aus) 56.42
1990	Lisa-Marie Vizaniari (Aus) 56.38
1994	Daniela Costian (Aus) 63.72

Javelin

1934	Gladys Lunn (Eng) 32.18
1938	Robina Higgins (Can) 38.28
1950	Charlotte MacGibbon-Weeks (Aus) 38.84
1954	Magdalena Swanepoel (SAf) 43.82
1958	Anna Pazera (Aus) 57.40
1962	Susan Platt (Eng) 50.24
1966	Margaret Parker (Aus) 51.38
1970	Petra Rivers (Aus) 52.00
1974	Petra Rivers (Aus) 55.48
1978	Tessa Sanderson (Eng) 61.34
1982	Suzanne Howland (Aus) 64.46
1986	Tessa Sanderson (Eng) 69.80
1990	Tessa Sanderson (Eng) 65.72
1994	Louise McPaul (Aus) 63.76

Pentathlon

(Scored on 1971 tables.)

1970	Mary Peters (NI) 4515 *(5148 on tables used)*
1974	Mary Peters (NI) 4455
1978	Diane Konihowski (Can) 4768

Heptathlon

(Scored on 1984 tables.)

1982	Glynis Nunn (Aus) 6254
1986	Judy Simpson (Eng) 6282w
1990	Jane Flemming (Aus) 6695
1994	Denise Lewis (Eng) 6325

10 kilometres walk

1990	Kerry Saxby (Aus) 45:03
1994	Kerry Junna-Saxby (Aus) 44:25

Badminton

Men's singles

1966	Tan Aik Huang (Mal)
1970	Jamie Paulson (Can)
1974	Punch Gunalan (Mal)
1978	Padukone Prakash (Ind)
1982	Syed Modi (Ind)
1986	Steve Baddeley (Eng)
1990	Rashid Sidek (Mal)
1994	Rashid Sidek (Mal)

Men's doubles

1966	Tan Aik Huang & Yew Cheng Hoe (Mal)
1970	Ng Boon Bee & Punch Gunalam (Mal)
1974	Derek Talbot & Elliot Stuart (Eng)
1978	Ray Stevens & Michael Tredgett (Eng)
1982	Razif Sidek & Beng Teong Ong (Mal)
1986	Billy Gilliland & Dan Travers (Sco)
1990	Jalani Sidek & Razif Sidek (Mal)
1994	Cheah Soon Kit & Ong Ewe Hock (Mal)

Mixed doubles

1966	Roger Mills & Angela Bairstow (Eng)
1970	Derek Talbot & Margaret Boxall (Eng)
1974	Derek Talbot & Gillian Gilks (Eng)
1978	Michael Tredgett & Nora Perry (Eng)
1982	Martin Dew & Karen Chapman (Eng)
1986	Mike Scandolera & Audrey Tuckey (Aus)
1990	Chan Chi Choi & Amy Chan (HK)
1994	Chris Hunt & Gillian Clark (Eng)

Women's singles

1966	Angela Bairstow (Eng)
1970	Margaret Beck (Eng)
1974	Gillian Gilks (Eng)
1978	Sylvia Ng (Mal)
1982	Helen Troke (Eng)
1986	Helen Troke (Eng)
1990	Fiona Smith (Eng)
1994	Lisa Campbell (Aus)

Women's doubles

1966	Helen Horton & Ursula Smith (Eng)
1970	Margaret Boxall & Susan Whetnall (Eng)
1974	Margaret Beck & Gillian Gilks (Eng)
1978	Nora Perry & Anne Statt (Eng)
1982	Claire Backhouse & Johanne Falardeau (Can)
1986	Gillian Clark & Gillian Gowers (Eng)
1990	Fiona Smith & Sara Sankey (Eng)
1994	Joanne Muggeridge & Joanne Wright (Eng)

Team

1978	England
1982	England
1986	England
1990	England
1994	England

Bowls

	Men's singles	Men's pairs	Men's fours
1930	Robert Colquhoun (Eng)	Tommy Hills & George Wright (Eng)	England
1934	Robert Sprot (Sco)	Tommy Hills & George Wright (Eng)	England
1938	Horace Harvey (SAf)	Lance Macey & William Denison (NZ)	New Zealand
1950	James Pirret (NZ)	Robert Henry & Phil Exelby (NZ)	South Africa
1954	Ralph Hodges (Zim)	William Rosbotham & Percy Watson (NI)	South Africa
1958	Phineas Danilowitz (SAf)	John Morris & Richard Pilkington (NZ)	England
1962	David Bryant (Eng)	Robert McDonald & Hugh Robson (NZ)	England
1970	David Bryant (Eng)	Norman King & Peter Line (Eng)	Hong Kong
1974	David Bryant (Eng)	John Christie & Alex McIntosh (Sco)	New Zealand
1978	David Bryant (Eng)	Eric Liddell & Clementi Delgado (HK)	Hong Kong
1982	William Wood (Sco)	John Watson & David Gourlay (Sco)	Australia
1986	Ian Dickison (NZ)	George Adrain & Grant Knox (Sco)	Wales
1990	Rob Parella (Aus)	Trevor Morris & Ian Schuback (Aus)	Scotland
1994	Richard Corsie (Sco)	Rex Johnson & Cameron Curtis (Aus)	South Africa

	Women's singles	Women's pairs	Women's fours
1986	Wendy Line (Eng)	Freda Elliott & Margaret Johnstone (NI)	Wales
1990	Geua Vada Tau (PNG)	Marie Watson & Judy Howat (NZ)	Australia
1994	Margaret Johnstone (NI)	Sarah Gourlay & Frances White (Sco)	South Africa

Women's triples

1982	Zimbabwe

Boxing

Light-flyweight – 48kg

1970	James Odwori (Uga)
1974	Stephen Muchoki (Ken)
1978	Stephen Muchoki (Ken)
1982	Abraham Wachire (Ken)
1986	Scott Olson (Can)
1990	Justin Juko (Uga)
1994	Abudrahaman Ramadhani (Ken)

Flyweight – 51kg

1930	Jacob Smith (SAf)
1934	Patrick Palmer (Eng)
1938	Johannes Joubert (SAf)
1950	Hugh Riley (Sco)
1954	Richard Currie (Sco)
1958	Jackie Brown (Sco)
1962	Robert Mallon (Sco)
1966	Sulley Shittu (Gha)
1970	David Needham (Eng)
1974	David Larmour (NI)
1978	Michael Irungu (Ken)
1982	Michael Mutua (Ken)
1986	John Lyon (Eng)
1990	Wayne McCullough (NI)
1994	Paul Shepherd (Sco)

Bantamweight – 54kg

1930	Hyman Mizler (Eng)
1934	Freddy Ryan (Eng)
1938	William Butler (Eng)
1950	Johannes van Rensburg (SAf)
1954	John Smillie (Sco)
1958	Howard Winstone (Wal)
1962	Jeffery Dynevor (Aus)
1966	Edward Ndukwu (Nig)
1970	Sulley Shittu (Gha)
1974	Pat Cowdell (Eng)
1978	Barry McGuigan (NI)
1982	Joe Orewa (Nig)
1986	Sean Murphy (Eng)
1990	Sabo Mohammed (Nig)
1994	Robert Peden (Aus)

Featherweight – 57kg

1930	F R Meachem (Eng)
1934	Charles Catterall (SAf)
1938	Anadale Henricus (Sri)
1950	Henry Gilliland (Sco)
1954	Leonard Leisching (SAf)
1958	Wally Taylor (Aus)
1962	John McDermott (Sco)
1966	Philip Waruinge (Ken)
1970	Philip Waruinge (Ken)
1974	Edward Ndukwa (Nig)
1978	Azumah Nelson (Gha)
1982	Peter Konyegwachie (Nig)
1986	Billy Downey (Can)
1990	John Irwin (Eng)
1994	Casey Patton (Can)

Lightweight – 60kg

1930	James Rolland (Sco)
1934	Leslie Cook (Aus)
1938	Harry Groves (Eng)
1950	Ronald Latham (Eng)
1954	Piet van Staden (Zim)
1958	Dick McTaggart (Sco)
1962	Eddie Blay (Gha)
1966	Anthony Andeh (Nig)
1970	Abayomi Adeyemi (Nig)
1974	Ayub Kalule (Uga)
1978	Gerard Hamil (NI)
1982	Hussein Khalili (Ken)
1986	Asif Dar (Can)
1990	Godfrey Nyakana (Uga)
1994	Mike Strange (Can)

Light-welterweight – 63.5kg

1954	Mickey Bergin (Can)
1958	Henry Loubscher (SAf)
1962	Clement Quartey (Gha)
1966	James McCourt (NI)
1970	Muhamad Muruli (Uga)
1974	Obisia Nwakpa (Nig)
1978	Winfield Braithwaite (Guy)
1982	Christopher Ossai (Nig)
1986	Howard Grant (Can)
1990	Charlie Kane (Sco)
1994	Peter Richardson (Eng)

Welterweight – 67kg

1930	Leonard Hall (SAf)
1934	David McCleave (Eng)
1938	Bill Smith (Aus)
1950	Terence Ratcliffe (Eng)
1954	Nicholas Gargano (Eng)
1958	Joseph Greyling (SAf)
1962	Wallace Coe (NZ)
1966	Eddie Blay (Gha)
1970	Emma Ankudey (Gha)
1974	Muhamad Muruli (Uga)
1978	Michael McCallum (Jam)
1982	Christopher Pyatt (Eng)
1986	Darren Dyer (Eng)
1990	David Defiagbon (Nig)
1994	Neil Sinclair (NI)

Light-middleweight – 71kg

1954	Wilfred Greaves (Can)
1958	Grant Webster (SAf)

1962	Harold Mann (Can)
1966	Mark Rowe (Eng)
1970	Tom Imrie (Sco)
1974	Lotti Mwale (Zam)
1978	Kelly Perlette (Can)
1982	Shawn O'Sullivan (Can)
1986	Dan Sherry (Can)
1990	Richie Woodhall (Eng)
1994	Jim Webb (NI)

Middleweight – 75kg

1930	Frederick Mallin (Eng)
1934	Alf Shawyer (Eng)
1938	Denis Reardon (Wal)
1950	Theunis van Schalkwyk (SAf)
1954	Johannes van der Kolff (SAf)
1958	Terry Milligan (NI)
1962	Cephas Colquhoun (Jam)
1966	Joe Darkey (Gha)
1970	John Conteh (Eng)
1974	Frankie Lucas (SVI)
1978	Philip McElwaine (Aus)
1982	Jimmy Price (Eng)
1986	Rod Douglas (Eng)
1990	Christopher Johnson (Can)
1994	Ron Donaldson (Can)

Light-heavyweight – 81kg

1930	Joe Goyder (Eng)
1934	George Brennan (Eng)
1938	Nicholaas Wolmarans (SAf)
1950	Donald Scott (Eng)
1954	Piet van Vuuren (SAf)
1958	Tony Madigan (Aus)
1962	Tony Madigan (Aus)
1966	Roger Tighe (Eng)
1970	Fatai Ayinla (Nig)
1974	William Knight (Eng)
1978	Roger Fortin (Can)
1982	Fine Sani (Fij)
1986	James Moran (Eng)
1990	Joseph Akhasamba (Nig)
1994	Dale Brown (Can)

Heavyweight – over 81kg

1930	Victor Stuart (Eng)
1934	Pat Floyd (Eng)
1938	Thomas Osborne (Can)
1950	Frank Creagh (NZ)
1954	Brian Harper (Eng)
1958	Daniel Bekker (SAf)
1962	George Oywello (Uga)
1966	William Kini (NZ)
1970	Benson Masanda (Uga)

1974	Neville Meade (Eng)
1978	Julius Awome (Eng)
1982	Willie DeWit (Can)

Heavyweight – 91kg

1986	James Peau (NZ)
1990	George Onyango (Ken)
1994	Omaar Ahmed (Ken)

Super-heavyweight – over 91kg

1986	Lennox Lewis (Can)
1990	Michael Kenny (NZ)
1994	Duncan Dokiwari (Nig)

Cycling

Men

Sprint

1934	Ernest Higgins (Eng)
1938	Edgar Gray (Aus)
1950	Russell Mockridge (Aus)
1954	Cyril Peacock (Eng)
1958	Dick Ploog (Aus)
1962	Thomas Harrison (Aus)
1966	Roger Gibbon (Tri)
1970	John Nicholson (Aus)
1974	John Nicholson (Aus)
1978	Kenrick Tucker (Aus)
1982	Kenrick Tucker (Aus)
1986	Gary Neiwand (Aus)
1990	Gary Neiwand (Aus)
1994	Gary Neiwand (Aus)

1000 metres time trial

1934	Edgar Gray (Aus) 1:16.4
1938	Robert Porter (Aus) 1:15.2
1950	Russell Mockridge (Aus) 1:13.4
1954	Dick Ploog (Aus) & Alfred Swift (SAf) 1:12.5
1958	Neville Tong (Eng) 1:12.1
1962	Peter Bartels (Aus) 1:12.9
1966	Roger Gibbon (Tri) 1:09.6
1970	Harry Kent (NZ) 1:08.69
1974	Dick Paris (Aus) 1:11.85
1978	Jocelyn Lovell (Can) 1:06.00
1982	Craig Adair (NZ) 1:06.954
1986	Martin Vinnicombe (Aus) 1:06.23
1990	Martin Vinnicombe (Aus) 1:05.572
1994	Shane Kelly (Aus) 1:05.386

4000 metres individual pursuit

1950	Cyril Cartwright (Eng) 5:16.3
1954	Norman Sheil (Eng) 5:03.5
1958	Norman Sheil (Eng) 5:10.2
1962	Maxwell Langshaw (Aus) 5:08.2
1966	Hugh Porter (Eng) 4:56.6
1970	Ian Hallam (Eng) 5:01.41
1974	Ian Hallam (Eng) 5:05.46
1978	Michael Richards (NZ) 4:49.74
1982	Michael Turtur (Aus) 4:50.990
1986	Dean Woods (Aus) 4:43.92
1990	Garry Anderson (NZ) 4:44.610
1994	Rodney McGee (Aus) 4:31.371

4000 metres team pursuit

1974	England 4:40.50
1978	Australia 4:29.43
1982	Australia 4:26.090
1986	Australia 4:26.94
1990	New Zealand 4:22.76
1994	Australia 4:10.485

Tandem sprint

1970	Gordon Johnson & Ron Jonker (Aus) 11.43
1974	Geoffrey Cooke & Ernest Crutchlow (Eng) 10.74
1978	Jocelyn Lovell & Gordon Singleton (Can) 15.52

10 miles track

1934	Robert McLeod (Can) 24·26.2
1938	William Maxfield (Eng) 24:44.0
1950	William Heseltine (Aus) 23:23.4
1954	Lindsay Cocks (Aus) 21:59.5
1958	Ian Browne (Aus) 21:40.2
1962	Douglas Adams (Aus) 22:10.8
1966	Ian Alsop (Eng) 21:46.0
1970	Jocelyn Lovell (Can) 20:46.72
1974	Stephen Heffernan (Eng) 20:51.25
1978	Jocelyn Lovell (Can) 20:05.81
1982	Kevin Nichols (Aus) 19:56.559
1986	Wayne McCarney (Aus) 19:40.61
1990	Gary Anderson (NZ) 19:44.20
1994	Stuart O'Grady (Aus) 18:50.520

Points

| 1990 | Robert Burns (Aus) |
| 1994 | Brett Aitken (Aus) |

100 kilometres road team time trial

1982	England 2:09:27
1986	England 2:13:16
1990	New Zealand 2:06:46.5
1994	Australia 1:53·19.133

Road race

Raced over 100km 1938-54, 193km (120 miles) 1958-66, 164.6km 1970, 183km 1974, 188km 1978, 184km 1982, 169km 1986, 173km 1990.

1938	Hendrik Binneman (SAf) 2:53:29.6
1950	Hector Sutherland (Aus) 3:13:06.4
1954	Eric Thompson (Eng) 2:44:08.1
1958	Ray Booty (Eng) 5:16:33.7
1962	Wesley Mason (Eng) 5:20:26.2
1966	Peter Buckley (IOM) 5:07:52.5
1970	Bruce Biddle (NZ) 4:38:05.8
1974	Clyde Sefton (Aus) 5:07:16.87
1978	Philip Anderson (Aus) 4:22:34.41
1982	Malcolm Elliott (Eng) 4:34:40.06
1986	Paul Curran (Eng) 4:08:50
1990	Graeme Miller (NZ) 4:34:00.19
1994	Mark Rendell (NZ) 4:46:07

Women

Sprint

1990	Louise Jones (Wal)
1994	Tanya Dubnicoff (Can)

3000 metres individual pursuit

1990	Madonna Harris (NZ) 3:54.670
1994	Kathy Watt (Aus) 3:48:52.2

Road race

Over 72km 1990.

1990	Kathy Watt (Aus) 1:55:11.60
1994	Kathy Watt (Aus) 2:48:04

Points

1994	Yvonne McGregor (Eng)

50 kilometres team time trial

1994	Australia 1:04:03.20

Fencing

Men

	Foil	Épée	Sabre
1950	René Paul (Eng)	Charles-Louis de Beaumont (Eng)	Arthur Pilbrow (Eng)
1954	René Paul (Eng)	Ivan Lund (Aus)	Michael Amberg (Eng)
1958	Raymond Paul (Eng)	William Hoskyns (Eng)	William Hoskyns (Eng)
1962	Alexander Leckie (Sco)	Ivan Lund (Aus)	Ralph Cooperman (Eng)
1966	Allan Jay (Eng)	William Hoskyns (Eng)	Ralph Cooperman (Eng)
1970	Mike Breckin (Eng)	William Hoskyns (Eng)	Alexander Leckie (Sco)

	Team foil	Team épée	Team sabre
1950	England	Australia	England
1954	England	England	Canada
1958	England	England	England
1962	England	England	England
1966	England	England	England
1970	England	England	England

Women

	Foil – individual		Foil – team
1950	Mary Glen-Haig (Eng)	1966	England
1954	Mary Glen-Haig (Eng)	1970	England
1958	Gillian Sheen (Eng)		
1962	Melody Coleman (NZ)		
1966	Janet Wardell-Yerburgh (Eng)		
1970	Janet Wardell-Yerburgh (Eng)		

Gymnastics

Men

	All-round	Team
1978	Philip Delesalle (Can)	Canada
1990	Curtis Hibbert (Can)	Canada
1994	Neil Thomas (Eng)	Canada

	Rings	Parallel bars	Horizontal bars
1990	Curtis Hibbert (Can)	Curtis Hibbert (Can)	Curtis Hibbert (Can) & Alan Nolet (Can)
1994	Lee McDermott (Eng)	Peter Hogan (Aus)	Alan Nolet (Can)

	Floor exercises	Pommel horse	Vault
1990	Neil Thomas (Eng)	Brennon Dowrick (Aus)	James May (Eng)
1994	Neil Thomas (Eng)	Brennon Dowrick (Aus)	Bret Hudson (Aus)

Women

	All-round	Team	Asymmetrical bars
1978	Elfi Schlegel (Can)	Canada	-
1990	Lori Strong (Can)	Canada	Monique Allen (Aus)
1994	Stella Umeh (Can)	England	Rebecca Stoyal (Aus)

	Beam	Floor exercises	Vault
1990	Lori String (Can)	Lori String (Can)	Nicky Jenkins (NZ)
1994	Salli Willis (Aus)	Annika Reeder (Eng)	Stella Umeh (Can)

Rhythmic gymnastics – individual

1990 Mary Fuzesi (Can) won overall, ribbon and hoop; Angela Walker (NZ) won rope

1994 Kasumi Takahashi (Aus) won all five gold medals: all-around, hoops, ball, clubs and ribbon

Rhythmic gymnastics – team

1994 Canada

Judo

Men (1990)

60kg	Carl Finney (Eng)
65kg	Brent Cooper (NZ)
71kg	Roy Stone (Eng)
78kg	David Southby (Eng)
86kg	Densign White (Eng)
95kg	Ray Stevens (Eng)
95+kg	Elvis Gordon (Eng)
Open	Elvis Gordon (Eng)

Women (1990)

48kg	Karen Briggs (Eng)
52kg	Sharon Rendle (Eng)
56kg	Loretta Cusack (Sco)
61kg	Diane Bell (Eng)
66kg	Sharon Mills (Eng)
72kg	Jane Morris (Eng)
Over 72+kg	Sharon Lee (Eng)
Open	Sharon Lee (Eng)

Rowing

Men

Single sculls

1930	Bobby Pearce (Aus) 8:03.6
1938	Herbert Turner (Aus) 8:24.0
1950	Mervyn Wood (Aus) 7:46.8
1954	Donald Rowlands (NZ) 8:28.2
1958	Stuart Mackenzie (Aus) 7:20.1
1962	James Hill (NZ) 7:39.7
1986	Steven Redgrave (Eng) 7:28.29

Double sculls

1930	Elswood Bole & Bob Richards (Can) 7:48.0
1938*	William Bradley & Cecil Pearce (Aus) 7:29.4
1950	Mervyn Wood & Murray Riley (Aus) 7:22.0
1954	Mervyn Wood & Murray Riley (Aus) 7:54.5
1958	Michael Spracklen & Geoffrey Baker (Eng) 6:54.4
1962	George Justice & Nicholas Birkmyre (Eng) 6:52.4
1986	Pat Walter & Bruce Ford (Can) 6:19.43

* No medals awarded.

Coxless pairs

1950	Walter Lambert & Jack Webster (Aus) 7:58.0
1954	Robert Parker & Reginald Douglas (NZ) 8:23.9
1958	Robert Parker & Reginald Douglas (NZ) 7:11.1
1962	Stewart Farquharson & James Lee-Nicholson (Eng) 7:03,7
1986	Steven Redgrave & Andrew Holmes (Eng) 6:40.48

Coxless fours

1930	England	7:04.6
1958	England	6:34.4
1962	England	6:31.1
1986	Canada	6:00.56

Coxed fours

1930	New Zealand	8:02.0
1938	Australia	7:16.8
1950	New Zealand	7:17.2
1954	Australia	7:58.3
1958	England	6:46.5
1962	New Zealand	6:48.2
1986	England	6:08.13

Eights

1930	England	6:37.0
1938	England	6:29.0
1950	Australia	6:27.0
1954	Canada	6:59.0
1958	Canada	5:51.1
1962	Australia	5:53.4
1986	Australia	5:44.42

Lightweight single sculls

1986	Peter Antonie (Aus)	7:16.43

Lightweight coxless fours

1986	England	6:25.86

Women (1986)

Single sculls: Stephanie Foster (NZ) 7:43.22

Double sculls: Stephanie Foster & Robin Clarke (NZ) 7:21.52

Coxless pairs: Kathryn Barr & Andrea Schreiner (Can) 7:34.51

Coxed fours: Canada 6:50.13

Eights: Australia 6:43.69

Lightweight single sculls: Adair Ferguson (Aus) 7:45.49

Lightweight coxless fours: England 6:54.70

Shooting

Men

Small-bore rifle (.22 rifle)

1966   Gilmour Boa (Can) 587
1974   Yvonne Gowland (Aus) 594
1978   Alister Allan (Sco) 1194

Small-bore rifle – prone

1982   Alan Smith (Aus) 1184
1986   Alan Smith (Aus) 599
1990   Roger Harvey (NZ) 591
1994   Stephen Petterson (NZ) 698.4

Small-bore rifle – prone, pairs

1982   Malcolm Cooper & Mike Sullivan (Eng) 1187
1986   Michael Ashcroft & Gale Stewart (Can) 1175
1990   Stephen Pettersson & Roger Harvey (NZ) 1185
1994   Stephen Pettersson & Lindsay Arthur (NZ) 1181

Small-bore rifle – three positions

1982   Alister Allan (Sco) 1146
1986   Malcolm Cooper (Eng) 1170
1990   Mart Klepp (Can) 1157
1994   Michel Dion (Can) 1234.2

Small-bore rifle – three positions, pairs

1982   Malcolm Cooper & Barry Dagger (Eng) 2301
1986   Malcolm Cooper & Sarah Cooper (Eng) 2278
1990   Jean-François Senecal & Mart Klepp (Can) 2272
1994   Wayne Sorensen & Michel Dion (Can) 2300

Full-bore rifle

(.303 rifle 1966, 7.62mm rifle from 1974)
1966   Lord (John) Swansea (Wal) 394
1974   Maurice Gordon (NZ) 387.26
1978   Desmond Vamplew (Can) 391
1982   Arthur Clarke (Sco) 387
1986   Stan Golinski (Aus) 396
1990   Colin Mallett (Jersey) 394
1994   David Calvert (NI) 398

Full-bore rifle – pairs

1982   Keith Affleck & Geoffrey Ayling (Aus) 572
1986   Alain Marion & William Baldwin (Can) 583
1990   Simon Belither & Andrew Tucker (Eng) 580
1994   Albert Bowden & Geoffrey Grenfell (Aus) 593

Free pistol (.22 single-shot)

1966   Charles Sexton (Eng) 544
1974   Jules Sobrian (Can) 549
1978   Yvon Trempe (Can) 543
1982   Tom Guinn (Can) 553
1986   Greg Yelavich (NZ) 551
1990   Phillip Adams (Aus) 554
1994   Michael Gault (Eng) 654.1

Free pistol – pairs

1982   Phillip Adams & John Tremelling (Aus) 1077
1986   Tom Guinn & Claude Beaulieu (Can) 1099
1990   Phillip Adams & Bengt Sandström (Aus) 1106
1994   Phillip Adams & Bengt Sandström (Aus) 1104

Centre-fire pistol

1966   James Lee (Can) 576
1982   John Cooke (Eng) 580
1986   Robert Northover (Eng) 583
1990   Ashok Pandit (Ind) 583
1994   Jaspal Rana (Ind) 581

Centre-fire pistol – pairs

1982   Noel Ryan & Alexander Taransky (Aus) 1151
1986   Phillip Adams & Roderick Hack (Aus) 1165
1990   Phillip Adams & Bruce Quick (Aus) 1155
1994   Jaspal Rana & Ashok Pandit (Ind) 1168

Rapid-fire pistol (.22 semi-automatic)

1966   Anthony Clark (Eng) 585
1974   William Hare (Can) 586
1978   Jules Sobrian (Can) 587
1982   Solomon Lee (HK) 583
1986   Pat Murray (Aus) 591
1990   Adrian Breton (Guernsey) 583
1994   Michael Jay (Wal) 670.2

Rapid-fire pistol – pairs

1982   Peter Heuke & Alexander Taransky (Aus) 1160
1986   Brian Girling & Terry Turner (Eng) 1169
1990   Bruce Farrell & Patrick Murray (Aus) 1153
1994   Patrick Murray & Robert Dowling (Aus) 1148

Air pistol

1982   George Darling (Eng) 576
1986   Greg Yelavich (NZ) 575
1990   Bengt Sandström (Aus) 580
1994   Jean-Pierre Huot (Can) 672.4

Air pistol – pairs

1982   Phillip Adams & Gregory Colbert (Aus) 1128
1986   Paul Leatherdale & Ian Reid (Eng) 1143
1990   Atteequr Rahman & Abdus Sattar (Ban) 1138
1994   Michelangelo Giustiniano & Bengt Sandstrom (Aus) 1137

Air rifle

1982   Jean-François Senecal (Can) 574
1986   Guy Lorion (Can) 588
1990   Guy Lorion (Can) 583
1994   Chris Hector (Eng) 685.9

Air rifle – pairs

1982   Alister Allan & Bill McNeil (Sco) 1137
1986   Guy Lorion & Sharon Bowes (Can) 1167
1990   Guy Lorion & Mart Klepp (Can) 1163
1994   Jean-François Senecal & Wayne Sorensen (Can) 1166

Open Olympic trap (clay pigeon)

1974	John Primrose (Can) 196
1978	John Primrose (Can) 186
1982	Peter Boden (Eng) 191
1986	Ian Peel (Eng) 195
1990	John Maxwell (Aus) 184
1994	Manaher Singh (Ind) 141

Open Olympic trap – pairs

1982	Jim Ellis & Terry Rumbel (Aus) 190
1986	Ian Peel & Peter Boden (Eng) 185
1990	Kevin Gill & Ian Peel (Eng) 181
1994	Thomas Hewitt & Samuel Allen (NI) 188

Open skeet

1974	Harry Willsie (Can) 194
1978	John Woolley (NZ) 193
1982	John Woolley (NZ) 197
1986	Nigel Kelly (IOM) 196
1990	Kenneth Harman (Eng) 187
1994	Ian Hale (Aus) 144

Open skeet – pairs

1982	Brian Gabriel & Fred Altmann (Can) 191
1986	Joe Neville & Kenneth Harman (Eng) 195
1990	Ian Marsden & James Dunlop (Sco) 189
1994	Antonis Andreou & Christos Kourtellas (Cyp) 189

Running target

1990	Colin Robertson (Aus) 539
1994	Bryan Wilson (Aus) 657.9

Running target – pairs

1990	Paul Carmine & Tony Clarke (NZ) 1091
1994	Mark Bedlington & Matthew Bedlington (Can) 1088

Women

Small-bore rifle – prone

1994	Shirley McIntosh (Sco) 586

Small-bore rifle – prone, pairs

1994	Kim Frazer & Sylvia Purdie (Aus)

Small-bore rifle – three positions

1994	Sharon Bowes (Can) 666.4

Small-bore rifle – three positions, pairs

1994	Sharon Bowes & Christina Ashcroft (Can) 1143

Air rifle

1994	Fotini Theofanous (Cyp) 488.7

Air rifle – pairs

1994	Pushpannali Ramanayake & Mali Wickremasinghe (Sri) 771

Air pistol

1994	Helen Smith (Can) 474.2

Air pistol – pairs

1994	Annette Woodward & Christine Trefry (Aus) 747

Sport pistol

1994	Christine Trefry (Aus) 679.4

Sport pistol – pairs

1994	Annette Woodward & Christine Trefry (Aus)

Swimming and Diving

Men

50 metres freestyle

1990	Andrew Baildon (Aus) 22.76
1994	Mark Foster (Eng) 23.12

100 yards freestyle

1930	Munroe Bourne (Can) 56.0
1934	George Burleigh (Can) 55.0

110 yards freestyle

1938	Bob Pirie (Can) 59.6
1950	Peter Salmon (Can) 1:00.4
1954	Jon Henricks (Aus) 56.5
1958	John Devitt (Aus) 56.6
1962	Richard Pound (Can) 55.8
1966	Mike Wenden (Aus) 54.0

100 metres freestyle

1970	Mike Wenden (Aus) 53.06
1974	Mike Wenden (Aus) 52.73
1978	Mark Morgan (Aus) 52.70
1982	Neil Brooks (Aus) 51.14
1986	Greg Fasala (Aus) 50.95
1990	Andrew Baildon (Aus) 49.80
1994	Stephen Clarke (Can) 50.21

200 metres freestyle

1970	Mike Wenden (Aus) 1:56.69
1974	Stephen Badger (Aus) 1:56.72
1978	Ron McKeon (Aus) 1:52.06
1982	Andrew Astbury (Eng) 1:51.52
1986	Robert Gleria (Aus) 1:50.57
1990	Martin Roberts (Aus) 1:49.58
1994	Kieren Perkins (Aus) 1:49.31

400 yards freestyle

1930	Noel Ryan (Aus) 4.39.8

440 yards freestyle

1934	Noel Ryan (Aus) 5:03.0
1938	Bob Pirie (Can) 4:54.6
1950	Garrick Agnew (Aus) 4:49.4
1954	Gary Chapman (Aus) 4:39.8
1958	John Konrads (Aus) 4:25.9
1962	Murray Rose (Aus) 4:20.0
1966	Robert Windle (Aus) 4:15.0

400 metres freestyle

1970	Graham White (Aus) 4:08.48
1974	John Kulasalu (Aus) 4:01.44
1978	Ron McKeon (Aus) 3:54.43
1982	Andrew Astbury (Eng) 3:53.29
1986	Duncan Armstrong (Aus) 3:52.25
1990	Ian Brown (Aus) 3:49.91
1994	Kieren Perkins (Aus) 3:45.77

1500 yards freestyle

1930	Noel Ryan (Aus) 18:55.4
1934	Noel Ryan (Aus) 18:25.4

1650 yards freestyle

1938	Robert Leivers (Eng) 19:46.4
1950	Graham Johnston (SAf) 19:55.7
1954	Graham Johnston (SAf) 19:01.4
1958	John Konrads (Aus) 17:45.4
1962	Murray Rose (Aus) 17:18.1
1966	Ron Jackson (Aus) 17:25.9

1500 metres freestyle

1970	Graham Windeatt (Aus) 16:23.82
1974	Steve Holland (Aus) 15:34.73
1978	Max Metzker (Aus) 15:31.92
1982	Max Metzker (Aus) 15:23.94
1986	Jason Plummer (Aus) 15:12.62
1990	Glen Housman (Aus) 14:55.25
1994	Kieren Perkins (Aus) 14:41.66

4 x 110 yards freestyle relay

1962	Australia 3:43.9
1966	Australia 3:35.6

4 x 100 metres freestyle relay

1970	Australia 3:36.02
1974	Canada 3:33.79
1978	Canada 3:27.94
1982	Australia 3:24.17
1986	Australia 3:21.58
1990	Australia 3:20.05
1994	Australia 3:20.89

4 x 200 yards freestyle relay

1930	Canada 8:42.4
1934	Canada 8:40.6

4 x 220 yards freestyle relay

1938	England 9:19.0
1950	New Zealand 9:27.7
1954	Australia 8:47.6
1958	Australia 8:33.4
1962	Australia 8:13.4
1966	Australia 7:59.5

4 x 200 metres freestyle relay

1970	Australia 7:50.77
1974	Australia 7:50.13
1978	Australia 7:34.83
1982	Australia 7:28.81
1986	Australia 7:23.49
1990	Australia 7:21.17
1994	Australia 7:20.80

100 yards backstroke

1930	John Trippett (Eng) 1:05.4
1934	Willie Francis (Sco) 1:05.2

110 yards backstroke

1938	Percy Oliver (Aus) 1:07.9
1950	Jacobus Wiid (SAf) 1:07.7
1954	John Brockway (Wal) 1:06.5
1958	John Monckton (Aus) 1:01.7
1962	Graham Sykes (Eng) 1:04.5
1966	Peter Reynolds (Aus) 1:02.4

100 metres backstroke

1970	Bill Kennedy (Can) 1:01.65
1974	Mark Tonelli (Aus) 59.65
1978	Glenn Patching (Aus) 57.90
1982	Michael West (Can) 57.12
1986	Mark Tewksbury (Can) 56.45
1990	Mark Tewksbury (Can) 56.07
1994	Martin Harris (Eng) 55.77

220 yards backstroke

1962	Julian Carroll (Aus) 2:20.9
1966	Peter Reynolds (Aus) 2:12.0

200 metres backstroke

1970	Mike Richards (Wal) 2:14.53
1974	Brad Cooper (Aus) 2:06.31
1978	Gary Hurring (NZ) 2:04.37
1982	Cameron Henning (Can) 2:02.88
1986	Sandy Goss (Can) 2:02.55
1990	Gary Anderson (Can) 2:01.69
1994	Adam Ruckwood (Eng) 2:00.79

110 yards breaststroke

1962	Ian O'Brien (Aus) 1:11.4
1966	Ian O'Brien (Aus) 1:08.2

100 metres breaststroke

1970	Bill Mahony (Can) 1:09.0
1974	David Leigh (Eng) 1:06.52
1978	Graham Smith (Can) 1:03.81
1982	Adrian Moorhouse (Eng) 1:02.93
1986	Victor Davis (Can) 1:03.01
1990	Adrian Moorhouse (Eng) 1:01.49
1994	Phil Rogers (Aus) 1:02.62

200 yards breaststroke

1930	Jack Aubin (Can) 2:38.4
1934	Norman Hamilton (Sco) 2:41.4

220 yards breaststroke

1938	John Davies (Eng) 2:51.9
1950	David Hawkins (Aus) 2:54.1
1954	John Doms (NZ) 2:52.6
1958	Terry Gathercole (Aus) 2:41.6
1962	Ian O'Brien (Aus) 2:38.2
1966	Ian O'Brien (Aus) 2:29.3

200 metres breaststroke

1970	Bill Mahony (Can) 2:30.29
1974	David Wilkie (Sco) 2:24.42
1978	Graham Smith (Can) 2:20.86
1982	Victor Davis (Can) 2:16.25
1986	Adrian Moorhouse (Eng) 2:16.35
1990	John Cleveland (Can) 2:14.96
1994	Nick Gillingham (Eng) 2:12.54

110 yards butterfly

1962	Kevin Berry (Aus) 59.5
1966	Ron Jacks (Can) 1:00.3

100 metres butterfly

1970	Byron MacDonald (Can) 58.44
1974	Neil Rogers (Aus) 56.58
1978	Dan Thompson (Can) 55.04
1982	Dan Thompson (Can) 54.71
1986	Andrew Jameson (Eng) 54.07
1990	Andrew Baildon (Aus) 53.98
1994	Scott Miller (Aus) 54.39

220 yards butterfly

1958	Ian Black (Sco) 2:22.6
1962	Kevin Berry (Aus) 2:10.8
1966	David Gerrard (NZ) 2:12.7

200 metres butterfly

1970	Tom Arusoo (Can) 2:08.97
1974	Brian Brinkley (Eng) 2:04.51
1978	George Nagy (Can) 2:01.99
1982	Phil Hubble (Eng) 2:00.98
1986	Anthony Mosse (NZ) 1:57.27
1990	Anthony Mosse (NZ) 1:57.33
1994	Danyon Loader (NZ) 1:59.54

200 metres individual medley

1970	George Smith (Can) 2:13.72
1974	David Wilkie (Sco) 2:10.11
1978	Graham Smith (Can) 2:05.25
1982	Alex Baumann (Can) 2:02.25
1986	Alex Baumann (Can) 2:01.80
1990	Gary Anderson (Can) 2:02.94
1994	Matthew Dunn (Aus) 2:02.28

440 yards individual medley

1962	Alex Alexander (Aus) 5:15.3
1966	Peter Reynolds (Aus) 4:50.8

400 metres individual medley

1970	George Smith (Can) 4:48.87
1974	Mark Treffers (NZ) 4:35.90
1978	Graham Smith (Can) 4:27.34
1982	Alex Baumann (Can) 4:23.53
1986	Alex Baumann (Can) 4:18.29
1990	Rob Bruce (Aus) 4:20.26
1994	Matthew Dunn (Aus) 4:17.01

3 x 100 yards medley relay

1934	Canada 3:11.2

3 x 110 yards medley relay

1938	England 3:28.2
1950	England 3:26.6
1954	Australia 3:22.0

4 x 110 yards medley relay

Butterfly leg added.

1958	Australia 4:14.2
1962	Australia 4:12.4
1966	Canada 4:10.5

4 x 100 metres medley relay

1970	Canada 4:01.10
1974	Canada 3:52.93
1978	Canada 3:49.76
1982	Australia 3:47.34
1986	Canada 3:44.00
1990	Canada 3:42.45
1994	Australia 3:40.41

Springboard diving

1930	Alfred Phillips (Can)
1934	J Briscoe Ray (Eng)
1938	Ron Masters (Aus)
1950	George Athans (Can)
1954	Peter Heatly (Sco)
1958	Keith Collin (Eng)
1962	Brian Phelps (Eng)
1966	Brian Phelps (Eng)
1970	Donald Wagstaff (Aus)
1974	Donald Wagstaff (Aus)
1978	Chris Snode (Eng)
1982	Chris Snode (Eng)
1986	Shaun Panayi (Aus)
1990	3m Craig Rogerson (Aus)
	1m Russell Butler (Aus)
1994	3m Michael Murphy (Aus)
	1m Jason Napper (Can)

Highboard diving

1930	Alfred Phillips (Can)
1934	Tommy Mather (Eng)
1938	Doug Tomalin (Eng)
1950	Peter Heatly (Sco)
1954	William Patrick (Can)
1958	Peter Heatly (Sco)
1962	Brian Phelps (Eng)
1966	Brian Phelps (Eng)
1970	Donald Wagstaff (Aus)
1974	Donald Wagstaff (Aus)
1978	Chris Snode (Eng)
1982	Chris Snode (Eng)
1986	Craig Rogerson (Aus)
1990	Robert Morgan (Wal)
1994	Michael Murphy (Aus)

Water polo

1950	Australia

Women

50 metres freestyle
1990	Lisa Curry-Kenny (Aus) 25.80
1994	Karen Van Wirdum (Aus) 25.90

100 yards freestyle
1930	Joyce Cooper (Eng) 1:07.0
1934	Phyllis Dewar (Can) 1:03.0

110 yards freestyle
1938	Evelyn de Lacy (Aus) 1:10.1
1950	Marjorie McQuade (Aus) 1:09.0
1954	Lorraine Crapp (Aus) 1:05.8
1958	Dawn Fraser (Aus) 1:01.4
1962	Dawn Fraser (Aus) 59.5
1966	Marion Lay (Can) 1:02.3

100 metres freestyle
1970	Angela Coughlan (Can) 1:01.22
1974	Sonya Gray (Aus) 59.13
1978	Carol Klimpel (Can) 57.78
1982	June Croft (Eng) 56.97
1986	Jane Kerr (Can) 57.62
1990	Karen Van Wirdum (Aus) 56.48
1994	Karen Pickering (Eng) 56.20

200 metres freestyle
1970	Karen Moras (Aus) 2:09.78
1974	Sonya Gray (Aus) 2:04.27
1978	Rebecca Perrott (NZ) 2:00.63
1982	June Croft (Eng) 1:59.74
1986	Susie Baumer (Aus) 2:00.61
1990	Hayley Lewis (Aus) 2:00.79
1994	Susan O'Neill (Aus) 2:00.86

400 yards freestyle
1930	Joyce Cooper (Eng) 5:25.4

440 yards freestyle
1934	Phyllis Dewar (Can) 5:45.6
1938	Dorothy Green (Aus) 5:39.7
1950	Joan Harrison (SAf) 5:26.4
1954	Lorraine Crapp (Aus) 5:11.4
1958	Ilsa Konrads (Aus) 4:49.4
1962	Dawn Fraser (Aus) 4:51.4
1966	Kathy Wainwright (Aus) 4:38.8

400 metres freestyle
1970	Karen Moras (Aus) 4:27.38
1974	Jenny Turrall (Aus) 4:22.09
1978	Tracey Wickham (Aus) 4:08.45
1982	Tracey Wickham (Aus) 4:08.82
1986	Sarah Hardcastle (Eng) 4:07.68
1990	Hayley Lewis (Aus) 4:08.89
1994	Hayley Lewis (Aus) 4:12.56

800 metres freestyle
1970	Karen Moras (Aus) 9:02.45
1974	Jaynie Parkhouse (NZ) 8:58.49
1978	Tracey Wickham (Aus) 8:24.62
1982	Tracey Wickham (Aus) 8:29.05
1986	Sarah Hardcastle (Eng) 8:24.77
1990	Julie McDonald (Aus) 8:30.27
1994	Stacey Gartrell (Aus) 8:30.18

4 x 100 yards freestyle relay
1930	England 4:32.8
1934	Canada 4:21.8

4 x 110 yards freestyle relay
1938	Canada 4:48.3
1950	Australia 4:44.9
1954	South Africa 4:33.9
1958	Australia 4:17.4
1962	Australia 4:11.0
1966	Canada 4:10.8

4 x 100 metres freestyle relay
1970	Australia 4:06.41
1974	Canada 3:57.14
1978	Canada 3:50.28
1982	England 3:54.23
1986	Canada 3:48.45
1990	Australia 3:46.85
1994	England 3:46.23

4 x 200 metres freestyle relay
1986	Australia 8:12.09
1990	Australia 8:08.95
1994	Australia 8:08.06

100 yards backstroke
1930	Joyce Cooper (Eng) 1:15.0
1934	Phyllis Harding (Eng) 1:13.8

110 yards backstroke
1938	Pat Norton (Aus) 1:19.5
1950	Judy-Joy Davies (Aus) 1:18.6
1954	Joan Harrison (SAf) 1:15.2
1958	Judy Grinham (Eng) 1:11.9
1962	Linda Ludgrove (Eng) 1:11.1
1966	Linda Ludgrove (Eng) 1:09.2

100 metres backstroke
1970	Lynne Watson (Aus) 1:07.10
1974	Wendy Cook (Can) 1:06.37
1978	Debra Forster (Aus) 1:03.97
1982	Lisa Forrest (Aus) 1:03.48
1986	Sylvia Hume (NZ) 1:04.00
1990	Nicole Livingstone (Aus) 1:02.46
1994	Nicole Stevenson (née Livingstone) (Aus) 1:02.68

220 yards backstroke
1962	Linda Ludgrove (Eng) 2:35.2
1966	Linda Ludgrove (Eng) 2:28.5

200 metres backstroke
1970	Lynne Watson (Aus) 2:22.86
1974	Wendy Cook (Can) 2:20.37

1978	Cheryl Gibson (Can) 2:16.57
1982	Lisa Forrest (Aus) 2:13.36
1986	Georgina Parkes (Aus) 2:14.88
1990	Anna Simcic (NZ) 2:12.32
1994	Nicole Stevenson (Aus) 2:12.73

110 yards breaststroke

| 1962 | Anita Lonsbrough (Eng) 1:21.3 |
| 1966 | Diana Harris (Eng) 1:19.7 |

100 metres breaststroke

1970	Beverley Whitfield (Aus) 1:17.40
1974	Catherine Gaskell (Eng) 1:16.42
1978	Robin Corsiglia (Can) 1:13.56
1982	Kathy Bald (Can) 1:11.89
1986	Allison Higson (Can) 1:10.84
1990	Keltie Duggan (Can) 1:10.74
1994	Samantha Riley (Aus) 1:08.02

200 yards breaststroke

| 1930 | Celia Wolstenholme (Eng) 2:54.8 |
| 1934 | Claire Dennis (Aus) 2:50.2 |

220 yards breaststroke

1938	Doris Storey (Eng) 3:06.3
1950	Elenor Gordon (Sco) 3:01.7
1954	Elenor Gordon (Sco) 2:59.2
1958	Anita Lonsbrough (Eng) 2:53.5
1962	Anita Lonsbrough (Eng) 2:51.7
1966	Jill Slattery (Eng) 2:50.3

200 metres breaststroke

1970	Beverley Whitfield (Aus) 2:44.12
1974	Pat Beavan (Wal) 2:43.11
1978	Lisa Borsholt (Can) 2:37.70
1982	Anne Ottenbrite (Can) 2:32.07
1986	Allison Higson (Can) 2:31.20
1990	Nathalia Giguere (Can) 2:32.16
1994	Samantha Riley (Aus) 2:25.53

110 yards butterfly

1958	Beverley Bainbridge (Aus) 1:13.5
1962	Mary Stewart (Can) 1:10.1
1966	Elaine Tanner (Can) 1:06.8

100 metres butterfly

1970	Diane Lansley (Eng) 1:07.90
1974	Patti Stenhouse (Can) 1:05.38
1978	Wendy Quirk (Can) 1:01.92
1982	Lisa Curry (Aus) 1:01.22
1986	Caroline Cooper (Eng) 1:02.12
1990	Lisa Curry-Kenny (Aus) 1:00.66
1994	Petra Thomas (Aus) 1:00.21

220 yards butterfly

| 1966 | Elaine Tanner (Can) 2:29.9 |

200 metres butterfly

| 1970 | Maree Robinson (Aus) 2:24.67 |
| 1974 | Sandra Yost (Aus) 2:20.57 |

1978	Michelle Ford (Aus) 2:11.29
1982	Michelle Ford (Aus) 2:11.89
1986	Donna McGinnis (Can) 2:11.97
1990	Hayley Lewis (Aus) 2:11.15
1994	Susan O'Neill (Aus) 2:09.96

200 metres individual medley

1970	Denise Langford (Aus) 2:28.89
1974	Leslie Cliff (Can) 2:24.13
1978	Sharron Davies (Eng) 2:18.37
1982	Lisa Curry (Aus) 2:16.94
1986	Suzanne Landells (Aus) 2:17.02
1990	Nancy Sweetnam (Can) 2:15.61
1994	Elli Overton (Aus) 2:15.59

440 yards individual medley

| 1962 | Anita Lonsbrough (Eng) 5:38.6 |
| 1966 | Elaine Tanner (Can) 5:26.3 |

400 metres individual medley

1970	Denise Langford (Aus) 5:10.74
1974	Leslie Cliff (Can) 5:01.35
1978	Sharron Davies (Eng) 4:52.44
1982	Lisa Curry (Aus) 4:51.95
1986	Suzanne Landells (Aus) 4:45.82
1990	Hayley Lewis (Aus) 4:42.65
1994	Elli Overton (Aus) 4:44.01

3 x 100 yards medley relay

| 1934 | Canada 3:42.0 |

3 x 110 yards medley relay

1938	England 3:57.7
1950	Australia 3:53.8
1954	Scotland 3:51.0

4 x 110 yards medley relay
Butterfly leg added.

1958	England 4:54.0
1962	Australia 4:45.9
1966	England 4:40.6

4 x 100 metres medley relay

1970	Australia 4:30.66
1974	Canada 4:24.77
1978	Canada 4:15.26
1982	Canada 4:14.33
1986	England 4:13.48
1990	Australia 4:10.87
1994	Australia 4:07.89

Springboard diving

1930	Oonagh Whitsett (SAf)
1934	Judy Moss (Can)
1938	Irene Donnett (Aus)
1950	Edna Child (Eng)
1954	Ann Long (Eng)
1958	Charmian Welsh (Eng)
1962	Susan Knight (Aus)
1966	Kathy Rowlatt (Eng)

1970	Beverley Boys (Can)
1974	Cindy Shatto (Can)
1978	Janet Nutter (Can)
1982	Jenny Donnet (Aus)
1986	Debbie Fuller (Can)
1990	3m Jenny Donnet (Aus)
	1m Mary De Piero (Can)
1994	3m Annie Pelletier (Can)
	1m Annie Pelletier (Can)

Highboard diving

1930	Pearl Stoneham (Can)
1934	Elizabeth Macready (Eng)
1938	Lurline Hook (Aus)
1950	Edna Child (Eng)
1954	Barbara McAulay (Aus)
1958	Charmian Welsh (Eng)
1962	Susan Knight (Aus)
1966	Joy Newman (Eng)
1970	Beverley Boys (Can)
1974	Beverley Boys (Can)
1978	Linda Cuthbert (Can)
1982	Valerie Beddoe (Aus)
1986	Debbie Fuller (Can)
1990	Anna Dacyshyn (Can)
1994	Anne Montminy (Can)

Synchronized swimming – solo

1986	Sylvie Frechette (Can)
1990	Sylvie Frechette (Can)
1994	Lisa Alexander (Can)

Synchronized swimming – duet

1986	Carolyn Waldo & Michelle Cameron (Can)
1990	Katherine Glen & Christine Larsen (Can)
1994	Lisa Alexander & Erin Woodley (Can)

Synchronized swimming – team

1986	Canada

Weightlifting

Three lifts 1950–70, two from 1974. Separate medals also awarded for each lift – snatch, clean and jerk from 1990. All weights are for totals in kilograms (originally measured in pounds 1950–66). The weight categories changed in 1994.

Up to 52kg – flyweight

1970	George Vasiliades (Aus) 290
1974	Precious McKenzie (Eng) 215
1978	Ekambaram Karunakaran (Ind) 205
1982	Nick Voukelatos (Aus) 207.5
1986	Greg Hayman (Aus) 212.5
1990	Chandersekaran Raghavan (Ind) 232.5

54kg

1994	Badathala Adisekhar (Ind) 237.5

Up to 56kg – bantamweight

1950	Tho Fook Hung (Mal) 297
1954	Maurice Megennis (Eng) 281
1958	Reginald Gaffley (SAf) 299
1962	Chua Phung Kim (Sin) 322
1966	Precious McKenzie (Eng) 319.5
1970	Precious McKenzie (Eng) 335
1974	Michael Adams (Aus) 222.5
1978	Precious McKenzie (NZ) 220
1982	Geoffrey Laws (Eng) 235
1986	Nick Voukelatos (Aus) 245
1990	Rangaswamy Punnuswamy (Ind) 247.5

59kg

1994	Marcus Stephen (Nauru) 262.5

Up to 60kg – featherweight

1950	Koh Eng Tong (Mal) 310.5
1954	Rodney Wilkes (Tri) 313
1958	Tan Ser Cher (Sin) 310.5
1962	George Newton (Eng) 326.5
1966	Kum Weng Chung (Wal) 337
1970	George Perrin (Eng) 342.5
1974	George Vasiliades (Aus) 237.5
1978	Michel Mercier (Can) 237.5
1982	Dean Willey (Eng) 267.5
1986	Raymond Williams (Wal) 252.5
1990	Chandra Sharma (Ind) 257.5

64kg

1994	Sevdalin Marinov (Aus) 277.5

Up to 67.5kg – lightweight

1950	James Halliday (Eng) 344.5
1954	Verdi Barberis (Aus) 347
1958	Tan Howe Liang (Sin) 358
1962	Carlton Goring (Eng) 351.5
1966	Hugo Gittens (Tri) 367
1970	George Newton (Eng) 372.5
1974	George Newton (Eng) 260
1978	Bill Stellios (Aus) 272.5
1982	David Morgan (Wal) 295
1986	Dean Willey (Eng) 315
1990	Paramjit Sharma (Ind) 295

70kg

1994	Moji Oluwa (Nig) 295

Up to 75kg – middleweight

1950	Gerard Gratton (Can) 360.5
1954	James Halliday (Eng) 362.5
1958	Blair Blenman (Bar) 360.5
1962	Tan Howe Laing (Sin) 390
1966	Pierre St Jean (Can) 404.5
1970	Russell Perry (Aus) 412.5
1974	Tony Ebert (NZ) 275
1978	Sam Castiglione (Aus) 300
1982	Stephen Pinsent (Eng) 312.5
1986	Bill Stellios (Aus) 302.5
1990	Ron Laycock (Aus) 310

76kg

1994	David Morgan (Wal) 327.5

Up to 82.5kg – light-heavyweight

1950	James Varaleau (Can) 369.5
1954	Gerry Gratton (Can) 403.5
1958	Phil Caira (Sco) 396.5
1962	Phil Caira (Sco) 408
1966	George Vakakis (Aus) 419.5
1970	Nicolo Ciancio (Aus) 447.5
1974	Tony Ford (Eng) 302.5
1978	Robert Kabbas (Aus) 322.5
1982	Newton Burrowes (Eng) 325
1986	David Morgan (Wal) 350
1990	David Morgan (Wal) 347.5

83kg

1994	Kiril Kounev (Aus) 352.5

Up to 90kg – middle-heavyweight

1954	Keevil Daly (Can) 399
1958	Manoel Santos (Aus) 403.5
1962	Louis Martin (Eng) 469.5
1966	Louis Martin (Eng) 462
1970	Louis Martin (Eng) 457.5
1974	Nicolo Ciancio (Aus) 330
1978	Gary Langford (Eng) 335
1982	Robert Kabbas (Aus) 337.5
1986	Keith Boxell (Eng) 350
1990	Duncan Dawkins (Eng) 357.5

91kg

1994	Harvey Goodman (Aus) 362.5

Up to 100kg – sub-heavyweight

1978	John Burns (Wal) 340
1982	Oliver Orok (Nig) 350
1986	Denis Garon (Can) 360
1990	Andrew Saxton (Eng) 362.5

99kg

1994	Andrew Callard (Eng) 347.5

Up to 110kg – heavyweight

1950	Harold Cleghorn (NZ) 408
1954	Doug Hepburn (Can) 471.5
1958	Ken McDonald (Eng) 455.5
1962	Arthur Shannos (Aus) 465
1966	Donald Oliver (NZ) 497
1970	Russell Prior (Can) 490
1974	Russell Prior (Can) 352.5
1978	Russell Prior (Can) 347.5
1982	John Burns (Wal) 347.5
1986	Kevin Roy (Can) 375
1990	Mark Thomas (Eng) 357.5

108kg

1994	Nicu Vlad (Aus) 405

Over 110kg – super-heavyweight

1970	Ray Rigby (Aus) 500
1974	Graham May (NZ) 342.5
1978	Jean-Marc Cardinal (Can) 365
1982	Dean Lukin (Aus) 377.5
1986	Dean Lukin (Aus) 392.5
1990	Andrew Davies (Wal) 402.5

Over 108kg

1994	Stefan Botev (Aus) 360

Wrestling

48kg – light-flyweight

1970	Ved Prakash (Ind)
1974	Mitchell Kawasaki (Can)
1978	Ashok Kumar (Ind)
1982	Ram Chander Sarang (Ind)
1986	Ron Moncur (Can)
1994	Jacob Isaac (Nig)

52kg – flyweight

1950	Bert Harris (Aus)
1954	Louis Baise (SAf)
1958	Ian Epton (SAf)
1962	Mohammad Niaz (Pak)
1966	Mohammad Nazir (Pak)
1970	Sudesh Kumar (Ind)
1974	Sudesh Kumar (Ind)
1978	Ray Takahashi (Can)
1982	Mahabir Singh (Ind)
1986	Chris Woodcroft (Can)
1994	Selwyn Tam (Can)

57kg – bantamweight

1930	James Trifunov (Can)
1934	Edward Melrose (Sco)
1938	Ted Purcell (Aus)
1950	Douglas Mudgeway (NZ)
1954	Geoffrey Jameson (Aus)
1958	Mohammad Akhtar (Pak)
1962	Siraj-ud-Din (Pak)
1966	Bishambar Singh (Ind)
1970	Sadar Mohd (Pak)
1974	Premnath (Ind)
1978	Satbir Singh (Ind)
1982	Brian Aspen (Eng)
1986	Mitch Ostberg (Can)
1994	Robert Dawson (Can)

62kg – featherweight

1930	Clifford Chilcott (Can)
1934	Robert McNab (Can)
1938	Roy Purchase (Aus)
1950	John Armitt (NZ)
1954	Abraham Geldenhuys (SAf)
1958	Abraham Geldenhuys (SAf)
1962	Ala-ud-Din (Pak)

1966	Mohammad Akhtar (Pak)
1970	Mohammad Saeed (Pak)
1974	Egon Beiler (Can)
1978	Egon Beiler (Can)
1982	Bob Robinson (Can)
1986	Paul Hughes (Can)
1994	Marty Calder (Can)

68kg – lightweight

1930	Howard Thomas (Can)
1934	Richard Garrard (Aus)
1938	Richard Garrard (Aus)
1950	Richard Garrard (Aus)
1954	Godfrey Pienaar (SAf)
1958	Mohammad Ashraf (Pak)
1962	Mohammad Akhtar (Pak)
1966	Mukhtiar Singh (Ind)
1970	Udey Chand (Ind)
1974	Jagrup Singh (Ind)
1978	Zsigmund Kelevitz (Aus)
1982	Jagminder Singh (Ind)
1986	David McKay (Can)
1994	Chris Wilson (Can)

74kg – welterweight

1930	Reg Priestley (Can)
1934	Joseph Schleimer (Can)
1938	Thomas Trevaskis (Aus)
1950	Henry Hudson (Can)
1954	Nicholas Laubscher (SAf)
1958	Mohammad Bashir (Pak)
1962	Mohammad Bashir (Pak)
1966	Mohammad Bashir (Pak)
1970	Mukhtiar Singh (Ind)
1974	Raghunath Pawar (Ind)
1978	Rajinder Singh (Ind)
1982	Rajinder Singh (Ind)
1986	Gary Holmes (Can)
1994	David Hohl (Can)

82kg – middleweight

1930	Mike Chepwick (Can)
1934	Terry Evans (Can)
1938	Terry Evans (Can)
1950	Maurice Vachon (Can)
1954	Hermanus van Zyl (SAf)
1958	Hermanus van Zyl (SAf)
1962	Mohammad Faiz (Pak)

1966	Mohammad Faiz (Pak)
1970	Harish Rajindra (Ind)
1974	David Aspin (NZ)
1978	Richard Deschatelets (Can)
1982	Chris Rinke (Can)
1986	Chris Rinke (Can)
1994	Justin Abdou (Can)

90kg – light-heavyweight

1930	Bill McIntyre (Can)
1934	Mick Cubbin (SAf)
1938	Edward Scarf (Aus)
1950	Patrick Morton (SAf)
1954	Jacob Theron (SAf)
1958	Jacob Theron (SAf)
1962	Anthony Buck (Eng)
1966	Robert Chamberot (Can)
1970	Mohammad Faiz (Pak)
1974	Terry Paice (Can)
1978	Stephen Danier (Can)
1982	Clark Davis (Can)
1986	Noel Loban (Eng)
1994	Scott Bianco (Can)

100kg – heavyweight

1930	Earl McCready (Can)
1934	Jack Knight (Aus)
1938	Jack Knight (Aus)
1950	James Armstrong (Aus)
1954	Kenneth Richmond (Eng)
1958	Lila Ram (Ind)
1962	Mohammad Niaz (Pak)
1966	Bhim Singh (Ind)
1970	Edward Millard (Can)
1974	Claude Pilon (Can)
1978	Wyatt Wishart (Can)
1982	Richard Deschatelets (Can)
1986	Clark Davis (Can)
1994	Greg Edgelow (Can)

Over 100kg – super-heavyweight

Limit 130kg from 1986

1970	Ikram Ilahi (Pak)
1974	Bill Benko (Can)
1978	Robert Gibbons (Can)
1982	Wyatt Wishart (Can)
1986	Wayne Brightwell (Can)
1994	Andrew Borodow (Can)

Commonwealth Games Medals by Nation 1930-94

	Nation	Gold	Silver	Bronze	Total
1	England	451	413	417	1281
2	Australia	484	426	365	1275
3	Canada	327	343	345	1015
4	New Zealand	99	137	181	417
5	Scotland	62	77	120	259
6	South Africa	62	48	52	162
7	Wales	37	47	66	150

	Nation	Gold	Silver	Bronze	Total
8	India	43	47	38	128
9	Kenya	42	29	41	112
10	Nigeria	30	38	39	107
11	Northern Ireland*	20	22	37	79
12	Jamaica	22	18	20	60
13	Pakistan	20	13	13	46
14	Ghana	12	16	13	41
15	Malaysia	12	13	11	36
	Uganda	8	13	15	36
17	Zambia	3	11	18	32
18	Trinidad & Tobago	7	11	13	31
19	Zimbabwe	3	10	17	30
20	Hong Kong	5	2	9	17
21	Tanzania	3	5	6	14
22	Bahamas	3	6	4	13
	Guyana	2	5	6	13
24	Singapore	4	1	4	9
	Fiji	2	2	5	9
26	Sri Lanka	3	4	1	8
	Western Samoa	-	2	6	8
28	Cyprus	3	2	2	7
29	Nauru	4	2	-	6
	Barbados	1	3	2	6
	Guernsey	1	3	2	6
32	Isle of Man	2	-	3	5
	Papua-New Guinea	1	3	1	5
34	Bermuda	1	1	2	4
	Jersey	1	-	3	4
36	Malawi	-	-	3	3
	Swaziland	-	1	2	3
38	St Vincent	1	-	1	2
	Bangladesh	1	-	1	2
	Namibia	1	-	1	2
	Botswana	-	-	2	2
42	Gambia	-	-	1	1
	Malta	-	-	1	1
	Norfolk Island	-	-	1	1
	Seychelles	-	-	1	1
	Tonga	-	-	1	1
TOTAL		1566	1558	1650	4774

* Ireland in 1930.

Most gold medals – men

9   Bill Hoskyns (Eng) fencing – 3 individual épée and 6 team golds 1958-70
9   Michael Wenden (Aus) swimming – 4 individual and 5 relay golds 1966-74

Most gold medals – women

7   Marjorie Jackson (Aus) athletics – 4 individual and 3 relay 1950-4
7   Raelene Boyle (Aus) athletics – 5 individual and 2 relay 1970-82

Most gold medals at one Games

6   Graham Smith (Can) swimming – 4 individual and 2 relay 1978
5   Decima Norman (Aus) athletics – 3 individual and 2 relay 1938
5   Hayley Lewis (Aus) swimming – 4 individual and 1 relay 1990

Most medals – men

14   Phillip Adams (Aus) shooting – 6 gold, 7 silver, 1 bronze 1982-90

| 13 | Michael Wenden (Aus) swimming – 9 gold, 3 silver, 1 bronze 1966-74 |
| 13 | Ivan Lund (Aus) fencing – 3 gold, 6 silver, 4 bronze 1950-62 |

Most medals – women

| 9 | Raelene Boyle (Aus) athletics – 7 gold, 2 silver 1970-82 |
| 8 | Dawn Fraser (Aus) swimming – 6 gold, 2 silver 1958-62 |

Most medals at one Games

| 8 | Ralph Hutton (Can) swimming – 1 gold, 5 silver, 2 bronze 1966 |
| 7 | Elaine Tanner (Can) swimming – 4 gold, 3 silver 1966 |

Pan-American Games

The Pan-American Games are multi-sport competitions open to athletes from North, Central and South American nations. They have been held every four years from 1951, when the Games were opened in Buenos Aires by the Argentinian President, Juan Perón, in front of a crowd of 100,000. They had been originally planned for 1942, but were delayed due to the outbreak of war.

A record 37 sports were contested at the Games in 1995, when there were over 5000 competitors from a record 42 nations affiliated to the controlling body, the Pan-American Sports Organization.

Venues

1951	Buenos Aires, Argentina		1979	San Juan, Puerto Rico
1955	Mexico City, Mexico		1983	Caracas, Venezuela
1959	Chicago, USA		1987	Indianapolis, USA
1963	São Paulo, Brazil		1991	Havana, Cuba
1967	Winnipeg, Canada		1995	Mar del Plata, Argentina
1971	Cali, Colombia		1999	Winnipeg, Canada
1975	Mexico City, Mexico			

Athletics

Games best performances after 1995 (w denotes wind-assisted; m denotes manual timing):

Men

	min sec	Name	Year
100 metres	10.06	Leandro Peñalver (Cub)	1983
200 metres	19.86	Don Quarrie (Jam)	1971
400 metres	44.45	Ronnie Ray (USA)	1975
800 metres	1:46.02	José Luiz Barbosa (Bra)	1995
1500 metres	3:40.5m	Don Paige (USA)	1979
5000 metres	13:31.40	Arturo Barrios (Mex)	1987
10,000 metres	28:20.37	Bruce Bickford (USA)	1987
Marathon	2hr 12:42	Jorge Gonzalez (PR)	1983
3000 metres steeple	8:14.41	Wander Moura (Bra)	1995
110 metres hurdles	13.20	Renaldo Nehemiah (USA)	1979
400 metres hurdles	48.49	Winthrop Graham (Jam)	1987
4 x 100 metres relay	38.31	USA	1975
4 x 400 metres relay	2:59.54	USA	1987
20 kilometres walk	1hr 22:53	Jefferson Pérez (Ecu)	1995
50 kilometres walk	3hr 47:55	Carlos Mercenario (Mex)	1995
	metres		
High jump	2.40	Javier Sotomayor (Cub)	1995
Pole vault	5.75	Pat Manson (USA)	1995
Long jump	8.75	Carl Lewis (USA)	1987
Triple jump	17.89	João Carlos de Oliveira (Bra)	1975
Shot	20.52	C J Hunter (USA)	1995
Discus	67.32	Luis M Delis (Cub)	1983
Hammer	77.24	Jud Logan (USA)	1987
Javelin (old)	84.16	Duncan Atwood (USA)	1979
Javelin (new)	79.28	Emeterio González (Cub)	1995
	pts		
Decathlon	8024	Bruce Jenner (USA)	1975

Women

	min sec	Name	Year
100 metres	11.05	Evelyn Ashford (USA) (in semi)	1979
	11.05	Chryste Gaines (USA)	1995
200 metres	22.24w	Evelyn Ashford (USA) (& 22.45 in semi)	1979
400 metres	49.61	Ana Quirot (Cub)	1991
800 metres	1:58.71	Ana Quirot (Cub)	1991
1500 metres	4:05.7m	Mary Decker (USA)	1979
3000 metres	8:53.6m	Jan Merrill (USA)	1979
10,000 metres	33:00.00	Marty Cooksey (USA)	1987
Marathon	2hr 43:36	Olga Avalos (Mex)	1991
100 metres hurdles	12.81	LaVonna Martin (USA)	1987
	12.68w	Aliuska López (Cub)	1995
400 metres hurdles	54.23	Judi Brown King (USA)	1987
4 x 100 metres relay	42.90	USA	1975
4 x 400 metres relay	3:23.35	USA	1987
10 kilometres walk	46:31.93	Graciela Mendoza (Mex)	1995

	metres		
High jump	1.96	Coleen Sommer (USA)	1987
Long jump	7.45	Jackie Joyner (USA)	1987
Triple jump	14.09	Laiza Carrillo (Cub)	1995
Shot	19.34	María Sarria (Cub)	1983
Discus	65.58	Maritza Martén (Cub)	1987
Hammer	58.92	Alexandra Givan (USA)	1995
Javelin	64.78	Dulce M García (Cub)	1983

	pts		
Heptathlon	6266	Jamie McNeair (USA)	1995

Most individual event wins

4   Osvaldo Suárez (Arg) 5000m 1955, 1963; 10,000m 1955, 1959
4   João Carlos de Oliveira (Bra) long jump and triple jump 1975 and 1979
4   Ana Quirot (Cub) 400m and 800m 1987, 1991

Swimming

Games best performances after 1995:

Men

Event	min sec	Name	Year
50 metres freestyle	22.55	Tom Williams (USA)	1987
100 metres freestyle	49.31	Gustavo Borges (Bra)	1995
200 metres freestyle	1:48.49	Gustavo Borges (Bra)	1995
400 metres freestyle	3:50.38	Sean Killion (USA)	1991
1500 metres freestyle	15:20.90	Alex Kostich (USA)	1987
4 x 100 metres freestyle relay	3:18.68	USA	1995
4 x 200 metres freestyle relay	7:21.61	USA	1995
100 metres backstroke	54.74	Jeff Rouse (USA)	1995
200 metres backstroke	1:59.34	Rick Carey (USA)	1983
100 metres breaststroke	1:02.28	Steve Lundquist (USA)	1983
200 metres breaststroke	2:15.50	Marion González (Cub	1991
100 metres butterfly	53.45	Anthony Nesty (Sur)	1991
200 metres butterfly	1:58.85	Craig Beardsley (USA)	1983
200 metres individual medley	2:00.92	Ronald Karnaugh (USA)	1991
400 metres individual medley	4:18.55	Curtis Myden (Can)	1995
4 x 100 metres medley relay	3:40.42	USA	1983

Women

50 metres freestyle	26.01	Kristen Topham (Can)	1991
100 metres freestyle	55.62	Angel Martino (USA)	1995
200 metres freestyle	1:58.43	Cynthia Woodhead (USA)	1979

400 metres freestyle	4:10.56	Cynthia Woodhead (USA)	1979
800 metres freestyle	8:34.72	Tami Bruce (USA)	1987
4 x 100 metres freestyle relay	3:44.71	USA	1995
4 x 200 metres freestyle relay	8:07.30	USA	1995
100 metres backstroke	1:01.71	Barbara Bedford (USA)	1995
200 metres backstroke	2:13.65	Katie Welch (USA	1987
100 metres breaststroke	1:10.36	Lisa Flood (Can)	1995
200 metres breaststroke	2:28.69	Dorsey Tierney (USA)	1991
100 metres butterfly	1:00.53	Jill Sterkel (USA)	1979
200 metres butterfly	2:09.77	Mary T Meagher (USA)	1983
200 metres individual medley	2:15.66	Joanne Malar (Can)	1995
400 metres individual medley	4:43.64	Joanne Malar (Can)	1995
4 x 100 metres medley relay	4:08.17	USA	1995

Most individual event wins

Men: 4 Steve Furniss (USA) 200m and 400m individual medley 1971, 1975
Women: 4 Cynthia Woodhead (USA) 100m, 200m and 400m freestyle 1979, 200m freestyle 1983, Tracy Caulkins (USA) 200m and 400m individual medley 1979, 1983

Leading Nations at all Sports 1951-95

	Gold	Silver	Bronze	Total
USA	1426	1016	670	3012
Cuba	580	415	354	1349
Canada	217	394	505	1116
Argentina	206	224	275	705
Brazil	134	171	236	541
Mexico	108	150	318	576
Venezuela	38	104	145	287
Chile	28	51	82	161
Colombia	25	64	107	196
Puerto Rico	14	57	84	155

Major International and Continental Games

All-African Games

The first African Games, covering ten sports, were contested 18-25 July 1965.

Venues

1965	Brazzaville, Congo
1973	Lagos, Nigeria
1978	Algiers, Algeria
1987	Nairobi, Kenya
1991	Cairo, Egypt
1995	Harare, Zimbabwe

Asian Games

The first Asian Games were held in New Delhi, India on 8-11 March 1951, when ten nations took part. These multi-sport Games have been held at four-yearly intervals since 1954. In 1990 new records were set, with some 6000 competitors at 29 sports, including two demonstration ones, from 36 nations, of which 25 won medals. Those figures were exceeded in 1994, when there were about 6800 competitors from 43 nations, of which 32 won medals.

Venues

1951	New Delhi
1954	Manila
1958	Tokyo
1962	Djakarta
1966	Bangkok
1970	Bangkok
1974	Teheran
1978	Bangkok
1982	New Delhi
1986	Seoul
1990	Beijing
1994	Hiroshima
1998	Bangkok

A precursor of the Asian Games was the Far Eastern Games, first held in 1913 in Manila, with China, the Philippines and two Japanese athletes taking part. These Games were held every two years to 1927 and then in 1930 and 1934.

Central American and Caribbean Games

First held in 1926 in Mexico City, and at four-yearly intervals since except for 1942. The 17th Games were staged in Maracaibo, Venezuela in 1998.

Goodwill Games

First staged in 1986 in Moscow, run principally by the Turner Broadcast System, not only as an important televised sports meeting, but also to promote goodwill between the USA and the USSR following the boycott by the USA of the 1980

Olympic Games, and by the USSR of the 1984 Olympic Games. The second Goodwill Games were staged in Seattle in 1990 at 21 sports, the third in St Petersburg and Moscow, Russia in 1994, and the fourth in New York in 1998.

Pan-Arab Games

These Games were instituted by decree of the Arab League in 1951, and first held in 1953. Thereafter they were staged every four years until 1965, with a gap until 1985 (18 sports).

South-East Asia Games

First held in Bangkok, Thailand in 1959, these Games have subsequently been held bienially except for 1963. At the 15th Games in 1989, in Kuala Lumpur, Malaysia, 24 sports were contested, including, among more familiar ones, the regional sports of *sepak takrwa* and *silat olahraga*, a martial art. The 19th Games were held in 1997 in Jakarta, Indonesia.

World Games

A four-yearly international championship for sports not on the Olympic programme, the World Games were first held at Santa Clara, USA in 1981. Subsequent festivals have been held in London 1985, Karlruhe, F R Germany 1989, The Hague, Holland 1993 and Lahti, Finland 1997. In 1997 the following sports were contested: sports aerobics, aikido, bowling, field archery, casting, dance sort, faustball, ju-jitsu, karate, korfball, life-saving, military pentathlon, pétanque (and demonstration of *boules lyonnais*), powerlifting, roller skating (figure and speed), underwater swimming, trampolining, tug-of-war, women's water skiing. The next Games are scheduled for Akita, Japan in 2001.

World Student Games

The Universiade or World Student Games, organized by the Fédération Internationale du Sport Universitaire (FISU), is well established as one of the world's most important sports meetings, although it has been some-what under-regarded in the UK and perhaps in the USA.

The first 'International Universities' Games were held in Warsaw, organized by the Confédération Internationale des Étudiants (CIE). From 1951 to 1962 rival Games were staged by FISU and the UIE. The latter, Communist inspired, were known as the World Youth Games from 1954 and these had the higher standards. From 1963, however, the Games merged and are now held bienially.

Ten sports are usually contested at the summer Games: association football, athletics, basketball, fencing, gymnastics, judo, swimming, tennis, volleyball and water polo.

Venues
(From 1951-61: U - UIE, F - FISU)

1924	Warsaw
1927	Rome
1928	Paris
1930	Darmstadt
1933	Turin
1935	Budapest
1937	Paris
1939	Monaco
1947	Paris
1949	Budapest
1951	Berlin (U) & Luxembourg (F)
1953	Bucharest (U) & Dortmund (F)
1954	Budapest (U)
1955	Warsaw (U) & San Sebastian (F)
1957	Moscow (U) & Paris (F)
1959	Vienna (U) & Turin (F)
1961	Sofia (F)
1962	Helsinki (U)
1963	Porto Alegre
1965	Budapest
1967	Tokyo
1970	Turin
1973	Moscow
1975	Rome (unofficial)
1977	Sofia
1979	Mexico City
1981	Bucharest
1983	Edmonton
1985	Kobe
1987	Zagreb
1989	Duisberg★
1991	Sheffield
1993	Buffalo
1995	Fukuoka
1997	Catania
1999	Palma de Mallorca

★ Restricted schedule of athletics, men's basketball, fencing and rowing after São Paulo withdrew.

Winter sports are staged at the Winter Universiade, of which the 18th was in 1997. There are also separate World University Championships at various other sports.

Awards

L'Equipe Champion des Champions

The French daily sports newspaper *L'Equipe* annually selects its world sports man or woman of the year.
Winners:

1976	Alberto Juantorena (Cub, athletics)
1977	Rosemarie Ackermann (GDR, athletics)
1978	Henry Rono (Ken, athletics)
1979	Sebastian Coe (UK, athletics)
1980	Eric Heiden (USA, ice skating)
1981	Sebastian Coe (UK, athletics)
1982	Paolo Rossi (Ita, football)
1983	Carl Lewis (USA, athletics)
1984	Carl Lewis (USA, athletics)
1985	Sergey Bubka (USSR, athletics)
1986	Diego Maradona (Arg, football)
1987	Ben Johnson (Can, athletics)
1988	Florence Griffith-Joyner (USA, athletics)
1989	Greg LeMond (USA, cycling)
1990	Ayrton Senna (Bra, motor racing)
1991	Carl Lewis (USA, athletics)
1992	Michael Jordan (USA, basketball)
1993	Noureddine Morceli (Mor, athletics)
1994	Romario (Bra, football)
1995	Jonathan Edwards (UK, athletics)
1996	Michael Johnson (USA, athletics)
1997	Sergey Bubka (Ukr, athletics)

Jesse Owens International Award

Presented annually in the February following the year of achievement to the international athlete (in Olympic sports) who best personifies the qualities of the great Olympian Jesse Owens, who won four gold medals in 1936.
Winners:

1981	Eric Heiden (USA, speed skating)
1982	Sebastian Coe (UK, athletics)
1983	Mary Slaney (USA, athletics)
1984	Edwin Moses (USA, athletics)
1985	Carl Lewis (USA, athletics)
1986	Saïd Aouita (Mor, athletics)
1987	Greg Louganis (USA, diving)
1988	Ben Johnson (Can, athletics)
1989	Florence Griffith-Joyner (USA, athletics)
1990	Roger Kingdom (USA, athletics)
1991	Greg LeMond (USA, cycling)
1992	Mike Powell (USA, athletics)
1993	Wang Junxia (Chn, athletics)
1994	Johan Olav Koss (Nor, ice skating)
1995-6	Michael Johnson (USA, athletics)

Sports Illustrated Sportsman of the Year

The American magazine has awarded this title annually since 1954 to the sports man or woman who 'symbolizes in character and performance the ideals of sportsmanship'.
Winners:
(USA unless shown; T & F denotes Track and Field Athletics)

1954	Roger Bannister (UK, T & F, miler)
1955	Johnny Podres (baseball)
1956	Bobby Joe Morrow (T & F, sprinter)
1957	Stan Musial (baseball)
1958	Rafer Johnson (T & F, decathlon)
1959	Ingemar Johansson (Swe, boxing)
1960	Arnold Palmer (golf)
1961	Jerry Lucas (basketball)
1962	Terry Baker (football)
1963	Pete Rozelle (NFL commissioner)
1964	Ken Venturi (golf)
1965	Sandy Koufax (baseball)
1966	Jim Ryun (T & F, miler)
1967	Carl Yastrzemski (basketball)
1968	Bill Russell (basketball)
1969	Tommy Seaver (baseball)
1970	Bobby Orr (Can, ice hockey)
1971	Lee Trevino (golf)
1972	Billie Jean King (tennis) & John Wooden (basketball coach)
1973	Jackie Stewart (UK, motor racing)
1974	Muhammad Ali (boxing)
1975	Pete Rose (baseball)
1976	Chris Evert (tennis)
1977	Steve Cauthen (horse racing)
1978	Jack Nicklaus (golf)
1979	Willie Stargell (baseball) & Terry Bradshaw (football)
1980	US Olympic ice hockey team
1981	Ray Leonard (boxing)
1982	Wayne Gretzky (Can, ice hockey)
1983	Mary Decker (T & F, distance)
1984	Edwin Moses (T & F, 400m hurdler) & Mary Lou Retton (gymnastics)
1985	Kareem Abdul-Jabbar (basketball)
1986	Joe Paterno (football coach)
1987	'Athletes who care'
1988	Orel Hershiser (baseball)
1989	Greg LeMond (cycling)
1990	Joe Montana (football)
1991	Michael Jordan (basketball)
1992	Arthur Ashe (tennis)
1993	Don Shula (football coach)
1994	Johan Olav Koss (Nor) & Bonnie Blair (ice skating)

1995   Cal Ripken, Jr (baseball)
1996   Tiger Woods (golf)
1997   Dean Smith (basketball coach)

BBC Sports Personality of the Year

Inaugurated in 1954, this prestigious annual award
is presented to the British sports man or woman
who gains the most votes from television viewers.
Winners:
1954   Chris Chataway (athletics)
1955   Gordon Pirie (athletics)
1956   Jim Laker (cricket)
1957   Dai Rees (golf)
1958   Ian Black (swimming)
1959   John Surtees (motorcycling)
1960   David Broome (show jumping)
1961   Stirling Moss (motor racing)
1962   Anita Lonsbrough (swimming)
1963   Dorothy Hyman (athletics)
1964   Mary Rand (athletics)
1965   Tommy Simpson (cycling)
1966   Bobby Moore (football)
1967   Henry Cooper (boxing)
1968   David Hemery (athletics)
1969   Ann Jones (tennis)
1970   Henry Cooper (boxing)
1971   Princess Anne (three-day event)
1972   Mary Peters (athletics)
1973   Jackie Stewart (motor racing)
1974   Brendan Foster (athletics)
1975   David Steele (cricket)
1976   John Curry (ice skating)
1977   Virginia Wade (tennis)
1978   Steve Ovett (athletics)
1979   Sebastian Coe (athletics)
1980   Robin Cousins (ice skating)
1981   Ian Botham (cricket)
1982   Daley Thompson (athletics)
1983   Steve Cram (athletics)
1984   Jayne Torvill & Christopher Dean (ice skating)
1985   Barry McGuigan (boxing)
1986   Nigel Mansell (motor racing)
1987   Fatima Whitbread (athletics)
1988   Steve Davis (snooker)
1989   Nick Faldo (golf)
1990   Paul Gascoigne (football)
1991   Liz McColgan (athletics)
1992   Nigel Mansell (motor racing)
1993   Linford Christie (athletics)
1994   Damon Hill (motor racing)
1995   Jonathan Edwards (athletics)
1996   Damon Hill (motor racing)
1997   Greg Rusedski (tennis)

British Sports Bodies

British Olympic Association
1 Wandsworth Plain,
London SW18 1EH
Tel: 0181 871 2677
Fax: 0181 871 9104
Chairman: Craig Reedie,
Chief Executive: S Clegg
Founded 1905.

British Universities Sports Association
8 Union Street,
London SE1 1SZ
Tel: 0171 357 8555
Fax: 0171 403 1218
Chairman: Alison Odell,
Chief Exceutive: G Gregory-Jones

Central Council of Physical Recreation
Francis House, Francis Street,
London SW1P 1DE
Tel: 0171 828 3163
Fax: 0171 630 8820
Chairman: David Oxley,
General Secretary: M Denton
Founded 1935.

Commonwealth Games Council for England
Tavistock House, Tavistock Square,
London WC1H 9JZ
Tel: 0171 388 6643
General Secretary: Miss A Hogbin

Commonwealth Games Federation
Walkden House, 3-10 Melton Street,
London NW1 2EB
Tel: 0171 383 5596
Hon Secretary: D Dixon

English Sports Council
16 Upper Woburn Place,
London WC1H 0QP
Tel: 0171 273 1500
Fax: 0171 333 5740
Chairman: Sir Rodney Walker,
Chief Executive: Derek Casey
Founded 1997 (formerly
The Sports Council).

Scottish Sports Council
Caledonia House, South Gyle,
Edinburgh EH12 9DQ
Tel: 0131 317 7200
Fax: 0131 317 7202
Chairman: Graeme Simmord,
Chief Executive: F A L Alstead

Sports Council for Northern Ireland
House of Sport, 2a Upper
Malone Road, Belfast
BT9 5LA
Tel: 01232 381222
Fax: 01232 682757
Chief Executive: E McCartan

Sports Council for Wales
National Sports Centre for Wales,
Sophia Gardens, Cardiff CF1 9SW
Tel: 01222 300500
Fax: 01222 300600
Chairman: Ossie Wheatley,
Chief Executive: Dr Huw Jones

United Kingdom Sports Council
Walkden House, 10 Melton Street,
London NW1 2EB
Tel: 0171 380 8000
Fax: 0171 380 8010
Chairman: Sir Rodney Walker,
Chief Executive: David Chesterton

Angling

National Federation of Anglers
Halliday House, Egginton
Junction, Derbyshire DE65 6GU
Tel: 01283 734735
Fax: 01283 734799
President: K W Ball, Chief
Administration Officer: W J Hall
Founded 1903.

Archery

Grand National Archery Society
National Agriculture Centre, Seventh
Street, Stoneleigh Park, Kenilworth,
Warwickshire CV8 2LG
Tel: 01203 696631
Fax: 01203 419662
Chairman: Michael Shepherd,
Chief Executive: J S Middleton
Founded 1861.

Athletics

Athletics Association of Wales
Morfa Stadium, Landore,
Swansea SA1 7DF
Tel: 01792 456237
Fax: 01792 474916
President: Hedydd Davies,
Chief Executive: David Turner
Founded 1991.

British Athletics
Athletics House, 30a Harborne Road,
Edgbaston, Birmingham B15 3AA
Tel: 0121 456 5098
Fax: 0121 456 5898
Chief Executive: David Moorcroft,
Information Officer: W Adcocks

Northern Ireland Athletic Federation
Athletics House, Old Coach Road,
Belfast BT9 5PR
Tel: 01232 602707
Fax: 01232 309939
Chairman: Adrienne Smyth,
Secretary: John Allen
Founded 1989.

Race Walking Association
Hufflers, Heard's Lane, Shenfield,
Brentwood, Essex CM15 0SF
Tel: 01277 220687
Fax: 01277 212380
President: Beryl Randle, Hon.
General Secretary: P J Cassidy

Scottish Athletics Federation
Caledonia House, South Gyle,
Edinburgh EH12 9 DQ
Tel: 0131 317 7320
Fax: 0131 317 7321
Chairman: Peter Carter,
Administrator: Neil Park
Founded 1992.

Badminton

Badminton Association of England Ltd
National Badminton Centre,
Bradwell Road, Loughton Lodge,
Milton Keynes MK8 9LA
Tel: 01908 268400
Fax: 01908 566922
E-mail: info@badeng.powernet.co.uk
Chairman: John Havers,
Chief Executive: Steve Baddeley
Founded 1893.

Scottish Badminton Union
Cockburn Centre, 40 Bogmoor
Place, Glasgow G51 4TQ
Tel: 0141 445 1218
Fax: 0141 425 1218
President: R E Conway,
Chief Executive: Anne Smillie
Founded 1908.

Welsh Badminton Union
Fourth Floor, 3 Westgate Street,
Cardiff CF1 1ND
Tel: 01222 222082
Fax: 01222 394282
E-mail:
welsh@welshbadminton.force9.co.uk
Chairman: Clyd Davies, Coaching
Development Manager: L Williams
Founded 1928.

Baseball

British Baseball Federation
66 Belvedere Road, Hessle,
North Humberside HU13 0YQ
Tel: 01482 643551
Fax: 01482 640224
Chairman: S R Herbert,
Secretary: Ms W Macadam
Founded 1890.

Basketball

Basketball Association of Wales
Connies House, Rhymney River,
Cardiff CF3 7YZ
Tel: 01222 454395
Administrator: F M Daw

English Basketball Association
48 Bradford Road, Stanningley,
Leeds LS28 6DF
Tel: 0113 236 1166
Fax: 0113 236 1022
President: Keith Mitchell,
Chief Executive (Acting): S Kirkland
Founded 1936.

Scottish Basketball Association
Caledonia House, South Gyle,
Edinburgh EH12 9DQ
Tel: 0131 317 7260
Fax: 0131 317 7489
E-mail: sba@basketball-scotland.com
Chairman: W D McInnes, Chief
Executive Officer: Sadie Mason
Founded 1947.

Billiards and Snooker

**World Ladies' Billiards and
Snooker Association**
27 Oakfield Road, Clifton,
Bristol BS8 2AT
Tel: 0117 974 4491
Fax: 0117 974 4931
Chairman: Ms M Fisher,
Company Secretary: M D Blake

**World Professional Billiards and
Snooker Association**
27 Oakfield Road,
Bristol BS8 2AT
Tel: 0117 974 4491
Fax: 0117 974 4931
Chairman: Rex Williams,
Chief Executive: M D Blake

Bobsleigh

British Bobsleigh Association
The Chestnuts, 85 High Street,
Codford, Warminster, Wilts
BA12 0ND
Tel: 01985 850064
Fax: 01985 850064
E-mail: bba@dial.pipex.com
Chairman: Gen. Rob McAfee,
General Secretary: Ms H Alderman

Bowling

**British Tenpin Bowling
Association**
114 Balfour Road, Ilford,
Essex IG1 4JD
Tel: 0181 478 1745
Fax: 0181 514 3665
Founded 1961.

Bowls

British Isles Bowls Council
2 Pentland Avenue, Gowkshill,
Gorebridge, Midlothian EH23 4PG
Tel: 01875 821105
Fax: 01875 821105
President & Hon. Secretary:
John Philip Darling
Founded 1962.

British Isles Indoor Bowls Council
9 Highlight Lane, Barry CF62 8AA
Tel & Fax: 01446 733978
President: Gareth Humphreys,
Hon. Secretary: J R Thomas
Founded 1979.

**British Isles Women's Bowling
Council**
2 Case Gardens, Seaton,
Devon EX12 2AP
Tel & Fax: 01297 21317
Hon. Secretary: Mrs Nancie Colling
Founded 1972.

**British Isles Women's Indoor
Bowls Council**
101 Skyline Drive, Lambeg,
Lisburn, Co. Antrim,
N Ireland BT27 4HU
Tel: 01846 663516
Chairman & Hon. Secretary:
Doreen Miskelly
Founded 1982.

English Bowling Association
Lyndhurst Road, Worthing,
W Sussex BN11 2AZ
Tel: 01903 820222
Fax: 01903 820444
Secretary: G D Shaw
Founded 1903.

**English Indoor Bowling
Association**
David Cornwell House,
Bowling Green, Leicester Road,
Melton Mowbray, Leics LE13 0DA
Tel: 01664 481900
Fax: 01664 481901
President: M Willis, National
Secretary: David N Brown
Founded 1971.

**English Women's Bowling
Association**
2 Case Gardens, Seaton,
Devon EX12 2AP
Tel & Fax: 01297 21317
Chairman: Mrs J Clark, Hon.
Secretary: Mrs Nancie Colling
Founded 1931.

**English Women's Indoor Bowling
Association**
3 Scirocco Close, Moulton Park,
Northampton NN3 6AP
Tel: 01604 494163
Fax: 01604 494434
President: Mrs E Read,
Secretary: Mrs M E Ruff
Founded 1951.

Boxing

**Amateur Boxing Association
of England Ltd**
Crystal Palace Sports Centre,
London SE19 2BB
Tel: 0181 778 0251
Fax: 0181 778 9324
Chairman: Com. R Robertson
Secretary: C Brown
Founded 1880.

**British Amateur Boxing
Association**
96 High Street, Lochee,
Dundee DD2 3AY
Tel: 01382 611412
Chief Executive: F Hendry

**British Boxing Board of Control
Ltd**
Jack Petersen House, 52a Borough
High Street, London SE1 1XW
Tel: 0171 403 5879
Fax: 0171 378 6670
President: Leonard 'Nipper' Read,
General Secretary: John Morris
Founded 1929.

Canoeing

British Canoe Union
John Dudderidge House,
Adbolton Lane, West Bridgford,
Nottingham NG2 5AS
Tel: 0115 982 1100
Fax: 0115 982 1797
President: A Woods,
Chief Executive: P Owen
Founded 1936.

Cricket

England and Wales Cricket Board
Lord's Cricket Ground, St John's
Wood, London NW8 8QZ
Tel: 0171 432 1200
Fax: 0171 289 5619
Chairman: Lord Maclaurin of
Knebworth, Chief Executive:
Tim Lamb
Founded 1997.

Marylebone Cricket Club (MCC)
Lord's Cricket Ground,
London NW8 8QN
Tel: 0171 289 1611
Secretary: R D V Knight

Croquet

Croquet Association
c/o The Hurlingham Club,
Ranelagh Gardens,
London SW6 3PR
Tel: 0171 736 3148
Fax: 0171 736 3148
E-mail: caoffice@croquet.uk.org
Chairman: W H Arliss,
Secretary: Paul Campion
Founded 1897.

Curling

Royal Caledonian Curling Club
English Curling Association,
Little Wethers, Sandy Lane,
Northwood, Middlesex HA6 3HA
Tel: 01772 634154
Fax: 01895 201001
Secretary: Eric Hinds
Founded 1838.

Cycling

British Cycling Federation
National Cycling Centre, Stuart
Street, Manchester M11 4DQ
Tel: 0161 230 2301
Fax: 0161 231 0591
E-mail:
101701.2260@compuserve.com
President: Brian Cookson,
Chief Executive: Peter King
Founded 1959.

Road Time Trials Council
77 Arlington Drive, Pennington,
Leigh, Lancs WN7 3QP
Tel: 01942 603976
Fax: 01942 262326
Chairman: Peter McGrath,
National Secretary: Philip Heaton
Founded 1937.

Darts

British Darts Organization
2 Pages Lane, Muswell Hill,
London N10 1PS
Tel: 0181 883 5544
Fax: 0181 883 0109
E-mail:
101776.666@compuserve.com
Chairman: Sam Hawkins,
Gen. Secretary/Director: O A Croft
Founded 1973.

Diving

Great Britain Diving Federation
PO Box 222, Batley,
W Yorks, WF17 8XD
Tel: 01924 422322
Director of Administration: J Cryer

Equestrian

British Equestrian Federation
British Equestrian Centre, Stoneleigh
Park, Kenilworth, Warks CV8 2RH
Tel: 01203 698871
Fax: 01203 696484
President: John Tulloch

British Horse Trials Association
British Equestrian Centre, Stoneleigh
Park, Kenilworth, Warks CV8 2RN
Tel: 01203 698856
Fax: 01203 697235
Chairman: Michael Allen,
Director: Maj. T Taylor

Fencing

British Fencing Association
1 Baron's Gate, 33-35 Rothschild,
London W4 5HT
Tel: 0181 742 3032
Fax: 0181 742 3033
Chairman: James Chambers,
General Secretary: Miss G Kenneally
Founded 1902.

Fives

Eton Fives Association
74 Clarence Road, St Albans,
Herts AL1 4NG
Tel: 01727 837099
Secretary: R Beament
Founded 1931.

Rugby Fives Association
The Old Forge, Sutton Valence,
Maidstone, Kent ME17 3AW
Tel: 01622 842278
E-mail: michael.beaman@which.net
President: J I Cooper,
General Secretary: Michael Beaman
Founded 1927.

Football (Association)

Football Association
16 Lancaster Gate, London W2 3LW
Tel: 0171 402 7151
Fax: 0171 402 0486
Chairman: K St J Wiseman,
Chief Executive: R H G Kelly
Premier League: P Leaver
Founded 1863.

Football Association of Wales
3 Westgate Street, Cardiff CF1 1DD
Tel: 01222 372325
Fax: 01222 343961
E-mail: info@faw.co.uk
President: J O Hughes,
Secretary General: D G Collins
Founded 1876.

Football League Ltd
319 Clifton Drive South,
Lytham St Annes, Lancs FY8 1JG
Tel: 01253 729421
Fax: 01253 724786
Chairman: D R Sheepshanks,
Chief Executive: R C Scudamore

Irish Football Association
20 Windsor Avenue, Belfast BT9 6EE
Tel: 01232 669458
Fax: 01232 667620
President: Jim Boyce, General
Secretary: D I Bowen
Founded 1886.

Irish Football League
96 University Street,
Belfast BT7 1HE
Tel: 01232 242888
Fax: 01232 330773
Chairman: G McConkey,
Secretary: H Wallace
Founded 1890.

Scottish Football Association
6 Park Gardens, Glasgow G3 7YF
Tel: 0141 332 6372
Fax: 0141 332 7559
E-mail: info@scottishfa.co.uk
President: John C McGinn,
Chief Executive: Jim Farry
Founded 1873.

Scottish Football League
188 West Regent Street,
Glasgow G2 4RY
Tel: 0141 248 3844
Fax: 0141 221 7450
E-mail: sfl@sol.co.uk
Chairman: J Oliver,
Secretary: P Donald

Women's Football Association
16 Lancaster Gate,
London W2 3LW
Tel: 0171 262 4542
Fax: 0171 402 0486

Gliding

British Gliding Association
Kimberley House, 47 Vaughan Way,
Leicester LE1 4SE
Tel: 0116 253 1051
Fax: 0116 251 5939
E-mail: bga@ad.com
Secretary/Administrator: Barry Rolfe
Founded 1929.

Golf

Ladies' Golf Union
The Scores, St Andrews,
Fife KY16 9AT
Tel: 01334 475811
Fax: 01334 472818
President: Miss B A B Jackson,
Secretary: Julie Hall
Founded 1893.

Royal and Ancient Golf Club of St Andrews
Golf Place, St Andrews,
Fife KY16 9JD
Tel: 01334 472112
Fax: 01334 477580
Secretary: Michael Bonallack
Founded 1754.

Gymnastics

British Gymnastics
Ford Hall, Lilleshall National Sports
Centre, Newport, Shropshire
TF10 9NB
Tel: 01952 820330
Fax: 01952 820621
E-mail: info@baga.co.uk
President: William Slater,
General Secretary: D Minnery
Founded 1888.

Handball

British Handball Association
60 Church Street, Radcliffe,
Manchester M26 8SQ
Tel & Fax: 0161 724 9656
Founded 1967.

Hang Gliding

Hang Gliding and Paragliding Association
The Old School Room,
Loughborough Road,
Leicester LE4 5PJ
Tel: 0116 261 1322
Fax: 0116 261 1323

Hockey

All-England Women's Hockey Association
The Stadium, Silbury Boulevard,
Milton Keynes MK9 1NR
Tel: 01908 689290
Fax: 01908 689286
Founded 1895.

English Hockey Association
The Stadium, Silbury Boulevard,
Milton Keynes MK9 1NR
Tel: 01908 689290
Chief Executive: S P Baines

The Hockey Association
Norfolk House, 102 Saxon Gate
West, Milton Keynes MK9 2EP
Tel: 01908 241100
Fax: 01908 241106
Founded 1886.

Scottish Hockey Union
48 The Pleasance,
Edinburgh EH8 9TJ
Tel: 0131 650 8170
Chairman: P Monaghan

Welsh Hockey Union
80 Woodville Road, Cathays,
Cardiff CF2 4ED
Tel: 01222 233257
Fax: 01222 233258
Chairman: Roger Harris,
Executive Secretary: John G Williams
Founded 1897.

Horse Racing

British Horse Racing Board
42 Portman Square,
London W1H 0EN
Tel: 0171 396 0011
Fax: 0171 935 3626
Chairman: Peter Savill,
Chief Executive: R T Ricketts
Founded 1993.

Jockey Club
42 Portman Square,
London W1H 0EN
Tel: 0171 486 4921
Fax: 0171 487 1148
Senior Steward: Christopher Spence
Founded 1972.

Ice Hockey

British Ice Hockey Association
2nd Floor Suite, 517 Christchurch
Road, Boscombe, Bournemouth
BH1 4AG
Tel: 01202 303946
Fax: 01202 398005
E-mail: biha@mcmail.com
President: F W L Meredith,
General Secretary: D Pickles
Founded 1936.

Ice Skating

National Ice Skating Association of UK Ltd
First Floor, 114-116 Curtain Road,
London EC2A 3AH
Tel: 0171 613 1188
Fax: 0171 613 4616
E-mail:
NISA@iceskating.demon.co.uk
President: Sally-Anne Stapleford,
Chief Executive: Ms C Godsall
Founded 1879.

Judo

British Judo Association
7A Rutland Street,
Leicester LE1 1RB
Tel: 0116 255 9669
Fax: 0116 255 9660
E-mail: britjudo@aol.com
Chairman: Lesley-Anne Alexander,
President: Charles Palmer
Founded 1949.

Karate

English Karate Governing Body
12 Princes Avenue, Woodford Green,
Essex IG8 0LN
Tel: 0181 599 0711

Kendo

British Kendo Association
Security House, Littleton Drive,
off Coxborough Lane, Huntingdon,
Staffs WS12 4TS
Tel: 01543 466334
Fax: 01543 505882
Founded 1939.

Korfball

British Korfball Association
47 Garth Road, Morden,
Surrey SM4 4JX
Chairman: Terry Daniels

Lacrosse

English Lacrosse Association
4 Western Court, Bromley Street,
Digbeth, Birmingham B9 4AN
Tel: 0121 773 4422
Fax: 0121 753 0042
E-mail: lacrosseuk@aol.com
Chairman: Meg Black,
President: Tony Malkin, Chief
Executive Officer: D Shuttleworth
Founded 1996 (merger of English
Lacrosse Union (men, founded 1892)
and All-England Women's Lacrosse
Association (founded 1912)).

Lugeing

Great Britain Luge Association
11 Highfield House, Hampton
Bishop, Hereford HR1 4JN
Tel: 01432 271982
General Secretary: J G Evans

Martial Arts

Martial Arts Development Commission
PO Box 381, Erith,
Kent DA8 1TF
Tel: 01322 431440
Office Administrator: Mrs E Jewell

Modern Pentathlon

Modern Pentathlon Association of Great Britain
8 The Commons, Shaftesbury,
Dorest SP7 8JU
Tel: 01747 540519
Fax: 01747 855593

Motor Cycling

Auto-Cycle Union Ltd
ACU House, Wood Street,
Rugby, Warwickshire CV21 2YX
Tel: 01788 566400
Fax: 01788 573585
E-mail: admin@acu.org.uk
Chairman: E P Bartlett,
Chief Executive: Geoff Wilson
Founded 1903.

Motorcycle Circuit Racing Control Board
PO Box 72, Castle Donington,
Derbyshire DE74 2ZQ
Tel: 01332 853822
Manager: D R Barnfield

Scottish Auto-Cycle Union Ltd
Block 2, Unit 6, Whiteside
Industrial Estate, Bathgate,
W Lothian EH48 2RX
Tel: 01506 630262
Fax: 01506 634072
Chairman: Robert T Young,
Secretary: Adam Brownlie
Founded 1913.

Motor Racing

RAC Motor Sports Association Ltd
Motor Sports House, Riverside Park,
Colnbrook, Slough SL3 0HG
Tel: 01753 681736
Fax: 01753 682938
E-mail: racmsa@compuserve.com
Chief Executive: J R Quenby
Founded 1979.

Mountaineering

British Mountaineering Council
177-179 Burton, West Didsbury,
Manchester M20 2BB
Tel: 0161 445 4747
General Secretary: R Payne

Netball

All-England Netball Association Ltd
Netball House, 9 Paynes Park,
Hitchin, Herts SG5 1EH
Tel: 01462 442344
Fax: 01462 442343
Chairman: Mrs J Bourne,
Chief Executive: Mrs E M Nicholl
Founded 1926.

Northern Ireland Netball Association
House of Sport, 2a Upper Malone
Road, Belfast BT9 5LA
Tel: 01232 381222
Secretary: Mrs R McWhinney

Scottish Netball Association
24 Ainslie Road, Hillington
Business Park, Hillington,
Glasgow G52 4RU
Tel: 0141 570 4016
Fax: 0141 570 4017
President: Moira Ord,
Administrator: Ms M Martin
Founded 1947.

Welsh Netball Association
50 Cathedral Road, Cardiff CF1 9LL
Tel: 01222 237048
Fax: 01222 226430
E-mail: welshnetball@comail.com
President: Miss P Nicholas, Chief
Executive Officer: Mrs S J Holvey

Orienteering

British Orienteering Federation
Riversdale, Dale Road North, Darley
Dale, Matlock, Derbyshire DE4 2HX
Tel: 01629 734042
Fax: 01629 733769
E-mail: bof@bof.cix.co.uk
General Secretary: D Locke
Founded 1967.

Polo

Hurlingham Polo Association
Winterlake, Kirtlington, Kidlington,
Oxon OX5 3HG
Tel: 01869 350044
Fax: 01869 350625
E-mail: hpapolo@patrol.iway.co.uk
Chairman: Hon. Mark Vestey,
Secretary: J W M Crisp
Founded 1925.

Pool

English Pool Association
44 Jones House, Penkridge Street,
Walsall WS2 8JX
Tel & Fax: 01922 635587

Racketball

British Racketball Association
50 Tredegar Road, Wilmington,
Dartford DA2 7AZ
Tel: 01322 272200
Fax: 01322 289295
Secretary: Ian Wright

Rackets and Real Tennis

Tennis and Rackets Association
c/o The Queens Club, Palliser Road,
West Kensington, London W14 9EQ
Tel: 0171 386 3447
Fax: 0171 385 7424
Chairman: C J Swallow,
Chief Executive: Brig. A D Myrtle
Founded 1907.

Roller Hockey

National Roller Hockey Association of England
136 Canterbury Road, Herne Bay,
Kent CT6 5RX
President: Ron Barker

Roller Skating

British Federation of Roller Skating
Lilleshall National Sports Centre,
Newport, Shropshire TF10 9AT
Tel: 01952 825253
Fax: 01952 825228
President: Margaret Brooks

Rowing

Amateur Rowing Association Ltd
The Priory, 6 Lower Mall,
Hammersmith, London W6 9DJ
Tel: 0181 748 3632
Fax: 0181 741 4658
President: Martin Brandon-Bravo,
National Manager: Mrs R Napp
Founded 1882.

**Scottish Amateur Rowing
Association**
18 Daniel McLauchlin Place,
Kirkintilloch, Glasgow G66 2LH
Tel & Fax: 0141 775 0522
E-Mail: sara@colloquium.co.uk
Chairman: Iain Somerside,
Secretary: Miss R Clarke
Founded 1881.

**Welsh Amateur Rowing
Association**
Lyndhurst, 77 Hereford Road,
Monmouth, Monmouthshire
NP5 4JZ
Tel: 01600 714244
Chairman: R J Jenkins,
Secertary: M C Hargaden
Founded 1985.

Rugby League

**British Amateur Rugby League
Association**
West Yorkshire House, 4 New North
Parade, Huddersfield HD1 5JP
Tel: 01484 544131
Fax: 01484 519985
Chairman: Michael J Morrissey,
Chief Executive: M F Oldroyd
Founded 1973.

Rugby Football League
Red Hall, Red Hall Lane,
Leeds LS17 8NB
Tel: 0113 232 9111
Fax: 0113 232 3838
Chairman: Sir Rodney Walker,
Chief Executive: J N Tunnicliffe
Founded 1895.

Rugby Union

Irish Rugby Football Union
62 Lansdowne Road, Ballsbridge,
Dublin 4, Republic of Ireland
Tel: 00 353 1 668 4601
Fax: 00 353 1 660 5640
Chairman: N A Murphy,
Secretary: P R Browne
Founded 1874.

Rugby Football Union
Rugby House, Rugby Road,
Twickenham, Middlesex TW1 1DS
Tel: 0181 892 2000
Fax: 0181 892 9816
Chairman: Brian Baister
Founded 1871.

**Rugby Football Union for
Women (England)**
133 Rice Mews, St Thomas,
Exeter EX2 9AY
Tel: 01635 278177
Secretary: Ms S Eakers

Scottish Rugby Union
Murrayfield, Edinburgh EH12 5PJ
Tel: 0131 346 5000
Fax: 0131 346 5001
E-mail: feedback@sru.org.uk
Chairman: Charlie Ritchie,
Chief Executive: Bill Watson
Founded 1873.

Scottish Women's Rugby Union
111 Bavelaw Crescent, Penicuik,
Midlothian EH26 9AX
Tel: 01968 673355

Welsh Rugby Union
PO Box 22, Hodge House,
St Mary Street, Cardiff CF1 1DY
Tel: 01222 781700
Fax: 01222 781722
Chairman: G S Griffiths,
Secretary: Dennis Gethin
Founded 1881.

Welsh Women's Rugby Union
140 Wolseley Street, Pilwenlly,
Newport NP9 2HP
Tel: 01633 220249
Secretary: Ms F Margerison

Women's Rugby Football Union
Newbury Sports Arena, Monks Lane,
Newbury, Berks RG14 7RW
Tel: 01635 42333
Fax: 01635 43016
Secretary: Veronica Wilson

Sailing

Royal Yachting Association
RYA House, Romsey Road,
Eastleigh, Hants SO50 9YA
Tel: 01703 627400
Fax: 01703 629924
E-mail: admin@rya.org.uk
Chairman: Ken Ellis,
Secretary-General: R Duchesne
Founded 1875.

Shooting

**Clay Pigeon Shooting Association
Ltd**
Earlstrees Court, Earlstrees Road,
Corby, Northants NN17 4AX
Tel: 01536 443566
Fax: 01536 443438
Chairman: Geoff Taylor,
Director: E G Orduna
Founded 1928.

National Rifle Association
Bisley Camp, Brookwood,
Woking, Surrey GU24 0PB
Tel: 01483 797777
Fax: 01483 797285
E-mail: c1@nra.org.uk
Chairman: J P de Havilland,
Chief Executive: Col. Colin Cheshire
Founded 1860.

**National Small-Bore Rifle
Association**
Lord Roberts House, Bisley Camp,
Brookwood, Woking,
Surrey GU24 0NP
Tel: 01483 476969
Chairman: G D Pound,
Secretary: Lt-Col. J D Hoare
Founded 1901.

Skiing

**British Skiing and Snowboard
Federation**
258 Main Street, East Calder,
Livingston, W Lothian EH53 0EE
Tel: 01506 884343
Fax: 01506 882952
E-mail: britski@easynet.co.uk
President: John Ritblat,
Chief Executive: M Jardine
Founded 1981.

Speedway

Speedway Control Board Ltd
ACU Headquarters, Wood Street,
Rugby, Warwickshire CV21 2YX
Tel: 01788 540096
Fax: 01788 552308
E-mail: scb@bhb.globalnet.co.uk
Manager: D Hughes
Founded 1934.

Squash

Scottish Squash
Caledonia House, South Gyle,
Edinburgh EH12 9DQ
Tel: 0131 317 7343
Secretary: N Brydon

Squash Rackets Association
PO Box 1106, London W3 0ZD
Tel: 0181 746 1616
Fax: 0181 746 9580
E-mail: pn85@dial.pipex.com
President: Jonah Barrington,
Chief Executive: S H Courtney
Founded 1928.

Welsh Squash
PO Box 56, Penarth,
Cardiff CF64 1XP
Tel: 01222 704096
Fax: 01222 350306
Chairman: Alan James,
Administrator: Diane Selley

Swimming

Amateur Swimming Association
Harold Fern House, Derby Square,
Loughborough, Leics LE11 5AL
Tel: 01509 618700
Fax: 01509 618701
President: John Leech,
Chief Executive: D Sparkes
Founded 1869.

Scottish Amateur Swimming Association
Holmhills Farm, Greenlees Road,
Cambuslang, Glasgow G72 8DT
Tel: 0141 641 8818
Fax: 0141 641 4443
E-mail: scotswim@aol.com
President: Robin Dale, Administrative Manager: Mrs E Mackenzie
Founded 1888.

Welsh Amateur Swimming Association
Roath Park House, Ninian Road,
Cardiff CF2 5ER
Tel & Fax: 01222 488820
Chairman: A Roberts
Founded 1887.

Sub-Aqua

British Sub-Aqua Club
1 Telfords Quay, Ellesmere Port,
Cheshire L65 4FY
Tel: 0151 350 6255
Chief Executive Officer: D Roberts

Table Tennis

English Table Tennis Association
Queensbury House, Havelock Road,
Hastings, E Sussex TN34 1HF
Tel: 01424 722525
Fax: 01424 422103
Chairman: Alan Ransome,
Chief Executive: R Yule
Founded 1926.

Taekwondo

British Taekwondo Council
58 Wiltshire Lane, Pinner,
Middlesex HA5 2LU
Tel: 0181 429 0878
Fax: 0181 866 4151

Tennis

Lawn Tennis Association
The Queens Club, Barons Court,
West Kensington, London W14 9EG
Tel: 0171 381 7000
Fax: 0171 381 5965
President: Geoffrey Cass,
Chief Executive: John Crowther,
Secretary: J C U James
Founded 1888.

Trampolining

British Trampoline Federation Ltd
146 College Road, Harrow,
Middlesex HA1 1BH
Tel: 0181 863 7278
Secretary: R C Walker
Founded 1963.

Triathlon

British Triathlon Association
PO Box 26, Ashby de la Zouch,
Leicester LE65 2ZR
Tel: 01530 414234
Fax: 01530 560279

Tug-of-War

Tug-of-War Association
57 Lynton Road, Chesham,
Bucks HP5 2BT
Tel: 01494 783057
Fax: 01494 772040
Hon. Secretary: P J Craft
Founded 1958.

Volleyball

British Amateur Volleyball Association
English Volleyball Association,
27 South Road, West Bridgford,
Nottingham NG2 7AG
Tel: 0115 981 6324
Fax: 0115 945 5429
President: Andrew Barstow
Founded 1955.

Scottish Volleyball Association
48 The Pleasance,
Edinburgh EH8 9TJ
Tel: 0131 315 4997
Fax: 0131 557 4314
President: David Munro,
Executive Officer: Gillian Anderson
Founded 1965.

Welsh Volleyball Association
9 St Dennis Road, Heath,
Cardiff CF4 4NA
Tel: 01222 758427
Secretary: Ms T Shaw

Water-skiing

British Water Ski Federation
390 City Road, London EC1V 2QA
Tel: 0171 833 2855
Fax: 0171 837 5879
E-mail: Gill@bwsf.co.uk
President: Alan Goggin,
Executive Officer: Gillian Hill
Founded 1951.

Weightlifting

British Amateur Weightlifters' Association
3 Iffley Turn, Oxford OX4 4DU
Tel: 01865 200339
Fax: 01865 249281
Hon. Secretary: W Holland
Founded 1911.

Wrestling

British Amateur Wrestling Association
41 Great Clowes Street, Salford,
Manchester M7 9RQ
Tel: 0161 832 9209
Fax: 0161 833 1120
Secretary: P Tomlinson
Founded 1904.